Lecture Notes in Computer Science 4738

Commenced Publication in 1973
Founding and Former Series Editors:
Gerhard Goos, Juris Hartmanis, and Jan van Leeuwen

W0018282

Ana Paiva   Rui Prada
Rosalind W. Picard (Eds.)

Affective Computing and Intelligent Interaction

Second International Conference, ACII 2007
Lisbon, Portugal, September 12-14, 2007
Proceedings

 Springer

Volume Editors

Ana Paiva
INESC-ID / Instituto Superior Técnico – Taguspark
Avenida Prof. Cavaco Silva, 2780-990 Porto Salvo, Portugal
E-mail: ana.paiva@inesc-id.pt

Rui Prada
INESC-ID / Instituto Superior Técnico – Taguspark
Avenida Prof. Cavaco Silva, 2780-990 Porto Salvo, Portugal
E-mail: rui.prada@gaips.inesc-id.pt

Rosalind W. Picard
MIT Media Laboratory
20 Ames Street, Cambridge, MA 02139, USA
E-mail: picard@media.mit.edu

Library of Congress Control Number: 2007934295

CR Subject Classification (1998): I.4, I.5, I.3, H.5.1-3, I.2.10, J.4, K.3

LNCS Sublibrary: SL 6 – Image Processing, Computer Vision, Pattern Recognition, and Graphics

ISSN   0302-9743
ISBN-10   3-540-74888-1 Springer Berlin Heidelberg New York
ISBN-13   978-3-540-74888-5 Springer Berlin Heidelberg New York

Springer is a part of Springer Science+Business Media

springer.com

© Springer-Verlag Berlin Heidelberg 2007
Printed in Germany

Typesetting: Camera-ready by author, data conversion by Scientific Publishing Services, Chennai, India
Printed on acid-free paper   SPIN: 12122028   06/3180   5 4 3 2 1 0

Preface

This volume contains the proceedings of the 2nd International Conference on Affective Computing and Intelligent Interaction (ACII 2007) held in Lisbon, Portugal, September 12–14, 2007.

The 1st International Conference on Affective Computing and Intelligent Interaction was held in Beijing, China, in 2005. Following its success, in 2007 ACII was organized by the Humaine Network of Excellence as a meeting point for researchers studying and developing the role of emotion and other affective phenomena in many different areas. Among these areas, ACII 2007 featured papers in affective human–computer and human–robot interaction, computer graphics for recognizing and expressing emotions, emotion-based AI architectures, robotics, vision, speech, synthetic characters, games, educational software, and others. By investigating new theories and mechanisms through which we can create machines that are able to recognize, model and express emotions and other affective phenomena, we hope to contribute towards the creation of machines that allow for the establishment of sustainable and affective relations with humans.

ACII 2007 received a total of 151 papers. From these, 57 were accepted as long papers and 4 as short papers. Due to the high quality of papers, the conference also included poster presentations, which are published as extended abstracts in this volume. Although this is a new multidisciplinary field, the number and quality of submitted and accepted papers was evidence of its rapid maturation.

This year the ACII also featured a Doctoral Consortium, which received 20 papers that were published separately from these proceedings.

We would like to thank a number of people who contributed and helped to guarantee the high quality of the papers, in particular the Program Committee consisting of distinguished researchers who worked hard to meet the tight deadlines we had set for ourselves. Special thanks go to Patricia Lima (from the GAIPS group at INESC-ID) for her extremely efficient work in the organization of the event and to Roddy Cowie (the Humaine coordinator) without whom the organization of the conference would not have been possible.

We hope that the readers of this volume find it helpful, inspiring, and above all, an important reference for the area of affective computing and intelligent interaction.

September 2007

Ana Paiva
Rosalind Picard
Ruth Aylett
Stefanos Kolias
Andrew Ortony
Jianhua Tao
Rui Prada

Organization

ACII 2007 was organized by the Humaine Network of Excellence (funded by the European Commission, http://emotion-research.net/), the GAIPS (Intelligent Agents and Synthetic Characters) group of INESC-ID, and IST (Instituto Superior Técnico) in Portugal in cooperation with ACM/SIGART, ACM/SIGCHI and ACM/SIGGRAPH.

Organizing Committee

Conference Co-chairs	Ana Paiva (Portugal)
	Rosalind Picard(USA)
Program Chairs	Ruth Aylett (UK)
	Stefanos Kolias (Greece)
	Andrew Ortony (USA)
	Jianhua Tao (China)
Local Organization	Rui Prada (Portugal)
Publicity Co-chairs	Lola Cañamero (UK)
	Nick Campbell (Japan)
Tutorials Co-chairs	Jonhatan Gratch (USA)
	Kristina Höök (Sweden)
Doctoral Consortium Co-chairs	Fiorella de Rosis(Italy)
	Roddy Cowie (UK)
Demos Co-chairs	Paolo Petta (Austria)
	Carlos Martinho (Portugal)

Program Committee

Anton Nijolt (Netherlands)
Antonio Camurri (Italy)
Brian Parkinson (UK)
Carlos Martinho (Portugal)
Catherine Pelachaud (France)
Christian Becker (Germany)
Christian Peter (Germany)
Christine Lisetti (France)
Chung-Hsien Wu (China)
Cindy Mason (USA)
Cristiano Castelfranchi (Italy)
Cristina Connati (Canada)
Daniel Thalmann (Switzerland)

Darryl Davis (UK)
David House (Sweden)
Diane Litman (USA)
Dirk Heylen (Netherlands)
Elisabeth André (Germany)
Ellen Cowie (UK)
Eugénio de Oliveira (Portugal)
Eva Hudlicka (USA)
Fiorella de Rosis (Italy)
Gerard Bailly (France)
Graça Gaspar (Portugal)
Hatice Gunes (Australia)
Helen Pain (UK)

Helmut Prendinger (Japan)
Henry Lieberman (USA)
Hongxun Yao (China)
Hugo Liu (USA)
Ian Horswill (USA)
Isabel Trancoso (Portugal)
Jean-Claude Martin (France)
Jianhua Tao (China)
Jonathan Gratch (USA)
Juan Velasquez (USA)
Julia Hirschberg (USA)
Keikichi Hirose (Japan)
Kerstin Dautenhahn (UK)
Kim Binsted (USA)
Kristina Höök (Sweden)
Laurence Devillers (France)
Lola Canãmero (UK)
Luís Botelho (Portugal)
Luís Caldas de Oliveira (Portugal)
Luís Morgado (Portugal)
Magy Seif El-Nasr (USA)
Maja Pantic (UK)
Marc Shröder (Germany)

Maria Cravo (Portugal)
Matthias Scheutz (USA)
Nadia Bianchi-Berthouze (UK)
Nadia Magnenat-Thalmann
    (Switzerland)
Nick Campbell (Japan)
Niels Ole Bernsen (Denmark)
Oliviero Stock (Italy)
Paolo Petta, (Austria)
Phoebe Sengers (USA)
Rada Mihalcea, (USA)
Rana el Kaliouby (USA)
Roberto Bresin (Sweden)
Roddy Cowie (UK)
Rodrigo Ventura (Portugal)
Ruth Ayllet (UK)
Stacy Marsella (USA)
Stefan Kopp (Germany)
Susanne Kaiser (Switzerland)
Tanja Bänziger (Switzerland)
Thomas Rist (Germany)
Thomas Wehrle (Switzerland)
Zhiliang Wang (China)

Additional Reviewers

Andreas Wichert (Portugal)
António Serralheiro (Portugal)
Carmen Banea (USA)
Celso de Melo (Portugal)
Christopher Peters (France)
Claudia Costa Pederson (USA)
Diamantino Caseiro (Portugal)
Dan Cosley (USA)
Daniel Moura (Portugal)
David Matos (Portugal)
Emiliano Lorini (Italy)
Giovanni Pezzulo (Italy)
Guilherme Raimundo (Portugal)
Hronn Brynjarsdottir (USA)
I. Wassink (Netherlands)
João Dias (Portugal)

Joseph Zupko (USA)
Kirsten Boehner (USA)
Louis-Philippe Morency (USA)
Lucian Leahu (USA)
Luís Sarmento (Portugal)
Luísa Coheur (Portugal)
Magalie Ochs (France)
Marco Vala (Portugal)
Mei Si (USA)
Michele Piunti (Italy)
R. Rienks (Netherlands)
Radoslaw Niewiadomski (France)
Ronald Poppe (Netherlands)
T.H. Bui (Netherlands)
Thurid Vogt (Germany)
Vincent Wan (UK)

Sponsoring Institutions

Humaine Network of Excellence
YDreams
Microsoft Research
MindRaces European Project
Fundação Calouste Gulbenkian
Fundação para a Ciência e a Tecnologia
CALLAS European Project
FLAD Fundação Luso-Americana para o Desenvolvimento

Organized by:

FP6 IST Humaine Network of Excellence
INESC-ID (Instituto de Engenharia de Sistemas e Computadores - Investigação
    e Desenvolvimento em Lisboa)
IST- Instituto Superior Técnico

Table of Contents

Affective Facial Expression and Recognition

Affective Body Expression and Recognition

Affective Speech Processing

Affective Text and Dialogue Processing

Recognising Affect Using Physiological Measures

Computational Models of Emotion and Theoretical Foundations

Affective Databases, Annotations, Tools and Languages

Affective Sound and Music Processing

Affective Interactions: Systems and Applications

Evaluating Affective Systems

Posters

Expressive Face Animation Synthesis Based on Dynamic Mapping Method*

Panrong Yin, Liyue Zhao, Lixing Huang, and Jianhua Tao

National Laboratory of Pattern Recognition (NLPR)
Institute of Automation, Chinese Academy of Sciences, Beijing, China
{pryin,lyzhao,lxhuang,jhtao}@nlpr.ia.ac.cn

Abstract. In the paper, we present a framework of speech driven face animation system with expressions. It systematically addresses audio-visual data acquisition, expressive trajectory analysis and audio-visual mapping. Based on this framework, we learn the correlation between neutral facial deformation and expressive facial deformation with Gaussian Mixture Model (GMM). A hierarchical structure is proposed to map the acoustic parameters to lip FAPs. Then the synthesized neutral FAP streams will be extended with expressive variations according to the prosody of the input speech. The quantitative evaluation of the experimental result is encouraging and the synthesized face shows a realistic quality.

1 Introduction

Speech driven face animation aims to convert incoming audio stream into a sequence of corresponding face movements. A number of its possible applications could be seen in multimodal human-computer interfaces, visual reality and videophone. Till now, most of their work was still focused on the lips movement [1][2][3]. Among them, Rule-based method [2] and Vector Quantization method [3] are two direct and easily realized ways. But the results from them are usually inaccurate and discontinuous due to limited rules and codebooks. Neural network is also an effective way for the audio-visual mapping. For instance, Massaro [1] trained a neural network model to learn the mapping from LPCs to face animation parameters, they used current frame, 5 backward and 5 forward time step as the input to model the context. Although the neural network has merits of moderate amount of samples and smooth synthesized result, it is deeply influenced by the initial parameters setting, and it is easier to be bogged down into local minimum. Hidden Marcov Model (HMM) is also widely used in this area because of its successful application in speech recognition. Yamamoto E. [3] built a phoneme recognition model via HMM, and directly mapping recognized phonemes to lip shapes. The smoothing algorithm was also used. The HMMs can only be generated based on phonemes, the work has to be linked to a specific language, furthermore, the synthesized lip sequence is also not very smooth.

---

* The work is supported by the National Natural Science Foundation of China (No. 60575032) and the 863 Program (No. 2006AA01Z138).

A. Paiva, R. Prada, and R.W. Picard (Eds.): ACII 2007, LNCS 4738, pp. 1–11, 2007.

Most of those systems are based on phonemic representation (phoneme or viseme) and appear limited efficiency due to the restriction of algorithms. In order to reduce the computing complexity and make the synthesized result smoother, some researchers have applied dynamic mapping method to reorder or concatenate existing audio-visual units to form new visual sequence. For instance, Bregler(Video Rerite) [6] reorders existing mouth frames based on recognized phonemes. Cosatto [7] selects corresponding visual frames according to the distance between new audio track and stored audio track, and concatenates the candidates to form a smoothest sequence.

While lip shapes are closely related to speech content (linguistic), facial expression is a primary way of passing non-verbal information (paralinguistic) which contains a set of message related to the speaker's emotional state. Thus, it would be more natural and vivid for the talking head to show expressions when communicating with the human. In Pengyu Hong' research [4], he not only applied several MLPs to map LPC cepstral parameters to face motion units, but also used different MLPs to map the estimated motion units to expressive motion units. Ashish Verma [12] used optical flow between visemes to generate face animations with different facial expressions. Yan Li [16] adopted 3 sets of cartoon templates with 5 levels of intensity to show expression synchronized with face animation.

Although some work has been done for the expressive facial animation from the speech, the naturalness of synthesized results is still an open question. In our work, we design a framework of speech driven face animation system based on the dynamic mapping method. To investigate the forming process of facial expression, the correlation between neutral facial deformation and expressive facial deformation is firstly modeled by GMM. Then we combine the VQ method and frame-based concatenation model to facilitate the audio-visual mapping, and keep the result as much realistic as possible. In the training procedure, we cluster the training audio vectors according to the phoneme information, and use a codebook to denote phoneme categories. The number of phonemes in database determines the size of the codebook. During the synthesizing, we apply a hierarchical structure by the following steps.

First: each frame of the input speech is compared to the codebook, then we get three different candidate codes.

Second: for each candidate code, there are several phoneme samples. The target unit (the current 3 frames) of the input speech together with its context information is shifted within the speech sequence of a tri-phone under so as to find out the most matched sub-sequence.

Third: the visual distance between two adjacent candidate units is computed to ensure that the concatenated sequence is smooth.

Last: the expressive variation that is predicted from the *k-th* GMM, which is determined by the prosody of the input speech, will be imposed on the synthesized neutral face animation sequence.

Figure 1 shows a block diagram of our expressive talking head system. In the rest of the paper, section 2 introduces the data acquisition, section 3 analyses the trajectories of expressive facial deformation and GMM modeling process, section 4 focuses on the realization of lip movement synthesis from speech, section 5 gives the experimental result, and section 6 is the conclusion and future work description.

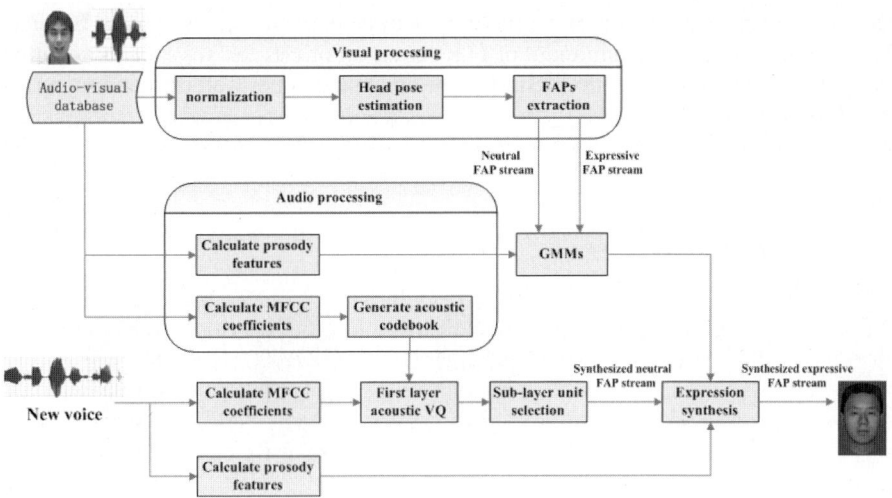

Fig. 1. Expressive speech driven face animation system framework

2 Data Acquisition and Preprocessing

For establishing audio-visual database, a digital camera and a microphone on the camera were used to collect the facial movement and speech signal synchronously. The training database used in our work consists of 300 complete sentences and about 12000 frame samples. The speaker was directed to articulate the same content of text with neutral accent and with natural intensity expressions respectively. Here, we choose 3 emotional states – angry, happy and surprise.

Once the training data is acquired, audio and visual data will be analyzed separately. For visual representation, our tracking method is implemented in an estimation-and-refining way, and this method is applied in each successive image pair. 20 salient facial feature points (Fig. 2(a)) including two nostrils (*p1* and *p2*), six brow corners (*p3, p4, p5, p6, p7* and *p8*), eight eye corners (*p9, p10, p11, p12, p13, p14, p15* and *p16*), and four mouth corners (*p17, p18, p19* and *p20*) are used to represent the facial shape. They are initialized in the first frame interactively, and the KLT is used to estimate the feature points in the next frame. Assume $X = (x^1, y^1, x^2, y^2, \cdots, x^N, y^N)^T$ are the positions of feature points in the current frame, and dX are the estimated offset by KLT, we try to refine the initial tracking result $X + dX$ by applying the constraints of Point Distribution Models (PDM). Figure 2(b) shows some examples of expressive facial image. Then after coordinate normalization and affine transformation, 19 FAPs (see Table 1) related to lip and facial deformation will be extracted.

For audio representation, the Mel-Frequency Cepstrum Coefficients (MFCC) which gives an alternative representation to speech spectra is calculated. The speech signal, sampled at 16 kHz, is blocked into frames of 40 ms. 12-dimentional MFCC coefficients are computed for every audio frame, and one visual frame corresponds to one audio frame. Furthermore, global statistics on prosody features (such as pitch, energy and so on) responsible for facial expressions will be extracted in our work. F0 range, the maximum of F0s, the minimum of F0s, the mean of F0s and the mean of energy, which have been confirmed to be useful for emotional speech classification, are selected for each sample.

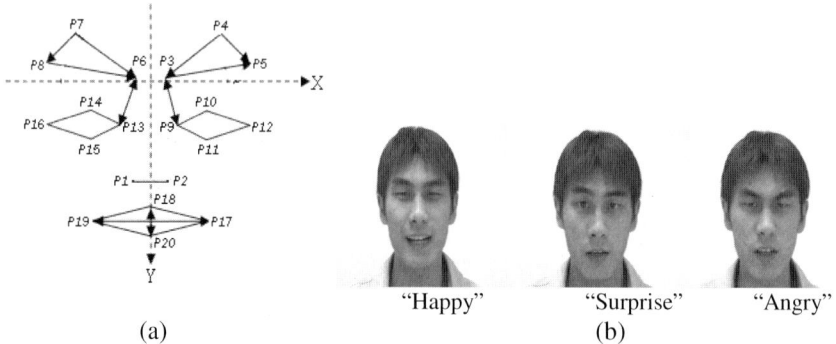

| | "Happy" | "Surprise" | "Angry" |

(a)   (b)

Fig. 2. (a) Facial feature points and (b) Expressive facial image

Table 1. FAPs for visual representation in our system

Group	FAP name	Group	FAP name
2	Open_jaw	8	Stretch_r_cornerlip_o
4	Raise_l_i_eyebrow	8	Stretch_l_cornerlip_o
4	Raise_r_i_eyebrow	8	Lower_t_lip_lm_o
4	Raise_l_m_eyebrow	8	Lower_t_lip_rm_o
4	Raise_r_m_eyebrow	8	Raise_b_lip_lm_o
4	Raise_l_o_eyebrow	8	Raise_b_lip_rm_o
4	Raise_r_i_eyebrow	8	Raise_l_cornerlip_o
8	Lower_t_midlip_o	8	Raise_r_cornerlip_o
8	Raise_b_midlip_o		

3 Neutral-Expressive Facial Deformation Mapping

In our work, the problem of processing facial expression is simplified by taking advantage of the correlation between the facial deformation without expressions and facial deformation with expressions that account for the same speech content. Here, we choose 3 points for following analysis: p4(middle point of right eyebrow), p18(middle of upper lip), p19(left corner of the mouth).

Figure 3 shows the dynamic vertical movement of p4 for "jiu4 shi4 xia4 yu3 ye3 qu4" in neutral and surprise condition and the vertical movement of p18 in neutral and happy condition. It is evident from Fig.3(a) that facial deformations are strongly affected by emotion. Although the trajectory of vertical movement of right eyebrow in surprise condition is following the trend of that in neutral condition, the intensity is much stronger and the time duration tends to be longer. On the other hand, the lip movement is not only influenced by the speech content, but also affected by the speech emotional rhythm. The action of showing expressions will deform the original mouth shape. From Fig.3(b) and Fig.3(c), we can see that p18 which is on the upper lip moves up more under happy condition, and p18 and p19 have similar vertical trajectories because of their interrelate relationship on the lip.

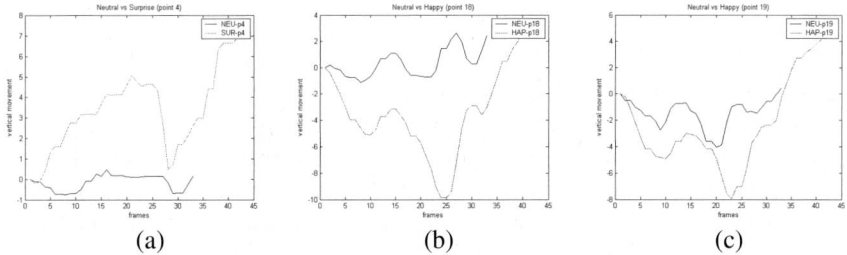

(a)   (b)   (c)

Fig. 3. Movements of (a) p4, (b) p18 and (c) p19 under different emotional states

Since the degree of expressive representation is in a continuous space, it is not reasonable to simply classify the intensity of expression into several levels. Therefore, for estimating natural expressive facial deformation from neutral face movements, some GMMs are used to model the probability distribution of the neutral-expressive deformation vectors. Each emotion category corresponds to a GMM. To collect training data, these N vector and E vector sequences are firstly aligned with Dynamic Time Warping (DTW). Then, we cascade neutral facial deformation features with the expressive facial deformation features to compose the joint feature vector: $Z_{ik}=[X_k, Y_{ik}]^T$, $i \in [0,1,2,3,4,5]$, $k=1,...,N$. Therefore, the joint probability distribution of the neutral-expressive deformation vectors is modeled by GMM, which is a weighted sum of Q Gaussian functions:

$$P(Z) = \sum_{q=1}^{Q} w_q N(Z; \mu_q; \Sigma_q), \quad \sum_{q=1}^{Q} w_q = 1. \tag{1}$$

Where $N(Z; \mu_q; \Sigma_q)$ is the Gaussian distributed density component, μ_q and Σ_q are the q-th mean vector and q-th covariance matrix, w_q is the mixture weight and Q is the number of Gaussian functions in the GMM. GMMs' parameters: (w,μ,Σ) (Equation.2) can be obtained by training with Expectation-Maximization(EM) algorithm.

$$\mu_q = \begin{bmatrix} \mu_q^X \\ \mu_q^Y \end{bmatrix}, \quad \Sigma_q = \begin{bmatrix} \Sigma_q^{XX} & \Sigma_q^{XY} \\ \Sigma_q^{YX} & \Sigma_q^{YY} \end{bmatrix}, \quad q = 1,...,Q. \tag{2}$$

After the GMMs are trained with the training data, the optimal estimate of expressive facial deformation (Y_{ik}) given neutral facial deformation (X_k) can be obtained according to the transform function of conditional expectation (Equation.3).

$$\overline{Y_{ik}} = E\{Y_{ik} / X_k\} = \sum_{q=1}^{Q} P_q(X_k)[\mu_q^Y + \Sigma_q^{YX}(\Sigma_q^{XX})^{-1}(X_k - \mu_q^X)]. \tag{3}$$

Where $p_q(X_k)$ is the probability that the given neutral observation belongs to the mixture component (Equation.4).

$$p_q(X_k) = \frac{w_q N(X_k; \mu_q; \Sigma_q)}{\sum_{p=1}^{Q} w_p N(X_k; \mu_p; \Sigma_p)} \ . \tag{4}$$

4   Lip Movement Synthesized from Speech

Dynamic concatenation model applied in our previous work [8] has output a result of natural quality and could be easily realized. Considering searching efficiency and automatic performance of system, we introduce hierarchical structure and regard every three frames as a unit instead of a phoneme in our previous work. Unlike Cossato's work [7], in our approach, every three frames of the input speech are not directly compared with existing frames in corpus, because the frame-based corpus would be too large to search. Therefore, we break the mapping process (see Fig.4) into two steps: finding out approximate candidate codes in codebooks and finding out approximate sub-sequence by calculating cost with context information.

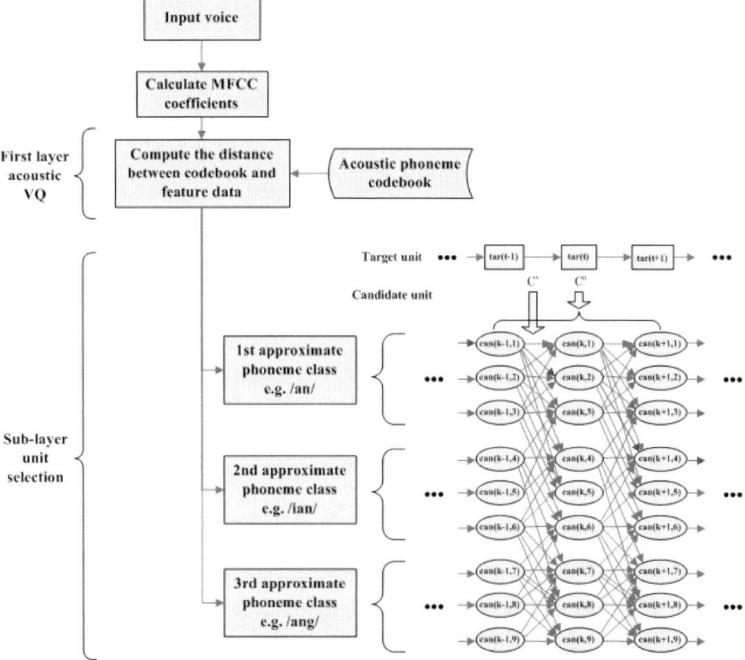

Fig. 4. Hierarchical structure of improved dynamic concatenation model

4.1 Phoneme Based Acoustic Codebook

For higher efficiency, a phoneme based codebook is produced in training process. The training audio vectors are clustered according to the phoneme information. Every code in the codebook corresponds to a phoneme. The number of phonemes in database determines the size of the codebook. There are totally 48 codes including the SIL part in sentences. When coming to the synthesizing process, the distance between each frame of the input speech and the codebook is calculated. The most 3 approximate phoneme categories represented by candidate codes will be listed, so that mistakenly choosing similar phoneme by choosing only one code can be avoided. The first layer cost $COST^1$ can be obtained by Equation.5.

$$COST^1 = \left\{ dist(k); \quad k = \arg\min_n \left\| \overrightarrow{a}^t - codebook(n) \right\| \right\}. \tag{5}$$

4.2 Cost Computation

For each candidate code, there are several phoneme samples. Then more detailed audio-visual unit mapping is employed to synthesize continuous FAP streams. Sub-layer cost computation is based on two cost functions:

$$COST^2 = \alpha C^a + (1-\alpha)C^v. \tag{6}$$

where C^a is the voice spectrum distance, C^v is the visual distance between two adjacent units, and the weight "α" balances the effect of the two cost functions.

In the unit selection procedures, we regard every 3 frames of the input speech as a target unit. In fact, the process of selecting candidate units is to find out the most approximate sub-sequence within the range of the candidate phoneme together with its context. The voice spectrum distance (see Fig.5) not only accounts for the context of target unit of the input speech, but also considers the context of the candidate phoneme. The context of target unit covers former m frames and latter m frames of the current frame. The context of candidate phoneme accounts for a tri-phone, which covers the former phoneme and the latter phoneme. When measuring how close the candidate unit compared with the target unit, the target unit with its context is shifted from the beginning to the end of the tri-phone. In this way, all the positions of sub-sequence within the tri-phone could be considered. Finally, the sub-sequence with the minimum average distance is output, thus the candidate unit is selected. So the voice spectrum distance can be defined by Equation.7:

$$C^a = \sum_{t=curr-p}^{p} \sum_{m=-6}^{6} w_{t,m} \left| a_{t,m}^{tar} - a_{t,m}^{can} \right|. \tag{7}$$

The weights w_m are determined by the method used in [10], we compute the linear blending weights in terms of target unit's duration. $\left| a_{t,m}^{tar} - a_{t,m}^{can} \right|$ is the Eucilidian distance of the acoustic parameter of two periods of frames. For the sake of reducing the complexity of Viterbi search, we set a limit of sequence candidate number for every round selection.

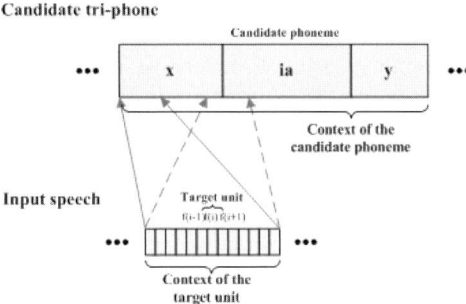

Fig. 5. Voice spectrum cost

Not only should we find out the correct speech signal unit, but also the smooth synthesized face animation should be considered. The concatenation cost measures how closely the mouth shapes of the adjacent units match. So the FAPs of the last frame of former candidate unit are compared with that of the first frame of current candidate unit (Equation.8).

$$C^v = v(can_{r-1}, can_r) \tag{8}$$

Where $v(can_{r-1}, can_r)$ is the Euclidian distance of the adjacent visual features of two candidate sequence.

Once the two costs $COST^1$ and $COST^2$ are computed, the graph for unit concatenation is constructed. Our approach finally aims to find the best path in this graph which generates minimum COST (Equation.9), Viterbi is a valid search method for this application.

$$COST = \sum_r^{n/3} COST^1(r) * COST^2(r). \tag{9}$$

Where n indicates the total number of frames in the input speech, and r means the number of target units contained in the input speech.

5   Experimental Result

When the speech is input, the system will calculate MFCC coefficients and prosody features respectively. The former one is used to drive content related face movement, the latter one is used to choose the appropriate GMM. Once the neutral FAP stream is synthesized by improved concatenation model, the chosen GMM will predict expressive FAP stream based on the neutral FAP stream. Fig.6 shows the examples of synthesized FAP stream results and Fig.7 shows the synthesized expressive facial deformation of 3 points (3 FAPs related) compared with the recorded deformation.

In Fig.6(a) and Fig.6(b), we compare the synthesized FAP 52 stream with recorded FAP stream from validation set and test set respectively. In Fig.6(a), the two curves (smoothed synthesized sequence and recorded sequence) are very close, because the validation speech input is more likely to find out the complete sequence of the same sentence from corpus. In Fig.6(b), the input speech is much different from those used in training process. Although the two curves are not so close, the slopes of them are similar in most cases. To reduce the magnitude of discontinuities, the final synthesized result is smoothed by curve fitting.

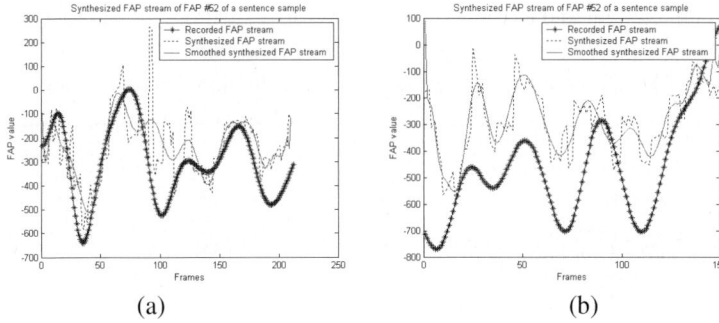

Fig. 6. Selected synthesized FAP streams from (a) validation sentence and (b) test sentence

In Fig.7, the synthesized expressive trajectories appear good performance of following the trend of recorded ones. It is noticed that the ends of synthesized trajectories do not well estimate the facial deformation, this is mainly because that the longer part of expressive training data is a tone extension, so the features of end part of two aligned sequences do not strictly correspond.

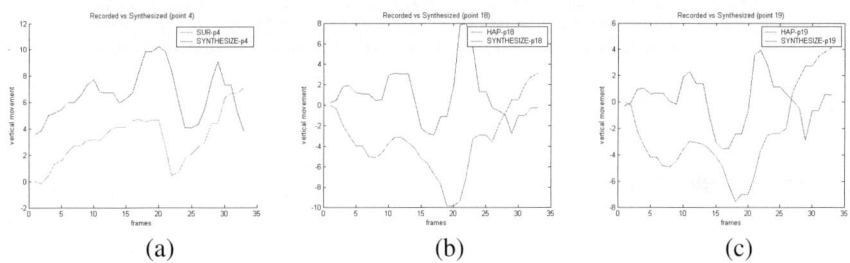

Fig. 7. Synthesized expressive trajectories of (a) p4, (b) p18 and (c) p19 under different emotional states

For quantitative evaluation, correlation coefficient (Equation.10) is used to represent the deviation similarity between recorded FAP stream and synthesized stream. The coefficient is closer to 1, the result is better follow the trends in original values.

$$CC = \frac{1}{T}\sum_{t=1}^{T}\frac{(\hat{f}(t)-\hat{\mu})(f(t)-\mu)}{\hat{\sigma}\sigma} \ .$$

(10)

Where $f(t)$ is the recorded FAP stream, $\hat{f}_{(t)}$ is the synthesis, T is the total number of frames in the database, and μ and σ are corresponding mean and standard deviation.

From Table 2, we can see that estimates for p4 are generally better than those of other points on lips. The eyebrows movements are observed to be mainly affected by expressions, while lip movements are not only influenced by the speech content, but also extended with emotional exhibition. The trajectories of p18 and p19 are determined by both content and expression, thus they have smaller correlation coefficients.

Table 2. The average correlation coefficients for different expressions

Correlation Coefficients	p4	p18	p19
Improved dynamic concatenation model (Neutral)	0.782	0.723	0.754
GMM for Surprise	0.737	0.656	0.688
GMM for Happy	0.729	0.725	0.701

At last, a MPEG-4 facial animation engine is used to access our synthesized FAP streams qualitatively. The animation model displays at a frame rate of 30 fps. Fig.8 shows some frames of synthesized talking head compared with recorded images.

Fig. 8. Some frames of synthesized talking head

We have tried different voices on our system. The synthesized result is well matched their voices, and the face animation seems very natural. Although Chinese voice of a man is used in the training process, our system can adapt to other languages as well.

6 Conclusion and Future Work

In the present work, we analyze the correlation between neutral facial deformation and expressive facial deformation and use GMM to model the joint probability distribution. In addition, we also make some improvements to the dynamic mapping method in our previous work. By employing a hierarchical structure, the mapping process can be broke into two steps. First-layer acoustic codebook gives a general classification for the input speech frames. Sub-layer frame-based cost computation ensures that most approximate candidate sequence is selected. Through this method, the unit searching speed is largely enhanced, the artificial operation in animation process is avoided and the synthesized result keeps natural and realistic. But our work is presently limited to some typical emotions. The affective information represented by speaker in natural spiritual state is still a challenged work. In the future, more work will be done to investigate into how dynamic expressive movement is related to prosody features. It also needs to align FAP sequences with better strategy and finding more appropriate parameters to smooth the synthesized trajectories.

References

1. Massaro, D.W., Beskow, J., Cohen, M.M., Fry, C.L., Rodriguez, T.: Picture My Voice: Audio to Visual Speech Synthesis using Artificial Neural Networks. In: Proceedings of AVSP'99, Santa Cruz, CA, August, pp. 133–138 (1999)
2. Ezzat, T., Poggio, T.: MikeTalk: A Talking Facial Display Based on Morphing Visemes. In: Proc. Computer Animation Conference, Philadelphia, USA (1998)
3. Yamamoto, E., Nakamura, S., Shikano, K.: Lip movement synthesis from speech based on Hidden Markov Models. Speech Communication 26, 105–115 (1998)
4. Hong, P., Wen, Z., Huang, T.S.: Real-time speech-driven face animation with expressions using neural networks. IEEE Trans on Neural Networks 13(4) (2002)
5. Matthew Brand. Voice Puppetry. In: Pro of SIGGRAPH'99. p21-28
6. Bregler, C., Covell, M., Slaney, M.: Video Rewrite: Driving Visual Speech with Audio, ACM SIGGRAPH (1997)
7. Cosatto, E., Potamianos, G., Graf, H.P.: Audio-visual unit selection for the synthesis of photo-realistic talking-heads. In: IEEE International Conference on Multimedia and Expo, ICME, vol. 2, pp. 619–622 (2000)
8. Yin, P., Tao, J.: Dynamic mapping method based speech driven face animation system. The First International Conference on Affective Computing and Intelligent Interaction (2005)
9. Tekalp, A.M., Ostermann, J.: Face and 2-D mesh animation in MPEG-4, Signal Processing. Image Communication 15, 387–421 (2000)
10. Wang, J.-Q., Wong, K.-H., Pheng, P.-A., Meng, H.M., Wong, T.-T.: A real-time Cantonese text-to-audiovisual speech synthesizer, Acoustics, Speech, and Signal Processing. Proceedings (ICASSP '04) 1, 653–656 (2004)
11. Arun, K.S., Huang, T.S., Blostein, S.D.: Least-square fitting of two 3-D point sets. IEEE Trans. Pattern Analysis and Machine Intelligence 9(5), 698–700 (1987)
12. Verma, A., Subramaniam, L.V., Rajput, N., Neti, C., Faruquie, T.A.: Animating Expressive Faces Across Languages. IEEE Trans on Multimedia 6(6) (2004)
13. Tao, J., Tan, T.: Emotional Chinese Talking Head Syste. In: Proc. of ACM 6th International Conference on Multimodal Interfaces (ICMI 2004), State College, PA (October 2004)
14. Gutierrez-Osuna, R., Kakumanu, P.K., Esposito, A., Garcia, O.N., Bojorquez, A., Castillo, J.L., Rudomin, I.: Speech-Driven Facial Animation with Realistic Dynamics. IEEE Trans. on Multimedia 7(1) (2005)
15. Huang, Y., Lin, S., Ding, X., Guo, B., Shum, H.-Y.: Real-time Lip Synchronization Based on Hidden Markov Models. ACCV (2002)
16. Li, Y., Yu, F., Xu, Y.-Q., Chang, E., Shum, H.-Y.: Speech-Driven Cartoon Animation with Emotions. In: Proceedings of the ninth ACM international conference on Multimedia (2001)
17. Rao, R., Chen, T.: Audio-to-Visual Conversion for Multimedia Communication. IEEE Transactions on Industrial Electronics 45(1), 15–22 (1998)

Model of Facial Expressions Management for an Embodied Conversational Agent

Radosław Niewiadomski and Catherine Pelachaud

IUT de Monreuil, Université Paris 8, France
{niewiadomski,pelachaud}@iut.univ-paris8.fr

Abstract. In this paper we present a model of facial behaviour encompassing interpersonal relations for an Embodied Conversational Agent (ECA). Although previous solutions of this problem exist in ECA's domain, in our approach a variety of facial expressions (i.e. expressed, masked, inhibited, and fake expressions) is used for the first time. Moreover, our rules of facial behaviour management are consistent with the predictions of politeness theory as well as the experimental data (i.e. annotation of the video-corpus). Knowing the affective state of the agent and the type of relations between interlocutors the system automatically adapts the facial behaviour of an agent to the social context. We present also the evaluation study we have conducted of our model. In this experiment we analysed the perception of interpersonal relations from the facial behaviour of our agent.

Keywords: Embodied conversational agents, social context, facial expressions.

1 Introduction

Human facial behaviour is influenced by many social and cultural aspects. In a series of experiments it was proved that people modify spontaneous facial expressions in interpersonal relations [6,9,13,14,19,20]. For this purpose they often use different types of display strategies like showing fake, inhibited, or masked expressions etc. The ability to control emotional expressions (i.e. suppress, substitute, or simulate expressions of emotions) is part of emotional skills and competences often called *emotional intelligence* [10] . By analogy to human beings, we expect that embodied conversational agents (ECA)[1] can also benefit from these emotional skills. Emotionally effective and socially competent agents are more likely to build a successful relationship with a human user. According to Reeves and Nass [17] people have some implicit expectations about the social and emotional behaviour of the electronic media. Because of that, computers have to respect social rules and, in particular, rules of interpersonal relations. The violation of social norms (such as being impolite) by the computer is viewed as a social incompetence and is offensive [17]. In this paper we aim at improving

---

[1] An ECA is a virtual humanoid able to communicate verbally and not verbally.

A. Paiva, R. Prada, and R.W. Picard (Eds.): ACII 2007, LNCS 4738, pp. 12–23, 2007.

the facial communication of embodied agents. We introduce an architecture that uses a variety of facial expressions (like fake or masked expressions) to manifest relations between the embodied agent and the user. We expect that by improving the expressive skills of an ECA we can contribute to successful communication between humans and computers. In order to build the architecture we need an agent that is able to:

- express different types of facial expressions,
- know which factors influence facial behaviour,
- know how they influence facial behaviour.

In a previous paper[4] we proposed a model for generation of different types of facial expressions. Psychologists (e.g. [9]) classified facial expressions according to meaning, role, and appearance. Facial expressions do not always correspond to felt emotions: they can be fake (showing an expression of an unfelt emotion), masked (masking a felt emotion by an unfelt emotion), superposed (showing a mixed of felt emotions), inhibited (masking the expression of emotion with the neutral expression), suppressed (de-intensifying the expression of an emotion), or exaggerated (intensifying the expression of an emotion) (see [15] for detailed discussion). We call *complex facial expressions* the expressions that are different from the spontaneous facial displays of simple emotional states (e.g. display of anger or sadness). They can be displays of some combinations of emotions as well as expressions of emotions, which are modified according to some social rules. We model complex facial expressions using a face partitioning approach. It means that different emotions are expressed on different areas of the face. More precisely, each facial expression is defined by a set of eight facial areas (brows, upper eyelids,...). Then the complex facial expressions are composed of the facial areas of input expressions using a set of rules [4].

In this paper we focus on facial expression management. We aim at determining factors that influence the facial behaviour in interpersonal relations and at building the model of the facial behaviour management for an ECA. Depending on some parameters that define interpersonal relations and the emotional state of the agent our algorithm modifies agent's default (i.e. "spontaneous") facial behaviour. It means that in certain social contexts our agent will use some *complex facial expressions* instead of *simple* ones. Thus we need to find rules between factors that influence the facial behaviour in interpersonal relations and the occurrence of particular type of complex facial expressions. Our rules of facial behaviour management are mostly based on the results of the annotation of a video-corpus we have made for this purpose.

The remaining part of this paper is structured as follows. In next section we present an overview of existing architectures that model certain aspects of social interaction, while section 3 presents the theory of politeness, which is used in our model. Section 4 is entirely dedicated to the study of the video corpus we made in order to gather information about facial behaviour in interpersonal relations. Then, in section 5, the details of our model are presented while, in section 6, we present the evaluation study we conducted. Finally we discuss future works in section 7.

2   State of Art

The social context was often implemented in the agent's domain. First of all, different architectures modify with success the verbal content of a communicative act. Usually they adapt the style of linguistic act to the requirements of the situation by implementing some forms of polite behaviour [2,12,21]. There exists also a system that models the closeness in relations by the use of adequate messages [7]. Also other forms of communication like posture and gaze are used by some agents in interpersonal relations [3]. Surprisingly, the facial behaviour was rarely considered in this context. Among others Prendinger et al. modelled "social role awareness" in animated agents [16]. They introduced a set of procedures called "social filter programs". These procedures are a kind of rules for facial expression management. Defining social filter programs Prendinger et al. considered both social conventions (politeness) and personalities of interlocutors. The social filter program defines the intensity of an expression as the function of a social threat (power and distance), user personality (agreeableness, extroversion), and the intensity of emotion. As a result, it can either increase, decrease the intensity of facial expression, or even totally inhibit it.

The agent called Reflexive Agent [8] is also able to adapt its expressions of emotions according to the situational context. This agent analyses various factors in order to decide about either displaying or not its emotional state: emotional nature factors (i.e. valence, social acceptance, emotion of the addressee) and scenario factors (i.e. personality, goals, type of relationship, type of interaction). In particular the Reflexive Agent uses *regulation rules* that define for which values of these factors the concrete emotion can (or cannot) be displayed [8]. Although many factors that are related to the management of facial displays are considered in this model, it allows to apply only one type of complex facial expressions i.e. inhibition.

The solutions presented above do not allow human users to perceive the difference between different facial expressions; e.g. they do not allow distinguishing between spontaneous and fake smiles. As a consequence these applications deprive facial expressions of their communicative role. Instead we aim at building an agent that will modify the facial expressions depending on the relation it has with the interlocutors. These changes need to be perceivable and interpretable by human interlocutors.

3   Politeness Strategies

Brown and Levinson proposed a computational model of politeness in language [5]. According to this theory, any linguistic act like request or promise can threaten the "face" of the speaker and/or hearer. Politeness consists in taking remedial actions to counterbalance the negative consequences of these face threatening acts.

Brown and Levinson proposed the classification of all actions that prevent face threatening. They defined five different strategies of politeness: bald, positive and negative politeness, off-record, and "don't do the action". These strategies are ordered according to the impact they have on avoiding threatening situations. The fist one - bald strategy - does nothing to minimize threats to the face, while the fifth one - "don't do the action" - allows the speaker to surely avoid threatening the face but, at the same time, it precludes the communication of his intentions.

The decision about strategy to be used depends on the level of threat of an action (FTA). Brown and Levinson proposed to estimate FTA of an action by using three variables: the social distance, the power relation, and the absolute ranking of imposition of an action. Social distance refers to the degree of intimacy and the strength of the relation, while social power expresses the difference in status and the ability to influence others. The last parameter depends on the objective importance of an action in a specific culture or situation. It can be the cost in terms of services, time or goods. FTA value is calculated as the sum of these three values. Finally, the more antagonistic a given act is (higher FTA value), the more likely a high ordered strategy is to be chosen [5].

4 Video-Corpus

Our model of facial expressions is mostly based on the results of annotation of a video-corpus. For this purpose we decided to re-use the approach proposed by Rehm and André [18]. They analysed the relationship between different types of gestures and politeness strategies in verbal acts. They built a video-corpus called SEMMEL that contains various examples of verbal and nonverbal behaviour during face threatening interactions. They found that nonverbal behaviour is indeed related to politeness strategies. However, the facial expressions had not been considered. Inspired by the encouraging results of Rehm and André's experiment, we decided to analyse the SEMMEL video-corpus in order to find relations between politeness strategies and facial behaviour.

4.1 Annotation Scheme and Results

We used 21 videos with eight different protagonists. The overall duration of the analysed clips is 6 minutes and 28 seconds. In this study we used the original annotation of politeness strategies proposed by Rehm and André (strategy.basic track). They considered four politeness strategies: bald, positive politeness, negative politeness, and off-record strategy [18]. In our study the facial expressions (and corresponding emotional states) were annotated by a native speaker annotator. In our annotation scheme we considered four types of facial expressions: expression of the true emotional state, inhibited, masked, and fake expression. Because of a relatively small number of examples analysed so far we decided to consider only one feature of an emotional state: i.e. valence. Thus we distinguished between positive, negative emotions, and a neutral state. As a consequence, we did not consider separate emotional states and expressions corresponding to them, but some *patterns* of facial behaviour. For example, a

Table 1. The occurrence of different patterns of facial expressions

Pattern	Strategy				All
	bald	positive	negative	off-record	
negative masked	0	0	1	4	5
negative inhibited	0	0	1	2	3
negative expressed	0	2	0	2	4
fake negative	0	0	0	0	0
neutral expression	4	8	34	7	53
fake positive	0	5	16	6	27
positive masked	0	0	0	0	0
positive inhibited	0	0	2	0	2
positive expressed	2	3	1	2	8
All	6	18	55	23	102

pattern called "positive masked" describes any facial expression that occurs in a situation in which any positive emotion is masked by another one. The following patterns of facial expressions were considered in the annotation process: negative masked, negative inhibited, negative expressed, fake negative, neutral expression, fake positive, positive masked, positive inhibited, positive expressed. We analysed the frequency of the occurrence of each of them. The detailed results of our annotation are presented in Table 1. We can see that different types of facial expressions are not evenly distributed along different strategies of politeness. Some expressions are more often used with one type of politeness behaviour and other with another one. The "neutral expression" pattern was the most often observed (52% of all cases) and "fake positive" pattern was observed in 26.5%. Some patterns were not observed at all. None of "positive masked" expressions or "fake negative" expressions was annotated. We use this information to build our model of facial behaviour in interpersonal relations.

5   Facial Expression Management Model

In this section we explain how our embodied agent adapts its expressive behaviour to the situation. In more detail, basing on the results of annotation study presented in the previous section we establish a set of rules that models relations between different types facial expressions and the social context. In particular for each strategy of politeness we established the most characteristic pattern of facial expression according to the annotation results. The pairs (politeness strategy, pattern of facial expressions) were used to define the rules that our agent will apply in order to modify its facial behaviour.

5.1   Variables

Different sources show that two variables, social distance (SD), social power (SP), are important factors that describe interpersonal relations. According to

[22] all personality traits relevant to social interaction can be located in two dimensional space defined by the orthogonal axes of dominance and affiliation. So two variables: dominance (corresponding to SP) and affiliation (corresponding to SD) are sufficient to describe interpersonal relations. Moreover Brown and Levinson include SP and SD in their theory of politeness (see section 3). Power (SP) and social distance (SD) are two factors that influence human expressions according to various studies about facial behaviour [6,13,20].

Facial behaviour management is also conditioned by emotional factors. In particular, facial behaviour depends on the valence (Val) of emotion [6,14]. Negative emotions are more often masked or inhibited, while positive emotions are often pretended.

Thus, in our model, we consider three variables to encompass the characteristics of interaction and features of emotional state of the displayer, namely: social distance (SD), social power (SP), and valence of emotion (Val).

5.2   Rules

We consider three different emotional states: negative, positive, and neutral emotional state. For each of them we looked for the pattern of facial behaviour that corresponds the best to each politeness strategy. The choice is based on the frequency of the co-occurrence of strategy j and pattern i in the annotated video clips (see Table 1). In more details, for each strategy of politeness j (j=1..4) and the emotional state k (k=1..3) we choose the pattern i (i=1..10) such that the value a(i,j,k):

$$a(i, j, k) = \frac{x_{ijk}}{\sum_{z=1}^{4} x_{izk}}$$

is maximal (the value x_{ijk} expresses the co-occurrence of i-th pattern of a facial behaviour and the strategy j in the emotional situation k). In the situations in which the data gathered in the annotation study was insufficient to make a choice, we used also the conclusions from other experiments [6,13,14]. In Table 2 we can see which pattern of facial expression i will be used for each type of emotion (positive, neutral, negative) and strategy of politeness.

Table 2. Facial behaviour and strategies of politeness

face threat	bald	positive	negative	off-record
positive emotion	positive expressed	positive expressed	positive inhibited	positive expressed
neutral state	neutral expressed	fake positive	neutral expressed	fake positive
negative emotion	negative expressed	negative expressed	negative inhibited	negative masked

5.3   Processing

The values of social power (SP) and distance (SD) and the label of an emotional state E_i are the inputs of our model. SP and SD take values from the interval $[0,1]$. The emotional state is described by an emotional label from a finite set of labels. This set contains emotions whose expressions can be displayed by the agent. The label that identifies the neutral state is also considered as a valid input. The valence $Val(E_i)$ of an emotion E_i can be found using any dimensional model of emotions. We use the data proposed in [1]. In our model any emotional state can be either positive or negative (the neutral category concerns only the neutral state).

Brown and Levinson introduced the concept of the level of threat of a linguistic act (FTA). This value is used to choose between different politeness strategies (see section 3). Let w be a variable that is a counterpart of the FTA in our model. We establish this value as the difference: $w = SD - SP$ which takes values in the interval $[-1,1]$. We use w to choose the pattern of facial behaviour. Following the approach proposed by Walker et al. [21] we define for each strategy an interval of acceptable values. For this purpose we split the interval of all possible values of w into four equal parts: $w \in [-1, -0.5]$ (very low) is associated with the bald strategy, $w \in (-0.5, 0]$ with positive politeness, $w \in (0, 0.5]$ with negative politeness, while $w \in (0.5, 1]$ (very high) with the off-record strategy. Finally our facial management rules are of the type: *if Val(E_i) is {positive | negative | zero} and w is {very low | low | high | very high} then the expression of E_i is {expressed | fake | inhibited | masked}*.

Using Table 2 we decide on the facial expression pattern of an emotion E_i. In the case of negative masked or fake positive pattern we use the expression of fake joy or masked joy. Finally, for any emotional state E_i, values of social distance SD and of social power SP, by using our rules, we can generate an adequate facial expression using an approach presented in [4].

6   Evaluation

Our experiment consists in checking whether subjects are able to guess the social context of the situation from the facial expressions displayed by the agent. We aim at verifying if the agent that follows our rules of facial behaviour management behaves in accordance with human expectations. As a result we expect that our subjects are aware of certain rules of facial behaviour in interpersonal relations and that these rules are concordant with the rules of our model.

6.1   Scenario Set-Up

Our evaluation study consists in showing subjects a set of animations that we generated using the Greta agent [4] and a model of complex facial expressions [15]. Each of them presents the same sequence of events. The verbal content is identical and animations can be distinguished only by the facial behaviour of the agent. Our intention is to demonstrate that facial behaviour is different in different social contexts. The subjects were also told a short story with different versions whose variations correspond to situations of different interpersonal relations. Subjects' task was to match each animation to one story variation.

Scenario. For the purpose of the experiment we prepared a short scenario that was presented to the participants at the beginning of the experiment. Our scenario describes a sequence of events that happens at an airport departure lounge. Two persons are playing cards. During the game different events take place. One person, we called her the protagonist, wins the first turn, but then she discovers that her opponent is cheating, finally she looses another turn. The sequence of events is favourable for diversification of emotional reactions. The protagonist of the events is played by the Greta agent. Her opponent is not visible to the subject. Three different types of relations are considered in three variations of the story presented to the subjects: interaction with a friend (A), interaction with a stranger (B), and interaction with a superior (C). These cases were chosen in order to emphasise the differences between different types of interpersonal relations. The first situation illustrates relations between two persons that are close to each other. The second situation is a typical example of a relation in which the social distance is high (Greta interacts with a stranger). Finally, in the last case our intention was to model a situation of submission. The distance is high and the opponent has a power over the displayer. We assume that these relations are constant during the interaction i.e. the values of power and distance do not change.

Animations. For the purpose of the experiment we generated five different animations. Three of them correspond to different politeness strategies (positive politeness, negative politeness, and off-record in turn, see Table 2). The animations used in the experiment were constructed as follow:

- Animation A1 - corresponds to low social distance and low or neutral power (negative and positive expressions are expressed freely, the fake joy is used instead of the neutral expression);
- Animation A2 - corresponds to high social distance and neutral power (positive expressions are inhibited, while negative ones are masked);
- Animation A3 - corresponds to high social distance and high dominance of the observer over the displayer (negative expressions are masked, positive expressions are displayed, fake joy is used instead of the neutral expression);
- Animation A4 - negative expressions are masked by happiness, fake expression of sadness is used;
- Animation A5 - negative expressions are expressed freely, fake expression of anger is used, happiness is masked by anger.

Animations A1-A5 differ only in facial behaviour. The agent's utterances do not change between animations, even if in the real-life verbal communication is usually modified according to the values of power and distance (see section 3). In this experiment we aimed at measuring the effect of facial expressions only, thus we had to avoid the influence that different verbal messages might have on the subjects' evaluation. For this purpose we decided to use "neutral-style" utterances, which are identical for all animations. The subjects were informed about this fact before the experiment. In Figure 1 some examples that illustrate the variety of facial reactions displayed by the agent at the same instant in different animations are presented. In particular, the first row includes the reactions of the agent when she discovers the dishonesty of her opponent, while in the second row we can see the agent's reactions when loosing a turn.

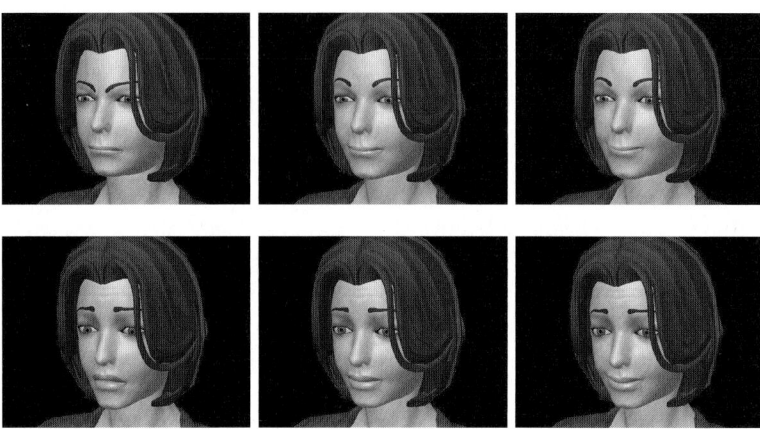

Fig. 1. Examples of different facial expressions displayed by the agent at the same instant in different animations

6.2   Procedure

20 persons (8 men and 12 women) participated in the experiment. The animations were presented in a random order. Firstly, the participants watched all the animations. They could also re-view them if they found it necessary. After seeing all animations they matched each video with one of the situations A), B), or C). The same animation could not be attributed to more than one situation. It means that two animations had to be rejected. After the session participants were also asked to justify their choices.

6.3   Results

In order to evaluate our algorithm we established the frequency of occurrence of the expected answers among the subjects' answers. Let us enumerate the expected matchings in our test:

- ANS1 - The animation A1 is attributed to the situation A,
- ANS2 - The animation A2 is attributed to the situation B,
- ANS3 - The animation A3 is attributed to the situation C.

First, we have counted the number of completely right answers. Six out of twenty participants (30%) identified all three animations correctly (i.e. ANS1–ANS3 were satisfied). The number of persons whose answers were all incorrect was,

Table 3. Matrix of confusions of subjects' answers (subjects' answers are in columns)

	A1	A2	A3	Other	Accuracy
A1	11	4	0	5	55%
A2	1	9	2	8	45%
A3	5	0	12	3	60%
Other	4	7	6	23	58%

however, similar (25%). Then we measured the number of persons who gave the majority of responses correctly. Thus, in this condition it was sufficient that at least two answers from three satisfy ANS1 – ANS3. As a result the majority of participants (55%) answered the majority of responses correctly. Finally, we also measured the number of good responses in general. ANS3 was recognized the most while ANS2 was the less one. Table 3 presents the number of good responses and the confusion matrix for each answer.

6.4   Discussion

The aim of this experiment was to verify the rules of facial behaviour management model. The overall tendency observed was concordant with our expectations as there were more correct answers than incorrect ones. The accuracy of answers exceeded significantly the chance level in all cases. The majority of subjects answered in most cases in accordance with our rules. At the same time, the probability of accidental good matchings was small. Moreover, in all cases the predicted answers occurred more often than any other answer. It means that matchings ANS1 – ANS3 were in general confirmed by our subjects. On the other hand, many persons provided answers different from our expectations. In particular, the percentage of the participants that answered all questions differently to our expectations is relatively high.

7   Conclusion

In this paper we described an architecture that uses facial expressions in order to express interpersonal relations of an ECA. The agent is able to mask, hide or even simulate the expression of its emotions taking into account the social context. Its facial expressions reflect the management of the display of its emotions. We presented also the evaluation study of our model of facial behaviour in interpersonal relations. We studied if subjects were able to guess the social context from the facial expressions generated by our model. The results indicate that our rules are plausible for subjects, at least from the European culture.

In future we plan to consider the inter-cultural differences, other types of facial expressions (like suppression or exaggeration), as well as other factors which influence the facial behaviour in interpersonal relations. So far, for sake of simplicity, we have considered neither the personality of displayer, the circumstances of interaction (see [19,11]) nor the features of the emotional state of a displayer other than valence (e.g., the intensity and the dominance value). For instance, in our model, as sadness and anger have the same valence, the expression of sadness is processed in the same way as the expression of anger. We believe that all these elements need to be integrated in order to create a more reliable and socially competent embodied agent.

Acknowledgement. We are very grateful to Elisabetta Bevacqua and Maurizio Mancini for implementing the Greta system. Part of this research is supported by the EU FP6 Network of Excellence HUMAINE (IST-2002-2.3.1.6) and by the EU FP6 Integrated Project Callas (FP6-2005-IST-5).

References

1. Albrecht, I., Schröder, M., Haber, J., Seidel, H.: Mixed feelings: expression of non-basic emotions in a muscle-based talking head. Virtual Reality 8(4), 201–212 (2005)
2. André, E., Rehm, M., Minker, W., Buhler, D.: Endowing spoken language dialogue systems with emotional intelligence. In: André, E., Dybkjaer, L., Minker, W., Heisterkamp, P. (eds.) Affective Dialogue Systems, pp. 178–187. Springer, Heidelberg (2004)
3. Ballin, D., Gillies, M.F., Crabtree, I.B.: A framework for interpersonal attitude and non-verbal communication in improvisational visual media production, First European Conference on Visual Media Production (CVMP), pp. 203–210 (2004)
4. Bevacqua, E., Mancini, M., Niewiadomski, R., Pelachaud, C.: An expressive ECA showing complex emotions. In: Proceedings of the AISB Annual Convention, Newcastle, UK, pp. 208–216 (2007)
5. Brown, P., Levinson, S.C.: Politeness: some universals on language usage. Cambridge University Press, Cambridge (1987)
6. Buck, R., Losow, J., Murphy, M., Costanzo, P.: Social facilitation and inhibition of emotional expression and communication. Journal of Personality and Social Psychology 63(6), 962–968 (1992)
7. Cassell, J., Bickmore, T.: Negotiated Collusion. Modeling Social Language and its Relationship Effects in Intelligent Agents 13(1-2), 89–132 (2003)
8. De Carolis, B., Pelachaud, C., Poggi, I., De Rosis, F.: Behavior Planning for a Reflexive Agent. In: Proceedings of IJCAI 2001, Oporto, Portugal (April 2001)
9. Ekman, P., Friesen, W.V.: The Repertoire of Nonverbal Behavior's: Categories, Origins, Usage and Coding. Semiotica 1, 49–98 (1969)
10. Goleman, D.: Inteligencja Emocjonalna, Media Rodzina, Poznan (1997)
11. Gross, J.J., Oliver, P., Richards, J.M.: The Dissociation of Emotion Expression from Emotion Experience. a Personality Perspective, Personality and Social Psychology Bulletin 26(6), 712–726 (2000)
12. Johnson, W.L., Rizzo, P., Bosma, W., Kole, S., Ghijsen, M., van Welbergen, H.: Generating Socially Appropriate Tutorial Dialog, ISCA Workshop on Affective Dialogue Systems, pp. 254–264 (2004)
13. La France, M., Hecht, M.A.: Option or Obligation to Smile: The Effects of Power and Gender and Facial Expression. In: Philippot, P., Feldman, R.S., Coats, E.J. (eds.) The Social Context of Nonverbal Behavior (Studies in Emotion and Social Interaction), Cambridge University Press, pp. 45–70. Cambridge University Press, Cambridge (2005)

14. Manstead, A.S.R., Fischer, A.H., Jakobs, E.B.: The Social and Emotional Functions of Facial Displays. In: Philippot, P., Feldman, R.S., Coats, E.J. (eds.) The Social Context of Nonverbal Behavior (Studies in Emotion and Social Interaction), pp. 287–316. Cambridge University Press, Cambridge (2005)

15. Niewiadomski, R.: A model of complex facial expressions in interpersonal relations for animated agents, Ph.D. dissertation, University of Perugia (2007)

16. Prendinger, H., Ishizuka, M.: Social role awareness in animated agents. In: Proceedings of the fifth international conference on Autonomous agents, Montreal, Quebec, Canada, pp. 270–277 (2001)

17. Reeves, B., Nass, C.: The media equation: how people treat computers, television, and new media like real people and places. Cambridge University Press, Cambridge (1996)

18. Rehm, M., André, E.: Informing the Design of Embodied Conversational Agents by Analysing Multimodal Politeness Behaviors in Human-Human Communication, Workshop on Conversational Informatics for Supporting Social Intelligence and Interaction (2005)

19. Wagner, H., Lee, V.: Facial Behavior Alone and in the Presence of Others. In: Philippot, P., Feldman, R.S., Coats, E.J. (eds.) The Social Context of Nonverbal Behavior (Studies in Emotion and Social Interaction), pp. 262–286. Cambridge University Press, Cambridge (2005)

20. Wagner, H.L., Smith, J.: Facial expression in the presence of friends and strangers. Journal of Nonverbal Behavior 15(4), 201–214 (1991)

21. Walker, M., Cahn, J., Whittaker, S.: Linguistic style improvisation for lifelike computer characters. In: Proceedings of the AAAI Workshop on AI, Alife and Entertainment (1996)

22. Wiggins, J.S., Trapnell, P., Phillips, N.: Psychometric and geometric characteristics of the Revised Interpersonal Adjective Scales (IAS-R). Multivariate Behavioral Research 23(3), 517–530 (1988)

Facial Expression Synthesis Using PAD Emotional Parameters for a Chinese Expressive Avatar

Shen Zhang[1,2], Zhiyong Wu[2], Helen M. Meng[2], and Lianhong Cai[1]

[1] Department of Computer Science and Technology
Tsinghua University, 100084 Beijing, China
[2] Department of Systems Engineering and Engineering Management
The Chinese University of Hong Kong, HKSAR, China
zhangshen05@mails.tsinghua.edu.cn, john.zy.wu@gmail.com
hmmeng@se.cuhk.edu.hk, clh-dcs@tsinghua.edu.cn

Abstract. Facial expression plays an important role in face to face communication in that it conveys nonverbal information and emotional intent beyond speech. In this paper, an approach for facial expression synthesis with an expressive Chinese talking avatar is proposed, where a layered parametric framework is designed to synthesize intermediate facial expressions using PAD emotional parameters [5], which describe the human emotional state with three nearly orthogonal dimensions. Partial Expression Parameter (PEP) is proposed to depict the facial expression movements in specific face regions, which act as the mid-level expression parameters between the low-level Facial Animation Parameters (FAPs) [11] and the high-level PAD emotional parameters. A pseudo facial expression database is established by cloning the real human expression to avatar and the corresponding emotion states for each expression is annotated using PAD score. An emotion-expression mapping model is trained on the database to map the emotion state (PAD) into facial expression configuration (PEP). Perceptual evaluation shows the input PAD value is consistent with that of human perception on synthetic expression, which supports the effectiveness of our approach.

Keywords: Facial expression, PAD emotional model, partial expression parameter, talking avatar.

1 Introduction

Facial expression is one of the most common and effective way for human to express emotions, and it plays a crucial role in face to face communication in that it can convey non-verbal information and intended emotion beyond speech. For expressive visual speech synthesis [1], the facial expression together with head movement is referred as visual prosody [2]. Our long-term plan is to create a Chinese expressive talking avatar for text-to-audio-visual-speech (TTAVS) synthesis [1], which leads to two questions: First, how should the emotional state be described? Second, what is the relationship between inner emotion and facial expression? Previous research on facial expression [1,3,8] are usually limited to six basic emotion categories (i.e. happy, sad, surprise, angry, disgust and fear). However, according to Mehrabian's theory [5], human emotion is not limited to

A. Paiva, R. Prada, and R.W. Picard (Eds.): ACII 2007, LNCS 4738, pp. 24–35, 2007.
© Springer-Verlag Berlin Heidelberg 2007

isolated categories but can be described along three nearly rthogonal dimensions: pleasure-displeasure (P), arousal-nonarousal (A) and dominance-submissiveness (D), namely the PAD emotional model which is proven to be appropriate in describing universal emotions. Ruttkay et al.[6] have proposed the *"Emotion Disc"* and *"Emotion Square"* to generate continuum of facial expression with 2-dimensional navigation. Albrecht et al. [12] have extended the work of MPEG-4 based facial expression synthesis [13], and designed a method to generate mixed expressions, where a two dimension *"Activation-Evaluation"* emotion space is adopted. Kshirsagar et al. [14] have proposed a multi-layered approach including high-level description of emotion intensity over time, mid-level configuration of static facial expressions, and low-level FAPs definitions. However, there are few quantitative results on explicit mapping between emotion dimension such as PAD, and low-level facial expression parameters such as MPEG-4 FAPs [11].

In this paper, a layered framework is proposed to synthesize facial expression using PAD emotional parameters for a Chinese expressive talking avatar. The PAD parameters are adopted as high-level description of emotion state. The MPEG-4 Facial Animation Parameters (FAPs) [11] are used for direct control of mesh deformation on avatar. Different with Kshirsagar's mid-level FAPs configuration of static expression [14], the Partial Expression Parameters (PEPs), which model the correlations among FAPs within local face region, are proposed as mid-level expression parameters to depict common expression movements, such as eyebrow-raise, mouth-open etc. The PAD-PEP mapping model and PEP-FAP translation model are then established for converting high-level PAD emotional parameters to mid-level PEP parameters and then to low-level FAP parameters.

The rest of this paper is as follows. Section 2 introduces the overall architecture of the layered framework for facial expression synthesis. Detailed information about Partial Expression Parameter (PEPs) and the PEP-FAP translation model are presented in section 3. Section 4 introduces the creation of a pseudo facial expression database on three-dimensional avatar. Section 5 presents the design of emotion-expression mapping function that models the correlation between PAD and PEP. The synthetic result and perceptual evaluation is discussed in Section 6. Finally we conclude our work and discuss the future direction.

2   Layered Framework for Facial Expression Synthesis

For geometric facial animation on 3D avatar, we adopt the Facial Animation Parameters (FAPs) provided by MPEG-4 standard [11]. FAP is designed to control the face model points to generate various facial movements. However, it is too complicated for expression synthesizer to manipulate the FAPs directly since they only define the motions (e.g. translations and rotations) of single feature points on the avatar, while ignore the high correlations between different FAPs within the same face region. This motivates us to propose a new parameter to capture the FAP correlations. Based on our previous work on FAP-driven facial expression synthesis [1,9], we propose the Partial Expression Parameters (PEPs) to depict the common expression movement within specific face regions, such as mouth-bent, eye-open and eyebrow-raise etc. The PEPs capture the correlation among different FAPs, and thus reduces the complexity of FAP-driven expression synthesis [1].

With PAD as high-level emotion description, PEP as mid-level expression configuration and FAP as low-level animation parameter, a layered framework for PAD-driven facial expression synthesis is proposed as shown in Figure 1, where the PAD-PEP mapping model is trained on a pseudo facial expression database with PAD and PEP annotations, and the PEP-FAP translation model is defined experimentally using a home-grown expression editor [9].

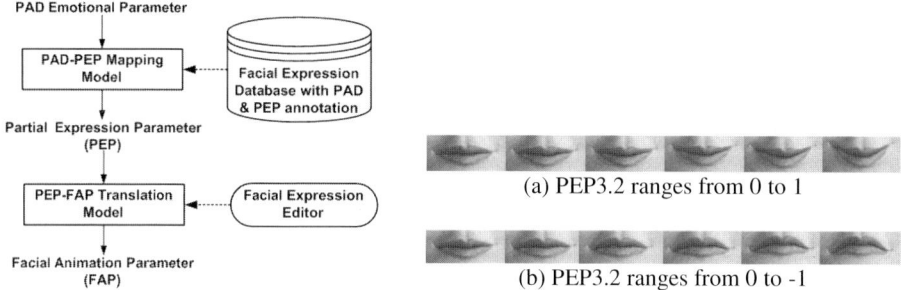

(a) PEP3.2 ranges from 0 to 1

(b) PEP3.2 ranges from 0 to -1

Fig. 1. Layered framework for PAD-driven facial expression synthesis

Fig. 2. Partial expression movement of mouth-bent with PEP 3.2 ranging in [-1, 1]

3   PEP-FAP Translation Model

3.1   Partial Expression Parameter (PEP)

The PEPs are designed to capture the correlation among FAPs in specific face region for facial expression synthesis. The selection of each PEP features is based on our observation of Japanese Female Facial Expression (JAFFE) database [8] as well as our previous work on FAPs manipulation [1,9]. Detailed partial expression description for PEP can be found in Table 1. The value of the PEP is a scalar ranging in [-1, 1] to simulate the continuous facial expression change. For better understanding, the partial expression movement of *mouth-bent* (PEP 3.2) is illustrated in Figure 2 with its value ranging from -1 to +1.

3.2   PEP-FAP Translation Template

Previous research on FAPs correlation [7] indicates that there are high correlations among different FAPs, and this cross-correlation property has been successfully exploited to interpolate the unknown FAP value from a set of decided FAPs. This motivates us to implement the linear PEP-FAP translation templates experimentally. For each PEP parameter, we define its associated FAP group and key-FAP as shown in Table 2. The mathematical form of the linear PEP-FAP translation template is then defined in Equation 1. For the i-th PEP parameter in region R (P_i^R), the FAP that best represents the corresponding partial expression movement is selected as the key-FAP (F_k) The value of key-FAP is determined by (P_i^R) directly. The value of non-key FAP (F_j) is linear correlated with the key-FAP (F_k) with the coefficient α_k^j The F_k^{max} is the maximum value of F_k. F_k^{max} and α_k^j are experimentally defined using a home-grown facial expression editor [9].

$$\begin{cases} F_k = P_i^R \cdot F_k^{max} & (P_i^R \in [-1,+1]) \\ F_j = \alpha_k^j \cdot F_k & (\alpha_k^j \in [-1,+1], \ k \neq j) \end{cases} \qquad (1)$$

Table 1. PEP definition with partial expression description

Face Region	PEP code (Left/Right)	Partial Expression Description	
		[0,-1]	[0,1]
Eye-brow	1.1(L/R)	Eyebrow lower down	Eyebrow raise up
	1.2(L/R)	Relax Eyebrow	Squeeze Eyebrow
	1.3(L/R)	In the shape of "\ /"	In the shape of "/ \"
Eye	2.1(L/R)	Close eye-lid	Open eye-lid
	2.2(L/R)	(Eyeball) look right	(Eyeball) look left
	2.3(L/R)	(Eyeball) look up	(Eyeball) look down
Mouth	3.1	Close mouth	Open mouth
	3.2	Mouth-corner bent down	Mouth-corner bent up
	3.3	Mouth sipped	Mouth protruded (pout)
	3.4	Mouth stretched in	Mouth stretched out
Jaw	4.1	Jaw move up	Jaw lower down
	4.2	Jaw move right	Jaw move left

Table 2. Related FAP group and key FAP for each PEP parameter

Face Region	PEP Code	FAP Number	Key FAP	Related FAP Group
	1.1	6	F33	[F33,F31,F35,F34,F32,F36]
Eye-brow	1.2	2	F37	[F37,F38]
	1.3	6	F31	[F31,F35, F33, F32, F36, F34]
	2.1	4	F19	[F19,F21,F20,F22]
Eye	2.2	2	F23	[F23,F24]
	2.3	2	F25	[F25,F26]
	3.1	12	F5	[F5,F10,F11,F52,F57,F58, F4,F8,F9,F51,F55,F56]
Mouth	3.2	4	F12	[F12,F13,F59,F60]
	3.3	2	F16	[F16,F17]
	3.4	4	F6	[F6,F7,F53,F54]
Jaw	4.1	1	F3	[F3]
	4.2	1	F15	[F15]

4   Pseudo Facial Expression Database on Avatar

In order to capture the relationship between PAD emotional parameters and PEP parameters, a pseudo facial expression database is created. Here, the "*pseudo*" indicates that the database is not realistic human expression but the cartoon-like expression on the avatar as shown in Figure 3. We choose the Japanese Female Facial Expression (JAFFE) database [8] as reference to build up our pseudo database.

4.1 JAFFE Expression Database

The JAFFE expression database contains 213 expression images with 10 Japanese females posing three or four examples for each of seven basic expressions, *Neutral*, *Happy*, *Sad*, *Surprise*, *Angry*, *Disgust* and *Fear*. For each image we annotated 18 facial points manually according to MPEG-4 facial definition points (FDPs) [11] as shown in Figure 4(a) and 4(b). These facial points are then used to extract the PEP parameters for creating the pseudo facial expression database on avatar.

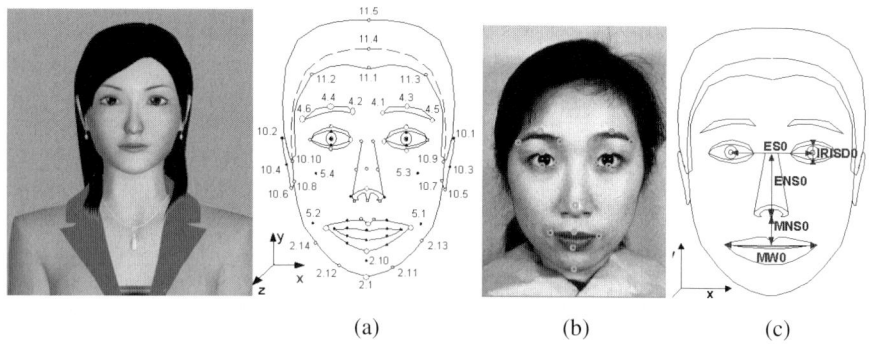

(a)   (b)   (c)

Fig. 3. Avatar front view   **Fig. 4.** Annotated facial points (b), FDPs (a) and FAPU (c)

4.2 PEP Extraction for Pseudo Facial Expression Database

Based on the above facial points annotation result, 12 PEP parameters are then extracted by measuring the movement of facial points as defined in Table 3. The other 6 PEPs are not extracted because the depth information is lacked (PEP 2.2 and 2.3 for

Table 3. PEP measurement by facial point movement

Face Region	PEP code	PEP Measurement	Units (FAPU)
Eye-brow	1.1(L/R)	4.3.y(L) and 4.4.y(R)	ENS
	1.2(L/R)	4.1.x(L) and 4.2.x(R)	ES
	1.3(L/R)	atan(|4.1.y-4.5.y|/|4.1.x-4.5.x|) (L) atan(|4.2.y-4.6.y|/|4.2.x-4.6.x|) (R)	AU
Eye	2.1(L/R)	|3.9.y-3.13.y| (L) |3.10.y-3.14.y| (R)	IRISD
	2.2(L/R)	Not-extracted	AU
	2.3(L/R)	Not-extracted	AU
Mouth	3.1	|8.1.y-8.2.y|	MNS
	3.2	|(8.3.y+8.4.y)/2-(8.1.y+8.2.y)/2|	MNS
	3.3	Not-extracted	MNS
	3.4	|8.3.x-8.4.x|	MW
Jaw	4.1	2.1.y	MNS
	4.2	2.1.x (Not-extracted)	MW

Table 4. Sample number of 7 expressions (labels in the first row) in each PEP clustering center (C_i in the first column)

	HAP	SUP	ANG	NEU	SAD	FEAR	DIS	Total
C1	**25**	1	2	0	1	0	0	29
C2	4	**20**	1	0	0	3	1	29
C3	2	0	**18**	0	9	4	*12*	45
C4	0	6	1	**30**	0	0	0	37
C5	0	0	0	0	**15**	9	2	26
C6	0	3	0	0	4	**11**	2	20
C7	0	0	8	0	2	5	**12**	27
Total	31	30	30	30	31	32	29	213

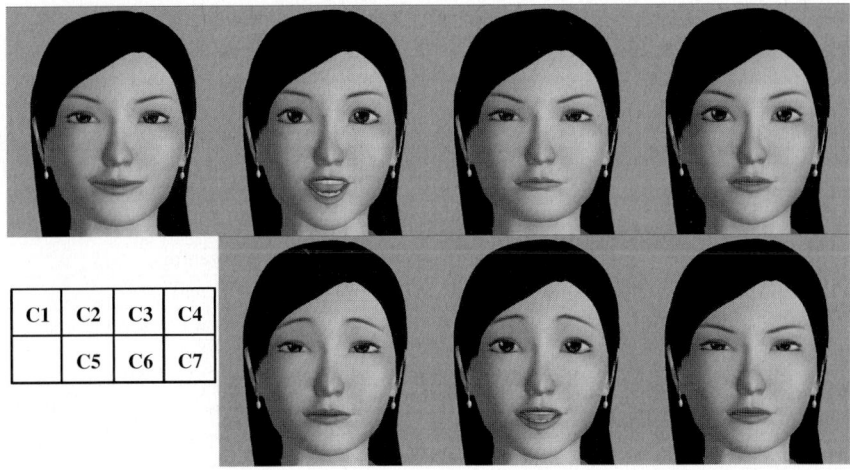

Fig. 5. Synthetic expressions for PEP value of clustering center in Table 4

eye-ball movement, PEP 3.3 for mouth movement in z-direction) or the movement is not obvious (PEP 4.2 for horizontal jaw movement) in the database. The FAPU shown in Figure 4(c) is utilized to normalize the extracted PEP to eliminate the individual difference caused by face shape of different subjects. By applying the extracted PEP on avatar, we create the pseudo expression database which has similar synthetic expressions as JAFFE.

A *k-means clustering* experiment is then conducted on the pseudo database to check the validation of the cloned facial expressions. The clustering result is presented in Table 4, which states the number of seven intended expression in each PEP clustering group. The synthetic expression of each clustering center is illustrated in Figure 5. According to the clustering result, the extracted PEP can distinguish the basic expressions to some extent in that the PEP configuration for the same expression will nearly be clustered into the same group with the exception of *Angry* and *Disgust*. This may be understandable because that some commonalities of facial movements are shared for *Angry* and *Disgust* as reported in [1], which causes the current PEP features cannot completely distinguish the two expressions.

5 PAD-PEP Mapping Model

5.1 PAD Annotation for Pseudo Expression Database

As the layered framework for PAD-driven facial expression synthesis in section 2 proposed, the PAD-PEP mapping model is learned from a facial expression database with PAD and PEP annotation. The above pseudo facial expression database already contains the PEP values, thus the PAD values for each synthetic expression in the pseudo database need to be annotated for training the PAD-PEP mapping model.

Based on the PAD model proposed by Mehrabian [5], the Chinese version of abbreviated PAD emotion scales is provided [4] so that the P, A and D values can be evaluated by a 12-item questionnaire as shown in Table 5. The abbreviated PAD scale has been proved as a versatile psychological measuring instrument which is capable of adapting to a variety of applications including emotion annotation.

Table 5. 12-item PAD questionnaire for expression annotation and evaluation

Emotion		-4	-3	-2	-1	0	1	2	3	4	Emotion	
Angry	(愤怒的)										Activated	(有活力的)
Wide-	(清醒的)										Sleepy	(困倦的)
Controlled	(被控的)										Controlling	(主控的)
Friendly	(友好的)										Scornful	(轻蔑的)
Calm	(平静的)										Excited	(激动的)
Dominant	(支配的)										Submissive	(顺从的)
Cruel	(残忍的)										Joyful	(高兴的)
Interested	(感兴趣的)										Relaxed	(放松的)
Guided	(被引导的)										Autonomous	(自主的)
Excited	(兴奋的)										Enraged	(激怒的)
Relaxed	(放松的)										Hopeful	(充满希望
Influential	(有影响力)										Influenced	(被影响的)

For each synthetic expression image in the pseudo expression database, we annotate the P, A and D value using the 12-item questionnaire. During annotation, the annotator is required to describe the synthetic expression using 12 pairs of emotional words as given in Table 5. For each pair of the emotional words, which are just like two ends of a scale, the annotator should choose one of them that better describes the synthetic expression with a 9 level score varying from -4 to +4. The P, A and D values are then calculated from this questionnaire using the method described in [5]. Before annotating, the annotator is trained by expert of psychology on using the PAD questionnaire.

The annotation results are summarized in Table 6, with the corresponding distribution in PAD emotional space shown in Figure 7. We can see that the PAD annotations for each basic emotion category are distributed in nearly different areas with the exception of *Angry* and *Disgust*. This result is consistent with the clustering result of PEP configuration as described in section 4.2

Table 6. Average PAD annotation for the pseudo expression database

Intent	MEAN		
Emotion	P	A	D
ANG	-0.59	0.08	0.47
DIS	-0.59	-0.01	0.40
FEAR	-0.08	0.18	-0.39
HAP	0.63	0.40	0.29
NEU	0.03	-0.04	-0.07
SAD	-0.28	-0.12	-0.37
SUP	0.41	0.55	0.19

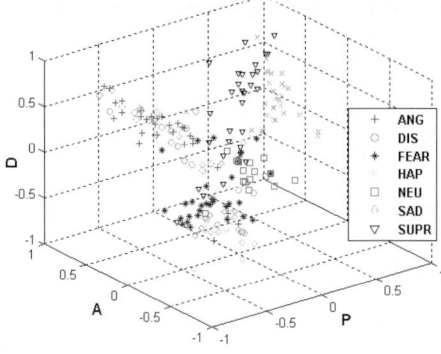

Fig. 7. Distribution of PAD annotations for the pseudo expression database

5.2 PAD-PEP Mapping Model

Different from the previous work on facial expression manipulation, our work focuses on exploring the relationship between high-level emotion description and mid-level expression configuration, in other words, our goal is to implement a mapping function to convert the PAD into PEP. The pseudo expression database containing the PAD annotation as well as PEP configuration is used to train the PAD-PEP mapping model.

In order to find a proper emotion-expression mapping function between PAD and PEP, we have tried the polynomial function with the first and second order as well as non-linear exponential function. As the experimental result reveals, it is the second order polynomial function that receive the best fitting result, and the mathematic form is shown in Equation 2.

$$PEP = \alpha \cdot E^2 + \beta \cdot E + \delta \tag{2}$$

Where **PEP** is the PEP vector of expression configuration, and **E** is the PAD vector $[P, A, D]$, E^2 is also a vector with each element the square value of its counterpart in **E** respectively, i.e. $[P^2, A^2, D^2]$, α and β are the corresponding coefficient matrix, δ is the constant offset vector. It should be noticed that, each dimension of **PEP** vector is estimated respectively with the same mathematic form as equation 3 shown. The PEP_i is the i-th dimension in **PEP** vector, and all the corresponding function coefficients are indicated with the subscript i and P-A-D dimensions.

$$PEP_i = [\alpha_{Pi}, \alpha_{Ai}, \alpha_{Di}] \begin{bmatrix} P^2 \\ A^2 \\ D^2 \end{bmatrix} + [\beta_{Pi}, \beta_{Ai}, \beta_{Di}] \begin{bmatrix} P \\ A \\ D \end{bmatrix} + \delta_i \tag{3}$$

6 Experiments

6.1 Experiments on PAD-PEP Mapping Function

The pseudo expression database consists of only 213 expression samples, which are extracted from the JAFFE database consisting of 10 subjects and 7 expressions. In order to reduce the limitation caused by the small database, we adopt the K-fold cross-validation method to train the PAD-PEP mapping function. For the test set, we select 10*2=20 expression image samples by randomly selecting 2 different expressions for all 10 subjects. The training set, which consists of the rest 193 expression image samples, is then divided into 10 subsets with each subset covering all 10 subjects and each subject with 1-2 expressions. By such division scheme, we are able to capture the common facial expression movement shared by different people as much as possible in the PAD-PEP mapping function.

The coefficients of the PAD-PEP mapping function is estimated using the least square errors method. It should be noticed that each dimension of PEP (e.g. PEP_i) is estimated separately with the same form as shown in equation 3, which means that we finally have 12 sets of coefficients corresponding to 12 PEP parameters.

Table 7. Correlation coefficients for evaluating PAD-PEP mapping function

PEP code	Validation set (k=10)			Test set
	Min	Max	Avg	
1.1L	0.56	0.88	0.77	0.74
1.1R	0.52	0.86	0.77	0.77
1.2L	0.13	0.82	0.43	0.51
1.2R	0.13	0.64	0.44	0.62
1.3L	0.63	0.89	0.79	0.80
1.3R	0.56	0.91	0.77	0.82
2.1L	0.53	0.84	0.75	0.60
2.1R	0.51	0.85	0.76	0.62
3.1	0.36	0.89	0.65	0.52
3.2	0.24	0.93	0.71	0.75
3.4	0.06	0.77	0.52	0.78
4.1	0.36	0.83	0.57	0.66
Average	0.38	0.84	0.66	0.69

In the K-fold cross-validation training process (k=10), there are 10 iterations corresponding to 10 validating subset. For each iteration, we calculate the correlation coefficients between real and estimate data on current validating subset as criteria to evaluate the fitting performance of the trained function. The minimum, maximum and average value of correlation coefficient is summarized in Table 7. The trained function with the average fitting performance among all the 10 iterations is chosen as the final result and used to evaluate the test set.

From table 7, we can see that the performance of mapping function on test set is acceptable with correlation coefficient be around 0.70. There is still some space for performance to be improved. This may be explained as that the pseudo expression database consists only 10 subjects with 7 basic expressions, which is insufficient for training the mapping function to capture common expression patterns among different people. The possible solution is either to increase the number of the subjects or to collect more expression images for a specific subject.

6.2 Synthetic Expression and Perceptual Evaluation

A series of perceptual evaluation is conducted to evaluate the performance of the layered framework for expression synthesis. The synthetic expressions for the 6 basic emotion words (*happy*, *surprise*, *sad*, *scared*, *angry*, and *disgusting*) and some other candidate emotion words with corresponding PAD value are shown in Figure 8. 14 subjects are then invited in the evaluation to finish the 12-item PAD questionnaire as shown in Table 5 for each synthetic facial expression image. Another emotion labeling experiment is also conducted where the subjects are required to select one word that best describe the synthetic expression from 14 candidate emotion words, which are *Happy*, *Optimism*, *Relax*, *Surprise*, *Mildness*, *Dependent*, *Bored*, *Sad*, *Scared*, *Anxious*, *Scornful*, *Disgusting*, *Angry*, and *Hostile*.

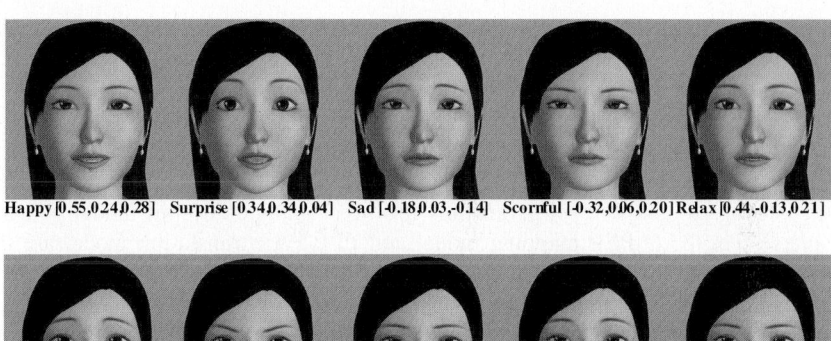

Happy [0.55,0.24,0.28]   Surprise [0.34,0.34,0.04]   Sad [-0.18,0.03,-0.14]   Scornful [-0.32,0.06,0.20] Relax [0.44,-0.13,0.21]

Scared [-0.19,0.26,-0.13] Angry [-0.40,0.22,0.12] Disgust [-0.36,0.08,0.13] Optimism [0.50,0.21,0.35] Hostile [-0.42,0.20,0.22]

Fig. 8. PAD-driven synthetic expression for selected emotions (Emotion [P,A,D])

Table 8. Result of PAD evaluation and emotion labeling. (The PAD value of *Hostile* is [-0.42, 0.20, 0.22]).

PAD-driven synthetic expression	Original PAD of emotion words			Evaluation PAD of Synthetic image			Expression Label (with voting percent)
	P	A	D	P	A	D	
Happy	0.55	0.24	0.28	0.42	0.12	0.10	Happy (67%)
Surprise	0.34	0.34	0.04	0.36	0.45	-0.05	Surprise (100%)
Sad	-0.18	0.03	-0.14	-0.01	-0.26	-0.27	Sad (42%)
Scared	-0.19	0.26	-0.13	0.01	-0.04	-0.25	Sad (50%)
Angry	-0.40	0.22	0.12	-0.17	0.02	-0.08	Hostile (58%)
Disgust	-0.36	0.08	0.13	-0.56	0.15	0.44	Disgusting (50%)

The PAD values for each basic emotion word and the PAD perception values for synthetic expression are summarized in Table 8. A voting method is applied to determine the emotion category for each synthetic facial expression image based on the result of expression labeling. The PAD correlation coefficients between emotion words and synthetic expression are 0.89(P), 0.68(A) and 0.70(D) respectively, this result is consistent with the reliability and validity of Chinese version of abbreviated PAD emotion scales reported in [4]. Confusion between *Sad* and *Scared* as well as *Angry* and *Hostile* is found in expression labeling experiment, it is because that the input PAD value for each of the two confused words are very close as shown in Table 8, which originates from the confusion in human understanding between these emotion words and thus leads to the similarity between synthetic expressions.

The experimental results indicates that the PAD emotional parameters can be used in describing the emotion state as well as facial expression; and the proposed layered framework is effective for PAD-driven facial expression synthesis.

7   Conclusion and Further Work

This paper proposes a layered framework for facial expression synthesis on a Chinese expressive avatar. The synthetic facial expression is controlled by the high-level PAD emotional parameters, namely the Pleasure-Arousal-Dominance, by which the human emotion can be described with three independent orthogonal dimensions. The mid-level Partial Expression Parameter (PEP) is proposed to depict the facial expression movement in a specific local face region. The MPEG-4 Facial Animation Parameter (FAP) is adopted as low-level parameters for direct manipulation of model points on the avatar. The PAD-PEP mapping model and PEP-FAP translation model are then implemented to translate the PAD parameters to PEP parameters and then to FAP parameters for facial expression synthesis.

The proposed approach is effective in facial expression synthesis, which enriches the avatar with emotions. Together with our previous work on expressive head movement synthesis [10], we can generate a more engaging avatar for expressive visual speech synthesis. Further work will focus on combining these works to develop a text-driven expressive talking avatar for TTAVS synthesis.

Acknowledgments. This work is supported by the research fund from the National Natural Science Foundation of China (NSFC) under grant No. 60433030 and the joint fund of NSFC-RGC (Hong Kong Governments Research Grants Council) under grant No. 60418012 and N-CUHK417/04. This work is affiliated with the Microsoft-CUHK Joint Laboratory for Human-centric Computing and Interface Technologies. We also thank Sirui Wang from Institute of Psychology, Chinese Academy of Science for providing the 14 typical emotion words and corresponding PAD values in the perceptual evaluation.

References

1. Wu, Z.Y., Zhang, S., Cai, L.H., Meng, H.M.: Real-time Synthesis of Chinese Visual Speech and Facial Expressions using MPEG-4 FAP Features in a Three-dimensional Avatar. In: Proc. Int. Conf. on Spoken Language Processing, pp. 1802–1805 (2006)
2. Graf, H.P., Cosatto, E., Strom, V., Huang, F.J.: Visual Prosody: Facial Movements Accompanying Speech. In: Fifth IEEE Int. Conf. on Automatic Face and Gesture Recognition, pp. 381–386 (2002)

3. Du, Y.Z., Lin, X.Y.: Emotional facial expression model building. Pattern Recognition Letters 24(16), 2923–2934 (2003)
4. Li, X.M., Zhou, H.T., Song, S.Z., Ran, T., Fu, X.L.: The Reliability and Validity of the Chinese Version of Abbreviated PAD Emotion Scales. In: Int. Conf. on Affective Computing and Intelligent Interaction (ACII), pp. 513–518 (2005)
5. Mehrabian, A.: Pleasure-arousal-dominance: A General Framework for Describing and Measuring Individual Differences in Temperament. Current Psychology. Developmental, Learning, Personality, Social 14, 261–292 (1996)
6. Ruttkay, Z., Noot, H., Hagen, P.: Emotion Disc and Emotion Squares: Tools to Explore the Facial Expression Space. Computer Graphics Forum 22(1), 49–53 (2003)
7. Lavagetto, F., Pockaj, R.: An Efficient Use of MPEG-4 FAP Interpolation for Facial Animation at 70 bits/Frame. IEEE Transactions on Circuits and Systems for Video Technology 11(10), 1085–1097 (2001)
8. Lyons, M., Akamatsu, S., Kamachi, M., Gyoba, J.: Coding. facial expressions with gabor wavelets. In: Proc. of the 3rd IEEE Conf. on Face and Gesture Recognition, pp. 200–205 (1998)
9. Zhang, S., Wu, Z.Y., Cai, L.H.: Region-based Facial Expression Synthesis on a Three-dimensional Avatar. In: China Conference on Human Computer Interaction(CHCI) (2006)
10. Zhang, S., Wu, Z.Y., Meng, H.M., Cai, L.H.: Head Movement Synthesis based on Semantic and Prosodic Features for a Chinese Expressive Avatar. In: IEEE Int. Conf. on Acoustics, Speech and Signal Processing (ICASSP) (2007)
11. Motion Pictures Expert Group, ISO/IEC 14496-2: 1999/Amd. 1: 2000(E). International Standard, Information Technology – Coding of Audio-Visual Objects. Part 2: Visual; Amendment 1: Visual Extensions
12. Albrecht, I., Schröder, M., Haber, J., Seidel, H.P.: Mixed feelings: expression of non-basic emotions in a muscle-based talking head. Virtual Reality 8(4), 201–212 (2005)
13. Tsapatsoulis, N., Raousaiou, A., Kollias, S., Cowie, R., Douglas-Cowie, E.: Emotion recognition and synthesis based on MPEG-4 FAPs MPEG-4 facial animation—the standard implementations applications, pp. 141–167. Wiley, Hillsdale (2002)
14. Kshirsagar, S., Escher, M., Sannier, G., M.-Thalmann, N.: Multimodal Animation System Based on the MPEG-4 Standard. In: Multimedia Modelling 99, Ottawa, Canada, pp. 215–232 (1999)

Reconstruction and Recognition of Occluded Facial Expressions Using PCA

Howard Towner and Mel Slater

Department of Computer Science, University College London
Gower Street, London, WC1E 6BT, UK

Abstract. Descriptions of three methods for reconstructing incomplete facial expressions using principal component analysis are given, projection to the model plane, single component projection and replacement by the conditional mean – the facial expressions being represented by feature points. It is established that one method gives better reconstruction accuracy than the others. This method is used on a systematic reconstruction problem, the reconstruction of occluded top and bottom halves of faces. The results indicate that occluded-top expressions can be reconstructed with little loss of expression recognition – occluded-bottom expressions are reconstructed less accurately but still give comparable performance to human rates of facial expression recognition.

1   Introduction

Facial expression is a key modality in human interaction and non-verbal communication. Facial expression can represent the internal emotional state of a person, their mental state or be used to communicate goals or intentions. Humans have evolved a capacity for controlling their own facial expressions and recognising the facial expressions of others.

Automatic facial expression analysis is a flourishing area of research in computer science. Problems that have been tackled have been the tracking of facial expression in static images and video sequences, transfer of expressions to novel faces or repurposing of a person's expression to a virtual model, and recognition of facial expression. These recognition tasks have focussed on the classification of emotional expressions[1], classification of complex mental states[2] or the automatic recognition of FACS action units[3].

A problem that is frequently encountered in each of these tasks is that of partial occlusions. Occlusions can introduce errors into the predicted expression or result in an incorrect expression being transferred to a virtual head. One type of partial occlusion is a temporary occlusion caused by a part of the face being obscured momentarily by an object or as a result of a person moving their head so that not all features of the face can be seen by a camera. Another type of occlusion is a systematic occlusion, which can be caused by a person wearing something such as a head-mounted display, which causes the features of the upper half of the face to be invisible. These types of occlusions are potentially more damaging since they result in whole features of relevance to judging facial expression being obscured.

A. Paiva, R. Prada, and R.W. Picard (Eds.): ACII 2007, LNCS 4738, pp. 36–47, 2007.
© Springer-Verlag Berlin Heidelberg 2007

2 Background

A facial expression can be represented as a set of feature points retrieved from points across that face, for example, eye, brows, mouth. Ways in which principal component analysis (PCA) can be employed with this data is to train a PCA model with multiple sets of these points, obtained when a person is making multiple expressions or from a set of people making different expressions.

A PCA model is built using a set of related training data. This PCA model can then be used on a novel example not contained in the training data, and this example can be reconstructed using a simple mathematical operation, a transpose of a matrix. This computation, however, requires that the observed example is complete and that no values are missing. The PCA model and reconstruction are robust to some small amounts of missing data and certain types of occlusions, and in these situations a configuration of observed and missing variables replaced by arbitrary values can be reconstructed accurately[4]. However, it can also be the case that missing feature points or pixels can cause widespread errors so that not only is the occluded data reconstructed incorrectly but so is the observed data[5].

For this reason a number of techniques have been developed that use only those values in the novel example that are observed or are known with confidence [6], together with their corresponding values in the PCA model. Situations in which this has been applied have been with facial images where a number of pixels have been removed, Everson and Sirovich[7] demonstrated that this results in a high level of reconstruction accuracy. An alternative method was also described by Nelson et al.[6] and Hu and Buxton[8] that uses all the information contained in the PCs, corresponding to both the observed and occluded variables.

Studies that looked at the human classification of static images or videos identified that untrained observers can correctly differentiate between the six basic facial expressions[9] with a high accuracy rate. Bassili[10] reports human recognition rates of over 80% for all expressions except disgust which was sometimes confused with anger.

Studies have also been concerned with human recognition of limited facial expressions. Typically, images or videos of the top or bottom half of the face are presented for judgement and the recognition rates are compared with each other and with the full face recognition for the same faces. Studies[10,11,12] showed that the facial expressions of half faces were less accurately classified than full face ones with facial expressions from the lower half of the face being more accurately identified than facial expressions from the upper half of the face; however, some specific expressions were more accurately predicted from the upper half of the face than the lower – such expressions termed recognizable-top by Calder[12] – examples being sadness and fear.

A common procedure for expression recognition is to build a model that represents each expression in some common way. The particular representation is used as input to some classification method which uses this representation to predict the most likely facial expression. Such a study was conducted by Michel and el Kaliouby[14] who used the positions of feature points obtained from video tracking as input to a support vector machine, and then use this model to test unseen data. They report classification accuracy of about 90%.

Studies that have investigated partial occlusions have typically looked at how robust an expression recognition system could be given the presence of occlusions. Two general techniques have been used for the recognition of occluded facial expressions. The first assumes the presence of occlusion and trains a model with only the data that is expected to be present. An example of this approach is that of Buciu, Kotsia, and Pitas[15] who remove pixels from facial images, train a model based on these images and then test their system on other images with the same pixels removed. The other approach is to build a set of local models for training a recognition system. For a particular facial expression the local regions that correspond to the visible regions are weighted accordingly[16].

Our approach was to use a model, as represented by the technique of principal component analysis (PCA), built from a set of facial expressions to estimate the value of the missing data. Facial expression is represented by a set of feature points obtained from across the face. Three techniques described by Nelson, Taylor and MacGregor[6] were identified as being suitable for replacing missing data using PCA, projection to the model plane, single component projection and replacement by the conditional mean; these were tested to see which provided the best reconstruction. The observed feature points are used to estimate the positions of the missing points together with information contained in the PCA representation. To analyse the efficacy of these methods we use real facial expressions and reconstructions of these when occluded, evaluated using residual errors and automatic classification of emotional meaning.

3   Methods

Principal component analysis (PCA)[17] provides a compact representation of a set of related data. As applied to a set of facial feature points it transforms N example expression vectors containing $2 \times k$ feature points to a PCA representation that consists of a mean facial expression vector $\overline{X}$ of size $1 \times 2k$ and a set of t principal component vectors also of size $1 \times 2k$. These principal components are combined in a matrix Φ. The effect of applying PCA to a data set in this way is to reduce the number of variables needed to represent a face from $2k$ to a smaller number t and to allow facial expressions not contained in the training data to be estimated. A facial expression E can be represented by this principal component representation as shown in Equation 1. A fuller description of the derivation of PCA can be found in Jolliffe[17].

$$E = \overline{X} + \Phi w \tag{1}$$

To illustrate the occluded face examples we divide an example into two sets, Y the observed data, of size n feature points and Z the missing data, of size m feature points, $n + m = k$. Equation 2 illustrates how these relate to the standard projection equation used in PCA, Equation 1.

$$E = \begin{pmatrix} Y \\ Z \end{pmatrix}$$

$$= \begin{pmatrix} \overline{Y} \\ \overline{Z} \end{pmatrix} + \begin{pmatrix} \Psi \\ \Theta \end{pmatrix} w \tag{2}$$

where the matrix Ψ has the rows of the complete eigenvector matrix Φ corresponding to the observed variables and is of size $2n \times t$ and similarly Θ consists of all the other rows with the occluded variables, of size $2m \times t$.

These equations cannot be solved in the standard PCA way as they are incomplete and the observed matrix of principal component variables Ψ is not orthogonal. Instead, there are a number of alternative methods for computing an estimate for the example E. Three of these methods were described by Nelson et al.[6].

The first is projection to the model plane. This has two forms, Equations 3 and 4. Equation 3 solves for the weights in Equation 2 when there are less missing variables m than numbers of principal component variables t and Equation 4 solves for the case where m is greater than t. This method uses the observed data and the corresponding variables in the principal component matrix Φ to compute the value of the weights w.

$$w = (\Psi^T \Psi)^{-1} \Psi^T (Y - \overline{Y}) \tag{3}$$

$$w = \Psi^T (\Psi \Psi^T)^{-1} (Y - \overline{Y}) \tag{4}$$

A second solution for the weights w in Equation 2 was described by Nelson et al, which involves successively fitting each eigenvector, in decreasing order of magnitude of eigenvalue, so as to minimise the distance between the estimated observed data and its principal component description – this is called single component projection. Firstly, the mean is subtracted from the example. Then a scalar is calculated that when multiplied by the next eigenvector will result in the closest approximation to the observed example possible – as calculated by the mean squared error. By successive fitting in this way a vector of scalar values w is produced that when applied in Equation 1 can be used to estimate the full example E.

The third method described by Nelson et al. was the replacement by the conditional mean. Equation 5 uses the eigenvector variables for the observed data Ψ as well as the eigenvector variables for the missing data Θ, to solve for the full estimate, with Λ being a diagonal matrix containing the eigenvalues λ.

$$\hat{Z} = \overline{Z} + \Theta \Lambda \Psi^T (\Psi \Lambda \Psi^T)^{-1} (Y - \overline{Y}) \tag{5}$$

The Equation that this technique uses is the same as that described by Hu and Buxton[8] who use it to estimate the value of 3D body silhouettes from 2D posture values. A full description of the derivation of these methods is given in Nelson, Taylor and MacGregor[6].

4   Results

To evaluate the success of estimating the feature points of a facial expression using these techniques a set of feature points were extracted from a database of facial expression videos. The database used was the Cohn-Kanade[13] database for facial expression analysis. This contains over 450 short video sequences taken from multiple subjects adopting a variety of facial expressions and has been used in a number of studies on facial tracking and facial expression analysis[3]. Each of the image sequences contains a subject adopting one facial expression, and is captured in black and white images from a front-on position.

The software used for capture of the feature points was the commercially available FaceStation package[18]. This tracks largely front-on expressions and registers the positions of 22 feature points. These can then be inputted into 3D Studio Max[19] to animate a 3D head model. For our purposes the feature points were kept in the format in which they were outputted from the face tracking software and were represented by a set of 2D normalised points. The 22 feature points are shown in Figure 4 in an example of tracking.

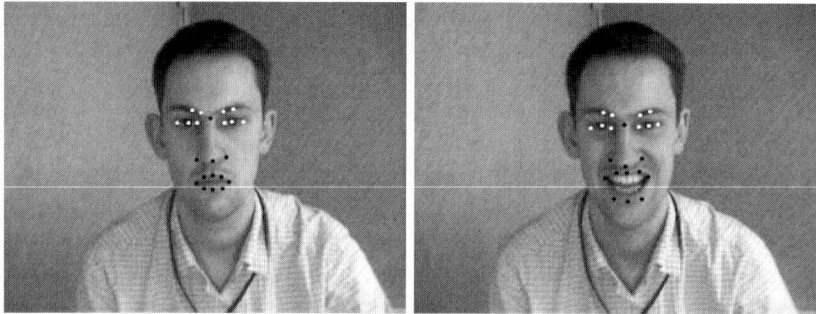

Fig. 1. Example of tracking points used in analysis, black points from lower half of face and white points from upper half of face

Once a set of feature points was obtained representing every tracked face in the database the Procrustes alignment procedure was applied to every individual frame in the set – the particular form we used being described by Cootes et al.[20]. The subsequent PCA procedures were performed with the fully aligned set.

To evaluate the efficacy of the PCA approaches to approximating missing data the scheme used was to train a subset of tracked and aligned feature points and then to use the rest of this set as test data. A configuration of points is removed from the test data and the complete set of feature points is estimated using the occluded PCA methods. This approach allows the estimated points to be compared directly with the original, correct points. Each facial expression is represented by a configuration of feature points for each frame, and the missing points are computed separately for each frame.

4.1   Reconstruction with Random Points Missing

We wanted to test the three techniques previously described on real facial expressions to determine the one that worked most effectively. To establish this a random set of feature points were removed from each facial expression in the test set and reconstructed using each of these techniques. This was repeated using different numbers of missing feature points. For each specific number of feature points 25 random sets of points were used to test reconstruction accuracy. The mean squared error was computed between the correct locations of the feature points and their estimates for each number of missing points.

A PCA model was first created that represented all the frames in 150 expressions. The feature points were then removed at random from the remaining 307 facial expressions.

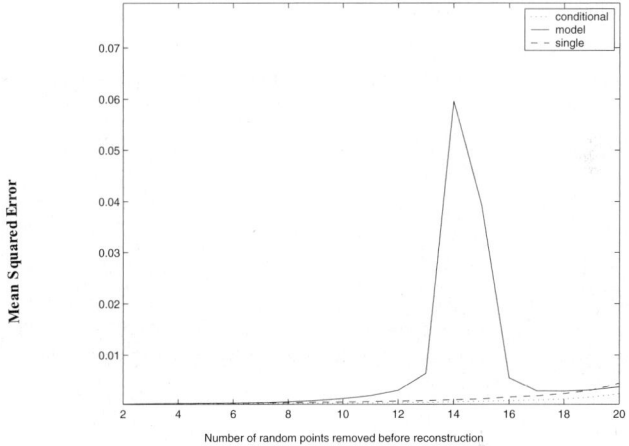

Fig. 2. Comparison of the mean squared error between original configurations of feature points and reconstructions. This is with 2-20 feature points removed randomly across the configurations.

Figure 2 shows the mean squared error computed between the correct positions of the complete configuration of feature points and the estimated set. The replacement by the conditional mean method produces the best results at all values of randomly missing data.

Another observation from Figure 2 is the peak that occurs for the projection to the model plane method when the number of points that are observed is equal to 14. This is the case when the number of variables used in projection to the model plane is 16 (2 times 8 missing feature points). This is the closest case to that where the number of observed variables is equal to the number of variables used to model the data (the number of PCs). This is the point in the graph where the case changes from the over-determined case to the under-determined one and a different form of the least squares estimator is used (Equations 3 and 4).

Inspection of the reconstruction accuracy for different cases reveals that for some instances of data removal the resulting matrix for which the inverse is calculated becomes close to singular, as represented by the condition number. This has the effect of producing poor reconstruction and hence giving poor reconstruction accuracy. This gives a further justification for using the replacement by the conditional mean method for reconstruction of highly occluded facial expressions and for considering the number of PCs used to model the facial expressions.

4.2   Analysis with Systematic Data Missing

After removing random feature points from across the faces it was determined that the replacement by the conditional mean technique produced estimates with low reconstruction errors, even when a large number of points were removed. However, we felt it important to establish how well the method could be deployed in a different situation, as well as establishing what the effect of the errors was on the overall impact of a facial expression.

Initially, we investigated the effect of less random, more systematic occlusions. We performed a similar analysis as previously, except simulating random occlusions from the top and bottom of the face. From 2 to 12 feature points were removed from the top and bottom of the face – the top half of the face represented by feature points on the eyes, eyebrows and nose and the lower half represented by feature points on the mouth and nose. Which feature points were removed was again chosen at random. 25 different sets of random points were removed from each of the 300 facial expressions in the test set, and each facial expression was reconstructed using the replacement by the conditional mean method. The mean squared error between the correct configuration and the reconstruction was computed.

Figure 3 demonstrates that random data taken from across the face is more accurately reconstructed than more systematic data. For small levels of occlu-

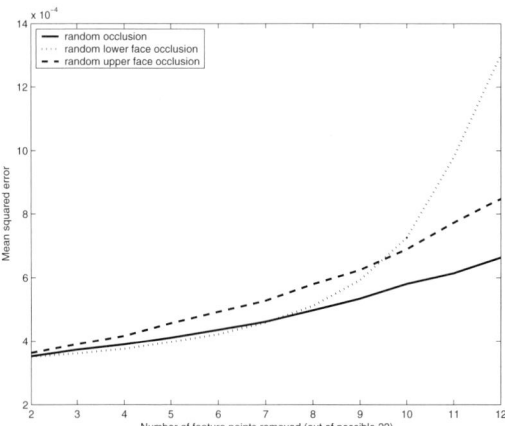

Fig. 3. Performance of replacement by conditional mean method when random sets of feature points are removed from across facial expressions

sions there is little difference in reconstruction accuracy. However, when upwards of 8 feature points are missing, both the upper and lower face cases show poorer performance, with missing data from the lower half showing the worst accuracy.

4.3   Classification of Expression

The previous Sections demonstrated that replacement by the conditional mean was the best technique, of the ones attempted, for reconstruction of facial expressions' feature point configurations, and that systematic missing data was less accurately estimated than random data. As well as establishing this we wanted to assess the effect on the emotional meaning of the reconstructed feature points, to gain an understanding other than the mean squared error.

To establish the performance of the algorithm under these conditions a classification problem was undertaken comparable with previous studies[14], but using the estimations of occluded expressions as our test data. This task was the classification of a facial expression in terms of the six basic emotional labels. An SVM was initially trained to automatically classify the complete set of feature points by facial expression. Once trained, the same SVM was used but this time with a full set of feature points provided by reconstruction of partially occluded facial expressions.

The two cases we used for our systematic data were produced by removing the top and bottom sets of feature points. The feature points for the top half consisted of 10 points located on the eyes and eyebrows and the feature points for the bottom half consisted of 8 points on the mouth and 4 on the nose (these sets are highlighted in Figure 4).

The faces were classified into the six basic emotion categories according to a set of combinations given by Pantic and[21] Rothkrantz[] of the FACS activated action units, a set of rules also employed by Buciu et al.[15] – 376 video sequences were classified in this way. The metric used was the positions of the feature points of the maximum expression in the video sequence after alignment: The maximum expression was calculated as that which provided the greatest value for the Euclidean distance between the neutral configuration of the points and each other configuration produced during the expression.

The support vector machine (SVM) package libsvm[22] was used for this classification exercise. The training data used was a 180 sample set of feature vectors – 30 examples for each expression. The approach that was used is very similar to that used by Michel and Kaliouby[14] who used the same classification approach, the same dataset and the same set of points on the face – we extend this by using the SVM trained for the full set of feature points to test the reconstructed feature points.

Table 1 shows a Confusion Matrix for the SVM using the full set of feature points taken from the facial expressions. It demonstrates that expressions are estimated well from a feature point representation using the classification method. The training data consists of 180 expressions, the full 376 facial expressions are used to give classification rates for the SVMs.

Table 1. Confusion Matrix for complete facial expression comparing number of expression labels correctly predicted with SVM, rows contain correct expression, columns give predicted expression

T/ P	surprise	anger	happy	fear	sad	disgust	correct %
surprise	75	0	1	0	0	0	99
anger	0	31	0	0	1	1	94
happy	0	3	84	7	2	2	86
fear	3	1	4	52	3	0	82
sad	1	9	1	0	61	1	84
disgust	0	0	0	0	0	33	100

Table 2. Overall classification rates for all expressions in correct emotional category using an SVM. The top row shows the overall accuracy rate for correctly classified expressions each using a separate SVM. The second row shows the accuracy rate for the reconstruction, tested on the SVM trained for the full feature points case.

Data used	All feature points	Lower feature points	Upper feature points
Feature points alone	90%	85%	75%
Estimates after reconstruction		82%	70%

As well as training an SVM for the full set of feature points we also trained one specifically for feature points taken from the top and bottom halves of the face. This was so we could establish the discriminative quality these feature points contain. This was consistent with studies such as those of Buciu[15] who trained classifiers with occluded data. Table 2 compares the results of recognising reconstructed facial expressions with the SVM trained for the full set of expressions, and also with the results from the occluded feature point SVMs. These are consistent with each other. They demonstrate that the feature points from the lower half of the face contain more information than those from the upper half and provide better recognition. The classifier trained for the occluded points alone, without reconstruction show improved classification rates. This we attribute to using an SVM that is trained specifically to classify a particular set of feature points, and this classifier locating different features for discriminating samples from the full feature points data. As such, Table 2 gives an indication as to the best reconstruction performance that could be achieved using the set of feature points used. We also observe that the classification of the occluded feature points doesn't give an estimate for the missing data, especially when varying amounts of data are missing.

Tables 3 and 4 show the effect of using all the expressions that had been used with the SVM of full feature points: these expressions had had the top or bottom points removed and then been reconstructed using the replacement by the conditional mean. Inspection of the Confusion Matrices shows that for each expression the full feature points give better classification than the estimates using the lower points, and these in turn are superior to the estimates using the upper points.

Table 3. Confusion Matrix for expression classification from estimated occluded upper faces comparing number of expression labels correctly predicted with SVM, rows contain correct expression, columns give predicted expression

T/P	surprise	anger	happy	fear	sad	disgust	correct %
surprise	75	0	1	0	0	0	99
anger	0	23	0	0	6	4	70
happy	0	1	72	12	5	8	73
fear	3	2	6	49	3	0	78
sad	0	8	2	0	60	3	82
disgust	0	0	0	1	1	31	94

Table 4. Confusion Matrix for expression recognition from estimated occluded lower face comparing number of expression labels correctly predicted with SVM, rows contain correct expression, columns give predicted expression

T/P	surprise	anger	happy	fear	sad	disgust	correct %
surprise	63	0	2	7	4	0	83
anger	0	16	3	0	9	5	48
happy	3	0	66	18	9	2	67
fear	4	1	10	44	4	0	70
sad	3	3	5	3	54	5	74
disgust	0	5	6	2	0	20	60

More detailed inspection reveals that sadness, surprise and fear are the facial expressions that are most robust to the occlusions used. Calder et al.[12] identify that surprise is recognisable from both the top and bottom halves of the face, and this is consistent with our results, which show the best classification accuracy in all conditions. However, with the top half removed there is no change in classification accuracy indicating that the expression of the lower half of the face is distinctive for the surprise expression. Both Bassili[10] and Calder et al.[12] identify sadness and fear as recognisable-top expressions, most readily recognisable from the eyes and eyebrows. This is consistent with our classification results, which show the smallest drop in classification for these expressions when the bottom half is missing. Disgust shows a marked decrease in recognition accuracy when the bottom half is removed, a decrease not seen with the top half removed. This is consistent with both Bassili's and Calder's label of disgust as a recognisable-bottom expression. Happiness was also described as a recognisable-bottom expression and does show a greater decrease with the bottom half removed but there is a smaller difference between the classification change that results. The anger expression is the one that shows the least relation with Bassili's and Calder's labels. It shows the largest decrease in classification accuracy for both occluded top and bottom halves.

5   Conclusion

We have described three techniques that take a previously trained PCA model and used this to estimate the configurations of occluded feature points in a representation of facial expression. After having established that one technique, replacement by the conditional mean, gives superior estimation performance to the other two techniques for randomly generated missing data, we carried out an analysis for the performance of this technique with systematic data taken from the top and bottom of the face. Using a classification approach with the emotional labels for the facial expressions reconstructed we were able to identify how successfully the facial expression could be estimated from occluded data. We established that in both cases the reconstruction techniques allowed better than chance classification of expressions. We also confirmed that more expression information is contained in the lower half of the face.

The results from all our analyses demonstrate that occlusions of systematic data from the top and bottom halves of the face has an impact on the reconstruction of facial expression. This is most profound for data that is missing from the lower half of the face. This is suggestive that for some facial expressions with this amount of occlusion it will be difficult to correctly estimate the missing data because the observed data is consistent with a number of configurations of feature points. However, reconstruction produces configurations that are recognised with better than chance accuracy and at rates that are comparable with human performance.

Acknowledgements

This research was conducted as part of the EngD research programme, and funding was provided by the EPSRC and BT Group Plc.

References

1. Hong, H., Neven, H., von der Malsburg, C.: Online facial expression recognition based on personalized galleries. In: Proceedings of the Second International Conference on Automatic Face and Gesture Recognition, pp. 354–359 (April 1998)
2. Kaliouby, R.E., Robinson, P.: Real-time inference of complex mental states from facial expressions and head gestures. In: Conference on Computer Vision and Pattern Recognition Workshop, vol. 10 (2004)
3. Tian, Y., Kanade, T., Cohn, J.F: Recognizing action units for facial expression analysis. IEEE Transactions on Pattern Analysis and Machine Intelligence 23(2) (February 2001)
4. Edwards, J., Taylor, C.J, Cootes, T.F: Interpreting face images using active appearance models. International Conference on Face and Gesture Recognition, pp. 300–305 (1998)
5. Leonardis, A., Bischof, H.: Dealing with occlusions in the eigenspace approach. IEEE Conference on Computer Vision and Pattern Recognition, 453–458 (1996)

6. Nelson, P.R.C, Taylor, P.A, MacGregor, J.F.: Missing data methods in pca and pls: Score calculations with incomplete observations. Chemometrics and Intelligent Laboratory Systems 35, 45–65 (1996)
7. Everson, R., Sirovich, L.: Karhunen-loève procedure for gappy data. Journal of the Optical Society of America A 12, 1657–1664 (1995)
8. Hu, S., Buxton, B.: Statistical personal tracker. In: BMVA Symposium on Spatiotemporal Image Processing (March 2004)
9. Ekman, P.: Are there basic emotions? Psychological Review 99(3), 550–553 (1992)
10. Bassili, J.N.: Emotion recognition: The role of facial movement and the relative importance of upper and lower areas of the face. Journal of Personality and Social Psychology 37(11), 2049–2058 (1979)
11. Baron-Cohen, S., Wheelwright, S., Jolliffe, T.: Is there a "language of the eyes"? evidence from normal adults, and adults with autism or asperger syndrome. Visual Cognition 4(3), 311–331 (1997)
12. Calder, A.J, Young, A.W, Keane, J., Dean, M.: Configural information in facial expression perception. Journal of Experimental Psychology: Human Perception and Performance 26(2), 527–551 (2000)
13. Kanade, T., Cohn, J., Tian, Y.: Comprehensive database for facial expression analysis. In: Proceedings of the International Conference on Face and Gesture Recognition, pp. 46–53 (March 2000)
14. Michel, P., Kaliouby, R.E.: Real time facial expression recognition in video using support vector machines. In: Proceedings of the 5th International Conference on Multimodal Interfaces, pp. 258–264 (2003)
15. Buciu, I., Kotsia, I., Pitas, I.: Facial expression analysis under partial occlusion. In: IEEE International Conference on Acoustics, Speech and Signal Processing, vol. 5, pp. 453–456. IEEE Computer Society Press, Los Alamitos (2005)
16. Bourel, F., Chibelushi, C.C., Low, A.A.: Recognition of facial expressions in the presence of occlusion. In: 12th British Machine Vision Conference, vol. 1, pp. 213–222 (2001)
17. Jolliffe, I.T.: Principal Component Analysis. Springer Series in Statistics. Springer, Heidelberg (1986)
18. Facestation, http://www.eyematic.com
19. Autodesk. 3d studio max, http://www.autodesk.com/3dmax
20. Cootes, T.F, Taylor, C. J, Cooper, D.H, Graham, J.: Active shape models – their training and application. Computer Vision and Image Understanding 61(1), 38–59 (1995)
21. Pantic, M., Rothkrantz, L.J.M: Expert system for automatic analysis of facial expressions. Image and Vision Computing 18, 881–905 (2000)
22. Chang, C.-C., Lin, C.-J.: LIBSVM: A Library for Support Vector Machines, Software (2001), available at http://www.csie.ntu.edu.tw/~cjlin/libsvm

Recognizing Affective Dimensions from Body Posture

Andrea Kleinsmith and Nadia Bianchi-Berthouze

UCL Interaction Centre, University College London, London, WC1E 7DP, UK
a.kleinsmith@cs.ucl.ac.uk, n.berthouze@ucl.ac.uk

Abstract. The recognition of affective human communication may be used to provide developers with a rich source of information for creating systems that are capable of interacting well with humans. Posture has been acknowledged as an important modality of affective communication in many fields. Behavioral studies have shown that posture can communicate discrete emotion categories as well as affective dimensions. In the affective computing field, while models for the automatic recognition of discrete emotion categories from posture have been proposed, to our knowledge, there are no models for the automatic recognition of affective dimensions from static posture. As a continuation of our previous study, the two main goals of this study are: i) to build automatic recognition models to discriminate between levels of affective dimensions based on low-level postural features; and ii) to investigate both the discriminative power and the limitations of the postural features proposed. The models were built on the basis of human observers' ratings of posture according to affective dimensions directly (instead of emotion category) in conjunction with our posture features.

1 Introduction

The role of computers and other technologies in many facets of today's society explains the importance of creating systems to be capable of interacting well with humans. Affective communication may be used to provide developers with a rich source of information for achieving this goal. Posture in particular has been recognized as an important modality for affective communication [20][1][8] [5]. In fact, cognitive neuroscience studies have shown the importance of body posture over facial expressions in cases of incongruent affective displays [7].

Behavioral studies have shown that posture can communicate both affective dimensions and discrete emotion categories [17][5]. In the affective computing field, models for the automatic recognition of discrete emotion categories from static body postures have been proposed [2][5][15]. Other studies have shown that body motions extracted from dance sequences [3][24][14] can convey emotion in terms of discrete categories effectively. To our knowledge, what are missing still are models for the automatic recognition of affective dimensions from posture as there are for motion [4]. This is important as a single label may not reflect the complexity of the affective state conveyed by the posture. Indeed, Ekman

A. Paiva, R. Prada, and R.W. Picard (Eds.): ACII 2007, LNCS 4738, pp. 48–58, 2007.

and Friesen [10] initially posit that while they consider the face to be the fore-most modality for expressing discrete emotion categories, the body is better at communicating dimensions of affect.

While affective posture recognition systems continue to focus on discriminating between emotion categories, our previous work [18] has attempted to understand if we can go beyond these categories and recognize levels of affective dimensions. Using a multidimensional scaling technique, affective dimensions were extracted that support the categorical evaluation of affective posture. The extracted dimensions are arousal, valence, and action tendency. The goals of the new study are: i) to build automatic recognition models to discriminate between levels of affective dimensions based on low-level postural features; and ii) to investigate both the discriminative power and the limitations of the postural features proposed.

The remainder of the paper is organized as follows: Section 2 describes the affective dimension recognition survey and the automatic recognition models built upon the survey data and our low-level postural features. The models and the statistically determined most relevant features of each are evaluated in Section 3. Section 4 provides a discussion on some further testing that was carried out and future directions to be explored.

2   Affective Dimension Recognition

2.1   Human Recognition of Affective Dimensions

As our goal is to build posture recognition models based on affective dimensions, an online survey was conducted to collect data from human observers. To carry out the survey, the same set of affective posture images that were used in the previous study were used in the current study. The reader is directed to [17] for a detailed explanation of the posture collection and stimulus preparation processes.

The survey was conducted online as a series of webpages. The stimuli comprised 111 affective posture images, and were presented separately (one posture per page), in a randomized order that differed for each participant (called observers hereafter). Five anonymous observers, two males and three females participated in the study. In contrast to the previous study, in the current survey, human observers judged postures according to affective dimensions directly

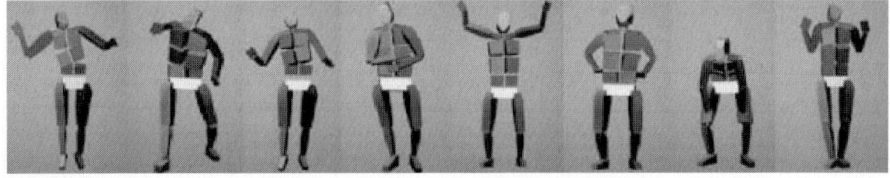

Fig. 1. Examples of the affectively expressive avatars reconstructed from motion capture data

instead of judging postures according to discrete emotion categories only. Specifically, observers were asked to rate each posture according to a seven-point Likert scale for each of four affective dimensions: *valence* (pleasure), *arousal* (alertness), *potency* (control), and *avoidance* (avoid/attend to). Valence, arousal, and potency (or dominance) were chosen based on psychological research throughout the last century which asserts that these three dimensions cover the majority of affect variability [25][23][6] [22]. Furthermore, valence and arousal were two of the dimensions identified in our initial study, and we consider potency a form of action tendency, which was the third dimension we identified previously.

Next, we analyzed the observers' data to determine the level of agreement between observers in rating the affective dimensions. Using the normalized observers' rating for each posture for each dimension, the estimated marginal means for each observer were calculated for each dimension. Results showing differences between observers across the four affective dimensions are presented in Figure 2. The *x-axis* denotes the four affective dimensions and the *y-axis* denotes the estimated marginal means for each observer. As we can see, the greatest variability occurs with observer two across the arousal, potency, and avoidance dimensions. According to the means, across all observers, the arousal dimension contains the least amount of variability while the greatest amount of variability occurs for the *avoidance* dimension. Cronbach's α was used to test the reliability of the observers' agreements across the four dimensions. The results reflect the above findings with arousal showing the highest reliability ($\alpha = 0.85$, r $= 0.55$), and avoidance showing the lowest reliability ($\alpha = 0.35$, r $= 0.11$).

Next, we calculated the average percentage of error across all observers for each dimension, considering each observer's rating for each posture separately. The results obtained show an average error of 19% for valence, 15% for arousal, 19% for potency, and 25% for avoidance. We consider these differences to reflect the variability that may typically occur in human-human affective communication.

2.2   Automatic Recognition of Affective Dimensions

To build automatic affective dimension recognition models, each static posture is associated with a vector of 24 postural configuration features (explained below), and four values indicating the observers' normalized average ratings for each affective dimension: *valence, arousal, potency,* and *avoidance.* The same features were used to build emotion category recognition models in previous studies [2][16][9].

The postures are described according to the 24 features introduced in our previous research [2][8], which are listed in Table 1, and shown in Figure 3. These features, calculated using the numerical data obtained from the motion capture, were chosen because they are low-level and context-independent. Precisely, direction and volume of the body were described by projecting each marker on the three orthogonal planes and measuring the lateral, frontal, and vertical extension of the body, body torsion, and the inclination of the head and shoulders.

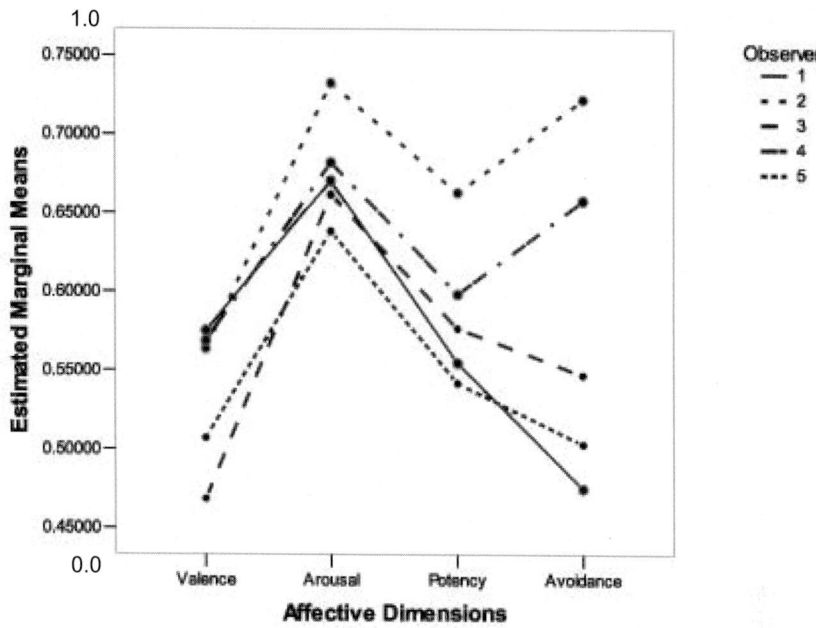

Fig. 2. Results of observer ratings for each affective dimension. The affective dimensions comprise the x-axis, and the estimated marginal means for each observer comprise the y-axis.

Table 1. The table lists the set of posture features proposed. The Code column indicates the feature codes used in the paper. The following short-cuts are used: L: Left, R: Right, B: Back, F: Front.

Code	Posture Features	Code	Posture Features
V4	$Orientation_{XY}$: B.Head - F.Head axis	V5	$Orientation_{YZ}$: B.Head - F.Head axis
V6	$Distance_z$: R.Hand - R.Shoulder	V7	$Distance_z$: L.Hand - L.Shoulder
V8	$Distance_y$: R.Hand - R.Shoulder	V9	$Distance_y$:L.Hand - L.Shoulder
V10	$Distance_x$: R.Hand - L.Shoulder	V11	$Distance_x$:L.Hand - R.Shoulder
V12	$Distance_x$: R.Hand - R.Elbow	V13	$Distance_x$:L.Hand - L.Elbow
V14	$Distance_x$: R.Elbow - L.Shoulder	V15	$Distance_x$: L.Elbow - R.Shoulder
V16	$Distance_z$: R.Hand - R.Elbow	V17	$Distance_z$:L.Hand - L.Elbow
V18	$Distance_y$: R.Hand - R.Elbow	V19	$Distance_y$:L.Hand - L.Elbow
V20	$Distance_y$: R.Elbow - R.Shoulder	V21	$Distance_y$:L.Elbow - L.Shoulder
V22	$Distance_z$: R.Elbow - R.Shoulder	V23	$Distance_z$:L.Elbow - L.Shoulder
V24	$Orientation_{XY}$: Shoulders axis	V25	$Orientation_{XZ}$: Shoulders axis
V26	$Orientation_{XY}$: Heels axis	V27	$3D - Distance$: R.Heel - L.Heel

A backpropagation algorithm was used to build a separate model for each affective dimension. One reason for choosing backpropagation is its effective handling of data comprising continuous values. Although other algorithms may perform better, finding one is not the goal. Instead, the goal is to examine our set

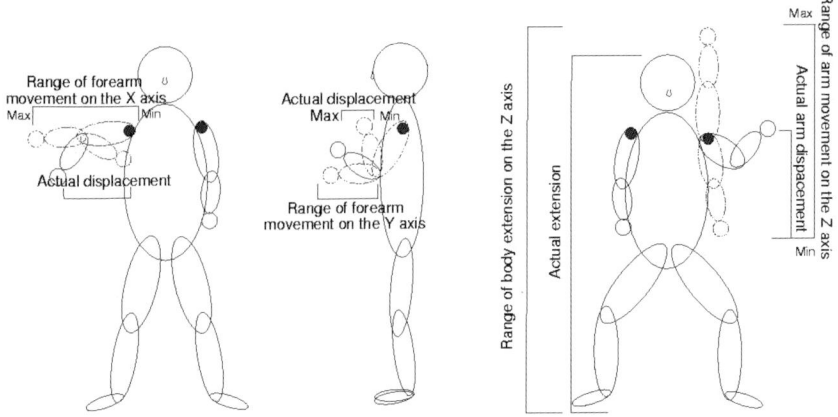

Fig. 3. Visual representation of some of the postural configuration features. These features were computed in the frontal view by projecting 3D motion captured data on the 3 orthogonal planes to measure direction and volume of the body according to the lateral, frontal, and vertical extensions of the body, and body orientation.

of features, and to determine whether or not they are effective for discriminating between levels of affective dimensions from posture. Furthermore, backpropagation is a well accepted algorithm used in recognition tasks.

The topology of the backpropagation network was determined empirically. It consists of one input layer with 24 nodes (corresponding to the 24 posture features), one hidden layer with 12 nodes (the number of input nodes/2), and an output layer with one node (corresponding to the observers' ratings for each dimension, separately). Both the learning rate and the momentum were set to 0.01. Each network was trained with 10,000 epochs, and tested using five fold cross-validation. The performance error obtained for each of the backpropagation models, shown in Table 2, is 21% for both the *valence* and *arousal* dimensions, and 19% for both the *potency* and *avoidance* dimensions. Comparable to the results of the human observers discussed in Section 2.1, these results using backpropagation are quite promising.

Table 2. Performance levels of backpropagation for the 111 postures for each affective dimension model using the complete set of 24 posture features

Affective Dim. Models	Error %: 24 Features
Valence	21%
Arousal	21%
Potency	19%
Avoidance	19%

3   Grounding Affective Dimensions into Posture Features

In the first part of this paper, we proposed a set of low-level postural features and tested the possibility of building models for recognizing levels of affective dimensions. As mentioned above, these results are quite promising as they are similar to the level of agreement between our observers. This second part of the paper tackles two issues. One, we look at how humans may use postural features to discriminate between levels of affective dimensions. Two, we assess the limitations of our features and hence, which features may be necessary to add in future studies. To answer the first question, we extract the most relevant features for each affective dimension by applying non-linear mixture discriminant analysis (MDA) [19][12] to the postures for which agreement between the observers was high. To answer the second question, we examine the postures for which agreement between the observers was very low and discuss them according to models presented in other studies.

MDA was applied to each of the four affective dimensions separately. MDA is a statistical technique used to discriminate between two or more categories or groups. Mixtures of Gaussian distributions are used to model the groups. Moreover, the separation between groups is maximized while the variance within the groups is minimized. Postures that received an average observer rating of < 3.8 were labeled *low*. Postures that received an average rating between $3.8 - 4.2$ were labeled *neutral*. Finally, postures that received an average rating of > 4.2 were labeled *high*. Given that the majority of the postures were labeled as either *low* or *high*, the number of subclasses used by the MDA algorithm for classification was two for low-rated postures, one for neutral-rated postures, and two for high-rated postures. Furthermore, in order to discern the most discriminating feature sets, only the postures which obtained high agreement between observers (> 0.80) were used. Thus, after discarding the low agreement postures from the original 111, 91 postures remained for the valence dimension, 101 postures remained for the arousal dimension, 93 postures remained for the potency dimension, and 68 postures remained for the avoidance dimension. The MDA algorithm allows us to ascertain the most relevant features because it uses an iterative process to create the models based on linear combinations of the most discriminating features.

Separate models were built to discriminate between pairs of affective dimension levels (e.g., low vs. high, low vs. neutral, etc.). The models obtained are shown in Table 3. The last column of the Table reports the percentage of classification error for the models. The remaining columns report the features used by the discrimination functions of each model. The number in each entry of the Table represents the rank of importance of the features. Lower numbers correspond to higher discriminative power. For conciseness, we report in this Table only the features selected by at least one of the four models.

An examination of the Table shows that the head ($V5$) is important for distinguishing between low and high for all dimensions and high and neutral for all dimensions except arousal. For arousal, to distinguish between high and neutral, and low and neutral levels, openness of the body seems to be important as these models rely on at least one vertical, frontal, and lateral feature. In the

Table 3. Important features for discriminating between pairs the affective dimension levels are presented. The last column contains the percentage of error for each model. The following short-cuts are used: Dim: Dimension, H: High, L: Low, N: Neutral.

Affective Dim. Model	Head V5	Vertical					Frontal						Lateral					Heels		MDA Error
		V6	V7	V16	V22	V23	V8	V9	V19	V20	V21	V24	V10	V11	V13	V14	V15	V26	v27	Error
Valence HL	3	1																	2	16%
Arousal HL	1	2				5							3			4				5%
Potency HL	3		2	1			4							5	6					3%
Avoidance HL	4		1		2									3						7%
Valence HN	4					1				2								3		27%
Arousal HN			1		4		3							2						9%
Potency HN	4	3		1			5				2			8			6		7	19%
Avoidance HN	2				5	1							4	3						14%
Valence LN		3					1	2												28%
Arousal LN		3		1					4	5					2					12%
Potency LN	3	4		1											2					20%
Avoidance LN		1											2							18%

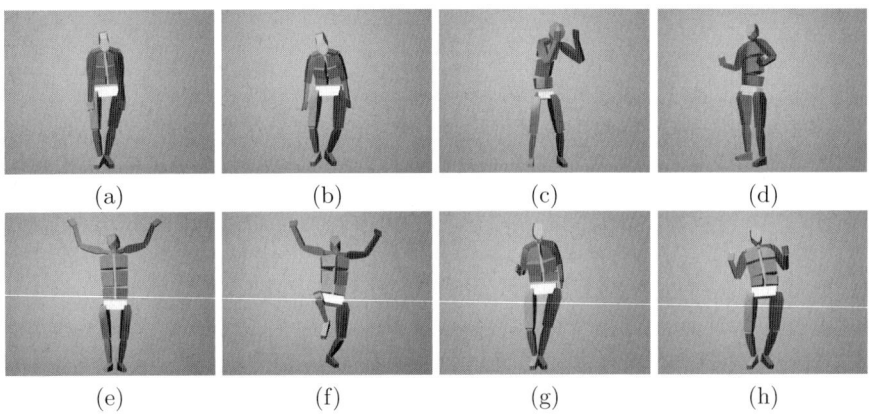

Fig. 4. Examples of the 3D affectively expressive avatars for low and high **valence** subclasses. (a)(b) Low subclass 1, (c)(d) Low subclass 2, (e)(f) High subclass 1 (g)(h) High subclass 2.

case of potency, the most discriminating feature for all three models is *V16*, the vertical extension of the arm. Frontal features do not play a role in any of the avoidance models. Similarly, lateral features are not represented in any of the valence models.

A visual examination of the the labels assigned to the subclasses for low- and high-rated avatars for all four dimensions indicates that the relevant features identified by MDA do aid in discriminating between postures. Refer to Figures 4, 5, 6, and 7 for examples. Low subclasses of valence (Figure 4(a-d)) appear to be separated by the vertical extension of the arm (*V6*) and the 3D distance between the heels (*V27*). In one subclass (Figure 4(a,b)), the arms are stretched down alongside the body and the heels remain close together (the body is quite closed), while in the other subclass (Figure 4(c,d)), the arms are raised to face level and the heels are further apart. Whether the arms are raised well

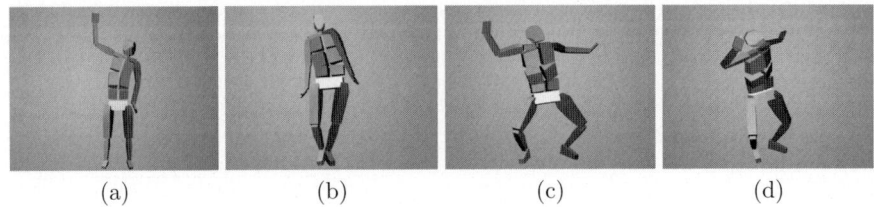

Fig. 5. Examples of the 3D affectively expressive avatars for high **arousal** subclasses. (a)(b) High subclass 1 (c)(d) High subclass 2.

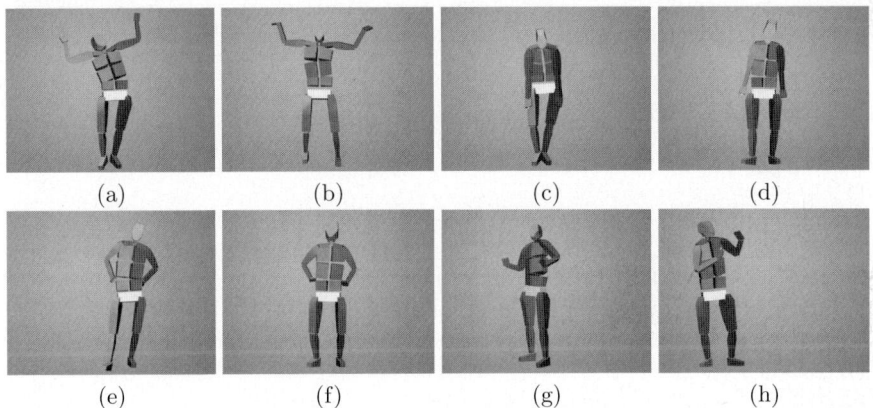

Fig. 6. Examples of the 3D affectively expressive avatars for low and high **potency** subclasses. (a)(b) Low subclass 1, (c)(d) Low subclass 2, (e)(f) High subclass 1 (g)(h) High subclass 2.

above the head (Figure 4(e,f)) or fall within the torso area ($V6$) (Figure 4(g,h)) seems to separate postures within the two high subclasses of valence.

Lateral features ($V10$ and $V14$) are used for distinguishing between high levels of arousal. As we can see from Figure 5, the body in one subclass (Figure 5(c,d)) is significantly more open laterally than in the other high subclass (Figure 5(a,b)).

In the case of potency, the vertical ($V7$ and $V16$) and lateral ($V11$ and $V13$) openness of the body seem to classify postures within the two low-rated subclasses (Figure 6(a-d)). In the high subclasses of potency, the vertical ($V7$ and $V16$) and frontal ($V9$) extension of the arms are the most distinguishing features. In one high subclass (Figure 6(e,f)), hands rest on the hips, whereas in the other high subclass (Figure 6(g,h)), the arms are more raised and extended out in front of the body.

Vertical ($V7$ and $V23$) and lateral ($V10$ and $V11$) features are important for distinguishing between two levels of low avoidance, as well as two levels of high avoidance. In particular, arms are folded across the body or near the face for one low subclass (Figure 7(a,b)), while in the other low subclass (Figure 6(c,d)), the arms are stretched down along the side of the body. In the case of high subclasses,

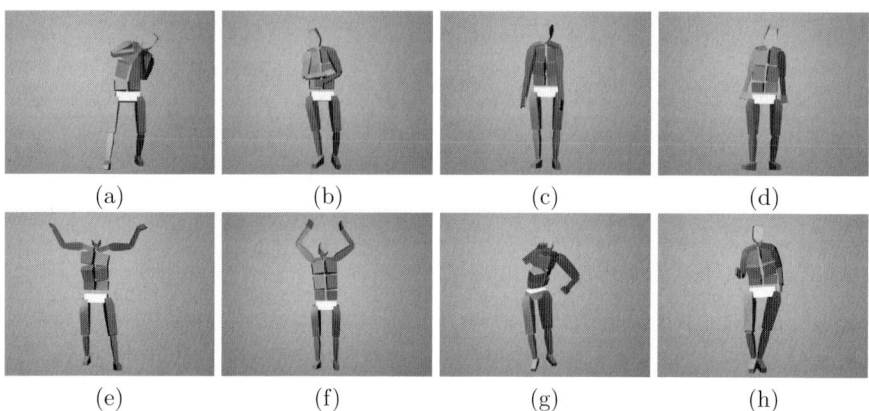

Fig. 7. Examples of the 3D affectively expressive avatars for low and high **avoidance** subclasses. (a)(b) Low subclass 1, (c)(d) Low subclass 2, (e)(f) High subclass 1 (g)(h) High subclass 2.

one subclass (Figure 6(e,f)) contains postures in which the arms are raised and open laterally, while postures in which the arms rest at torso level both vertically and laterally are represented in the second high subclass (Figure 6(g,h)).

Interestingly, an examination of the misclassified postures reveals a possible inconsistency in perception by the observers, and not in classification by the automatic recognition models. In the majority of the cases, the postures actually seem to be classified correctly by MDA when considering postural features.

4   Discussion

The results presented in this paper are quite interesting and promising. Our set of low-level posture configuration features seem quite suitable for building automatic recognition models for affective dimensions. In fact, backpropagation was used for further evaluation using reduced feature sets to build a new set of affective dimension models. These models were built with the set of features determined by MDA to be the most discriminating features for each separate affective dimension, and tested on the entire set of 111 postures. The reduced number of features required a reduction in the number of nodes for both the input layer and the hidden layer of the architecture. Specifically, there were five nodes in the input layer and three nodes in the hidden layer for the valence, potency, and avoidance models; and four nodes in the input layer and two nodes in the hidden layer for the arousal model. The results obtained from testing are positive and lend further support to the effectiveness of our features, as a marked decrease can be seen in the error percentages across all four dimensions. There was a 12% error percentage for valence, 10% for both arousal and potency, and 11% in the case of avoidance.

While the recognition models presented here were tested with standing postures, the low-level, context-independent nature of our features has also been assessed with a combination of standing and seated postures. In that situation, our affective posture recognition system [16] was used to classify posture according to nine affective categories (*angry, confused, fear, happy, interest, relaxed, sad, startled,* and *surprised*) chosen to represent different types of emotion situations. On average, 70% of the postures were correctly classified.

However, there are more situations and conditions to examine. As mentioned in Section 3, other types of features, (e.g., amplitude, speed of movement, direction, etc.) may be necessary for achieving better recognition of some affective states such as fear [5][16]. Indeed, an evaluation of the postures that were discarded due to low agreement on affective dimension ratings between observers reveals that fear and surprise were the most frequently chosen emotion categories.

Moreover, currently unrepresented static features may add to the performance of the models. In fact, a 1932 behavioral study by James [13] found that Approach-Withdrawal (leaning direction) and Expansion-Contraction of the body are important for attributing attitude to static posture. This importance of leaning direction also has been evidenced by more recent studies [11][21].

References

1. Argyle, M.: Bodily Communication. Methuen & Co. Ltd. London (1988)
2. Bianchi-Berthouze, N., Kleinsmith, A.: A categorical approach to affective gesture recognition. Connection Science 15, 259–269 (2003)
3. Camurri, A., Hashimoto, S., Suzuki, K., Trocca, R.: Kansei analysis of dance performance. In: IEEE Int'l Conf. on Systems, Man and Cybernetics, pp. 327–332 (1999)
4. Camurri, A., Volpe, G., De Poli, G., Leman, M.: Communicating Expressiveness and Affect in Multimodal Interactive Systems. IEEE Multimedia 12, 43–53 (2005)
5. Coulson, M.: Attributing emotion to static body postures: recognition accuracy, confusions, and viewpoint dependence. Jour. of Nonv. Behav. 28, 117–139 (2004)
6. Davitz, J.: Auditory correlates of vocal expression of emotional feeling. In: Davitz, J. (ed.) The Communication of emotional Meaning, pp. 101–112. McGraw-Hill, New York (1964)
7. de Gelder, B., Snyder, J., Greve, D., Gerard, G., Hadjikhani, N.: Fear fosters flight: A mechanism for fear contagion when perceiving emotion expressed by a whole body. Proc. of the National Academy of Science 101(47), 16701–16706 (2003)
8. de Silva, P.R., Bianchi-Berthouze, N.: Modeling human affective postures: An information theoretic characterization of posture features. Journal of Computer Animation and Virtual Worlds 15, 269–276 (2004)
9. de Silva, P., Kleinsmith, A., Bianchi-Berthouze, N.: Towards unsupervised detection of affective body posture nuances. In: Tao, J., Tan, T., Picard, R.W. (eds.) ACII 2005. LNCS, vol. 3784, pp. 32–39. Springer, Heidelberg (2005)
10. Ekman, P., Friesen, W.: Head and body cues in the judgment of emotion. A reformulation, Perceptual and Motor Skills 24, 711–724 (1967)
11. Harrigan, J., Rosenthal, R.: Physicians head and body positions as determinants of perceived rapport. Journal of of Applied Social Psychology 13(6), 496–509 (1983)
12. Hastie, T., Tibshirabi, R.: Discriminant analysis by Gaussian mixture. Journal of the Royal Statistical Society B:58, 155–176 (1996)

13. James, W.T.: A study of the expression of bodily posture. Journal of General Psychology 7, 405–437 (1932)
14. Kamisato, S., Odo, S., Ishikawa, Y., Hoshino, K.: Extraction of motion characteristics corresponding to sensitivity information using dance movement. Journal of Advanced Computational Intelligence and Intelligent Informatics 8(2), 167–178 (2004)
15. Kapoor, A., Picard, R., Ivanov, Y.: Probabilistic combination of multiple modalities to detect interest. Proc. of the 17th International Conference on Pattern Recognition 3, 969–972 (2004)
16. Kleinsmith, A., Fushimi, T., Bianchi-Berthouze, N.: An incremental and interactive affective posture recognition system. In: Ardissono, L., Brna, P., Mitrović, A. (eds.) UM 2005. LNCS (LNAI), vol. 3538, Springer, Heidelberg (2005)
17. Kleinsmith, A., de Silva, P., Bianchi-Berthouze, N.: Cross-cultural differences in recognizing affect from body posture. Interacting with Computers 18, 1371–1389 (2006)
18. Kleinsmith, A., de Silva, P., Bianchi-Berthouze, N.: Grounding affective dimensions into posture features. In: Proceedings of the First International Conference on Affective Computing and Intelligent Interaction, pp. 263–270. Springer, Heidelberg (2005)
19. Lachenbruch, P.A.: Discriminant Analysis, NY, Hafner (1975)
20. Mehrabian, A., Friar, J.: Encoding of attitude by a seated communicator via posture and position cues. Journal of Consulting and Clinical Psychology 33, 330–336 (1969)
21. Mehrabian, A.: Inference of attitude from the posture, orientation, and distance of a communicator. Journal of Consulting and Clinical Psychology 32, 296–308 (1968)
22. Mehrabian, A., Russell, J. (eds.): An Approach to Environmental Psychology. MIT Press, Cambridge (1974)
23. Osgood, C., Suci, G., Tannenbaum, P.: The measurement of meaning. University of Illinois Press, Chicago (1957)
24. Woo, W., Park, J., Iwadate, Y.: Emotion analysis from dance performance using time-delay neural networks. Proc. of the JCIS-CVPRIP 2, 374–377 (2000)
25. Wundt, W.: Outlines of psychology. Wilhelm Englemann, Leipzig (1907)

Detecting Affect from Non-stylised Body Motions

Daniel Bernhardt and Peter Robinson

Computer Laboratory, University of Cambridge,
15 JJ Thomson Avenue, Cambridge, CB3 0FD, UK

Abstract. In this paper we present a novel framework for analysing non-stylised motion in order to detect implicitly communicated affect. Our approach makes use of a segmentation technique which can divide complex motions into a set of automatically derived motion primitives. The parsed motion is then analysed in terms of dynamic features which are shown to encode affective information. In order to adapt our algorithm to personal movement idiosyncrasies we developed a new approach for deriving unbiased motion features. We have evaluated our approach using a comprehensive database of affectively performed motions. The results show that removing personal movement bias can have a significant benefit for automated affect recognition from body motion. The resulting recognition rate is similar to that of humans who took part in a comparable psychological experiment.

1 Introduction

The human body has evolved not only to perform sophisticated tasks, but also to communicate affect and inter-personal attitudes. One possible distinction can be made between affect communicated through non-stylised and stylised motions. In a stylised motion the entirety of the movement encodes a particular emotion. Stylised motions normally originate from laboratory settings, where subjects are asked to freely act an emotion without any constraints. They also arise from stylised dance. This paper, however, concerns itself with the more subtle aspects of *non-stylised* motions. We will examine how affect is communicated by the manner, in which every-day actions, such as knocking or walking, are performed.

After reviewing relevant related work in the next section, we discuss the segmentation of a complex motion into a sequence of meaningful motion primitives in Sect. 3. Sect. 4 then describes a set of dynamic features which captures the segments' affective information. In order to disambiguate affective cues from personal movement idiosyncrasies we make use of a statistical normalisation procedure. Sect. 5 introduces the experimental validation results which are based on an existing motion database of acted every-day motions. A concluding discussion is given in Sect. 6.

A. Paiva, R. Prada, and R.W. Picard (Eds.): ACII 2007, LNCS 4738, pp. 59–70, 2007.

2 Background

What makes a walk happy? How does an angry knock differ from a sad one? Indeed, are the visual cues from the body alone sufficient to judge a person's affect? Early research by Ekman suggested that people make greater use of the face than the body for judgements of emotion in others [1]. More recent results from psychology suggest, however, that emotional body language does constitute a significant source of affective information. In an experimental study Bull established that body positions and movements are consistently displayed and recognised during phases of interest/boredom and agreement/disagreement [2]. In a more recent study Pollick et al. examined the accuracy with which human observers could distinguish basic emotions from point-light arm movements [3]. They found that despite the impoverished nature of the displays, the recognition rates were significantly above chance level.

It is surprising that despite the apparent interest of psychologists in natural, non-stylised motions, research in affective computing has for a long time focused on stylised body movements. Only very recently, Kapoor et al. investigated *natural* behaviour in a computer-based tutoring environment. They demonstrated a correlation between frustration and various non-verbal cues including body posture [4]. Earlier, Camurri et al. had developed a vision-based library to analyse expressive body gestures based on both shape and dynamic cues. In recently reported results, they show correlations between affect expressed through stylised dance and dynamic measures such as quantity of motion and body contraction [5]. In a different study Kapur et al. showed how very simple statistical measures of stylised motions' dynamics can be used to distinguish between four basic emotions [6]. Our work builds on these latter dynamic approaches, gaining its main affective information from quantities such as limb velocity and acceleration.

However, the nature of non-stylised movements means that we will need to look more deeply into the structure of the motions involved. We need to understand which elements are governed by affect and which are confounded by other factors such as idiosyncrasies in personal movement (movement bias), gender or activity. This is a problem which animators have faced for a long time in order to create compelling and realistic motion sequences. As John Lasseter put it [7]:

> One character would not do a particular action the same way in two different emotional states. [...] No two characters would do the same action in the same way.

There has been a large body of recent work on the subject, which normally aims to provide better means for animators to control the expressions of their characters. Many of the approaches work on the notion of affective transforms applied to an underlying basic or neutral animation. In many cases these transforms change the spatial amplitude and speed of motions [8,9,10]. An interesting concept, as suggested by Rose et al., is the notion of motions being composed of a verb (a basic motion concept, such as walking) and an adverb which modifies the basic motion in various ways (e.g. happily, sadly, uphill or downhill) [11].

The idea of viewing body language as analogous to natural language is not a new one. Ray Birdwhistell argued that complex motions can be broken down into an ordered system of isolable elements which he called kinemes [12]. The notion of a universal set of kinemes or motion primitives is a compelling one as it gives structure to the otherwise vast complexity of human motion — a goal which the Facial Action Coding System [13] has achieved so successfully for the face. It is this segmentation into motion primitives which will help us to discard the structural information of non-stylised motions, leaving the essentially dynamic cues which we will use to distinguish different affects.

3   Motion Analysis

For this work we used a motion-captured database recorded at the Psychology Department, University of Glasgow [14]. It gave us access to a collection of knocking, throwing, lifting and walking motions performed by 30 individuals (15 male and 15 female) in neutral, happy, angry and sad affective styles. Most of our quoted results are based on the approximately 1200 knocking motions from the database.

The skeletal structure of the recorded bodies is represented by 15 joints, positioned relative to a world frame. In order to obtain a rotation- and scale-invariant representation, we transform the joint positions into a body-local coordinate system and normalise them with respect to body size. Let f stand for the dimension of time, measured in frames. We denote the time-varying signal of normalised joint positions as the matrix $\boldsymbol{\Psi}$. We can also represent the motion in terms of the joint rotations over time, $\boldsymbol{\Theta}$. A particular body configuration at frame f can be represented as a row vector, denoted as $\boldsymbol{\psi}_f$ or $\boldsymbol{\theta}_f$. The gth positional or rotational degree of freedom at frame f is written as $\psi_{f,g}$ or $\theta_{f,g}$ respectively. We will also make use of the dot notation (e.g. $\dot{\theta}_{f,g}$) to denote derivatives with respect to time. Finally, projecting a body configuration vector onto a subspace is written as the linear operator $P(\cdot)$, e.g. $P_{\mathrm{rh}}(\boldsymbol{\psi}_f)$ denotes the position of the right hand relative to the body-centred coordinate system at time frame f.

3.1   Motion Segmentation

The goal of motion segmentation is to parse high-dimensional body movements into a sequence of more basic primitives. In general, this is a hard problem which is of interest to researchers from many different areas, including gesture recognition and robotics. Our approach is based on the work by Fod et al. [15]. It makes use of an objective function $E(f)$ which is a measure for the overall motion energy (activation) at time frame f. In many ways this concept of energy is analogous to that employed in the segmentation of speech into phonemes or words [16]. Let $\dot{\theta}_{f,g}$ denote the angular speed of the gth rotational degree of freedom at time frame f. Then we can define the body's motion energy as a weighted sum of the rotational limb speeds.

$$E(f) = \sum_{k=1}^{n} w_k \dot{\theta}_{f,k}^2 \qquad (1)$$

In essence, E will be large for periods of energetic motion and will remain small during periods of low motion energy. Fig. 1 shows E for repeated knocking. Fig. 2 illustrates how the observed energy peaks coincide with actions such as arm raises or individual forward and backward movements during the knock. Local minima in E can be observed whenever the trajectory of the right arm changes direction. We can use these insights to segment a complex motion as follows.

1. Compute E for the whole motion sequence.
2. Threshold the signal at a threshold t. Mark all frames f for which $E(f) > t$.
3. Find all connected regions of marked frames and regard them as individual motion segments.
4. Extend the segments to the preceding and succeeding local minima of E.

Obviously, our choice of t has a major impact on the nature of the segments. Fod et al. use empirically derived thresholds. If this method is to be used in a general framework, however, we need an automatic way of finding an optimal t. We propose the following solution. For every pair (E, t_n) we obtain a number of segments by thresholding E at t_n. Let $numseg_E(t_n) = s_n$ be the function which computes the number of segments s_n for any such pair. Fig. 3 shows $numseg$ for the motion in Fig. 1 and sampled at various thresholds. Our goal is to find a threshold which will exhibit all major motion segments (energy peaks) while filtering out small scale motions due to low-level signal noise. We note that noise is mainly registered during periods of low energy (e.g. between frames 250–300

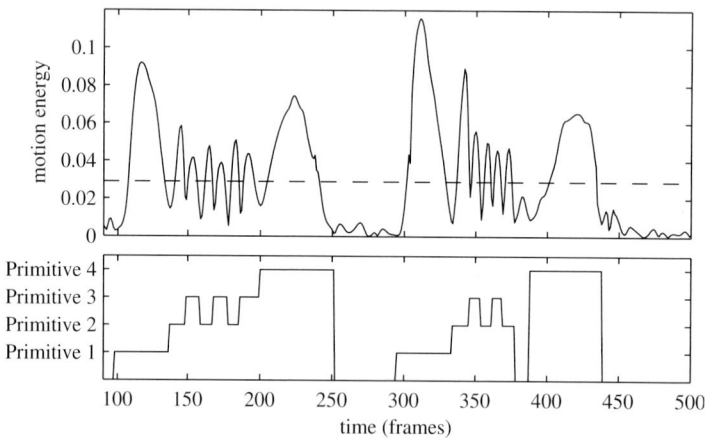

Fig. 1. Objective function $E(f)$ (top) with automatically calculated optimal segmentation threshold $t_{opt} = 0.029$ for part of a repeated knocking motion. The bottom shows the parse of the above motion sequence into four motion primitives and periods of no motion.

and 450–500 in Fig. 1). Let t_0 be an empirical noise threshold. Then the optimal threshold t_{opt} is defined as the threshold which maximises the number of major motion segments.

$$t_{opt} = \underset{t}{\operatorname{argmax}}\{numseg_E(t)\} \qquad \text{subject to } t_{opt} > t_0. \qquad (2)$$

3.2   Motion Primitives

Ideally, we would like to group the extracted segments into semantically meaningful clusters representing primitive motions. One approach to define such primitives would be to use a comprehensive list as devised by Bull or Birdwhistell to transcribe their psychological or anthropological observations [2,12]. Due to their

Primitive 1   Primitive 2   Primitive 3   Primitive 4

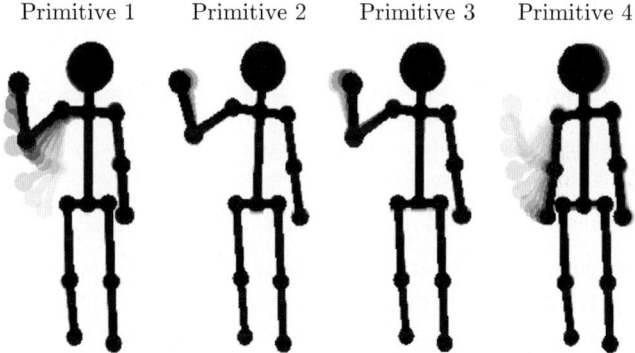

Fig. 2. Four phases of a knocking motion exhibiting distinct peaks of motion energy. Our algorithm detects each of the phases as a separate motion segment. Each segment is labelled with one of four automatically derived motion primitives. The primitives coincide with the semantically meaningful basic actions "Raise arm", "Knock", "Retract", "Lower arm".

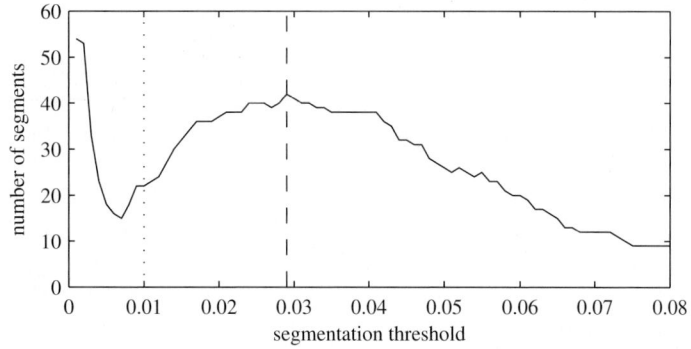

Fig. 3. $numseg_E(t)$ for a repeated knocking motion sampled for thresholds between 0.001 and 0.08. The diagram also shows t_{opt} (dashed) and t_0 (dotted).

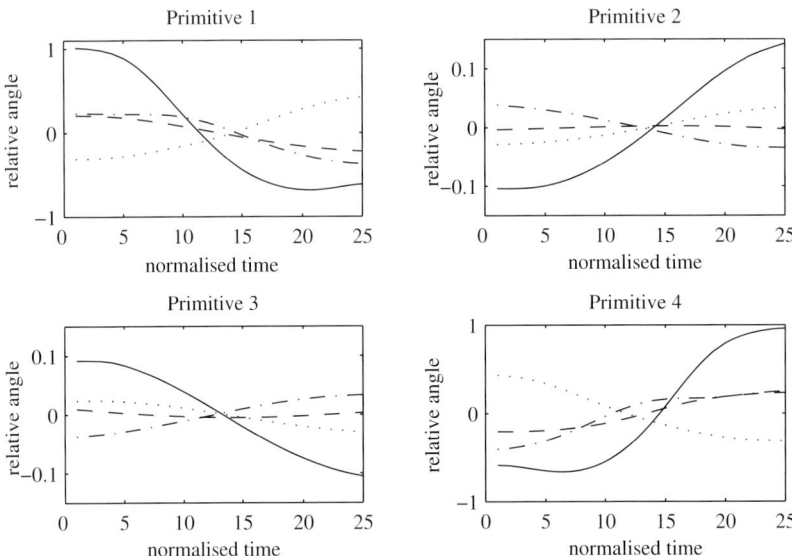

Fig. 4. Four motion primitives derived by k-means clustering. Dashed/dotted curves visualise rotations in the right shoulder, solid line visualises rotation in the right elbow. All other degrees of freedom are omitted as they exhibit no significant motion.

generality, however, these sets are large. Many of the listed primitives are irrelevant for any particular context. Indeed, context often governs the *affective and social meaning* of movements [12]. We therefore adopt a more context-dependent approach to the definition of motion primitives. It is based on the clustering of a set of example motions which are representative for a certain context. For our current scenario the context is very specific (knocking) and therefore the number of motion primitives is rather small. In more complex scenarios such as "everyday activities" or "interpersonal conversations" we would expect to require a larger set of primitives to represent all observed movements well.

Consider the database of affective knocking motions described above. After segmenting the movements, we need to find a representation for the segments which allows us to compare and cluster them. We therefore consider the *joint angles* of the motions and time-normalise them. This is done by resampling each segment at 25 equally spaced intervals. We also subtract the segments' means in order to capture the *relative* motion rather than the absolute body configurations. Next, we wish to group the segments into semantically distinct categories. We hypothesised that the knocking motions can be divided into four basic phases: lift arm, repeatedly knock and retract, lower arm. We therefore used a simple k-means clustering algorithm with $k = 4$. In a completely unsupervised scenario without any prior knowledge of the number of motion primitives, we would choose a clustering technique which automatically determines an optimal number of clusters such as hierarchical or Markov clustering. The following steps summarise our algorithm to compute a set of motion primitives from a set of example motions:

1. Segment the set of motions as described in Sect. 3.1.
2. Time-normalise all segments. Subtract sample means.
3. Cluster the normalised segments.
4. The clusters (or cluster centroids) represent the motion primitives.

The four derived motion primitives for the set of knocking motions are visualised in Fig. 4. The four degrees of freedom of the right arm are represented as four separate curves.

Having defined our primitives, we can now *parse* a new motion by following steps 1 and 2 as outlined above and replacing steps 3 and 4 by an assignment to the closest cluster centroid (most similar primitive). Fig. 1 illustrates how a repeated knocking motion (energy curve shown on top) has been parsed into a sequence of primitives (bottom). The motion is parsed in a semantically meaningful fashion. Fig. 2 shows that primitives 1 and 4 correspond to the larger scale motions of raising and lowering the right arm while primitives 2 and 3 capture the smaller scale knocking motions. We will now turn to the analysis of the dynamic and affective parameters of the segmented motions.

4   Affect Recognition

Angry movements in the analysed database tend to look energetic and forceful while sad knocks appear relatively slow and slack. Similar observations are true for the other classes of motions such as throwing and walking. This role of dynamic movement qualities such as velocity and acceleration in affect recognition has been stressed by several authors [3,5,6]. Never before, however, has the analysis of dynamics been attempted at the level of motion primitives. We propose this solution as a more flexible and well-founded alternative to the use of fixed or sliding windows as used in other recent works [5,6].

We are using four statistical measures as features for affect recognition. They are computed over a whole motion segment such as an arm raise. For the analysed knocking motions only the right arm exhibits significant movement. Therefore all dynamic features are currently based on the right arm. Consider a motion segment $\boldsymbol{\Psi}$ of length n. Remembering that $P_{\mathrm{rh}}(\boldsymbol{\psi}_f)$ denotes the position of the right hand, we can define the features as follows.

1. Maximum distance of hand from body $d_h = \max_{f=1}^n \|P_{\mathrm{rh}}(\boldsymbol{\psi}_f)\|$

2. Average hand speed $\bar{s}_h = \frac{1}{n}\sum_{f=1}^n \|P_{\mathrm{rh}}(\dot{\boldsymbol{\psi}}_f)\|$

3. Average hand acceleration $\bar{a}_h = \frac{1}{n}\sum_{f=1}^n \|P_{\mathrm{rh}}(\ddot{\boldsymbol{\psi}}_f)\|$

4. Average hand jerk $\bar{j}_h = \frac{1}{n}\sum_{f=1}^n \|P_{\mathrm{rh}}(\dddot{\boldsymbol{\psi}}_f)\|$

We can also compute analogous features $d_e, \bar{s}_e, \bar{a}_e, \bar{j}_e$ based on the elbow motion. For any person p and motion segment m this gives us the feature vector $\phi_{\boldsymbol{p,m}} = (d_h, \bar{s}_h, \bar{a}_h, \bar{j}_h, d_e, \bar{s}_e, \bar{a}_e, \bar{j}_e)$.

4.1 The Problem of Individual Movement Bias

According to Lasseter's view quoted in Sect. 2, the two major factors affecting observable motion qualities are emotion and individual style. In Sect. 5 we shall show that our data does indeed reveal some global correlation between the above features $\phi_{p,m}$ and the different emotion classes. Fig. 5(a), however, shows that the between-class variability of the two very different emotion classes sad and angry is smaller than we would hope. The hand speed distribution for sad knocks (black) overlaps heavily with that of angry knocks (white). In order to be separable through a pattern recognition approach, the two distributions should show a large between-class variability while exhibiting a small within-class variability. This exemplifies the problem of individual movement bias. Different people tend to display the same emotion in very different ways, thus impeding classification.

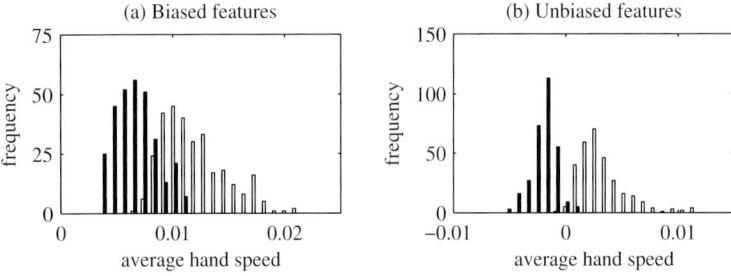

Fig. 5. Biased and unbiased feature distributions for sad knocks (black) and angry knocks (white)

Our approach to this problem is a normalisation procedure based on the following intuition. It seems a reasonable assumption that a person's motion idiosyncrasies influence his or her movements in a consistent fashion — after all we expect them to be governed by gender, physical build and other constant factors. Even dynamic factors such as mood might be changing slowly enough to be assumed temporarily constant. We therefore propose to model individual motion bias as an additive constant signature $\bar{\phi}_p$ which influences the motion features introduced above. We obtain an estimate of the unbiased motion features $\hat{\phi}_{p,m}$ by subtracting the personal bias.

$$\hat{\phi}_{p,m} = \phi_{p,m} - \bar{\phi}_p \qquad \text{for any motion } m \qquad (3)$$

An important problem is how to estimate $\bar{\phi}_p$. If we do not "know" a person, i.e. have no history of his or her movements, we may need to take an a priori guess, maybe conditioned on gender or other cues. However, if we have a history, we can compute $\bar{\phi}_p$ from all the observed motions. In our case, we take an average over all the knocking motions in the database in order to learn about a person's motion bias. Note that this operation does not tell us anything about affect-specific factors as all motions are treated equally and different affects are represented at equal frequencies in the database. Fig. 5(b) illustrates how this normalisation improves the between-class variability for the two shown classes considerably. Sect. 5 gives a more rigorous account of the improvements achieved when taking movement bias into consideration.

4.2   Machine Learning

We can use the biased or unbiased motion features to train a classifier which distinguishes the four emotions neutral, happy, angry and sad. We decided to use support vector machines (SVMs) with a polynomial kernel as they tend to exhibit good generalisation performance. The suitability of SVMs for this domain was demonstrated by Kapur et al. [6]. In order to solve the general problem of recognising the affect of a motion sequence, we train a family of binary SVMs $M_{x,y}^z$. The classifier $M_{x,y}^z$ aims to find the maximum margin between affect classes x and y for motion primitives of type z. Once these binary classifiers have been trained, we can classify a new motion as follows:

1. Segment motion into a list of primitives as described in Sect. 3.
2. Let the first segment in the list be of primitive type z. Apply all pairwise SVMs $M_{x,y}^z$. Classify the segment according to a majority vote.
3. Remove segment from the list and repeat from step 2 until list is empty.
4. Classify whole motion by majority vote of individual segment classifications.

5   Experimental Results

With the conducted experiments we aimed to answer three questions:

1. What recognition rate can be achieved with our approach?
2. How does movement bias (see Sect. 4.1) affect the recognition performance?
3. How do our results compare to related results found in the literature?

We used the knocking motions from our database to run Leave-One-Subject-Out cross-validation (LOSO-CV) tests. Overall, we used approximately 1200 motion samples with an equal proportion for each of the considered emotions neutral, happy, angry and sad. For each iteration of the cross-validation the system was therefore trained on around 1160 samples and validated on 40 samples. In different tests we found that the system does considerably better if we add some of the remaining 40 samples to the training set or perform a subject-independent cross-validation. In contrast to those tests, the figures we quote here are representative for the generalisation performance of our system for an unknown person.

The confusion matrices for LOSO-CV using biased and unbiased features are shown in Table 1. Note that angry and sad knocks are classified more reliably than neutral and happy ones. The most significant factor which negatively affects recognition rates (sensitivity) is the confusion between neutral and happy knocks. In answer to question 2 above, we find that using unbiased features improves the

Table 1. Confusion matrices for LOSO-CV using biased features (left) and unbiased features (right). The classification procedure distinguished between four emotions: neutral (neu), happy (hap), angry (ang) and sad. All average and affect-specific sensitivities are above chance level (0.25).

Truth	classified as					classified as			
	neu	hap	ang	sad		neu	hap	ang	sad
neu	**0.379**	0.229	0.127	0.265		**0.742**	0.199	0.007	0.052
hap	0.281	**0.411**	0.179	0.129		0.278	**0.653**	0.056	0.013
ang	0.176	0.203	**0.591**	0.030		0.013	0.063	**0.924**	0.000
sad	0.214	0.139	0.023	**0.624**		0.066	0.010	0.000	**0.924**
	average sensitivity: **0.501**					average sensitivity: **0.811**			

overall recognition rate considerably from 50% to 81%. Our informal observations from Sect. 4.1 have hence been confirmed.

We can obtain a measure for the more objective recognition efficiency η if we normalise the achieved sensitivity by the sensitivity expected by chance (sometimes referred to as generality [17]).

$$\eta = \frac{\text{achieved sensitivity}}{\text{sensitivity expected by chance}} \tag{4}$$

In our case we would expect a classifier which assigns one of the four affect classes at random to achieve a sensitivity of 25%. Therefore the efficiencies of our classifiers for biased and unbiased features are $\eta_b = 2.0$ and $\eta_{ub} = 3.24$ respectively. We can use these measures to compare our results to those of related experiments in the next section.

6   Discussion and Future Work

For our discussion we consider the results of two other related experiments. We were using part of a database which was created by Pollick et al. for psychological work. In one particular study they examined how accurately *human subjects* could classify affect from knocking motions displayed as point-light or full video stimuli [3]. The only major difference from our experimental setup was their forced choice between five rather than our four emotional states (afraid being the additional class). They report that humans achieved a recognition rate of 59% for point-light and 71% for full video stimuli. These figures illustrate that even humans are far from perfect at classifying affect from non-stylised body motions. We can calculate the efficiency $\hat{\eta}$ achieved by humans as defined in Eq. 4. For point-light and video displays humans exhibit efficiencies of $\hat{\eta}_{pl} = 2.95$ and $\hat{\eta}_v = 3.55$ respectively.

One of the major contributions of our work derives from the fact that classifying affect from non-stylised motions is harder than from stylised ones. This is demonstrated by the experiments performed by Kapur et al. [6]. They recorded stylised emotions and compared the accuracy of various machine learning techniques as well as human performance. For the task of distinguishing four basic

Table 2. Comparison of results from our and related experiments

experiment	Kapur et al. [6]		Pollick et al. [3]		Our results (Sect. 5)	
motions	stylised		non-stylised		non-stylised	
classifier	human	SVM	human		SVM	
features	biased		pt.-light	video	biased	unbiased
# emotions	4	4	5	5	4	4
sensitivity	93%	84%	59%	71%	50%	81%
efficiency	**3.72**	**3.34**	**2.95**	**3.55**	**2.0**	**3.24**

emotions from point-light displays, humans achieved a recognition rate of 93% ($\eta = 3.72$). This is considerably higher than human performance reported by Pollick et al. for non-stylised movements ($\hat{\eta}_{pl} = 2.95$). For SVMs the recognition rate was lower at 83.6% ($\eta = 3.34$). These results are summarised in Table 2.

We have shown that using unbiased dynamic features based on motion primitives boosts the recognition rate considerably. Our computational approach exhibits a better efficiency than humans for classifying affect in non-stylised movements from point-light displays. The performance of our approach is also comparable to that of Kapur et al. This is significant since their stylised motion data contained solely affective information. For our non-stylised motions, on the other hand, only certain subtle aspects communicate affect while most of the motion signal is governed by the independent semantic meaning of the motion.

We are currently working on overcoming various limitations of our approach. In the version presented here, the algorithm only considers the right arm for extracting affect-related dynamic features. Incorporating features from other body parts will help us to analyse motions such as walking, which are not primarily based on arm movements. Furthermore, the torso and head can be expected to hold valuable cues even for heavily arm-based actions [9]. One challenge which needs to be addressed in this direction is the generalisation of motion segments to multiple body parts. One could either compute segments for each body part individually or attempt to capture more subtle relationships between limbs by defining segments in terms of the simultaneous motion of multiple body parts.

Another limitation which might have to be addressed in the future is the assumption that motion primitives are clearly separable by local motion energy minima. For very smooth and cyclic motions, for example, it might be possible to exhibit the basic cycle periods of a motion as segments. Furthermore, it might not be sufficient to employ a single segmentation threshold t_{opt} if we analyse a series of movements which are very different in terms of exhibited motion energy. This problem might be solved by recomputing t_{opt} either regularly or, alternatively, whenever we detect a significant change in motion energy.

Finally, we are investigating better ways to estimate the personal movement signature $\bar{\phi}_p$. Ultimately, we would like to be able to predict $\bar{\phi}_p$ from as few and unconstrained example motions as possible.

References

1. Ekman, P.: Differential communication of affect by head and body cues. Journal of Personality and Social Psychology, 726–735 (1964)
2. Bull, P.E.: Posture and Gesture. Pergamon Press 16 (1987)
3. Pollick, F.E., Paterson, H.M., Bruderlin, A., Sanford, A.J.: Perceiving affect from arm movement. Cognition 82, 51–61 (2001)
4. Kapoor, A., Burleson, W., Picard, R.W.: Automatic prediction of frustration. International Journal of Human-Computer Studies (2007)
5. Camurri, A., Lagerlöf, I., Volpe, G.: Recognizing emotion from dance movement: comparison of spectator recognition and automated techniques. International Journal of Human-Computer Studies 59(1-2), 213–225 (2003)
6. Kapur, A., Kapur, A., Virji-Babul, N., Tzanetakis, G., Driessen, P.F.: Gesture-based affective computing on motion capture data. In: Affective Computing and Intelligent Interaction, pp. 1–7 (2005)
7. Lasseter, J.: Principles of traditional animation applied to 3D computer animation. In: SIGGRAPH '87: Proceedings of the 14th annual conference on Computer graphics and interactive techniques, pp. 35–44 (1987)
8. Amaya, K., Bruderlin, A., Calvert, T.: Emotion from motion. In: Graphics Interface '96, Canadian Human-Computer Communications Society, pp. 222–229 (1996)
9. Zhao, L., Badler, N.I., Costa, M.: Interpreting movement manner. In: CA '00: Proceedings of the Computer Animation, pp. 98–103 (2000)
10. Polichroniadis, T.P.: High Level Control of Virtual Actors. PhD thesis, Computer Laboratory, University of Cambridge (2001)
11. Rose, C., Cohen, M.F., Bodenheimer, B.: Verbs and adverbs: Multidimensional motion interpolation. IEEE Computer Graphics and Applications 18, 32–40 (1998)
12. Birdwhistell, R.L.: Kinesics and Context: Essays on Body Motion Communication. University of Pennsylvania Press (1970)
13. Ekman, P., Friesen, W.V.: Facial action coding system. Consulting Psychologists Press (1978)
14. Ma, Y., Paterson, H.M., Pollick, F.E.: A motion capture library for the study of identity, gender, and emotion perception from biological motion. Behavior Research Methods 38, 134–141 (2006)
15. Fod, A., Matarić, M.J., Jenkins, O.C.: Automated derivation of primitives for movement classification. Autononmous Robots 12(1), 39–54 (2002)
16. Wang, D., Lu, L., Zhang, H.J.: Speech segmentation without speech recognition. In: Proc. of IEEE International Conference on Acoustics, Speech and Signal Processing, pp. 468–471. IEEE Computer Society Press, Los Alamitos (2003)
17. Huijsmans, N., Sebe, N.: Extended performance graphs for cluster retrieval. In: Proceedings of the International Conference on Computer Vision and Pattern Recognition, vol. 1, pp. 26–32 (2001)

Recognising Human Emotions from Body Movement and Gesture Dynamics

Ginevra Castellano[1], Santiago D. Villalba[2], and Antonio Camurri[1]

[1] Infomus Lab, DIST, University of Genoa[*]
[2] MLG, School of Computer Science and Informatics, University College Dublin
ginevra.castellano@unige.it, santiago.villalba@ucd.ie

Abstract. We present an approach for the recognition of acted emotional states based on the analysis of body movement and gesture expressivity. According to research showing that distinct emotions are often associated with different qualities of body movement, we use non-propositional movement qualities (e.g. amplitude, speed and fluidity of movement) to infer emotions, rather than trying to recognise different gesture shapes expressing specific emotions. We propose a method for the analysis of emotional behaviour based on both direct classification of time series and a model that provides indicators describing the dynamics of expressive motion cues. Finally we show and interpret the recognition rates for both proposals using different classification algorithms.

1 Introduction

One critical aspect of human-computer interfaces is the ability to communicate with users in an expressive way [1]. Computers should be able to recognise and interpret users' emotional states and to communicate expressive-emotional information to them. Recently, there has been an increased interest in designing automated video analysis algorithms aiming to extract, describe and classify information related to the emotional state of individuals. In this paper we focus on video analysis of movement and gesture as indicators of an underlying emotional process.

Our research aims to investigate which are the motion cues indicating differences between emotions and to define a model to recognise emotions from video analysis of body movement and gesture dynamics. The possibility to use movement and gesture as indicators of the state of individuals provides a novel approach to quantitatively observe and evaluate the users in an ecological environment and to respond adaptively to them. Our research is grounded in the Component Process Model of emotion (CPM) proposed by Scherer [2], and explores the component of the model representing motor activation in emotion. Specifically, the CPM describes a relationship between the results of different event appraisals (such as novelty, intrinsic pleasantness, goal conduciveness etc.)

---

[*] Part of this work was carried out in the context of the EU Project HUMAINE (Human-Machine Interaction Network on Emotion)(IST-2002-507422).

A. Paiva, R. Prada, and R.W. Picard (Eds.): ACII 2007, LNCS 4738, pp. 71–82, 2007.

and the response patterning with respect to physiological arousal, action tendency, subjective feeling and, in particular, motor expression.

In this paper we present an approach for the recognition of four acted emotional states (anger, joy, pleasure, sadness) based on the analysis of body movement and gesture expressivity. According to research showing that distinct emotions are often associated with different qualities of body movement (see for example [3]), we use non-propositional movement qualities (e.g. amplitude, speed and fluidity of movement) to infer emotions, rather than trying to recognise different gesture shapes expressing specific emotions, to investigate the role of movement expressivity versus shape in gesture. We propose a method for the analysis of emotional behaviour based on direct classification of time series and on a model that provides indicators describing the dynamics of expressive motion cues. Finally we show and interpret the recognition rates for both proposals using different classification algorithms.

2   Motivations and Related Work

Research aiming to endow computers with the ability to mimic human emotional intelligence and to recognise emotions communicated by others through body movement needs to be grounded in neuroscience and psychology. Psychological studies on visual analysis of body movement show that human movement differs from other movements because it is the only visual stimulus we have experience of both perceiving and producing [4]. Understanding the human processing mechanism of the stimuli coming from the so called "biological movement" [5], the one produced by animals in general and humans in particular, would lead to better designed computational models of emotion based on visual analysis of affective body language. Further, theories linking the response to motion visual stimuli to mirror motion-visual neurons would allow a deeper understanding of how we comprehend others' emotions and develop empathy [6]. Finally, several studies from psychology focus on the relationships between emotion and movement qualities, and investigate expressive body movements [7,8,9].

In human-computer interaction a central role is played by automated video analysis techniques aiming to extract physical characteristics of humans and use them to infer information related to the emotional state of individuals. Modelling emotional behaviour starting from automatic analysis of movement and gesture is currently still a poorly explored field though. Most of the previous studies, in fact, focus on emotion recognition based on audio and facial expression data. Nevertheless, some attempts were made in the direction of designing systems able to analyse expressive body movements and use this information to recognise emotions.

Burgoon et al. [10] proposed an approach for analysing cues from multiple body regions for the automated identification of emotions displayed in videos. Camurri et al. [11] classified expressive gestures in human full-body movement (dance performances). They identified cues deemed important for emotion recognition, like quantity of motion and contraction/expansion of the body, and showed how these cues could be tracked by automated recognition techniques. Kapur et al. [12] used full-body skeletal movements data obtained with a technology based on the VICON motion capturing system to classify four emotional states. Bianchi-Berthouze and Kleinsmith [13] proposed a model that can self-organise postural features into affective categories to give robots the ability to incrementally learn to recognise affective human postures through interaction with human partners. Other studies show that expressive gesture analysis and classification can be obtained by means of automatic image processing [14] and that the integration of multiple modalities (facial expressions and body movements) is successful for multimodal emotion recognition. Gunes and Piccardi [15] for example fused facial expression and body gesture information at different levels for bimodal emotion recognition. Further, el Kaliouby and Robinson [16] proposed a vision-based computational model to infer acted mental states from head movements and facial expressions.

3   Experimental Setup and Data Collection

Our work is based on a corpus of 240 gestures collected during the Third Summer School of the HUMAINE (Human-Machine Interaction Network on Emotion) EU-IST project, held in Genoa in September 2006. Ten participants (six male and four female) were asked to act eight emotional states (anger, despair, interest, pleasure, sadness, irritation, joy and pride) equally distributed in the valence-arousal space. In this study we focus mainly on four emotions: anger, joy, pleasure and sadness (see Table 1).

Table 1. The emotions in the space valence-arousal

	positive-valence	negative-valence
high-arousal	joy	anger
low-arousal	pleasure	sadness

We asked the participants to perform the same gesture (raising and lowering the arms in the coronal plane, starting with the arms down by the side while standing in the rest position) trying to express the different emotional conditions. We chose this experimental setup because we are interested in investigating the role of movement expressivity versus shape in gesture. For this reason, we decided to use the same gesture, whose shape does not appear to convey any obvious emotional expression or meaning, while expressing different emotions. In this way we evaluate whether it is possible to recognise the emotions based only on expressivity. The gesture was repeated three times for each emotion, so that we collected 240 posed gestures.

During the experiment, subjects' full-bodies were recorded by a DV camera (25 fps) viewed from the front. A uniform dark background was used in order to make the silhouette extraction process easier. Further, a long sleeved shirt was worn by all the participants in order to make the hand tracking feasible with our available technical resources.

3.1   Feature Extraction

Our approach to video analysis of gesture and body movement allows the silhouette and body parts to be tracked without the need for markers. We used the EyesWeb platform [17] to extract the whole silhouette and the hands of the subjects from the background. The EyesWeb Expressive Gesture Processing Library [18] was used to compute five different expressive motion cues: quantity of motion and contraction index of the body, velocity, acceleration and fluidity of the hand's barycentre.

The quantity of motion (QoM) is a measure of the amount of detected motion, computed with a technique based on silhouette motion images (SMIs). These are images carrying information about variations of the silhouette shape and position in the last few frames (see Figure 1).

$$SMI[t] = \sum_{i=0}^{n} Silhouette[t-i]\} - Silhouette[t] \tag{1}$$

The SMI at frame t is generated by adding together the silhouettes extracted in the previous n frames and then subtracting the silhouette at frame t. The resulting image contains just the variations that happened in the previous frames.

Fig. 1. A measure of QoM using SMIs (the shadow along the arms and the body) and the tracking of the hand

QoM is computed as the area (i.e., number of pixels) of a SMI, normalised in order to obtain a value usually ranging from 0 to 1. That can be considered as an overall measure of the amount of detected motion, involving velocity and force.

$$QoM = Area(SMI[t,n])/Area(Silhouette[t]) \tag{2}$$

The contraction index (CI) is a measure, ranging from 0 to 1, of the degree of contraction and expansion of the body. CI can be calculated using a technique related to the bounding region, i.e., the minimum rectangle surrounding the body: the algorithm compares the area covered by this rectangle with the area currently covered by the silhouette.

Velocity (Vel) and acceleration (Acc) are related to the trajectory followed by the hand's barycentre in a 2D plane. Fluidity gives a measure of the uniformity of motion, so that fluidity is considered maximum when, in the movement between two specific points of the space, the acceleration is equal to zero. It is computed as the Directness Index [18] of the trajectory followed by the velocity of hand's barycentre in the 2D plane.

Due to technical and time constraints during the recordings our data became noisy somehow. Since we didn't use markers the hand-tracking was difficult, even in our controlled environment. We lost 14 full videos and some frames at the end of a small number of other videos. This is only a reflection of the current limitations of technology that a deployed recognition system should be able to handle. Missing and noisy data, though, are expected as inputs to a production system.

The gestures are then described by the profiles over time of expressive motion cues. In order to compare the gestures from all the subjects, the data were normalised considering the maximum and the minimum values of each motion cue in each actor. We used these normalised time series as inputs for the recognition experiment described in section 4.2.

A further processing step converted these temporal series into a fixed set of indicators or meta-features (see Figure 2) conveying information about the dynamics of the gesture expressivity over time.

Starting from the temporal profiles of each cue, information about its shape was calculated. Automatic extraction of the selected features was made using new software modules developed in EyesWeb. This process was made for each motion cue, so that each gesture is characterised by a set of 80 (5x16)

- **Initial and Final Slope**: slope of the line joining the first value and the first relative extremum, slope of the line joining the last value and the last relative extremum.
- **Initial (Final) Slope of the Main Peak**: slope of the line joining the absolute maximum and the preceding (following) minimum.
- **Maximum, Mean, Mean / Max, Mean / Following Max**: the maximum and mean values and their ratio, ratio between the two first biggest values.
- **Maximum / Main Peak Duration, Main Peak Duration / Duration**: ratio between the maximum and the main peak duration, ratio between the peak containing the absolute maximum and the total gesture duration.
- **Centroid of Energy, Distance between Max and Centroid**: location of the barycentre of energy, distance between the maximum and the barycentre of energy.
- **Shift Index of the Maximum, Symmetry Index**: position of the maximum with respect to the centre of the curve, symmetry of the curve relative to the maximum value position.
- **Number of Maxima, Number of Maxima preceding the Main One**: number of relative maxima, number of relative maxima preceding the absolute one.

Fig. 2. The features computed from the expressive motion cues

meta-features. These are the inputs for the classifiers used in the experiment described at section 4.3.

4   Emotion Recognition and Experimental Results

Our emotion recognition system is based on gesture dynamics captured from video via computer-vision techniques (see figure 3). We face a time-series classification problem, which can be solved in several ways. Two of the possible approaches are [19]:

- Use of techniques that specifically deal with temporal classification, working directly over the series data. Hidden Markov Models or Dynamic Time Warping are examples of this. We follow this approach in the recognition experiment described in section 4.2.
- Representing the problem in such a way as to allow the application of propositional concept learners (the more widespread and best understood classification techniques). This approach constructs a set of features trying to best describe the series. This is the direction we follow in the recognition experiment described in section 4.3.

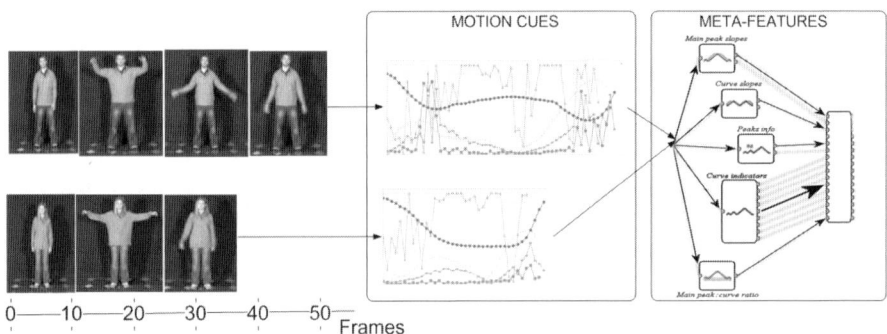

Fig. 3. Representing gesture videos as cue-time-series and meta-features. Several of the usual problems in series classification, such as scaling, misalignment and different duration are present.

4.1   Performance Estimation Procedure

Credibility is the main concern when evaluating the generalisation capability of a learning system [20]. In our case the small size of our dataset poses a challenge to both error estimation and overfitting (over-representation of the system performance) avoidance.

All the quantitative results presented here were obtained using leave one out cross validation (LOOCV). LOOCV allows us to train with the greatest amount of data each time, which increases the chance that the classifier is accurate and that both train and test data are representative. Since no random sampling is involved its results are deterministic. Standard 10-fold cross validation estimation was exhibiting a big, undesirable variance.

We also followed the sometimes overlooked principle of not allowing the learning machines to see in any way the testing data during the training phase. We found extremely easy to memorise our data and introduce overfitting artifacts by full-dataset pre-discretisation and pre-feature-selection, leading to fallacious error estimations. Supervised discretisation and feature selection were performed as an integral part of the whole classification system, that is, for each iteration of the LOOCV.

4.2 A Lazy Classifier Based on Dynamic Time Warping

Dynamic Time Warping (DTW)[21] is a well known algorithm for measuring similarity between two sequences which may vary in phase or speed. It computes both a distance between series and a *warping path* or correspondence between pairs of points from the two series. In the last decade DTW has emerged as a common solution for time series alignment and comparison. It has already been applied to gesture temporal alignment for the same gesture performed with different styles [22].

Once we have a distance measure between time series, a world of possibilities is presented. For example, we can apply clustering algorithms, or use the distance matrix as input for Kernel-based algorithms (e.g. SVMs) or other dissimilarity based classifiers. In this study we used simple a nearest neighbour [20] based on DTW distance (1NN-DTW) as the classifier for our system. A new gesture is assigned to the emotion of the gesture in the training set to a minimum distance, its nearest neighbour. Different from the other alternatives, this simple approach allows us to interpret the results in a more straightforward way and, furthermore, it has proven effective.

There are several perspectives from which the recognition system should be evaluated. Table 2 shows the results for the dataset containing the eight original emotions and those with a reduced set containing only four emotions (anger, joy, pleasure, sadness). We evaluated the performance of the system trained using only the personal set of gestures (i.e. training one classifier per subject, "personal

Table 2. LOOCV errors for the 1NN-DTW classifier. Cues per rows, in columns experiment for 4 / 8 emotions, personal (PS) versus universal (US) classifiers. In the case of the personal space the error rate is averaged over all subjects.

Cue ↓	4 Emotions (PS)	4 Emotions (US)	8 Emotions (PS)	8 Emotions (US)
Acceleration	0.54	0.57	0.73	0.77
CI	0.41	0.42	**0.53**	**0.59**
Fluidity	0.56	0.56	0.80	0.82
QoM	**0.34**	**0.37**	0.57	0.63
Velocity	0.40	0.43	0.64	0.65

space") and the universal set (i.e. an inter-subject enabled classifier using the universal set of gestures, "universal space"). From the results presented in table 2 we draw several conclusions.

- Our system is not able to discriminate successfully between the 8 emotions. We think that this is due not only to the increased complexity for the learning task, but also to inherent lacks in the task definition. Maybe it's just that those emotions are indistinguishable from the gesture at hand or that our features are not relevant.
- For the gesture considered QoM is the clear winner in the 4-emotions case.
- As it is the case in the real world, it's desirable for the classifier to get the knowledge of the actual subject nuances. No "universal" classifier can be flexible enough as to adapt to the modes of all subjects. By inspecting the nearest neighbour for each gesture, the 1NN classifier allows to measure an indicator in the universal space that we call the doubleHit / hit ratio. It is the percentage of correctly classified gestures (*hits*) that, furthermore, are correctly classified in the subject space (*doubleHits*). These values are of 69% and 77% for 4 and 8 emotions, that is, most of the emotion hits correspond to a gesture from the same subject. These results seem not coming by pure chance since, in fact, the more a universal system becomes a good predictor of the subject (41% and 35% respectively) the less the doubleHit / hit ratio. What we understand from those numbers is that the personalisation aspect is crucial. An hypothetic scenario would be starting from an universal recognitor and then to do a progressive fine tuning towards each specific subject.

4.3   A Simple Meta-features Approach

Design of a good set of features to describe the considered problem domain is one of the key steps, if not the key, towards successful generalisation. A paradigmatic example comes from speech recognition, a mature biometric-based tough recognition problem. Features constructed to capture several aspects of speech, relying on models of human vocal tract and human sound perception, enable speaker-independent systems with a high word recognition rate.

A meta-feature is an abstraction of some substructure that is observed within the data [19]. For time series several meta-features have been proposed [19,23]. By means of meta-features calculation we intend to present our data in a format that is appropriate for feature-vector-based classifiers.

We decided to use several simple holistic meta-features (see Figure 2), in the hope that they were neither too naive nor myopic as to extract useful information from our movement cues time series. If useful those meta-features (from now on simply "features") would provide interpretable results, allowing for a more comprehensible classification system. Further, since their calculation requires few computational efforts, they would be easily used to enable a real time recognition system.

We used Weka [20], an open source suite of machine learning tools for data mining, as the basis for classification. We adopted a comparative approach between three different classifiers.

- A simple 1-nearest-neighbor (1NN). It's the natural counterpart to the DTW-1NN approach presented in section 4.2.
- A decision-tree. We use J48, Quinlan's C4.5 implementation in Weka.
- A Bayesian Network. One of the state of the art techniques for emotion recognition [24]. After a first exploration of the different implementations we chose Hidden Naive Bayes (HNB) [25]. The rationale behind its better performance, compared to other Bayesian network architectures, is its more suitable handling of the independence assumption, given that our features are obviously non independent.

For HNB it is necessary to discretise the features. Using weka supervised discretisation module with the Kononenko's MDL criterion to evaluate the quality of the intervals exhibited a great improvement over using Weka's default setting. To be fair, we also tried the other two classifiers with the features discretised in this way. Our feature set is of high dimensionality for our training set size, so we performed two simple minded feature selection processes with a shallow forward search using both, a correlation based and a wrapper approach, to measure the merit of each features subset [20]. In all cases we used the default values for the classifiers parameters. The results are shown in table 3.

Table 3. LOOCV error rates for our meta-features experiment applied to the 4-emotions dataset. In columns the different preprocessing steps (All= no preprocessing, CB-FS= Correlation Based Feature Selection, Wr-FS = Wrapper Feature Selection, D = Discretisation).

Dataset →	All	CB-FS	Wr-FS	D-ALL	D-CB-FS	D-Wr-FS
HNB	-	-	-	47.22	37.92	51.85
J48	**52.78**	47.22	48.15	56.48	48.15	47.22
1NN	53.70	**43.52**	**37.04**	44.44	**32.41**	**44.44**

The three chosen classifiers produce in different levels interpretable results which allowed us to confirm some of the hypotheses coming from the previous analysis. One of them is that the same cues remain the winners with our metafeatures, since the constructed trees and the selected features show a strong bias towards the choice of QoM based features, with a minor role played by CI. In particular, the maximum of QoM seems to be one of the most significant features: it discriminates between "high arousal" emotions (anger and joy) and "low arousal" emotions (pleasure and sadness), with the first ones showing higher values for the maximum of QoM. Further, the mean of CI discriminates between "positive" and "negative" emotions: pleasure and joy show low values for mean of CI, whereas anger and sadness show high values for this feature. Another obvious conclusion is that we are generating irrelevant and redundant features. A classifier such as 1NN, which is very sensitive to the presence of noise, gets a strong improvement when the dimensionality is reduced.

Finally we report one of the confusion matrices in table 4.

Table 4. Confusion matrix of the HNB classifier used after a Correlation based Feature Selection Process (D-CB-FS)

Ang	Joy	Ple	Sad	←true class
0.9	0.1	0	0	Anger
0.2	**0.44**	0.28	0.08	Joy
0.0	0.21	**0.62**	0.17	Pleasure
0.08	0.08	0.36	**0.48**	Sadness

This table highlights that "negative" emotions (anger and sadness) were confused with the correspondent "positive" emotion with the same arousal characteristics. That suggests that arousal plays an important role in the recognition of emotion by movement and gesture and this is confirmed by the decision trees structure, that shows that QoM discriminates between "high" and "low arousal" emotions. Nevertheless, "positive" emotions (joy and pleasure) were misclassified with the correspondent "positive" emotion with opposite arousal characteristics. It seems that also valence plays a role in the recognition process. This is also confirmed from the decision trees structure, where it is evident that joy and pleasure have lower values of CI, i.e., the generated movements are more expanded than those of anger and sadness.

5   Conclusions and Future Work

We have presented an approach for automated video analysis of human gesture dynamics for emotion recognition. Since we do not use markers, this approach allows us to analyse human emotional behaviour in ecological environments in a non-intrusive way. We used movement expressivity to infer emotions and, in particular, we proposed a method for the analysis of emotional behaviour based on both direct classification of time series and a model that provides descriptors of the dynamics of expressive motion cues. We presented and analysed the classification results of our approach, finding that QoM is the most significant cue in differentiating between the emotions, with a minor role played by CI.

With this study we investigated the role of movement expressivity versus shape in gesture. To the best of our knowledge our experiments are novel. No other publication have addressed the same problem of out-of-context intra-gesture emotion classification using dynamic movement information. Results showed how expressive motion cues allow to discriminate between "high" and "low arousal" emotions and between "positive" and "negative" emotions. This result appears interesting because, since we considered gestures with the same shape, we can conclude that movement expressivity allows to differentiate the four emotions considered.

Our work is applicable to several different scenarios and the final scope is to complement other modalities in a multimodal fusion recognition system. For this purpose though, it's necessary to collect more data to feed these kind of systems. Since with the small datasets available no definitive conclusions can be drawn nor a robust system can be constructed; we plan further recordings with a larger and more representative set of subjects and gestures.

We plan to extend the meta-features based system to a broader feature space considering local features of the time series, as proposed in [23]. More classification schemes and better model selection are to be explored, which constitutes a work in progress. A cleverer cue fusion is also in study.

Last but not least, the base assumption behind our system is that the subjects were actually expressing the requested emotion. Future work includes perceptive tests to verify how the acted emotions are perceived by humans. Neglecting further discussion about this, how to construct a pervasive recognition system based on "real-life" emotion data is still a challenging open question.

Acknowledgments

We would like to thank Gualtiero Volpe for his advice and useful discussion.

References

1. Picard, R.W.: Affective Computing. The MIT Press, Cambridge (1997)
2. Scherer, K.R.: On the nature and function of emotion: a component process approach. In: Scherer, K.R., Ekman, P. (eds.) Approaches to emotion, pp. 293–317. Hillsdale, NJ: Erlbaum (1984)
3. Pollick, F., Paterson, H., Bruderlin, A., Sanford, A.: Perceiving affect from arm movement. Cognition 82, 51–61 (2001)
4. Shiffrar, M., Pinto, J.: The visual analysis of bodily motion. In: Prinz, W., Hommel, B. (eds.) Common mechanisms in perception and action: Attention and Performance, pp. 381–399. Oxford University Press, Oxford (2002)
5. Giese, M.A., Poggio, T.: Neural mechanisms for the recognition of biological movements. Nature Reviews Neuroscience 4, 179–192 (2003)
6. Rizzolatti, G., Fogassi, L., Gallese, V.: Mirrors in the mind. Scientific American 295, 54–61 (2006)
7. Boone, R.T., Cunningham, J.G.: Children's decoding of emotion in expressive body movement: the development of cue attunement. Developmental psychology 34, 1007–1016 (1998)
8. De Meijer, M.: The contribution of general features of body movement to the attribution of emotions. Journal of Nonverbal Behavior 13, 247–268 (1989)
9. Wallbott, H.G.: Bodily expression of emotion. European Journal of Social Psychology 28, 879–896 (1998)
10. Burgoon, J.K., Jensen, M.L., Meservy, T.O., Kruse, J., Nunamaker, J.F.: Augmenting human identification of emotional states in video. In: Intelligence Analysis Conference, McClean, VA (2005)
11. Camurri, A., Lagerlof, I., Volpe, G.: Recognizing emotion from dance movement: comparison of spectator recognition and automated techniques. International Journal of Human-Computer Studies 59, 213–225 (2003)
12. Kapur, A., Kapur, A., Babul, N.V., Tzanetakis, G., Driessen, P.F.: Gesture-based affective computing on motion capture data. In: ACII, pp. 1–7 (2005)
13. Bianchi-Berthouze, N., Kleinsmith, A.: A categorical approach to affective gesture recognition. Connection Science 15, 259–269 (2003)

14. Balomenos, T., Raouzaiou, A., Ioannou, S., Drosopoulos, A.I., Karpouzis, K., Kollias, S.D.: Emotion analysis in man-machine interaction systems. In: Machine Learning for Multimodal Interaction, pp. 318–328 (2004)
15. Gunes, H., Piccardi, M.: Bi-modal emotion recognition from expressive face and body gestures. Journal of Network and Computer Applications In Press, Corrected Proof
16. el Kaliouby, R., Robinson, P.: Generalization of a vision-based computational model of mind-reading. In: ACII, pp. 582–589 (2005)
17. Camurri, A., Coletta, P., Massari, A., Mazzarino, B., Peri, M., Ricchetti, M., Ricci, A., Volpe, G.: Toward real-time multimodal processing: Eyesweb 4.0. In: AISB 2004 Convention: Motion, Emotion and Cognition (2004)
18. Camurri, A., Mazzarino, B., Volpe, G.: Analysis of expressive gesture: The Eyesweb Expressive Gesture processing library. In: Camurri, A., Volpe, G. (eds.) GW 2003. LNCS (LNAI), vol. 2915, pp. 460–467. Springer, Heidelberg (2004)
19. Kadous, M.W.: Temporal Classification: Extending the Classification Paradigm to Multivariate Time Series. PhD thesis, School of Computer Science & Engineering, University of New South Wales (2002)
20. Witten, I.H., Frank, E.: Data Mining: Practical Machine Learning Tools and Techniques, 2nd edn. Morgan Kaufmann Series in Data Management Systems. Morgan Kaufmann, San Francisco (2005)
21. Keogh, E., Ratanamahatana, C.A.: Exact indexing of dynamic time warping. Knowledge and Information Systems 7(3), 358–386 (2005)
22. Heloir, A., Courty, N., Gibet, S., Multon, F.: Temporal alignment of communicative gesture sequences. Computer Animation and Virtual Worlds 17(3-4), 347–357 (2006)
23. Rodríguez, J.J., Alonso, C.J., Maestro, J.A.: Support vector machines of interval-based features for time series classification. Knowledge-Based Systems 18(4-5), 171–178 (2005)
24. Sebe, N., Cohen, I., Cozman, F.G., Gevers, T., Huang, T.S.: Learning probabilistic classifiers for human-computer interaction applications. Multimedia Systems V10(6), 484–498 (2005)
25. Zhang, H., Jiang, L., Su, J.: Hidden naive bayes. In: AAAI 2005, The Twentieth National Conference on Artificial Intelligence and the Seventeenth Innovative Applications of Artificial Intelligence, pp. 919–924 (2005)

Person or Puppet? The Role of Stimulus Realism in Attributing Emotion to Static Body Postures

Marco Pasch and Ronald Poppe*

Human Media Interaction Group, University of Twente
P.O. Box 217, 7500 AE Enschede, The Netherlands
{m.pasch,poppe}@ewi.utwente.nl

Abstract. Knowledge of the relation between body posture and the perception of affect is limited. Existing studies of emotion attribution to static body postures vary in method, response modalities and nature of the stimulus. Integration of such results proves difficult, and it remains to be investigated how the relation can be researched best. In this study we focus on the role of stimulus realism. An experiment has been conducted where computer generated body postures in two realism conditions were shown to participants. Results indicate that higher realism not always results in increased agreement but clearly has an influence on the outcome for distinct emotions.

Keywords: Nonverbal behavior, emotion recognition, body postures.

1 Introduction

Recognizing a person's affective state is one of the big challenges within the field of affective computing [11]. In order to achieve truly intelligent Human-Computer Interaction, we need to know how humans perceive each other. We communicate our affective states in many ways, most obviously through the tones of our voices and our choice of words. But also nonverbal signals, such as facial expressions, gestures and body postures, give clues about one's affective state. Of these channels, especially facial expressions have received a great deal of attention. It has been researched how individual facial muscles contribute to an expression [13], and how certain express-ions are perceived in terms of affect [6]. Body postures have received significantly less attention. However, the ability of the body to display affect has often been mentioned [1].

In this paper, we investigate how body postures are perceived by human observers in terms of affective attributions. This kind of research is not new, and dates back at least to James' study on the expression of body posture [8]. On an abstract level, perception research is characterized by human observers rating stimuli on a number of labels. From the various studies, we know that at least some emotions can be perceived with above-chance level agreement. However, proper consolidation of the findings of these studies is difficult due to the many factors involved while performing this kind of research. We discuss these factors subsequently.

First, there is no general agreement on how to specify emotional affect, and this is reflected in the choice of emotion labels used throughout perception literature. Ekman's

---

* Corresponding author.

A. Paiva, R. Prada, and R.W. Picard (Eds.): ACII 2007, LNCS 4738, pp. 83–94, 2007.

model of six basic emotions [4] is used widely (e.g. by Ekman and Friesen [5], and Coulson [2]), albeit sometimes with a lower number of labels (Kleinsmith et al. [9], De Silva and Bianchi-Berthouze [3]). Other studies use a more elaborate list of emotions (e.g. Wallbott [16], Kudoh and Matsumoto [10], Grammer et al. [6]).

The postures that are used in perception literature are another factor that is of influence. The human body is complex with a large number of degrees of freedom, usually represented by joint rotations. Even if each joint could assume only a few rotations, the total number of postures would be far too large to evaluate. Therefore, studies use only a small subset of all physically feasible postures. James [8] used a large number of body part positions, which he combined to generate more complex deformations. James did not choose the postures with a specific form of affect in mind. Similarly, Kudoh and Matsumoto [10] asked participants to describe postures that occur in everyday conversations. Pictures of spontaneously performed postures are used by Ekman and Friesen [5], who induced the emotional state, and Grammer et al. [6], who measured participants' self-reported affect. In contrast, studies by Kleinsmith et al. [9], and De Silva and Bianchi-Berthouze [3] used prototypical postures, each of which depicted a clearly defined emotion. These postures can be performed by actors (e.g. Wallbott and Scherer [17], Kleinsmith [9], Pitterman and Nowicki [12]), or defined manually (e.g. Coulson [2]).

The methodology also varies, according to the purpose of the study. James' study was investigative, and the responses to each stimulus were open-ended. Although these responses are more informative compared to a forced-choice methodology, there is clearly a degree of subjectivity in interpreting and analyzing the responses of multiple observers. Winters [18] has looked into the different kinds of response modality, and observed that the choice of methodology has a large effect on the outcomes of the perception agreement.

A final factor of influence is the type of stimulus that is used to portray the postures. The DANVA-POS set, as collected and described by Pitterman and Nowicki [12], consists of photographs of persons in various sitting and standing postures. To make sure facial expressions do not influence the perception, all faces have been erased using a black marker. James [8] also used photographs, but of a mannequin. This allowed him to have more control over the postures, and visual appearance between stimuli was guaranteed. Moreover, factors such as age, sex and ethnicity would not play a role in the attribution. Schouwstra and Hoogstraten [14] used drawings as stimuli, but it remains unclear how much detail was preserved. Computer-generated stimuli were recently used by Coulson [2], Grammer et al. [7] and De Silva and Bianchi-Berthouze [3]. These stimuli have the advantage that parameters such as visual appearance, posture, viewpoint, detail, and lighting, can be completely controlled. While stimulus control is important, it is also necessary to know how all these parameters influence the outcomes of perception research.

In this study, we investigate the effect of stimulus realism on the attribution of emotion to static body postures. To this end we replicated the experiment of Coulson [2], who used computer-generated stimuli of a mannequin. Elimination of the factors age, sex and ethnicity is useful to prevent possible biases. However, when using mannequins, the degree of realism and detail is minimal. Wallbott [15] observed that, when the spatial resolution of the stimuli is decreased, so is the affect recognition rate. The same might be the case when presenting mannequins instead of more detailed stimuli. More details give more clues towards the position of body parts, e.g. the angle of the head. Another factor is the rate of realism. In James' [8] experiment, observers occasionally experienced the emotion that was attributed to the postural expression. Sometimes, this effect was accompanied by mimicking the presented posture. We expect that the kinesthetic effect will be less when using mannequins. On the other hand, mimicking the posture might be more necessary when using the mannequin stimuli, since the observer has less clues about the depth of the body parts, and consequently of the precise posture.

To investigate the role of realism on the attribution, we add a realism condition to the experiment. We acknowledge that in performing the experiment, the specific choices for response modality, emotion labels and the posture set itself have a large influence of the outcome of the experiment. Coulson [2] mentions that some postures look unnatural, and the choice of postures is arbitrary. Also, as Winters [18] observes, the use of a forced-choice methodology is likely to introduce noise in the responses. However, Coulson's systematic description of the postures and his findings allow us to replicate his experiment and investigate the differences between the two realism conditions. Our study is therefore not aimed at investigating how postures, or posture features, define the attribution of emotion. We rather investigate if, and how, the level of realism influences the attribution. This way, we hope to be able to make suggestions on how to improve the current state of perception research.

The paper is organized as follows. In Section 2 we specify our research questions. Section 3 describes our method, and results are presented and discussed in Section 4. We summarize our contribution and give pointers to future research in Section 5.

2 Research Questions

We investigate if and how stimulus realism influences the way the affective state of an observed subject is perceived. Our initial assumption is that realism does play a role in the attribution of emotions to static body postures. A realistic figure contains more body features and shows them more detailed. It is thus possible that the viewer perceives more visual cues. Also, the kinesthetic effect will be larger when observing more realistic stimuli. Our first hypothesis is thus formulated:

H$_1$: *Realistic stimuli obtain a higher consensus level than abstract stimuli when attributing emotion to static body postures.*

It is important to note that the consensus level here is the level of agreement between the observed and rated stimuli, and the emotion label that was defined beforehand. This predefined label is not necessary the label that is most often reported. However, since we use prototypical postures, we expect this effect to be small.

Previous studies have found that different basic emotions are attributed with different levels of consensus (e.g. Coulson [2], Ekman and Friesen [5]). We expect that this also holds for different levels of realism. Some emotions will be perceived with the same accuracy, disregarding the realism condition. Others will be influenced by the realism, and difference in detail. Our second hypothesis is presented:

H$_2$: *Stimulus realism has an effect on the consensus levels for different emotion labels when attributing emotion to static body postures.*

3 Method

3.1 Participants

A total of 48 participants were recruited for the experiment (16 female, 32 male). All participants were university students or staff members, with an average age of 29 years (range 22 to 54 years). There was no gratification given.

3.2 Stimuli

In this study, we replicate the experiment of Coulson as reported in [2]. He uses a simplified model of the human body. For the lower body, only the weight transfer is modeled. Furthermore, six joint rotations are regarded in the upper body (head bend, chest bend, abdomen bend, shoulder adduction, shoulder swing, and elbow bend). The corresponding descriptions of body postures are given in Table 1.

Table 1. Joint rotations for each of the emotion labels (reprinted from Coulson [2])

	Abdomen twist	Chest bend	Head bend	Shoulder ad/abduct	Shoulder swing	Elbow bend	Weight transfer	No. of postures
Anger	0	20, 40	-20, 25	-60, -80	45, 90	50, 110	Forwards	32
Disgust	-25, -50	-20, 0	-20	-60, -80	-25, 45	0, 50	Backwards	32
Fear	0	20, 40	-20, 25, 50	-60	45, 90	50, 110	Backwards	24
Happiness	0	0, -20	0, -20	50	0, 45	0, 50	Forwards, Neutral	32
Sadness	0, -25	0, 20	25, 50	-60, -80	0	0	Backwards, Neutral	32
Surprise	0	-20	25, 50	50	-25, 0, 45	0, 50	Backwards, Neutral	24

We use two realism conditions, a realistic and an abstract condition. The latter one is our control condition, and contains all stimuli from Coulson's experiment. For both conditions, images of postures were generated with Poser 6 (e-Frontier), a 3D figure animation tool. For the realistic condition the default character "James" was used, a young male. To avoid the interference of facial expressions, all facial features were removed by replacing the face with a skin-textured sphere. For the control condition, Poser's mannequin figure was chosen in accordance with Coulson's study. We used the same three viewpoints: from the front, the left hand side, and from a position above and behind the left shoulder. Figure 1 illustrates our stimuli set by showing 6 identical postures depicting happiness in both realism conditions and seen from the three viewpoints.

3.3 Procedure

For each realism condition, 176 postures were rendered from three viewpoints, resulting in a total of 528 stimuli images per condition. The images for each of the realism conditions were split into three stimulus sets of 176 images. Each set

Fig. 1. The same posture in both realism conditions, and shown from the three viewpoints

contained all postures, each viewed from exactly one angle, and each viewpoint occurring in one third of the stimuli. Within a subset, stimuli images were shown in a semi-random order, according to Coulson's study. Our experimental design is a 2 x 3 x 6 x 3 design, with realism condition and subset as between-subjects variables, and emotion label and viewpoint as within-subjects variables.

Participants were instructed to choose the emotion label they thought could be attributed best to the posture shown on screen. The realism condition and stimulus set that a participant had to judge were assigned at random. Upon clicking the start button, the participant was shown the first image. Judgments could be made by pressing one of the six labeled buttons below the image, each corresponding to one of the six emotion labels. These were ordered alphabetically and their location on screen did not change during the experiment. A click on one of the buttons advanced the experiment to the next image. There was no time limit imposed, and participants were told to take a break whenever they thought was necessary. The time between the first and last judgment was measured for verification purposes. Each participant processed a stimulus set of 176 images.

4   Results and Discussion

First, we check whether fatigue affected the participants' judgments over the course of the experiment. A paired t-test between the performance of each participant in the first and second half of the experiment fails to reach significance ($t(48) = -0.036$, n.s.).

We conduct repeated measures ANOVA, with realism condition and stimulus subset as between-subjects variables, and viewpoint and emotion as within-subject variables. First we notice that there is no significant main effect for stimulus subset. However, there is a marginal interaction effect between viewpoint and subset, and the interaction between viewpoint, condition and subset is significant ($F(4, 42) = 2.811$, $p < .05$). These effects can be explained since realism condition, viewpoint and subset are correlated. This is an inconvenient result of our efforts to keep the number of stimuli for each participant manageable.

Table 2. Agreement scores broken down by realism condition, viewpoint and emotion label

	Realistic condition				Abstract condition			
	Front	Side	Rear	Average	Front	Side	Rear	Average
Anger	35%	30%	31%	32%	34%	43%	41%	39%
Disgust	7%	12%	7%	9%	23%	29%	20%	24%
Fear	35%	33%	39%	36%	18%	24%	27%	23%
Happiness	64%	53%	55%	57%	78%	56%	52%	62%
Sadness	64%	50%	59%	58%	28%	74%	59%	54%
Surprise	18%	42%	36%	32%	13%	22%	14%	16%
Average	**38%**	**37%**	**38%**	**38%**	**34%**	**43%**	**37%**	**38%**

To evaluate our first hypothesis, we look at the main effect for realism condition. We observe that this effect is not significant ($F(1, 42) = 0.203$, n.s.), which can be understood by looking at the average scores of both conditions in Table 2. The averages over all emotions and all viewpoints are 38% for both conditions. However, we clearly see different scores between the two realism conditions for the different emotions. Indeed, there is an interaction effect between realism condition and emotion, thus confirming our second hypothesis. We discuss the differences in scores between emotions later. First, we report the other significant findings in our ANOVA.

There is a significant main effect for emotion ($F(5, 210) = 39.080$, $p < .001$), which can be seen in Table 2 as well. This effect is in agreement with findings by, amongst others, Coulson [2]. We discuss this later.

Also consistent with Coulson's study is the significance of the main effect for viewpoint ($F(2, 84) = 7.471$, $p < .01$). Also, interestingly, there is an interaction effect for viewpoint and condition ($F(2, 42) = 10.347$, $p < .001$). In Table 2, we see that in the abstract condition the side viewpoint scores much better than in the realistic condition. Also, the front viewpoint has a slightly lower score.

The interaction between viewpoint and emotion is also significant ($F(10, 42) = 8.349$, $p < .001$), as well as the second order interaction between emotion, viewpoint and realism condition ($F(10, 42) = 8.949$, $p < .001$). Tables 4 and 5 show the consensus levels (i.e. level of agreement with the predefined emotion label) for the realistic condition and abstract condition, respectively. In Table 6 the difference in the consensus levels between the two conditions is presented.

Since the abstract condition was a replication of Coulson's [2] study, we check whether there are differences between the results. If we turn to Tables 5 and 7, overall we notice small differences. An exception is sadness from a frontal view where we can see a bigger difference. When taking a closer look at our results, we can observe that the postures of our abstract character depicting sadness from a frontal view were often perceived as happiness or surprise. This appears unusual as sadness and happiness/surprise can be seen as quite opposing emotions. Figure 2 shows 4 postures that are predefined to depict sadness. While the two leftmost postures were perceived by the majority of observers as sad, the two rightmost ones received a majority vote for happiness or surprise. A pattern that we can observe is that in all these postures the arms have a above-zero value for the shoulder abduction parameter.

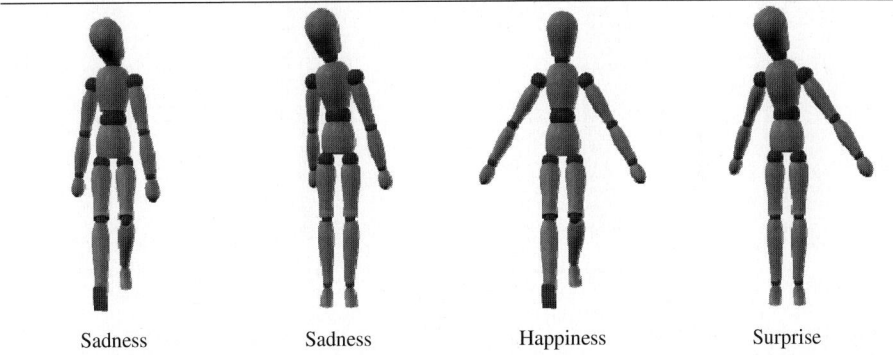

| Sadness | Sadness | Happiness | Surprise |

Fig. 2. Postures with predefined emotion label sadness with corresponding majority votes

It is possible that our replicated posture set deviates from Coulson's original set. Coulson reports the best scoring postures for each emotion label. For sadness, the posture has a chest bend of 40 degrees, which is not within the specified range (see Table 1). The fact that we use 20 as the maximum results in a head that is effectively less bent down. This is less visible in the front view, which could explain the lower consensus levels for this view.

We now focus on the scores for the different emotion labels. Overall, we observe that all findings are above chance level ($F(1,42) = 350,709$, $p < .001$) when performing ANOVA with the scores corrected for chance (16,7% for each emotion). From here we look at each emotion separately. Anger shows good consensus levels in both conditions but scores better in the abstract condition as can be seen in Table 6. The same is true for disgust, though none of the postures for disgust in the realistic condition, and only few in the abstract condition, reach consensus levels over 50% (see Tables 4 and 5). The deviation between the realism conditions is also smaller here. Fear reaches high consensus in the realistic condition, but consensus is poor for abstract stimuli, so fear is clearly recognized better in the realistic condition. For happiness we find very high consensus levels in both conditions but still see a clear advantage towards the abstract condition. For sadness we have to distinguish the results for each viewpoint. When seen from the front, there is a clear advantage towards the realistic condition. Seen from the side, the abstract condition shows higher consensus levels. From the rear, the consensus levels of both conditions are almost identical. An example for the deviation between the viewpoints for sadness can be seen in Figure 3, which shows the same posture in both conditions seen from the front and the side with the corresponding consensus levels. In the side view of the abstract condition the right hand can be seen, while it is covered in the realistic condition. This excess in information is a possible explanation for the higher consensus level of the abstract condition.

Realistic Condition		Abstract Condition	
Front	Side	Front	Side

| 100% | 50% | 50% | 100% |

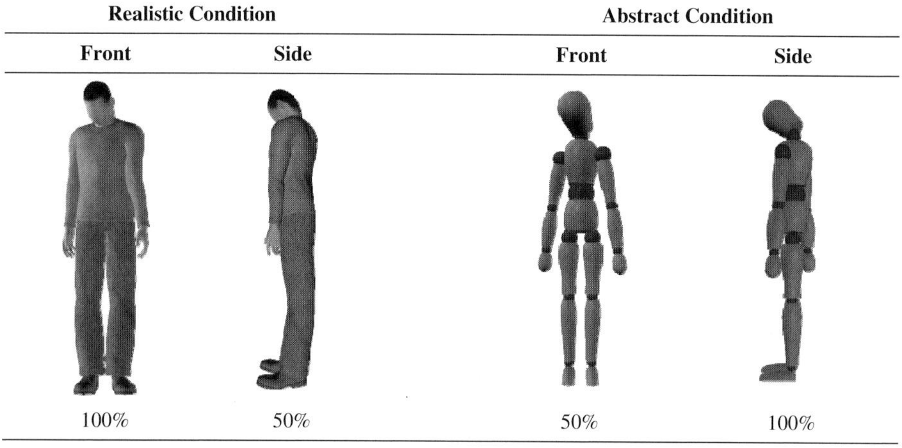

Fig. 3. Example of deviation in agreement levels of a posture seen from different viewpoints

We expect that certain emotion labels are more confused than others. In Table 3, we summarized these confusions for both conditions. In general, happiness and sadness are often chosen, whereas especially disgust received a minority of the votes. These results are not surprising, and have been reported repeatedly in literature. The fact that disgust and surprise are often expressed with movement, rather than static body postures is a viable explanation.

If we focus on the difference in the two realism conditions, we see large differences in the attribution of postures that are predefined to express disgust and surprise. Disgust is often confused with happiness and surprise in the realistic condition. In the abstract condition, fear and happiness are often chosen, besides the correct label. These findings could be partly explained by the fact that the chest bend for disgust, happiness and surprise can be negative, which indicates a more rising posture. This could be more visible in the realistic condition.

We discussed the confusion between sadness, surprise and happiness earlier. Another interesting observation is the difference between the attributions for fear. Fear is recognized better in the realistic condition, and is often confused with anger in the abstract condition. If we look at Table 1, we notice that the postures for anger and fear are quite alike. The only differences are the head bend and the weight transfer. In the front view, it is difficult to distinguish between the different parameters. This effect is probably especially present in the abstract condition.

Table 3. Confusion matrix for both realism conditions

			Observed				
Predefined	Anger	Disgust	Fear	Happiness	Sadness	Surprise	**Recall**
Anger	**247 - 299**	56 - 74	209 - 166	24 - 49	197-159	35 - 21	**32 - 39%**
Disgust	91 - 72	**66 - 185**	82 - 134	189 - 154	34-54	306 - 169	**9 - 24%**
Fear	106 - 175	29 - 49	**205 - 132**	8 - 34	208-173	20 - 13	**36 - 23%**
Happiness	107 - 101	19 - 37	39 - 30	**439 - 476**	34-10	130 - 114	**57 - 62%**
Sadness	53 - 35	139 - 68	50 - 82	32 - 70	**443-412**	51 - 101	**58 - 54%**
Surprise	58 - 77	49 - 31	48 - 36	223 - 336	14-3	**184 - 93**	**32 - 16%**
Total	662 - 759	358 - 444	633 - 580	915 - 1119	930-811	726 - 511	
Precision	**37 - 39%**	**18 - 42%**	**32 - 23%**	**48 - 43%**	**48 - 51%**	**25 - 18%**	

First value is the realistic condition, second value is abstract condition. Recall values are percentage of the total number of samples (576 for fear and surprise, 768 for others)

We did not look at how distinct anatomical features can be used to explain the attribution of the posture to a certain emotion. Such an analysis is not within the scope of our research as reported here. The interested reader is referred to Coulson [2] who performed such an analysis. Attempts to describe the relation from posture to emotion label functionally are reported by Wallbott [16] and De Silva and Bianchi-Bertouze [3].

5 Conclusion and Future Work

Computer-generated body postures in two realism conditions were used to assess the role of stimulus realism for the attribution of emotion to static body postures. We replicated an experiment by Coulson [2], who used a mannequin character as stimulus and used this test set as abstract realism condition. We further added a realistic condition by using the same posture descriptions for a more realistic, human-like character, whose facial features were removed to avoid a bias through facial expressions.

We expected the realistic condition to result in higher agreement rates than the abstract condition as we expected that observers could perceive more visual cues and could identify with the figure more easily. Our results show that overall there is no difference between the realism conditions. However, there are differences for individual emotion labels. Anger, disgust, and happiness are recognized with a higher level of agreement when displayed by an abstract character, while fear and surprise are recognized better when displayed by a realistic character. For sadness, the realistic condition yields a higher consensus level in the front view while in the side view, the abstract condition shows higher agreement with the predefined emotion label. We can therefore conclude that realism does influence the perception and should therefore be taken into account when performing research into perception of affect from postures.

By introducing the realism condition, however, we also introduced other variables that are likely to have an effect on the attribution. For example, hiding the facial features is an arbitrary choice. Though not reported by participants, the lack of facial features makes the character less realistic and it is possible that the removed face makes the character look intimidating. It remains to be investigated how the interaction between facial and postural features in this kind of research affects the emotion attribution.

Former studies of body postures relied on abstract characters in an attempt to discard sex, age and ethnicity. By employing a realistic character, we bring these factors back into the equation. In this study we used a young male computer-generated character. It is possible that a different sex, age, and ethnicity of the character would have led to different scores. Investigating the precise role of these factors appears eligible. Also, research by Kudoh and Matsumoto [10] and Kleinsmith et al. [9] has demonstrated that differences in attributions exist between people of different cultures. Although the postures we used are prototypical, it should be analyzed whether ethnicity of the participants influences their perception.

We hope to fuel the discussion on how research into the perception of affect from postures can best be conducted. We have shown that realism plays an important role in the attribution, but there are clearly many more factors. Proper consolidation of our research is possible only if agreement is reached over methodology, emotion labels and postures. When advantage is taken of the multidisciplinary nature of the research, interesting results are to be expected.

Acknowledgments

This research was partly funded by the EU Project HUMAINE (IST-507422), and is part of the ICIS program. ICIS is sponsored by the Dutch government under contract BSIK03024. We thank Mark Coulson for providing the data which allowed us to rebuild the stimuli, and for the detailed information of his results. We further wish to thank Matthijs Poppe for his useful comments regarding the design and analysis of the experiment.

References

1. Cook, M.: Perceiving others: the psychology of interpersonal perception. Methuen, London (1979)
2. Coulson, M.: Attributing emotion to static body postures: recognition, accuracy, confusions, and viewpoint dependence. Journal of Nonverbal Behaviour 28(2), 117–139 (2004)
3. De Silva, P.R., Bianchi-Berthouze, N.: Modeling human affective postures: an information theoretic characterization of posture features. Computer Animation and Virtual Worlds 15(3-4), 269–276 (2004)
4. Ekman, P.: Basic emotions. In: Dalgleish, T., Power, M. (eds.) Handbook of Cognition and Emotion, John Wiley & Sons, Sussex (1999)
5. Ekman, P., Friesen, W.V.: Head and body cues in the judgment of emotion: a reformulation. Perceptual and Motor Skills 24(3), 711–724 (1967)
6. Ekman, P., Friesen, W.V., Ellsworth, P.: Emotions in the human face: guidelines for research and an integration of findings. Pergamon Press, New York (1972)
7. Grammer, K., Fink, B., Oberzaucher, E., Atzmüller, M., Blantar, I., Mitteroecker, P.: The representation of self reported affect in body posture and body posture simulation. Collegium antropologicum 28(2), 159–173 (2004)

8. James, W.T.: A study of expression of body posture. Journal of General Psychology 7, 405–437 (1932)
9. Kleinsmith, A., De Silva, P.R., Bianchi-Berthouze, N.: Cross-cultural differences in recognizing affect from body posture. Interacting with Computers 18(6), 1371–1389 (2006)
10. Kudoh, T., Matsumoto, D.: Crosscultural examination of the semantic dimensions of body posture. Journal of Personality and Social Psychology 48(6), 1440–1446 (1985)
11. Picard, R.W.: Affective computing. MIT Press, Cambridge (1997)
12. Pitterman, H., Nowicki Jr, S.: A test of the ability to identify emotion in human standing and sitting postures: the diagnostic analysis of nonverbal accuracy-2 posture test (DANVA-POS). Genetic, Social, and General Psychology Monographs 130(2), 146–162 (2004)
13. Rinn, W.E.: The neuropsychology of facial expression: a review of the neurological and psychological mechanisms for producing facial expression. Psychological Bulletin 95(1), 52–77 (1984)
14. Schouwstra, S.J., Hoogstraten, J.: Head position and spinal position as determinants of perceived emotional state. Perceptual and Motor Skills 81(2), 673–674 (1995)
15. Wallbott, H.G.: Effects of distortion of spatial and temporal resolution of video stimuli on emotion attributions. Journal of Nonverbal behavior 16(1), 5–20 (1992)
16. Wallbott, H.G.: Bodily expression of emotion. European journal of Social Psychology 28(6), 879–896 (1998)
17. Wallbott, H.G., Scherer, K.R.: Cues and channels in emotion recognition. Journal of Personality and Social Psychology 51(4), 690–699 (1986)
18. Winters, A.: Perceptions of body posture and emotion: A question of methodology. The New School Psychology Bulletin 3(2), 35–45 (2005)

Appendix A: Consensus Levels

Table 4. Consensus levels for the realistic condition

	Anger			Disgust			Fear			Happiness			Sadness			Surprise		
	Front	Side	Rear	Front	Side	Rear	Front	Side	Rear	Front	Side	Rear	Front	Side	Rear	Front	Side	Rear
50%	10	8	10	0	0	0	13	6	8	26	20	19	23	19	24	0	15	8
60%	6	3	2	0	0	0	2	3	5	21	14	16	23	12	18	0	6	3
70%	5	0	1	0	0	0	1	0	2	15	11	10	17	5	11	0	2	0
80%	3	0	0	0	0	0	0	0	0	8	7	7	10	4	7	0	0	0
90%	0	0	0	0	0	0	0	0	0	3	1	2	4	1	1	0	0	0

Number of stimuli reaching consensus levels between 50% and 100% for the emotions across viewpoints

Table 5. Consensus levels for the abstract condition

	Anger			Disgust			Fear			Happiness			Sadness			Surprise		
	Front	Side	Rear	Front	Side	Rear	Front	Side	Rear	Front	Side	Rear	Front	Side	Rear	Front	Side	Rear
50%	10	19	15	4	4	4	1	2	4	30	22	19	8	31	25	0	2	0
60%	8	7	9	0	2	1	1	1	0	27	16	15	2	28	15	0	0	0
70%	4	2	2	0	0	0	0	0	0	25	13	13	0	18	10	0	0	0
80%	1	0	0	0	0	0	0	0	0	16	8	5	0	13	5	0	0	0
90%	0	0	0	0	0	0	0	0	0	6	2	1	0	4	2	0	0	0

Number of stimuli reaching consensus levels between 50% and 100% for the emotions across viewpoints

Table 6. Deviation in consensus levels between realistic and abstract condition

	Anger			Disgust			Fear			Happiness			Sadness			Surprise		
	Front	Side	Rear	Front	Side	Rear	Front	Side	Rear	Front	Side	Rear	Front	Side	Rear	Front	Side	Rear
50%	0	-11	-5	-4	-4	-4	12	4	4	-4	-2	0	15	-12	-1	0	13	8
60%	-2	-4	-7	0	-2	-1	1	2	5	-6	-2	1	21	-16	3	0	6	3
70%	1	-2	-1	0	0	0	1	0	2	-10	-2	-3	17	-13	1	0	2	0
80%	2	0	0	0	0	0	0	0	0	-8	-1	2	10	-9	2	0	0	0
90%	0	0	0	0	0	0	0	0	0	-3	-1	1	4	-3	-1	0	0	0

Deviation = Consensus levels of realistic condition minus consensus levels of abstract condition

Table 7. Consensus levels as reported by Coulson [2]

	Anger			Disgust			Fear			Happiness			Sadness			Surprise		
	Front	Side	Rear	Front	Side	Rear	Front	Side	Rear	Front	Side	Rear	Front	Side	Rear	Front	Side	Rear
50%	18	12	10	0	0	0	0	4	2	49	28	24	25	43	36	4	4	1
60%	16	8	4	0	0	0	0	2	0	35	25	20	20	39	29	0	1	0
70%	10	3	1	0	0	0	0	0	0	24	16	12	12	26	18	0	1	0
80%	2	1	0	0	0	0	0	0	0	7	7	8	5	12	8	0	0	0
90%	1	0	0	0	0	0	0	0	0	1	2	2	0	3	1	0	0	0

Motion Capture and Emotion:
Affect Detection in Whole Body Movement

Elizabeth Crane and Melissa Gross

Division of Kinesiology, University of Michigan
401 Washtenaw Ave, Ann Arbor, MI, USA
{bcrane,mgross}@umich.edu

Abstract. Bodily expression of felt emotion was associated with emotion-specific changes in gait parameters and kinematics. The emotions angry, sad, content, joy and no emotion at all were elicited in forty-two undergraduates (22 female, 20 male; 20.1±2.7 yrs) while video and whole body motion capture data (120 Hz) were acquired. Participants completed a self-report of felt emotion after each trial. To determine whether the walkers' felt emotions were recognizable in their body movements, video clips of the walkers were shown to 60 undergraduates (29 female, 31 male; 20.9±2.7 yrs). After viewing each video clip, observers selected one of 10 emotions that they thought the walker experienced during the trial. This study provides evidence that emotions can be successfully elicited in the laboratory setting, emotions can be recognized in the body movements of others, and that body movements are affected by felt emotions.

Keywords: Affect Detection, Motion Capture, Posture, Whole body movement, Emotion, Kinematics.

1 Introduction

Affective body movement provides important visual cues used to distinguish expression of emotion [1, 2]. The effects of emotion on body movement have been studied primarily in actors portraying emotions, and the emotion-related effects have been described qualitatively, e.g., "heavy-footed" for angry gait [3]. Wallbott [4] developed a coding scheme for studying body movement that included descriptive characteristics of upper body, shoulders, head, arms, hands, and movement quality judgments. By coding body movement, he provided evidence for distinct movement patterns and postural behavior associated with emotions. Although qualitative descriptions provide clues about the kinematics of movement behavior, they do not provide sufficient information needed to develop applications that can reliably detect and/or synthesize affective behavior in body movement. Atkinson [1] recently established that emotion is conveyed through whole-body gestures based on both form and motion signals. His unique studies using point light and full form displays of gestures were able to identify the contributions of form and motion in emotion perception. Thus, research on emotion recognition that focuses on static body poses [5-7] may not provide complete information about the emotion signal. Pollick [2] quantified expressive arm movements in terms of velocity and acceleration suggesting

A. Paiva, R. Prada, and R.W. Picard (Eds.): ACII 2007, LNCS 4738, pp. 95–101, 2007.
© Springer-Verlag Berlin Heidelberg 2007

which aspects of movement are important in recognizing emotions. Studies employing fMRI have also established the significance of dynamic information for detecting emotion from whole body movement [8, 9].

While these studies strongly suggest that emotion is associated with detectable differences in body movement patterns, generalizations about the underlying kinematic qualities associated with emotion have been limited because of methodological issues. First, the studies typically lack rigorous checks to ensure that emotions were felt rather than portrayed. In fact, many of the studies used actors to display emotional movements. We do not currently have enough evidence to know if movement associated with felt emotions is quantitatively different from movement in which emotion is portrayed, even if recognition rates suggest no difference. Second, emotion recognition studies often use forced choice paradigms that may artificially inflate the recognition rates, leading to potential false positive results, confounding a quantitative description of movement qualities associated with a particular emotion. Finally, the methods used to identify the effect of different emotions on body movement have been flawed, both because simultaneous posture and limb movements have not been quantified and because the movement task has not been controlled between emotions. The purpose of this paper is to demonstrate how motion capture technology can be used to address some of the limitations in previous studies by quantifying the effect of emotion on whole body movement. Particular attention is given to emotion elicitation, emotion recognition, and kinematic description of emotion in whole body movement.

2 Methodology

We developed methods to assess: (1) the effectiveness of emotion elicitation in the laboratory setting, (2) observer recognition of emotion, and (3) the kinematic changes in body movements during walking associated with felt and recognized emotions.

2.1 Emotion Elicitation

Two negative emotions (anger and sad), two positive emotions (content and joy), and neutral emotion were elicited in 42 university students (22 female, 20 male; 20.1± 2.7 yrs). The emotions were selected based on their intensity and valance. For example, joy and contentment are both considered positive emotions with high and low intensity, respectively. Joy and anger are both high intensity emotions with opposite valence. Balancing the emotions in this way is important so that differences attributed to emotions are not inappropriately confounded by differences in valence or intensity.

An autobiographical memories paradigm was used to elicit emotions [10]. Prior to data collection, each participant completed a worksheet asking them to describe a time in their own life when they felt a specific emotion. For example, for joy, they were asked to complete the following information:

Think of a time in your life when you felt exhilarated, for instance, when you felt euphoric or very playful, or felt like you wanted to jump up and down. Using only a few words, please indicate: a) ....where you were: b) ...who you were with: c) ....what caused the feeling/what was it about?

Participants were told that the information provided on the worksheet was for their use only. After reading their notes and recalling an emotion, participants walked at a self-selected pace for approximately 5 meters while video and whole body motion capture data (120 Hz) were acquired. Participants performed three trials for each emotion in a block. During data collection, emotions were referred to as numbers so as not to bias the results. The emotion order was randomized for each participant.

To validate that the emotion was actually felt by the walker and not just portrayed, after each trial participants rated the intensity of 8 emotions (4 target; 4 non-target) using a questionnaire. The four non-target emotions were selected based on their similarity, in terms of valance and intensity, to the target emotions. The non-target emotions acted as distracter emotions decreasing the odds of selecting the correct emotion by chance. The feelings questionnaire included the four target emotions (e.g., anger - "I felt angry, irritated, annoyed.") and four non-target "distracter" emotions (e.g., fear - "I felt scared, fearful, afraid."). A 5-item Likert scale (0 = not at all; 1 = a little bit; 2 = moderately; 3 = a great deal; 4 = extremely) was used to score intensity. Intensity scores of two ("moderately") or greater were considered a "hit" (the subject felt the emotion). Neutral trials were considered "felt" if all 8 scores were less than two.

2.2 Emotion Recognition

To determine whether the walkers' felt emotions were recognizable in their body movements, video clips of the walkers with blurred faces were randomized and shown to 60 undergraduates (29 female, 31 male; 20.9±2.7 yrs). Because of the large number of clips (42 walkers each displaying 5 emotions = 210 clips), the video clips were divided between two observer groups so that each walker-emotion video clip was seen by 30 observers and each observer saw a maximum of 110 video clips (22 walkers and 5 emotions). To achieve a balanced design, a full set of clips (1 clip for each emotion) was used for each walker even when one of the emotions was not felt. After viewing each video clip, observers selected one of 10 emotions (4 target, 4 non-target, neutral/no emotion, and none of the above) that they thought the walker experienced during the trial.

A clip was recognized if the felt emotion agreed with the observer-selected emotion. Agreement was coded as a binomial variable (agreement = 1, disagreement = 0). A generalized linear mixed model with crossed random effects was used to model the binomial response variable (agreement) with a logit link. Fixed effects of emotion, walker gender, observer gender, walker age, observer age, video sequence and observer group were tested. A likelihood ratio test was used to determine if the variance of the random observer effect was significantly greater than zero. Recognition rates were calculated for each clip included in the study. A clip was considered recognized if agreement occurred at a rate better than chance ($>10\%$). In addition, an overall recognition rate for each emotion was calculated.

2.3 Motion Capture

Motion capture can be used to refer to many methods used for quantifying human motion. A commonly used type of motion capture, and the one used in this study, is optoelectronic stereophotogrammetry. This method of motion capture relies on passive retro-reflective markers placed on specific anatomical landmarks on the body. The position of each marker is tracked using high-speed video cameras and the centroid position of each marker is calculated for each instant in time.

The retro-reflective markers demarcate the body so that it can be represented as a number of linked segments. Each segment represents a bony segment of the musculo-skeletal system. For further simplification we assume that each segment is a rigid body as defined in classical mechanics. For a review of this assumption see [11]. In this study, the body was modeled with head/neck, thorax/abdomen, pelvis, upper arm, forearm, hand, thigh, shank, and foot segments. Relative movement between these segments was calculated to determine angular joint kinematics for neck, shoulder, elbow, wrist, hip, knee, and ankle. Two-dimensional joint kinematics were also calculated for additional postural information. These variables included lumbar and thoracic curves as well as shoulder elevation/depression and protraction/retraction.

In the kinematic analyses only trials in which the target emotion was both felt and recognized were included. The data were filtered using a 6 hz Butterworth filter and time was normalized. Joint angle data were aggregated and means and ranges of motion were computed for each walker and emotion. A linear mixed model with random walker effects and fixed effect of emotion was used to model the mean and range of motion of joint angles, gait velocity, stride length and cadence.

3   Results

3.1   Emotion Elicitation

Walkers felt the target emotions in more than 93% of trials. The criterion for a "felt" emotion was met or exceeded in 100% of the anger and joy trials, 95% of the content, 98% of the sad trials, and 69% of the neutral trials. In all of the trials where neutral was not felt, the emotion(s) selected were content and/or joy. Interestingly, 77% of the neutral trials that were not felt were recognized by observers as neutral at rates better than chance.

3.2   Emotion Recognition

Recognition rates depended on emotion. Target emotions were recognized at levels greater than chance in 83% of neutral trials, 76% of sad trials, 74% of content trials, 67% of joy trials, and 62% of anger trials. Because not all recognized trials were felt, the percentage of both felt and recognized was slightly decreased in content (69%), sad (74%) and neutral (57%) trials. In 67% of the gait trials (140 of 210 trials), the emotion felt by the walkers and recognized by the observers was same. Among the felt emotion trials, sad was most recognized (74%) and anger was least recognized (62%). Some walkers reported feeling above-threshold levels of contentment in neutral trials. Consequently, neutral trials were least often felt (69%) compared to 100% of trials felt for anger and joy and 95% of content trials. Recognition rates for each emotion were different for each walker. Recognition rates for the most recognized trials for individual walkers were 93.3%, 73.3%, 66.7%, 53.3% and 53.3%, for sad, anger, joy, content and neutral trials, respectively.

Emotion agreement between walker and observer for each video clip was not affected by walker gender, observer gender, walker age, observer age, video sequence or observer group (p > .05). Agreement was affected by emotion, however, since sad was 137% more likely to result in agreement than neutral (p < .000). The variance of the random observer effect was significantly greater than zero (p < .000) so observer effects were included in all observer recognition statistical analyses.

3.3 Kinematics

Emotion affected walking movement speed. The fastest speeds occurred in anger and joy trials, which had similar velocities (1.43 and 1.44 m/s, respectively). Gait speed was significantly slower in sad trials (1.07 m/s) than in anger or joy trials. Gait velocity was similar in neutral and low-activation emotion trials (content and sad). Emotion-dependent velocity differences were due primarily to changes in cadence rather than stride length. That is, the significant difference in gait speed between anger and sad trials was achieved by increasing step frequency in anger trials while stride length remained essentially the same.

Preliminary analyses indicated that both posture and limb motions changed with emotion. In sad trials, the head was oriented downward; the head/neck segment was 7.4, 11.6, 10.9 and 9.7 degrees more flexed than in anger, joy, content and neutral trials, respectively. The amplitude of upper extremity motion was less in sad trials than in trials with other emotions. Shoulder and elbow ranges of motion were significantly less in sad (19.4 and 22.6 deg) than in anger (27.5 and 36.1 deg), content (26.1 and 31.2 deg) and joy (28.4 and 37.2 deg) trials. Hip range of motion was slightly but significantly reduced in sad trials compared to anger, content or joy trials (7.0, 3.2, 5.8 deg, respectively).

Body motion was affected by emotion valence and activation level. For example, the amplitude of elbow flexion was also greater in the high activation emotion trials (anger and joy) than in neutral trials (4.0 and 3.0 deg, respectively).

4 Conclusion

This study provides evidence that emotions can be successfully elicited in the laboratory setting, emotions can be recognized in the body movements of others, and that body movements are affected by felt emotions. Measures were taken to ensure that the emotion signal in the movement was both felt and recognized. The self-report questionnaire used by the walkers in this study indicated that the autobiographical memories task is an effective method for eliciting positive and negative emotions with varying intensities in a laboratory setting. The lower recognition rate for neutral trials, however, may be due to not including a no emotion/neutral item on the questionnaire. In this case, participants may have felt the need to score the closest emotion, content, rather than indicating no feeling intensity for any of the emotions. In future studies we will add a no emotion/neutral category and a "none of the above" category to reduce the possibility that walkers select content when they feel neutral. The "none of the above category" will also reduce the likelihood that a walker will score a listed emotion because it is close to the emotion they truly felt. Because so few emotions were recognized but not felt, we do not have sufficient data to determine if movement associated with felt emotions is quantitatively different from movement in which emotion is portrayed. Until future studies address this issue, the authors advocate for providing a measure of felt emotion.

By using a carefully balanced observer questionnaire, which offered target emotions, distracter emotions, no emotion/neutral, and none of the above as options, we feel confident that our recognition rates are not inflated. Therefore, we have decreased the chance of confounding our quantitative description of movement qualities associated with a particular emotion.

Bodily expression of felt and recognized emotions was associated with emotion-specific changes in gait parameters and kinematics. Whole body motion capture allowed for the quantification of simultaneous posture and limb movements. The use of a single movement task (walking) emphasized that the emotion signal is evident in the kinematics and not solely dependent on gesticulatory behavior. Additionally, studying a single movement allows us to compare the movement kinematics. The authors, however, are not suggesting that emotion recognition is not improved with gestures or that some movements may lend themselves to some emotions more than others. These issues need to be addressed in future studies.

Future work is underway to extend what we have learned about posture and limb movements while walking with emotion. This includes analyses that assess the coordinative structure of the movement.

Acknowledgments. Barbara Fredrickson for her guidance on working with emotions and Brady West for his statistical help.

References

1. Atkinson, A.P., Tunstall, M.L., Dittrich, W.H.: Evidence for distinct contributions of form and motion information to the recognition of emotions from body gestures. Cognition 104, 59–72 (2007)
2. Pollick, F.E., Paterson, H.M., Bruderlin, A., Sanford, A.J.: Perceiving affect from arm movement. Cognition 82, 51–61 (2001)
3. Montepare, J.M., Goldstein, S.B., Clausen, A.: The identification of emotions from gait information. Journal of Nonverbal Behavior 11, 33–42 (1987)
4. Wallbott, H.G.: Bodily expression of emotion. European Journal of Social Psychology 28, 879–896 (1998)
5. Coulson, M.: Attributing emotion to static body postures: Recognition accuracy, confusions, and viewpoint dependence. Journal of Nonverbal Behavior 28, 117–139 (2004)
6. de Gelder, B., Snyder, J., Greve, D., Gerard, G., Hadjikhani, N.: Fear fosters flight: A mechanism for fear contagion when perceiving emotion expressed by a whole body. PNAS 101, 16701–16706 (2004)

7. Sprengelmeyer, R., Young, A.W., Schroeder, U., Grossenbacher, P.G., Federlein, J.: Knowing no fear. Proceedings of the Royal Society B. Biological Sciences 266, 2451–2451 (1999)
8. de Gelder, B.: Toward a biological theory of emotional body language. Biological Theory 1, 130–132 (2006)
9. Grezes, J., Pichon, S., de Gelder, B.: Perceiving fear in dynamic body expressions. NeuroImage 35, 959–967 (2007)
10. Healy, H., Williams, M.G., Dalgleish, T., Power, M.J.: Autobiographical memory. Handbook of cognition and emotion, pp. 229–242. John Wiley & Sons Ltd, Chichester (1999)
11. Cappozzo, A., Della Croce, U., Leardini, A., Chiari, L.: Human movement analysis using stereophotogrammetry: Part 1: theoretical background. Gait & Posture 21, 186–196 (2005)

Does Body Movement Engage You More in Digital Game Play? and Why?

Nadia Bianchi-Berthouze, Whan Woong Kim, and Darshak Patel

UCLIC, University College London, 31-32 Alfred Place, London WC1E7DP, UK
{n.berthouze,zchaar0}@ucl.ac.uk, panhoong@gmail.com

Abstract. In past years, computer game designers have tried to increase player engagement by improving the believability of characters and environment. Today, the focus is shifting toward improving the game controller. This study seeks to understand engagement on the basis of the body movements of the player. Initial results from two case-studies suggest that an increase in body movement imposed, or allowed, by the game controller results in an increase in the player's engagement level. Furthermore, they lead us to hypothesize that an increased involvement of the body can afford the player a stronger affective experience. We propose that the contribution of full-body experience is three-fold: (a) it facilitates the feeling of presence in the digital environment (fantasy); (b) it enables the affective aspects of human-human interaction (communication); and (c) it unleashes the regulatory properties of emotion (affect).

Keywords: Engagement, body movement, gaming, affective states.

1 Introduction

The new generation of games starts to offer control devices that allow for a more natural type of interaction. For example, Guitar Hero, introduced by RedOctane for the Playstation, comes with a guitar-shaped device with tilt-in sensors that require guitar-player-like movements for controlling the game. "Wii" controller, introduced by Nintendo, is equipped with a motion capture and gyroscopic device. Instead of using cursor keys and buttons to hit a tennis ball, the Wii remote will allow players to act as if they were actually handling a tennis racket. Similarly, Sony has introduced a new Dual Shock controller for their PlayStation 3, which also includes a gyroscopic device. The aim of these devices is to allow the player to control the game through natural movements. These new games, or rather, these new types of devices, not only have the ability to capture the interest of a larger audience (as they may allow for a faster learning curve), they could also facilitate the engagement of the player along all the 4 factors proposed by Lazzaro [14].

Whilst this recent trend suggests that game designers expect these new consoles to result in more intuitive and natural games, engagement is still a novel area in game research, and the relationship between engagement and body movement has not been studied. Recent studies in cognitive and affective sciences have shown the important role played by the body over the mind: *"thought grows from action and that activity is*

A. Paiva, R. Prada, and R.W. Picard (Eds.): ACII 2007, LNCS 4738, pp. 102–113, 2007.

the engine of change" [35]. On this view, the way our body interacts with the environment is affecting the way we perceive the environment.

This study, therefore, seeks to further our understanding of the relationship between body movement and the engagement experience in computer games, by testing the hypothesis that an increase in body movement imposed, or allowed, by the game controller can result in an increase of the player's engagement level. But first, let us briefly review the literature on engagement in game and engagement in general.

2   Engagement

The degree of involvement in technology is currently described using a variety of terms: immersion, engagement, presence or fun, to name just a few. The concept of presence or immersion, and their measurement, has mostly been studied in the context of virtual environments (e.g., [1-5]). In the context of games, however, the definition of engagement, and its related terms, is still unclear.

According to Malone [6], the qualitative factors for engaging game play are challenge, curiosity, fantasy and flow. Csikszentmihalyi's [7] theory of "flow" depicts a state of mind in which a person feels so engaged by an activity that his/her actions and awareness merge. Also known as optimal experience, this phenomenon is closely linked with motivation and attention, and is essential in games. An optimal level of challenge is necessary to maintain motivation in game players. When skills improve, a new level of challenge is required for challenge to meet the improved skill level [8]. Douglas and Hargadon [9] mentioned that flow is involved in both immersion and engagement.

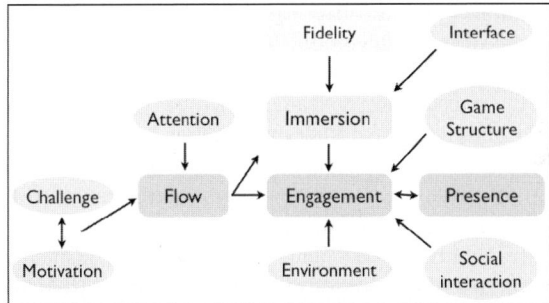

Fig. 1. Engagement model summarizing the various theories. The figure is modified from Chen et al. [11]'s figure, which focused mainly on game usability.

While Brown and Cairns [10] defined the relationship of engagement as the first step in immersion then to engrossment and then to full immersion, Chen et al. [11] used fidelity, immersion, and engagement. While these cannot be compared directly, both introduce three steps in a person's level of involvement. Brown and Cairns suggested that control of the game is a barrier in their definition of engagement to move to the next level, and game structure is a barrier for engrossment. Chen et al. [11] also consider similar aspects of the aural and visual interface to influence fidelity and game structure to influence immersion. Then, Brown and Cairns claimed that "full immersion is presence", with Smith et al. [4] adding that environmental factors affect this relationship.

Finally, engagement was also described in terms of three categories: participation, narration and co-presence of others, thus stating the social aspect of engagement [12]. Figure 1 depicts a schematic representation of the various theories linked to engagement. Although the specifics of the figure could be argued, what we would like to stress is the fact that most theories of engagement have focused purely on its mental aspects. Tellingly, Koster [13] defined "fun" as the act of mastering the game mentally. One aim of this paper is to suggest that body movements should play an important role in engagement.

3   Social and Regulatory Properties of Body Movement

In a qualitative study, Lazzaro [14] used facial expressions and surveys of players to identify four factors characterizing fun: hard fun (similar to the challenge factor of Malone), easy fun (similar to the curiosity factor of Malone), altered states (closely related to Malone's fantasy factor) and socialization (the people factor). The significance of this study is that it associated bodily expressions of affects to engagement. The choice of facial expressions to characterize engagement was not surprising given the traditional view that facial expression is the most powerful modality for expressing affective states. With their 7-38-55 rule, for example, the oft-quoted Mehrabian and Friar [15] stressed how important the non-verbal component (55% for facial expression and 38% for voice tone) of communication was in communicating affect when compared to the purely verbal component (7%).

In recent years, however, this idea has been questioned by psychology studies showing body posture to be a very good indicator for certain categories of emotions, see [16-19]) for examples. And accordingly, recent studies (see [20-25] for some examples) have set to establish a framework for grounding the recognition of affective states into body postures. Our own studies, in particular, have proposed a general description of posture based on angles and distances between body joints and used it to create an affective posture recognition system that maps the set of postural descriptors into affective categories. In addition to classification rates that favourably compared with those obtained using facial expressions, we also showed how posture could provide for the discrimination of affective categories across cultures [26], thus showing posture as a very powerful communicative modality.

But interestingly, another line of work suggests another important role of body posture. And that is that changes in posture can induce changes in affective states or have a feedback role affecting motivation and emotion. A study by Riskind and Gotay [27], for example, revealed how *"subjects who had been temporarily placed in a slumped, depressed physical posture later appeared to develop helplessness more readily, as assessed by their lack of persistence in a standard learned helplessness task, than did subjects who had been placed in an expansive, upright posture."* Furthermore, it was shown that posture had also an effect on verbally reported self-perceptions. This is not surprising, as others have reported similar regulatory properties with other forms of non-verbal expressions of affects. Richards and Gross [28], for example, showed that simply keeping a stiff upper lip during an emotional event had effect on the memory of the event, and generally, exacted a cognitive toll as great as intentional cognitive avoidance. As a result, the field of pain management, for example, is becoming increasingly interested in the relation between pain and emotion [29], as various studies suggest that problems in regulating and expressing emotions are linked to increased pain and distress.

4 Body Movement and Engagement

These two facets of bodily activity in general (posture, movement) provide the theoretical justification for our hypothesis on the existence of a (possibly bilateral) relationship between engagement and body movement. The question we specifically address here is whether an increase in task-related body movement imposed, or allowed, by the game controller will result in an increase of the player's engagement level. To address this question, we conducted two separate experiments. In the first experiment the participants played a same computer game using two different controllers that imposed different amount of task-related movement. To rule out the possibility that the shape of the controllers itself may be a confounding factor, a second experiment was performed in which the participants used the same controller with the difference that the amount of body motion imposed in the two conditions depended upon how the controller was used.

4.1 Experiment 1

Method
Fourteen participants (aged 25±4.4) were asked to play Guitar Hero, a music game for PlayStation. This game sees the player "play" the song by pressing a number of colour-coded buttons in sequence. The timeliness of each input contributes to the score of the player. Each participant was asked to play the game in two conditions. In the "pad" condition, the player was given a standard PlayStation DualShock controller, which only involved button pressing. In the "guitar" condition, the player was given a guitar-shaped controller that featured not only five fret buttons but also a strut bar and a whammy bar so that the device feels like, and plays like, a real guitar. With this controller, raising the guitar upward increases the player's "star power", which further encourages him/her to use full-body movements.

All participants were beginners and had no prior exposure to any such game. Before playing the game, the tendency of the participant to get immersed -- a potential predictor of engagement [10] -- was assessed using a revised version (GITQ)[1] of the Immersive Tendency Questionnaire (ITQ) proposed by Witmer and Singer [5]. This questionnaire was used with the assumption that engagement is the first step towards immersion. After filling the questionnaire, the participants were let to familiarize themselves with the game and the game controllers for a period of 5 minutes. The participants were fitted with a lightweight (6kgs) exoskeleton -- GIPSY by Animazoo (UK) -- on their upper body, arms and head, so as to provide angular measurements for each of the upper-body joints. In addition, a video camera was placed in front of the participant to record his/her body movements during play.

---

[1] http://www.cs.ucl.ac.uk/staff/n.berthouze/Questionnaire/GITQ-RevFromWitmer98.pdf

Each participant was asked to play for 20 minutes in each condition, with each condition played over two different days. The order in which each participant played each condition was counterbalanced. After each condition, the engagement level of the participant was assessed using a revised version [2] of the Gaming Engagement Questionnaire (GEQ) by Chen et al. [11].

Results

Since both GEQ and GITQ are based on the theoretical work by Sheridan [1] who suggested that the factors that underline the concept of presence could be grouped into 4 categories (Control, Sensory, Distraction and Realism), it is reasonable to think of the tendency to get immersed as a predictor for engagement. To investigate how individual differences in immersive tendency actually related to the degree of engagement experienced, three correlation coefficients were calculated: (a) the Pearson's coefficient for the "dual-pad" condition (condition D thereafter), (b) the Pearson's coefficient for the "guitar" condition (condition G thereafter) and (c) the Pearson's coefficient when both conditions were pooled (condition D+G thereafter).

In the pooled condition, a significant correlation of $r=.610$ ($p<.01$) was obtained, thus justifying our prediction. When considering each condition separately, however, we found that this correlation was mostly accounted for by a significant correlation obtained in the G condition, $r=.810$ ($p<.01$) since the D condition showed a non-significant correlation of $r=.426$ ($p=.146$). The significance of this finding will be discussed later in the section.

To investigate the role played by the game controller in the engagement level of the participant, we performed a paired t-test on the engagement scores of the participants in each condition. The test revealed that players in the G condition returned significantly higher engagement scores ($t=3.659$, $p<.001$). This finding is corroborated by an analysis of the video recordings of the players. Such analysis showed a higher incidence of task related movements (such as keeping the beat using head and body) in the G condition that, at least qualitatively, correlates with a higher engagement. This analysis is discussed in section 4.

The amount of body movements in each condition was quantified by a measure (denoted Gypsy score thereafter) computed as the normalized sum of the total angular movement over the entire duration of the song. Concretely, a sum of angular differences between each consecutive frame was computed, summed up over all frames (60 frames per second), and normalized by the number of frames in a song to account for differences in song duration.

Prior to looking into any correlations between movement and engagement, a comparison of means between conditions D and G was done on the GITQ, GEQ and Gypsy scores. Since these scores have interpersonal differences, using absolute values might not be appropriate [30]. To standardize the scores, the Gipsy score X_n was z-transformed, i.e., demeaned and divided by the standard deviation : $Z_n=(X_n-\mu)\div$. Significant differences were obtained in both GEQ scores ($t=-3.659$, $p<.001$) and Gypsy scores ($t=-3.264$, $p=.002$), both obtaining higher values in the G condition. A similar

---

[2] Items that did not relate to gaming and engagement were excluded and some of the terminology was modified to suit measuring people playing games. http://www.cs.ucl.ac.uk/staff/n.berthouze/Questionnaire/GEQ-RevFromChen2005.pdf

significant difference was not found in GITQ scores (t=-.768, p=.444). This lack of significance in the GITQ scores was reasonable since the participant's tendency to immersion should not be affected by any of the variables, including the change in game controller. Thus, these findings demonstrate significant differences between conditions.

In light of those findings, the correlations obtained earlier between the two questionnaires become significant. They suggest that providing the participants with either a more natural game controller, or affording them more movement facilitates this relationship. Given a similar GITQ score and the fact that engagement is considered the first step in immersion [10], the higher correlation obtained in the G condition demonstrates that the guitar-shaped controller enhanced the level of engagement the participants experienced.

4.2 Experiment 2

Method
To remove the possibility that the shape of the controller (and hence its novelty), rather than the movements it afforded and elicited, could be a factor in the increased engagement level, we carried out a similar experiment with the main difference that only the guitar-shaped controlled was used. In one condition (here again called D for consistency), the guitar-shaped controller was used as a dual-pad controller, i.e., the participants were taught all of those features that are controlled solely with the hands (i.e., fret buttons, strut bar and whammy bar). In the second condition (here again called G for consistency), instead, the participants were also informed about the tilt sensor in the neck of the guitar to acquire "star power". Eighteen participants (mean age of 20 and standard deviation of 0.77) took part in the experiment. All participants were beginner. Each group of 9 participants was asked to play one condition only since using the guitar knowing about the tilt-sensor feature but not being allowed to use it would have been too unnatural. Each participant was asked to play for 10 minutes after which his/her engagement level was assessed using the same revised version of the Gaming Engagement Questionnaire (GEQ) as mentioned earlier.

Results
After confirming that the GEQ score were normally distributed, they were analysed using a t-test. The test revealed that players in the G condition returned significantly higher engagement scores (t=5.123, p<.001) supporting the finding of the previous experiment, i.e., that the body movement imposed in the G condition appears to affect the engagement level.

To better understand how the conditions affected the engagement level, we measured the amount of motion of the players in two different ways. The first measures were computed using the data collected with the motion capture system. For the second type of measurements, we asked 3 observers (students from the Psychology department) to rate the amount of movement of each player over a 7-degree scale (10 minutes of video for each player). The observers were informed of the two experiment conditions and instructed not to consider in their evaluation the interval in which the players are raising their arms to get "star power". To examine the validity of these two types of measures, the average of the observers' scores was computed and correlated with the motion capture scores. A strong correlation was found between the two types of measurements (Pearson = 0.858, p < 0.001).

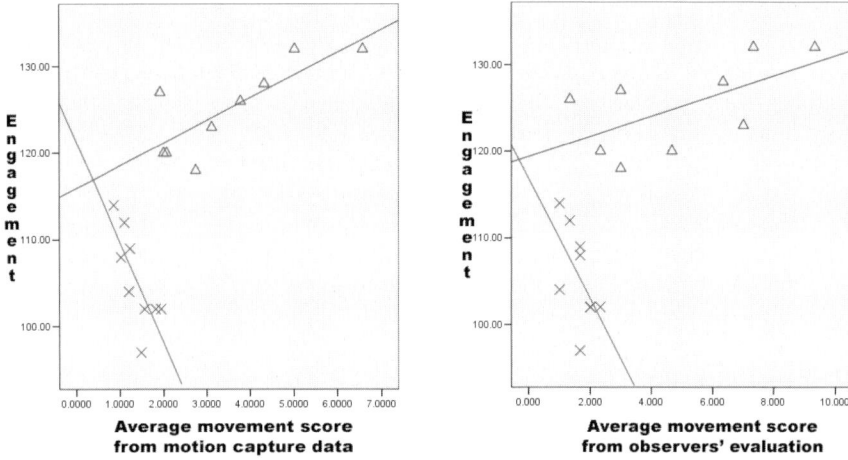

Fig. 2. Movement vs. engagement score. On the left, the amount of movement is computed on the data collected with the motion capture. On the right, it is computed as the average of the scores of 3 observers. We can observe a positive correlation for the G condition (Δ), and a negative correlation for the D condition (X).

We then computed the correlation between amount of movement and engagement scores. The left panel in Figure 2 shows the relation between amount of movement computed on the motion capture data and the engagement score, whereas the right panel depicts the relation between engagement score and movement as evaluated by the 3 observers. Both graphs reveal a positive trend in the G condition and a negative one in the D condition. The trend in the D condition (Pearson's coefficient = - .766, p=.016 for the left panel) seems to confirm the results of other studies that showed that attention in computer games is correlated with a decrease of body motion [36, 37].

In contrast, the trend in the G condition (Pearson's coefficient = .799, p = .01 for the left panel) appears to contradict such result as the amount of motion is positively correlated to the level of engagement in the player. We would like to suggest that conditions D and G simply involve two different levels and types of engagement. In condition D, players may be driven by a desire to win the game (hard fun), leading to an increased focus on the display. In condition G, instead, engagement may also derive from the feeling of becoming a guitar player (fantasy) and from the higher level of arousal and positive experience that it generates.

5 Affective Experience

To confirm the hypothesis that this increased involvement of body movement affects the fantasy and the affective experience of the player, we selected from the videos collected in experiment 1, the clips that showed body movement that could either be related to affective expressions (see Figure 3) or be task-related movements (excluding the movement of raising the neck of the guitar). Twenty seven video clips, portraying 12 of the 14 participants, were obtained. As expected from the previous section, the number of clips that could be extracted from the G condition was much higher than in the D condition. Each clip included 2 seconds prior to the main motion and 2 seconds afterwards so as to provide some context. In total, the clips lasted about 5 to 8 seconds, depending on how long the expressional movements or gestures were (1 to 4 seconds). To provide a reference for the type of affective experience that may occur in non-computer games, ten clips of affective body movements from players playing a social board game were added to this pool.

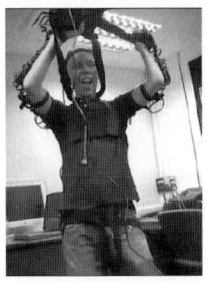 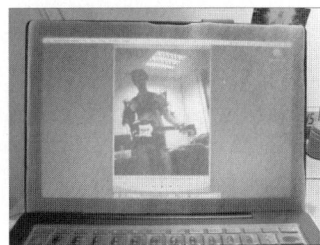

Fig. 3. Left: Example of body movement in the selected clips. Right: Experimental setting. A semi-transparent sheet was used to blur any facial information.

6 observers (students from the Psychology department) were asked to rate the body movements displayed in the video clips according to three affective dimensions (valence, arousal and power of control) on an 11-point scale. They were also asked to select, within a list of 22 affective words, the word that they felt best described the subject's emotions. The design of this list (excited, aroused, happy, content, relaxed, satisfied, bored, depressed, sad, miserable, frustrated, annoyed, angry, alarmed, surprised, frightened, disgusted, hateful, amused, disappointed, calm, joyful) was made on the basis of the Circumplex model of affect by Russell [31], a list of words proposed by Bowen [32] and by Peter and Herbon [30], and from a pilot study we conducted. In addition, the observers were also encouraged to select their own word if they could find a more appropriate one. The observers were allowed no more than 4 viewings of each clip and each session took approximately 30 to 40 minutes.

The randomized 37 clips were shown to the 6 observers using an Apple MacBook 2.0Ghz laptop computer with a 13.3" wide-screen display. To remove any possible confounds of sound and facial expressions, the clips were shown in mute and with a semitransparent sheet covering the display. The relatively low resolution of the clips (320x240 pixels) and the relative opaqueness of the material resulted in clearly visible body movements but blurred facial expressions (see Figure 3, right).

5.1 Results

Means and standard deviations were calculated for each clip's dimensions of arousal, valence and control. The scores were in the range [-5,5]. Mean scores were used to minimize individual differences and investigate the general consensus as a whole. It showed arousal, valence and control/power mean values to range from approximately

- 2.5 to 3. All clips had a standard deviation of less than 2.5, except for five clips. The third dimension was found to essentially correlate with arousal (possibly because of a misunderstanding by the observers) and was therefore discarded.

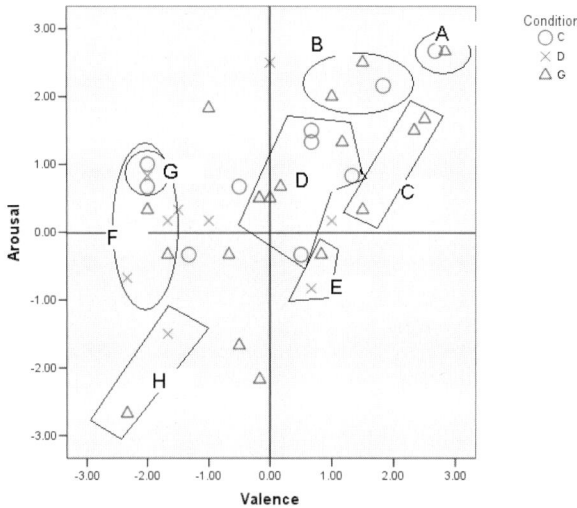

Fig. 4. Projection of the clips into the arousal and valence space and their clustering according to body gestures. O = social board game, X = D condition and Δ = G condition. Each cluster is denoted by a letter. The descriptions of the gestures in each cluster are in Table 1.

Table 1. Typical body movements observed in the clips corresponding to the clusters depicted in Figure 4 and the emotion labels used by the observers

Cluster	Body gestures	Affective Labels
A	Raising arms up to mid air	Excited, joyful, happy
B	Shaking body in a rhythmic fashion (dancing)	Excited, content, aroused
C	Thumbs-up and arm bent	Happy, satisfied, joyful
D	Leaning back and shaking body	Amused, excited, happy, content, surprised, satisfied
E	Shaking head	Relaxed, content satisfied
F	Dropping arms	Disappointed, frustrated, calm
G	Shaking/shivering body while leaning back	Disappointed, frustrated
H	Very little movement	Bored, disappointed

Figure 4 shows the projection of the clips in the arousal/valence space. We analyzed that data in terms of whether adjacent clips in that coordinate system would show similarities in the associated body movements. Our analysis revealed 8 clusters, as shown in Table 1. Looking at the type of movement associated to each cluster, we can see that the high-arousal/high-valence quadrant contains movements that are related to positive emotions and to music-player movements. The opposite quadrant instead contains movements that can be related to negative emotion expressed possibly when the player made mistakes. What is interesting to notice here is that most of the clips for the D condition fall in the low-valence quadrants (predominantly around low/neutral levels of arousal). The clips from the G conditions fall mainly in the high-valence/high-arousal quadrant but still have a good representation in the low-valence/low-arousal quadrant. This supports our hypothesis that in the G condition, the affective experience is not only related to the performance in the game, but also to the enjoyment derived from the music-player role assumed by the player.

To rule out the possibility that the extraction of the clips could be biased, we repeated the experiment by asking 3 new observers to rate the complete videos of 6 participants (3 videos for each condition) randomly selected. The observers were asked to indicate the starting time and ending time of each negative or positive affective expressions or task-related movement (e.g., dancing, keeping the rhythm). The results showed a significant difference with a larger presence of positive affective expressions ($p < 0.0001$) as well as rhythmic movements such as dancing ($p < 0.005$) in the G condition.

6 Discussion

The significance of the findings reported in this paper must be qualified by the rather small size of the pool of subjects. Nevertheless, our studies indicate statistically significant relations between body movement and engagement which raise interesting questions.

Our main finding is that body movements appear not only to increase the players' level of engagement but also to modify the way they get engaged. The combined results demonstrate in fact that the controller itself plays a critical role in creating a more complete experience. By inducing body movement, the device resulted in a higher sense of engagement in the players and mediated a feeling of presence in the digital world. The players appeared to quickly enter in the role suggested by the game, here, a musician, and started to perform task related motions that were not required by the game itself. Gaming was no longer only a question of challenge; it was the experience itself that rewarded the players. A further analysis of the game scores of the participants could shed more light on the different type of engagement in the two conditions. Nonetheless, this is an important finding that supports the factor of fantasy of Malone [6] and Lazzaro [14] in their description of engagement. It also comes in contrast with the predominant view that the feeling of presence can only be induced by virtual reality environment. Another important observation is that the involvement of body movements appeared to address another of Malone's factor, i.e., the affective aspect of the game. As discussed in our section on the regulatory properties of body movements, the body movements also appeared to play a role in determining the players' affective state and hence in increasing the players' level of engagement.

In the G condition, task-related body movements (i.e., raising the guitar upward) resulted in the player displaying more excitement. It must be noted, however, that the resulting increased "star power" could also be a contributing factor. However, even within the same G condition, the engagement scores were positively correlated with the amount of movement of the player, thus supporting our hypothesis.

Describing the effect of interface on emotion and engagement, Brown and Cairns [10] claimed that there needs to be an invisibility of controls for total immersion to take place. With respect to human-machine interaction, this study opens the door to the development of systems, which, by involving bodily activity, can induce specific affective states and therefore improve user engagement. By looking at the relationship between engagement, behaviour and affective states in game play, we will be able to ground their relationship in a gaming context and be able to suggest a model for application in future games. By increasing the non-verbal response of the player, we are providing the game designer with a huge amount of information that could allow the creation of more social and entertaining games. Indeed, the experience of the player itself could be used as an input to the game. The impact of such approach could extend beyond the realm of gaming. Edutainment, for example, stands to benefit from methods aiming to support and facilitate task related movements in the user. Recent studies have shown that the use of body motion during cognitive processes supports these cognitive processes [38] even if the gestures performed are not necessary to the accomplishment of the task [33, 34].

References

1. Sheridan, T.B.: Musings on telepresence and virtual presence: Teleoperators and Virtual Environments 1(1), 120–125 (1992)
2. Barhield, W., Weghorst, S.: The sense of presence within virtual environments: A conceptual framework. In: Proceedings of the Fifth International Conference on Human-Computer Interaction, vol. 2, pp. 699–704 (1993)
3. Witmer, B.G., Singer, M.J.: Measuring immersion in virtual environments (ARI Technical Report 1014), U.S. Army Research Institute for the Behavioral and Social Sciences Alexandria, VA (1994)
4. Smith, S., Marsh, T., Duke, D., Wright, P.: Drowning in immersion. In: Proceedings of UK-VRSIG'98: UK Virtual Reality Special Interest Group (1998)
5. Witmer, B.G., Singer, M.J.: Measuring presence in virtual environments: A presence questionnaire. Presence 7, 225–240 (1998)
6. Malone, T.W.: What makes computer games fun? Byte 6, pp. 258–277 (1981)
7. Csikszentmihalyi, M.: Flow. Harper Collins Publishers, New York (1990)
8. Berieter, C., Scardamalia, M.: Surpassing ourselves: An inquiry into the nature and implications of expertise. Chicago, IL: Open Court (1992)
9. Douglas, Y., Hargadon, A.: The pleasure principle: Immersion, engagement, flow. In: Proceedings of the eleventh ACM on Hypertext and hypermedia, pp. 153–160. ACM Press, New York (2000)
10. Brown, E., Cairns, P.A: A grounded investigation of game immersion. CHI 2004, ACM Conference on Human Factors in Computing, pp. 1297–1300. ACM Press, CHI (2004)
11. Chen, M., Kolko, B., Cuddihy, E., Medina, E.: Modelling and measuring engagement in computer games. Paper presented at the annual conference for the Digital Games Research Association (DiGRA), Vancouver, Canada (2005)
12. Haywood, N., Cairns, P.: Engagement with an interactive museum exhibit. In: Proceedings of HCI 2005, Springer, London (2005)
13. Koster, R.: A Theory of Fun for Game Design. Paraglyph Press (2005)
14. Lazzaro, N.: Why we play games: Four keys to more emotion without story. Technical report, XEO Design Inc (2004)

15. Mehrabian, A., Friar, J.: Encoding of attitude by a seated communicator via posture and position cues. Journal of Consulting and Clinical Psychology 33, 330–336 (1969)
16. Coulson, M.: Attributing emotion to static body postures: recognition accuracy, confusions, and viewpoint dependence. Journal of Nonverbal Behavior 28(2), 117–139 (2004)
17. Bull, E.P.: Posture and Gesture. Pergamon, Oxford (1987)
18. Graham, J.A., Ricci-Bitti, R., Argyle, M.: A crosscultural study of the communication of emotion by facial and gestural cues. Journal of Human Movement Studies 1, 68–77 (1975)
19. Argyle, M.: Bodily communication, Routledge (1988)
20. Bianchi-Berthouze, N., Kleinsmith, A.A.: categorical approach to affective gesture recognition. Connection Science 15(4), 259–269 (2003)
21. de Silva, R., Bianchi-Berthouze, N.: Modeling human affective postures: An information theoretic characterization of posture features. Journal of Computational Agents and Virtual Worlds 15(3-4), 269–276 (2004)
22. De Silva, R., Kleinsmith, A., Bianchi-Berthouze, N.: Towards unsupervised detection of affective body nuances. In: Tao, J., Tan, T., Picard, R.W. (eds.) ACII 2005. LNCS, vol. 3784, pp. 29–32. Springer, Heidelberg (2005)
23. Picard, R.E., Vyzas, E., Healy, J.: Toward machine emotional intelligence: Analysis of affective physiological state. IEEE Transactions on Pattern Analysis and Machine Intelligence 23(10), 1175–1191 (2001)
24. Fagerberg, P., Stahl, A.: Designing gestures for affective input: an analysis of shape, effort and valence. Proceedings of Mobile Ubiquitous and Multimedia, Norrkoping. Sweden (2003)
25. Camurri, A., De Poli, G., Leman, M., Volpe, G.: Communicating expressiveness and affect in multimodal interactive systems. IEEE Multimedia Magazine 12(1), 43–53 (2005)
26. Kleinsmith, A., De Silva, R., Bianchi-Berthouze, N.: Cross-cultural differences in recognizing affect from body posture. Interacting with Computers, vol. 18(6) (2006 in press)
27. Riskind, J.H., Gotay, C.C.: Physical posture: Could it have regulatory or feedback effects on motivation and emotion? Motivation and Emotion 6(3), 273–298 (1982)
28. Richards, J.M., Gross, J.J.: Personality and emotional memory: How regulating emotion impairs memory for emotional events. J. of Research in Personality 40(5), 631–651 (2005)
29. Keefe, F.J., Lumley, M., Anderson, T., Lynch, T., Carson, K.L.: Pain and emotion: New research directions. Clinical Psychology 57(4), 587–607 (2001)
30. Peter, C., Herbon, A.: Emotion representation and physiology assignments in digital systems. Interacting with Computers 18, 139–170 (2006)
31. Russell, J.A.: A circumplex model of affect. Journal of personality and social psychology 39, 1161–1178 (1980)
32. Bowen, H.: Can video games make you cry? GameInformer Magazine (2005)
33. Clark, A.: Being there. Putting Brain, Body, and World together again. MIT Press, Cambridge, Mass (1997)
34. Singer, M.A., Goldin-Meadow, S.: Children learn when their teacher's gestures and speech differ. Psychological Science 16(2), 85–89 (2005)
35. Thelen, E.: Time-scale dynamics in the development of an embodied cognition. In: Port, R., van Gelder, T. (eds.) In Mind In Motion, MIT Press, Cambridge, MA (1995)
36. Rugel, R.P., Cheatam, D., Mitchell, A.: Movement and inattention in learning-disable and normal children. Journal of Abnormal Child Psychology 6(3), 325–337 (1978)
37. Farrace-Di Zinno, A.M, Douglas, G., Houghton, S., Lawrence, V., West, J.: Whiting, Body Movements of Boys with Attention Deficit Hyperactivity Disorder (ADHD) during computer video game play, British Journal of Educ. Technology 32(5), 607–618 (2001)
38. Rambusch, J.: The embodied and situated nature of computer game play. In: Proceedings of the workshop on Cognitive Science of Games and Gameplay, CogSci'06 (2006)

A Systematic Comparison of Different HMM Designs for Emotion Recognition from Acted and Spontaneous Speech

Johannes Wagner, Thurid Vogt, and Elisabeth André

Multimedia concepts and applications
Augsburg University, Germany
johannes.wagner@student.uni-augsburg.de,
{vogt,andre}@informatik.uni-augsburg.de

Abstract. In this work we elaborate the use of hidden Markov models (HMMs) for speech emotion recognition as a dynamic alternative to static modelling approaches. Since previous work on this field does not yet define a clear line which HMM design should be prioritised for this task, we run a systematic analysis of different HMM configurations. Furthermore, experiments are carried out on an acted and a spontaneous emotions corpus, since little is known about the suitability of HMMs for spontaneous speech. Additionally, we consider two different segmentation levels, namely words and utterances. Results are compared with the outcome of a support vector machine classifier trained on global statistics features. While for both databases similar performance was observed on utterance level, the HMM-based approach outperformed static classification on word level. However, setting up general guidelines which kind of models are best suited appeared to be rather difficult.

1 Introduction

For the recognition of emotions from speech, many feature extraction strategies and a number of classification approaches have been explored. These have been mainly static modelling approaches that compute global statistics of relevant features over an "emotion unit", e. g. a word or an utterance [14,2]. However, the temporal structure within the expression of emotions becomes largely lost by this kind of modeling, though it has been noted as an important feature type [4]. In contrast, hidden Markov models (HMMs) offer a dynamic modelling approach which provides a better consideration of the temporal structure but up to now has been used relatively scarcely (e. g. [8,13,5]). This may partly be due to the set of parameters of an HMM (model topology, number of states, output probabilities) which is crucial to its performance though an optimal configuration for emotion recognition is still disputed. In this paper, we address the lack of a systematic analysis of the suitability of different HMM configurations and examine all combinations of the most common settings of the individual parameters.

Furthermore, HMMs have so far been tested mainly on acted emotions or on small spontaneous emotion databases with few speakers. We explore their

A. Paiva, R. Prada, and R.W. Picard (Eds.): ACII 2007, LNCS 4738, pp. 114–125, 2007.

use on an acted emotions corpus (BERLIN [3]) and on a spontaneous emotions corpus of considerable size (AIBO [1]) to see whether HMMs are also suitable for spontaneous speech and if differences exist in good model parameters for acted and spontaneous emotion.

In the following we will first introduce HMMs as a modelling technique for emotion recognition, discuss some previous work on this topic and elaborate on our goals. After describing our experimental setting in terms of databases, features and HMM modelling environment, we will present our results along with a thorough interpretation of the findings.

2   HMMs in Speech Emotion Recognition

2.1   Static Versus Dynamic Modelling

A main characteristic of human speech is its dynamic structure. In classification tasks the sampled speech signal is represented as a time series of observations, usually multi-dimensional vectors of relevant features. The length of a single observation is usually around 10–25 ms and as long as the observations are kept in the original sequence, the dynamic information within a segment is captured.

Since many classification methods only handle single observations, a common strategy is the use of global statistics instead of the sequence itself. Popular methods requiring this intermediate step are support vector machines, neural networks or Naïve Bayes, referred to as static or discriminative classifiers. Although experiments set up on these methods have shown reasonable results, as a drawback the temporal structure of the sequences is discarded and consequently also affective information incorporated within the temporal activity of speech.

As an alternative, dynamic modelling methods exist which do not suffer from this drawback. Such a method is discussed within the scope of this work: the so called hidden Markov models (HMMs), which are capable of processing sequences with dynamic length. An HMM is a stochastic finite automaton, where the probability to pass to the next state only depends on the previous state. Additionally, each state produces an output with a certain probability. Only this output can be observed, the under-lying state sequence is "hidden" and has to be inferred from the observations. Thus, an HMM is characterised by the transition probabilities between its states which determine the connectivity of the model, the output probabilities of the states which are usually mixtures of Gaussian distributions, and the number of states in the model. In order to build an HMM classifier, transition and output probabilites are estimated from a training set of data instances.

Transferred to emotion recognition, the output is the observed sequence of feature vectors and the state sequence represents the emotion to be recognised. Obviously, temporal changes in the features can be captured well by this kind of classifier and this is one of the reasons why HMMs are an established modelling technique for automatic speech recognition. Common topologies there have been forward directed networks with no or only short jumps. For emotion recognition, also topologies with backward jumps and more connectivity have been considered (see Fig. 1). Still, it has not yet been systematically investigated which

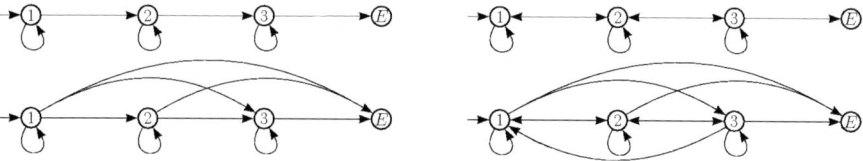

Fig. 1. Different topologies of a 3-state HMM. Top: linear model with only forward connections and model with additional backward connections. Bottom: left-right and fully connected (ergodic) model.

kind of networks are best suited to model the emotional cues and why. Finding reasonable answers to these questions is of main interest to this work.

2.2   Previous Work

Kwon *et al.* [8] used continuous HMMs with left-right topology and up to 5 states to model on word level a neutral and 3 stress styles. They report an average recognition accuracy of 70.1%, which was superior to the performance of a SVM classifier (67.1%). For a second database containing short commands or greetings with several words in 5 basic emotions an average result of 40.8% was achieved, this time inferior to the SVM classifier (42.3%). Based on this observation the authors suggest the use of HMM-based classifiers in applications with short utterances, but discriminative classifiers in case of variable-length utterances. They also report that performance of the HMM-based classifier was improved mostly by increasing the number of states.

Performance of global statistics versus instantaneous features was also addressed by Schuller *et al.* [13]. Utterances collected from 5 speakers in 7 emotional states — acted and spontaneous — were modelled using HMMs with up to 64 states and up to 4 mixtures per state. Again a left-right topology was used with an additional jump limit of two states at most. Performance was compared to the outcome of a Gaussian mixture model (GMM) trained on global statistics of the utterances. While the latter achieved an average recognition accuracy of 86.8%, classification with instantaneous features reached only 77.8%. As a possible reason for this difference the authors quote the elimination of unvoiced parts in the utterances, leading to a loss of temporal information on durations of voiced sounds. Again, adding more states generally improved HMM-based classification. A similar approach is also reported by Jiang *et al.* [6], with the difference that HMM- and GMM-likelihoods were combined to form a final decision.

Beside a single HMM with five states modelled with unimodal Gaussian densities, Fernandez *et al.* [5] also tested several variants such as autoregressive HMMs or hidden Markov decision trees. Experiments were based on utterances recorded from 4 subjects in a driving simulator under different stress situations. Best recognition rates are reported with a mixture of HMMs consisting of several single networks which were trained each on a different cluster of the data. In a subject-dependent task a mean recognition rate of 61.20% for the four stress levels was achieved. In a second approach based on global statistics, a support vector machine and a neural network could only reach 46.70% and 50.57%, resp.

While the approaches mentioned above are all based on continuous HMMs, Nwe *et al.* [10] run experiments on discrete HMMs. Short acted utterances in 6 archetypal emotions obtained from 12 non-professional speakers were modelled by HMMs with up to 8 states. The choice of an ergodic topology instead of a left-right structure was deduced from the assumption that emotional cues contained in an utterance may not occur strictly sequentially. Best results were achieved for 4 states. Other approaches with discrete HMMs are reported by Pao *et al.* [11], Kang *et al.* [7] and Nogueiras *et al.* [9], all carried out on acted speech.

All these reports prove that HMMs provide a suitable method to model emotional cues in speech. If tested, results were comparable or even superior to classification based on global statistics. However, there is not yet a clear line which HMM design should be prioritised, since the used networks differ greatly in respect of the number of states, topology and model densities. If within the same approach different network configurations were compared, often only the number of states was considered, while little is known about the effect of the other parameters. On the other hand, the previous approaches are mainly based on acted speech collected from a small number of subjects, so it is still vague to what extent HMMs are also applicable to spontaneous speech.

2.3 Scope of This Work

In this work we try to overcome the before mentioned limitations by working with a considerable larger set of HMMs. Furthermore, two databases are evaluated: one containing acted speech from 10 adults, similar to the ones used in previous approaches, and a second one recorded within a more realistic setting gathering spontaneous speech from 51 children. To draw a comparison which kind of network configuration is preferable for each segmentation level, experiments are carried out on word and utterance level, respectively. In respect to previous work, we especially investigate the following assumptions:

A1: In the case of continuous models, performance is improved when the number of mixtures per state is increased, that is, detailed density modelling [13]. A comparison with discrete models has not been drawn yet.

A2: High network connectivity is beneficial for modelling the presented sequences of emotional cues [10,11].

A3: Increasing the number of states, that is, detailed temporal modelling, leads to better recognition results [8,13,6,10,9].

A4: HMM-based classifiers are less useful in applications with utterances of variable length [8].

3   Experimental Settings

3.1   Databases

Our experiments were conducted on two different databases, one with acted emotions and one with elicited spontaneous emotions.

The Berlin database of emotional speech [3] contains recordings of 10 non-professional actors (5 male/5 female) in 6 emotional states (joy, anger, boredom, disgust, sadness, fear) as well as a neutral state. There are in total 493 utterances with 4827 words in it. We used a 5-fold cross validation strategy for evaluation, with always 8 speakers in the training and 2 (1 male/1 female) in the test set. This database has been labelled on utterance level; for word level investigations, each word obtained the label of the pertaining utterance. In the following this database is referred to as BERLIN-W (words) and BERLIN-U (utterances).

The German Aibo Emotion Corpus [1] contains spontaneous emotions and has been collected in a Wizard-of-Oz setting to elicit emotions. It covers speech of 51 children (31 girls/20 boys) interacting with Sony's robot dog Aibo and was recorded at two schools. The most prominent emotional states where angry, emphatic (as a pre-stage to anger), motherese (or baby-talk) and neutral. We evaluated a subcorpus of the original corpus with a relatively balanced class distribution. Additionally to word segmentation, a segmentation into chunks exists, which have been extracted from the dialogue turns by a manually revised pause segmentation, so in total 4543 chunks and 16427 words were analysed. Labels were originally assigned to words; these were mapped onto chunks using a modified majority-voting strategy, where the impact of neutral was weakened. For a detailed description of the selection of the subcorpus and the mapping of word-based labels onto chunks or turns see [2]. This corpus was evaluated by taking one school (Ohm, 26 speakers) for training and the other (Mont, 25 speakers) for testing. In the following AIBO-W (words) and AIBO-U (utterances) are used as abbreviations for this database.

3.2   Networks

Since the number of HMM networks is theoretically infinite, first a meaningful subset of representative networks was determined.

We compared discrete and continuous networks modelled by one of the following probability distributions: discrete with size 64 or 256, and continuous consisting of 1, 4 or 8 Gaussian mixtures. As a further constraint all states of a network had to be modelled by the same number of distributions. In the following d64, d256, c01, c04 and c08 are used as abbreviations for the corresponding networks.

Next, we compared four different topologies: a linear model with only forward transition (F) and a left-right model (Fj), which are both commonly used in speech recognition, as well as a model with also backward transitions (FB) and a fully connected network (FjBj). The latter is known as an ergodic model and assumed to be notably beneficial in modelling emotional cues [10,11]. Example diagrams for each network type have been previously shown in Figure 1.

In simple word recognition tasks the number of states usually corresponds roughly to the number of phonemes within a word, that is 2 to 10 states [12]. Hence, networks with 5 and 10 states were included as a promising length for recognition on word level. Additionally — since we also try to recognize emotions based on utterance level — longer networks with 15, 20 and 25 states are considered, as well. Networks with only a single state, which is equivalent to a GMM, were also tested in order to get an impression how much recognition gain is actually added by temporal modelling. In the following the state number of a network is coded with sXX.

Based on these parameters a set of 120 HMMs can be built, each coded by the concatenation of the introduced abbreviations. For example, c04-Fj-05 stands for a continuous left-right model with 5 states and 4 Gaussian mixtures.

3.3   Feature Extraction and Evaluation

Since the modelling task was of main interest to this work, we used a relatively simple feature set consisting of 13 MFCC coefficients including the 0th cepstral parameter, which represents the energy within the frame. First and second derivation were also added, resulting in 39 features in total. MFCCs are commonly used in speech recognition to encode the spectral information of speech. In particular, they are known for their good approximation of the human auditory perception. Feature extraction, as well as evaluation was done using the Hidden Markov Model Toolkit[1] (HTK) developed by the Cambridge University Engineering Department. For each emotion we trained a separate model and classified an unknown sequence into the model that gave highest probability.

4   Results

4.1   Recognition Rates Achieved with HMMs

Each of the 120 networks was trained and tested on both databases and for both segmentation types, namely words and utterances. Sole exception: on word level results for F and FB networks with 15 or more states were discarded, since too many samples would have been refused[2]. Throughout the following chapter performance of a network is measured according to the classwise averaged recognition result CL, that is the mean of the recognition rates achieved for each emotional class.

First of all, it should be mentioned that finding general tendencies was rather difficult, since on the one hand quite different parameters sometimes gained the same results, whereas on the other hand a slight parameter change sometimes caused a very different performance. However, to get an impression of the results, Table 1 lists for each domain performance of the worst and best networks, as well as the average result of all networks. In the first place, the broad margin of at least 10 % between worst and best performing networks is remarkable. This clearly shows that the network design is a crucial aspect, which has considerable impact on recognition accuracy. Before we discuss more accurately the influence of each parameter, we also want to note that there is an obvious difference of

---

[1] http://htk.eng.cam.ac.uk/

[2] Networks without skipping transition can only process a sample if it has at least as many frames as the network has states.

Table 1. Worst, best and average CL in % through all networks

Words

	worst network		best network		avg
AIBO	**43.53**	d64-FjBj-s25	**56.50**	c08-FB-s10	**52.18**
BERLIN	**33.32**	d64-Fj-s15	**50.53**	c08-FjBj-s10	**42.29**

Utterances

	worst network		best network		avg
AIBO	**44.73**	d256-FjBj-s20	**55.80**	c04-FjBj-s15	**50.85**
BERLIN	**48.97**	d256-F-s20	**73.92**	c08-F-s05	**61.36**

performance according to the segmentation level of both databases: while average recognition results for BERLIN is about 10% better for utterances than words, it is the other way round for AIBO. An explanation for this finding will be given in the next chapter.

First, we address assumption $A1$, i. e. the impact of the probability density. Therefore, the mean CL among all networks (grey bar), as well as the average of the 3 best performing networks (white bar), is presented in Figure 2. A general improvement in performance can be observed for HMMs modelled with a continuous probability density compared to discrete HMMs, even though the difference is more obvious for BERLIN than for AIBO. It also appears that among the continuous HMMs c04 and c08 networks slightly outperform those models with only a single mixture, that is c01. However, there seems to be no general improvement when increasing the number of mixtures from 4 to 8 in continuous networks or using a larger codebook than 64 in the discrete case.

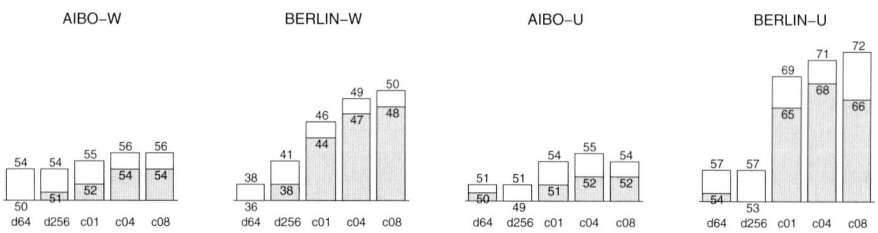

Fig. 2. Averaged CL among all networks modelled by the same probability density

Next we examine assumption $A2$, namely topology. Again, average CLs are shown in Figure 3. The results imply that none of the tested connectivity levels seem to be superior to the others. In particular, the hypothesis that additional connectivity is more suitable in modelling emotional cues is not supported.

According to assumption $A3$, average CLs according to different state numbers are given in Figure 4. Even though, differences are again small, networks of length 5 or 10 seem to be generally more profitable on word level. This supports our assumption that here similar network sizes as in word-based speech

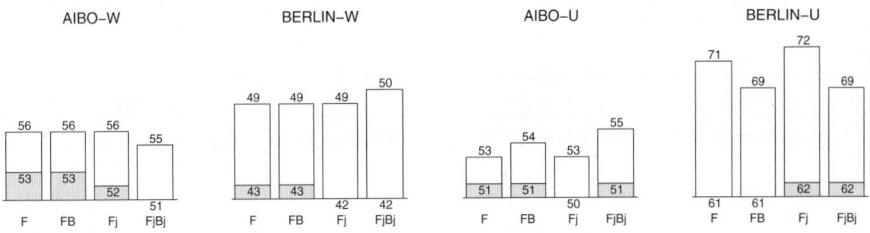

Fig. 3. Averaged CL among all networks modelled by the same topology

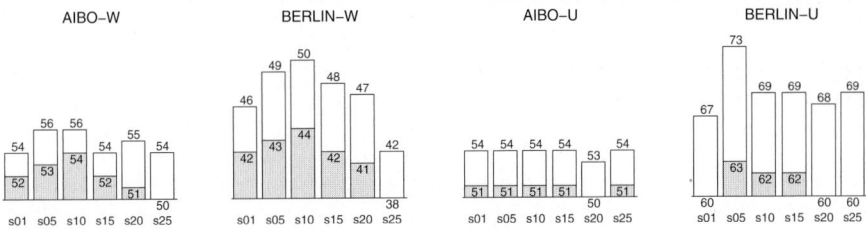

Fig. 4. Averaged CL among all networks modelled by the same number of states

recognition should be used. With regard to utterances, different tendencies for both databases can be observed: while networks with 5–15 states work best for BERLIN-U, performance for AIBO-U stays almost steady along all tested sizes. As a general tendency, results do not improve for models with 15 or more states.

To sum up, we can draw the following conclusions concerning *A1–3*:

- HMMs modelled by continuous densities outperform discrete networks.
- A pool of 4 mixtures seems to be sufficient.
- Ergodic models are not necessarily more suitable.
- HMMs with 5 to 10 states appear to be most beneficial.
- There seems to be no improvement for networks with 15 or more states.

Futhermore, results show that a good network design seems to be relatively independent of the source of speech (acted vs. spontaneous) and the segmentation level (word vs. utterance).

4.2   Interpretation of the Presented Results

As already mentioned, a remarkable difference of recognition accuracy between words and utterances can be observed for both databases. This difference follows from the different annotation strategies that have been used. While AIBO is labelled word-wise and therefore obviously adequately for evaluation on word level, words in BERLIN receive their label from the pertaining utterance. The latter certainly involves that some words do not carry the affective information they are labelled with. On the other hand, mapping labels from words to utterances — as done in AIBO — is also error prone.

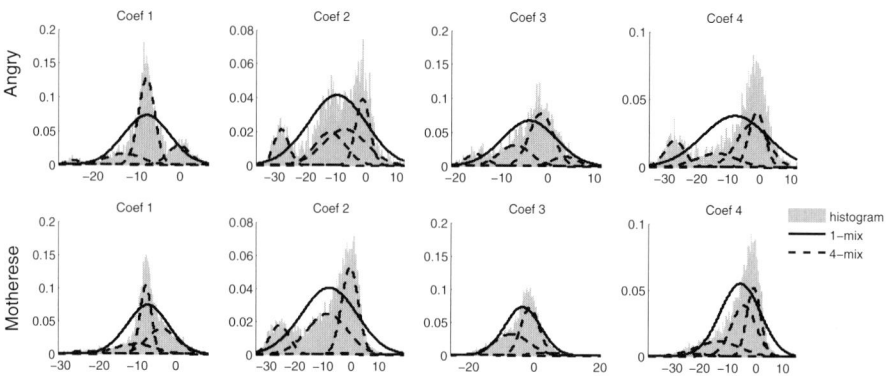

Fig. 5. Histograms and mixtures for four MFCC coefficients during motherese and angry

The output probability distribution of the HMM states defines how accurate the emotional cues are captured. Figure 5 shows histograms for the first 4 MFCC coefficients collected from all chunks of a single AIBO speaker during angry and motherese. The chart reveals that distributions belonging to the same coefficient differ only slightly between both emotions. However, a pool of 4 mixtures (dotted lines) allows a better modulation of these differences than a single Gaussian mixture (solid line). If we think of the additional distortion introduced by quantization, this also explains why discrete modelling is even less profitable.

The observation that performance of a network is more or less independent of its level of connectivity implies that additional backward and forward transitions do not significantly improve its capability to model emotional cues. Figure 6 shows transition probabilities for the c08-FB-s05 and c08-Fj-s05 networks trained with neutral words from AIBO-W. Indeed — compared to forward transitions — the probability associated with backward transitions is rather small in the FB network. Similarly, for the Fj network the transition probabilities become smaller the further the connected states are apart from each other. For both networks, the probability to remain in the same state is always the highest. This induces that successive frames tend to stay in the same state and that in case of a change usually the right neighbour is taken, just like we would expect it for an F network.

Figure 7 shows output probability densities of the 1st MFCC coefficient for states of different networks which were trained with emphatic words or utterances from AIBO. From these charts we can explain our findings according to the size of a network. For instance, we have seen that increasing the number of states to 15 or more states gave no further gain to the recognition performance. The reason is that in long networks successive states tend to show increasingly similar densities. Hence, at some point additional states do not improve temporal modelling anymore. For instance, in the network at the top of Figure 7 state 3 to 6 could be merged to a single state. In contrast, for the network shown below, which has only 5 instead of 15 states, all densities differ clearly. However, if the

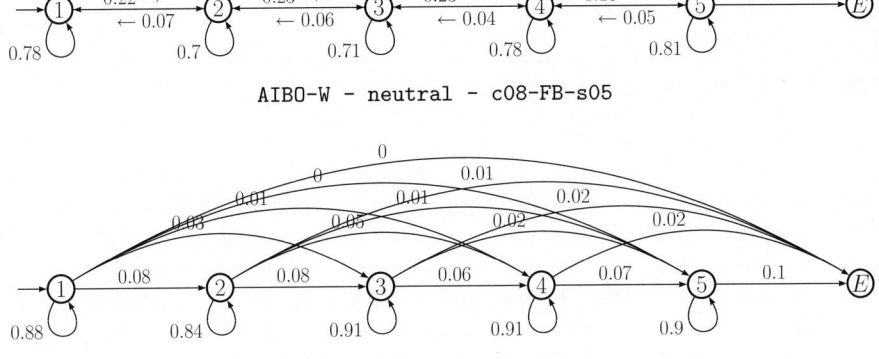

AIBO-W - neutral - c08-FB-s05

AIBO-W - neutral - c08-Fj-s05

Fig. 6. Transition probabilities of a trained network with different topologies

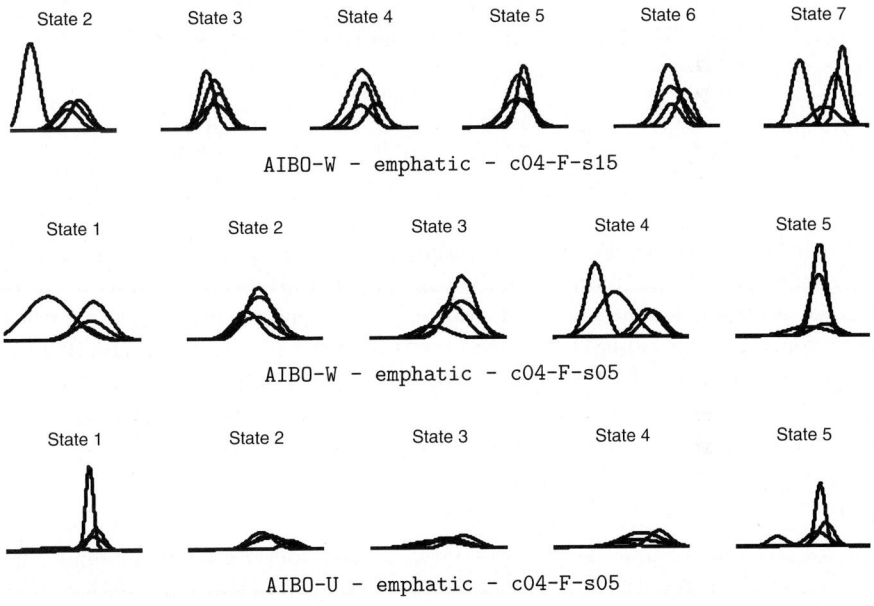

AIBO-W - emphatic - c04-F-s15

AIBO-W - emphatic - c04-F-s05

AIBO-U - emphatic - c04-F-s05

Fig. 7. Output probability densities of a single feature for states of different networks

same network is trained on utterances (bottom of Figure 7), we get again similar densities for state 2 to 4. A sign that in this case the network could be pruned even further. Indeed, this corresponds with the fact that temporal modelling did hardly gain any profit for AIBO-U. In our opinion the reason is that the utterances in this corpus range from single words to long phrases, and are therefore too inhomogeneous in respect of their length that a single network could effectively represent their temporal structure. This also explains why temporal modelling was more successful for BERLIN-U: here utterances are exclusively whole sentences of similar length.

4.3   Comparison with a Static Classifier

For comparison purposes, we also carried out experiments with features based on global statistics. A feature set composed of 1053 MFCC and 137 energy features[3] was calculated and used to train a support vector machine (SVM). To get a fair rating for the HMM-based approach, we discarded all discrete networks, as well as continuous networks with a single Gaussian density and 15 or more states and averaged outcomes among the remaining HMMs. Results are listed in Table 2 and show that on word level — independent of the database — HMMs are more than 10 % superior to the SVM approach. If we compare the values on utterance level, HMMs are still slightly better for AIBO, but inferior for BERLIN. This supports the assumption posited by Kwon et al. [8] that HMM-based classifiers are less applicable in applications with utterances of variable length (A_4).

Table 2. CL in % for the SVM and HMM-based approach

Words	SVM	HMM	Utterances	SVM	HMM
AIBO	**43.7**	**55.5**	AIBO	**51.2**	**52.5**
BERLIN	**36.6**	**48.6**	BERLIN	**73.3**	**69.5**

At this point we would like to mention, that performance with static modelling can be significantly improved when other feature types, such as duration or pitch features, are added. For instance, in combination with automatic feature selection, we could achieve a best recognition rate of 77.4% for BERLIN-U [14]. Using an optimised set of 381 features, involving also spectral and lexical features, Batliner et al. [2] report 58.7% recognition accuracy for turns in AIBO.

5   Conclusion

Our results confirm that HMMs provide a suitable method to model emotional cues in speech. Compared to classification based on global statistics, performance was similar on utterance level and clearly superior on word level. This applied for acted and spontaneous speech. From this we conclude that HMMs are also applicable in realistic settings.

Our results also show the difficulty to set up general guidelines which kind of networks is best suited. Tests based on a large set of networks could, for instance, not support the assumption that ergodic models are generally more suitable in modelling emotional cues. Solely, continuous networks gave significantly better results compared to discrete HMMs. According to the source of speech (acted vs.

---

[3] To achieve comparable results we obtained global statistics only for those feature types also used in our approach with HMMs.

spontaneous) and the segmentation level (word vs. utterance) similar tendencies were observed.

In [8], Kwon *et al.* state that HMM-based classifiers are less applicable for utterances of variable length. Our experiments prove this assumption insofar as temporal modelling appeared to be less profitable when the modelled samples were very diverse in respect of their length.

In our future work we will investigate this assumption more accurately by using a pool of networks which are trained with samples of similar sizes. Likewise, multiple networks can be used to represent nuances of the same emotion, such as cold and hot anger. Furthermore, it seems reasonable to combine dynamic and static classification to get the benefits of both approaches.

Acknowledgements. This work was partially funded by the EU network of excellence HUMAINE and the EU projects eCIRCUS and CALLAS.

References

1. Batliner, A., Hacker, C., Steidl, S., Nöth, E., D'Arcy, S., Russell, M., Wong, M.: You stupid tin box — children interacting with the AIBO robot: A cross-linguistic emotional speech corpus, LREC, Lisbon, Portugal (2004)
2. Batliner, A., Steidl, S., Schuller, B., Seppi, D., Laskowski, K., Vogt, T., Devillers, L., Vidrascu, L., Amir, N., Kessous, L., Aharonson, V.: Combining Efforts for Improving Automatic Classification of Emotional User States, IS-LTC, Ljubljana, Slov (2006)
3. Burkhardt, F., Paeschke, A., Rolfes, M., Sendlmeier, W.F., Weiss, B.: A Database of German Emotional Speech, Interspeech, Lisbon, Portugal (2005)
4. Cowie, R., Douglas-Cowie, E., Tsapatoulis, N., Votsis, G., Kollias, S., Fellenz, W., Taylor, J.G.: Emotion Recognition in Human-Computer Interaction. IEEE Signal Processing Magazine 18(1), 32–80 (2001)
5. Fernandez, R., Picard, R.W.: Modeling drivers' speech under stress. Speech Communication 40(1-2), 145–159 (2003)
6. Jiang, D.-N., Cai, L.-H.: Speech emotion classification with the combination of statistic features and temporal features, ICME, Taipei, Taiwan (2004)
7. Kang, B.-S., Han, C.-H., Lee, S.-T., Youn, D.-H., Lee, C.: Speaker dependent emotion recognition using speech signals, ICSLP, Beijing, China (2000)
8. Kwon, O.-W., Chan, K.-L., Hao, J., Lee, T.-W.: Emotion Recognition by Speech Signals, Eurospeech, Geneva, Switzerland (2003)
9. Nogueiras, A., Moreno, A., Bonafonte, A., Mari, J.B.: Speech emotion recognition using hidden Markov models, Eurospeech, Aalborg, Denmark (2001)
10. Nwe, T.L., Foo, S.W., De Silva, L.C.: Speech emotion recognition using hidden Markov models. Speech Communication 41(4), 603–623 (2003)
11. Pao, T.-L., Chen, Y.-T., Yeh, J.-H., Liao, W.-Y.: Detecting Emotions in Mandarin Speech. Comp. Ling. and Chinese Lang. Proc. 10(3), 347–362 (2005)
12. Rabiner, L.R.: A Tutorial on Hidden Markov Models and Selected Applications in Speech Recognition. Proc. IEEE 77(2), 257–286 (1989)
13. Schuller, B., Rigoll, G., Lang, M.: Hidden Markov model-based speech emotion recognition, ICME, Baltimore, USA (2003)
14. Vogt, T., André, E.: Comparing Feature Sets for Acted and Spontaneous Speech in View of Automatic Emotion Recognition. ICME (2005)

On the Necessity and Feasibility of Detecting a Driver's Emotional State While Driving

Michael Grimm[1], Kristian Kroschel[1], Helen Harris[2], Clifford Nass[2],
Björn Schuller[3], Gerhard Rigoll[3], and Tobias Moosmayr[4]

[1] Universität Karlsruhe (TH), Institut für Nachrichtentechnik,
76128 Karlsruhe, Germany
grimm@int.uni-karlsruhe.de
[2] Stanford University, Department of Communication,
Stanford, CA 94305-2050, USA
[3] Technische Universität München, Institute for Human-Machine Communication,
80290 München, Germany
[4] BMW Group, Forschungs- und Innovationszentrum, Akustik,
Komfort und Werterhaltung, 80788 München, Germany

Abstract. This paper brings together two important aspects of the human-machine interaction in cars: the psychological aspect and the engineering aspect. The psychologically motivated part of this study addresses questions such as *why* it is important to automatically assess the driver's affective state, which states are important and how a machine's response should look like. The engineering part studies *how* the emotional state of a driver can be estimated by extracting acoustic features from the speech signal and mapping them to an emotion state in a multidimensional, continuous-valued emotion space. Such a feasibility study is performed in an experiment in which spontaneous, authentic emotional utterances are superimposed by car noise of several car types and various road surfaces.

1 Introduction

In recent years there has been a growing number of speech-driven applications in the car [1]. Therefore, current research on improvements of both comfort and safety in the car needs to pay attention to the speech interface between the driver and the infotainment system of the car. This paper focuses on one major aspect of the human factors: the driver's emotion.

In a previous study it was found that matching the emotional state of the driver and the expressiveness of a synthetic voice has a major impact on the driving performance [2,3]. Thus, it is necessary to automatically recognize the emotional state of a person while driving. This led us to the following experiment: Spontaneous emotional utterances were superimposed with car noise of several scenarios. The emotion conveyed in these utterances was automatically estimated using a set of 20 selected acoustic features. For the representation of the emotion, a three-dimensional emotion space concept was applied. Thus, an emotion

A. Paiva, R. Prada, and R.W. Picard (Eds.): ACII 2007, LNCS 4738, pp. 126–138, 2007.

is described in terms of three continuous-valued primitives (attributes), namely valence (positive vs. negative), activation (calm vs. excited), and dominance (weak vs. strong).

There are only a few other works on emotion recognition in the car. Jones and Jonsson [4] presented a method to detect five emotional states of drivers in a driving simulator. They use neural network classifiers but did not investigate the impact of the car noise. Schuller *et al.* [5] also based their experiment on driving simulator data, recognizing four different emotions using Support Vector Machines. However, preliminary studies on emotional speech superimposed by white noise showed that the recognition performance depends very much on the signal-to-noise ratio [6]. Thus, we study the impact of car noise on the emotion recognition in this paper.

The rest of the paper is organized as follows. Section 2 discusses the impact of the driver's emotion on the communication with the car and its importance regarding the safety. Section 3 presents the data used for the automatic emotion recognition experiment. Section 4 introduces the car noise conditions. Section 5 details the classification of emotions from the speech signal. Section 6 presents the recognition results. Section 7 summarizes the study and outlines future work.

2   The Role of Emotion in Driving Experiments

No human thought or action takes place in a vacuum. Temperaments, moods, and emotions shape how people view the world and how they react to it. Although temperaments and personality traits display more stability over time, and predict nuances of behavior, moods and emotions are easier to detect and classify in a real-time scenario. Furthermore, emotional states are more readily mapped to behavioral consequences.

2.1   Emotional States and Driving Behavior

In the context of driving, three distinct groups of emotional states have emerged as states of interest. The first state is defined by a slightly positive valence and a moderate level of arousal, closely associated with the emotional state of *happy*. The optimal state, thought of as a *flow* state [7], involves a moderate level of arousal, allowing for attention, focus, and productivity. A state of high arousal or extreme positive valence can potentially lead to distraction. States of a positive affect have also been shown to improve performance in non-driving contexts [8,9,10].

The second state of interest is characterized by an extreme level negative valence and high arousal, usually classified as anger. Frustration is distinguished from anger by the degree of negativity and arousal. Often, frustration is referred to as a gateway emotion that leads to anger, and ultimately to aggression and road rage [11]. With an increasing number of vehicles on the roadways, drivers encounter more frustration-inducing scenarios. As a result, road rage is now an escalating problem, and is the primary cause of many accidents and driving fatalities.

The third state is characterized by very low arousal and sometimes accompanied by a slight negative valance; when broadly defined, this state encompasses both sadness and drowsiness. A sad or negative state degrades task performance, and within the car this state is manifested as inattention.

Given these implications of driving under the influence of particular emotional states, it is unquestionably important to be able to identify such states at drivers. However, once the state of the driver is known, what is the best strategy to improve driver emotion and optimize driving behavior?

2.2   Appropriate Responses to Driver Emotion

Previous research has experimentally tested social responses to driver emotion. Nass and colleagues used a 2 (inducement emotion) x 2 (voice interface emotion) between-subject factorial design [3]. Without the benefit of a naturalistic setting and real-time assessment of driver emotion, researchers relied on the method of using emotionally-charged clips to induce emotion [12,13]. Two five minute videos, one inducing the state of *happy*, and the other for *sad/subdued* were created from a pre-tested image database. Half of the participants in the study were induced to be *happy*, and the other half were *sad/subdued*; the effectiveness of the inducement method was verified by self-report data from the Differential Emotional Scale (DES) [14].

In keeping with the factorial design, half of the participants from each inducement group drove through a simulated driving course while engaged in conversation with a *happy* voice interface; the other half interacted with the *sad/subdued* voice. The voice interface was actually a series of brief questions and comments, played at exactly the same time in the simulator for every participant. The same female voice talent recorded both the *happy* and *sad/subdued* versions of the script; there was no difference in content between the two versions, only a distinction in intonation and expression.

Contrary to common beliefs that *happy* is always best, results from the study showed that matching the voice emotion to the driver emotion proved more beneficial to emotion than simply presenting all drivers with a *happy* voice. This surprising result reveals the importance of designing socially appropriate in-car voice interfaces. Drivers who were induced to be *sad/subdued* expected their conversation partner to be aware of their state and respond accordingly, in a more subdued manner. Thus, the ability to detect driver emotion is not only helpful in predicting driver behavior, but necessary for designing smart, adaptive, and beneficial driver interfaces.

In order to implement socially appropriate interfaces [15,16], several hurdles must be overcome before the technology and knowledge can be integrated in vehicles. Future research must continue to explore the implications of addressing the driver with an in-car voice interface. Some first steps have been made, but the studies that have been completed only begin to touch upon the range of human emotional states, not to mention the effects of individual differences. However, suitable interactions cannot occur without first an adequate classification of emotions along the valence, activation, and dominance dimensions, as well as a robust capability to detect such emotions. The field of psychology, among others, provides a significant body of work to aid in distinguishing emotions. The work presented here further contributes to the future of intelligent in-car interface design by demonstrating the feasibility of detecting emotions in variety of contexts and under challenging noise conditions.

3   Data and Evaluation

For this study we used the VAM corpus, a database consisting of 947 spontaneous emotional utterances in German, which was first used in [17]. These utterances were recorded from 47 speakers in a talk-show on TV. The emotions arose from spontaneous, unscripted discussions, mainly on family issues or friendship questions.

The mean utterance duration was 3.0 s. The mean Signal-to-Noise Ratio was 19.2 ± 3.0 dB, reflecting the relatively good recording conditions of the close talk microphones. All signals were sampled at 16 kHz and 16 bit resolution.

The emotional content was manually labeled by a group of 18 human evaluators. An appropriate value for each emotion primitive was assigned to each utterance by means of the Self Assessment Manikins [18,19,20]. One out of five icons per primitive could be selected. The choice was then mapped to a scale of [-1,+1].

The average standard deviation in the human evaluator's ratings was 0.31, and the average inter-evaluator correlation was 0.6. This shows moderate to high inter-evaluator agreement for a rather difficult task of labeling spontaneous, non-acted emotions.

4   Noise Scenario

Robust automatic speech recognition (ASR) under the influence of car noise is still being researched [21]. Also, emotion recognition in the car is much more demanding than in clean speech. To study the feasibility, several noise scenarios of approx. 30 seconds were recorded in the car while driving. The microphone was mounted in the middle of the instrument panel, which is the standard for ASR applications in the car. The recorded noise was a superposition of several influences: noise from the wheels/suspension, the combustion engine, interior squeak and rattle noise, and wind noise. The influence of the signal path between the speaker and the microphone was neglected.

4.1   Choice of Vehicles

For this study we used four different cars as itemized in Table 1. Although the soft top of both convertibles was closed during the recordings, the interior noise was noticeable higher than in comparable sedans. While the engine noise dominates during the acceleration of the sportive M5, the similarly constructed 5 series Touring is more gentle and comfortable. The supermini unifies convertible,

Table 1. Choice of Vehicles

Notation	Vehicle	Derivative	Class
530i	BMW 5 series	Touring	Executive Car
645Ci	BMW 6 series	Convertible	Executive Car
M5	BMW M5	Sedan	Executive Sports Car
Mini	MINI Cooper S	Convertible	Supermini

hard suspension and sportive engine, and it thus provides the most demanding noise scenario.

4.2   Road Surfaces

Just as the vehicle type, the road surface affects the interior noise. We recorded the interior noise in all cars on the following surfaces:

- Smooth city road, 50 km/h (CTY)
- Highway, 120 km/h (HWY)
- Big cobbles, 30 km/h (COB)

The lowest noise levels were found with a constant driving over a smooth city road at 50 km/h and medium relovution. Higher noise levels were measured at a highway drive due to the increased wind noise. The worst scenario was found in the recordings on a road with big cobbles. The wind noise resided in lower levels but the rough surface involved dominant wheel/suspension noise as well as buzzes, squeaks and rattles.

4.3   Signal-to-Noise Ratio

The car noise signal of the different scenarios was chopped to fit the length of each utterance and then overlaid additively. To determine the noise conditions quantitatively, the Signal-to-Noise Ratio (SNR) was calculated for each utterance in the speech database and each noise scenario,

$$SNR = 10 \log_{10} \frac{P_{\text{sig}}}{P_{\text{N,car}} + P_{\text{N,mic}}}. \tag{1}$$

In addition to the car noise $P_{\text{N,car}}$, the recording noise $P_{\text{N,mic}}$ in the speech signal was taken into account and compared to the signal power P_{sig}. The signal power was measured in voiced segments only, whereas the recording noise power was measured in speech pauses only. Due to the varying signal power in the speech recordings, and due to the varying durations of the noise segments, the result was a Gaussian-like distribution, which is shown in Figure 1.

It can be summarized that the road surface has a major impact on the scenario. The SNR for the CTY scenarios was best with a mean value of 11 dB. It was followed by the HWY scenarios (4 dB) and the COB scenarios (-5 dB).

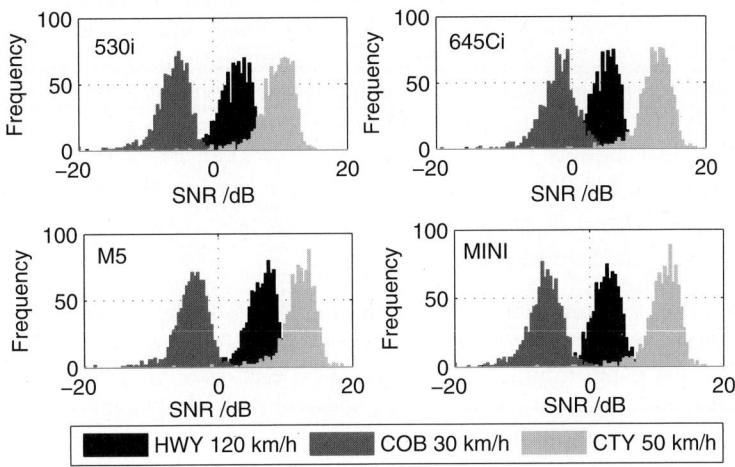

Fig. 1. Signal-to-Noise Ratio distribution in the experiment

The vehicle has a minor influence. Still, the M5 and the 645Ci resulted in 2 dB better result than the 530i or the Mini for the CTY scenarios. On the highway (HWY), the M5 outperformed the 645Ci by 2 dB and the 530i or Mini by 3 and 4 dB, respectively. Interestingly, on the cobbled road (COB), the 645Ci outperformed the M5 by 2 dB and the 530i or Mini by 4 and 5 dB, respectively.

5   Classification

For the automatic estimation of the emotion conveyed in the speech signal, a two-step procedure was applied. First, a set of characteristic prosodic features was extracted from the speech signal. Second, these features were mapped to the values of the three emotion primitives using multidimensional regression techniques and a training set to determine the parameters of the regression curve. The details of the emotion estimation system are described in [22].

5.1   Acoustic Features

We used a set of 20 prosodic features selected by Sequential Forward Selection from a total of 137 features. These features include

- pitch related features
- energy related features
- features related to duration and timing
- spectral features using Mel Frequency Cepstral Coefficients (MFCCs)

The pitch and energy related features are the statistics, such as mean value, standard deviation, range, and quartiles of the fundamental frequency F0 and the energy as well as their first and second derivatives, respectively. Together with the temporal features, which are, e.g., speaking rate and mean speaking pause duration, such characteristics describe the intonation of the utterance. The spectral characteristics describe the sentence-dependent voice characteristics in several subbands selected to match the perception characteristics of the human ear. Similar feature sets were used in a number of other studies on emotion recognition in speech [23]. All features were normalized to the range of [0,1].

5.2   Estimation Technique

As a classifier, we used kernel-based Support Vector Regression (SVR) [22]. Such method was shown to give superior results compared to other classifiers [5,22]. The algorithm minimizes the structural risk, in contrast to many other classification techniques minimizing the empirical risk only [24,25]. A radial basis function ($\sigma = 3.5$) was used as kernel. Parameter optimization was achieved by a grid search on a logarithmic scale and a subsequent search in the region of minimum error. The output of the SVR consists of one real-valued estimate for each emotion primitive [22].

We performed two different experiments for the automatic emotion estimation:

(a) train the algorithms with undisturbed speech and test them with the noisy speech, and
(b) use noisy speech for both training and testing.

While the first method allows for a more convenient training procedure and less effort to create training data, the latter one might provide better training conditions to the algorithms due to the same nature of training and test data.

6   Results

All results were calculated from 10-fold cross-validation experiments. The automatic emotion estimation under noise was compared to the reference given by the human evaluators. For each scenario the mean linear error was calculated. The accuracy of the tendency in the estimates was measured by the correlation between the estimates and the average ratings of the human evaluators (Pearson's empirical correlation coefficient).

The results for clean speech for both, training and testing, were added for comparison as a baseline. This baseline shows that, provided acoustically good conditions, emotion primitives estimation is possible with a mean error of 0.14 and a correlation of 0.42, 0.81 and 0.82 for valence, activation, and dominance, respectively. While the correlation coefficient for valence is only moderate, which is due to a very flat distribution, the emotion primitives activation and dominance were estimated with high reliability in clean speech.

Table 2. Results of experiment (a)—training with clean speech and testing with noisy speech: mean linear error. Baseline clean speech (CS) added for comparison.

	Valence			Activation			Dominance		
	HWY	COB	CTY	HWY	COB	CTY	HWY	COB	CTY
530i	0.15	0.17	0.13	0.18	0.24	0.16	0.18	0.20	0.15
645Ci	0.14	0.15	0.13	0.18	0.22	0.15	0.16	0.20	0.14
M5	0.13	0.16	0.13	0.18	0.25	0.16	0.18	0.21	0.13
Mini	0.14	0.17	0.13	0.20	0.25	0.17	0.18	0.22	0.14
CS	0.13			0.15			0.14		

Table 3. Results of experiment (a)—training with clean speech and testing with noisy speech: correlation coefficient between estimates and manual emotion labels. Baseline clean speech (CS) added for comparison.

	Valence			Activation			Dominance		
	HWY	COB	CTY	HWY	COB	CTY	HWY	COB	CTY
530i	(0.34)[1]	(0.14)	(0.43)	0.74	0.52	0.79	0.67	0.50	0.76
645Ci	(0.41)	(0.30)	(0.45)	0.75	0.57	0.81	0.70	(0.48)	0.78
M5	(0.39)	(0.19)	(0.46)	0.74	(0.46)	0.79	0.68	(0.40)	0.80
Mini	(0.35)	(0.10)	(0.45)	0.69	(0.40)	0.77	0.61	(0.38)	0.76
CS	(0.42)			0.82			0.81		

6.1 Experiment (a)—Training with Clean Speech and Testing with Noisy Speech

The results of experiment (a) are reported in Tables 2 and 3, respectively. The performance of the emotion estimation mainly depends on the road surface and therefore on the SNR. In experiment (a), the mean error increased by 2% for the CTY scenario, which is almost neglectable. For the HWY and the COB scenarios, the mean error increased notably by 18% and dramatically by 44%, respectively.

The correlation coefficients have to be read skeptically for valence, since the statistical confidence was only moderate for this primitive ($p \geq 10^{-3}$). For the statistically significant correlation coefficients, however, a moderate (CTY: -4%) to remarkable (HWY: -14%, COB: -40%) decrease was observed.

Thus, in the CTY scenario, the emotion recognition still works fine, almost independent of the vehicle type. On the highway (HWY) there is a notable decay in performance, but the recognition is still feasible. There is a clearly better result for the executive cars over the supermini in this case. On the cobbled road, the automatic recognition is not feasible any more. In this scenario, the 6 series convertible outperformed the other vehicles, but, still the results imply that the recognition is hardly possible.

---

[1] All correlation coefficients in brackets are only moderately statistically significant at $p \geq 10^{-3}$.

6.2   Experiment (b)—Training and Testing with Noisy Speech

The results of experiment (b) are reported in Tables 4 and 5, respectively. In experiment (b), the results were better, which was probably the case because the calculated regression hyperplane could adapt to the noise scenarios. Still, the mean error increased by 2% and 7% for the CTY and the HWY scenarios, respectively, which implies that in this case the emotion recognition is sill possible with a mean error of 0.13 to 0.16. However, for the COB scenarios, the mean error increased by 16% indicating that emotion recognition is possible, but with a notable decay in performance. The correlation coefficients emphasize the fact that providing noisy data at the training state is very helpful.

Table 4. Results of experiment (b)—both training and testing with noisy speech: mean linear error. Baseline clean speech (CS) added for comparison.

	Valence			Activation			Dominance		
	HWY	COB	CTY	HWY	COB	CTY	HWY	COB	CTY
530i	0.14	0.14	0.13	0.16	0.18	0.16	0.15	0.17	0.14
645Ci	0.14	0.14	0.13	0.16	0.17	0.16	0.15	0.16	0.14
M5	0.13	0.14	0.13	0.16	0.18	0.16	0.15	0.17	0.14
Mini	0.14	0.15	0.13	0.16	0.19	0.16	0.15	0.17	0.14
CS	0.13			0.15			0.14		

Table 5. Results of experiment (b)—both training and testing with noisy speech: correlation coefficient between estimates and manual emotion labels. Baseline clean speech (CS) added for comparison.

	Valence			Activation			Dominance		
	HWY	COB	CTY	HWY	COB	CTY	HWY	COB	CTY
530i	(0.38)	(0.32)	(0.43)	0.79	0.73	0.81	0.75	0.69	0.79
645Ci	(0.40)	(0.37)	0.44	0.79	0.78	0.81	0.76	0.71	0.79
M5	0.44	(0.34)	(0.43)	0.79	0.75	0.80	0.76	0.69	0.79
Mini	(0.39)	(0.35)	0.45	0.79	0.72	0.80	0.77	0.67	0.79
CS	(0.42)			0.82			0.81		

6.3   Discussion

It was found that experiment (b) gave clearly better results. In this case the noisy speech was already provided at the training step and thus the feature representation used for the determination of the regression hyperplane was more significant with respect to the test data. However, for the practical application, it is difficult to gather emotionally labeled training samples of the driver under different noise conditions. It is much easier to provide a large set of emotional training data if these can be gathered from clean speech. Therefore the question is, whether the good results achieved with noisy training data could also be achieved by a combination of providing clean speech training data and introducing filter techniques before extracting the acoustic features.

6.4   Noise Reduction

A preliminary analysis of the noise signals revealed that these signals were highly concentrated in the low-frequency bands. They almost vanished in frequency bands above 130 Hz. However, cutting the noisy speech at 130 Hz is not reasonable since the fundamental frequency of several male speakers in our corpus were (locally) as low as 60 Hz. Therefore, we decided for a compromise and used a highpass filter that combined a very narrow stop band of 48 Hz and a rather wide transition band of 272 Hz. Thus, a great part of the noise was suppressed. In the critical frequency range of [48 Hz, 130 Hz], the noise was at least damped while still providing the crucial frequency information on the fundamental frequency of the speaker. For the implementation of the filter we used a FIR filter of order 155 using the Parks-McClellan algorithm [26]. Such high filter order was necessary because of the very low cut-off frequency, which was only 0.006 times the sampling frequency.

Table 6. Results of emotion estimation in noisy, highpass filtered speech: mean linear error. Baseline clean speech (CS) added for comparison.

	Valence			Activation			Dominance		
	HWY	COB	CTY	HWY	COB	CTY	HWY	COB	CTY
530i	0.13	0.13	0.13	0.16	0.17	0.17	0.15	0.15	0.15
645Ci	0.13	0.13	0.13	0.16	0.17	0.16	0.15	0.15	0.15
M5	0.13	0.13	0.13	0.17	0.16	0.16	0.15	0.15	0.15
Mini	0.13	0.13	0.13	0.16	0.16	0.16	0.15	0.15	0.15
CS	0.13			0.15			0.14		

Table 7. Results of emotion estimation in noisy, highpass filtered speech: correlation coefficient between estimates and manual emotion labels. Baseline clean speech (CS) added for comparison.

	Valence			Activation			Dominance		
	HWY	COB	CTY	HWY	COB	CTY	HWY	COB	CTY
530i	(0.43)	0.44	(0.43)	0.79	0.79	0.78	0.77	0.77	0.77
645Ci	(0.43)	0.44	0.46	0.80	0.78	0.79	0.77	0.77	0.77
M5	0.45	0.44	(0.43)	0.79	0.79	0.79	0.77	0.77	0.77
Mini	0.45	0.44	(0.45)	0.79	0.79	0.79	0.77	0.77	0.77
CS	(0.42)			0.82			0.81		

The results of such highpass pre-processing were very promising. Tables 6 and 7 show the individual errors and correlation coefficients. The error was almost the same as the baseline: 0.13, 0.16, and 0.15 for valence, activation and dominance, respectively. It increased on average only by 6%, which indicates that the automatic emotion recognition is still possible. Furthermore, it was observed that the results now were almost the same for all vehicles. This can be explained by the fact that the more demanding noise scenario in the Mini, for example, was caused by more noise energy, but in the same frequency bands than with comparable executive cars.

7   Conclusion and Outlook

This paper reports current research on the emotion in human-computer interaction in the car. The first part of this study stressed the fact that detecting the driver's emotional state is indeed important. Such knowledge reveals information on the communication between the driver and the car instruments, and, in addition, can be used to design the car's answer in a way to provide best conditions for safe driving.

We presented results of emotion recognition in the speech when the signal is superimposed by car noise. Several vehicle types and road surfaces were tested. The results were calculated on a continuous-valued, three-dimensional description basis for emotions consisting of the three emotion primitives valence, activation and dominance, each normalized to [-1,+1].

The results show that although sedan and executive type cars provide 2-3 dB better SNR than superminis, the road surface has more impact on the results than the car type. With our speech corpus consisting of spontaneous, unscripted emotional utterances, we observed that the automatic emotion recognition results correlated with the SNR, which was found to be 10 to 12 dB for city scenarios, 2 to 6 dB for the highway, and -7 to -2 dB for cobbled roads. The emotion recognition still worked fine for city and highway (only when noisy data was provided for training already) with a degradation of 2 and 7%, respectively. On rough cobbled roads the emotion recognition did not give acceptable results any more.

As an improvement pre-filtering was proposed for the highly relevant case of only clean speech training data being available. The application of a highpass filter with cut-off frequency as low as 48 Hz led to remarkable improvements. In this case the degradation from clean speech experiments was only 6% and emotion recognition was feasible with error rates of 0.13, 0.16, and 0.15 for valence, activation, and dominance, respectively.

While these results are based on a manual superposition of clean speech utterances and recorded noise signals of the cars, our future work will investigate the application of such an emotion recognition within the car in real time. Additionally, the emotion recognition results might be used to formulate behavior rules for the car's infotainment system once they are provided as a human-in-the-loop feedback signal.

Acknowledgment

This work was supported by grants of the Collaborative Research Center (SFB) 588 "Humanoid Robots" of the Deutsche Forschungsgemeinschaft (DFG).

References

1. Hitzenberger, L.: Man Machine Interaction in Car Information Systems. In: Proceedings of the First International Conference on Language Resources and Evaluation, Granada, pp. 179–182 (1998)
2. Jonsson, I.M., Nass, C., Harris, H., Takayama, L.: Matching In-Car Voice with Driver State: Impact on Attitude and Driving Performance. In: Proceedings of the Third International Driving Symposium on Human Factors in Driver Assessment, Training and Vehicle Design, pp. 173–181 (2005)
3. Nass, C., Jonsson, I.M., Harris, H., Reaves, B., Endo, J., Brave, S., Takayama, L.: Improving Automotive Safety by Pairing Driver Emotion and Car Voice Emotion. In: Proc. CHI (2005)
4. Jones, C., Jonsson, I.M.: Automatic recognition of affective cues in the speech of car drivers to allow appropriate responses. In: Proc. OZCHI (2005)
5. Schuller, B., Lang, M., Rigoll, G.: Recognition of Spontaneous Emotions by Speech within Automotive Environment. In: Proc. 32. Deutsche Jahrestagung für Akustik (DAGA), Braunschweig, Germany, pp. 57–58 (2006)
6. Schuller, B., Arsic, D., Wallhoff, F., Rigoll, G.: Emotion Recognition in the Noise Applying Large Acoustic Feature Sets. In: Proc. Speech Prosody, Dresden, Germany (2006)
7. Csikszentmihalyi, M.: Flow: The Psychology of Optimal Experience. Harper & Row, New York (1991)
8. Hirt, E., Melton, R., McDonald, H., Harackiewicz, J.: Processing goals, task interest, and the mood-performance relationship: A mediational analysis. Journal of Personality and Social Psychology 71, 245–261 (1996)
9. Groeger, J.: Understanding Driving: Applying Cognitive Psychology to a Complex Everyday Task. Psychology Press, Philadelphia, PA (2000)
10. Isen, A., Rosenzweig, A., Young, M.: The influence of positive affect on clinical problem solving. Medical Decision Making 11(3), 221–227 (1991)
11. Galovski, T., Blanchard, E.: Road rage: A domain for psychological intervention? Aggression and Violent Behavior 9(2), 105–127 (2004)
12. Gross, J., Levenson, R.: Emotion elicitation using films. Cognition & Emotion 9, 87–108 (1995)
13. Detenber, B., Reeves, B.: A bio-informational theory of emotion: Motion and image size effects on viewers. Journal of Communication 46(3), 66–84 (1996)
14. Izard, C.: Patterns of Emotions. Academic Press, New York (1972)
15. Nass, C., Gong, L.: Social aspects of speech interfaces from an evolutionary perspective: Experimental research and design implications. Communications of the ACM 43, 36–43 (2000)
16. Nass, C., Brave, S.: Wired for Speech: How Voice Activates and Enhances the Human-Computer Relationship. MIT Press, Cambridge, MA (2005)
17. Grimm, M., Kroschel, K.: Rule-based emotion classification using acoustic features. In: Proc. 3rd International Conference on Telemedicine and Multimedia Communication (ICTMC) (2005)

18. Lang, P.: The Cognitive Psychophysiology of Emotion: Anxiety and the Anxiety Disorders. Lawrence Erlbaum, Hillsdale, NJ (1985)
19. Grimm, M., Kroschel, K.: Evaluation of natural emotions using self assessment manikins. In: Proc. ASRU, pp. 381–385 (2005)
20. Grimm, M., Mower, E., Kroschel, K., Narayanan, S.: Primitives-based evaluation and estimation of emotions in speech. Speech Communication Journal, accepted for publication (2007)
21. Setiawan, P., Suhadi, S., Fingscheidt, T., Stan, S.: Robust Speech Recognition for Mobil Devices in Car Noise. In: Proc. Interspeech, Lisbon, Portugal (2005)
22. Grimm, M., Kroschel, K., Narayanan, S.: Support vector regression for automatic recognition of spontaneous emotions in speech. In: Proceedings of IEEE International Conference on Acoustics, Speech, and Signal Proccessing (ICASSP) (Accepted for Publication) (2007)
23. Cowie, R., Douglas-Cowie, E., Tsapatsoulis, N., Votsis, G., Kollias, S., Fellenz, W., Taylor, J.: Emotion recognition in human-computer interaction. IEEE Signal Processing Magazine 18(1), 32–80 (2001)
24. Vapnik, V.: The Nature of Statistical Learning Theory. Springer, New York (1995)
25. Smola, A., Schölkopf, B.: A tutorial on support vector regression. Technical report, NeuroCOLT2 (1998)
26. Kammeyer, K.D., Kroschel, K.: Digitale Signalverarbeitung, 4th edn., Teubner Stuttgart (1998)

Frame vs. Turn-Level: Emotion Recognition from Speech Considering Static and Dynamic Processing

Bogdan Vlasenko[1], Björn Schuller[2], Andreas Wendemuth[1], and Gerhard Rigoll[2]

[1] Cognitive Systems, IESK, Otto-von-Guericke University, Magdeburg, Germany
[2] Institute for Human-Machine Communication, Technische Universität München, Germany
Bogdan.Vlasenko@e-technik.uni-magdeburg.de, Schuller@tum.de

Abstract. Opposing the pre-dominant turn-wise statistics of acoustic Low-Level-Descriptors followed by static classification we re-investigate dynamic modeling directly on the frame-level in speech-based emotion recognition. This seems beneficial, as it is well known that important information on temporal sub-turn-layers exists. And, most promisingly, we integrate this frame-level information within a state-of-the-art large-feature-space emotion recognition engine. In order to investigate frame-level processing we employ a typical speaker-recognition set-up tailored for the use of emotion classification. That is a GMM for classification and MFCC plus speed and acceleration coefficients as features. We thereby also consider use of multiple states, respectively an HMM. In order to fuse this information with turn-based modeling, output scores are added to a super-vector combined with static acoustic features. Thereby a variety of Low-Level-Descriptors and functionals to cover prosodic, speech quality, and articulatory aspects are considered. Starting from 1.4k features we select optimal configurations including and excluding GMM information. The final decision task is realized by use of SVM. Extensive test-runs are carried out on two popular public databases, namely EMO-DB and SUSAS, to investigate acted and spontaneous data. As we face the current challenge of speaker-independent analysis we also discuss benefits arising from speaker normalization. The results obtained clearly emphasize the superior power of integrated diverse time-levels.

Keywords: Emotion Recognition, Frame-Level Analysis, Turn-Level Analysis, Model Fusion, LOSO, Feature Selection.

1 Introduction

Apart from a few attempts to classify emotions within speech dynamically [1,2], current approaches usually employ static feature vectors derived on a turn or frame level. In [2] the latter has also been shown superior to dynamic modeling. This derives mostly from the fact, that by (usually statistical) functional application to the Low-Level-Descriptors (LLD) as e.g. pitch, energy, or spectral coefficients an important information reduction takes place, which avoids phonetic (respectively spoken-content) over-modeling. Yet, it is also considered received knowledge that thereby important temporal information is lost due to a high degree of abstraction. This led to first successful attempts to integrate information on diverse time levels [3-6].

Apart from this several works point at the high influence of emotional variability within speech on the recognition of speakers [7,8]. We therefore investigate how

A. Paiva, R. Prada, and R.W. Picard (Eds.): ACII 2007, LNCS 4738, pp. 139–147, 2007.
© Springer-Verlag Berlin Heidelberg 2007

reliably a state-of-the art speaker recognition engine using MFCC, Cepstral Mean Substraction (CMS), and Gaussian Mixture Models (GMM) can recognize emotions instead of speakers. As such processing operates on a per-frame basis, we finally use this to accomplish the initially introduced thought of combining different temporal layers for emotion recognition within speech.

For testing we will use two public databases providing acted and spontaneous samples of emotional speech.

The paper is structured as follows: Section 2 and 3 deal with frame- and turn-level analysis of speech with respect to emotion. In section 4 two optimization strategies, namely speaker normalization and feature space optimization, are discussed. Section 5 introduces the fusion of the two approaches. Finally, in the sections 6-8 data, results and conclusions are presented.

2   Frame-Level Analysis (FL)

We consider using a speaker recognition system to recognize emotion from speech in the first place. Likewise, instead of the usual task to deduce the most likely speaker (from a known speaker set) ω_k form a given sequence X of M acoustic observations x [9], we will recognize the current emotion. This is usually solved by a stochastic approach following eq. 1,

$$\omega_k = \arg\max_{\Omega} P(\omega \mid X) = \arg\max_{\Omega} \frac{P(X \mid \omega)P(\omega)}{P(X)}. \tag{1}$$

where $P(X \mid \omega)$ is called the speaker acoustic model, $P(\omega)$ is the prior speaker information and ω speaker model given the set of reference models $\Omega = \{ \omega_1, \dots, \omega_N \}$.

The vectors in a sequence, X, are independent and identically distributed random variables. This allows to express $P(X \mid \omega)$ as

$$P(X \mid \omega) = \prod_{t=1}^{M} p(x_t \mid \omega). \tag{2}$$

where $P(x_t \mid \omega)$ is the likelihood of single frame x_t given model ω. This is a fundamental equation of statistical theory and is widely used in speech and speaker recognition systems using frame level analysis.

A typical state-of-the-art system uses single state HMMs as speaker acoustic model, also known as GMMs. This state is associated with an emission-probability $P(X \mid s)$ which for continuous variables x is replaced with its probability density function (PDF). These PDFs are realized using weighted sums of elementary Gaussian PDFs (Gaussian Mixtures, which leads to the name GMM).

A GMM is a weighted sum of N component densities and is given by the form

$$P(x \mid \Omega) = \sum_{i=1}^{N} c_i b_i(x). \tag{3}$$

where x is a M-dimensional random vector, $b_i(x)$, i=1,...,N, is the component density and c_i, i = 1,... , N, is the mixture weight. Each component density is a M-variate Gaussian function of the form

$$b_i(x) = \frac{1}{(2\pi)^{M/2}|\Sigma_i|^{1/2}} \cdot \exp\left(-\frac{1}{2}(x-\mu_i)^T \Sigma_i^{-1}(x-\mu_i)\right). \tag{4}$$

with mean vector μ_i and covariance matrix Σ_i. The mixture weights satisfy the stochastic constraint that

$$\sum_{i=1}^{N} c_i = 1. \tag{5}$$

The complete Gaussian mixture model is parameterized by the mean vectors, covariance matrices and mixture weights from all component densities. These parameters are collectively represented by the notation

$$\Omega = \{c_i, \mu_i, \Sigma_i\}, i = 1,..., N. \tag{6}$$

In our emotion recognition system, each emotion is represented by such a GMM and is referred to by its model Ω.

For a sequence of T test vectors $X = x_1, x_2, \cdots, x_T$, the standard approach is to calculate the GMM likelihood as in Eq. (2) which can be written in the log domain as

$$L(X \mid \Omega) = \log p(X \mid \Omega) = \sum_{i=1}^{T} \log p(x_t \mid \Omega). \tag{7}$$

The GMM parameters are estimated by the EM-algorithm using training material for other speakers and a number of 1 to 120 Gaussian mixtures to approximate the original PDFs [10]. However, we also consider multiple states, herein, as in some speaker recognition systems, to better model dynamics. These are trained accordingly.

Speech input is processed using a 25ms Hamming window, with a frame rate of 10ms. As in typical speaker recognition we employ a 39 dimensional feature vector per each frame consisting of 12 MFCC and log frame energy plus speed and acceleration coefficients. Cepstral Mean Substraction (CMS) and variance normalization are applied to better cope with channel characteristics. The priors are chosen as an equal distribution among emotion classes.

3 Turn-Level Analysis (TL)

In order to represent a typical state-of-the-art emotion recognition engine operating on a turn-level, we use a set of 1,406 acoustic features basing on 37 Low-Level-Descriptors (LLD) as seen in table 1 and their first order delta coefficients [11]. These 37x2 LLDs are next smoothened by Low-pass filtering with an SMA-filter.

Opposing the formerly introduced dynamic modeling, such systems derive statistics per speaker turn by a projection of each uni-variate time series, respectively LLD, X onto a scalar feature x independent of the length of the turn. This is realized by use of a functional F, as depicted in eq. 8.

$$F : X \rightarrow x \in \mathbb{R}^1. \tag{8}$$

19 functionals are applied to each contour on the turn-level covering extremes, ranges, positions, first four moments and quartiles as seen in table 1. Note, that three functionals are related to position, known as duration in traditional phonetic terminology, as their physical unit is msec.

For classification we use Support Vector Machines (SVM) with linear Kernel and 1-vs.-1 multi-class discrimination. One could consider the use of GMM here, as well. Yet, SVM have proven the preferred choice in many works to best model static acoustic feature vectors [11].

Table 1. Overview of applied Low-Level-Descriptors and functionals for turn-wise analysis

Low-Level-Descriptors (2x37)	Functionals (19)
Pitch	Mean
Energy	Standard Deviation
Envelope	Zero-Crossing-Rate
Formant 1-5 Amplitude	Quartile 1
Formant 1-5 Bandwidth	Quartile 2
Formant 1-5 Frequency	Quartile 3
MFCC Coefficient 1-16	Quartile 1 - Minimum
Harmonics-to-Noise-Ratio HNR	Quartile 2 - Quartile 1
Shimmer	Quartile 3 - Quartile 2
Jitter	Maximum - Quartile 3
Delta Pitch	Centroid
Delta Energy	Skewness
Delta Envelope	Kurtosis
Delta Formant 1-5 Amplitude	Maximum Value
Delta Formant 1-5 Bandwidth	Relative Maximum Position
Delta Formant 1-5 Frequency	Minimum Value
Delta MFCC Coefficient 1-16	Relative Minimum Position
Delta Harmonics-to-Noise-Ratio	Maximum Minimum Range
Delta Shimmer	Position of 95% Roll-Off-Point
Delta Jitter	

4 Optimization Strategies

Next, two optimization strategies are considered: First, speaker normalization (SN) by feature normalization with the whole individual speaker context. Second, feature-space optimization by correlation-based exclusion of highly correlated features (FS).

We investigate the benefits of speaker normalization, as we intend to analyze emotion independent of the speaker, herein. SN is thereby realized by a normalization of each feature x by its mean and standard deviation for each speaker individually. Thereby the whole speaker context is used. This has to be seen as an upper benchmark for ideal situations, where a speaker could be observed with a variety of emotions. Yet, it is not necessary to know the actual emotional state of observed utterances at this point.

As a high number of features is used throughout static modeling, feature space optimization seems a must in view of performance and real-time-capability. In order to optimize a set of features rather than combining attributes of single high relevance, we use a correlation-based analysis, herein. Thereby features of high class-correlation and low inter-feature correlation are kept [12]. This does not employ the target-classifier in the loop. Likewise it mostly reduces correlation within the feature space rather than evaluation of the benefit of single attributes. Still, this leads to a very compact representation of the feature space, which usually leads to an improvement of accuracy while reducing feature extraction effort at the same time.

5   Time-Level Combination

So far the two individual approaches to emotion recognition based on information processing directly on the frame-level, or on a higher turn-level, have been introduced. In order to fuse these two approaches it seems beneficial to keep utmost amounts of information for the final decision process. However, an early feature fusion is not feasible, as frame-level processing results in a dynamic number of frames. We therefore decided to include final GMM scores within the static acoustic feature vector. The process of speaker normalization and feature space optimization is extended to the likewise obtained new feature vector x'. Fig. 1 depicts the overall processing flow from an input audio file via the two streams to the final result. Overall feature selection having the GMM scores within the space reveals their high importance, as they are kept among high ranks.

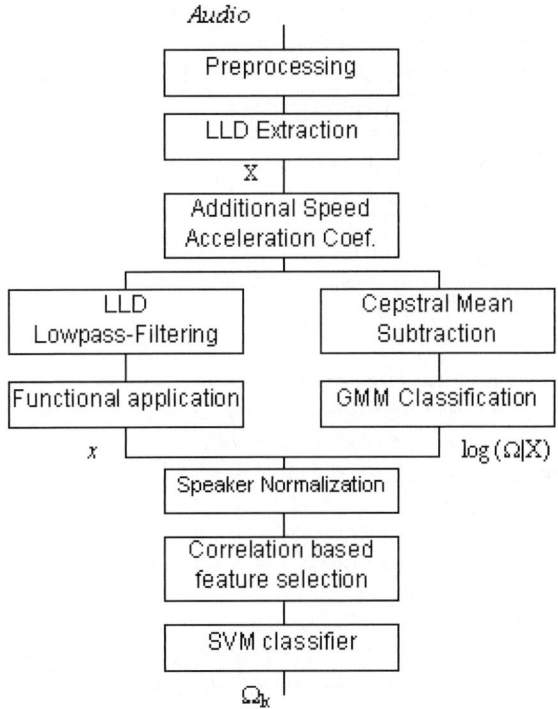

Fig. 1. Processing flow for the combined frame- and turn-level analysis

6   Acted and Spontaneous Data

To demonstrate effectiveness of each single approach and the fusion on acted and spontaneous data, we decided first for the popular studio recorded Berlin Emotional Speech Database (EMODB) [13], which covers the 'big six' emotion set (MPEG-4) besides boredom instead of surprise, and added neutrality. 10 (5f) professional actors speak 10 German emotionally undefined sentences. 494 phrases are marked as min.

60% natural and min. 80% assignable by 20 subjects. 84.3% accuracy are reported for a human perception test.

Second, we selected the Speech Under Simulated and Actual Stress (SUSAS) database [14] as a reference for spontaneous recordings. As additional challenge speech is partly masked by field noise. It consists of five domains, encompassing a wide variety of stresses and emotions. We decided for the 3,663 actual stress speech samples recorded in subject motion fear and stress tasks, as acted samples are already covered by EMODB in this work. 7 speakers, 3 of them female, in roller coaster and free fall actual stress situations are contained in this set. Two different stress conditions have been collected: medium stress, and high stress. Within the further samples also neutral samples, fear during freefall and screaming are contained as classes. Likewise a total of five emotions, respectively speaking styles, are covered. SUSAS samples are constrained to a 35 words vocabulary of short aircraft communication commands. All files are sampled in 8 kHz, 16 bit. The recordings are partly overlaid with heavy noise and background over-talk. However, this resembles realistic acoustic recording conditions, as also given in many related scenarios of interest such as automotive speech interfaces or public transport surveillance.

7   Experimental Results

Results are presented for each modeling technique individually (TL and FL), and for the combination of these two. Thereby the effects of speaker normalization SN and feature space optimization FS as described are shown, too.

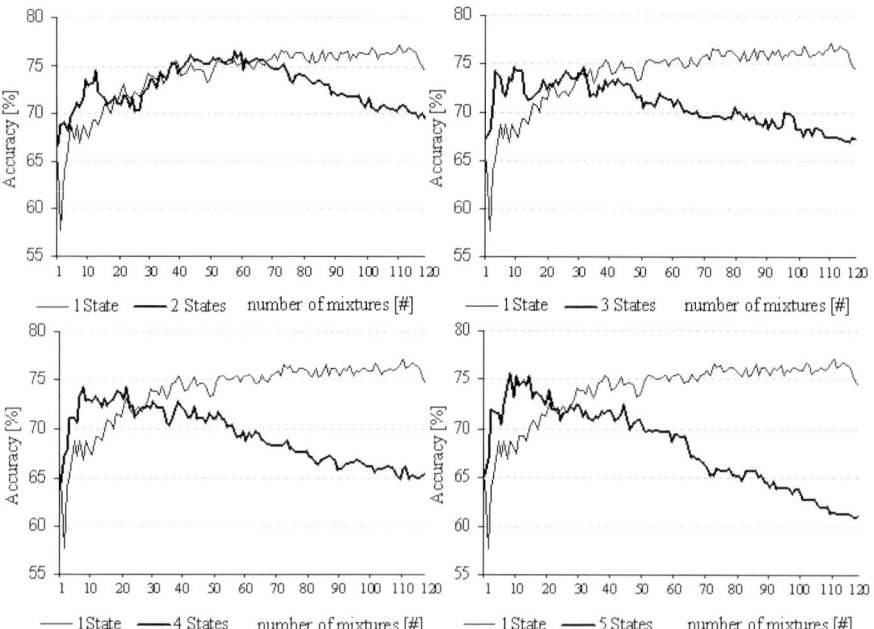

Fig. 2. Accuracy depending on the number of mixtures and number of HMM states, LOSO evaluation, database EMODB

As can be seen in fig. 2. single state HMM show the most stable and robust results.

For EMODB, we provide results of a leave-one-speaker-out (LOSO) evaluation to face the challenge of speaker independence. For SUSAS we decided for 10-fold stratified cross validation (SCV), as only 7 speakers are contained in the chosen spontaneous subset. On the other hand this is possible, as roughly 500 phrases are available per speaker.

Table 2. Combination of turn level and frame level analysis, databases EMODB with LOSO evaluation and speaker dependent 10-fold SCV for SUSAS. TL and FL abbreviate turn and frame levels. SN and FS represent speaker adaptation and feature selection. (√) indicates that the technique has been applied.

Accuracy [%]	SN	FS	EMODB	SUSAS
TL	-	-	74.9	80.8
TL	√	-	79.6	80.8
TL	√	√	83.2	83.3
FL	-	-	77.1	67.1
TL+FL	√	-	81.6	81.3
TL+FL	√	√	89.9	83.8

During feature selection the original 1,406 features have been reduced to 76 for EMODB. For SUSAS 71 features have been selected on the whole dataset, and 33-107 features were observed as optimum for the individual speakers. This underlines the brute-force nature of the creation of a >1k feature space in order to find a very compact robust final set. Tab. 1 shows the summarized results.

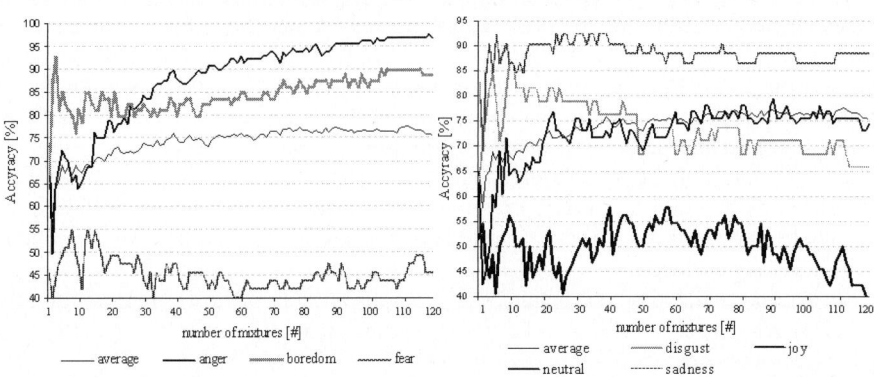

Fig. 3. Accuracy depending on the number of mixtures, LOSO evaluation, database EMODB

In the following the influence of the chosen number of mixtures for frame-level analysis is illustrated in detail for EMODB and SUSAS overall results and for each emotional state independently. As can be seen in fig. 3, a surprisingly high number of mixtures (>60) compared to the size of the database seems beneficial. Yet, not all emotions benefit from increase of mixtures, as e.g. fear. A similar behavior is observed for the SUSAS database (fig. 4)

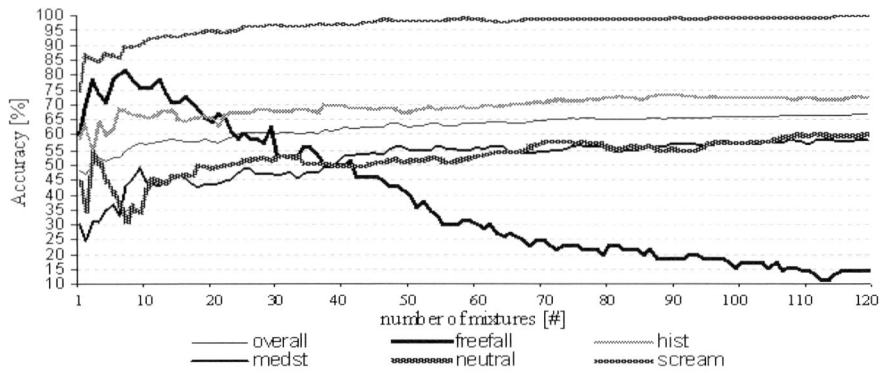

Fig. 4. Accuracy depending on the number of mixtures, mean of speaker-dependent 10-fold SCV evaluation, database SUSAS

where freefall is represented by very few samples and therefore is highly negatively influenced by the increase of mixtures. This comes, as classes with sparse data suffer from over-adaptation with respect to high accuracy. Also, this derives from the fact that no prior information was used in eq. 1. This however allows for more comparability between FL and TL modeling. In general ~50 mixtures seem optimal.

8   Discussion and Future Work

Within this paper we introduced speaker recognition motivated emotion recognition on a frame-level and its fusion with turn-level-based emotion recognition. The results presented do not allow for a direct comparison between these two, as a different number of LLDs has been used. Still, even using a typical speaker recognition system shows surprisingly high performance for the recognition of emotion within speech though it should be noted that FL clearly falls behind TL for the SUSAS database. When investigating the optimal number of mixtures to be used, it seems favorable to provide a minimum of 50 mixtures. However, some emotions may be negatively influenced by too high a number of mixtures. Considering dynamical modeling, no gain could be observed for use of several HMM states, as long as an adequate number of mixtures is provided.

Speaker normalization and feature space optimization both clearly help to improve overall results. Thereby it has to be noted that less than 10% of the original feature space suffices to get an optimum performance.

The highest accuracy is however obtained by the suggested fusion of both approaches. This is in particular true for EMODB. For SUSAS it is not too clear, whether the extra effort is justified.

It has to be mentioned that for both databases results in the order of human perception can be reported. This is true, even though speaker independence and spontaneous data in noisy environment have been faced, yet once at a time.

In future work we plan to investigate phonetic unit bound HMM models. Furthermore, a combination of functional application on syntactical unit motivated chunks combined with dynamic modeling capabilities of an HMM seem a promising variant. Finally, the findings have to be verified on datasets without limited predefined spoken content.

Acknowledgements

The work has been conducted in the framework the NIMITEK project (Sachsen-Anhalt Federal State funding). Bogdan Vlasenko acknowledges support by a graduate grant of the Federal State of Sachsen-Anhalt.

References

1. Polzin, T.S., Waibel, A.: Detecting emotions in speech, Cooperative Multimodal Communication, 2nd Int. Conf. 98, CMC (1998)
2. Schuller, B., Rigoll, G., Lang, M.: Hidden Markov Model-Based Speech Emotion Recognition. In: Proc. ICASSP 2003, IEEE, Hong Kong, China, vol. II, pp. 1–4 (2003)
3. Lee, Z., Zhao, Y.: Recognition emotions in speech using short-term and long-term features. In: Proc. ICSLP, pp. 2255–2558 (1998)
4. Jiang, D.N., Cai, L.-H.: Speech emotion classification with the combination of statistic features and temporal features. In: Proc. ICME 2004, IEEE, Taipei, Taiwan, pp. 1967–1971 (2004)
5. Murray, L.R., Arnot, I.L.: Toward the simulation of emotion in synthetic speech: A review of the literature of humans vocal emotion. JASA 93(2), 1097–1108 (1993)
6. Schuller, B., Rigoll, G.: Timing Levels in Segment-Based Speech Emotion Recognition. In: Proc. INTERSPEECH 2006, ICSLP, ISCA, Pittsburgh, PA, pp. 1818–1821 (2006)
7. Klasmeyer, G., Johnstone, T., Bänziger, T., Sappok, C., Scherer, K.R.: Emotional Voice Variability in Speaker Verification. In: Proc. ITRW on Speech and Emotion, ISCA, Newcastle, UK (2000)
8. Shahin, I.: Enhancing speaker identification performance under the shouted talking condition using the second order circular Hidden Markov Models. Speech Communication 48(8), 1047–1055 (2006)
9. Reynolds, D.: Speaker identification and verification using Gaussian mixture speaker models. Speech Communication 17, 91–108 (1995)
10. Young, S., Evermann, G., Kershaw, D., Moore, G., Odell, J., Ollason, D., Povey, D., Valtchev, V., Woodland, P.: The HTK-Book 3. Cambridge University, Cambridge, England (2002)
11. Schuller, B., Seppi, D., Batliner, A., Maier, A., Steidl, S.: Towards More Reality in the Recognition of Emotional Speech. In: Proc. ICASSP 2007, Honolulu, Hawaii (2007)
12. Witten, I.H., Frank, E.: Data Mining: Practical machine learning tools with Java implementations, p. 133. Morgan Kaufmann, San Francisco (2000)
13. Burkhardt, F., Paeschke, A., Rolfes, M., Sendlmeier, W., Weiss, B.: A Database of German Emotional Speech. In: Proc. INTERSPEECH 2005, ISCA, Lisbon, Portugal, pp. 1517–1520 (2005)
14. Hansen, J.H.L., Bou-Ghazale, S.: Getting Started with SUSAS: A Speech Under Simulated and Actual Stress Database. In: Proc. EUROSPEECH-97, Rhodes, Greece, vol. 4, pp. 1743–1746 (1997)

Characterizing Emotion in the Soundtrack of an Animated Film: Credible or Incredible?

Noam Amir and Rachel Cohen

Department of Communication Disorders, Tel Aviv University, Israel
`noama@post.tau.ac.il`

Abstract. In this study we present a novel emotional speech corpus, consisting of dialog that was extracted from an animated film. This type of corpus presents an interesting compromise between the sparsity of emotion found in spontaneous speech, and the contrived emotion found in speech acted solely for research purposes. The dialog was segmented into 453 short units and judged for emotional content by native and non-native English speakers. Emotion was rated on two scales: Activation and Valence. Acoustic analysis gave a comprehensive set of 100 features covering F0, intensity, voice quality and spectrum. We found that Activation is more strongly correlated to our acoustic features than Valence. Activation was correlated to several types of features, whereas Valence was correlated mainly to intensity related features. Further, ANOVA analysis showed some interesting contrasts between the two scales, and interesting differences in the judgments of native vs. non-native English speakers.

Keywords: Emotion, speech, animated film, Activation, Valence.

1 Introduction

Emotion in speech has been the subject of an increasing amount of research in recent years. The further this subject is studied, the more it becomes apparent that it is extremely multifaceted and that it is impossible to draw sweeping conclusions. Personal and situational context have a large influence on emotions that individuals experience and on their degree of control and inhibition in expressing them. In this study we propose a relatively novel paradigm for obtaining emotional speech, examine cross cultural judgment of the emotional content, and analyze the acoustic correlates of emotion in this context.

1.1 Obtaining Emotional Speech

Several popular paradigms for obtaining emotional speech have appeared in the literature, ranging from speech acted purely for the purposes of research [1] to speech taken from real-life situations [2]. The degree to which results based on acted speech can be carried over to situations arising in daily life is debatable. On the one hand, a major advantage of speech acted for the purposes of research is that the textual and emotional content can be monitored closely. Real life data, on the other hand, can be difficult to obtain and often sparse in emotional expression. One middle route which has

A. Paiva, R. Prada, and R.W. Picard (Eds.): ACII 2007, LNCS 4738, pp. 148–158, 2007.

been experimented with is elicited emotion, i.e. placing non-actors in situations that give rise to emotion [3]. This "Wizard of Oz" approach has proven to be useful, though results can vary depending on the participants and the methods used to elicit emotions.

In this study we present an alternative which has been explored very little, which is acted speech that has been acted for the benefit of a wide commercial audience rather than a specific study, namely animated films. To our knowledge, few such studies have appeared; one examined the expression of intense fear [4], and another examined humor [16]. Acted speech taken from films has several advantages: it is intended to convey emotion to an audience, therefore it is performed convincingly, also enabling us to use performances by world-class actors. This type of speech emulates many real-life situations in their proper context, rather than being created in a research laboratory. Nevertheless, due to the nature of films, lasting approximately 1.5 hours, a reasonable amount of emotional interaction and expression must take place in order to make the film interesting and credible. Overall, it is more reasonable to expect that the emotion expressed in a film will be closer to real life situations, with their associated richness in texture and variety, than emotions uttered in order to fit specific simple emotional labels. On the downside, film is often accompanied by overlying music, which creates an atmosphere of its own and can interfere with the acoustic analysis. Not all emotions can be expected to be uttered by all characters, and of course there remains the question if the emotional expression is truly similar to what is found is real-life situations. It is interesting to note, however, that analysis of this type of speech has an application within its own paradigm. The process of creating an animated film involves first recording the soundtrack and then adding the animation. Animators create the visual part of the film so that it follows the soundtrack, and acoustic analysis that evaluates the emotional content of the soundtrack can be a tool that could help in synchronizing the audio and visual cues of emotional expression.

1.2 Segmentation and Labeling

Beyond obtaining the speech material, segmenting and labeling a database of emotional speech are also major issues. As of yet there is no standard procedure for either of these, and in fact they also depend to a great extent of the type of database being analyzed.

Several approaches for segmentation have been used on databases that contain continuous speech, from the word level [3] to stretches between pauses referred to by Cowie et al [5] as "tunes", to turns [6]. Ideally one would like to segment a stretch of speech into the shortest segment that expresses one clear emotion coherently, though this is more emblematic than could be expected. Thus, efforts based on this idea have adopted mostly ad-hoc methods rather than the rigorous criteria that can be used to define tunes or turns. Examples of this approach appear in [8] and [9]. This type of approach has been adopted in the present study, borrowing the notion of "intonation units" or "prosodic units" (PU) from linguistics [9,10]. Though we acknowledge this to be a somewhat fuzzy term, we believe that an informed segmentation into such units can serve as a very reasonable basis for further analysis, at least till clearer criteria may emerge from the literature.

Emotional labeling could well be considered one of the most controversial issues in this field of research. The so called "big six" (anger, fear, sadness, disgust, surprise, neutral or any other similar set) [15] might be appropriate for very prototypical acted emotions, but as the speech data moves towards being more real-life oriented, so the emotions become more complex and also more context specific. Two major trends to overcome this obstacle is the use of data-driven categories [5, 11] or psychological scales [12]. Due to the wide variety of emotions in our data, and the fact that its application could eventually be geared towards use as an animation tool, we chose to perform labeling using two psychological scales that have appeared rather frequently: Activation and Valence.

1.3 Acoustic Analysis

Acoustic features indicating the expression of emotion in speech have also been discussed widely. Recent studies have been employing very large features sets based on a large range of paralinguistic information, such as F0, intensity, duration, voice quality, spectrum [11, 13], and linguistic information also [6]. Few studies have as yet conducted a comprehensive comparison of the relative importance of each type of feature. Indeed, most probably this will also prove to be dependent on context, personal style and culture. Though we present several novel features here, this is not the focus of our study. We do employ a comprehensive set of nonlinguistic features covering the classes mentioned above, to compare their relevant importance in the current context.

Normalization of various features is also a subject that is still contentious. Though different speakers have different average F0 values, it is not clear whether the excursions from this mean should be considered purely in relation to this mean value, or whether at the extremities of the F0 range values are less dependant on the mean. We therefore employ both normalized and unnormalized F0 values. Intensity features, on the other hand, must necessarily be normalized, since there is no control for microphone distance and postproduction gain adjustments.

1.4 Goals of This Study

Our overall aim was to study the expression of emotions in an animated film, segmented into PUs, and labeled using two psychological scales: Activation and Valence. A further objective was to carry out a cross cultural comparison of emotional labeling, comparing judgments of native Hebrew speakers and native American-English speakers. Using a comprehensive set of acoustic features, we wished to examine which were significant in conveying emotional data as reflected by each labeling scale. Finally, we also wished to determine whether the segmentation into PUs was indeed appropriate to this research, by determining whether acoustic features specific to this segmentation (such as length, initial and final pitch, initial and final intensity) would prove valuable in evaluating emotional expression.

2   Methods

2.1 Speech Material

All of the speech material was taken from an animated film, "The Incredibles" (Pixar, 2004). This kind of film contains extreme or "fullblown" emotions along with a

the large number of acoustic features, a complete description of the results is beyond the scope of this paper. We therefore summarize the most important results. One way to assess the overall results is to note the types and amounts of acoustic features that were significant in a given ANOVA. This is summarized in Table 2.

The above table gives an indication of how the acoustic features performed in distinguishing between the different classes. Though some of the features are certainly correlated to some extent, some observations can be made from this table and from further information supplied by the statistical analysis.

The number of significant features is similar, around 60, for all judgments of **Activation**: for both English and Hebrew speaking judges, and for both PN and EM divisions.

For both PN and EM divisions, features that were significant in rating Activation were of all types: pitch, intensity, voice quality and spectrum. Only one duration feature was used, which was the overall length of the PU – this feature also figures prominently in the above table. What is not visible here is that the class averages of some of the features, for English speaking listeners, were often further apart than for Hebrew speakers. An example is presented in figure 3.

For **Valence**, results were more varied. Using the PN division, a much smaller number of features was found significant, for both speaker groups: 23 and 25 for Hebrew and English speaker respectively, out of which more than half were intensity related, and voice quality features were nearly absent. Using the EM division, However, 61 features were found to be significant in distinguishing between groups for English speaker ratings, vs. only 49 features for the Hebrew speaker's ratings.

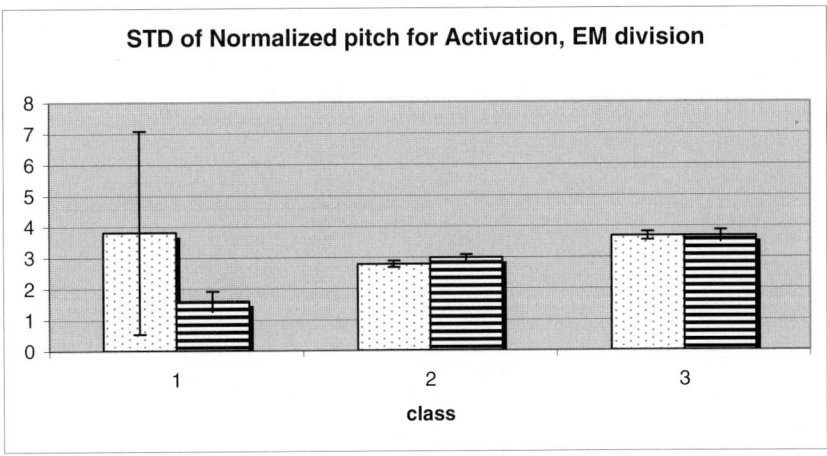

Fig. 3. Behavior of one acoustic feature – STD of normalized pitch - across the three classes of Activation in the EM division. Mean and STD for Hebrew speakers (*dotted columns*), and for English speakers (*striped columns*). Class 1 is for judgments between -3 and -1.5, class 2 is for judgments between -1.5 and 1.5, class 3 is for judgments between 1.5 and 3. Note that means for the English speakers are more distinctly separated across classes, and that STD is smaller.

4 Discussion and Conclusions

Agreement between judges: our initial expectation was that agreement would be higher between native English speaking listeners than between native Hebrew speakers. In practice, statistical measures of agreement gave very similar results on both groups. In fact, histograms of the judgments after partitioning into PN and EM divisions, also showed them to be very similar. Yet this does not mean that both groups judged the *same* PUs similarly. In fact, we did find evidence of higher agreement between native English speakers, though it was found to be manifested in subtler ways, as discussed below in connection with the ANOVA results.

Correlation analysis, reveals that the acoustic features reflect Activation much more readily than they reflect Valence: more features were correlated with Valence, and the correlation values themselves were higher. This is not surprising, since it is well known that emotions exhibiting high degrees of Activation, yet opposing Valence, are readily confused when taken out of context, e. g. anger and joy [15]. It is interesting to observe that the most strongly correlated feature for Valence was the upper quartile of *normalized* pitch, whereas for Valence it was the minimum of *unnormalized* pitch. This suggests that important information may be carried both by normalized and unnormalized pitch. On the whole, intonation was far from being the sole conveyer of emotion, and maybe not the major one. Many intensity related features were also correlated with Activation, and furthermore nearly *only* intensity features were correlated with Valence.

ANOVA: The eight ANOVAs enable interesting comparisons between the different listener groups, the different subdivisions of the emotional scales, and the two different scales themselves.

As already indicated by correlation analysis, ANOVA further corroborates that Activation is more robustly indicated by acoustic features than Valence. Many features, across the board, were significant in indicating Activation, regardless of the listeners group or the judgment groupings (EM and PN).

Valence proved to be much more sensitive then than Activation, in two distinct ways. First, the number of significant features was much lower for PN than for EM, for both listener groups. This indicates that grouping all positive values of Valence into one bin and all negative ones into another bin makes these two bins hard to distinguish from each other. This could be due to a large variance in *judgments* when Valence levels are small, or to the fact that important differences in *acoustic features* occur over a small range of Valence values. Valence in general is not as directly connected to arousal states as Activation, and therefore needs to be examined with a finer comb, and maybe not on a scale that is completely independent of Activation.

Many more features became significant for Valence using the EM division, and furthermore this brought to light differences between the listener groups. Though on the one hand Hebrew speaker vs. English speaker histograms were similar, only 49 acoustic features were significant for Hebrew speakers' judgments of Valence in EM, 61 features were significant for the English speakers. Evidently the English speakers were more attuned to the Valence content, causing more features to "line up" with their judgments.

Finally, we find it noteworthy that features directly related to the segmentation into PUs were found to be significant. Of course nearly all the features are implicitly related to the segmentation method, but some of them are more explicitly related to this, e.g. segment length, initial and final pitch, initial and final intensity. These features were significant in nearly all the ANOVA analyses, strengthening the case for the segmentation strategy we employed. Segmentation in general is still an open point, and will probably be explored further in many future studies.

Further work: The results presented here are clearly not the final word on this database. Several further directions are currently being explored.

First, interdependency between the activation and Valence scales can be assessed by combining judgments on the two separate scales into quadrants in the 2-D activation/Valence plane. This has been carried out before, however our results with the PN scheme indicate that it might be justifiable to group points that are relatively near to the origin as a neutral class, rather than belonging to a specific quadrant.

Second, it seems that spectral features merit further examination, since they were represented here by only three features. Several approaches to extracting spectral features have been examined in depth on this corpus, to be reported elsewhere.

Third, many current studies go beyond correlation and ANOVA-type analyses described here, performing automatic classification into emotional classes. We are currently in the process of carrying this out on the present database.

Fourth, we note that the division of the scales into several groups was somewhat arbitrary. Using classification techniques it could be possible to find more meaningful repartitioning schemes, which would increase the classification rates, which in turn would probably give further insights into the relationship between acoustics and emotional content.

Finally, at this point we have not compared the "density" of emotions in this database to what is found in databases of spontaneous speech. Such and endeavor raises various methodological difficulties, since it is difficult to find two databases that were labeled with the same methodology. Nevertheless, this is a topic that should be looked into in the future.

In conclusion, it appears that the paradigm proposed here is a very interesting one for assessing emotions in speech. As a compromise between purely spontaneous speech and speech acted purely for research purposes, it can provide researchers with large amounts of emotionally-rich speech.

References

1. Whiteside, S.: Simulated emotions: an acoustic study of voice and perturbation Measures. In: Proceedings of International Conference on Spoken Language Processing (ICSLP), Sydney (1998)
2. Amir, N., Ziv, S., Cohen, R.: Characteristics of authentic anger in Hebrew speech. In: Proceedings of Eurospeech, Geneva (2003)
3. Batliner, A., Fischer, K., Huber, R., Spilker, J., Nöth, E.: Desperately seeking emotions or: actors, wizards, and human beings. In: Proceedings of the ISCA Workshop on Speech and Emotion, Belfast (2000)

4. Clavel, C., Vasilescu, I., Devillers, L., Ehrette, T., Richard, G., Vasilescu, I., Devillers, L., Ehrette, T., Richard, G.: Fear-type emotions of the safe corpus: annotation issues. In: Proc. 5th Int. Conf. on Language Resources and Evaluation (LREC), Genoa (2006)
5. Cowie, R., Douglas-Cowie, E., Tsapatsoulis, N., Votsis, G., Kollias, S., Fellenz, W., Taylor, J.G.: Emotion recognition in human-computer interaction. IEEE Signal Processing Magazine, 32–81 (2001)
6. Batliner, A., Steidl, S., Schuller, B., Seppi, D., Laskowski, K., Vogt, T., Devillers, L., Vidrascu, L., Amir, N., Kessous, L., Aharonson, V.: Combining Efforts for Improving Automatic Classification of Emotional User States. In: Proceedings of IS-LTC 2006, Ljubliana, pp. 240–245 (2006)
7. Devillers, L., Vidrascu, L., Lamel, L.: Challenges in real-life annotation and machine learning based detection. Neural Networks 18(4), 407–422 (2005)
8. Stone, M., DeCarlo, D., Oh, I., Rodriguez, C., Stere, A., Lees, A., Bregler, C.: Speaking with hands: Creating animated conversational characters from recordings of human performance. In: Proceedings of Siggraph (2004)
9. Du Bois, J.W., Schuetze-Coburn, S., Cumming, S., Paolino, D.: Outline of Discourse Transcription. In: Edwards, J., Lampert, M. (eds.) Talking Data: transcription and coding in discourse research, pp. 45–90. Lawrence Erlbaum Associates Publishers, Hillsdale, New Jersey, Hove and London (1993)
10. Chafe, W.: Discourse, Consciousness, and Time: the Flow and Displacement of Conscious Experience in Speaking and Writing, pp. 53–70. The University of Chicago Press, Chicago (1994)
11. Schröder, M., Cowie, R., Douglas-Cowie, E., Westerdijk, M., Gielen, S.: Acoustic correlates of emotion dimensions in view of speech synthesis. In: proceedings of Eurospeech. Aalborg, pp. 87–90 (2001)
12. Savvidou, S., Cowie, R., Douglas-Cowie, E., FEELTRACE,: FEELTRACE: validating a tool for continuous measurement of perceived emotional content. In: Proceedings of the ISCA Workshop on Speech and Emotion, Belfast (2000)
13. Liscombe, J., Venditti, J., Hirschberg, J.: Classifying subject ratings of emotional speech using acoustic features. In: Proceedings of Eurospeech, Geneva, pp. 725–728 (2003)
14. Praat software, http://www.praat.org
15. Murray, I.R., Arnott, J.L.: Toward the simulation of emotion in synthetic speech: A review of the literature on human vocal emotion. Journal of the Acoustic Society of America. 93(2), 1097–1108 (1993)
16. Purandare, A., Litman, D.: Prosody analysis and automatic recognition for F*R*I*E*N*D*S. In: Proceedings of EMNLP, Sydney (2005)
17. Cohen, J.: A coefficient of agreement for nominal scales. Educational and Psychological Measurement 20, 37–46 (1960)
18. Landis, J.R., Koch, G.G.: The Measurement of observer agreement for categorical data. Biometrics 33, 159–174 (1977)

Time- and Amplitude-Based Voice Source Correlates of Emotional Portrayals

Irena Yanushevskaya, Michelle Tooher, Christer Gobl, and Ailbhe Ní Chasaide

Phonetics and Speech Laboratory, School of Linguistic, Speech and Communication Sciences,
Trinity College Dublin, Ireland
{yanushei,mtooher,cegobl,anichsid}@tcd.ie

Abstract. A detailed analysis of glottal source parameters is presented for emotional portrayals which included both low and high activation states: *neutral, bored, sad,* and *happy, surprised, angry.* Time- and amplitude-based glottal source parameters, F0, RG, RK, RA, OQ, FA, EE, and RD were analysed. The results show statistically significant differentiation of all emotions in terms of all the glottal parameters analysed. Results furthermore suggest that the dynamics of the individual parameters are likely to be important in differentiating among the emotions.

Keywords: Voice source parameters, emotion, inverse filtering, LF model.

1 Introduction

The communication of emotion has been a major focus of many in the speech research community over recent years [1]. However, there has been limited analysis of how the voice source varies in emotionally coloured speech, so that we lack a true understanding of how the encoding of emotion is reflected in voice source parameters.

It has been suggested that acoustic correlates of emotion can be described in terms of f0 contour, utterance timing, intensity and voice quality, e.g. [2]. In [1, 4] f0 and temporal characteristics, among other measures, are reported to be correlated with the activation levels of emotions. However, it was also proposed that discrete emotions cannot in fact be modelled using features such as f0 and temporal characteristics alone. [3, 4] comment on the limitations with respect to the acoustic parameters studied in the vocal communication of emotions research and suggest that in order to understand encoding and communication of emotions, more weight must be given to voice quality. The results of listening tests of synthesised tokens of an utterance with different voice qualities, reported in [5], showed that such voice quality differences alone are capable of imparting differences in affective colouring. In some analytic studies [6, 7], a global glottal parameter, NAQ, an amplitude parameter derived in the time domain, has been considered in relation to emotional speech. NAQ claims to provide a similar but more robust measure of the closing phase of a glottal pulse than time-domain parameters. Short vowel segments of acted emotional speech [6], as well as a large corpus of naturally occurring speech [7] have been analysed using the NAQ parameter. In [6], NAQ was found to vary with respect to emotion and gender of the speaker. In [7], NAQ showed consistent voice quality variation to signal

A. Paiva, R. Prada, and R.W. Picard (Eds.): ACII 2007, LNCS 4738, pp. 159–170, 2007.

paralinguistic information. [8] tested acoustic correlates of emotional speech through formant synthesis and perception tests, and concluded that a combination of parameters is needed to convey emotions. Tests reported in [9] showed that the inclusion of spectral measures, such as drop-off of spectral energy above 1000Hz, spectral flatness measures, and the Hammarberg Index, was beneficial to sinusoidal modelling of expressive speech, whereas inclusion of jitter, shimmer and HNR was found to be relatively unimportant. [10] attempted to simulate seven basic emotions, using prosodic parameters (F0, duration, intensity) and voice quality measures (aspiration noise, jitter, shimmer, OQ, SQ, RQ) suggested in the literature. However, they commented on the lack of published data relating to measurements of the glottal source variation in emotional speech.

The present study focuses on glottal source parameters rather than other measures traditionally employed to quantify vocal expression of emotions, such as, for example, jitter, shimmer and energy distribution of the spectrum [1, 4]. Although the scope is quite limited in terms of the quantity of data and the nature of the emotionally coloured speech analysed, the study aims to contribute towards a more detailed specification of the voice source in the expression of emotion. The data analysed here involved a number of emotion-portraying utterances of a male speaker. The current analysis methods impose many constraints on the type of data we can work with and on the recording materials and conditions. Therefore, it was necessary to work with portrayed rather than naturally occurring emotions, and the results reported here make no claim that these portrayals are representative of truly occurring emotional states. Rather, the study focuses on the more limited objective of detailing how these instances of emotion portrayal are differentiated in terms of glottal source parameters. We are particularly interested in those parameters which may be used for resynthesis, and would hope eventually to be able to synthesise narrations (e.g., of children's stories) where such emotional portrayals would be appropriate.

2 Data and Methodology

The recorded data consisted of repetitions of a short all-voiced utterance 'We were aWAY a YEAR ago' produced by a male speaker of Irish English. The speaker's neutral mode of phonation corresponded to modal voice of Laver's taxonomy [11]. The recording was made in a semi-anechoic chamber; the distance from the microphone was kept constant at 30 cm. The signal was recorded directly to computer, at the sampling frequency 44.1 kHz.

With the help of short frame stories[1], the speaker portrayed the following basic emotions: *sad, happy, bored, surprised, disgusted, angry, afraid* as well as the *neutral* state. In the course of the recording, the speaker was advised to keep the peaks of prominence (accents) on the same syllables in all repetitions. For each portrayed emotion, four repetitions were recorded. On the basis of the following auditory

---

[1] E.g., when portraying 'sad' the speaker had to admit that even though going away on holidays was possible a year ago, dire financial circumstances would not allow such a trip any time soon; in 'neutral' an elderly lady who had left her reading glasses at home asked him to read a product label in a shop for her, etc.

analysis, one repetition was selected for the instrumental analysis; two major factors influencing the choice being the overall quality of the signal and the authenticity of the emotional portrayal. To confirm that the recorded portrayals indeed represented the targeted emotions, a listening test was conducted.

2.1 Listening Test

The stimuli for the listening test consisted of the 7 portrayals of emotions (*happy, sad, bored, angry, surprised, disgusted,* and *afraid*) and three repetitions of the *neutral* utterance. The stimuli were presented to the listeners on a computer screen in randomised order, 5 randomised lists were generated. 16 volunteers participated in the listening test. The participants were asked to listen to each of the sound files as many times as they wanted, to ascertain which emotion is expressed in each one, and to mark their choice by clicking the radio button next to the emotion label listed next to the sound file. The emotive labels included *happy, sad, bored, angry, surprised, disgusted, afraid* and *no emotion*. A blank box was also added to the list of labels so that the listeners could provide their own emotive label should none of the available labels prove adequate. The results of the listening test are presented in Table 1.

Table 1. Results of the perception test (%). Emotions recognised as targeted in 70% or more cases are shown in bold type.

Target \ Perceived as	Sad	Happy	Bored	Surprised	Disgusted	Angry	Afraid	Neutral	Other
Sad	58	-	8	-	1	-	6	21	6
Happy	-	46	-	5	5	12	2	28	2
Bored	18	-	**71**	-	-	-	1	9	1
Surprised	-	6	-	**93**	-	-	1	-	-
Disgusted	1	1	12	6	24	-	-	51	5
Angry	-	1	1	1	2	**91**	-	2	2
Afraid	56	1	1	-	2	1	28	6	5
Neutral	8	3	6	-	6	2	2	**71**	2

The analysis of the listening test showed that the targeted emotion was recognised at a level of 70% or higher in only 4 out of 8 portrayals. The most readily recognised were *surprised* (93%) and *angry* (91%), followed by *bored* and *neutral* (both with 71% 'correct' recognition). *Bored* was perceived as *sad*, but only in 18% of cases. *Sad* received relatively lower recognition rates: only in 58% of cases did the listeners recognise it as such. *Sad* was identified as *neutral* in 21% of cases. *Afraid*, recognised as such in only 28% of cases, was most readily perceived as *sad* (56%). *Disgusted* got the lowest recognition rates compared to the other emotions, only 24% listeners identified it as such, and it was identified primarily as *neutral* (51%). As *disgust* is more often than not expressed in affect bursts rather than in longer utterances and with facial expression acting as a strong recognition cue, its low recognition rates were somewhat expected. *Happy* was also among the emotions that received relatively low recognition rating, 46%, and it was confused principally with *neutral* (28%) or *angry* (12%).

The utterances that were recognised by the listeners as conveying the targeted emotions in more than 70% of all cases were selected for the further analysis involving inverse filtering. Furthermore, despite the relatively lower recognition rates, both *sad* and *happy* were also included in the glottal source parameter analysis, in order to represent a broader range of affective states.

2.2 Data Analysis: Inverse Filtering and Glottal Source Parameters

The selected six utterances (*angry, surprised, bored, sad, happy* and *neutral*) were inverse filtered. Prior to inverse filtering, each sound file was resampled at a sampling frequency of 10 kHz and high-pass filtered using a phase linear high-pass filter with a cut-off frequency of 40 Hz, to ensure the correct zero pressure line.

Each utterance was initially inverse filtered using automatic inverse filtering software based on closed phase covariance LPC, to obtain a first estimate of the differentiated glottal flow. Subsequent manual, interactive fine-tuning of the inverse filter was performed, pulse by pulse, for all utterances. The details of the system are described in [12]. The number of pulses in the utterances varied across the different utterances/emotions, e.g. there were 81 pulses in *bored* and *neutral*, 86 in *sad*, 96 in *surprised*, 105 in *happy* and 129 in *angry*. It should be noted that that the last syllable [ɡo] was excluded from the analysis due to the difficulties the presence of the obstruent posed for the software.

The same interactive software [12] was used to manually fit the LF model to obtain measures of glottal source parameters. The LF model is a well established parametric voice source model, which is described in detail in [13] and [14]. The model matching procedure for extracting data on source parameters is advantageous in that it provides a means for optimisation in both the time and frequency domains. A further reason to use the model is that the LF model is incorporated in the KLSYN88 [15] formant synthesiser, which facilitates the task of resynthesis of emotionally coloured speech.

The following glottal source parameters were included in the analysis: F0, EE, RK, RG, RA, FA, OQ and RD. Note that the first five parameters are sufficient to characterise the basic glottal pulse shape.

F0 is the fundamental frequency and is calculated as the inverse of the glottal pulse duration, T_0. EE is a measure of the strength of the main glottal excitation. RK is a measure of the symmetry/skew of the glottal pulse. A higher RK value indicates a more symmetrical glottal pulse. RG is the glottal frequency FG normalised to F0, i.e. RG = FG/F0, where FG is the characteristic frequency of the glottal pulse during the open phase. RA is T_a normalised to T_0, where T_a is a measure of the effective duration of the return phase after the main excitation, prior to full or maximum glottal closure. Acoustically, its importance lies in its relation to spectral tilt. FA is a parameter related to RA, as it is also a measure capturing spectral tilt. It is inversely proportional to T_a and the FA value indicates the frequency in the source spectrum at which there may be additional downward tilt. Thus, a high FA value indicates a source spectrum with relatively strong higher harmonics. OQ is the duration of the glottal open phase in relation to the duration of the whole glottal period. The OQ value, which can be derived from the parameters RG and RK, is linked to the strength of the lowest harmonics of the source spectrum. RD is a global waveshape parameter [14], which is

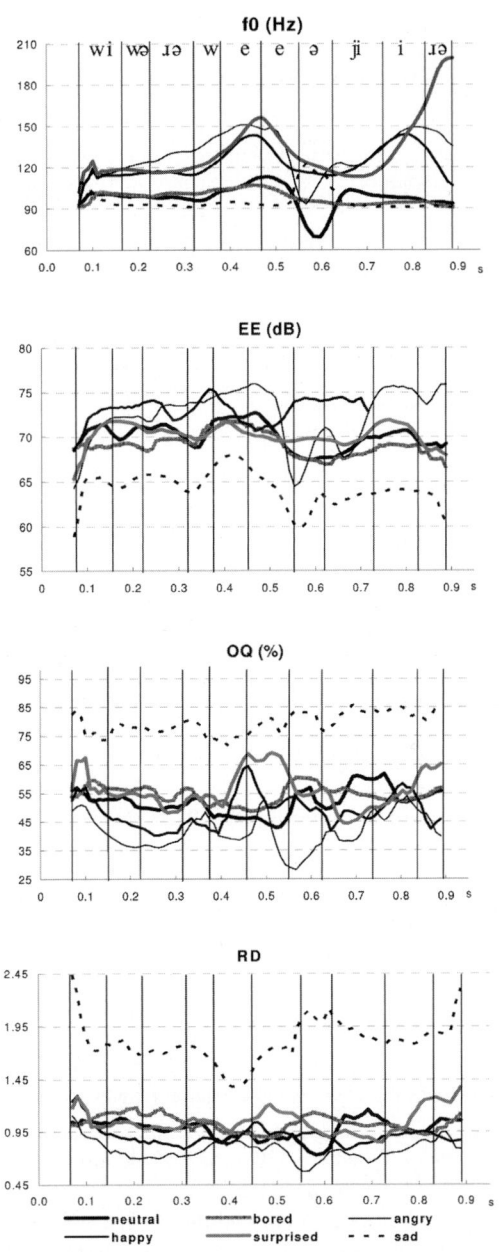

Fig. 1. Dynamics of glottal parameters

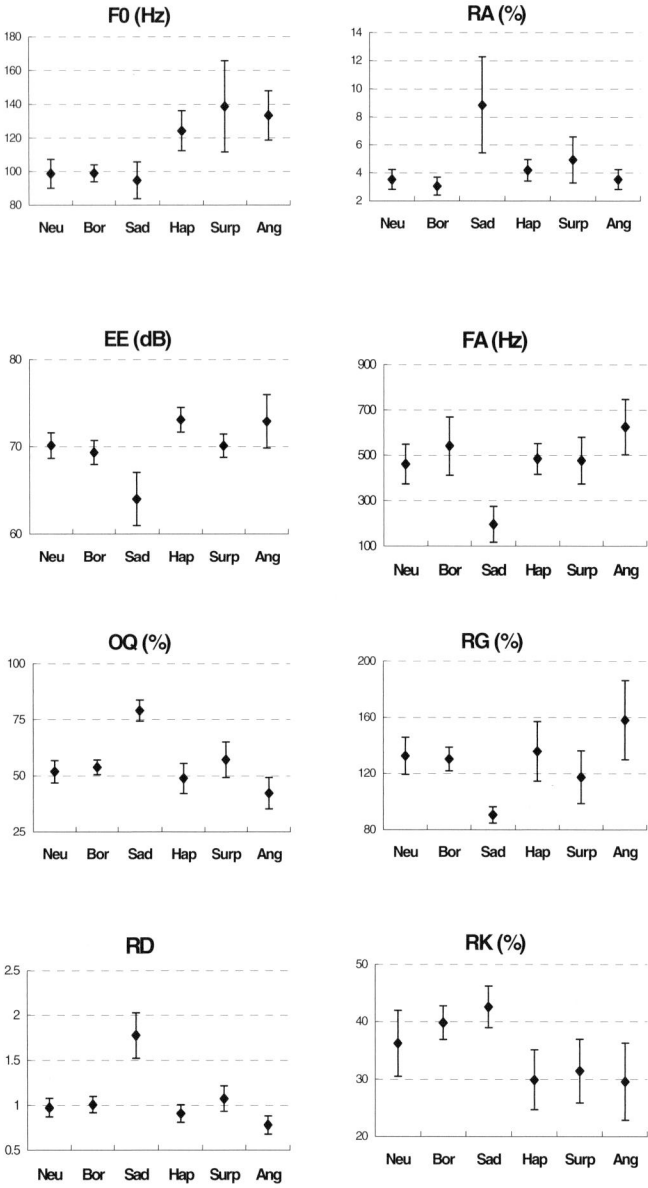

Fig. 2. Mean and standard deviation of glottal parameters across emotions

derived from F0, EE and UP, where UP is the peak amplitude of the glottal flow pulse. It has been suggested that there is a high correlation between the RD value and voice quality variation on the tense to lax continuum [16]. Note that RD is essentially the same as the NAQ parameter [6]. For more detailed descriptions of these parameters and their spectral correlates, see [5, 12].

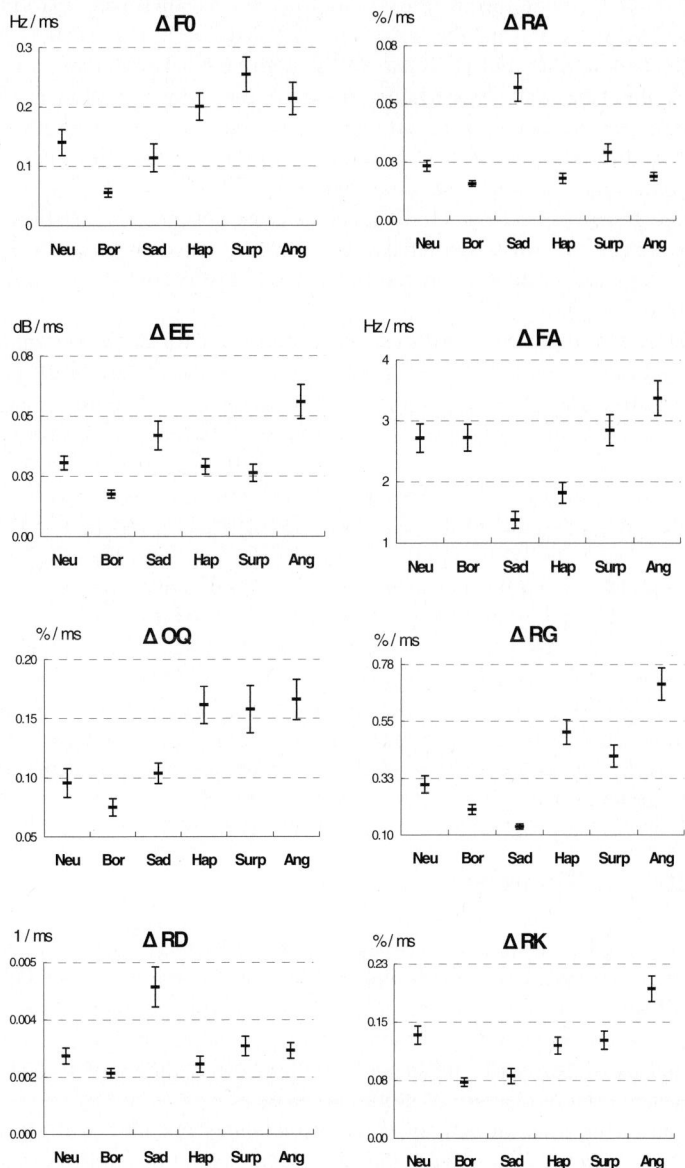

Fig. 3. Mean and standard error of the rate of change of parameters across emotions

2.3 Statistical Analysis and Data Processing for Presentation of Results

In order to aid visual inspection of the parameter dynamics of each emotion-coloured utterance (Fig. 1), the time axis of each utterance was normalised to that of *neutral*. A number of anchor points were chosen in the *neutral* utterance marking syllable boundaries. For vowels from the accented syllables, additional anchor points were placed at their midpoints. For each part of the utterance between these anchor points, 11 in total, the time axis was scaled to be of the same duration as that of the corresponding *neutral* one. As the utterances also had a different number of pulses, linear interpolation was performed in order to plot all emotive utterances to the same time axis points as that of the *neutral* utterance.

To reduce noise caused by small pulse to pulse parameter variation, a moving average of parameters was calculated. The frame spanned 3 pulses with a 1 pulse frame-shift. This served to smooth the plots, while preserving the overall parameter dynamics (see Fig. 1).

For each of the analysed utterances, mean and standard deviation values of each parameter were calculated (see Fig. 2). To explore parameter variability as a function of emotion, a one-way ANOVA with subsequent Tukey's HSD test was conducted (see Table 2). There was a statistically significant difference at the $p<0.05$ level in parameter values for all emotions ($p < 0.0001$): F0 [$F (5, 573)=161.31$; $\eta_p^2=0.58$], EE [$F (5, 573)=220.32$; $\eta_p^2=0.68$], OQ [$F (5, 573)=401.41$; $\eta_p^2=0.78$], RD [$F (5, 573)=588.53$; $\eta_p^2=0.84$], RA [$F (5, 573)=158.59$; $\eta_p^2=0.58$], RG [$F (5, 573)=142.51$; $\eta_p^2=0.55$], RK [$F (5, 573)=103.19$; $\eta_p^2=0.47$], FA [$F (5, 573)=195.34$; $\eta_p^2=0.63$]. High partial eta squared (η_p^2) values are suggestive of significant effect size: over 50% of the variance in mean parameter values is explained by emotion.

The mean values for parameters in Fig. 2 only give a very global picture of variation found for the different emotions. To better capture the parameter dynamics across the duration of the utterance, the rate of change in each parameter was obtained by calculating the first order difference from the smoothed parameter values. Fig. 3 shows the mean and standard error of the absolute rate of change for the analysed glottal parameters.

3   Results and Discussion

ANOVA results showed statistically significant differences among all emotions in terms of all glottal parameters measured. Table 2 details the results of Tukey's HSD test. Fig.1 illustrates the dynamics of the parameters across emotions. Fig. 2 shows the mean and standard deviation for each of the parameters across emotions. Fig. 3 complements by showing the mean and standard error values of the absolute first order difference (rate of change) of glottal parameters.

According to the level of activation, affective states fall into two distinct groups; low activation: *neutral*, *bored* and *sad*, and high activation: *happy*, *surprised* and *angry*. To facilitate the discussion, we will focus the analysis on each of these activation groups with respect to the measured parameters.

Statistical analysis (Table 2) showed that parameters F0, OQ, RD and RK, have relatively high potential to differentiate between high and low activation groups within this dataset. RK is one of the glottal parameters that best differentiates between activation groups, and between emotions within the low activation group. The results observed for F0 were somewhat expected, as F0 is an established correlate of affect,

Table 2. Significance level of the difference in parameters across emotions (* represents p<0.05; p values showing no significant difference between activation groups are in bold type)

F0	neu	bor	sad	hap	surp	RA	neu	bor	sad	hap	surp
bor	1.00					bor	0.52				
sad	0.57	0.50				sad	*	*			
hap	*	*	*			hap	**0.09**	*	*		
surp	*	*	*	*		surp	*	*	*	*	
ang	*	*	*	*	0.08	ang	*	**0.38**	*	*	*

EE	neu	bor	sad	hap	surp	FA	neu	bor	sad	hap	surp
bor	0.26					bor	*				
sad	*	*				sad	*	*			
hap	*	*	*			hap	**0.79**	*	*		
surp	**1.00**	**0.25**	*	*		surp	**0.97**	*	*	1.00	
ang	*	*	*	0.99	*	ang	*	*	*	*	*

OQ	neu	bor	sad	hap	surp	RG	neu	bor	sad	hap	surp
bor	0.34					bor	0.99				
sad	*	*				sad	*	*			
hap	*	*	*			hap	**0.92**	**0.39**	*		
surp	*	*	*	*		surp	*	*	*	*	
ang	*	*	*	*	*	ang	*	*	*	*	*

RD	neu	bor	sad	hap	surp	RK	neu	bor	sad	hap	surp
bor	0.85					bor	*				
sad	*	*				sad	*	*			
hap	*	*	*			hap	*	*	*		
surp	*	*	*	*		surp	*	*	*	0.40	
ang	*	*	*	*	*	ang	*	*	*	1.00	0.12

for example [1]. OQ and RD, a global waveshape parameter, differentiated between all emotions, apart from *neutral* and *bored*. The RD data were compared with the NAQ (essentially the same global parameter as RD) values in [6]. In [6], NAQ values for all emotions barring *angry* were higher than *neutral*. Similar patterns were observed here for RD, except *happy* was also lower than *neutral*.

EE, RA, FA and RG were not significantly different for emotions from the two different activation groups. For example, EE of *surprised* is not significantly different from that of *bored* and *neutral*, and RA for *angry* and *bored* yielded similar values. Overlap between emotion groups in EE, RA, FA and RG suggests that no one parameter can provide sufficient information about the voice source in certain affective states and that these parameters in particular should be considered in conjunction with other glottal parameters.

Analysis of parameter values suggests that within-group emotion differentiation is parameter specific, some parameters distinguishing between emotions more clearly than others. Emotion differentiation is also activation-group specific. Within the high activation group, emotions are differentiated in terms of OQ, RD, RA and RG, whereas within the low activation group the only differentiator is RK. All parameters except RK showed no statistically significant difference between *bored* and *neutral*, which in itself is noteworthy.

It is obvious not only from the means in Fig. 2, but also from the smoothed parameter trajectories in Fig. 1, that parameter values of *angry* and *sad* almost always appear as extremes (highest and lowest), each representative of the most extreme emotion within their relevant activation group. It is interesting to note that these affective states have been associated with very different voice qualities, which is supported by the combination of parameters found here.

It is often the case that when parameters show no emotion differentiation in terms of mean values, it is the parameter dynamics that distinguish emotions. It is especially evident in the example of *bored* and *neutral* that yield similar mean values for the majority of parameters (except RK), but show very different rates of change, parameters for *neutral* being of more dynamic nature. Within the high activation group, for example, *angry* is not differentiated from *happy* and *surprised* in terms of mean RK, but it shows markedly higher rate of change for this parameter.

In emotion research literature, there has been an increasing awareness that to achieve affective sounding speech synthesis, we must adequately represent the contribution of the voice source. The results presented here show that we must take into account how the voice source parameters vary, not only in broad terms but also in terms of their dynamics. It goes without saying that ultimately this information needs to be combined with other variables such as speech rate, duration, etc., which are also important in the signalling of emotion. Similar suggestions were made earlier, e.g. [8].

A summary of parameter combinations for each emotion that could also serve as a first approximation of parameter settings for each affect is shown in Table 3. Parameter levels are calculated as a percentage difference relative to *neutral*. These parameters can be readily converted into synthesis parameters, for example those of the KLSYN88 [15] formant synthesiser. Note that the combination of parameter settings is different for each emotion and we would tentatively conclude that the voice source difference between affective states will not be captured by a single measure or a combination of static parameters. Rather, a combination of dynamically varying parameters needs to be considered.

Table 3. Suggested levels for LF-parameters for synthesis: summary* (shaded are other parameters considered in the paper)

Affect		F0	EE	RG	RK	RA	OQ	FA	RD
Low activation	Neutral	M	M	M	**M**	M	M	M	M
	Bored	M	M	M	H	L	M	H	M
	Sad	M	L	LL	H	**HH**	HH	LL	**HH**
High activation	Happy	**H**	M	H	L	H	**L**	M	L
	Surprised	**HH**	M	L	L	HH	**H**	M	H
	Angry	**HH**	**M**	H	L	M	**L**	**HH**	L

* LL = [< -25%] (very low), L = [-25%, -5%] (lower than *neutral*), M = [-5%, 5%] (within the *neutral* range), H = [5%, 25%] (higher than *neutral*), HH = [> 25%] (very high). Bold type shows parameters demonstrating high dynamic variation.

4 Conclusion

Glottal parameters were analysed for emotion-portraying utterances, with the aim of 1) describing how glottal parameters can vary across the emotions, and 2) identifying which glottal parameters or combination of such may be more important for the resynthesis of emotion. The parameters chosen were a combination of those that give an overall picture of the glottal pulse and those that can be incorporated into synthesis of emotive speech. As already mentioned, the analysis is on limited data, and results can only be considered tentative. The parameters demonstrate unequal potential in emotion differentiation. Parameters that differentiate between activation groups are F0, RK, RD and OQ. Four out of eight parameters analysed – RA, FA, RG, and EE demonstrate overlap between the activation groups. *Bored* and *neutral* show similar parameter values, except for RK and FA. *Sad* is significantly different from all other emotions in terms of all parameters except F0 (F0 *sad* is similar to *neutral* and *bored*).

In the high activation group, there is good within-group differentiation in terms of the mean values of RA, RG, RD and OQ, but no differentiation in F0 (*angry* and *surprised*), RK (all high activation emotions), EE (*angry* and *happy*) and FA (*happy* and *surprised*). It is obvious that parameter dynamics should be considered, as they further demonstrate differences among emotions. For example, *neutral* and *bored* are not differentiated in terms of mean values of all parameters except one (RK), but are well differentiated in terms of the rate of change. Glottal parameters can be used to describe voice quality patterns pertaining to various emotions, especially those that prove to demonstrate good differentiation between high and low activation emotions. However, one cannot expect to reproduce emotion in synthesis by setting voice source parameter values to static values, the dynamics must also be considered.

The results presented here are only preliminary, and much further work will be required that will include analysis of more speech samples obtained from more speakers, with a broader range of affective states, where arousal differences within emotions of the same family are taken into account in the emotion elicitation process. One aim of the present research is to provide data for the synthesis of narrated stories, capable of generating at least a small repertoire of narrator's emotions, something we hope to explore in future work.

Acknowledgments. The research was funded by the EU Sixth Framework Network of Excellence HUMAINE and by the Irish Research Council for Science and Engineering Technology-EMBARK initiative.

References

1. Juslin, P., Scherer, K.R.: Vocal Expression of Affect. In: Harrigan, J., Rosenthal, R., Scherer, K.R. (eds.) The New Handbook of Methods in Nonverbal Behavior Research, pp. 65–135. Oxford University Press, Oxford (2005)
2. Murray, I., Arnott, J.: Toward the Simulation of Emotion in Synthetic Speech: A Review of the Literature on Human Vocal Emotion. Journal of the Acoustical Society of America 93, 1097–1108 (1993)
3. Scherer, K.R.: Vocal Communication of Emotion: A Review of Research Paradigms. Speech Communication 40, 227–256 (2003)
4. Banse, R., Scherer, K.R.: Acoustic Profiles in Vocal Emotion Expression. Journal of Personality and Social Psychology 70(3), 614–636 (1996)
5. Gobl, C., Ní Chasaide, A.: The Role of Voice Quality in Communicating Emotion, Mood and Attitude. Speech Communication 40, 189–212 (2003)

6. Airas, M., Alku, P.: Emotions in Short Vowel Segments: Effects of the Glottal Flow as Reflected by the Normalised Amplitude Quotient. In: André, E., Dybkjær, L., Minker, W., Heisterkamp, P. (eds.) ADS 2004. LNCS (LNAI), vol. 3068, pp. 13–24. Springer, Heidelberg (2004)
7. Campbell, N., Mokhtari, P.: Voice Quality: the 4th Prosodic Dimension. In: Proceedings of the 15th International Congress of Phonetic Sciences, pp. 2417–2420 (2003)
8. Burkhardt, F., Sendlmeier, W.F.: Verification of Acoustical Correlates of Emotional Speech using Formant-Synthesis. In: Proc. ISCA Workshop (IRTW) on Speech and Emotion, pp. 151–156 (2000)
9. Drioli, C., Tisato, G., Cosi, P., Tesser, F.: Emotions and Voice Quality: Experiments with Sinusoidal Modelling. ITRW VOQUAL'03, Switzerland, pp. 127–132 (2003)
10. Cabral, J.P., Oliveira, L.C.: EmoVoice: a System to Generate Emotion in Speech. Interspeech 2006, Pittsburgh (2006)
11. Laver, J.: The Phonetic Description of Voice Quality. Cambridge University Press, Cambridge (1980)
12. Gobl, C., Ní Chasaide, A.: Techniques for Analysis the Voice Source. In: Hardcastle, W.J., Hewlett, N. (eds.) Coarticulation: Theory, Data and Techniques, pp. 300–320. Cambridge University Press, Cambridge (1999)
13. Fant, G., Liljencrants, J., Lin, Q.: A Four Parameter Model of Glottal Flow. STL-QPSR, Speech, Music and Hearing, Royal Institute of Technology, Stockholm 1, 1–13 (1985)
14. Fant, G.: The LF-model Revisited: Transformations and Frequency Domain Analysis. STL-QPSR, Speech, Music and Hearing, Royal Institute of Technology, Stockholm 156, 2–3 (1995)
15. Klatt, D.H., Klatt, L.C.: Analysis, Synthesis and Perception of Voice Quality Variations among Male and Female Talkers. Journal of the Acoustical Society of America 87, 820–856 (1990)
16. Fant, G.: The Voice Source in Connected Speech. Speech Communication 22, 125–139 (1997)

Temporal Organization in Listeners' Perception of the Speakers' Emotions and Characteristics: A Way to Improve the Automatic Recognition of Emotion-Related States in Human Voice

Valérie Maffiolo[1], Noël Chateau[1], and Gilles Le Chenadec[2]

[1] France Telecom Orange Labs, Technologies, 2 av. P. Marzin, 22300 Lannion, France
[2] CRIL Technology- Alyotech - rue Galilée, 22300 Lannion, France
{valerie.maffiolo,noel.chateau}@orange-ftgroup.com,
le.chenadec@free.fr

Abstract. We propose to improve the automatic detection and characterization of emotion-related expressions in human voice by an approach based on human auditory perception. In order to determine the temporal hierarchical organization in human perception of the speakers' emotions and characteristics, a listening test has been set up with seventy-two listeners. The corpus was constituted of eighteen voice messages extracted from a real-life application. Message segments of different temporal length have been listened to by listeners who were asked to verbalize their perception. Fourteen meta-categories have been obtained and related to age, gender, regional accent, timbre, personality, emotion, sound quality, expression style and so on. The temporal windows of listening necessary for listeners to perceive and verbalize these categories are defined and could underlie the building of sub-models relevant to the automatic recognition of emotion-related expressions.

Keywords: Voice, expressions of emotion, perception, anthropomorphic characteristics, listening test, temporal organization.

1 Context

Developing an effective system able to automatically detect and characterize spontaneous and natural expressions of emotion in the human voice is by no means the least difficult [1]. Most of the studies conducted in this framework deal with systems including two phases: learning and classifying. In both phases, the same pre-processing is done on the vocal signal in order to extract features allowing the extraction of information carried by the vocal signal. The first phase consists in learning the relations existing between the features' values extracted from a corpus of vocal signals and emotional labels. Particularly, this automatic learning of a mathematical model allows the identification of features (and theirs values) which characterize the expressions of the aimed emotion. During the phase of classification, the learned model is applied to the features' values extracted from a new vocal signal to estimate the presence and the nature of emotion.

A. Paiva, R. Prada, and R.W. Picard (Eds.): ACII 2007, LNCS 4738, pp. 171–178, 2007.
© Springer-Verlag Berlin Heidelberg 2007

Up to now learning processes come up against two main problems: the identity of the features to be extracted and the method to combine these features.

Expressions of emotion in human voice are of two main types: linguistic (ex: lexical, syntax or related to dialogs) and paralinguistic (often related to acoustics)[2]. Thus, learning systems are based on either linguistic features, or acoustic, or a mix of both types. Taking into account linguistic features alone allows the determination of certain emotions, when the speaker's state is explicitly formulated ("I am not happy") or implicitly formulated "No, I have more than enough, I don't agree"). Nevertheless, it is often necessary to disambiguate simple sentences as "Here you are" with the acoustic information to understand the emotion expressed.

The great majority is the systems based on only acoustic features [3] though the use of acoustic features alone present inconvenient. Indeed, a purely acoustic system cannot distinguish linguistic intonation (related to words and sentence's structure) and paralinguistic intonation (related to the speaker's state, his/her regional accent, etc.). It is not able to detect the presence of emotion except when the global intonation leaves the framework of the linguistic intonation. Note that joy and anger express themselves through the same acoustic features, it is particularly difficult to distinguish them on this basis alone [4]. The features related to the context are complementary to the two other types but are less used even if the type of interaction (human-human, human-machine, professional or familial context; etc.) influences the expressions of emotions and their characterization [5].

In order to take into account both linguistic and paralinguistic information, some systems are based on the combination of both types of features [6, 7, 8]. This combination rests on either the fusion of decisions or the fusion of features. The first approach consists in learning a model on acoustic features then another model on linguistic features and in taking the decision from the decisions stemmed from the two models. This approach does not allow taking into account explicitly the interactions between linguistic and acoustic features. The second approach deals with a mixed representation of the signal containing both linguistic and acoustic features and seems to be the most promising.

A common problem among the techniques of learning and classifying is the choice of the length of the temporal window on which features' values are calculated. In literature, most authors use a unique segmentation according to a chosen syntactical unit (phonemes, syllables, words, silence, etc.) by using an automatic speech recognition tool. Certain authors use systems combining the outputs of acoustic models based on features from which the values are calculated on different temporal windows [9]. The latter agree with Laver [10] who underlines that "*the description of paralinguistic features making up tone of voice is almost always relevant to the description of phonetic voice quality features, because the main difference between vocal paralinguistic features and voice quality's phonetic component is the time scale involved and not so much the identity of the features used.*" Thus it is not so much the identity of features that is important in the differentiation of the characteristics of a voice as the temporal window on which the features are observed.

2   Our Approach

On this basis, we propose to tackle the building of a learning and classification process of emotional expressions in the human voice by an approach based on the auditory human perception. In the mediated human-human interaction or human-machine interaction, in the case they are constructed on the vocal modality, the speaker gives his/her interlocutor (human or system), through his/her voice, a lot of information. Indeed, the voice is a conveyor of expression of the speaker's characteristics (age, gender, timbre, personality, geographical origin, social background, etc.), the emotional and cognitive states (he/she is afraid, he/she doubts), the communicative acts (he/she wants to seduce, convince, etc.) and the context (he/she speaks loudly because there is noise, he/she speaks slowly because the quality of the network is not good, he/she is involved in a human-machine interaction, etc.). Several works are interested in all these characteristics but most of the time these latter are studied independently of the others [11, 12] or co-articulated for only one dimension of emotion [13]. Nevertheless there is definitely interdependency between all these elements. In the listening of a voice, a listener can say that this is a female speaker. Later, during the listening, the listener can say that her timbre is nasal. And later, his/her characterization of the speaker's emotion will integrate the fact that she is a female speaker with a nasal timbre. Consequently, the determination of the speaker's gender and timbre takes part in the perception and characterization of the speaker's emotion. Thus, it is of prime importance to take into account the way information conveyed by features (that is to say the speaker's characteristics described by features) appears in the temporality of the perception and interacts between them. In other words, it is relevant to build a speaker-model and to study the speaker's characteristics that are recognized and the temporal hierarchy on which they are organized in the perception.

The present paper reports the experiment we have set up in order to determine the temporal hierarchical organization of the speakers' characteristics and emotional states in the auditory human perception. In a first section, the corpus studied is described. Section 4 presents the setup of the listening test put in place. Section 5 presents and discusses the results obtained concerning the temporal organization in the perception of the speakers' emotions and characteristics. In the last section, we present our future works.

3   A Real-Life Corpus

The corpus underlying our study is composed of recordings of two thousand customers' messages posted on an answering machine. More precisely, France Telecom has developed a method to evaluate the quality of its mobile-phone customer care service (CCS): every day, a sample panel of customers who have called the CCS is set up. Subsequently to their calls, those customers belonging to the sample panel receive an SMS asking them to call back a free number. When calling this number, they are asked to give their opinion on the CCS quality by leaving a message on an answering machine. Often, customers talk about their problems which have motivated their calls to the CCS. Consequently, several emotional phases often appear in a same message: e.g., calm when it concerns the satisfaction regarding the quality of the welcome of the CCS but also anger when it concerns a problem encountered with the product bought.

This corpus constitutes a spontaneous and real-life corpus but also a difficult study case as it presents an important variability in vocal quality (due to the recording (wind, traffic, external discussions, etc.) and transmission (terminal used, quality of the channel, etc.) conditions) and in speaker's expressions (all the speakers are different and are free to express themselves in their own words and in their own way).

4   Experimental Setup

The aim of the experiment is to determine which speaker's characteristics and emotional cognitive states are perceived in human voice and verbalized by human subjects and at which moment in the listening.

Eighteen messages have been extracted from the corpus, representing a variety of voice timbres, of regional accent, of expressions (emotional and others). All were comprised of fourteen to eighteen words. Each message has been split into multiple segments. For example if a message comprised fourteen words, it was segmented in fourteen segments, each segment beginning by one of the word constituting the message. All the segments stopped at the end of the message. The longest segment begins at the first word of the message. The shortest segment begins at the last word of the message.

Eighteen groups of four listeners have taken part in the experiment. The subjects were asked to listen to several voice segments. For each segment, the subjects heard a pair of sequences that is first, the beginning of the segment called sequence of reference, followed by the same sequence extended. The subjects controlled the length of the second sequence of the pair by clicking on an "extension" button. Each extension corresponded to 25% of the length of the reference sequence. At the first listening of the segment, the reference sequence had a length of 100 ms. Each extension allowed subjects to hear some more voice and produced richest impressions. At each step they perceived new elements in the voice, subjects were asked to freely and verbally comment in writing the global impression they had while listening to the extended sequence in comparison with the reference sequence. They had the possibility to listen to the pair again by clicking on the "listen again" button. The global impression could be related to the speaker (age, gender, regional accent, social milieu, etc.), to his/her attitude (ironic, uneasy, insistent, etc.), to his/her emotions (angry, happy, etc.), to what or who the speaker made subjects think of (the postman, noise of rattle, etc.), or to the sound environment (noisy, private conversation, fun fair, etc.). If they perceived nothing else than the previous listening, subjects extended the second sequence of the pair. If they noted a comment in the "comment" box, the reference sequence of the next pair was the extended sequence of the previous pair. From extension to extension, subjects reached the end of the segment. Then they moved on to the next segment corresponding to another message. The messages were randomly presented to subjects.

The difference between the groups of subjects depends, for a given message, on the segment heard that is characterized by its starting word. Thus the groups didn't hear the same length of segment. Those who started the listening of the segment at the first word of the message had a longer time of listening. Moreover the number of groups being superior to the number of words of certain messages, some groups didn't hear the messages in question.

5   Results and Discussion

5.1   Analysis of Comments

The seventy-two subjects have produced 7755 verbal comments. The analysis of these comments led to a set of fourteen meta-categories listed in Table 1. Categories are related to speaker's characteristics (*age, gender, timbre, personality, regional accent, social background, family status, occupation*), or to speaker's *emotion-related states* (cf. Table 2), or to the *expressive style* (that is the way of speaking as elocution, tone of voice, hesitation, etc.), or to the *sound quality* (often related to the quality of the network), or to *hedonism* (pleasant, charming, kind, nice voice) and *effect on listener* (stressful, anxiety provoking, soothing, etc.). The *fuzzy set* gathers the categories *soft, calm* and *aggressive* which can be linked to different categories cited above, for example, *personality* or *expressive style*.

Table 1. Occurrences of categories

Categories	Occurrences	Categories	Occurrences
Expressive style	1568	Fuzzy set	375
Emotion-related states	1396	Social background	357
Gender	1210	Occupation	264
Age	1060	Hedonism	193
Regional accent	474	Sound quality	118
Personality	417	Family status	44
Timbre	398	Effect on listener	21

Table 2 gives details about occurrences of emotion-related states. Among all the emotion-related categories, many expressions of negative emotion-related states

Table 2. Occurrences of emotion-related categories

Displeased	222	Weary	40
Angry	217	Various labels	40
Satisfied	149	Sad	34
Pleased	136	Surprised	32
Anxious	134	Stressed	30
Unsatisfied	88	Frightened	18
Questioning	80	Impatient	16
Happy	66	Ironical	10
Neutral	42		
Disappointed	42		

appear through ten categories. There are also three positive emotion-related states: satisfied, pleased and happy. This result may be explained, on the one hand, by the emotional nature of the corpus itself, and on the other hand, by the difference concerning the diversity of words available in the French language to talk about negative emotions versus positive emotions.

5.2   Determination of the Temporal Organization

This section concerns the analysis of the temporal organization of the fourteen meta-categories. Fig. 1 shows two statistical features (mean duration and standard deviation normalized to the mean) of the temporal windows necessary for listeners to perceive and verbalize each category.

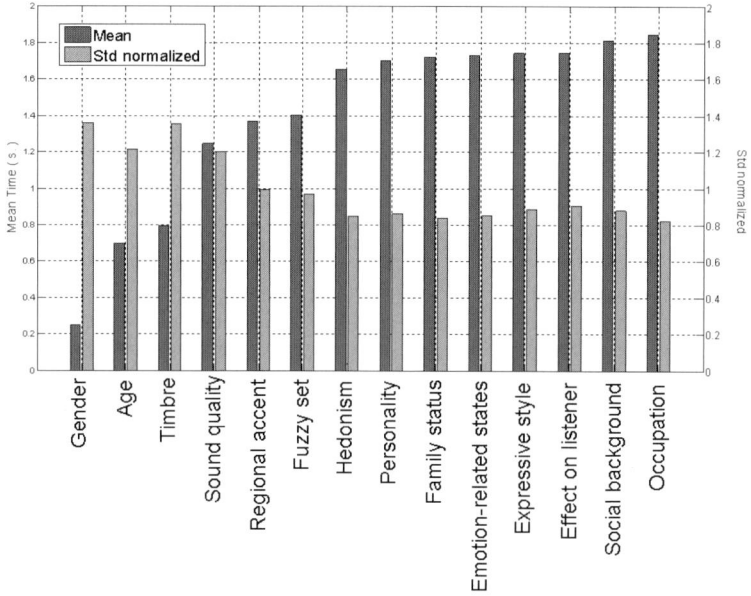

Fig. 1. Mean duration and normalized standard deviation of temporal windows for each category

The first speaker's characteristic which is cited by listeners whatever the message and the segment, is an inference of the speaker's *gender*. This characteristic is perceived and cited approximately from 250 ms of listening. The following characteristics perceived and cited are *age* and *timbre* which last less than one second. *Sound quality*, *accent* and *fuzzy set* have a mean duration between 1.2 s and 1.4 s. The other characteristics can be gathered in a group characterized by a mean duration between 1.6 s. and 1.8s. In this last group, are the *emotion-related states* with a 1.7 s. mean duration.

The normalized standard deviation associated with *gender* is approximately 1.3 which means there is a large variation in the arising of comments related to *gender* all through the listening. Analyzing the other characteristics, note that the larger the mean duration of temporal windows is, the smaller the variation.

This analysis clearly highlights that various characteristics are conveyed by speech signals and that listeners can perceive them from different temporal windows. With the aim to build an automatic system, these temporal windows may be useful to build sub-models dedicated to the estimation of all the characteristics perceived by the listeners.

6   Future Works

For each message, as listeners advanced in the listening of the voice segments, sometimes they went back over some categories either to confirm their previous perception or to contradict it. For example, listeners often went back to the category "age", to precise the age of the speaker as they listened to more segments: "he is old", "approximately sixty", "rather forty". In a further step, we will analyze confirmations and contradictions observed in comments in order to precise the temporal windows necessary to determine certain categories. The backgrounds of listeners will be taken into account in order to determine if gender, age, occupation affect the results. We will also have to analyze the link between categories in order to verify the existence of a hierarchical organization of speaker's characteristics that is, if recurrent sequences of characteristics exist, allowing the detection of some emotion-related states.

To build an automatic classification process of emotional expressions in the human voice, the approach adopted in our work is a global approach of perceptive and semantic integration, based on a low-level machine learning of multi-windows multi-features and combined to a high-level fusion of semantic information. We consider that this approach is independent of culture but the characteristics and their temporal hierarchical organization in the auditory human perception depends on the context of application and are given by expertise. For this, we have set up a listening test. Afterwards, the features' values conveying a given speaker's characteristic will be measured on a temporal window having at the most the length of the temporal window relevant to characterize this characteristic from the human perception viewpoint. In the model, the fusion of the high-level information will be organized from this hierarchy. A decision on a characteristic will take part in the decision on the next characteristic in the temporal hierarchy. The decision taken on the latter could modify the decision on the previous characteristic.

To sum up, the development of an effective system able to automatically detect and characterize spontaneous and natural expressions of emotions in the human voice cannot be done: 1) without building and combining sub-models of estimation of speaker's characteristics (age, gender, timbre, etc.) and mental states, 2) without combining the decisions of each sub-models according to the interdependency of the speaker's states and characteristics and according to their temporal hierarchical organization in auditory human perception, 3) without basing these sub-models on features of different natures and extracted from different length of temporal windows given by the temporal hierarchical organization, and 4) without taking into account relations between the current states of the sub-models and their previous states [14].

References

1. Scherer, K.R.: Vocal communication of emotion: A review of research paradigms. Speech Communication 40, 227–256 (2003)
2. Cowie, R., Douglas-Cowie, E., Tsapatsoulis, N.: Emotion recognition in human-computer interaction. IEEE Signal Processing Magazine 18(1), 32–80 (2001)
3. Ververidis, D., Kotropoulos, C.: Emotional speech recognition: Resources, features, and methods. Speech Communication 48, 1162–1181 (2006)
4. Scherer, K.R., Johnstone, T., Klasmeyer, G.: Vocal expression of emotion. In: Davidson, R., Scherer, K., Goldsmith, H. (eds.) Handbook of Affective Sciences, pp. 433–456. Oxford Press (2003)
5. Petty, R.E., Fabrigar, L.R., Wegener, D.T.: Emotional factors in attitudes and persuasion. In: Davidson, R., Scherer, K., Goldsmith, H. (eds.) Handbook of Affective Sciences, pp. 752–772. Oxford Press (2003)
6. Batliner, A., Fischer, K., Hunber, R.: How to find trouble in communication. Speech Communication 40, 117–143 (2003)
7. Schuller, B., Rigoll, G., Lang, M.: Speech emotion recognition combining acoustic features and linguistic information in a hybrid support vector machine - belief network architecture. In: Proceedings ICASSP 2004., Montreal, Canada, vol. 1, pp. 577–580 (2004)
8. Batliner, A., Steidl, S., Schuller, B., Seppi, D., Laskowski, K., Vogt, T., Devillers, L., Vidrascu, L., Amir, N., Kessous, L., Aharonson, V.: Combining efforts for improving automatic classification of emotional user states. In: Erjavec, T., Gros, J. (eds.) Language Technologies, IS-LTC, Ljubljana, Slovenia, pp. 240–245. Infornacijska Druzba (Information Society) (2006)
9. Lee, C.M., Yildirim, S., Bulut, M.: Emotion Recognition based on Phoneme Classes. In: Proceedings ICSLP, Jeju Island, Corea (2004)
10. Laver, J.: The analysis of vocal quality: from the classical period to the twentieth century. In: Asher, R.E, Henderson, E.J.A (eds.) Towards a history of phonetic, Edinburgh University Press (1981)
11. Chateau, N., Maffiolo, V., Blouin, C.: Analysis of emotional speech in voice mail message: The influence of speaker's gender. In: Proceedings Interspeech-ICSLP, Corea, pp. 885–888 (2004)
12. Grimm, M., Kroschel, K., Narayanan, S.: Modelling Emotion Expression and Perception Behaviour in Auditive Emotion Evaluation. In: Proceedings Prosody (2006)
13. Tato, R., Kemp, T., Marasek, K.: Method for detecting emotions involving subspace specialists, Brevet n° US 2003/0069728 A1 (2003)
14. Maffiolo, V., Chateau, N., Le Chenadec, G.: Procédé d'estimation de l'état mental d'une personne, Brevet n° 06581-FR (2007)

'You are Sooo Cool, Valentina!' Recognizing Social Attitude in Speech-Based Dialogues with an ECA

Fiorella de Rosis[1], Anton Batliner[2], Nicole Novielli[1], and Stefan Steidl[2]

[1] Intelligent Interfaces, Department of Informatics, University of Bari
Via Orabona 4, 70126 Bari, Italy
{derosis,novielli}@di.uniba.it
[2] Lehrstuhl für Mustererkennung, Universität Erlangen-Nürnberg
Martensstrasse 3, 91058 Erlangen - F.R. of Germany
{batliner,steidl}@informatik.uni-erlangen.de

Abstract. We propose a method to recognize the 'social attitude' of users towards an Embodied Conversational Agent (ECA) from a combination of linguistic and prosodic features. After describing the method and the results of applying it to a corpus of dialogues collected with a Wizard of Oz study, we discuss the advantages and disadvantages of statistical and machine learning methods if compared with other knowledge-based methods.

1 Introduction

This work is part of a research project that is aimed at adapting the behavior of an ECA (that we named Valentina) to the 'social' attitude of its users. To make suggestions effective, knowledge of the user characteristics (preferences, values, beliefs) is needed: this knowledge may be acquired by observing the users' behavior during the dialogue to infer a dynamic, consistent model of their mind. Affect proved to be a key component of such a model (Bickmore and Cassell, 2005). Adaptation may be beneficial if the user characteristics are recognized properly but detrimental in case of misrecognition; this is especially true for affective features, for which consequences of misrecognition (and misreactions) may be dangerous. An example:

The user: "You are not very competent Valentina!" (by smiling)
The ECA: "Thanks!" (by reciprocating smile).

Recognition of the affective state should therefore consider on the one hand the aspects that may improve interaction if properly recognized and, on the other hand, the features that available methods enable recognizing with an acceptable level of accuracy. Affective states vary in their degree of stability, ranging from long-standing features (personality traits) to more transient ones (emotions). Other states, such as *interpersonal stance*[1], are in a middle of this scale: they are initially influenced by individual features like personality, social role and relationship between the

---

[1] To Scherer, *interpersonal stance* is *"characteristic of an affective style that spontaneously develops or is strategically employed in the interaction with a person or a group of persons, coloring the interpersonal exchange in this situation (e.g. being polite, distant, cold, warm, supportive, contemptuous)":* http://emotion-research.net/deliverables/D3e%20final.pdf

A. Paiva, R. Prada, and R.W. Picard (Eds.): ACII 2007, LNCS 4738, pp. 179–190, 2007.

interacting people but may be changed, in valence and intensity, by episodes occurring during interaction. This general concept was named differently in recent research projects, each considering one of its aspects: *empathy* (Paiva, 2004), *engagement, involvement, sympathy* (Hoorn and Konijn, 2003, Yu et al., 2004). A popular term among e-learning researchers is *social presence*, which received several definitions, from the general one *"the extent to which the communicator is perceived as 'real'"* (Polhemus et al., 2001) to the more ECA-specific one *"the extent to which individuals treat embodied agents as if they were other real human beings"* (Blascovich, 2002). The concept of social presence refers to the nature of interaction with other people in a technologically mediated communication (Rettie, 2003). In reasoning about the social response of users to ECAs, we prefer to employ the term *social attitude*. To distinguish warm from cold social attitude, we refer to Andersen and Guerrero's definition of *interpersonal warmth* (1998) as *"the pleasant, contented, intimate feeling that occurs during positive interactions with friends, family, colleagues and romantic partners...[and]... can be conceptualized as... a type of relational experience, and a dimension that underlines many positive experiences."*

Researchers proposed a large variety of markers of social presence related to nonverbal behavior, such as body distance, memory, likeability, physiological data, task performance and self-report (Bailenson et al., 2005). Polhemus et al. (2001) suggested various text-based indicators: *personal address and acknowledgement* (using the name of the persons to which one is responding, restating their name etc.), *feeling* (using descriptive words about how one feels), *paralanguage* (features of language which are used outside of formal grammar and syntax), *humor, social sharing* (of information non related to the discussion), *social motivators* (offering praise, reinforcement and encouragement), *negative responses* (disagreement with the other's comment), *self-disclosure* (sharing personal information). Additional dimensions have been suggested by Andersen e Guerrero (1998): *sense of intimacy* (use of a common jargon), attempt to establish a *common ground, benevolent or polemic attitude* towards the system failure, *interest* to protract or close interaction.

We studied social attitude and the factors affecting it by observing the verbal behavior of subjects interacting with an ECA in a Wizard of Oz (WoZ) simulation study. In a previous work (de Rosis et al., 2006), we described how social attitude can be recognized from language and how its evolution during the dialogue can be modeled with dynamic oriented graphs. In that context, we described the 'signs' through which, according to the psycholinguistic theories proposed above, social attitude may be displayed, and discussed the difficulty of recognizing them by means of simple keyword analysis. The corpus of dialogues on which the methods were developed and tested were collected with studies in which users interacted with the ECA by means of keyboard and mouse. Subsequently, we decided to study whether and how changing the interaction mode to speech and touch-screen influenced the user attitude towards the ECA (de Rosis et al., submitted). We collected a new corpus of dialogues with a new set of WoZ studies and extended our method of social attitude recognition in two directions: by refining language analysis with a bayesian classifier rather than a keyword analyzer and by incorporating acoustic analysis.

In this paper, we will describe the results of this research. After proposing a method to recognize social attitude from speech and language, we will discuss the advantages and disadvantages of statistical and machine learning methods (now prevailing in affect recognition) if compared with other knowledge-based methods.

2   Corpus Description

We collected, with a WoZ study, thirty speech-based dialogues (with 907 moves overall) from subjects between 21 and 28 years of age, equidistributed by gender and background (in computer science or in humanities). After a first analysis of the data, we noticed that different signs of social attitude could be observed by looking at their prosodic or their linguistic characteristics. Especially when the moves were long, they could be differentiated into several parts (segments), each showing different combinations of acoustic and linguistic signs: cf. the discussion on adequate units of analysis in (Batliner et al., 2003; Nicholas et al., 2006, Liscombe et al., 2005). Some examples:

> "Vabbé (Come on, with a neutral prosody), meglio così insomma" (So much the better, all in all!, with a light laughter)

> "Mmm (with a prosody of 'I'm thinking') caffè d'orzo, biscotti e cornetto vuoto" (barley coffee, biscuits and an empty croissant, with a neutral prosody)

Table 1. Our markup language for signs of social attitude

Signs with definition
Linguistic signs
Friendly self-introduction: The subjects introduce themselves with a friendly attitude (e.g. by giving their name or by explaining the reasons why they are participating in the dialogue).
Colloquial style: The subject employs a current language, dialectal forms, proverbs etc.
Talks about self: The subjects provide more personal information about themselves than requested by the agent.
Personal questions to the agent: The subject tries to know something about the agent's preferences, lifestyle etc., or to give it suggestions in the domain.
Humor and irony: The subjects make some kind of verbal joke in their move.
Positive or negative comments: The subjects comment the agent's behavior, experience, domain knowledge, etc.
Friendly farewell: This may consist in using a friendly farewell form or in asking to carry-on the dialogue.
Acoustic signs
Agreement: The dialogue segment displays a prosody of agreement with the system.
Friendly prosody: The dialogue segment displays a friendly prosody.
Laughter: The dialogue segment displays a smile or laughter.
Neutral: The dialogue segment does not display any affective prosody.
Negative prosody: The dialogue segment displays a negative prosody.
I'm thinking: The dialogue segment displays, in its prosody, a reflection attitude.

We therefore decided to preprocess the corpus as follows:

a. we isolated the subset of moves which appeared to be clearly 'neutral' from both the linguistic and the acoustic viewpoint (e.g., a *'yes'* or *'no'* with no particular prosody);

b. as 'neutral' moves were prevailing in the corpus, we extracted a sample set, to include it in the analysis as representative of 'neutral' cases;

c. we integrated this sample of neutral moves with all 'potentially non neutral' moves in the dialogues; this combination of the two sets was the corpus we used in our analysis;

    d. we segmented manually the moves in the corpus into 'acoustically homogeneous' segments, by adopting an 'optimal chunking' method: a segment was isolated from the move when a clear switch in prosody was detected. Very long segments resulting from this preliminary chunking were then segmented again according to pauses which were identified, in the transcript, with full points, semicolons and dots;

    e. three PhD students labelled independently the corpus with an acoustic-oriented and a linguistic-oriented markup language (Table 1). Acoustic labelling was done at the segment-level, linguistic labelling at the move-level; overlapping between linguistic signs was allowed.

These are the reasons why we decided to label our corpus according to linguistic and acoustic criteria at different grain size:

a. Linguistic analysis is aimed at recognizing in a user move the information to employ in selecting the next system move.

Example 1a:

    S: Hi' my name is Valentina...

    U: What should I do? (neutral)

    S: To start, I'm going to ask you some information about your eating habits. What did you eat at dinner, yesterday?

Example 1b:

    S: Hi, my name is Valentina.

    U: Hi Valentina, my name is Carlo and I'm happy to interact with you (friendly self-introduction)

    S: Hi Carlo, good to hear your interest! I hope you'll find our dialogue useful. I'll, first of all, ask you some information about your eating habits. OK?

Example 2a:

    S: Do you believe your weight is correct?

    U: No (neutral)

    S: Will you tell me something more? Which is your weight and height?

Example 2b:

    S: Do you believe your weight is correct?

    U: No, I am a bit overweight, I would like to loose some kilos (talks about self)

    S: Good that you care for your fitness! ...

At the same time, as far as the dialogue goes on, linguistic signs discovered in the dialogue history contribute to build a dynamic image of the social attitude of the user towards the ECA that is used, as well, in adapting the dialogue (de Rosis et al., 2006).

b. Acoustic analysis is aimed at enriching the linguistic connotation of moves with information about their prosody (intonation). When the segment corresponds to an entire move, acoustic parameters just refine the linguistic description. When several acoustically different segments are isolated in a single move, the variation of prosody within a move may help in interpreting its meaning and reducing the risk of errors. In the next Section, we will see some examples of this kind of recognition. Our corpus includes 1020 segments overall, with the frequency of labels (majority agreement among raters) that is shown in the second column of Table 2: we omit from this table the linguistic sign of 'humour and irony' (with a low frequency) and will illustrate columns 3 and 4 of this table in the next Section. In last coloumn we provide Cohen's

Kappa statistics as an estimates of interrater reliability. Overall, our markup language proved to be quite reliable (Di Eugenio, 2000), although some of the signs we wanted to label were rather fuzzy from the conceptual viewpoint.

Table 2. Prevalence of linguistic and acoustic signs of social attitude in our corpus

Linguistic labels	Frequency	Recall	Precision	Kappa
Friendly self-introduction	2%	99.5	37.5	0.87
Friendly farewell	3%	99.5	38.9	0.65
Colloquial style	3%	75.9	11.7	0.70
Question about the agent	6%	85.2	30.9	0.56
Talks about self	16%	78.5	48.9	0.64
Positive comment	5%	4.3	66.7	0.42
Neutral-l	56%	48.4	94.9	0.53
Negative comment-l	3%	24.0	60.0	0.42
Acoustic labels				
Agreement	5 %	47.1	21.4	0.96
Friendly prosody	14 %	24.5	20.9	0.83
Laughter	9 %	44.7	23.8	0.98
I'm thinking	21 %	57.5	62.4	0.91
Neutral-p	43 %	32.6	58.8	0.76
Negative comment-p	9 %	19.6	12.4	0.94

3 Sign Recognition Method

3.1 Acoustic Analysis of Segments

For each segment, we first computed a voiced-unvoiced decision. For each voiced sub-segment, a prosodic feature vector consisting of 73 features (69 for duration, energy, and pitch, and 4 for jitter/shimmer) was computed; subsequently, minimum, maximum, and mean values were calculated for each segment, resulting in a total of 219 acoustic features. This approach is fully independent of linguistic (word) information: we do not need any word segmentation, and we do not use acoustic features such as Mel Frequency Cepstral Coefficients (MFCCs). These features on the one hand have proved to be competitive for classifying affective speech, on the other hand implicitly contain word information, so that a strict separation of linguistic and acoustic modelling would no longer have been possible. As classifier, we used Linear Discriminant Analysis; with Principal Component Analysis, the 219 features were reduced to 50 features. As we are faced with a strong sparse data problem - very few speakers, and some of the classes could be observed only for some of the speakers - we decided in favour of leave-one-case-out; our classification is thus not speaker-independent.

Results of this analysis are described, in terms of recall and precision, in the third and fourth column of Table 2, lower part. I'm thinking seems to be the best sign to recognize; Negative comment-p, Agreement and Friendly prosody the most difficult ones. However, I'm thinking is not a specific sign of social attitude: it is rather a sign of 'doubt' or of a reflexive personality trait. We thought how to possibly compact the six signs, to increase the recall rate. A plausible combination might assemble all 'positive' signs (Agreement, Friendly prosody), the 'non positive' ones (Neutral-p and Negative comment-p) and leave separate the sign of doubt (I'm thinking): this would produce a 42% recall for the 'positive' signs and a 62% for the 'non positive' ones. This idea was confirmed by a careful analysis of results of acoustic analysis of individual moves, in which we could notice that the distinction between Agreement and Friendly prosody was quite fuzzy.

3.2 Linguistic Analysis of Moves

As we anticipated in the Introduction, we improved our original keyword-based recognition method by applying a bayesian classifier. An input text is categorized as 'showing a particular sign of social attitude' if it includes some word sequences belonging to *semantic categories* which are defined as 'salient' for the considered sign. More in detail: bayesian classification enables associating with every string (segment or full move) a value of a-posteriori probability for every sign of social attitude. Given: the set S of signs of social attitude that may be displayed in the language, with $S = \{s_1,..., s_j,...,s_n\}$; a set C of semantic categories of word sequences in the language, with $C = \{c_1,..., c_h,...,c_m\}$; a mapping between signs and categories, according to which the categories $c_h, c_k,...,c_z$ are considered 'salient' for the sign s_j. (E.g., the categories 'Greetings', 'Self-introduction', and 'Ciao' are defined as salient for the Friendly self-introduction sign); a combination $V(c_h, c_k...,c_z)$ of truth values for the categories $c_h, c_k,...,c_z$, denoting their presence in a given sentence. (E.g., the combination (0,1,1) for the set $\{c_1, c_2,...,c_3\}$ denotes that 'Greetings' is absent while 'Self-introduction' and 'Ciao' are present in a sentence, like in "Hi, my name is Carlo"); prior probabilities $P(s_j)$ of the sign s_j in the sentences of the language and $P(V(c_h, c_k,...,c_z))$ for the combination of truth values $V(c_h, c_k,...,c_z)$ in the language (E.g. 4 % of sentences in the language include a 'Self-introduction' and a 'Ciao' and no 'Greetings'); a conditional probability $P(V(c_h, c_k,...,c_z)| s_j)$ for the combination $V(c_h, c_k,...,c_z)$ in the sentences displaying the sign s_j. (E.g., 85 % of the sentences showing a sign of Friendly self-introduction include a 'Self-introduction' and a 'Ciao' and no 'Greetings'), and given: result of the lexical analysis of the string m_h, as a combination of truth values for all the elements in $(c_1,...,c_h,...,c_m)$, the probability that the string m_h displays the sign s_j may be computed as $P(s_j|V(c_h, c_k,...,c_z)) = P(V(c_h, c_k,...,c_z)| s_j) * P(s_j) / P(V(c_h, c_k,...,c_z))$.

Notice that this formula does not assume the conditional independence of semantic categories given a sign. All parameters (prior and conditional probabilities) are extimated as observed frequencies in the annotated corpus.

The recognition performance of the various signs in our corpus are shown, again in terms of recall and precision, in the third and fourth column of Table 2, upper part. This table clearly shows that Positive and Negative comments are the most difficult signs to recognize, while the recall for the other signs is quite good: we will come back to this problem in the next session and will describe, in the Discussion, how we are working at improving the recognition of these features.

4 Integration of Acoustic and Linguistic Features

We did two types of integration: a) combination of both features at the segment level, and b) linguistic analysis at the move level, integrated with acoustic features at the segment level. Let us describe the two methods in more detail.

4.1 Linguistic and Acoustic Analysis at the Segment Level

Prior to describing how we combined the two sets of features we show, in Table 3, the confusion matrix for acoustic analysis. This table shows that confounding with Neutral-p is the main source of reduction of recall for all signs; negative prosody (NegativeComment-p) is often confounded also with Friendly prosody and Laughter.

Table 3. Confusion matrix for acoustic signs

	Agr	Frint	Laughter	I'mThinking	Neutral-p	NegativeComment-p
Agreement	**47.1**	7.8	11.8	3.9	17.6	11.8
Friendly prosody	12.9	**24.5**	12.2	7.2	26.6	16.5
Laughter	10.6	9.4	**44.7**	7.1	17.6	10.6
I'm thinking	5.1	5.6	11.2	**57.5**	9.8	10.7
Neutral-p	9.1	19.4	13.7	10.3	**32.6**	15.0
Negativecomment-p	10.9	21.7	16.3	12.0	19.6	**19.6**

To integrate acoustic with linguistic features, we assigned to the segments the same linguistic labels that were assigned by raters to the whole move. An example: the following move: "No! / La frutta... qualche frutta / Ma non tutte."(No! / Fruits... some fruits / But not all fruits) was divided into three segments, all labelled as Negative comment-l and Familiar style, as the whole move was labelled.

Differently from acoustic analysis, our bayesian classifier does not force us to select only one sign, but enables us to consider cases of presence of multiple signs; as a matter of fact, some segments displayed several linguistic signs of social attitude at the same time: see the previous example, but also the following one:

"Vabbé, ma non mangio cose fritte ogni giorno!" (OK, but I don't eat fried food every day!): a Talk about self and a Negative comment-l, with a Familiar style.

However, to produce a confusion matrix for linguistic analysis (in Table 4) to compare with the matrix for the acoustic one, we selected, for every segment, only the sign with maximum probability value. As a consequence, if data in the diagonal of this table are compared with the recall data in Table 2, one may notice a reduction of recall for all signs.

We analysed, in particular, the segments belonging to the most problematic category: negative prosody. An accurate analysis of these segments enabled us to understand the nature of this data.

Table 4. Confusion matrix for linguistic signs

	Fsi	Ffwell	Collst	Qagt	Talks	PosC	Neut-l	NegC-l
Friendly self-introduction	**64.3**	28.6	0.0	0.0	7.1	0.0	0.0	0.0
Friendly farewell	0.0	**70.8**	12.5	0.0	4.2	0.0	12.5	0.0
Colloquial style	0.0	0.0	**57.1**	14.3	14.3	0.0	14.3	0.0
Question about the agent	0.0	0.0	0.0	**72.2**	22.2	0.0	5.6	0.0
Talks about self	0.0	0.0	5.4	1.2	**74.7**	1.2	12.7	4.8
Positive comment	0.0	7.1	25.0	14.3	10.7	**25.0**	17.9	0.0
Neutral-l	0.0	1.1	9.8	6.6	24.4	3.4	**49.5**	5.1
Negative comment-l	0.0	0.0	20.4	16.7	24.1	1.9	20.4	**16.7**

As displayed in Table 3, the recognition rate of these segments was quite low (less than 20%). If the result of linguistic analysis was added to the acoustic one, the recognition rate of 'acoustically and linguistically negative' cases increased to 31%: a slight increase, then. But, by looking deeper into the segments, we found that cases in which the subjects expressed their negative attitude both linguistically and acoustically were really 'extreme' cases. An example:

"Madò, ma ci metti di tempo a rispondere!" (My god, it takes you a lot to answer!): acoustically and linguistically negative.
Comment: the subject seems to be really bored by the ECA's behavior.

In the majority of cases, on the contrary, the segments that were annotated as 'showing acoustic signs of negative attitude' displayed multiple (and apparently inconsistent) results of acoustic and linguistic analysis. This was not an inconsistency though, but rather a realistic description of the subjects' behavior when reacting negatively to an ECA's move. Some examples:

"Cioè, ma non c'entra con quello che ti ho detto!" (But this has'n got anything to do with what I said!): acoustically: a Laughter; linguistically: a Negative comment and a Talk about self.
Comment: the subject expresses his negative evaluation of the ECA's behavior with a bit of irony and politeness.

"Eh però, quando tu parli di frutta secca non mi parli di dosi!" (Hey, but when you talk about dried fruits, you don't say anything about doses!); acoustically: a Friendly prosody; linguistically: a Negative comment and a Question about the agent.
Comment: again, the subject expresses friendly his negative evaluation of the ECA's behavior.

"No, mi auguro di no!" (No, I hope no!); acoustically: neutral prosody; linguistically: a Negative comment-l and a Colloquial style.
Comment: in this case, the subject expresses his negative evaluation of the ECA's behavior linguistically, but with a neutral prosody and by smoothing it with a colloquial style.

To summarise: apparently, our subjects tended to express their negative attitude towards an ECA's move by avoiding to be rude: they smoothed their negative comments by introducing some bit of politeness in the prosody (in the form of laughter or smiling), or in the language (in the form of colloquial style or other).

To integrate acoustic with linguistic signs, we then decided to compact the 8x6 combinations of labels into a lower number of categories, suited to adaptation purposes. The first need of adaptation is to distinguish, as accurately as possible, between a 'negative', 'neutral' or 'warm' attitude of the user. We labelled the corpus of segments with an automatic rule-based annotation which compacted the raters' acoustic and linguistic labelling into four-categories, according to the following rules (rules are applied subsequently until one of them is satisfied):

IF (Neutral-p or I'mThinking) and Neutral-l THEN NEUTRAL

A segment is labelled as Neutral if it was acoustically labelled as Neutral–p or I'm thinking, and linguistically as Neutral-l;

IF (NegativeComment-p or NegativeComment-l) THEN NEGATIVE

A segment is labelled as Negative if it was labelled as such either acoustically or linguistically;

IF ((¬Neutral-p ∧ ¬I'mThinking) xor (¬Neutral-l)) ∧¬NegativeComment-p ∧ ¬NegativeComment-l
THEN LIGHT-WARM

A segment is labelled as Light-warm if it was annotated either acoustically or linguistically as displaying some positive sign

IF (¬Neutral-p ∧ ¬I'mThinking ∧ ¬NegativeComment-p ∧ ¬Neutral-l ∧ ¬NegativeComment-l)
THEN WARM

A segment is labelled as Warm if it was annotated both acoustically and linguistically as displaying some positive sign.

For every segment, we had a 'probability value' for each of the 8+6 signs. We processed this dataset with K2 learning algorithm (k-fold cross validation, with k=number of segments with WEKA) and got a recall of 90.05%; results of this analysis are displayed in Table 5. The higher level of accuracy in the recognition of the four categories (if compared with tables 3 and 4) is due, on one hand, to reduction of the number of features from 14 to 4 and, on the other hand, to integration of linguistic and acoustic analysis. Due to space issues, we only provide results for the combination of the two categories of signs, while we omit the separate confusion matrices. A positive aspect of this recognition method is that the only non negligible confusion is between Light-warm and Warm attitude: a kind of confounding that is not very dangerous for adaptation. Notice that again, due to sparse data, this cross-validation was not performed speaker-independently.

Table 5. Confusion matrix for the combination of acoustic and linguistic features

	Negative	Neutral	Light-warm	Warm	Recall	Precision
Negative	232 (94 %)	11 (4 %)	1 (.5 %)	4 (1.5 %)	.94	.94
Neutral	2 (1 %)	174 (95 %)	8 (4 %)	0	.95	.84
Light-warm	10 (3 %)	23 (6 %)	317 (85 %)	21 (6 %)	.85	.92
Warm	3 (1 %)	0	19 (9 %)	201 (90 %)	.90	.89

4.2 Acoustic Analysis as Complementary to the Linguistic One

This is an ongoing work that we performed, so far, only on a subset of the moves. Every move was first analyzed to recognize linguistic signs of social attitude; this information was then integrated with the recognized prosodic signs in every 'acoustically significant' segment of the move. This analysis, together with possible information about the context in which the move was uttered by the subject (previous ECA's move) enabled us to have a deeper insight into the subject's attitude towards the ECA and its suggestions. Some examples:

"E i dolci? Fanno proprio male i dolci?" ("How about sweets? Do sweets harm?"). This is a linguistically neutral move which, in its first segment, does not show any particular affective prosody. In the second one, however, some light laughter is shown. This variation of prosody seems to display a little embarrassment of the subject in admitting her preferences.

"No, finora non ho avuto questi problemi; il fegato funziona, e i reni pure". ("No, so far I had no problem; my liver works, my kidneys too."). This move comes after a system's information of the possible negative consequences of the dietary habits declared by the subject. In the move, the subject talks about self, initially with a negative prosody, then with a neutral one, and finally with a friendly prosody. Overall, this change of prosody during the move seems to display the subject's intention to smooth her objection to the system's remark.

"Vabbé, ma non mangio cose fritte ogni giorno: ogni tanto, una volta a settimana!" ("OK, but I don't eat fried food every day: from time to time, once a week!"). The context of this move is similar to that of the previous example: information about negative effects of fried food. The subject replies by describing his eating habits with a colloquial style but introduces, at the same time, a negative prosody in the beginning of the move, probably to show his disagreement with the ECA's evaluation.

These examples demonstrate that analysis at the move level which integrates linguistic interpretation of the utterance with recognition of the *variation of prosody* during the utterance itself might provide more information than a simple integration of the two kinds of features at the segment level. Rather than machine learning methods, rule-based recognition criteria including consideration of the context seem to be more appropriate to this task.

5 Discussion and Future Work

As we said in the Introduction, recognition of the affective state should consider on one hand the aspects that may improve interaction and, on the other hand, those that available methods enable recognizing with a reasonable level of accuracy. In this paper, we proposed two methods for recognizing social attitude of users in speech-based human-ECA dialogues; in the first one, we showed how integrating linguistic and acoustic features at the segment level enables distinguishing between 'levels of social attitude' (negative, neutral, light or strong warm) with a good level of accuracy (90%). In the second one we proposed, with some examples, how combining language analysis at the move level with acoustic analysis at the segment level might enable deeper and more refined understanding of the user attitude towards the ECA. Research about this second method is still ongoing, and we plan to produce some results in the near future.

Our research builds upon a consolidated experience in the domain. Several studies investigated how to assess affective situations from spoken language, by combining prosodic information with language features: in all these studies, language features had a supporting role to prosodic ones, which were the main recognition factors. Lee et al. (2002) found that, by adding language features to acoustic information, the recognition rate of 'negative' and 'non negative' emotions increased considerably. Ang et al. (2002) integrated prosodic features with a trigram model to discriminate 'neutral' from 'annoyed and frustrated' conditions in call center dialogues. Litman and Forbes-Riley (2003) combined prosodic features with lexical items to recognize the valence of emotions in spoken tutoring dialogues, by finding that the combined feature set outperformed the speech-only set. In attempting to recognize fear, anger, relief and sadness in human-human medical dialogues, Devillers and Vidrascu (2006) separated linguistic analysis from paralinguistic one, by obtaining a better performance with lexical cues than with acoustic features. In working with WoZ data, Batliner et al. (2003) demonstrated that the combination of prosodic with linguistic and conversational data yielded better results than the use of prosody only, for recognizing 'troubles in communication', that is the beginning of emotionally critical phases in a dialogue.

Language analysis methods that may be applied in the recognition of affective features range from simple keyword recognition to more sophisticated approaches. Statistical machine learning methods are now a very popular approach in this domain, after the initial rule-based methods that were applied, e.g., to recognize doubt (Carberry et al., 2002). Statistical methods have their advantages in enabling a quick analysis of the data distributions. However, in building criteria that may be applied to adapt conversational systems to the user attitude, a deeper inspection of the corpus, with some reasoning on the patterns they display, may insure more careful adaptation. Patterns discovered may be formalized, again in terms of decision rules. In the near future, we plan to continue this work by collecting more dialogues, to overcome the sparse data problem. In addition, we are focusing our present activity on the recognition of positive and negative comments with sentiment analysis methods. The main idea is to consider the language processing methods which have been applied to opinion extraction, to reflect on their limits and on how beliefs may be inferred gradually, in conditions of uncertainty and by carefully considering various forms of context (de Rosis and Novielli, 2007).

Acknowledgements. This work was financed, in part, by HUMAINE, the European Human-Machine Interaction Network on Emotion (EC Contract 507422). We sincerely acknowledge Irene Mazzotta for cooperating to the WoZ studies in which the corpus of dialogues analyzed in this paper was collected.

References

Andersen, P.A., Guerrero, L.K.: Handbook of Communication and Emotions. Research, theory, applications and contexts. Academic Press, New York (1998)

Ang, J., Dhillon, R., Krupsky, A., Shriberg, E., Stolcke, A.: Prosody-based automatic detection of annoyance and frustration in human-computer dialog. In: ICSLP, pp. 2037–2040 (2002)

Bailenson, J.N., Swinth, K.R., Hoyt, C.L., Persky, S., Dimov, A., Blascovich, J.: The independent and interactive effects of embodied agents appearance and behavior on self-report, cognitive and behavioral markers of copresence in Immersive Virtual Environments. PRESENCE 14(4), 379–393 (2005)

Batliner, A., Fischer, K., Huber, R., Spilker, J., Nöth, E.: How to Find Trouble in Communication. In: Speech Communication 40, 117–143 (2003)

Bickmore, T., Cassell, J.: Social Dialogue with Embodied Conversational Agents. In: van Kuppevelt, J., Dybkjaer, L., Bernsen, N. (eds.) Advances in Natural, Multimodal Dialogue Systems, pp. 1–32. Kluwer Academic, New York (2005)

Blascovich, J.: Social influences within immersive virtual environments. In: Schroeder, R. (ed.) The social life of avatars, pp. 127–145. Springer, London (2002)

Carberry, S., Lambert, L., Schroeder, L.: Towards recognizing and conveying an attitude of doubt via natural language. Applied Artificial Intelligence 16(7), 495–517 (2002) de Rosis, F., Novielli, N.: From language to thought: inferring opinions and beliefs from verbal behavior. In: AISB '07, Mindful Environments Workshop (2007)

de Rosis, F., Novielli, N., Carofiglio, V., Cavalluzzi, A., De Carolis, B.: User modeling and adaptation in health promotion dialogs with an animated character. In: Journal of Biomedical Informatics, Special Issue on 'Dialog systems for health communications 39(5), 514–531 (2006)

de Rosis, F., Novielli, N., Mazzotta, I.: Factors affecting the social attitude of users towards an ECA and how it is Worded. Submitted.

Devillers, L., Vidrascu, L.: Real-life emotions detection with lexical and paralinguistic cues on human-human call center dialogs. In: INTERSPEECH, pp. 801–804 (2006)

Di Eugenio, B.: On the usage of Kappa to evaluate agreement on coding tasks. In: LREC2000: Second International Conference on Language Resources and Evaluation, pp. 441–444 (2000)

Hoorn, J.F., Konijn, E.A.: Perceiving and Experiencing Fictional Characters: An integrative account. Japanese Psychological Research 45(4), 250–268 (2003)

Lee, C.M., Narayanan, S.S., Pieraccini, R.: Combining acoustic and language information for emotion recognition. In: ICSPL, pp. 873–876 (2002)

Liscombe, J., Riccardi, G., Hakkani-Tür, D.: Using context to improve emotion detection in spoken dialogue systems. In: Interspeech (2005)

Litman, D., Forbes-Riley, K., Silliman, S.: Towards emotion prediction in spoken tutoring dialogues. In: HLT/NAACL, pp. 52–54 (2003)

Nicholas, G., Rotaru, M., Litman, D.J.: Exploiting word-level features for emotion prediction. In: IEEE/ACL Workshop on Spoken Language Technology (SLT) (2006)

Paiva, A. (ed.): Empathic Agents. Workshop in conjunction with AAMAS (2004)

Polhemus, L., Shih, L.-F., Swan, K.: Virtual interactivity: the representation of social presence in an on line discussion. Annual Meeting of the American Educational Research Association (2001)

Rettie, R.: Connectedness, awareness and social presence. In: PRESENCE, online proceedings (2003)

Yu, C., Aoki, P.M., Woodruff, A.: Detecting user engagement in everyday conversations. In: ICSLP, pp. 1329–1332 (2004)

Assessing Sentiment of Text by Semantic Dependency and Contextual Valence Analysis

Mostafa Al Masum Shaikh[1], Helmut Prendinger[2], and Ishizuka Mitsuru[1]

[1] Department of Information and Communication Engineering, University of Tokyo,
7-3-1 Hongo, Bunkyo-ku, 113-8656 Tokyo, Japan
mostafa@mi.ci.i.u-tokyo.ac.jp, ishizuka@i.u-tokyo.ac.jp
[2] Digital Contents and Media Sciences Research Division, National Institute of Informatics,
2-1-2 Hitotsubashi, Chiyoda-ku, 101-8430 Tokyo, Japan
helmut@nii.ac.jp

Abstract. Text is not only an important medium to describe facts and events, but also to effectively communicate information about the writer's (positive or negative) sentiment underlying an opinion, and an affect or emotion (e.g. happy, fearful, surprised etc.). We consider sentiment assessment and emotion sensing from text as two different problems, whereby sentiment assessment is a prior task to emotion sensing. This paper presents an approach to sentiment assessment, i.e. the recognition of negative or positive sense of a sentence. We perform semantic dependency analysis on the semantic verb frames of each sentence, and apply a set of rules to each dependency relation to calculate the contextual valence of the whole sentence. By employing a domain-independent, rule-based approach, our system is able to automatically identify sentence-level sentiment. Empirical results indicate that our system outperforms another state-of-the-art approach.

1 Introduction

Sensing of affective information would benefit the development of text based affective user interfaces because the words people use to express their feelings can be important clues to their mental, social, and physical state [15]. Examples of such applications are the affective text analyzer [2,5,18], the affective email-client [9], empathic chat, information and tutoring tools, computational humor [20], affective lexicon [22], affective information recognizer [12,7], and psycholinguistic analysis [6,15]. We expect that more are likely to appear with the increase of textual resources on the internet (e.g. blogs, reviews etc.). We are interested in identifying positive and negative sentiment as well as emotions (e.g. happiness, sadness etc.) conveyed through text. Our approach relies on the semantic relationship between the structure of natural language and contextual valence of the words used in a given text. The scope of this paper, however, is limited to sentiment assessment.

There are four main factors that distinguish our work from others. First, we have integrated semantic processing of input text by dependency analysis on semantic verb-frame(s) of each sentence. Second, cognitive and commonsense knowledge resources have been utilized to assign a prior valence to a set of words, which

A. Paiva, R. Prada, and R.W. Picard (Eds.): ACII 2007, LNCS 4738, pp. 191–202, 2007.

leverage scoring for new words. Third, a set of rules to calculate contextual-valence has been implemented to support word sense disambiguation. Finally, instead of using machine learning or relying on text corpora, we followed a rule-based approach to assess the valence of each semantic verb frame in a sentence, and then assign an overall valence to the whole sentence(s) by applying dedicated rules. This paradigm of content analysis allows assessing sentiments from texts of any genre (e.g. movie or product review, news articles, blogs, etc.) at the sentence level.

2   Background and Related Work

Sentiment has been studied at three different levels: word, sentence, and document level. There are methods to estimate positive or negative sentiment of words [21,1], phrases and sentences [7,26], and documents [5]. Previous approaches for assessing sentiment from text are based on one or a combination of the following techniques: keyword spotting, lexical affinity [22,8], statistical methods [15], a dictionary of affective concepts and lexicon, commonsense knowledgebase [9], fuzzy logic [19], knowledge-base from facial expression [3], machine learning [7,25], domain specific classification [13], and valence assignment [16,26,18].

Some researchers proposed machine learning methods to identify words and phrases that signal subjectivity. For example, Wiebe and Mihalcea [23] stated that subjectivity is a property that can be associated with word senses, and hence word sense disambiguation can directly benefit subjectivity annotations. Turney [21] and Wiebe [24] concentrated on learning adjectives and adjectival phrases, whereas Wiebe et al. [25] focused on nouns. Riloff et al [17] extracted patterns for subjective expressions as well.

According to a linguistic survey [15], only 4% of the words used in written texts carry affective content. This finding shows that using affective lexicons is not sufficient to recognize affective information from text. It also indicates the difficulty of employing methods like machine learning, keyword spotting, and lexical affinity (see [9] for a detailed criticism). Statistical methods are well suited for psycholinguistic analysis (e.g. [15]) of persons' attitudes, social-class, standards etc. from documents rather than individual sentences. Fuzzy logic based approaches assess input text by spotting regular verbs and adjectives that have pre-assigned affective categories (centrality and intensity), but ignore their semantic relationships. Similar to machine learning, this technique cannot be used for analyzing smaller text units such as sentences.

A number of researchers have explored to automatically learn words and phrases with prior positive or negative valence (e.g., [6,21,26]). By contrast, we begin with a lexicon of words by calculating prior valences using WordNet [2] and ConceptNet [10], and assign the contextual valence [16] of phrases by applying a set of rules. Kim and Hovy [7], Hu and Liu [5], and Wilson et al [26] multiply or count the prior valences of opinion bearing words of the sentence. They also consider local negation to reverse valence but they do not perform a deep analysis (e.g. semantic dependency), as our approach does. Nasukawa and Yi [13] classify the contextual valence of sentiment expressions (as we do) and also expressions that are about specific items based on manually developed patterns and domain specific corpora, whereas our approach is domain independent. The use of domain specific corpora for sentiment classification of text has shown very promising results regarding sentiment analysis of product-reviews and blogs, but it requires special tuning of data in order to build category-specific classifiers for each text-domain (e.g. product review or movie review).

3 Our Approach

We propose a pipelined architecture with the following phases: Parse, Process, and Assess. Briefly, the Parse phase implements semantic parsing, i.e., it performs dependency analysis on the words and outputs triplet(s) of subject, verb, and object according to each semantic verb frame of the input sentence(s). In the Process phase rules are applied to assign contextual-valences to the triplet(s). Finally, in the Assess phase an overall valence is assigned to each input sentence(s).

3.1 Semantic Parsing

For each input sentence the Semantic Parsing Module outputs triplet(s) consisting of a subject or agent, a verb, and an object. Each member of the triplet may or may not have associated attribute(s) (e.g. adjective, adverb etc.). We first obtain XML-formatted syntactic and functional dependency information of each word of the input text using the Machinese Syntax parser [11] and this output constitutes the basis for further processing to generate the triplet(s). Since a triplet is initiated for each occurrence of a verb in the sentence, semantic parsing may extract more than one such triplet if multiple verbs are present in the sentence.

Basically a triplet encodes information about "who is associated with what and how" with a notion of semantic verb frame [2] analysis. For example, the input sentence *"Eight members of a Canadian family vacationing in Lebanon were killed Sunday in an Israeli air raid that hit a Lebanese town on the border with Israel, Canadian and Lebanese officials said."* produces three triplets as shown in Table 1.

Table 1. Triplet output of Semantic Parsing for the sentence given above

Senses processed by SenseNet	
Triplet 1	[[['Subject-Name:', 'raid', 'Subject-Type:', 'concept', 'Subject-Attrib:', ['A ABS: Israeli', 'N NOM SG: air']], ['Action-Name:', 'kill', 'Action Status:', 'Past Particle', 'Action-Attrib:', ['passive', 'time: Sunday', 'place: Lebanon']], ['Object-Name:', 'member', 'Object-Type:', 'person', 'Object-Attrib:', ['NUM: eight', 'A ABS: Canadian', 'N NOM: family', 'N NOM: vacationing']]]
Triplet 2	[[['Subject-Name:', 'raid', 'Subject-Type:', 'concept', 'Subject-Attrib:', []], ['Action-Name:', 'hit', 'Action-Status:', 'Past ', 'Action-Attrib:', []], ['Object-Name:', 'town', 'Object-Type:', 'N NOM', 'Object-Attrib:', ['A ABS: Lebanese', 'place: border', 'N NOM: Israel']]]
Triplet 3	[[['Subject-Name:', 'official', 'Subject-Type:', 'Object', 'Subject-Attrib:', ['A ABS: Canadian', 'A ABS: Lebanese']], ['Action-Name:', 'say', 'Action-Status:', 'Past ', 'Action-Attrib:', []], ['Object-Name:', '', 'Object-Type:', '', 'Object-Attrib:', []]]]

3.2 The Knowledgebase

A common approach to sentiment assessment is to start with a set of lexicons whose entries are assigned a prior valence indicating whether a word, out of context, evokes something positive or something negative [26]. Our system maintains a list of scored verbs, adjectives, adverbs, nouns and named entities. For instance, 'destroy' usually bears a negative connotation, whereas 'develop' has a positive connotation. Cognitive and commonsense knowledge resources have been utilized to assign prior valence to the lexicon entries, and the resources also leverage scoring of new words, as explained in the following paragraphs.

Scoring a list of Verbs, Adjectives and Adverbs. A group of eight judges have manually counted the number of positive and negative senses of each word of our selected list[1] of verbs, adjectives, and adverbs according to the contextual explanations of each sense found in WordNet 2.1 [2]. A judge's score of a verb is stored in the format: verb-word [Positive-Sense Count, Negative-Sense Count, Prospective Value, Praiseworthy Value, Prior Valence]. The Prior Valence, Prospective and Praiseworthy values indicate the lexical affinity of a word with respect to "good" or "bad", "desirable" or "undesirable", and "praiseworthiness" or "blameworthiness", respectively. Prospective and Praiseworthy values of the words are not used in this system (we use it for the detailed emotion analysis).

We will explain the scoring procedure by an example. For the word 'kill' WordNet 2.1 outputs 15 senses as a verb and each of the senses is accompanied by at least an example sentence or explanation to clarify the contextual meaning of the verb. Each judge reads each meaning of the sense and decides whether it evokes positive or negative sentiment. E.g., for the word "kill", one judge has considered 13 senses as negative and 2 senses as positive, which are stored in the scoring sheet. In this manner we collected the scores for all the listed words.

Formula 1 assigns a prior valence (i.e., a value between -5 to 5) to each selected word. A subset of verbs (e.g. like, love, hate, kiss etc.) from the verb list is marked by a tag named *<affect>* to indicate these verbs have strong affective connotation regarding preference or dislike. This subset is formed according to WordNet-Affect [22].

$$c(w) = \frac{\sum_{i=1}^{m}((\frac{p_i - n_i}{N_i}) * 5.0))}{m} \tag{1}$$

Here, $c(w)$ = Prior Valence of word w, whereby $-5 \leq c(w) \leq +5$
m = Number of judges (8)
p_i = The number of positive senses assigned by i-th judge, for word w
n_i = The number of negative senses assigned by i-th judge, for word w
N_i = Total number of senses counted by i-th judge for word w

To measure inter-agreement among judges, we used Fleiss' Kappa statistic [4]. The Kappa value for the prior valence assignment task for 723 verbs, 205 phrasal verbs, 237 adjectives related to shape, time, sound, taste/touch, condition, appearance and 711 adjectives related to emotional affinity and 144 adverbs is reliable (κ=0.914).

---

[1] http://www.englishclub.com/vocabulary/

3.2 Correlation Analysis

Pearson correlation coefficients were calculated between judgment averages per PU for each scale, and the full set of acoustic features. It is beyond the scope of this paper to present a full table of results, so we shall present several representative results.

Activation: Though many of the acoustic features gave statistically significant correlation with Activation judgments, 30 features gave correlations that were higher in absolute value than 0.4: 18 were related to pitch, 10 to intensity, and 2 to LTAS. The correlation coefficients were consistently higher for the English speaker's judgments than for the Hebrew speakers. The highest correlation was the upper quartile of normalized pitch, at 0.70, for English speaking listeners, and 0.59 for Hebrew speakers. Voice quality features are conspicuously absent from this group.

Valence: Correlations with Activation, though significant, were far weaker. Only 12 acoustic features had absolute values above 0.25. Only 1 of these is related to pitch – unnormalized pitch minimum. The other 11 are all related to intensity.

3.3 Judgment Groupings and ANOVA

The fine grained judgments carried out by the judges are a potential source of confusion, since personal scales of different judges can easily differ in this type of task. We therefore grouped judgments into more coarse rating classes, in order to highlight the major differences between the different scales and judge groups. Judgments of each group were first averaged, and then assigned to classes, using two partitionings of the range from -3 to 3. **Positive/Negative (PN)** division distinguished between positive and negative average judgments on each scale. **Extreme/Mild (EM)** division distinguished

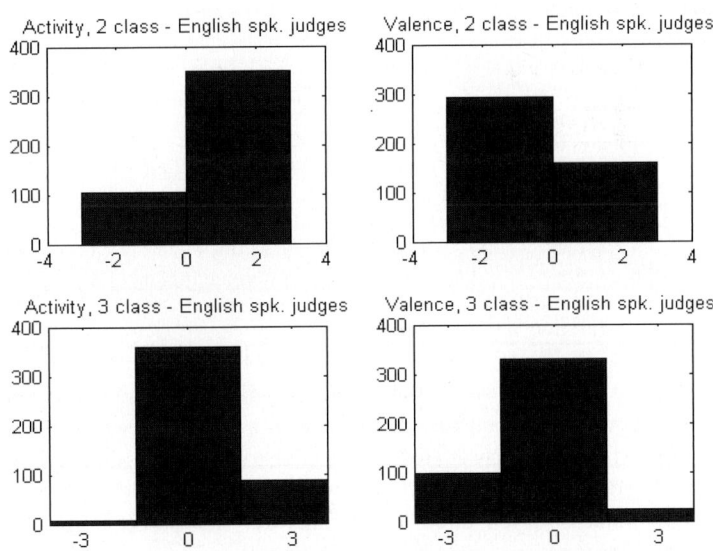

Fig. 1. Distributions of Activation and Valence for English speakers, after scales were repartitioned into 2 and 3 classes

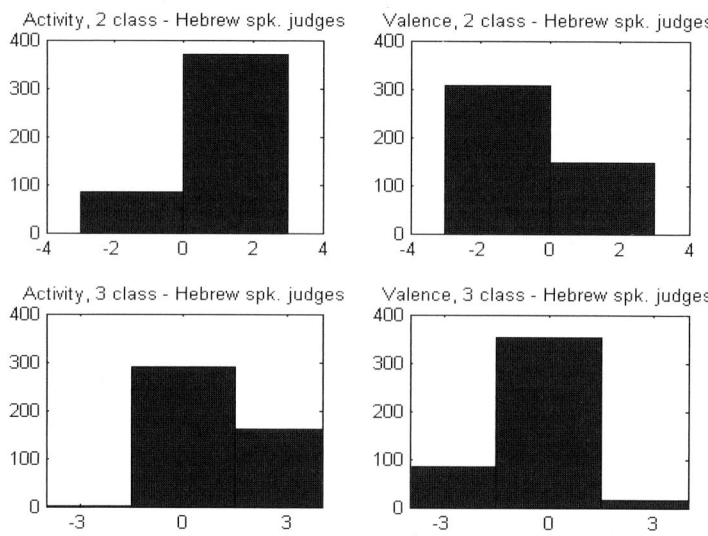

Fig. 2. Distributions of Activation and Valence for Hebrew speakers, after scales were repartitioned into 2 and 3 classes

Table 2. Number of significant features in each ANOVA analysis and breakdown into feature groups

	Hebrew speakers		English speakers	
	Activation	Valence	Activation	Valence
PN (2 classes)	**Total: 56** 24 – pitch 17- intensity 2 – LTAS 12 – voice quality 1 - duration	**Total: 23** 9 – pitch 13- intensity 1 – LTAS	**Total: 59** 26 – pitch 18- intensity 3 – LTAS 11– voice quality 1 - duration	**Total: 25** 8 – pitch 13- intensity 3 – LTAS 1- voice quality
EM (3 classes)	**Total: 59** 28 – pitch 19- intensity 3 – LTAS 8 – voice quality 1 - duration	**Total: 49** 24 – pitch 16- intensity 3 – LTAS 5 – voice quality 1 - duration	**Total: 60** 26 – pitch 21- intensity 3 – LTAS 9 – voice quality 1 - duration	**Total: 61** 28 – pitch 21- intensity 3 – LTAS 8– voice quality 1 - duration

between judgments near zero and extreme judgments. After some experimentation, it was decided to set the class boundaries at -1.5 and 1.5, giving three possible regions on each scale. The different judgments are not evenly distributed across these divisions. For both groups of judges there are relatively few PUs that received high judgments of Valence or low values of Activation. Histograms for each partitioning scheme, each scale, and each listener group appear in Figures 1 and 2.

One way ANOVA was then carried out for each of the divisions (PN and EM), for each group of judges, and for each scale, giving eight different analyses. Considering

variety of less extreme emotions. The actors participating in the soundtrack of the film are world famous actors such as Holly Hunter, Samuel Jackson and others, which ensures that a high degree of acting quality can be expected. Employing professional actors of such renown would probably be outside the budget of most researchers in the field of emotional speech.

A professional teacher of animation techniques selected 11.75 minutes of dialog from the film. These included a bare minimum of background music, and included speech from 8 characters ("Bob", "Helen", "Violet", "Flash", "Frozone", Frozone's wife, "Syndrome" and "Mirage") – 4 male and 4 female. Speech was segmented into PUs using guidelines appearing in the literature on corpus linguistics [9]. The net result was 453 PUs which were split into separate soundfiles. F0 detection was carried out using Praat software [14] and corrected manually by one of the researchers.

2.2 Subjective Evaluation

Subjective evaluation was performed by two groups of subjects. The first group was composed of 8 native American-English speakers (ages 19-28 years, mean age 24.9, 5 men and 3 women, 5 had seen the film). The second group was composed of 9 native Hebrew speakers who had acquired English as a second language in the course of secondary and higher education (ages 25-33 years, mean age 27.7, 5 men and 4 women, 3 had seen the film). Subjects heard the 453 PUs in random order, judging the emotional content per unit on two separate scales – activation and Valence. Both scales contained discrete values between -3 and 3. Since some of the PUs were quite short, for example the word "I" surrounded by long pauses, the judges were also presented with a 3 selection forced choice question: whether each unit was too long, too short, or appropriate in length for evaluating emotional content. A Matlab program with a graphic user interface was written for this purpose, so that subjects could advance through the task at their own pace. They were allowed to replay each PU at their discretion.

2.3 Acoustic Analysis

Each of the PUs was subjected to an extensive acoustic analysis, eventually extracting a set of 100 acoustic features which can be grouped in several subgroups:

Intonation features: this set of features was based on the manually corrected pitch contour. Raw statistics (mean, median, STD, min, max) were calculated per PU. Next, pitch was normalized using the following procedure: all PUs that were judged by all judges, or all except one, to have values of Activation and Valence between -1 and 1, were taken to represent "neutral". The average pitch over these neutral utterances for one speaker was taken as the baseline pitch value for this speaker. From this normalized pitch we then calculated once more the above raw statistics, in semitones. Several regressions/curve fitting algorithms were also applied: linear regression, parabolic regression, and DCT regression using 5 coefficients. Curve fitting was applied using the stylization algorithm described in Praat software. Coefficients taken from these algorithms were also used as features. Finally, two measures of microprosody were derived by calculating the Mean Square Error (MSE) between the DCT regression and the measured contour, and the Praat stylization and the measured contour.

Intensity features: the intensity contour was calculated and normalized using the same procedure as for pitch. An identical set of features was then extracted as for the pitch contour.

Voice quality features: Standard clinical measures of voice quality were calculated using Praat software: jitter, shimmer, NHR, HNR, autocorrelation.

Spectral features: Spectral features were calculated from the Long Term Average Spectrum (LTAS), taken also from Praat. These were slope, frequency of maximum, and standard deviation.

2.4 Statistical Analysis

Several analyses were applied to the data. We first examined the agreement between judgments, both intra- and inter-groups, for each scale separately. We then carried out correlation analysis to see which acoustic parameters were correlated with the subjective judgments. Finally we grouped the judgments into coarser categories and used one way ANOVA to examine which acoustic parameters could distinguish between groups. Several groupings were experimented with.

3 Results

3.1 Agreement Between Judges

Intra group agreement between judgments was performed using two common measures: the Kappa statistic [17] and Kendall's coefficient of concordance [18]. 10 PUs that were judged by 4 or more judges in each group as being too short for judging were excluded from the complete group of 453 PUs. Results are summarized in table I:

Table 1. Agreement between judges in both groups, for both scales

	Hebrew speakers		English speakers	
	Activation	Valence	Activation	Valence
Kappa	0.103	0.098	0.101	0.125
Kendall	0.5261	0.489	0.481	0.56

Kappa is a more severe measure, resulting here in slight agreement between judges for all cases. Kendall's coefficient is a more forgiving measure, resulting here in moderate agreement in all cases, with no major differences between the two groups of listeners (the commonly accepted scale for interpreting the numerical values is: 0.01-0.2: slight agreement, 0.21-0.4: fair agreement, 0.41-0.6: moderate agreement, 0.61-0.8: substantial agreement, 0.81-0.99: almost perfect agreement).

Averages for each scale were calculated separately for each group. These were compared using a Kruskal-Wallis test, which indicated that the means for the two groups were significantly different for the Activation scale, whereas they were not significantly different for the Valence scale.

Moreover, our scoring resembles to the EVA function [6] score that assigns values to a word based on the minimal-path lengths from adjectives 'good' and 'bad'. A word not present in the annotated list is scored by calculating the average valence of its already scored synonyms.

Scoring of Nouns. Since manual scoring is a tedious job and there exist more nouns than the above lists, we employed ConceptNet [10] to assign prior valence to nouns. ConceptNet is a large semantic network of commonsense knowledge which encompasses the spatial, physical, social, temporal, and psychological aspects of everyday life. A value from [-5,5] is assigned as the valence to an input noun or concept. (Here we use noun and concept synonymously.) To assign valence to a concept, the system collects all concepts which are semantically connected to other concepts and from other concepts to the input concept found in the ConceptNet. The returned entries are separated into two groups depending on their semantic relations. The entries of the first group correspond to relationships like 'IsA', 'DefinedAs', 'MadeOf', 'PartOf', etc. and the second group entries corresponds to relations like, 'CapableOf', 'UsedFor', 'CapableOfReceivingAction', etc. Of the two groups, the first one basically indicates other associated concepts, and the second one indicates the actions that the input concept can either perform or receive. The first list is searched against the scored list of nouns and the first 5 unique concepts which are found in the target list are taken from the matching list. An average score of those matched 5 concepts is retuned as the valence of the non-scored concept. If the first procedure fails to assign a valence, a similar procedure is performed for verbs.

Let us look at an example. In the case of the noun 'doctor', the system initially failed to find a prior valence in the existing scored list of nouns. Here, the following two lists are obtained by applying the explained procedures and ConceptNet.

Possible_concept_list = ['person', 'smart person', 'human', 'conscious being', 'man', 'wiley bandicoot', 'clever person', 'dentist', 'pediatrician', 'surgeon', 'physician', 'veterinarian', 'messy handwriting', 'study medicine', 'job']

Possible_action_list = ['examine', 'help', 'look', 'examine patient', 'help sick person', 'wear', 'prescribe medicine', 'treat', 'prescribe', 'wear white coat', 'look at chart', 'save life', 'heal person', 'take care'] (the list is truncated due to space limitations)

In this case the system first processed the 'Possible_concept_list', and failed to assign a value. Therefore, the second list, 'Possible_action_list', is processed and from that list the system returned the value 4.21 by averaging the scores of the verbs, 'examine (4.50)'; 'help (5.00)'; 'wear (2.57)'; 'prescribe (4.27)' and 'treat (4.69)'. Hence the value 4.21 is assigned as the prior valence for the concept 'doctor' and stored in the database for future use. We scored about 4500 concepts using this procedure. This list is maintained to speed up processing time since otherwise the system has to invoke ConceptNet every time.

Scored-list of Named Entity. The system also maintains a list of scored named entities. The information of an entity is stored as the following format: Named-entity [Role, Concept, Genre, General-Sentiment, Prior-Valence]. The field 'Role' indicates any of the values from the list *{Company, Concept, Country, Object, Other, Person, Product, Service, Team}* and 'Concept' stores a ConceptNet keyword to represent the concept of the entity. 'Genre' indicates any of the 15 genres (e.g. Politics, Sports,

Technology etc.) taken from the Yahoo! news domain. 'General-Sentiment' contains either a negative (-1) or positive (+1) value based on the value of the prior valence towards the named entity. We did not use any named entity recognizer to identify a named entity, and make the simplifying assumption that anything for which ConceptNet fails to assign valence is a named entity. To assign General-Sentiment we have developed a tool that can extract sentiment from Opinmind [28]. For example, ConceptNet fails to assign a valence to "George Bush" or "Asimov". From Opinmind we get -1 (37% positive, 63% negative) and +1 (97% positive, 3% negative) for those two entities, which is stored as: George Bush {Person, President, Politics, -1, (+1.85, -3.15)}; Asimov {Product, Machine, Science, +1, (+4.85, -0.15)}. Initially a list of 2000 entries is manually created and scored using Opinmind. Usually the value of 'General Sentiment' is idiosyncratic and arguable. If the valence-sign of the 'Concept' and 'General-Sentiment' (e.g. President [+3.533], George Bush [-1]) differs from each other, the system considers this as an ambiguity and assigns neutral valence to the sentence referring that named entity.

3.3 Contextual-Valence and Sentiment Assessment

Before we explain the algorithm, we first discuss its underlying data structure.

Input. The smallest input to the system is a sentence S. A paragraph P, containing one or more sentences can also be processed by the system.

Processing elements. We assume the input is a Paragraph P, containing n sentences, such that $P = \{S_1, S_2,...,S_i,..., S_n\}$ and $1 \leq i \leq n$. As a sentence S_i may have one or more verbs, the semantic parser may output one or more triplet(s) for S_i. We represent S_i as a set of m triplets T, i.e., $S_i=\{T_1, T_2,...T_j,..., T_m\}$, whereby $1 \leq j \leq m$. A triplet T_j has the following form: ⟨*actor, action, concept*⟩. The triplet elements *actor* and *concept* have the following form, ⟨*name, type, attribute*⟩. The *action* has the form ⟨*name, status, attribute*⟩ . An *attribute* is either an empty set or non-empty set of words. For example, the input S '*The President called the space shuttle Discovery on Tuesday to wish the astronauts well, congratulate them on their space walks and invite them to the White House.*' , the following four triplets are obtained for the four verbs.

T_1 = ⟨⟨*President, Concept, {the}*⟩, ⟨*call, past, {time: tuesday}*⟩, ⟨*discovery, Named-Entity, {the, space, shuttle}*⟩⟩

T_2 = ⟨⟨*President, Concept, {the}*⟩, ⟨*wish, infinitive, {dependency}*⟩, ⟨*astronaut, Concept, {the, adv: well}*⟩⟩

T_3 = ⟨⟨*President, Concept, {the}*⟩, ⟨*congratulate, infinitive, {dependency}*⟩, ⟨*astronaut, Concept, {dependency, goal: space walk}*⟩⟩

T_4 = ⟨⟨*President, Concept, {the}*⟩, ⟨*invite, infinitive, {dependency}*⟩, ⟨*astronaut, Concept, {dependency, place: white house}*⟩⟩

Knowledgebase. The knowledge-base of the system has been discussed in Section 3.2. Using that data source, the system builds the following computational data-structure that is consulted to process the input text. The verbs are classified into two groups, affective verb (AV) and non-affective verb (V) group. The verbs having the tag <*affect*> in the knowledge-base are members of AV. Both AV and V are further partitioned into positive (AV_{pos}, Vpos) and negative (AV_{neg}, Vneg) groups on the basis of their prior valences. Similarly, adjectives (*ADJ*), adverbs (*ADV*), concepts (*CON*) also have positive and negative groups indicated by ADJ_{pos}, ADJ_{neg}; ADV_{pos}, ADV_{neg}; and CON_{pos}, CON_{neg}; respectively. For a named entity (*NE*) the system creates three kinds of lists, namely ambiguous named entity (NE_{ambi}), positive named entity (NE_{pos}) and negative named entity (NE_{neg}). The named entity that has a different sign for the valence of 'concept' and 'general sentiment' fields is a member of NE_{ambi}.

Algorithm. The core algorithm underlying our system can be summarized as follows.
Input: P={S₁, S₂, ... Sₙ} // a Paragraph which is a set of sentences
Output: V = {V, V₁, V₂, ... Vₙ} // indicates valence for paragraph and each sentence
Pseudo Code for Processing:

```
Begin
for each Sᵢ in P do //assume 1 ≤ i ≤ n
  tripletSetᵢ = getSemanticParsing (Sᵢ)
          //the output of Semantic Parser is a set of Triplets for each sentence.
  for each triplet Tⱼ, in tripletSetᵢ do   //we assume 1 ≤ j ≤ m, m triplets
    actorValence = ContextualValenceAttrib (actorPriorValence, actorAttributes)
    actionValence =ContextualValenceAttrib (actionPriorValence, actionAttributes)
    objectValence = ContextualValenceAttrib (objectPriorValence, objectAttributes)
    actionObjectPairValence=setActionObjectPairVal (actionValence, objectValence)
    tripletValence = setTripletValence (actorValence, actionObjectPairValence)
    tripletValence = handleNegationAndConditionality (tripletValence, Tⱼ)
    tripletDependency = if the token "dependency" is found then 'true' else 'false'
    tripletResultⱼ = {tripletValence, tripletDependency}
  loop until all triplets are processed
  contextualValence = processTripletLevelContextualValence (tripletSetᵢ)
```

$$sentimentScore = \text{average}(\sum_{k=1}^{m} abs(contextualValence_k))$$

```
  valenceSign = get ResultantValenceSign(contextualValence)
  SentenceValenceᵢ =  sentimentScore * valenceSign
loop until all sentences are processed
valence = getParagraphValence (SentenceValence)
outputValence = valence ∪ {SentenceValence}
End
```

Here are some example rules to compute contextual valence using attributes (e.g., adjectives and adverbs).

- ADJ_{pos}+(CON_{neg} or NE_{neg})→ neg. Valence (e.g., strong cyclone; nuclear weapon)
- ADJ_{pos}+ (CON_{pos} or NE_{pos})→ pos. Valence (e.g., brand new car; final exam)
- ADJ_{neg} +(CON_{pos} or NE_{pos})→ neg. Valence (e.g., broken computer; terrorist gang)
- ADJ_{neg} + (CON_{neg} or NE_{neg})→ neg. Valence (e.g., ugly witch; scary night)

So we notice that the sign of the valence is toggled by the adjectives when there is a negative scored adjective qualifying a CON_{pos} or NE_{pos}. In other cases the sign of respective *CON* or *NE* is unchanged. The resultant valence (i.e., actor valence or object valence) is also intensified than the input *CON* or *NE* due to *ADJ*.

For adverbs the following rules are applied. We have some adverbs tagged as *<except>* to indicate exceptional adverbs (e.g., hardly, rarely, seldom etc.) in the list. For these exceptional adverbs we have to deal with ambiguity as explained below.

- ADV_{pos} + (AV_{pos} or V_{pos})→ pos. Valence (e.g., write nicely; sleep well)
- ADV_{pos} + (AV_{neg} or V_{neg})→ neg. Valence (e.g., often miss; always fail)
- ADV_{neg} + (AV_{pos} or V_{pos})→ neg. Valence (e.g., rarely complete; hardly make)
- ADV_{neg} + AV_{pos} → pos. Valence (e.g., badly like; love blindly)
- ADV_{neg} + (AV_{neg} or V_{neg})→ ambiguous (e.g., hardly miss; kill brutally)

Hence, the rules to resolve the ambiguity are:

- ADV_{neg} (except) + (AV_{neg} or V_{neg})→ pos. Valence (e.g., rarely forget; hardly hate)
- ADV_{neg} (not except)+(AV_{neg} or V_{neg})→ neg. Valence (e.g., suffer badly; be painful)

The contextual valence of Action-Object pairs is computed based on the following rules taking the contextual valence of action and object into consideration.

- Neg. Action Valence + Pos. Object Valence → Neg. Action-Object Pair Valence (e.g., kill innocent people, miss morning lecture, fail the final examination, etc.)
- Neg. Action Valence + Pos. Object Valence → Pos. Action-Object Pair Valence (e.g., quit smoking, hang a clock on the wall, hate the corruption, etc.)
- Pos. Action Valence + Pos. Object Valence → Pos. Action-Object Pair Valence (e.g., buy a brand new car, listen to the teacher, look after you family, etc.)
- Pos. Action Valence + Neg. Object Valence → Neg. Action-Object Pair Valence (e.g., buy a gun, patronize a famous terrorist gang, make nuclear weapons, etc.)

We are aware that the above rules are naive and there are exceptions to the rules. In the sentences *"I like romantic movies"* and *"She likes horror movies"* the rules fail to detect both as conveying positive sentiment because "romantic movies" and "horror movies" are considered positive and negative, respectively. In order to deal with such cases we have a list of affective verbs (AV_{pos}, AV_{neg}) that uses the following rules to assign contextual valence for an affective verb.

- AV_{pos} + (pos. or neg. Object Valence) = pos. Action-Object Pair Valence (e.g., I like romantic movies. She likes horror movies.)
- AV_{neg} + (neg. or pos. Object Valence) = neg. Action-Object Pair Valence (e.g., I dislike digital camera. I dislike this broken camera.)

The rules for computing valence of a triplet are as follows. Pronouns (e.g. I, he, she etc.) and proper names (not found in the listed named-entity) are considered as positive valenced actors with a score 2 out of 5. The rules are:

- (CON_{pos} or NE_{pos})+ Pos. Action-Object Pair Valence→ Pos. Triplet Valence (e.g., the professor explained the idea to his students.)
- (CON_{pos} or NE_{pos}) + Neg. Action-Object Pair Valence→ Neg. Triplet Valence (e.g., John rarely attends the morning lectures.)
- (CON_{neg} or NE_{neg}) + Pos. Action-Object Pair Valence→ Tagged Negative Triplet Valence (e.g., the robber appeared in the broad day light.) to process further.
- (CON_{neg} or NE_{neg}) + Neg. Action-Object Pair Valence→ Neg. Triplet Valence (e.g., the strong cyclone toppled the whole city.)

For example, the input sentence *"The robber arrived with a car and mugged the store-keeper."* outputs two 'tagged negative triplet valence' values for the actor (robber) where the 'action-object pair valence' for ["arrive, car"] and ["mug, store-keeper"] are positive and negative, respectively. For such cases where a negative valenced actor is associated with at least one 'negative action-object pair valence', the tagged output is marked with a highly negative valence.

But if a negative valenced actor is associated with all positively scored 'action-object pair valence' the 'tagged negative triplet valence' is toggled to positive. For example, "The kidnapper freed the hostages and retuned the money." gives two tagged negatives scores (i.e.; -8.583 and -9.469) for two positive "action-object pair valence" (i.e., ['free, hostage'] and ["return", "money"]). Hence, the system finally assigns a positive valence because the negative valenced actor is not associated with any negative 'action-object pair valence". This implies that an action done by a negative-role actor is not necessarily always negative. We also consider the cases of negation and conditionality as discussed in [5,26].

3.4   Sentiment Assessment

In the previous section we described how valence is assigned to a 'Triplet'. Here we explain how sentiment is assessed for a sentence. The data structure 'tripletResult' has a field named 'tripletDependency' to indicate inter-dependency between Triplets. If interrelated Triplets are found, the function *setContextualValence* is invoked to set the contextual valence for those Triplets. If there is no dependency then the variable 'ContextualValence' is kept the same as the 'tripletValence' of that triplet. But if there are two negatively valenced inter-dependent triplets, their valences are averaged and the sign of the 'tripletValence' is changed to positive.

For example, the sentence *"It is difficult to take bad picture with this camera."* produces two dependant triplets ['it', 'is', 'difficult'] and ['camera', 'take' 'bad-picture'] and both produce negative valences (-10.00 and -11.945) but the final valence is set to positive (10.973). The average of the absolute values of 'contextualValence' is assigned as the 'sentimentScore' for a sentence, S. The 'valenceSign' is set either +1 or -1 according to the sign of the valence whose value is the maximum among 'contextualValence'.   The value of 'sentimentScore' is multiplied with 'valenceSign' to get 'sentenceValence' and it is the valence we get for a sentence. According to the scoring system the range of 'sentenceValence' is ±15.

4   System Evaluation

We evaluated our system to assess the accuracy of sentence-level sentiment recognition when compared to human-ranked scores (as "gold standard") for two data-sets. The first one, Data-Set I, was created by collecting 200 sentences from internet based sources for reviews of products, movies, and news (Yahoo! News, 2006), and email correspondences. It was scored by 23 human judges according to positive, negative, or neutral sentiment affinity by an online survey[2]. The second set, Data-Set II, is the sentence polarity dataset v1.0[3] first used by Pang and Lee [14]. A summary of our data sets is given in Table 2.

Table 2. Input Data-Sets

Sentences	Data-Set I	Data-Set II
Number of Positive Sentences (x)	90	5331
Number of Negative Sentences (y)	87	5331
Number of Neutral Sentences (z)	23	0
Fleiss' kappa (κ)	0.782	

For Data-Set I the number of positive, negative, and neutral sentences has been decided according to the average scores assigned by the judges. The agreement (κ=0.782) among the judges can be seen as reliable.

We have performed two types of comparisons. First we compared system performance with human ratings, and then with a similar, state-of-the-art system [9] for both data sets. Three types of experiments (E1C1; E2C2; E3C3) are conducted considering three conditions where the ranges for a neutral sentiment are respectively ±16.66%, ±23.33% and ±30.00%. The motivation behind this is to set-up the decision logic to classify neutral sentences. On both data sets, the accuracy measure for positive sentences (P1) is the percentage of the number of positive sentences that both humans and our system identified as positive. Similarly P2 and P3 are obtained for negative and neutral sentences. The system's overall accuracy is computed as the average of P1, P2 and P3. There is no P3 score for Data-Set II (see Table 3). The results of all the experiments obtained an average of 0.654 and 0.673 as Human-System agreement (i.e., the Cohen's kappa score for Data-Set I and Data-Set II).

Table 4 shows the results for the performance comparison between our system and Liu's system [9]. Although Liu's system does not directly assess sentiment of text, it appears to have outstanding performance to analyze emotion from text of smaller input size (e.g. a sentence). We consider Liu's system [9] because like ours, it is a rule based system, and it seems to be the best performing system for sentence-level emotion sensing. On the practical side, it is freely available on the internet, so we could use it for comparison. In order to compare the output of Liu's system to our scoring model, we considered fearful, sad, angry, and disgust emotions as belonging to the negative sentiments and happy and surprise as belonging to the positive sentiments. These are the emotions that Liu's system can recognize, and for each sentence a vector containing the percentage value afferent to each emotion is returned. We took the highest percentage value from the positive and negative emotion group for each input sentence of our data sets. This resulted in an average accuracy of 81.64% for our system, and 71.75% for Liu's system, when compared to the scores of the human judges as "gold standard".

---

[2] http://ita.co.jp/research/survey/ (one can login using a guest username).
[3] Introduced in Pang and Lee at ACL 2005. at http://www.cs.cornell.edu/People/pabo/movie-review-data/

Table 3. System Accuracy Metrics using Data-Set I and Data-Set II

Run #	Data-Set I					Data-Set II				**Row**
	P1	P2	P3	**Avg.**	κ	P1	P2	**Avg.**	κ	**Avg.**
E1C1	88.88	86.21	60.86	**78.65**	0.649	79.47	85.81	**82.64**	0.653	**80.65**
E2C2	85.55	79.31	78.26	**81.04**	0.701	84.93	83.87	**84.40**	0.689	**82.72**
E2C3	76.66	70.11	91.30	**79.36**	0.613	87.07	80.43	**83.74**	0.677	**81.55**

Table 4. Accuracy Comparison Metrics [Liu's system doesn't apply any condition]

Run #	Data-Set I		Data-Set II	
	Our Sys	Liu's Sys	Our Sys	Liu's Sys
E1C1	78.65%	70.83%	82.64%	72.67%
E2C2	81.04%	70.83%	84.40%	72.67%
E2C3	79.36%	70.83%	83.74%	72.67%
Avg.	**79.68%**	**70.83%**	**83.59%**	**72.67%**

5   Conclusion

The system described in this paper proposes a method to recognize sentiment at the sentence level. The system first performs semantic processing and then applies rules to assign contextual valence to the linguistic components in order to obtain sentence-level sentiment valence. The system is robust because we have employed both cognitive and commonsense knowledge to assign prior valences to the words and developed the rules. A study demonstrated the accuracy of the system when compared to human performance, but also, that it outperforms a state-of-the-art system (under simplifying assumptions). In future we plan to compare our results with other machine learning approaches.

In general terms this research aims at giving computer programs a skill known as "emotional intelligence" with the ability to understand human emotion and to respond to it appropriately. We plan to extend the sentiment recognition system into a full-fledged emotion recognition system, which may classify named emotions rather than positive or negative sentiments. We also intend to take into account user-specific preferences (e.g. personal opinions about particular entities) that might help the system to analyze subjective statements in a personalized manner.

References

1. Esuli, A., Sebastiani, F.: Determining the semantic orientation of terms through gloss analysis. In: Proc. CIKM, pp. 617–624 (2005)
2. Fellbaum, C. (ed.): WordNet: An Electronic Lexical Databases. MIT Press, Cambridge, Massachusetts (1999)
3. Fitrianie, S., Rothkrantz, L.J.M.: Constructing Knowledge for Automated Text-Based Emotion Expressions. In: Proc. CompSysTech (2006)

4. Fleiss, J.L.: Measuring nominal scale agreement among many raters. Psychological Bulletin 76(5), 378–382 (1971)
5. Hu, M., Liu, B.: Mining and summarizing customer reviews. In: Proc. KDD (2004)
6. Kamps, J., Marx, M.: Words with Attitude. In: Proc. 1st Intl. WordNet Conf. (2002)
7. Kim, S.M., Hovy, E.H.: Identifying and Analyzing Judgment Opinions. In: Proc. HLT-NAACL 2006, ACL, pp. 200–207 (2006)
8. Kim, S.M., Hovy, E.H.: Automatic Detection of Opinion Bearing Words and Sentences. In: Companion Volume to the Proceedings of the 2nd IJCNLP (2005)
9. Liu, H., Lieberman, H., Selker, T.: A Model of Textual Affect Sensing using Real-World Knowledge. In: Proc. IUI, Miami, FL, January 12-15, pp. 125–132. ACM, New York (2003)
10. Liu, H., Singh, P.: ConceptNet: A Practical Commonsense Reasoning Toolkit. In: Liu, H., Singh, P. (eds.) ConceptNet: A Practical Commonsense Reasoning Toolkit, BT Technology Journal, vol. 22(4), pp. 211–226. Kluwer Academic Publishers, Dordrecht (2004)
11. Machinese Syntax, the official website (2005), http://www.connexor.com/connexor/
12. Mihalcea, R., Liu, H.: A corpus-based approach to finding happiness, Computational approaches for analysis of weblogs. In: AAAI Spring Symposium (2006)
13. Nasukawa, T., Yi, J.: Sentiment Analysis: Capturing Favorability Using Natural Language Processing. In: Proc. K-CAP, pp. 70–77. ACM Press, New York (2003)
14. Pang, B., Lee, L.: Seeing stars: Exploiting class relationships for sentiment categorization with respect to rating scales. In: Proc. ACL, pp. 115–124 (2005)
15. Pennebaker, J.W., Mehl, M.R., Niederhoffer, K.: Psychological aspects of natural language use: Our words, our selves. Annual Review of Psychology 54, 547–577 (2003)
16. Polanyi, L., Zaenen, A.: Contextual valence shifters. In: Shanahan, J., Qu, Y., Wiebe, J. (eds.) Computing Attitude and Affect in Text: Theory and Applications, The Information Retrieval Series, vol. 20, pp. 1–10 (2004)
17. Riloff, E., Wiebe, J., Wilson, T.: Learning Subjective Nouns Using Extraction Pattern Bootstrapping. In: Proc. CoNLL-2003 (2003)
18. Shaikh, M.A.M., Prendinger, H., Ishizuka, M.: SenseNet: A Linguistic Tool to Visualize Numerical-Valance Based Sentiment of Textual Data. In: Proc. ICON, pp. 147–152 (2007)
19. Subasic, P., Huettner, A.: Affect Analysis of Text Using Fuzzy Semantic Typing. IEEE Transactions on Fuzzy Systems 9(4), 483–496 (2001)
20. Stock, O., Strapparava, C.: Getting Serious about the Development of Computational Humor. In: Proc. IJCAI, pp. 59–64 (2003)
21. Turney, P.: Thumbs Up or Thumbs Down? Semantic Orientation Applied to Unsupervised Classification of Reviews. In: Proc. 40th Annual Meeting of the ACL, pp. 417–424 (2002)
22. Valitutti, A., Strapparava, C., Stock, O.: Developing Affective Lexical Resources. PsychNology Journal 2(1), 61–83 (2004)
23. Wiebe, J., Mihalcea, R.: Word Sense and Subjectivity. In: Proc. ACL-06, pp. 1065–1072 (2006)
24. Wiebe, J.: Learning subjective adjectives from corpora. In: Proc. AAAI (2000)
25. Wiebe, J., Wilson, T., Cardie, C.: Annotating expressions of opinions and emotions in language. Language Resources and Evaluation 39(2-3), 165–210 (2005)
26. Wilson, T., Wiebe, J., Hoffmann, P.: Recognizing Contextual Polarity in Phrase-Level Sentiment Analysis. In: Proc. HLT/EMNLP. ACL, pp. 347–354 (2005)
27. Opinmind, http://www.opinmind.com/

How Rude Are You?: Evaluating Politeness and Affect in Interaction

Swati Gupta, Marilyn A. Walker, and Daniela M. Romano

Department of Computer Science, University of Sheffield, Regent Court, 211 Portobello street,
Sheffield, UK, S1 4DP
{s.gupta,m.walker,d.romano}@dcs.shef.ac.uk

Abstract. Recent research on conversational agents emphasises the need to build affective conversational systems with social intelligence. Politeness is an integral part of socially appropriate and affective conversational behaviour, e.g. consider the difference in the pragmatic effect of realizing the same communicative goal with either "Get me a glass of water mate!" or "I wonder if I could possibly have some water please?" This paper presents POLLy (Politeness for Language Learning), a system which combines a spoken language generator with an artificial intelligence planner to model Brown and Levinson's theory of politeness in collaborative task-oriented dialogue, with the ultimate goal of providing a fun and stimulating environment for learning English as a second language. An evaluation of politeness perceptions of POLLy's output shows that: (1) perceptions are generally consistent with Brown and Levinson's predictions for choice of form and for discourse situation, i.e. utterances to strangers need to be much more polite than those to friends; (2) our indirect strategies which should be the politest forms, are seen as the rudest; and (3) English and Indian native speakers of English have different perceptions of politeness.

1   Introduction

Recent research suggests that computers are perceived as social actors, who must exhibit social intelligence and awareness, rather than merely as computational machines that perform tasks assigned to them by the user [1,7,11,17,18,20,26]. This social role awareness involves the ability to behave in a socially correct manner, where an integral part of this behaviour is conversation, the ability to communicate appropriately, according to the situation and the feelings of the interlocutors. For example, consider the difference in the pragmatic effect of realizing the same communicative goal with either "Get me a glass of water mate!" or "I wonder if I could possibly have some water please?".

According to theories in sociolinguistics, choices of these different forms are driven by sociological norms among human speakers [6,9] *inter alia*, and work on computational models for conversational agents has recently begun to build on these sociolinguistic theories. Walker et al. [26] were the first to utilize and implement Brown & Levinson's [6] theory of politeness, henceforth B&L, in conversational agents, in order to provide interesting variations of character and personality in an

A. Paiva, R. Prada, and R.W. Picard (Eds.): ACII 2007, LNCS 4738, pp. 203–217, 2007.
© Springer-Verlag Berlin Heidelberg 2007

interactive narrative application. Other work has explored building affective conversational systems that are considerate of the emotions of the user and which exhibit appropriate emotions [2,17], and work has shown that the expression and recognition of personality is strongly linked to positive and negative affect [14,15]. But politeness is an integral part of affective conversational behaviour, as impoliteness exhibits negative feelings towards the hearer, and may hurt the hearer's feelings or make the hearer angry.

This paper presents POLLy (Politeness for Language Learning), a system which combines a spoken language generator with an AI Planner to model B&L's theory of politeness in task-oriented dialogue. The value of politeness strategies based on B&L has been demonstrated in several conversational applications, e.g. tutorial dialogue [11,12,18], animated presentation teams [1,21], and real estate sales [7]. Recent research also shows that human tutors employ politeness strategies while interacting with students and that pedagogical agents that use polite language provide affective scaffolding to the instructors and contribute to the learners' motivational state to help them learn difficult concepts [11,19,27]. André et al. [3] use politeness strategies to mitigate face threats resulting from dialogue acts and investigate how the user's affective response to the system can be improved. Roman et al. [22] found that politeness plays a role in dialogue summarization since human summarizations tend to report politeness as a result of their point of view (which interlocutor they are asked to empathize with or if they are supposed to act as an observer). This was most evident for reporting impolite behaviour. This bias could be for saving the face of the interlocutor they empathize with, which is directly related to the notion of self-esteem. Morand & Ocker [16] suggest how politeness contributes to the study of role relations in computer-mediated communication. They point out that in task-oriented speech acts, emotion work appears in the form of politeness and the degree, type and tactics of politeness provide important cues regarding actors' relational orientations towards each other. Reeves and Nass [20] also observed that users are polite to the computers because they are considerate about the computer's feelings, and are not likely to speak in a manner that might hurt its feelings. Thus, previous work suggests that computers should reciprocate with humans by being polite, as social behaviours are not accomplished in isolation from the responses to them, and sociological norms dictate that humans expect reciprocity.

Here, we explore the effect of politeness in natural conversation by evaluating the use of different politeness strategies in task-oriented dialogues in a collaborative task domain of cooking, where subjects are asked to collaborate with another person to make a recipe [10,24,25]. We show that: (1) politeness perceptions of POLLy's output are generally consistent with B&L's predictions for choice of form and for discourse situation, i.e. utterances to strangers need to be more polite than those to friends; (2) our indirect strategies which should be the politest forms, are seen as the rudest; and (3) English and Indian speakers of English have different perceptions of politeness. Section 1 describes POLLy's architecture and functionality. Section 2 describes an evaluation of users' perceptions of automatically generated task-oriented polite language and Section 3 presents the experimental results. Section 4 sums up and compares our results with previous work.

2   POLLy's Architecture and Theoretical Basis

POLLy consists of two parts: an AI Planner based on GraphPlan [5] and a Spoken Language Generator (SLG), as illustrated in Figure 1. GraphPlan is a classic STRIPS-style planner which, given a goal, e.g. cook pasta, produces a plan of the steps involved in doing so. POLLy then allocates the plan steps to two agents as a shared collaborative plan to achieve the cooking task, with goals to communicate about the plan via speech acts (SAs) needed to accomplish the plan collaboratively, such as Requests, Offers, Informs, Acceptances and Rejections [10,24,25].

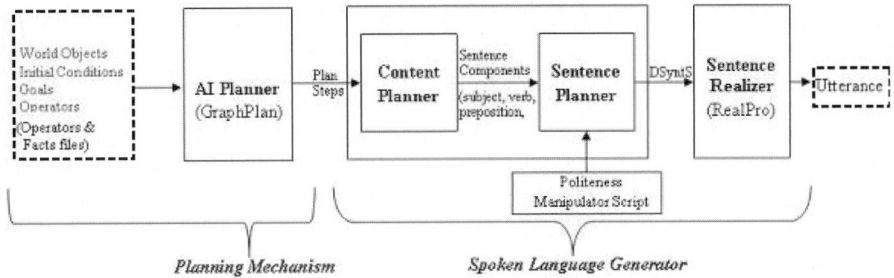

Fig. 1. POLLy's Architecture

The SLG then generates variations of the dialogue based on B&L's theory of politeness that realizes this collaborative plan, as in [1,26]. This is explained in more detail below and an example dialogue is shown in Table 2. When this dialogue is embedded in our virtual reality environment [23], the human English language learner will be able to play the part of one of the agents in order to practice politeness in a real-time immersive environment.

2.1   Brown and Levinson's Theory

B&L's theory states that speakers in conversation are rational actors who attempt to realize their speech acts (SAs) to avoid threats to one another's **face**, which consists of two components. **Positive face** is the desire that at least some of the speaker's and hearer's goals and desires are shared by other speakers. **Negative face** is the want of a person that his action be unimpeded by others. Utterances that threaten the conversants' face are called Face Threatening Acts (FTAs). B&L predict a universal of language usage that the choice of linguistic form can be determined by the predicted Threat Θ as a sum of 3 variables:

1. P: power that the hearer has over the speaker;
2. D: social distance between speaker & hearer;
3. R: a ranking of imposition of the speech act.

Linguistic strategy choice is made according to the value of the Threat Θ. We follow Walker et al.'s [26] four part classification of strategy choice. The **Direct strategy** is used when Θ is low and executes the SA in the most direct, clear and unambiguous way.

It is usually carried out either in urgent situations like "Please Help!", or where the face threat is small as in informing the hearer "I have chopped the vegetables" or if the speaker has power over the hearer, "Did you finish your homework today?". The **Approval strategy** (Positive Politeness) is used for the next level of threat Θ - this strategy is oriented towards the need for the hearer to maintain a positive self-image. Positive politeness is primarily based on how the speaker approaches the hearer, by treating him as a friend, a person whose wants and personality traits are liked, and by using friendly markers "Could you please chop the vegetables mate?" or stating optimism "I'm sure you won't mind washing the dishes!" The **Autonomy Strategy** (Negative Politeness) is used for greater face threats, when the speaker may be imposing on the hearer, intruding on their space or violating their freedom of action. These face threats can be mitigated by apologizing, "I know I'm asking you for a big favour but could you please wash the dishes?" or by minimizing imposition, "I just want to ask you if you could close the door." The **Indirect Strategy** (Off Record) is the politest strategy and is therefore used when Θ is greatest. It depends on speaking in an indirect way, with more than one attributable intention so that the speaker removes himself from any imposition. For example by using metaphor and irony, rhetorical questions, understatement, or hints such as "Its cold in here," which implies a request to close the door, or being vague like "Someone should have cleaned the table." Table 1 lists the B&L strategies used in the evaluation experiment in Section 3.

Table 1. The individual B&L strategies used for Request and Inform speech acts

B&L	Request Speech Act		Inform Speech Act	
	Strategy Forms	**Strategy Names**	**Strategy Forms**	**Strategy Names**
Direct	Do X.	RD1Imperative	X	ID1DirectAssert
	Do X please.	RD2ImperativePlz	-	-
	You must do X.	RD3ImperativeInsist	-	-
	You could do X.	RD4AsModAbility	-	-
Approval	Could you please do X mate?	RAp1QModAbility	Do you know that X?	IAp1QKnowledge
	If you don't mind you can do X.	RAp2AsModAbility	Do you know that X mate?	IAp2QueryKNowledgeAddress
	Would it be possible for you to do X?	RAp3AsPossible	-	-
	I'm sure you won't mind doing X.	RAp4AsOptimism	-	-
Autonomy	Could you possibly do X for me?	RAu1QModAbility	It seems that X.	IAu2AsAppear
	I know I'm asking you for a big favour but could you please do X?	RAu2ApologizeQModAbility	I am wondering if you know that X.	IAu1AsConfuse
	I'm wondering whether it would be possible for you to do X.	RAu3AsConfusePossibility	-	-
	Would you not like to do X?	RAu1QOptimism	-	-
Indirect	X is not done yet.	RI1AsNegation	-	-
	X should have been done.	RI2AsModRight	-	-
	Someone should have done X.	RI3AsModRightAbSub	-	-
	Someone has not done X yet.	RI4AsNegationAbsSub	-	-
	Where X is a task request. For example 'You could chop the onions,' or 'Would it be possible for you to clean the spill on the floor?'	*These strategies are applied to the various tasks requests X.*	*Where X is an inform event, like 'Do you know that the milk is spoilt mate?' or 'I'm wondering if you know that you have burnt the pasta.'*	*These strategies are applied to the various inform events X.*

2.2 Planning Mechanism

Planning is the process of generating a sequence of actions that can achieve a pre-specified goal. In particular, our planner generates the sequence of actions that are to be performed for cooking pasta. The information needed to create dialogic utterances for the agents in a dialogue are extracted from the plan. The planner output can be in any form depending upon the planner used, but a mapping between the components of the plan and the lexicalized entries for the syntactic structure of the utterance realizing that plan component is required. This mapping is typically referred to as a generation dictionary. Given a generation dictionary (a mapping) the dialogue generation component of the system can be used with any planner.

The AI planner GraphPlan [5] has been used for POLLy. GraphPlan applies the Planning Graph Analysis approach to a STRIPS-like planning domain where the operators have preconditions, add effects, and delete effects which are actually conjuncts of propositions that have parameters that can be instantiated to objects in the world. Thus a planning problem consists of a STRIPS-like domain, a set of objects, a set of propositions or initial conditions and a set of problem goals required to be true at the end of a plan. Graphplan takes the objects, initial conditions, goals and operator definitions as input (see Figures 1, 2 and 3) and creates a plan for cooking pasta. The facts file shown in Figure 3 defines the objects of the world, the initial conditions that need to be true and the final goals that have to be achieved. The operators file shown in Figure 2 contains the operator definitions with their parameters, preconditions and effects where the parameters are initialised with the objects of the world as defined in the facts file.

An excerpt from the output plan is:

Step 1: place_pan_burner
Step 2: turn-on_burner
Step 3: boil_pasta_pan
Step 4: chop_vegetables_knife
Step 5: place_pan_burner
Step 6: add_oil_pan

```
(operator chop
        (params (<v> V) (<k> K))
        (preconds (available <v>)
                  (available <k>))
        (effects (chopped <v>)
                 (del available <v>)
                 (del not-chopped <v>)
                 (not-placed pan1 burner1)))
(operator cook
        (params (<v> V) (<p2> P2))
        (preconds (chopped <v>)
                  (ingredients-added other-ingredients <v>))
        (effects (cooked <v>)
                 (del chopped <v>)))
```

```
(vegetables V)
(knife K)
(pasta P1)
(water W)
....
(preconds
                (available vegetables)
                (available knife)
                (available pasta)
                (available water)
                .............)
(effects
                (ready pasta))
```

Fig. 2. Excerpt of the operators file   **Fig. 3.** Excerpt of the facts file

In our plan operators, lexicalization is directly encoded in the plan, so the generation dictionary is not needed, i.e. lexical entries such as place, pan, burner, etc are directly picked up from the plan steps by the language generator.

2.3 SLG (Spoken Language Generation)

The SLG is based on a standard architecture [8] with three components: Content planning, utterance planning and surface realization. See Figure 1. The politeness strategies are implemented through a combination of content selection and utterance planning. The linguistic realizer RealPro is used for realization of the resulting utterance plan [13], and the content planning and utterance planning components produce outputs that can be transformed into RealPro input, which we discuss first.

The **Surface Realizer** RealPro takes a dependency structure called a Deep-Syntactic Structure (DSyntS) as input and realizes it as a string. DSyntS are unordered *trees* with labelled nodes and arcs where the nodes are lexicalized. Only meaning bearing lexemes are represented and not function words. An example of a DSyntS for the utterance "I have chopped the vegetables." is given below. The attributes to all the nodes are explicitly specified, such as tense, or article. The two nodes are specified with relations I and II, where I is the subject and II is the object.

```
"chop" [ lexeme: "chop" class: "verb" taxis: "perf" tense: "pres" ]
    (
        I  "<PRONOUN>" [ lexeme:"<PRONOUN>" number: "sg" person:"1st" rel: "I" ]
        II "vegetable" [ lexeme: "vegetable" article: "def" class: "common_noun" number: "pl" rel: "II"]
    )
```

`"cook" [ lexeme: "cook" class: "verb" tense: "pres" mood:"imp"]`
`(`
  `II "vegetable" [ lexeme: "vegetable" article: "def" class: "com`
    `mon_noun" number: "pl" rel: "II" ]`
`)`
This would be realized simply as *"Cook the vegetables."* It is transformed to create utterances which vary in politeness according to B&L.
<div align="center">**Base DSyntS**</div>
	`"wonder" [ lexeme:"wonder" class:"verb" tense:"pres" ]`
	`(`
	  `I "<PRONOUN>" [ lexeme: "<PRONOUN>" number:"sg"`
	    `person:"1st" rel:"I" ]`
	  `II "be" [ lexeme:"be" class:"verb" mood:"cond" tense:"pres"`
	    `rel:"II" ]`
	  `(`
	    `II "possible" [ lexeme:"possible" rel:"II" ]`
	    `I "it" [ lexeme:"it" rel:"I" ]`
	    `III "cook" [ lexeme:"cook" class:"verb" mood:"inf-to" ques`
	      `tion:"+" rel:"III" ]`
	    `(`

`"cook" [ lexeme:"cook" class:"verb" mood:"cond" question:"+" ]`
`(`
  `I "<PRONOUN>" [ lexeme:"<PRONOUN>" number:"sg"`
    `person:"2nd" rel:"I" ]`
  `II "vegetable" [ lexeme:"vegetable" article:"def" class:"com`
    `mon_noun" number:"pl" rel:"II" ]`
  `ATTR "like_to" [ lexeme:"like_to" class:"adverb" rel:"ATTR"]`
  `ATTR "mate" [ lexeme:"buddy" rel:"ATTR" ]`
`)`
Realized as "Would you like to cook the vegetables mate?"
<div align="center">**Base DSyntS manipulated to create a polite DSyntS (the RAu9QOptimism strategy)**</div>
	`II "vegetable" [ lexeme:"vegetable" article:"def"`
	        `class:"common_noun" number:"pl" rel:"II" ]`
	      `I "<PRONOUN>" [ lexeme:"<PRONOUN>"`
	        `number:"sg" person:"2nd" rel:"I" ]`
	    `)`
	  `ATTR "whether" [ lexeme:"whether" rel:"ATTR" ]`
	  `ATTR "perhaps" [ lexeme:"perhaps"`
	    `class:"adverb"rel:"ATTR" ]`
	  `)`
	`)`
	Realized as "I wonder whether it would perhaps be possible for you to cook the vegetables."
	<div align="center">**Base DSyntS manipulated to create another polite DSyntS (the RAu7AsConfusePossibility strategy)**</div>

Fig. 4. Transformation from base DSyntS to RAu9QOptimism and RAu7AsConfusePossibility strategies for the CookVeg task

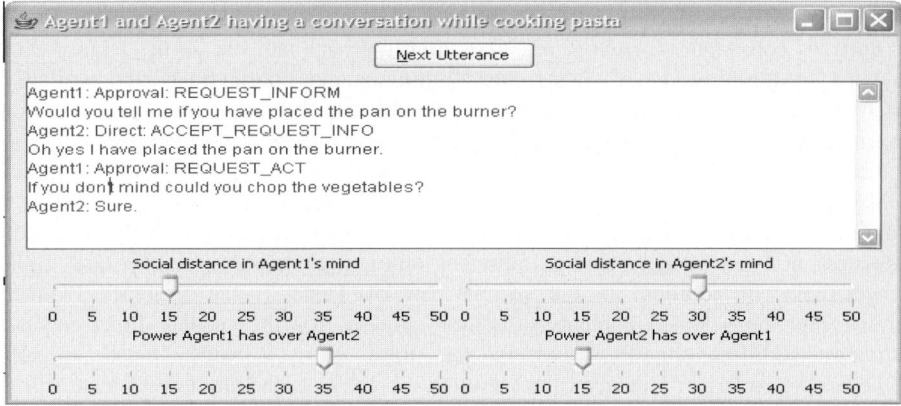

Fig. 5. A screenshot of the textual interface

The **Content Planner** interfaces to the AI Planner, selecting content from the preconditions, steps and effects of the plan. According to B&L, direct strategies are selected from the steps of the plan, while realizations of preconditions and negating the effects of actions are techniques for implementing indirect strategies. For instance, in case of the first direct request strategy RD1Imperative (stands for Request SA, Imperative direct strategy) in Table 1, which is realised as 'Do X', task X is selected from the steps of the plan and since it is a request SA and imperative strategy, it is realized simply as 'Do X'. Similarly, in case of the first indirect strategy RI1AsNegation (Request SA, Assert Negation Indirect strategy) which is realized as 'X is not done yet', the content is selected by the negation of effects of the action of doing X. The content planner extracts the components of the utterances to be created, from the plan and assigns them their respective categories, for example, lexeme get/add under category verb, or knife/oil under direct object, and sends them as input to the Sentence Planner.

The **Sentence Planner** then converts the utterance components to the lexemes of DSyntS nodes to create basic DsyntS for simple utterances [4], which are then transformed to create variations as per B&L's politeness strategies. At the moment our interface is text based, but our plan is to embed it in Sheffield's virtual reality environment. A screenshot of our textual interface is in Figure 5. The Sentence Planner creates SAs of two kinds: Initiating SAs such as request, inform, suggest, and offer and Response SAs such as inform SA and acceptance and rejection of requests or suggestions. To generate a conversation, first the initiating SAs are created followed by response SAs. The subject is implicitly assumed to be first person singular (I) in case of offer, inform, accept and reject, second person singular (you) in request_act and request_inform and first person plural (we) in case of suggest and accept_suggest. Each SA has multiple variants for realizing its politeness strategies, some of which are shown in Table 1.

For realizing these B&L strategies, a number of transformations on the basic DSyntS were implemented that were hypothesized to vary the politeness of a utterance. These politeness transformations are divided into four categories: **Address** form which means a friendly manner of addressing someone like 'mate'. **Abstracting the subject** by saying 'someone should have washed the dishes' instead of addressing the hearer directly. **Softeners** like 'if you don't mind,' 'if you know,' 'please' and 'possibly'. **Additives** consisted of *Apologizing* like admitting impingement as in "I know I'm asking you for a big favour", using *must* "You must take out the trash" and explicitly stating that you are asking a favour as in "Could you chop the onions for me?" For example if we want variations for a Request_act SA in which one agent requests the other to cook vegetables, the Content Planner sends the verb (cook) and the direct object (vegetable) to the Sentence Planner which then creates a base DsyntS. Figure 4 shows the RAu9QOptimism transformation for the CookVeg task (which stands for Request act speech act, Query optimism autonomy strategy for the task cook vegetables). In addition, in the second row of Table 1, the Sentence Planner transforms the selected content by adding 'please' for the second direct request strategy RD2ImperativePlz, and in the third row, it adds 'must' to the RD3ImperativeInsist. Under indirect strategy in Table 1, the strategy of abstracting the subject by saying 'someone' instead of addressing the hearer directly is shown as RI4AsNegationAbsSub. An example run of a dialogue generated by the system for two agents cooking pasta is given in Table 2.

Table 2. An example run of the system for two agents cooking pasta with vegetables

Agent	Utterance	SA and Politeness Strategy
Agent1	Could you tell me if you have placed the pan on the burner?	Approval: REQUEST_INFORM
Agent2	*Oh yes, I have placed the pan on the burner.*	*Direct: ACCEPT_REQUEST_INFO*
Agent1	Have you turned-on the burner mate?	Approval: REQUEST_INFORM
Agent2	*I am not sure.*	*Direct: REJECT_REQUEST_INFO*
Agent2	*Could I boil the pasta in the pan for you?*	*Autonomy: OFFER*
Agent1	Alright if it is not a problem.	Autonomy: ACCEPT_OFFER
Agent2	*Do you know that I have chopped the vegetables with the knife?*	*Approval: INFORM*
Agent1	Ok.	Direct: ACCEPT_INFORM
Agent2	*Do you know that I have added the oil to the pan my friend?*	*Approval: INFORM*
Agent1	Yeah.	Direct: ACCEPT_INFORM
Agent1	I have added the vegetables to the pan.	Direct: INFORM
Agent2	*Alright.*	*Direct: ACCEPT_INFORM*
Agent1	Could I add the other-ingredients to the vegetables?	Approval: OFFER
Agent2	*That is nice of you but no please do not bother yourself.*	*Approval: REJECT_OFFER*
Agent2	*I am wondering whether you would like to cook the vegetables in the pan.*	*Autonomy: REQUEST_ACT*
Agent1	Please do not mind but I can not do that.	Autonomy:REJECT_REQUEST_ACT

3 Experimental Method

We conducted an experiment to study the perception of politeness by subjects in different discourse contexts, with subjects who were native speakers of English, but from two different cultural backgrounds: 11 were British and 15 were Indians, most of them students of mixed gender with an age between 20 to 30 years. Subjects were administered a web-based questionnaire and presented with a series of collaborative cooking tasks. They were asked to rate various utterances automatically generated by POLLy as though the utterance ***had been said to them by their partner*** in the process of cooking a recipe together. The subjects were asked to rate how polite they perceived their partner to be, on a five point Likert-like scale: Excessively Overpolite, Very Polite, Just Right, Mildly Rude or Excessively Rude. All of the tasks were selected to have relatively high R (ranking of imposition) as per B&L's theory. Requests were to 'chop the onions', 'wash the dishes', 'take out the rubbish' and 'clean the spill on the floor.' The events for the propositional content of the Inform SAs were "You have burnt the pasta", "The milk is spoilt", "You have broken the dish" and "The oven is not working". The subjects rated a total of 84 utterances spread over these eight different tasks as shown in Table 3. There was also a text box for subjects to write optional comments.

There were five experimental variables: (1) Speech act type (request vs. inform); (2) B&L politeness strategy (direct, approval, autonomy, indirect); (3) discourse context (friend vs. stranger); (4) linguistic form of the realization of the B&L strategy; (5) cultural background (Indian vs. British). The politeness strategies were selected from strategies given by B&L for each level of politeness, and are shown in Table 1. We did not manipulate the power variable of B&L.

For each task, subjects were told that the discourse situation was either cooking with a **Friend**, or with a **Stranger**. This was in order to implement B&L's D variable representing social distance. A friend has a much lower social distance than a stranger, thus Θ should be much greater for strangers than friends.

The speech acts tested were: **Request** and **Inform**. The ranking of imposition R for speech acts has Requests with higher R than Inform, so Θ should be greater for requests, implying the use of a more polite B&L strategy.

For the Request speech act, each subject judged 32 example utterances, 16 for each situation, Friend vs. Stranger. There were 4 examples of each B&L strategy, direct, approval, autonomy, indirect. The B&L strategies for requests are given in Table 1.

Table 3. Distribution of the 84 utterances used in the experiment

			B&L Strategies					
			Direct	Approval	Autonomy	Indirect	Total	
Speech Act	**Situation**	**Tasks**						
Request	**Friend**	chop onions	4	4	4	4	16	64
		clean spill on floor	4	4	4	4	16	
	Stranger	wash dishes	4	4	4	4	16	
		take out rubbish	4	4	4	4	16	
Inform	**Friend**	oven not working	1	2	2	0	5	20
		burnt the pasta	1	2	2	0	5	
	Stranger	milk is spoilt	1	2	2	0	5	
		broken the dish	1	2	2	0	5	

For the Inform speech act, subjects judged 10 example utterances for each situation, friend and stranger, with 5 B&L strategies, used to inform the hearer of some potentially face-threatening event. Of the five, there was one direct, two approval and two autonomy utterances. No Indirect strategies were used for Inform SAs because those given by B&L of hints, being vague, jokes, tautologies are not implemented in our system. The B&L strategies for Informs are also in Table 1. The distribution of the utterances used in the experiment is in Table 3.

4 Results and Observations

We calculated an ANOVA with B&L category, situation (friend/stranger), speech act, syntactic form, politeness formula and the nationality of subjects as the independent variables and the ratings of the perception of politeness by the subjects as the dependent variable. Results are in Tables 4, 5, and 6 and are discussed below.

Table 4. Mean values of situation and utterance forms in relation to the speech acts

		Request	Inform
Situation	Friend	2.8	3.2
	Stranger	2.3	2.8
Utterance Form	Imperative	1.9	NA
	Assertion	2.4	3.2
	Queries	3.3	3.0
	Direct Assertion	NA	2.4

Table 5. Overall mean values of the utterance forms and politeness formulas

		Overall Score
Utterance Form	Imperative	1.8
	Assertion	2.5
	Queries	3.2
	Direct Assertions	2.4
Politeness Formula	AddressForm	3.1
	AbstractSubject	2.0
	Softeners	3.3
	Additives	3.0

Table 6. Mean values of the politeness ratings of SAs and situations for B&L's strategies and their overall mean score

		Direct	Approval	Autonomy	Indirect	Overall
Speech Act	Request	2.0	3.0	3.4	1.8	2.6
	Inform	2.4	3.0	3.2	NA	3.0
Situation	Friend	2.3	3.3	3.6	2.0	3.0
	Stranger	1.8	2.8	3.1	1.7	2.4

B&L strategies Effect: The four B&L strategies (Direct, Approval, Autonomy and Indirect) had a significant effect on the interpretation of politeness (df=3, F=407.4, p<0.001). See Table 6. The overall politeness ratings from least polite to most polite were Indirect, Direct, Approval and then Autonomy strategy. See the graph in Figure 6. It must be noted that as opposed to our findings, B&L posit that the indirect strategy is the politest. This may be so because the indirect realizations that our generator produces from the AI planner are the effect-not-achieved forms like the indirect request strategies (RI1AsNegation, RI2AsModRight, RI3AsModRightAbSub and RI4AsNegationAbsSub) as shown in Table 1, which sound like a complaint or sarcasm. Other Indirect strategies given by B&L like giving hints, being vague, sarcasm or jokes are situation dependent and require general knowledge that we have not yet implemented.

Situation Effect (Friend/Stranger): Figure 7 and Table 4 show that politeness ratings averaged over the four B&L's strategies for friend, which is 3 or 'just right', is more than that for a stranger, which is a little above 2 or 'mildly rude'. Table 6 shows that utterances spoken by a friend are rated as more polite than those spoken by a stranger, for all four B&L strategies (df=1, F=123.6, p<0.001). This shows the effect of B&L's social distance variable, i.e. when social distance is large, a politer utterance is appropriate but if we use an utterance that assumes too much social distance, , the utterance is regarded as too polite.

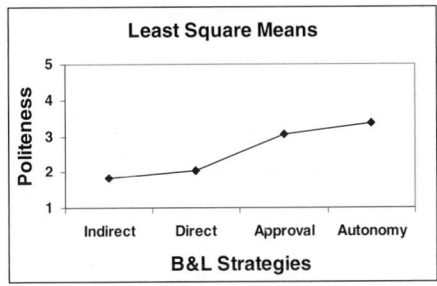
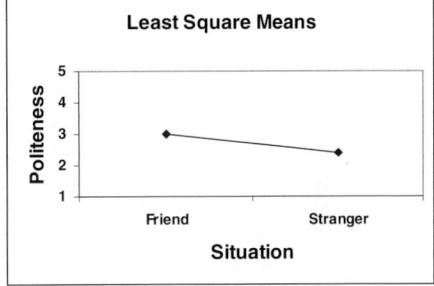

Fig. 6. The effect of B&L Strategies on politeness. 1 = Excessively Rude, 5 = Overly Polite.

Fig. 7. The effect of situation on politeness. 1 = Excessively Rude, 5 = Overly Polite.

SA Effect (Request/ Inform): Inform SA was rated as more polite than Request SA (df=1, F=61.4, p<0.001) as shown in Figure 8. This is in line with what B&L say about face threat, that speech acts such as Requests carry more face threat than speech acts such as Inform as they impede upon the hearer's freedom of action and thus require more face redressing or politeness strategies.

Utterance Form Effect: We divided the utterances into four categories, used for B&L strategy realizations, as per their syntactic forms. *Queries* are those that interrogate the listener, like the Approval strategy RAp1QModAbility for requests, "Could you please wash the dishes mate?" *Assertions* in case of a request SA refer to utterances that make a request by asserting something, such as asserting that the precondition holds or asserting the ability of the hearer as in the Approval strategy RAp2AsModAbility, "If you don't mind you can chop the onions." For the inform SA, Assertions refer to polite declaratives that use some politeness formulas or additives with autonomy and approval strategies. On the other hand *Direct Assertions* refer to utterances that directly assert something without using much politeness and are used to realize the direct form of the Inform SA, like the ID1DirectAssert strategy, "You have burnt the pasta." Lastly, *Imperatives* are those utterances that directly command the user to perform some action, like the RD3ImperativeInsist strategy, "You must clean the spill on the floor".

In case of requests, Queries were rated as the politest followed by Assertions and then Imperatives (df=2, F=279.4, p<0.001). In case of the Inform SA, Assertions are considered to be the most polite, followed by Queries and then Direct Assertions (df=2, F=36.0, p<0.001). The overall order of politeness ratings is in Figure 9 with politeness scores in Tables 4 and 5.

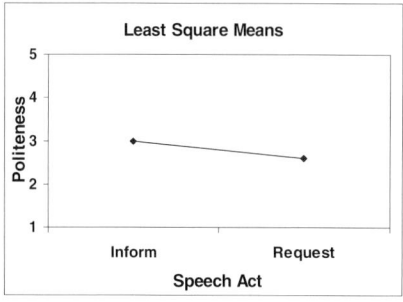

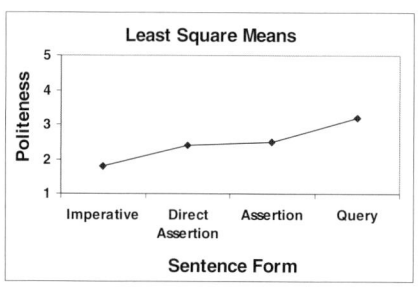

Fig. 8. The effect of speech act on politeness. 1 = Excessively Rude, 5 = Overly Polite.

Fig. 9. The effect of utterance form on politeness. 1 = Excessively Rude, 5 = Overly Polite.

Nationality Effect: We found that the politeness interpretations of Indian and British subjects were significantly different. Indians perceived the utterances as overall much more polite than the British did, as shown in Figure 10. This was most evident when the partner was a Friend (df=1, F=6.0, p<0.01), and for Requests (df=1, F=6.37, p<0.01) whereas perceptions were almost equal for strangers. This demonstrates a cultural effect, namely that Indian native speakers of English are more informal in their communication, especially when they are talking to a friend. Although the overall degrees of politeness of the four B&L strategies was rated higher by Indians, the order of the ranking of the strategies was the same for both Indians and British (indirect being the least polite, followed by approval, autonomy and direct) which shows that broad universality is still preserved.

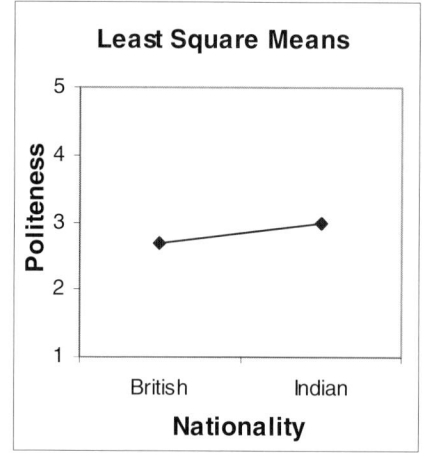

Fig. 10. The effect of nationality on politeness. 1 = Excessively Rude, 5 = Overly Polite.

Politeness Formula Effect: We observed that utterances with the address form 'mate', which is more specific to the British culture, were rated more polite than those without it (df=1, F= 49.8, p<0.001). Abstracting the subject (used in indirect strategy) made the utterance less polite (df=1, F=125.0, p<0.001) and adding Softeners notably increased politeness (df=4, F=104.0, p<0.001). In case of additives, apologies were rated to be most polite, followed by those that explicitly asked for a favour and utterances that used an insisting adverb such as `must' were least polite (df=3, F=185.6, p<0.001). Average ratings of politeness formulas are in Table 5.

5 Discussion and Conclusion

We presented an implementation of a system, called POLLy, that combines a general AI planner with a spoken language generator, for generating polite language as per the theory of Brown and Levinson, and demonstrated how to extract language from a plan to automatically generate task-oriented conversations [24,25]. One of the strengths of B&Ls theory is the assumption that conversational agents are rational actors, who make explicit use of planning representations, with content selection for discussing actions based on the steps, preconditions and effects of the plan. The general approach is very similar to that of Walker et al's [26] application of B&L to conversational agents for interactive narrative, but while they used a planner representation, they did not integrate a planner and their approach was not evaluated. Here, we have presented an experiment which shows that the B&L strategies have a significant effect on humans' perception of politeness. The utterances evaluated by our subjects were produced by POLLy and there was no human moderator, whereas the evaluation experiment of Cassell & Bickmore was Wizard-of-Oz [7]. As far as cultural differences are concerned, our experiment showed strong differences in the perception of politeness by Indian and British native speakers of English in the case of SAs with B&L's high ranking of imposition such as requests, and in situations where B&L's social distance variable was lower, such as when talking to a friend. In contrast, Johnson et al. [12] showed that the perceptions of politeness of American and German speakers in the domain of tutorial dialogues were identical. André et al. [1] proposed the idea of animated presentation teams for presenting information to the user but they investigated only personality and not politeness and their NLG was template based. Our generator is to be applied in the domain of teaching English as a Second Language (ESL). Previously, Porayska-Pomsta [18] applied B&L's theory in the tutorial domain for modelling teacher's corrective responses, with a generator was based on case-based reasoning, selecting utterances from human-human dialogues rather than building a generator based on B&L. Johnson et al. [11] also had a similar approach for generating socially appropriate tutorial dialogue, with a template-based NLG component, for a language training system that provides training in a foreign language and culture. Their goals are similar to ours, but their language courses have a strong task-based focus, on skills needed to cope with specific situations such as introducing yourself, obtaining directions and arranging meetings. Rehm and Andre [21] have shown that the interpretation of politeness strategies is affected by the gestures used in an embodied conversational agent, and we have not yet carried out experiments on an embodied agent.

One apparent limitation of our work to date, is that an examination of the utterances in the example run in Table 2 suggests that the language is somewhat inappropriate. This is because this system presents a design for a plug-in that can be used in different applications and for demonstration purpose we have kept the utterance generation random. Because of this random nature, there arise two problems. One, because of the random retrieval of utterances from the set of DSyntS for each B&L category, some of the sequences seem inconsistent in a particular context. Each set of utterances under a specific category includes the various realizations given by B&L and these realizations may not always be appropriate in every context; a limitation of B&L's theory is that its equation it does not take the context into account. Second, random selection may result in a repetition of the type of strategy realization.

In future work, we aim to modify the language generator to make it more robust, explore B&L's power variable, as well as the interplay of the three sociological variables and integrate POLLy into a virtual reality environment for learning politeness while learning English as a second language.

References

1. André, E., Rist, T., Mulken, S.: The automated design of believable dialogues for animated presentation teams. In: Embodied Conversational Agents, pp. 220–255. MIT Press, Redmond, Washington (2000)
2. André, E., Dybkjær, L., Minker, W., Heisterkamp, P. (eds.): ADS 2004. LNCS, vol. 3068. Springer, Heidelberg (2004)
3. André, E., Rehm, M., Minker, W., Buhler, D.: Endowing spoken language dialogue systems with emotional intelligence. In: André, E., Dybkjær, L., Minker, W., Heisterkamp, P. (eds.) Affective Dialogue Systems, pp. 178–187. Springer, Heidelberg (2004)
4. Berk, L.M.: English syntax: from word to discourse. Oxford University Press, Oxford (1999)
5. Blum, A., Furst, M.: Fast Planning Through Planning Graph Analysis. Artificial Intelligence 90, 281–300 (1997)
6. Brown, P., Levinson, S.: Politeness: Some Universals in Language Usage. Cambridge University Press, Cambridge u.a (1987)
7. Cassell, J., Bickmore, T.W.: Negotiated Collusion: Modeling Social Language and its Relationship Effects in Intelligent Agents. User Model. User-Adapt.Interact. 13(1-2), 89–132 (2003)
8. Dale, R., Reiter, E.: Building Natural Language Generation Systems. Studies in Natural Language Processing. Cambridge University Press, Cambridge (1995)
9. Goffman, E.: The presentation of self in everyday life. Doubleday Press (1959)
10. Grosz, B.J., Sidner, C.L.: Plans for discourse. In: Cohen, P.R., Morgan, J.L., Pollack, M.E. (eds.) Intentions in Communication, pp. 417–444. MIT Press, Cambridge, MA (1990)
11. Johnson, L.W., Rizzo, P., Bosma, W.E., Ghijsen, M., van Welbergen, H.: Generating socially appropriate tutorial dialog. In: ISCA Workshop on Affective Dialogue Systems, pp. 254–264 (2004)
12. Johnson, L., Mayer, R., André, E., Rehm, M.: Cross-cultural evaluation of politeness in tactics for pedagogical agents. In: Proc. of the 12th Int. Conf. on Artificial Intelligence in Education (2005)
13. Lavoie, B., Rambow, O.: RealPro – a fast, portable sentence realizer. In: Proceedings of the Conference on Applied Natural Language Processing (ANLP'97), Washington DC (1997)

14. Mairesse, F., Walker, M.A.: Words Mark the Nerds: Computational Models of Personality Recognition through Language. In: Proceedings of the 28th Annual Conference of the Cognitive Science Society (CogSci 2006) (2006)
15. Mairesse, F., Walker, M.A.: PERSONAGE: Personality Generation for Dialogue. In: Proceedings of the 45th Annual Meeting of the Association for Computational Linguistics. ACL (2007)
16. Morand, D.A., Ocker, R.J.: Politeness theory and Computer-Mediated communication: A Sociolinguistic Approach to Analyzing Relational Messages. In: Proceeding of the 36th Hawaii International Conference on System Sciences, HICSS (2003)
17. Piwek, P.: An Annotated Bibliography of Affective Natural Language Generation. Technical Report ITRI-02-02. University of Brighton (2002)
18. Porayska-Pomsta, K.: Influence of Situational Context on Language Production: Modelling Teachers' Corrective Responses. PhD Thesis. School of Informatics, University of Edinburgh (2003)
19. Porayska-Pomsta, K., Pain, H.: Providing Cognitive and Affective Scaffolding through Teaching Strategies. In: Proceedings of the 7th International Conference on Intelligent Tutoring Systems (ITS) (2004)
20. Reeves, B., Nass, C.: The Media Equation. University of Chicago Press (1996)
21. Rehm, M., Andre, E.: Informing the Design of Agents by Corpus Analysis. Conversational Informatics. In: Nishida, T. (ed.) (2007)
22. Roman, N., Piwek, P., Carvalho, A.: Politeness and Bias in Dialogue Summarization: Two Exploratory Studies. In: Qu, Y., Wiebe, J. (eds.) Simple Program Schemes and Formal Languages, vol. 20, Springer, Heidelberg (2006)
23. Romano, D.M.: Virtual Reality Therapy. Developmental Medicine & Child Neurology. Journal 47(9), 580 (2005)
24. Sidner, C.L.: An artificial discourse language for collaborative negotiation. In: Proc. 12th National Conf. on AI, pp. 814–819 (1994)
25. Walker, M.A.: The effect of resource limits and task complexity on collaborative planning in dialogue. Artificial Intelligence Journal 85, 1–2 (1996)
26. Walker, M., Cahn, J., Whittaker, S.J.: Improving linguistic style: Social and affective bases for agent personality. In: Proc. Autonomous Agents'97, pp. 96–105. ACM Press, New York (1997)
27. Wang, N., Johnson, W.L., Rizzo, P., Shaw, E., Mayer, R.: Experimental evaluation of polite interaction tactics for pedagogical agents. In: Proceedings of IUI '05 (2005)

Textual Affect Sensing for Sociable and Expressive Online Communication

Alena Neviarouskaya[1], Helmut Prendinger[2], and Mitsuru Ishizuka[1]

[1] University of Tokyo, Department of Information and Communication Engineering, Japan
`lena@mi.ci.i.u-tokyo.ac.jp, ishizuka@i.u-tokyo.ac.jp`
[2] National Institute of Informatics, Japan
`helmut@nii.ac.jp`

Abstract. In this paper, we address the tasks of recognition and interpretation of affect communicated through text messaging. The evolving nature of language in online conversations is a main issue in affect sensing from this media type, since sentence parsing might fail while syntactical structure analysis. The developed Affect Analysis Model was designed to handle not only correctly written text, but also informal messages written in abbreviated or expressive manner. The proposed rule-based approach processes each sentence in sequential stages, including symbolic cue processing, detection and transformation of abbreviations, sentence parsing, and word/phrase/sentence-level analyses. In a study based on 160 sentences, the system result agrees with at least two out of three human annotators in 70% of the cases. In order to reflect the detected affective information and social behaviour, an avatar was created.

Keywords: Affective sensing from text, affective user interface, avatar, emotions, online communication, language parsing and understanding, text analysis.

1 Introduction

Emotions and feelings accompany us throughout the span of our lives and colour the way we build and maintain the basis for interactions with people in a society. This phenomenon also takes place in the virtual communities, where *"you can't kiss anybody and nobody can punch you in the nose, but a lot can happen within those boundaries. To the millions who have been drawn into it, the richness and vitality of computer-linked cultures is attractive, even addictive."* [24]. The online world of computer-mediated communication is such an environment where people can remain in touch virtually with their relatives and friends to exchange experiences, share opinions and feelings, and satisfy their social need of interpersonal communication. Since affect is an important component of effective social interaction, consideration of human emotions while constructing human-human online environments and human-computer systems [7] might enrich their interactivity and expressiveness. Affect-driven software may even benefit a person's well-being, as demonstrated in the research on simulating user-adapted persuasion dialogs about healthy eating [8].

In the past decade, issues of recognition, interpretation and representation of affect have been extensively investigated by researchers in the field of affective computing.

A. Paiva, R. Prada, and R.W. Picard (Eds.): ACII 2007, LNCS 4738, pp. 218–229, 2007.

A wide range of modalities have been considered, including affect in speech, facial display, posture, and physiological activity [21]. Recently, textual information is gaining increased attention by researchers interested in studying different kinds of affective phenomena, including sentiment analysis, subjectivity and emotions.

The focus of our work is on textual affect sensing and visualization in virtual communication environments, specifically, in Instant Messaging (IM), where people tend to use an informal style of writing. The evolving language observed in online communication poses a challenge for text processing tasks. We have thus taken into account the peculiarity of this communication medium (details are given in [18]) when designing our rule-based Affect Analysis Model. In order to make the user's experience in online communication enjoyable, exciting and fun, we have developed a system for the recognition and interpretation of affect conveyed through text, and complementary, the visual reflection of affective states and communicative behaviour through the use of a 2D cartoon-like avatar.

The remainder of the paper is structured as follows. Section 2 discusses related work. Section 3 describes the basis for text classification. The developed Affect Analysis Model and preliminary experimental results are discussed in Section 4 and Section 5, respectively. In Section 6, we briefly discuss and conclude the paper.

2   Related Work

In order to analyse affect communicated through written language, researchers in the area of natural language processing proposed a variety of approaches, methodologies and techniques.

WordNet-Affect, a linguistic resource for the lexical representation of affective knowledge, was created by Strapparava and Valitutti [26] with the aim to support applications relying on language recognition and generation. [25] described automatic textual emotion recognition and its visualization by kinetic typography (text animation). In order to analyse affective content, the authors were using not only affective words from WordNet-Affect, but also an affective lexicon derived from the evaluation of the semantic similarity between generic terms and affective concepts.

Kamps and Marx [10] investigated measures for affective or emotive aspects of meaning obtained from the structure of the WordNet lexical database. To classify sentiment and affect represented in text, methods employing Pointwise-Mutual Information calculation were introduced [23,28]. An approach to analysing affect content in free text using fuzzy logic techniques was proposed by Subasic and Huettner [27]. [2] presented a method for extracting sentiment-bearing adjectives from Word-Net using the Sentiment Tag Extraction Program. Kim and Hovy [11] developed an automatic algorithm for classifying opinion-bearing and non-opinion-bearing words, and described a method for the detection of sentence-level opinion.

Statistical language modelling techniques have been applied by researchers to analyse moods conveyed through online diary posts [12,14,15]. However, the main limitation of those "bag-of-words" approaches to textual affect classification is that they neglect the negation constructions and syntactical relations in sentences. Pang et al. [20] reported promising results on the classification of film reviews into "positive" and "negative" by using support vector machines. In contrast to classifying documents by their overall sentiment, Wilson et al. [30] presented experiments in which they automatically distinguish prior and contextual polarity of individual words and phrases in sentiment expressions.

Some researchers employed a keyword spotting technique to recognize emotion from text [19] or expressed in a multi-modal way (for example, speech signals along with textual content [31]). However, the use of a simple word-level analysis model cannot handle cases where affect is expressed by phrases requiring complex phrase/sentence-level analyses, since words are interrelated and influence each other's affect-related interpretation (like in the sentence "*I use the ability to breathe without guilt or worry*"), or when a sentence carries affect through underlying meaning (for example, "*I punched my car radio, and my knuckle is now bleeding*").

Advanced approaches targeting at textual affect recognition performed at the sentence-level are described in [5,13,16]. The lexical, grammatical approach introduced by Mulder et al. [16] focused on the propagation of affect towards an object. Boucouvalas [5] developed the Text-to-Emotion Engine based on word tagging and analysis of sentences. However, the proposed system employs the parser that generates emotional output only if an emotional word refers to the person himself/herself and the sentence is in present continuous or present perfect continuous tense. We think that such limitations greatly narrow the potential of textual emotion recognition. An approach for understanding the underlying semantics of language using large-scale real-world commonsense knowledge was proposed by Liu et al. [13], who incorporated the created affect sensing engine into an affectively responsive email composer called EmpathyBuddy.

3   Foundation for Affective Text Classification

Here we address the basis of affective text classification as an important first task for the development of an automatic emotion recognition system.

3.1   Emotion and Communicative Function Categories

Why do people prefer to communicate and interact with a person who is expressive? In face-to-face communication, displayed emotions signal that the speaker is more sociable, open and humorous. All types of expressive means (such as gaze, intonation, facial expressions, gestures, body postures and movements etc.) potentially carry communicative power and promote better understanding [1,22].

Thus we believe that interaction in online conversations might benefit from the automation of multiple expressive channels, so that the user does not have to worry about visual self-presentation or misunderstandings as in standard IM systems, but can focus on the content of the conversation. Thus, we aim at recognizing and visualizing not only emotions in text messages, but also communicative functions. Both can then be "acted out" by our avatar. Since the purpose of affect recognition in an IM system is to relate text to avatar emotional expressions, emotional categories were confined to those that can be visually expressed and easily understood by users. For affect categorization, we have decided to use the subset of emotional states defined by Izard [9]: 'anger', 'disgust', 'fear', 'guilt', 'interest', 'joy', 'sadness' ('distress'), 'shame', and 'surprise'. As to communicative functions, 'greeting', 'thanks', 'posing a question', 'congratulation', and 'farewell' form the basis for communicative behaviour identification.

3.2 Affect Database

In order to support the handling of abbreviated language and the interpretation of affective features of emoticons, abbreviations, and words, a special database was created using MySQL 5.0 [17].

While accumulating affect database entries, we collected 364 emoticons, both of American and Japanese style (for example, ":">" and "=^_^=" for 'blushing'), and the 337 most popular acronyms and abbreviations, both emotional and non-emotional (for example, "BL" for 'belly laughing', "cul8r" for 'see you later', and "bc" – 'because'). From the source of affective lexicon, WordNet-Affect [26], we have taken 1627 words: adjectives, nouns, verbs, and adverbs. We added not only words that refer directly to emotions, mood, traits, cognitive states, behaviour, attitude, sensations, but also words that carry the potential to elicit affective states in humans to our database (for example, "beautiful", "disaster", "break", "deceive", "violate" etc.). In addition to affect-related words, we were taking into account words standing for communicative functions listed in the previous subsection. Since interjections, such as "alas", "wow", "yay", "ouch", etc. are specific indicators of communicated emotion caused by unexpectedness, a long-awaited joyful event, or pain, they were collected as well. Moreover, we included 112 modifiers (e.g. "very", "extremely", "slightly", "hardly", "less", "not" etc.) into our database because they influence the strength of related words and phrases in a sentence.

Emotion categories and intensities were manually assigned to affect-related entries of the database by three independent annotators. Intensity values range from 0.0 to 1.0, and describe the intensity degree of affective states from 'very weak' to 'very strong'. Annotators conformed to our guideline with the description of emotional state gradation within intensity levels. For example, 'cheerful', 'glad', 'happy', 'joyful' and 'elated' all correspond to the 'joy' emotional state, but to a different degree of intensity. Emoticons and emotional abbreviations were transcribed and related to named affective states, whereby each entry was assigned to only one category (examples are listed in Table 1). The inter-rater agreement was calculated using Fleiss' Kappa statistics. The Kappa coefficients for emoticons and abbreviations are 0.94 and 0.93, respectively, showing good annotation reliability.

Since some affective words may express more than one emotional state, annotators could relate words to more than one category. For instance, in the annotation of the word "frustrated", both 'anger' and 'sadness' emotions are involved, with intensities 0.2 and 0.7, respectively (Table 2).

Assignments of emotion labels to the same word might differ among annotators. We only considered emotion categories that occur in the assignments of at least two annotators. The most frequent emotion labels in resulting sets were 'joy' and 'sadness' (34.3% and 30.0% of overall number of affective words, respectively) whereas the least frequent was 'guilt' (3.1%). The distribution of affective words with one, two, and three emotion labels is 67%, 29%, and 4%, respectively.

Table 1. Examples of emoticons and abbreviations taken from affect database

Symbolic representation	Meaning	Category	Intensity
:-)	happy	Joy	0.6
:-o	surprise	Surprise	0.8
:-S	worried	Fear	0.4
\(^O^)/	very excited	Joy	1.0
(~_~)	grumpy	Anger	0.3
m(._.)m	bowing, thanks	Thanks	-
JK	just kidding	Joy	0.3
4gv	forgive	Guilt	0.6
PPL	people	-	-

Table 2. Examples of words taken from affect database

Affective word	Part of speech	Category	Intensity
cheerfulness	Noun	Joy	0.3
astonished	Adjective	Surprise	1.0
frustrated	Adjective	Anger	0.2
		Sadness	0.7
dislike	Verb	Disgust	0.4
remorsefully	Adverb	Guilt	0.8
		Sadness	0.5

In intensity estimation, variance of data from the mean was taken into consideration. If the variance was not exceeding a predetermined threshold, the resulting intensity was measured as the average of intensities given by three annotators. Otherwise, the intensity value responsible for exceeding the threshold was removed, and only the remaining values were taken into account. Regarding the emotion intensity annotations of affective words, we observed interesting statistics within each of the nine emotion categories. Fig. 1 shows the percentage of cases with valid variance of given intensities within each emotion category.

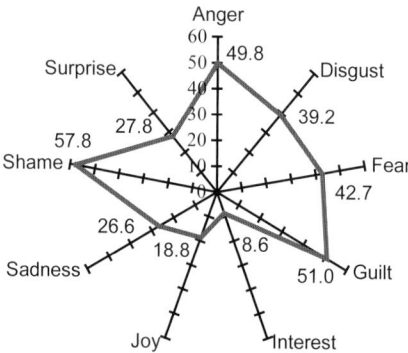

Fig. 1. The percentage of cases with valid variance of intensities within each emotion category

As seen from the diagram, annotators easily agreed in intensity assignments to 'shame', 'guilt', and 'anger' categories, in contrast to frequent disagreement in cases of 'interest', 'joy', and 'sadness'. We can only speculate that disagreement is related to the huge diversity of 'joyful' and 'sad' synonymous words with different emotional colorations, and due to the fuzziness of the 'interest' concept (some of psychologists do not consider 'interest' as an emotional state at all).

Adverbs of degree have an impact on neighbouring verbs, adjectives, or another adverb, and are used to mark that the extent or degree is either greater or less than usual [4]. In [3], authors use adverbs of degree to modify the score of adjectives in sentiment analysis. In our work, such adverbs along with some of prepositions constitute the set of modifiers. Two annotators gave coefficients for intensity degree strengthening or weakening (from 0.0 to 2.0) to them, and the result was averaged (see Table 3).

Table 3. Examples of modifier coefficients

Modifier	Category	Coefficient
perfectly	adverb of affirmation	1.9
seemingly	adverb of doubt	0.6
immensely	strong intensifying adverb	1.8
slightly	weak intensifying adverb	0.2
hardly	negation	0.0

4   Affect Analysis Model

The algorithm for analysis of affect in text consists of five stages: (1) symbolic cue analysis, (2) syntactical structure analysis, (3) word-level analysis, (4) phrase-level analysis, and (5) sentence-level analysis. The working flow of the Affect Analysis Model is presented in Fig. 2.

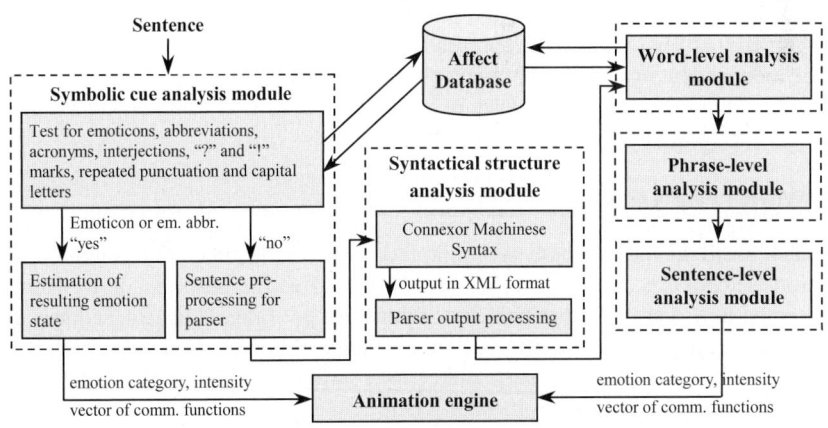

Fig. 2. Working flow of the Affect Analysis Model

4.1 Symbolic Cue Analysis

In the *first stage*, the sentence is tested for occurrences of emoticons, abbreviations, acronyms, interjections, "?" and "!" marks, repeated punctuation and capital letters.

If there is an emoticon or abbreviation related to an emotional state, no further analysis of affect in text is performed based on the simplifying assumption that the emoticon (or abbreviation) dominates the affective meaning of the entire (simple or compound) sentence. It is known that people type emoticons and emotional abbreviations to show actual feeling, or to avoid misleading the other participants, for instance, after irony, joke, or sarcasm (e.g. *"Thank you so much for your kind encouragement :-("*). On the other hand, if there are multiple emoticons or emotion-relevant abbreviations in the sentence, we determine the prevailing (or dominant) emotion based on the following two (tentative) rules: (1) when emotion categories of the detected emoticons (or abbreviations) are the same, the higher intensity value is taken for this emotion; (2) when they are different, the category (and intensity) of the emoticon occurring last is dominant.

If there are no emotion-relevant emoticons or abbreviations in a sentence, we prepare the sentence for parser processing: emoticons and abbreviations standing for communicative function categories are excluded from the sentence; and non-emotional abbreviations and acronyms are replaced by their proper transcriptions found in the database (e.g. *"I m* [am] *stressed bc* [because] *i have frequent headaches"*). In such a way, the problem of correct processing of abbreviated text by syntactical parser is settled.

4.2 Syntactical Structure Analysis

The *second stage* is devoted to syntactical structure analysis. The used Connexor Machinese Syntax parser [6] returns exhaustive information for analysed sentences, including word base forms, parts of speech, dependency functions, syntactic function tags, and morphological tags. From the parser output, we can read off the characteristics of each token and the relations between words in a sentence. While handling the parser output, we represent the sentence as a set of primitive clauses (either independent or dependent). Each clause might include Subject formation, Verb formation and Object formation, each of which may consist of main element (subject, verb, or object) and its attributives and complements.

4.3 Word-Level Analysis

For each word in the database we built (see Sect. 3.2), either the communicative function category is taken as a feature or the affective features of a word are represented as a vector of emotional state intensities e = [anger, disgust, sadness, fear, guilt, interest, joy, shame, surprise]. For example, e("rude")=[0.2,0.4,0,0,0,0,0,0,0]; e("brotherly")=[0,0,0,0,0,0,0.2,0,0]; and e("love")=[0,0,0,0,0,0.8,1,0,0]. In the case of a modifier, the system identifies its coefficient.

Since the database contains words only in their dictionary form, one important system function at this stage is to increase the intensity of the emotional vector of an adjective (or adverb) if it is in comparative or superlative form (e.g. "gladder", "gladdest").

4.4 Phrase-Level Analysis

In the *fourth stage*, phrase-level analysis is performed. The purpose of this stage is to detect emotions involved in phrases, and then in Subject, Verb, and Object formations. Words in a sentence are interrelated and, hence, each of them can influence the overall meaning and affective bias of a statement.

We have defined general types of phrases, and rules for processing them with regard to affective content:

- adjective phrase ("extremely sad"): modify the vector of adjective;
- noun phrase: output vector with the maximum intensity within each corresponding emotional state in analysing vectors (e.g. e("brotherly love")= =[0,0,0,0,0,0.8,1,0,0]);
- verb plus adverbial phrase: output vector with the maximum intensity within each corresponding emotional state in analysing vectors;
- verb plus noun phrase: if verb and noun phrase have opposite valences ("break favourite vase", "enjoy bad weather"), consider vector of verb as dominant; if valences are the same ("like honey", "hate crying"), output vector with maximum intensity in corresponding emotional states;
- verb plus adjective phrase: output vector of adjective phrase.

The rules for modifiers are as follows:

- adverbs of degree multiply or decrease emotional intensity values;
- negation modifiers such as "no", "not", "never", "any", "nothing" and connector "neither...nor" cancel (set to zero) vectors of the related words, i.e. "neutralize the emotional content";
- prepositions such as "without", "except", "against", "despite" cancel vectors of related words (e.g. statement "*despite his endless demonstrations of rude power*" is neutralized due to preposition).

Statements with prefixed words like "think", "believe", "sure", "know", "doubt" or with modal operators such as "can", "may", "must", "need", "would" etc. are not considered by our system because they express a modal attitude towards the proposition. Conditional clause phrases beginning with "if", "even if", "when", "whenever", "after", "before", and "although", "even though", etc. are disregarded as well (e.g. "*I eat when I'm angry, sad, bored...*", or "*If only my brain was like a thumbdrive, how splendid it would be.*").

There might be several emotional vectors within each of the Subject, Verb, or Object formations. During this stage, we apply the described rules to phrases detected within formation boundaries. Finally, each formation can be represented as a unified vector encoding its emotional content.

4.5 Sentence-Level Analysis

In the *fifth and final stage*, the overall emotion of a sentence and its resulting intensity degree are estimated. The emotional vector of a simple sentence (or of a clause) is generated from Subject, Verb, and Object formation vectors.

The main idea here is to first derive emotion vector of Verb-Object formation relation. It is estimated based on the "verb plus noun phrase" rule described above. In order to apply this rule, we automatically determine valences of Verb and Object formations using their unified emotion vectors (particularly, non-zero-intensity emotion categories). The estimation of the emotion vector of a clause (Subject plus Verb-Object formations) is then performed in the following manner: if valences of Subject formation and Verb formation are opposite (e.g. Subject formation = "my darling", Verb formation = "smashed", Object formation "his guitar"; or Subject formation = "troubled period", Verb formation = "luckily comes to an end"), we consider the vector of the Verb-Object formation relation as dominant; otherwise, we output the vector with maximum intensities in corresponding emotional states of vectors of Subject and Verb-Object formations.

It is important to note that the developed system enables the differentiation of the strength of the resulting emotion depending on the tense of a sentence and availability of first person pronouns. In our approach, the emotional vector of a simple sentence (or of a clause) is multiplied by the corresponding empirically determined coefficient of intensity correction (details are given in [18]).

For compound sentences, we defined two rules: (1) with coordinate connectors "and" and "so": output the vector with the maximum intensity within each corresponding emotional state in the resulting vectors of both clauses; (2) with coordinate connector "but": the resulting vector of a clause following after the connector is dominant (e.g. *"They attacked, but we luckily got away!"*).

After the dominant emotion of the sentence is determined (according to the highest intensity in the resulting vector), the relevant parameters are sent to the animation engine of our avatar.

5   System Evaluation

For system evaluation, we collected 160 sentences from a corpus of online diary-like blog posts [29]. Three annotators labeled the sentences with one of nine emotion categories discussed in Sect. 3.1 (or neutral) and a corresponding intensity value. The annotations from human raters are considered as "gold standard" for the evaluation of algorithm performance. The measured Fleiss' Kappa coefficient was low (0.58), and suggests that persons' comprehension, interpretation and evaluation of emotions are individual and might depend on personality type and emotional experience.

When comparing system results with human raters' annotations, we found that the percentage of cases where the dominant emotion category obtained by our algorithm matches with at least one of three raters' annotation is 79.4% (from which 84.3% are categorized as emotional, and 15.7% - neutral) of all sentences. In view of the variety of considered emotions (9 categories and neutral), the accuracy of our system seems reasonably high. In 70%, system output agrees with at least two annotators.

We also evaluated the system performance with regard to intensity estimation. The percentage of emotional sentences according to the measured distance between

Table 4. Percentage of emotional sentences according to the range of intensity difference between human annotations and output of algorithm

Range of intensity difference	[0.0 – 0.2]	(0.2 – 0.4]	(0.4 – 0.6]	(0.6 – 0.8]	(0.8 – 1.0]
Percentage of sentences %	68.2	26.2	4.7	0.9	0.0

intensities given by human raters (averaged values) and those obtained by Affect Analysis Model is shown in Table 4. As seen in the table, our system achieved satisfactory results for emotion intensity estimation.

6   Discussion and Conclusions

In this paper, we describe a rule-based approach to affect sensing from text at a sentence-level. A preliminary evaluation of the Affect Analysis Model algorithm shows promising results regarding its capability to recognize affective information in text from an existing corpus of informal online communication.

The salient features of the proposed algorithm are: (1) analysis of nine emotions on the level of individual sentences (which remains a challenge for machine learning based approaches); (2) the ability to handle the evolving language of online communications; (3) consideration of syntactic relations and dependences between words in a sentence; (4) basis on database of affective words, interjections, emoticons, abbreviations and acronyms, modifiers; (5) analysis of negation, modality, and conditionality; and (6) emotion intensity estimation. Moreover, we implemented a test interface with an avatar based on the Affect Analysis Model (see Fig. 3).

On the other hand, the system strongly depends on the created source of lexicon, affect database. This limits its performance if indirectly emotion-related words occur in analysed sentence (e.g. *"Oh yes, not forgetting, they had a mini chocolate fountain!"*). Furthermore, the Affect Analysis Model does not yet disambiguate word meanings (e.g. word "kill" is typically associated with negative emotions, but the phrase "to kill the audience" conveys 'surprise') and it fails to process expression-modifiers such as "to no end", "to death" (e.g. *"I love my ipod to death "*), etc.

We also encountered the problem of annotating sentences in isolation, i.e, without context. For example, the sentence *"There are no other terms that could really put me in a better position"* was rated as 'sad' by two annotators, as 'joy' by one, and as

Fig. 3. Test application of Affect Analysis Model

'neutral' by our system, whereas originally it belongs to a 'sad' monologue. Therefore, when analysing text messages in IM, we should also take into account the emotion dynamics throughout the conversation, or its "overall mood".

In our future study we will investigate those issues and explore the possibilities to overcome current limitations of the system.

Acknowledgments. We would like to acknowledge and thank Dr. Alessandro Valitutti and Dr. Diego Reforgiato for their kind help while affect database creation. We wish also to express our gratitude to Dzmitry Tsetserukou, Shaikh Mostafa Al Masum and Manuel M. Martinez who have contributed to annotations of affect database entries and sentences for their efforts and time.

References

1. Allwood, J.: Bodily Communication Dimensions of Expression and Content. In: Multimodality in Language and Speech Systems, pp. 7–26. Kluwer Academic Publishers, Netherlands (2002)
2. Andreevskaia, A., Bergler, S.: Mining WordNet for Fuzzy Sentiment: Sentiment Tag Extraction from WordNet Glosses. In: Proceedings of EACL'06, Italy (2006)
3. Benamara, F., Cesarano, C., Picariello, A., Reforgiato, D., Subrahmanian, V.: Sentiment Analysis: Adjectives and Adverbs are Better than Adjectives Alone. In: Proceedings of ICWSM'07,, OMNIPRESS, Boulder, Colorado (2007)
4. Biber, D., Johansson, S., Leech, G., Conrad, S., Finegan, E., Quirk, R.: Longman Grammar of Spoken and Written English. Pearson Education Limited (1999)
5. Boucouvalas, A.C.: Real Time Text-to-Emotion Engine for Expressive Internet Communications. In: Being There: Concepts, effects and measurement of user presence in synthetic environments, pp. 306–318. IOS Press, Amsterdam (2003)
6. Connexor Oy, http://www.connexor.com/
7. Cowie, R., Douglas-Cowie, E., Tsapatsoulis, N., Votsis, G., Kollias, S., Fellenz, W., et al.: Emotion Recognition in Human-Computer Interaction. IEEE Signal Processing Magazine 1, 32–80 (2001)
8. De Rosis, F., Mazzotta, I., Miceli, M., Poggi, I.: Persuasion Artifices to Promote Wellbeing. In: Proceedings of First International Conference on Persuasive Technology for Human Well-being, Netherlands, pp. 84–95 (2006)
9. Izard, C.E.: Human Emotions. Plenum Press, New York, NY (1977)
10. Kamps, J., Marx, M.: Words with Attitude. In: Proceedings of BNAIC'02, pp. 449–450 (2002)
11. Kim, S.-M., Hovy, E.: Automatic Detection of Opinion Bearing Words and Sentences. In: Proceedings of IJCNLP'05 (2005)
12. Leshed, G., Kaye, J.: Understanding How Bloggers Feel: Recognizing Affect in Blog Posts. Extended Abstracts of CHI'06, 1019–1024 (2006)
13. Liu, H., Lieberman, H., Selker, T.: A Model of Textual Affect Sensing using Real-World Knowledge. In: Proceedings of IUI'03, pp. 125–132 (2003)
14. Mihalcea, R., Liu, H.A: Corpus-based Approach to Finding Happiness. In: Proceedings of the AAAI Spring Symposium on Computational Approaches to Weblogs (2006)
15. Mishne, G.: Experiments with Mood Classification in Blog Posts. In: Proceedings of the First Workshop on Stylistic Analysis of Text for Information Access (2005)

16. Mulder, M., Nijholt, A., den Uyl, M., Terpstra, P.: Lexical Grammatical Implementation of Affect. In: Proceedings of the 7th International Conference on Text, Speech and Dialogue, pp. 171–178. Springer, Heidelberg (2004)
17. MySQL 5.0, http://www.mysql.com/
18. Neviarouskaya, A., Prendinger, H., Ishizuka, M.: Analysis of Affect Expressed through the Evolving Language of Online Communication. In: Proceedings of IUI'07, pp. 278–281. ACM Press, New York (2007)
19. Olveres, J., Billinghurst, M., Savage, J., Holden, A.: Intelligent, Expressive Avatars. In: Proceedings of WECC'98, pp. 47–55 (1998)
20. Pang, B., Lee, L., Vaithyanathan, S.: Thumbs up? Sentiment Classification Using Machine Learning Techniques. In: Proceedings of the Conference on Emprirical Methods in Natural Language Processing (2002)
21. Picard, R.: Affective Computing. The MIT Press, Cambridge, MA (1997)
22. Poggi, I., Pelachaud, C.: Performative Faces. Speech Communication 26, 5–21 (1998)
23. Read, J.: Recognising Affect in Text using Pointwise-Mutual Information. Master thesis, University of Sussex (2004)
24. Rheingold, H.: The Virtual Community: Homesteading on the Electronic Frontier. Wesley Publishing, Menlo Park, CA (1993)
25. Strapparava, C., Valitutti, A., Stock, O.: Dances with Words. In: Proceedings of IJCAI'07, Hyderabad, India, pp. 1719–1724 (2007)
26. Strapparava, C., Valitutti, A.: WordNet-Affect: an Affective Extension of WordNet. In: Proceedings of LREC'04, pp. 1083–1086 (2004)
27. Subasic, P., Huettner, A.: Affect Analysis of Text Using Fuzzy Semantic Typing. In: IEEE Transactions on Fuzzy Systems 9(4), 483–496 (2001)
28. Turney, P.D.: Thumbs Up or Thumbs Down? Semantic Orientation Applied to Unsupervised Classification of Reviews. In: Proceedings of ACL'02, USA (2002)
29. Weblog Data Collection. BuzzMetrics, Inc., http://www.nielsenbuzzmetrics.com
30. Wilson, T., Wiebe, J., Hoffmann, P.: Recognizing Contextual Polarity in Phrase-level Sentiment Analysis. In: Proceedings of HLT/EMNLP-2005, Vancouver, Canada (2005)
31. Chuang, Z.-J., Wu., C.-H.: Multi-Modal Emotion Recognition from Speech and Text. In: Computational Linguistic and Chinese Language Processing 9(2), 45–62 (2004)

Lexical Affect Sensing: Are Affect Dictionaries Necessary to Analyze Affect?

Alexander Osherenko and Elisabeth André

Multimedia Concepts and Applications, Faculty of Applied Informatics
University of Augsburg, Germany
{osherenko,andre}@informatik.uni-augsburg.de

Abstract. Recently, there has been considerable interest in the automated recognition of affect from written and spoken language. In this paper, we investigate how information on a speaker's affect may be inferred from lexical features using statistical methods. Dictionaries of affect offer great promise to affect sensing since they contain information on the affective qualities of single words or phrases that may be employed to estimate the emotional tone of the corresponding dialogue turn. We investigate to what extent such information may be extracted from general-purpose dictionaries in comparison to specialized dictionaries of affect. In addition, we report on results obtained for a dictionary that was tailored to our corpus.

Keywords: Lexical Modality, Lexical Affect Sensing, Emotion Detection, Spontaneous Dialogues, Affect Dictionaries.

1 Introduction

Recently, there has been considerable interest in the automated recognition of affect from written and spoken language. The driving force behind this work is the observation that a computer system is more likely to be accepted by the human user if it is able to recognize his or her emotions and respond accordingly. Psychological studies reveal that the user's emotional state significantly affects his or her phrasing. For instance, if someone is in a state of high arousal, his or her phrasing tends to be more stereotypical and less diversified [6]. Weintraub observed in an experiment that speakers that were considered as more emotional used few non-personal references and a fair number of expressions of feeling [15]. In this paper, we investigate how information on a speaker's affect may be inferred from lexical features.

Dictionaries of affect offer great promise to lexical affect sensing since they contain information on the affective qualities of single words or phrases that may be employed to estimate the emotional tone of the corresponding dialogue turn. Dictionaries of affect are usually composed drawing on human common-sense knowledge about affect words or employing rating tools, such as semantic differential scales. Examples include the Whissell's Dictionary of Affect Language (DAL) [16], the LIWC2001 Dictionary [10] or the WordNet-Affect Database of ITS-IRST [14].

A number of approaches to affect sensing take advantage of the information included in affect dictionaries either exclusively or in addition to other features.

A. Paiva, R. Prada, and R.W. Picard (Eds.): ACII 2007, LNCS 4738, pp. 230–241, 2007.
© Springer-Verlag Berlin Heidelberg 2007

Prendinger and colleagues [9] make use of the emotional senses in WordNet to estimate the emotional content of words in a document. Shaikh and colleagues [13] introduce an approach to affect sensing that is based on manually collected sentiment verbs and adjectives from WordNet. Zhang and colleagues rely on the Heise dictionary and WordNet to extract affect from speech in e-drama [19]. Nasukawa and Yi [8] conduct a sentiment analysis using a dictionary consisting of 3,513 affective adjectives, adverbs and nouns.

Affect dictionaries have also been proven useful to discriminate deceptive from non-deceptive speech. For instance, Hirschberg and colleagues [3] make use of the LIWC and DAL dictionaries to extract features from speech. They observe that the pleasantness score as well as the occurrence of positive emotion words seem to be a promising factor in predicting deception. Deceptive speech tends to have a greater pleasantness score and a greater proportion of positive emotion words than truthful speech.

Mairesse and Walker [7] aim at identifying a speaker's personality by means of a conversational analysis using the LIWC dictionary [10] as well as the MRC psycholinguistic database [1]. They observe that emotional stability is best predicated by features extracted from MRC while LIWC features show a better performance for other personality traits.

In this paper, we concentrate on affect recognition for spontaneous utterances based on the affective qualities of words. We investigate to what extent such information may be extracted from general-purpose dictionaries or dictionaries of affect. In particular, we focus on the following questions:

1. Do we get higher recognition rates if we restrict ourselves to word features that convey emotional content?
2. Do emotive annotations in dictionaries improve affect sensing for dialogue turns?
3. Are common words more useful to affect sensing than less common words?
4. Are dictionaries of affect more useful to affect sensing than general-purpose dictionaries?

In this paper, we answer these questions by evaluating two dictionaries of affect as well as one general-purpose dictionary. In addition, we create our own dictionary based on the corpus we investigate – a corpus containing transcriptions of spontaneous speech.

2 Dictionaries

In this study, we consider two affect dictionaries, the Whissell's Dictionary of Affect Language (DAL) [16] and the Linguistic Inquiry and Word Count Dictionary (LIWC) [10], as well as word frequency lists that are based on the general-purpose British National Corpus (BNC) and word frequency lists extracted from our own affect corpus.

DAL contains 8,742 words of different inflection that are characterized by their emotional connotation along three dimensions: evaluation, activation and imagery. Scores for the evaluation range from 1 (unpleasant) to 3 (pleasant), for the activation range from 1 (passive) to 3 (active), for imagery range from 1 (difficult to form a mental picture of this word) to 3 (easy to form a mental picture). The scores have been determined by human judgment. In the following, the original scale is mapped from 1 to 3 to -1 to 1 for better readability.

The LIWC affect dictionary contains 2,251 word patterns that represent words ending with a wildcard e.g. the pattern *abandon** describes all inflections of word *abandon*. Unlike DAL, the LIWC does not characterize words by using continuous scales, but classifies entries categorically – there are word patterns of 68 different categories in LIWC. We are mostly interested in the category Affective or Emotional Processes (*Affect*) with 617 patterns referring to affective or emotional processes. *Affect* is subcategorized into positive emotions (*Posemo*) and negative emotions (*Negemo*). *Posemo* again has two subcategories: positive feelings (*Posfeel*), optimism and energy (*Optim*) while *Negemo* has three subcategories – anxiety or fear (*Anx*), anger (*Anger*), sadness (*Sad*). For example, the word *afraid* got the labels *Affect*, *Negemo* and *Anx*.

The DAL or LIWC dictionaries are compiled specifically for emotional analysis. In contrast, the BNC frequency list is a general-purpose list based on a 100 million word collection obtained from a wide range of written and spoken language sources representing contemporary British English [4]. Each word in the list is indicated with its frequency in the BNC corpus e.g. the word *children* occurs in the corpus 46,577 times. We compose several smaller frequency lists (*BNC-threshold*) out of the original BNC frequency list by discarding words for which the BNC frequency does not exceed the specified threshold. For instance, BNC-650 contains the subset of 8,603 words from the BNC corpus whereas each of words occurs more than 650 times in the whole 100M-word BNC. Additionally, we examine frequency lists (*SAL-n*) that are calculated based on the studied affect corpus SAL (see Section 4).

3   Corpus

In our study, the affective meaning of dialogue utterances from the SAL corpus is explored [5]. The freely available SAL corpus contains audio-visual data of four users communicating with one of four psychologically different characters: optimistic and outgoing (Poppy), confrontational and argumentative (Spike), pragmatic and practical (Prudence), depressing and gloomy (Obadiah) that try to draw the user into their own emotional state. The corpus includes 27 dialogues (672 turns) each of them annotated with FEELTRACE data by three annotators *dr*, *em*, *jd* [2]. The fourth annotator *cc* annotated only 23 out of 27 dialogues (569 turns). The FEELTRACE data are specified as coordinates in Osgood's Evaluation/Activation (E/A) space and are mapped onto 5 affect segments (see Fig. 1).

We extracted a subcorpus from SAL by using a majority vote strategy. A turn is only considered for the subcorpus if the FEELTRACE data of at least two judges correspond to the same affect segment at the end of the turn. Hence, 35 out of 672 utterances had to be discarded due to missing agreement between annotators. For

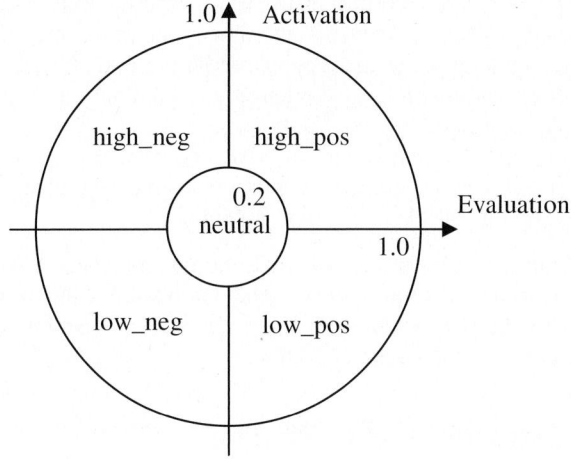

Fig. 1. Affect segmentation in the E/A space

remaining 637 utterances a majority vote could be obtained resulting in the following affect distribution – *high_neg*: 182 utterances, *low_neg*: 112 utterances, *neutral*: 139 utterances, *low_pos*: 24 utterances, *high_pos*: 180 utterances. Example utterances from the SAL corpus with the majority vote are shown in Fig. 2.

```
[1 - Affect segment: neutral] (Breath intake) Well,
I'll be able to have fun when I've done all the work,
but you see I have a very, er, heavy, difficult couple
of months ahead of me.

[2 - Affect segment: high_pos] (Laugh) I'm damn awful.
How are you (laugh)?

[3 - Affect segment: low_pos] Yup.

[4 - Affect segment: high_neg] Yes, that's not very
pleasant, is it?

[5 - Affect segment: low_neg] Erm, that's probably
true.
```

Fig. 2. Examples of SAL utterances

Note that utterance 1 is annotated as *neutral* even though it contains the words *fun, heavy, difficult* that usually indicate highly affective utterances, utterance 2 is annotated as *high_pos* despite of the words *damn* and *awful*, utterance 3 is annotated as *low_pos* despite of no affect words at all, utterance 4 is annotated as *high_neg* despite of the word *pleasant*, utterance 5 as *low_neg* despite of the word *true*. Furthermore, utterances 4 and 5 are very similar regarding their grammatical and lexical form, but still got different annotations (*high_neg* vs. *low_neg*). Summing up, the properties of utterances in the SAL corpus may be characterized as follows:

1. *Genre.* The SAL corpus consists of transcripted spontaneous spoken utterances. The spontaneous utterances in SAL may be grammatically incorrect and often contain repairs, repetitions and inexact words.
2. *Length of emotional text.* The length of a dialogue turn in SAL is variable and may consist of one word only.
3. *Annotations.* An annotation in SAL indicates the affect experienced by several test persons conversing with one of the SAL characters. Test persons and annotators in SAL are different people.

Due to the properties above, the SAL corpus presents a great challenge to computer-aided affect sensing if it is based on lexical features only. In contrast, human annotators relied in addition to linguistic features also on visual and acoustic features in order to annotate dialogue turns.

4   Feature Extraction and Evaluation

Features are computed automatically for dialogue turns making use of frequency lists as well as the affective qualities of words extracted from various dictionaries. In particular, we concentrate on the following features:

- *WORD FEATURES:* Each word in the dictionary represents a word feature to which a frequency value is assigned. The frequency value represents how many times the word occurs in a dialogue turn. The use of word features is based on the assumption that the frequency of certain words is characteristic of the affective tone of the dialogue turn. The number of word features depends on the size of the dictionary. For example, when using LIWC, we obtain 2,251 word features.
- *LIWC FEATURES:* For each LIWC category, we compute how frequently it occurs in the dialogue turn by counting the number of words that correspond to the category. Depending on whether we rely on all categories or just the affect-related categories, we obtain sets with 68 (CAT-68) or 8 features (CAT-8) respectively.
- *DAL FEATURES:* We compute the averaged scores for the emotive connotations (evaluation, activation, imagery). In sum, we get a set with three features (EA-AVG).

We did not normalize word or category counts with respect to text length since an earlier experiment did not show a significant effect of normalization on the recognition rate.

To find the most relevant features for emotion recognition, we conducted several experiments with subsets of features. In particular, we explored the following options for feature reduction.

Selection of the most frequent words as features
This option is based on the assumption that more common words are more suitable to discriminate between different emotional states expressed by a dialogue turn. Since the available dictionaries differ very much in size, we apply different selection strategies for them:

- For BNC, we extract 56 sets of word features: BNC-650, BNC-1400, ..., BNC-72800 where *BNC-n* contains words with at least *n* occurrences in the BNC corpus. The values of *n* are selected in the manner that facilitates the comparison with the number of features in DAL. The frequency word list for the BNC corpus is freely available under [http://www.kilgarriff.co.uk/BNC_lists/all.al.gz].
- For SAL, we extract 95 sets of word features *SAL-n* (*n*=1...95) where *SAL-n* contains the *m/n* most frequent words from the SAL corpus and *m* = 2,051 is the number of words in SAL.

Selection of words with higher emotional expressivity
This option is based on the assumption that words that have higher activation and evaluation values or that can be categorized as emotion words are more discriminative than other words. We employ different strategies for the two available dictionaries:

- For DAL, we extract 40 sets of word features DAL-1, DAL-2, ..., DAL-40 and corresponding DAL features (EA-AVG) where *DAL-n* contains all words from DAL with $\sqrt{activation^2 + evaluation^2} \geq \frac{n-1}{n}$. The distribution of the E/A space is illustrated in Fig. 3. For example, the complete set of DAL word features lies within the outmost circle while the dotted area corresponds to word features with higher emotional expressivity. Fig. 3 shows circle 3 (DAL-3) containing the word *brutality*.

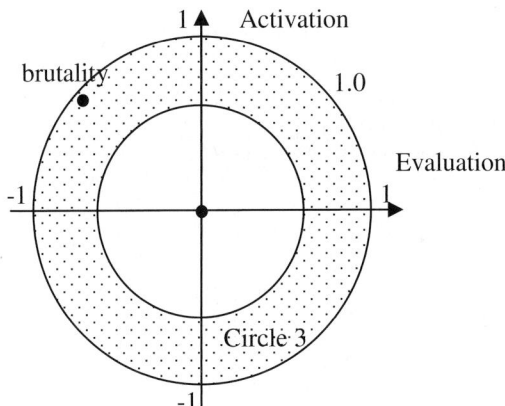

Fig. 3. Extraction of words from DAL

- For LIWC, we extract 2 sets of word features LIWC-68 and LIWC-8 where LIWC is the original set of 2,251 word features and LIWC-8 only contains 617 word features that correspond to the affect-related categories.

5 Results

Classification is done using SVM from the WEKA data mining toolkit [18]. Figures 4-6 and Table 1 below show the 10-fold cross-validation results that are

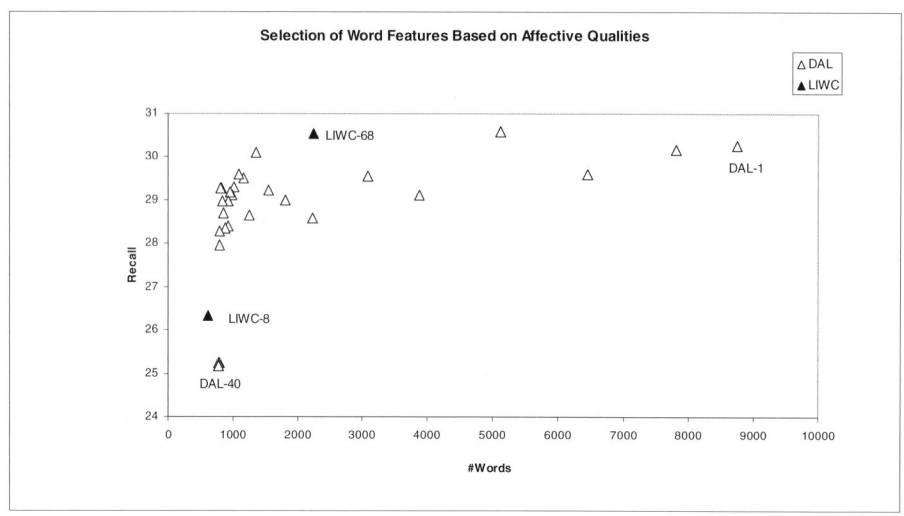

Fig. 4. Selection of Word Features Based on Affective Qualities

averaged over affect classes. The recall, precision, and fMeasure measures are expressed in percent.

We examine the aforementioned subsets of features with respect to their relevance to affect recognition in dialogue turns. In Fig. 4, we reduce the number of word features originating from the DAL and the LIWC dictionary based on their affective qualities. In Fig. 5, we reduce the number of word features based on their frequency. Here, we start from the general-purpose BNC corpus and frequency lists generated from the SAL corpus. In Fig. 6, we compare word features lists with and without features based on affective annotations/categories: word features from DAL that are selected according to their evaluation and activation values, the complete set of LIWC words with and without affective categories and a reduction of the LIWC words to affective LIWC words with and without affective categories. In Table 1, we list the affect sensing results based on features from affective annotations from DAL (EA-AVG), from LIWC (CAT-8, CAT-68) and their combinations. The first column indicates the number of features, the second column the names of the feature sets.

The recognition rates for the feature sets examined in this paper range from 21.70% recall (EA-AVG) to 36.20% recall (SAL-19). Compared to choice by chance for a 5-class problem (20%), the recognition rates are rather low. But as we have seen in Section 4, the corpus presents a great challenge to affect recognition since speakers do not always use expressive words that can be directly mapped onto emotions.

We obtained the best results for SAL-19 (recall 36.20%) – one of the dictionaries which was directly extracted from our corpus. We combined SAL-19 with the best LIWC categories and part of speech (POS) features from the BNC tagset, but it didn't improve recognition rates (36.20% vs. 32.84%).

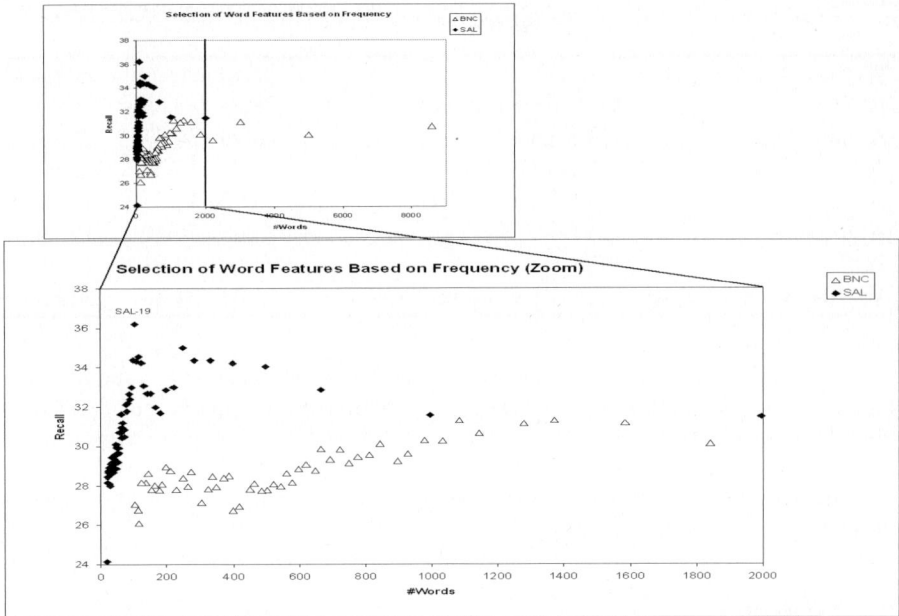

Fig. 5. Selection of Word Features Based on Frequency

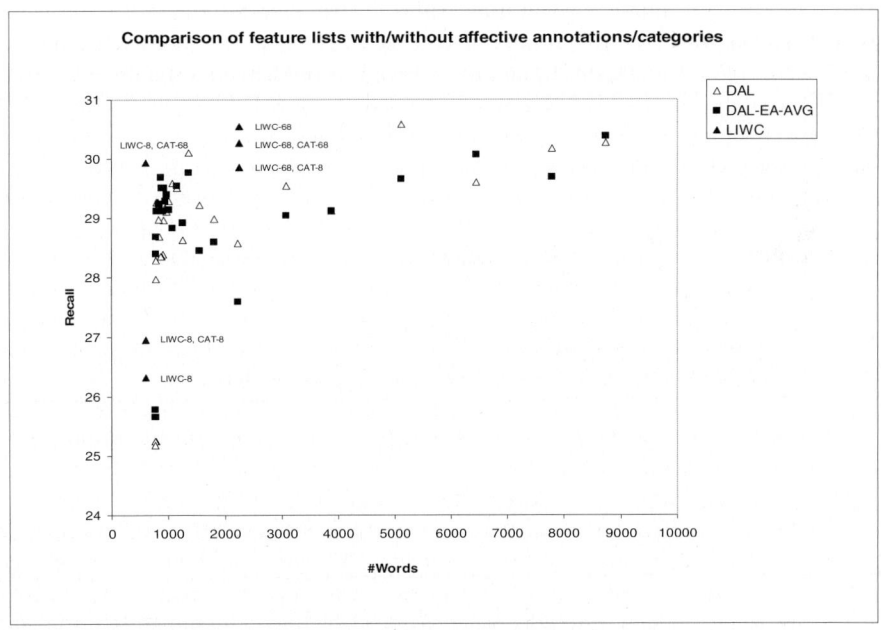

Fig. 6. Comparison of feature lists with/without affective annotation/categories

Table 1. Results of affect sensing using exclusively affective annotations/categories

#Features	Features	Recall	Precision	fMeasure
A: 71	CAT-68 + EA-AVG	28.54	28.89	26.42
A: 68	**CAT-68**	**28.90**	**30.37**	**26.83**
A: 3	EA-AVG	21.70	13.60	14.61
A: 11	CAT-8 + EA-AVG	23.92	14.57	16.72
A: 8	CAT-8	24.46	25.40	17.76
POS: 48	POS	24.20	22.01	19.76
W: 104, A: 68, POS: 48	**SAL-19, CAT-68, POS**	**32.84**	**34.46**	**32.66**

We assumed that classification results depend on the coverage – the ratio of words found both in the employed dictionary (or subdictionary) and the corpus divided by the number of words in the corpus. However, we did not find any distinct influence of the coverage on the classification rate.

In the following, we examine the recognition results in more detail to shed light on the questions addressed in Section 1.

6 Discussion

Results in the previous section allow for answering the questions in the introduction:

1. **Do we get higher recognition rates if we restrict ourselves to word features that convey emotional content?** Fig. 4 shows that a reduction of word features to the most expressive ones does not lead to a significant change in recognition results. For instance, we achieve a recall rate of 30.27 % for a set with nearly 9,000 word features (DAL-1) which slowly degrades to 25.18% (DAL-40) when restricting ourselves to a much smaller set of 779 more expressive word features that are selected based on their activation and evaluation values in the Whissell dictionary. Obviously, the choice of word features based on their emotional expressivity does not have a great impact on recognition rate, but may provide a useful criterion of feature reduction without risking a severe degradation of recognition rates. For instance, we get nearly the same recognition rates for sets with about 9000 word features and for sets with between 1300 and 1500 more expressive features.

2. **Do emotive annotations in dictionaries improve affect sensing for dialogue turns?** As Fig. 6 shows, the classification results do not change significantly when augmenting word features by features that are based on affective annotations from the DAL or affective categories of the LIWC dictionary. Obviously, affect-related features do not include discriminative information that is not yet included in the word counts. On the other hand, the results do not degrade dramatically when relying exclusively on affective annotations (see Table 1). For example, when using the affective annotations from the LIWC only (CAT-68) we get similar results, but just need to consider 68 features as opposed to several hundreds of features. A reduction of features is of major importance when analysing affect in a real-time application.

3. **Are common words more useful to affect sensing than less common words?** Fig. 5 shows that a reduction of the BNC lists based on their frequency does not lead to a dramatic change in recognition rates. Based on our experiments, it is hard to say whether a reduction of features should be based rather on the frequency of words or their expressive qualities. A comparison of Fig. 4 and Fig. 5 shows that datasets that are chosen on the basis of the expressed affect may be outperformed by datasets with words that are derived from the investigated corpus and chosen on the basis of frequencies. Nevertheless, a reduction of word features based on frequencies has to be taken with care. For instance, Wiebe and colleagues [17] found that rare words, especially hapax legomena (words occurring only once in a corpus) can be successfully used for affect sensing. According to their studies, we should not entirely exclude rare words from further consideration. However, as long as we do not have concrete knowledge regarding the predictive power of specific words, a reduction of word features based on their frequency seems to be reasonable.

4. **Are dictionaries of affect more useful to affect sensing than general-purpose dictionaries?** Our experiments show that general-purpose dictionaries may provide similar results as affect dictionaries for similar numbers of features. For instance, we achieve a recall of about 30% with the BNC and the DAL datasets when using around 5000 features. The best result – a recall of 36.20% – has been obtained for SAL-19 which just contains 104 word features resp. Here, we have to consider, however, that SAL-1 to SAL-95 have been specifically tailored to our corpus.

7 Conclusion

In this paper, we investigated the potential benefits of several dictionaries for affect sensing in dialogue. Our results indicate that lexical affect sensing may also be successfully conducted with a general-purpose dictionary. Obviously, affective annotations/categories in dictionaries do not provide much more information on the affective qualities of a dialogue turn in addition to word counts. On the other hand, the affective annotations seem to provide a good means to reduce the number of features for classification tasks. For example, when just considering the 68 affective word categories of LIWC, we get similar results as when using several thousands word features taken from an affect dictionary or a general-purpose dictionary. Such a reduction is of high significance when sensing affect in real-time.

We showed classification results for the SAL corpus as a corpus that presents a great challenge to affect sensing due to its properties, but we assume that our findings are also applicable for other "less difficult" corpora. For example, we studied a corpus with 215 movie reviews [www.reelviews.net] distributed over 5 emotional classes (40 movie reviews with zero rating, 25 movie reviews with four-star-rating, and 50 movie reviews each with other three ratings) and revealed similar trends (Fig. 7).

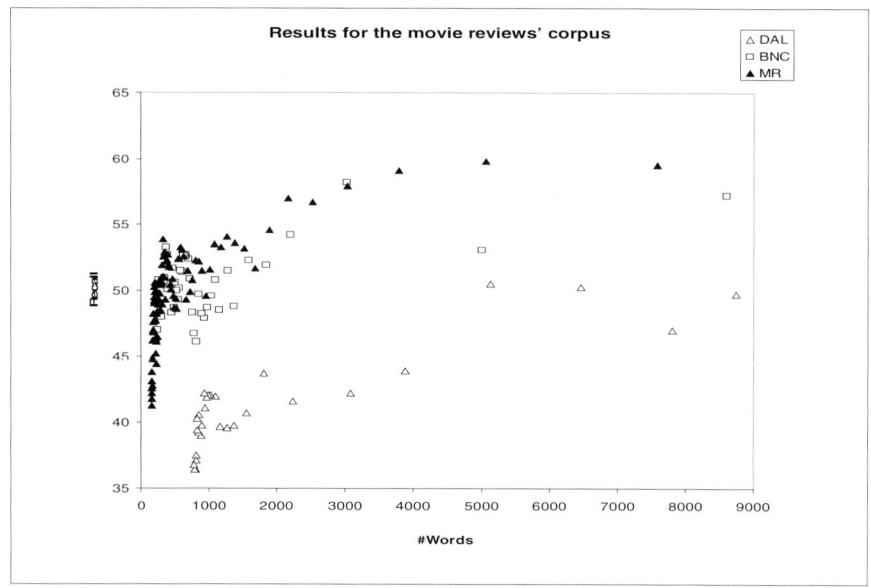

Fig. 7. Results for the movie reviews' corpus

MR in Fig. 7 represents word features' sets extracted from the frequency list of the movie reviews' corpus (an equivalence of the SAL feature sets). Noticeable is a significantly higher recognition rates compared with that in the SAL corpus (greater than 35%).

Of course, the results should be taken with care since our experiments are based on two corpora only. In our future work, we will therefore investigate to what extent the results may be generalized for other corpora. Furthermore, we will have a look at additional affect dictionaries, such as the WordNet-Affect Database.

Acknowledgments

This work was partially financed by the European Network of Excellence HUMAINE and the European CALLAS IP.

We are greatly indebted to Thurid Vogt for her useful comments and suggestions.

References

1. Coltheart, M.: The MRC psycholinguistic database. Quarterly Journal of Experimental Psychology 33A, 497–505 (1981)
2. Cowie, R., Douglas-Cowie, E., Savvidou, S., McMahon, E., Sawey, M., Schröder, M.: 'FEELTRACE': An instrument for recording perceived emotion in real time. In: Proceedings of the ISCA Workshop on Speech and Emotion, Northern Ireland, pp. 19–24 (2000)

3. Hirschberg, J., Benus, S., Brenier, J.M., Enos, F., Friedman, S., Gilman, S., Girand, C., Graciarena, M., Kathol, A., Michaelis, L., Pellom, B., Shriberg, E., Stolcke, A.: Distinguishing Deceptive from Non-Deceptive Speech, URL (2005), http://www.speech. cs.cmu.edu/awb/jss/IS051364.PDF
4. Kilgarriff, A.: Putting Frequencies in the Dictionary. International Journal of Lexicography 10(2), 135–155 (1997)
5. Kollias, S.: ERMIS Project. URL (2007), http://www.image.ntua.gr/ermis/
6. Langenmayr, A.: Sprachpsychologie. Hogrefe, Göttingen (1997)
7. Mairesse, F., Walker, M.: Words Mark the Nerds: Computational Models of Personality Recognition through Language. In: Proceedings of the 28th Annual Conference of the Cognitive Science Society (CogSci 2006), Vancouver, pp. 543–548 (July 2006)
8. Nasukawa, T., Yi, J.: Sentiment analysis: capturing favorability using natural language processing. In: Proceedings of the 2nd international Conference on Knowledge Capture, Sanibel Island, FL, USA (October 23 - 25). K-CAP '03, ACM Press, New York (2003)
9. Neviarouskaya, A., Prendinger, H., Ishizuka, M.: Analysis of Affect Expressed through the Evolving Language of Online Communication. In: Proc. of IUI 2007, pp. 278–281. ACM Press, New York (2007)
10. Pennebaker, J.W., Francis, M.E., Booth, R.J.: Linguistic Inquiry and Word Count (LIWC): LIWC2001. Erlbaum Publishers, Mahwah, NJ (2001)
11. Pennebaker, J.W., Mehl, M.R., Niederhoffer, K.: Psychological aspects of natural language use: Our words, our selves. Annual Review of Psychology 54, 547–577 (2003)
12. Riloff, Ellen, Patwardhan, Siddharth, Wiebe, Janyce.: Feature Subsumption for Opinion Analysis. In: Proceedings of EMNLP-06, the Conference on Empirical Methods in Natural Language Processing. Sydney, AUS: Association for Computational Linguistics, pp. 440–448 (2006)
13. Shaikh, S., Islam, Md.T., Ishizuka, M., Prendinger, H.: Implementation of Affect Sensitive News Agent (ASNA) for affective classification of news summary. In: Proceedings International Conference on Computer and Information Technology (ICCIT-06), Dhaka, Bangladesh (2006)
14. Valitutti, A., Strapparava, C., Stock, O.: Developing Affective Lexical Resources. PsychNology Journal 2(1), 61–83 (2004)
15. Weintraub, W.: Verbal Behavior in Everyday Life. Springer, Heidelberg (1989)
16. Whissell, C.M.: The dictionary of affect in language. In: Plutchik, R., Kellerman, H. (eds.) Emotion: Theory, Research, and Experience, pp. 113–131. Academic Press, New York (1989)
17. Wiebe, J., Wilson, T., Bruce, R., Bell, M., Martin, M.: Learning Subjective Language. Computational linguistics 30(3), 277–308 (2004)
18. Witten, I.H., Frank, E.: Data Mining: Practical Machine Learning Tools and Techniques, 2nd edn. Morgan Kaufmann, San Francisco (2005)
19. Zhang, L., Barnden, J.A., Hendley, R.J., Wallington, A.M.: Exploitation in Affect Detection in Open-Ended Improvisational Text. In: Proceedings of the Workshop on Sentiment and Subjectivity in Text, ACM Press, New York (2006)

Affective Text Variation and Animation for Dynamic Advertisement

Carlo Strapparava, Alessandro Valitutti, and Oliviero Stock

FBK-irst, I-38050, Povo, Trento, Italy
{strappa,alvalitu,stock}@itc.it

Abstract. The largest part of the advertising market is already electronic. This means there is an opportunity for automatizing some of the production processes, such as producing and rendering catchy language expressions. A system is described that produces creative, affective variations of familiar textual expressions and animates them according to the affective contents. The textual variations are based on lexical semantics techniques such as an algorithm that looks for affective similarity, and on concepts such as optimal innovation, realized through assonant substitutions. Animation results from the realization of a scripting language for kinetic typography. The combination of affective variation and automatic affective perceptual rendering of key elements in the resulting expression is meant to guarantee effectiveness in advertising communication.

1 Introduction

Advertising requires getting the attention of the message recipient, and then reinforcing his attention and ensuring memorization. Surprise is an important component of the reinforcement phase, and creative variation of familiar expressions is often used for this purpose. A very effective tool is when variation is so to say "affectively charged". In addition to the introduction of this creative novel language expression, it is very important that the perceptual aspect is taken into consideration. Traditionally, we had a video, or a person speaking, but also typographic tools to emphasize or characterize otherwise text portions. With web-based advertisement (recent data show that most advertisements are web-based already now) we tend to have new means for communicating. This paper is about automatizing the process. In modern advertising practice, it is common of "creatives" to be recruited and hired in pairs formed by a copywriter and an art director. They work in a creative partnership to conceive, develop and produce effective advertisement. While the copywriter is mostly responsible for the textual content of the creative product, the art director focalizes efforts on the graphical presentation of the message. Advertising messages may be very synthetic but, at the same time, rich of emotional meaning and persuasive power.

In this paper we explore the development of a computational tool for ad production, composed of two parts. The first consists of the selection and creative affective variation of familiar common sense expressions (e.g. proverbs, idioms,

A. Paiva, R. Prada, and R.W. Picard (Eds.): ACII 2007, LNCS 4738, pp. 242–253, 2007.

clichés, movie titles, famous citations, etc.). The second step consists of the presentation of the headline through an affective text animation based on kinetic typography. Kinetic typography is one of several multimodal options for perceptual rendering. In contrast to synthesized speech, talking heads or ECAs it does not require the attribution to the computer of human qualities. It just adds dynamism to texts in more or less sophisticated ways, basically just introducing evocative movements to the traditional typographic elements: characters, words. The reader has this additional perceptual dimension in his processing.

1.1 Surprise Induction and Optimal Innovation

An important characteristic of an advertising message is its ability to induce surprise in the recipient. The surprise increases the level of emotional arousal and induces positive (or negative) attitudes toward the object being advertised. The surprise factor allows the message to capture attention and make it easy to memorize. These aspects of an ad increase the probability to induce some wanted behaviours, for example the purchase of some product, the choice of a specific brand, or the click on some specific web link. In the last case, it is crucial to make the recipient curious about the subject referred by the URL.

In order to develop a strategy for surprise induction, we considered an interesting property of pleasurable creative communication that was named by Rachel Giora as the *optimal innovation hypothesis* [1]. According to this assumption, when the novelty is in a complementary relation to salience (familiarity), it is "optimal" in the sense that it has an aesthetics value and "induce the most pleasing effect".

Therefore the simultaneous presence of novelty and familiarity makes the message potentially surprising, because this combination allows the recipient's mind to oscillate between what is known and what is different from usual. For this reason, an advertising message must be original but, at the same time, connected to what is familiar [2]. Familiarity causes expectations, while novelty violates them, and finally surprise arises.

1.2 Familiar Expression Variation

To produce creative messages capable of inducing valenced attitudes towards some target-topic, we started from the idea of "familiar expression variation". With this term we indicate an expression (sentence or phrase) that is obtained as a linguistic variation (e.g. substitution of a word, morphological or phonetic variation, etc.) of an expression recognized as familiar by recipients. In this work we limited the variation to word substitutions, compatible with the optimal innovation hypothesis. The "innovation" is provided by the substitution with words both semantically similar to the target topic and emotionally loaded, and the "optimality" is guaranteed by the assonance with the given familiar expression (i.e. old and new words have to be assonant).

We used in this process part of our experience in computational humor [3], in which we exploited incongruity theory to produce funny variations of given acronyms. In this work we extend this approach, affectively loading lexical entries for the variation production and generating automatically typographical animations that are coherent with the emotions we want to communicate. We employed the *affective weight* function developed in our previous work [4] for finding an affective category most appropriate for the text fragment.

The paper is structured as follows. In Section 2 we introduce the resources used in the system, in particular (i) WORDNET-AFFECT, an extension of the WordNet database in which some affective labels are assigned to a number of synsets; (ii) an affective semantic similarity, based on a Latent Semantic Analysis (i.e. *affective weight* function), which gives us an indication of the affective weight of generic terms; (iii) databases of familiar expressions and assonance tools; and (iv) a kinctic typography scripting language used for the final sentence animation. Section 3 describes the algorithm to variate familiar expressions and Section 5 displays some examples. Conclusions and future works are reported in Section 6.

2   Resources

2.1   Affective Semantic Similarity

We deal with the use of words in texts, and in particular their co-occurrences with words with explicit affective meaning. As claimed by Ortony et al. [5], we have to distinguish between words directly referring to emotional states (e.g. "fear", "cheerful") and those having only an indirect reference that depends on the context (e.g. words that indicate possible emotional causes as "killer" or emotional responses as "cry"). We call the former *direct affective words* and the latter *indirect affective words* [4]. In order to manage affective lexical meaning, we (i) organized the direct affective words and synsets inside WORDNET-AFFECT, an affective lexical resource based on an extension of WORDNET, and (ii) implemented a selection function (named *affective weight*) based on a semantic similarity mechanism automatically acquired in an unsupervised way from a large corpus of texts (100 millions of words), in order to individuate the indirect affective lexicon[1].

WORDNET-AFFECT *and the Emotional Categories.* WORDNET-AFFECT is an extension of the WordNet database [6], including a subset of synsets suitable to represent affective concepts. Similarly to what was done for domain labels [7], one or more affective labels (*a-labels*) are assigned to a number of WordNet synsets. In particular, the affective concepts representing an emotional state are individuated by synsets marked with the a-label EMOTION. There are also other a-labels for those concepts representing moods, situations eliciting emotions, or emotional responses. WORDNET-AFFECT is freely available for research purpose at http://wndomains.itc.it. See [8] for a complete description of the resource.

---

[1] In particular, we used the British National Corpus is a very large (over 100 million words) corpus of modern English, both spoken and written (see http://www.hcu.ox.ac.uk/bnc/). Of course, it is possible to add and/or consider specific corpora to get a more domain oriented similarity.

We extended WORDNET-AFFECT with a set of additional a-labels (i.e. the *emotional categories*), hierarchically organized, in order to specialize synsets with a-label EMOTION. In a second stage, we introduced some modifications, in order to distinguish synsets according to emotional valence. We defined four additional a-labels: POSITIVE, NEGATIVE, AMBIGUOUS, NEUTRAL. The first one corresponds to "positive emotions", defined as emotional states characterized by the presence of positive edonic signals (or pleasure). It includes synsets such as `joy#1` or `enthusiasm#1`. Similarly the NEGATIVE a-label identifies "negative emotions" characterized by negative edonic signals (or pain), for example `anger#1` or `sadness#1`. Synsets representing affective states whose valence depends on semantic context (e.g. `surprise#1`) were marked with the tag AMBIGUOUS. Finally, synsets referring to mental states that are generally considered affective but are not characterized by valence, were marked with the tag NEUTRAL.

Computing Lexical Affective Semantic Similarity. There is an active research direction in the NLP field about sentiment analysis and recognition of semantic orientation from texts (e.g. [9,10,11]). In our opinion, a crucial issue is to have a mechanism for evaluating the semantic similarity among generic terms and affective lexical concepts. To this aim we estimated term similarity from a large scale corpus. In particular we implemented a variation of Latent Semantic Analysis (LSA). LSA yields a vector space model that allows for a *homogeneous* representation (and hence comparison) of words, word sets, sentences and texts. For representing word sets and texts by means of a LSA vector, we used a variation of the *pseudo-document* methodology described in [12]. This variation takes into account also a *tf-idf* weighting schema (see [13] for more details). In practice, each document can be represented in the LSA space by summing up the normalized LSA vectors of all the terms contained in it. Also a synset in WORDNET (and then an emotional category) can be represented in the LSA space, performing the pseudo-document technique on all the words contained in the synset. Thus it is possible to have a vectorial representation of each emotional category in the LSA space (i.e. the *emotional vectors*), and consequently we can compute a similarity measure among terms and affective categories. We defined the *affective weight* [14] as the similarity value between an emotional vector and an input term vector (e.g. we can check how a generic term is similar to a given emotion).

For example, the noun "gift" is highly related to the emotional categories: LOVE (with positive valence), COMPASSION (with negative valence), SURPRISE (with ambiguous valence), and INDIFFERENCE (with neutral valence).

In summary, the vectorial representation in the Latent Semantic Space allows us to represent, in a *uniform* way, emotional categories, generic terms and concepts (synsets), and eventually full sentences.

2.2 Database of Familiar Expressions

The base for the strategy of "familiar expression variation" is the availability of a set of expressions that are recognized as familiar by English speakers.

We considered three types of familiar expressions: proverbs, movie titles, clichés. We collected 1836 familiar expressions from the Web, organized in three types: common use proverbs (628), famous movie titles (290), and clichés (918). Proverbs were retrieved in some of many web sites in which they are grouped (e.g. http://www.francesfarmersrevenge.com/stuff/proverbs.htm or www.many things.org/proverbs). We considered only proverbs of common use. In a similar way we collected clichés, that are sentences whose overuse often makes them humorous (e.g. home sweet home, I am playing my own game). Clichés are mostly collected from the web sites http://www.clichesite.com and http://www.find cliches.com. Finally, movie titles were selected from the Internet Movie Database (www.imdb.com). In particular, we considered the list of the best movies in all sorts of categories based on votes from users.

2.3   Assonance Tool

To cope with this aspect we got and reorganized the CMU pronouncing dictionary (http://www.speech.cs.cmu.edu/cgi-bin/cmudict) with a suitable indexing. The CMU Pronouncing Dictionary is a machine-readable pronunciation dictionary for North American English that contains over 125,000 words and their transcriptions.

Its format is particularly useful for speech recognition and synthesis, as it has mappings from words to their pronunciations in the given phoneme set. The current phoneme set contains 39 phonemes; vowels may carry lexical stress.

3   Algorithm

In this section, we describe the algorithm developed to perform the creative variation of an existing familiar expression.

1. **Insertion of an input concept.** The first step of the procedure consists of the insertion of an input concept. This is represented by one or more words, a set of synonyms, or a WordNet synset. In the latter case, it is individuated through a word, the part of speech (noun, adjective, verb, or adverb), and the sense number, and it corresponds to a set of synonyms. Using the pseudo-document representation technique described above, the input concept is represented as a vector in the LSA vectorial space. For example, say that a cruise vacation agency seeks to produce a catchy message on the topics "vacation" and "beach".

2. **Generation of the target-list.** A list (named *target-list*) including terms that are semantically connected (in the LSA space) with the input concept(s) is generated. This target list represents a semantic domain that includes the input concept(s).For example, given the vector representing "vacation", "beach", the LSA returns a list "sea", "hotel", "bay", "excursion", etc.

3. **Association of assonant words.** For each word of the target-list one or more possible *assonant words* are associated. Then a list of word pairs

(named *variation-pairs*) is created. The list of variation-pairs is filtered according to some constraints. The first one is syntactic (elements of each pair must have the same part of speech). The second one is semantic (i.e. the second element of each pair must not be included in the target-list), and its function is to realize a semantic opposition between the elements of a variation pair. Finally, to each variation pair an *emotion-label* (representing the emotional category most similar to the substituting word) is provided with the corresponding affective weight. Some possible assonant pairs for the example above are: *(bay, day), (bay, hay), (hotel, farewell)*, etc.

4. **Creative variation of familiar expressions.** In this step, the algorithm gets in input a set of familiar expressions (in particular, proverbs and movie titles) and, for each of them, generates all possible variations. The list of variated expressions is ordered according to the global affective weight.

Following the example, a resulting ad is *Tomorrow is Another Bay* as a variation of the familiar expression *Tomorrow is Another Day*. Note that still for moment, the final choice among the best resulting expressions proposed by system is left to human selection.

At this point, the variated expression is animated with kinetic typography, as explained in the next section. In particular, words are animated according to the underlying emotion to emphasize the affective connotation.

4   Affective Animation

Kinetic typography is the technology of text animation, i.e. text that uses movement or other changes over time. The advantage of kinetic typography consists in a further communicative dimension, combining verbal and visual communication, and providing opportunities to enrich the expressiveness of static texts. According to [15], kinetic typography can be used for three different communicative goals: capturing and directing attention of recipients, creating characters, and expressing emotions. A possible way of animating a text is mimicking the typical movement of humans when they express the content of the text (e.g. "Hi" with a jumping motion mimics exaggerated body motion of humans when they are really glad).

We explore the idea to have a link between lexical semantics of texts (automatically discerned through NLP techniques) and some kinetic properties exploited for animating the words. In particular, kinetic typography allows us to make the indirect affective meaning explicit in order to automatically augment the affective expressivity of texts.

A first step was the individuation of an appropriate tool for the authoring and visualization of text animations. We wanted to act in an environment that allows us to realize animations in a very simple manner and to represent them in a easily exportable format. Functionalities for the automated composition of animations were our specific concern. To this aim we considered the Kinetic Typography Engine (KTE), a Java package developed at the Design School of Carnegie Mellon University [15]. It allows us to create a potentially wide range of animations. Taking this engine as a starting point, we first realized a development environment for the creation and the visualization of text animations. Our model for the animation representation is a bit simpler than the KTE model. The central assumption consists of the representation of the animation as a composition of elementary animations (e.g. linear, sinusoidal or exponential variation). In particular, we consider only one operator for the identification of elementary animations (K-BASE) and three composition operators: kinetic addition (K-ADD), kinetic concatenation (K-JOIN), and kinetic loop (K-LOOP).

The K-BASE operator selects an elementary animation (named *elementary kinetic behavior*) as a temporal variation of some kinetic property. Elementary kinetic behaviors correspond to a subset of dynamic variations implemented in KTE, for example linear variation (*linear*), sinusoidal variation (*oscillate*), and exponential variation (*exponential*).

Table 1. Some elementary kinetic behaviors

linear	linear variation
oscillate	sinusoidal variation
pulse	impulse
jitter	sort of "chaotic" vibration
curve	parabolic variation
hop	parabolic variation with small impulses at the endpoints
hop-secondary	derivative of hop, used as secondary effect to simulate elastic movements

The kinetic addition (K-ADD) of two animations with the same start time is obtained by adding, for each kinetic property of text, the corresponding dynamical variation of each single animation. The kinetic concatenation (K-JOIN) consists in the temporal shifting of the second animation, so that the ending time of the first is the starting time of the second. The kinetic loop (K-LOOP) concatenates an animation with itself a fixed number of times. In the development environment it is possible to freely apply these operators for the real time building of new animations. Compositional structure of animations can be represented in XML format and then easily exported. Finally, an interpreter allows us to generate in real time the animation starting from its structural representation.

After building the development tool, we selected a set of emotional categories and, for each of them, we created the corresponding text animations.

In particular, we focused on five emotional categories: joy, fear, surprise, anger, sadness (i.e. a subset of Ekman emotions [16]).

The kinetic animation to associate to a fixed emotion can be realized imitating either emotional and physiological rensponses (*analogous motion* technique), or tone of voice. We consider only animations of the first type, i.e. we represent each emotion with an animation that simulates a particular emotional behavior. In particular, JOY is represented with a sequence of hops, FEAR with palpitations, ANGER with a strong tremble and blush, SURPRISE with a sudden swelling of text, and finally SADNESS with text deflaction and getting squashed. Thus we

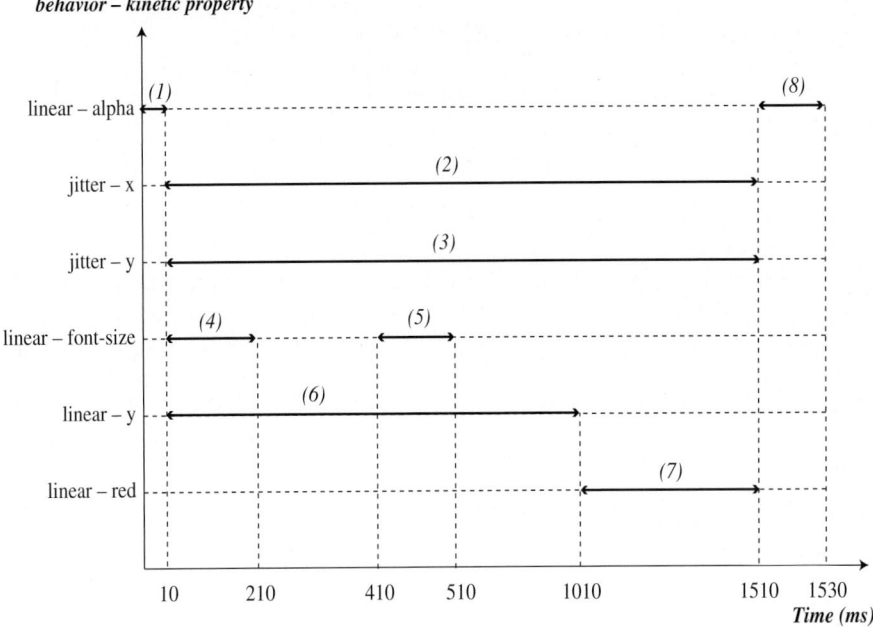

Fig. 1. Kinetic behavior description for "anger" emotion

annotated the corresponding emotional categories in WORDNET-AFFECT with these kinematic properties.

Figure 1 displays in detail the behavior of the anger emotion, showing the time-dependent composition graph of the basic animations. The string appears (1) and disappears (8) with a linear variation of the alpha property (that defines the transparency of a color and can be represented by a float value). The animation is contained between these two intervals and its duration is 1500 ms. The first component is a tiny random variation of the position (2) (3), represented by x and y kinetic properties, with jitter behavior. The second component consists of an expansion of the string (4) and a subsequent compression (5). The third component is given by a slow rise up (6). The last component, before disappearing, is a color change to red (7). The whole behavior is then described and implemented using the scripting language introduced above.

As it is difficult to enjoy the animations on *static* paper, please visit the web page `http://tcc.itc.it/people/strapparava/affective-KT` where some downloadable affective animations are available.

In a previous work [17] we conducted an exploratory evaluation of memorization, affective coherence and pleasantness of automatically animated existing news headlines. The system checked for the affective content of the headline, and consequently animated in a coherent way the text. We asked the users to annotate a set of generated animations choosing from the following emotional labels: joy, fear, anger, sadness, surprise, and possibly no-label. The agreement with the automatic annotation was about 72%. Regarding the memorization, all

Fig. 2. Jittering *anger*

the users were able to recognize the animated headlines faster with respect to static ones, with a mean of 47.5% less time in finding the animated headlines. Finally 80% of the users declared they really appreciated the animated titles. In addition, we created a set of "inconsistent" animations (e.g. some titles animated with a kinetic script not related to the respective emotional category). We repeated the first experiment. It is interesting to note that in this case the users performance in finding the headlines among a list of 50 news titles was even worse than the case of static headlines[2].

5   Examples

In this section we show some examples of creative variations.

Starting from an input concept (e.g. *disease*) we can obtain, using the semantic similarity, a list of related terms (Table 2).

Table 2. Input word: "disease"

Name	POS	Similarity to the input
symptom	noun	0.971
therapy	noun	0.969
metabolism	noun	0.933
analgesic	noun	0.899
suture	noun	0.851
thoracic	adjective	0.782
extraction	noun	0.623

Using the affective weight function, it is possible to check for their affective characterization (in Table 3 only four emotions are displayed), selecting those affectively coherent with the input term. Subsequently, the system searches for assonant words (Table 4) and checks for affective opposition with the original words (Table 5).

---

[2] We also asked the users to annotate these inconsistent animations. The general feeling reported was that of an annoying disorientation, in addition to the fact that the agreement was quite low (14% with the emotion of the text and 46% with the "wrong" emotion suggested by the animation, thus showing a small bias towards the latter).

Table 3. Affective weight

Name	fear	joy	anger	sadness
disease	0.357	0.201	0.135	0.679
symptom	0.423	0.293	0.164	0.685
therapy	0.374	0.315	0.170	0.691
metabolism	0.372	0.258	0.082	0.552
analgesic	0.280	0.241	0.173	0.526
suture	0.237	0.299	0.227	0.490
thoracic	0.157	0.135	0.134	0.448
extraction	0.126	0.245	0.177	0.366

Table 4. Phonetic associations

Name	Assonant Words
suture	*future*
thoracic	Jurassic
extraction	abstraction, attraction, contraction, diffraction, distraction, inaction, reaction, retraction, subtraction, transaction

Table 5. Affective difference

Name	fear	joy	anger	sadness
suture	0.237	0.299	0.227	**0.490**
future	0.467	**0.571**	0.417	0.462

Table 6. More Examples

Input Words	Varied Expression	Word Substitution
vacation, beach	Tomorrow is another bay	day → bay
disease	Back to the Suture	future → suture
	Thoracic Park	jurassic → thoracic
	Fatal Extraction	attraction → extraction
crash	Saturday Fright Fever	night → fright
fashion	Jurassic Dark	park → dark

At this point, the system retrieves familiar expressions that include the word to be substituted.

Table 6 shows the final word substitution in several examples. The system can then automatically animate the resulting expression emphasizing the novel affective connotation through kynetic typography techniques.

6   Conclusion

We have described a system that produces creative, affective variations of familiar expressions and animates them according to the affective contents. The textual variations are based on lexical semantics techniques such as an algorithm that looks for affective similarity, and on concepts such as optimal innovation, realized through assonant substitutions. Animation results from the realization of a scripting language for kinetic typography. The combination of affective variation and automatic affective perceptual rendering of key elements in the resulting expression is meant to guarantee effectiveness. As for applied prospects for this approach we should point out that we are talking about a very important area. Internet is a fundamental medium for advertising already now. Internet advertising was about 9.4 billion $ (8,000 million euro) in 2004 according to Kagan Research LLC. And growth is very fast: Google advertisement revenues went from 0 to 3,400 million euro in five years according to Business Week.

The future will probably include two important factors: a) reduction in time to market and extension of possible occasions for advertisement; b) more attention to the wearing out of the message and for the need for planning variants and connected messages across time and space; c) contextual personalisation, on the basis of audience profile and perhaps information about the situation. Leaving alone questions of privacy as far as this paper is concerned (but of course advertisement and promotion can be for a good cause and for social values!), all three cases call for a strong role for computer-based intelligent technology for producing novel appropriate advertisements.

Acknowledgments

This work was developed in the context of HUMAINE Network of Excellence and partially sponsored by MUR FIRB-project number RBIN045PXH.

References

1. Giora, R.: On Our Mind: Salience, Context and Figurative Language. Oxford University Press, New York (2003)
2. Pricken, M.: Creative Advertising. Thames & Hudson (2002)
3. Stock, O., Strapparava, C.: Getting serious about the development of computational humour. In: Proceedings of the 18th International Joint Conference on Artificial Intelligence (IJCAI-03), Acapulco, Mexico (August 2003)
4. Strapparava, C., Valitutti, A., Stock, O.: The affective weight of lexicon. In: Proceedings of the Fifth International Conference on Language Resources and Evaluation (LREC 2006), Genoa, Italy (May 2006)
5. Ortony, A., Clore, G.L., Foss, M.A.: The psychological foundations of the affective lexicon. Journal of Personality and Social Psychology 53, 751–766 (1987)
6. Fellbaum, C.: WordNet. An Electronic Lexical Database. The MIT Press, Cambridge (1998)

7. Magnini, B., Cavaglià, G.: Integrating subject field codes into wordnet. In: Proc. of the 2nd International Conference on Language Resources and Evaluation (LREC2000), Athens, Greece (2000)

8. Strapparava, C., Valitutti, A.: WordNet-Affect: an affective extension of WordNet. In: Proc. of 4th International Conference on Language Resources and Evaluation (LREC 2004), Lisbon (May 2004)

9. Turney, P., Littman, M.: Measuring praise and criticism: Inference of semantic orientation from association. ACM Transactions on Information Systems (TOIS) 21(4), 315–346 (2003)

10. Liu, H., Lieberman, H., Selker, T.: A model of textual affect sensing using real-world knowledge. In: Proc. of the Seventh International Conference on Intelligent User Interfaces (IUI 2003), Miami (2003)

11. Mihalcea, R., Liu, H.: A corpus-based approach to finding happiness. In: Proc. of Computational approaches for analysis of weblogs, AAAI Spring Symposium 2006, Stanford (March 2006)

12. Berry, M.: Large-scale sparse singular value computations. International Journal of Supercomputer Applications 6(1), 13–49 (1992)

13. Gliozzo, A., Strapparava, C.: Domains kernels for text categorization. In: Proc. of the Ninth Conference on Computational Natural Language Learning (CoNLL-2005), Ann Arbor (June 2005)

14. Valitutti, A., Strapparava, C., Stock, O.: Lexical resources and semantic similarity for affective evaluative expressions generation. In: Proc. of the First International Conference on Affective Computing & Intelligent Interaction (ACII 2005) (October 2005)

15. Lee, J., Forlizzi, J., Hudson, S.: The kinetic typography engine: An extensible system for animating expressive text. In: Proc. of ACM UIST 2002 Conference, ACM Press, New York (2002)

16. Ekman, P.: Biological and cultural contributions to body and facial movement. In: Blacking, J. (ed.) Anthropology of the Body, pp. 34–84. Academic Press, London (1977)

17. Strapparava, C., Valitutti, A., Stock, O.: Dances with words. In: Proceedings of the 20th International Joint Conference on Artificial Intelligence (IJCAI-07), Hyderabad, India (January 2007)

Entertainment Modeling in Physical Play
Through Physiology Beyond Heart-Rate

Georgios N. Yannakakis and John Hallam

Maersk Mc-Kinney Moller Institute
University of Southern Denmark
Campusvej 55, Odense M, DK-5230
{georgios,john}@mmmi.sdu.dk

Abstract. An investigation into capturing the relation of physiology, beyond heart rate recording, to expressed preferences of entertainment in children's physical gameplay is presented in this paper. An exploratory survey experiment raises the difficulties of isolating elements derived (solely) from heart rate recordings attributed to reported entertainment and a control experiment for surmounting those difficulties is proposed. Then a survey experiment on a larger scale is devised where more physiological signals (Blood Volume Pulse and Skin Conductance) are collected and analyzed. Given effective data collection a set of numerical features is extracted from the child's physiological state. A preference learning mechanism based on neuro-evolution is used to construct a function of single physiological features that models the players' notion of 'fun' for the games under investigation. Performance of the model is evaluated by the degree to which the preferences predicted by the model match those expressed by the children. Results indicate that there appears to be increased mental/emotional effort in preferred games of children.

1 Introduction

The principal goal in the reported work is to construct a user model of a class of game-playing experience. Specifically, the aim is that the model can predict the answers to which variants of a given game are more or less "fun." This approach is referred to as *Entertainment Modeling*. Entertainment generated by a physical game experience is captured through features extracted from the player's physiological state and feature selection is used for choosing the appropriate set of features that successfully predict expressed entertainment preferences. Game play experiences might very well be identified through features extracted from user-game interaction. Furthermore, game play behavior could be video recorded and emotions could be recognized by experts or automatically through face gesture detection; however, these approaches are not the focus of this work.

In this work the entertainment model is constructed using preference learning techniques applied to statistical features derived from physiological signals measured during play. The output of the constructed model is a real number in the range $[0, 1]$ such that more enjoyable games receive higher numerical output. This basic approach of entertainment modeling is applicable to a variety

A. Paiva, R. Prada, and R.W. Picard (Eds.): ACII 2007, LNCS 4738, pp. 254–265, 2007.

of games, both computer [1] and physical [2,3,4] using features derived from physiological data and/or from the interaction of player and opponent measured through game parameters.

Even though entertainment is a highly complicated mental state it is correlated with sympathetic arousal [5] which can be captured through specific physiological signals such as heart rate variability (HRV) and skin conductivity [6]. While the emotional impact on a subject's physiological state during computer game playing is well reported in the literature (see [5] among others), there are no corresponding studies in the physical play domain. Motivated by the lack of entertainment modeling approaches grounded on a player's physiological state in physical interactive games, the Playware [7] physical interactive game platform has been used for recoding Heart Rate (HR) signals of children during play [8,3]. Herein, results and conclusions derived from this exploratory experiment (56 children participants) are presented. The complexity of isolating the elements of physical activity from expressed entertainment in physical games is outlined through this experiment. This problem is handled, in part, through a carefully designed control experiment of physical activity reported in [4].

As a sequel to the exploratory experiment, a new set of experiments for capturing entertainment preferences through physiology in physical play is presented here. This experiment expands the investigation of the physiological state's relation to entertainment preferences from HR to Blood Volume Pulse (BVP) and Skin Conductance (SC) signals. Moreover, the number of child participants is increased to 72 allowing for safer conclusions given our aims. A statistical analysis reveals that features extracted from HR and BVP that correspond to both physical and mental/emotional effort correlate significantly with expressed preferences. Moreover, preference learning (neuro-evolution) attempts on single features indicate that the energy of the high frequency band (derived through power spectral analysis) of HRV constitutes the feature that performs best in predicting expressed preferences on unknown data. This feature, which is suppressed during mental or emotional stress [9,10], is highly anti-correlated to reported entertainment indicating high parasympathetic heart activity on preferred games. Results also suggest that collecting physiological signals beyond HR, such as BVP, may provide more meaningful features for capturing entertainment preferences of children in physical play.

2   Related Work

Physiological condition measures have been used extensively for emotion recognition in children and adults within the affective computing research area. Mandryk *et al.* [5] examine the correlations between physiological signals (galvanic skin response, electromyography in jaw, respiration and cardiovascular measures) in reported adult user experiences in computer games. The preliminary experiments of Rani *et al.* [11] for appropriately adjusting the level of challenge in the game of 'Pong' based on recorded physiological signals in real-time and subject's self-reports of their emotional experiences during gameplay is closely related to our work. That study, however, is primarily focused on the anxiety level detection in real-time and is limited by the number of human participants. Physiological state (HR, SC) prediction models have also been proposed for potential entertainment augmentation in computer games [12].

Working on the same basis as Mandryk *et al.* [5], Ravaja *et al.* [13] examined whether the nature of the game opponent influences the physiological state of players. In addition, Hazlett's [14] work is focused on the use of facial electromyography to distinguish positive and negative emotional valence during interaction with a racing video game.

All aforementioned studies are focused on the use of physiology for capturing user experiences (e.g. "fun", engagement or excitement) applied within the computer and edutainment games framework. The work reported here is novel in that it examines the physiological state (HR, BVP, SC) correlates of reported "fun" in physical activity games, attempts to isolate physiological signal features attributed to reported entertainment in such physically demanding games and proposes a way of constructing a subjective model (a predictor of user preferences) of reported "fun" grounded in statistical features of physiological signal dynamics.

3   Test-Bed Physical Games

The Playware [7] prototype playground consists of several building blocks (i.e. tangible tiles) that allow for the game designer (e.g. the child) to develop a significant number of different games within the same platform. The overall technological concept of Playware is based on intelligent physical identities (tiles) that incorporate processing power, communication, input and output, focusing on the role of the morphology-intelligence interplay in developing game platforms [7,2,4].

Two games were designed on Playware and used for the experiments presented here: 'Bug-Smasher' and 'Space-Invaders'. Bug-Smasher is developed on a 6×6 square tile topology. During the game, different 'bugs' (colored lights) appear randomly on the game surface and disappear sequentially after a short period of time by turning a tile's light on and off respectively. The child's goal is to smash as many bugs as possible by stepping on the lighted tiles. Bug-smasher has been used as a test-bed in previous work; further details can been found in [2,8,4].

On the other hand, Space-Invaders' design is based on the classical arcade game released by Taito in 1978. The game is implemented on a 5×10 tile topology. During the game, different alien spaceships (colored lights) appear on the top side of the game topology and move towards the bottom row of the game where the player's loaded 'guns' are placed. The child's goal is to shoot the alien spaceships down by firing at them. A shot is fired by pressing the lighted tiles indicating the guns. Further details on the Space-Invaders game can be found in [3,4].

4   Experiment Setup

According to the experimental design proposed in [4], the test-bed game under investigation is played in variants. For this purpose, different states (e.g. 'Low',

'High') of quantitative estimators of qualitative entertainment factors (e.g. challenge) are used. The combination of states/number of entertainment factors generates a pool of dissimilar games for the designer to investigate.

By experimental design (see [1,2]), each subject plays against k of the selected n variants of the selected game in all permutations of pairs. (k equal 2 and n equals 8 and 9 in the preliminary/exploratory and the main experiment respectively in this paper.) Thus, C_k^n is the required number of subjects to cover all combinations of k out of n game variants. More specifically, each child plays games in pairs (game A and game B) — differing in the levels/states of one or more of the selected entertainment factors — for a selected time window. Each time a pair of games ('game pair') is finished, the child is asked whether the first game was more "fun" than the second game (pairwise preference). Children are not interviewed but are asked to fill in a questionnaire, minimizing the interviewing effects reported in [5]. To minimize any potential order effects we let each child play the aforementioned games in the inverse order too. Statistical analysis of the effect of order of game playing on children's judgement of entertainment indicates the level of randomness in children's preferences (see [4]). Randomness is apparent when there is a different preference in the pair (A, B); i.e. $A \succ B$ and $B \succ A$.

All subjects are given the same instructions by an experimenter who is unaware of the purpose of the experiment, minimizing experimenter expectancy effects [15]. The playing time window chosen (90 seconds in this paper) is a compromise between effective data collection (long enough subject-game interaction to support a relative judgement) and not overstretching children on excessive periods of energetic physical play.

Emotion, such as entertainment, capture is considered, in general, a hard problem mainly because understanding emotion is hard [16]. Capturing reports of playing experiences or emotions is still tough since data obtained embed experimental noise and subjectivity. As previously mentioned, a pairwise preference scheme (2-alternative forced choice: 2-AFC) is used in self-reports of children. 2-AFC offers several advantages for a subjective entertainment capture: it minimizes the assumptions made about subjects' notions of "fun" and allows a fair comparison between the answers of different humans. Since the focus is to construct a model relating reported entertainment preferences to individual playing features that generalizes over the reports of different players 2-AFC is preferred to a ranking approach [5]. Forcing the choice of subjects generates experimental noise, in that the subject may have no significant preference for one or other of the game variants played yet must nevertheless express a preference; however, insignificant order effects provide evidence that the experimental noise generated in this way is random. Previous studies [2] have shown that reported fun cannot be captured solely on the basis of game variants since individuality (e.g. through physiological measures) is required for effectively modeling expressed preferences of entertainment.

Note that in the presented studies subjects played all their assigned games on the same day, mitigating day-dependence effects on their physiology [16].

Moreover, experiments held meet three of the five factors for eliciting genuine emotion in the most natural setup (*ibid.*): the experiments took place in a setup close to the *real-world* since children played in their school classroom, our emphasis was on internal *feelings* and subjects were not aware of the purpose of the experiment (*other-purpose*).

5   Machine Learning

The proposed approach to entertainment modeling is based on selecting a minimal subset of individual features and constructing a quantitative user model that predicts the subject's reported entertainment preferences. The assumption is that the entertainment value y of a given game, which models the subject's internal response to playing the game, that is, how much "fun" it is, is an unknown function of individual features which a machine learning mechanism can learn. The subject's expressed preferences constrain but do not specify the values of y for individual games but we assume that the subject's expressed preferences are consistent.

Any machine learning which is based on learning a target output is inapplicable since target outputs are unknown. By the use of a ranking approach numerical values for the y variable could be made available; however, ranking is an undesired method for the self-report design of comparative "fun" analysis for the disadvantages mentioned earlier. Preference learning [17] is the only applicable type of machine learning for this constrained classification problem. There are several techniques that learn from a set of pairwise preferences such as algorithms based on support vector machines and perceptron modeling [18]. However, given the high level of subjectivity of human preferences and the highly-noisy nature of input data, we believe that more complex non-linear functions such as Artificial Neural Networks (ANN) serve our purposes better. Thus, feedforward multi-layered Neural Networks for learning the relation between the selected player features (ANN inputs) and the "entertainment value" (ANN output) of a game are used in the experiments presented here. Even though ANNs may achieve high training performance are not, in general, easily interpreted; however, a small (input) feature set and/or the inclusion of rules in the ANN structure (e.g. fuzzy-ANN [1]) could make interpretation a much easier task [4]. Since there are no prescribed target outputs for the learning problem (i.e. no differentiable output error function), ANN training algorithms such as back-propagation are inapplicable. Learning is achieved through artificial evolution. Details on the neuro-evolution mechanism used can be found in [3]. Other preference learning approaches are considered for comparison as a direction for future work.

6   Exploratory Experiment

Fifty six normal-weighted (based on their body mass index) children whose ages covered a range between 8 and 10 years participated in this exploratory experiment. The 56 children were split into two groups of 28 children and each group was assigned to play either Bug-Smasher or Space-Invaders according to the protocol presented in section 4. To investigate the interplay between entertainment and physical activity we asked all 56 children to participate in an additional experiment: each child was asked to run around a 3m×3m space for 90 seconds. The assumption here is that this exercise (physical activity control) task is a non-entertaining activity for the child since children were not asked whether it was "fun" or not and it was not compared to any physical game task. Further details on the experimental protocol used can be found in [3].

In this experiment the following statistical parameters are extracted from HR signals recorded while children playing: the average HR $E\{h\}$, the standard deviation of HR $\sigma\{h\}$, the maximum HR $\max\{h\}$, the minimum HR $\min\{h\}$, the correlation coefficient R_h between HR recordings and the time t in which data were recorded, the autocorrelation (lag equals 1) of the signal ρ_1^h and the approximate entropy $(ApEn_h)$ [19] of the signal which quantifies the unpredictability of fluctuations in the HR time series. In addition, three different regression models were used to fit (least square fitting) the HR signal: linear, quadratic and exponential. The additional features were the parameters of the three regression models mentioned above. The computation of HRV features was not possible given the data provided by the available recording apparatus since the detected RR intervals are opaquely converted into HR estimates by the wireless POLAR s610i ECG device used.

Statistical analysis showed that average HR appears to be the only feature examined that is significantly correlated to reported entertainment ($r = 0.4146$, p $= 0.0057$). This interplay between engagement, physical activity and entertainment demonstrated in [8,3] is consistent with the significant correlation between the average response time of children interacting with Playware games and reported entertainment [2]. (This is unsurprising, since one would expect a more enjoyable game to induce greater physical effort from the player.)

6.1   Feature Selection and Preference Learning

Given the selected features (ANN input) and the expressed preferences of entertainment ANNs are evolved by following the approach presented in [3] and evaluated through the leave-one-out cross-validation method. The two feature selection methods (n Best Feature Selection and Sequential Forward Selection) described in [3] are applied and compared. The initial subset (ANN input) for both methods includes the feature that performs best in the single feature experiment: $ApEn$ [3].

The best cross-validation performance (80.66%; average of 88%, 78% and 76%) is achieved when the ANN input contains $ApEn$ and $E\{h\}$. More HR signal features added in the feature subset do not yield significantly higher classification accuracy [3]. The relation between $ApEn$, $E\{h\}$ and the game's predicted entertainment value (y) given by the highest performing ANN found is illustrated in Fig. 1. Note that the three fittest ANNs generated, each trained on different portions of 2/3 of total data, exhibit the same qualitative features of the surface illustrated in Fig. 1.

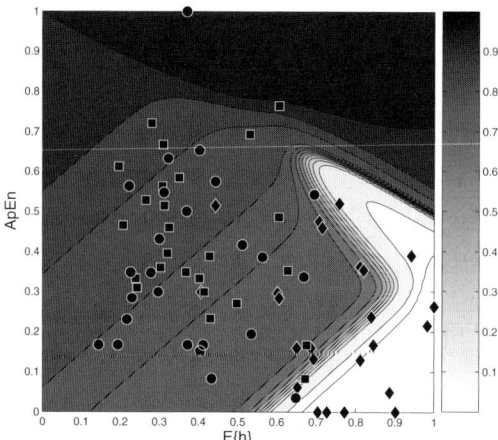

Fig. 1. Evolved ANN that yields the best classification accuracy on unknown data (88.00%): ANN output y (entertainment; the darker the higher) with regards to $E\{h\}$ and $ApEn$. Points plotted correspond to the 75 data of the validation set including 25 preferred (entertaining) games (squares), 25 non-preferred (non-entertaining) games (circles) and 25 exercise trials (diamonds).

According to Fig. 1, a physical activity is not entertaining when high $E\{h\}$ values ($E\{h\} > 0.7$) are combined with lower than average $ApEn$ values ($ApEn < 0.5$). Given the experiments presented in this paper, this is a common situation in pure exercise physical activities which are not considered entertaining by children according to our assumption. Highly entertaining games are the ones that correspond to a combination of very high $E\{h\}$ and $ApEn$ values ($E\{h\} > 0.6$, $ApEn > 0.7$).

HR signals obtained show that the running task appears to involve much more physical effort (high $E\{h\}$ values) than the physical effort required in a physical game, and further that the physical effort involved is different in kind (low $ApEn$ values; high regularity of the HR signal). It follows that the exercise/running control experiment may generate HR dynamics rather easy to separate from game-play HR dynamics, and allows one to distinguish entertaining game-play from exercise purely on the artificial basis of the kind of physical activity taking place. It is therefore, in retrospect, not a good control for physical activity effects in game play.

Thus, it is likely that constructed user models would be less effective for distinguishing more and less enjoyable games based on the degree rather than the kind of physical activity they engender. To deal with this and control for any elements of physical activity in the physiological measurements, an objectively (by human-verification) non-entertaining form of physical activity needs to be tested. Preliminary results have shown that user ANN models able to predict children's preferred game variants given suitable HR dynamics feature representations can indeed be constructed and that such models not only distinguish game-play from game-like non-entertaining physical activity but also generalize (to some extent) over children's individual preferences [4].

7 Player's Physiology Beyond Heart-Rate

This section presents an initial analysis of data collected through an additional larger survey experiment using the experimental protocol presented in section 4. In this experiment physiology data collection expands to blood volume pulse and skin conductance signal recordings. The ProComp Infiniti biosensing system by Thought Technology is used for this set of experiments. Seventy two children participated each playing a pair of variants of the Bug-Smasher game in both orders (see section 4).

The features extracted from the obtained signals include the fifteen statistical parameters of the HR signal presented in previous studies (see section 6 and [8]). The additional features for each signal type are as follows:

HR. The initial HR recording h_{in}, the last HR recording h_{last}, the time when maximum HR occurred t_{max}^h, the time when minimum HR occurred t_{min}^h, the difference $t_{max}^h - t_{min}^h$.

BVP. The average BVP $E\{b\}$, the standard deviation of BVP $\sigma\{b\}$, the maximum BVP $\max\{b\}$, the minimum BVP $\min\{b\}$, the average inter-beat amplitude $E\{IBAmp\}$, the mean of the absolute values of the first and second differences of the raw BVP [16] ($\delta_{|1|}^b$ and $\delta_{|2|}^b$ respectively) and the following HRV parameters:

  - HRV - time domain: the standard deviation of RR intervals $\sigma\{RR\}$, the fraction of RR intervals that differ by more than 50 msec from the previous RR interval $pRR50$, the root-mean-square of successive differences of RR intervals RMS_{RR} [10].
  - HRV - frequency domain: the frequency band energy values derived from power spectra obtained using discrete Fourier transformation; energy values are computed as the integral of the power of each of the following four frequency bands (see [10,20] among others): Ultra Low Frequency (ULF) band: $[0.0, 0.0033]$ Hz; Very Low Frequency (VLF) band: $(0.0033, 0.04]$ Hz; Low Frequency (LF) band: $(0.04, 0.15]$ Hz and High Frequency (HF) band: $(0.15, 0.4]$ Hz.

SC. All extracted features used for the HR signal. Additional features include the mean of the first and second differences of the raw SC (δ_1^s and δ_2^s respectively) and the mean of the absolute values of the first and second differences of the raw SC ($\delta_{|1|}^s$ and $\delta_{|2|}^s$ respectively).

7.1 Statistical Analysis

The correlation coefficients between children's expressed preferences and recorded physiological signal features are obtained through $c(\overrightarrow{z}) = \sum_{i=1}^{N_s}\{z_i/N_s\}$, where N_s is the total number of game pairs where physiological signals were properly recorded ($N_s = 115$ for HR and BVP and $N_s = 85$ for SC) and $z_i = 1$, if the subject chooses as the more entertaining game the one with the larger value of the examined feature and $z_i = -1$, if the subject chooses the other game in the game pair i.

Table 1. Correlation coefficients between reported entertainment and individual physiological features. For reasons of space, the three highest absolute correlation coefficient values for each physiological signal type are ranked and presented here. γ_s is the parameter of the quadratic regression $(s_Q(t) = \beta_s t^2 + \gamma_s t + \epsilon)$ on the SC signal which quantifies the rotation angle with respect to the x-axis of the quadratic curve. Statistically significant effects appear in bold.

HR	$c(\vec{z})$	BVP	$c(\vec{z})$	SC	$c(\vec{z})$
$E\{h\}$	**0.224**	$\delta^b_{|1|}$	**0.216**	$E\{s\}$	0.167
$\max\{h\}$	**0.209**	$\delta^b_{|2|}$	**0.216**	γ_s	0.119
$\min\{h\}$	0.179	HF	**-0.216**	$\sigma\{s\}$	-0.119

Within the HR signal extracted features, significant correlations are observed between average and maximum HR and reported entertainment preferences (see Table 1). These effects are consistent with the significant correlations of both $E\{h\}$ and $\max\{h\}$ on physiological data obtained from previous experiments using the Bug-Smasher game [8,4]. Within the class of features extracted from the BVP signal, significant effects are observed on the mean of the absolute values of both the first and the second differences of the raw signal $(\delta^b_{|1|}, \delta^b_{|2|})$ and on the energy of the HF band. On the contrary no significant effect appears in the class of SC features.

Obtained effects demonstrate that the higher the $\delta^b_{|1|}$ and $\delta^b_{|2|}$ values, the steeper the BVP signal and the higher the expressed "fun" preferences of children. Moreover, the lower the energy of the HRV HF band — which is driven by respiration and appears to derive mainly from vagal activity [10] — the more children appear to be entertained. Specifically, the energy of the HF range, representing quicker changes in HR, is primarily due to parasympathetic activity of the heart which is decreased during mental or stress load [9,10]. This derives the conclusion that high mental or stress load appear to be the main factors that guide a child to prefer a game variant more than another.

The obtained statistically significant effects assume a linear relation between the respective features and reported entertainment which may (or may not) provide insight into the appropriate set of features on which to build a successful non-linear model of reported entertainment using preference learning. However, no safe conclusion can be derived for the appropriate feature subset before the proposed methodology is applied.

7.2   Best Feature Selection

Given the 85 pairs of preferred/non-preferred game comparisons, ANNs are evolved by following the neuro-evolution approach presented in [3]. The data is partitioned into 2/3 training and 1/3 validation data subsets and the leave-one-out cross-validation technique is used to obtain the average classification performance of the ANNs. In an attempt to minimize the ANN's size, it was determined that ANN architectures with 10 hidden neurons, are capable of successfully obtaining solutions of high fitness. As observed from Table 2, there is some consistency between features linearly related to reported entertainment and features that predict entertainment preferences based on a non-linear function (ANN). More specifically, all five features that correlate highly with reported entertainment (see Table 1) appear in Table 2. Moreover, one may notice that the five highest performing features are extracted from BVP with HF energy being the highest performing feature (66.67%; average of 71.43%, 67.86%, 60.71%). Given that the average performance of 30 randomly generated ANNs (10 for each validation set) is 48.80%, the p-value for the HF energy performance to occur is 0.043.

The single feature experiments suggest that collecting physiological signals beyond HR, such as BVP, may provide more meaningful features (e.g. HF, $\delta^b_{|1|}$, $\delta^b_{|2|}$) for capturing entertainment preferences of children in physical play. The best performance obtained equals 66.67%, which appears to be rather low. However, the reported complexity of classifying emotions through physiological state [16], the augmented signal noise recorded during physical play (especially through the BVP sensor) and the binomial-distributed probability of this performance to occur at random (0.043) suggest that the evolved ANNs are successful predictors of children's reported entertainment preferences based on a single feature extracted from physiological state.

Table 2. The ten highest performing features ranked by cross-validation performance from left to right

Feature	HF	min{b}	LF	$\delta^b_{|1|}$	$\delta^b_{|2|}$	max{h}	σ{RR}	h_{in}	E{h}	min{h}
Performance	66.67	63.10	63.10	63.10	61.90	60.71	60.71	60.71	59.52	59.52

8   Conclusion

This paper explored the interplay between physiological signals and children's entertainment preferences in physical play. More specifically, the quantitative impact of children's reported entertainment on HR, BVP and SC signal statistics was investigated through action games developed on the Playware playground. The statistical effects obtained from the survey experiment presented here provide some first insights for the physiology of entertainment. Higher average and maximum HR, steeper blood volume signals and quicker changes in HR appear to correlate with higher levels of reported entertainment in children of the age group examined. The single feature experiments projected the impact of HF energy of HRV on reported entertainment indicating that there appears to be increased mental and stress load in preferred games.

However, more complete conclusions will be derived when multi-feature selection is applied and the non-linear function between the selected feature subset and subject's preferences on 'fun' is generated. Even though HRV frequency bands provide indications about the interplay between affect, reported entertainment and physical activity, additional physical activity control experiments (see [4]) will be required to isolate elements of physiology that correspond solely to entertainment preferences.

The proposed approach can be used for adaptation of the game's entertainment features (challenge, curiosity) according to the player's individual playing and physiological features in real-time in physical games. The key to this is the observation that the models (e.g. ANNs) relate features to an entertainment value. It is therefore possible in principle to infer what changes to game features (given embedding of the features in the model) will cause an increase in the entertainment value of the game, and to adjust game parameters to make those changes. For further discussion on this future direction the reader may refer to [1,2].

Acknowledgments

This work was supported in part by the Danish Research Agency, Ministry of Science, Technology and Innovation (project no: 274-05-0511).

References

1. Yannakakis, G.N., Hallam, J.: Towards Capturing and Enhancing Entertainment in Computer Games. In: Antoniou, G., Potamias, G., Spyropoulos, C., Plexousakis, D. (eds.) SETN 2006. LNCS (LNAI), vol. 3955, pp. 432–442. Springer, Heidelberg (2006)
2. Yannakakis, G.N., Hallam, J.: Game and Player Feature Selection for Entertainment Capture. In: Proceedings of the IEEE Symposium on Computational Intelligence and Games, pp. 244–251. IEEE Computer Society Press, Los Alamitos (2007)
3. Yannakakis, G.N., Hallam, J.: Preliminary Studies for Capturing Entertainment through Physiology in Physical Play. Technical Report TR-2007-5, Maersk Institue, University of Southern Denmark (2007)
4. Yannakakis, G.N., Hallam, J., Lund, H.H.: Entertainment Capture through Heart Rate Activity in Physical Interactive Playgrounds. User Modeling and User-Adapted Interaction, Special Issue: User Modeling and Affective Computing (to appear, 2007)
5. Mandryk, R.L., Inkpen, K.M., Calvert, T.W.: Using Psychophysiological Techniques to Measure User Experience with Entertainment Technologies. Behaviour and Information Technology (Special Issue on User Experience) 25, 141–158 (2006)
6. Zuckerman, M.: Sensation Seeking in Entertainment. In: Phychology of Entertainment, pp. 367–387. Lawrence Erlbaum Associates Publishers (2006)
7. Lund, H.H., Klitbo, T., Jessen, C.: Playware technology for physically activating play. Artifical Life and Robotics Journal 9, 165–174 (2005)

8. Yannakakis, G.N., Hallam, J., Lund, H.H.: Capturing Entertainment through Heart-rate Dynamics in the Playware Playground. In: Harper, R., Rauterberg, M., Combetto, M. (eds.) ICEC 2006. LNCS, vol. 4161, pp. 314–317. Springer, Heidelberg (2006)

9. Rowe, D.W., Sibert, J., Irwin, D.: Heart Rate Variability: Indicator of User State as an aid to Human-Computer Interaction. In: Proceedings of Conference on Human Factors in Computing Systems, pp. 480–487 (1998)

10. Goldberger, J.J., Challapalli, S., Tung, R., Parker, M.A., Kadish, A.H.: Relationship of heart rate variability to parasympathetic effect. Circulation 103, 1977–1983 (2001)

11. Rani, P., Sarkar, N., Liu, C.: Maintaining optimal challenge in computer games through real-time physiological feedback. In: Proceedings of the 11th International Conference on Human Computer Interaction (2005)

12. McQuiggan, S., Lee, S., Lester, J.: Predicting User Physiological Response for Interactive Environments: An Inductive Approach. In: Proceedings of the 2nd Artificial Intelligence for Interactive Digital Entertainment Conference, pp. 60–65 (2006)

13. Ravaja, N., Saari, T., Turpeinen, M., Laarni, J., Salminen, M., Kivikangas, M.: Spatial Presence and Emotions during Video Game Playing: Does It Matter with Whom You Play? Presence Teleoperators & Virtual Environments 15, 381–392 (2006 in press)

14. Hazlett, R.L.: Measuring emotional valence during interactive experiences: boys at video game play. In: CHI '06: Proceedings of the SIGCHI conference on Human Factors in computing systems, pp. 1023–1026. ACM Press, New York (2006)

15. Rosenthal, R.: Covert communication in laboratories, classrooms, and the truly real world. Current Directions in Psychological Science 12, 151–154 (2003)

16. Picard, R.W., Vyzas, E., Healey, J.: Toward Machine Emotional Intelligence: Analysis of Affective Physiological State. IEEE Trans. Pattern Anal. Mach. Intell. 23, 1175–1191 (2001)

17. Doyle, J.: Prospects for preferences. Computational Intelligence 20, 111–136 (2004)

18. Fiechter, C.N., Rogers, S.: Learning subjective functions with large margins. In: ICML '00: Proceedings of the Seventeenth International Conference on Machine Learning, pp. 287–294. Morgan Kaufmann Publishers Inc., San Francisco, CA, USA (2000)

19. Pincus, S.M.: Approximate entropy as a measure of system complexity. Proc. Natl. Acad. Sci. 88, 2297–2301 (1991)

20. Goldberger, A.L., Amaral, L.A.N., Glass, L., Hausdorff, J.M., Ivanov, P.C., Mark, R.G., Mietus, J.E., Moody, G.B., Peng, C.K., Stanley, H.E.: PhysioBank, PhysioToolkit, and PhysioNet: Components of a new research resource for complex physiologic signals. Circulation 101, 215–220 (2000)

Comprehension of Users' Subjective Interaction States During Their Interaction with an Artificial Agent by Means of Heart Rate Variability Index

Takanori Komatsu[1], Sho'ichiro Ohtsuka[2], Kazuhiro Ueda[3], and Takashi Komeda[2]

[1] Future University-Hakodate, 116-2 Kamedanakano, Hakodate 041-8655, Japan
komatsu@fun.ac.jp
[2] Shibaura Institute of Technology, 307 Fukasaku, Minuna, Saitama 330-8570, Japan
komeda@se.shibaura-it.ac.jp
[3] The University-Tokyo, 3-8-1 Komaba, Muguro, Tokyo 153-8902, Japan
ueda@gregorio.c.u-tokyo.ac.jp

Abstract. The purpose of this study is to investigate whether users' subjective interaction states which indicate whether they feel comfortable interacting with artificial agents can be comprehended by means of biological index. As a biological index, we focused on the heart rate variability and used an RSA ratio for the time period when the respiratory sinus arrhythmia (RSA) value is higher than the Mayer wave sinus arrhythmia (MWSA) value divided by the total interaction period. To clarify the effectiveness of this RSA ratio, we conducted two experiments to measure this index among participants who played a simple cooperation game with an artificial agent, which either responded as the participant desired or responded randomly. The results showed that the RSA ratio determined the subjective interaction state which indicated whether they felt comfortable or uncomfortable with their interactions with the agents.

1 Introduction

Many researchers have been working on developing interactive artificial agents such as home care robots (Ishiguro *et al.*, 2001; Wakamaru, 2005) and life-like agents (Prendinger and Ishizuka, 2004; Takahashi, Bartneck, Katagiri and Arai, 2005). Many approaches to research are being utilized to create such agents: for example, one involves implementing learning mechanisms into the agent, such as reinforcement learning or neural network modules, and the other involves creating agents with friendly and familiar appearances. We focus on a different approach; that is, we assume that these agents need to express certain outputs based on the users' subjective interaction state, pertaining to whether they feel comfortable or uncomfortable with their interactions with the other agents. To

A. Paiva, R. Prada, and R.W. Picard (Eds.): ACII 2007, LNCS 4738, pp. 266–277, 2007.

tackle this research approach, we need to clarify the users' subjective interaction states in a real-time manner.

Questionnaires or interviews are normally conducted to assess the users' subjective interaction states. However, it is nearly impossible to capture these states in a real-time manner because the participants are intensely focusing on certain tasks involving the agent. Therefore, asking them to fill in a questionnaire or take part in an interview would interfere with these tasks and their interactions. In ergonomic studies, much focus has been placed on clarifying the users' mental workloads by measuring their biological signals, such as skin conductance response, brain waves, or heart rate variability (Ohsuga, 2001; Picard and Sheirer, 2001). Ohsuga (Ohsuga, Terashima, Shimano, and Toda, 1993) conducted an experiment that required participants to perform mental calculation tasks over certain durations, thereby adding to their mental workloads. The participants' heart rate variability was then measured. The results were that she observed significant differences in the measured signals between resting and task conditions. Actually, it can be said that she succeeded in revealing the relationship between the participants' mental workloads and the measured heart rate variability. However she did not focus on the relationship between a self assessment of the participants' subjective interaction states and the measured heart rate variability.

We then investigated whether certain biological index could determine users' subjective interaction states whether they feel comfortable or uncomfortable during their interaction with agents. Specifically, we focused on heart rate variability as a biological index and conducted experiments to evaluate this index's effectiveness in determining the users' subjective interaction states.

2   Heart Rate Variability as a Biological Index

Many kinds of biological signals from participants interacting with agents can be enumerated, such as brain waves, skin conductivity, and the electrical activity of the heart. For measuring brain waves, participants would require dozens of electrodes to be fastened on their heads. Unfortunately, this places strong physical constraints on them. This method does have some advantages over measuring skin conductivity because it provides detailed information on their physiological state and because the measuring instruments are rather simple. However, these measured data is easily affected by environmental disturbances and their physical conditions, thereby making it difficult to measure the data stably over a long period of time. For an electrocardiogram, which is the classic method for measuring the electrical activity of the heart, participants would need to wear about three electrodes. This would enable us to measure the data stably over the long term and to avoid any undue physical constraint on the participants during our experiment. We therefore decided to use electrocardiogram readings as the biological signal in our study.

Specifically, we focused on the heart rate variability that can be acquired from the electrocardiogram data because this variability is generally stable against

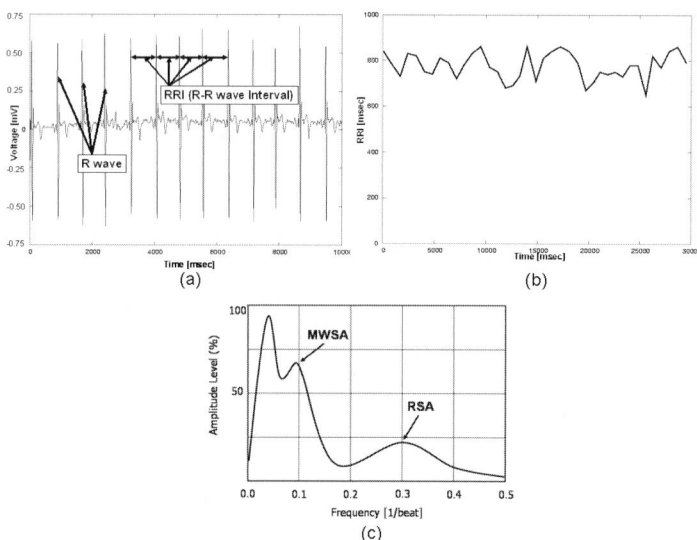

Fig. 1. (a) Voltage of heartbeats acquired from electrocardiogram, (b) Time course of RRI, and (c) Frequency analysis of time-course RRI

various forms of environmental disturbance. The voltage of heartbeats can be acquired from the measured electrocardiogram data (Figure 1a). This figure shows the R waves corresponding to each heartbeat. The interval time between R waves (R-R wave Interval: RRI) can then be calculated. The time-course variability of the RRI and the spectrum of this time-course variability are shown in Figures 1b and 1c, respectively. In Figure 1c, the depicted curve has three peaks around 0.3, 0.1, and 0.25 [1/beat]. The peak around 0.3 [1/beat] is called the respiratory sinus arrhythmia [$msec^2$] (RSA), and the one around 0.1 [1/beat] is called the Mayer wave sinus arrhythmia [$msec^2$] (MWSA). In general, the RSA represents the effects of the breathing cycle controlled by the parasympathetic nervous system, and its value increases when subjects are relaxing. The MWSA represents the effects of blood pressure controlled by both the parasympathetic and sympathetic nervous systems, and its value increases when subjects are under stress (for example, Taguchi 1998; Ebe, Okuwa, and Inagaki, 1999).

In this study, we conducted psychological experiments to determine the effects on the MWSA and RSA values, as determined by an electrocardiogram, of participants who were interacting with an artificial agent in two different interactive conditions: one was a smooth condition in which an agent behaved according to the users' instructions, the other was a random condition in which the agent behaved randomly; its actions were based on a random number table. We hypothesized that the participants would feel comfortable with the interaction with the agents in the smooth condition, while they would feel less comfortable or uncomfortable in the random condition.

3   Experiment 1

3.1   Purpose and Settings

This experiment was intended to allow us to observe the MWSA and RSA values of the participants in smooth or random experimental conditions and to analyze how these values reflect the participants' subjective interaction states. We introduced a simple cooperation game; participants were asked to play "Pong" (Figure 2). In this game, ten points were awarded to the participant each time the game paddle succeeded in hitting the ball, and ten points were deducted each time the game paddle missed it. Specifically, the experimenter gave the instruction to the participants that the participant's role was to give verbal instructions to the game paddle agent which can understand their verbal instructions. The goal of the participants was then to work together with this game paddle agent to get the highest possible score in the game. In this game, the experimenter actually operated the game paddle because it is quite difficult to realize the game paddle agent which can understand the given verbal instruction perfectly. The participants did not know that the experimenter was the one moving the game paddle.

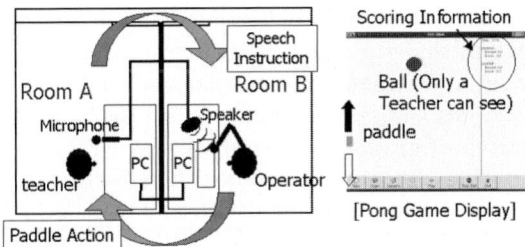

Fig. 2. Experimental setting

3.2   Participants

18 university students (5 men and 13 women; 18 - 21 years old) participated in this experiment, and they were randomly divided into the following two experimental groups.

- **Smooth condition** (9 participants): These participants experienced smooth interaction with the game paddle. In this condition, the experimenter moved the paddle according to the verbal instructions given by the participants. It is expected that these participants would feel comfortable during the game playing.
- **Random condition** (9 participants): These participants experienced disrupted or incoherent interaction with the paddle. In this condition, the experimenter moved the game paddle according to a table of random numbers: an odd number indicated "go left" while an even one indicated "go right." It is expected that these participants would feel uncomfortable during the game playing.

Each participant played the game for about 10 minutes. Meanwhile, the data on the electrocardiogram and the total game score were recorded. After the game, the experimenter had interviews with the participants regarding their subjective feelings about the game, e.g., whether they noticed the game paddle was operated by someone. The electrocardiogram data was then analyzed using Atsumi's method (Atsumi, 1994) in order to calculate the RSA and MWSA values. Specifically, we used an RSA ratio as a biological index that was calculated by dividing the duration when the RSA was higher than the MWSA by the total duration of the experiment.

3.3   Results

Figure 3 and 4 depicts the transition in game score and MWSA and RSA values of the typical participant in each of the experimental conditions. Figure 3 shows that the participant in the smooth condition had a higher RSA value (bold line) than a MWSA value (dashed line) in most parts of the experiment, and the game score kept positive values. Also, in Figure 4, the participant in the random condition showed that the RSA values seemed to be lower than the MWSA values and that the latter values were frequently bursting. The game score continuously decreased. These figures indicated that the game score increased in smooth condition and that the score decreased in random condition. Thus, the experimental condition was set as the experimenter indented.

The results of the participants' interviews were that eight participants in the smooth condition reported that they enjoyed playing the game and felt comfortable doing so, while seven in the random condition reported that they did not enjoy playing it and were irritated with the game paddle, which did not

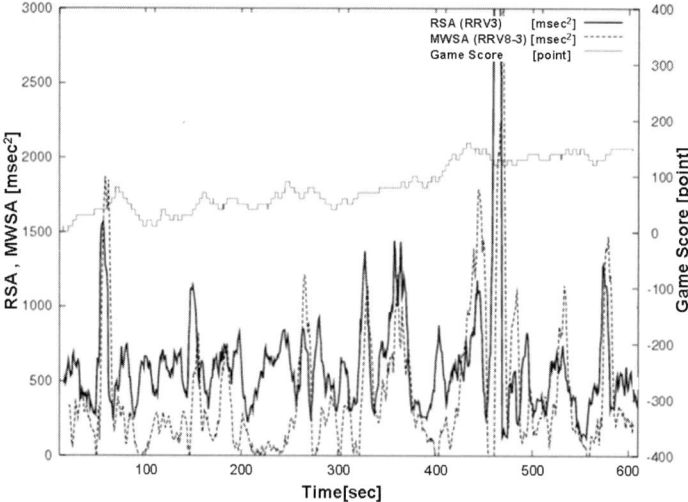

Fig. 3. Typical transition of game score and RSA and MWSA for a participant in smooth condition

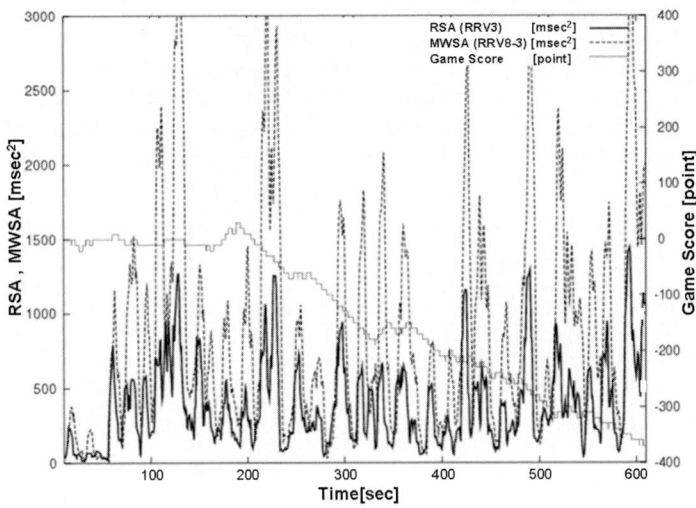

Fig. 4. Typical transition of game score and RSA and MWSA for a participant in random condition

Table 1. Results of Experiment 1

	Smooth condition (9 participants)	Random condition (9 participants)
Game score	32.3 (points)	-228.9 (points)
RSA ratio	69.1 (%)	44.4 (%)

behave as they intended. We then expected that the RSA value would be higher than the MWSA when the participants felt comfortable with playing the game and that these values also could reflect the participants' subjective interaction states whether they felt comfortable or uncomfortable with their experimental tasks.

Table 1 shows the RSA ratios and game scores for each experimental condition. First, the game scores in both conditions were analyzed with an (interactive conditions: smooth or random) ANOVA. The results of the ANOVA revealed a significant difference in the game scores between the two factors $(F(1, 8) = 7.05, p < .05(*))$. The RSA ratios were also analyzed with an (same interactive conditions) ANOVA, and the results revealed a significant difference in the RSA ratios $(F(1, 8) = 6.32, p < .05(*))$. The significant differences in the game scores indicate that the participants in the smooth condition achieved significantly higher scores than the ones in the random conditions. Also, the significant differences in the RSA ratio indicate that the participants in the smooth condition had a higher RSA ratio than the ones in the random condition.

The results of this experiment can be summarized as follows.

- **Smooth condition:** The game score continuously increased, and the participants' RSA ratio showed higher values than the ones in the random condition. The participants also reported that they enjoyed playing the game.
- **Random condition:** The game score continuously decreased, and the participants' RSA ratio showed lower values than the ones in the smooth condition. The participants also reported that they were irritated when playing the game.

Thus, it can be said that the RSA ratio could reflect the participants' subjective interaction states.

4   Experiment 2

4.1   Purpose and Settings

Based on the results of experiment 1, we conducted a second experiment to observe how the RSA ratio changes under dynamic experimental conditions with the "Pong" video game. Specifically, we prepared two experimental conditions: one was a smooth-random condition where the agent at first behaved according to the participants' instructions but then started behaving randomly. The other was a random-smooth condition where the agent at first behaved randomly but then started behaving according to the participant's instructions. The purpose of this experiment was to determine whether the RSA ratio reflected the participants' subjective interaction states, even though they were in dynamic interaction and not in a stable interaction like in experiment 1. The artificial agent interacting with users would require in changing its behaviors according to the users' interaction states or task achievement levels, so that it can be said that it is quite important to determine whether the RSA ratio reflected the participants' subjective interaction states in dynamic interaction.

4.2   Participants

18 university students (9 men and 9 women; 18 - 21 years old) participated in this experiment. They had not participated in experiment 1, and they were randomly divided into the following two experimental conditions.

- **Smooth-random condition** (9 participants): These participants first experienced smooth interaction with the game paddle and then experienced disrupted or incoherent interaction. In this condition, the experimenter first moved the game paddle according to the participants' instruction and then changed midway to moving it randomly. It is expected that these participants would feel comfortable at first and then change to feel uncomfortable.
- **Random-smooth condition** (9 participants): These participants first experienced disrupted or incoherent interaction with the game paddle and then experienced smooth interaction. In this condition, the experimenter

first moved the game paddle randomly and then changed midway to moving according to the participants' instructions. It is expected that these participants would feel uncomfortable at first and then change to feel comfortable.

Each participant played the game for about 15 minutes, and the behavior of the game paddle (smooth or random condition) was changed after 7.5 minutes game time. During the experiment, the data on the electrocardiogram was recorded in the same way as they were in experiment 1. Also, the experimenter had interviews with the participants after the game.

4.3   Results

Figure 5 and 6 depict the transition in game score and MWSA and RSA values of the typical participants in each experimental condition. In Figure 5, the participants in the smooth-random condition had higher RSA values than MWSA values, and their game score increased in the first 7.5 minutes (first half). In the remaining 7.5 minutes (second half), their RSA values became smaller than their MWSA values, and their game score decreased. In the latter condition (random condition), we observed that their MWSA values were frequently bursting. In Figure 6, the participants in the random-smooth condition had higher MWSA values than RSA values, and their game score decreased in the first half. Also, their MWSA values were frequently bursting. In the second half, their game score increased. However, their MWSA values were still smaller than their RSA values, and we also observed bursts in the MWSA values.

Table 2 shows the average of the RSA ratio and game scores in each experimental condition. First, the game scores in both conditions were analyzed with a 2 (interactive condition: smooth or random) X 2 (session order: first or second half)

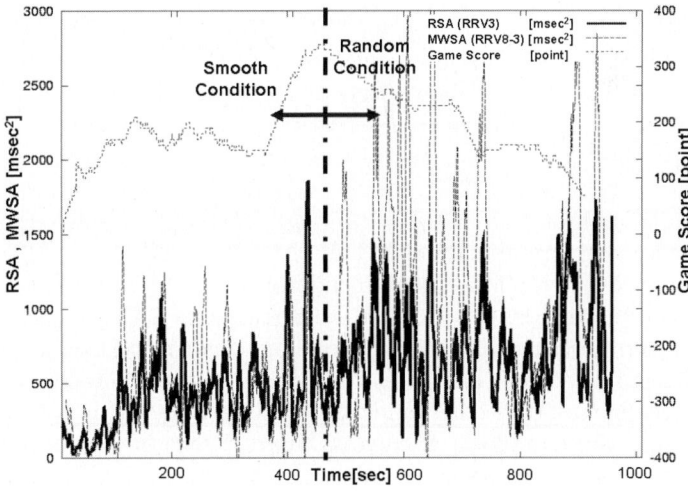

Fig. 5. Typical transition of game score and RSA and MWSA for a participant in smooth-random condition

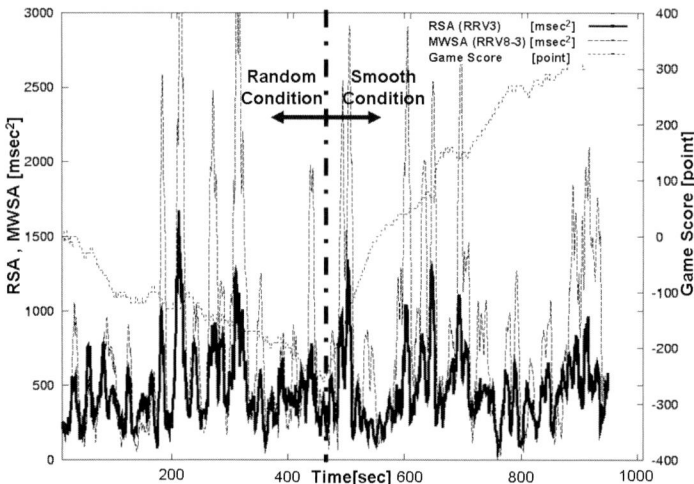

Fig. 6. Typical transition of game score and RSA and MWSA for a participant in random-smooth condition

Table 2. Results of experiment 2

	smooth-random (9 participants)		random-smooth (9 participants)	
	Score	RSA ratio	Score	RSA ratio
first half	227.5 (points)	55.8 (%)	-152.3 (points)	40.2 (%)
second half	-82.5 (points)	47.3 (%)	338.9 (points)	39.8 (%)

mixed ANOVA (Figure 7a). The results of the ANOVA revealed significant differences in the interaction between two factors ($F(1,15) = 65.77, p < .01(**)$) and a significant tendency in the main effects of the session order factor ($F(1,15) = 3.36, p < .075(+)$). The following were observed in the second half, the significant differences in the simple main effect of the game score in the first half between both conditions ($F(1,15) = 42.11, p < .01(**)$), the game score in the second half between both conditions ($F(1,15) = 22.38, p < .01(**)$), the game score of the smooth-random condition in the first half ($F(1,15) = 19.70, p < .01(**)$), and the game score of the random-smooth condition ($F(1,15) = 49.44, p < .01(**)$). The results of this analysis showed that the participants in the smooth condition acquired higher scores than those in the random condition. Thus, it is said that the experimental condition was set as the experimenter indented.

Next, the RSA ratios in both conditions were analyzed with a 2 (interactive condition: smooth or random) X 2 (session order: first or second half) mixed ANOVA (Figure 7b). The results of the ANOVA revealed significant differences in the main effect of session order ($F(1,15) = 4.55, p < .01(**)$) and a significant tendency in the interaction between the two factors ($F(1,15) = 4.26, p < .075(+)$). Also, we observed a significant tendency in the simple main effect of

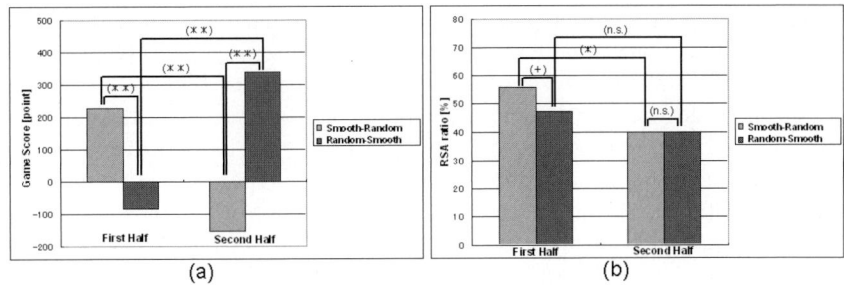

Fig. 7. (a) Acquired game score in each experimental condition, and (b) Acquired RSA ratio in each experimental condition

the RSA ratio in the first half between conditions ($F(1, 15) = 1.15, p < .075(+)$) and a significant difference in the simple main effect of the RSA ratio in the smooth-random group between session orders ($F(1, 15) = 8.22, p < .05(*)$). The results of this analysis showed that the RSA ratio of the participants in the smooth-random condition had higher values in the first half (smooth condition) but lower values in the second half (random condition), and that the RSA ratio of the participants in the random-smooth condition had lower values in the first half (random condition), but this value did not change even in the second half (smooth condition).

The results of this experiment can be summarized as follows.

- **Smooth-random condition:** In the first half (smooth condition), the game score increased, and the participants' RSA ratio showed higher values. In the second half (random condition), the game score started decreasing, and their RSA ratio became lower than that in the first half.
- **Random-smooth condition:** In the first half (random condition), the game score decreased, and the participants' RSA ratio showed lower values. In the second half (smooth condition), the game score started increasing. However, the RSA ratio did not change and was still low.

The results of the experiment 1 showed that the participants in smooth condition showed the higher RSA ratio and that the ones in random condition did the lower RSA ratio. However, the results of the experiment 2 showed that the participants in random-smooth condition showed the lower RSA ratio even in the smooth condition in which the game scores increased (second half). At a glance, this result in experiment 2 seemed to contradict the ones of the experiment 1, so that we focused on the results of the participants' interviews.

An analysis of the participants' interviews revealed that nine participants in the smooth-random condition reported that they enjoyed playing the game in the first half, but immediately after the second half began, they started wondering why the game paddle would no longer behave as they intended. Thus, it can be said that the participants who felt comfortable at first and then change to feel uncomfortable showed the higher RSA ratio at first and then change to the lower

RSA ratio. In the random-smooth condition, eight participants reported that they were irritated with the game paddle because it would not behave as they intended, and this feeling persisted for all 15 minutes of the game. Interestingly, they also reported that they believed the game paddle still behaved randomly in the second half, even though the game paddle actually behaved as they intended and their game score actually increased. Therefore, they did not notice that the experimental condition had changed, even though all participants in the smooth-random condition did. Thus, it can be said that the participants who felt uncomfortable persistently showed the lower RSA ratio persistently.

To sum up, the RSA ratio had a lower value when the participants were irritated with the game paddle (even if the game score would increase), while it had a higher value when they enjoyed playing the game. Thus, it was strongly confirmed that the RSA ratio reflects the participants' subjective interaction states.

5   Discussion and Conclusion

The results of the two experiments suggest that the RSA ratio reflects the participants' subjective interaction states and that this RSA ratio would be useful as a biological index to clarify such interaction states. Actually, this information would be equivalent to that acquired from the participants' interviews. However it is impossible to acquire the participants' opinions during engaged interaction with an agent; otherwise, this would interfere with and disrupt their interactions. On the other hand, the RSA ratio can be acquired without such interference, so utilizing this RSA ratio presents a strong advantage in clarifying the users' subjective interaction states. Actually, the RSA ratio in this experiment was not calculated in an on-line manner (real-time manner). However, such a calculation can be done easily by means of Atsumi's method (Atsumi, 1994). Therefore, the results of our experiments can contribute to comprehending the participants' subjective interaction states stably and readily, and to realize the interactive artificial agents who could choose and express appropriate behaviors according to the users' subjective interaction states.

One of the unsolved issues of this study is that the results of the two experiments did not reveal the threshold RSA value, e.g., when the observed RSA value exceeds the threshold RSA value, a user feels comfortable, while, when the observed value does not exceed the threshold, s/he feels uncomfortable. One of the reasons that we could not determine such a threshold value is that wide differences were found in the acquired RSA value between participants. In experiment 2, one participant had an RSA ratio ranging from 0.12 (random condition) to 0.33 (smooth condition), while another had one from 0.63 (random condition) to 0.84 (smooth condition). Therefore, the RSA values of users who are in stable or neutral conditions would need to be measured to determine their standard RSA values. The relative differences between these standard RSA values and the measured ones would be a much more stable index for comprehending users' subjective interaction states while eliminating the individual differences.

References

1. Ishiguro, H., Ono, T., Imai, M., Maeda, T., Kanda, T., Nakatsu, R.: Robovie: an interactive humanoid robot. International Journal of Industrial Robot 28(6), 498–503 (2001)
2. Wakamaru (2005), `http://www.wakamaru.net`
3. Prendinger, H., Ishizuka, M.: Life-like Characters. Tools Affective Functions, and Application. Springer, Berlin (2004)
4. Takahashi, T., Bartneck, C., Katagiri, Y., Arai, N.: TelMeA: Expressive Avatars In Asynchronous Communications. International Journal of Human-Computer Studies 62(2), 193–209 (2005)
5. Ohsuga, M., Terashima, H., Shimono, F., Toda, M.: Quantitative evaluation of stress response (In Japanese). The Japanese Journal of Ergonomics 29(6), 353–356 (1993)
6. Ohsuga, M.: Assessment of phasic work stress using autonomic indices. International Journal of Psychophysiology 40(3), 211–220 (2001)
7. Picard, R.W., Scheirer, J.: The Galvactivator: A Glove that Senses and Communicates Skin Conductivity. In: Proceedings of the 9th International Conference on Human-Computer Interaction, pp. 1538–1542 (2001)
8. Taguchi, T.: Evaluation of Fatigue during Car Driving. The R&D Review of Toyota CRDL (In Japanese) 33(4), 25–31 (1998)
9. Ebe, K., Okuwa, M., Inagaki, H.: Evaluation of Driver's Mental Workload Due to Visual and Auditory Cognition. The R&D Review of Toyota CRDL (In Japanese) 34(4), 55–62 (1999)
10. Atsumi, B.: Evaluation of Mental Condition on Drivers by Analysis of Heart Rate Variability. In: proceedings of 1994 JSAE Annual Congresses (In Japanese), pp. 133–136 (1994)

Facial Activation Control Effect (FACE)

Toni Vanhala[1] and Veikko Surakka[1,2]

[1] Research Group for Emotions, Sociality, and Computing,
Tampere Unit for Human-Computer Interaction,
FIN-33014 University of Tampere, Finland
Toni.Vanhala@cs.uta.fi
http://www.cs.uta.fi/hci/ESC
[2] Tampere University Hospital, Department of Clinical Neurophysiology,
P.O. Box 2000, FIN-33521 Tampere, Finland
Veikko.Surakka@uta.fi

Abstract. The present study was the first in line of a series of experiments investigating the possibilities of using voluntarily produced physiological signals in computer-assisted therapy. The current aim was to find out whether computer-guided voluntary facial activations have an effect on autonomous nervous system activity. Twenty-seven participants performed a series of voluntary facial muscle activations, while wireless electrocardiography and subjective experiences were recorded. Each task consisted of activating either the *corrugator supercilii* muscle (activated when frowning) or the *zygomaticus major* muscle (activated when smiling) at one of three activation intensities (i.e. low, medium, and high). Our results showed a voluntary facial activation control effect (FACE) on psychological (i.e. level of experience) and physiological activity. Different muscle activations produced both task-specific emotional experiences and significant changes in heart rate and heart rate variability. Low intensity activations of both muscles were the most effective, easy to perform, and pleasant. We conclude that the FACE can clearly open the route for regulating involuntary physiological processes.

Keywords: Electrocardiography, Electromyography, Heart rate patterns, Physiological computing, Wireless monitoring.

1 Introduction

Computer systems have recently been successfully applied to the treatment of emotional disorders, including fear of flying, panic disorders, and social phobia [1]. A traditional method for treating emotional disorders (e.g. phobias) is systematic desensitization [2]. This desensitization is performed by exposing the person gradually to the subject of his or her fear. For example, a spider phobic is first instructed to imagine a spider. Then, he or she views pictures of a spider. Next, a toy spider is introduced to the therapy. Finally, the patient is asked to approach and hold a real spider in hand. Similarly, in computer-assisted exposure therapy the patient is gradually exposed to a computer-generated representation of his or her phobia, for example, a virtual spider. In some cases,

A. Paiva, R. Prada, and R.W. Picard (Eds.): ACII 2007, LNCS 4738, pp. 278–289, 2007.
© Springer-Verlag Berlin Heidelberg 2007

physiological measurements are collected and shown to the person herself or himself [1]. This way, a person can become aware of unconscious physiological responses and processes, which markedly improves the results of treatment [3].

There is presently considerable interest for using physiological signals in human-computer interaction. Physiological data can be considered to be one of the most important sources of information for affective computing, that is, computing that relates to, arises from, or deliberately influences emotions [4,5]. The potential advantage of monitoring of physiological activity is the possibility to derive a continuous and relatively accurate estimate of the cognitive and emotional state of a person [6].

Physiological measures of emotion have been studied extensively [6,7,8,9]. It can be argued that facial activity could be one of the most reliable measures for distinguishing emotional reactions, as the facial musculature system is very fine grained and well represented in the brain's motor cortex [10]. A well-tried measure of emotional state is facial electromyography (EMG) which reflects the electrical activity of facial muscles. Specifically, the activity of *corrugator supercilii* muscle (activated when frowning) has been shown to increase during negative emotions and to decrease during positive emotions [8]. The activity of *zygomaticus major* muscle (activated when smiling) varies with emotional valence in the opposite manner.

Based on facial EMG, Partala and others [11,12] were able to develop automatic systems that classified emotional experiences into three categories: negative, neutral, and positive. These systems achieved classification accuracies of about 70% when participants viewed pictures and approximately 80% when video stimuli were used. Picard and others [13] were able to classify emotional experiences to eight classes with an accuracy of 81% by combining EMG measurements with three other physiological signals.

Other physiological measures that could be used in estimating affective processes include heart rate which varies between different emotional stimulations [7,9,14]. Previous studies have associated HCI events with distinct heart rate responses that could be used, for instance, to evaluate interfaces [15]. Further, heart rate measurements are quite comfortable and easy to perform due to recent advances in technology. Wireless, wearable, and unobtrusive physiological measurement devices are more convenient and less restricted than traditional measurements in general [16,17]. For example, an ordinary looking office chair embedded with electromechanical film can now be used to measure emotion-related heart rate changes discreetly and non-invasively [7].

Heart rate can be analysed also in the frequency domain. Common method for spectral analysis of heart rate variability (HRV) is to compute the power of different frequency bands from heart rate measurements lasting at least 30 seconds [18,19]. Although the limits of these frequency bands vary somewhat from study to study, they are known to reflect some specific underlying processes [6,9,20]. For example, the low frequency (LF) HRV is known to reflect sympathetic activity of the autonomous nervous system (ANS) which raises blood pressure by increasing heart rate and constricting blood vessels [6,9]. Elevated LF HRV is associated with several cardiovascular diseases and it increases, for example, when a person experiences anger [20,21]. High frequency (HF) HRV is best associated with parasympathetic cardiovascular activity and it is suppressed during sustained attention and experiences of happiness and fear [19,22,23]. Thus, HRV seems to reflect both cognitive and emotion related processing.

Compared to the extensive research on spontaneous physiological activity, little attention has been paid to voluntary physiological activity and its effects in affective computing. Most previous research on voluntary activity has focused on new interface modalities. For example, Surakka and others [24] constructed a system for pointing and selecting objects using gaze and voluntary facial muscle activations. As another well-known example, people can learn to produce input signals to a computer with voluntarily controlled brain activity [25].

Voluntarily produced physiological changes can also induce specific emotional experiences and affect ANS functioning. In their work on directed voluntary facial activations, Levenson and others [14] instructed participants to produce facial configurations associated with a set of basic emotions. They found that these activations produced corresponding emotional experiences as well as emotion specific patterns of ANS activity. For example, expressions of anger, fear, and sadness were associated with significantly greater heart rate acceleration than disgust. More recently, Coan and others [26] found that facial configurations associated with withdrawal (i.e. disgust, fear, and sadness) were associated with relatively less activity in the left frontal brain than approach related emotions (i.e. joy and anger). We note that these previous studies used facial configurations composed of several facial muscle activations and previous research on the effects of controlled activations of a single facial muscle is still lacking.

In summary, previous research suggests that monitoring of voluntary physiological activity is a promising method for HCI. However, research on the effects of simple, computer-guided voluntary physiological activations is needed. The present work is our first in a series of investigations on the effects of voluntary activations and their applications in therapy. For the present purpose, twenty-seven participants performed a series of voluntary facial muscle activations, while EMG, wireless ECG, and ratings of valence and task difficulty were registered. The aim was to study how computer-guided activations of a single facial muscle might modulate involuntary electrocardiographic (ECG) activity.

2   Methods

2.1   Participants

27 students (4 female) participated in the experiment for partial fulfilment of a computer science course. All participants had normal or corrected-to-normal vision and normal heart functioning according to their own report. The participants' age ranged from 19 to 39 years old (median = 24 years).

Due to technical problems, the acquisition of EMG data failed for two participants and they could not begin the experiment. Thus, the analysis of subjective ratings data included data from 25 participants. Data from 23 participants was used in physiological data analyses after excluding two additional participants with failed ECG registrations.

2.2 Equipment

Experimental tasks were presented on a 19" CRT monitor with a resolution of 1024×768 pixels and a refresh rate of 75 Hz at a distance of approximately 100 centimetres. The ECG signal was registered with a prototype wireless measurement patch with slightly adjustable inter-electrode distances ([16,27]; Fig. 1). The patch contained a signal amplifier and it was attached to the chest of the participant with Blue Sensor ECG electrodes. Electrodes were placed directly on the skin without preparation. For male subjects, a reference electrode was placed at the end of the sternum. The second electrode was placed 90 mm above this location. The final electrode was placed on the left side of the chest at a distance of 90 mm from the reference and 125 mm from the second electrode. For female subjects, the second electrode was placed at the end of the sternum and the reference electrode below it. Thus, the orientation of the patch was the same for both sexes, but its placement was lower for female than for male participants. The inter-electrode distances were the same for both sexes. A cable running beneath the participant's clothing connected the patch to a radio frequency transmitter that was placed on her or his thigh. The strap shown in Fig. 1 was not used. The acquired ECG data was buffered and sent to a desktop computer with 30 millisecond long intervals.

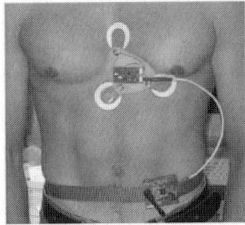

Fig. 1. Wireless ECG measurement and amplification patch attached to the chest with self-adhesive electrodes and connected to a radio frequency transmitter

Facial muscle activity was measured with electromyography (EMG) from above the *corrugator supercilii* and the *zygomaticus major* muscle sites. The electrodes were attached to the left side of the face according to the guidelines of Fridlund and Cacioppo [28]. A pair of electrodes was placed above and below the right eye in order to register eye blinks. The ground electrode was placed over the mastoid bone. The skin was cleaned and slightly abraded prior to the attachment of electrodes. Ag-AgCl electrodes were used and all inter-electrode impedances were below $10\,k\Omega$.

The EMG signal was amplified and filtered with a Grass®Model15™differential amplifier (-30 dB cut-off). The sampling rate was 2 kHz and the recording passband was from 10 to 1000 Hz. Blinks were filtered with a passband of 0.3 to 30 Hz. The ECG was sampled at 500 Hz with a passband of 0.07 to 192 Hz.

2.3   Facial Activation Tasks

A screen displaying the level of the EMG activity of the *corrugator supercilii* and the *zygomaticus major* muscles was shown to the participant (Fig. 2). The intensity of facial activation was displayed with a bar within one of two rectangles, both of which extended from 600 pixels high to 200 pixels wide. The activity of the corrugator muscle was displayed on the left and the activity of the zygomaticus muscle on the right. The bar within the rectangle was 66 pixels wide. The height of the bar varied with the intensity of the activation: the greater the EMG power, the higher the bar. The level of EMG activity was defined as the total activity during a window of 1000 samples (i.e., 500 milliseconds). Total activity was estimated by the sum of rectified EMG samples.

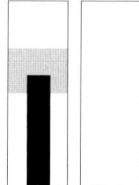

Fig. 2. Display of muscle activation intensity (EMG power)

The participants were to contract their facial muscles separately from each other at three different intensity levels. The required intensity was indicated with the grey area on one of the rectangles, as exemplified in Fig. 2. The task was to hold the intensity of the activation at one of three intensity levels for the duration of the task. The target and current levels of activity were shown only for the muscle that was to be used in the current task. When the current activation intensity was within the target range, the task started.

Experimental tasks lasted 30 seconds and each was preceded by a 30 second interval. This was specifically planned as per the requirements of HRV analyses [18,19]. The screen was blank white during the interval. After the interval, an instruction for the following task was presented in 48 point Serif font. The instruction specified the muscle and the target intensity level of activation for the next task and asked the participant to breathe calmly. After five seconds, the instruction was removed and another interval of five seconds was followed by another task.

2.4   System Calibration

The system was adapted for each individual subject by measuring the minimum and maximum levels of electrical muscle activity during a separate calibration session. The participant was given a mirror to help in monitoring her or his own facial behaviour and was instructed to practise the activation of both facial muscles. A screen similar to the one displayed during tasks was presented to the participant during the calibration (Fig. 2). However, the target level of activation intensity was not displayed and the displayed range of activity was dynamically adjusted according to the registered minimum and maximum levels of activity during the calibration session.

The participant was guided to produce a number of maximal activations during the calibration, while relaxing between them. The lower 80 percent of the registered range of activity was later displayed during experimental tasks and used as the effective range when computing target activity levels for different experimental tasks. The effective range of activity was divided into four equal sections. From top to bottom, the first, the second, and the third section were used as the target ranges for high, medium, and low intensities of activity, respectively. The calibration session ended after several maximal activations had been produced and the participant felt confident in her or his ability to voluntarily activate both muscles.

2.5   Procedure

First, the laboratory was introduced to the participant. The participant was told a cover story that the purpose of the experiment was to find out facial muscles suited for voluntary control of a computer interface. It was also told that the purpose of registering heart activity was to isolate a source of artefacts.

Then, the electrodes were attached to the participant's face and chest. Next, system calibration was performed. After the calibration session, each of the six facial activation tasks was trained once. The tasks and preceding intervals were only 10 seconds long during this training session. The participant was instructed to relax and breathe calmly between tasks. After each task, the participant was to rate how she or he felt during the task with two bipolar scales: emotional valence and task difficulty. The rating scales varied from unpleasant to pleasant and difficult to easy in a scale of 1 to 9.

After the completion of six practice tasks, the experimenter left the room. An interval of one minute preceded the first task. During the experiment, each of the six different tasks was presented five times for a total of 30 tasks. Subjective ratings were collected after each task. The order of tasks was randomized. The participant was debriefed after the last task was completed.

2.6   Data Analysis

The mean heart rate (HR) was computed for the 30 seconds during each task. First, the peaks of R waves were detected from the electrocardiographic data using the algorithm of Pan and Tompkins [29]. The R wave is a part of the QRS complex that signifies the end of a cardiac cycle in an electrocardiographic signal. Then, the derived R to R intervals (RRI) were processed with a tachometer in order to produce an instantaneous heart rate signal that was uniformly sampled at 5 Hz. Third, measurements containing artefacts were identified and removed from the HR data as follows. Standard deviation of heart rate was computed both for all HR data (δ_{all}) and HR data from each subject ($\delta_{subject}$). If $\delta_{subject}$ was larger than $\delta_{all}/2$, HR data from the subject was discarded from further analysis. Visual inspection confirmed the validity of the used criterion. Data from 17 participants was left for HR and heart rate variability (HRV) analysis after this procedure. Finally, the mean heart rate change (compared to baseline) was computed for each participant and task. Data from 5 seconds before the onset of each task was used as the baseline.

The variability of the heart rate was computed for both during the task and during the 30 second long interval preceding it. HRV was indexed by the power of the heart rate signal in two frequency bands: Low Frequency (LF) from 0.04 to 0.15 Hz and High Frequency (HF) from 0.15 to 0.40 Hz. First, a non-uniformly sampled heart rate signal was computed from the RRI data. Then, the power spectral density was estimated using the Lomb periodogram [29,30]. Finally, the sum of squared power spectral values was computed for both frequency bands. HRV data from six tasks was excluded from further analysis, as the spectral density did not contain a sample for both bands.

3 Results

3.1 Heart Rate

Figure 3 illustrates the averaged heart rate responses to each task, suggesting that the heart rate decelerates compared to the baseline during low and medium intensity activations of both muscles, while remaining close to baseline during their high intensity activations. The results of statistical analysis support this observation. A one-way ANOVA for heart rate data during *zygomaticus major* activations showed a significant main effect for the intensity level $F(2,32) = 8.4$, $p < .01$. Bonferroni corrected post hoc pairwise comparisons for the heart rate during *zygomaticus major* activations showed significant differences between low and high $t(16) = 3.2$, $p < .05$ and medium and high intensity levels $t(16) = 3.1$, $p < .05$. Similarly, a one-way ANOVA for heart rate data during *corrugator supercilii* activations showed a significant main effect for the intensity level $F(2,32) = 5.2$, $p < .05$. Bonferroni corrected post hoc pairwise comparisons for the heart rate during *corrugator supercilii* activations showed significant differences between low and high intensity activations $t(16) = 3.4$, $p < .05$. Other pairwise comparisons did not reach significance.

3.2 Heart Rate Variability

Table 1 shows that both LF HRV and HF HRV were suppressed during every task as compared to baseline. For HRV data, 30 seconds of data both before and after task onset were included in analysis. A two-way 3×2 ANOVA (intensity level × time) for LF HRV data during *zygomaticus major* activations showed a significant main effect of the time $F(1,16)=12.5$, $p<.01$. The main

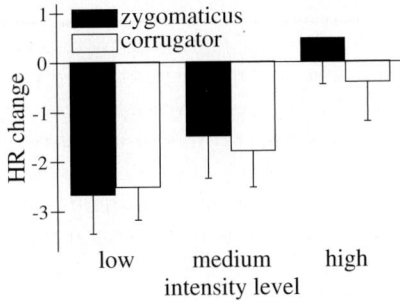

Fig. 3. Averaged heart rate changes from baseline and standard error of the mean (S.E.M.) in beats per minute during different voluntary facial activations

effect of intensity level was not statistically significant and neither was the interaction of the main effects. Post hoc pairwise comparisons showed statistically significant changes from baseline during low $t(16) = 3.1$, $p < .01$, medium $t(16) = 2.9$, $p < .05$, and high $t(16) = 4.4$, $p < .001$ intensity activations. A two-way 3×2 ANOVA (intensity level × time) for LF HRV data during *corrugator supercilii* activations showed a significant main effect of the time $F(1,16)=17.5$, $p<.001$. Post hoc pairwise comparisons showed statistically significant changes from baseline during low $t(16) = 5.1$, $p < .001$, medium $t(16) = 3.4$, $p < .01$, and high $t(16) = 2.6$, $p < .05$ intensity activations.

Table 1. Mean LF and HF HRV changes from baseline for different facial activations

	corrugator supercilii			*zygomaticus major*		
	low	medium	high	low	medium	high
LF	-7.3***	-5.4**	-4.9*	-6.6**	-8.7*	-6.0***
HF	-3.7**	-3.5**	-3.0**	-4.5**	-4.1	-2.7**

*p < .05 **p < .01 ***p < .001

A two-way 3×2 ANOVA (intensity level × time) for HF HRV data during *zygomaticus major* activations showed a significant main effect of the time $F(1,16) = 12.4$, $p < .01$. There were no other significant effects. Post hoc pairwise comparisons showed statistically significant changes from baseline during low intensity activations $t(16) = 3.2$, $p < .01$ and high intensity activations $t(16) = 2.7$, $p < .05$. A two-way 3×2 ANOVA (intensity level × time) for HF HRV data during *corrugator supercilii* activations showed a statistically significant main effect of the time $F(1,16) = 6.6$, $p < .05$. Again, there were no other significant effects. Pairwise comparisons showed statistically significant changes from baseline during low $t(16) = 3.2$, $p < .01$, medium $t(16) = 3.6$, $p < .01$, and high $t(16) = 3.2$, $p < .01$ intensity activations.

3.3   Subjective Experiences

Figure 4 shows a somewhat linear trend so that the higher the required activation intensity the less positive the ratings of valence were for both muscles. It can also be seen that the mean valence ratings of each task are close to neutral or positive. One-way ANOVA for valence ratings of *zygomaticus major* activations showed a statistically significant main effect of the intensity level $F(2,48) = 16.8$, $p < .001$. Bonferroni corrected post hoc pairwise comparisons showed significant differences between low and medium intensity activations $t(24) = 3.8$, $p < .01$ and low and high intensity activations $t(24) = 5.3$, $p < .001$. The difference between medium and high intensity *zygomaticus major* activations was not significant.

A one-way ANOVA for valence ratings of *corrugator supercilii* activations showed a statistically significant main effect of the intensity level $F(2,48) = 24.1$, $p < .001$. Bonferroni corrected post hoc pairwise comparisons showed statistically significant differences between low and medium intensity activations $t(24) = 5.6$, $p < .0001$, low and high intensity activations $t(24) = 5.5$, $p < .0001$, and medium and high intensity activations $t(24) = 3.6$, $p < .01$.

For ratings on the ease of task Fig. 5 shows a curvilinear trend so that participants rated the medium intensity level activations as close to neutral, and

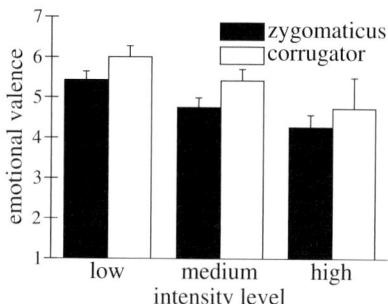

Fig. 4. Mean (and S.E.M.) of valence ratings during different voluntary facial activations

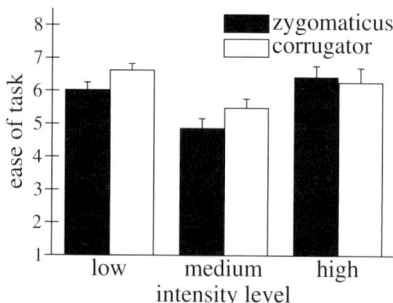

Fig. 5. Mean (and S.E.M.) of ease of task ratings during different voluntary facial activations

both low and high level activations of both muscles were rated to be on the more easy side of the scale. A one-way ANOVA for the ease of task ratings of *zygomaticus major* activations showed a statistically significant main effect of the intensity level $F(2,48) = 14.5$, $p < .001$. Bonferroni corrected post hoc pairwise comparisons showed statistically significant differences between low and medium intensity activations $t(24) = 4.5$, $p < .001$, and medium and high intensity activations $t(24) = 4.4$, $p < .01$.

A one-way ANOVA for task difficulty ratings of *corrugator supercilii* activations showed also a statistically significant main effect of the intensity level $F(2,48) = 14.5$, $p < .001$. Bonferroni corrected post hoc pairwise comparisons showed a statistically significant difference between the low and medium intensity activations $t(24) = 6.1$, $p < .0001$. Other pairwise comparisons were not statistically significant.

4 Discussion

Our results showed that voluntary activations of facial muscles significantly affected physiological processes controlled by ANS as well as produced task-specific subjective experiences. Heart rate decelerated markedly during each task except high intensity activations of the muscles. Heart rate has been previously found to decelerate during both cognitive and emotion related processing [7,9,31].

HRV analyses revealed that LF HRV was significantly suppressed during all voluntary activations. Also HF HRV was suppressed during all activations, although medium intensity *zygomaticus major* activations did not result in a significant effect. As LF HRV reflects sympathetic and HF HRV reflects parasympathetic ANS activity, it seems that the facial activation control effect (FACE) attenuated the activity of both branches of the ANS.

The ratings of emotional valence showed a linear trend so that the higher the required intensity the less pleasant the rating. A different curvilinear pattern was evident for both muscles in the ratings of the ease of the task. Activations with low or high intensity level were rated as more easy, while medium intensity activations were rated as neutral. There was no statistically significant difference between the experienced difficulty of low and high intensity activations. The pattern in difficulty ratings is consistent with our intuition that medium intensity activations require most concentration and control in simultaneous excitation and inhibition of muscle activity.

In summary, all voluntary facial activations produced significant changes in physiological activity by suppressing both LF and HF HRV and decelerating heart rate. However, the effect was clearest for low intensity activations of both muscles which produced greater mean heart rate decelerations and most of the largest LF and HF HRV suppressions. Low intensity activations were also rated as easier than medium intensity activations and as easy as high intensity activations of both muscles. The low intensity activations were also rated as most pleasant for both muscles. As a conclusion, voluntarily controlled moderate intensity activations of facial muscles seemed to be the most effective, pleasant, and easy as a method for regulating human psychological (i.e. the level of experience) and physiological systems. Importantly, the results showed that a voluntarily controlled physiological system affected ANS activity which is in the hard core of many emotional disorders [2,3]. These results give clear encouragement for continuing our efforts in studying the possibilities of using the FACE in computer-assisted therapy.

Acknowledgements. This research was supported by the Graduate School in User-Centered Information Technology and the Academy of Finland (project numbers 1202183 and 1115997).

References

1. Wiederhold, B.K., Bullinger, A.H.: Virtual reality exposure for phobias, panic disorder, and posttraumatic disorder: A brief sampling of the literature. In: Proceedings of HCII 2005, Lawrence Erlbaum Associates CD-ROM (2005)
2. Weiten, W.: Psychology: Themes and variations, 7th edn. Thomson Higher Education (2007)
3. Wiederhold, B.K., Wiederhold, M.D.: Three-year follow-up for virtual reality exposure for fear of flying. CyberPsychology and Behavior 6, 441–445 (2003)
4. Allanson, J., Fairclough, S.H.: A research agenda for physiological computing. Interacting with Computers 16, 857–878 (2004)
5. Picard, R.W.: Affective Computing. MIT Press, Cambridge (1997)
6. Wilhelm, F.H., Pfaltzl, M.C., Grossman, P.: Continuous electronic data capture of physiology, behavior and experience in real life: towards ecological assessment of emotion. Interacting with Computers 18, 171–186 (2006)
7. Anttonen, J., Surakka, V.: Emotions and heart rate while sitting on a chair. In: Proceedings of CHI 2005, pp. 491–499 (2005)
8. Larsen, J.T., Norris, C.J., Cacioppo, J.T.: Effects of positive and negative affect on elctromyographic activity over the zygomaticus major and corrugator supercilii. Psychophysiology 40, 776–785 (2003)
9. Bradley, M.M.: Emotion and Motivation. In: Handbook of Psychophysiology, 2nd edn., pp. 602–642. Cambridge University Press, Cambridge (2000)
10. Schieber, M.H.: Constraints on somatotopic organization in the primary motor cortex. Journal of Neurophysiology 86, 2125–2143 (2001)
11. Partala, T., Surakka, V., Vanhala, T.: Real-time estimation of emotional experiences from facial expressions. Interacting with Computers 18, 208–226 (2006)
12. Partala, T., Surakka, V., Vanhala, T.: Person-independent estimation of emotional experiences from facial expressions. In: Proceedings of IUI 2005, ACM Press, pp. 246–248. ACM Press, New York (2005)
13. Picard, R.W., Vyzas, E., Healey, J.: Toward machine emotional intelligence: Analysis of affective physiological state. IEEE Transactions on Pattern Analysis and Machine Intelligence 23, 1175–1191 (2001)
14. Levenson, R.W., Ekman, P.: Difficulty does not account for emotion-specific heart rate changes in the directed facial action task. Psychophysiology 39, 397–405 (2002)
15. Ward, R.D., Marsden, P.H.: Physiological responses to different web page designs. International Journal of Human-Computer Studies 59, 199–212 (2003)

16. Vehkaoja, A., Lekkala, J.: Wearable wireless biopotential measurement device. In: Proceedings of the IEEE EMBS 2004, pp. 2177–2179. IEEE Computer Society Press, Los Alamitos (2004)
17. Teller, A.: A platform for wearable physiological computing. Interacting with Computers 16, 917–937 (2004)
18. Jennings, J.R., Berg, W.K., Hutcheson, J.S., Obrist, P., Porges, S., Turpin, G.: Publication guidelines for heart rate studies in man. Psychophysiology 18, 226–231 (1981)
19. Brownley, K.A., Hurwitz, B.E., Schneiderman, N.: Cardiovascular psychophysiology. In: Handbook of Psychophysiology, 2nd edn., pp. 224–264. Cambridge University Press, Cambridge (2000)
20. Matthews, G., Wells, A.: The cognitive science of attention and memory. In: Handbook of Cognition and Emotion, pp. 171–192. Wiley, Chichester (1999)
21. Malliani, A., Pagani, M., Lombardi, F., Cerutti, S.: Cardiovascular neural regulation explored in the frequency domain. Circulation 84, 482–492 (1991)
22. Weber, E.J.M., Van der Molen, M.W., Molenaar, P.C.M.: Heart rate and sustained attention during childhood: age changes in anticipatory heart rate, primary bradycardia, and respiratory sinus arrythmia. Psychophysiology 31, 164–174 (1994)
23. Rainville, P., Bechara, A., Naqvi, N., Damasio, A.R.: Basic emotions are associated with distinct patterns of cardiorespiratory activity. International Journal of Psychophysiology 61, 5–18 (2006)
24. Surakka, V., Illi, M., Isokoski, P.: Gazing and frowning as a new technique for human-computer interaction. ACM Transactions on Applied Perception 1, 40–56 (2004)
25. Birbaumer, N.: Breaking the silence: Brain-computer interfaces (BCI) for communication and control. Psychophysiology 43, 517–532 (2006)
26. Coan, J.A., Allen, J.J.B., Harmon-Jones, E.: Voluntary facial expression and hemispheric asymmetry over the frontal cortex. Psychophysiology 38, 912–925 (2001)
27. Puurtinen, M., Hyttinen, J., Malmivuo, J.: Optimizing bipolar electrode location for wireless ECG measurement – analysis of ECG signal strength and deviation between individuals. International Journal of Bioelectromagnetism 1, 236–239 (2005)
28. Fridlund, A.J., Cacioppo, J.T.: Guidelines for human electromyographic research. Psychophysiology 23, 567–589 (1986)
29. PhysioNet: Physiotoolkit, 03.20.2007 (2003), http://www.physionet.org/physiotools
30. Laguna, P., Moody, G.B., Mark, R.G.: Power spectral density of unevenly sampled data by least-square analysis: performance and application to heart rate signals. IEEE Transactions on Biomedical Engineering 45, 698–715 (1998)
31. Öhman, A., Hamm, A., Hugdahl, K.: Cognition and the Autonomic Nervous System: Orienting, Anticipation, and Conditioning. In: Handbook of Psychophysiology, 2nd edn., pp. 533–575. Cambridge University Press, Cambridge (2000)

Music, Heart Rate, and Emotions in the Context of Stimulating Technologies

Jenni Anttonen[1] and Veikko Surakka[1,2]

[1] Tampere Unit for Computer-Human Interaction (TAUCHI), Department of Computer Sciences, University of Tampere, FIN-33014 Tampere, Finland
{jenni.anttonen,veikko.surakka}@cs.uta.fi
[2] Department of Clinical Neurophysiology, Tampere University Hospital,
P.O. Box 2000, FIN-33521 Tampere, Finland

Abstract. The present aim was to explore heart rate responses when stimulating participants with technology primarily aimed at the rehabilitation of older adults. Heart rate responses were measured from 31 participants while they listened to emotionally provoking negative, neutral, and positive musical clips. Ratings of emotional experiences were also collected. The results showed that heart rate responses to negative musical stimuli differed significantly from responses to neutral stimuli. The use of emotion-related physiological responses evoked by stimulating devices offers a possibility to enhance, for example, emotionally stimulating or otherwise therapeutic sessions.

Keywords: Emotions, music, heart rate, physiology, stimulating technologies.

1 Introduction

1.1 Technologies to Enhance the Quality of Life of Older Adults

People live longer and the proportion of older adults in the population grows. This fact has led different fields of research to consider how they could help in dealing with the substantial increase in the need for old age care in the future. In human-computer interaction (HCI), the research efforts have focused mostly on designing assistive technologies to promote the functional independence of older adults, for example, health monitoring technologies, smart environments that help in household maintenance, or memory aids that remind of taking one's medication [e.g. 20]. In addition to promoting functional independence, a central issue in achieving good results in old age care is supporting social and emotional well-being. For example, feelings of loneliness and social isolation are common among older adults living in the Western societies [8, 15]. Therefore, technologies that promote older adults' social and emotional interactions seem promising [e.g. 13].

A typical example of such technologies is the Message center that was designed to enhance digital communication with friends and family [26]. Some studies have dealt with the need of the family members to know if their older family member is doing alright at home. So called lifestyle monitoring systems visualize relevant information of the older adult's daily activities to keep the family members aware of them [5, 21]. Yet another line of research has been the development of relational computer agents

A. Paiva, R. Prada, and R.W. Picard (Eds.): ACII 2007, LNCS 4738, pp. 290–301, 2007.

with whom older adults can interact and form social and emotional human-computer relationships [4].

There have also been efforts to design emotionally stimulating technologies as being exposed to different kinds of social and emotional stimuli is an essential factor in the maintenance and improvement of well-being and functionality. People with dementia typically suffer from deterioration in short-term memory, which severely reduces their ability to communicate. However, long-term memory is often preserved and can be accessed through appropriate stimulation. One challenge in the interaction with people who have dementia is that it is challenging for relatives and nursing staff to keep up the interaction and the responsibility of the interaction relies heavily on the relative or caregiver [e.g. 12]. Stimulating technologies are known to be able to evoke meaningful social and emotional interactions. This leads to activation of long-term memory, which in turn is central for the maintenance of cognitive and other functionality.

One example of stimulating technologies is the Computer Interactive Reminiscence and Conversation Aid (CIRCA) that provides access to multimedia content through a touch-screen interface [12]. Gowans and others' observed sessions where people with dementia, their caregivers, and their relatives used the device to enhance interaction. They found that people with dementia were able to participate in the conversation more equally when the computer system was used and the system elicited memories and stories that the caregivers had not heard before. Also, the conversation atmosphere was more relaxed because the system provided a context and stimulation so that the caregivers did not have to continually prompt the people with dementia. Perhaps surprisingly, the people with dementia enjoyed interacting with the system and were also able to operate the system themselves. Another example is the Nostalgia device that plays old news and music and thereby increases social communication and triggers old memories in the listeners [22].

The Sound Vitamins Concept® (see Fig. 1) is a Finnish example of technology that is designed to evoke emotional experiences and social interactions[1]. It is an auditory application that is used in the rehabilitation of older adults to maintain interaction and mental, physical, and social functionality. It includes music and spoken programs such as physical exercises, stories, sing-along, spiritual programs, and quizzes. It is mostly used in group sessions in old age homes but it can also be used independently in the home environment. The effects of regular group sessions with the Sound Vitamins Concept® were evaluated in a Finnish study [24]. It was found that the system had a beneficial effect on mental and social functionality and on the reconstruction of social networks and social roles for people who had better functionality. For people with lowered functionality especially the music content and physical exercises evoked nonverbal behaviors and provided an opportunity for reciprocal communication and successful interaction between the older adult and nursing staff.

It seems that music is a profoundly emotion evoking stimulus and pieces of music are often associated with strong emotional memories. For these reasons, music is often used in stimulating and therapeutic purposes. It has been shown that despite dementia people may be able to recognize familiar music from the past and even sing

---

[1] The Sound Vitamins Concept® is a registered trademark of Audio Riders Oy, Finland.

along with the music [7]. Shared experiences through music make it possible to relate to other humans leading to reciprocal interactions.

Because emotions involve changes in physiology, experience, and behavior, one way to enhance emotional communication with people who have difficulties to express themselves is to use physiological measures, such as heart rate. It has been found that autonomic nervous system activity is related to emotional processing and, therefore, measures of autonomic activity can be used to make inferences about emotional responses [e.g. 9]. In the absence of visible emotional expressions, monitoring of subtle emotion-related physiological responses could provide opportunities to get information about emotional reactions. This information could offer an important contact point for the nursing staff or a therapist to activate the person further and the older adult would have a possibility to communicate emotional reactions at some level.

Fig. 1. The EMFi chair and the loudspeaker and control panel of the Sound Vitamins Concept®

Today, physiology can be measured with unobtrusive devices that can be brought into the older people's environment. The EMFi chair (see Fig. 1) is an example of an unobtrusive measurement technology that can be used to detect emotion-related heart rate variations without attaching any sensors to the subjects [1]. It is a normal looking office chair that is embedded with electromechanical film (EMFi) sensors that are used for ballistocardiographic heart rate measurement. In a previous experiment, we presented six-second long auditory, visual, and audiovisual stimuli with emotionally negative, neutral, and positive contents to 24 participants while their heart rates were measured with the EMFi chair. In line with other findings [e.g. 6], the results showed significantly different heart rate responses to negative and positive emotional stimulation [1].

As older people understandably do not want institutional looking equipment to their homes [e.g. 5] the EMFi technology could also be embedded, for example, in a cozy armchair. By combining the EMFi chair with a stimulating technology like the Sound Vitamins Concept®, it might be possible to create a physiologically sensing auditory environment for the rehabilitation of older adults.

2 Heart Rate Responses to Music

Emotional experiences can be measured using valence and arousal scales [18]. The valence scale ranges from unpleasant to pleasant and the arousal scale ranges from calm to aroused. The center of both scales is neutral. The scales form a two-dimensional space where different emotions can be located. When emotion psychophysiology has been studied in relation to musical stimuli, most of the studies have dealt with physiological changes in response to the arousal dimension (i.e. exciting and relaxing music). Bartlett [2] provided a review of studies investigating physiological responses to music, including studies with heart rate measurements. Some studies in Bartlett's review and also a later study by Iwanaga and Moroki [14] showed that arousing music increased heart rate whereas calming music decreased heart rate. However, there were also studies where this effect was not found or studies that suggested the opposite. Much of the ambiguousness of the results across studies is likely to be due to varying methodologies and varying musical stimuli [2].

The effect of the emotional valence of musical stimuli on heart rate responses has not been studied much although there is considerable evidence that during perception the cardiac response is associated with the valence dimension of emotions [e.g. 19]. It has been found that heart rate decelerates in response to emotional auditory stimuli and that the deceleration is more profound with negative than with positive stimuli [e.g., 6]. As heart rate responses are related to emotional valence, the ambiguity in the results of the studies investigating heart rate responses to music might also result from not controlling the valence of the musical stimuli carefully enough.

We were able to locate seven studies that had examined the effect of the valence of musical stimuli on heart rate responses. In studies by Kallinen [16], Krumhansl [17], and Nyklíček and others [23], there were significant differences between heart rate responses to positive and negative musical stimuli. The results of these three studies showed a larger decrease in heart rate during negative than positive music. These were in line with Bradley and Lang's [6] study with auditory stimuli (e.g. a baby crying). In the study by Etzel and others [10], the averaged heart rate responses to happy and sad music were similar to the above mentioned studies although the differences were not significant. In studies by Baumgartner and others [3], Gomez and Danuser [11], and Witvliet and Vrana [27], there were no significant valence effects for heart rate responses and the mean heart rate responses to positive and negative music were not described. In sum, four out of seven studies reviewed here suggested that the valence of the emotional experience during music listening affects heart rate in a way that is congruent, for example with Bradley and Lang's study [6].

The aim of this study was to examine the possibilities of using a stimulating technology together with a heart rate measurement technology which could open interesting possibilities, for example, in the rehabilitation of older adults. We studied heart rate measures during music listening with young adults in a bit more loosely controlled experiment than usual. For example, many aspects of the stimuli, such as mode, tempo, and length, could not be very tightly controlled. In the experiment, 15 emotionally negative, neutral, and positive musical stimuli from the Sound Vitamins Concept® system were presented to 31 participants while their heart rates were measured with the EMFi chair. Also, the emotional experiences evoked by the musical stimuli were measured on valence and arousal scales.

3   Methods

3.1   Participants

31 (13 female) voluntary young adults participated in the experiment. The mean age of the participants was 26 years, with a range from 20 to 38.

3.2   Stimuli

15 auditory stimuli from the Sound Vitamins Concept® system were used in the experiment. The stimuli were carefully selected excerpts of Finnish evergreen songs with lyrics, many of them generally familiar to everybody. The songs were selected so that they included prospectively 5 emotionally negative, 5 emotionally neutral, and 5 emotionally positive stimuli. While selecting the songs, we made an effort to include songs with slower and faster tempos in each emotional category. The excerpts consisted of one strophe and one repetition of the chorus. The music excerpts lasted between 37 and 77 seconds, with an average duration of 56 seconds.

3.3   Equipment

Heart rate (beats/min) was measured with the EMFi chair. The sampling rate of the EMFi chair was 500 Hz. The heart rate signal was digitized to a PC computer with a Windows XP operating system using a Quatech DAQP-16 digitizing card. We used the E-Prime© experiment generator running on a PC computer with a Windows XP operating system to control the stimulus presentation and the rating of the stimuli [25]. The stimuli were presented through loudspeakers at a constant comfortable volume level.

3.4   Experimental Procedure

When the participant arrived, the sound attenuated and electromagnetically shielded laboratory was introduced to the participant. Then, the participant was seated on the EMFi chair. We attached a photoplethysmography (PPG) sensor to the participant's earlobe and told as a cover story that the ear sensor measured skin temperature. The PPG sensor was functional but the data was not analyzed because we showed earlier that the EMFi chair measures heart rate reliably [1]. The participant was asked to sit comfortably and listen to the stimuli carefully. We also asked the participant to keep the eyes focused on the computer screen during the whole experiment. The experiment was started 30 seconds after the experimenter had left the room. The musical stimuli were separated with 10-second inter-stimulus intervals. The presentation order of the stimuli was randomly varied for each participant. The computer screen was light grey during the whole experiment. The stimulus presentation lasted approximately 17 minutes.

When the stimulus presentation was finished, the earlobe sensor was detached and the rating of the stimuli was begun. The participant was asked to rate his or her own emotional experience instead of the emotion he or she thought the musical clip was intended to express. Each stimulus was rated with two nine-point (1-9) rating scales: valence (unpleasant - pleasant) and arousal (calm - aroused). The scales appeared on the display and the ratings were given with the keyboard. The use of the scales was explained to the participant who then rated two practice stimuli that were not used in the actual experiment. The stimulus was presented first, and after that the valence and arousal scales appeared in this order. The scales changed as the participant gave a rating and a beep indicated that the rating had been recorded. The order of the stimuli in the rating phase was randomly varied for each participant. The whole experimental session lasted approximately 30 minutes. In the end, the participant was debriefed about the purpose of the study and the measurements that had been done.

3.5 Data Analysis

First, artifacts (large, sudden changes in heart rate data caused e.g. by body movements) were detected and removed from the heart rate data with an algorithm developed by Mikko Koivuluoma at the Digital Media Institute at the Tampere University of Technology. As a result, 29 % of the heart rate data was discarded as artifacts. Then, the heart rate data was baseline corrected using a 5-second pre stimulus baseline. For the statistical analyses, stimuli that included ≥ 50 % missing values (due to artifact removal) during the baseline period or during the stimulus presentation period were discarded from further analyses. At this point, 222 out of 450 stimuli (49 %) were discarded. Next, a mean value of heart rate during the listening of each musical clip was calculated for each participant resulting in 15 mean values (one value for each stimulus) per participant.

We assumed that past experiences and personal musical taste affects the emotional experience during music listening to the extent that the stimuli cannot be categorized a priori into positive, neutral, and negative. Therefore, the musical stimuli were categorized post hoc into negative, neutral, and positive individually for each participant according to the participant's valence rating for each stimulus. The musical clips with valence ratings 1, 2, and 3 were classified as negative, the clips with ratings 4, 5, and 6 were classified as neutral, and the clips with ratings 7, 8, and 9 were classified as positive. Thus, the same musical clip could be classified as positive for one participant and negative for another participant if they had rated them accordingly. Then, the heart rate data was categorized into negative, neutral, and positive according to which category the participant's valence rating of the emotional experience associated with each stimulus fell. Finally, a mean value for each participant and each emotional valence category was calculated resulting in 3 mean values (negative, neutral, and positive) per participant.

To check possible effect of arousal, the musical stimuli were also categorized into low arousal (1-3), neutral (4-6), and high arousal (7-8) according to the participant's arousal rating for each stimulus. Based on this, the heart rate data was categorized into low arousal, neutral, and high arousal in a similar way than above.

The data were analyzed with one-way repeated measures analyses of variance (ANOVAs) and associated post hoc pairwise comparisons. All the reported p-values in the post hoc pairwise comparisons were Bonferroni corrected.

4 Results

4.1 Subjective Ratings

The valence ratings of the stimuli showed that, out of the 15 musical clips, the participants rated on average 3.6 clips as negative, 6.6 clips as neutral, and 4.8 clips as positive. The mean ratings of valence were 2.4 for negative, 5.0 for neutral, and 7.5 for positive stimuli. The mean ratings of arousal were 5.0 for negative, 4.0 for neutral, and 5.1 for positive stimuli (see Fig. 2).

ANOVA showed a significant effect for valence ratings $F(2,52) = 954.05, p < 0.00$. Post hoc pairwise comparisons showed that the valence ratings of negative musical clips were significantly lower than the valence ratings of neutral musical clips $t(26) = 22.02, p < 0.00$. The valence ratings of neutral musical clips were significantly lower than the valence ratings of positive musical clips, $t(29) = 23.54$ $p < 0.00$. Also, the valence ratings of negative musical clips were significantly lower than the valence ratings of positive musical clips $t(27) = 43.68, p < 0.00$.

ANOVA showed a significant effect also for arousal ratings $F(2,52) = 10.66$, $p < 0.00$. Post hoc pairwise comparisons showed that the arousal ratings of negative musical clips were significantly higher than the arousal ratings of neutral musical clips $t(26) = 3.95$ $p < 0.01$. The arousal ratings of positive musical clips were significantly higher than the valence ratings of neutral musical clips $t(29) = 3.41$, $p < 0.01$. Importantly, there was no significant difference between the arousal ratings of negative and positive musical clips.

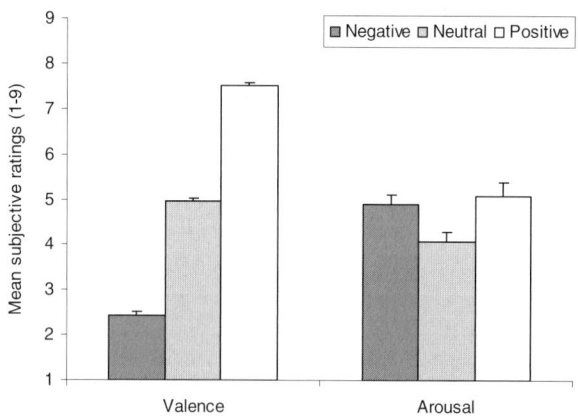

Fig. 2. Mean ratings of valence and arousal and standard errors of the means (S.E.M.) for all musical stimuli

4.2 Heart Rate Measures

The heart rate changes from the baseline averaged over the whole stimulus presentation period were -0.27 beats/min for negative, 2.13 beats/min for neutral, and 1.06 beats/min for positive musical stimuli (Fig. 3). ANOVA showed a significant valence effect for mean heart rate responses $F(2,40) = 4.01$, $p < 0.05$. Post hoc pairwise comparisons showed that the mean heart rate responses to negative musical clips were significantly lower than the mean heart rate responses to neutral musical clips $t(20) = 3.78$, $p < 0.05$. There were no significant differences between responses to negative and positive or between neutral and positive musical clips.

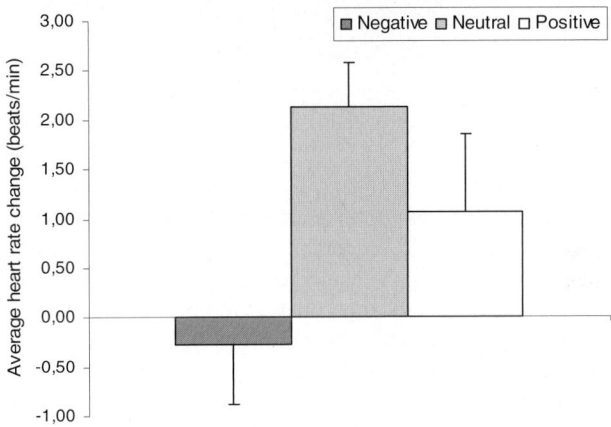

Fig. 3. Mean heart rate responses (beats/min) and standard errors of the means (S.E.M.) by valence

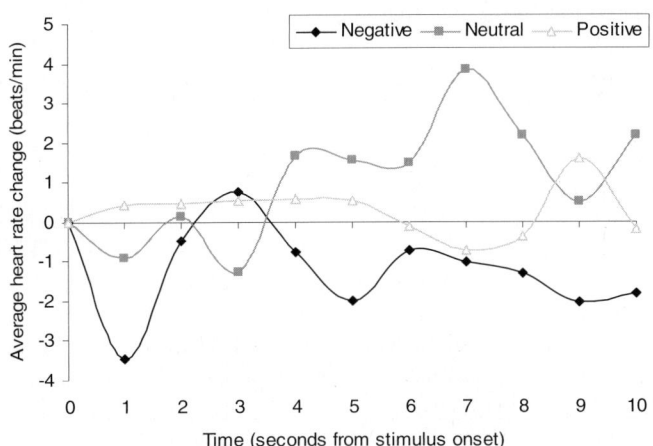

Fig. 4. Mean heart rate responses (beats/min) by valence during the first 10 seconds from the stimulus onset

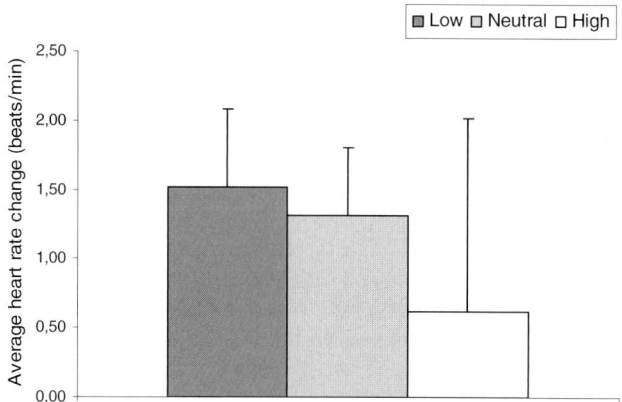

Fig. 5. Mean heart rate responses (beats/min) and standard errors of the means (S.E.M.) by arousal

We examined the mean heart rate responses to negative, neutral, and positive musical stimuli during the first 10 seconds more closely (Fig. 4). The mean heart rate responses to negative musical clips decelerated deeply during the 1st second and then the response peeked above the baseline on the 3rd second and after that decelerated below the baseline again. The mean heart rate responses to positive musical clips stayed quite near the baseline, and the mean responses to neutral musical clips decelerated first slightly and then accelerated after the 4th second. The responses are more clearly distinct from the 4th second onwards.

To check that the effect on heart rate is due to the valence of the musical stimuli, we also categorized the stimuli according to the participant's arousal ratings. When the heart rate data was analyzed in response to the arousal of the stimuli, the mean heart rate changes from the baseline during the whole stimulus presentation period were 1.51 beats/min for low arousal, 1.31 beats/min for neutral, and 0.62 beats/min for high arousal musical stimuli (Fig. 5). ANOVA showed no significant arousal effect for mean heart rate responses $F(2,28) = 0.019$, ns.

5 Discussion

The results of the subjective ratings showed that there were some inter-individual differences in the evoked emotional experiences during music listening as we had anticipated. The same piece of music was sometimes experienced as negative by one and as positive by another participant possibly as a result of different interpretations or previous experiences and memories related to a song. The results of the heart rate data showed that the mean responses to negative musical stimuli were significantly different than the mean responses to neutral stimuli. There was no significant arousal effect on the heart rate responses which supports the assumption that heart rate responses during perception were more dependent on the stimuli's emotional valence.

In previous research, a decelerating response to emotionally negative and positive auditory stimuli has been observed and the deceleration has been greater for negative than for positive stimuli [1, 6, 17, 23]. Our present results are parallel to the earlier findings in respect to negative stimulation. However, the response to positive musical clips remained in the proximity of the baseline when examined during the first 10 second of stimulus presentation. A decelerating heart rate response has been generally associated with perception of emotional stimuli [19] and a similar result has also been obtained with acoustic stimuli [6]. However, heart rate has been observed to accelerate during imagery and recall of emotional memories [19]. So, because music, at least intuitively, provokes memories easily it is possible that emotional processing during musical stimuli is somehow different than during the perception of visual and non-musical auditory stimuli.

One possible explanation for our partly different results could be the length of stimuli used in this experiment (between 37 and 77 seconds). In most studies, the length of stimulus exposure has been significantly shorter, for example, when using IADS stimulation stimulus duration of 6 seconds is typical. However, studies with musical stimuli seem to have had relatively long stimulus exposure times, usually beginning from 30 seconds, as shorter excerpts would not seem reasonable. It is also possible that other attributes of music affect the emotional response together with the valence of the musical stimulus. We did not try to control aspects like structure (tempo, major/minor mode etc.), musical preference, familiarity, or past experiences [e.g. 2]. Also, unlike most studies with musical stimuli our stimuli had lyrics.

When measuring heart rate during music listening, a note of caution needs to be mentioned: people tend to move a little, and body movements result in changes in heart rate. The heart rate measurement method of the EMFi chair is sensitive for body movements as the EMFi sensors sense changes in pressure. Thus, one of the aims of this study was to investigate the suitability of the EMFi chair in measuring heart rate responses during music listening and more generally using heart rate measurements in a less tightly controlled experiment. In the experimental sessions, some participants sang along with the songs and moved their body when they listened to the music. This resulted in a very high percentage of artifacts in the heart rate data (29 %). However, the results showed that although the percentage of artifacts and discarded stimuli were high, the remaining data was enough to differentiate negative heart rate responses from neutral ones. This is encouraging from the perspective of using heart rate measurements in real life applications.

The participants of the present study were healthy (and mobile) young people. Thus, future work should involve research with older adults. In the case of using EMFi chair measurements with stimulating technologies for older adults with lower physical functionality it is likely that there will be less artifacts that are caused by body movements during music listening. One of the primary goals of using the EMFi chair with stimulating technologies is particularly to get information on the emotional responses of older adults with lowered functionality who have difficulties to communicate their emotions otherwise.

The study provided an encouraging exploration into using physiological measures with stimulating technologies that are aimed at the rehabilitation of older adults. The results were partly promising suggesting that it may be possible to perceive responses to negatively stimulating pieces of music. Further, this suggests a possibility for an emotional contact even though it is through negative emotions. For example, in therapy in many cases it would be essential to deal with to negative emotional reactions. By embedding physiological sensors into a comfortable chair it would be possible to make inferences on a person's emotional responses and this information could be utilized when stimulating older adults with music.

Acknowledgments. The authors would like to thank the participants of the study and Arvo Laitinen, Eija Lämsä, and Tommi Harju from Audio Riders Oy. The EMFi chair is a product of a collaborative project, thus we also wish to thank Laurentiu Barna, Timo Flyktman, Mikko Koivuluoma, Jukka Lekkala, and Alpo Värri. This research was supported by the Finnish Funding Agency for Technology and Innovation (project number 20553), the Academy of Finland (project numbers 177857 and 1202183), and UCIT graduate school.

References

1. Anttonen, J., Surakka, V.: Emotions and heart rate while sitting on a chair. In: Proc. of CHI'05, pp. 491–499 (2005)
2. Bartlett, D.L.: Physiological responses to music and sound stimuli. In: Hodges, D.A. (ed.) Handbook of Music Psychology, Texas, USA, pp. 343–385. IMR Press, San Antonio (1996)
3. Baumgartner, T., Esslen, M., Jäncke, L.: From emotion perception to emotion experience: emotions evoked by pictures and classical music. Int. J. of Psychophysiology 60, 34–43 (2006)
4. Bickmore, T.W., Picard, R.W.: Establishing and maintaining long-term human-computer relationships. ACM TOCHI, 12(2), 293–327 (2005)
5. Blythe, M.A., Monk, A.F., Doughty, K.: Socially dependable design: the challenge of ageing populations for HCI. Interacting with Computers 17(6), 672–689 (2005)
6. Bradley, M.M., Lang, P.J.: Affective reactions to acoustic stimuli. Psychophysiology 37, 204–215 (2000)
7. Cuddy, L.L., Duffin, J.: Music, memory, and Alzheimer's disease: is music recognition spared in dementia, and how can it be assessed? Medical hypotheses 64(2), 229–235 (2005)
8. Dykstra, P.A., van Tilburg, T.G., de Jong Gierveld, J.: Changes in older adult loneliness: results from a seven-year longitudinal study. Research on Aging 27, 725–747 (2005)
9. Ekman, P., Levenson, R.W., Friesen, W.V.: Autonomic nervous system activity distinguishes among emotions. Science 221, 1208–1209 (1983)
10. Etzel, J.A., Johnsen, E.L., Dickerson, J., Tranel, D., Adolphs, R.: Cardiovascular and respiratory responses during musical mood induction. Int. J. of Psychophysiology 61(1), 57–69 (2006)
11. Gomez, P., Danuser, B.: Affective and physiological responses to environmental noises and music. Int. J. of Psychophysiology 53, 91–103 (2004)
12. Gowans, G., Campbell, J., Alm, N., Dye, R., Astell, A., Ellis, M.: Designing a multimedia conversation aid for reminiscence therapy in dementia care environments. In: Proc. of CHI'04, pp. 825–836 (2004)
13. Hirsch, T., Forlizzi, J., Hyder, E., Goetz, J., Stroback, J., Kurtz, C.: The ELDer project: Social and emotional factors in the design of eldercare technologies. In: Proc. of Universal Usability, pp. 72–79 (2000)
14. Iwanaga, M., Moroki, Y.: Subjective and physiological responses to music stimuli controlled over activity and preference. J. of Music Therapy 36(1), 26–38 (1999)

15. Jylhä, M.: Old age and loneliness: cross-sectional and longitudinal analyses in the Tampere Longitudinal Study of Aging. Canadian J. on Aging 23(2), 157–168 (2004)
16. Kallinen, K.: Emotion related psychophysiological responses to listening music with eyes-open versus eyes-closed: electrodermal (EDA), electrocardiac (ECG), and electromyographic (EMG) measures. In: Proc. of Music Perception & Cognition, pp. 299–301 (2004)
17. Krumhansl, C.L.: An exploratory study of musical emotions and psychophysiology. Canadian J. of Experimental Psychology 51(4), 336–352 (1997)
18. Lang, P.J., Bradley, M.M., Cuthbert, B.N.: A motivational analysis of emotion: Reflex-cortex connections. Psychological Science 3(1), 44–49 (1992)
19. Lang, P.J., Greenwald, M.K., Bradley, M.M., Hamm, A.O.: Looking at pictures: affective, facial, visceral, and behavioral reactions. Psychophysiology 30, 261–273 (1993)
20. Mynatt, E.D., Rogers, W.A.: Developing technology to support the functional independence of older adults. Ageing International 27(1), 24–41 (2002)
21. Mynatt, E.D., Rowan, J., Jacobs, A., Craighill, S.: Digital family portraits: Supporting peace of mind for extended family members. In: Proc. of CHI'01, pp. 333–340 (2001)
22. Nilsson, M., Johansson, S., Håkansson, M.: Nostalgia: an evocative tangible interface for elderly users. In: Proc. of CHI'03, pp. 964–965 (2003)
23. Nyklíček, I., Thayer, J.F., Van Doornen, L.J.P.: Cardiorespiratory differentiation of musically-induced emotions. J. of Psychophysiology 11(4), 304–321 (1997)
24. Saarela, M.: Sävelsirkku. Ääniohjelmat vuorovaikutuksen ja toimintakyvyn ylläpitäimisen apuvälineinä vanhustyössä. Vanhustyön keskusliiton raportti, 3/1999 (1999)
25. Schneider, W., Eschman, A., Zuccolotto, A.: E-Prime User's Guide. Pittsburgh, Psychology Software Tools, Inc. (2002)
26. Wiley, J., Sung, J.-y., Abowd, G.: The message center: Enhancing elder communication. In: Proc. of CHI'06, pp. 1523–1528 (2006)
27. Witvliet, C.V., Vrana, S.R.: The emotional impact of instrumental music on affect ratings, facial EMG, autonomic measures, and the startle reflex: effects of valence and arousal. Psychophysiology Supplement, vol. 91 (1996)

A Multi-method Approach to the Assessment of Web Page Designs

S.J. Westerman, E.J. Sutherland, L. Robinson, H. Powell, and G.Tuck

Institute of Psychological Sciences,
University of Leeds, Leeds LS2 9JT, U.K.
s.j.westerman@leeds.ac.uk

Abstract. This study used self-report, facial EMG, galvanic skin response, and eye tracking to assess users' participants' responses to two charity web sites. For each site, page content and colour of presentation (colour versus black & white) were manipulated. Results support the utility and diversity of these measures. Each provided information about users' responses to web page designs, with a good deal of variation in sensitivity to experimental manipulations. In combination the data from these measures allowed further inferences to be drawn, supporting a multi-dimensional view of user experience and the need for multi-method approaches to evaluation.

1 Introduction

In recent years there has been increasing emphasis on developing methods of assessing multiple dimensions of users' responses to computer interfaces. In part this has been driven by proposals for 'affective computing' systems [1] and associated requirements for measuring the user's state in ways that are not intrusive to task performance. In part these developments are being driven by a broadening conception of user experience [2][3] that goes beyond 'traditional' descriptions of user satisfaction (e.g., [4]). In this paper we report a study that uses multiple methods to assess users' responses to different web page designs. In the following sections we introduce each of these methods and briefly consider associated strengths and weaknesses.

1.1 Self-report

The application of self-report measures has a long history in the study of HCI. Initially this approach was predominantly used to provide measures of user acceptance of technology (e.g., [5]) and satisfaction (see [6]). More recently, it has been expanded to accommodate broader views of user experience (see e.g., [2][3]) and multiple scale measures have been developed to reflect a diversity of constructs (see e.g., [7][8][9]; see also [10]). There are several important advantages associated with self-report methods of assessment. It is a very accessible method for researchers, no expensive equipment is required. It can provide an unparalleled breadth of view on user experience, including qualitative 'scoping' of design issues and user strategies, and quantitative assessments of performance demands and users' attitude, including

A. Paiva, R. Prada, and R.W. Picard (Eds.): ACII 2007, LNCS 4738, pp. 302–313, 2007.

measures of workload, usability, flow, trust, and hedonic quality. It also engages the user in the research and development processes; an important component of participatory design. However, self-report does have drawbacks (see [11]). The reliance on introspection means that potentially important unconscious influences [12] may not be reflected (e.g., [13]). The method is also disruptive of task performance and cannot provide a continuous record of the users' experience in the way that other types of measures can (see below).

1.2 Psychophysiology

Several psychophysiological methods have been explored as means of assessing users' responses to manipulations of the human-computer interface. Unlike self-report measures, these are thought to be able to assess non-conscious responses [14], they are relatively unintrusive on task performance, and also allow continuous monitoring of users' responses over extended periods of time. Two measures that have been used successfully in an HCI context, and that are examined in the study reported here are Galvanic Skin Response and Facial EMG.

Recordings of Galvanic Skin Response (GSR) provide an assessment of arousal in the autonomic nervous system (ANS) of the user. Several studies have been found it to be sensitive to interface/interaction manipulations (e.g., [15][16]). However, these have tended to be relatively 'gross' manipulations. Moreover, it is generally thought that GSR is not sensitive to the valence component of affect. In contrast, facial EMG recordings hold the promise of being able to access valence of affect but are somewhat more 'invasive' for the participant in their application. Typically assessments are made of of corrugator and zygomaticus activity ('frown' and 'smile' muscles), with corrugator activity producing more promising results (see e.g., [17][18][19]).

Although psychophysiological methods have some advantages over self report, there are also associated drawbacks. The set up process required for psycho-physiological recording can be time consuming and inconvenient/constraining for the participant, typically requiring the recording of a baseline (although see e.g., [19]). These measures require sophisticated equipment (unlike questionnaire measures). They are also subject to external influences, particularly from factors that produce ANS activation (e.g., room temperature, social evaluation). Interpretation can be problematic, partly because of the potential for external influences, and partly because of the previously mentioned insensitivity of some measures, e.g., GSR, to the valence dimension of affect (cf. [20]). Currently, more extensive testing of psycho-physiological methods is required in HCI settings. Many existing assessments have incorporated experimental manipulations that are fairly gross in magnitude and designed to induce user frustration (see [21]). Psychophysiological methods need to be tested in a wider range of computer-based scenarios.

1.3 Eye Tracking

Eye tracking is becoming an increasingly popular and accessible means of assessing alternative interface designs. Current eye tracking systems are relatively non-intrusive of task performance, being sufficiently sophisticated in design to permit a good deal of head movement by the user whilst maintaining accurate recording. A range of measures can be derived, including scan paths/sequences, scan path lengths, fixation durations, and gaze time (see [22][23][24]).

Eye tracking is particularly useful for gathering information on the strategies that users' adopt during computer-based task performance (e.g., [25]) and which aspects of the interface 'capture' attention (e.g., [26]). This information can be used to identify and correct design features that lead to user error, to design for natural performance sequences, and to position information so that it is more likely to be noticed (see e.g., [26][27]). However, as with the other methods, described above, there are also a number of practical and theoretical difficulties and limitations associated with the use of eye tracking in the context of HCI. Interpretation of results can be complicated by the fact that eye movements are determined in both a 'bottom up' (by features of the interface design) and 'top down' (by task requirements and goals) manner [22]. Moreover, gaze location does not inevitably imply attention to that location [23][25] although this is the premise on which eye tracking tends to be based. Eye tracking is also limited in the range of user responses that it can detect. With eye tracking the emphasis is firmly on assessing user attention as it relates to information content and format [28]. Following from these characteristics, eye movements can be strongly influenced by sequencing effects, and this has implications with regard to the influence of experimental controls, i.e., counterbalancing (see [24]). Eye tracking has not generally been found to be associated with affective responses, although the early period of stimulus viewing (<500ms) may hold some promise (see e.g., [29]).

1.4 Experimental Aims

From this brief review we can see that there is no single perfect method to assess HCI. We argue here that a combination of methods will provide a more complete account of user experience. In this paper we report a study that examined four methods of assessing web page designs: i) self-report – a questionnaire measure developed on the basis of psychometric principles; ii) facial electromyagraph (EMG) recording; iii) Galvanic Skin Response (GSR); and iv) eye tracking. The goal was to determine how these methods relate to different aspects of user response. It may be, for example that two different methods provide similar information about the users' experience and therefore one is redundant. Alternatively, it may be that different methods tell different parts of the story of user experience and that information can be 'triangulated'. In this circumstance it would be important to establish 'boundaries' for methods so that they can be combined and deployed efficiently and effectively. The results of the reported study bear on this important issue.

2 Method

2.1 Participants

Forty participants were recruited for this study (mean age = 21.15 years, sd=2.39). There were equal numbers of men and women.

2.2 Procedure

Participants were required to view two pages selected from two charity web sites that provide help and support on multiple sclerosis. Participants' 'task' was to decide which charity they would prefer to donate to. To standardise their experience as far as possible, web pages were presented as isolated pages, and participants were not able to navigate to other parts of the web site. Web sites and web pages were selected on the basis of their similarity of content, but substantially different graphic designs varied. Each participant viewed one web site in colour and the other in black & white. One web page from each site provided rather general information, presented in a predominantly prose style, the other provided more detailed facts, presented predominantly in a 'bullet point' style. All orders of presentation were counter-balanced.

While participants were viewing the websites their eye movements were recorded using a Tobii X50 eye tracker. This is a relatively unobtrusive process. The Tobii eye tracker tracks the positions of both eyes making the system relatively robust with regard to head movement of the user. Measures of total viewing time and mean fixation durations are reported here. For the purposes of analysis a filter, with the parameters 30 pixels and 60 msecs, was set to identify fixations. This seemed appropriate for the mixture of textual and pictorial content that was present in the web sites.

Facial EMG and Galvanic Skin Responses (GSR) were recorded using a Biopac system (Biopac Systems, Inc., Santa Barbara, CA). For facial EMG, electrodes were placed over the corrugator and zygomaticus muscles. Signals were amplified, using a high band-pass filter of 30Hz and a low band pass filter of 500 Hz, integrated and rectified across 25 samples. Scores were standardized within individuals to remove effects of individual differences in reactivity (see Winkielman & Cacioppo, 2001). GSR was recoded using a finger electrode transducer. Baseline recordings for GSR and facial EMG were taken prior to task performance.

After viewing each website participants completed an extensive (95 items) psychometric questionnaire in which they provided ratings of various aspects of their perceptions. Detailed results of these analyses are reported elsewhere [30]. Due to the length of the questionnaire, these were completed with reference to each website rather than each page. Only results for the scales assessing 'positive affect', 'flow', and 'cognitive evaluations' are reported here.

3   Results

3.1   Psychometrics

A series of 2 x 2 ANOVAs was used to test effects of web site and colour on psychometric ratings. The main effect of web site was not significant for the 'Positive Affect' scale, $F_{(1,33)}=1.07$. However, there was a significant effect of the colour manipulation, $F_{(1,33)}=10.35$, $p<.01$, such that higher positive affect was reported following viewing a web site in colour (see Table 1).

Table 1. Ratings of 'Positive affect' ratings for different levels of web site and colour of presentation variables

	Web Site A		Web Site B	
	Mean	SD	Mean	SD
B&W	7.58	2.72	6.94	2.88
Colour	10.50	6.17	9.41	4.23

Table 2. Ratings of 'Flow' ratings for different levels of web site and colour of presentation variables

	Web Site A		Web Site B	
	Mean	SD	Mean	SD
B&W	33.29	7.78	28.71	7.56
Colour	32.71	9.33	32.12	7.49

There was a main effect of web site on participants' ratings for the 'Flow' scale, $F(1,32)=4.27$, $p<.05$, such that participants experienced greater 'flow' when viewing the web site A (see Table 2). The effect of colour was not significant, $F(1,32)=1.27$. There was no significant effect of web site, $F(1,31)=3.09$, or colour, $F(1,31)=2.55$, for the 'Cognitive Evaluations' scale.

3.2 Psychophysiology

A 2 x 2 x 2 ANOVA was used to examine effects of web site, web page, and colour manipulations for each of the psychophysiological measures.

Table 3. GSR readings for web site, page, and colour conditions

	Web site A				Web site B			
	About page		Facts page		About page		Facts page	
	Mean	SD	Mean	SD	Mean	SD	Mean	SD
B&W	-0.34	0.68	-0.45	0.79	-0.22	0.80	-0.14	0.85
Colour	0.09	0.97	0.27	0.83	0.51	0.91	0.28	0.76

For GSR the effects of web site, $F(1,34)=0.84$, and 'page', $F(1,34)=0.04$, were not significant. However, there was an effect of 'colour', $F(1,34)=5.93$, $p<.05$, such that GSR was greater when the web sites were presented in colour (see Table 3).

Table 4. Corrugator facial EMG recordings for web site, page, and colour conditions

	Web site B				Web site B			
	About page		Facts page		About page		Facts page	
	Mean	SD	Mean	SD	Mean	SD	Mean	SD
B&W	-0.24	0.90	0.12	0.85	-0.25	0.77	-0.03	0.90
Colour	-0.17	0.75	0.45	0.94	-0.13	0.91	0.26	0.81

When considering corrugator activity, the effect of web site, F(1,34)=0.14, and 'colour', F(1,34)=0.96, were not significant. However, there was a significant effect of 'page', F(1,34)=11.70, p<.01, such that participants' corrugator EMG activity was greater for the 'Facts' page than for the 'About' page. There were no significant effects of the experimental manipulations for zygomaticus activity.

3.3 Eye Tracking

Two measures were taken from the eye tracking data, for inclusion here: i) the total time spent looking at each web page; and, ii) the mean fixation duration. The results for a measure of the number of fixations paralleled those of total time spent viewing, so are not reported. Gaze duration was also explored but rejected.

For total viewing time there was a main effect of site, F(1,34)=89.42, such that participants spent longer viewing at web site A. There was also a significant effect of web page, F(1,34)=102.89, p<.001, such that participants spent longer looking at the 'About' web page, and a significant interaction between these variables (see Figure 1), F(1,34)=32.61, p<.001, such that the effects of the 'page' manipulation were greatest for web site A, with the longest viewing time being for the 'About' page of this site. The effects of the colour manipulation were not significant, F(1,34)=2.33.

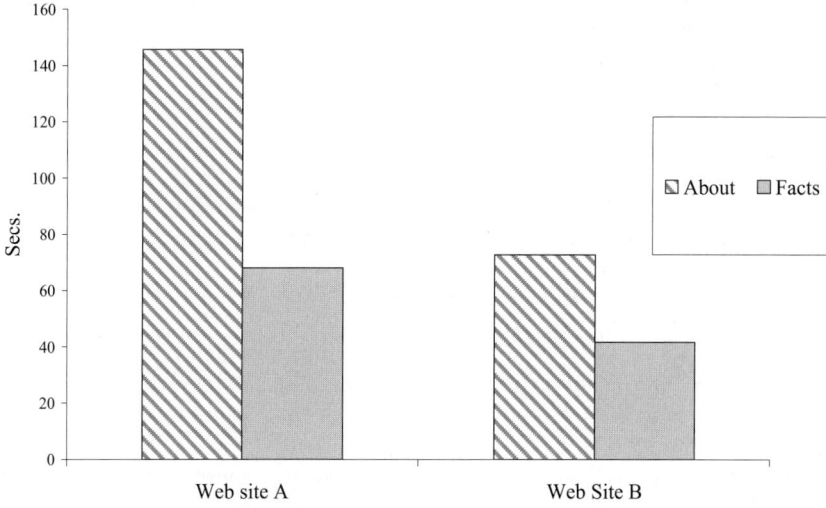

Fig. 1. Interaction between manipulations of 'Web Site' and 'Page' for total time viewing (seconds)

Table 5. Mean fixation duration (msecs) for each page for each web site, page, and colour condition

| | Web site A | | | | Web site B | | | |
| | About page | | Facts page | | About page | | Facts page | |
	Mean	SD	Mean	SD	Mean	SD	Mean	SD
B&W	221.08	62.21	204.77	56.36	182.76	71.91	179.70	66.39
Colour	177.15	57.59	172.08	64.54	214.08	65.31	210.67	57.60

For mean fixation duration, the main effect of web site was not significant, $F(1,34)=0.27$. However, there was a significant effect of 'page', $F(1,34)=6.93$, $p<.05$, such that fixation durations were somewhat longer when participants were viewing the 'About' page (see Table 5). The effects of colour, for this variable, were not significant, $F(1,34)=0.38$.

3.4 Correlations Between Different Methods of Assessment

To examine correlations between psychometric, psychophysiological, and eye tracking measures it was necessary to combine scores for the two web pages for the psychophysiological and eye tracking measures. Then, for all measures a difference score was then calculated by subtracting values for Web Site B from those for Web Site A. This measure was taken to reflect users' preferences for one web site over the other and provided a means of standardising scores for individuals. These values were then correlated to examine the extent to which different measures were accounting for similar variance. Correlations between psychophysiological measures are presented in Table 6. As can be seen, associations were generally weak. However, there was a significant negative association between GSR and total viewing time. Longer viewing times were associated with reduced GSR.

Table 6. Correlations between difference measures (between responses to websites) for facial EMG, GSR, and eye tracking

	Zygomaticus	GSR	Total viewing time	Mean fixation duration
Corrugator	-0.12	-0.04	0.12	0.03
Zygomaticus		-0.12	0.20	-0.13
GSR			-0.35 *	-0.17
Total viewing time				-0.04

Correlations between psychometric measures and psychophysiological and eye tracking data are presented in Table 7. Generally, associations were weak and non significant. However, GSR was positively correlated with ratings for Positive Affect.

Table 7. Correlations between psychophysiological and psychometric difference measures (between websites)

	Cognitive evaluation	NA	PA	Flow
Corrugator	0.11	-0.14	0.04	0.04
Zygomaticus	-0.08	0.14	0.03	0.04
GSR	0.37	-0.10	0.39 *	0.20
Total viewing time	-0.31	0.30	-0.25	-0.12
Mean fixation duration	-0.12	0.18	-0.13	0.01

Note: * $p<.05$.

4   Discussion

The reported study examined users' responses to two different charity web sites using four different methods of measurement: self-report, galvanic skin response (GSR), facial EMG, and eye tracking. For each site the type of page ('About' versus 'Facts') and colour of presentation (colour versus black and white) were manipulated. An important question, examined here, is whether these different methods of measuring users' responses to interface designs are sensitive to the same experimental manipulations, indicating a high degree of redundancy of measurement. In this case, when planning an empirical test of users' experiences, it would be sufficient to select the most sensitive method. Conversely, if methods differ with regard to the types of interface manipulations to which they are sensitive, or in the type of information they provide on users' responses, the use of multiple measures would provide added value to a programme of testing. In the following section we discuss the sensitivity of each method of measurement to the experimental manipulations. In the subsequent section we focus on the overlap between methods, discussing inter-method correlations and the patterning of results.

4.1   Sensitivity of Methods of Measurement to the Experimental Manipulations

Consistent with recent approaches to describing computer users' experiences [31][32] a multi-factorial model was adopted to guide self-report assessment. Full details are provided in [30], with only a limited range of the factors assessed reported here. These include scales for 'positive affect', 'flow', and 'cognitive evaluations'. Results support the existence of separate psychological constructs with different scales being sensitive to different experimental manipulations. Scores for the 'positive affect' scale were influenced by the manipulation of web site colour, with participants reporting greater positive affect when a web site was presented in colour rather than black and white. The potential for colour manipulations, including hue, saturation, and brightness, to influence affective response is well established [33]. In contrast, the self-report scale for 'flow' was sensitive to the manipulation of website content, with ratings being relatively higher for web site A. This perhaps indicates the greater 'task orientation' of this psychological construct, with users being engaged by, and engrossed in, the material contained in web site A. When considering the 'cognitive evaluations' scale, although the trend suggested a preference for web site A, there were no significant differences between ratings for the different web sites, pages, or colour manipulations. This scale contains evaluations relating to overall perceptions of quality, and may reflect the combined effects of a range of constructs including those encompassed by positive affect and flow. If each are 'pulling' in different directions this might produce sufficient measurement 'noise' to prevent significant differences being identified. For example, it may be that there are positive and negative aspects associated with each interface manipulation. This would illustrate the importance of a fine-grained multi-factorial assessment.

When considering the psychophysiological measures tested, GSR was sensitive to differences in the colour of presentation, with higher GSR recordings being produced when the websites were presented in colour rather than in black and white. This is broadly consistent with previous research in other areas, see e.g., [34][35], that has found effects on GSR of manipulations of hue, although see also [36][37] for arguments relating to limitations of these effects. For facial EMG, there was a reliable difference in corrugator activity between the two types of 'web pages' ('About' versus 'Facts'). Corrugator activity was greater when participants were viewing the 'facts' page, as opposed to the 'about' page. In contrast, Zygomaticus activity seems to be a less potent measure of users' responses to design factors [21]. In this instance it was not sensitive to any of the experimental manipulations.

Finally, with regard to eye movement, total viewing time was longer for web site A. There was also a significant effect of 'page type', with participants spending longer viewing the 'About' pages. An interaction between these variables indicated that this difference was greatest for website A. Effects of colour of presentation were not significant. There was a similar effect of page type for fixation durations, but effects of web site were not significant.

4.2 Patterns of User Response

Generally, it would seem that these methods of measurement are able to detect users' reactions that arise from interface manipulations and that, to some extent, different methods are sensitive to different manipulations. An independence of methods is supported by the correlational analyses. Correlations between the three psycho-physiological measures were all weak and non significant. In the case of zygomaticus activity, given that this was not able to detect any of the experimental interface manipulations, unreliability of measurement cannot be excluded as a possible explanation. However, this does not apply to GSR or corrugator activity.

Correlations between the pyschophysiological measures and the eye tracking measures were also generally weak. However, there was a significant negative correlation between GSR activity and total viewing time. One possible artefactual explanation is that GSR decreased as viewing time increased because participants became more relaxed with the stimuli. Consistent with this position, corrugator activity was greater for the 'Facts' pages, which were viewed for relatively shorter durations than the 'About' pages. The association between GSR and viewing time could reflect efforts associated with forming assessments of the designs during the early phases of viewing. If this is the case, there are obvious implications with regard to experimental controls that should be applied when using psychophysiological methods of assessment in usability studies.

Positive affect and GSR were both sensitive to the manipulation of colour of presentation. Both were greater when the web sites were presented in colour, as opposed to black and white. This is not unusual in the context of empirical assessments of responses to colour. However, in the context of affective computing GSR has typically been used as an index of users' frustration with an interface (see e.g., [15]), with increased GSR coinciding with increased frustration, a condition in which positive affect would often be relatively low. In this study GSR is elevated in an interface condition for which the user experiences greater positive affect. There was also a significant positive correlation between these two measures (see Table 7). It would seem that, in this study, the positive affective state induced by a colourful (as opposed to black and white) presentation leads to increased ANS activity. This illustrates one of the difficulties, as mentioned above, of some psychophysiological measures. In isolation they give no indication as to the valence of the users' response. Without the combination of measurement methods it not be possible to disambiguate the users' response.

As mentioned above, facial EMG recording of corrugator activity was sensitive to the different types of web pages shown to participants ('About' versus 'Facts'). Activity was greater when viewing the 'Facts' page, although total viewing time and fixation duration were greater for the 'About' page. These are potentially useful results in disambiguating the nature of the corrugator response. Given that fixation duration may be an index of processing effort [38] this would suggest that, in this instance, corrugator response is not the result of increased cognitive effort (cf., [21]). Longer fixation duration may result from the more densely packed, prose style nature of the 'About' pages in contrast to the 'bullet point' style of the 'Facts' pages. A somewhat speculative explanation of these effects on corrugator muscle activity is that the layout of the 'Facts' pages tended to place relatively greater emphasis on some consequences/issues relating to multiple sclerosis that induced a negative affective response. At least at a qualitative level, some of the text contained on the 'Facts' pages seemed more 'hard hitting'. As with GSR, it is possible that elevated corrugator activity can be produced by more than one cause [21]. It is only by the use of multiple measurements that disambiguation is possible.

Self-reported ratings of 'flow' and viewing duration were both sensitive to the manipulation of web site (A versus B). Ratings for flow were greater after users experienced web site A, and this site was viewed for longer. A simple artefactual explanation for longer viewing would be an imbalance in the amount of information contained on the two sites. However, in combination, these results suggest that users seem to be more 'engaged' with web site A. Even if it was the case that web site A had somewhat more demanding content, ratings of 'flow', would lead to the conclusion that it was also a more engaging design. As with the other combinations of factors, as described above, it is only through conjoint consideration of different measures that this inference can be drawn.

4.3 Conclusion

In this study four different methods for assessing users' responses to different web site designs were tested. Each was sensitive to at least one interface manipulation, with some differentiation between methods in the specific manipulations that produced differences in responses. This indicates that the design of user testing programmes must involve the careful selection of measurement methods, based on the nature of the interface elements that are being evaluated, and that there may be advantages associated with the use of more than one method. In the reported study, there was also a degree of 'overlap' in method-manipulation sensitivity and, in more than one instance, it was only through the 'triangulation' of methods, considering results in combination, that a clear picture of the nature of users' responses could be obtained. These data further indicate that multiple measures of assessment can provide added value to the process of user testing.

Acknowledgements. This work was partly supported by the EC funded HUMAINE Network of Excellence.

References

1. Picard, R.W.: Affective Computing. MIT Press, Cambridge (1997)
2. Dillon, A.: Beyond usability: Process, outcome, and affect in human-computer interactions. The Canadian, Journal of Information and Library Science 26(4), 57–69 (2001)
3. Hassenzahl, M., Tractinsky, N.: User experience - a research agenda. Behaviour & Information Technology 25, 91–97 (2006)
4. ISO 9241-11: Ergonomic Requirements for Office Work with Visual Display Terminals (VDTs). Part 11: Guidance on Usability. International Organization for Standardization, Geneva (1998)
5. Davis, F.D.: Perceived usefulness, perceived ease of use, and user acceptance of information technology. MIS Quarterly 13, 318–340 (1989)
6. Bailey, J.E., Pearson, S.W.: Development of a tool for measuring and analysing computer user satisfaction. Management Science 29, 530–545 (1983)
7. Hassenzahl, M.: The interplay of beauty, goodness, and usability of interactive products. Human-Computer Interaction 19, 319–349 (2004)
8. Huang, M.-H.: Designing website attributes to induce experiential encounters. Computers in Human Behavior 19, 425–442 (2003)
9. Huang, M.-H.: Web performance scale. Information & Management 42, 841–852 (2005)
10. Hornbaek, K.: Current practice in measuring usability: Challenges to usability studies and research. International Journal of Man-Machine Studies 64, 79–102 (2006)
11. Annett, J.: Subjective rating scales: Science or art? Ergonomics 45, 966–987 (2002)
12. Veryzer, R.W.: A nonconscious processing explanation of consumer response to product design. Psychology & Marketing 16, 497–522 (1999)
13. Nisbett, R.E., Wilson, T.D.: Telling more than we can know: Verbal reports on mental processes. Psychological Review 84, 231–259 (1977)
14. Winkielman, P., Cacioppo, J.T.: Mind at ease puts a smile on the face: Psychophysiological evidence that processing facilitiation elicits positive affect. Journal of Personality and Social Psychology 81, 989–1000 (2001)
15. Scheirer, J., Fernandez, R., Klein, J., Picard, R.W.: Frustrating the user on purpose: A step toward building an affective computer. Interacting with Computers 14, 93–118 (2002)
16. Ward, R.D., Marsden, P.H.: Physiological responses to different web page designs. International Journal of Human-Computer Studies 59, 199–213 (2003)
17. Branco, P., Firth, P., Encarnação, M., Bonato, P.: Faces of emotion in human-computer interaction. In: CHI 2005, pp. 2–7. ACM Press, New York (2005)
18. Hazlett, R.: Measurement of user frustration: A biologic approach. In: CHI 2003, April 5-10, ACM, New York (2003)
19. Hazlett, R.L., Benedek, J.: Measuring emotional valence to understand the users' experience of software. International Journal of Human-Computer Studies 65, 306–314 (2007)
20. Russell, J.A.: Core affect and the psychological construction of emotion. Psychological Review 110, 145–172 (2003)
21. Westerman, S.J., Gardner, P.H., Sutherland, E.J.: Taxonomy of Affective Systems Usability Testing. HUMAINE EC Network of Excellence project report D9g (2006)
22. Duchowski, A.T.: Eye Tracking Methodology: Theory and Practice. Springer, London (2003)
23. Liversedge, S.P., Findlay, J.M.: Saccadic eye movements and cognition. Trends in Cognitive Sciences 4, 6–14 (2000)

24. Pan, B., Hembroke, H.A., Gay, G.K., Granka, L.A., Feusner, M.K., Newman, J.K.: The determinants of web page viewing behaviour: An eye tracking study. Proceedings of Eye Tracking Research and Applications. SIGGRAPH, pp. 147–154. ACM, New York (2004)
25. Rudmann, D.S., McConkie, G.W., Zheng, X.S.: Eye tracking in cognitive state detection for HCI. In: Proceedings of ICMI'03, pp. 159–163 (2003)
26. Goldberg, J.H., Stimson, M.J., Lewenstein, M., Scott, N., Wichansky, A.M: Eye tracking in web search tasks: Design implications. In: Proceedings of ETRA'02., pp. 51–58. ACM, New York (2002)
27. Bojko, A.: Using eye tracking to compare web page designs: A case study. Journal of Usability Studies 3, 112–120 (2006)
28. Rayner, K.: Eye movements in reading and information processing: 20 years of research. Psychological Bulletin 124, 372–422 (1998)
29. Calvo, M.G., Lang, P.J.: Gaze patterns when looking at emotional pictures: Motivationally biased attention. Motivation and Emotion 28, 221–243 (2004)
30. Westerman, S.J., Sutherland, E.J., Powell, H., Robinson, L., Tuck, G.: Users' responses to alternative website designs: A framework and psychometric assessment (Unpublished manuscript)
31. Dillon, A.: Beyond usability: Process, outcome, and affect in human-computer interactions. The Canadian, Journal of Information and Library Science 26(4), 57–69 (2001)
32. Hassenzahl, M., Tractinsky, N.: User experience - a research agenda. Behaviour & Information Technology 25, 91–97 (2006)
33. Valdez, P., Mehrabian, A.: Effects of colour on emotions. Journal of Experimental Psychology: General 123(4), 394–409 (1994)
34. Wilson, G.D.: Arousal properties of red versus green. Perceptual and Motor Skills 23, 947–949 (1966)
35. Jacons, K.W., Hustmyer, F.E.: Effects of four psychological primary colours on GSR, heart rate and respiration rate. Perceptual and Motor Skills 38, 763–766 (1974)
36. Calwell, J.A., Jones, G.E.: The effects of exposure to red and blue light on physiological indices and time estimation. Perception 14, 19–29 (1985)
37. Robinson, W.S.: Colours, arousal, functionalism, and individual differences. Psyche, 10, 2 (2004), http://psyche.cs.monash.edu.au/
38. Renshaw, J.A., Finlay, J.E., Tyfa, D., Ward, R.D.: Understanding visual influence in graph design through temporal and spatial eye movement characteristics. Interacting with Computers 16, 557–578 (2004)

Rational Agents That Blush

Paolo Turrini[1], John-Jules Ch. Meyer[2], and Cristiano Castelfranchi[3]

[1] University of Siena, Italy
[2] University of Utrecht, The Netherlands
[3] ISTC-CNR, Italy

"Video meliora proboque; deteriora sequor"
(Ovidius, Metam. VIII, 18-21)

1 Introduction

A student, supported by his classmates, throws a piece of chalk at the teacher who is writing on the blackboard. The teacher rapidly turns back and promptly catches him in the act. The student blushes and suddenly realizes how bad it was what he did.

What happened to the guy? Why did he decide to throw the piece of chalk? And why, after a few seconds, he would have liked that what he did had never happened? Aim of this work is to provide a formal characterization of those emotions that deal with normative reasoning, such as shame and sense of guilt, to understand their relation with rational action and to ground their formalization on a cognitive science perspective. In order to do this we need to identify *when* agents feel ashamed or guilty and *what* agents do when they feel so. We will also investigate how agents can induce and silence these feelings in themselves, i.e. the analysis of defensive strategies they can employ. We will argue that agents do have control over their emotions and we will analyze some operations they can carry out on them. After presenting a cognitive model of shame and guilt as social emotions, we will provide a formal representation of them and their dynamics in terms of basic notions such as beliefs, goals and violations, following the rational action approach of [26] [25] [13] and the cognitive approach in [16] [3].

Related Work. As witnessed by [6] the study of emotions has recently gained much attention in the fields of artificial intelligence [21] [13], evolutionary computation [22] and multi agent systems [19], due to the encounter between computer science tools and neuro, cognitive and social sciences analyses [5] [18] [9]. Ours is a cognitive perspective: even though we agree that it is important to study emotions from a computational and emergentist point of view, we argue that in

A. Paiva, R. Prada, and R.W. Picard (Eds.): ACII 2007, LNCS 4738, pp. 314–325, 2007.
© Springer-Verlag Berlin Heidelberg 2007

order to build an anatomy of emotions it is as important to understand them in terms of their interaction with other cognitive ingredients[1].

The most influential cognitive paradigm for studying and constructing cognitive agents with emotions has been that by Ortony, Clore and Collins [18]. Nevertheless, in [18] the characterizations of feelings related to norms are not deeply investigated:

> "In order to feel shame one must have violated a standard one takes to be important, as moral standards are. Such violations are held to be inexcusable. This is not necessary for a person who is feeling guilty.(...)
> In fact, we do not think that there is a distinct emotion of feeling guilty. Rather, we view feelings of guilt as mixtures of distinct emotions such as shame and regret, perhaps accompanied by certain cognitive states, such as the belief that one was, at least technically, responsible." (p. 142-143)

Many expressions here would need to be explicated further: why are violations only in case of shame held to be inexcusable? What is a mixture of emotions? And a technical responsibility? If we find the distinction between shame and guilt and all the other related feelings as meaningful at all, we need to have clear-cut definitions that relate those feelings to agents' mental states and to precisely understand their functioning.

We will pursue a formal investigation on emotions, as done for instance in [19], but adding a closer look to the formal properties of our notions, that we construct in a well known logical framework such as KARO [26] [25] [13]. From a cognitive point of view we will follow the analysis of [16] that grounds emotional displays like blushing and feelings like loneliness or pride on complex multiagent interaction. We claim that such model overcomes the oversimplifications in [18] while keeping a semiformal approach that eases a proper formal investigation.

2   A Cognitive Model for Shame and Sense of Guilt

Shame and sense of guilt are seen as social emotions. They are social because they: are socially acquired (through values and norms internalization); have social targets (the victim, for instance, in case of sense of guilt) and referents (the

---

[1] Many criticisms have been moved to cognitivists theories, some of which can be hardly addressed in this context. Nevertheless we would like to point out how several ones are based on what we think is a misconception of the use of formal models of cognition. In the study of normative emotions of [22] it is argued that "logic does not provide an adequate foundation" to the study of human behaviour and "the necessary abandonment of logical models for the explanation and simulation of human social behaviour" is advocated. Even though we share the worries in [22] w.r.t. representing humans as perfect reasoners, we claim that an anti-logical position in modelling interaction is simply wrong: emotions can be studied as mechanisms that act on human cognition. But mechanisms do have a logic. What is more, the recent breakthroughs of logical models in the study of social interaction and information flow [23] have shown that formal semantics can lead to the construction of rigorous models of complex phenomena such as emotions (as in [13]).

holders of a value); achieve social functions (like regulation)[2]. Miceli and Castelfranchi [16] emphasize how the perceived causal responsibility (see also [4]), that is the belief of having had the capacity to avoid a damage or a violation, is a crucial notion for distinguishing these feelings: "when ashamed, one sees oneself as incompetent or inadequate with respect to some goal; when guilty, one sees oneself as endowed with negative power." ([16],295)[3].

Internalization. When agents use values or norms as input for their decisions to comply with what prescribed, we say that these values or norms have been internalized. An internalized norm, thus, drives agents' behaviour towards obedience. Psychological research has shown that internalization can be induced, by *significant others* expectations [8] and commands [10]; the importance of implementing the role of significant others for judgment formation is therefore already acknowledged as crucial in pedagogical activity and interaction design [11]. In this article the dynamics of internalization will be taken into account w.r.t. the way changing significant others influences the set of world states agents label as good and acceptable, and what the consequences of these are in terms of feeling guilty and ashamed.

Normativity comes from outside. Shame and sense of guilt are associated with violation of normative standards. As emphasized in [3] agents may not fulfill others' expectations, and, even worse, they can go against others' values. Agents are continuously judged in this respect. But, following [8], they do not fear such evaluation from all others, but only from a particular subset of them, those ones on which they are dependent, they care about, and whose standards they have the goal to meet: the significant others.

It goes without saying that agents that have not internalized at all a value cannot feel guilty or ashamed w.r.t. that value. Therefore the situation in which only significant others share a norm that is not internalized is a severe conditioning factor for agents' emotional reaction.

We may observe, due to difference in personality traits, a pride reaction in some agents, while instead others may show feelings of loneliness and exclusion [17]. On the other side, others not sharing a value or a norm for which the agents has perception of negative power does not necessarily cancel its perception of

---

[2] The paper takes a cognitive approach which is quite different from the believability approach (see for instance [11]). We believe that the appropriate *affective interaction* should be based on mental contents and interpretations, not just on a superficial reaction. Complex agents, such as human beings, react to the ascribed mind. For example, to a shameful face we can respond in many different ways, depending on our interpretation of the grounding mental content. "Yes I think that what you said/did is ridiculous/ugly!"; "Why do you care about their judgment?! They have stupid prejudices"; "This feature of yours is very special and nice; you should be proud of it!"; "You are wrong, they appreciate you the way you are", etc.

[3] In Maria Miceli's words shame is the perception of oneself being a dull knife, whereas feeling guilty is the perception of oneself being a sharp knife [17].

wrongdoing. Instead more personal feelings can come up, like sense of guilt and shame towards the self. The interplay is sketched in Table 1.

When agents realize that some significant others do not share fundamental values or norm their being significant is rapidly questioned. We believe that the different opinions that an agent and its significant others have concerning a relevant value can be associated with phenomena like cognitive dissonance and the processes that lead to its resolution [10].

Table 1. Multi Agent Perspective

	Others Don't Share		Others Share	
	Internalized Norm / Value	Not Internalized Norm / Value	Internalized Norm / Value	Not Internalized Norm / Value
Negative Power	Sense of Guilt towards the self	Indifference	Sense of Guilt	Pride / Loneliness
Inadequacy	Shame towards the self	Indifference	Shame	Pride / Loneliness

2.1   Controlling Emotions

The most interesting intuition that the cognitive approach in [16] [3] [2] gives is that human beings do have some control of their emotions. "In particular, people can react to their own emotions defending themselves from the disturbing or blamed ones. They try to repress, deny, and manipulate them." [2].

We are going to push this intuition further by looking at both *control via belief manipulation* and *control via goal manipulation*. The first type of control will act on an agent belief base in order to eliminate those beliefs that induce in the self the emotion (for instance, justifications), while the second will act with the same purpose on the agent motivational base (for instance, apologies). But how would these strategies work? Elaborating on Miceli and Castelfranchi's proposal in [16], the different types of reaction can be related to basic psychological types of agents, such as high self esteem (HSE) and low self esteem (LSE) ones. HSE people might try to question the basis on the grounds of which they are blamed or they feel bad; they will react actively by trying to produce justificatory beliefs for their actions. Instead LSE agents will tend to apologise and find excuses, as they are more unlikely to question the values which they are accused to go against. In this sense HSE agents will tend to react with pride to the above mentioned situation, while LSE agents will react with for instance feeling lonely or rejected. We distinguish a typical LSE reaction, "I did not know", that we classify as an excuse by claiming ignorance of the relevant effects of a dangerous action that has been carried out, from a typical HSE reaction, "It was not that bad", that is a justification on a presumed violation. It claims that what others may think as wrong is not really so. We argue that these mechanisms can be formally modeled. For lack of space, we leave the formal treatment of offensive moves, precisely analyzed in [14], to future work.

2.2   Feeling Ashamed

Shame is not necessarily a moral emotion, because the needs not to be, e.g., poor, ugly, fat, bald are not moral, although they involve a normative standard. As argued in [2] feeling ashamed always involves a believed negative self evaluation (concerning one's inadequacy) related to somebody whose judgment agents care about. As far as the behaviour is concerned, the goal of an ashamed person is to reduce exposure [3]. This may be translated into various actions, either minimizing the importance of a value (agents that are proud of something), which is an HSE agent's typical reaction, or minimizing their active contribution to a damage by declaring submission and imperfection, which are typical LSE agents' reactions. Emotional displays of shame are admission of imperfection, that instantiate for instance with blushing. Blushing is not a confession of guilt [2] but it still has a precise communicative function [3]. We can be caught doing something that looks bad w.r.t. others (even though we know they are wrong) and yet blush.

2.3   Feeling Guilty

The feeling of guilt is usually linked to the conviction of having actively injured someone or broken some moral imperative or norm [2]. It is associated to the evaluation of having negative power against a given value, i.e. a perception of responsibility. Looking at agent types reactions and beliefs of responsibility, it is intuitively clear how difficult it is to both feel ashamed and guilty at the same time for the very same thing. Either agents believe to be a dull knife or a sharp knife. Nevertheless the complex transitions between the two feelings are common in everyday life, by means of a belief revision [26] concerning responsibility .

   As far as reactive behaviour is concerned, one first goal of agents that feel guilty is that of reparation, which triggers the agent to care about the damaged person, and to expiate, to pay in some sense for what has been done. A very interesting property of agents that feel guilty is to regret doing something. But what is regret? It is the desire (very easy to frustrate) of not having done something we actually did. Regret acts as a situation marker [5]: not only do we feel guilty about a situation but we also associate to that situation a further punishment, due to the desire frustration, in order to recognize the preconditions that caused us to feel guilty[4].

3   A Language for Rational Agents with Emotions

Emotional Multiagent Karo. The reconstruction of cognitive agents that feel guilty and ashamed needs some further concepts with respect to those already in [13]. We need to reason about agents' values, and their mismatch with others' perceived ones; operations that act directly on the agent emotional state, i.e. allow changing perception of situations in order not to feel bad; finally,

---

[4] This is an interesting link with the notion of sadness as formalized in [13].

in order to reason about multiagent interaction we need to extend dynamic deontic logic to the multiagent case. The works in [12] [20] and [7] provide a solid basis for addressing this issue. We will introduce in such a framework a set of violation constants V_i indexed with agents, that will label worlds that are bad for particular agents, as well as different dynamics for different types of agents.

3.1 The Language

Action Expression. The actions that agents perform can have different form. We classically consider a set of atomic actions from which all the others can be obtained compositionally. For easing notation, we will not consider parallel execution and nondeterministic choice for complex actions and events, while action negation (i.e. refraining) will be limited for technical reasons ([12]) to the atomic case. Finally the planning component in emotions requires the treatment of the notion of action composition. The set of action expressions Act is the smallest set containing all actions of the following form:

$$\alpha ::= b \,|\, skip \,|\, \mathbf{kick}(x, \phi) \,|\, \mathbf{welcome}(x, \phi) \,|\, \mathbf{replace}(x, y, \phi) \,|\, \alpha_1; \alpha_2 \,|\, \alpha_1^n$$

where $b = a|\bar{a}$ is an atomic action or its negation; $\phi \in \Pi_0$, where Π_0 is the set of atomic propositions; $x, y \in Agt$, which is the set of agents; $kick$, $welcome$, $replace$ actions will be used for updating evaluations and will be dealt as special actions later on in the paper. The set of events Evt has the following grammar:

$$\xi ::= X : \alpha \,|\, \xi_1; \xi_2 \,|\, \xi_1^n$$

To ease reading, we skip the technical construction of action interpretation and we send the reader to [12] for a thorough account of the single agent case, which inspired in turn the multiagent extension contained in [20] and ours.

As soon as the reader encounters expressions of the form $x[\![\xi]\!]_R y$, where x, y are couples model-world, we ask him or her to attach to them the informal reading of "state y is an effect of the execution of event ξ in state x".

For convenience, we sometimes view $[\![\xi]\!]_R$ as a functional relation.

Syntax. Our language is given by the following syntax:

$$p(p \in \Pi_0) \,|\, V_i(i \in Agt) \,|\, \neg\phi \,|\, \phi \wedge \psi \,|\, \mathbf{Aut}_{i,j}\phi \,|\, \mathbf{B}_i\phi \,|\, \mathbf{D}_i\phi \,|\, \mathbf{P}\phi \,|\, [\xi]\phi \,|\, \mathbf{A}_i\alpha \,|\, \mathbf{Com}_i(\alpha) \,|\, DONE_X(\alpha)^5$$

We moreover use the following abbreviations: $\phi \vee \psi := \neg(\neg\phi \wedge \neg\psi)$; $\phi \rightarrow \psi := \neg\phi \vee \psi$; $\phi \leftrightarrow \psi := (\phi \rightarrow \psi) \wedge (\psi \rightarrow \phi)$; $\langle\xi\rangle\phi := \neg[\xi]\neg\phi$; $\mathbf{I}_i(\alpha, \phi) := \mathbf{B}_i(\neg\phi \wedge \mathbf{D}_i\phi \wedge \langle\alpha\rangle\phi \wedge \mathbf{A}_i\alpha)$, the last with the informal reading of "possible intention".

Structure. The structures interpreting the language $\mathcal{L}$ are given by a class of E-KAROUS[6] models in which each model M is of the following shape:

$$M = <Agt, W, Act, \sigma, \{B_i | i \in Agt\}, \{D_i | i \in Agt\}, Aut>$$

In which Agt is a finite nonempty set of agents. We take $Agt = Agt_h + Agt_l$. It is partitioned into Agt_h which will represent the HSE agents and Agt_l, the LSE agents. $Agt_h \cap Agt_l = \emptyset$; W is a finite nonempty set of worlds; Act is the set of basic actions; $\sigma : \Pi_0 \cup \{V_i | i \in Agt\} \rightarrow 2^W$ is the augmented valuation function, that assigns each atom to a set of worlds, with the intended meaning that they are those worlds in which the atom is true. $\{B_i | i \in Agt\}$ is an epistemic accessibility relation; Each $B_i \subseteq W \times W$ is composed by couples $\{w, w'\}$ in such a way that the world w' represents an epistemic alternative for agent i at world w. We indicate with $[w]_{B_i}$ the set of epistemic alternatives for agent i at world w. $\{D_i | i \in Agt\}$ is defined as B_i for desired worlds. Aut is a function g such that $g : Agt \times Agt \times (\mathcal{M} \times W) \rightarrow 2^{L_0}$. This function associates to each agent a set of agents that point to a group of propositions. The idea is that such agents indicate which situations are to be considered bad by the agent. As the function ranges over a powerset we can have more agents that point to a proposition. We say that those agents block the proposition. We now label as $Sig_{(i,M,w)} = \{j | \exists \phi s.t. \phi \in Aut(i, j, (\langle M, w \rangle))\}$ the set of significant others for agent i at the situation $\langle M, w \rangle$. This set comprises those agents that block at least a proposition in a given situation for agent i. Moreover we impose an order $<$ that links couples model-world with events, in such a way to induces a tree on transitions that guarantees linear past and branching future[7].

Semantics. The formulas of our language $\mathcal{L}$ are interpreted as follows:

- $M, w \models p$ iff $w \in \sigma(p)$;
- Propositional cases are usual;
- $M, w \models V_i$ iff $w \in \sigma(V_i)$;
- $M, w \models \mathbf{Aut}_{i,j}\phi$ iff $\phi \in Aut(i, j, (\langle M, w \rangle))$;
- $M, w \models \mathbf{B}_i\phi$ iff $M, w' \models \phi$ for all w' s.t. wB_iw';
- $M, w \models \mathbf{D}_i\phi$ iff $M, w' \models \phi$ for all w' s.t. wD_iw';
- $M, w \models \mathbf{P}\phi$ iff $\exists(\langle M', w' \rangle)$ s.t $(\langle M', w' \rangle) < (\langle M, w \rangle)$ and $M', w' \models \phi$;
- $M, w \models [\xi]\phi$ iff $M', w' \models \phi$ for all $(\langle M', w' \rangle)$ s.t. $(\langle M, w \rangle)[\![\xi]\!]_R(\langle M', w' \rangle)$;
- $M, w \models \mathbf{A}_i\alpha$ iff $\alpha \in c(\langle M, w \rangle)(i)$; $M, w \models \mathbf{Com}_i(\alpha)$ iff $\alpha \in Ag(\langle M, w \rangle)(i)$[8]
- $M, w \models \mathbf{Sig}_{j,i}$ iff $j \in Sig_{(i,M,w)}$; $M, w \models DONE_X(\alpha)$ iff $\exists(\langle M', w' \rangle)$ s.t. $(\langle M', w' \rangle) < (\langle M, w \rangle) \, and \, (\langle M', w' \rangle)[\![X : \alpha]\!]_R(\langle M, w \rangle)$.

---

[6] E-KAROUS is a fancy transformation of KARO to an emotional multiagent shape, resembling moreover the name of a person that did not pay much attention to the suggestions of the friends.

[7] We point to [1] for a formal characterization of such constraint.

[8] The behaviour of Ag and c functions is described in details in [24]. The first updates the agent's agenda concerning commitments, the second returns the set of actions the agent has the internal ability to carry out.

Constraints on the models. We denote with $[\![\phi]\!]_M$ the set A such that $A = \{w|M, w \models \phi\}$. We constrain our models in the following way:

- For all $w \in W$, $[w]_{B_i} \neq \emptyset$; $w' \in [w]_{B_i} \Rightarrow [w']_{B_i} = [w]_{B_i}$
- $[\![\mathbf{Sig}_{i,j}]\!]_M \subseteq [\![\mathbf{Bel}_j\mathbf{Sig}_{i,j}]\!]_M$; $W\backslash[\![\mathbf{Sig}_{i,j}]\!]_M \subseteq W\backslash[\![\mathbf{Bel}_j\mathbf{Sig}_{i,j}]\!]_M$
- $[\![V_i]\!]_M \subseteq [\![\mathbf{Bel}_iV_i]\!]_M$; $W\backslash[\![V_i]\!]_M \subseteq W\backslash[\![\mathbf{Bel}_iV_i]\!]_M$

Proposition 1. *The following propositions are valid in E-KAROUS models:*

- $\models B_i\top$; $\models \neg B_i\phi \rightarrow B_i\neg B_i\phi$; $\models B_i\phi \rightarrow B_iB_i\phi$;
- $\models Sig_{i,j} \rightarrow B_j Sig_{i,j}$; $\models \neg Sig_{i,j} \rightarrow B_j\neg Sig_{i,j}$
- $\models V_i \rightarrow B_iV_i$; $\models \neg V_i \rightarrow B_i\neg V_i$

The first three entries are standard for $S4$ models of beliefs [1], forbidding logical inconsistency and allowing positive and negative introspection. The fourth and fifth add positive and negative introspection for significant others. It makes sense to claim that if agents have some agent as significant other then they believe so, and vice versa for those that are not significant others. The last two items state that the positive and negative perception of the own valuations is valid.

3.2 Changing Friends

In [26] non standard actions such as those that induce mind changing are described. In the same fashion we would like to describe those actions that update the authority relations among agents. In particular agents should be able to resolve their cognitive dissonance by eliminating significant others or welcoming new ones.

We describe functions the transition function $[\![]\!]_R$ for actions *welcome, kick, replace* leaving the treatment of the capability function c ([24]) that tells us when agents have the internal ability to perform these actions, to future work. These are special actions that transform the models in a peculiar way. The first updates the set of relevant others by adding a new agent. Violation states are updated as specified. The second deletes an agent from such set. The third first deletes some agents and after adds new ones to the set.

Definition 1. *For some E-KAROUS model*
$M = < Agt, W, Act, \sigma, \{B_i|i \in Agt\}, \{D_i|i \in Agt\}, Aut >$ *with $w \in W$ and $\phi, \psi \in L_0$ be given. We define: All $\langle M', w' \rangle \in [\![i : \textbf{welcome}(\phi, j)]\!]_R(\langle M, w \rangle)$ are such that:*
$M' = < Agt, W, Act, \sigma', \{B_i|i \in Agt\}, \{D_i|i \in Agt\}, Aut' >$ *with*

- $\models Aut'(i', j', (\langle M', w' \rangle)) = Aut(i', j', (\langle M, w \rangle))$ *if $i \neq i'$ or $j \neq j'$ or $w' \neq w$;*
  $\models Aut'(i, j, (\langle M', w' \rangle)) = \{\phi\}$; $\models \sigma'(V_i) \cap [\![\phi]\!]_{M'} = \emptyset$; $\models \sigma'(\psi) = \sigma(\psi)$ *for $\psi \neq V_j$*

Definition 2. $\langle M', w' \rangle \in [\![i : \textbf{kick}(\phi, j)]\!]_R(\langle M, w \rangle)$ *are such that:*
$M' = < Agt, W, Act, \sigma', \{B_i|i \in Agt\}, \{D_i|i \in Agt\}, Aut' >$ *with*

$-\models Aut'(i',j',(\langle M',w'\rangle)) = Aut(i',j',(\langle M,w\rangle))$ if $i \neq i'$ or $j \neq j'$ or $w' \neq w$;
$\models Aut'(i,j,(\langle M',w'\rangle)) = \{\emptyset\}$; $\models \sigma'(V_i) = \sigma(V_i)\backslash\sigma(V_k)$; $\models \sigma'(\psi) = \sigma(\psi)$
for $\psi \neq V_j$

Definition 3. $[\![i:\mathbf{replace}(\phi,j,k)]\!]_R(\langle M,w\rangle) = [\![(i:\mathbf{kick}(\phi,j);\mathbf{welcome}(\phi,k)]\!]_R$ $(\langle M,w\rangle)$.

Proposition 2. *The following propositions are valid in E-KAROUS models:*

- $\models \mathbf{Sig}_{ik} \leftrightarrow [i:\mathbf{welcome}(\phi,j)]\mathbf{Sig}_{ik};\models [i:\mathbf{welcome}(\phi,j)]\mathbf{Sig}_{ij}$
- $\models [i:\mathbf{welcome}(\phi,j)](\phi \leftrightarrow \neg V_i); \models \psi \rightarrow [i:\mathbf{welcome}(\phi,j)]\psi$
- $\models \mathbf{Sig}_{ik} \leftrightarrow [i:\mathbf{kick}(\phi,j)]\mathbf{Sig}_{ik}; \models [i:\mathbf{kick}(\phi,j)]\neg\mathbf{Sig}_{ij}$
- $\models [i:\mathbf{kick}(\phi,j)](\phi \leftrightarrow V_i); \models \psi \rightarrow [i:\mathbf{kick}(\phi,j)]\psi$
- $\models \mathbf{Sig}_{ij} \rightarrow [i:\mathbf{replace}(\phi,j,k)]\mathbf{Sig}_{ik}; \models [i:\mathbf{replace}(\phi,j,k)]\neg\mathbf{Sig}_{ij}$
- $\models [i:\mathbf{replace}(\phi,j,k)](\phi \leftrightarrow V_i); \models \psi \rightarrow [i:\mathbf{replace}(\phi,j,k)]\psi$

The first four items deal with the welcoming operation. The first of them says that welcoming a new agent does not affect the perception of others; the second simply that welcoming causes an agent to be a significant other; the third that the reason of welcome is not seen as bad by the agent; the fourth that the evaluation of the other propositions do not change. The kicking operations behaves dually, while replacing can be obtained by composing the other two.

4   The Dynamics of Guilt and Shame

4.1   Sense of Guilt

An agent feels guilty when it observes that what he actively caused was violation for some of his significant others[9]. This means that the agent has the intention to do π for achieving goal ϕ but he believes the actual world state he actively chose (that he could avoid) satisfies a violation condition for some agent j which happens to be a significant other.

For the heavy use of refraining actions, we limit the treatment to atomic cases. With technical extensions, as suggested in [12], it is possible to address complex actions. Taken $a, b \in Act$, with $a \neq b$,

$$\mathbf{I}_i(\pi,\phi) \wedge \mathbf{Com}_i(\pi) \wedge \mathbf{I}_i(\pi',\phi) \wedge \mathbf{Com}_i(\pi') \wedge$$
$$\wedge\, a \preceq \pi \wedge b \preceq \pi' \wedge \mathbf{Sig}_{j,i} \wedge \mathbf{B}_i(V_j \wedge DONE_i(a) \wedge \mathbf{P}(\mathbf{A}_i(b)\wedge <i:b> \neg V_j)) \rightarrow$$
$$guilty(i,a,j).\text{[10]}$$

---

[9] Following [15] we can say that an agent i evaluates as morally wrong the formula ϕ iff $M \models \phi \leftrightarrow V_i$ for some model M. We can also say that an action α is wrong for i iff $M \models [X:\alpha]V_i$, for any actor X. Things get more interesting if we move to a local level, in which actions can be evaluated as bad $M,w \models [i:\alpha]V_i$ or they can be always safe $M,w \models [i:\alpha^n]\neg V_i$ (values), or even the only possible cure $M,w \models [i:\alpha^n]\neg V_i \wedge [i:\overline{\alpha}^n]\neg V_i$ or a safe resort at our disposal $M,w \models [i:\overline{\alpha}^n;\alpha]\neg V_i \wedge [i:\overline{\alpha}^n;\overline{\alpha}]\neg V_i$. Of course feeling guilty or ashamed for having challenged a value of other agents can be much more painful and dangerous, but we are not going to go that further with the distinctions, which are in principle possible.

[10] In KARO framework a classical deliberation cycle is assumed [13]. In our case deliberation is a program that updates beliefs, desires, commitments and status of significant others by means of the above defined revision actions.

This means that our agent believed he could in fact avoid the violation state for his significant other and yet pursue his plan π, in that he had a choice w.r.t. to the action to carry out.

Reactions to sense of guilt are influenced by the level of self esteem agents have. We can distinguish two categories, Agt_h, high self esteem agents, which will react providing justifications to their actions and in extreme cases changing the significance they attribute to people. On the other side, Agt_l, low self esteem people will try to find excuses for their actions and to generate reparation goals, that is to perform an action in such a way to avoid further violations. Both agents could also generate the goal of feeling regret, that is to feel bad concerning a past event. With abuse of notation we will write in the object language $i \in Agt_h$ to mean that agent i is a high self esteem agent.

$$\mathbf{I}_i(\pi, \phi) \wedge \mathbf{Com}_i(\pi) \wedge i \in Agt_h \wedge \mathbf{B}_i(V_j) \wedge$$
$$\wedge \, guilty(i, a, j) \rightarrow [deliberate_i](\neg\mathbf{Sig}_{j,i}) \vee \mathbf{B}_i(\neg V_j) \vee \mathbf{D}_i \neg DONE_i(a)$$

So either i will update authority relations by cancelling j, or he will believe the present state is not violation for j or he will merely wish so (but still believing it, so frustrating his desire). On the other hand...

$$\mathbf{I}_i(\pi, \phi) \wedge \mathbf{Com}_i(\pi) \wedge i \in Agt_l \wedge \mathbf{B}_i(V_j) \wedge guilty(i, a, j) \rightarrow$$
$$\rightarrow [deliberate_i](\mathbf{I}_i(\pi', \phi) \wedge \mathbf{Com}_i(\pi') \wedge$$
$$\wedge \, \mathbf{B}_i[i : \pi']\neg V_j) \vee \mathbf{B}_i(\neg\mathbf{P}[i : \bar{a}]\neg V_j)) \vee (\mathbf{D}_i \neg DONE_i(a))$$

The low self esteem agent either will commit to a plan that escapes from violation state, or he will find excuses for his wrongdoing, namely he will generate the belief that what it did was unavoidable, or he will wish that he did not do what he actually did (regret).

4.2   Shame

Shame is the believed lack of a relevant feature, that is the believed incapacity to achieve a value that is important for the agent or for its significant others. If only the first is present we will talk of shame towards the self. We are going to formalize shame by considering an agent that believes it is possible to get over a violation state but that there is no capability for him/her to do so.

$$\mathbf{Sig}_{j,i} \wedge \mathbf{B}_i(\mathbf{A}_{Agt}(a) \wedge \mathbf{A}_{Agt}(\bar{a}) \wedge V_j \wedge [i : a]V_j \wedge [i : \bar{a}]V_j \wedge [Agt \backslash \{i\} : a]\neg V_j) \rightarrow$$
$$shame(i, a, j)$$

So avoiding V_j is a "norm" or a standard to which i is not able to comply.

What do ashamed agents do? We distinguish LSE reactions and HSE reactions. Similarly with sense of guilt, the first types of reactions will tend to manipulate the belief base in such a way to remove the belief of incapacity, and moreover they will try to repair to their incapacity, which can be done in various way, for instance adopting a goal of the significant other.

$$shame(i, a, j) \wedge i \in Agt_l \rightarrow [deliberate_i]\mathbf{B}_i(\neg[i : \cup Act_i]V_j) \wedge (\mathbf{B}_i(\mathbf{D}_j \phi \rightarrow ([i :$$
$$\pi]\phi \rightarrow \mathbf{I}_i(\pi, \phi)) \wedge \mathbf{I}_i(\rho, \phi) \wedge \mathbf{Com}_i(\pi) \wedge \mathbf{B}_i[i : \rho] \bigvee_{k \in Agt} \mathbf{B}_k[i : \cup Act_i]V_j$$

The agent openly communicates to others the own incapacity [3], that is, he blushes. The second type of reactions will try to update authority relations, in such a way not to perceive their incapacity as wrong. This is a typical pride reaction.

$$shame(i, a, j) \land i \in Agt_h \to [deliberate_i] \neg \mathbf{Sig}_{j,i}$$

5   Conclusion and Future Work

In this paper we provided a formal language to describe sense of guilt and shame as social emotions. In order to do this we grounded our work on the cognitive theory of Castelfranchi and Miceli, the psychological theory of significant others by Higgins, the rational action theory in the KARO framework by Meyer and colleagues. The cognitive science perspective has allowed us to build an anatomy of these emotions in terms of basic cognitive ingredients such as Beliefs, Goals and Values. We described formally the operations that allow agents to change their evaluations together with the people they take as references, and we connected these to shame, sense of guilt and their dynamics.

Much work still needs to be done. Apart from what already pointed throughout the paper, we would like to: investigate further the theory of cognitive dissonance and to give a formal characterization of the role of emotions in its resolution; to shed more light on the characterization of emotions by studying the logical models we used to talk about them: could we rewrite the conditions that trigger these emotions without recurring to past reasoning, but only as in [13] reasoning about the resulting conditions after an action execution? Finally we would like to investigate the connection of feeling ashamed and guilty with other feelings like happiness and sadness already formally described in [13] and the agent types defensive and offensive strategies in [16] and [14].

Acknowledgments. The authors thank Maria Miceli, Frank Dignum, Rosaria Conte, Davide Grossi for the inspiring discussions over norms and emotions; a further special thanks to the anonymous reviewers for their precise remarks and to Davide Grossi for the Ovidius quote.

References

1. Blackburn, P., de Rijke, M., Venema, Y.: Modal Logic. Cambridge Tracts in Theoretical Computer Science (2001)
2. Castelfranchi, C.: Cognitive anatomy of shame and guilt: Differences, functions, defensive moves. EABCT, Manchester (2004)
3. Castelfranchi, C., Poggi, I.: Blushing as a discourse: Was darwin wrong? In: Shyness and Embarrassment: Perspectives from Social Psychology, pp. 230–251 (1990)
4. Conte, R., Paolucci, M.: Responsibility for societies of agents. JASSS (2004), http://jasss.soc.surrey.ac.uk/7/4/3.html
5. Damasio, A.: Descartes' Error: Emotion, Reason and the Human Brain. NY G.P. Putnam's Sons (1999)

6. de Sousa, R.: Emotion. In: Stanford Encyclopedia of Philosophy (2003)
7. Grossi, D., Royakkers, L.M.M., Dignum, F.: Organizational structure and responsibility. Forthcoming (2007)
8. Higgins, E.T.: Self-discrepancy: A theory relating self and affect. Psychological Review 94, 319–340 (1987)
9. Oatley, K., Jenkins, J.M.: Understanding Emotions. Blackwell, Oxford (1996)
10. Festinger, L., Carlsmith, J.M.: Cognitive consequences of forced compliance. Journal of Abnormal and Social Psychology 58, 203–210 (1959)
11. Marsella, S.C., Johnson, W.L., Labore, C.: Interactive pedagogical drama. In: Sierra, C., Gini, M., Rosenschein, J.S. (eds.) Proceedings of the Fourth International Conference on Autonomous Agents, pp. 301–308. ACM Press, New York, USA (2000)
12. Meyer, J.J.C.: A different approach to deontic logic: Deontic logic viewed as a variant of dynamic logic. Notre Dame J. of Formal Logic 29(1), 109–136 (1988)
13. Meyer, J.J.Ch.: Reasoning about emotional agents. In: Mántaras, R.L.d., Saitta, L. (eds.) Proc.16th European Conf. on Artif. Intell (ECAI 2004), pp. 129–133. IOS Press, Amsterdam (2004)
14. Miceli, M.: How to make someone feel guilty: Strategies for guilt inducement and their goals. Journal for the Theory of Social Behaviour 22, 81–104 (1992)
15. Miceli, M., Castelfranchi, C.: A cognitive approach to values. Journal for the Theory of Social Behaviour 19, 169–194 (1989)
16. Miceli, M., Castelfranchi, C.: How to silence one's conscience: Cognitive defenses against the feeling of guilt. Journal for the Theory of Social Behaviour 28, 287–318 (1998)
17. Miceli, M.: Personal communication (2006)
18. Ortony, A., Clore, G.L., Collins, A.: The cognitive structure of Emotions. Cambridge University Press, Cambridge (1988)
19. Pitt, J.: Digital blush: towards shame and embarrassment in multi-agent information trading applications. Cognition, Technology and Work 6, 23–36 (2004)
20. Royakkers, L.M.M.: Extending deontic logic for the formalization of legal rules. Kluwer Academic Publishers, Dordrecht (1998)
21. Sloman, A.: Motives, mechanisms and emotions. In: Boden, M. (ed.) The Philosophy of Artificial Intelligence, pp. 231–247 (1990)
22. Staller, A., Petta, P.: Introducing emotions into the computational study of social norms: A first evaluation. Journal of Artificial Societies and Social Simulation, 4(1) (2001), http://www.soc.surrey.ac.uk/JASSS/4/1/2.html
23. van Benthem, J.: Where is logic going, and should it? In: Bencivenga, E. (ed.) What is to be Done in Philosophy? (2005)
24. van der Hoek, W., van Linder, B., Meyer, J.-J.C.: A logic of capabilities. In: Matiyasevich, Y.V., Nerode, A. (eds.) LFCS 1994. LNCS, vol. 813, pp. 366–413. Springer, Heidelberg (1994)
25. van der Hoek, W., van Linder, B., Meyer, J.-J.C.: An integrated modal approach to rational agents. In: Proc. of PRR97, Practical Reasoning and Rationality (1997)
26. van Linder, B., van der Hoek, W., Meyer, J.J.C.: Actions that make you change your mind. Knowledge and Belief in Philosophy and Artificial Intelligence, 103–146 (1995)

Wishful Thinking Revision*

César F. Pimentel and Maria R. Cravo

Instituto Superior Técnico, Dep. Eng. Informática, GIA
Av. Rovisco Pais, 1049-001 Lisboa, Portugal
cesar.pimentel@dei.ist.utl.pt, mrcravo@gia.ist.utl.pt

Abstract. Wishful thinking is an affective bias towards more pleasant interpretations/beliefs. We model wishful thinking effects, to some extent, with a belief revision theory: *Wishful Thinking Revision*. By modeling tendencies to believe in goals, "disliked situations" appear as "contradicting beliefs" (the target of belief revision). Furthermore, the current set of beliefs is selected according to an assessment of preference that accounts for rational factors, as well as an affective factor: "likeability".

1 Introduction

One of the most commonly known influences of affects on human reasoning and belief is *wishful thinking*, i.e., a bias that shifts one's interpretations/beliefs towards "liked" scenarios and away from "disliked" ones. Generally speaking, what one likes (as opposed to what one dislikes) is defined as what satisfies or facilitates one's current desires, goals, and even commitments. If we aim at building agents that mimic human reasoning and belief maintenance, wishful thinking is one of the essential and most intuitive affective aspects to be modeled.

Wishful thinking is a widely known phenomenon, sometimes referred to by other names or as part of other, more general, concepts. In [5], the authors describe *Motivational Force* as the phenomenon where motivation (i.e., the desire for pleasure or for getting rid of discomfort) guides one's thoughts and alters one's beliefs' resistance to change. Quoting Frijda and Mesquita, "The motivational source of the beliefs does much to explain their resistance against change. Abandoning a belief may undermine one's readiness to act, and one may feel one cannot afford that". According to the *Law of Lightest Load* [4], "Whenever a situation can be viewed in alternative ways, a tendency exists to view it in a way that minimizes negative emotional load". Castelfranchi discusses how belief acceptance is influenced by "likeability" [3]. In [16], Paglieri models likeability as the degree of goal satisfaction that data represents. In his approach, likeability is one of the data properties that interfere in the process of "belief selection".

Throughout this paper we simply use the term *wishful thinking*, encompassing the tendency for: a) *Wishful thinking* (in the strict sense), as the belief in something because it is liked; b) *Denial*, as the rejection of a belief because it is

---

* This work was partially supported by IDMEC (Institute of Mechanical Engineering
- Intelligent Systems Center - Lisbon) and the EC project HUMAINE.

A. Paiva, R. Prada, and R.W. Picard (Eds.): ACII 2007, LNCS 4738, pp. 326–337, 2007.

disliked. Denial/wishful thinking, as "two sides of the same coin", are recognized as strategies of cognitive coping (see, e.g., [13], [2] and [10]). Note that wishful thinking is often present, biasing belief strength and resistance to change, but only in exceptional cases causes a change of what is believed.

One of the main motivations in the field of *Affective Computing* is the study of human emotions by modeling them [17]. Although human wishful thinking is mediated by emotions, our aim is to model some of its effects on beliefs, without modeling the involved emotions explicitly. In our model, the degree of *likeability* of a given belief scenario is defined by a measure of belief in goal satisfactions.

In this paper, we present a *belief revision theory*, i.e., a theory that determines which beliefs should be held and which should not, when one has to maintain a consistent set of beliefs. Since the seminal work of Alchourrón, Gärdenfors and Makinson [1], several belief revision theories have been developed. Typically, these theories assume the existence of an order among beliefs, that supports the choice of which to keep and which to reject, to obtain a consistent set of beliefs. Our theory is called *Wishful Thinking Revision* (or simply, WTR), given that it aims at modeling wishful thinking influences, to some extent.

WTR complements the conventional tasks of a belief revision theory with two functionalities, that are advantageous in the context of an autonomous agent:

- In order to choose the preferred set of beliefs, at any given moment, WTR does not depend on an external order among beliefs. It generates its own intuitive criteria to determine the preferred set of beliefs, with full autonomy.
- As is common knowledge, "belief is a matter of degree" [8]. You may "believe" that by using regular mail, the letter you are about to send will be safely delivered to its destination. However, if your envelope carries money instead of just a simple letter, you will most likely not "believe" in that safe delivery, and prefer to send it via registered mail. WTR models this relative notion of belief by means of a function that determines belief strength.

To model intuitive criteria guiding these two functionalities, WTR follows an approach consistent with the *Foundations Theories* (see [8]). Shortly put, these theories claim that the choice of which beliefs to hold and which to reject (in belief revision) is based on the reasons that originated each belief. Note also that WTR is a non-prioritized revision, i.e., a revision that does not necessarily accept the newly arrived information as true (see [7]).

There is a distinction between a belief's subjective credibility (above referred to as strength) and a belief's resistance to change (i.e., resistance to abandonment). Isaac Levi [11] refers to the former as certainty and to the latter as unchangeability (see also [7]). The ordering of beliefs used by conventional revision theories implicitly relates to the notion of resistance to change. It is our conviction that resistance to change is better associated to sets of beliefs, rather than to individual beliefs. For instance, the resistance to change of belief "My mother boarded flight 17" is lowered with the presence of belief "Flight 17 crashed" (due to wishful thinking). However, if the latter is abandoned, the former may go back to having a high resistance to change. WTR chooses the preferred set of beliefs according to values of preference attributed to sets of beliefs.

2   Representations and Assumptions

Commonsense refers to *belief* as a proposition that one holds as true with at least some degree of strength, that makes the information reliable for reasoning and action [15]. The representation of a *belief*, in this paper, has a broader meaning, including any small "inclination" to believe. Additionally (in section 4), we define the commonsense concept of belief, as an inclination to believe with a minimum degree of strength.

We assume that agents have an internal state containing, among other things, the agent's knowledge base, the agent's goals, the subjective credibility the agent associates to each other agent, and a wishful thinking coefficient. We also assume that agents have reasoning capabilities, based on some monotonic logic(s). Given an agent ag, we represent the language of the logic used by that agent by $\mathcal{L}_{ag}$, and the derivability relation by $\vdash_{ag}$. We assume that all agents are uniquely identified by their name, and represent the set of names of the agents by $\mathcal{N}$, where $\mathcal{N} \cap \{\texttt{Obs}, \texttt{WT}, \texttt{Der}\} = \emptyset$.

The knowledge base of agent ag, $KB(ag)$, is a set of supports. These are triplets $<F, \tau, \alpha>$, where: $F \in \mathcal{L}_{ag}$, $\tau \in \{\texttt{Obs}, \texttt{WT}, \texttt{Der}\} \cup \mathcal{N}$, and $\alpha \subseteq \mathcal{L}_{ag}$. Given a support $<F, \tau, \alpha>$, we say that F is its formula, τ its origin tag, and α its origin set. Let $\mathcal{A} = <F, \tau, \alpha>$; We define $form(\mathcal{A}) = F$, $ot(\mathcal{A}) = \tau$, and $os(\mathcal{A}) = \alpha$. The origin tag indicates how the formula got in the knowledge base: $\texttt{Obs}$ means that the proposition represented by the formula was observed by the agent; $\texttt{WT}$ means that it originated, by wishful thinking, from one of the agent's goals; $\texttt{Der}$ means that it was derived from other formulas; Finally, if the origin tag is the name of an agent, this means that the formula was communicated by that agent. These four kinds of supports are referred to as, respectively, *observation*, *wishful thinking*, *derivation* and *communication* supports. We point out that the same formula may have more than one support in the knowledge base.

Observation, communication and wishful thinking supports are all called *non-derivation supports*. Formulas that occur in derivation supports are known as *derived formulas*, and formulas that occur in non-derivation supports are known as *hypotheses*. Notice that a formula can be both a derived formula and a hypothesis. If $\mathcal{A}$ is a derivation support, its origin set is the set of hypotheses underlying this specific derivation of $form(\mathcal{A})$. If $\mathcal{A}$ is a non-derivation support, its origin set is $\{form(\mathcal{A})\}$. This way of recording dependencies among formulas is inspired in the one used in systems known as ATMS's, *Assumption based Truth Maintenance Systems* [9] [12].

Goals refer to what one wants to be true, and consist of one's main compass for affective orientation. For the purpose at hand, we represent by $Goals(ag)$ the set of goals of agent ag. If g is a goal, then $GDesc(g) \in \mathcal{L}_{ag}$ is the goal's description, and $GImp(g) \in]0, 1[$ is the goal's importance.

Each agent associates a subjective credibility to each other agent, a number in the interval $]0, 1]$. This may start as a default value, and evolve depending on the interactions between the two agents. For the purpose at hand, it is enough to say that we represent by $Cred(ag_1, ag_2)$ the credibility attributed to agent ag_2 by agent ag_1.

The wishful thinking coefficient of agent ag, represented by $wt(ag)$, is a number, in the interval $[0, 1[$, indicating to what measure ag is susceptible to wishful thinking. This coefficient is assumed to reflect the agent's personality traits (e.g., increasing with *extraversion* and decreasing with *conscientiousness*).

WTR assumes that there is one wishful thinking support, $<GDesc(g), \texttt{WT}, \{GDesc(g)\}>$, in the knowledge base of agent ag, for each goal $g \in Goals(ag)$, unless $wt(ag) = 0$, in which case no support of this type should exist. The management of derivation supports is out of the scope of WTR, provided that, given agent ag, for any derivation support, $<F, \texttt{Der}, \alpha> \in KB(ag)$, the following conditions hold: 1) $\alpha \vdash_{ag} F$, 2) $\neg \exists \alpha' \subset \alpha : \alpha' \vdash_{ag} F$ (so that origin sets are minimal), and 3) $F \notin \alpha$ (self derivations are redundant). An agent that always generates every possible derivation is known as a *logically omniscient* agent. WTR accounts for both logically omniscient and non-omniscient agents.

A set of hypotheses is called a *context*. When ψ is the context believed by agent ag, ag's *belief space* (i.e., the set of all ag's beliefs) is defined as $BS(\psi, ag) = \{F : <F, \tau, \alpha> \in KB(ag) \land \alpha \subseteq \psi\}$. Notice that, for logically omniscient agents, this set corresponds to $\{F : \psi \vdash_{ag} F\}$ (i.e., all the logical consequences of ψ). We say that a context, ψ, is *consistent*, as far as agent ag knows, $Cons(\psi, ag)$, if and only if $\forall F \in BS(\psi, ag) : \neg F \notin BS(\psi, ag)$. Notice that for logically omniscient agents, this corresponds to saying $\psi \nvdash_{ag} \perp$. As we can see, given an agent that is not logically omniscient: a) not all logical consequences of a believed context are necessarily beliefs, and b) a consistent context, according to our definition, may not be logically consistent. This happens because such kind of agent does not necessarily derive everything that is possible, and is naturally ignorant concerning what was not yet concluded.

3   The Revision Process

In this section we present the belief revision process, i.e., the process that determines an agent's beliefs at a given moment. We divide the hypotheses of an agent, ag, in two (possibly intersecting) sets:

$\beta_0 = \{F : \exists(\mathcal{A} \in KB(ag))form(\mathcal{A}) = F \land ot(\mathcal{A}) \in \mathcal{N} \cup \{\texttt{Obs}\}\}$ is the *collected data*, i.e., all the hypotheses originating from the world (via observations and communications).

$\gamma_0 = \{F : \exists(\mathcal{A} \in KB(ag))form(\mathcal{A}) = F \land ot(\mathcal{A}) = \texttt{WT}\}$ is the set of *wishful thoughts*, i.e., all the hypotheses originating from goals (via wishful thinking).

WTR is responsible to determine, at a given moment, what *consistent* subset of $\beta_0 \cup \gamma_0$ is believed. Such subset is obviously a context, since the elements of $\beta_0 \cup \gamma_0$ are hypotheses. We write β^γ to represent the believed context. We distinguish two (possibly intersecting) subsets of β^γ: 1) $\beta = \beta^\gamma \cap \beta_0$ is the set of *base beliefs*, i.e., of collected data that is believed, and 2) $\gamma = \beta^\gamma \cap \gamma_0$ is the set of *wishful beliefs*, i.e., of wishful thoughts that are believed. Figure 1 depicts the main sets involved in the revision process, and the support dependencies.

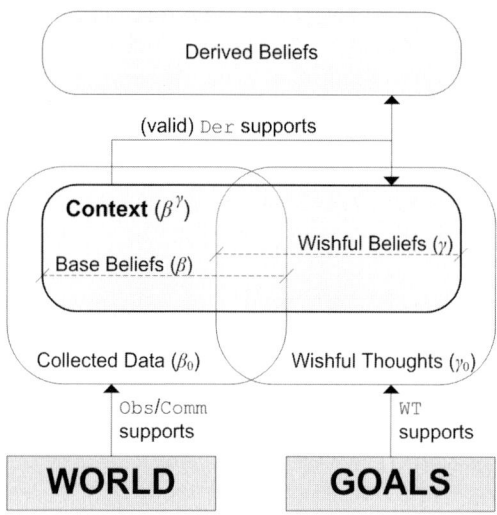

Fig. 1. WTR: Main sets and support dependencies

We point out that, since a believed context must be consistent, a conflict between collected data and wishful thoughts is addressed as any "regular" contradiction. Hence, WTR treats, in a uniform fashion, "disliked situations" and "conflicting collected data". In fact, in this paradigm, a contradiction can have, on each side of the conflict, "combined forces" from collected data and/or from wishful thinking. Wishful thinking "forces" are of a weaker nature and, usually, not enough to singlehandedly overthrow collected data, but can easily be the element that "turns the tide" in a conflict among collected data.

WTR determines the preferred context, β^γ, from $\beta_0 \cup \gamma_0$, in three steps: 1) Determining the candidate contexts (described in section 3.1); 2) Determining the preference of each candidate context (described in section 3.2); 3) Choosing a context (described in section 3.3).

3.1   Determining the Candidate Contexts

A candidate context is a consistent subset of $\beta_0 \cup \gamma_0$ (because an agent with inconsistent beliefs is ineffective). We remind that a consistent context, in WTR, is a context where no contradiction has been derived (see section 2). Furthermore, only maximal sets are considered candidates, i.e., if ψ_1 is a candidate and $\psi_2 \subset \psi_1$, then ψ_2 is not a candidate, because ψ_1 should be preferred to ψ_2. The reason for this preference is that, the fact that the formulas in $\psi_1 \setminus \psi_2$ are not inconsistent with ψ_2 means that there is no reason against them (neither rational nor affective). Because there are reasons to believe these formulas (since they are in $\beta_0 \cup \gamma_0$) and no reasons against, they should be believed (if ψ_2 is believed).

Given these criteria, we define the set of candidate contexts as: $Cand(\beta_0, \gamma_0, ag) = \{\lambda \subseteq \beta_0 \cup \gamma_0 : Cons(\lambda, ag) \wedge (\neg \exists \varphi \subseteq \beta_0 \cup \gamma_0 : Cons(\varphi, ag) \wedge (\lambda \subset \varphi))\}$.

3.2   Determining the Preference of Each Candidate Context

In order to determine the preference of a context, a more basic measure is necessary: the *strength* of a given belief, i.e., its subjective credibility. This strength is determined according to what originated/supports the belief and, for that reason, we also refer to it as *causal strength*.

If F is a belief of agent ag, when ag's believed context is β^γ (i.e., $F \in BS(\beta^\gamma, ag)$), the causal strength attributed to F is given by $CauStr(F, \beta^\gamma, ag) \in]0, 1]$. The value of 1 represents the causal strength of a belief considered an *absolute certainty* (also simply called *certainty*), i.e., a belief without doubt. With respect to WTR, certainties can only be overthrown by other conflicting certainties.

The set of valid supports for a formula F, when β^γ is the context believed by the agent, ag, is given by $Sups(F, \beta^\gamma, ag) = \{<F, \tau, \alpha> \in KB(ag) : \alpha \subseteq \beta^\gamma\}$. It is trivial to conclude that $Sups(F, \beta^\gamma, ag) \neq \emptyset$ if and only if $F \in BS(\beta^\gamma, ag)$.

Causal strength of a belief combines the causal strength conveyed by each of that belief's valid supports. Given a support, $\mathcal{A}$, valid when β^γ is the context believed by agent ag, $SuppStr(\mathcal{A}, \beta^\gamma, ag) \in]0, 1]$ is the strength conveyed by $\mathcal{A}$. So, the value of $CauStr(F, \beta^\gamma, ag)$ is a combination of the support strength (determined by function $SuppStr$) of each of the supports in $Sups(F, \beta^\gamma, ag)$.

We claim no specific definition for $CauStr$, however, we postulate that: 1) If there is a support in $Sups(F, \beta^\gamma, ag)$ with support strength of 1 (a certainty), then $CauStr(F, \beta^\gamma, ag) = 1$; 2) Otherwise, having one more support in $Sups(F, \beta^\gamma, ag)$, or having a higher strength of a support in $Sups(F, \beta^\gamma, ag)$, increases $CauStr(F, \beta^\gamma, ag)$.

We claim no specific definition for $SuppStr$, however, we postulate that: 1) $SuppStr(<F, ag', \{F\}>, \beta^\gamma, ag)$ increases with $Cred(ag, ag')$; 2) $SuppStr(<F, \text{WT}, \{F\}>, \beta^\gamma, ag)$ increases with the importance of the goal with description F, and with $wt(ag)$; 3) $SuppStr(<F, \text{Der}, \emptyset>, \beta^\gamma, ag) = 1$ (F is a tautology); 4) $SuppStr(<F, \text{Der}, \alpha>, \beta^\gamma, ag)$ remains the same if a certainty is added to α, decreases if a non-certainty is added to α, and increases if the strength (in context $\beta^\gamma \setminus \{F\}$, to disregard derivation cycles) of an element in α increases.

Finally, the preference of a context accounts for several factors. The most important factor is the number of absolute certainties among the base beliefs. This factor has priority over all other factors, following from the definition of certainty. Apart from certainties, the number and strength of the other (uncertain) base beliefs also influences the preference of the context. Since causal strength combines strength conveyed by all four kinds of supports, this factor reflects that combined effect. The fact that base beliefs can also have derivation supports means that context preference captures, to some extent, a measure of interconnection among these beliefs. The third factor is likeability, measured in terms of a) the number and strength of beliefs in goal achievements (wishful beliefs), in combination with the importance of the corresponding goals, and b) the number and strength of beliefs in negations of goal achievements, in combination with the importance of the corresponding goals. The influence of likeability is regulated by the wishful thinking coefficient.

The *context preference* that an agent, ag, attributes to a context, β^γ, is given by $CtxPrf(\beta^\gamma, ag) \in \mathbb{R}^+$. Since we want the number of certainties among base beliefs to have precedence over other factors, we define context preference as that number, added to a value in $]0,1[$ that accounts for the remaining factors. This added value is given by $LessSigPrf(\beta^\gamma, ag) \in]0,1[$ (*Less Significative Preference*):

$$CtxPrf(\beta^\gamma, ag) = \#\{F \in \beta : CauStr(F, \beta^\gamma, ag) = 1\} + LessSigPrf(\beta^\gamma, ag),$$

where β is obtained from β^γ and ag, as defined in the beginning of section 3. $LessSigPrf(\beta^\gamma, ag)$ is a mapping to $]0,1[$ of $LSP(\beta^\gamma, ag) \in \mathbb{R}$. Zero preference is mapped to 0.5, positive preference ($\mathbb{R}^+$) is mapped to the interval $]0.5,1[$, and negative preference ($\mathbb{R}^-$) is mapped to the interval $]0,0.5[$. The mapping is a continuous increasing function (to preserve the order of preference):

$$LessSigPrf(\beta^\gamma, ag) = \frac{LSP(\beta^\gamma, ag)}{1 + 2 \times |LSP(\beta^\gamma, ag)|} + 0.5.$$

LSP combines the preference conveyed by the uncertainties in the belief base, given by $UncertPrf(\beta^\gamma, ag) \in \mathbb{R}_0^+$, with the preference conveyed by likeability, given by $LkbPrf(\beta^\gamma, ag) \in \mathbb{R}$. This combination is defined as an average of the two components, weighted according to the wishful thinking coefficient:

$$LSP(\beta^\gamma, ag) = (1 - wt(ag)) \times UncertPrf(\beta^\gamma, ag) + wt(ag) \times LkbPrf(\beta^\gamma, ag).$$

The set of uncertainties among the base beliefs of context β^γ, for agent ag, is given by $Uncert(\beta^\gamma, ag) = \{F \in \beta : CauStr(F, \beta^\gamma, ag) \neq 1\}$, where β is obtained from β^γ and ag, as defined in the beginning of section 3.

We claim no specific definition for $UncertPrf$, however, we postulate that: 1) When $Uncert(\beta^\gamma, ag) = \emptyset$, then $UncertPrf(\beta^\gamma, ag) = 0$; 2) The value of $UncertPrf(\beta^\gamma, ag)$ increases when there is one more belief in $Uncert(\beta^\gamma, ag)$, or when the strength of one of the beliefs in $Uncert(\beta^\gamma, ag)$ increases (remaining an uncertainty).

If β^γ is the context believed by agent ag, the set of goals that ag believes to be achieved is given by $Achv(\beta^\gamma, ag) = \{g \in Goals(ag) : GDesc(g) \in \beta^\gamma\}$, and the set of goals ag believes not to be achieved is given by $NotAchv(\beta^\gamma, ag) = \{g \in Goals(ag) : \neg GDesc(g) \in BS(\beta^\gamma, ag)\}$.

We claim no specific definition for $LkbPrf$, however, we postulate that: 1) When $Achv(\beta^\gamma, ag) = NotAchv(\beta^\gamma, ag) = \emptyset$, then $LkbPrf(\beta^\gamma, ag) = 0$; 2) $LkbPrf(\beta^\gamma, ag)$ increases when there is one more goal in $Achv(\beta^\gamma, ag)$, or when a goal in $Achv(\beta^\gamma, ag)$ has its importance increased or is believed with greater strength; 3) $LkbPrf(\beta^\gamma, ag)$ decreases when there is one more goal in $NotAchv(\beta^\gamma, ag)$, or when a goal in $NotAchv(\beta^\gamma, ag)$ has its importance increased or its negation is believed with greater strength; 4) The more important the goal, the greater the impact (on likeability) of changing the strength of belief in its achievement or its negation.

3.3   Choosing a Context

Once determined a value of preference for each candidate context, choosing the one with the highest value of preference is the obvious procedure, i.e.:

$$\beta^{\gamma} = arg \max_{\psi \in Cand(\beta_0, \gamma_0, ag)} CtxPrf(\psi, ag).$$

However, although improbable, it is possible that several candidates share the same highest value of preference (i.e., a tie). This is likely to occur if humans take part in defining variables (such as goal importance, agent credibility, observation strength, etc), because humans have the tendency to round numbers.

WTR does not define a specific way to solve ties, but we suggest two approaches. Consider that $\mathcal{P}$ is the set of preferred contexts (i.e., those that share the highest value of preference). One approach, inspired by Fuhrmann's theory [6], is to find the intersection of the preferred contexts, i.e., $\beta^{\gamma} = \bigcap_{\psi \in \mathcal{P}} \psi$. This solution might be adopted by a cautious agent. Another intuitive approach is to represent the disjunction of the "realities" expressed by the preferred contexts. In other words, if δ is the intersection returned by the previous approach, the second approach chooses $\beta^{\gamma} = \delta \cup \{\bigvee_{\psi \in \mathcal{P}} (\bigwedge_{F \in \psi \setminus \delta} F)\}$. In order to use this approach, one must define an appropriate support for the new belief (the disjunction).

4   Degrees of Belief

As explained in section 2, WTR calls belief to any small "inclination" to believe. Yet, as Paglieri puts it, "beliefs are *data accepted as reliable* (...) considered as 'safe ground' for reasoning and action" [15]. So, for commonsense, a belief must have *a minimum* degree of subjective credibility/strength that makes it reliable for reasoning and action. We point out that this minimum degree of strength depends on the particular reasoning/action, i.e., on the *aim* that requires the belief. Mainly, it depends on an assessment of: a) The eventual losses when the aim is followed, based on a false belief; b) The eventual gains when the aim is followed, based on a true belief; c) The difficulty of acquiring more information regarding the credibility of the belief. E.g., assume that today is Saturday and one knows that a given shop is open on Saturdays. For the purpose of answering a non-compromising question from another agent, one may answer "yes, I believe the shop is open". However, if one plans to travel 200 Km to make a purchase in that shop, one may consider oneself relatively ignorant concerning whether it is open or not. The information is not strongly supported and the potential losses are high (to make a long trip in vain). One may consider making a phone call to better support the information, and if that phone call is not possible, one may simply decide not to go. Hence, for commonsense, belief is a relative concept.

This commonsense notion of belief naturally emerges from WTR, following a straightforward approach, provided that one knows the appropriate thresholds dictated by the aims at stake. We remind that function *CauStr* (defined in section 3.2) models subjective credibility of beliefs. If β^γ is the context believed by agent ag, and $t_{aim} \in [0, 1]$ is the threshold defined by some aim (denoted by aim) that requires a belief, $F \in BS(\beta^\gamma, ag)$, then, F is also *a belief regarding aim*, if and only if $CauStr(F, \beta^\gamma, ag) \geq t_{aim}$.

5   An Example

In this section, we present an example of a concrete WTR operation, and illustrate its behavior with a sequence of simple scenarios. In order to have a concrete WTR, one must define functions $CauStr$, $SuppStr$, $UncertPrf$ and $LkbPrf$, in accordance with the behavior postulated in section 3.2, regarding these functions. Having these postulates in mind, we define:

$$CauStr(F, \beta^\gamma, ag) = 1 - \prod_{\mathcal{A} \in Sups(F, \beta^\gamma, ag)} (1 - SuppStr(\mathcal{A}, \beta^\gamma, ag)).$$

$$SuppStr(<F, \tau, \alpha>, \beta^\gamma, ag) =$$

$$\begin{cases} 1, & \text{if } \tau = \texttt{Obs}; \\ GImp(g)^{(1-wt(ag))/wt(ag)}, & \text{if } \tau = \texttt{WT}, \text{ where } F = GDesc(g); \\ \prod_{F_i \in \alpha} CauStr(F_i, \beta^\gamma \setminus \{F\}, ag), & \text{if } \tau = \texttt{Der}; \\ Cred(ag, \tau), & \text{if } \tau \in \mathcal{N}. \end{cases}$$

$$UncertPrf(\beta^\gamma, ag) = \sum_{F \in Uncert(\beta^\gamma, ag)} CauStr(F, \beta^\gamma, ag).$$

$$LkbPrf(\beta^\gamma, ag) = (\sum_{g \in Achv(\beta^\gamma, ag)} CauStr(GDesc(g), \beta^\gamma, ag) \times GImp(g))$$

$$- \sum_{g \in NotAchv(\beta^\gamma, ag)} CauStr(\neg GDesc(g), \beta^\gamma, ag) \times GImp(g).$$

Notice that this particular definition of $SuppStr$ models observations as absolute certainties, but this does not have to be the case for every concretization of WTR.

Assume an agent, ag, that reasons using first order logics ($\mathcal{L}_{ag} = \mathcal{L}_{FOL}$ and $\vdash_{ag} = \vdash_{FOL}$) and whose wishful thinking coefficient is $wt(ag) = 0.3$.

Scenario 1. The agent has the single goal of having her mother alive with an extremely high importance (0.95), i.e., $Goals(ag) = \{g\}$, where $GImp(g) = 0.95$ and $F_{al} = GDesc(g) = alive(Mother)$. *David* (another agent) tells ag that her mother boarded flight number 17 ($F_{17} = inFlight(Mother, 17)$). ag thinks of *David* as having a not too high credibility ($Cred(ag, David) = 0.5$).

Later on, ag watches a news report announcing that flight number 17 crashed, leaving no survivors. We refer to (part of) the news report about the plane crash

Table 1. An abbreviated description of each of the three scenarios

Scenario:	1	2	3
$wt(ag)$:	0.3	0.3	0.3
$KB(ag)$:	$<F_{al}, \mathtt{WT}, \{F_{al}\}>$ $<F_{17}, David, \{F_{17}\}>$ $<F_{cr}, Reporter, \{F_{cr}\}>$ $<\neg F_{al}, \mathtt{Der}, \{F_{17}, F_{cr}\}>$	$<F_{al}, \mathtt{WT}, \{F_{al}\}>$ $<F_{17}, David, \{F_{17}\}>$ $<F_{cr}, Reporter, \{F_{cr}\}>$ $<\neg F_{al}, \mathtt{Der}, \{F_{17}, F_{cr}\}>$ $<F_{17}, Bruno, \{F_{17}\}>$	$<F_{al}, \mathtt{WT}, \{F_{al}\}>$ $<F_{17}, David, \{F_{17}\}>$ $<F_{cr}, Reporter, \{F_{cr}\}>$ $<\neg F_{al}, \mathtt{Der}, \{F_{17}, F_{cr}\}>$ $<F_{17}, Bruno, \{F_{17}\}>$ $<\neg F_{17}, Susan, \{\neg F_{17}\}>$
β_0:	$\{F_{17}, F_{cr}\}$	$\{F_{17}, F_{cr}\}$	$\{F_{17}, F_{cr}, \neg F_{17}\}$
γ_0:	$\{F_{al}\}$	$\{F_{al}\}$	$\{F_{al}\}$
β^γ:	$\{F_{al}, F_{cr}\}$	$\{F_{17}, F_{cr}\}$	$\{F_{al}, F_{cr}, \neg F_{17}\}$

as $F_{cr} = \forall(x)\ inFlight(x, 17) \rightarrow \neg alive(x)$. Assume that, if *Reporter* is the agent who communicates the crash, then $Cred(ag, Reporter) = 0.8$. *ag* easily concludes that F_{17} and F_{cr} imply $\neg F_{al}$ (i.e., that her mother died). See table 1 for a short description of scenario 1.

Clearly, believing all three hypotheses would cause an inconsistency (i.e., $Cons(\beta_0 \cup \gamma_0, ag)$ does not hold). There are three candidate contexts: $Cand(\beta_0, \gamma_0, ag) = \{\{F_{al}, F_{17}\}, \{F_{al}, F_{cr}\}, \{F_{17}, F_{cr}\}\}$. The context preference ($CtxPrf$) of each of these candidates is, respectively, 0.7733, 0.8096 and 0.8071 (approximately). Hence, the chosen context is $\beta^\gamma = \{F_{al}, F_{cr}\}$.

ag is in denial concerning her mother's death, mainly due to the low credibility of *David* (who communicated F_{17}), and to the very high goal importance of having her mother alive (0.95). High values of importance are typical of preservation goals such as those related to life and health (see, e.g., [14]). But the personality of the agent is also responsible for this denial; If, for instance, the wishful thinking coefficient would be 0.2 (instead of 0.3), the preferred context would be $\{F_{17}, F_{cr}\}$ (no denial).

Scenario 2. After the events of the previous scenario, *Bruno* ($Cred(ag, Bruno) = 0.8$) also tells *ag* that her mother boarded flight 17 (see table 1). Still, $Cand(\beta_0, \gamma_0, ag) = \{\{F_{al}, F_{17}\}, \{F_{al}, F_{cr}\}, \{F_{17}, F_{cr}\}\}$. Now, the context preferences are, respectively, 0.8192, 0.8096 and 0.8316 (approximately). Hence, $\beta^\gamma = \{F_{17}, F_{cr}\}$.

ag is no longer in denial because now there are two agents (one of them quite credible) saying that her mother boarded flight 17. Notice that F_{17} was exactly the "weakest link"; If *Bruno* would have communicated F_{cr} instead, *ag* would remain in denial given the low strength of F_{17}.

Scenario 3. After the events of the previous scenario, *Susan* ($Cred(ag, Susan) = 0.6$) tells *ag* that her (*ag*'s) mother did *not* board flight 17, i.e., $\neg F_{17}$ (see table 1). Now, the candidate contexts are $Cand(\beta_0, \gamma_0, ag) = \{\{F_{al}, F_{17}\}, \{F_{al}, F_{cr}, \neg F_{17}\}, \{F_{17}, F_{cr}\}\}$, with preferences, respectively, 0.8192, 0.8557 and 0.8316 (approximately). Hence, $\beta^\gamma = \{F_{al}, F_{cr}, \neg F_{17}\}$.

Susan's communication was just what *ag* wanted to hear to deny (again) her mother's death. The choice of context was based on the combined influence of rational factors with wishful thinking: By itself, $Susan$'s communication ($\neg F_{17}$) is weaker than F_{17}, since $CauStr(\neg F_{17}, \beta_0 \cup \gamma_0, ag) = 0.6$ and $CauStr(F_{17}, \beta_0 \cup \gamma_0, ag) = 0.9$; Alone, the "affective" preference for having $Mother$ alive was not enough to override the evidences of her death (as it is shown in scenario 2).

We point out that WTR is guided by an order among contexts that does not necessarily have a correspondence to some order among hypotheses. For instance, suppose that, because $\neg F_{17} \in \beta^\gamma$ and $F_{17} \notin \beta^\gamma$, we would conclude that $\neg F_{17}$ is preferred over F_{17}. Notice that this preference is a consequence of the mutual presence of F_{al} and F_{cr} (that make F_{17} "unwanted"). If we consider contexts $\{F_{al}, F_{17}\}$ and $\{F_{al}, \neg F_{17}\}$ (neither includes F_{cr}), we observe that the first has higher context preference than the second. This would imply that F_{17} is preferred over $\neg F_{17}$, which is the opposite of what we initially concluded.

Since $F_{al} \in BS(\beta^\gamma, ag)$, one may question the degree to which ag believes her mother is alive. Note that $CauStr(F_{al}, \beta^\gamma, ag) \simeq 0.8872$. First consider ag is asked that question, merely for curiosity, assuming a corresponding threshold of $t_{curiosity} = 0.2$. Since $CauStr(F_{al}, \beta^\gamma, ag) \geq t_{curiosity}$, ag would answer "Yes, I believe my mother is alive" (assuming ag answers according to what she actually thinks/feels). Second, consider ag had previously planned to buy a new expensive TV for her mother, assuming a corresponding threshold of $t_{TV} = 0.9$. Since $CauStr(F_{al}, \beta^\gamma, ag) < t_{TV}$, ag would consider herself ignorant about her mother's state and would not buy the TV (yet).

6   Conclusions and Future Work

We present a belief revision theory that generates its own criteria to determine the preferred set of beliefs, modeling rational reasons, as well as wishful thinking influences: WTR. The supports of beliefs are used to determine their subjective credibility and overall context preference, in consonance with the foundations theories. Beliefs are represented as ranging down from the weak inclination to believe, up to the absolute certainty, where a belief can be credible enough regarding some aim, and not credible enough regarding another. Wishful thinking is modeled as follows: By representing inclinations to believe in one's goals, "disliked" beliefs are seen as "contradictory" towards one's goals, thus evoking revision; Furthermore, the determination of context preference incorporates a likeability bias, regulated by a personality parameter.

The criteria behind the determination of context preference, in WTR, are similar to those guiding the process of belief selection in Paglieri's *Data-oriented Belief Revision* (DBR) [15]. An important distinction is that DBR's selection is belief-oriented, while WTR's is context-oriented. Our approach attempts to model how preference of a belief is dependent on the remaining beliefs (e.g., with respect to likeability), as we discuss in section 5.

Although WTR is intended to incorporate an autonomous (computational) agent, some work must be done to reduce eventual computational costs. As the agent's knowledge base grows, so does the cost of computing context preference. We propose that, when the revision process is triggered, only part of the knowledge base is considered: that which is *relevant* to the event that triggered revision. In Paglieri's approach [15] [16], *relevance* is the property that determines which of the stored data is selected, as active data, for belief revision.

References

1. Alchourrón, C.E., Gärdenfors, P., Makinson, D.: On the logic of theory change: partial meet functions for contraction and revision. The Journal of Symbolic Logic 50(2), 510–530 (1985)
2. Carver, C.S., Scheier, M.F., Weintraub, J.K.: Assessing coping strategies: a theoretically based approach. Journal of Personality and Social Psychology 56(2), 267–283 (1989)
3. Castelfranchi, C.: Guarantees for autonomy in cognitive agent architecture. In: Woolridge, M., Jennings, N. (eds.) Intelligent Agents. LNCS (LNAI), vol. 890, pp. 56–70. Springer, Heidelberg (1995)
4. Frijda, N.H. (ed.): The Laws of Emotion, Mahwah, N.J. Lawrence Erlbaum Associates (2007)
5. Frijda, N.H., Mesquita, B.: Beliefs through emotions. In: Frijda, N.H., Mesquita, B. (eds.) Emotions and Beliefs - How Feelings Influence Thoughts, pp. 45–77. Cambridge University Press, Cambridge, UK (2000)
6. Fuhrmann, A.: Theory Contraction through Base Contraction. Journal of Philosophical Logic 20(2), 175–203 (1991)
7. Hansson, S.O.: Ten philosophical problems in belief revision. Journal of Logic and Computation 13(1), 37–49 (2003)
8. Harman, G.: Change in View: Principles of Reasoning, p. 21. MIT Press, Cambridge, USA (1986)
9. de Kleer, J.: An Assumption-Based Truth Maintenance System. Artificial Intelligence 28(2), 127–162 (1986)
10. Lazarus, R.S., Folkman, S.: Stress, appraisal and coping. Springer, Heidelberg (1984)
11. Levi, I.: The Fixation of Belief and Its Undoing. Cambridge University Press, Cambridge (1991)
12. Martins, J.P., Shapiro, S.C.: A Model for Belief Revision. Artificial Intelligence 35(1), 25–79 (1988)
13. McCrae, R.R., Costa Jr, P.T.: Personality, coping, and coping effectiveness in an adult sample. Journal of Personality 54, 385–405 (1986)
14. Ortony, A., Clore, G.L., Collins, A.: The Cognitive Structure of Emotions. Cambridge University Press, New York, N.Y (1988)
15. Paglieri, F.: Data-oriented Belief Revision: Toward a unified theory of epistemic processing. In: Onaindia, E., Staab, S. (eds.) Proceedings of STAIRS 2004: 2nd Starting AI Researchers Symposium, pp. 179–190. IOS Press, Amsterdam (2004)
16. Paglieri, F.: See what you want, believe what you like: Relevance and likeability in belief dynamics. In: Cañamero, L. (ed.) Proceedings of AISB (Artificial Intelligence and the Simulation of Behaviour) 2005 Symposium Agents that want and like: Motivational and emotional roots of cognition and action, Hatfield, AISB, pp. 90–97 (2005)
17. Picard, R.: What does it mean for a computer to "have" emotions? MIT Media Laboratory Technical Report N. 354 (2001)

An Empathic Rational Dialog Agent

Magalie Ochs, Catherine Pelachaud, and David Sadek

France Télécom, R&D, France
{magalie.ochs,david.sadek}@orange-ftgroup.com
Laboratoire LINC, Université Paris 8, France
c.pelachaud@iut.univ-paris8.fr

Abstract. Recent research has shown that virtual agent able to express empathic emotions enhances human-machine interaction. In this paper, we present the capabilities that virtual agent should have to be empathic toward a user. Moreover, we propose a computational representation of emotions which may be experienced by a user during a human-machine dialog. This semantically grounded formal representation enables a rational dialog agent to identify from a dialogical situation the empathic emotion and its intensity that he should express.

Keywords: Computational model of emotion, empathy, rational dialog agent.

1 Introduction

A growing interest in using virtual agents expressing emotions as interfaces to computational systems has been observed in the last few years. Recent research has shown that virtual agent's expressions of empathic emotions enhance users' satisfaction, engagement, perception of virtual agents, and performance in task achievement whereas the expression of self-emotions seems to have few impact on the interaction [Klein et al., 1999, Prendinger and Ishizuka, 2005].

In our research, we are particularly interested in the use of virtual dialog agents as information system communicators. Users interact with agents in natural language to find out information on a specific domain. We aim to give such agents the capability of expressing empathic emotions towards users during dialog, and thus to improve interaction [Prendinger and Ishizuka, 2005].

Introducing empathy into a virtual dialog agent means to give him the ability to identify the emotions potentially felt by a user during interaction. This requires that the virtual dialog agent knows the emotions that may be elicited during the interaction and the circumstances under which they may appear.

In this paper, we first introduce theoretical foundations on empathy that enable us to highlight the capacity that a virtual agent should have to be empathic. We then present some existing empathic virtual agents and the methods used to construct them. We attempt to identify, based on the Appraisal Theories of emotion and on the results of an analysis of real human-machine emotional dialogs, user's emotions that may be elicited during dialogs, their type, intensity and conditions of elicitation. Finally, we propose a formalization of emotions and empathy that enables a rational dialog agent to be empathic.

A. Paiva, R. Prada, and R.W. Picard (Eds.): ACII 2007, LNCS 4738, pp. 338–349, 2007.

2 The Empathy in Virtual Agents

Empathy: Theoretical Foundations. Empathy is generally defined as "the capacity to put yourself in someone else shoes to understand her emotions" [Pacherie, 2004]. In other words, to empathize with other means to simulate in her own mind a situation experienced by another one, to imagine oneself instead of the latter (with the same beliefs and goals), and then to deduce her felt emotions. For instance, Bob can imagine that Fred is happy because he won a thousand dollar and instead of Fred, Bob would be happy. This process of simulation may lead one to feel an emotion, called *empathic emotion*. For example, Bob may feel happy for Fred[1]. In the literature, it is not clear if an empathic emotion is equivalent to a non empathic one. In the OCC model [Ortony et al., 1988], such emotions are distinguished (for instance *happy for* emotion is different from *happy*). We follow this approach. The authors of the OCC model describe only two types of empathic emotion: *happy for* and *sorry for*. However, other research suggests that the type of an empathic emotion toward a person is similar to the type of the emotion of the latter [Hakansson, 2003]. Indeed, by empathy, someone may for instance feel fear for another person. Therefore, there exists as many types of empathic emotion as types of non empathic one.

The process of empathy may elicit no emotion. One can understand another's emotions without feeling an empathic one. As highlighted in [Paiva et al., 2004], people experience more empathic emotion with persons with whom they have some similarities (for example the same age) or a particular relationship (as for example a friendship). According to the OCC model [Ortony et al., 1988], the intensity of the empathic emotion depends on the degree to which the person is liked and deserves or not deserves the situation. People tend to be more pleased (respectively displeased) for others if they think the situation is deserved (respectively not deserved). Therefore, the intensity of an empathic emotion may be different from the intensity of the emotion that the person thinks the other feels. For instance, Bob can imagine that Fred is incredibly happy because he won a thousand dollars but Bob is not very happy for him because he does not think that Fred deserves it.

Contrary to the phenomenon of emotional contagion, the perception of an individual's expression of emotion is not necessary to elicit empathic emotions. Indeed, empathic emotions may be triggered even if the person does not express or feel emotion [Poggi, 2004].

Some characteristics of empathy have already been integrated in virtual agents. We present some of such agents and the methods used to construct the latter.

Existing Empathic Virtual Agents. Empathy in human-machine interaction can be considered in two ways: a user can feel empathic emotions toward a virtual agent (for instance in *FearNot!* [Paiva et al., 2004]) or a virtual agent can express

---

[1] We consider only empathic emotions *congruent* with the person's emotions (for instance, we do not take into account an emotion of joy elicited by the sadness of another person).

empathic emotions toward a user. In our research, we focus on the empathy of a virtual agent toward users.

Based on the OCC model, most of empathic virtual agents consider only two types of empathic emotions: *happy-for* and *sorry-for*. The *happy-for* (respectively *sorry-for*) emotion is elicited by an agent when a goal of another agent (virtual agent or user) is achieved (respectively failed). In [Elliot, 1992], the empathic virtual agent has a representation of the others agents' goals. He deduces these goals from their emotional reactions. Consequently, the agent knows the others' goals only if they have been involved in an emotion elicitation. Therefore, the other agents' goals representation might be incomplete. Finally, the virtual agent triggers an empathic emotion toward another agent only if he has sympathy for him (represented by numerical value). In [Reilly, 1996], the virtual agent expresses *happy-for* (respectively *sorry-for*) emotion only if he detects a positive (respectively negative) emotion expression in his interlocutor. The agent's empathic emotions are in this case elicited by the perception of the expression of an emotion of another agent. In the same way, in [Prendinger and Ishizuka, 2005], the virtual agent expresses empathy according to the user's emotions (frustration, calm or joy) recognized through physiological sensors. However, an empathic emotion can be elicited even if this emotion is not felt or expressed by the interlocutor [Poggi, 2004].

Another approach consists in observing real interpersonal mediated interactions in order to identify the circumstances under which an individual expresses empathy and how it is displayed. The system *CARE* (*Companion Assisted Reactive Empathizer*) has been constructed to analyze user's empathic behavior during a treasure hunt game in a virtual world [McQuiggan and Lester, 2006]. The results of this study are domain-dependent. The conditions of empathic emotion elicitation in the context of a game may not be transposable in another context (as for example the context in which a user interacts with a virtual agent to find out information on a specific domain).

Our method to create empathic virtual agent is based both on a theoretical and empirical approaches. It consists to identify through psychological cognitive theories of emotion and through the study of real human-machine emotional dialogs the situations that may elicit users' emotions.

3   The Users' Emotions During Human-Machine Dialogs

An empathic virtual dialog agent should express emotions in the situations that may potentially elicit a user's emotion. His empathic emotion depends on the user's potentially felt emotion. The agent should therefore know the conditions of emotion elicitation and the type and intensity of such elicited emotions.

3.1   The Emotion Elicitation

Theoretical Foundations. According to the *Cognitive Appraisal Theories* [Scherer, 2000], emotions are triggered by a subjective interpretation of an event. This interpretation corresponds to the evaluation of a set of variables (called *appraisal variables*). When an event occurred (or is anticipated) in the environment, the individual evaluates the latter by valuing a set of variables. The values of these variables determine the type and the intensity of the elicited emotion. In our work, we focus on the goal-based emotions. We consider the following appraisal variables (extracted from [Scherer, 1988]):

- *The consequence of the event on the individual goal*: According to Lazarus [Lazarus, 1991], an event may trigger an emotion only if the person thinks that it affects one of her goals. The consequences of the event on the individual goal determine the elicited emotion. For instance, fear is triggered when a survival goal is threatened or risks to be threatened. Generally, failed or threatened goals elicit negative emotions whereas achieved goals trigger positive ones.
- *The causes of the event*: the causes of an event that lead to emotion elicitation may influence the type of the elicited emotion. For instance, a goal failure caused by another agent may trigger anger.
- *The consistency of consequences with the expectations*: the elicited emotion depends on the consistency between the current situation (*i.e.* the consequences of the occurred event on the individual's goals) and the situation expected by the individual.
- *The potential to cope with consequences*: the coping potential represents the capacity of an individual to deal with a situation that has led to a threatened or failed goal. It may influence the elicited emotion.

The interpretation of an event (*i.e.* the evaluation of appraisal variables and then the elicited emotion) depends principally on the individual's goals and beliefs (on the event, its causes, its real and expected consequences, and on her coping potential). That explains the different emotional reactions of distinct individuals in front of a same situation.

In a dialog context, an event corresponds to a communicative act. Consequently, according to the Appraisal Theory of emotion [Scherer, 2000], a communicative act may trigger a user's emotion if it affects one of her goals. To identify more precisely the dialogical situations that may lead a user to feel emotion, we have analyzed real human-machine dialogs that have led a user to express emotions. We present in the next section the results of this study.

The Analysis of Users' Emotions Elicitation in Human-Machine Interaction. We have analyzed real human-machine dialogs that have led a user to express emotions. The analyzed dialogs have been derived from two vocal applications developed at France Telecom R&D (*PlanResto* and *Dialogue Bourse*). The users interact orally with a virtual dialog agent to find out information on a specific domain (on stock exchange or on restaurants in Paris). First, the dialogs have been annotated with the label *negative_emotion* by two annotators[2]. The annotations have been done based on vocal and semantic cues of user's emotions.

---

[2] Unfortunately, we could not analyze the situations that have led to the users's expression of a positive emotion.

In the dialogs transcribed in text, the tag *negative_emotion* represents the moment where user expresses negative emotion. Secondly, these dialogs have been annotated with a particular coding scheme in order to highlight the characteristics of the dialogical situations that may elicit emotions in a human-machine context (for more details on the coding scheme see [Ochs et al., 2007]). The analysis of the annotated dialogs has enable us to identify more precisely the characteristics of a situation that may lead to a *negative* emotion elicitation in human-machine interaction:

- *The consequence of the event on the individual goal* : an event may trigger a user's negative emotion when it involves:
  - the failure of a user's intention[3]
  - a belief conflict on an intention: the user thinks that the virtual agent thinks the user has an intention different from her own one.
- *The cause of the event* that seems to elicit a user's negative emotion is in some cases the dialog agent.
- *The consistency of consequences with the expectations*: in the emotional situations, the user's expectations seem to be inconsistent with the situation that she observes.
- *The potential to cope with consequences*: after the failure of her intention, the user tries sometimes to achieve it in another way (coping potential). In some cases, the user seems not to be able to cope with the situation.

The appraisal variables determine the type and intensity of the elicited emotion. By combining the results of the study on human-machine emotional dialogs and the Appraisal Theory, we can deduce the type and the intensity of the emotions that a user may experience during human-machine dialogs.

3.2   The Type and Intensity of Users' Emotions

The Types of Emotions. To identify the types of emotions a user may feel during human-machine interaction, we explore the work of Scherer [Scherer, 1988] and try to correlate his descriptions of the conditions of elicitation of emotion type to the characteristics of emotional dialogical situations introduced above.

A positive emotion is generally triggered when a goal is completed. More precisely, if the goal achievement was expected, an emotion of **satisfaction** is elicited; while, if it was not expected, an emotion of **joy** appears [Scherer, 1988]. In the human-machine dialogs, a user's goal achievement corresponds to the successful completion of her intention. The user may experience satisfaction when the achievement of her intention was expected. She may feel joy when it was not expected.

A goal failure generally triggers a negative emotion. If a situation does not match with an individual's expectations, an emotion of **frustration** is elicited

---

[3] In the human-machine dialogs studied, we have observed, more particularly, the users' and agents' intentions. An intention is defined as a persistent goal (for more details see [Sadek, 1991]).

[Scherer, 1988]. Consequently, the user may experience frustration when one of her intentions failed. An emotion of **sadness** appears when the individual cannot cope with the situation. On the other hand, if she can cope with the situation, an emotion of **irritation** is elicited [Scherer, 1988]. The user may feel sadness when she does not know any other action that enables her to carry out her failed intention. If an action can be achieved by the user to complete her intention, she may experience irritation. When the goal failure is caused by another person, an emotion of **anger** may be elicited. In the dialogs analysis described above, this situation may correspond to a user's intention failure caused by the dialog agent due to a belief conflict. The user may experience anger toward the agent when a belief conflict with the dialog agent has led to a goal failure.

Of course, we cannot deduce the exact emotion felt by the user from this description of emotion type. Other elements (as for example the mood, the personality, and the current emotions) influence the elicitation of an emotion. However, that enables us to provide virtual agent with some information on the dialogical situations that *may* trigger a user's emotion.

The Intensity of Emotions. The intensity of an elicited emotion may be computed from the value of *intensity variables*. In the context of human-machine dialog, we consider the following variables (extracted from the OCC model [Ortony et al., 1988]).

The *degree of certainty*[4] of an information represents the likelihood for an individual that an information is true. According to our analysis of human-machine emotional dialogs, in the case of an intention failure, the intensity of negative emotion seems to be *proportional* to the degree of certainty of the user. The more the user was certain about the achievement of her intention by the event just occurred, the more the intensity of the negative elicited emotion (and more particularly the emotion of frustration [Scherer, 1988]) is high when the intention failed. Conversely, we suppose, based on the OCC model [Ortony et al., 1988], that the intensity of positive emotion is *inversely proportional* to the degree of certainty. We assume that the more the user was uncertain to complete her intention by the event just occurred the more the positive elicited emotion is high.

The *effort* invested by an individual to perform her goal influences the intensity of elicited emotions. Generally, a greater effort invested implies a more intense emotion [Ortony et al., 1988]. We then suppose that the intensity of an emotion is proportional to the effort invested by the user. In the case of anger (elicited by an intention failure caused by another agent because of a belief conflict), we assume that the intensity depends both on the effort invested by the user to try to carry out her intention and on the effort invested by the agent to complete the intention that the agent thinks the user has.

Not much research has highlighted the influence of *coping potential* on the intensity of an elicited emotion. We suppose that the intensity of the emotions

---

[4] Called *unexpectedness* in the OCC model [Ortony et al., 1988].

of sadness and irritation (which depend on the coping potential [Scherer, 1988]) are higher when the user does not know any action to complete her intention that has just failed. In other words, we assume that the intensity of sadness and irritation are *inversely proportional* to the coping potential.

Based on [Elliot, 1992, Reilly, 1996], we distinguish the *importance for the user to achieve her intention* from *the importance not to have her intention failed*. The intensity of positive (respectively negative) emotion is proportional to the importance to achieve her intention (respectively not to have her intention failed). Typically, in the context of human-machine dialog, we can suppose that the intensity of positive elicited emotion by the achievement of the user's intention to be understood by the agent is lower than the intensity of negative emotion triggered by the fact that the agent does not understand the user's intention.

The description of the relations between the value of these variables on the intensity of emotions enables a virtual agent to evaluate approximatively the importance of the intensity of user's elicited emotion.

The conditions of elicitation of different types of emotion that a user may experience during human-machine dialogs and the impact of the intensity variables on the intensity of such emotions described in this section enable us to model empathic virtual dialog agent.

4   The Empathic Rational Dialog Agent

Before describing the computational representation of the elements that enables us to create an empathic rational dialog agent, we present briefly the concept of rational dialog agent.

4.1   The Concept of Rational Dialog Agent

To create a virtual dialog agent, we use a model of rational agent based on a formal theory of interaction (called *Rational Interaction Theory*) [Sadek, 1991]. This model uses a BDI-like approach [Cohen and Levesque, 1990]. The implementation of this theory has given rise to a rational dialog agent (named the *Jade Semantic Agent (JSA)*) that provides a generic framework to instantiate intelligent agents able to dialog with others [Louis and Martinez, 2005].

The *mental state* of a rational agent is composed of two mental attitudes: *belief* and *intention*, formalized with the modal operators B and I as follows (p being a closed formula denoted a proposition): $B_i p$ means "agent i thinks that p is true". $I_i p$ means "agent i intends to bring about p". Based on his mental state, a rational agent acts to realize his intentions. Several others operators have been introduced to formalize the occurring action, the agent who has achieved it, and temporal relation. For instance, the formula $Done(e, p)$ means that the event e has just taken place and p was true before that event e occurred ($Done(e) \equiv Done(e, true)$). For more details see [Sadek, 1991].

4.2 The Agent's Representation of Users' Beliefs and Intentions During the Dialog

An empathic virtual agent should be able to adopt the user's perspective during dialog in order to identify her potentially felt emotions. The user's elicited emotions depend mostly on her beliefs and her intentions (see Section 3.1). Consequently, an empathic virtual agent has to know the user's beliefs and intentions during dialogs to infer the user's elicited emotions. Based on the Speech Acts Theory [Searle, 1969], the virtual dialog agent can deduce the user's beliefs and intentions related to the dialog from the communicative act that the user expresses. Researchers in philosophy have observed that language is not only used to describe something or to give some statement but also to do something with intention, *i.e.* to act [Searle, 1969]. Then, a *communicative act* (or *speech act*) is defined as the basic unit of language used to express an intention. Based on the *Speech Acts Theory* [Searle, 1969], we suppose that a user's intention during human-machine dialog is to achieve the *perlocutory effects* of the performed communicative act. The *perlocutory effects* describe the intention that the user wants to see achieved through the performed communicative act. For instance, the *perlocutory effect* of the act to inform agent i of proposition p is that agent i knows proposition p. In addition, we suppose that the user has the intention that her interlocutor knows her intention to produce the *perlocutory effects* of the performed communicative act. This intention corresponds to the *intentional effect* of the act [Sadek, 1991]. For instance, the *intentional effect* of the act to ask agent i some information p, is that agent i knows that the speaker has the intention to know information p. In a nutshell, when the user performs a communicative acts, the rational dialog agent can infer that (1) the user has the *intention* to achieve the intentional end perlocutory effects of the act and (2) the users *believes* that she can achieve the intentional and perlocutory effects of the act that she expresses. A rational dialog agent has a representation of communicative acts in terms of their intentional and perlocutory effects. That enables him to deduce the user's intentions and beliefs from the communicative acts that the user expresses.

4.3 The Computational Representation of Emotion and Empathy

In order to identify the user's potentially elicited emotions (its type and intensity) from the user's beliefs and intentions, the rational dialog agent has to know the conditions of elicitation of the different types of emotion. He should then be able to approximate the intensity of the elicited emotion. To provide these capabilities to a rational dialog agent, we propose a computational representation of the intensity variables and of the conditions of elicitation of the different emotion types. In the following, the variables i and j denote the agents who entertain dialog (in a human-machine dialog they represent the virtual agent and the user).

The Agent's Representation of the Intensity Variables. We propose to formalize the intensity variables introduced before (see Section 3.2) as follows:

- The *degree of certainty* of an agent i about the feasibility of an intention ϕ by an event e is noted $deg\_certainty(i, e, \phi)$ and varies in the interval $[0, 1]$. It is equal to the probability of the agent i to achieve his intention ϕ by the occurrence of the event e.
- The *effort* invested by an agent i to attempt to complete an intention ϕ is noted $effort(i, \phi)$. It represents the percentage of energy invested by i to attempt to carry out ϕ.
- The *coping potential* of an agent i after the failure of an intention ϕ, noted $coping\_potential(i, \phi)$ varies in the interval $[0, 1]$. It represents the probability for the agent i that there exists an action that enables him to complete his intention ϕ.
- The importance for the agent i to achieve his intention ϕ is noted $imp\_a(i, \phi)$. The importance for the agent i not to have his intention ϕ failed is noted $imp\_f(i, \phi)$. The values of importance, which vary in the interval $[0, 1]$, should be set by the programmer.

Based on the approach of Gratch [Gratch, 2000], we define the intensity of an emotion as the product of the value of variables that contribute to that emotion. We then introduce the following intensity function:

$f\_intensite(d\_c, p\_r, effort, imp) = d\_c * p\_r * effort * imp$ in which d_c, p_r, $effort$, and imp represent the value respectively of the degree of certainty, the coping potential, the effort and the importance of the intention. We use this function in the next section to compute the intensity of an elicited emotion.

The Agent's Representation of the Conditions of Emotion Elicitation.
To represent the conditions of emotion elicitation, we first introduce the following definitions:

- The *achievement of an intention* ϕ of an agent i by an event e is represented by the formula[5]: $achiev\_intention_i(e, \phi) \equiv^{def} B_i(Done(e, I_i\phi) \wedge \phi)$. This formula means that the agent i thinks the event e has enabled him to achieve his intention ϕ.
- The *failure of an intention* ϕ of an agent i after the occurred event e is represented by the formula: $failure\_intention_i(e, \phi) \equiv^{def} B_i(Done(e, I_i\phi \wedge B_i(Done(e) \Rightarrow \phi)) \wedge \neg\phi$. This formula means that the agent i thinks that the event e has not enabled him to achieve his intention ϕ that he thought to produce by e.
- The *belief conflict* between the agents i and j on an intention ϕ after the occurred event e is represented by the formula: $belief\_conflict_i(e, \phi, j) \equiv^{def} B_i(Done(e, \neg B_j(I_i(\phi)) \wedge \neg I_i(\phi)) \wedge B_j(I_i(\phi)) \wedge \neg I_i(\phi))$. This formula means that the agent i has the belief (that he had not before the event e) that the agent j thinks that agent i has another intention ϕ other than his own one.

---

[5] The logic used does not enable us to represent the action that has caused the achievement or failure of an intention.

Based on the description of emotions elicitation introduced before (see Section 3.2), we propose the following rules[6]:

- An emotion of *joy* of an agent i with an intensity c about an intention ϕ is triggered by the achievement, not expected by i, of the intention ϕ:

$$achiev\_intention_i(e, \phi) \wedge (deg\_certainty(i, e, \phi) \leq 0.5) \Rightarrow Joy_i(c, \phi)$$
$$c = f\_intensite(1 - deg\_certainty(i, e, \phi), 1, effort(i, \phi), imp\_a(i, \phi))$$

- An emotion of *satisfaction* of an agent i with an intensity c about an intention ϕ is triggered by the achievement, expected by i, of the intention ϕ:

$$achiev\_intention_i(e, \phi) \wedge (deg\_certainty(i, e, \phi) > 0.5) \Rightarrow Satisfaction_i(c, \phi)$$
$$c = f\_intensite(1 - deg\_certainty(i, e, \phi), 1, effort(i, \phi), imp\_a(i, \phi))$$

- An emotion of *frustration* of an agent i with an intensity c about an intention ϕ is triggered by the failure, unexpected by i, of the intention ϕ:

$$failure\_intention_i(e, \phi) \wedge (deg\_certainty(i, e, \phi) > 0.5) \Rightarrow Frustration_i(c, \phi)$$
$$c = f\_intensite(deg\_certainty(i, e, \phi), 1, effort(i, \phi), imp\_f(i, \phi))$$

- An emotion of *sadness* of an agent i with an intensity c about an intention ϕ is elicited by the failure of the intention ϕ that i does not think to be able to achieve by another way:

$$failure\_intention_i(e, \phi) \wedge (coping\_potential(i, \phi) \leq 0.5) \Rightarrow Sadness_i(c, \phi)$$
$$c = f\_intensite(1, 1 - coping\_potential(i, \phi), effort(i, \phi), imp\_f(i, \phi))$$

- An emotion of *irritation* of an agent i with an intensity c about an intention ϕ is triggered by the failure of the intention ϕ which i thinks to be able to achieve by another way:

$$failure\_intention_i(e, \phi) \wedge (coping\_potential(i, \phi) > 0.5) \Rightarrow Irritation_i(c, \phi)$$
$$c = f\_intensite(1, 1 - coping\_potential(i, \phi), effort(i, \phi), imp\_f(i, \phi))$$

- An emotion of *anger* of an agent i against j with an intensity c about an intention ϕ is triggered by the failure of the intention ϕ caused by the agent j because of a belief conflict on an intention ψ:

$$failure\_intention_i(e, \phi) \wedge belief\_conflict_i(e, \psi, j) \Rightarrow Anger_i(c, \phi, j)$$
$$c = f\_intensite(1, 1, (effort(i, \phi) + effort(j, \psi))/2, imp\_f(i, \phi))$$

Given this formalization, a negative elicited emotion by an intention failure is a combination of frustration and sadness or irritation (and eventually anger).

This formalization enables a rational dialog agent to deduce from the dialogical situation and the user's beliefs and intentions, the user's potential felt emotions and their intensity[7].

---

[6] The value 1 of a parameter of the intensity function means that this parameter has no impact on the computation of the intensity of the emotion.

[7] However, a rational dialog agent is not able to deal with external event of the dialog. Consequently, the emotions that may be elicited by such events cannot be deduced by the agent.

The Agent's Empathic Emotions. When the virtual dialog agent thinks another agent has an emotion, she may *have* an empathic emotion toward the latter. It depends on different factors as for instance the relation between such agents. Moreover, the intensity of the empathic emotion is not necessary similar to the intensity of the emotion that the agent thinks another agent has (see Section 2). To illustrate it, we introduce a *degree of empathy* (noted $degree\_empathy_i(j)$). It represents the degree to which the agent i has empathic emotions toward the agent j. It is null when the agent i has no empathic emotion toward the agent j. We propose the following function to compute the intensity of an empathic emotion of an agent i toward another agent j: $f\_empathy_i(j, intensity) = degree\_empathy_i(j) * intensity$ where $intensity$ represents the intensity of the emotion that the agent i thinks the agent j has.

The rule on the elicitation of an empathic emotion is then described by the following formula (the empathic emotion of the type $emotion$ and of intensity c' of the agent s toward the user u about an intention ϕ is noted $emotion_{s,u}(c', \phi)$):

$$B_s(emotion_u(c, \phi)) \Rightarrow emotion_{s,u}(c', \phi) \text{ with } c' = f\_empathy_s(u, c)$$

This formula means that the virtual agent s has an empathic emotion of the type *emotion* toward the user u if he thinks u has an emotion of the same type. Given the formalization of emotion elicitation described above, the agent s thinks the the user u has an emotion if he thinks that an event e has affected an intention ϕ of u. Then, the empathic emotion of s is related to ϕ. The intensity of this emotion may be null if the degree of empathy of the virtual agent s toward toward the user u is null.

5 Conclusion and Perspectives

In this paper, we have proposed a computational representation of different emotions that may be experienced by a user during a human-machine dialog. That enables a rational dialog agent to identify the empathic emotions to express during the interaction. We are currently implementing an empathic rational dialog agent. A subjective evaluation will be performed to verify the believability of the conditions of the agent's empathic emotions elicitation and the impact on the user's satisfaction and perception of such an agent.

References

[Cohen and Levesque, 1990] Cohen, P.R, Levesque, H.J: Intention is choice with commitment. Artificial Intelligence 42(2-3), 213–232 (1990)

[Elliot, 1992] Elliot, C.: The Affective Reasoner: A process model of emotions in a multi-agent system. PhD thesis, Northwestern University (1992)

[Gratch, 2000] Gratch, J.: Emile: Marshalling passions in training and education. In: Proceedings of the Fourth International Conference on Autonomous Agents (2000)

[Hakansson, 2003] Hakansson, J.: Exploring the phenomenon of empathy. PhD thesis, Department of Psychology, Stockholm University (2003)

[Klein et al., 1999] Klein, J., Moon, Y., Picard, R.: This computer responds to user frustration. In: Proceedings of the Conference on Human Factors in Computing Systems, pp. 242–243. ACM Press, New York (1999)

[Lazarus, 1991] Lazarus, R.S.: Emotion and adaptation. Oxford University Press, New York (1991)

[Louis and Martinez, 2005] Louis, V., Martinez, T.: An operational model for the fipa-acl semantics. In: Proceedings of AAMAS (2005)

[McQuiggan and Lester, 2006] McQuiggan, S., Lester, J.: Learning empathy: A data-driven framework for modeling empathetic companion agents. In: Proceedings of AAMAS (2006)

[Ochs et al., 2007] Ochs, M., Pelachaud, C., Sadek, D.: Emotion elicitation in an empathic virtual dialog agent. In: Prooceedings of the Second European Cognitive Science Conference (EuroCogSci) (2007)

[Ortony et al., 1988] Ortony, A., Clore, G.L, Collins, A.: The cognitive structure of emotions. Cambridge University Press, United Kingdom (1988)

[Pacherie, 2004] Pacherie, E.: L'empathie. In: chapter L'empathie et ses degrés, pp. 149–181. Editions Odile Jacob (2004)

[Paiva et al., 2004] Paiva, A., Dias, J., Sobral, D., Woods, S., Hall, L.: Building empathic lifelike characters: the proximity factor. In: Proceedings of the AAMAS Workshop on Empathic Agents (2004)

[Poggi, 2004] Poggi, I.: Emotions from mind to mind. In: Proceedings of the AAMAS Workshop on Empathic Agents (2004)

[Prendinger and Ishizuka, 2005] Prendinger, H., Ishizuka, M.: The empathic companion: A character-based interface that addresses users' affective states. International Journal of Applied Artificial Intelligence 19, 285–297 (2005)

[Reilly, 1996] Reilly, S.: Believable Social and Emotional Agents. PhD thesis, Carnegie Mellon University (1996)

[Sadek, 1991] Sadek, D.: Attitudes mentales et interaction rationnelle: vers une théorie formelle de la communication. PhD thesis, Université Rennes I (1991)

[Scherer, 1988] Scherer, K.: Criteria for emotion-antecedent appraisal: A review. In: Hamilton, V., Bower, G., Frijda, N. (eds.) Cognitive perspectives on emotion and motivation, pp. 89–126. Kluwer Academic Publishers, Dordrecht (1988)

[Scherer, 2000] Scherer, K.: Emotion. In: Hewstone, M., Stroebe, W. (eds.) Introduction to Social Psychology: A European perspective, pp. 151–191. Oxford Blackwell Publishers, Oxford (2000)

[Searle, 1969] Searle, J.R.: Speech Acts. Cambridge University Press, United Kingdom (1969)

Basing Artificial Emotion on Process and Resource Management

Stefan Rank[1] and Paolo Petta[1,2]

[1] Austrian Research Institute for Artificial Intelligence
Freyung 6/6, A-1010 Vienna, Austria
stefan.rank@ofai.at
[2] Institute of Medical Cybernetics and Artificial Intelligence
Medical University of Vienna
Freyung 6/2, A-1010 Vienna, Austria
paolo.petta@MeduniWien.ac.at

Abstract. Executable computational process models of emotion are based on specific sets of modelling primitives. Motivated by the requirements of a specific scenario and concepts used by emotion theories, we propose as building blocks explicitly bounded resources and concurrent processes acquiring and using them. Our approach is intended for the incremental modelling of a growing collection of emotional episodes, with a clear delineation of technically necessary simplifications of the natural phenomena. An episode of disgust is used to discuss the approach, which is realised using real-time cooperative microthreading technology.

Keywords: Affective agent architectures, appraisal theories, computational modelling, design criteria, disgust, embodiment, real-time systems.

1 Introduction

The contribution of this paper is the proposal to use explicitly bounded resources and concurrent processes as building blocks for computational modelling of emotion in a virtual world (section 3). This approach acknowledges that ongoing "always on" interaction of the agent with its environment[1] is fundamental, and that physical and material constraints are important. These tenets can be put to use in a virtual agent situated in a virtual world without sacrificing the benefits of dealing with an environment under the control of the modeller (as opposed to the real world). Further, we argue that this approach can be used to cover phenomena as described by current theories of emotion, while making explicit the symbolic and computational shortcuts necessary to achieve a certain depth of modelling. This furthers the line of research of Tabasco [20]: at first, we did away with reification of emotions; we now in particular aim at deconstructing the notion of static appraisal frames, to be replaced by coordination mechanisms in a concurrent model. We have to emphasise that the proposal of using processes

---

[1] Terminology used in this paper: *agents* (virtual bodies plus control architectures) are embedded in *their environment*; agents and environment form the virtual *world*.

A. Paiva, R. Prada, and R.W. Picard (Eds.): ACII 2007, LNCS 4738, pp. 350–361, 2007.

and resources as abstractions concerns the runtime of models. At design time, there may well be more suitable, higher-level abstractions.

Models of artificial emotion are a crucial element for building intelligent agents in social virtual worlds [13], and can also provide valuable benefits for theorising in emotion psychology [5,10]. Human emotions, however, are extremely complex phenomena involving cognitive, perceptual, and expressive competences. Attempts at operationalising mechanisms of emotion for an artificial system in a virtual world need to choose from a range of approaches differing in scope, detail, and fidelity of simulation—both of the system itself and the environment it is embedded in. The structure of current computer systems and the abstractions that are easily available in current programming languages often bias the structure of computational models: A single locus of control, widespread use of symbols for internal state and communication, absence of timing constraints, and conceptually unbounded use of resources are typical symptoms.

In early cognitive architectures, such features of implementations have posed difficulties for their application in robotic scenarios, and the concept of embodiment is often used to argue for the need of a different approach for agents in the real world [4]. More generally, the particular scenario of use, including the motivation for modelling emotion, determines the requirements that a particular implementation needs to meet [23]. For the purpose of the present paper, we assume the scenario of modelling a specific emotional phenomenon, disgust, in a virtual world similar to a computer game (section 2). In section 4, we illustrate our approach by sketching the resources and processes involved in the modelling of a specific episode of disgust.

2   Requirements Analysis

Affective agent architectures are used to construct agents for environments, such as (serious) computer games, that require autonomy and believable interaction with humans. A foundation for such affective agents are computational models of emotion that are executable in real-time. The context of virtual worlds and real-time interaction restricts the set of usable techniques. Furthermore, there are many approaches, based on abstractions readily available in mainstream programming languages, that fail to meet the requirements of our specific scenario, as described in this section. The scenario includes (the modelling of) two or more virtual characters in a three-dimensional world that can be manipulated by a human user. This world is to be a test-bed for the incremental modelling of a growing collection of specific emotion phenomena in a grounded fashion, explicating all simplifications considered as technically necessary. This section details the requirements that impinge on our choice of basic building blocks for such simulations.

Cognitive architectures often use a single control structure and a small set of general representation schemes. An example is Soar and emotion models based on it [12,16] which use, at the core, a single execution cycle and a central hierarchical data structure modified by operators. Similarly, logic-based agents employ propositions and an inference mechanism. Such mechanisms and representations have their uses, and the present proposal is not aimed at replacing them with a single "better" mechanism. Rather, we try to identify building blocks for our approach that allow the use of diverse resourceful [18] methods, while providing the features that we deem fundamental: fidelity of simulation, compatibility with theories of emotion, tractability, and the explication of modelling shortcuts.

Fidelity of simulation. The agent is to be simulated as a physical system with resource bounds in both space and time. The simulation of the physical system *"emotional mind"* in a digital computer that is inherently serial calls for mechanisms that approximate the analogue and massively parallel nature of emotional agents acting in the real world, i.e., living beings. Further, all the resources in the model are part not only of the agent but also of the (simulated) world and thus not under the exclusive control of the agent. As an example of an external influence, consider a physics simulation that is part of the environment: Given its continuous effect on the agent, it warrants inclusion of adaptive action monitoring processes in the agent. Similarly, simulated visual perception has to be actively directed to focus on specific parts of the environment, and processes internal to the agent are bounded in terms of e.g. available processing time. Fidelity of simulation also implies that robotic architectures, where physical and material constraints cannot be abstracted, are a relevant source of insights. Arzi-Gonczarowski [1] argues for transferring the issues of embodied grounding that are relevant in creating particular but approximate models of intelligence for robots to the theoretical foundations for general accounts of intelligence. Similarly, Aylett [2] presents an example of applying the striving for applicability in the real world, as in robotic architectures, to virtual worlds.

Emotion processes in psychology. The building blocks chosen should allow assembly of simple models that are compatible with the rich descriptions of emotion processes in the psychological literature. Two specific accounts of appraisal theories of emotion [6] are considered here: Scherer's component process model [25] and Frijda's description of the laws of emotion [7,8] are both well suited for a process-oriented modelling approach. The following two aspects of these theories have a main impact on the choice of modelling primitives.

First, emotions are an inherently temporal phenomenon. They are events over time, vary over time, and include constituent processes at different time scales [8]. Descriptive accounts of emotion that disregard the temporal development of emotion episodes are of limited use in real-time environments. The chosen modelling primitives should support modelling the temporal characteristics of emotional mechanisms. Second, both theories assume that the normal operation of a (human) agent involves many parallel processes, mostly unsynchronised and not reflected in overt behaviour. This can be inferred from the descriptions of the internal changes making up emotion: Scherer characterises emotion as an episode of interrelated, synchronised changes in several organismic subsystems; Frijda [8] highlights the control precedence of the action readiness associated with an emotion, i.e. the tendency to override other activities. Multiple action readinesses can be aroused in response to concurrent formation of appraisal patterns and while only one may initially instigate overt action, others can surface later. Further, the primary effect of control precedence is counteracted by simultaneously active regulation processes. The emotion episode modelled in section 4 includes examples of such processes.

Tractability. The requirement of the model of emotion to run on mainstream hardware entails simplifications of the modelled phenomena and the use of standard engineering methods to create a modular and parsimonious architecture. These design properties are worthwhile modelling goals in themselves that do not necessarily need to correspond to features of the modelled system.

Explication of shortcuts. In addition to tractability concerns, modelling activities may introduce further simplifications. One of our aims is the clear delineation and characterisation of any such shortcuts deemed necessary. Two prominent examples unavoidable in current designs of broad virtual agents regard sensing and acting, and common-sense reasoning. Subsequent modelling efforts may refine the model by selectively reducing the amount of simplifications.

Sociality. Emotional phenomena combine aspects internal to the organism, such as the synchronisation of subsystems, with external aspects of social behaviour, including dispositions and roles [19]. As another consideration explicitly included from the start, the social aspect of emotion has no direct impact on our choice of building blocks, but it motivates starting points for models of specific emotional phenomena to be refined incrementally. Disgust was chosen as an example, as the notion encompasses both, an emotion with comparatively straightforward elicitors—core disgust—as well as a distinctly social phenomenon in the form of socio-moral disgust [24].

A further possible aim for designing a model of emotion could be correspondence with current knowledge about brain anatomy [9]. We currently exclude such considerations, to constrain the scope of our effort.

3   Building Blocks for Artificial Emotion

We use concurrent processes directly to model the activities within an agent, thereby avoiding the use of parameterised states to model effects that arise immediately from interactions of processes over time. The resource bounds of the modelled agent are represented explicitly by distinct resources that need to be acquired explicitly by processes for use.

3.1   Processes

A process models one concurrent strand of activity in the agent[2]. It can be active, i.e. allocated a "processing time" resource, or dormant. A change to the dormant state is triggered by waiting: for a specific resource; for communication from another process; or for the notification of a change in an observed process. A process can request control of resources. A process can start or stop another process, and transfer its processing time and other resources to it. Similarly, a (meta-level) process can act as a scheduler for other processes. Processes can actively observe and inspect the status of other processes, their communication patterns, their resource use, or they may request to be notified of such changes.

Building on these capabilities of processes, we can model what Frijda [8] calls competences: a behaviour system that includes sensitivities for triggering activation, and criteria for well-functioning used in system monitoring. Such competences in turn form the basis for on-line appraisal processes and major concerns of an agent.

3.2   Resources

A resource is an abstraction for the limited control an agent has over the part of the world that constitutes it. Processing time is an abstract resource that limits the number and the speed of concurrently running processes. In the context of a simulation on a serial computer, this translates to how frequently and then for how long a process is allowed to run. Communication channels are a specific form of resource that allow direct communication between processes. Further, communication can be used as a means for synchronisation to model interdependencies between processes. Scherer assumes that parallel appraisal processes usually complete in a specific sequence because of such interdependencies [25].

Resources at the boundary to the agent's environment group sensors and actuators, reflecting the fact that the agent is always interacting with the environment rather than receiving or sending [3]. These are subject to influences from both, the environment and the agent. Internal resources and processes are only indirectly affected by the environment through communication links (we thus exclude scenarios involving drug use and brain surgery, while conceptually internal effects of e.g. hormones may be modelled as processes). They can be shielded explicitly, i.e. decoupled, from the environment to form emulators [14] or prediction machines [18].

3.3   Configurations

Figure 1 shows a notation for processes, resources, and their interactions. Given a system configuration of dormant and active concurrent processes, a first issue regards the starting configuration. This question is obviously important for designing and running an artificial system. Translated to the context of adult humans, the question is equivalent to obtaining a snapshot of a mind at a specific moment. A starting point for our incremental modelling approach is to assume that there is at least one active process per resource on the boundary to the environment, that tries to identify changes (i.e., sensors are active by default).

---

[2] We use the computer science term 'processes' rather than 'threads', as usually threads indicate strands of control that share global data, while processes communicate by message passing only.

There also is one process for each sensitivity of the major concerns [8] of the agent, which in turn creates specific monitoring processes that operationalise the motivation to act on opportunities and threats.

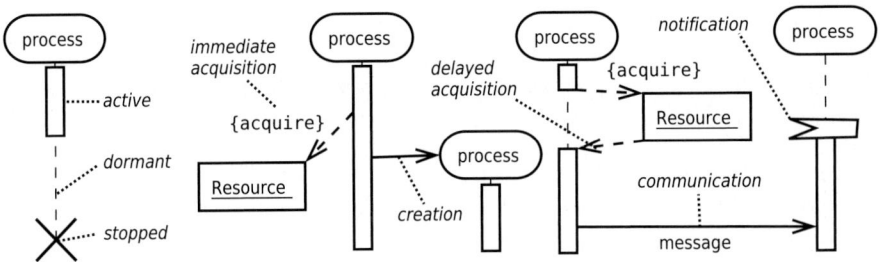

Fig. 1. Notation for some possible interactions of processes and resources, adapted from UML (time flows downwards, comments are indicated with dotted lines)

Based on these building blocks, the following architectural questions need to be answered for any specific scenario:

- What (types of) processes and resources are there, and how many instances of the different types exist? (e.g. regulation, monitors, schedulers)
- What processes run periodically and most frequently? Which processes compete on which resources? Which processes monitor what of other processes?

The current implementation uses cooperative microthreading, with complete control over scheduling and significantly less overhead than operating system threads or processes; the set of resources is static over the lifetime of an agent. The next section presents a first iteration for a specific scenario.

4 A Disgusting Example

As mentioned earlier, disgust was chosen as a first testing ground for the proposed modelling approach because this emotion word subsumes response dispositions aimed at protecting the body (core-disgust, [15]), and social and personal values (socio-moral disgust, [28]). Disgust is assumed to have evolved from a distaste response, but the current form of human disgust is largely social. It seems to require inculturation since it is not present in infants, and is a rather common topic of adolescent humour [24]. According to Frijda [7], the expression of disgust reduces sensory contact with distasteful substances in the mouth and tends toward expelling those substances (p.11). The associated action tendency is labelled "Rejecting (closing)", with the function of protection and the end state "Removal of object" (p.88). The appraisal pattern predicted by Scherer [25] involves low levels of familiarity, predictability, and need relevance; very low intrinsic pleasantness; medium urgency; and a very high outcome probability.

The actual example described below is a blend of core-disgust and the use of a disgust expression for social signalling. The short episode describes the interaction between two simulated agents and a single object in the environment: a mother, a child, and a pile of dog poop made of chocolate.

4.1   The Disgust Episode

We will describe a possible set of processes active in the mother during the following short scene:

> The child notices the dog poop and moves towards it. The mother notices that the child moves, that there is dog poop, and that the child is moving towards it. Finally, the mother moves towards the child to grab it and strongly expresses disgust even though in the meantime she has noticed the true nature of the "dog poop".

Figure 2 is a sequence diagram of the interactions between processes inside the "mother-agent" during this short episode[3].

1) Initially, there are several processes active in the mother-agent. One process, look-after-child, is responsible for satisfying the mother's concern for the well-being of the child. This process is active periodically to look for matches with its sensitivities, as are other concern-relevant processes: protect-child, teach-child, and a regulation process regulate-conflicts.
2) The process look-after-child acquires the resource Eyes, actively looks for the child, and detects that the child is moving[4], a novel and unexpected event. It spawns a process to interpret that movement.
3) Interpret-move uses the resource Eyes to find a target object in the direction of movement. It spawns a process to identify the object and another one to predict what the child will be doing.
4) As soon as identify-object has a first identification (*dog poop*) it starts an evaluation process. Similarly, the prediction process, after using a Child Predictor resource and the current result of the identify-object process, spawns a process to evaluate the predicted action.
5) The evaluation of the *dog poop* appraises it as unfamiliar and intrinsically unpleasant. The resulting relational action tendency (not shown in the diagram due to lack of space) triggers the process for expressing disgust and receding from the object as coping action. Each of these processes starts by acquiring the relevant resources, Face and Legs.
6) The evaluation of the predicted action (the child taking the *dog poop*) has identified a threat: possible harm for the child. The process protect-child,

---

[3] The example is constructed to illustrate the potential of modelling with concurrent processes. It is not directly based on examples from the psychological literature.

[4] Another possibility would be that some other process that uses the Eyes detects the movement. Look-after-child is then notified because it was monitoring any changes involving the "child object".

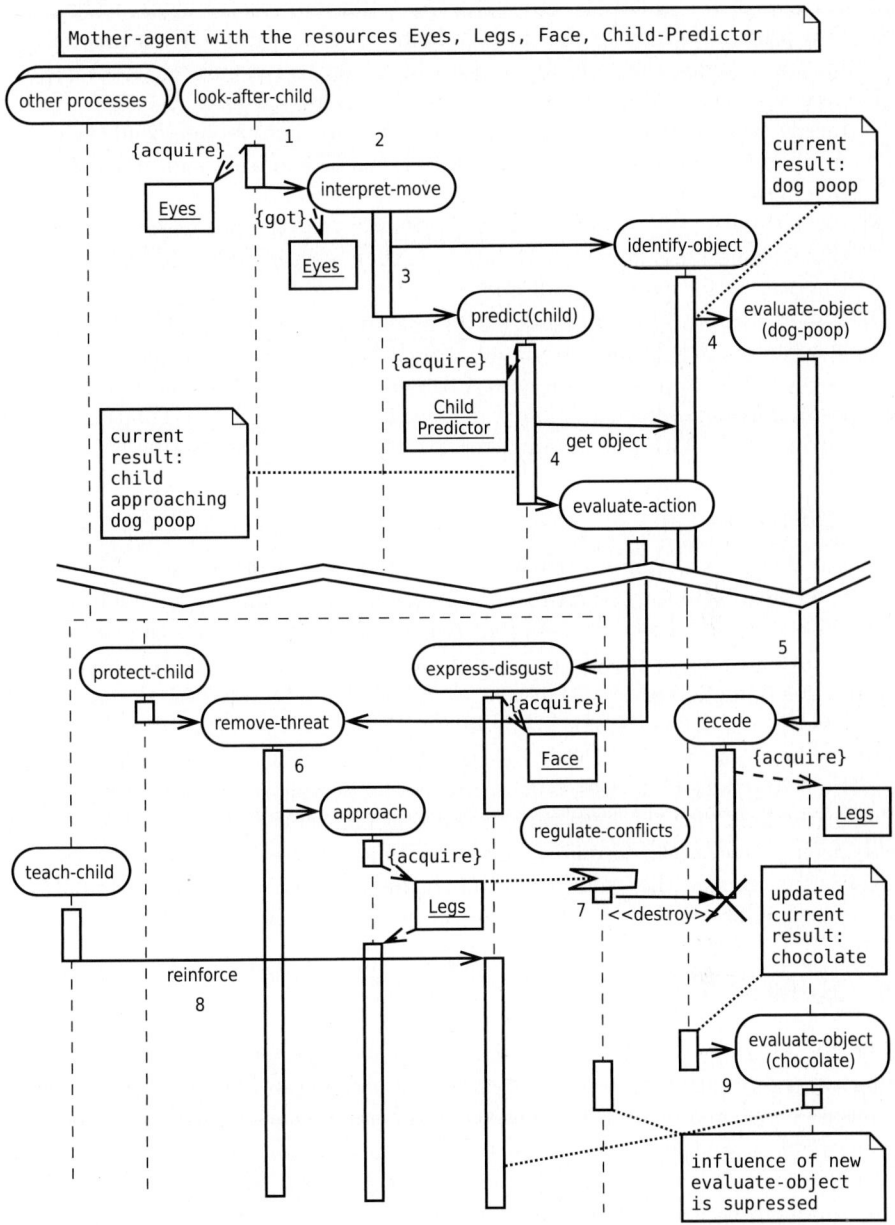

Fig. 2. Processes in the mother-agent during the disgust episode. See Fig.1 for the notation used. Action tendencies not shown due to lack of space, see main text.

because of its sensitivity for threat constellations, reacts by creating a new process to remove the threat which, in turn, instantiates a process for approaching the child (again part of an action readiness).

7) The approach process tries to acquire the Legs but fails, because the recede process controls this resource. The process regulate-conflicts is notified by the action monitoring provisions of approach and arbitrates by ending the process recede.

8) Concurrently, the process teach-child detects that the processes remove-threat and express-disgust are related via the object involved. It reinforces the process for expressing disgust.

9) Finally, the object identification process finds new evidence (the *dog poop* is actually made of *chocolate*) and restarts the evaluation process. Consequences this might normally have (overt signs of alleviation and humour, related internal process reconfiguration) are suppressed by regulation as incompatible with the ongoing, reinforced, expression of disgust.

4.2   Shortcuts

Several shortcuts have been taken in this process-based description of a disgust episode. Most notably, the intricacies of sensing and acting in the environment have been simplified to a process that employs a resource. Predicting actions of others and forming expectations by internal simulation has also been abstracted into a ready-made resource. Further, any knowledge required and used by the processes is not accounted for in the model. As an example, the identification of objects has to access some body of prior knowledge. This might be modelled as exclusive and specific to this type of process or as a shared (set of) resource(s). The same holds for the detection of the relation between threat, disgust, and *dog poop* based on the examination of (relations between) active processes. We expect that during the evolution of our framework and building of simulations of increasing detail shared knowledge will be introduced as resources.

5   Related Work

The APOC framework [27] is intended to provide a universal formalism for (primarily robotic) agent architectures, based on building blocks called components that are connected by four different types of communication links. A component consists of an update function that updates the internal state and continuously produces output (in discrete steps) based on previous state and inputs. Further, a component can control an external process, thereby encapsulating an asynchronous physical or computational activity. The premises of APOC are similar to those of our proposal, but the framework differs not only in the intended application area—robotics versus virtual environments—but also in conceptual focus. While our proposal focuses on the dynamic run-time properties of the simulated system, APOC is geared towards modelling data flow and, although dynamically self-modifying architectures are possible, APOC's formalism specifies a relatively static architectural layout for instantiated architectures.

In [30], Sloman argues again that what is generally called emotion needs to be defined more rigorously in terms of architectural components. Sloman's H-CogAff architecture was used to propose three different classes of emotion, based on the architectural layout of many concurrently active tasks and interactions between them. Our approach is similar in spirit, but complementary. By incrementally modelling specific emotional phenomena, building on psychological theories and their implied dynamic run-time requirements, we aim to inform the architectural requirements for human-level competencies. Another high-level architectural account of the human mind very similar to H-CogAff has been proposed by Minsky [18]. The basic notion of Minsky's work is that the mind consists of many resources ("agents" in earlier publications) that can be activated or suppressed. The distinctive feature of the human mind is its "resourcefulness", i.e. the ability to selectively activate and suppress sets of resources suitable for a situation while dynamically switching between them and recognising opportunities and needs for switching (even during the same situation). EM-ONE [29] is an implementation by Push Singh based on Minsky's theory that focuses on common-sense thinking in a physical scenario with two agents. The present proposal rather tries to model emotional phenomena while clearly delineating that certain capabilities, such as common-sense thinking, have to be simplified.

EMA [12] is a computational model of appraisal that implements checks posited by appraisal theories based on a symbolic representation of the agent's interpretation of its relationship to the environment. In [17], the authors apply EMA to a relatively fast-paced emotional episode (captured on video) to model the dynamics of the situation. They argue that each appraisal check is always a fast and parallel process, while other cognitive and perceptual processes alter the central subjective interpretation at different speeds. Our approach aims to avoid fixed appraisal processes, but rather models appraisals and related processes as ongoing activities that can start and be refined before, while, and after symbolic representations are formed or altered (possibly by other appraisal processes).

6   Conclusion and Future Work

We have presented an incremental approach to modelling emotional episodes based on concurrent processes. The concept of a resource is used to explicitly model boundedness. These building blocks are motivated by the needs of modelling a physical system, by the characterisation of emotion by psychological theories, and by practical implementation concerns. A major goal of the work is to make explicit shortcuts necessary to arrive at an executable model of emotion in an interesting virtual scenario. Implementation efforts are currently underway based on a game-like scenario allowing for human interaction with a virtual environment inhabited by agents based on our affective architecture building on earlier work [21,22]. Therein, possibilities to operationalise the theoretical concept of relational action tendencies will be identified and evaluated. Future work includes the incremental addition of models suitable for further emotional episodes, building architectural abstractions as the need arises. To verify consistency of the models, they will be integrated in the same game-like scenario. Further work will investigate modelling of effects in social interactions as process and resource dependencies across agents.

Acknowledgements. The Austrian Research Institute for AI is supported by the Austrian Federal Ministries for Science and Research and for Transport, Innovation and Technology. This research is funded by the EU FP6 Network of Excellence HUMAINE (Contract 507422) with support from the Austrian Funds for Research and Technology Promotion for Industry (FFF 808818/2970 KA/SA). This publication reflects only the authors' views. The EU is not liable for any use that may be made of the information contained herein.

References

1. Arzi-Gonczarowski, Z.: From Embodiments Back to their Models: An Affective Abstraction. The Intersection of Cognitive Science and Robotics: From Interfaces to Intelligence, Papers from the 2004 AAAI Fall Symposium, 76–81 (2004)
2. Aylett, R.: Behavioural Virtual Agents. In: Wooldridge, M.J., Veloso, M. (eds.) Artificial Intelligence Today. LNCS (LNAI), vol. 1600, pp. 1–12. Springer, Heidelberg (1999)
3. Bickhard, M.H.: Motivation and Emotion: An Interactive Process Model. Department of Philosophy, Lehigh University, Bethlehem PA USA [2007-04-19] (1999), http://www.lehigh.edu/~mhb0/motemotion.html
4. Chrisley, R., Ziemke, T.: Embodiment. In: Nadel, L. (ed.) Encyclopedia of Cognitive Science, pp. 1102–1108. Nature Publishing Group, Macmillan, London (2003)
5. Cleeremans, A., French, R.M.: From Chicken Squawking To Cognition: Levels of Description and the Computational Approach in Psychology. Psychologica Belgica 36(1-2), 5–29 (1996)
6. Ellsworth, P.C., Scherer, K.R.: Appraisal Processes in Emotion. In: Davidson, R.J., Scherer, K.R., Goldsmith, H.H. (eds.) Handbook of Affective Sciences, pp. 572–595. Oxford University Press, Oxford/New York (2003)
7. Frijda, N.H.: The Emotions. Cambridge University Press, Editions de la Maison des Sciences de l'Homme, Paris (1986)
8. Frijda, N.H.: The Laws of Emotion. Lawrence Erlbaum Associates, Mahwah NJ USA/London UK EU (2007)
9. Granger, R.: Engines of the Brain: The Computational Instruction Set of Human Cognition. In: Cassimatis, N., et al. (eds.) Achieving Human-Level Intelligence through Integrated Systems and Research, AI Magazine 27(2), 15–32 (2006)
10. Gratch, J., Marsella, S., Mao, W.: Towards a Validated Model of "Emotional Intelligence". In: Proceedings of the Twenty-First National Conference on Artificial Intelligence, pp. 1613–1616. AAAI Press, Menlo Park CA USA (2006)
11. Gratch, J., Marsella, S., Petta, P. (eds.) Agent Construction and Emotion: Modelling the Cognitive Antecedents and Consequences of Emotion. In: Trappl R. (ed.): Cybernetics and Systems 2006. Austrian Soc. for Cybernetic Studies, Vienna (2006)
12. Gratch, J., Marsella, S.: A Domain-independent Framework for Modeling Emotion. Cognitive Systems Research 5(4), 269–306 (2004)
13. Gratch, J., Marsella, S.: The Architectural Role of Emotion in Cognitive Systems. In: Gray, W.D. (ed.) Integrated Models of Cognitive Systems, pp. 230–242. Oxford University Press, New York (2007)

14. Grush, R.: The emulation theory of representation: Motor control, imagery, and perception. Behavioral and Brain Sciences 27(3), 377–396 (2004)
15. Lawrence, A.D., Calder, A.J.: Homologizing Human Emotions. In: Evans, D., Cruse, P. (eds.) Emotions, Evolution and Rationality, pp. 15–50. Oxford University Press, Oxford (2004)
16. Marinier, R.P., Laird, J.E.: A Cognitive Architecture Theory of Comprehension and Appraisal. In: [11], pp. 589–594 (2006)
17. Marsella, S., Gratch, J.: EMA: A Computational Model of Appraisal Dynamics. In: [11], pp. 601–606 (2006)
18. Minsky, M.: The Emotion Machine: Commonsense Thinking, Artificial Intelligence, and the Future of the Human Mind. Simon & Schuster, New York (2006)
19. Parkinson B.: Putting Appraisal in Context. In: [26], pp. 173–186 (2001)
20. Petta, P.: The Role of Emotions in a Tractable Architecture for Situated Cognizers. In: Trappl, R. (ed.) Emotions in Humans and Artifacts, pp. 251–288. MIT Press, Cambridge, MA, USA/ London, UK, EU (2003)
21. Rank, S.: Toward Reusable Roleplayers Using an Appraisal-based Architecture. Payr, S. (ed.) Educational Agents and (e-)Learning, Applied Artificial Intelligence 19(3-4), 313–340 (2005)
22. Rank, S., Petta, P.: Appraisal for a Character-based Story-World. In: Panayiotopoulos, T., et al. (eds.) Intelligent Virtual Agents. 5th International Working Conference, Kos Greece EU, pp. 495–496. Springer, Berlin (2005)
23. Rank, S., Petta, P.: Comparability is Key to Assess Affective Architectures. In: [11], 643–648 (2006)
24. Rozin, P., Haidt, J., McCauley, C.R.: Disgust. In: Lewis, M., Haviland, J.M. (eds.) Handbook of Emotions, 2nd edn., pp. 637–653. Guilford Press, New York (2000)
25. Scherer, K.R.: Appraisal considered as a process of multilevel sequential checking. In: [26], 92–120 (2001)
26. Scherer, K.R., Schorr, A., Johnstone, T. (eds.): Appraisal Processes in Emotion: Theory, Methods, Research. Oxford University Press, Oxford/New York (2001)
27. Scheutz, M., Andronache, V.: The APOC Framework for the Comparison of Agent Architectures. In: Jones, R.M (ed.) Intelligent Agent Architectures: Combining the Strengths of Software Engineering and Cognitive Systems: Papers from the 2004 AAAI Workshop, pp. 66–73. AAAI Press, Menlo Park CA USA (2004)
28. Simpson, J., Carter, S., Anthony, S.H., Overton, P.G.: Is Disgust a Homogeneous Emotion? Motivation and Emotion 30(1), 31–41 (2006)
29. Singh, P.: EM-ONE: An Architecture for Reflective Commonsense Thinking. Department of Electrical Engineering and Computer Science, Massachusetts Institute of Technology, Cambridge MA USA, PhD Thesis (2005)
30. Sloman, A.: What Are Emotion Theories About? In: Hudlicka, E., Cañamero, L. (eds.) Architectures for Modeling Emotion: Cross-Disciplinary Foundations, Papers from the 2004 AAAI Spring Symposium, March 22-24, pp. 128–134. AAAI Press, Menlo Park CA USA (2004)

The Benefits of Surprise in Dynamic Environments: From Theory to Practice[⋆]

Emiliano Lorini[1,2] and Michele Piunti[1,3]

[1] ISTC - CNR, Rome, Italy
[2] IRIT, Toulouse, France
[3] Università degli studi di Bologna - DEIS, Bologna, Italy
{emiliano.lorini,michele.piunti}@istc.cnr.it

Abstract. Artificial agents engaged in real world applications require accurate resource allocation strategies. For instance, open systems may require artificial agents with the capability to filter out all information which are irrelevant with respect to the actual intentions and goals. In this work we develop a model of surprise-driven belief update. We formally define a strategy for epistemic reasoning of a BDI-inspired agent, where surprise is the causal precursor of a belief update process. According to this strategy, an agent should update his beliefs only with inputs which are surprising and relevant with respect to his current intentions. We also compare in practice the performances of agents using a surprise-driven strategy of belief update and agents using traditional reasoning processes.

> *"A wealth of information creates a poverty of attention,*
> *and a need to allocate that attention efficiently"*
> [H. A. Simon talks at Johns Hopkins & CIOS Conf. in Tokyo, Fall 1969].

1   Introduction

Realistic cognitive agents are by definition resource-bounded [1], hence they should not waste time and energy in reasoning out and reconsider their knowledge on the basis of every piece of information they get. They need some filter mechanism which is responsible: 1) for signaling the inconsistency between beliefs and an incoming input which is relevant with respect to the current task; 2) for the revision of beliefs and expectations on the basis of the incoming relevant information. Our claim is that one of the main functions of surprise in cognitive agents is exactly this. In this work we will develop a computational model of a cognitive agent where a surprise-based filter of belief change is implemented. The computational model we will present consists in the operationalization of two general hypothesis. On one hand, we suppose that at each moment an agent is focused and allocates his attention on a particular task that he is trying to solve and on a certain number of intentions which represent the pragmatic solutions that the agent has selected in order to accomplish the task [2]. The agent ignores all incoming inputs which are not relevant with respect to the current task on which he is focused

---

[⋆] This research is supported by the European Project MindRACES (IST-511931).

A. Paiva, R. Prada, and R.W. Picard (Eds.): ACII 2007, LNCS 4738, pp. 362–373, 2007.

and only considers those information which are relevant. On the other hand, we suppose that if a relevant input turns out to be incompatible with respect to the pre-existent beliefs of the agent, surprise arises. The surprise reaction is a causal precursor of a belief update process. In fact, a surprise with a certain intensity relative to the incoming relevant input "signals" to the agent that things are not going as expected and that beliefs must be reconsidered. Other authors [3,4] have attributed to surprise a precise and crucial functional role in mind by stressing that it is perhaps the most important causal precursor of a process of belief change.[1] The main objective of this paper is to clarify such a functional role of surprise in mind by integrating a surprise-based mechanism of belief update into a $belief - desire - intention$ (BDI) computational model [7,8]. The BDI is a well-established framework which is aimed at describing an agent's mental process of deciding moment by moment on the basis of current beliefs, which action to perform in order to achieve some goals.[2] The computational model of surprise-based belief change presented in this paper has also the ambition to bridge the existing gap between formal and computational models of belief change and psychological models of belief dynamics. Indeed, most of the authors in the tradition of belief change theory have been mainly interested in finding rationality principles and postulates driving belief change (this is for instance the main purpose of the classical AGM theory [10]) without investigating the causal precursors of this kind of process (they have implicitly assumed that when an agent perceives some fact such a perception is always a precursor of a belief change).

The paper is organized as follows. In section 2 we provide the abstract model of a BDI cognitive agent by formalizing his informational attitudes (volatile beliefs and expectations which change over time and the stable knowledge about the dependencies of objects in the environment) and motivational attitudes (intentions and desires). In section 3 we apply the abstract model of a BDI cognitive agent to a specific foraging scenario. In section 4 the cognitive architectures of two general typologies of BDI agents are designed. The first typology corresponds to a standard BDI agent [7,8]. The second typology corresponds to a BDI agent endowed with a surprise-based filter of belief update (we call it $BDIS$ agent). In section 5 we report the results of some simulative studies in the scenario described in section 3. We compare the performances of the BDI agent and $BDIS$ agent in different conditions of environmental dynamism.

2   The Abstract Model of an Agent's Mental State

The abstract model of an agent's mental state is made of a set of $n \leq 1$ random variables **VAR** $= \{X_1, ..., X_n\}$. We suppose that each random variable $X_i \in$ **VAR** takes values from the set $Val_{X_i} = \{x_1, ..., x_r\}$, with $r > 1$. For each set Val_{X_i} we define the corresponding set $Inst_{X_i} = \{(X_i = x_1), ..., (X_i = x_r)\}$ of all possible instantiations

---

[1] Other functional roles have been attributed to surprise. For instance, some authors conceive surprise as a shortcut for attention [5]. The felt feedback of surprise is responsible for redirecting attention towards the unexpected and surprising stimuli, and for concentrating cognitive resources on them. According to other authors surprise is responsible for a shift from an automatic level of performance to a deliberate level [6].

[2] The idea to introduce emotions in a BDI system is not new. See for example [9].

of random variable X_i. Besides, we write $Inst = \bigcup_{X_i \in \mathbf{VAR}} Inst_{X_i}$ to denote the set of all possible instantiations of all random variables.

We have a set $\Gamma \subseteq Inst$ of perceived data which fixes the value of certain variables that an agent perceives at a certain moment. For example, $\Gamma = \{(X_i = x_i)\}$ means "an agent sees that the observable variable X_i has value x_i". We denote with $\Gamma_{Var} = \{X_i \in \mathbf{VAR} | \exists x_i \ s.t. (X_i = x_i) \in \Gamma\}$ the subset of $\mathbf{VAR}$ which includes the variables that an agent observes at a certain moment, that is, all those variables which have (at least) one instantiation in Γ. Here we suppose that for all $X_i \in \Gamma_{Var}, Inst_{X_i} \cap \Gamma$ is a singleton, that is, we suppose that an agent cannot perceive two different instantiations of the same variable. We use the notation $\Gamma(X_i)$ to denote that singleton, that is, for any $X_i \in \Gamma_{Var}, Inst_{X_i} \cap \Gamma = \Gamma(X_i)$.

We also use a simple bayesian network K which represents the joint probability distribution over the set of random variables $\mathbf{VAR}$. A bayesian network is a directed acyclic graph (DAG) whose nodes are labeled by the random variables in $\mathbf{VAR}$ and the edges represents the causal influence between the random variables in $\mathbf{VAR}$. Given an arbitrary random variable X (i.e. an arbitrary node) in the bayesian network K we denote with $anc(X)$ the ancestors of X. Formally, Z is an ancestor of X in the bayesian network K if there is a directed path from Z to X in K. Moreover, given an arbitrary random variable X in the bayesian network K, we denote with $par(X)$ the parents of X in the bayesian network. Formally, Z is a parent of X in the bayesian network K if Z is an ancestor of X in K which is directly connected to Z. Finally, we associate to each random variable X in K a conditional probability distribution $P(X | par(X))$, where each conditional probability distribution can be represented in terms of a conditional probability table. The bayesian network K encodes the agent's causal knowledge of the environment. Here we suppose that this part of the agent's knowledge is stable and can not be reconsidered.

In our general model, we also encodes the agent's beliefs and expectations that can change over time, i.e. the agent's volatile expectations and beliefs [11]. Given a random variable $X_i \in \mathbf{VAR}$, we denote with $\sum_{X_i}$ the set of all possible probability distributions over the random variable X_i. Then, we denote with $\prod_{X_i \in \mathbf{VAR}} \sum_{X_i}$ the set of all possible combinations of probability distributions over the random variables in $\mathbf{VAR}$. Besides, we denote with $\sigma, \sigma', ... \in \prod_{X_i \in \mathbf{VAR}} \sum_{X_i}$ specific combinations $\{\sigma_1, ..., \sigma_n\}, \{\sigma'_1, ..., \sigma'_n\}, ...$ of probability distributions over each random variables in $\mathbf{VAR}$. Given a certain σ, every $\sigma_i \in \sigma$ corresponds to a set $\sigma_i = \{[(X_i = x_1) = a_1], ..., [(X_i = x_r) = a_r]\}$ of probability assignments $a_1, ..., a_r \in [0, 1]$ to each possible instantiations of the variable X_i. Now, we denote with $B = \bigcup_{\sigma_i \in \sigma} \sigma_i, B' = \bigcup_{\sigma'_i \in \sigma'} \sigma'_i, ...$ specific configurations of beliefs of the agent, and with $BEL = \{\bigcup_{\sigma_i \in \sigma} \sigma_i | \sigma \in \prod_{X_i \in \mathbf{VAR}} \sum_{X_i}\}$ the set of all possible configurations of beliefs of the agent. Given a specific configuration of beliefs $B = \bigcup_{\sigma_i \in \sigma} \sigma_i$, we write $B(X_i = x_j) = a_j$ if and only if $[(X_i = x_j) = a_j] \in \sigma_i$. Thus, $B(X_i = x_j) = 0.4$ means that given the configuration of beliefs B the agent assigns probability 0.4 to the fact that variable X_i takes value x_j. We denote with $B(X_i = x_j)$ the number $a_j \in [0, 1]$ such that $B(X_i = x_j) = a_j$.

We also model motivational attitudes by denoting with INT the set of potential intentions of an agent. Here we suppose that every instantiation of a variable in $\mathbf{VAR}$ is a potential intention of the agent, that is, we suppose that $INT = Inst$. Thus every instantiation of a variable corresponds to a result that the agent can intend to achieve. We denote with $I, I', ... \in 2^{INT}$ specific sets of intentions of the agent. Given a specific set I of intentions of the agent, we denote with $I_{Var} = \{X_i \in \textbf{VAR} | \exists x_i \ s.t. (X_i = x_i) \in I\}$ the subset of **VAR** which includes all intended variables, that is, all those variables which have (at least) one instantiation in I. As for intentions, we specify a set $DES = Inst$ of potential desires. We denote with $D, D', ... \in 2^{DES}$ specific sets of desires of the agent.

We specify a set MER of means-end rules and a set PR of planning rules. A means-end rule in MER is a desire-generation rule in the style of [12] of the form: $\psi_1, ..., \psi_s | \lambda_1, ..., \lambda_j \implies \varphi_1, ..., \varphi_t$. Such a rule is responsible for generating t desires $\varphi_1, ..., \varphi_t$ when the agent has s beliefs $\psi_1, ..., \psi_s$ and j intentions $\lambda_1, ..., \lambda_j$. The set MER of means-end rules corresponds to the function $options : BEL \times 2^{INT} \mapsto 2^{DES}$. This function returns a specific set D of desires, given a specific configuration B of beliefs and a specific set I of intentions. A planning rule in PR is a plan-generation rule of the form: $\psi_1, ..., \psi_s | \lambda_1, ..., \lambda_j \implies \varphi_1, ..., \varphi_t$. Such a rule is responsible for generating t plans $\varphi_1, ..., \varphi_t \in \Pi$, where Π is the repertoire of actions of our agent, when the agent has s beliefs $\psi_1, ..., \psi_s$ and j intentions $\lambda_1, ..., \lambda_j$. The set PR of planning rules corresponds to a function: $plan : BEL \times 2^{INT} \mapsto 2^{\Pi}$. This function returns a set π of plans, given a specific set B of beliefs and specific set I of intentions.

To summarize, a mental state of an agent is defined in our abstract model as a tuple $(B, D, I, K, MER, PR, \Pi)$, where each element in the tuple is defined as before.

3   From the Abstract Model to the Experimental Scenario

Our experimental scenario is represented by the 8×8 grid in Fig. 1a. An agent moves in the grid being driven by the goal of finding fruits of a certain color, according to the ongoing season. Indeed, agents look for fruits of different colors in different seasons of the year. We suppose that there are three different seasons and related colors of fruits and trees: the red season, the blue season and the green season. Agents are intrinsically motivated to look for and to eat red fruits during the red season, blue fruits during the blue season and green fruits during the green season. Environmental dynamics are characterized by periodic season cycles: after s_t rounds the season changes on the basis of a periodic function and the intrinsic motivation of an agent changes accordingly. Fruits of any color occupy cells (i, j) (with $1 \leq i \leq 16$ and $1 \leq j \leq 4$), whilst trees of any color occupy macro areas i of size 2×2 (with $1 \leq i \leq 16$) in the grid depicted in Fig. 1a. We suppose that at each moment for every color there is exactly one fruit and tree of that color in the grid. We suppose an objective dependence between trees and fruits in the grid. Indeed, a fruit of a certain color is a sign of the presence of a fruit of the same color in the immediate neighborhood. Agents exploit these signs during their search of fruits. We suppose that a tree of any color is randomly placed in a macro area i of size 2×2. Given a tree of a certain color in a macro area i of size 2×2, a fruit of the same color is randomly placed by the environment simulator in one of the four cells inside the macro area i. For example, if a red tree is in the macro area 1 of the grid then for each cell $(1, 1)$, $(1, 2)$, $(1, 3)$ and $(1, 4)$ there is 0.25 of probability that a red fruit is located in that cell. Fruits and trees change periodically their positions in the grid. More

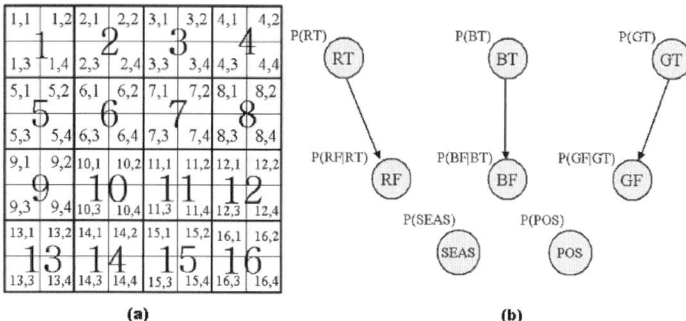

Fig. 1. (a) The Environment grid; (b) The Bayesian Network

precisely, the dynamism factor δ indicates how many seasons have to pass before a tree location changes. We impose constraints on the perceptual capabilities of agents and the related set Γ of perceived data by supposing that an agent sees only those fruits which are in the cells belonging to the same macro-area in which the agent is. For example, if the agent is in cell $(6, 1)$, he only see those fruits which are in the cells belonging to the macro area 6. Moreover we suppose that an agent sees only those trees which are situated in the same macro-area in which the agent is or in the four neighbouring macro areas on the left, right, up or down. For example, if the agent is in cell $(6, 1)$, he only see those trees which are in macro areas $2, 5, 7, 10$.

The knowledge of our agents is encoded by means of 8 random variables **VAR** $=$ $\{SEASON, POS, RF, BF, GF, RT, BT, GT\}$. RF, BF, GF take values from the sets $Val_{RF} = Val_{BF} = Val_{BF} = \{(i, j)|1 \leq i \leq 16, 1 \leq j \leq 4\}$, whilst RT, BT, GT take values from the set $Val_{RT} = Val_{BT} = Val_{BT} = \{i|1 \leq i \leq 16\}$. Finally, $Val_{SEAS} = \{red, blue, green\}$ and $Val_{POS} = \{(i, j)|1 \leq i \leq 16, 1 \leq j \leq 4\}$. Variables RF, BF, GF specify respectively the position of a red/blue/green fruit in the grid depicted in Fig. 1a. Variables RT, BT, GT specify respectively the position of a red/blue/green tree in the grid. For example, $RT = 13$ means "there is a red tree in the macro area 13". Variable $SEAS$ specifies the current season. For example, $SEASON = blue$ means "it is time to look for blue fruits!". Finally, Variable POS specifies the position of the agent in the grid. We suppose that the variables in **VAR** are organized in the bayesian network K as follows: $par(POS) = \{\emptyset\}$, $par(SEAS) = \{\emptyset\}$, $par(RT) = \{\emptyset\}$, $par(BT) = \{\emptyset\}$, $par(GT) = \{\emptyset\}$, $par(RF) = \{RT\}$, $par(BF) = \{BT\}$, $par(GF) = \{GT\}$. This leads to the bayesian network K depicted in Fig. 1b. Since there are 64 possible positions of a fruit in the grid and 16 possible positions of a tree in the grid, each conditional probability table associated with $P(RF|RT)$, $P(BF|BT)$ and $P(GF|GT)$ has $64 \times 16 = 1024$ entries. We suppose that the knowledge of an agent about the dependencies between trees and fruits perfectly maps the objective dependencies between trees and fruits. Hence, we only specify for each tree of a certain color (RT, BT or GT) and arbitrary macro area $i \in \{1, ..., 16\}$ in the grid in which a tree can appear, the 4 conditional probabilities that a fruit of the same color appears in one cell in that macro area. We suppose for each of them the same value 0.25. All other conditional probabilities have value 0, that is, given a tree of

certain color which appears in an arbitrary macro area $i \in \{1, ..., 16\}$, the probability that there is a fruit of the same color outside that macro area is zero. More precisely, we have that:

for all $1 \leq i \leq 16$ $P(RF = (i,1)|RT = i) = P(RF = (i,2)|RT = i) = P(RF = (i,3)|RT = i) = P(RF = (i,4)|RT = i) = 0.25$;
for all $1 \leq i,j \leq 16$ if $j \neq i$ then $P(RF = (j,1)|RT = i) = P(RF = (j,2)|RT = i) = P(RF = (j,3)|RT = i) = P(RF = (j,4)|RT = i) = 0$.

Means-end rules in MER are exploited by agents for solving the general task of finding a fruit of a certain color in the grid. Agents are endowed with three general classes of means-end rules. The first class includes means-end rules of the following form. For $i \in Val_{SEAS}$: $[(SEAS = i) = 1] \Longrightarrow SEAS = i$.

Such means-end rules are responsible for changing the intrinsic motivation of an agent, according to the season change, that is: if an agent is certain that it is time to look for fruits of kind i (red, blue or green), then he should form the desire to look for fruits of kind i.[3] The second class includes means-end rules of the following form. For

$1 \leq i \leq 16$: $[(RT = i) = 1]\,|SEAS = red \Longrightarrow RT = i$,
$[(BT = i) = 1]\,|SEAS = blue \Longrightarrow BT = i$,
$[(RT = i) = 1]\,|SEAS = green \Longrightarrow GT = i$.

Such means-end rules are responsible for orienting the search of an agent towards a certain macro area, according to the current season (i.e. an intention to find fruits of a certain color) and his beliefs about the position of trees in the grid. For example, if an agent is certain that there is a red tree in the macro area 3 of the grid (i.e. $[(RT = 3) = 1]$) and intends to find a red fruit (i.e. $SEAS = red$), then he should form the desire to reach that position of a red tree (i.e. $RT = 3$). Finally, agents are endowed with means-end rules of the following form. For $1 \leq i \leq 16$ and $1 \leq j \leq 4$:

$[(RF = (i,j)) = 1]\,|SEAS = red \Longrightarrow RF = (i,j)$,
$[(BF = (i,j)) = 1]\,|SEAS = blue \Longrightarrow BF = (i,j)$,
$[(RF = (i,j)) = 1]\,|SEAS = green \Longrightarrow GF = (i,j)$.

Such means-end rules are responsible for orienting the search of an agent towards a certain cell, according to the current season (i.e. an intention to find fruits of a certain color) and his beliefs about the position of fruits in the grid. For example, if an agent intends to find a blue fruit (i.e. $SEAS = blue$) and he is certain that there is a blue fruit in cell $(10,1)$ of the grid (i.e. $[(BF = 10,1) = 1]$), then he should form the desire to move towards that position of the blue fruit (i.e. $BF = (10,1)$). Our agents have a reduced repertoire of actions $\Pi = \{MoveDown, MoveUp, MoveLeft, MoveRight\}$. Indeed, at each round they can only move from one cell to the next one. Planning rules encode approaching policies which depend on the agent's current intentions and his actual position in the grid. Agents have both planning rules for reaching macro areas in the grid (given their current positions) and planning rules for reaching cells in the

---

[3] In our experimental setting agents are always notified of the fact the season has changed. Therefore, at the beginning of a new season, an agent is certain that it is time to look for fruits of a different color and forms the desire to look for fruits of a different color.

grid (given their current positions). The latter planning rules are exploited for the local search of a fruit of a certain color inside a macro area. Examples of these planning rules are the following:

$$[(POS = (15,1)) = 1] | RT = 3 \Longrightarrow MoveUp,$$
$$[(POS = (10,2)) = 1] | RF = 10,4 \Longrightarrow MoveDown.$$

For instance, according to first planning rule, if an agent intends to reach position 3 of a red tree and is certain to be in cell $(15,1)$ then he should form the plan to move up.[4]

4   Surprise-Based Filter of Belief Update

Our general aim in this section is to model two different typologies of agents. The first type of agent corresponds to a standard BDI agent whose control loop is described in the right column of Table 1. The second type of agent, whose control loop is described in the left column of Table 1, is a BDI agent endowed with a surprise-based filter of belief update. We call this second type of agent $BDIS$ agent. The formal description of the control loop of the standard BDI agent is similar to [7,8]. In lines 1-2 the beliefs and intentions of the agent are initialized. The main control loop is in lines 3-10. In lines 4-5 the agent perceives some new facts Γ and updates his beliefs according to a function bu. In line 6 the agent generates new desires by exploiting his means-end rules. In line 7 he deliberates over the new generated desires and his current intentions according to the function $filter$.[5] Finally, in lines 8-9 the agent generates a plan for achieving his

Table 1. The two typologies of agents

$\mathcal{BDIS}$ agent control loop	$\mathcal{BDI}$ agent control loop
1. $B := B_0$;	1. $B := B_0$;
2. $I := I_0$;	2. $I := I_0$;
3. while (true) do	3. while (true) do
4. get new percept Γ;	4. get new percept Γ;
5. if $\mathbf{S}(I, \Gamma, B) > \Delta$ then	5. $B := bu(\Gamma, B)$;
6. $B := bu^*(\Gamma, B, I)$;	6. $D := options(B, I)$;
7. end-if	7. $I := filter(B, D, I)$;
8. $D := options(B, I)$;	8. $\pi := plan(B, I)$;
9. $I := filter(B, D, I)$;	9. $execute(\pi)$;
10. $\pi := plan(B, I)$;	10. end-while
11. $execute(\pi)$;	
12. end-while	

---

[4] In our experimental setting agents have always access to their current position in the grid.

[5] Space restrictions prevent a formal description of the function $filter$ here (see [7] for a detailed analysis). Let us only note that this function is responsible for updating the agent's intentions with his previous intentions and current beliefs and desires (i.e. $filter : BEL \times 2^{INT} \times 2^{DES} \mapsto 2^{INT}$).

intentions by exploiting his planning rules and he executes an action of the current plan. The main difference between the standard BDI agent and the $BDIS$ agent is the belief update part in the control loop. We suppose that a process of belief update is triggered in the $BDIS$ agent only if the agent perceives a fact and evaluates this as incompatible with respect to the knowledge he has about the things he intends to achieve (line 5 in the control loop of the $BDIS$ agent). In this sense, the $BDIS$ is endowed with a cognitive mechanism of surprise-based belief change. In fact, this mechanism filters out all perceived facts that are irrelevant with respect to the current intentions. Thus, the $BDIS$ agent only updates his beliefs by inputs which are surprising and relevant with respect to his current intentions. Differently, at each round the standard BDI agent updates his beliefs indiscriminately: for any fact he perceives, he updates his beliefs whether the perceived fact is relevant with respect to his intentions or not. In order to model the triggering role of surprise in the $BDIS$ agent, we specify a local surprise function noted by $s(Y = y, \Gamma, B)$. Suppose that $(Y = y) \in I$ then:

$$s(Y=y,\Gamma,B)=\begin{cases} 1 - B(\Gamma(Y)) \\ Condition\ A: [if\ Y \in \Gamma_{Var}] \\ \\ |B(Y=y) - P(Y = y|\{X_i = x_i|X_i \in par(Y), X_i = x_i \in \Gamma\})| \\ Condition\ B: [if\ par(Y) \subseteq \Gamma_{Var}\ and\ Y \notin \Gamma_{Var}] \\ \\ 0 \\ Condition\ C: [if\ par(Y) \not\subseteq \Gamma_{Var}\ and\ Y \notin \Gamma_{Var}] \end{cases}$$

$$(1)$$

According to this function, the degree of local surprise due to the percept Γ and intended fact $Y = y \in I$ is: a) equal to the degree of unexpectedness of the percept Γ, when the intended variable Y is also a perceived variable in Γ_{Var} (i.e. there exists an instantiation of Y which is an element of Γ);[6] b) equal to the degree of discrepancy between the intended fact $Y = y$ and the percept Γ, defined by the absolute value of the difference between the probability assigned to $Y = y$ (i.e. $B(Y = y)$) and the conditional probability that $Y = y$ is true given that the perceived instantiations of the parents of Y are true (i.e. $P(Y = y|\{X_i = x_i|X_i \in par(Y), X_i = x_i \in \Gamma\})$), when the intended fact $Y = y$ is not an instantiation of a perceived variable in Γ_{Var} and the parents of Y in the bayesian network K are perceived variables in Γ_{Var};[7] c) 0, when the intended fact $Y = y$ is not an instantiation of a perceived variable in Γ_{Var} and not all Y's parents in the bayesian network K are perceived variables in Γ_{Var}. This third condition corresponds to the irrelevance of the incoming input Γ with respect to the agent's intention $Y = y$. Under this third condition, the agent simply ignores the input, hence he is not surprised by what he perceives.

We define a global surprise function $S(I, \Gamma, B)$ which returns the maximum value of local surprise for each intended fact $Y = y \in I$.

$$S(I, \Gamma, B) = \max_{Y=y\in I} s(Y = y, \Gamma, B) \qquad (2)$$

---

[6] According to this function, the degree of unexpectedness of the percept Γ is inversely proportional to the probability assigned by the agent to the perceived instantiation of the intended variable Y, i.e. $B(\Gamma(Y))$. This is similar to the notion of unexpectedness studied in [13].

[7] This corresponds to a sort of surprise based on an inferential process.

This function is used in the control loop of the $BDIS$ agent: if the new percept Γ is responsible for generating a degree of global surprise higher than Δ (with $\Delta \in [0, 1]$) then a process of belief update is triggered and the $BDIS$ agent adjusts his beliefs with the perceived data Γ according to a function bu^*. The belief update function bu^* of the $BDIS$ agent takes in input the set of intentions I, the belief configuration B and the percept Γ and returns an update belief configuration B', that is $bu^* : 2^{Inst} \times BEL \times 2^{INT} \mapsto BEL$. More precisely, suppose that $bu^*(\Gamma, B, I) = B'$ then for all $Y \in \mathbf{VAR}$:

1. if $Y \in I_{Var}$ and $Y \in \Gamma_{Var}$ then
   $B'(\Gamma(Y)) = 1$ and $\forall (Y = x_i) \in Inst_Y / \Gamma(Y), B'(Y = x_i) = 0$
2. if $Y \in I_{Var}$ and $par(Y) \subseteq \Gamma_{Var}$ and $Y \notin \Gamma_{Var}$ then
   $\forall (Y = y) \in Inst_Y, B'(Y = y) = P(Y = y| \{X_i = x_i| X_i \in par(Y),$
   $X_i = x_i \in \Gamma\})$
3. otherwise,
   $\forall (Y = y) \in Inst_Y, B'(Y = y) = B(Y = y)$

According to the previous formal characterization of the function bu^*, the $BDIS$ agent only reconsiders the probability distributions over intended random variable $Y \in I_{Var}$. In fact, we suppose that the $BDIS$ agent only reconsiders those beliefs which are directly related with his intentions, since he allocates his attention on the current task he is trying to solve. More precisely: if Y is both an intended random variable in I_{Var} and a perceived variable in Γ_{Var}, then the updated probability distribution over Y assigns probability 1 to the perceived instantiation $\Gamma(Y)$ of variable Y and probability 0 to all the other instantiations of variable Y (condition 1); if Y is an intended random variable in I_{Var}, it is not a perceived variable in Γ_{Var} but its parents in the bayesian network are perceived variables in Γ_{Var}, then the updated probability distribution over Y assigns to each instantiations $Y = y$ of variable Y a probability which is equal to the conditional probability that $Y = y$ is true given that the perceived instantiations of the parents of Y are true (i.e. $P(Y = y| \{X_i = x_i| X_i \in par(Y), X_i = x_i \in \Gamma\}))$ (condition 2). In all other cases the probability distribution over Y is not updated.

Space restrictions prevent a formal description of the belief update function bu of the standard BDI agent. Let us only say that function bu (differently from the function bu^* of the $BDIS$ agent) updates indiscriminately all beliefs of the agent, that is, at each round the standard BDI agent reconsiders the probability distributions over all random variables $Y \in \mathbf{VAR}$ (even those variables which are not intended).[8]

5   Experimental Results and Experimental Setting

In order to compare traditional and surprise driven strategies for belief update, we run the standard BDI agent and the $BDIS$ agent in simulative experiments in the foraging scenario. Each reported experiment consists of 10 runs using different randomly generated initial conditions in a discrete world. Season length s_t is set to 15 rounds. Random initial placements of agents and entities (fruits, trees) are used for all experiments. The

---

[8] Function bu has the same three conditions of function bu^* specified above. The only difference is that in the three conditions of bu the requirement $Y \in I_{Var}$ is not specified.

threshold Δ of belief update in the $BDIS$ agent is set to 1. Thus, the $BDIS$ agent revises his beliefs only if a tree or a fruit of a certain color is perceived in a completely unexpected position in the grid.

Given that environmental dynamics are independent from the agent activities, we expect that to higher dynamism correspond higher costs of belief change (and, on the contrary, to lower dynamism correspond lower costs of belief change). More than absolute performance relying on the agent score (i.e. number of eaten fruits), we are interested in monitoring the ratio between belief update costs and the absolute performance in terms of eaten fruits. As in [14,15], in our experiments we evaluate the computational efforts for epistemic activities. For each trial we define the *belief change cost* of an agent as the total amount of belief change operations performed by the agent (i.e. the total number of modifications of the belief base of the agent during the all trial). Obviously, if the input belief set and the output belief set of the belief update function bu (viz. bu^*) are the same, that is $bu(\Gamma, B) = B$ (viz. $bu^*(\Gamma, B, I) = B$), then this does not count as a belief change operation. We define the *cost ratio c* of an agent in terms of *belief change cost* divided by the total amount of achieved task (number of eaten fruits). Namely, c represents the unit of cost spent for each achieved goal.

Because of the distributions, the *cost ratio* of an agent presents a fluctuating course before converging, hence each individual trial has to be sufficiently long for the effectiveness to become stable. In order to measure the effectiveness in function of time, we define a standard trial length of 600 rounds. We define the characterization of an agent by averaging his cost ratio progresses for 10 trials. Experiments are conducted in environments with three different levels of dynamism.

Static World: Fig. 2a shows the cost ratios of the two typologies of agents in a static environment ($\delta = 3$, a tree changes its location every 3 seasons, 45 rounds). The standard BDI agent attains an average of 25.9 eaten fruits on each trial, while $BDIS$ achieves an average performance of 21.7. Both agents show a comparable progress in terms of cost ratio. On the long term they stabilize their knowledge through a low frequency of belief change activities. Considering the low dynamism, once agents have overcome their transitory progress the result of effectiveness converges towards a value $c = 0.2$.

Medium World: Fig. 2b shows the cost ratios of the two typologies of agents in an environment with medium dynamism ($\delta = 2$, a tree changes its location every 2 seasons, 30 rounds). In terms of eaten fruits the BDI agent attains better performances (31.9) than the $BDIS$ (25.7). On the long term, cost performance converges to a value lower than 0.3 for both agents, even if the BDI wastes more resources for belief change. Despite of a lower number of eaten fruits, the $BDIS$ agent is able to maintain a better cost ratio along the experiments.

Dynamic World: Fig. 2c shows the cost ratios of the two typologies of agents in a highly dynamic environment ($\delta = 1$, a tree changes its location at each season change, 15 rounds). Due to his epistemic activity, the BDI agent is able to maintain a more consistent and complete knowledge of the environment. In so doing, he strongly overcomes the $BDIS$ agent in terms of achieved goals (25.9 average number of eaten fruits against 21.7) but, accordingly, he faces with higher epistemic costs, even beyond the transitory phase. The cost ratios of the two agents highlight a difference in performance:

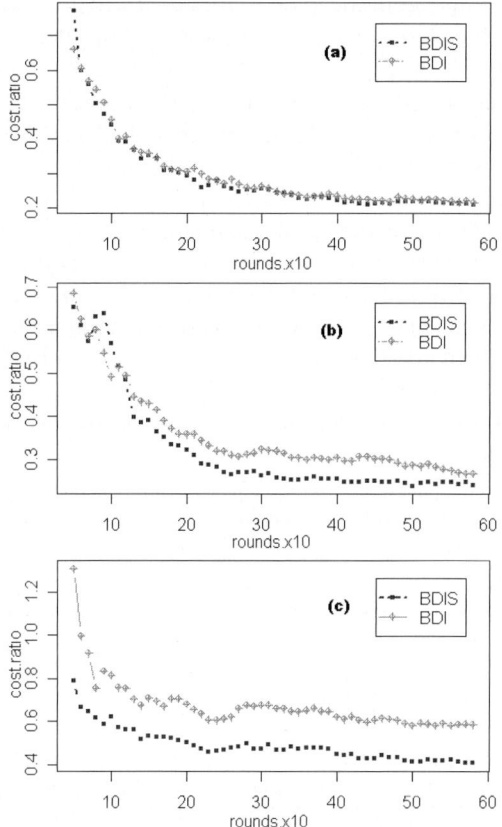

Fig. 2. Cost performance measured in static (a), medium (b) and dynamic (c) environments

the $BDIS$ cost ratio converges to a value of about 0.4 which is two orders of magnitude lower than the BDI cost ratio (0.6). The results of the experiments show that the more an agent spends his resources for belief change, the more his beliefs will be correct thereby enabling the agent to eat more fruits. On the other side, the results of the experiments show that in a very dynamic environment, the higher costs sustained for belief update are not compensated by an enhancement of the performance (i.e. number of eaten fruits).

6   Discussion and Future Works

The mechanism of surprise-based belief update modeled in this paper enables agents to process perceived data according to their ongoing intentions. Hence, agents acquire the capability to divide the overall set of perceived data in a *relevant* subset and a *irrelevant* one. The possibility to build agents which can filter out all irrelevant information they get will be a critical issue for forthcoming cognitive systems (e.g. agents engaged

in a information retrieval task in the context of open system applications). We are actually working on a generalization of the model by introducing a more sophisticated belief and expectation processing. As in [16], our aim is to have *uncertainty* in deliberation by using prediction models (i.e. forward models) and introducing a quantitative dimension of goal importance (i.e. utilities of the expected outcome). Besides, we think that the model presented in this paper provides a novel understanding of the issue of intention reconsideration [14]. Since the persistence of an intention over time depends on the persistence of those beliefs which support this intention (i.e. beliefs are reasons for intending [2]), a surprised-based filter of belief update should affect persistence of intentions in an indirect way, that is, an agent should revise his intentions only if he is surprised by some perceived facts (since only in condition of surprise the agent's beliefs change). We would like to explore such an intriguing issue in a future work.

References

1. Cherniak, C.: Minimal rationality. MIT Press, Cambridge (1986)
2. Bratman, M.: Intentions, plans, and practical reason. Harvard University Press, Cambridge (1987)
3. Meyer, W.U., Reisenzein, R., Schützwohl, A.: Towards a process analysis of emotions: The case of surprise. Motivation and Emotion 21, 251–274 (1997)
4. Lorini, E., Castelfranchi, C.: The cognitive structure of surprise: looking for basic principles. Topoi: an International Review of Philosophy 26(1) (2007)
5. Itti, L., Baldi, P.: Bayesian surprise attracts human attention. In: Advances in Neural Information Processing Systems, pp. 1–8. MIT Press, Cambridge (2006)
6. Ortony, A., Norman, D.A., Revelle, W.: Effective functioning: A three level model of affect, motivation, cognition, and behavior. In: Fellous, J.M., Arbib, A. (eds.) Who Needs Emotions? The Brain Meets the Machine, Oxford University Press, New York (2005)
7. Wooldridge, M.: An Introduction to Multiagent Systems. John Wiley & Sons, Chichester (2002)
8. Rao, A.S., Georgeff, M.: An abstract architecture for rational agents. In: Proc. of the 3th Int. Conf. on Principles of Knowledge Representation and Reasoning (KR'92) (1992)
9. Pereira, D., Oliveira, E., Moreira, N., Sarmento, L.: Towards an architecture for emotional BDI agents. In: Bento, C., Cardoso, A., Dias, G. (eds.) EPIA 2005. LNCS (LNAI), vol. 3808, Springer, Heidelberg (2005)
10. Alchourron, C., Gardenfors, P., Makinson, D.: On the logic of theory change: Partial meet contraction and revision functions. The Journal of Symbolic Logic 50, 510–530 (1985)
11. Casati, R., Pasquinelli, E.: How can you be surprised? the case for volatile expectations. Phenomenology and the Cognitive Sciences 6(1-2), 171–183 (2006)
12. Kaelbling, L.P., Rosenschein, S.J.: Action and planning in embedded agents. In: Maes, P. (ed.) Designing autonomous agents, pp. 35–48. MIT Press, Cambridge (1990)
13. Ortony, A., Partridge, D.: Surprisingness and expectation failure: Whats the difference? In: Proc. of the 10th Int. Joint Conf. on Artificial Intelligence (IJCAI) (1987)
14. Schut, M.C., Wooldridge, M., Parsons, S.D.: The theory and practice of intention reconsideration. Journal of Experimental and Theoretical Artificial Intelligence 16(4), 261–293 (2004)
15. Kinny, D., Georgeff, M., J., H.: Experiments in optimal sensing for situated agents. In: Proc. of the 2nd Pacfic Rim. Int. Conf. on AI (PRICAI-92) (1992)
16. Piunti, M., Castelfranchi, C., Falcone, R.: Surprise as shortcut for Anticipation: clustering Mental States in reasoning. In: Proc. of IJCAI-07 (2007)

Modulatory Influence of Motivations on a Schema-Based Architecture: A Simulative Study

Giovanni Pezzulo and Gianguglielmo Calvi

ISTC-CNR, Via S. Martino della Battaglia, 44 - 00185 Rome, Italy
giovanni.pezzulo@istc.cnr.it, gianguglielmo.calvi@noze.it

Abstract. We analyze the role of motivations in living organisms, and the nature of their influences on behavior with the aim to propose a design methodology for schema-based agent architectures. We propose that motivations have a modulatory influence on behavior, and in our design methodology they regulate the allocation of resources to the sensorimotor system and schemas. We describe an agent architecture incorporating this principle and we highlight its performance in a simulative study[1].

1 Introduction

Neurobiological evidence suggest that the organism's motivational system is its first and foremost source of activity, that it determines the architecture and organization of its brain, and that an organism without feelings is severely limited in its adaptivity, survivability, and autonomy [4]. In a living organism the motivational system is shaped for maintaining in acceptable bounds bodily variables that are crucial for survival: internal signals, feelings and drive stimuli, carry on information related to the needs of the organism, and motivate the organism to look for appropriate external stimuli. We can say then that in a living system actions are selected in order to satisfy motivations, and not to respond to external stimuli as such: a machine is run by stimuli, an agent acts according to its motivations. Since in order to fully understand living organisms and their autonomy it is crucial to focus on their internal context, here we propose that this methodology should be adopted in the design of artificial systems, too. Contrary to the typical emphasis on inputs and outputs, we then focus first and foremost on the motivational dimension of agents, we then investigate the relations between motivations and behavior with the aim to provide a design methodology for incorporating motivations in a schema-based agent architecture.

How Do Motivations Impact on Behavior? What is special about the "processing" of motivations? why do feelings and drives stimuli are different from external stimuli and affordances? Here we suggest that the motivational system has a way of influencing the sensorimotor system that is distinct from the effects of the stimuli from the environment: it *modulates* behavior in a very broad, often

---

[1] Work supported by the EU-funded project **MindRACES** (FP6-511931).

A. Paiva, R. Prada, and R.W. Picard (Eds.): ACII 2007, LNCS 4738, pp. 374–385, 2007.

unselective way ('energizing' effect in [8]), and produces qualitative effects only indirectly. According to [9]: "The manner in which the nervous system responds to the inputs from the external environment can be called neuro-transmissory whereas the manner in which it responds to influences from the rest of the body can be called neuro-modulatory." This fact has rarely been acknowledged in AI (with exceptions, see later); but treating motivational and perceptual influences in the same way we risk to have 'hyper-rational' models of emotions and motivations, and ultimately to reduce them to appealing labels.

Including Motivations in Agents' Design. Our design methodology consists in introducing in a schema-based agent architecture [1,2] a motivational component which interacts that other components of the architecture in an energizing, modulatory and unselective way. This means that while specific behavioral responses exist for stimuli and affordances in the environment, this is not the case for feelings and motivational influences. Motivations and emotions have directing and energizing effects, and produce behavioral consequences such as selecting stimuli, orienting attention, facilitating action, etc. However, these specific behavioral responses are not designed but emerge from the interaction between the motivational and the sensorimotor system (either immediately, or indirectly, by learning the value of actions and objects). Different responses such as 'fight, flee or freeze' do not depend on three specific modules or schemas, but on the influences of different internal contexts over the same sensorimotor system.

Our work is related to similar schema-based architectures (e.g., [1,2]; see also [14]). However, in our design methodology the motivational system influences the sensorimotor system by *regulating the allocation of resources* for action selection and execution. Similar approaches are 'hormonal modulation of behavior' in [3], and the idea that emotions are 'selectors of resources' [7]. We also emphasize the distributed and decentralized nature of resources allocation, and the fact that by manipulating the allocation of resources in the sensorimotor system qualitatively different behaviors can be produced. In this perspective, the main influence of motivations on behavior is 'covert', but indirectly it results in 'overt' actions such as the selection of a specific behavior or an attentional switch.

2   The Computational Model: The Mantis Architecture

We have implemented a schema-based agent architecture in which the sensorimotor and motivational systems interact. We have used the cognitive modeling framework AKIRA (http://www.akira-project.org/), the AKIRA Schema Library (AKSL) [12], and the 3-D engine Irrlicht (http://irrlicht.sourceforge.net/). The architecture is based on earlier work [10] and is inspired by the ethological model of the praying mantis reported in [2].

Fig. 1 shows the main components of the model: the **motivational system** (the drives) and the **sensorimotor system** (Perceptual and Motor Schemas). The architecture also includes several **routines** for preprocessing of data, two *sensors* and two **actuators**, the camera and wheels.

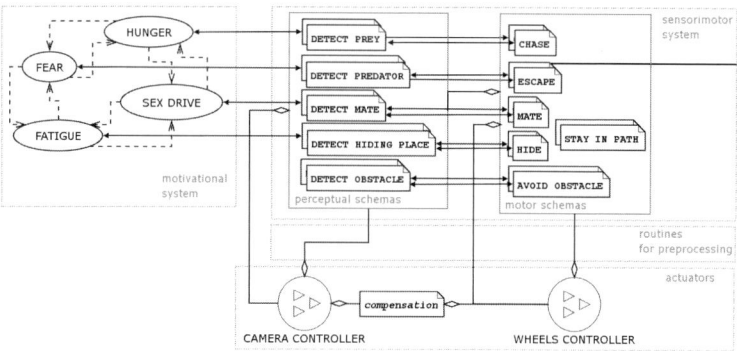

Fig. 1. The components of the mantis architecture

2.1   The Sensorimotor System: Schemas and Actuators

The architecture includes two kinds of schemas: perceptual schemas realize behaviors such as *escape from predator* and *avoid obstacle*, while motor schemas realize behavior such as *find prey* and *detect obstacle*. Each schema has also an activity level that represents its reliability and usefulness with respect to the external context, as well as its relevance with respect to the motivational context. Depending on the activity level, each schema can influence more the other schemas, by sending them activation or by inhibiting them, receive more or less promptly stimuli from the sensors, and send motor commands with higher or lower firing rate to the actuators.

The whole mantis architecture includes five kinds of perceptual schemas: *detect prey, detect predator, detect mate, detect hiding place, detect obstacle*; and six kinds of motor schemas: *stay in path* (the default behavior), *chase, escape, mate, hide, avoid obstacle*. For each kind of schema, there are five schema instances, that are specialized for different contextual conditions. For example, two *find prey* schemas can be specialized for dealing with slow or fast preys.

Perceptual and motor schemas can be *coupled*. The functioning of two sample coupled schemas, *detct prey* and *chase prey*, is illustrated in Figure 2. The perceptual schema receives as input perceptual information from the camera. As

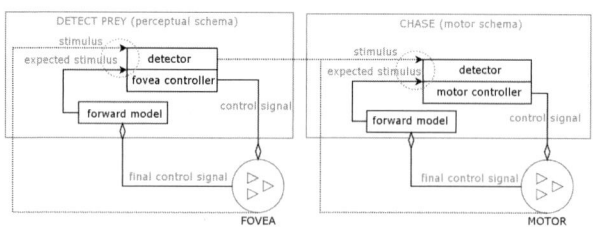

Fig. 2. A coupled perceptual and motor schema

indicated by the dotted circle, sensed stimuli are compared with sensory information that is predicted by the forward model, and the error is used for setting the reliability value of the schema (explained later on). The detector thus sends sensory stimuli to the controller (inverse model), which in turn generates a motor command and sends it to the camera motor (via motor routines), and (optionally) sensory information (e.g. the position of the detected prey) to the coupled motor schema. The motor schema receives as input the activity level of the coupled perceptual schema, proprioceptive information about the current state of the wheels' motor, and optionally additional sensory information from the perceptual schema. Like in the perceptual schema, sensed and predicted stimuli are compared and reliability values are assigned. Sensory information is conveyed to the controller, which sends motor commands to the wheels' motor. Notice that in both schemas, in order to generate predictions, the forward models receive an efference copy of the (final) motor commands received by the camera or wheel motors, and learn to predict their sensory effects.

Activity Level. Schemas have an *activity level* reflecting their relevance with respect to external and motivational context. Activity level results in fact from the sum of four parameters. **(1) Absolute value.** Schemas have a varying level of activation that depends on their absolute relevance. For example, schemas such as *escape from predator* are more relevant in absolute than *avoid obstacle* and, ceteris paribus, influence more the agent's conduct. **(2) Reliability.** The expectations produced by forward models are compared with actual stimulus, and schemas predicting well gain activation, like in other schema-based architectures [15]. The rationale is that schemas predicting well are well attuned with the current context; for example, if a slow prey is being chased, schemas specialized for finding and chasing slow prey will generate appropriate predictions. It is important to remark that success in prediction also entails success in action (the converse is not always true); in the above example, if the active schemas continue to generate good predictions, eventually the slow prey will be successfully chased (otherwise they would have generated bad predictions). **(3) Learned links.** Energetic links are learned between schemas with differential Hebbian learning [6], that favor connections betweens components that are active in the same time span. Schemas (for the same or for different behaviors) that are active in the same context are likely to evolve strong links and are thus able to prime each other. For example, it is likely that during escaping behavior schemas for avoiding obstacles are useful while ones for chasing preys are not. **(4) Motivational context.** Schemas receive activation from related drives via links that are learned with differential Hebbian learning.

Another factor impacts on activation level: there is a limited amount of resources that can be accessed by schemas, called the *energy pool*. Since schemas compete for acccessing resources, currently active schemas also inhibit other ones (e.g. *escape* inhibits *chase* and vice versa).

The Actuators. Commands received by the schemas are fused by the actuators, the camera and wheels controllers. We adopted an emergent action selection scheme, which favors the most active schemas of the same kind, see [12]. Since more active schemas send motor commands more frequently (with an higher firing rate), they influence more the overall behavior of the agent. This does not mean that other active schemas do not have an influence. For example, when the agent is chasing a prey, occasionally (if *detect predator* is active) it can do a saccade in search of a predator. Our action selection mechanism favors *clean switching*: it permits to switch among behaviors, but avoids to activate 'intermediate' ones (e.g., do a saccade in the middle between a predator and a prey). The final behavior is emergent, since it is not encoded in any schema, but depends on the continuous interactions between schemas, the internal context (drives) and the external one (stimuli).

2.2   The Motivational System: Drives

The agent model includes a motivational system composed of four drives: *hunger, sex drive, fatigue* and *fear*[2]; see Fig. 1. All drives have an activity level that changes dynamically and is inversely proportional to their degree of satisfaction, that ranges from zero to one for each drive. Drives have also inhibitory links to each other, representing the fact that the motivational system has limited resources and drives compete.

Hunger receives three kinds of feelings. The first represents the need for food of the organism. This is provided by a biological clock (a shortcut for the fact that the body monitoring system notifies the need of food at regular intervals). When such feeling is received, the level of hunger increases. The second represents the anticipated pleasure of receiving food. This is received when the activity level of *detect prey* schemas increases, and slightly raises hunger. This mechanism is adaptive, since it permits to maintain persistence during a chase. The third represent the satisfaction of the need of food. It is notified (by the body monitoring system) when the prey is successfully chased (i.e., when a *chase* schema succeeds) and then food is obtained.

Sex drive functions like *hunger*, with a different biological clock. It is related to *detect mate* and *mate*, not to *detect prey* and *chase*.

Fatigue receives two kinds of feelings. The former represents the consummation of resources for moving, and augments the level of fatigue whenever the agent moves (i.e., whichever schema is used for moving). The second represents the recovery, and restores the initial level of fatigue when the agent successfully rests. The level of fatigue impacts also on the amount of computational resources available to the schemas. In order to act effectively, the agent has to rest (possibly in hiding places) when it is fatigued.

Fear receives two kinds of feelings. The former represents the anticipated pain of being captured by a predator; it is received when the activity level of *detect predator* increases and increases the level of fear. The latter represents

---

[2] In our schema-based model, like in similar ones [2], *fear* is considered as a motivational variable that influences predator avoidance. An alternative view is that fear is the feeling originating from the drive to avoid predators and other dangers.

the anticipated pleasure of escaping the predator; it is received when the activity level of *detect predator* decreases (or remains low) and decreases the level of fear.

Drives send activation to schemas satisfying their conditions; for example, *hunger* makes schemas such as *detect prey* and *chase* more active. Drives that are far from satisfaction are able to send more activation to related schemas, and vice versa. At the same time, schemas activation level feedbacks on related drives (e.g. *detect prey* and *chase* send activation to *hunger*). This characteristic, called *hysteresis* [13] or persistence, permits to maintain behavior elicited by a stimulus after it has disappeared (otherwise an organism that loses visual contact with a predator would stop escaping it).

3   Experimental Set-Up

We have tested the mantis architecture in a simulated predator-and-prey scenario designed with the 3D simulator Irrlicht. The scenario consists in a 3D open space, with hills and valleys that partially occlude vision, with coordinates that vary between -10000 and +10000 in the three axes. We have introduced from one to five predators, preys, mates, obstacles and hiding places. Each of these entities is defined by three features: color, size, and shape, that range between zero and one. As an average, entities have 30% of overlapping features.

We have implemented the agent architecture described here by using the AKSL library [12], which is based on the multi-thread framework AKIRA [11]. Each component, schema or drive, is implemented by using a single thread of execution whose activity level is dynamically set. The amount of resources available to schemas is limited; since schemas compete for gaining activation, this means that the most active ones also inhibit the other ones. For all the simulations described here, we have set this limit to 5.0.

Drives. Drives have an activity level that varies between zero and one. A Fuzzy Cognitive Map [6], a hybrid neural network - fuzzy system, calculates dynamically the amount of resources assigned to each drive (and to its thread of execution) on the basis of the input they receive from the body monitoring system and the sensorimotor system. All their inhibitory links are set to -0.6. The weighs of the links from and to the schemas are learned with differential Hebbian learning. As described earlier, two drives (*hunger* and *sex drive*) depend on a 'biological clock'. *Hunger* is increased by 0.05 every seconds, while *sex drive* is set to one after exactly one and two minutes from the beginning of the simulation. Fatigue is increased by 0.01 every ten seconds.

Sensors and Actuators. A simulated camera which can monitor an angle of 90° in front of the agent collects the estimated position in the three axis ($< x_e, y_e, z_e >$) of one feature per time in the visual field and conveys it to the perceptual schemas. The input was modified by randomly adding or subtracting 5% of its value as noise. Preprocessing units, the routines, are used for conveying sensory information only to percetual schemas which are specialized in the appropriate subregion of the feature (e.g., to *detect prey* schemas that are specialized for small preys). Each schema only receives information by a subset of routines, which is pre-determined. The camera and wheels motors collect motor commands sent asynchronously and with different firing rates from perceptual and motor schemas respectively, and fuse them for obtaining the next fixation point of the camera $< x_n f, y_n f, z_n f >$ and the next position of the agent $< x_n p, y_n p, z_n p >$.

Schemas. Each schema has a fixed cycle which is however executed at a speed which depends on its current activity level (calculated anew at the beginning of each cycle). The activity level is set by summing up the four parameters introduced above: absolute value, reliability, learned links, and motivational context. The values are then normalized, and so each schema has an activity level which varies between zero and one. For each cycle, the three components of each schema illustrated in fig. 2 perform one single operation.

The *detector* collects the estimated position $< x_e, y_e, z_e >$ of the features it is specialized to deal with (from one to three) from the camera (the case of perceptual schemas) or the coupled perceptual schema (the case of motor schemas). It also collects the predicted position generated by the forward model $< x_p, y_p, z_p >$. It compares them, and the error in prediction $(1 - || < x_e, y_e, z_e > - < x_p, y_p, z_p > ||)$ is used for determining the reliability value of the schema. The detector of the perceptual schemas fed $< x_e, y_e, z_e >$ to the detector of the coupled motor schema, too.

The *inverse model* receives the estimated and predicted position of the feature(s), and generates a motor command to send to the effector, representing the next fixation point of the camera $< x_n f, y_n f, z_n f >$ (the case of perceptual schemas) and the next position of the agent $< x_n p, y_n p, z_n p >$ (the case of motor schemas). For eight schemas (*detect prey, detect predator, detect mate, detect hiding place, detect obstacle, chase, mate, hide*) the inverse model generates the appropriate motor command for minimizing the distance between $< x_e, y_e, z_e >$ and $< x_p, y_p, z_p >$. For two schemas (*escape* and *avoid obstacle*) it generates the appropriate motor command for maximizing their distance.

The *forward model* receives an efference copy of the final motor command executed by one actuator and generates the prediction $< x_p, y_p, z_p >$[3].

---

[3] For example, the *detect prey* schema specialized for small preys (i.e., a subregion of the size feature) receives the information that a small entity is in front of the agent, and predicts that a small entity will be next sensed on the left. The sensed and expected position (generated by the forward model) are then used for generating a command to the camera to move left, in order to maintain the prey in sight. *Detect prey* feds the sensed position to the coupled *chase prey* schema, too, which predicts the next position of the prey and generates appropriate motor commands to reach it. At the same time, other perceptual schemas such as *detect obstacle* receive the information that a small entity is in front of the agent (and, indirectly, other motor schemas, too). Arguably, they generate different predictions about the next position of the small entity (if it is an obstacle, it remains in place). Schemas' reliability, that is their accuracy in predicting, serves to calculate their activity level and then their influence on the final agent's behavior, since more active schemas read more quickly from the sensors and send more motor commands to the effectors.

Learning. The drives were entirely designed by hand, as above described. We have also designed by hand about one hundred schemas specialized for processing different subregions of the features of the entities. For example, we designed several *detect prey* schemas detecting and predicting different subregions of color and/or size and/or shapes of preys. All the schemas had the same absolute value: 0.1. The mantis architecture, shown in figure 1, was then developed through a two-stages learning process. In the former phase the objective is to learn the inverse and forward models of each schema, and to store only the most reliable ones. In the latter phase the objective is to permit to all the schema to operate together, and to learn the schema-schema and drive-schema links.

First stage. In the former stage each schema learned its inverse and forward models individually in a simple environment having a limited number of entities (from one to five preys, predators, mates, obstacles or hiding places of the same kind). Basically the task of a forward model is to learn to predict the trajectory of an entity which is defined by one to three (subregions of) features. Each predator, prey and mate moves with a specific trajectory in the environment; circular and oval trajectories having different amplitudes were used. Notice that several factors contribute to make these trajectories difficult to learn. First of all, the environment is 3D: trajectories that are circular in 2D are much more complex with hills and valleys since even the values in the z axis varies over time. Moreover, the agent has a limited visual field, the target can be partially occluded by obstacles, and there is noise. The task of the inverse model is instead to learn to generate appropriate motor commands for minimizing or maximizing the distance between the sensed and predicted positions. Again, several factors contribute to make this task more complex, the most significant one being the complexity of the 3D environment.

The inverse and forward models inside each schema are realized by using feed-forward neural networks. The inverse models have three input nodes for each feature the schema is specialized to deal with, representing the position in the three axis of the features, plus three input nodes representing the predicted position of the entity in the three axis, calculated by the forward model. They have three output nodes, representing the motor commands to send to the effector: the next fixation point of the camera (the case of perceptual schemas) and the next position of the agent (the case of motor schemas) in the three axis. The forward models have three input nodes for each feature the schema is specialized to deal with, representing the position in the three axis of the features, plus three input nodes representing the final motor command executed by the effector. They have three output nodes, representing the predicted position of the entity in the three axis. The networks were trained with the cascade-correlation algorithm [5] that estimates autonomously during learning the best number of neurons in the hidden layer. They learned via a free interaction of the agent with the entities in the environment. One example was sampled every twelve, with a total of thirty-six; the learning stopped when the error of at least one forward model (the euclidean distance between the actual and predicted position in 3D, $0.1 * 10^{-6}$) was less than 0,0000001 (positions vary between -10000 and

+10000 in the three axes). After learning we selected only the five more reliable perceptual and motor schemas of each kind (i.e., those predicting better): five *detect prey*, five *chase*, five *detect predator*, etc. In total we selected 55 schemas.

Second stage. In the second stage all the previously selected schemas were integrated in an unique architecture having also the motivational system (the drives). The challenge is now to coordinate them in a complex environment. The agent architecture interacted freely with all the entities of the environment in 3-minutes simulations. In this phase the inverse and forward models did not learn any more, but drives and schemas which were active in the same span of time evolved energetic links (in addition to those shown in Fig. 1) with differential Hebbian learning [6]; see [11] for the details. As a result, schemas which operate on the same entities learns to prime each other, and activation is conveyed in a context-sensitive way from less to more relevant schemas.

Notice that the learned schema-schema and drive-schema links have weighs which concur to determine the activity level of the schemas (they correspond to the 'learned links' and 'motivational context' parameters). This means that the same schemas can have different roles and importance in different agent architectures depending on the arrangement of the whole system.

3.1   Study 1: Adaptive Advantages of the Motivational System

Which are the adaptive advantages of having drives? We have argued that motivations make pragmatic activity more efficient, and we tested this prediction in a set of simulations in the above described scenario.

We have compared in the same environmental conditions two agent architectures. The former (Mantis) is the previously described one, having a full fledged motivational and sensorimotor systems. In the latter (Mantis-wf) the energetic links from the motivational system to the sensorimotor system are removed, then they can not influence one another –in a sense, AG2 is deprived of its feelings.

We have conducted 100 real-time, 3-minutes simulations for each of three experimental conditions: (1) the environment only contains one entity of each kind (one predator, one prey, one mate, one obstacle, and one hiding place); (2) the environment contains three entities of each kind; (3) the environment contains five entities of each kind. We have then estimated the performance and adaptivity of each agent (Mantis vs. Mantis-wf) in the environment by measuring how much their four drives are satisfied throughout the simulations. The value of each drive ranges from zero (totally unsatisfied) to one (totally satisfied), and represents a poor or a good level of vital bodily variables. Three analysis of variance (ANOVA) with mean drives satisfaction (calculated as the mean value of $1 - (fatigue + fear + hunger + sex\ drive)/4$) during the simulations) as dependent variable were carried out, one for each experimental condition.

In the first experimental condition *Mantis* had a mean satisfaction of 0,818, while *Mantis-wf* had 0,427. In the second experimental condition *Mantis* had 0,835 and *Mantis-wf* had 0,415. In the third experimental condition *Mantis* had 0,843 and *Mantis-wf* had 0,403. In all conditions Mantis performs significantly better than Mantis-wf ($p <, 00001$ with ANOVA in all cases). An agent deprived of its feelings can not select the right affordances in its environment, and its performance is very poor. This fact derives from many converging factors. First of all, Mantis-wf is almost totally driven by the presence of stimuli and affordances, which can appear quite randomly. This could be appropriate if the agent had only one need, but it is extremely maladaptive if its drives and necessities change with time, as it is the case in living organisms. Another relevant factor is that drives make pragmatic activity much more efficient, for example by providing persistence: even if the visual contact is lost, the agent does not change objective too often (i.e. energetic resources are not transferred too often among schemas of different kinds). We illustrate this phenomenon in a second study.

3.2   Study 2: Persistence Provided by Motivations

In this study we have compared three identical agent architectures, AG1, AG2 and AG3, all having full fledged motivational and sensorimotor systems, like Mantis. Our aim is to analyze the role of motivations in the selection of alternative actions and in determining persistence. We have tested AG1, AG2 and AG3 individually in the same task, illustrated in Figure 3 (for the sake of simplicity, we have illustrated it in 2D, although the environment is 3D). Each agent has two tasks: catching a static prey (square, center) and, at the same time, escaping a moving predator (double circle, top left) that enters in their visual field shortly after the beginning of the simulation. We have set their levels of *hunger* differently. AG1 and AG2 have respectively an initial value of 0.6 and 0.3, and these values are allowed to vary during the simulation (as previously explained). AG3 has instead an unrealistically high (and maladaptive) value, since it is allowed to recruit all the activity level of the motivational system, and its value is not allowed to change during the simulation.

As Figure 3 shows, only AG1 captures the prey and escapes the predator. AG2 only escapes the predator, while AG3 is captured. Both AG1 and AG2 detect the predator at instant 1, and they switch accordingly their behavior, avoiding

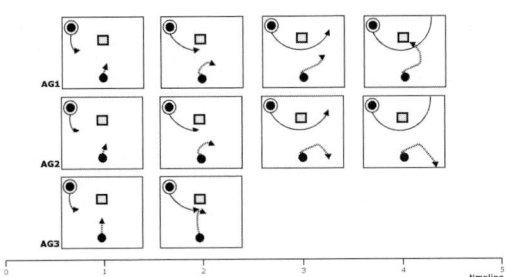

Fig. 3. Different trajectories of AG1, AG2 and AG3 (full circle, bottom) when capturing a prey (square, center) and escaping a predator (double circle, top left)

to go in its direction. The difference in behavior between AG1 and AG2 depends on their different motivational levels, that provide different levels of persistence. While AG2 loses persistence after the detour caused by the predator, AG1 is able to come back again to the prey, and to fulfill both the tasks. After the detour, AG1 and AG2 lose visual contact with the prey. The stimulus can not be used to trigger *detect prey* and *chase*. If the energy provided by the motivational state is poor, as in AG2, there is no way to remain committed; and for this reason AG2 continues going in the opposite direction. On the contrary, in AG1 the value of *hunger* is high, and it continues fueling the *detect prey* and *chase* schemas even in the period in which they are unsuccessful, since they lack visual stimuli. AG1 remains committed to the initial motivation of capturing the prey, and when the danger represented by the predator is passed, it can fulfill it. In this case, it is possible for AG1 to maintain a 'virtual' visual contact with the prey since *detect prey* contains a predictive component (the forward model) that continues to simulate the position of the prey even when the visual contact is lost. In order to do that, however, energetic resources have to be assigned to the schema even if it is temporarily not relevant for the external context (since there are no prey-like stimuli). The energizing influence of *hunger* produces covert behavior (instant 2), and later on overt effects (instant 3). The difference in behavior between AG3 and the other two agents depends instead on the fact that, since it is totally focused on detecting the prey, it detects the predator only at instant 2, when it is too late; and it is captured. Our study shows that qualitatively different responses to similar stimuli, chase, escape or freeze, can be obtained without three specialized schemas by varying the internal, motivational context. Here AG3 freezes because of the contradictory motor commands received from *chase* and *escape*. But the most important aspect is that the epistemic activity of AG3 is channelized by its motivations, and a maladaptive value of *hunger* makes AG3 unable to deal with the dangers in its environment [4].

4   Conclusion

We have proposed that motivations have a way of influencing behavior that can be called modulatory, since they do not trigger specific behavioral responses (as stimuli do) but influence indirectly the sensorimotor system by governing the allocation of its resources, and motivations determine which affordances in the environment are exploited. As suggested by [8], motivations have a *directing* and an *energizing* effect on behavior, but in our view the directing effect is a byproduct of the energizing one. We have then sketched a methodology for designing artificial agents that focuses on modulatory influences of motivations on behavior. In order to illustrate the effects of this design methodology, we have implemented an agent architecture which has a sensorimotor system, including perceptual and motor schemas, and a motivational system, including drives. We have then analyzed its behavior in two studies. In study 1 we have reported the significant adaptive advantages of having a fully functioning motivational apparatus that interacts with the sensorimotor system and channelizes the agent's behavior. Motivations provide *values* to the agent: an agent acts (and learns to act) for satisfying its drives. The affordances in the environment are selected and used only if they are relevant for the agent's current needs. In study 2 we have highlighted two points. (1) Motivations can provide persistence (hysteresis). Thanks to its motivational state, AG1 is able to capture the prey even after losing perceptual contact with it. (2) Epistemic activity is channelized by motivations. The motivational state of AG3 do not only determine its behavior (going quickly toward the prey). Since its *detect prey* perceptual schemas have almost total control over the camera, only information relative to the prey is gathered and processed, and AG3 detects the predator only when it is too late.

References

1. Arbib, M.: Schema theory. In: Shapiro, S. (ed.) Encyclopedia of Artificial Intelligence, 2nd edn., vol. 2, pp. 1427–1443. Wiley, Chichester, UK (1992)
2. Arkin, R., Ali, K., Weitzenfeld, A., Cervantes-Pérez, F.: Behavioral models of the praying mantis as a basis for robotic behavior. Robotics and Autonomous Systems. 32(1), 39–60 (2000)
3. Avila-Garcia, O., Canamero, L.: Hormonal modulation of perception in motivation-based action selection architectures. In: Canamero, L., Evans, D. (eds.) Agents that Want and Like: Motivational and Emotional Roots of Cognition and Action. Workshop of the AISB05 Convention (2005)
4. Damasio, A.: Looking for Spinoza: Joy, Sorrow, and the Feeling Brain. Harcourt (2003)
5. Fahlman, S.E., Lebiere, C.: The cascade-correlation learning architecture. In: Advance in neural information processing systems, vol. 2, pp. 524–532. Morgan Kaufmann Publishers Inc., Seattle, Washington, USA (1990)
6. Kosko, B.: Neural Networks and Fuzzy Systems. Prentice-Hall, Englewood Cliffs (1992)
7. Minsky, M.: The emotion machine (in preparation)
8. Niv, Y., Joel, D., Dayan, P.: A normative perspective on motivation. Trends in Cognitive Science 8, 375–381 (2006)
9. Parisi, D.: Internal robotics. Connection Science 16(14), 325–338 (2004)
10. Pezzulo, G., Calvi, G.: A schema based model of the praying mantis. In: Nolfi, S., Baldassarre, G., Calabretta, R., Hallam, J.C.T., Marocco, D., Meyer, J.-A., Miglino, O., Parisi, D. (eds.) SAB 2006. LNCS (LNAI), vol. 4095, pp. 211–223. Springer, Heidelberg (2006)
11. Pezzulo, G., Calvi, G.: Designing modular architectures in the framework akira. Multiagent and Grid Systems 3(1), 65–86 (2007)
12. Pezzulo, G., Calvi, G.: Schema-based design and the akira schema language: An overview. In: Butz, M., et al. (eds.) Anticipatory Behavior in Adaptive Learning Systems: Advances in Anticipatory Processing. LNCS (LNAI), vol. 4520, Springer, Heidelberg (2007)
13. Snaith, M., Holland, O.: An investigation of two mediation strategies suitable for behavioural control in animals and animats. In: Nolfi, S., Baldassarre, G., Calabretta, R., Hallam, J.C.T., Marocco, D., Meyer, J.-A., Miglino, O., Parisi, D. (eds.) SAB 2006. LNCS (LNAI), vol. 4095, pp. 255–262. Springer, Heidelberg (2006)
14. Tyrrell, T.: Computational Mechanisms for Action Selection. PhD thesis, University of Edinburgh (1993)
15. Wolpert, D.M., Kawato, M.: Multiple paired forward and inverse models for motor control. Neural Networks 11(7-8), 1317–1329 (1998)

Designing an Emotional and Attentive Virtual Infant

Christopher Peters

LINC lab, University of Paris 8,
Paris, France
peters@iut.univ-paris8.fr
http://iut.univ-paris8.fr/greta

Abstract. This paper outlines the design of a model amalgamating computational visual attention and emotion approaches for the purposes of driving expressive attentive and emotional behaviour in an embodied, situated real-time virtual infant. The themes of emotion and attention underlie all aspects of our model: from perception, to memory, internal state and behaviour expressivity. The model is focused on some of the earliest stimulus evaluation checks related to appraisal theory: perceptual attention focuses and refines the details of relevant and potentially relevant stimuli, reducing uncertainty in order to discover reward and heed danger. In the process, the agents internal state is modified and feeds back to modulate the ongoing allocation of attention and processing of stimuli. Changes in internal state are expressed through a repertoire of prototypical infant gaze, face and body behaviours. This represents, to our knowledge, the first attempt to marry all of these concepts in a real-time 3D embodied agent system.

1 Introduction

Emotion and attention are two fundamental aspects of critical importance to human-machine interaction. For a machine to be able to fluently interact with and adapt to its environment and the humans within it, it must be seen to act in a manner that is sensitive to the emotional and attentive states of others and do so in a way that is congruent with the notion that it too may possess some human-like emotional and attentive states (even if it does not). In our view, such capabilities are necessary building blocks for the creation of more complex agent interaction behaviours, involving engagement and empathy for example.

In this paper, we propose a design for a model of perception, inner state representation and behaviour for a real-time autonomous agent that resembles a human infant. We have chosen this appearance since a primary intended purpose of the model is to conduct user evaluation testing of emotion- and attention-related behaviours in 3D agents. We feel that the scope of capabilities and level of sophistication of behaviour presented here is more appropriate to an infant rather than an adult humanoid appearance.

A. Paiva, R. Prada, and R.W. Picard (Eds.): ACII 2007, LNCS 4738, pp. 386–397, 2007.

The virtual infant, situated in a 3D virtual environment, perceives its surroundings through an orientable virtual vision sensor, which at each update creates the initial input to a perception pipeline (see Section 3). As visible stimuli are attended to and their representations progress through the pipeline, they are progressively appraised [22] in relation to their *relevance* so that more details are revealed about them, such as their reward and threat values. The output of the pipeline, a *relevance master map*, represents an overview of relevant parts of the scene for influencing internal attentive and emotional state, as modelled by the dimensions of *valence, arousal* and *spread of focus* (Section 4). This state feeds back to modulate appraisal and feeds forward in order to control expressive behaviour. The agent is capable of expressing attentive gaze behaviours in order to orient its focus towards objects and locations of relevance, and has a repertoire of prototypical facial and bodily infant expressions, such as smiling, cry-face and body stilling (see Section 5). Before we look at the design in more detail, we first consider previous work in some similar areas.

2   Background

A number of relatively detailed visual attention models have been proposed for application to humanoid agents in virtual environments (see for example [5], [19], [11]), usually for the purposes of controlling autonomous gaze and looking behaviours. Although each model has its own respective strengths and weaknesses, they all share a common and conspicuous omission: they do not cater for the role of affect. When considering the domain of computational emotion modelling, a number of works are of relevance for constructing emotion-enabled agents. Of particular interest are those models of a more holistic nature that study interrelationships between a number of components rather than treating them in isolation. These models are for use in practical interactive systems, for example simulations intended for use with robots [4] or for entertainment purposes [9]. A number of these systems are directed especially towards infant-like behaviour, for example infant-carer relationships [20], or use infant representations to visualise their internal workings [25]. In general, however, these systems do not focus in great detail on the role of visual attention in emotion. In this respect, computational models of appraisal processing [13] are a particularly promising avenue of research for weaving together these two important strands of emotion and attention processing. It is in this respect that we focus on how an agents perceptual model can incorporate aspects of appraisal processing.

3   Perceptual Modelling

Perceptual modelling deals with the transformation of stimuli perceived by the agent through synthetic senses into useful internal presentations that can be used to inform its reasoning processes and guide behaviour. In this Section we deal specifically with visual perception, although others have created models for multiple synthetic modalities [6]. In our model, the first step in perceptual modelling involves tagging all objects in the virtual environment with a number of attributes. The most basic of these are stimulus valence and arousal. These were chosen since they encapsulate low-level emotion and attention related information about the stimulus: for example, it has been noted [16] that when the visual cortex is processing affective stimuli, a category of stimuli judged to be of neutral valence but high arousal (labelled in the study as *interesting*) received enhanced activation, in addition to stimuli with a high valence but neutral arousal.

The virtual infant perceives stimuli in a snapshot manner through an orientable synthetic vision sensor, locked to its gaze direction [18]. This sensor captures two types of renderings from the point of view of the agent. The first of these, a *full-coloured* rendering, contains spatial information: that is, the colour of each element of the visual field including the contribution of textures, lights, special effects and so on. The second, *false-coloured* rendering, renders objects in the visual field according to unique predefined colours that allow elements of the scene to be queried for their associated object: this could be thought of as a fast method of scene segmentation allowing object-specific processing to take place. By combining the full-coloured and false-coloured representations, the agent obtains a view dependant perception of the scene in both a spatial and object-based manner. These two maps form the initial input into the visual perception pipeline, which is a branched pipeline structure consisting of a number of different stages. At each stage in the pipeline, visual information may be refined, filtered, transformed or otherwise operated on and the results transferred to different branches in order to allow the partitioning of processed data. For example, social stimuli can be partitioned into an area that will later be processed for eye direction (see Section 3.3), an operation that does not make sense for other types of objects. In the perception pipeline, refinement, filtering and transformation of perceived data involves attention (determined by the gaze direction and inner attentional state of the agent: see Section 4.1) which is required to conduct successive appraisals, as described next.

3.1   Appraisal Processing

In our model, appraisal processing has the function of revealing attributes of stimuli in the agents memory. It relates primarily to reductions in uncertainty - when uncertainty is reduced below an appropriate threshold a corresponding appraisal is considered to have been conducted, after which attention allocation can be readapted. Here, we are particularly focused on appraisals related to relevance [21]. Although it is a category encompassing only a few of the large number of total theorised SECs [22] in the component process model of emotion, relevance represents an interesting crossroads between emotion and attention: it is a common subjective reason as to why a diverse range of stimuli may elicit and engage ones attention and emotions. In studying this, we highlight *potential relevance* as an especially important concept. When dealing with perceptual attention, which relevance is a factor in eliciting, the question is raised of how one can judge the relevance of something if attention has not yet been elicited to it. Potential relevance helps solve this conundrum by representing fast, bottom-up pre-attentive processing that can cue the presence of objects worthy of further study. We focus on a number of categories that, when combined, result in an assessment of the overall relevance and potential relevance for the contents of the scene. Each of these different categories are represented in the perception pipeline by *Synthetic Perceptual Maps* and are described in more detail next.

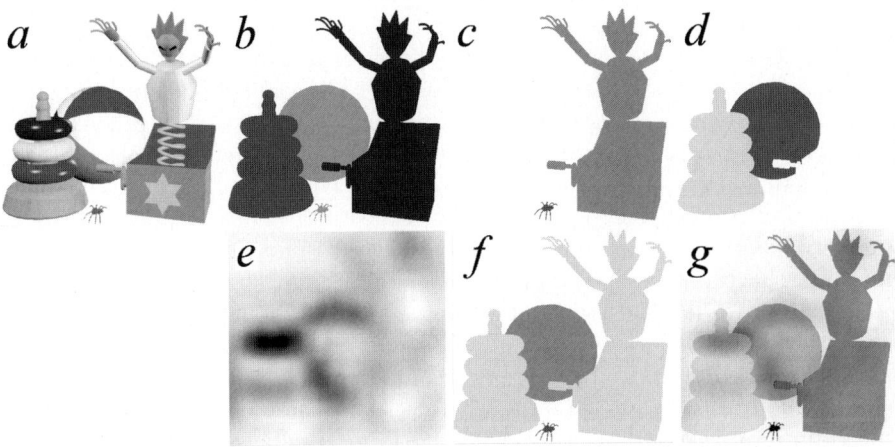

Fig. 1. Depiction of synthetic perceptual maps based on test (a) full-coloured and (b) false-coloured renderings used as input. (c) illustrates the threat map, (d) reward map, (e) saliency map, (f) uncertainty map and (g) a combined, weighted relevance master map. In each map, darker regions indicate regions of higher strength for the results of that particular operation: in this case, the spider (bottom-center) is the most relevant visible object due to its potential threat level and uncertainty.

3.2   Synthetic Perceptual Maps

We introduce *Synthetic Perceptual Maps* (see Figure 1) as a robust method for allowing information obtained through synthetic senses to be represented and operated on using a homogenous representation. For the visual modality, synthetic perceptual maps are a virtual analogy of topographic retinotopic maps that represent the visual world as seen through the eyes of a viewer. They are rectangular, 2D grey-scale maps corresponding to the agents field-of-view, where the value of a location in the map represents the strength of some particular feature or resultant operation based on the corresponding spatial location. There are four general categories in our model that are represented by synthetic perceptual maps and contribute to the overall relevance of scene elements. These are: salience, threat/potential threat, reward/potential reward and uncertainty.

Salience relates to basic feature contrast between spatial scene elements, such as colour or orientation opponency (Figure 1(e)). It is the only process that can operate in our model in the complete absence of attention allocation - that is, if no visible stimuli have been appraised, then salience is the sole indicator of relevance. This map is created solely from the spatial representation of the scene (i.e. the full-colour rendering (Figure 1(a)) and does not consider object semantics. Salience calculation is based on a model of bottom-up attention from computational neuroscience [10] that has been adapted by us for use with agents [18]. The output is a saliency perceptual map.

Both *reward* and *threat* (Figures 1(c) and (d)) and their potentials are represented in reward and threat perceptual maps. Our design for the detection of emotional aspects of stimuli in visual processing is inspired by work in neuroscience indicating emotional modulation of the visual cortex at very early stages of processing [2] and studies positing threat to be a vital factor in quickly grabbing attention and eliciting emotional expression [12]. Unlike the saliency map which is spatial in nature, these maps are based on object representations of the scene (that is, they utilise the false-colour rendering (Figure 1(b)). The value of each element occupied spatially by the object is set to its appraised threat / reward value (or the potential threat / reward value if the reward / threat appraisals have not yet taken place for the object in question). Reward and potential reward is linked to the pleasantness of the stimulus, as derived from the basic stimulus characteristics of arousal and valence. Threat and potential threat are also derived from these basic characteristics.

Uncertainty is also applied on a per object basis based on the corresponding uncertainty value stored in memory. In this form, it acts to inhibit objects that have been previously attended to and ensures shifts in the focus of attention. The uncertainty map (Figure 1(f)) is also used for establishing the *scene uncertainty* (see Section 4.2), a global metric for determining the virtual infants motivation towards undertaking explorative behaviour.

Each of these maps is weighted and combined into the final *relevance master map* (Figure 1(g)), which is the last stage in the visual perception pipeline. The relevance master map greatly influences the focus and spread of attention allocation over the visual field, and thus, somewhat indirectly, also influences changes in inner state (Section 4). Weighting and combination of the maps allows the establishment of a goal hierarchy for attention to adhere to so that not all factors are treated equally: for example, using this design, one can ensure that threat is always treated as a dominant factor over reward, and that negatively valenced stimuli receive enhanced modulation over positively valenced or neutral stimuli. As a further example, in this model when two stimuli are equally threatening/rewarding, the more salient one will attract more attention.

NEGATIVE EXPRESSIONS				Threat Potential	POSITIVE EXPRESSIONS				Reward Potential
Gaze Direction	Facial Expression				Gaze Direction	Facial Expression			
Directed	Anger			High	Directed	Joy			High
Averted		→		Low	Averted		→		Medium
Directed	Fear			Medium	Directed	Calmness and other			Medium
Averted				High	Averted	positive			Low

Fig. 2. Two tables denoting some examples of the mapping from gaze and facial expression onto assessments for the existence of threat or reward in the environment

3.3   Social Stimuli

In order to demonstrate how the design can accommodate more sophisticated stimuli and appraisals, we include here the case of social stimuli, such as people and faces. These stimuli contain extra characteristics: the perceived *facial expression* and *gaze direction*. Faces and facial expression are known to be strong indicators of emotion and attractors of visual attention [27]. Gaze is an important component in emotional appraisal of faces that is sometimes overlooked: indeed the amygdala is sensitive to eye gaze [26], and can act to disambiguate the threat source during expressions of anger and fear [1]. Appraisal results based on the gaze direction and facial expression (see Figure 2) can be incorporated directly into the reward and threat maps described in Section 3.2. Gaze direction is categorised as either looking directly towards the agent or else classified as 'away'. The facial expression of the other is deemed to fall into a small number of broad discrete categories: happy, sad, angry, neutral, surprise or interest. As with other stimuli, arousal and valence information is also available about the facial expression as part of the basic stimulus characteristics.

4   Modelling of Internal State

At the core of the virtual agent is a representation of its fundamental internal state, controlling its perception and behaviour. The internal state is based on three dimensions: *valence, arousal* and *spread of focus*.

Valence, or hedonic tone, relates to liking, pleasure and preference on one hand, or dislike, aversion and distress on the other. The valence of the virtual infant is related to the valence of stimuli it has been perceiving. Functionally, its key purpose in the model is to determine the type of expressive behaviours of the agent.

Arousal, relates to the degree to which the agent is awake, alert and ready to act. We focus here on cognitive aspects of arousal and liken it to a 'power lever' that can be turned up, endogenously or exogenously, in order to increase the amount of resources the agent has available for allocation to tasks such as appraisal. Arousal only effects the amount of resources available for allocation, but not the allocation strategy itself.

Spread of Focus, refers to the way in which the agent is allocating available cognitive resources (as determined by arousal) towards the processing of single or multiple concepts. It could be thought of as the degree to which attention is distributed over a wide area of the scene or multiple objects (i.e. a wide focus), or narrowed in to zoom on a specific area or single object (i.e. narrow focus). The spread of focus has an impact on the depth of processing, which is also dependant on arousal.

Valence and arousal together are indicative of the agents emotional state, while arousal and focus are indicative of its attentional state. Arousal thus acts as a key link in our model between emotion and attention, ensuring that any change in attentional state has emotional consequences and vice versa. For example, if appraisal of a threatening stimulus arouses the agent emotionally, the increase in arousal makes available more attentional resources with which to further appraise the threat.

The emotional state of the infant is determined by the dimensions of valence and arousal (see Figure 3). Both the valence and arousal tend naturally towards a rest position when there are no particularly new or interesting stimuli visible. The valence of the inner state is influenced by the valence of appraised stimuli, so if the agent has been perceiving negatively valenced stimuli its state will be influenced towards a negative valence. The valence is primarily used to influence the types and intensities of facial expressions made by the infant - stimuli that it finds pleasant invoke positive expressions, such as smiling, while negatively valenced stimuli invoke negative reactions, such as cry-faces (see Section 5).

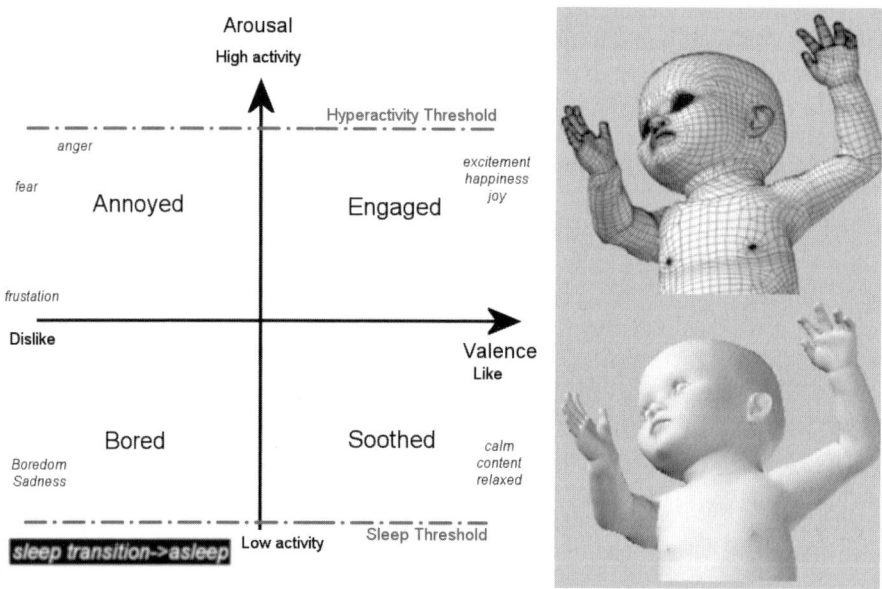

Fig. 3. Left: The inner emotional state, represented by the dimensions of valence and arousal. Right: The 3D model used for the representation of the virtual infant.

We model the effects of arousal in a general way inspired by the Yerkes-Dodson law, which predicts reduced performance when the arousal level is too high or too low: the agent performs best in terms of observing and appraising the environment at moderate levels of arousal. At extreme levels it becomes either hyperactive or falls into a state of sleep, in both situations being unresponsive to visual stimuli until its arousal returns to moderate levels. The infant will tend towards entering these states when the scene uncertainty is extremely low or when there are a large number of threatening or rewarding stimuli in the environment - although behaviour is different in each case.

4.1   Attention Allocation

The attentional state of the virtual infant is determined by its arousal and spread of focus, which attempt to allocate resources in the best manner to satisfy the relevance master map (see Section 3.2). These variables are important because they determine the extent to which resources are available for deployment: in our model, attention has the function of reducing the uncertainty associated with stimuli, which in turn results in their appraisal (see Section 3). Here, arousal can be regarded as a 'power lever' dictating the amount of pooled cognitive resources available for allocation towards appraising elements of relevance. Assuming the field-of-view and other variables are the same, a highly aroused agent will be able to conduct its appraisals (i.e. reduce uncertainty) in a quicker manner than one that is less aroused. In this work we assume that all resources made available according to the level of arousal are always allocated towards enhancing perceptual attention.

In contrast, spread of focus specifies how those available resources are allocated over the perceptual field. A narrow spread of focus therefore characterises an agent diverting its attentive resources to focus on a single stimulus, while one with a wide spread of focus divides its attention more evenly over the entire scene in a parallel manner. Given the same available resources, a focus may be spatially narrow, but deep in terms of depth of processing, or spatially wide but shallow in terms of depth of processing. In nearly all situations, all locations within the field-of-view will receive some degree of attention, although at a much reduced rate compared with those inside the foci of attention.

4.2   Memory and Scene Uncertainty

As mentioned, each object in the scene has an associated value in the agents memory corresponding to the level to which it has been appraised. As stimuli are attended to, this value is reduced leading to successive appraisals. An important metric for helping to define the behaviour of the agent is the *scene uncertainty*: this is a measure of the total uncertainty for all objects in the visual field. When the scene uncertainty is extremely low, the arousal of the infant falls and in some cases the infant may transition into sleep. In contrast, when it is high, the infants arousal increases and it is more motivated towards undertaking explorative gaze behaviours. The uncertainty metric is also used for determining the intensity of orienting behaviours: When the contrast is high between the uncertainty value of a perceived stimulus and the scene uncertainty value, orienting response behaviours are more intense.

5   Behaviour

Behaviour generation consists of changes in facial expression, bodily movements and gaze direction, controlled by a hierarchical finite state machine, or *HFSM*, which is derived from the virtual infants internal state and conducts transitions according to changes in this state. While the infant can have a wide variety of internal states, it has a more discrete behaviour repertoire for expressing them, as outlined next. These behaviours represent the infants only method for expressing its internal state to the outside world. Although the repertoire is limited, it is dynamic to an extent. As an example, the intensity of a smile is linked to the internal valence, meaning that the agent is capable of making a large number of varying smiles. In general, the main behaviours are based on findings that in infants, more emotionally positive and negative faces are characterised by similar, although not identical, factors of stronger lip movement, eye constriction and wider mouth opening, with greater mouth opening has been associated strongly with higher arousal. The categories of behaviours are:

- **Smiles** are generally used to express positive emotions in infants, where lip corners pull up obliquely towards the cheekbones. In smiles with eye constriction (Duchenne), the cheeks raise toward the eyes and tightens the skin lateral to the eyes. They may occur with both a closed or an open mouth. Between 1 and 6 months, smiling with eye constriction and with mouth opening are both more likely during positive naturalistic interaction [15]. For infant smiles, it has been found [7][14] that the co-occurrence of the three factors of greater lip movement, mouth opening and eye constriction are strongly related to the perception of the intensity of the negative emotion. Individually, greater eye constriction and stronger lip corner movement have been rated as expressing greater positive emotion. It is greatest in smiles involving both mouth opening and eye constriction and is less strong when the smile involves only one of these features.
- **Cry-faces** are regarded as a prototypical infant response to negative stim-uli, encompassing the expression of discrete states such as anger, distress or pain. They are typically characterised by a lowering of the brows, raising of the upper lip and in some cases, nose wrinkling. Cry faces also involve lip-stretching, although unlike smiles, movement is *lateral* (rather than oblique). Cheek raising can produce eye constriction (also active during smiles), but tightening of the eyelids is active only in cry faces. There is also at least a minimal degree of mouth opening (jaw drop). Although the source of mouth opening is similar in cry and smile faces, cry faces involve some mouth open-ing combined with lip stretching in order to produce a characteristic square mouth formation.

  For infant cry-faces, it has been found [7] that the co-occurrence of the three factors of greater lip movement, mouth opening and eye constriction are strongly related to the perception of the intensity of the negative emo-tion. Individually, greater eye constriction and greater mouth opening are particularly linked with the perception of expression of greater negative emo-tion. Other facial features such as brow movements might also impact the perceived intensity of negative expressions. In our work, cry-faces will be sig-nalled according to internal valence, with intensity determining the strength and combination of these factors.
- **Orienting response** and **behavioural freezing** ('stilling'), encapsulating interruption of exploratory behaviour, decrease in general activity level, gaze

fixation ('attention immobility'), postural rigidity and facial sobriety (shows no excessive or extreme qualities of emotion). The facial expression of surprise, involving movement of the brows, opening of the eyes, and opening of the mouth of jaw, is rarely seen in infants [23]. The degree of orienting response is dependant on the uncertainty contrast, as described in Section 4.2.

– **Predefined behaviours**, unlike the previous behaviours listed here, have no dynamic aspect. They are prerecorded keyframed animations that are replayed at runtime as required. These include animations for *sleeping, hyperactivity* and accompanying behaviours for facial expressions such as shaking the arms or legs.

5.1   Behavioural Output and Scenario

The attentive state of the virtual infant is reflected primarily through changes in its gaze direction and orienting behaviours towards relevant stimuli. As mentioned (see Section 4), these behaviours are dependant on the agents arousal, spread of focus and the relevance master map. In situations where the agent has moderate or high arousal and low spread of focus, it will appear to be have great interest in specific aspects of the environment, studying them in great deal as it selectively attends to and appraises them - depending on the contrast with the uncertainty of the rest of the scene, this initially results in a degree of 'stilling' or freezing of facial expression and body movements while the stimulus is initially appraised. In situations where the agent is moderately or highly aroused, but has a distributed spread of focus, it will appear interested in all of its surroundings, appearing very explorative as it looks around, while conducting only limited appraisals. Of course, during this process, it is possible that a sufficiently potentially relevant stimulus will grab attention and start to reduce the spread of focus. When the agent is not so aroused, automated looking behaviours are inhibited to the point where, if arousal falls below the sleep threshold, a predefined sleep animation is played.

The model described in this paper and a scenario to demonstrate it are under construction using the Torque game engine [8]. The infant is being represented with a 3D model (see Figure 3: Right). The scenario demonstrating the virtual baby will be a bed and playroom, with the infant seated in a high chair. The user will be able to interactively present predefined stimuli into environment, such as toys, some of which are shown in Figure 1.

6   Conclusions and Future Work

We have presented the design of a virtual infant capable of a number of attention and emotion related behaviours. An infant-like appearance has been adopted as we feel it better suits the demonstration our agents capabilities and evaluate its potential. During evaluations, human perceivers may have a tendency to be expectant of appropriate cognitive and linguistic capabilities that current technology has trouble providing for adult humanoid characters. Given the lack of cognitive and linguistic capabilities in our agent, this choice of appearance could provide a better fit for its behavioural capabilities and thus help reduce disparity between expected behaviour and appearance allowing more focus on the core qualities relating to artificially generated emotion and attention behaviours.

Important future work that we are considering includes the construction of a novelty detection module. Such a module would fit well into the proposed design, feeding into the relevance calculations. For example, recent findings suggest that the pure novelty of a stimulus can serve as a reward in its own right [3]. Finally, we are also evaluating the use of Baby FACS [17] as a possible method for informing the animation of the virtual infants face, and EARL [24] as a global representation method for use when transferring emotion attributes, such as those relating to stimulus appraisals and the state of the internal emotion model, internally between model components.

Acknowledgements

The author would like to thank Catherine Pelachaud for her support throughout this research and the reviewers for their valuable commentary. This work has been funded by the Network of Excellence HUMAINE: IST-2002-2.3.1.6 / Contract no. 507422 (http://emotion-research.net/).

References

1. Adams, R., Gordon, H., Baird, A., Ambady, N., Kleck, R.: Effects of gaze on amygdala sensitivity to anger and fear faces. Science 300(5625), 1536 (2003)
2. Adolphs, R.: Emotional vision. Nature Neuroscience 7(11), 1167–1168 (2004)
3. Bunzeck, N., Duzel, E.: Absolute coding of stimulus novelty in the human substantia nigra/vta. Neuron 51, 369–379 (2006)
4. Cañamero, D.: Modeling motivations and emotions as a basis for intelligent behavior. In: Johnson, W.L., Hayes-Roth, B. (eds.) Proceedings of the First International Conference on Autonomous Agents (Agents'97), pp. 148–155. ACM Press, New York (1997)
5. Chopra, S., Badler, N.: Where to look? automating attending behaviors of virtual human characters. Autonomous Agents and Multi-Agent Systems 4(1/2), 9–23 (2001)
6. Conde, T., Thalmann, D.: An artificial life environment for autonomous virtual agents with multi-sensorial and multi-perceptive features. Computer Animation and Virtual Worlds 15(3-4), 311–318 (2004)
7. Dinehart, L., Messinger, D., Acosta, S., Cassel, T., Ambadar, Z., Cohn, J.: Adult perceptions of positive and negative infant emotional expressions. Infancy 8(3), 279–303 (2005)
8. The Torque Game Engine, http://www.garagegames.com/
9. Grand, S., Cliff, D.: Creatures: Entertainment software agents with artificial life. Autonomous Agents and Multi-Agent Systems 1(1), 39–57 (1997)
10. Itti, L.: Models of Bottom-Up and Top-Down Visual Attention. PhD thesis, Pasadena, California, Jan (2000)

11. Kim, Y., Hill Jr, R.W., Traum, D.R.: A computational model of dynamic perceptual attention for virtual humans. In: 14th Conference on Behavior Representation in Modeling and Simulation (BRIMS) (2005)
12. LeDoux, J.: The Emotional Brain. Touchstone, New York (1996)
13. Marsella, S., Gratch, J.: Ema: A computational model of appraisal dynamics. In: Trappl, R. (ed.) Cybernetics and Systems 2006, pp. 601–606. Austrian Society for Cybernetic Studies, Vienna (2006)
14. Messinger, D.: Positive and negative: Infant facial expressions and emotions. Current Directions in Psychological Science 11(1), 1–6 (2002)
15. Messinger, D., Fogel, A.: All smiles are positive, but some smiles are more positive than others. Developmental Psychology 37(5), 642–653 (2001)
16. Mourao-Miranda, J., Volchan, E., Moll, J., de Oliveira-Souza, R., Oliveira, L., Bramati, I., Gattass, R., Pessoa, L.: Contributions of stimulus valence and arousal to visual activation during emotional perception. NeuroImage 20(4), 1955–1963 (2003)
17. Oster, H.: Baby facs: Facial action coding system for infants and young children. In: Unpublished monograph and coding manual, New York University (1999)
18. Peters, C.: Bottom-Up Visual Attention for Autonomous Virtual Human Animation. PhD thesis, Trinity College, Dublin, Ireland (2004)
19. Peters, C., Sullivan, C.O'.: Bottom-up visual attention for virtual human animation. In: Proceedings of Computer Animation for Social Agents (CASA) 2003 (2003)
20. Petters, D.: Simulating infant-carer relationship dynamics. In: Hudlicka, E., Cañamero, L. (eds.) Architectures for Modeling Emotion: Cross-Disciplinary Foundations, Technical Report SS-04-02, pp. 114–121. AAAI Press, Menlo Park (2004)
21. Scherer, K.: An emotion's occurrence depends on the relevance of an event to the organism's goal/need hierarchy. Oxford University Press, New York/Oxford (1994)
22. Scherer, K.: Appraisal processes in emotion: Theory, methods, research, chapter Appraisal considered as a process of multilevel sequential checking, pp. 92–120. Oxford University Press, New York (2001)
23. Scherer, K., Zentner, M., Stern, D.: Beyond surprise: The puzzle of infants' expressive reactions to expectancy violation. Emotion 4(4), 389–402 (2004)
24. Schroeder, M., Pirker, H., Lamolle, M.: Proceedings of lrec'06 workshop on corpora for research on emotion and affect. In: Deviller, L., Martin, J.-C., Cowie, R., Douglas-Cowie, E., Batliner, A. (eds.) Cybernetics and Systems 2006, Genoa, Italy, pp. 88–92 (2006)
25. Velásquez, J.D.: Modeling emotions and other motivations in synthetic agents. In: Proceedings of the Fourteenth National Conference on Artificial Intelligence (AAAI-97). Providence, RI, pp. 10–15 (1997)
26. Vuilleumier, P.: Staring fear in the face. Nature 433(6), 22–23 (2005)
27. Vuilleumier, P., Schwartz, S.: Emotional facial expressions capture attention. Neurology 56, 153–158 (2001)

A Bottom-Up Investigation of Emotional Modulation in Competitive Scenarios

Lola Cañamero and Orlando Avila-García[*]

Adaptive Systems Research Group
School of Computer Science, University of Hertfordshire
College Lane, Hatfield, Herts AL10 9AB, UK
L.Canamero@herts.ac.uk, newoavila@hotmail.com

Abstract. In this paper, we take an incremental, bottom-up approach to investigate plausible mechanisms underlying emotional modulation of behavior selection and their adaptive value in autonomous robots. We focus in particular on achieving adaptive behavior selection in competitive robotic scenarios through modulation of perception, drawing on the notion of biological hormones. We discuss results from testing our architectures in two different competitive robotic scenarios.

1 Introduction

One of the main problems for autonomous robots is behavior selection or "what to do next" [12]. Motivation-based architectures [12,4,17,2] integrate a combination of internal and external factors to select the appropriate behavior and satisfy the robot's needs in real time. However, these architectures are not always sufficiently adaptive to rapid environmental changes. Previous work [5] postulated the use of second-order mechanisms, akin to some of the functions of emotions in biological systems, that act on other elements in the architecture for improved performance in dynamic, unpredictable, and dangerous environments. In that architecture and others that have followed a similar approach, the adaptive functions of emotions are predefined by the designer. While this nowadays widespread design practice can produce efficient behavior selection, it leaves unanswered the question of which are the underlying mechanisms and how they integrate and interact with other elements to achieve adaptive behavior. In the work presented here, we take an incremental approach to investigate plausible mechanisms underlying emotional modulation of behavior selection and their adaptive value. We are particularly interested in how such modulation can achieve different functionalities from the same architecture by interacting with other elements, rather than including emotions as additional components. In this paper, we focus on discussing how behavior selection can be made adaptive (i.e., its output biased) to different environmental situations (two different competitive robotic scenarios) by modulating different sensory channels—perception of external and internal stimuli. Drawing on the notion of biological hormones,

---

[*] Currently with OpenCanarias S.L.

A. Paiva, R. Prada, and R.W. Picard (Eds.): ACII 2007, LNCS 4738, pp. 398–409, 2007.

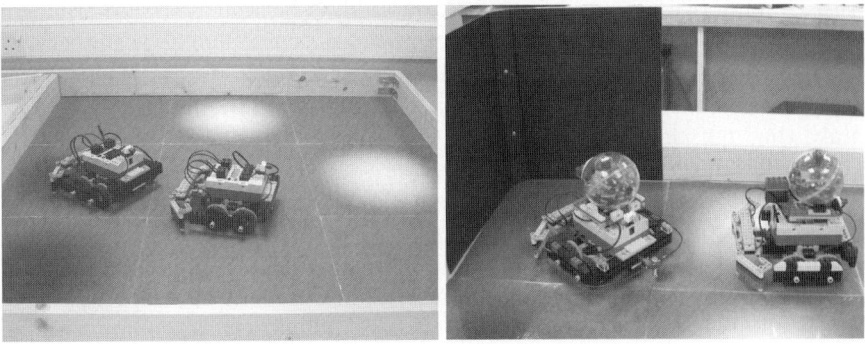

Fig. 1. Experimental setups used to carry out the studies: a Competitive Two-Resource Problem scenario (left), and a "prey-predator" scenario showing the prey robot inside the nest and the predator outside (right)

we have modeled two of the functionalities ascribed to them in order to improve the adaptation of motivation-based architectures to different problems. To achieve different functionalities from the same architecture, we have taken inspiration from neuroscience models of hormonal control [9,10], in particular regarding the following ideas: (a) Sensory inputs enhance the release of hormones that act at different levels of the nervous system; (b) they act as gain-setting sensitization processes that bias the output of the organism in particular directions; and (c) after modulation, the organism responds to particular sensory stimuli with an altered output appropriate to the new situation. We have tested our "hormone-like" mechanisms in two dynamic and unpredictable competitive robotic scenarios depicted in Figure 1, and show how they improve adaptation and performance using quantitative indicators based on the notion of viability. Finally, we analyze the results in terms of interesting behavioral phenomena that emerge from the interaction of these artificial hormones with the rest of architectural elements and the environment, and that resemble "emotional" behavior in biological systems confronted to similar situations.

2 Behavior Selection Architecture

Following [5], in our architecture behavior selection results from the interactions of a number of elements integrated through an artificial physiology and in interaction with the environment.

The physiology consists of (1) survival-related, homeostatically controlled essential variables and (2) hormones. *Essential variables* are abstractions representing the level of internal resources that the robot needs in order to survive. They must be kept within a range of permissible values for the robot to remain viable or "alive," thus defining a physiological space [14] or viability zone [1,13] within which survival (continued existence) is guaranteed, whereas transgression of these boundaries leads to "death." *Hormones* can be seen as second-order control mechanisms that affect the behavior of other elements of the arhitecture.

Motivations are abstractions representing tendencies to act in particular ways as a function of internal and external factors [18]. Internal factors are mainly (but not only) physiological deficits ($0 \leq d_i \leq 1$) or bodily needs—traditionally known as "drives"—that set urges to action to maintain the state of the controlled physiological variables within the viability zone. External factors are environmental stimuli, commonly termed "incentive cues" in Ethology, ($0 \leq c_i \leq 1$) that allow to satisfy bodily needs through behavior execution. In our implementation, each motivation performs homeostatic control of one physiological variable. We have used the equation proposed in [2] to combine cue and physiological deficit when computing motivational intensities:

$$m_i = d_i + (d_i \times \alpha c_i) \qquad (1)$$

In addition to physiological deficits (d_i) and incentive cues (c_i), this equation introduces a weighting factor ($0 \leq \alpha \leq 1$) that affects the relevance given to the external cue.

Behaviors are coarse-grained subsystems (embedding simpler actions) that implement behavioral competencies similar to [12,5]. Following a classical distinction in ethology [15], motivated behavior can be consummatory—"goal-achieving" and needing the presence of an incentive stimulus to be executed—or appetitive—"goal-directed" search for a particular incentive stimulus. In addition to modifying the external environment, the execution of a behavior has an impact on (increases or decreases) the level of specific physiological variables. Therefore, behaviors take part in the homeostatic control to maintain the state of the physiological variables within the viability zone.

Behavior Selection is performed in a continuous loop consisting of three main steps: (1) The deficit of the physiological variables (internal needs) and the intensity of the external stimuli are calculated; (2) motivational intensities are computed combining (perception of) deficits and external stimuli ponderated by the weight α, following equation 1; (3) the behavior that (best) satisfies the motivation with the highest intensity is executed, modifying the physiology and possibly the position of the robot relative to external stimuli in the environment.

3   Competition for Resources

In previous work [2] we analyzed different motivation-based behavior selection architectures within a static Two-Resource Problem (TRP), in which a single robot must maintain appropriate levels of two internal variables by consuming two resources available in the external environment. The TRP constitutes the minimal scenario to test behavior selection mechanisms, and it has become a standard testbed for behavior selection both in animals—see e.g., [17]—and autonomous agents and robots—e.g., [4,7,3]. Its simplicity, although not devoid of problems, favors a systematic analysis of results. The particular implementation of the TRP in [2] used a Lego Mindstorms robot (see Figure 1, left, for a similar arena, although the TRP uses only one robot), with the need to maintain temperature and energy levels by consuming heat (white gradients on the floor of the arena) and food (black gradients), respectively. The robot had two motivations: m_{cold} to increase temperature, which can be satisfied by executing the consummatory behavior b_{warmup}, and $m_{fatigue}$ to increase energy, which can be achieved by executing the consummatory behavior b_{feed}. In addition, the robot had a reflex obstacle avoidance behavior b_{avoid}, and the appetitive behavior b_{search}. The execution of all behaviors affects both essential variables[1].

To measure results in TRP, we used different performance indicators based on the notion of viability, in particular: *Life Span*, defined as the time that the robot survived in each run ($LS = t_{life}/t_{run}$); *Overall Comfort*, the average level of satisfaction of the physiological variables during a run ($OvC = \sum_{i=1}^{t_{life}}(1 - \overline{d_i})/t_{life}$); and *Physiological Balance*, the homogeneity with which physiological needs are satisfied during a run ($PhB = \sum_{i=1}^{t_{life}}(1 - \sigma^2(d_i))/t_{life}$). We also noted that, when doing behavior selection in TRP, the robot executed regular cycles of activities rather than isolated behaviors, and those activity cycles were reflected in the physiological space of the robot, as shown in Figure 2: from the initial state, the robot would start looking for a given resource, e.g. heat (arrow noted as A in the figure), then consume it until satiated (B), then start looking for the other resource (C), consume it until satiated (D), and start all over again. The position of the cycles in the physiological can be changed: the same cycle (i.e., with the same shape and duration of each activity) would be executed closer to the ideal state, therefore preserving viability "better", or father away from it (and therefore in a "less viable" way) depending on the value of α, the parameter that weighed the significance of external stimuli in equation 1, as depicted on Figure 2 (right). The regular shape of those activity cycles reflects the fact that behavior selection in TRP was static and highly predictable.

The Competitive Two-Resource Problem[2] (CTRP) is an extension of this problem that consists in the introduction of two robots in the same environment simultaneously performing their own TRP, as depicted in Figure 1 (left). The robots do not explicitly communicate or compete; however, the fact that they have to use the same resources to satisfy their needs introduces competition for those resources, as both robots might need access to the same resource at the same time. Therefore, new forms of environmental complexity—availability and accessibility of resources—appear due to the interaction between robots, breaking the predictability and symmetry of TRP. The question that needs to be examined here is to what extent the architecture used for the TRP can solve the CTRP.

---

[1] At each execution cycle, b_{warmup} increases temperature by 0.3 units while decreasing energy by 0.1 units, b_{feed} increases energy by 0.3 units while decreasing temperature by 0.1 units, and b_{avoid} and b_{search} decrease each variable by 0.2 units.

[2] We refer the reader to [3] for an in-depth technical quantitative analysis of this scenario, while here we focus on a qualitative discussion of the adaptive value of hormonal modulation and its significance from the point of view of emotion.

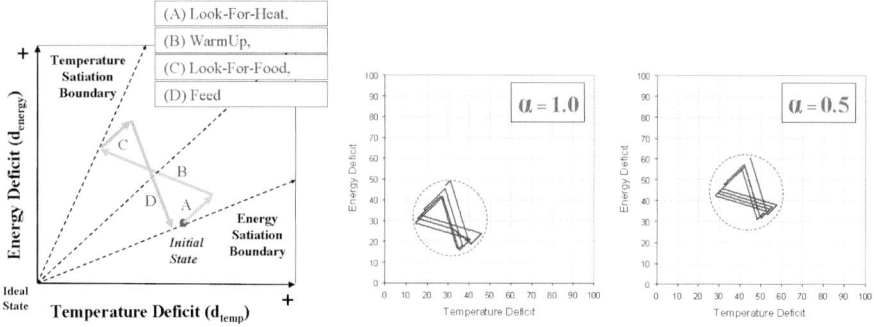

Fig. 2. Activity cycles in TRP. Left: cycle as reflected in the physiological space. Right: position of cycles in the physiological space as a function of α.

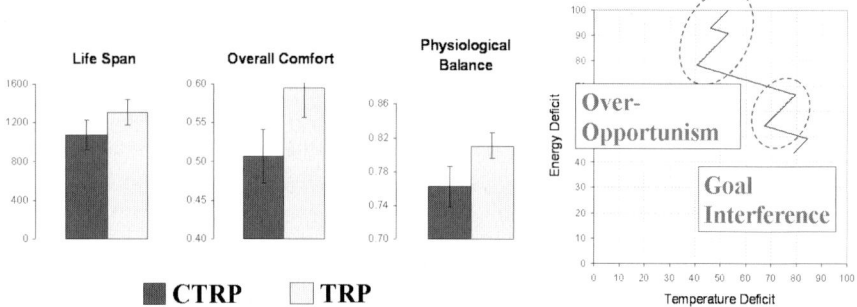

Fig. 3. Decreased performance in the CTRP, as measured by viability indicators (left) and activity cycles (right)

Analysis showed that the new forms of complexity dramatically decrease the performance of that behavior selection architecture, as clearly reflected by the different viability indicators and the activity cycles depicted in Figure 3. In particular, analysis of the activity cycles shows that the cycles easily loose the regularity and symmetry they showed in TRP, as illustrated in Figure 3 (right), and that the robot very often dies from two problems that the behavior selection mechanism used within the TRP presents when used in the CTRP. First, the robot can fall in a pathological sequence of opportunistic activities—consuming the same resource—that eventually can drive it to death due to over-opportunism. Second, when one robot is located on top of a resource—i.e., consuming it—the other robot might bump into it and push it out of the resource. This will result in the interruption of the ongoing consummatory activity and to death due to goal interference.

The next step in our incremental design approach is to analyze what needs to be added to the architecture to be able to solve those problems. A solution to the "over-opportunism" problem requires shifting attention away from less needed resources when the robot is in a high risk of death (RoD), that we define as the inverse of the distance between physiological state (d_{temper}, d_{energy}) and lethal boundaries. A solution to the "goal interference" problem requires that the robot in need of an occupied resource does not avoid the "intruder" as if it were a mere obstacle. Both problems can be solved by altered perception of external stimuli, i.e., by modulation of exteroception.

3.1 Modulation of Exteroception

Rather than adding more structural elements to our architecture, our solution consists in trying to achieve additional functionality from the same architecture. A single "hormone-like" modulatory mechanism can alter perception in both cases, with a twofold effect. First, by acting on the parameter α of equation 1— i.e., by biasing the relevance given to external cues—the hormone reduces the perception of both incentive cues, therefore reducing opportunistic activities when there is any risk of death. Second, by cancelling the perception of obstacles $s_{obstacle}$ (carried out using the bumper sensor), and hence the avoidance reflex behavior, when the robot is facing the competitor, the hormone potentiates the competition skills of the robot by enhancing its capacity to push the other robot out the resources and not to be interrupted. To achieve this twofold functionality, the concentration of hormone will be a function of the risk of death (RoD) and the perception of the competitor, given by $0 \leq s_{competitor} \leq 1$. Hormone concentration is computed as:

$$c_g = RoD + s_{competitor} \tag{2}$$

The relation between hormone concentration and the cancellation of the perception of incentive cues and obstacles is as follows. To achieve the first functionality, the cancellation of α is directly proportional to the increment in hormone concentration, i.e., when RoD increases, α decreases: $\alpha = min(1 - c_g, 0)$ The second functionality is obtained by cancelling the perception of $s_{obstacle}$—i.e., bumpers—when the competitor is in front of the robot. For this mechanism to be efficient, two conditions must be fulfilled to make a coherent pushing of the other robot. First, the robot must avoid getting engaged in fights when it has high RoD. Second, it must only bump blindly into the other robot, not against the walls of the arena. To produce that effect the cancellation of the bumpers must be at hormonal levels $c_g \simeq 1$ and $c_g \simeq 2$.

It is worth noting that the motivation-based behavior selection architecture has suffered no modification; the only difference with respect to the TRP is the fact that now one of its parameters (α, cfr. equation 1) is modulated by the hormonal feedback mechanism.

3.2 Experiments and Results

We tested the robots for a total of 16 runs of 1200 steps (approximately 5 minutes) each, one step representing a loop of the behavior selection mechanism that takes $260ms$ in the 16MHz onboard microcontroller. As shown in Figure 4,

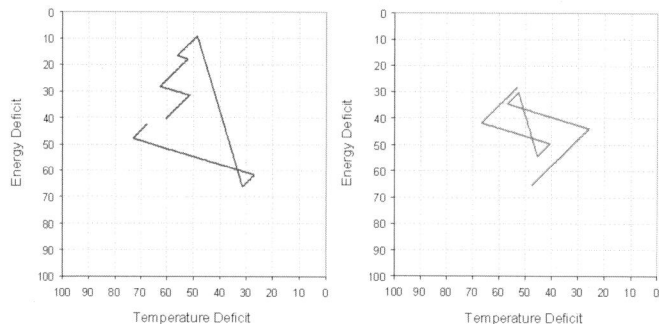

Fig. 4. Activity cycles in CTRP in unmodulated architecture (left) and with modulation of exteroception (right)

the robot with hormone-like mechanism recovers the stability and viability of activity cycles. We refer the reader to [3] for a detailed quantitative analysis, while we focus here on various interesting functionalities that emerged as a result of modulating the exteroception of the robot. The first functionality is to stop consuming resources when the robot detects its competitor approaching. This could be interpreted by an external observer as abandonment of a situation (waiting for the other robot at the resource) in which competing is disadvantageous. Instead, the robot will leave the resource and go straightforward towards the competitor until it reaches it; at that moment, two things can happen. If there is some level of RoD, the bumpers of the robot will not be cancelled and it will avoid the competitor, showing a behavior that an observer could interpret as "fear" after evaluating the competitor. On the contrary, if there is no RoD, the hormonal system will cancel the bumpers and the robot will push the competitor unconditionally—as if it showed some sort of "aggression" against it. If we study the whole picture as external observers, such behavioral phenomena could well be interpreted as some sort of "protection of resources".

4   Prey-Predator Scenario

The previous scenario involved no active interaction between the two robots. It therefore seems natural to ask whether an active relation between the robots would introduce additional complexity, and how the previous behavior selection architecture would cope with it. We thus designed a prey-predator scenario (Figure 1, right) that we call the Hazardous 3-Resource Problem (H3RP). In H3RP, a "predator" robot actively chases and can damage a "prey" robot by hitting a home-made contact sensor in the form of a ring. To make this interaction possible, we had to introduce new elements in the environment—a nest in one of the corners of the arena, in which the prey can "hide" and recover from damage—and in the architecture of the prey, namely: (a) a third physiological variable, integrity, which is a metaphor of the essential need any organism has to keep its tissue—the boundary between the organism and its environment—intact and that is unpredictably reduced by the attacks of the predator; (b) a new motivation m_{damage} to decrease the integrity deficit; and (c) an appropriate consummatory behavior $b_{recover}$ to satisfy the new need.

Initial experiments showed very quickly that a purely motivation-based behavior selection mechanism does not perform well within the new framework, since the prey invariably died as a consequence of predator attack (see the right graph of Figure 6 for quantitative results of additional experiments). The main cause seemed to be the inability of the prey to react timely to the attack of the predator, which was perceived in close proximity only. In other words, the behavior selection mechanism paid low attention to the new motivation to recover integrity, even when the predator is in sight. The probability to lose integrity rises when the predator is around, therefore it would be advantageous for the prey robot to "anticipate" that loss and start "preparing in advance" to recover integrity.

In the animal world, exposure to predators triggers what has been termed "predator-induced stress" or "predator-stress" for short, characterized by high levels of corticoids or "stress hormones" and a number of responses related to increased attention to and avoidance of the predator. Such reactions occur not only in the presence of a predator. Prey animals use unconditioned and conditioned predator cues to assess risk of predation, and they even seem to be able to perceive risks in the absence of such cues [6]. An example of the latter is the phenomenon known as "risk of permanence"—maintained levels of vigilance after predator's disappearance. Risk of predation strongly influences prey decision-making (for example, when and where to feed, vigilance, or the use of nest), which in this circumstances can be considered as a mechanism to allow an animal to manage predator-induced stress [11]. Risk of predation has been proposed to increase the animal's level of "apprehension," i.e. the reduction in attention to other activities (e.g. foraging) as a result of increasing the time spent executing defense-related activities such as vigilance or refuge use [8].

4.1 Modulation of Interoception

We have again applied "hormonal" modulation to our behavior selection architecture to achieve such "anticipatory" behavior, this time exploiting the temporal dynamics of hormonal decay to produce long-term modulatory effects triggered by short-term exposure to a stimulus [10].

To achieve this, a simple solution consists in using one of the existing sensors of the prey robot to detect the predator from a distance. Given the morphology of the robot, this sensor must be the same as that used to locate the nest. The problem of using that sensor is that it is fixed, pointing forwards. Since the predator does not pass in front of the prey very often and only does it for very brief periods, the additional stimulus ($s_{predator}$) will be too weak to make any difference. However, long-term hormonal modulation acts as a mechanism for predation risk assessment in the absence of predator cues. Hormone concerntration makes the system more sensitive to integrity deficit after the detection of the predator. Hormonal secretion follows the detection of the stimulus $s_{predator}$ and increases the *perceived* integrity deficit. Due to the hormone's temporal dynamics, modulation will be acting in the system long time after the predator has disappeared. Hormone concentration modifies again one of the sensory inputs of the architecture—interoceptive in this case—biasing behavior selection.

We have modeled hormonal temporal dynamics—release and dissipation—using an artificial endocrine system similar to that proposed in [16] and described by equations 3 and 4. A gland g releases hormone as a function of the intensity of the external stimulus predator ($s_{predator}$) at a constant releasing rate β_g:

$$r_g = \beta_g \cdot s_{predator} \tag{3}$$

Hormone concentration[3] suffers two opposite forces over time: it increases with the release of hormone by the gland, and dissipates or decays over time at a constant rate γ_g:

$$c(t+1)_g = max[(c(t)_g \cdot \gamma_g) + r_g, 100] \tag{4}$$

In this implementation, the hormone increases the perception of the integrity deficit ($d_{integrity}$), i.e., the higher the hormone concentration, the higher the reading of the $d_{integrity}$ interoceptor:

$$d_{integrity}^{new} = max(d_{integrity} + \delta_g \cdot c_g, 1) \tag{5}$$

Factor δ_g determines how susceptible to hormonal modulation the interoceptor ($d_{integrity}$) is. We use $\delta_g = 0.005$, which implies that the level of perceived $d_{integrity}$ is increased by 0.5 when hormonal concentration is maximum ($c_g = 100$). In other words, although the level of integrity is at its ideal value ($d_{integrity} = 0$), the interoceptor will perceive a level of 0.5 if hormone concentration is maximum. Note that there is a constraint to avoid the level of integrity deficit to be perceived beyond the maximum possible value ($d_{integrity} = 1$).

4.2   Experiments and Results

We tested the robot for 16 runs of 1600 steps each, i.e., each architecture (non-modulated and modulated) was tested for almost two hours in H3RP.

The prey robot presented higher viability levels in terms of life span, at the cost of overall comfort, when equipped with the modulatory mechanism, as shown in Figure 5. Long-term hormonal modulation acts as a mechanism for predation risk assessment in the absence of predator cues. It can be regarded as increasing the level of "apprehension" of the prey robot after short-term predator exposure, and this is reflected in an increment of the motivation to recover and of the execution time of recover-related (consummatory and appetitive) activities—the robot spends more time looking for the nest and recovering integrity in it—at the cost of other activities, namely feed and warmup, as reflected in Figure 6

---

[3] We constrained hormonal concentration to a maximum of $c_g = 100$ in order to keep more control on the hormone's dynamics and thus facilitate the analysis of results.

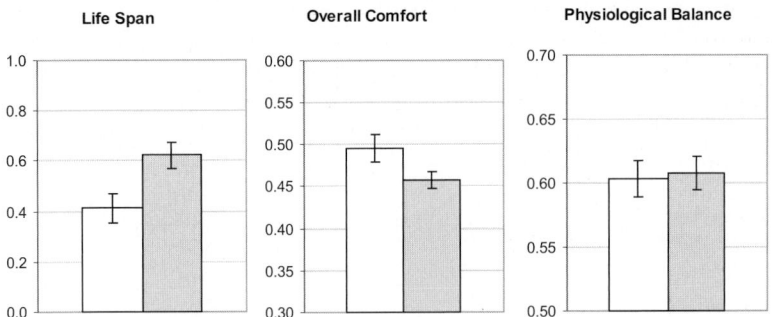

Fig. 5. Average performance of non-modulated (light bars) and modulated (dark bars) architecutres in terms of LifeSpan, Physiological Balance, and Overall Comfort. Bars show standard error of the mean.

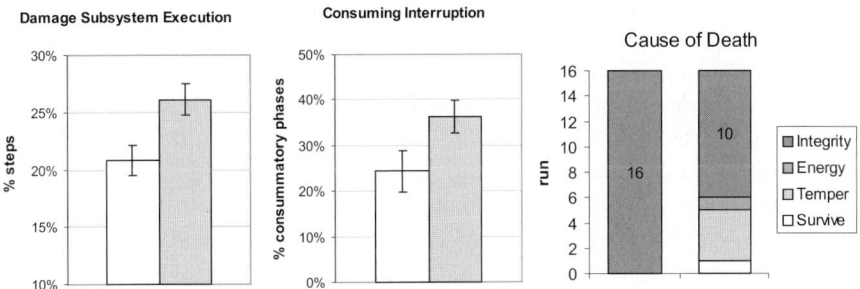

Fig. 6. Comparison between non-modulated (bars on the left of each graph) and modulated (bars on the right) architectures in terms of execution time of recover subsystem (left), average number of interruptions of consummatory feed and warmup behaviors (center), and causes of death in the 16 runs (right). Bars show standard mean error.

(left). This increment in the execution time of recover-related activities is statistically highly significant. Another important phenomenon is the interruption of ongoing consummatory feeding or warming-up activities (Figure 6, center). When the robot is under the effect of the hormone it will abandon the resource and go to the nest before the motivation has been satiated. The prey robot, when equipped with the hormonal mechanism, presents statistically higher levels of interruption of ongoing feeding or warming-up activities. Finally, analysis of the causes of death (Figure 6, right) shows substantial differences with respect to the non-modulated architecture.

5   Conclusion

We have discussed a bottom-up study of plausible mechanisms underlying emotional modulation of behavior selection and their adaptive value, in particular

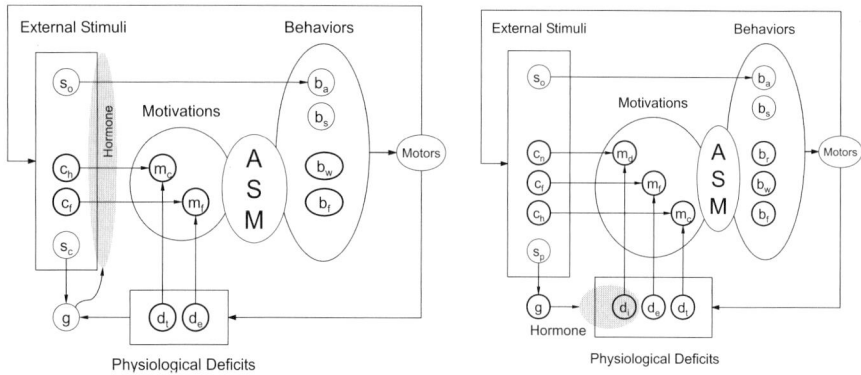

Fig. 7. Hormonal modulation of exteroception (left) and of interoception (right)

how such modulation applied to a motivation-based architecture can achieve different functionalities found in biological emotions, to face different emotionally-relevant problems posed by different competitive scenarios. We have considered a first scenario in which obtaining resources in competition with others is the main survival-related problem, and a second scenario in which the attack of a predator constitutes the main threat. Drawing on the notion of biological hormones, we have focused on achieving adaptive behavior selection in these different competitive robotic scenarios by modulating perception of external stimuli in the first case, and of internal stimuli in the second, as depicted in Figure 7. In addition to improving behavior selection performance and adaptation, modulation has given rise to some emergent behavioral phenomena that could be interpreted by an external observer as "emotional," such as aggressive/defensive behavior in the first, "fleeing" and "apprehension" in the second. We suggest that such modulatory mechanisms provide a more principled integration of different behavior selection elements and functions, in addition to improving the adaptation of a robot to changing environments. The type of adaptation fostered by such mechanisms is different from other mechanism such as learning or evolution, for which "past solutions" are "overwritten" by new ones.

Current and future work includes the integration in the same architecture of both types of hormonal modulation presented here, to face a more complex prey-predator problem requiring interactions among both mechanisms. We will also continue our incremental study of plausible modulatory mechanisms underlying emotions by changing and complexifying the environment to give rise to other behavior selection problems.

Acknowledgments

Support was provided partly by the European project HUMAINE (FP6-IST–507422) and partly by a University of Hertfordshire studentship to Orlando Avila-García.

References

1. Ashby, W.R.: Design for a Brain. Chapman & Hall, London (1952)
2. Avila-García, O., Cañamero, L., te Boekhorst, R.: Analyzing the Performance of "Winner-Take-All" and "Voting-Based" Action Selection Policies within the Two-Resource Problem. In: Banzhaf, W., Ziegler, J., Christaller, T., Dittrich, P., Kim, J.T. (eds.) ECAL 2003. LNCS (LNAI), vol. 2801, pp. 733–742. Springer, Heidelberg (2003)
3. Avila-García, O., Cañamero, L.: Using Hormonal Feedback to Modulate Action Selection in a Competitive Scenario. In: Proc. Eight Intl. Conf. Simulation of Adaptive Behavior (SAB04), pp. 243–252. MIT Press, Cambridge, MA (2004)
4. Blumberg, B.: Old Tricks, New Dogs: Ethology and Interactive Creatures. Unpublished PhD Thesis. MIT Media Laboratory, Cambridge, MA (1997)
5. Cañamero, L.D.: Modeling Motivations and Emotions as a Basis for Intelligent Behavior. In: Johnson, W.L. (ed.) Proc. First Intl. Conf. on Autonomous Agents, pp. 148–155. ACM Press, New York (1997)
6. Curio, E.: Proximate and Developmental Aspects of Antipredator Behavior. Adv. Study Behav. 22, 135–238 (1993)
7. Girard, B., Cuzin, V., Guillot, A., Gurney, K.N., Prescott, T.J.: Comparing a Brain-Inspired Robot Action Selection Mechanism with "Winner-Takes-All". In: Proc. Seventh Intl. Conf.on Simulation of Adaptive Behavior, MIT Press, Cambridge (2002)
8. Kavaliers, M., Choleris, E.: Antipredator Responses and Defensive Behavior: Ecological and Ethological Approaches for the Neurosciences. Neuroscience and Biobehavioral Reviews 25, 577–586 (2001)
9. Kravitz, E.A.: Hormonal Control of Behavior: Amines and the Biasing of Behavioral Output in Lobsters. Science 241, 1175–1781 (1988)
10. Levitan, I.B., Kaczmarek, L.K.: The Neuron: Cell and Molecular Biology, 3rd edn. Oxford University Press, Oxford, UK (2002)
11. Lima, S.L.: Stress and Decision Making under the Risk of Predation: Recent Developments from Behavioral, Reproductive, and Ecological Perspectives. Adv. Study Behav. 27, 215–290 (1998)
12. Maes, P.: A Bottom-Up Mechanism for Behavior Selection in an Artificial Creature. In: Proc. First Intl.Conf. on Simulation of Adaptive Behavior (SAB90), pp. 238–246. MIT Press, Cambridge, MA (1991)
13. Meyer, J.-A.: The Animat Approach to Cognitive Science. In: Roitblat, H.L., Meyer, J.-A. (eds.) Comparative Approaches to Cognitive Science, pp. 27–44. MIT Press, Cambridge, MA (1995)
14. McFarland, D. (ed.) Motivational Control Systems Analysis. Academic Press, London (1974)
15. McFarland, D.: Animal Behaviour, 3rd edn. Addison Wesley Longman Ltd., Redwood City, CA, USA (1999)
16. Neal, M., Timmis, J.: Timidity: A Useful Emotional Mechanism for Robot Control? Informatica 27, 197–204 (2003)
17. Spier, E., McFarland, D.: Possibly Optimal Decision Making under Self-Sufficiency and Autonomy. J. Theor.Biol. 189, 317–331 (1997)
18. Toates, F.: Motivational Systems. Cambridge Univ. Press, Cambridge (1986)

Enthusiasm and Its Contagion:
Nature and Function

Isabella Poggi

Università Roma Tre, Dipartimento di Scienze dell'Educazione,
Via del Castro Pretorio 20,
00185 Roma, Italy
poggi@uniroma3.it

Abstract. The paper presents a conceptual analysis of enthusiasm in terms of a goal and belief model of emotions. Enthusiasm is an emotion of the same family of joy, felt when an Agent believes she will very likely achieve a goal she is pursuing, because she has the necessary internal resources to achieve it. The function of enthusiasm is to enhance energy and persistence in goal pursuit. Some positive and negative aspects of the contagion of enthusiasm are presented and some empirical studies about enthusiasm and its contagion briefly overviewed.

Keywords: Enthusiasm, contagion, sport, school, affective computing.

1 Introduction

This work aims at defining the emotion of enthusiasm, describing aspects of its expression and communication, and clearing its function according to a model of mind and social interaction in terms of goals and beliefs.

I start my analysis from the term "enthusiasm". Among the hypotheses about its etymology one is particularly evocative: the term might derive from Greek *en* = "inside" + *theòs* = "God": so, enthusiasm means having a God inside. In fact, as we feel enthusiasm, we feel omnipotent, just like a God.

Enthusiasm was mainly studied by philosophers, like Plato [19] who saw it as a state of mystic inspiration, Giordano Bruno [3] who stressed it as a state of creative insanity, and, importantly, by Kant [13], who connected it to the aesthetical experience of sublime, but also acknowledged its function in revolutions and other innovative events [14]. Strangely enough, in the psychological domain enthusiasm is hardly mentioned, with the exception of Greenson [11], who distinguished the trait of being an enthusiastic person from the transitory state of enthusiasm, a type of euphoria apparently similar to mania, but in which, though, the subject maintains a sense of reality. The person who feels enthusiasm is in a state of exultance, fervour, elation: a state quite close to others in the area of joy, exuberance, optimism. Our ideas take life thanks to enthusiasm, a peculiar type of joy that implies a complete transformation of personality, of the Self and of the way we perceive the world. In general, then, we can define enthusiasm as that fire, that charge, that spur which helps us focus all of our physical and mental efforts to reach high value goals.

A. Paiva, R. Prada, and R.W. Picard (Eds.): ACII 2007, LNCS 4738, pp. 410–421, 2007.

2   Emotions, Their Functions and Their Dimensions

According to a goal and belief model of mind and social interaction [7], [21], an emotion is a complex subjective state encompassing cognitive aspects (beliefs, ideas, images, attributions), feelings (positive or negative), physiological aspects (arousal, bodily changes), expressive aspects (skin color changes, acoustic characteristics of voice, voluntary and involuntary face and body movements), and finally motivation aspects (the activation of specific goals, like flee for fear, aggression for anger, helping for compassion). This whole subjective state is triggered when an adaptively important goal of the Agent is, or is likely to be, achieved or thwarted, since the adaptive function of emotions is to monitor the state of the individual's adaptive goals [10], [4].

Thus, emotions can be distinguished in terms of several dimensions [21].

a. MONITORED GOAL: since the function of emotions is to monitor the state of achievement / thwarting of adaptive goals, emotions differ from each other qualitatively according to the type of the monitored goal. For instance, fear monitors the goal of survival and physical well-being, shame monitors the goals of image and self-image, and so on.

b. VALENCE: the difference between positive and negative emotions (the "valence" dimension in [18]) is determined by the achievement / thwarting dimension. We feel positive emotions (e.g. joy, satisfaction, pride) when a goal of ours is achieved, and negative ones (sadness, anger, shame) when a goal is thwarted.

c. TIME: before / after / during: some emotions are felt after the goal is achieved or thwarted (for example, joy or sorrow), while others are felt during, or even before goal pursuit. For instance, enthusiasm is generally felt during the course of the action or event one thinks could lead to achieve a goal, or even before the start of it.

d. DEGREE OF CERTAINTY: certain / likely / possible: this dimension has to do with the previous one. If goal pursuit is over we are certain about its achievement or thwarting, but during or before pursuit we are uncertain about it. So we feel joy or sadness when we are sure of the achievement or thwarting (generally when it already occurred), but fear when the goal is likely to be thwarted, and hope when the achievement is likely or even simply possible [16].

e. ADDITIONAL COGNITIVE ELEMENTS: in some emotions the cognitive aspects encompass some peculiar elements as expectations, causal attributions, evaluations. For example, to feel disappointment it is not sufficient that a goal is thwarted; a necessary condition is that you expected, with a fair degree of certainty, that the goal should be achieved. Again, we feel compassion for someone if we think he is suffering due to external causes, but we are angry against him if we attribute him the cause of his misfortune.

f. POWER OF CONTROL: another relevant cognitive element to distinguish emotions is the Agent's self-evaluation, his/her self-attribution of a power of control (the "potency" dimension in [18]. I fear you if I think you have more power than I have, while I am more likely to be angry at you if I think I have the power to contrast you.

g. ARGUMENTAL STRUCTURE: individual / social: some emotions (like love, hate, envy, admiration) are "intrinsically social" in that they are felt necessarily *towards* someone else. Others (like joy, enthusiasm, sadness) are "individual" emotions since they do not require a second argument in their argumental structure. Other emotions, finally, can have, so to speak, both an individual and a social version: I can be afraid of the storm, or be afraid of my boss. Finally some emotions, like amusement or enthusiasm, are not "social" per se, but they are typically subject to contagion and amplification when expressed in public.

h. INTENSITY: similar emotions may differ in intensity; for example, fear vs. terror, annoyance vs. anger, rage or fury. This has to do with the arousal level, the physiological activation of the felt emotion, that is presumably determined in turn by the importance of the monitored goal.

3   The Mental Ingredients of Enthusiasm

On the basis of this view of emotions we can now define enthusiasm. The emotion of enthusiasm belongs to the same family of joy: it is felt about the achievement of goals, typically during or even before goal pursuit, and it is a very positive emotion coming with the assumption that the goal pursued is very likely to be achieved. It is an "individual" emotion, but typically one that is felt more intensely if shared with other people, and easily subject to contagion.

As seen above, an emotion includes motivational, expressive, physiological, cognitive aspects. Here we focus on the cognitive aspects of enthusiasm: its "mental ingredients". The "mental ingredients" of an emotion - the pieces of its "cognitive anatomy" [5] - are the beliefs that are represented in an Agent when she is feeling an emotion, and that constitute the cognitive aspects of it.

In these terms, A feel enthusiasm as he or she feels a pleasant feeling caused by the following beliefs:

1. A is pursuing goal G1
2. A believes that G1 is a very important goal
3. A believes that A has the resources necessary to achieve goal G1
4. A feels responsible for the achievement of G1
5. A believes with a high degree of certainty that A will achieve goal G1
6. A has the meta-goal Gm to pursue G1 with conviction, strength and persistency

Let us see these mental ingredients in detail.

Belief 1. Enthusiasm is felt during the pursuit of a goal, or even before its start. For example, you can feel enthusiasm while you are planning vacations with friends: the vacation has not yet started but in your imagination; and when you have to study schedules or buy tickets, it will not be so exciting; but at the moment you are making your plan, you are already pursuing the goal, and you feel the pleasure to do so.

In fact, the emotion that is felt when the final goal is achieved is not enthusiasm but exultance. Take the players during a football game: they feel exultance when the game is over and they have won, but enthusiasm at the moment of a goal; that is, this emotion may be felt when an intermediate goal G2 is achieved, not the final objective G1 of the whole plan but a sub-goal of it. Because the very reason why you feel enthusiasm, whether G2 is in fact achieved or not, is belief 3., your believing that you *can* achieve G1. So when a goal is made during the football game, you feel this particular kind of intense joy, just because your hope to win the game, and trust in your power to overcome, are high: you think the achievement of the final objective is very likely to occur.

Let us come to belief 2. You feel enthusiasm when the ultimate goal you are pursuing, G1, is a very important goal, one worth to be pursued. Yet, it is not only a goal that is more important than others: you do not feel enthusiasm for any type of goal, but only for some "high", "noble" goals. They are terminal goals, that is, ends in themselves, not means to further goals. So, what are the goals whose pursuit gives enthusiasm? My hypothesis is that they are generally:

1. aesthetic goals – I may feel enthusiasm, for example,
    a.   while seeing a wonderful landscape,
    b.   while listening to a beautiful performance of a music I love;
2. goals of altruism:
    a.   if a friend of mine has won a competition,
    b.   while organizing a party for disabled children;
3. goals of equity:
    a.   in great revolutions (Kant [13] celebrated enthusiasm in the French revolution);
4. epistemic goals:
    a.   in solving a scientific problem,
    b.   in creating a new musical group,
    c.   in founding a new journal;
    d.   as every scholar knows, typically, in doing research!

But one who is feeling enthusiasm does not only know he is pursuing a high or noble goal; he also thinks he has the necessary resources to pursue it successfully. In other words – belief 3. – A attributes himself the power to achieve G1.

Our power to achieve goals is determined by both internal resources – our own beliefs and capacities for action – and external resources – world conditions and actions by other people. In enthusiasm, the resources A believes he has are not external conditions not dependent on herself, but his own internal resources. This is what distinguishes enthusiasm from being trustful or hopeful. Trust [9] and hope [16] imply that you rely, respectively, upon other people or world conditions: in any case, external resources not dependent on your will or capacity. In enthusiasm, instead, the Agent relies only on himself. This is the idea of omnipotence, the sensation of having "a god inside" which names the emotion: a sense of self-efficacy [2].

This self-attribution of power has two effects. First, an effect of responsibilization of A (belief 4): A believes that the achievement of G1 does not depend so much on world conditions as on his own action: A feels responsible for the achievement of G1.

The notion of responsibility implies, at the same time, both a notion of power and one of duty, with the former causing the latter: to the extent to which an Agent is believed to have the power to have something (G1) happen, and this is something people have the goal to happen, over that Agent a goal (Gn) starts to hold (a norm, a duty) to have G1 happen [20]. If I think you have the power to have G1 occur, and G1 is a goal of mine, then I have you responsible for the occurrence of G1, you are the one on whom G1 depends.

Therefore, thanks to his belief that he has the resources necessary for the goal, the Agent who feels enthusiasm feels responsible for his achievement, and feels it depends on himself.

Going back to the examples above, one could object that a sense of internal power and of responsibility is not implied in cases 1a., 1b. and 2a. But I claim that also in such cases these elements can be present, and only if they are can one feel true enthusiasm, not just simply be happy or delighted. In all three cases, the goals attained are intermediate goals (G2) with respect to the final one (G1), and it is just their attainment that gives you a sense of inner power and responsibility to go on pursuing the final goal. For aesthetic goals, attaining perfection or a sense of harmony with the universe can be the ultimate goals (G1): thus, even seeing a beautiful landscape (1a.) may give you the impression that you are actively pursuing this goal of harmony, and that achieving it depends on you. In example 2b., your friend's success can be seen as a sub-goal G2 for a more general goal G1 that "we, the good ones, finally win".

The second effect of the self-attribution of power (belief 5) is that A believes with a high degree of certainty that he will achieve goal G1. In this sense, enthusiasm includes the hope to succeed; but the degree of certainty attributed to success in enthusiasm is much higher than in hope.

Let us now see the third effect of the self-attribution of power. Among the factors that determine the activation of a goal, that is, that make you include it in the decision making to choose what goals to pursue, two are particularly relevant. On the one side the value of the goal, on the other side its likeliness of realization [26]. In fact, if a goal is very important, but it is very difficult to achieve it, I will possibly prefer a goal less desirable, but easier to realize. I would like to buy a loft in Boston, but I may decide to buy a flat at Andover. Now, the likeliness we attribute to our achievement of a goal depends on how much we believe we have the necessary resources to achieve it. But if we feel enthusiasm, we feel we can succeed in the enterprise; and thus the pursued goal is re-activated; or better, a meta-goal Gm is activated to pursue it with particular persistency (belief 6).

Finally, this goal strengthening does not only have effects at the mental level: the strong arousal induced by enthusiasm triggers all the physiological resources of the Agent, and thus instils further resources for pursuit.

4 Enthusiasm, Exultance, Hope, Optimism

We can now compare enthusiasm with other emotions or mental states. First of all with exultance, that is partly similar and partly different. Both emotions are positive, that is, linked to some goal achievement, and both are characterized by a high level of arousal. But exultance is felt only after the goal is achieved, and not only for "high" or "noble" goals. I can exult because I won the lottery, or, maliciously, because my worst enemy was fired at work; in these cases enthusiasm can be felt rarely, or not at all. The differences between enthusiasm and exultance are therefore in the type of goals they monitor and in the temporal relation between emotion and goal pursuit.

Enthusiasm is also linked to hope and optimism. It is similar to hope because in both you believe the goal will be achieved with a high level of certainty; but this is even higher for enthusiasm than for hope: in the former you are almost sure that you will succeed. Moreover, hope leaves this certainty to external conditions, enthusiasm to internal resources.

And finally the relationship to optimism. An optimistic person tends to attribute achievements to herself and failures to external causes; this implies a self-attribution of internal power similar to that of enthusiasm (belief 3) [26], [25].

5 The Function of Enthusiasm

What is the function of enthusiasm? My hypothesis is that it works as the "gasoline of motivation". The great physiological activation sustained by this emotion provides the Agent with more physical and mental resources and a higher persistency: on the one side the meta-goal to go on pursuing the goal, on the other side the capacities to do so. Therefore enthusiasm is a strongly adaptive emotion, in that it sustains action, it gives it hope, multiplies resources and renews the motivation to act.

The conceptual analysis of this emotion carried on so far is coherent with its function, that in its turn accounts for many of the aspects seen above. That enthusiasm is an activating emotion and that it is felt "during" action is linked to its function of providing energy to action. Furthermore, it induces to action because, by letting you believe that the goal is more likely to be achieved, it re-activates it and sustains it: you are convinced you will succeed, then you do want to do it.

Finally, that enthusiasm is felt most often with other people depends on the fact that the self attribution of power increases with the number of people: the more we are, the easier we win.

6 Contagion

Emotions, by their very nature, tend to be communicated, expressed or anyway transmitted from an Agent to another. We can define as "emotion transmission" the case in which an Agent B comes to feel an emotion due to the fact that another Agent A is feeling the same or a similar emotion [21]. Emotional contagion is a form of emotion transmission, and, among other things, it has a learning function. To see and to hear that other people are feeling emotions, and what emotions they feel, during the process of socialization teaches us what emotions our culture allows or prescribes us to feel in this or that situation [1]. Thus the emotions, in their being a pre-cognitive form of evaluation (an appraisal) teach us to evaluate situations, to distinguish those that are disruptive or threatening from those that are fruitful or reassuring.

Enthusiasm is an emotion that typically gets transmitted through contagion, even more than anxiety or mirth do: to see or to hear other people's enthusiasm makes us feel so too, sometimes in an irresistible manner, and it causes an amplification effect that triggers a loop of more and more enthusiasm: when B comes to feel enthusiasm through contagion from A, both B and A express it, both reciprocally perceive each other's enthusiasm, and thus the emotion increases in both.

Emotional contagion takes place when A feels an emotion and expresses it through an expressive signal, B perceives the signal and reproduces it, even automatically, that is, not necessarily at a high level of awareness and intentionality, and this causes B to feel an emotion that is similar or identical to A's.

1. A's emotion → 2. A's expressive signal → 3. B's perception of A's signal → 4. B's reproduction of A's signal → 5. B's emotion

The causal link between step 3 and step 4 can be accounted for by the mirror neurons [24], that allow B to reproduce the same expressive signal performed by A. The link between steps 4 and 5 could be accounted for by the "facial feedback" hypothesis [8], [12], according to which not only the emotion can trigger the expression, but also the expression can trigger the emotion.

This account of contagion implies, among other things, that the whole process is not necessarily subject to conscious control, by either A or B. B may not be conscious that the enthusiasm she feels has been transmitted to her by A, as well as A may not have transmitted it consciously or deliberately. But obviously in some cases A consciously wants to transmit his enthusiasm: for example, a political leader may harangue the crowd while deliberately aiming to transmit his enthusiasm through contagion [15].

Now, the very fact that this process is sometimes so automatic and not subject to conscious control makes enthusiasm and its contagion a powerful weapon; but a double-edged weapon. That this highly activating emotion can be triggered in an automatic and irreflexive way, without checks by conscious rationality, can make it a route to fanatism, and an arm for people who want you to act out without thinking it over.

7   Enthusiasm as a Means for Social Influence

Emotion is by itself a device of learning and motivation, one evolved earlier than rational thought, mediated, also neurophysiologically, by more primitive structures, and therefore less flexible and more compelling, being less subject to the aware control. This makes all emotions, both positive and negative, a nearly irresistible weapon for social influence; we are often induced to do or not to do things by someone who makes an appeal to our fear, or finds a way to humiliate us, to shame us, to make us feel guilty, to elicit our compassion – or even by someone who seduces us and takes us by the arms of love [22] [17]. Enthusiasm, in its enhancing motivation, typically induces people to do things, so much so that transmitting it is a way to influence people.

Typically, a leader expresses enthusiasm and transmits it to his followers through contagion. This emotion makes them evaluate the goal to pursue as beautiful and noble, and then causes them to pursue it persistently; at the same time it gives them trust in their own capacity to achieve it, thus giving their action self-confidence, and a colour of intense pleasure. This is why the leader must transmit enthusiasm: to sustain the followers' action, to win discouragement, and thus lead them up to far and difficult goals. But at the same time the charisma of the leader, this capacity of transmitting enthusiasm, that is positive and productive in a positive leader, can be threatening and destructive in satanic leaders. In such cases, if enthusiasm is induced through contagion, a form of emotion transmission that escapes conscious control, it can act in a subtle way, while no defence will be opposed to it.

After this flash about the possible negative aspects of the contagion of enthusiasm, we now briefly present some empirical and observational studies about enthusiasm and its contagion.

8   Enthusiasm in Everyday Life

An empirical study [6] investigated some physiological, expressive and motivational aspects of enthusiasm. A questionnaire with open and multiple-choice questions was submitted to 132 subjects, 122 females and 10 males between 19 and 35 years old. They were asked to report cases in which they had felt enthusiasm and its causes, their own proprioceptive sensations and external expressions when they experienced this emotion themselves, and the external expressions of other people that they thought were feeling enthusiasm.

The proprioceptive sensations of enthusiasm reported are similar to those of joy, but with some further specific elements. Heart beat acceleration, a sense of energy, well-being, good mood, heat, excitation; subjects report they cannot stand still, they want to talk, to hop up and down, their movements are uncontrolled, they speak in a loud voice, sometimes they want to shout.

A parallel pattern is reported about others' external manifestations. Subjects can tell one is feeling enthusiasm from his or her facial expression, a merry behaviour, smile, eyes open wide, sparkling eyes, good mood and the tendency to talk a lot.

From the situations reported as causes of enthusiasm it results that the goals whose achievement most typically triggers this emotion are aesthetic goals, like attending a rock concert, or the goals of image and self-image, like succeeding in something only thanks to yourself. Enthusiasm is felt more often at the beginning or during an action or event than at the end of it. Moreover, in the activity performed you can typically find an element of novelty: you feel enthusiasm when you are doing something creative, but especially when you are doing something important, beautiful, something that is worth doing.

9   In Sport

An observational study was aimed at finding signals of the contagion of enthusiasm and its effects. In some sport events the visual and acoustic cues of enthusiasm and its contagion were singled out.

During a basket game in a primary school, a girl kicks to the air (a visual signal) while her school mate is going to the basket: this signal of excitation is participating in her mate's action, and expresses trust in the chance to win the game. Later, the mates incite the players. A cue of enthusiasm is the increased speed of incitations, while their increasing intensity, showing that more children are inciting, is a cue to contagion.

The same increase in speed and intensity shows in a ritual expression of enthusiasm through Kenyan bongos. In some sport events, Kenyan athletes come along with bongo players who scan the rhythm of the jumpers' run-up.

In sport, contagion and amplification of enthusiasm often occur. Through analysis of multimodal data three types of it can be distinguished:

a. from fan to fan: all fans stand up together, or they do the "hola", moving the bust left and right, by swaying as a single whole mass: the same visible expressive action is performed either simultaneously or in a synchronised way by many people: the action, and thus the emotion, are transmitted by contagion.

Fans identify themselves with the athlete, so that his goal to win is their goal too, and when they see he can succeed (they assume he has the internal resources to achieve it) they feel enthusiasm, and transmit it by contagion to each other: everyone communicates "we can" to the other, and all feel enthusiasm together. This typically happens when the athlete has given evidence that he has the power to win, for example, in football, after a goal.

The sport reporter is a particular case of deliberate and conscious contagion of enthusiasm: the rhythm with which he reports the game increases more and more: speech acceleration is an acoustic signal of enthusiasm through which the audience receives the contagion.

b. from fan to athlete: as the fans feel enthusiasm because they think the athlete can win, they transmit it to him through contagion, which thus works as an incitation. Inciting is a communicative act in which the fan F communicates to the athlete A that

1. F has the same goal as A, for A to succeed in the enterprise;
2. F believes that A has the internal resources to succeed;
3. F encourages A to pursue the goal, that is, he aims to give him trust in his power to achieve it

The assumption that one has the necessary resources (belief 2) is shared by enthusiasm and incitation. So when the fan communicates his enthusiasm to the athlete it is as if they were telling him; "you can, we will succeed". And since enthusiasm is contagious, by expressing it the fan wants to have the athlete feel it, to make him believe: "I can, I will succeed".

c. from athlete to fan: the long jump champion, before starting the run-up, starts scanning the rhythm by clapping hands over his head, thus asking the public to imitate his gesture to accompany his run-up: he is asking for participation and incitation. The fans imitate him, they start clapping hands following the acceleration of the run-up. Again the raised rhythm expresses enthusiasm and contagion.

10   At School

Another empirical study investigated enthusiasm and its contagion in school. A questionnaire was submitted to 275 between students and teachers, between 10 and 54 years old. Through open and multiple choice questions about their present or past experience at school, subjects were asked which emotions they used to feel toward school matters, and which emotions they thought their teachers felt toward the topics they used to teach. I will briefly report the results concerning the emotion of enthusiasm, the process of contagion of emotions in general, and the contagion of enthusiasm. First we must distinguish between "total" contagion, that is, contagion where the emotion reported by student B is exactly the same as the one attributed to teacher A, and "partial" contagion: the case in which the valence of A's and B's emotions is the same (for instance, both positive or both negative) but the specific quality of the two is different. Results show that "partial" contagion is very frequent, as much as 94%, while "total" contagion is not. It is quite rare that emotion X of Teacher A induces the very same emotion X in Student B. What often occurs is that B comes to feel an emotion Y, which is of the same valence of X, and similar to X in many respects, but not all. For example, if Subject B, as a student, attributes the emotion of "passion" for her discipline to his teacher A, it is quite frequent for B to report "interest" or "curiosity" for that discipline. That is, a sort of "dilution" seems to occur in the transmission of an emotion from teacher A to student B.

Another result is that (fortunately), partial contagion of negative emotions is less frequent than for negative ones. This might mean that the positive emotions toward a discipline that a teacher transmits to a student tend to remain longer than negative ones, as a durable disposition to that discipline: if a teacher instils curiosity for some contents, curiosity remains, while if one induces disgust this can be later overcome.

Coming to the specific data about enthusiasm, its presence is quite rare, and it is a bit more felt by students than attributed to teachers. Subjects attribute enthusiasm for the discipline to their teachers only in 20 cases out of 151 reported emotions (13%); while they report enthusiasm felt by themselves in 35 cases (23%). As to the question whether contagion of enthusiasm holds, the answer is very often negative: out of the 20 students who attribute enthusiasm to their teachers, only 2 report it themselves for the same discipline. This might mean that enthusiasm is more often self-induced than received by contagion; or else it would confirm that contagion, also for enthusiasm, can be felt unawarely, that is, even if one does not consciously find the same emotion in the other.

11 Conclusion

This paper investigated the emotion of enthusiasm, its function, and its transmission through contagion, first through a conceptual analysis based on a model of emotions in terms of goals and beliefs, then through some empirical and observational exploratory studies. The studies overviewed seem to confirm the conceptual analysis about the nature and function of this emotion and about its contagion in sport events, while the frequency and source of enthusiasm in school and in teacher - student interaction look less clear.

What's the use of analysing enthusiasm, for affective computing? Could computers be endowed with the capacity to express this emotion and induce it in users through contagion?

The preliminary findings about its acoustic and visual expression could help simulate it in Embodied Agents, while its conceptual analysis tells us that inducing enthusiasm can increase motivation: an important issue in Persuasive and Pedagogical

Agents. Yet, it is not that clear if contagion would work the same way when the expression comes from an Embodied Agent vs. by a Human. Moreover, whatever the use to which the contagion of enthusiasm could be applied, just due to the power of this emotion and its influence over people, both builders and users of an "Enthusiasm-inducing Agent" should be very careful and self-conscious about its exploitation.

Acknowledgments

Participation in the ACII 2007 Conference was supported by HUMAINE (European Project IST-507422).

References

1. Averill, J.: Anger and aggression: An Essay on Emotion. Springer, Heidelberg (1982)
2. Bandura, A.: Self-efficacy: The exercise of control. Freeman, New York (1997)
3. Bruno, G.: Eroici furori. Bari: Laterza (1995)
4. Castelfranchi, C.: Affective appraisal versus cognitive evaluation in social emotions and interactions. In: Paiva, A.C.R. (ed.) Affective Interactions. LNCS, vol. 1814, Springer, Heidelberg (2000)
5. Castelfranchi, C.: For a 'cognitive anatomy' of human emotions, and a mind-reading based affective interaction. Haifa HUMAINE Workshop (2007)
6. Checchi, M., Poggi, I.: L'entusiasmo. Congresso Nazionale della Sezione di Psicologia Sperimentale, AIP, Capri (1999)
7. Conte, R., Castelfranchi, C.: Cognitive and social action. University College, London (1995)
8. Darwin, C.: The Expression of the Emotions in Man and Animals. Appleton and Company, New York and London (1872)
9. Falcone, R., Castelfranchi, C.: The socio-cognitive dynamics of trust: does trust create trust? In: Falcone, R., Singh, M., Tan, Y.H. (eds.) Trust in Cyber-societies: Integrating the Human and Artificial Perspectives. LNCS (LNAI), vol. 2246, pp. 55–72. Springer, Heidelberg (2001)
10. Frijda, N.H.: The emotions. Cambridge University Press, Cambridge and New York (1986)
11. Greenson, R.R.: Explorations in psychoanalysis. International Universities press, New York (1978)
12. Hager, J.C., Ekman, P.: The Inner and Outer Meanings of Facial Expressions. In: Cacioppo, J.T., Petty, R.E. (eds.) Social Psychophysiology: A Sourcebook, The Guilford Press, New York (1983)
13. Kant, I.: Kritik der Urteilskraft. Leipzig (1790). Critique of judgement (Translated by J.H. Bernard. Mineola). Dover Publications, New York (1983)
14. Lyotard, J.F.: L'enthousiasme. Paris, Editions Galilée (1986)
15. Marcus, G.E., Mackuen, M.B.: Anxiety, Enthusiasm, and the Vote: The Emotional Underpinnings of Learning and Involvement During presidential Campaigns. The American Political Science Review 87(3), 672–685 (1993)
16. Miceli, M., Castelfranchi, C.: The mind and the future: The (negative) power of expectations. Theory & Psychology 12, 335–366 (2002)

17. Miceli, M., de Rosis, F., Poggi, I.: Emotional and non emotional persuasion. Applied Artificial Intelligence: an International Journal 20, 849–879 (2006)
18. Osgood, C.E., Suci, G.J., Tannenbaum, P.H.: The measurement of Meaning. University of Illinois Press, Urbana (1957)
19. Plato: Fedro, Fondazione Lorenzo Valla. Arnoldo Mondadori Editore, Roma (1998)
20. Poggi, I.: "Giustificarsi". In: Castelfranchi, C., D'Amico, R., Poggi, I. (eds.) Sensi di colpa, Giunti, Firenze, pp. 180–202 (1994)
21. Poggi, I.: Emotions from mind to mind. In: Paiva, A. (ed.) Empathic Agents, Workshop at the third AAMAS International Joint Conference, New York, July 19-23 (2004)
22. Poggi, I.: The goals of persuasion. Pragmatics and Cognition 13, 298–335 (2005)
23. Poggi, I.: La mente del cuore. Scienze cognitive ed Emozioni. Armando, Roma (2007)
24. Rizzolatti, G., Fogassi, L., Gallese, V.: Neurophysiological mechanisms underlying the understanding and imitation of action. Nature Reviews Neuroscience 2, 661–670 (2001)
25. Seligman, M.E.P.: Helplessness. Freeman, S.Francisco, CA (1975)
26. Weiner, B.: Human Motivation. Metaphors, Theories, and Research. Sage, Newbury Park, CA (1992)

Learning to Interact with the Caretaker: A Developmental Approach

Antoine Hiolle, Lola Cañamero, and Arnaud J. Blanchard

Adaptive Systems Research Group
School of Computer Science
University of Hertfordshire
College Lane, Hatfield, Herts AL10 9AB, UK
{A.Hiolle,L.Canamero,A.J.Blanchard}@herts.ac.uk

Abstract. To build autonomous robots able to live and interact with humans in a real-world dynamic and uncertain environment, the design of architectures permitting robots to develop attachment bonds to humans and use them to build their own model of the world is a promising avenue, not only to improve human-robot interaction and adaptation to the environment, but also as a way to develop further cognitive and emotional capabilities. In this paper we present a neural architecture to enable a robot to develop an attachment bond with a person or an object, and to discover the correct sensorimotor associations to maintain a desired affective state of well-being using a minimum amount of prior knowledge about the possible interactions with this object.

1 Introduction

The question of how autonomous robots could be integrated in our everyday life is gaining increasing attention. To that end, robots will have to be able to exhibit adaptive and complex behaviors, and our view is that they should be able to learn without the constant explicit instruction of a teacher, but that they should rather develop in interaction with humans and learn from this interaction [1]. Robots will need to constantly learn how to react in different situations and environments with a minimal quantity of prior knowledge present in their behavioral systems. A key element towards this goal is the integration of emotional and affective factors in these interactions [2,3] as a way to guide development and learning. Indeed adding emotional values to different contexts is a way to help robot during the decision-making process [4]. Moreover, in potentially dangerous situations, emotions have been proven to be helpful and even crucial for autonomous robots to survive in a competition for resources [5].

The design of architectures for autonomous robots to endow them with behavioral responses related to attachment bonds is a promising avenue, not only to improve human-robot interaction but also as a way to develop further cognitive and emotional capabilities. It is known that affective bonds are crucial during the development of human infants and young mammals [6]. According to Bowlby's theory [7], a secure attachment bond helps infants during their development. It

A. Paiva, R. Prada, and R.W. Picard (Eds.): ACII 2007, LNCS 4738, pp. 422–433, 2007.

is known to foster exploratory behaviors, which are essential for the infant to build a coherent and stable internal model of the environment. It is also needed for the physical development of some brain areas to be damage free, since the lack of a secure attachment could lead later to psychological disorders [8]. Moreover, from a human-robot interaction point of view, a robot that explores its environment with confidence thanks to its history of affective interactions with humans has the advantage of being self-driven since the robot would have an internal motivation urging it to discover and later understand its environment.

A successful robotic implementation of a model of attachment bonds and its implication in exploratory behavior was presented in [4,9]. This work took inspiration from the imprinting phenomenon first described by Konrad Lorenz in the case of birds [10]. During the early days of life, an attachment bond develops between young birds and persons or objects to which the animals have been exposed. As a consequence, the birds follow the movements of the imprinted object or person. In this early attachment experience, the imprinted object acts as a sort of security mechanism for birds during exploration; moreover, the simple fact of following the imprinted object helps them discover their environment faster and without any explicit teaching by the imprinted object or person.

Modeling this phenomenon with autonomous robots showed that they could benefit from the advantages provided by imprinting to guide their first steps in an unknown environment and as a mechanism to bootstrap affective interactions with humans. However, in our previous model, the robot had already hardcoded or "pre-wired" in its system the know-how to follow the imprinted object. From an epigenetic perspective of development, letting the robot discover and learn by itself how to maintain the imprinted perception—being at the "right" distance from the imprinted object in our case—would be a more plausible approach to model early attachment in humans and other complex mammals, which is closely related to imprinting in birds but slightly different. Indeed, in more complex species in which newborns are less developed when they leave the maternal environment, learning from experience and interactions with the environment plays a crucial role to achieve normal development.

In the remainder of this paper, we present such an architecture that allows a robot to imprint a person (or a moving object) present in front of it when it is turned on and then to learn, without any external reinforcement, how to follow the imprinted object. We tested this architecture using two types of robots—an Aibo and a Koala—and here we present and discuss in detail the results obtained in the latter experimental setting.

2   Robot Architecture

Our architecture follows a "Perception-Action" approach [11], which postulates that perception and action are tightly coupled and coded at the same level. Action is thus executed as a "side-effect" of wanting to achieve, improve or correct some perception. The perception-action loop can be seen in terms of homeostatic control, according to which behavior is executed to correct perceptual errors. Actions that allow to correct different perceptual errors are selected on the grounds

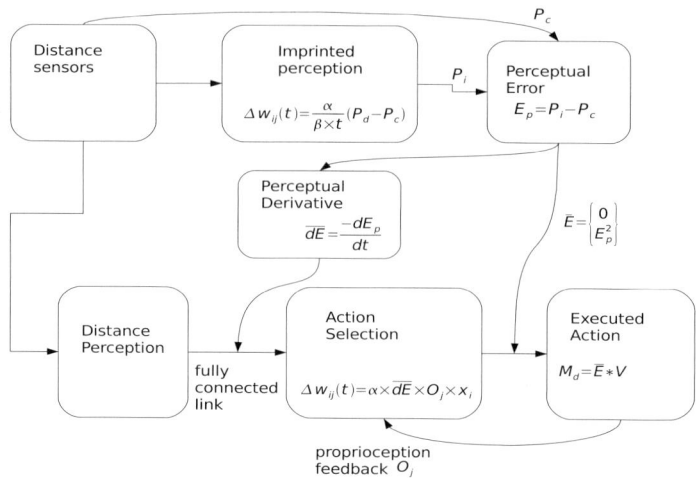

Fig. 1. Our action selection and learning architecture for imprinting

of sensorimotor associations that can be "hardcoded" by the designer (e.g., in a look-up table, as in [11,4]) or learned from experience by the robot, as it is our case here—our robot extracts sensory-motor associations led by its motivation to keep the imprinted object at a constant distance, and using a combination of associative learning and action selection. We have also taken inspiration from [12] regarding ideas on the relation between affective states and homeostasis. Figure 1 shows our architecture, implemented using a neural network consisting of neural groups that fulfill different functions, as explained in the remainder of this section.

2.1   Imprinting System

The imprinting system learns the value of the initial distance between the robot and the object in front of it. This neural group contains only one output neuron, which has its output equal to the learned distance value. The imprinting group learns using a modified Rescorla-Wagner conditioning rule [13] with a decreasing global learning rate to achieve stabilization, as follows:

$$w_{ij}(t) = w_{ij}(t-1) + \frac{\alpha}{(\beta \times t)} \times (P_d - P_c) \tag{1}$$

with:

$w_{ij}(t)$ the weight of the link between input neuron i of the distance perception system group and neuron j of the imprinting group.
α the learning rate here equal to 0.2
β the learning rate's decay rate equal to 0.05
P_d the current output of the ith neuron of the distance perception group
P_c the current output of the jth neuron of the imprinting group

When the global learning rate, $\frac{\alpha}{(\beta \times t)}$, reaches a value below 0.001, the output of the imprinting group remains unchanged until the end of the experiment, thus achieving stability in the computation of the perceptual error and its derivative.

2.2   Perceptual Categorization System

Our robot must learn to associate its relative position with respect to the imprinted object to the action to be taken to correct its perceptual error. For this, it must first calculate its perceptual error, then assess what type of error it is, to be able to choose the right corrective action.

Perceptual Error. To modulate the response of the system according to the discrepancy between the current perception and the imprinted one, we compute the current perceptual error (E_p) between the imprinted perception (a distance) and the current one as follows:

$$E_p = P_i - P_c \tag{2}$$

with:

P_c the current perception value (the current value of the distance sensors in the case of the Koala setup)

P_i the imprinted perception value (the value of the distance sensors during the imprinting phase)

We now use this value to evaluate a smooth derivative of the perceptive error as follows:

$$\frac{dE_p}{dt} = e(\tau_1) - e(\tau_2) \tag{3}$$

with: $e(\tau) = \frac{e(\tau-1) \times \tau + E_p}{\tau+1}$ the average value of E_p over τ time steps, $\tau_1 = 2$, and $\tau_2 = 4$.

The neuronal group computing these values has 2 output neurons, one for the opposite of the perceptual error, $\bar{E}$, and one for the smooth derivative of it, $d\bar{E}$. These two neurons have the following output functions:

$$\bar{E} = \begin{cases} 0 & \text{if } E_p^2 < \theta_1 \\ E_p^2 & \text{otherwise} \end{cases}$$

where θ_1 is chosen to provide an interval where the system considers its perception to be the correct one, i.e. the imprinted perception.

$$d\bar{E} = -\frac{dE_p}{dt}$$

Perceptual Categorization. Since we want our robot to be able to associate its relative position with respect to the imprinted object to the action to be taken to correct its perceptual error, we project the actual value of the distance sensors into three categories: too far from the object, too close to it, and correct distance (the one in which $\bar{E} = 0$). Therefore this neural group contains three neurons, one for each category. Although this categorization could have been achieved on line, by the system itself, we decided to use a fixed one in this case in order to focus on the problem that is our object of study here—the perception-action pairing. The output of this neural group is used as an input for the action selection one.

2.3 Action Selection

The task of the action selection module is to learn how to maintain the desired perception, the one learned by the imprinting module. Therefore, it needs to select the correct action according to the actual distance perception. To this end, the latter is fully connected to a Winner-Take-All (WTA) group of neurons. This group receives also two modulatory inputs from the perceptual error group, $d\bar{E}$ and $\bar{E}$, and proprioceptive feedback from a motor output group which displays the real action that has been executed. This signal acts as the teaching signal for the learning module. The input $d\bar{E}$ is used as a kind of reinforcer helping the system to learn associations between the active perceptual category and the action that has been produced. The association between a perceptual category and an action that makes the perceptive error decrease ($d\bar{E} > 0$) will be strengthened, whereas the association between a perception and an action that makes the perceptive error increase ($d\bar{E} < 0$) will be weakened. The initial weights between the perceptual categories and the WTA are initialized to small random values. The WTA group contains two output neurons, one for the action of going forward and one for going backward. Hence the WTA group learns using a modified Hebbian rule and produces outputs as follows:

$$w_{ij}(t) = w_{ij}(t-1) + \alpha \times d\bar{E} \times O_j \times x_i \tag{4}$$

with:

$w_{ij}(t)$ the weight of the link between input neuron i of the distance system group and neuron j of the WTA action selection group initialized with small random values.
α the learning rate, here equal to 0.2
$d\bar{E}$ the opposite of the derivative of the perceptual error
O_j the proprioceptive feedback from the motor output group
x_i the output value of the ith neuron of the (distance) perception group

The motor output group uses the output of the WTA to compute the speed of the robot. However, if the perceptual error is null, we want the system to remain static, as in [9]. For this, we use the value of $|\bar{E}|$ to modulate the value of the motor output. This value is a real integer, and will have the effect of going forward when positive, backward when negative. In order to avoid abrupt changes in the speed of the robot, we need to produce a smooth motor output; the value of the motor output is filtered as follows:

$$M(t) = M(t_1) + \alpha(M_d - M(t-1)) \tag{5}$$

with the selected motor output M_d computed as:

$$M_d = |\bar{E}| \times V \tag{6}$$

where V, the current direction of the robot, equals -1 when going backwards, 1 when going forward. This value is directly computed using the outputs of the WTA group.

2.4   Action Selection and Learning Algorithm

At the beginning of the "life" of the robot (for a short period after it is turned on) no action is taken in order to allow imprinting to take place. Then the system works in two phases. During the first phase, that we could call the action selection phase, all groups have their outputs updated and then an action is executed. During the second one, that we could call the learning phase, the perceptual error and its derivative are updated, and the action selection WTA group learns the consequences of its last action, the weights from the distance perceptual group are updated.

1st *Phase*:

1. The perceptual categorization neural group has its outputs matching the current distance sensors values, and the current position—too far, too close or correct—is compared with the desired perception.
2. The action selection neural group has its output updated, deciding which action is to be taken based on the current perception and the current perceptual error. If the error is null, the action is inhibited.
3. The motor neural group (labeled "Executed action" in Figure 1), executes the action, sending the new value of the speed—negative, positive or equal to zero—to the actuators.

2nd *Phase*:

4. The perceptual group has its outputs unchanged to match the previous perception state.
5. The perceptual error and derivative are updated.
6. The action selection group has its weights updated according to the previous learning rule.
7. Then the loop iterates again.

3 Experiments and Results

3.1 Experimental Setup

To test our system, we used two different types of robots and settings: an Aibo and a Koala. In both cases we used a one-dimensional task, in which the robot became imprinted to an experimenter playing the role of a caretaker placed in front of it. In the case of the Aibo, using the camera, the robot became imprinted to a ball held and moved by the experimenter and it learned to follow the ball with movements of its head, while attempting to correct the perceptual error— the difference between the actual position of the ball in its visual field, and the position it had when it was imprinted. In the case of the Koala, the experimenter was standing and moved forward and backwards in front of the robot; the Koala used its infrared sensors to detect the experimenter and had to learn to move with (follow or back up from) the experimenter while trying to maintain the distance at which it had been imprinted. In this paper we report our scenario and results using the Koala.

The experiment starts by turning on the robot in front of the caretaker, and none of them moves for a small period of time during which the initial imprinting takes place. After this phase, if the caretaker doesn't move, the perceptual error of the robot remains equal to 0 and therefore no movement is produced. Then after a few seconds, the caretaker moves away from the robot. The robot will then execute the action selected as winner output by the action-selection group. If the action executed makes the perceptual error decrease, then the robot will learn that this action is the correct one to execute in that situation—in this particular example approach the caretaker, resulting in a following behavior. If the action executed is not the correct one, after few timesteps the robot will choose to execute another action and, if it corrects the perceptual error, it will learn that it is the correct action to execute in that situation.

3.2 Results

During this experience, we recorded the values of the distance perception, the square error between the desired perception and the current one, the derivative of the latter and the values of the weights between the categorized perception and the action to do. Figure 2 shows an example in which the caretaker approached the robot, getting closer than the distance the robot was imprinted to. As we can see, the weight value, associated here with the action of backing up from the caretaker, increased correctly during the experiment. More specifically, if we look closer in the rectangular boxes labeled 1 in the figure, we can observe that the weight value increases when the derivative of the perceptual error is negative, which happens when the square perceptual error decreases—in this case, when the caretaker slowly approached the robot.

The caretaker then stopped moving, the robot went slowly backwards and, since the derivative of the error was negative, the association between this situation and the action of going backwards was strengthened, and the robot reached

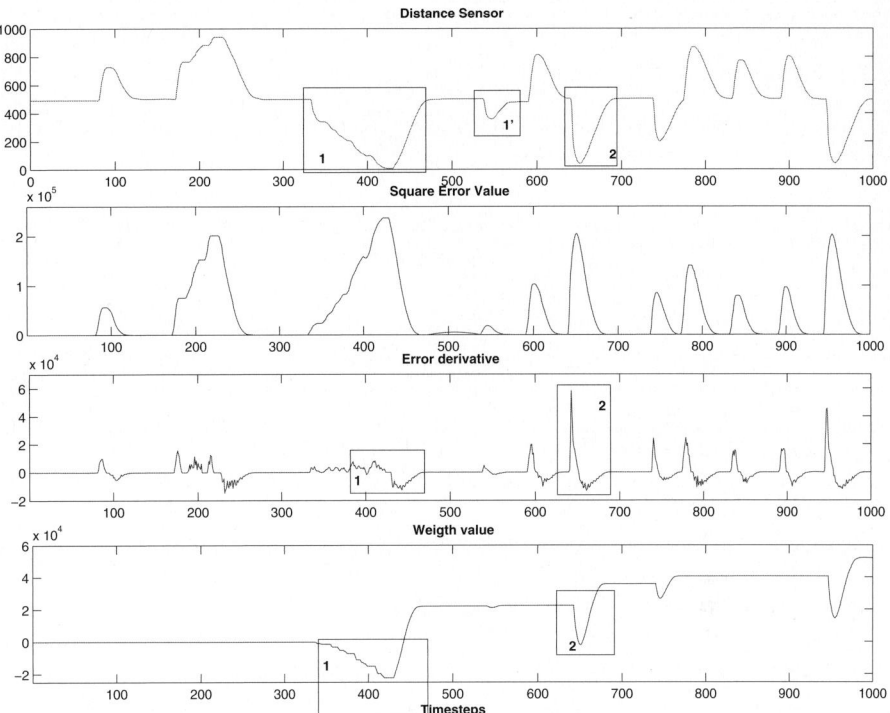

Fig. 2. Evolution of (from top to bottom): perception of the distance, square and derivative of the perceptual error, and the association weight between perception and action, producing in this case the behavior of backing up from the imprinted object as it gets too close

again the desired perception and stopped moving. When the caretaker tried again to move closer to the robot—the moment inside the rectangular box labeled 1′—the robot quickly reached the desired perception again, showing us that the correct association had been learned. The caretaker then moved closer to the robot again, but this time very quickly. We can see in the box labeled 2 that inducing this quick perturbation provoked a decrease in the association learned, the weight value decreases first. But since no other action had been associated as the correct action in that situation, the robot moved backward again, and the association is again reinforced with an even higher value than before. The same effects were observed with the opposite perturbation—the caretaker quickly moving away from the robot. It is interesting to note that our learning system is influenced by the intensity of the perturbation and its length. If the experimenter were to move further and further away from the robot, this system would not be able to learn how to follow it. But in a step-by-step manner, it learns with increasing accuracy the correlations between the perception it wants to reach and the correct action to do.

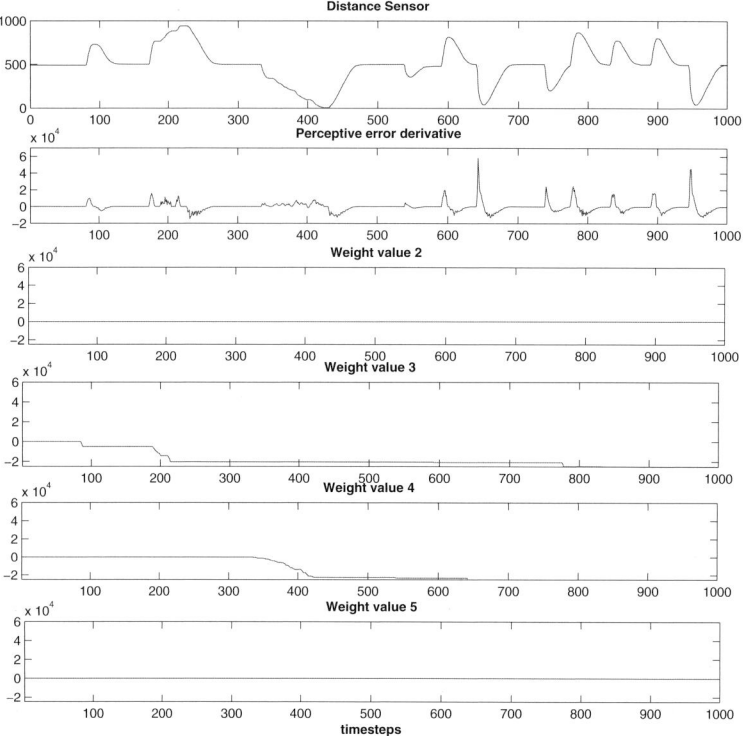

Fig. 3. Evolution of the perception of the distance, the derivative of the perceptual error, and the other association weights

In Figure 3, we can observe the evolution of the other association weight values during the experiment. The weights labeled 1 and 5 are those related to the correct perception category. Hence, no evolution is observed due to the modulation of the motor output by the square error. The remaining two weights are those related to the two other categories—being too far from or too close to the imprinted object. These association weights are linked to incorrect actions to produce in these two cases, and we can observe that their values are very negative, indicating that the system discovered that they are the opposite of the actions to do in these cases.

4   Discussion

This system described here allows a robot to learn how to maintain a desired perception, and therefore to follow its caretaker around, without any prior knowledge of how to do so, as opposed to having this knowledge "pre-wired" as in [4,1]. We have seen that it learns fast, without having to try the different actions several times as in other delayed reinforcement systems. However, our system cannot be easily compared to such architectures or to other learning-based systems. To our knowledge, only the architecture presented in [14], which learned new sensorimotor associations without explicit reinforcement in the case of a teacher-student interaction (a robot learning to imitate the arm movements of a human teacher), presents some similarities with ours. An internal reinforcement was built based on the prediction error of the rhythm of the interactions, and used to evaluate the confidence in the current sensorimotor associations of the system. If the rhythm of the interaction was correctly predicted the associations were strengthened, otherwise they were weakened. One major difference in the learning system was the introduction of noise on the weights of the untrusted associations to help the sytem explore and find the correct ones. With our architecture, each time a perturbation in the homeostasis of the system is induced by the experimenter, there is no way for the robot to distinguish whether this perturbation is a consequence of its own action or not. That is why the association weights decrease during this perturbation. If the task to learn was very sensitive to these perturbations, meaning that the weights of the associations had very close values, our system would have to learn again the association after each external perturbation. Adding a way for our robot to discriminate between perturbations due to external causes (e.g. the actions of the caretaker) or internal causes (typically the actions of the robot), although far from being a trivial problem, would be a natural future extension to our system from a developmental perspective.

This problem of external perturbations is also related to how caretakers respond to infants' demands. It seems natural that the experimenter acting as a caretaker would have to adapt his/her behavior to that of the robot. For example, if the caretaker were not to wait for the robot to learn how to follow him/her, we could say that the caretaker would not be responding correctly to the needs of the robot in terms of interactions. The appropriate behavior for the caretaker would be to wait for the robot to reach the desired perception and to have the time to learn how to reach that perception (i.e. which action to execute to do so in that situation), and to follow the caretaker at a constant distance, by trying different actions in a sort of "motor babbling", so that the robot can be in a good emotional state, without the distress of the absence of the caretaker. The interactions involved in this simple learning task are comparable to mother/infant interactions during the first year, and are particularly relevant to investigate Bowlby's notion of secure-insecure attachment [7] and its influence in the development of emotional and cognitive capabilities, such as openness towards the world and curiosity.

Our system uses the derivative of the perceptual error to directly modulate the associations that are to be strengthened. A similar approach has been used to orient a robot towards a situation were the robot could learn new affordances [15]. This system helped the robot exhibiting a behavior that could be termed "curiosity", since the robot remained in situation until nothing new could be learned and then switched to another task during which the consequences were not known by the system. Our system uses this notion to learn how to reach a desired perception related to the proximity to a caretaker in which its emotional state is satisfying.

5   Conclusion and Future Work

We have shown that the system presented in this paper is able to learn the consequences of its actions led only by the tendency to maintain a perception associated with the presence of a caretaker. We have applied this system to reproduce the imprinting phenomenon, going beyond previous work [4,1] as in this case the robot learns what to do to interact with the caretaker in order to maintain the imprinted perception, rather than assuming that knowledge is "pre-wired". In future work, further developing previous work [16], we plan to use this artificial affective bond to help the robot explore its environment with the assurance of having a familiar perception to comfort the robot in new situation that could be dangerous or stressful. In terms of cognitive architecture, to extend our system to more complex skills and learning tasks, we will introduce the use of multiple modalities for the recognition of and interaction with the caretaker.

This first experiment exhibits already some features characteristic of mother-infant interactions. In future work, we would like to explore how the quality of such interactions, particularly in terms of Bowlby's notion of secure-insecure attachment [7], influences further development. A first direction to explore in this respect would be to study the influence of factors such as a different learning rate or a different learning rule. Another direction would concern the influence of the quality of the robot-caretaker interactions on the development of emotional-cognitive capabilities such as curiosity. When the robot reaches its desired perception, it also moves towards a positive state of well-being, and this can be reflected by a "pleasure" parameter. Using associative learning applied not to sensory-motor associations but to emotional states, the robot could learn to associate this pleasure with the fact of choosing an action that makes its perceptual error decrease, and this could lead to the emergent property of being curious. Following this developmental approach should permit later on in the "life" of the robot to analyze how "personality" features such as curiosity (or the lack of it) can be related to early infancy experiences, particularly in terms of the interaction styles of the caretakers.

Acknowledgements

We are grateful to Rod Adams and Neil Davey for discussions on neural controllers for robots. This research is supported by the European Commission as part of the FEELIX GROWING project (http://www.feelix-growing.org) under contract FP6 IST-045169. The views expressed in this paper are those of the authors, and not necessarily those of the consortium.

References

1. Cañamero, L., Blanchard, A., Nadel, J.: Attachment bonds for human-like robots. International Journal of Humanoïd Robotics (2006)
2. Cañamero, L.: Building emotional artifacts in social worlds: Challenges and perspectives. Emotional and Intelligent II: The Tangled Knot of Social Cognition (2001)
3. Breazeal, C.: Emotion and sociable humanoid robots. International Journal of Human-Computer Studies 59, 119–155 (2003)
4. Blanchard, A., Cañamero, L.: From imprinting to adaptation: Building a history of affective interaction. In: Proc. of the 5th Intl. Wksp. on Epigenetic Robotics, pp. 23–30 (2005)
5. Avila-Garcia, O., Cañamero, L.: Using hormonal feedback to modulate action selection in a competitive scenario. In: Schaal, S., Ijspeert, J., Billard, A., Vijayakumar, S., Hallam, J., Meyer, J.A. (eds.) From Animals to Animats 8: Proceedings of the 8th International Conference on Simulation of Adaptive Behavior, pp. 243–252. The MIT Press, Cambridge, MA (2004)
6. Nadel, J., Muir, D.: Emotional Development. Oxford University Press, Oxford (2004)
7. Bowlby, J.: Attachment and loss, vol. 1. Basics Books, New York (1969)
8. Schore, A.N.: Effects of a secure attachment relationship on right brain development, affect, regulation, and infant mental health. Infant mental health Journal 22, 7–66 (2001)
9. Blanchard, A., Cañamero, L.: Modulation of exploratory behavior for adaptation to the context. In: Kovacs, T., Marshall, J. (eds.) Biologically Inspired Robotics (Biro-net) in AISB'06: Adaptation in Artificial and Biological Systems, vol. II, pp. 131–139 (2006)
10. Lorenz, K.: Companions as factors in the bird's environment. In: Studies in Animal and Human Behavior, volume 1, pp. 101–258. London: Methuen & Co., and Cambridge, Mass: Harvard University Press (1935)
11. Gaussier, P., Zrehen, S.: Perac: A neural architecture to control artificial animals. Robotics and Autonomous Systems 16, 291–320 (1995)
12. Panksepp, J.: Affective Neuroscience: The Foundations of Human and Animal Emotions. Oxford University Press, Oxford (1998)
13. Rescorla, R., Wagner, A.: A theory of pavlovian conditioning: Variations in effectiveness of reinforcement and nonreinforcement. In: Black, A., Prokasy, W. (eds.) Classical Conditioning II, pp. 64–99. Appleton-Century-Crofts, New York (1972)
14. Andry, P., Gaussier, P., Moga, S., Banquet, J.-P., Nadel, J.: Learning and communication in imitation: An autonomous robot perspective. IEEE Transactions on Man, Systems and Cybernetics, Part A: Systems and humans 31(5), 431–442 (2001)
15. Oudeyer, P.-Y., Kaplan, F.: Intelligent adaptive curiosity: a source of self-development. In: Berthouze, L., Kozima, H., Prince, C.G., Sandini, G., Stojanov, G., Metta, G., Balkenius, C. (eds.) Proc. of the 4th Intl. Wks. on Epigenetic Robotics, vol. 117, pp. 127–130. Lund University Cognitive Studies (2004)
16. Blanchard, A., Cañamero, L.: Developing affect-modulated behaviors: Stability, exploration, exploitation or imitation? Proc. of the 6th Intl. Wksp. on Epigenetic Robotics (2006)

Affective Adaptation of Synthetic Social Behaviour

Pablo Lucas dos Anjos, Ruth Aylett, and Alison Cawsey

Heriot-Watt University, School of Mathematical and Computer Sciences,
Edinburgh, EH14 4AS, United Kingdom
{anjos,ruth,alison}@macs.hw.ac.uk

Abstract. This research focuses on designing affective roles in agent-based social simulation (ABSS) focused on ethology. Synthetic agents are addressed as autonomous, intentional software entities capable of managing primate-like (hierarchical) social relationships in small-scale societies. The critique involves discussion of potential affective roles in socio-cognitive agent architectures, both in terms of individual action-selection and group organisation. With the diversity of social and emotional accounts, primate-like ABSS is put forward with individual behaviour related not only to reactivity or focused on function-optimisation.

Keywords: Multi-agent simulation, affective social regulation, and emergence.

1 Introduction

The first generation of ABSS systems was dominated by the implementation of arbitrarily defined rule-based autonomies with either reactive or logically determined behaviours. As function-optimisation approaches pervaded most designs of Multi-Agent Systems (MAS), it is only recently that agent designs have explored the inclusion of cognitive and emotional aspects in ethological models, thus allowing combinations of both symbolic (reasoning) and non-symbolic (behavioural) approaches to animal social behaviour.

Despite an increasing interest in bridging this gap, few Artificial Life (ALife) and MAS currently focus on modelling cognitive and affective capabilities for social entities. Instead, a great variety of available agent simulation frameworks are derived from the Belief-Desire-Intention (BDI) framework [9], which aims to provide agents with high-level deliberation capabilities like planning and symbolic representation. On the other hand, the majority of ALife systems focus on interaction dynamics, both from the perspective of single entities and MAS. These include, for example, models investigating the evolutionary characteristics of populations, and individual behaviour control commonly based on variations of the robotic subsumption architecture. We argue that the identification of systemic relations, from scenario to architectural characteristics, is important in integrating affective theories into synthetic action-selection and behavioural domain so as to mediate social interaction among autonomous agents.

Apart from one related example mediating agent cooperation and reciprocity [10], no architecture has yet been focused on primate-like social organisation using

A. Paiva, R. Prada, and R.W. Picard (Eds.): ACII 2007, LNCS 4738, pp. 434–439, 2007.

cognitive agents equipped with affect. Therefore this paper discusses a synthetic socio-cognitive approach to analysing individual dominant behaviour that is influenced by affective processes.

2   Affect in Primate-Like Social Interaction

Affect is known to play significant roles both in cognitive and physiological processes; for example triggering reactive, episodic responses or supporting long-term, intentional behaviour. This is especially notable in the human and animal primate domain, where individual behaviours directly influence group organisation and communities can be re-distributed by assessments of multiple dyadic relationships [1].

Individual affective states are important in relationships because interactions are highly contextual and capable of impacting primates both physiologically and psychologically. Evidence for such an impact ranges from physiological to cognitive studies, as suggested by mirror neurons [3] on the one hand and affective and appraisal theories [7, 8] on the other. Two types of social organisations have been considered: hunter-gatherer and fission-fusion. While the former relate to the socio-hierarchical primate nature and predominantly lone foraging; the latter is applied to human-like societies with non-hierarchical foraging and without domestication of edible resources or complex language abilities [4]. In these small-scale societies, individual short- and long-term memories can be decisive for assessing specific interactions and in decision-making [5]. Consequences include changes over time of group hierarchical organisation, mainly due to adaptation to social and environmental constraints. Thus with limited resources and behavioural capabilities, individuals may rearrange social patterns of interaction to adapt group hierarchy and maximise individual survival.

Observing natural human societies, one is able to identify that being too distant from loose (informal) social norms can impose difficulties for social interaction. Individual primate animals also recognise social relationship differences within their group. Primates present a simple mechanism for internalising emergent social patterns of interactions by social actions representing compliance or defiance [6, 11]. Sociologists and anthropologists amend this informal definition of an expected form of behaviour, by describing an informal social norm more precisely as a set of behavioural patterns confined within a well-defined social context. Social norms not necessarily motivated by specific functional purposes are often referred to as bottom-up social patterns, which can be tested via an individual's intentional attempt to match – or challenge– the expected form of social interaction [2]. For example, orchestrated by the highest ranked individual, a fission event may split the group into smaller sets aimed at task specialisation to locate dispersed food. All members may later re-organise into new groups with updated social ranks.

2.1   Affiliative and Affective Relationship Ranks

Real primate social structure is frequently analysed linearly, allowing studies of transitive hierarchical relationships. The dominance interaction is what determines an agent's ability to recognise the hierarchical position of another individual. This action is performed by assessing the other entity and information about interactions. Affiliative and rank-based social relationships are managed using an individual data structure to represent the agent's social and individual context. Illustrated in Figure 1, pre-defined kin and societal ranks are hierarchically tested by degrees of relatedness.

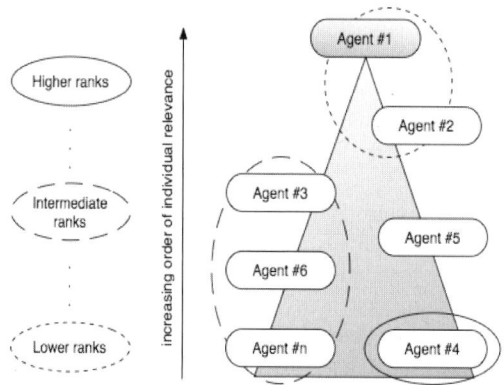

Fig. 1. Tracking individual kin and social relationships for Agent #1

In the case above, the initial physical position in the structure is given by the kinship distribution and agents may only alter their dominant rank in the society by social interaction. Agent #2 for example has the highest degree of individual relatedness to Agent #1, but has the lowest social rank in relation to Agent \#1's known group. While #4 is the highest ranked in this social group, its kin relation to Agent #1 is not very relevant; and agent #5 has not yet interacted with Agent #1 but is already mid-positioned due its pre-defined kinship. Other social subsets can also be differentiated by testing one's rank range, for example \#5 or another newcomer not yet included in this data structure.

As agents use non-reactive processes to assess their memory component, beliefs about individuals and their patterns of social interaction can be effectively distributed and only individually represented. Deviant social behaviour, particularly in small social groups, is argued as a feasible trigger for changing social organisation. More than an important mechanism for adaptive group structures, the intensity of positive and negative affective feedbacks may exemplify how individual actions can influence the behaviour and internal state of other entities. Agents may present different personality traits, such as a tendency to perform conflict avoidance, high tolerance or re-conciliation; interact with low tolerance or simply be careless about their own actions.

2.2 Specifying the Agent Architecture

Aiming to have action-selection and execution influenced by individual affect, behavioural synthesis is designed as a process to highlight social awareness. Appraisal and memory components are related to the input data, which contains the individual socio-affective relevance of kinship and estimated ranks. Hierarchical dominance simply examines submissive responses, like avoidance and cowering, during dyadic interactions; which also take kin differentiation into account. Figure 2 depicts the emotional state and behavioural synthesis linked in the agent architecture.

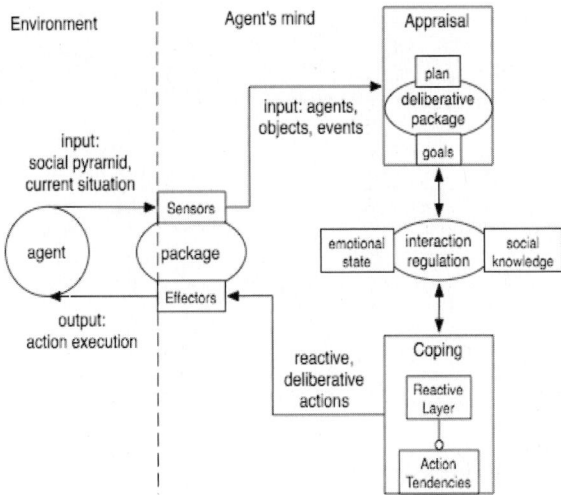

Fig. 2. A high-level representation of the agent architecture

Active and passive objects of change constitute the environment, where agents are able to move around in a grid-like representation and execute short reactive scripts. Occasionally sequences of actions, associated with future goals or intentions, can be deliberatively planned. For example in a fission-fusion society, entities assess whether such attempts to divide or reunite the group are genuine or deceitful actions. For that, it is assumed that only top-ranked individuals can genuinely perform such actions. By testing rank, physically close enough individuals can retrieve honest information from their social networks and act upon the available information and their internal state.

In the case of positive feedback, where the proponent has a higher rank within its social network, individuals with no short- (lower threshold) –or long- (higher threshold)– term conflict tendencies towards the believed top ranked individual will comply with the group dispersion (fission) or reunification (fusion). E.g. peacefully joining, or keeping away from its previous group – while others may challenge the current expected behaviour for that individual.

2.3 The Simulation and Agent Cycles

Figure 3 is a high-level illustration of the projected simulation cycle. With two main loops as the halting condition for agent survival and timeout verification, a chronological and another arbitrary stop condition can be combined. Dot-arrowed lines indicate processes that are part of an ongoing execution placed left. Boxes

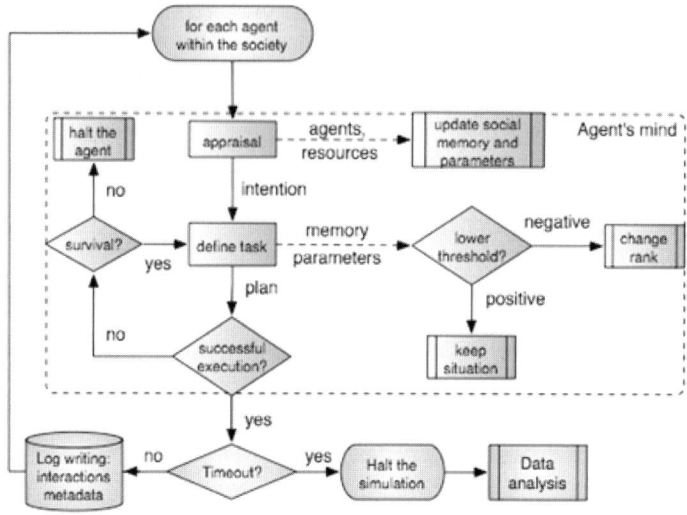

Fig. 3. The simulation cycle flow-chart

terminated with double lines are an execution in progress that can trigger internal memory and affective update procedures.

The current scenario being developed is based on a situation where fission-fusion episodes are expected due scattered concentrations of food. Primate-like autonomies can then move asynchronously onto adjacent horizontal, vertical or diagonal vacant places represented by a non-wrapping grid. For this particular setup, agents are initially located in arbitrary positions, occupying one cell each, while different amounts of food resources and obstacles are in fixed locations and cannot be moved during the simulation.

The long-term goal for each agent is to maintain its internal minimum food level, while managing its own social rank by complying, or challenging, interactions in the current social organisation. Such an approach, rather then replicating existing real world behaviour, is aimed at exploring novel social dynamics for strongly autonomous agents. These involve patterns of social interaction and hierarchical organisation created only by the collective outcome of entities intentionally selecting and executing actions resulting from their internal processing.

3   Final Considerations

If primate-like agents are expected to autonomously (i.e., purposively) adapt their social organisation, and patterns of interaction, a higher level of symbolic processing is argued as an inevitable requirement rather than merely a more complex communication schema. The architecture is designed to have lower and higher operation limits, acting as two oscillators for short and long term individual decision-making biases. Agents with different personalities (representing the long-term limit) and moods (standing for the short-term) are expected to behave differently. Thus, an impulsive character may have higher action readiness towards purely reactive behaviour than others. This proposed model is aimed at exploring which scenarios require or warrant the providing of affective functionalities for social organisation.

Acknowledgement

This work is supported by the EU 6th Framework Program, Network of Excellence Humaine [IST-2002-2.3.1.6 507422]. Sub-task: bridging the gap between micro and macro views of social interaction.

References

1. Dunbar, R.I.M.: Coevolution of neocortical size, group size and language in humans. Behavioral and Brain Sciences 16(4), 681–735 (1993)
2. Fiedler, K.: On the tusk, the measures and the mood: Research on affect and social cognition. In: Forgas, J.P. (ed.) Emotion and Social Judgements, Oxford (1991)
3. Rizzolatti, G., Craighero, L.: The mirror-neuron system. Annual Review of Neuroscience 27 (2004)
4. Steve Goodhall, Multi-Agent Simulation of Hunter-Gatherer Behavior, Master's thesis, Wayne State University, Fall (2002)
5. Henrich, R., Boyd, S., Bowles, C., Camerer, E., Fehr, H.: Cooperation, reciprocity and punishment in fifteen small-scale societies. In: American Economic Rev., vol. 91 (2001)
6. Huffman, M.A.: Acquisition of innovative cultural behaviors in non-human primates: a case study of stone handling, a socially transmitted behaviour in japanese macaques. In: Heyes, C.M., Galef Jr., B.G. (eds.) Social Learning in Animals, pp. 267–289. Academic Press, San Diego (1996)
7. LeDoux, J.: The Emotional Brain: The Mysterious Underpinnings of Emotional Life. Simon and Schuster, New York (1998)
8. Frijda, N.H.: The Emotions, Cambridge University Press, Editions de la Maison des Sciences de l'Homme, Paris, France (1986)
9. Pell, B., Pollack, M., Georgeff, M., Wooldridge, M., Tambe, M.: The belief-desire-intention model of agency (November 1999)
10. Staller, A., Petta, P.: Introducing emotions into the computational study of social norms. Journal of Artificial Societies and Social Simulation 4(1) (2001)
11. Whiten, A., Horner, V., de Waal, F B: Conformity to cultural norms of tool use in chimpanzees. Nature 437(7059), 737–740 (2005)

What Should a Generic Emotion Markup Language Be Able to Represent?

Marc Schröder[1], Laurence Devillers[2], Kostas Karpouzis[3],
Jean-Claude Martin[2], Catherine Pelachaud[4], Christian Peter[5], Hannes Pirker[6],
Björn Schuller[7], Jianhua Tao[8], and Ian Wilson[9]

[1] DFKI GmbH, Saarbrücken, Germany
[2] LIMSI-CNRS, Paris, France
[3] Image, Video and Multimedia Systems Lab, Nat. Tech. Univ. Athens, Greece
[4] Univ. Paris VIII, France
[5] Fraunhofer IGD, Rostock, Germany
[6] OFAI, Vienna, Austria
[7] Tech. Univ. Munich, Germany
[8] Chinese Acad. of Sciences, Beijing, China
[9] Emotion AI, Tokyo, Japan
http://www.w3.org/2005/Incubator/emotion

Abstract. Working with emotion-related states in technological contexts requires a standard representation format. Based on that premise, the W3C Emotion Incubator group was created to lay the foundations for such a standard. The paper reports on two results of the group's work: a collection of use cases, and the resulting requirements. We compiled a rich collection of use cases, and grouped them into three types: data annotation, emotion recognition, and generation of emotion-related behaviour. Out of these, a structured set of requirements was distilled. It comprises the representation of the emotion-related state itself, some meta-information about that representation, various kinds of links to the "rest of the world", and several kinds of global metadata. We summarise the work, and provide pointers to the working documents containing full details.

1 Introduction

As emotion-oriented computing systems are becoming a reality, the need for a standardised way of representing emotions and related states is becoming clear. For real-world human-machine interaction systems, which typically consist of multiple components covering various aspects of data interpretation, reasoning, and behaviour generation, it is evident that emotion-related information needs to be represented at the interfaces between system components.

The present paper reports on a joint effort to lay the basis for a future standard for representing emotion-related states in a broad range of technological contexts. After briefly revisiting previous work, we introduce the W3C Emotion Incubator group, before we describe two of its key results: a rich collection of use cases – scenarios where an emotion markup language would be needed –, and a compilation of the requirements resulting from these use cases.

A. Paiva, R. Prada, and R.W. Picard (Eds.): ACII 2007, LNCS 4738, pp. 440–451, 2007.
© Springer-Verlag Berlin Heidelberg 2007

1.1   Previous Work

Until recently, when markup languages provided for the representation of emotion, it was part of a more complex scenario such as the description of behaviour for embodied conversational agents (ECAs) [1]. The expressivity of the representation format was usually very limited – often, only a small set of emotion categories was proposed, such as the "big six" which according to Ekman [2] have universal facial expressions, and their intensity. When additional descriptions of an emotion were offered, these were closely linked to the particular context in which the language was to be used. As a result, these languages cannot generally be used outside the specific application for which they were built.

Two recent endeavours have proposed more comprehensive descriptions of emotion-related phenomena. The Emotion Annotation and Representation Language (EARL – [3]), developed in the HUMAINE network on emotion-oriented computing, has made an attempt to broaden the perspective on representing emotion-related information. The EARL is a syntactically simple XML language designed specifically for the task of representing emotions and related information in technological contexts. It can represent emotions as categories, dimensions, or sets of appraisal scales. As different theories postulate different sets of emotion words, dimensions and appraisals, the design is modular, so that the appropriate set of descriptors for the target use can be chosen. In addition, a set of attributes can represent intensity and regulation-related information such as the suppression or simulation of emotion. Complex emotions, which consist of more than one "simple" emotion, can also be represented. A detailed specification including an XML schema can be found at `http://emotion-research.net/earl`.

The HUMAINE database annotation scheme, developed independently of the EARL, has a slightly different focus. The HUMAINE team working on databases explored the annotation of a variety of emotional samples collected from different types of databases including induced, acted and naturalistic behaviours. A modular coding scheme [4] was defined to cover the requirements coming from these different data. This scheme enables the description at multiple levels of the emotional content and was applied to the annotation of French and English TV interviews. It is defined as a structured set of modular resources from which researchers can select what they need to match their own research requirements for the annotation of emotional data:

- Global emotion descriptors, used for representing emotion perceived in a whole clip: emotion words, emotion related states (e.g. attitudes), combination types, authenticity, core affect dimensions, context labels, key events and appraisal categories;
- Emotion descriptors varying over time: eight dimensional traces, such as the perceived variation of the level of acting during the clip;
- Signs of emotion: speech and language, gesture and face descriptors.

The conceptual coding scheme is implemented in XML in the Anvil tool format and is available for download from the HUMAINE web site[1].

---

[1] `http://emotion-research.net/download/pilot-db`

1.2   The W3C Emotion Incubator Group

The W3C Emotion Incubator group (http://www.w3.org/2005/Incubator/
emotion) was created to investigate the prospects of defining a general-purpose
Emotion annotation and representation language. The group consists of repre-
sentatives of 15 institutions from 11 countries in Europe, Asia, and the US. The
approach chosen for the group's work has been to revisit carefully the question
where such a language would be used, and what those use case scenarios require
from a language, before even starting to discuss the question of a suitable syntactic form for the language. In the following, the result of these two working
steps are summarised.

2   Use Cases

With the Emotion Incubator group taking a solid software engineering approach
to the question of how to represent emotion in a markup language the first
necessary step was to gather together as complete a set of use cases as possible
for the language. At this stage, we had two primary goals in mind: to gain an
understanding of the many possible ways in which this language could be used,
including the practical needs which have to be served; and to determine the
scope of the language by defining which of the use cases would be suitable for
such a language and which would not. The resulting set of final use cases would
then be used as the basis for the next stage of the design processes, the definition
of the requirements of the language.

The Emotion Incubator group is comprised of people with wide ranging in-
terests and expertise in the application of emotion in technology and research.
Using this as a strength, we asked each member to propose one or more use
case scenarios that would represent the work they, themselves, were doing. This
allowed the group members to create very specific use cases based on their own
domain knowledge. Three broad categories were defined for these use cases: Data
Annotation, Emotion Recognition and Emotion Generation. Where possible we
attempted to keep use cases within these categories, however, naturally, some
crossed the boundaries between categories.

A wiki was created to facilitate easy collaboration and integration of each
member's use cases[2]. In this document, subheadings of the three broad categories
were provided along with a sample initial use case that served as a template from
which the other members entered their own use cases and followed in terms of
content and layout. In total, 39 use cases were entered by the various working
group members: 13 for Data Annotation, 11 for Emotion Recognition and 15 for
Emotion Generation.

Possibly the key phase of gathering use cases was in the optimisation of the
wiki document. Here, the members of the group worked collaboratively within
the context of each broad category to find any redundancies (replicated or very
similar content), to ensure that each use case followed the template and provided

---

[2] http://www.w3.org/2005/Incubator/emotion/wiki/UseCases

the necessary level of information, to disambiguate any ambiguous wording (including a glossary of terms for the project), to agree on a suitable category for use cases that might well fit into two or more and to order the use cases in the wiki so that they formed a coherent document.

In the following, we detail each broad use case category, outlining the range of use cases in each, and pointing out some of their particular intricacies.

2.1 Data Annotation

The Data Annotation use case groups together a broad range of scenarios involving human annotation of the emotion contained in some material. These scenarios show a broad range with respect to the material being annotated, the way this material is collected, the way the emotion itself is represented, and, notably, which kinds of additional information about the emotion are being annotated.

One simple case is the annotation of plain text with emotion dimensions, notably valence, as well as with emotion categories and intensities. Similarly, simple emotional labels can be associated to nodes in an XML tree, representing e.g. dialogue acts, or to static pictures showing faces, or to speech recordings in their entirety. While the applications and their constraints are very different between these simple cases, the core task of emotion annotation is relatively straightforward: it consists of a way to define the scope of an emotion annotation and a description of the emotional state itself. Reasons for collecting data of this kind include the creation of training data for emotion recognition, as well as scientific research.

Recent work on naturalistic multimodal emotional recordings has compiled a much richer set of annotation elements [4], and has argued that a proper representation of these aspects is required for an adequate description of the inherent complexity in naturally occurring emotional behaviour. Examples of such additional annotations are multiple emotions that co-occur in various ways (e.g., as blended emotions, as a quick sequence, as one emotion masking another one), regulation effects such as simulation or attenuation, confidence of annotation accuracy, or the description of the annotation of one individual versus a collective annotation. In addition to annotations that represent fixed values for a certain time span, various aspects can also be represented as continuous "traces" – curves representing the evolution of, e.g., emotional intensity over time.

Data is often recorded by actors rather then observed in naturalistic settings. Here, it may be desirable to represent the quality of the acting, in addition to the intended and possibly the perceived emotion.

With respect to requirements, it has become clear that Data Annotation poses the most complex kinds of requirements with respect to an emotion markup language, because many of the subtleties humans can perceive are far beyond the capabilities of today's technology. We have nevertheless attempted to encompass as many of the requirements arising from Data Annotation, not least in order to support the awareness of the technological community regarding the wealth of potentially relevant aspects in emotion annotation.

2.2 Emotion Recognition

As a general rule, the general context of the Emotion Recognition use case has to do with low- and mid-level features which can be automatically detected, either offline or online, from human-human and human-machine interaction. In the case of low-level features, these can be facial features, such as Action Units (AUs) [5] or MPEG 4 facial action parameters (FAPs) [6], speech features related to prosody [7] or language, or other, less frequently investigated modalities, such as biosignals (e.g. heart rate or skin conductivity). All of the above can be used in the context of emotion recognition to provide emotion labels or extract emotion-related cues, such as smiling, shrugging or nodding, eye gaze and head pose, etc. These features can then be stored for further processing or reused to synthesise expressivity on an embodied conversational agent (ECA) [8].

In the case of unimodal recognition, the most prominent examples are speech and facial expressivity analysis. Regarding speech prosody and language, the CEICES data collection and processing initiative [9] as well as exploratory extensions to automated call centres are the main factors that defined the essential features and functionality of this use case. With respect to visual analysis, there are two cases: in the best case scenario, detailed facial features (eyes, eyebrows, mouth, etc.) information can be extracted and tracked in a video sequence, catering for high-level emotional assessment (e.g. emotion words). However, when analysing natural, unconstrained interaction, this is hardly ever the case since colour information may be hampered and head pose is usually not directed to the camera; in this framework, skin areas belonging to the head of the subject or the hands, if visible, are detected and tracked, providing general expressivity features, such as speed and power of movement [8].

For physiological data, despite being researched for a long time especially by psychologists, no systematic approach to store or annotate them is in place. However, there are first attempts to include them in databases [10], and suggestions on how they could be represented in digital systems have been made [11]. A main difficulty with physiological measurements is the variety of possibilities to obtain the data and of the consequential data enhancement steps. Since these factors can directly affect the result of the emotion interpretation, a generic emotion markup language needs to be able to deal with such low-level issues. The same applies to the "technical" parameters of other modalities, such as resolution and frame rate of cameras, the dynamic range or the type of sound field of the choosen microphone, and algorithms used to enhance the data.

Finally, individual modalities can be merged, either at feature- or decision-level, to provide multimodal recognition. In this case, features and timing information (duration, peak, slope, etc.) from individual modalities are still present, but an integrated emotion label is also assigned to the multimedia file or stream in question. In addition to this, a confidence measure for each feature and decision assists in providing flexibility and robustness in automatic or user-assisted methods.

2.3 Generation

We divided the 15 use cases in the generation category into a number of further sub categories, these dealt with essentially simulating modelled emotional processes, generating face and body gestures and generating emotional speech.

The use cases in this category had a number of common elements that represented triggering the generation of an emotional behaviour according to a specified model or mapping. In general, emotion eliciting events are passed to an emotion generation system that maps the event to an emotion state which could then be realised as a physical representation, e.g. as gestures, speech or behavioural actions.

The generation use cases presented a number of interesting issues that focused the team on the scope of the work being undertaken. In particular, they showed how varied the information being passed to and information being received from an emotion processing system can be. This would necessitate either a very flexible method of receiving and sending data or to restrict the scope of the work in respect to what types of information can be handled.

The first sub set of generation use cases were termed 'Affective Reasoner', to denote emotion modelling and simulation. Three quite different systems were outlined in this sub category, one modelling cognitive emotional processes, one modelling the emotional effects of real time events such as stock price movements on a system with a defined personality and a large ECA system that made heavy use of XML to pass data between its various processes.

The next sub set dealt with the generation of automatic facial and body gestures for characters. With these use cases, the issue of the range of possible outputs from an emotion generation systems became apparent. While all focused on generating human facial and body gestures, the possible range of systems that they connect to was large, meaning the possible mappings or output schema would be large. Both software and robotic systems were represented and as such the generated gesture information could be sent to both software and hardware based systems on any number of platforms. While a number of standards are available for animation that are used extensively within academia (e.g., MPEG-4 [6], BML [12]), they are by no means common in industry.

The final sub set was primarily focused on issues surrounding emotional speech synthesis, dialogue events and paralinguistic events. Similar to the issues above, the generation of speech synthesis, dialogue events, paralinguistic events etc. is complicated by the wide range of possible systems to which the generating system will pass its information. There does not seem to be a widely used common standard, even though the range is not quite as diverse as with facial and body gestures. Some of these systems made use of databases of emotional responses and as such might use an emotion language as a method of storing and retrieving this information.

3 Requirements

Each use case scenario naturally contains a set of implicit "needs" or requirements – in order to support the given scenario, a representation format needs to be capable of certain things. The challenge with the 39 use case scenarios collected in the Emotion Incubator group was to make those implicit requirements explicit; to structure them in a way that reduces complexity; and to agree on the boundary between what should be included in the language itself, and where suitable links to other kinds of representations should be used.

Work proceeded in a bottom-up, iterative way. From relatively unstructured lists of requirements for the individual use case scenarios, a requirements document was compiled within each of the three use case categories. These three documents differed in structure and in the vocabulary used, and emphasised different aspects. For example, while the Data Annotation use case emphasised the need for a rich set of metadata descriptors, the Emotion Recognition use case pointed out the need to refer to sensor data, the use case on Emotion Generation requested a representation for the "reward" vs. "penalty" value of things. The situation was complicated further by the use of system-centric concepts such as "input" and "output", which for Emotion Recognition have fundamentally different meanings than for Emotion Generation.

In order to allow for an integration of the three requirements documents into one, two basic principles were agreed.

1. The emotion language should not try to represent sensor data, facial expressions, etc., but define a way of interfacing with external representations of such data.
2. The use of system-centric vocabulary such as "input" and "output" should be avoided. Instead, concept names should be chosen by following the phenomena observed, such as "experiencer", "trigger", or "observable behaviour".

Based on these principles and a large number of smaller clarifications, the three use case specific requirements documents were merged into an integrated wiki document[3]. After several iterations of restructuring and refinement, a consolidated structure has materialised for that document; in the following, we report on the key aspects.

3.1   Core Emotion Description

The most difficult aspect of the entire enterprise of proposing a generic emotion markup is the question of how to represent emotions. Given the fact that even emotion theorists have very diverse definitions of what an emotion is, and that very different representations have been proposed in different research strands (see e.g. [13] for an overview), any attempt to propose a standard way of representing emotions for technological contexts seems doomed to failure.

The only viable way seems to be to give users a choice. Rather than trying to impose any of the existing emotion descriptions as the "correct" representation, the markup should provide the user with a choice of representations, so that an adequate representation can be used for a given application scenario.

---

[3] http://www.w3.org/2005/Incubator/emotion/wiki/UseCasesRequirements

This kind of choice should start with the possibility to explicitly state which type of affective or *emotion-related state* is actually being annotated. Different lists of such states have been proposed; for example, Scherer [14] distinguishes emotions, moods, interpersonal stances, preferences/attitudes, and affect dispositions.

For the emotion (or emotion-related state) itself, three types of representation are envisaged, which can be used individually or in combination. Emotion *categories* (words) are symbolic shortcuts for complex, integrated states; an application using them needs to take care to define their meaning properly in the application context. We do not intend to impose any fixed set of emotion categories, because the appropriate categories will depend on the application. However, we can draw on existing work to propose a recommended set of emotion categories, which can be used if there are no reasons to prefer a different set. For example, [4] proposes a structured list of 48 emotion words as a candidate for a standard list.

Alternatively, or in addition, emotion can be represented using a set of continuous *dimensional scales*, representing core elements of subjective feeling and of people's conceptualisation of emotions. The most well-known scales, sometimes by different names, are valence, arousal and potency; a recent large-scale study suggests that a more appropriate list may be valence, potency, arousal, and unpredictability [15]. Again, rather than imposing any given set of dimensions, the markup should leave the choice to the user, while proposing a recommended set that can be used by default.

As a third way to characterise emotions and related states, *appraisal scales* can be used, which provide details of the individual's evaluation of his/her environment. Examples include novelty, goal significance, or compatibility with one's standards. Again, a recommended set of appraisals may follow proposals from the literature (e.g., [16]), while the user should have the choice of using an application-specific set.

An important requirement for all three use cases was the fact that it should be possible to represent *multiple* and *complex* emotions. Different types of co-presence of emotions are envisaged: simultaneous emotions experienced due to the presence of several triggers (such as being sad and angry at the same time, but for different reasons); and regulation (such as trying to mask one emotion with another one, see below).

Emotions can have an *intensity*.

The concept of *regulation* [17] covers various aspects of an individual's attempts to feel or express something else than an emotion that spontaneously arises. On the behaviour level, that can lead to a difference between the "internal" and the "externalised" state. The various kinds of regulation which can be envisaged include: *masking* one state with another one; *simulating* a state which is not present; and *amplifying* or *attenuating* a state.

Finally, it is required that some *temporal aspects* of the emotion be represented, including a start time and duration, and possibly changes of intensity or scale values over time.

3.2   Meta Information About Emotion Description

Three additional requirements with respect to meta information have been elaborated: information concerning the degree of acting of emotional displays, information related to confidences and probabilities of emotional annotations, and finally the modalities involved. All of this information thereby applies to each annotated emotion separately.

Acting, which is particularly relevant for the Database Annotation use case, needs to cover the degree of naturalness, authenticity, and quality of an actor's portrayal of emotions, as e.g. perceived by test-subjects or annotators (an example of a database providing such information is [18]). In general, such attributes may be naturally quantified by use of a scale ranging from 0 to 1, to reflect for example the mean judgement among several test subjects or labellers.

Confidences and probabilities may generally be of interest for any of the three general use cases of annotation, recognition and synthesis. In the case of recognition, these are of particular importance within the multimodal integration of several input cues to preserve utmost information for a final decision process. Otherwise, a system reacting on emotions should be provided with additional information regarding the certainty of an assumed emotion to optimise the reaction strategy. In the case of database annotation, the mean inter-labeller agreement may be named as a typical example. More generally, it should be allowed to add such information to each level of representation, such as categories, dimensions, intensity, regulation, or degree of acting. Similar to the aforementioned meta information, confidences and probabilities may be represented by continuous scales, which preserves more information in a fusion scenario, or represented by symbolic labels as extra-low, low, medium, etc., which will often suffice to decide on a reaction strategy, e.g. in a dialogue.

The *modality* in which the emotion is reflected – observed or generated – is another example of a set that has to be left open for future additions. Typical generic modalities on a higher level are face, voice, body, text, or physiological signals; these can of course be further differentiated: parts of the face or body, intonation, text colour – the list of potential domain specific modalities is endless. Therefore, a core set of generally available modalities needs to be distinguished from an extensible set of application-specific modalities.

3.3   Links to the "Rest of the World"

In order to be properly connected to the kinds of data relevant in a given application scenario, several kinds of "links" are required.

One type of link which is required is a method for *linking to external media* objects, such as a text file containing the words of an utterance, an audio file, a video file, a file containing sensor data, technical description of sensor specifics, data enhancements applied, etc. This may for example be realised by a URL in an XML node.

A second kind of link deals with temporal linking to a *position on a time-line*. More specifically, this can be start and end times in absolute terms, or relative timings in relation to key landmarks on the time axis.

A mechanism should be defined for flexibly assigning meaning to those links. We identified the following initial set of meanings for such links to the "rest of the world": the *experiencer*, i.e. the person who "has" the emotion; the *observable behaviour* "expressing" it; the *trigger, cause, or eliciting event* of an emotion; and the *object or target* of the emotion, that is, what the emotion is "about". Note that trigger and target are conceptually different; they may or may not coincide. As an illustration, consider the example of someone incidentally spilling coffee on one's clothing: though the trigger might be the cloth-ruining event, the target would be the person spilling the coffee.

We currently think that the links to media are relevant for all these semantics. Timing information seems to be relevant only for the observable behaviour and the trigger of an emotion.

3.4 Global Metadata

Representing emotion, would it be for annotation, detection or generation, requires the description of the context not directly related to the description of emotion per se (e.g. the emotion-eliciting event) but also the description of a *more global context* which is required for exploiting the representation of the emotion in a given application. Specifications of metadata for multimodal corpora have already been proposed in the ISLE Metadata Initiative; but they did not target emotional data and were focused on an annotation scenario. The joint specification of our three use cases led to the identification of the following features required for the description of this global context.

For *person(s)*, we identified the following information as being potentially relevant: ID, date of birth, gender, language, personality traits (e.g. collected via personality questionnaires such as EPI for the annotation use case), culture, level of expertise as labeller. These pieces of information can be provided for real persons as well as for computer-driven agents such as ECAs or robots. For example, in the Data Annotation use case, it can be used for providing information about the subjects as well as the labellers.

Information about the *intended application* was also pointed out as being relevant for the exploitation of the representations of emotion (e.g. purpose of classification; application type – call centre data, online game, etc.; possibly, application name and version).

Furthermore, it should be possible to specify the *technical environment*. Within the document, it should be possible to link to that specification: for example, the modality tag could link to the particular camera properties, sensors used (model, configuration, specifics), or indeed any kind of environmental data.

Finally, information on the *social and communicative environment* will be required. For Data Annotation, this includes the type of collected data: fiction (movies, theatre), in-lab recording, induction, human-human interactions, human-computer interaction (real or simulated). All use cases might need the representation of metadata about the situational context in which an interaction occurs (number of people, relations, link to description of individual participants). Such information is likely to be global to an entire emotion markup document. It will be up to the application to use these in a meaningful way.

4   Conclusion and Outlook

In this paper, we have presented a consolidated list of requirements for a widely usable emotion markup language, based on a rich collection of use cases from a broad range of domains. This list aims at a balance between the aim of genericity and the fact that very different representations are required in different contexts. We are certain that the current list is not perfect; indeed, it is quite probably that we have missed out on some very relevant aspects. Despite these reservations, we believe that we have made reasonable progress towards a comprehensive list of requirements which can ultimately lead to a standard representation.

The next step will be to evaluate existing markup languages with respect to these requirements, in order to take stock of existing solutions for our needs. We also intend to sketch possible syntactic realisations of some of the key elements of the language.

Given the fact that the Emotion Incubator group is drawing to a close, serious work on a syntactic realisation will not be started within the lifetime of the group. Key design issues, such as the choice between XML and RDF formats, or the guiding principles of simplicity vs. non-ambiguity, deserve careful thinking. We are currently investigating possibilities for a follow-up activity, where an actual markup specification can be prepared.

Acknowledgements

The preparation of this paper was supported by the W3C and the EU project HUMAINE (IST-507422).

References

1. Prendinger, H., Ishizuka, M.: Life-like Characters. Tools, Affective Functions and Applications. Springer, Berlin (2004)
2. Ekman, P.: Facial expression and emotion. American Psychologist 48, 384–392 (1993)
3. Schröder, M., Pirker, H., Lamolle, M.: First suggestions for an emotion annotation and representation language. In: Proceedings of LREC'06 Workshop on Corpora for Research on Emotion and Affect, Genoa, Italy, pp. 88–92 (2006)
4. Douglas-Cowie, E.: et al.: HUMAINE deliverable D5g: Mid Term Report on Database Exemplar Progress (2006), http://emotion-research.net/deliverables
5. Ekman, P., Friesen, W.: The Facial Action Coding System. Consulting Psychologists Press, San Francisco (1978)
6. Tekalp, M., Ostermann, J.: Face and 2-d mesh animation in MPEG-4. Image Communication Journal 15, 387–421 (2000)

7. Devillers, L., Vidrascu, L., Lamel, L.: Challenges in real-life emotion annotation and machine learning based detection. Neural Networks 18, 407–422 (2005)
8. Bevacqua, E., Raouzaiou, A., Peters, C., Caridakis, G., Karpouzis, K., Pelachaud, C., Mancini, M.: Multimodal sensing, interpretation and copying of movements by a virtual agent. In: André, E., Dybkjær, L., Minker, W., Neumann, H., Weber, M. (eds.) PIT 2006. LNCS (LNAI), vol. 4021, Springer, Heidelberg (2006)
9. Batliner, A., et al.: Combining efforts for improving automatic classification of emotional user states. In: Proceedings IS-LTC 2006 (2006)
10. Blech, M., Peter, C., Stahl, R., Voskamp, J., Urban, B.: Setting up a multimodal database for multi-study emotion research in HCI. In: Proceedings of the 2005 HCI International Conference, Las Vegas (2005)
11. Peter, C., Herbon, A.: Emotion representation and physiology assignments in digital systems. Interacting With Computers 18, 139–170 (2006)
12. Kopp, S., Krenn, B., Marsella, S., Marshall, A., Pelachaud, C., Pirker, H., Thórisson, K., Vilhjálmsson, H.: Towards a common framework for multimodal generation in ECAs: The Behavior Markup Language. In: Gratch, J., Young, M., Aylett, R., Ballin, D., Olivier, P. (eds.) IVA 2006. LNCS (LNAI), vol. 4133, pp. 205–217. Springer, Heidelberg (2006)
13. Cornelius, R.R.: The Science of Emotion. Research and Tradition in the Psychology of Emotion. Prentice-Hall, Upper Saddle River, NJ (1996)
14. Scherer, K.R.: Psychological models of emotion. In: Borod, J.C. (ed.) The Neuropsychology of Emotion, pp. 137–162. Oxford University Press, New York (2000)
15. Roesch, E., Fontaine, J., Scherer, K.: The world of emotion is two-dimensional – or is it? Presentation at the HUMAINE Summer school, Genoa, Italy (2006)
16. Scherer, K.R.: On the nature and function of emotion: A component process approach. In: Scherer, K.R., Ekman, P. (eds.) Approaches to emotion, pp. 293–317. Erlbaum, Hillsdale, NJ (1984)
17. Gross, J.J. (ed.) Handbook of Emotion Regulation. Guilford Publications, New York (2006)
18. Burkhardt, F., Paeschke, A., Rolfes, M., Sendlmeier, W., Weiss, B.: A database of german emotional speech. In: Proc. Interspeech 2005, Lisbon, Portugal, ISCA, pp. 1517–1520 (2005)

Towards Knowledge-Based Affective Interaction: Situational Interpretation of Affect

Abdul Rehman Abbasi[1], Takeaki Uno[2], Matthew N. Dailey[1], and Nitin V. Afzulpurkar[1]

[1] Asian Institute of Technology, Bangkok, Thailand
{abdulrehman.abbasi,mdailey,nitin}@ait.ac.th
[2] National Institute of Informatics, Tokyo, Japan
uno@nii.ac.jp

Abstract. Human-to-computer interaction in a variety of applications could benefit if systems could accurately analyze and respond to their users' affect. Although a great deal of research has been conducted on affect recognition, very little of this work has considered what is the appropriate information to extract in specific situations. Towards understanding how specific applications such as affective tutoring and affective entertainment could benefit, we present two experiments. In the first experiment, we found that students' facial expressions, together with their body actions, gave little information about their internal emotion per se but they would be useful features for predicting their self-reported "true" mental state. In the second experiment, we found significant differences between the facial expressions and self-reported affective state of viewers watching a movie sequence. Our results suggest that the noisy relationship between observable gestures and underlying affect must be accounted for when designing affective computing applications.

Keywords: Affective tutoring, affective entertainer, facial expression analysis, gesture analysis, situation-specific affect interpretation.

1 Introduction

Imagine you tell a friend that you just lost your job, and he says nothing in reply. Further imagine that you cannot educe any emotion from his response. What would you think? Perhaps he did not understand what you wished to communicate, or perhaps, even worse, he has no feelings for you. In either case, the interaction was ineffective and unsuccessful. Emotions play an important role in successful and effective human-human relationships. In fact, in many situations, human "emotional intelligence" is more important than IQ for successful interaction [1]. There is also significant evidence that rational learning in humans is dependent on emotions [2], and that the computational systems interacting with humans would be more effective if they can negotiate human affect intelligently.

At present many "intelligent" systems lack the ability to adapt to the surrounding environment, especially to the emotional state of their users. Present

A. Paiva, R. Prada, and R.W. Picard (Eds.): ACII 2007, LNCS 4738, pp. 452–463, 2007.

day user would hardly consider a system intelligent if it lacked the ability to adapt to his expectations and to his feelings. Imagine how an intelligent tutoring system, acknowledging the user's affect and responding accordingly, could make the learning process more efficient and fruitful. For example, a distracted student reading a mathematical tutorial that is too difficult might feel a rise in interest, if the tutoring system were to realize his condition and start questioning interactively to secure his involvement. Similarly, people at leisure would appreciate an intelligent entertainment system that can tune itself according to the user's mood. For example, an exhausted salesperson who has worked all day might feel refreshed, if the entertainment system in his car were to notice and queue his favorite pop song. We now turn to the question how such a system might work.

1.1 Interpretation of Affect and Related Work

We assume, for simplicity, that a human's affective state at a particular point in time can be described by a set of mental states. Although we can never know with certainty another's affective state, we assume that it manifests stochastically as observable visual, conversational, and physiological clues, with noise, and that an observer's task is to infer the underlying affective state from those noisy features. Although physiological signals such as heart rate or fusion of evidence from multiple sensory modalities [3,4] can be effective, we focus on *facial expressions* due to their prominence and historical significance in the literature on emotion interpretation [5]. In contrast to an earlier study on emotional reactions by Landis [6], we also consider *body gestures* as additional features which are potentially associated with affective states in the first experiment. We discuss these two signals in more detail below.

There are many possible ways to analyze facial expressions. First, we might consider mapping directly from facial expressions to affective state. Early cross cultural studies, e.g. [7], suggested the existence of six universal emotion categories that correspond to particular facial expressions. Other researchers found evidence for a continuous multidimensional affect space in which fuzzy regions correspond to facial expressions [8]. An alternative approach is to use objective measurement systems such as the Facial Action Coding System (FACS) [9]. FACS groups facial muscle movements into "action units" that can be quantified by experienced observers. These action units or their combination correspond to particular emotions. There has been extensive work on automatic analysis of facial expressions [10,11,12], but it is still an open question how reliably we can infer underlying emotion from such analysis.

In our experience, most of the gestures related to affective state involve the face or hand. There has been a great deal of research on hand gesture analysis and using them for human-robot interaction [13]. An empirical study by Dadgostar et al.[14], describing presence of gestures in school children while learning through an intelligent tutoring system, relates them with students' skills. Here, we also focus on gestures that hold a relationship to the given situation.

Typically, hand tracking is a convincing approach to detect human gestures. The two main methods to hand tracking are appearance modeling and 3-D modeling [15]. Appearance methods use apparent hand features from two dimensional intensity images and are less complicated while 3-D methods track hand features in three dimensional space.

Extracting affect from the human face and body is a difficult problem because emotional display varies from person to person and is governed by cultural and social rules. Situational context is an important factor as well. Many existing emotion recognition systems recognize and interpret stereotypical posed expressions such as those in JAFEE [16], POFA [17], JACFEE [18], and the Cohn-Kanade database [19], but in real-life situations one rarely observes such exaggerated expressions [20]. Additionally, as evinced in the current study, there is not always a direct relationship between facial expression and affective state. In view of all these issues, how can we get the best possible estimate of a person's affect?

Our hypothesis is that situational context may be a key to understanding the relationship between observable gestures and underlying emotions. With this study, we are making a first attempt to test this hypothesis by exploring the relationship between expression and affect in two real-world situations.

1.2   Goals and Scope of Study

Since the relationship between emotion and observable gestures depends on the social and cultural context, the situational context must be considered by any system attempting to map from observable gestures to affective states. In the current study, we aim to i) develop a benchmark data set of observable gestures related to real-world applications, which will be made available on our website [21], and ii) to identify useful features that may be utilized in these applications. The features of interest are visually-observable gestures. For example, a student scratching her nose in response to a teacher's query might indicate recalling by the student in that situation. There have been some promising efforts to form databases of emotional stimuli elicited in context, e.g. [22], but to our knowledge, none have yet focused on specific applications of intelligent systems.

In the current study, we consider two possible applications i.e. an affective tutoring system and an affective entertainer. For each application, we recorded participants' spontaneous facial expressions during a possible real-world scenario. Because one gesture could have different meanings in different situations, interpretation of gesture should be conditional on the situation. We call this *situated or situational gesture interpretation.* In both experiments, we compared the self reported affective state description from the participants with their observable gestures. In the first experiment, we found few useful gestures from the participants during a class lecture situation, indicating a particular affective state. These gestures were occasionally accompanied by facial expressions as well. The affective states reported, were described by the participants in a post experiment interview. In the second experiment, we found facial expressions in response to a movie watching scenario. These expressions were compared to the self reported affective states, described by the participants in a post- experiment interview. We found a noisy relationship between the self reported affective states and the visually labeled facial expressions. We must be careful not to over generalize the current study's results, since the number of participants and situations were small, and the gesture labeling was performed by the experimenters. However, we believe the experiments demonstrate convincingly the need for considering situational context in affective computing application design.

The rest of paper is organized as follows: Section 2 describes the methodology for the conducted experiments. Section 3 presents the results. Section 4 concludes the discussion with suggestions and future work plan.

2   Methodology

We carried out two experiments involving a total of 17 participants. The goal of each experiment was to obtain a set of spontaneous facial expressions in a specific situational context then to correlate the participants' facial expressions with their self-reported affective states. In Picard's [23] terminology, this is an "opportunistic situation," for which the participants were not asked to portray some prescribed emotional displays rather they were exposed to a given event and their subsequent response was recorded. The two experiments involved a set of students in a classroom lecture and a set of viewers watching a movie.

In the first experiment, we recorded the activities of four students who were from different countries and educational backgrounds. Two video sessions of

Table 1. Gestures observed in Experiment 1

Observed event	Participants' self-reported affective state	Context
Head scratching	Recalling something	Teacher was asking a question
Lips drooping	Feeling dissatisfaction	Teacher was going a bit fast
Nose scratching	Feeling good	Teacher complimented the student
Smile with shrinking eyes	Successfully recalling	Taking test
Long smile	Enjoying the atmosphere	Participant had the best test among all
Smile with a nod	Just recalling something	Taking test
Ear scratching	Concentrating	Teacher was writing on board
Quick eye blinking	Tired	Teacher started next topic
Zipped lips	Bored	Teacher was writing
Finger / pen in the mouth	Trying to remember something	Teacher was writing
Brow raise	Indifferent to something	Other students watching participant's work
Closed eye smile	Happy	Completed the test
Head shaking	Denial	Teacher asked for any difficulty / problem
Wrinkles at forehead	Concentrating	Teacher was writing on board

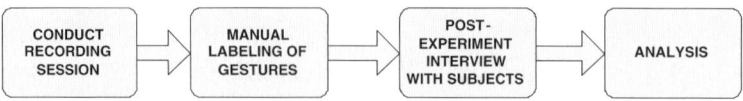

Fig. 1. Procedural steps for Experiment 1

Fig. 2. Recording setup for Experiment 1

more than two hours were recorded for these students. The experimenters manually labeled the participants' hand gestures into discrete categories (Refer to Table 1). These categories were determined through an initial preview by the experimenters. Later, a post-experiment interview was conducted to determine the actual affective state as reported by the participant. We then compared the gesture labels to the affective states. In the second experiment, 13 participants viewed a video sequence. This video sequence has 22 different clips from movies and other sources that could generate a variety of emotions among the viewers. Each session took 18 minutes, during which response by each of the 13 participants was recorded. Then a post-experiment interview was conducted to determine the affective state for each movie clip viewed. Finally, we reviewed the videos and compared the reported affective states to the facial expressions. Details of the experimental setup and subsequent analysis are provided in the following sections.

2.1   Experiment 1: Class Lecture Scenario for an Affective Tutoring System

We recruited students attending a preliminary Japanese language course at NII. Four students including two males and two females participated. They were briefed about the experiment, but in order to ensure spontaneous responses, we

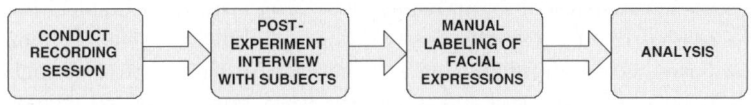

Fig. 3. Procedural steps for Experiment 2

did not inform them of the exact nature of the study. Their participation was voluntary. Fig. 1 shows the procedural steps involved in this experiment.

More than two hours of video recording was collected for the students in two sessions. Two passive cameras were used to record their activities as shown in Fig. 2.

During the first session, activities of two students were recorded, and in the second session, activities of the other pair of students were recorded. Once the recorded video was secured, the next phase was manual labeling of the observable gestures by the experimenters. At first we envisioned labeling facial expressions, but it turned out that the participants made very few identifiable expressions. On the other hand, their hand gestures were quit expressive, so we grouped them into the categories such as "Scratching nose" and so on (Refer to Table 1). This was followed by a post-experiment interview with each student. Each participant was shown his/her video footage and was asked about his/her feelings at the time of a particular gesture. The experimenters recorded participants' free-format responses. The gap between the recording and the interview session was not more than two days.

During the free format responses, the participants used a variety of ways to describe their feelings, so we normalized them using Geneva Affect Label Code (GALC) [24,25]. This code classifies such free form responses into well defined categories as it provides labels for 36 defined categories in English, French and German. For example, subjective description of "being tense" or "under pressure" was categorized as "tension." Finally, we grouped the participants' affective states with the corresponding images of gestures from the recorded video. Results for Experiment 1 are presented in Section 3.1.

2.2 Experiment 2: Movie Viewing Scenario for an Affective Entertainer System

13 volunteers were recorded, watching a movie sequence having a total of 22 clips of about 18 minutes in duration. Nine of the participants were male and the rest were female. These include seven Europeans, five Asians and one American. After the recording, one of the participants requested to withdraw him from the study, so we did not include his data for analysis.

As in Experiment 1, to ensure spontaneity participants were not aware of the exact nature of the study. The video clips were extracted from various sources including movies and web resources aimed to evoke variety of emotional reactions among the individuals. Each of the clips was purposefully chosen to generate a particular dominant feeling in the participant such as dislike, curiosity, happiness and so on. The procedural steps for this experiment are shown in Fig. 3.

Each session consisted of a participant watching a movie sequence. Each participant was recorded by a single passive camera. Following the experiment, each participant was asked about his/her felt emotion in the context of each scene. The free format affective state descriptions were normalized to single GALC [24,25] categories for each scene. For example, two participants each describing their feelings as "strange" and "amazing" were categorized by GALC [24,25] in a single well known category "surprise". The interview immediately followed the recording session. After the interview, the experimenters manually labeled the dominant facial expression in each scene from the video. Then, the reported information was compared with their facial response from the recorded video. The data collection therefore resulted in a dominant facial expression and a dominant felt emotion for each of the 22 video scenes, which were compared for correspondence.

3   Results

3.1   Experiment 1

For the four participants in this experiment, we labeled a total of 60 observable events involving some gesture from the recorded video. The distribution of the events was 26 (participant 1), 7 (participant 2), 16 (participant 3), and 11 (participant 4).

In the post-experiment interview, the participants were often unable to explain their affect in each and every event, but they were able to correlate some of their gestures to their feelings. For example, a participant scratching on her nose explained her behavior as feeling good during the lecture. Table 1 summarizes the significant gestures observed and Fig. 4 shows some of the images containing these gestures.

In addition to these gestures, we also observed a few notable phenomena:

- While experiencing extreme emotion, they either moved their hands or head or closed their eyes.
- Sometimes they leaned their head on their palms, when they felt stressed or depressed.

Fig. 4. Affective states of students from Experiment 1

Table 2. Number of participants with relevant expression description against each scene in Experiment 2

Expression Categories	1	2	3	4	5	6	7	8	9	10	11	12	13	14	15	16	17	18	19	20	21	22
Neutral	3	1	10	4	2	1	6	-	5	11	-	2	4	7	8	5	6	9	9	7	2	-
Happy	4	11	1	2	1	4	5	8	-	-	12	2	-	2	3	3	3	-	1	1	3	12
Surprised	4	-	-	2	-	3	1	1	-	1	-	1	2	-	-	-	1	2	1	1	3	-
In Pain	-	-	1	-	-	-	-	-	6	-	-	4	-	-	-	-	-	-	1	-	-	-
Fearful	1	-	-	-	1	-	-	-	1	-	-	-	-	-	-	-	-	1	-	-	-	-
Confused	-	-	-	1	1	-	-	-	-	-	-	-	1	-	-	-	-	1	-	-	-	-
Disappointed	-	-	-	-	-	2	-	-	-	-	-	-	1	1	-	-	-	-	-	-	1	-
Curious	-	-	-	1	-	2	-	1	-	-	-	-	2	2	1	2	2	-	-	-	3	-
Disgusted	-	-	-	2	7	-	-	2	-	-	-	3	2	-	-	2	-	-	-	2	-	-

- Their faces had a blank or neutral expression when they were unable to understand the lecture, rather than the expected confusion or disturbance.
- Some of their reflexes were without any reason, and participants were amazed to see their response and could not explain it.
- At times of extreme amusement, they closed their eyes and/or scratch on nose.

Furthermore, students' moods prior to a lecture had a notable influence on their level of interest and learning during class lecture. Students feeling happiness enjoyed the class and mostly comprehended the lecture very well. Three out of four subjects showed no sign of discomfort in front of camera and did not even feel its presence during lecture which was obvious from their video footage and was confirmed by them during the interview as well. Only one subject confessed that he occasionally felt a little bit stressed due to presence of camera.

For this experiment, it is worth mentioning that subjects behave differently during the proceedings but most of their responses were identical when the similar emotion was felt. We call this approach as *situated or situational affect interpretation,* and believe that it might be helpful in designing customized applications such as affective tutoring as it can help to correlate what physiological signal in combination with a particular facial expression indicates to a particular emotional state in a given situation.

Interestingly, for some gestures, subjects showed ignorance about their true state of mind even though they were provided with the context. We could not interpret these behaviors. This raises the question that if the subject him/her self can not explain a gesture, how can we hope to build a system to interpret gestures and predict affect?

As the research moves from simple perception to building system that perceive and act, we need to take uncertainty into account.

Fig. 5. Affective states of participants from Experiment 2

3.2   Experiment 2

For the second experiment, we analyzed the information from a slightly different perspective from Experiment 1. Here, in the post-experiment interview, participants were asked about their dominant feeling to each movie clip. Most of the time participants were comfortable describing their emotional state as their memory was fresh at that time. After the interviews, the experimenters independently labeled the subjects' dominant facial expressions to each scene, using the same labels. Note that these were experimenters' subjective impressions of the facial expressions and an objective measurement like FACS [9] would be preferred and is planned for our future work.

Finally, we compared the reported affective states to the corresponding labeled images, carrying the facial expressions. We found a variety of emotional responses for each participant, and Table 2 shows these responses for all the participants. The labeled and reported categories could be distinguished as Neutral, Happy, Surprised, In Pain, Fearful, Confused, Disappointed, Curious and Disgusted. Some of the relevant images showing these expressions are shown in Fig. 5.

Beyond the categories, we also observed that the intensity of the expression seemed to vary with time. For example, the longer the situation prevailed, the intensity of expression deepened.

Interestingly, we found that display of emotion also varied with the emotional valence. In most cases, subjects did not display negative expressions even though they admitted feeling such emotions during the situation. In general, for positive scenes (Scene No. 2, 11, 22 in Table 2), we observed unanimous agreement

Table 3. Correspondence, false detection, false negative and disagreement (participant B1)

Scene no.	Reported emotion (Actual/GALC)	Labeled facial response	Correspondence	False negative	False detection	Disagreement
1	Fear	Scared	1	-	-	-
2	Amusement	No reaction	-	1	-	-
3	Normal	No reaction	1	-	-	-
4	Normal	No reaction	1	-	-	-
5	Disgust	Disliked	1	-	-	-
6	Feeling stupid	Smile	1	-	-	-
7	Liked	Laughing	1	-	-	-
8	Amusement	Smile	1	-	-	-
9	Sympathy	No reaction	-	1	-	-
10	Nothing	No reaction	1	-	-	-
11	Nothing	Smile	-	-	1	-
12	Admiration	Disgust	-	-	-	1
13	Disgust	Disgust	1	-	-	-
14	Fear	Curious	-	-	-	1
15	Unimpressed	No reaction	-	1 -	-	
16	Disgust	Disliked	1	-	-	-
17	Unreal	Smile	-	-	-	1
18	Disgust	No reaction	-	1	-	-
19	Amusement	No reaction	-	1	-	-
20	Violent	Serious	1	-	-	-
21	Impressed	Curious	-	-	-	1
22	Happiness	Amused	1	-	-	-
Total	12	5	1	4		

for displaying facial expressions, from the participants. For the negative scenes (Scene No. 10 in Table 2), responses remained neutral.

A more significant observation was that the subjects' reported emotions often disagreed with their observable facial expressions. Besides this, there were a few instances when there was no facial expression observed for a reported emotion and vice versa. We summarize these observations in Table 3 for one of our participants.

The terms correspondence and disagreement can be defined as the events when there was an absolute agreement and disagreement between the facial expression and reported emotion respectively while a false negative is an instance, when there was no expression found for a reported emotion. Similarly, false detection represents the presence of a facial response without any emotional justification. These measures for all participants are also shown in Table 4.

From Table 4, we may infer that an overall agreement of about 56 percent was achieved between the reported emotions and their corresponding facial expressions while it shows a disagreement of about 15 percent. Similarly, for about

Table 4. Correspondence, false detection, false negative and disagreement (All participants)

Subject ID	B1	B2	B3	B4	B5	B6	B7	B8	B9	B10	B11	B12	Percentage occurences
Correspondence	12	13	11	15	13	14	17	9	9	9	10	15	55.70
False Negative	5	7	6	7	3	2	3	10	10	10	6	1	26.50
False Detection	1	0	0	0	3	1	0	0	0	0	1	1	02.65
Disagreement	4	2	5	0	3	5	2	3	3	3	5	5	15.15

27 percent of events there was no facial response even though an emotion was felt, while only 2 percent events caused an expression without an emotion.

4 Conclusion

Clearly, computer applications involved in teaching or entertaining humans could be improved if they could reliably estimate their users' emotions. Towards this goal, a great deal of research has focused on real-time extraction of facial expressions from video imagery. However, to be truly effective, affective applications should know *when they are probably right and when they are probably wrong.*

In two experiments, we have shown that facial expressions and body gestures correspond somewhat with underlying emotions and mental states. But it is crucial to realize how loose and noisy these correspondences really are in practice. One must be careful not to generalize our results too much, considering the small number of scenarios, the small subject sample sizes, and furthermore, the informal method of coding the subjects' gestures which is a limitation of the current work. However, in our future work, we plan a more dynamic fine-grained analysis.

Our findings lead us to recommend that prior to embedding emotion prediction models in their applications, researchers should perform situational extraction of emotions as early as possible in the system's life cycle. This will lead to effective knowledge-based affective computing applications whose knowledge is tuned to the particular contexts they are operating in.

Acknowledgments. We thank the students and researchers from the National Institute of Informatics, Japan for their voluntary participation in this study and appreciate Institute's support for this work. We are also grateful for the support of Thailand Research Fund through grant MRG4780209 to MND.

References

1. Pantic, M., Sebe, N., Cohn, J.F., Huang, T.: Affective multimodal human-computer interaction. In: Proc. ACM. Int. Conf. Multimedia, pp. 669–676. ACM Press, New York (2005)

2. Picard, R.W.: Affective Computing. MIT Press, Cambridge (2000)
3. Prendinger, H., Becker, C., Ishizuka, M.: A study in users' physiological response to an empathic interface agent. Int. J. of Humanoid Robotics 3(3), 371–391 (2006)
4. Kapoor, A., Burleson, W., Picard, R.W.: Automatic prediction of frustration. International Journal of Human-Computer Studies (In press 2007)
5. Darwin, C.: The Expression of the Emotions in Man and Animals. Oxford University Press, Oxford (1998)
6. Landis, C.: Studies of emotional reactions: I. A preliminary study of facial expression. Journal of Experimental Psychology 8 (1924)
7. Ekman, P., Friesen, W.: Constants across cultures in the face and emotion. Journal of Personality and Social Psychology 17(2), 124–129 (1971)
8. Russell, J.A., Bullock, M.: Fuzzy concepts and the perception of emotion in facial expressions. Social Cognition 4, 309–341 (1986)
9. Ekman, P., Friesen, W.: Facial Action Coding System (FACS) Manual. Consulting Psychologists Press, Palo Alto, Calif (1978)
10. Fasel, B., Luettin, J.: Automatic facial expression analysis: A survey. Pattern Recognition 36(1), 259–275 (2003)
11. Pantic, M., Rothkrantz, L.J.M.: Automatic analysis of facial expressions: The state of the art. IEEE PAMI 22(12), 1424–1445 (2000)
12. Tian, Y., Kanade, T., Cohn, J.F.: Facial expression analysis. In: Li, S.Z., Jain, A.K. (eds.) Handbook of Face Recognition, Springer, Berlin (2005)
13. Kim, K.K., Kwak, K.C., Chi, S.Y.: Gesture analysis for human-robot interaction. In: Proc. 8th International Conference on Advanced Communication Technology (ICACT), pp. 1824–1827 (2006)
14. Dadgostar, F., Ryu, H., Sarrafzadeh, A., Overmyer, S.P.: Making sense of student use of non-verbal cues for intelligent tutoring systems. In: Proc. OZCHI (2005)
15. Tao, J., Tieniu, T.: Affective computing: A review. In: Proc. 1st International Conference on Affective Computing and Intelligent Interaction, pp. 981–995 (2005)
16. http://www.kasrl.org/jaffe_download.html
17. Ekman, P., Friesen, W.: Pictures of Facial Affect. Consulting Psychologists Press, Palo Alto, Calif (1975)
18. Matsumoto, D., Ekman, P.: American-Japanese cultural differences in intensity ratings of facial expressions of emotion. Motivation and Emotion 13(2), 143–157 (1989)
19. Cohn-Kanade AU-Coded Facial Expression Database (CMU Database), http://www.cs.cmu.edu/~face/index2.htm
20. Sun, Y., Sebe, N., Lew, M.S., Gevers, T.: Authentic emotion detection in real-time video. In: Sebe, N., Lew, M.S., Huang, T.S. (eds.) Computer Vision in Human-Computer Interaction. LNCS, vol. 3058, pp. 94–104. Springer, Heidelberg (2004)
21. http://research.nii.ac.jp/SEMEX
22. Cowie, E.D., Cowie, R., Schröder, M.: A new emotion database: Considerations, sources and scope. In: Proc. ISCA ITRW on Speech and Emotion, pp. 39–44 (2000)
23. Picard, R.W., Vyzas, E., Healey, J.: Toward machine emotional intelligence: Analysis of affective physiological state. IEEE PAMI 23(10), 1175–1191 (2001)
24. http://www.unige.ch/fapse/emotion/resmaterial/GALC.xls
25. Scherer, K.R.: What are emotions? And how can they be measured? Social Science Information 44(4), 695–729 (2005)

Collection and Annotation of a Corpus of Human-Human Multimodal Interactions: Emotion and Others Anthropomorphic Characteristics

Aurélie Zara[1,2], Valérie Maffiolo[1], Jean Claude Martin[2], and Laurence Devillers[2]

[1] France Telecom Orange Labs, 2 av. P. Marzin, 22300 Lannion, France
[2] LIMSI-CNRS, BP 133, 91403 Orsay cedex, France
{aurelie.zara,valerie.maffiolo}@orange-ftgroup.com,
{devil,martin}@limsi.fr

Abstract. In order to design affective interactive systems, experimental grounding is required for studying expressions of emotion during interaction. In this paper, we present the EmoTaboo protocol for the collection of multimodal emotional behaviours occurring during human-human interactions in a game context. First annotations revealed that the collected data contains various multimodal expressions of emotions and other mental states. In order to reduce the influence of language via a predetermined set of labels and to take into account differences between coders in their capacity to verbalize their perception, we introduce a new annotation methodology based on 1) a hierarchical taxonomy of emotion-related words, and 2) the design of the annotation interface. Future directions include the implementation of such an annotation tool and its evaluation for the annotation of multimodal interactive and emotional behaviours. We will also extend our first annotation scheme to several other characteristics interdependent of emotions.

Keywords: Corpus collection, annotation, multimodal behaviours, human-human interaction.

1 Introduction

Interacting with computers elicits emotion from users. People feel amused when they are playing a game [1,2], frustrated or angry when the machine doesn't come up to their expectation. Taking expressions of emotion into account in human machine interaction may not only improve the machine's performances in assisting users but might also enhance computers' ability to make decisions [3]. Consequently, interest in virtual embodied agents able to express emotions [4], to react to users' expression of emotion [5] or even to have emotion, has grown in the past decade. This raises several questions: Which emotions are elicited from users when they interact with computers? How are these emotions expressed? How much does that depend on the application at hand? Which emotions should express a virtual agent and how should these emotions be expressed (regarding the application in which the interaction is studied)?

There has been a lot of research on emotions and their non-verbal expressions in face [6], voice [7,8] and body movements [9]. Yet, these studies are mostly based on

A. Paiva, R. Prada, and R.W. Picard (Eds.): ACII 2007, LNCS 4738, pp. 464–475, 2007.

acted basic emotions. Recent audio-visual corpora enabled to collect more spontaneous « real-life » behaviours in TV interviews [7,10], in-lab situations [11], or multimodal behaviours during sophisticated acting protocols [12]. Although these corpora allow spontaneity and naturalness, they are either limited with respect to multimodality (they contain few gestures or few body movements), or with respect to interaction (the video corpus does not show the full multimodal behaviours of the two people who interact). Some of these studies have also enlarged their investigations with other mental states [11,13], mood or attitudes [14]. Indeed, it has been shown that emotions and their expressions are interdependent to other characteristics proper to the human being:

- Emotions are interdependent of other mental states such as beliefs or intention (e.g. conflict of mental states can elicit negative emotions from a person) [15].
- Emotions influence attitudes, judgment and strategic communications [16].
- For a given situation, emotions and their modes of expression vary from one person to another, in accordance with his/her history, culture, social background and personality [17].

Furthermore, these anthropomorphic characteristics involve the same set of modalities as the expressions of emotion:

- Face reveals personality [18] and mental states such as beliefs (e.g. doubt: raised eyebrow) or intention (e.g. to implore: head aside, inner eyebrow up) [19].
- Eyes reflect cognitive activity (e.g. thinking: look up sideways) [20] and communicates the nature of the interpersonal relationship [21].
- Speech also gives cues about personality, social membership, beliefs (e.g. doubt: hesitation in speech), cognitive process such as comprehension and so on [22].
- Gestures are physical-symbolic representation of intention, beliefs and so on [23].

Therefore, it is necessary to consider both emotions and others anthropomorphic characteristics in the analysis of the multimodal behaviour. Several researches on virtual embodied agents have argued in favour of giving importance to anthropomorphic characteristics to enhance the believability of a virtual agent. According to Thomas and Johnson [24], characters that appear to think, have emotions and act of their own, can be considered as believable because these characteristics confer drawings with an illusion of life. A minority of virtual agents is currently able to express some of these characteristics and they only use a few modalities. One of them is GRETA which has been designed to show information about location and properties of concrete or abstract objects or events, beliefs, intentions, affective states and metacognitives actions with facial expressions and gaze directions [4].

The long-term goal of our work is to model the non-verbal behaviour of an agent endowed with anthropomorphic characteristics. A Wizard-of-Oz will be carried out to evaluate the impact of the expression of these characteristics on the interaction with a human in a game context. The first step is the identification of the relevant anthropomorphic characteristics for the virtual agent and the specification of the corresponding multimodal behaviours. For that, we selected a corpus-based approach for studying face-to-face human-human interaction in a game. Moreover, this approach allows us to collect strategies of interaction useful for the specification of

Wizard-of-Oz experiment (e.g. for the virtual agent, adopting appropriate emotional responses to some human behaviours according to the other anthropomorphic characteristics (for example personality) assigned to the virtual agent). We chose a game for the reason that several researchers consider games as a relevant means for eliciting emotional behaviours, especially in laboratory, and riding subjects of their inhibitions [1,2].

EmoTaboo is the name of the protocol we have established to collect a corpus of multimodal expressions of emotion during human-human interaction. The procedure is presented in section 2. A first phase of annotation using a multi-level coding scheme including emotion labels, mental states, and communication acts was carried out and is described in section 2. In order to reduce the influence of language via the predefined set of labels, we propose in section 3 a new annotation methodology based on a hierarchical structure of emotion-related words. We also explain our plans for implementing the corresponding user interface to be used by the coders. Future directions include the implementation of such an annotation tool and its evaluation for the annotation of multimodal interactive and emotional behaviours. We will also extend our first approach to several other characteristics interdependent of emotions.

2   The EmoTaboo Protocol

2.1   Procedure

The goal of the EmoTaboo protocol was to collect emotionally rich multimodal and interactive. EmoTaboo is an adaptation of the game Taboo. Our procedure involves interactions between two players. One of them has to guess a word that the other player is describing using his own speech and gestures, without uttering five forbidden words. The word to guess and the five forbidden words are written on a card. Each person had to make guess three series of words alternating roles (mime and soothsayer). The two players did not know each other. One of them was a naïve subject whereas the other player was instructed. This confederate knew all the cards in advance, and for each card, indications were given on how to induce emotions in the naïve subject. We involved a confederate in the protocol because we wanted to be sure to collect enough emotional interactions and we supposed that it would enable us to have a better control over the emotion elicitation situations. To ensure the engagement of the subjects in the task, the results of previous teams were displayed on a board in the room during the game, and a gift token was promised to the winner team. We used strategies for eliciting emotions at three different levels in the procedure: in the course of the game, in the choice of cards, and in the directions given to the confederate.

Strategies connected to the course of the game. The mime had ten seconds to read the card on which was written the word to make guess and the five forbidden words. Then he/she had two minutes to make guess the word. Thirty seconds before the end of the prescribed time, the experimenter announced the remaining time in order to motivate the players and to elicit stress. After these two minutes, the experimenter takes stock of the penalties, if the secret word wasn't found or if the team transgressed the game rules (e.g. using a forbidden word, describing the word using charades).

Strategies connected to the choice of cards. Game cards were provided to the players in ascending order of difficulty. Regarding the type of this game, we supposed that the emotions induced by game cards would include embarrassment, shame, amusement and surprise. To ensure their elicitation, we played on the knowledge of the word, the easiness to guess the word, and its evocation. We chose cards containing very uncommon words (e.g. "palimpsest") supposed to arouse embarrassment or shame, words evoking disgusting things (e.g. "putrid") or words with sexual connotation (e.g. "aphrodisiac").

Strategies connected the directives given to the instructed subject. For each card, the confederate had directions such as "do not find the word on purpose", "propose words with no relation at all with what is said by the naïve player". For each card, a list of emotions to elicit from the naïve subject was suggested (e.g. "temptation": negative emotions as disappointment, frustration, stress or positive emotions as pride, satisfaction). For each emotion an illustrative list of possible strategies was proposed (e.g. to induce anger, criticize the naïve player).

At the end of the procedure, subjects had to answer to a questionnaire (cf. section 2.3) about emotions felt by the naïve subject and another questionnaire evaluating the personality in terms of extraversion, neurosis and sincerity [25].

Fig. 1. The collected data features four viewpoints. The naive subject is on the left side, the confederate is on the right side.

We recorded ten pairs of players, each pair involving twenty cards. Naïve subjects were university students (four women and six men), confederates were close relations of the experimenter or laboratory staff (three women, five men). We collected about eight hours of videos with four different viewpoints corresponding to face close-up and upper body of both players (Fig. 1).

2.2 Representation of Emotions

Several studies define emotions using continuous abstract dimensions: Activation-Valence [7] or Intensity-Valence [26]. But these three dimensions do not always enable to obtain a precise representation of emotion. For example, it is impossible to distinguish fear and anger. According to the appraisal theory [27], the perception and the cognitive evaluation of an event determine the type and the intensity of the emotion felt by a person. Finally, the most widely used approach for the annotation of emotion is the discrete representation of emotion using verbal labels enabling to discriminate between different emotions categories. In most of these studies, the coders select one or several labels out of a set of emotion-related words. Some studies also propose a free text verbalization of emotions [28]. A few studies use taxonomy such as WordNet affect but in a language processing context [29,30].

In our experiment, we define two lists of emotion labels using a majority voting technique. A first list of labels was selected out of the fusion several lists of emotional labels defined within HUMAINE (European network on emotion http://emotion-research.net/). In a second step, several judges rated each emotion word of this list with respect to how much it sounded relevant for describing emotions induced by our EmoTaboo protocol. The most relevant words were used in a questionnaire used at the end of the game (cf. section 2.3). A similar approach was used to rate the relevance of each word of the merged list in the light of collected video data. We obtained the following twenty-one emotion labels that we used for manual annotation (cf. section 2.4): "Amusement", "Embarrassment", "Disappointment", "Excitement", "Impatience", "Frustration", "Annoyance", "Anxiety", "Effervescent happiness", "Nervousness", "Pride", "Satisfaction", "Stress", "Boredom", "Confidence", "Contentment", "Pleasure", "Surprise", "Cold Anger", "Sadness" and "Other".

2.3 Questionnaire Results: Reports by Naïve Subjects and Confederates

At the end of the game, each naïve subjects had to report emotions felt during the game, by recall, on a scale of intensity according to the twenty-one emotion labels. The confederate had to rate on the same scale the naïve subject's emotions he/she inferred. The goal of this questionnaire was to validate that subjects felt a great variety of emotions during the interaction and that these emotions were perceived by the confederate.

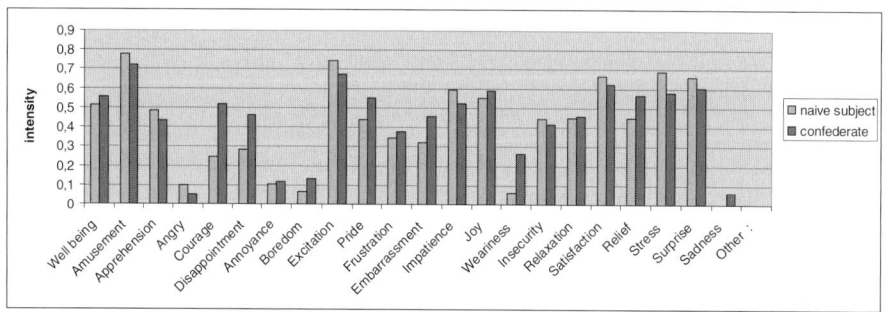

Fig. 2. Mean intensity of naïve subjects' emotion, reported by subjects themselves and confederates. Intensity is given in a scale 0-1.

Fig. 2 shows that emotions with highest intensity felt by the naïve subjects are "Amusement", "Excitation", "Satisfaction", "Surprise", "Stress" and "Impatience". For these emotions, the intensity inferred by the confederates is close but always lower.

We observe that confederates have significantly over-estimated the intensity of the naïve subjects' emotions "Courage", "Disappointment" and "Weariness". These differences are probably due to individual differences in the ability to categorize and verbalize felt or perceived emotional experiences [31]. It is also likely that subjects didn't evaluate emotions intensity but a combination of intensity and frequency of the emotion. Nevertheless, the analysis of the questionnaires highlights that subjects have felt emotions and these emotions have been perceived by the confederates. This suggests that our protocol EmoTaboo seems relevant for the collection of emotionally rich behaviours.

2.4   Corpus Analysis from the Viewpoints of Third Observers

In the eyes of the literature and first observations done of the corpus, we defined a first scheme to annotate emotion, cognitive states and processes (called mental states by Baron Cohen), strategic communication (including the strategies suggested in the instructions provided to the confederate and other strategies that we observed in the corpus such as "ironic") and contextual information (e.g. current card, current phase of the game). In order to represent complex emotion, the annotation procedure allowed the coders to choose at most five labels per segment [32]. For each emotion, we added two abstract dimensions: the intensity of the emotion and its valence [32]. Concerning cognitive states and processes, we selected an intermediate level in the taxonomy of Baron-Cohen [21]. These labels are: "Agreeing", "Concentrating", "Interested", "Disagreeing", "Thinking" and "Unsure". We also annotated speech acts, taken from DAMSL [33]. Videos were segmented in sequences of about 2 minutes corresponding to the guess of one word and annotated with the ANVIL software [34].

Table 1. Annotation of one sequence corresponding to the word palimpsest (body view)

Annotation Category (corresponding to a track in Anvil)	**Main results (% of the sequence annotated with a label of the corresponding category)**
Naïve subject's emotions	77% including: Amusement 29%; Stress 9%; Exasperation 7%, Embarrassment 7%.
Confederate's emotions	84% including: Embarrassment, 29%; Amusement, 21%; Stress, 11%; Satisfaction, 6%.
Naïve subject's cognitive states and processes	75% including: Uncertain 29%; Thinking 21%; Interested, 18%.
Confederate's cognitive states and processes	81% including: Interested, 41%; Thinking, 21%;
Strategic communication used by the naïve subjects	Joking, expressing self doubt, criticizing, sarcastic, encouraging, ironic, etc.
Strategic communication used by the confederates	Criticizing, disrespect, expressing doubt about partner, expressing self doubt, discouraging, etc.

First annotations, done by four coders on one sequence corresponding to the word "palimpsest", show the presence of emotional and cognitive states and processes in the corpus (cf. table 1). They suggest that the strategies used to elicit emotion (e.g. penalties, the choice of cards, the announcement of the remaining thirty seconds, some of directives given to the confederate) were effective and relevant for the specification of our future Wizard of Oz procedure because of their capacity to elicit emotions. A first analysis was also done on gesture and other modalities. It reveals that the corpus contains many and various multimodal behaviours [35].

2.5 Discussion

The corpus collected using the EmoTaboo protocol contains a great variety of emotions, felt and expressed by naïve subjects and confederates .Furthermore, these emotions can be considered as being emotions of everyday life and easily found in a human-machine interaction in close situations (e.g. frustration or irritation when the computer doesn't understand the user request). These emotions are expressed through various behaviours as well in categories (e.g. gestures categories) as in modalities (gesture, facial expressions, voice). Furthermore first annotations show that the expression of other characteristics such as cognitive states and processes are observed in the corpus.

Although the participation of a confederate appears to be effective to elicit emotions from the naïve player, it might constitute a bias in our experiment. Indeed, the use of strategies to elicit negative emotions from the naïve subject caused some embarrassment from the confederate. He was less spontaneous and natural and this is visible and annotated by the third observers (cf. Table 1). The study of the corpus cannot thus be done without taking into account this phenomenon.

First annotations have raised several questions. According to different coders, emotions-related words were not precise enough to capture the diversity of emotions expressed in the collected data. For example, some coders made distinctions between happiness and triumphant, and could not choose a label in adequacy with their perception because of the absence of such labels in the set of proposed ones. Consequently they annotated the emotion using the label with the closest meaning. We can assume that such annotations were low in accuracy. Our approach did not give the possibility to the coders to be as precise (or imprecise) as they wished in accordance with their level of certitude regarding their perception. A solution to this problem would be to allow the coder to propose a new label when there is no appropriate word in the defined list. But many emotional words are polysemic and we would not be able to discriminate the exact meaning used by the coder. Another solution would be to propose a larger list of emotion-related words, but this would increase the difficulty of annotation because of the length of the proposed list.

Moreover these first annotations have revealed that some emotion categories were missing and were not properly defined. For example, our initial list of strategic communications was a mix of cognitive states (e.g. self doubt, doubt about the partner), attitudes (e.g., offensive, perseverant), and communication strategies (e.g. criticizing, joking, ironic, sarcastic). Those considerations led us to revise our first annotation approach and to explore how people categorize and verbalize emotions and the influence of language on the perception of emotions.

3   Toward a New Approach for Annotating Emotions and Other Characteristics

3.1   "Emotional Granularity" and the Influence of the Language on the Perception of Emotion

When people report their emotional experiences in everyday life, some of them use discrete emotion labels such as "angry", "sad" etc. to represent the most general aspect of their feelings (typically pleasure and displeasure) whereas other people use more precise, differentiated terms, in a way that captures the distinctiveness in the words meaning [31]. Barrett called this phenomenon "*emotional granularity*". This is also observed when people describe their perception of others' emotions. Consequently people are not equal in categorizing and verbalizing their own emotions and their inferences of others' emotions. According to [37], the language also intrinsically shapes the inference of others' emotions from their behaviours. Through the results of three studies, the authors found that the accessibility in memory of emotion-related words influences participant's speed or accuracy in perceiving facial behaviours depicting emotion. Consequently coders with low "emotional granularity" might be slower in the processes of categorization of their perception and less accurate if they have to annotate with precise emotion-related words.

Moreover many studies on attention have shown that focalizing attention on a particular dimension (here some emotional terms) increases the capacity of discrimination of stimuli according to this dimension but also decreases this capacity on other dimensions. Tasks involving categorization processes are sensitive to this process [36]. We thus assume that presenting a restricted list of emotional-related words would encourage the coder to focalize his/her attention only on emotions for which related words are provided in the list.

3.2   On the Use of a Hierarchic Taxonomy for Manual Annotation

Our aim is to design a coding scheme which would allow coders to be as precise as they wish according to their confidence in their own judgment. In this way, we take for granted that people would be more accurate in the annotation task. Moreover, having precise information can be also useful for the specification of the virtual agent since it would enable to display a more appropriate behaviour according to a particular situation.

Ekman defined each emotion category (e.g. Surprise) as a family of emotion. He distinguishes four types of surprises depending on how the surprise is expressed using differently different parts of the face: questioning surprise (involving eyes and brows), astonished surprise (eyes and mouth), dazed or less interested surprise (brows and mouth) [8].

Many other studies have shown that emotion-related terms are organized in taxonomic structure which the form would be a circumplex shape [31,38,39,40]. According to Plutchik [39], a circumplex model enables to highlight continuous relations between emotion-related terms but also their discontinuity. In fact, terms can be grouped according to eight emotional concepts called primary emotions (fear, anger, joy, sadness, acceptance, disgust, anticipation, surprise) and seven concepts can be grouped in terms of pleasure and displeasure, excepted surprise. This conceptual and linguistic form of organisation is proposed by Plutchik to support the existence of analogous structure that it is supposed to exist within the framework of the experience of emotion. This taxonomic structure seems to be dependent on the language. Galati [40] underlined the existence of differences between Neolatin languages and English. Taxonomies of emotions in French were defined in [30,40]. A selection of the taxonomy presented in [40] is given in Table 2.

Table 2. Part of the semantic structure of French emotions lexicon [40]

pleasure	joy	Satisfaction, amusement, relief, well being, happiness…
displeasure	sadness	Despair, dissatisfaction, confusion, annoyance …
	anger	Irritation, contempt, consternation, aversion…
	fear	Anxiety, apprehension, embarrassment, discouragement …

Despite the fact that there is no evidence of a universal taxonomic structure of emotions [31], we believe that using this type of structure for helping the annotation task can answer the problems occurring during the annotation of anthropomorphic characteristics discussed in the previous sections. Whereas our first approach was to use a flat list, the structure that we propose for manual annotation would be hierarchic tree-network taxonomy. The top of the structure would describe general concepts (e.g. emotion-related states, attitudes, cognitive states) and leafs would represent precise concepts (e.g. jubilation, triumph, scepticism).

We propose two alternatives to the coder. The first one would allow the coder to have a direct access to the taxonomy. He/she would be able to navigate from general concepts (e.g. emotion, pleasure/displeasure) to more precise ones (e.g. triumphant). The second solution would be a completion system. The coder would be able to propose a label characterizing his/her perception. In this way, he/she wouldn't be influenced or disturbed by the organisation of concepts and it would ensure the validity of the proposed label (e.g. its spelling). Once the label chosen, the definition(s) and a part of the taxonomy corresponding to the label would be displayed to avoid meaning confusions and to enable the coder to validate his/her choice. Instead the coder might also choose another label that he/she estimates to be more appropriate (e.g. more precise term, more general term, synonym), in accordance with his/her degree of confidence.

This raises issues with respect to the ergonomics of such an annotation tool. We will thus investigate visualisation techniques used to display dictionaries or ontologies. Moreover, the use of a large number of labels will require the adaptation of statistical and inter-judge agreement algorithms. A solution would consist in taking into account the semantic distance in the taxonomy between emotion-related words.

4 Conclusion and Future Directions

The specification of multimodal behaviours of a virtual agent endowed with anthropomorphic characteristics in the context of a game requires the study of the human expressions of these characteristics in a closed context. In this framework, we presented the EmoTaboo protocol and explained how it enabled the collection of a corpus of dyadic interactions during a game. We illustrated the richness of the collected data with respect to expressions of emotions and other anthropomorphic characteristics. First experiments of annotation lead us to propose a new strategy of annotation. The new hierarchical approach of annotation would enable human judges to select labels at several possible levels of precision. We assume that this method is adapted to the annotation of any corpora requiring an interpretation from the judge.

To improve our first approach, we also suggest to reorganise categories and to add missing ones (we provide in brackets the general concepts associated to the category):

- Emotions (see for an example table 2) and their intensity (low, average, high).
- Cognitive states (e.g. interestedness, readiness, curiosity, certainty, doubt, preoccupation confusion) and cognitive processes (e.g. thinking, deciding, attention and inattention) adapted from [20,29].
- Attitudes (e.g. defensive, intolerance, paternalism) adapted from [27,29].
- Strategic communication (e.g. approval, disapproval, disrespect, Humour), corresponding to strategies used to elicit emotion, adapted from Wordnet (http://wordnet.princeton.edu/); and speech acts [33].
- Mood, adapted from [27,29,41].
- Personality [43] (e.g. Extraversion agreeableness, consciousness, neurosis, openness), adapted from theories of personality such as OCEAN [42].
- Contextual information such as (current card, game phase, etc.).

Future directions include the definition of a coding scheme for multimodal behaviours. This will enable us to compute relations between anthropomorphic characteristics and their multimodal expressions. From this corpus, a subject will be selected for his multimodal behaviour and his communication strategies as a model for the setting of the Wizard-Of-Oz, allowing the evaluation of the impact of the expression of anthropomorphic characteristics on a HMI in a game context.

References

1. Kaiser, S., Wehrle, T., Edwards, P.: Multi-modal emotion measurement in an interactive computer game. A pilot study. 8th Conference of the International Society for Research on Emotions (1993)
2. Wang, N., Marsella, S.: An Emotion Evoking Game. In: Gratch, J., Young, M., Aylett, R., Ballin, D., Olivier, P. (eds.) IVA 2006. LNCS (LNAI), vol. 4133, Springer, Heidelberg (2006)
3. Picard, R.: Affective Computing. MIT Press, Cambridge (1997)
4. Poggi, I., Pelachaud, C., de Rosis, F., Carofiglio, V., De Carolis, B.: GRETA. A Believable Embodied Conversational Agent. In: Stock, O., Zancarano, M. (eds.) Multimodal Intelligent Information Presentation, Kluwer, Dordrecht (2005)
5. Prendinger, H., Descamps, S., Ishizuka, M.: Scripting Affective Communication with Life-like Characters. In Web-based Interaction Systems. Applied Artificial, Intelligence Journal 16(7-8), 519–553 (2002)
6. Ekman, P.: Emotions revealed. Understanding faces and feelings. In: Weidenfeld & Nicolson (2003)

7. Douglas-Cowie, E., Campbell, N., Cowie, R., Roach, P.: Emotional speech - Towards a new generation of databases. In Speech Communication 40, 33–60 (2003)
8. Schröder, M.: Experimental study of affect burst. In Speech Communication. Special Issue following the ISCA Workshop on Speech and Emotion 40(1-2), 99–116 (2003)
9. Wallbott, H.G.: Bodily expression of emotion. In European Journal of Social Psychology 28, 879–896 (1998)
10. Martin, J.C., Abrilian, S., Devillers, L.: Annotating Multimodal Behaviors Occurring during Non Basic Emotions. 1st Int. Conf. Affective Computing and Intelligent Interaction (ACII'2005), Beijing, China (October 2005)
11. Le Chenadec, G., Maffiolo, V., Chateau, N., Colletta, J.: Creation of a corpus of multimodal spontaneous expressions of emotions in Human-Machine Interaction. 5th Int. Conference on Language Resources and Evaluation (LREC'2006), Genova, Italy, (May 2006)
12. Bänziger, T., Pirker, H., Scherer, K., GEMEP.: – Geneva Multimodal Emotion Portrayals: A corpus for the study of multimodal emotional expressions. Workshop "Corpora for research on emotion and affect (LREC'2006), Genova, Italy (May 2006)
13. Reidsma, D., Heylen, D., Ordelman, R.: Annotating emotion in meetings. 5th Int. Conf. on Language Resources and Evaluation (LREC'2006), Genova, Italy (May 2006)
14. Campbell N.: A Language-Resources Approach to Emotion: Corpora for the analysis of Expressive Speech. Workshop Corpora for research on Emotion and Affect (LREC'2006), Genova, Italy (May 2006)
15. Poggi, I.: Mind Markers. 5th International Pragmatics Conference, Mexico (July 1996)
16. Forgas, J.: Affective influences on attitudes and judgements. In: Davidson, R., Scherr, K., Goldsmith, H. (eds.) Handbook of Affective Studies, Oxford University Press, Oxford (2003)
17. Krone, H.W.: Individual differences in emotional reactions and coping. In: Davidson, R.J., Scherer, K.R., Goldsmith, H.H (eds.) Handbook of Affective Sciences, pp. 698–725. Oxford University Press, New York (2003)
18. Knutson, B.: Facial expressions of emotion influence interpersonal trait inferences. In Journal of Nonverbal Behavior 20, 165–182 (1996)
19. Baron-Cohen, S., Riviere, A., Fukushima, M., French, D., Hadwin, J., Cross, P., Bryant, C., Sotillo, M.: Reading the Mind in the Face. A Cross-cultural and Developmental Study, Visual Cognition 3, 39–59 (1996)
20. Baron-Cohen, S., Wheelwright, S., Jolliffe, T.: Is There a Language of the Eyes? Evidence from Normal Adults, and Adults with Autism or Asperger Syndrome. In Visual Cognition 4(3), 311–331 (1997)
21. Hall, J.A., Coats, E.J., Smith LeBeau, L.: Nonverbal behavior and the vertical dimension of social relations: A meta-analysis
22. Cowie, R., Douglas-Cowie, E., Tsapatsoulis, N.: Emotion recognition in human-computer interaction. In IEEE Signal Processing Magazine 18(1), 32–80 (2001)
23. Argyle, M.: Bodily communication. Second edition. London and New York, Routledge. Taylor & Francis. 0-415-05114-2 (2004)
24. Thomas, F., Johnson, O.: Disney Animation.The illusion of life. Abbeville Press (1981)
25. Eysenck H. J. and Eysenck S. B. G.: Manuel de l'Inventaire de Personnalité d'Eysenck. Paris. Les éditions du Centre de Psychologie Appliquée (1971)
26. Craggs, R., Wood, M.M.: A categorical annotation scheme for emotion in the linguistic content. Presented at Affective Dialogue Systems (ADS'2004), Kloster Irsee, Germany (2004)

27. Scherer, K.R.: Emotion. In: Stroebe, M.H.W. (ed.) In Introduction to Social Psychology: A European perspective, pp. 151–191. Blackwell, Oxford (2000)

28. Aubergé, V., Audibert, N., Rilliard, A.: Auto-annotation: an alternative method to label expressive corpora. In: LREC 2006 Workshop on Emotional Corpora, Genova, Italy, pp. 45–46 (2006)

29. Valitutti, A., Strapparava, C., Stock, O.: Developing affective lexical resources. Psychology 2(1), 61–83 (2004)

30. Mathieu, Y.Y.: Annotations of Emotions and Feelings in Texts. In: Tao, J., Tan, T., Picard, R.W. (eds.) ACII 2005. LNCS, vol. 3784, Springer, Heidelberg (2005)

31. Barrett, L.F.: Solving the emotion paradox: categorization and the experience of emotion. In Personality and Social Psychology Review 10(1), 20–46 (2006)

32. Devillers, L., Abrilian, S., Martin, J.C.: Representing real life emotions in audiovisual data with non basic emotional patterns and context features. In: Tao, J., Tan, T., Picard, R.W. (eds.) ACII 2005. LNCS, vol. 3784, Springer, Heidelberg (2005)

33. Core, M.G., Allen, J.F.: Coding Dialogues with the DAMSL Annotation Scheme, presented at AAAI Fall Symposium on Communicative Action in Humans and Machines, Menlo Park, California (1997)

34. Kipp, M.: Gesture Generation by Imitation - From Human Behavior to Computer Character Animation. Boca Raton, Florida: Dissertation.com (2004)

35. Zara, A., Martin, J.C., Devillers, L., Maffiolo, V., Le Chenadec, G.: Gestural expressions of emotion in human interactions. International Society for Gesture Studies Conference, Evanston United States (accepted 2007)

36. Lindquist, K.A., Barrett, L.F., Bliss-Moreau, E., Russel, J.A.: Language and the perception of emotion. In Emotion 6(1), 125–138 (2006)

37. Innes-Ker, A., Niedenthal, P.M.: Emotion concepts and emotional states in social judgment and categorization. Journal of Personality and Social Psychology 83, 804–816 (2002)

38. Russel, J.A.: A circumplex model of affect. In Journal of Personality and Social Psychology 45, 1281–1288 (1980)

39. Plutchik, R.: The emotion. Boston: University Press of America (1991)

40. Galati, D., Innes-Ker, A., Niedenthal, P.M.: Emotion concepts and emotional states in social judgment and categorization. Journal of Personality and Social Psychology 83, 804–816 (2002)

41. Gebhard, P., ALMA,: - A Layered Model of Affect Fourth International Joint Conference on Autonomous Agents and Multiagent Systems (AAMAS'05), Utrecht (2005)

42. Wiggins, J.S.: The Five-Factor Model of Personality. Theoretical perspectives, The Guildford Press (1996)

43. Martin, J. C,: Multimodal Human-Computer Interfaces and Individual Differences. Habilitation à diriger des recherches en Informatique. Université Paris XI (2006)

Using Actor Portrayals to Systematically Study Multimodal Emotion Expression: The GEMEP Corpus

Tanja Bänziger and Klaus R. Scherer

University of Geneva, Department of Psychology,
and Swiss Center for Affective Science
40 bd du Pont-d'Arve, 1205 Genève, Switzerland
Tanja.Banziger@pse.unige.ch, Klaus.Scherer@pse.unige.ch

Abstract. Emotion research is intrinsically confronted with a serious difficulty to access pertinent data. For both practical and ethical reasons, genuine and intense emotions are problematic to induce in the laboratory; and sampling sufficient data to capture an adequate variety of emotional episodes requires extensive resources. For researchers interested in emotional expressivity and nonverbal communication of emotion, this situation is further complicated by the pervasiveness of expressive regulations. Given that emotional expressions are likely to be regulated in most situations of our daily lives, spontaneous emotional expressions are especially difficult to access. We argue in this paper that, in view of the needs of current research programs in this field, well-designed corpora of acted emotion portrayals can play a useful role. We present some of the arguments motivating the creation of a multimodal corpus of emotion portrayals (Geneva Multimodal Emotion Portrayal, GEMEP) and discuss its overall benefits and limitations for emotion research.

Keywords: emotion*, expression*, portrayal*, actor*, emotional sensitivity, nonverbal communication, multimodality.

1 Introduction

During the past decades, there has been a steady growth of interest for the study of nonverbal communication of emotions (or affects) in the engineering and computer sciences. Consequently a number of questions that were previously mostly addressed by psychologists or ethologists have expanded to those disciplines. In this paper, we are tackling one of the fundamental problems every researcher – psychologist, ethologist, engineer, or computer scientist – is facing, when his work involves taking into account or studying emotional expressions (or their perception). We will address and discuss issues related to the source and the sampling of emotional expressive data, with a specific focus on the benefits and limitations associated to the utilization of acted emotion portrayals. Unfortunately there are no comprehensive reviews of prior work at hand in this field. Most research on facial, vocal or gestural/postural emotional expressions has been carried out on unimodal data - using audio recordings, static pictures, or videos from a large variety of sources. The focus and scope of this article does not allow us to review the very large number of disparate data sets that

A. Paiva, R. Prada, and R.W. Picard (Eds.): ACII 2007, LNCS 4738, pp. 476–487, 2007.

were used by different research groups over the past years. Instead and along with other reviews [1] we propose to consider emotional expressive data as belonging to one of three categories:

(1) Natural (or naturalistic) emotional expressions – expressions occurring in real-life settings (such as for example TV shows, interviews, or any interactions between humans or between humans and machines) and which are not directly influenced or controlled by the researcher. (2) Induced emotional expressions – expressions occurring in a controlled setting (often in the laboratory) and following an experimental manipulation designed to elicit an emotional response (such as the presentation of emotionally loaded pictures, movies, or music; scripted interactions; imagination/recall techniques). (3) Emotion portrayals – expressions produced by (amateur or professional) actors upon instructions by the researcher (the instructions may or may not include elements of emotional induction techniques).

Two fundamental notions are underlying the definitions of the three categories: 'spontaneity' and experimental 'control'. The commonly accepted view is that there is a tradeoff between those two aspects. 'Natural expressions' are considered to be the most 'spontaneous' (closest to 'genuine' emotions) and the least experimentally 'controlled' category. Unfortunately, researchers must rely only on post-hoc verbal report or observer inferences to assess the presence or absence of given emotions in this category. In contrast, 'acted portrayals' are considered to be the least 'spontaneous' and the most experimentally 'controlled' category. In this perspective, 'induced expressions' are often presented as the ideal "middle way"; keeping sufficient 'spontaneity' while at the same time allowing for sufficient experimental 'control'.

In this paper, we are taking a focus on 'acted portrayals'. The following section will develop some of the issues related to the long-standing debate opposing 'natural' to 'portrayed' emotional expressions. In particular, we want to highlight how acted portrayals can be used in the context of some central research issues pertaining to the study of nonverbal communication of emotion.

2   Acted Emotion Expressions: Pros and Cons

In this section, we will first introduce some of the central unsolved research questions regarding nonverbal communication of emotion. This will allow outlining the specific requirements the data ought to fulfill in this research field. We will attempt to demonstrate that acted emotion portrayals – provided that they are well "designed" – constitute an adequate material to address those specific requirements. Finally, we will take up some of the criticism that is commonly opposed to the use of acted portrayals and discuss the alleged and actual limitations of this kind of data.

2.1   Why Use Emotion Portrayals? and When?

It is well known and generally accepted that, most frequently, humans do make inferences regarding each other's emotional reactions and that they will use nonverbal signals to regulate their interactions. Emotions are communicated via facial, vocal, postural and gestural cues and, probably, via any combinations of those expressive modalities (channels). What still remains unclear could be summarized in broad lines as follows: (a) How does this communication operate? - What are the specific cues (expressive features) that are used and how are they used. (b) Which properties of emotional reactions can be inferred based on nonverbal expressions only, and (c) through which expressive channels? - What kind of information regarding the emotional state of a sender can be derived based on the aforementioned cues and to what extent do different expressive modalities (channels) carry different information.

In the following, we will briefly consider those three aspects. The available space doesn't allow for exhaustive reviews of the respective research questions. Hence we will schematize some of the issues and on occasion merely introduce some illustrations in order to outline the associated requirements on data.

(a) To examine which cues are underlying emotional communication

Studies on emotional expression usually focus either on production or on perception of expressions. For the first class of studies – production studies – the main goal is to describe the expressive features or cues (e.g. Facial Action Units, acoustic profiles, types of gestures) associated to underlying emotional states. Their primary aim is to "diagnose" the emotional state of an individual (sender) based on his or her nonverbal behavior. For the second class of studies – perception studies – the goal is primarily to understand which expressive features are associated to emotional attributions (inferences) in individuals witnessing the emotional expressions (receivers). Finding out which expressive cues correspond to which underlying emotional states in senders on one hand, and finding out which expressive cues influence the attributions of emotions in receivers on the other hand, and ultimately comparing the two set of cues, can be considered the ultimate goal of nearly every research program set to study the complete process of emotional communication [1] [2] [3].

(b) To examine which aspects of emotional reactions can be reliably communicated through nonverbal expressions

In production studies, researchers are looking for distinctive patterns of expressive features corresponding either to different emotion categories (such as fear, anger, joy, etc.) or different values on emotional dimensions (e.g. more or less emotional intensity, more or less negative-positive valence). In perception studies, the first goal is often to assess if a given category or dimensional characteristic (emitted intentionally or not by a sender) can be reliably recognized or, at least, discriminated from other emotional categories or other values on selected emotional dimensions by receivers. In both cases, the underlying conceptualization of potentially communicated expressive states is crucial for the study and for its results. In most studies, rather few categories or dimensions are examined; sometimes as little as two, and in many cases not more than 4 to 5 categories will be considered and compared in a single study. Obviously, this does not reflect the emotional and expressive variability people are confronted with in their daily lives (even in carefully selected situations). In the following, we will take two examples to develop and illustrate this point.

Many studies of facial expressions have been carried out with the - theoretically grounded - assumption that there are seven "basic emotion" categories, which are characterized, among other things, by prototypical facial expressions [4]. Those studies have confirmed that the seven "basic" categories ('anger', 'fear', 'sadness', 'disgust', 'contempt', 'surprise', 'happiness') are reliably communicated by a limited set of facial features (e.g. "true smiles" for 'happiness'). Only few studies have attempted to test if other categories could be reliably identified based on different configurations of facial features [5]. This question is especially salient when it comes to positive emotions. Proponents of basic emotion models have claimed that different positive feelings (such as pride, pleasure, amusement) are not reliably differentiated on the level of associated facial displays. This constitutes in fact the primary argument in support of the claim that there is only one "basic" emotion with positive valence (happiness), other positive states being considered variants of the basic form. In order to challenge this kind of assumption, an important requirement on data is to include sufficient variability on the level of the emotional states encoded in the nonverbal expressions, especially with respect to positive states.

Studies of vocal expressions often compare acoustic features or recognition rates for an even smaller number of categories. Reviews show that the majority of the results have been obtained for the following four categories: 'anger', 'fear', 'happiness', and 'sadness' [6]. There are of course fluctuations in the definition of those categories from one study to the next, but overall 'anger', 'fear' and 'happiness' are 'highly aroused' emotions in those studies ('rage', 'panic' and 'elation' are the "variants" that are most frequently studied), whereas 'sadness' is a low aroused emotion (almost exclusively 'depressed' variants of 'sadness' are considered) [1]. In the past 20 years, reviews of production studies in this field have repeatedly pointed to the fact that, outside isolated findings reported in single studies, the result that was most consistently replicated could be linked back to the arousal level [1] [6]. Emotionally high-aroused voice/speech, is louder, faster, higher pitched (etc) than low-aroused voice/speech. For single studies, this indicates that when hot 'anger' is clearly discriminated from (depressed) 'sadness', but less clearly distinguishable from (panic) 'fear', the difference between 'anger' and 'sadness' might be merely a matter of underlying arousal (and not the consequence of another qualitative difference between the categories). Hence it would seem important, for the study of vocal communication of emotion, that the data includes several states with comparable arousal, in order to disentangle emotion categories and arousal [7].

More generally, the use of emotion categories that are too broad and unspecific is detrimental to the progress of research in this field. Basic emotion categories (anger, fear, sadness, etc.) are rather unspecific. It is not difficult to understand, even only intuitively, that they might be used to designate a huge variety of potentially different states, which might be communicated using quite different displays (e.g. think of a "typical" vocal expression of cold anger and a "typical" vocal expression of hot anger). Overall, an important requirement on data is therefore to dispose of a very clear conceptualization (precise definitions) of the emotional states, which are represented in an expressive data set.

(c) To examine multimodal communication of emotion

Although everyday experience shows that much of spontaneously occurring emotional expression is multimodal, most studies investigating nonverbal communication of emotion have been carried out on single expressive modalities (using either facial, or vocal, or - less frequently – gestural and postural expressions). In line with the partitioning of the research field on the empirical level, only few emotion theories are explicit on the mechanisms that produce integrated multimodal emotion expression. Nevertheless, there is enough evidence to allow us to assume that when they are "driven" by an underlying emotional response, expressive behaviors in different channels (voice, face, body) ought to synchronize in order to build up an integrated expressive behavior [8].

On the other hand, perception studies on single modalities have repeatedly shown that some emotion categories are better communicated than others in specific modalities. For instance, 'happiness' and 'disgust' have been recurrently reported to be communicated very efficiently in static prototypical facial expressions; whereas the same categories are often difficult to recognize in vocal emotion portrayals [1]. In reviews of this research area, this kind of results have been described as supporting the notion of channel-specific communication, which might be interpreted as challenging the view of convergence (integration or synchronization) across modalities.

In fact, little data is currently available regarding multimodal expressions and an essential requirement for further studies would be to include simultaneously audio and video data of sufficient quality (i.e. low level of noise and parasite sounds; good camera angle and sufficient picture resolution to see detailed facial movements; view of the full body).

2.2 Principal Benefits of (Well-Designed) Emotion Portrayals

In line with the requirements outlined in the previous section, acted emotion portrayals feature a number of characteristics that ought to be fulfilled for the study of nonverbal communication of emotion.

In contrast to "natural" expressions, emotions (or rather "emotional intentions") underlying acted portrayals can be defined precisely, and independently of any attributions relying (in part or in total) on the expressions themselves. With "natural" expressions - which by definition occur outside the influence and control of the researcher - the emotions experienced by a sender can only be inferred by the researcher, based on their own judgments and/or based on judgments they collects from others. With induced expressions and with acted portrayals both perception of emotion and production processes can be addressed.

Furthermore acted portrayals offer the possibility to record very variable expressions for the same individuals, while they allow simultaneously to compare the expressions across individuals. When working with "natural" expressions on the other hand, in most cases just a few emotional reactions will be recorded only for a given individual. And given the variability of naturally occurring situations and events, the comparability of emotional reactions across individuals will tend to be reduced. In the end, emotions identified by the same verbal labels may actually be very different across individuals and confounds of senders and emotional states will even further complicate the comparison. With induced expressions, elements of the contextual variations across senders are controlled, introducing the possibility to compare the expressions across individuals for the same inductions. On the other hand, the number of differentiated emotional states one can expect to induce reliably is fairly low [9].Out of practical and ethical reasons strong emotional reactions cannot be induced by researchers, which leads to a reduction in the variability of emotions expressed in situations of emotional induction.

An essential requirement in this respect is that the categories selected for the portrayals are well defined. For this purpose scenarios describing the emotional states to be portrayed should be constructed and systematically used to instruct the actors. The selection of categories to be portrayed should be grounded on the specific research questions to be addressed.

Acted portrayals also offer the possibility to record multimodal expressions with very high quality, including constant speech across senders and portrayed emotions. It is comparably more difficult to achieve good quality and standard content when recoding senders unobtrusively either in "natural" situations or in situations of emotional induction. Also, empirical evidence has shown that detailed microanalyses of acted emotion portrayals can be profitably used to test empirical predictions, including differential testing of competing theories, and yield important insights for future research [5] [7] [10].

2.3 Alleged and Real Limitations of Emotion Portrayals

There are several objections commonly raised against the use of emotion portrayals. The account we propose here describes the main concerns that have been voiced.

Portrayals reflect stereotypes, not genuine emotions

It is often claimed that emotional expressions produced by actors reflect cultural stereotypes. A more or less explicit assumption in this reproach is that portrayals are exaggerated as compared to spontaneous expressions. They convey the expressive intention of the actor but not in a "realistic" way. The receiver will recognize the intention but will not necessarily believe that the sender is genuinely emotional. In cases where actors attempt to display expressive signs without invoking emotional feelings, portrayals might indeed be produced in the absence of genuine emotions. An assumption in this view is that actors who do this might be unable to mimic (simulate or fake) the more subtle signs habitually related to the emotion. In this perspective, without being necessarily exaggerated, the portrayals would lack essential features of genuine expressions.

In response to this objection, it can be said that actors can and should be encouraged to produce believable expressions by using acting techniques that are thought to stir genuine emotions through action. When portraying emotions, actors should not exaggerate or fake expressions but rather attempt to reactivate emotional experiences while and through acting. Furthermore, issue of the 'believability' of the portrayals should be addressed in the form of judgement studies designed to select credible portrayals.

It is also often argued that acted portrayals are hypercontrolled and not sufficiently spontaneous. Of course, this depends on the way in which the portrayals are elicited. If facial expressions are constrained, their production is indeed highly controlled. However, if Stansilavski or Acting Method techniques are used, it is expected that expressions emerge more spontaneously from the emotional state the actors has tried to produce. In addition, it should be noted that everyday expressions are also highly controlled by display rules or strategic self-presentation (see [7]).

Portrayals represent infrequent emotions

Actors have been traditionally requested to portray "basic" emotions, identified by labels such as: 'anger', 'fear', 'sadness', 'happiness', or 'disgust'. Taking a closer look at the literature it becomes apparent that most studies in which acted material was used were set to study rather "extreme" emotional states, which might be better labelled: 'rage', 'panic', 'depression', 'elation', or 'repulsion'. This range of very intense emotions is considered by some authors to be unrepresentative of the range of emotions that are likely to occur on a daily basis in ordinary interactions. This further led to the conclusion that portrayals are not representative of the range of emotional states that are of interest in specific applied contexts and therefore unsuited for research in corresponding fields (such as human-machine interactions).

We suggest that acted portrayals should clearly not be restricted to "basic emotions", especially in their extreme forms. Actors can be requested to portray states that are of interest in specific research contexts (for example "frustration" in response to a malfunctioning device or computer application). Portrayals produced by appropriately instructed actors could reflect a variety of "realistic" states in different contexts.

Portrayals are decontextualized

Portrayals are produced under conditions designed to remove contextual information, in order to record variations that can be related exclusively to the emotions portrayed. Senders are recorded under identical conditions while they portray a range of emotional states. They are typically seated in front of a uniform background, facing a (video) camera. In instances were vocal or dynamic facial expressions are recorded, the actors are usually requested to first appear inexpressive, then to produce an emotional expression, and finally to get back to their inexpressive "baseline". If vocal expressions are of interest to the researchers, the senders will usually be requested to portray emotions while pronouncing the same sentence in all conditions. While most researchers have favoured this type of controlled recording design, it is certainly true that receivers presented with a relatively large number of such portrayals will not be inclined to perceive them as "natural".

It is true that in most cases, emotional reactions are tightly linked to a specific context of occurrence (a situation/event that triggers the reaction). Portrayals would probably appear more "natural" if they were not produced in the complete absence of eliciting events. In everyday life, it is quite rare that a calm, inexpressive person suddenly becomes very emotional, without any apparent reason, and within a few seconds recomposes herself, appearing perfectly calm and inexpressive again. Furthermore, it is undoubtedly beneficial to formulate precise operational definitions of the emotions to be portrayed. This should include at least a rough description of the situation/event in which the reaction takes place. Hence the minimal "context" defined for a given portrayal could be composed of a scenario describing the situation in which the emotion is elicited and – as it is probably more easy for an actor to direct the portrayal at a designated receiver – a brief interpersonal interaction taking place in this situation.

For the construction of any corpus featuring emotional expressions it is essential to clearly define the range of emotions included. Many objections raised against emotion portrayals would probably lapse if the portrayed states would be better selected and clearly defined. For instance, the notion that acted portrayals are lacking "naturalness" (are stereotyped or exaggerated) might be largely derived from the insistence on recording portrayals reflecting extreme emotions.

3 Illustration: The Geneva Multimodal Emotion Portrayal (GEMEP) Corpus

This section outlines how some of the considerations developed above were used to create the GEMEP corpus, partly following the model of an earlier actor portrayal study [5] [7] [10]. In describing the new corpus, special emphasis is placed on some of the aspects outlined earlier in this paper. In particular, the selection and definition of the states portrayed in the corpus is outlined in detail.

The GEMEP corpus consists of more than 7'000 audio-video emotion portrayals, representing 18 emotions, portrayed by 10 different actors with the help of a professional theatre director [11].

3.1 Selection of Emotions to Be Portrayed

The affective states selected for portrayal were partly chosen to represent the states that are frequently studied in the literature dealing with facial and/or vocal expressions of affect. Some less frequently examined states were also included in order to address specific research questions. For example, a relatively large number of positive states – such as 'pride', 'amusement', 'elation', 'interest', 'pleasure', or 'relief' – was included in order to challenge the traditional view according to which only one rather undifferentiated positive state ('happiness') can be reliably communicated via facial cues. In a similar attempt, some states corresponding to the same *family* of emotional reactions were included with various arousal levels (e.g. 'irritated' and 'enraged' *anger*; 'anxious' and 'panic' *fear*). This fulfils at least two aims: (1) Reviews of studies describing acoustic profiles of emotional expressions have repeatedly reported differences in acoustic features of vocal expressions mostly related to arousal level. Controlling for arousal level within emotion category should allow to partly disentangle the influence of arousal level and emotion family on vocal expressions. (2) The inclusion of more than one type of *anger* (or *fear*) should result in increased variability of the expressions portrayed and should allow to include a range of variations that are more likely to occur in daily interactions, under the assumption, for example, that 'irritation' occurs more frequently than 'rage' and 'anxiety' more frequently than 'panic fear'.

A further attempt to increase the variability of the expressions was undertaken by requesting the actors to produce some of the emotions with less or more intensity than what corresponds to the most 'usual' intensity for a given emotion. An underlying assumption (which remains to be tested) is that the portrayals produced with less intensity might be closer to expressions that could occur in daily interactions, while the portrayals with more intensity might be more exaggerated (or more "stereotypical"). To this "regulation" of the intensity of portrayed states, we added a further request to partially mask some of the expressions (i.e. to portray a relatively unsuccessful deception attempt for some of the affective states).

The labels describing the states selected for portrayal are presented in Table 1. The 12 categories presented in the 4 cells of this table were portrayed by all 10 actors. The 6 additional categories presented under the table were split into two groups and were portrayed by 5 actors each.

Table 1. Selection of states portrayed

		Valence	
		positive	negative
Arousal	high	elation amusement pride	hot anger (rage) panic fear despair
	low	pleasure relief interest	cold anger (irritation) anxiety (worry) sadness (depression)

Additional states: shame   surprise   admiration
                          disgust   contempt   tenderness

Modulations of intensity and attempts of masking ("regulations") were produced only for the states represented in the four cells of Table 1 (i.e. not for the additional states represented under this table). Each actor produced the 3 "regulations" for 6 of the categories represented in the table. Actor 01, actor 03, actress 06, actress 07 and actor 08 portrayed "regulations" for 'amusement', 'hot anger', 'despair', 'pleasure', 'interest' and 'anxiety'. Actress 02, actor 04, actor 05, actress 09 and actress 10 portrayed "regulations" for 'elation', 'pride', 'panic fear', 'relief', 'cold anger' and 'sadness'.

3.2   Definition of Emotions and of Their "Context"

Short definitions of the emotional states and "scenarios"[1] were provided to the actors several weeks before the recordings took place. Three "scenarios" were created in order to instantiate each affective state. A "scenario" includes the essential features of a situation, which is assumed to elicit a given emotional reaction. Whenever possible, the scenarios included explicit references to one or more interaction partner(s). The actors were requested to improvise interactions with the director, in which they expressed a given affective state while pronouncing two pseudo-linguistic sentences (1. "ne kal ibam sud molen!"; 2. "kun se mina lod belam?"). The actors were further requested to express each affective state while uttering a sustained vowel, which allowed recording brief emotional expressions in the absence of articulatory movements. For each affective state, the director and the actors were trying different "scenarios" and – after a period of "rehearsal" – recorded one or more interactions until they were satisfied with their performance. There were no further expectations or

---

[1] Definitions and scenarios are currently available in French and can be requested from the first author.

instructions regarding realisation of the expressions (e.g. no instruction to smile or to frown, to gesture, or to shout). The director's goal was to encourage the actors to steer "genuine" emotional expressions but with no predefined visual/acoustic profile.

3.3   Technical Aspects and Description of the Corpus

The ten actors who contributed to this corpus are professional, French-speaking actors. They portrayed 15 affective states under the direction of (and in interaction with) a professional stage director. Three digital cameras were used for simultaneously recording: (a) facial expressions and head orientations of the actors, (b) body postures and gestures from the perspective of an interlocutor, (c) body postures and gestures from the perspective of an observer standing to the right of the actors (see Fig. 1). Sound was recorded using a separate microphone at each of the three cameras, plus an additional microphone positioned over the left ear of the actor, providing a separate speech recording with a constant distance to the actor's mouth.

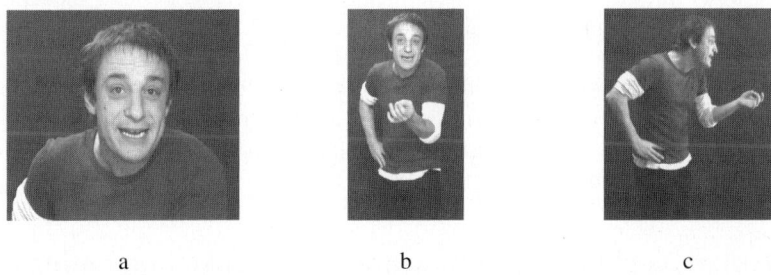

a   b   c

Fig. 1. Still frames illustrating the 3 camera angles used in the video recordings (actor 5)

Video and audio data was segmented on the level of single sentences. Recordings containing the two standard sentences (pseudo-speech) and the sustained vowel, as well as improvised sentences (in French) were extracted and saved in separate files. Over 7'300 such sequences, among them about 5'000 containing the pseudo-linguistic sentences and the sustained vowel, were extracted from the original interactions.

Expert ratings were carried out in order to select a reduced number of portrayals with standard speech content for subsequent analyses. Three research assistants (students in psychology) were requested to assess the technical quality of the recordings and the aptitude of the actors to convey the intended emotional impression, in both vocal and facial expressions. Although the three raters showed rather much disagreement in their judgments, this first assessment of the portrayals allowed to observe that some actors produce a higher proportion of "convincing" portrayals than other actors. Furthermore, there were also first indications that some emotions might be more easily conveyed in either facial or vocal displays.

Based on the assessments, a selection of portrayals, featuring an equal number of recordings for each actor and each portrayal category was established. Two portrayals for each condition and each actor (i.e. 126 portrayals per actor) were chosen in an iterative selection procedure by three research collaborators. Given the information provided by the expert ratings and their obvious limitations (low agreement, important rater biases, and limited number of raters) the selection had to be based on relatively complex decisions and could not be totally systematized.

In the next step of this project, rating studies involving lay participants will be carried out on this selection of recordings. Categorical and dimensional ratings will be obtained. The ratings will be obtained independently for (a) portrayals including facial and vocal cues (audio-video), (b) portrayals including only facial cues (video only), (c) portrayals including only vocal cues (audio only).

The data gathered in the rating studies will allow addressing a number of basic research questions in the domain of nonverbal communication of emotion. For instance, the possibility to differentiate a larger number of emotional categories than those which have been traditionally considered by psychologists interested in facial or in vocal expressions can be directly examined with the data we will obtain in the planned rating studies. The possibility for receivers to reliably differentiate positive emotional expressions (relief, pleasure, amusement, interest, tenderness, elation, pride, admiration), either in facial or in vocal expressions, is an especially interesting issue, as those positive categories have been especially neglected in past research efforts. Further questions to be addressed include issues related to multi-modal (facial plus vocal) versus uni-modal (facial only or vocal only) communication of emotion. The data will allow us to investigate the presence of modality specific communication for given emotion categories. Finally we will be able to compare the communication of emotion based on segments of "speech" (the two standard sentences) with communication based on a constrained "interjection" (the actors' attempts to communicate each emotion on a sustained vowel – aaa).

4 Potential Applications to Research in Affective Computing

Acted emotion portrayals allow recording a defined group of foreseen senders with good sound and picture quality, as well as maximal expressive variability. The otherwise uniform structure of acted portrayals makes them well suited for developing or testing automatic recognition systems or systems involving emotion synthesis. Automatic recognition based on auditive or on visual data ought to perform better with acted portrayals than with real-life data. In real-life situations, the range of expressions produced by a given sender will be scarcer and interfering variables more numerous. Hence acted portrayals could be used advantageously for the benchmarking and the comparison of various automatic recognition systems. The performance of automatic recognition systems trained and tested with acted portrayals should obviously also be compared with the performance of the same systems trained and tested in real-life settings.

The systematic analysis of expressive features used by actors could inform systems that attempt to (re)produce synthetic emotional expressions (e.g. Embodied Conversational Agents). Synthesis of emotional expression could in turn be used to test the influence of specific combinations of expressive features on emotional attributions. More importantly, multimodal actor portrayals could allow researchers to work on the integration of expressive modalities (voice, gestures, face) both with respect to emotion recognition and emotion synthesis. The accuracy of automatic recognition could for instance be compared for facial and vocal extractions. This would allow assessing the opportunity to analyse more than one expressive modality in order to improve the performance of automatic extraction.

Acknowledgments. This project is supported by the Swiss National Science Foundation, the Swiss Center for Affective Sciences and the European Network of Excellence HUMAINE.

References

1. Scherer, K.R.: Vocal communication of emotion: A review of research paradigms. Speech Communication 40, 227–256 (2003)
2. Juslin, P.N., Scherer, K.R.: Vocal expression of affect. In: Harrigan, J., Rosenthal, R., Scherer, K.R. (eds.) The new handbook of methods in nonverbal behavior research, pp. 65–135. Oxford University Press, Oxford, England (2005)
3. Brunswik, E.: Perception and the representative design of psychological experiments. University of California Press, Berkeley, CA (1956)
4. Ekman, P.: Emotions revealed. Times Books. New York (2003)
5. Scherer, K.R., Ellgring, H.: Are Facial Expressions of Emotion Produced by Categorical Affect Programs or Dynamically Driven by Appraisal? Emotion 7, 113–130 (2007)
6. Juslin, P.N., Laukka, P.: Communication of emotions in vocal expression and music performance: Different channels, same code? Psychological Bulletin 129, 770–814 (2003)
7. Banse, R., Scherer, K.R.: Acoustic profiles in vocal emotion expression. Journal of Personality and Social Psychology 70, 614–636 (1996)
8. Scherer, K.R., Ellgring, H.: Multimodal Expression of Emotion: Affect Programs or Componential Appraisal Patterns? Emotion 7, 158–171 (2007)
9. Westermann, R., Spies, K., Stahl, G., Hesse, F.W.: Relative effectiveness and validity of mood induction procedures: a meta-analysis. European Journal of Social Psychology 26, 557–580 (1998)
10. Wallbott, H.G.: Bodily expression of emotion. European Journal of Social Psychology 28, 879–896 (1998)
11. Bänziger, T., Pirker, H., Scherer, K.R., GEMEP,: - GEneva Multimodal Emotion Portrayals: A corpus for the study of multimodal emotional expressions. In: Proceedings of LREC'06 Workshop on Corpora for Research on Emotion and Affect, Genoa, Italy, pp. 15–19 (2006)

The HUMAINE Database: Addressing the Collection and Annotation of Naturalistic and Induced Emotional Data

Ellen Douglas-Cowie[1], Roddy Cowie[1], Ian Sneddon[1], Cate Cox[1], Orla Lowry[1],
Margaret McRorie[1], Jean-Claude Martin[2], Laurence Devillers[2], Sarkis Abrilian[2],
Anton Batliner[3], Noam Amir[4], and Kostas Karpouzis[5]

[1] Queen's University Belfast, Belfast, Northern Ireland, United Kingdom
e.douglas-cowie@qub.ac.uk
[2] LIMSI-CNRS, Spoken Language Processing Group, Orsay Cedex, France
[3] Lehrstuhl fur Mustererkennung, Universität Erlangen-Nurnberg, Germany
[4] Dept. of Communication Disorders, Tel Aviv University, Israel
[5] Institute of Communications & Computer Systems, National Technical University Athens

Abstract. The HUMAINE project is concerned with developing interfaces that
will register and respond to emotion, particularly pervasive emotion (forms of
feeling, expression and action that colour most of human life). The HUMAINE
Database provides naturalistic clips which record that kind of material, in multiple modalities, and labelling techniques that are suited to describing it.

1 Introduction

A key goal of the HUMAINE project was to provide the community with examples of
the diverse data types that are potentially relevant to affective computing, and the
kinds of labelling scheme that address the data. Data has been collected to show emotion in a range of contexts. The database proper is a selected subset of the data with
systematic labelling, mounted on the ANVIL platform [17]. It is designed to provide
a concrete illustration of key principles rather than to be used as it stands in machine
learning. Stage 1 (available via the HUMAINE portal at www.emotion-research.net)
contains 50 'clips' from naturalistic and induced data, showing a range of modalities
and emotions, and covering a balanced sample of emotional behaviour in a range of
contexts. Emotional content is described by a structured set of labels attached to the
clips both at a global level, and frame-by-frame, showing change over time. Labels
for a range of signs of emotion have also been developed and applied to a subset of
the clips: these include core signs in speech and language, and descriptors for gestures
and facial features that draw on standard descriptive schemes.

2 Background

Even in the early part of this decade, most databases of emotion were unimodal,
acted/posed, and focused on a few full blown emotions (e.g. [15], [16], [20], [29])

A. Paiva, R. Prada, and R.W. Picard (Eds.): ACII 2007, LNCS 4738, pp. 488–500, 2007.
© Springer-Verlag Berlin Heidelberg 2007

Labelling was at a very basic level. However, researchers were increasingly experimenting with data from a range of induced and more naturalistic settings (e.g. [1], [2], [3], [6], [10], [12]).The move was undoubtedly related to the recognition that systems trained on acted stereotypical data do not transfer to more everyday situations [5].

However, the early work on naturalistic data exposed a number of problems. 'Truly' natural data tended to be noisy, making machine analysis difficult, and there were problems with copyright. It also became apparent that labelling naturalistic data was far from straightforward, and that time needed to be spent on developing appropriate labelling schemes [9]. The call center datasets which had become popular held several attractions (genuine data, dialogue material and clear applications). But with these advantages came limitations. The frequency with which emotion is expressed was low, the nature of the interaction imposed constraints on the forms of utterances, raising major questions about generalisability, and the emotions tended to be from a narrow range, generally negative.

Work on a HUMAINE database began in response to that situation. Three priorities were identified as key to theoretical progress.

1. Range of content. The data should reflect the range of ways in which emotion in the broad sense ('pervasive emotion') enters into everyday life. That involves showing a wide emotional range (negative to positive, active to inert) across a range of contexts, involving action and interaction across a range of contexts. This involves, for instance, moving from emotion in monologue to emotion in sedentary interaction to emotion in action, again starting with data that is reasonably tractable and moving forward to more complex data.
2. Multimodality. The data should be fully multimodal; at least audiovisual, but also involving some physiological recordings and performance data. Again multimodality is approached in gradations, starting from audiovisual recording and adding other modalities where it makes sense.
3. Labelling. Labelling schemes based on the psychological literature should be developed to capture the emotional content. These should span a range of resolutions in time (whole passage to moment by moment). Sound schemes should also be developed to describe signs of emotion, particularly vocal and gestural.

These priorities are linked to each other and to wider issues. Multimodality provides incentives to achieve range (e.g to find situations where both prosody and choice of action are informative); the adequacy of a labelling scheme depends on its ability to cover diverse types of data; and so on. It is implicit in these goals that the data should be available to the community in general. This entails ethical clearance and full consent of the participants. It is also implicit that the data are likely to be 'provocative' rather than 'supportive' – putting technology in a better position to identify significant challenges rather than providing material that is ready for practical use. That has led to internal debate. Some argue that only databases relevant to specific applications are worth developing, others that considering only short term goals carries a high risk of falling into local minima. It is an issue that will only be resolved in the long term.

3 Resources

3.1 Basic Resources

The database is underpinned by a large collection of recordings, only some of which are labelled. In the long term as many of the recordings as possible will be made available. In the short term a selection of episodes from these recordings form the HUMAINE Database. The sections below describe the core characteristics of the material. For convenience the recorded material is split into two categories, 'naturalistic' and 'induced'.

Naturalistic data
Belfast Naturalistic Database [10]

Nature of material: The database consists of audiovisual sedentary interactions from TV chat shows and religious programs, and discussions between old acquaintances.

Technical info & availability: 125 subjects (2 sequences of 10-60 secs each, 1 neutral 1 emotional); selection of 30 sequences with ethical and copyright clearance available.

EmoTV Database (in French) [9]

Nature of material: The EmoTV Database consists of audiovisual interactions from TV interviews - both sedentary interactions and interviews 'on the street' (with wide range of body postures)

Technical info & availability: 48 subjects (51 sequences of 4-43 secs per subject in emotional state); copyright restrictions prevent release.

Castaway Reality Television Database

Nature of material: This consists of audiovisual recordings of a group of 10 taking part competitively in a range of testing activities (feeling snakes, lighting outdoor fires) on a remote island. The recordings include single and collective recordings and post-activity interviews and diary type extracts.

Technical info & availability: 10 tapes of 30 minutes each; copyright clearance

Emotional content: All of these were chosen to show a range of positive and negative emotions. Intensity is mostly moderate, though EmoTV and Castaway contain more intense material.

Induced data
Sensitive Artificial Listener: (http://emotion-research.net/deliverables/D5e_final.pdf)

Nature of material & induction technique: The SAL data consists of audiovisual recordings of human-computer conversations elicited through a 'Sensitive Artificial Listener' interface designed to let users work through a range of emotional states (like an emotional gym). The interface is built around four personalities – Poppy (who is happy), Obadiah (who is gloomy), Spike (who is angry) and Prudence (who is pragmatic). The user chooses which he/she wants to talk to. Each has a set of stock responses which match the particular personality. The idea is that Poppy/ Spike/ Obadiah/ Prudence draws the user into their own emotional state.

Emotional content: There is a wide range of emotions but they are not very intense.

Technical info & availability: Data has been collected for 4 users with around 20 minutes of speech each. SAL has also been translated into Hebrew (at Tel Aviv University) and Greek (at National Technical University of Athens, ICCS) and adjusted to suit cultural norms and expectations, and some initial data has been collected. The data has ethical permission and is available to the research community.

Activity Data/Spaghetti Data

Nature of material & induction technique: Audiovisual recordings of emotion in action were collected using two induction techniques developed in Belfast. In the first, volunteers were recorded engaging in outdoor activities (e.g mountain bike racing). The second used a more controlled environment where certain kinds of 'ground truth' could be established. It is called the Spaghetti method, because participants are asked to feel in boxes in which there were objects including spaghetti and buzzers that went off as they felt around. They recorded what they felt emotionally during the activity.

Emotional content: Method 1 elicited both positive and negative emotions with a high level of activation. Method 2 elicited a range of brief, relatively intense emotions - surprise, anticipation, curiosity, shock, fear, disgust.

Technical info & availability: Method 1 produced 'provocative' data which was very fast moving and had a noisy sound track. Method 2 produced data where the participants were reasonably static and stayed within fixed camera range, making it easier to deal with face detection. The audio output consists mainly of exclamations. There are now recordings of some 60 subjects. The data has ethical permission and is available to the research community.

Belfast Driving simulator Data [22]

Nature of material & induction technique: The driving simulator procedure consists of inducing subjects into a range of emotional states and then getting them to drive a variety 'routes' designed to expose possible effects of emotion. Induction involves novel techniques designed to induce emotions robust enough to last through driving sessions lasting tens of minutes. Standard techniques are used to establish a basic mood, which is reinforced by discussions of topics that the participants have preidentified as emotive for them. The primary data is a record of the actions taken in the course of a driving session, coupled with physiological measures (ECG, GSR, skin temperature, breathing). It is supplemented by periodic self ratings of emotional state.

Emotional content: 3 emotion-related conditions, neutral, angry, and elated

Technical info & availability: 30 participants; will be available pending completion of PhD on the data
EmoTABOO: developed by LIMSI-CNRS and France Télécom R&D:[30], [31], [21]

Nature of material & induction technique: EmoTABOO records multimodal interactions between two people during a game called Taboo..One person has to explain to the other using gestures and body movement a 'taboo' concept or word.

Emotional content: range of emotions including embarrassment, amusement

Technical info & availability: By arrangement with the LIMSI team.

Green Persuasive Dataset

Nature of material & induction technique: The dataset consists of audiovisual re-cordings of interactions where one person tries to persuade another on a topic with multiple emotional overtones (adopting a 'green' lifestyle).

Emotional content: Complex emotions linked to varied cognitive states and interper-sonal signals.

Technical info & availability: 8 interactions of about 30 mins each, and associated traces made by the interviewees to indicate how persuaded they felt from moment to moment. The data has ethical permission and is available to the research community.

DRIVAWORK (Driving under Varying Workload) corpus

Nature of material & induction technique The DRIVAWORK corpus has been col-lected at Erlangen, using a simulated driving task. There are three types of episode: participants are recorded relaxing, driving normally, or driving with an additional task (mental arithmetic). Recordings are video and physiological (ECG, GSR, skin tem-perature, breathing, EMG and BVP).

Emotional content: stress-related states rather than emotion per se.

Technical info & availability: Recordings are accompanied by self ratings and meas-ures of reaction time. There are 24 participants (a total of 15 hours). Availability by arrangement with Erlangen team.

3.2   Procedures for Selecting the Clips Used in the HUMAINE Database

Selection involves non-trivial issues. Two levels were used.

The first was the selection of sections from within a whole recording. A selected section is referred to as a 'clip'. The basic criterion used to set the boundaries of clips is that 'the emotional ratings based on the clip alone should be as good as ratings based on the maximum recording available' (i.e. editing should not exclude informa-tion that is relevant to identifying the state involved). In the case of relatively intense emotional episodes the extraction of a section/clip includes build up to and movement away from an emotional nucleus/explosion – lead in and coda are part of identifica-tion of the state.

The second stage of selection was deciding which clips should form the HUMAINE database proper. It is very easy to drift into using a single type of material which conceals how diverse emotion actually is. To counter that, the 50 clips were de-liberately selected to cover material showing emotion in action and interaction; in dif-ferent contexts (static, dynamic, indoor, outdoor, monologue and dialogue); spanning a broad emotional space (positive and negative, active and passive) and all the major major types of combination (consistent emotion, co-existent emotion, emotional tran-sition over time); with a range of intensities; showing cues from gesture, face, voice, movement, action, and words. and representing different genders and cultures.

4   Labelling

The labelling scheme emerged from sustained interaction with both theory and data. Early attempts (at QUB and LIMSI) dealt with the particular material for which they were developed, but failed to bring out issues that were salient in other sets, or to address theoretical issues that other HUMAINE partners considered important.

The resulting scheme provides ways of describing emotional content, the signs that convey it and relevant contextual factors, which can be applied to very diverse material, from induced to naturalistic emotion in action and interaction. It offers a range of labels, from relatively basic (and widely applicable) to more specialised (and probably application-specific). The emotion labels have been validated both theoretically and empirically (e.g. by measuring inter-labeller reliability). The labels for signs address multiple modalities – speech, language, gesture, face and physiological aspects (though some are only applied to a limited subset of clips). Information about many of the signs can be recovered automatically. Labels describing both signs and emotional content are designed to be time aligned rather than simply applied globally, since timing appears to be crucial in many areas.

The aim was to produce a system capable of dealing with most of the issues that an applied project might reasonably be expected to address. A scheme designed for a particular application will probably deal with a selected subset, but the HUMAINE scheme embodies a reasonable summary of the options that should be considered.

Specifications of database features are attached to the pilot database, which is available at http://emotion-research.net/deliverables/d5f-pilot-exemplar-database. What follows here picks out essentials and gives background information.

4.1   Development of Appropriate Emotion Descriptors and Labels

The emotion labelling scheme was developed mainly by QUB and LIMSI-CNRS. After much trial and error, two levels of description were included.

At the first level, global labels are applied to an emotion episode as a whole. Factors that do not vary rapidly (the person concerned, the context) are described here. It allows selection during the test process (e.g. identifying the emotion categories that are relevant). In the long term, it provides an index that can be used to identify clips that a particular user might want to consider. For instance, it will allow a user to find examples of the way anger is expressed in relatively formal interactions (which will not be the same as the way it is expressed on the football terraces).

Labelling at the second level is time-aligned. This is done using 'trace' type programs [8]. Unlike FEELtrace, from which they are derived, each of the current programs deals with a single aspect of emotion (e.g. its valence, its intensity, its genuineness). An observer traces his/her impression of that aspect continuously on a one dimensional scale while he or she watches the clip being rated. The data from these programs is imported into ANVIL as a series of continuous time-aligned traces.

The function of trace type labelling is to capture perceived flow of emotion. Focusing on that gives a rich picture in a reasonable time (roughly the duration of the clip times the number of traces). Different techniques are needed if it is critical to have fine timing or to know true rather than perceived emotion. They are usually much more time-consuming, and testing their validity raises difficult conceptual issues.

Emotion global descriptors

These cover eight main topics. Some simply summarise information associated with traces (e.g. range of intensities encountered, level of acting or masking encountered). Others are the outcome of long efforts to identify a minimal body of information that is needed to make sense of a clip that shows naturalistic material. That includes, for instance, understanding to what contexts the patterns observed might be generalized, and to which they should not. They are outlined here.

Emotion-related states: Full blown episodes of emotion make up very little of the emotion observed in naturalistic data. Descriptions of the types of state that do occur have been developed, taking Scherer's grid of design features [26] as a starting point. The categories included are Established (long term) emotion; Emergent emotion (full-blown); Emergent emotion (suppressed); Partial emotion; Mood; Stance towards person; Stance towards object/situation; Interpersonal bonds; Altered state of arousal; Altered state of control; Altered state of seriousness; Emotionless. Definitions are given in the guidelines for using the database on the HUMAINE portal.

Combination types: Again, 'pure' single emotions not the norm in naturalistic data [9], and so labels have been developed to describe the main types of combination that occur: unmixed, simultaneous combination (distinct emotions present at the same time), sequential combination (the person moves through a sequence of related emotions).

Context labels: Two broad types of context label are used. The first provides fairly factual data on the subject's personal characteristics; on technical aspects of recording; and on physical setting (degree of physical restriction, posture constriction, hand constriction and position of audience). The second deals with communicative context, including the purpose or goal of the communication (to persuade, to create rapport, to destroy rapport, or just pure expression of emotion); the social setting of the clip (for example, balanced interaction between two or more people, monologue directed to a passive listener); and social pressure (whether the person being rated is under pressure to be formal, as in a court, or to be freely expressive, as at a party).

Key Events: The labels in this set describe the key events with which the emotion is associated.. They identify both the focal key events that the person's feelings are about and other key types of event that contribute to the person feeling as they do. These include 'triggers' - events that prompt emotion about or towards another person/thing (e.g. OHP malfunction); 'causes' - long term influences on the person's state of mind (e.g crushing workload); and 'aspirations' – long term goal that shapes the way the person reacts (e.g retirement).

The global level also deals with two more standard types of descriptor.

Everyday emotion words: The sheer number of emotion words in everyday language [28] makes it a priority to find effective methods of selection. The HUMAINE Database selects at two levels. An outer set of 48 words is prespecified on the basis of studies [7], [4] that suggest they are important for labeling naturalistic material. From that set, individual raters then select those that are most relevant to the clip in question. That is a preliminary to tracing selected words to show the time-courses of the states that they describe.

Appraisal categories: Appraisal theory identifies emotional states with ways of evaluating significant events or people around. It provides an elegant framework, and pilot work tried to develop trace techniques based on it. Reliability was problematic for many of the categories [9]; not least because in naturalistic data, multiple aspects of the situation are likely to be appraised concurrently. However, appraisal-based descriptions are retained at global level, and those where reliability seems acceptable are also traced.

Emotion over time descriptors. Eight one-dimensional trace descriptors are used in the database. Many others have been explored, but were judged to be of less general interest or found not to give reliable ratings [9]. A key goal for analysis of the database is to establish whether the number can be reduced without losing information. The programs are as follows.

IntensTrace: This program deals with the intensity of the emotion raters believe the specified person is experiencing. Raters move a cursor on a scale that is displayed beside the clip as they watch it. Here and in the other programs, the layout of the scale is based on preliminary experiments. Definitions of the end points are displayed beside them ("zero emotion – totally emotionless" and "emotion at maximum intensity"). Intermediate descriptions are also displayed: 'distinctly unemotional', 'mild social emotion', and 'emotion in the full sense'. The markers are placed where average observers believe they naturally belong: the point of these is to minimize idiosyncratic departure from the average.

ActTrace: This deals with the extent to which the specified person is trying to give an impression of emotion that he/she does not actually feel. (i.e., there is an element of pretence or acting). The range is from "no attempt to simulate unfelt emotions" to "extreme attempt to simulate unfelt emotions".

MaskTrace: This is a converse of ActTrace: raters judge whether the specified person is trying to avoid showing emotions that they actually do feel. The idea that raters can judge how much emotion is being concealed can sound slightly paradoxical. In fact is is possible, because some signs of underlying emotion 'leak', and the effort of masking gives rise to its own signals (e.g. rigid posture).

ActivTrace: This deals with a quality that is sometimes called activation, sometimes arousal. It is basically how strongly the relevant person is inclined to take action, and it corresponds to a subjective sense of energy.

ValenceTrace: This asks tracers how positive or negative the specified person feels about the events or people at the focus of his or her emotional state.

PowerTrace: This asks tracers to rate how powerful the specified person feels, on a scale from 'absolutely no control over events' to 'completely in control of events'.

ExpectTrace: Tracers rate the extent to which the specified person has been taken unawares by the events at the focus of their emotional state. The range runs from "anticipated the events completely" to "taken completely unawares by the events".

WordTrace: In this case, raters choose an emotion word from the list of 48 (see above), and trace how the intensity of the chosen emotion varies through the clip. If the chosen word is 'fear', for instance, the end points of the scale are "absolutely no fear" and "pure uncontrolled fear" , and there are intermediate markers for "slight fear" and "strong fear".

The screen shot that follows conveys the net effect of putting traces together. The clip shows a participant feeling in a box, and suddenly triggering a buzzer. She gives a gasp, then a linguistic exclamation. The top trace, intensity, rises abruptly after the gasp. The rater does not judge that the response is acted, but there is a degree of masking at the beginning which breaks down abruptly at the unexpected event. Activation rises abruptly after a delay (during which the participant might be described as frozen).

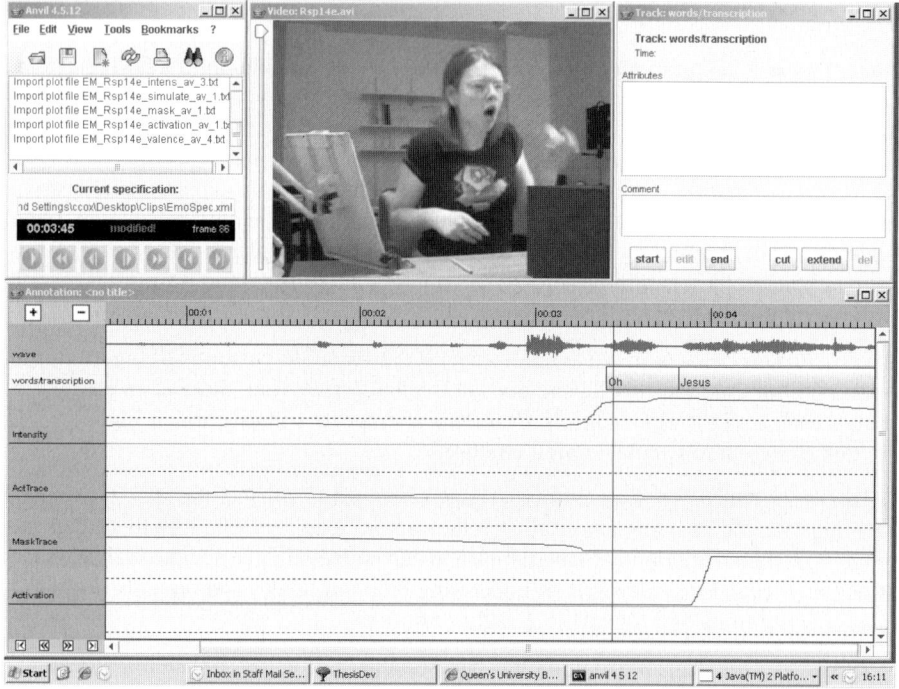

Fig. 1. Selected traces for a clip showing reactions to a sudden, surprising event

4.2 Labelling Signs of Emotion

Work on this part of the database has been highly interactive. The signal processing strand of HUMAINE has explored automatic extraction of parameters describing face and gesture, and identified the acoustic parameters that are most significant for recognition; and the teams building ECAs have helped to identify the parameters that needed to synthesise perceptually convincing gestures. In that sense, database research has a natural integrative function.

Speech and language descriptors: Three types of descriptor are used:

Transliteration. The core label here is the words spoken (see Figure 1). The data used in HUMAINE is largely interactive so both the words of the person observed and the words of any other interactants are transcribed. These are clearly differentiated. The words are time-aligned. Overlap is indicated. Future development will include the marking of pauses.

Largely automatically derived labels: The time waveform is displayed (see figure 1). It is first edited to suppress extraneous noises and the voices of other speakers (including sections of overlap). The edited .wav file is then used to derive a pitch contour for the person observed. This is derived using standard phonetic software, but hand edited to remove octave jumps and other errors (these are a substantial issue in emotional speech).

Work in the signal processing strand of HUMAINE will inform selection of a series of other automatically-derived labels, to be included in later versions of the database.

Auditory-based labels: These were developed by Douglas-Cowie on the basis of the Belfast Naturalistic Database [11] and then tested by another expert phonetician in further pilot work on a selection of clips from across the HUMAINE datasets. The original system contained many labels but for use in the HUMAINE database, these have been reduced to a core set of items which the tests indicate strongly characteristic of emotion and can be applied reliably. The labels address four descriptive categories and raters can assign a number of labels within these levels - Paralanguage (laughter, sobbing, break in voice, tremulous voice, gasp, sigh, exhalation, scream); Voice Quality (creak, whisper, breathy, tension, laxness); Timing (disruptive pausing, too long pauses, too frequent pauses, short pause + juncture, slow rate); Volume (raised volume, too soft, excessive stressing).

Gesture descriptors. The gesture coding scheme was developed at LIMSI-CNRS. It is a manual annotation scheme for coding expressive gestures in emotional corpora [21]. The following dimensions have been defined in the scheme:

- classical dimensions of gesture annotation ([23] [19] [18] [24]), to allow exploratory study of the impact of emotion on these dimensions:
- gesture units (e.g. to study how much gesture there is in an emotional corpus)
- phases (e.g. to study if the duration of these phases is emotion dependent)
- phrases / categories (e.g. to study the frequency of adaptators and compare it to other less emotionally rich corpora)
- lemmas adapted from a gesture lexicon [18] (e.g. Doubt=Shrug)

Face descriptors. Research in other parts of HUMAINE has developed procedures for extracting FAPs in a realistic timescale. They generate 17 FAPs which are suitable for automatic extraction, and which support reasonable levels of recognition. Fuller descriptions are given in [14]. The integration of this kind of data into Anvil has been carried out by the CNRS-LIMSI team using samples from EmTabou. Applying image processing techniques on video data like EmoTabou requires thorough comparison of manual annotation and image processing results. Some parts of the video cannot be processed because of factors like to hand-head occlusion or head movement and rotation, and even when there are no such obvious problems, mistakes can still arise.

Nevertheless, it is important that the database should acknowledge the role that automatic extraction can be expected to play in this area as techniques improve.

Physiological descriptors. Work on physiological descriptors is ongoing and will be expanded in later versions of the database. The physiological descriptors which will be incorporated in the database are those that apply to the physiological data from the driving experiments. Four basic channels are recorded: ECG (from which heart rate is derived); skin conductance; respiration; and skin temperature. There are many standard ways of deriving measures from these basic signals, involving differences, standard deviations, filtering, and various other operations. The approach in the database is generally to store the basic signals and leave users to derive other measures as and when they want to. Code that can be used to carry out standard transformations can be accessed via the portal from the Augsburg Biosignal Toolbox (AuBT), which was developed within the HUMAINE signal processing strand.

5 Conclusion

The HUMAINE Database workpackage set out to achieve a coherent set of responses to multiple challenges, involving both collection and annotation of diverse types of emotional material. This effort has included definition and testing of several coding schemes, and has influenced work in other areas of research (such as a W3C Incubator group on an Emotion Mark-Up language: Schröder et al., this conference).

It is a curious feature of the domain that the words commonly used to talk about it – affect, emotion, mood, anger, and so on – pull attention towards idealized landmarks and away from the everyday mixed cases between them. The obvious remedy is a collection of material that demonstrates by example what the everyday mixed cases look and sound like. The HUMAINE database makes a serious attempt to move in that direction. It is to be hoped that the effort will gather pace.

Acknowledgement. This research was supported by the EC FP6 Network of Excellence HUMAINE.

References

1. Abrilian, S., Devillers, L., Buisine, S., Martin, J.-C.: EmoTV1: Annotation of Real-life Emotions for the Specification of Multimodal Affective Interfaces. 11th Int. Conf. Human-Computer Interaction (HCII'2005), Las Vegas, USA. Electronic proceedings, LEA (2005)
2. Ang, J., Dhillon, R., Krupski, A., Shriberg, E., Stolcke, A.: Prosody-based automatic detection of annoyance and frustration in human–computer dialog. In: Proceedings ICSLP, Denver, Colorado (2002)
3. Batliner, A., Hacker, C., Steidl, S., Noth, E., Haas, J.: From emotion to interaction: Lessons learned from real human–machine dialogues. In: André, E., Dybkjær, L., Minker, W., Heisterkamp, P. (eds.) ADS 2004. LNCS (LNAI), vol. 3068, pp. 1–12. Springer, Heidelberg (2004)
4. Bänziger, T., Tran, V., Scherer, K.R.: The Geneva Emotion Wheel: A tool for the verbal report of emotional reactions. Bari, Italy (2005)

5. Batliner, A., Fischer, K., Huber, R., Spilker, J., Nöth, E.: How to find trouble in communication. Speech Communication 40, 117–143 (2003)
6. Campbell, N.: Recording and storing of speech data. In: Proceedings LREC (2002)
7. Cowie, R., Douglas-Cowie, E., Apolloni, B., Taylor, J., Romano, A., Fellenz, W.: What a neural net needs to know about emotion words. In: Mastorakis, N. (ed.) Computational Intelligence and Applications. World Scientific Engineering Society, pp. 109–114 (1999)
8. Cowie, R., Douglas-Cowie, E., Savvidou, S., McMahon, E., Sawey, M., Schröder, M.: 'Feeltrace': an instrument for recording perceived emotion in real time. In: Proceedings of the ISCA Workshop on Speech and Emotion, pp. 19–24 (2000)
9. Devillers, L., Cowie, R., Martin, J.-C., Douglas-Cowie, E., Abrilian, S., McRorie, M.: Real life emotions in French and English TV video clips: an integrated annotation protocol combining continuous and discrete approaches. 5th international conference on Language Resources and Evaluation (LREC 2006), Genoa, Italy (2006)
10. Douglas-Cowie, E., Campbell, N., Cowie, R.P.: Emotional speech: Towards a new generation of databases. Speech Communication 40(1–2), 33–60 (2003)
11. Douglas-Cowie, E., et al.: The description of naturally occurring emotional speech. In: Proceedings of 15th International Congress of Phonetic Sciences, Barcelona (2003)
12. France, D., Shiavi, R., Silverman, S., Silverman, M., Wilkes, D.: Acoustical properties of speech as indicators of depression and suicidal risk. IEEE Transactions on Biomedical Engineering 47(7) (2000)
13. Greasley, P., Sherrard, C., Waterman, M.: Emotion in language and speech: Methodological issues in naturalistic approaches. Language and Speech 43, 355–375 (2000)
14. Ioannou, S V., Raouzaiou, A T., Tzouvaras, V A., Mailis, T P., Karpouzis, K C., Kollias, S D: Emotion recognition through facial expression analysis based on a neurofuzzy network. Neural Networks 18, 423–435 (2005)
15. Juslin, P., Laukka, P.: Communication of emotions in vocal expression and music performance. Psychological Bulletin 129(5), 770–814 (2002)
16. Kienast, M., Sendlmeier, W.F.: Acoustical analysis of spectral and temporal changes in emotional speech. In: Cowie, R., Douglas, E., Schroeder, M. (eds.) Speech and emotion: Proc ISCA workshop. Newcastle, Co. Down, pp. 92–97 (September 2000)
17. Kipp, M,: Anvil - A Generic Annotation Tool for Multimodal Dialogue. 7th European Conference on Speech Communication and Technology (Eurospeech'2001), Aalborg, Danemark (2001), http://www.dfki.uni-sb.de/~kipp/research/index.html
18. Kipp, M.: Gesture Generation by Imitation. From Human Behavior to Computer Character Animation. Florida, Boca Raton (2004), http://www.dfki.de/~kipp/dissertation.html
19. Kita, S., van Gijn, I., van der Hulst, H.: Movement phases in signs and co-speech gestures, and their transcription by human coders. In: Wachsmuth, I., Fröhlich, M. (eds.) Gesture and Sign Language in Human-Computer Interaction. LNCS (LNAI), vol. 1371, Springer, Heidelberg (1998)
20. Leinonen, L., Hiltunen, T.: Expression of emotional-motivational connotations with a one-word utterance. Journ Acoustical Society of America 102(3), 1853–1863 (1997)
21. Martin, J.-C., Abrilian, S., Devillers, L.: Annotating Multimodal Behaviors Occurring during Non Basic Emotions. In: Tao, J., Tan, T., Picard, R.W. (eds.) ACII 2005. LNCS, vol. 3784, Springer, Heidelberg (2005), http://www.affectivecomputing.org/2005
22. McMahon, E., Cowie, R., Kasderidis, S., Taylor, J., Kollias, S.: What chance that a DC could recognise hazardous mental states from sensor outputs? In: Proc, DC Tales conference, Sanotrini (June 2003)
23. McNeill, D.: Hand and mind - what gestures reveal about thoughts. University of Chicago Press, IL (1992)

24. McNeill, D.: Gesture and Thought. The University of Chicago Press, Chicago (2005)
25. Sander, D., Grandjean, D., Scherer, K.: A systems approach to appraisal mechanisms in emotion. Neural Networks 18, 317–352 (2005)
26. Scherer, K R, et al.: Preliminary plans for exemplars: Theory HUMAINE deliverable D3c (2004), http://emotion-research.net/deliverables/D3c.pdf
27. Schröder, M., Devillers, L., Karpouzis, K., Martin, J.-C., Pelachaud, C., Peter, C., Pirker, H., Schuller, B., Tao, J., Wilson, I.: What should a generic emotion markup language be able to represent? In: Paiva, A., Prada, R., Picard, R.W (eds.) ACII 2007. LNCS, vol. 4738, pp. 440–451. Springer, Heidelberg (2007)
28. Whissell, C.: The dictionary of affect in language. In: Plutchnik, R. (ed.) Emotion: Theory and research, pp. 113–131. Harcourt Brace, New York (1989)
29. Yacoub, S., Simske, S., Lin, X., Burns, J.: Recognition of emotions in interactive voice response systems Proceedings of the Eurospeech, Geneva (2003)
30. Zara, A., Maffiolo, V., Martin, J.C., Devillers, L.: (submitted). Collection and Annotation of a Corpus of Human-Human Multimodal Interactions: Emotion and Others Anthropomorphic Characteristics. ACII (2007)
31. Zara, A.: Modélisation des Interactions Multimodales Emotionnelles entre Utilisateurs et Agents Animés.Rapport de stage de Master. Ecole Doctorale Paris XI. LIMSI-CNRS (8 September, 2006)

User-Centered Control of Audio and Visual Expressive Feedback by Full-Body Movements

Ginevra Castellano[1], Roberto Bresin[2], Antonio Camurri[1], and Gualtiero Volpe[1]

[1] InfoMus Lab, DIST - University of Genova
Viale Causa 13, I-16145, Genova, Italy
{Ginevra.Castellano,Antonio.Camurri,Gualtiero.Volpe}@unige.it
[2] KTH, CSC School of Computer Science and Communication,
Dept. of Speech Music and Hearing, Stockholm
roberto@kth.se

Abstract. In this paper we describe a system allowing users to express themselves through their full-body movement and gesture and to control in real-time the generation of an audio-visual feedback. The systems analyses in real-time the user's full-body movement and gesture, extracts expressive motion features and maps the values of the expressive motion features onto real-time control of acoustic parameters for rendering a music performance. At the same time, a visual feedback generated in real-time is projected on a screen in front of the users with their coloured silhouette, depending on the emotion their movement communicates. Human movement analysis and visual feedback generation were done with the EyesWeb software platform and the music performance rendering with pDM. Evaluation tests were done with human participants to test the usability of the interface and the effectiveness of the design.

Keywords: Affective interaction, expressive gesture, multimodal environments, interactive music systems.

1 Introduction

In human-computer interaction there is an increasing attention on the identification of new paradigms of expressive human-machine interaction, and on the design of interfaces combining information from several channels in a multimodal way. New results in these fields would lead to fully use the power and impact of human non-verbal expressive communication in experience-centric tasks and collaborative applications. Endowing computers with the ability of analysing, interpreting, and reacting to users' expressive gestures and behaviour is still an open issue ([1],[2],[3]).

Several studies in psychology of emotion show that the body is an important channel to communicate affect and that people naturally express emotions through the use of their motor skills (see for example [4],[5],[6],[7],[8],[9]). The focus of our research is on the non-verbal aspects of the communication process between humans and computers and in particular on forms of expressing emotions based on the use of human movements and gestures [10].

A. Paiva, R. Prada, and R.W. Picard (Eds.): ACII 2007, LNCS 4738, pp. 501–510, 2007.

In this paper we focus on the role of expressive intentions in the field of interactive music systems, i.e. systems able to process expressive gesture for the generation and control of matching musical signals ([11],[12]). The work presented here could also seen as an artistic application, since it also involves real-time generation of graphics and music performance driven by computer vision techniques [13]. However, the main focus of the paper is on how the user interacts with the environment with her body when multimodal feedback is provided, taking into account theories of embodied music cognition [14]. In this context, we want to develop interaction strategies which involve full-body movements and gestures at different levels of abstraction in an environment that can evolve and dialogue with the user. This leads to Multimodal Environments (MEs) which allow for creative, multimodal user interaction, by exhibiting real-time adaptive behaviour. We refer in particular to immersive environments enabling communication by means of full body movement, such as dance and expressive gestures, singing, and music playing. Users get a feedback from the environment in real-time in terms of sound, music, visual media, and changes in the environment.

The work presented in this paper is a contribution to the investigation of MEs with a special focus on expressive and emotional communication. We propose a system in which users can express themselves through their full-body movements and gestures which are used for controlling the real-time generation of an audio-visual feedback. The system analyses in real-time the user's full-body movements and gestures, extracts expressive motion features and classifies movement according to five different emotions (sadness, serenity, happiness, fear and anger). The values of the expressive motion features are mapped onto real-time control of acoustic parameters for rendering the expressivity in a musical performance. At the same time, the output of the classification drives the real-time generation of a visual feedback: users can see their silhouette projected on a screen in front of them, with different colours depending on the emotion communicated by their movements. This leads to the generation of an affective interaction, where users are immersed in an affective loop with the system [15].

Evaluation tests with subjects were done to evaluate the effectiveness of the designed interaction. During the evaluation phase, we addressed the following questions: (1) Is the designed audio-visual feedback suitable to reproduce the expressivity of the movement performed by subjects in the space? (2) Do the subjects understand the interaction? (3) Do subject feel in control of the musical and visual feedback? Do they become 'performers'? (4) Are there differences, at the perceptive level, between the visual and audio feedback?

This paper is divided into two main parts. The first part focuses on the design of the application. The second part deals with the usability evaluation with human participants, trying to give some answers to the above questions.

2 Overview of the System

The system presented in this paper is based on the integration of two different systems: EyesWeb [16], developed at DIST InfoMus Lab, and pDM (see [17],[18]), developed at KTH. EyesWeb is an open software platform for multimodal analysis and the development of interactive systems and MEs. pDM is a program for the real-time rendering of expressive music performance, allowing for different emotional characterizations by manipulating acoustic parameters such as sound level, tempo, and articulation.

The system integrating EyesWeb and pDM acquires input from a video camera, processes information related to the expressivity of human full-body movements, extracts expressive indicators, classifies movements in terms of emotions (sadness, serenity, happiness, fear and anger) and controls the expressive rendering of music performance and the visual feedback generation (see Figure 1).

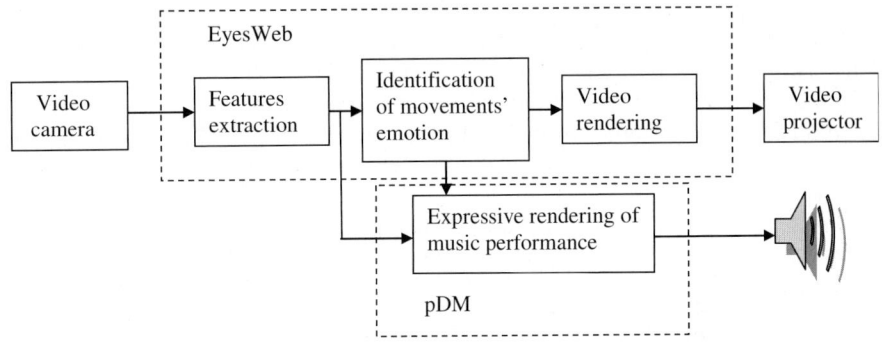

Fig. 1. Overview of the system

Human movement is being analysed with the EyesWeb platform and expressive motion features are being automatically extracted with the support of the EyesWeb Expressive Gesture Processing Library [19].Visual feedback generation was done with EyesWeb, and the music performance rendering with pDM.

3   Analysis of Human Full-Body Movement

Movement and gesture expressivity is a key element both in understanding and responding to users' behaviour. Several studies showed that the body is an important channel to communicate expressivity and people naturally express emotions through the use of their motor skills ([4],[5],[6],[7],[8],[9],[20]).

We focused on two expressive motion features: the Quantity of Motion (QoM) and the Contraction Index (CI). Both cues are global indicators of human movements from energy (QoM) and space (CI) perspectives.

QoM is an approximation of the amount of detected movement, based on Silhouette Motion Images (SMIs). A SMI is an image carrying information about variations of the silhouette shape and position in the last few frames.

$$SMI[t] = \left\{ \sum_{i=0}^{n} Silhouette[t-i] \right\} - Silhouette[t].$$

The SMI at frame t is generated by adding together the silhouettes extracted in the previous n frames and then subtracting the silhouette at frame t. The resulting image contains just the variations happened in the previous frames. QoM is computed as the area (i.e., number of pixels) of a SMI divided by the area of the current silhouette, i.e. normalized in order to obtain a value usually ranging from 0 to 1. It can be considered as an overall measure of the amount of detected motion, involving velocity and force.

$$QoM = \frac{Area(SMI[t,n])}{Area(Silhouette[t])}.$$

CI is a measure, ranging from 0 to 1, of how the user's body expands or contracts in the surrounding space. It can be calculated using a technique related to the bounding region, i.e., the minimum rectangle surrounding the user's body: the algorithm compares the area covered by this rectangle with the area currently covered by the silhouette. These two features are extracted and processed in order to control music and visual outputs. We are exploring relations between the emotions and other movement characteristics such as fluidity, impulsiveness, direction changes, amount of upward movements, symmetry and repetitivity.

4   Visual Feedback Generation Based on Emotional Communication

Visual feedback was designed to respond to the user's expressive motor behaviour. The user moves in a large space in front of the camera. The system identifies user's gestures and projects her silhouette on a wall in front of her by using different colours, which depend on the identified movement's expressivity. We focused on five emotions, each of them related to one specific combination of QoM and CI values: sadness, serenity, happiness, fear and anger.

According to theories from psychology on emotion in movements ([4],[5],[6],[7],[8],[9]) and from previous studies on expressivity ([10],[20],[21],[22]), we defined the following correspondence between emotion and movement characteristics (Table 1):

Table 1. Relations between emotion and movement characteristics

Emotion	Movement characteristics
Sadness	Slow (low QoM), contracted (high CI)
Serenity	Slow (low QoM), expanded (low CI)
Happiness	Fast (high QoM), expanded (low CI)
Anger	Very fast (very high QoM), expanded (low CI)
Fear	Fast (high QoM), contracted (high CI)

Applying results from previous studies on the association of colours to expressive music performance [23], we associated specific colours to the emotions communicated by the user's movement: violet to sadness, pink to serenity, yellow to happiness, red to anger, and blue to fear.

Figure 2 shows examples of the visual feedback as it was presented to the user.

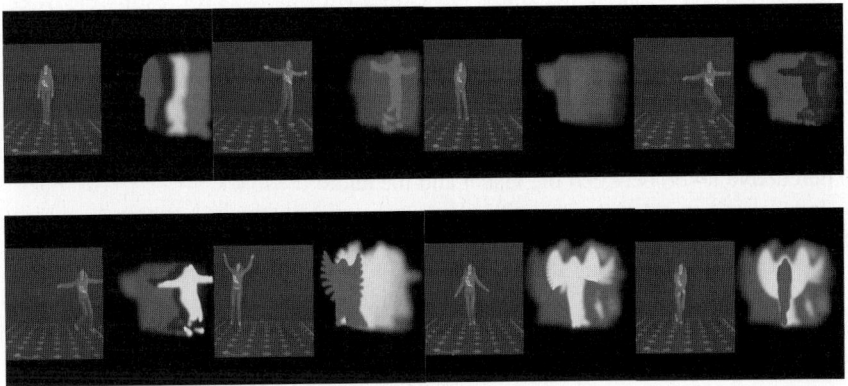

Fig. 2. The coloured silhouettes are examples of visual feedback as presented to the user. The current instant of time corresponds to the silhouette. Previous movements with different expressivity are still visible as traces left by the silhouette. The current input frame is shown on the left-hand side of each silhouette.

5   Acoustic Feedback Generation

Acoustic feedback was designed using pDM. It is a consolidated knowledge that sound level, tempo, and articulation accounts for more than 90% of the emotional expression in music performance (for an overview see [24]).

The values of QoM and CI provided by EyesWeb are used for controlling the real-time expressive performance of a musical score. The user can freely choose which score to control with her body gestures. QoM and CI are mapped onto tempo and sound level respectively. In this way the user's performance gets faster for faster movements (i.e. higher QoM values) and louder when the user is expanding her body (i.e. lower CI). Articulation is controlled by mapping the emotion detected in the user's movements to the articulation parameters in pDM. More *legato* articulation for emotions with lower activity (low QoM and contracted movements) and more *staccato* articulation for those characterized by higher energy (high QoM and expanded movements). Furthermore, articulation related to angry body movements was played less *staccato* than in happy movements.

More in detail, the overall expressivity in pDM was set to a set-up corresponding to a musically neutral performance (i.e. with values of phrasing, articulation, tempo and sound level corresponding to those typical of a neutral performance). It is the user with her QoM and CI who directly controls tempo and sound level. These two acoustic parameters have been demonstrated to be the most important, together with articulation, for the communication of emotion in expressive music performance [25].

Therefore the emotion in the resulting performance is a direct mapping of user's full body emotional behaviour in the space in front of the camera.

6 Usability Evaluation Tests with Subjects

An evaluation test was conducted in a lab setting with subjects for testing the usability of the interface and the effectiveness of the design. The questions which we addressed in this phase were the following: (1) Is the designed audio-visual feedback suitable to reproduce the expressivity of the movement performed by subjects in the space? (2) Do the subjects understand the interaction? (3) Do subject feel in control of the sound/colour generation? Do they become 'performers'? (4) Are there differences, at the perceptive level, between the visual and the audio feedback?

6.1 Subjects

A group of fourteen people (six male and eight female, from 20 to 51 years old, average age: 26.78), participated to the experiment. Each of them tried the system for the first time during the experiment.

6.2 Set Up

The experiment was realized in a square room with diffuse lights, in order to allow the system to track the participants' body. A computer running EyesWeb and pDM was connected through an Edirol FA-101 sound card to wireless headphones, which were worn by the subjects. A video camera Panasonic WVCP450/G, located in front of the users, was used for capturing the full-body movement of the participants and for providing EyesWeb with the visual input. 25fps non interlaced were used. A video-projector projected the visual feedback on the wall in front of the subjects. A second video camera Sony MiniDV "DCR PC1000E" / 3CMOS was used for recording possible comments of the participants as well as their movements from a frontal-lateral view.

6.3 Procedure

Subjects were asked to move in the space at disposal (a square with dimensions 2.80m X 3.60m, 1.75m far from the frontal video camera) and they were informed that they would be able to change audio and visual feedback by moving. They could hear the audio feedback with headphones and see the visual feedback on a wall in front of them. Subjects had the possibility to choose between two pieces of music to be rendered through their movements: 'We are the champions' by Queen and the Trio Sonata n. 3 by Johann Sebastian Bach. Six of them chose the Trio Sonata by Bach and eight the Queen's song. Subjects did not listen to the chosen piece before starting the experiment.

Participants were asked to move and to try obtaining a visual and audio feedback which they liked. That choice was done in order to induce them to be active and to allow them to achieve a full experience of the application. They were told that they were free to test the application as long as they wanted and they might signal the end of their trial by leaving the space in front of the video camera.

6.4 Methods for Evaluation

A triangulation between methods was used to evaluate the application; notes of the experimenter, video recordings, and interviews to the subjects were compared.

During the test, participants' behaviour was annotated by the experiments. Such notes were used after the test to compare results from the off-line analysis of the video recordings. Participants were interviewed at the end of the experiment. They had to answer the following questions:

1. Overall, what did you think about the system? What did you do? How?
2. Did the audio change by your movement? How?
3. Did the visual effects change by your movement? How?
4. Did you feel in control of the music interpretation?
5. Did you feel in control of the colours generation?
6. Do you think expressivity of your movement played an important role in the generation of the audio and visual feedback?
7. Did you feel immersed in the environment?

6.5 Results

From the qualitative analysis of the recordings and the notes, we can highlight some general observations.

1. People need a certain amount of time to become familiar with the application: the average time they needed was near to the four minutes.
2. Only the most active people obtained a full experience of the application.
3. Only one person talked during the test: sentences like "I want to become yellow!" and "Oh, perfect, done!" demonstrate the attempt to interact with the system to achieve some specific goal.
4. The most part of people (71.4%) continued looking at the wall with the visual effects; people that focused on the audio, did not make use of the arms while interacting with the interface.

We report in the following results from the analysis of the answers given by the subjects during the interviews.

1. Overall, what did you think about the system? What did you do? How?
Participants' main goal was to understand how the system worked. One person (student in philosophy) observed that the application was interesting from the artistic perception point of view and it was a good example of non-passive art: 'the presence of rules in the application makes the subject open to the world'.

2. Did the audio change by your movement? How?
Eleven people (78.6%) thought their movement changed the audio. Between them, one person understood the whole mapping, four understood the relationship between

quantity of motion/velocity and tempo in music, six didn't understand how the mapping worked.

3. Did the visual effects change by your movement? How?
Twelve people (85.7%) thought their movement changed the visual effects. Between them, one person understood the whole mapping (the same who understood the movement-audio mapping), six understood the relationship between quantity of motion/velocity and colours generation and five didn't understand how the mapping worked. Only one person thought the movement didn't change both audio and video.

4. Did you feel in control of the music interpretation?
The 7% of the participants felt in control of the music interpretation, the 36% felt in control in an acceptable way, the 57% didn't feel in control.

5. Did you feel in control of the colours generation?
The 28.6% of the participants felt in control of the colours generation, the 42.8% felt in control in an acceptable way, the 28.6% didn't feel in control.

6. Do you think expressivity of your movement played an important role in the generation of the audio and visual feedback?
The 35.7% of the participants answered *Yes*, the 35.7% answered *Enough*, the 28.6% answered *No*.

7. Did you feel immersed in the environment?
The 71.4% of the participants answered *Yes*, the 14.3% answered *Enough*, the 14.3% answered *No*.

7   Discussion

From the analysis of users' behaviour and their direct feedback we conclude that our system provided strong sensations of participation, interaction and immersion.

Most part of users perceived the changes in audio and colours generated by their movement and many of them understood the mappings we designed, with a prevalence for the understanding of the role played by the quantity of motion in colours generation and music performance rendering rather then by the contraction index. Nobody found out relationships between quantity of motion and articulation of the music performance. Further, most part of the users felt in control of the colours generation, while the control of the music rendering is less perceived. From the perceptive point of view, the tests highlighted the major role played by the visual channel. Users seem to understand better the effects which their movements have on the colour generation. The analysis of their answers highlights that they feel more in control of the visual feedback generation than of the audio feedback. This can be due to the fact that maybe some of the users were not used to listen to or did not know the music used during the experiment. Future tests will be designed in such a way that the participants get to know the music before starting the experiment, so that they can fully experience the system.

As it emerged from the interviews, users seem to understand the role that the expressivity plays in the interaction. Off-line analysis of the recorded videos demonstrates that the system provides users with a new way of expression, allowing them to communicate and interact with a computer in real-time and to obtain an appropriate feedback.

8 Conclusion

In this paper we presented a system allowing users to use their own body as an expressive interface, allowing the control of music expressivity with the body. Body expressivity is also used as channel for the communication of emotional, affective content: visual media generation and control become part of an affective analysis and synthesis loop involving the user in a perception-action process.

At the following link, ftp://infomus.dist.unige.it/Pub/ACII2007/, it is possible to see a concrete example of how the users can interact with the system.

Currently, our system is used for entertainment task and has been tested in a national exhibition. More generally, the results from this experiment confirm the general acceptance and engagement of users for experiences of participative listening [10] and visual affective interaction. This seems a promising perspective for future scenarios where the communication human-computer is based on non-verbal emotional channels. In order to further develop and validate the proposed system, in future experiments we will test it by giving mismatching feedback to the user for example by providing mismatching visual and/or audio feedback to the emotion of the user's body motion.

Acknowledgements. The research work has been realised in the framework of the EU-IST Project HUMAINE (Human-Machine Interaction Network on Emotion), a Network of Excellence (NoE) in the EU 6th Framework Programme (2004-2007) and the COST287 Action ConGAS (Gesture CONtrolled Audio Systems).

References

1. Picard, R.: Affective Computing. MIT Press, Boston, MA (1997)
2. Hashimoto, S., KANSEI,: KANSEI as the Third Target of Information Processing and Related Topics in Japan. In: Proc. International Workshop on KANSEI: The technology of emotion, Genova, pp. 101–104 (1997)
3. Cowie, R., Douglas-Cowie, E., Tsapatsoulis, N., Votsis, N., Kollias, N., Fellenz, W., Taylor, J.: Emotion Recognition in Human-Computer Interaction. IEEE Signal Processing Magazine 18(1), 32–80 (2001)
4. Scherer, K.R., Wallbott, H.G.: Analysis of Nonverbal Behavior. HANDBOOK OF DISCOURSE: ANALYSIS, vol. 2(11). Academic Press, London (1985)
5. Wallbott, H.G., Scherer, K.R.: Cues and Channels in Emotion Recognition. Journal of Personality and Social Psychology 51(4), 690–699 (1986)
6. DeMeijer, M.: The contribution of general features of body movement to the attribution of emotions. Journal of Nonverbal Behavior 13, 247–268 (1989)
7. Wallbott, H.G.: Bodily expression of emotion. European Journal of Social Psychology, Eur. J. Soc. Psychol. 28, 879–896 (1998)

8. Boone, R.T., Cunningham, J.G.: Children's decoding of emotion in expressive body movement: the development of cue attunement. Developmental Psychology 34, 1007–1016 (1998)
9. Pollick, F.E.: The Features People Use to Recognize Human Movement Style. In: Camurri, A., Volpe, G. (eds.) GW 2003. LNCS (LNAI), vol. 2915, pp. 20–39. Springer, Heidelberg (2004)
10. Camurri, A., De Poli, G., Leman, M., Volpe, G.: Toward Communicating Expressiveness and Affect in Multimodal Interactive Systems for Performing Art and Cultural Applications. IEEE Multimedia Magazine 12(1), 43–53 (2005)
11. Camurri, A.: Interactive Dance/Music Systems, Proc. Intl. Computer Music Conference ICMC-95. In: The Banff Centre for the arts, Canada, (September, 3-7), pp. 245–252. ICMA-Intl.Comp.Mus.Association (1995)
12. Camurri, A., Trocca, R.: Movement and gesture in intelligent interactive music systems. In: Battier, M., Wanderley, M. (eds.) Trends in Gestural Control of Music, Ircam Publ (2000)
13. Krueger, M.: Artificial Reality II. Addison-Wesley Professional, London, UK (1991)
14. Leman, M.: Embodied Music Cognition and Mediation Technology. MIT-Press, Cambridge, MA
15. Höök, K.: User-Centred Design and Evaluation of Affective Interfaces. In: From Brows to Trust: Evaluating Embodied Conversational Agents, Edited by Zsofia Ruttkay and Catherine Pelachaud, Published in Kluwer's Human-Computer Interaction Series (2004)
16. Camurri, A., Coletta, P., Massari, A., Mazzarino, B., Peri, M., Ricchetti, M., Ricci, A., Volpe, G.: Toward real-time multimodal processing: EyesWeb 4.0, in Proc. AISB 2004 Convention: Motion, Emotion and Cognition, Leeds, UK (March 2004)
17. Friberg, A.: pDM: an expressive sequencer with real-time control of the KTH music performance rules. Computer Music Journal 30(1), 37–48 (2006)
18. Friberg, A., Bresin, R., Sundberg, J.: Overview of the KTH rule system for music performance. Advances in Experimental Psychology, special issue on Music Performance 2(2-3), 145–161 (2006)
19. Camurri, A., Mazzarino, B., Volpe, G.: Analysis of Expressive Gesture: The Eyesweb Expressive Gesture Processing Library. In: Camurri, A., Volpe, G. (eds.) GW 2003. LNCS (LNAI), vol. 2915, Springer, Heidelberg (2004)
20. Camurri, A., Lagerlöf, I., Volpe, G.: Recognizing Emotion from Dance Movement: Comparison of Spectator Recognition and Automated Techniques, International Journal of Human-Computer Studies, pp. 213–225. Elsevier Science (July 2003)
21. Camurri, A., Castellano, G., Ricchetti, M., Volpe, G.: Subject interfaces: measuring bodily activation during an emotional experience of music. In: Gibet, S., Courty, N., Kamp, J.F. (eds.) Gesture in Human-Computer Interaction and Simulation, vol. 3881, pp. 268–279. Springer, Heidelberg (2006)
22. Dahl, S., Friberg, A. (forthcoming). Visual perception of expressiveness in musicians' body movements. Music Perception
23. Bresin, R.: What is the color of that music performance? In: In proceedings of the International Computer Music Conference - ICMC 2005, pp. 367–370 (2005)
24. Juslin, P., laukka, P.: Communication of emotions in vocal expression and music performance: Different channels, same code? Psychological Bulletin 129(5), 770–814 (2003)
25. Juslin, P.N.: Communicating Emotion in Music Performance: a Review and Theoretical Framework. In: Juslin, P.N., Sloboda, J.A. (eds.) Music and Emotion: Theory and research, pp. 309–337. Oxford: University Press, Oxford (2001)

Towards Affective-Psychophysiological Foundations for Music Production

António Pedro Oliveira and Amílcar Cardoso

Coimbra University, Department of Informatics Engineering, Portugal

Abstract. This paper describes affective and psychophysiological foundations used to help to control affective content in music production. Our work includes the proposal of a knowledge base grounded on the state of the art done in areas of Music Psychology. This knowledge base has relations between affective states (happiness, sadness, etc.) and high level music features (rhythm, melody, etc.) to assist in the production of affective music. A computer system uses this knowledge base to select and transform chunks of music. The methodology underlying this system is essentially founded on Affective Computing topics. Psychophysiology measures will be used to detect listener's affective state.

1 Introduction

Although emotions are essential to human life there is not yet a universal definition for them. According to Scherer [1] they may be conceived of as consisting of various components: cognitive appraisal, physiological activation, motor expression, behavior intentions, and subjective feeling. Emotional states can be described as particular configurations of these components. For a long time, Cognitive Sciences have been studying the foundations of emotions. More recently computational models have also been proposed. These contributions have been applied in several domains (e.g., robotics and entertainment). Music has been widely accepted as one of the languages of emotions. Nevertheless, only recently scientists have tried to quantify and explain how music influences our emotional states.

Our work intends to design a system to produce affective music by taking into account a knowledge base with mappings between emotions and music features. This work is being developed in two stages. Firstly, studies of the relations between emotions and musical features are examined, to try to select mappings useful in our computational context. Secondly, a computer system that uses these mappings to produce affective music is designed, implemented and assessed.

A possible application of this system will be music therapy as a way of emotional, cognitive and physical healing, as well as in the production of soundtracks for arts, movies, dance, deejaying, theater, virtual environments, computer games and other entertainment activities. The purpose of this system is the induction of an emotional experience in human listeners by using music. The next section makes a review of some of the most relevant contributions from Affective Computing and Music Therapy. Section 3 presents our methodology. Section 4

A. Paiva, R. Prada, and R.W. Picard (Eds.): ACII 2007, LNCS 4738, pp. 511–522, 2007.

presents our emotional representation. Section 5 shows how our affective music database will be organized. Section 6 presents how will be done the validation of the emotional output, and finally section 7 makes some final remarks.

2 Background

Affective computing systems need to recognize and/or express emotions. These activities are vital to an appropriate stimulation and interaction with users. They can be even more important if the system uses multiple modes of interfacing with the user. Multimodal interaction is very important because it stimulates the user through various senses.

One thing that has to be cleared up is what we understand by emotions, moods and other types of affect. We accept Scherer's suggestion [2] that there are affective states that result from the combination of 5 types of affect: emotions, moods, interpersonal stances, preferences and affect dispositions. The main differences between these states are their duration and intensity. This research like most of the works reviewed in this section focus on emotions. The next paragraphs are dedicated to the presentation of some relevant research to our work that deal with recognition and expression of emotions, particularly by using music as a stimulus. Other relevant works of Music Therapy and affective music generation are also presented.

2.1 Emotions Recognition

Friberg [3] designed an algorithm to analyse emotional expression in music performance and body motion. This is done by extracting musical features (tempo, sound level and articulation) and motion features (quantity of motion and gesture speed), and then by mapping them to emotions (anger, sadness and happiness) using an expression mapper (fuzzy sets). Taylor et al. [4] also worked in the analysis of emotional expression in music performance. To be more specific, a virtual character was designed to respond in real-time to the musical input. Appropriate behaviors are defined in the character to reflect the perception of the musical input. These characters are developed through the 3-layer framework ANIMUS. The first layer (perception) is responsible for the extraction of musical features (e.g., pitch, amplitude, tone and chord) from live musical input. The second layer (cognition) uses the major findings of music perception and cognition (e.g., harmonic structural rules), and Gestalt theory to organize these features. The third layer (expression) is responsible for the character animation using musical data obtained from the previous layers.

Haag et al. [5] presented a method of recognizing emotions (arousal and valence) using bio-signals. The subsequent bio-signals were used: Electromyography (EMG), electrodermal activity, skin temperature, Blood Volume Pulse (BVP), Electrocardiogram (ECG) and Respiration. Vyzas [6] used pattern recognition techniques to recognize emotional and cognitive states from physiological data. Like Haag et al., he used BVP, EMG, electrodermal activity and Respiration but also Heart Rate (HR). Each emotion was characterized by 24 features extracted from bio-signals. In the recognition process these features were subjected to dimensionality reduction techniques.

2.2   Emotions Expression

Leman and Camurri [7] developed the MEGA system for real-time communication of musical expressive gestures. Computational tools for non-verbal gesture-based communication of expressiveness were developed for this system: expressiveness extraction, synthesis of expressiveness and multimedia generation (e.g. audio and animation). This system envisioned the transmission of expressive parameters between several modalities: dance, music, audio, computer animation and robots. MEGASE (MEGA System Environment) is organized into 3 layers: low-level features (e.g. music signal and movements), non-verbal gesture representations and high-level symbolic descriptions.

Leman et al. [8] studied expressiveness in audio music. Expressiveness was recognized by extracting the following features: prominence, roughness, loudness, articulation, brightness, onset and tempo in musical audio. These features were mapped to a 3 dimensional affect space (valence, activity and interest). Castellano [9] studied the relationship between emotions induced by music and movement. This work was focused on the Component Process Model of emotion [10], namely motor activation as a component of emotional process. This work supports the idea that there is a close connection between emotions induced by music and motor activation (movement).

2.3   Music Therapy

Chiu and Kumar [11] reviewed works done on music therapy, in particular to find what physiologic mechanisms are affected by music. Effects on body of 4 music parameters were analysed. Tempos around 60 bpm (similar to heart rate) have a sooth effect, faster tempos evoke tension and slower tempos evoke suspense. High pitches induce tension and low pitches elicit tension. High volume can cause pain and low volume contributes to relaxation. Rhythm is seen as very important to assist the regulation of our body on: circadian rhythms of temperature and sleep, ultradian rhythms of autonomic system, metabolic processes, cerebral dominance, rhythms of respiration, peristalsis and heart rate. This study supported the idea that music listening is widely accepted as being helpful for music therapy.

Hilliard [12] reviewed 11 empirical studies of music therapy (MT) and its emergent role in hospice and palliative care. From this review it was found that the following variables are positively influenced by MT: pain, physical comfort, fatigue and energy, anxiety and relaxation, time and duration of treatment, mood, spirituality and quality of life.

Erkkila et al. [13] made a music analysis system to analyse improvisations in clinical music therapy. This work intends to develop models (statistical or neural nets) to estimate perceived musical qualities (activity, valence, tension, salience, congruence, etc.) given extracted musical features (texture, articulation, melody, rhythm, harmony, tonality and interaction between features). This tool and similar tools can help the musical interaction and experience shared by the client and therapist. The clinical relevance of the extracted features is still unknown.

Liljedahl et al. [14] developed 2 interactive music systems, which used REMUPP [15] to generate music to improve user's physical health. The Digiwall system uses music to help the user in the climbing activity and to foster the user to make music by physical motions. The Body Rest is a biofeedback system that encourages the control of users' physiology through visualization, muscle relaxation and other techniques. Biofeedback techniques are used to reduce stress, anxiety and harmful physiologic responses. Sensors are used to monitor and control heart rate, blood pressure, brainwave activity and respiration. The music generator used in this system uses mappings between musical parameters (tempo, instrumentation and rhythmic complexity) and physiological parameters (heart rate and heart rate variability). Body Rest system is presented with more detail by Fagerlönn [16]. It is a prototype used to induce relaxation by controlling heart rate using relaxing music. Results from this system supported the idea that heart rate is a stress indicator and that music of user's preference easily induces states of relaxation.

2.4   Affective Music Generation

Nakra [17] developed a system to synthesize music after analysing physiological and expressive gesture data using a wearable device. Sensors were used to measure muscle tension, respiration, heart rate, galvanic skin response (GSR) and temperature. Gestural and physiological data is used by musical software to map performer's gestures and breathing signals to real-time expressive effects by defining musical features (beats, tempo, articulation, dynamics and note length) in a musical score. In the same direction, Nakra and Picard [18] used this wearable system to monitor physiological data subjacent to emotional expressions of music performances.

Healey et al. [19] developed an interface of a wearable computer that perceives and responds to the user's affective state. This is done by the recognition and response to signals with emotional information. An algorithm is used to help in music selection with the objective to change user's current affective state to the intended state. This algorithm compares GSR of last 30 seconds of previous song with GSR of first 30 seconds of current song. Current affective state is predicted based on user preferences and physiological variables. These variables are measured based on Electromyogram, Photoplethysmograph (heart rate and vasoconstriction) and Galvanic Skin Response.

MAgentA [20] is an agent that automatically produces real-time background music (virtual DJ) for a virtual environment. Music is produced using rule-based algorithmic composition. The environment has an emotional state which is used by an affective composition algorithm. This algorithm is selected from a database of affective composition algorithms, which try to match elements of music with emotions. The emotional state is obtained using perception modules of the environment (cameras, etc.).

Chung and Vercoe [21] developed a system to generate real-time music based on intended listener's affective cues. Personal expression was analysed when listening to music, like head nodding, hand tapping, foot tapping, hand clapping, mock performing, mock conducting, dancing and other gestures. The goal of this system was to correlate musical parameters with changes in affective state. Music files are generated in real-time by music composition/production, segmentation and re-assembly of music. There is also a model to select music segments and remix them to induce an appropriate emotion. 4 Affective states (engaging, soothing, boring and annoying) are represented in a 2 Dimensional Emotion Space (valence and arousal). Musical parameters are also organized in a 2 Dimensional Space (rhythm and harmony). The analysis of listener's affective state was based on physiological data (skin arousal), physical data (foot tapping) and a questionnaire. Listener data is used to develop a probabilistic state transition model to infer the probability of changing from one affective state to another. Results from this system supports the ideas that: engaged and annoyed listeners tend to stay in the same affective state, soothed listeners tend to stay soothed but can become easily bored and engaged, and annoyed listeners tend to become engaged if induced to boredom.

3   Methodology

This section presents the methodology of our work: objectives, scope, proposed computational approach and architecture, and validation.

3.1   Objectives

The principal objective of this research is to build a computational model of music production that may express and induce intended emotions. This objective can be splited in the following two objectives:

1. Examine studies of the relations between emotions and musical features, to select mappings useful in our computational context;
2. Design, implement and assess a computer system that uses these mappings to control affective content in music production through the manipulation of structural and performance features.

Generally speaking, models of music perception and expression founded on research works from Music Perception, Music Cognition, Music Performance, Music Theory and Music Therapy were examined. With this knowledge, relations are established between musical features and emotions. Through a multidisciplinary review we intend to employ a holistic approach that bring together scientific, technological and artistic background into a computational model. Music manipulation algorithms will be used to create arrangements of pre-composed music with appropriate affective content. The plan of our work also includes the analysis of induced emotions.

There are also other objectives to be achieved: build a music base, compose music (instrumental mainly), extract music features (high level features from both audio and symbolic music) and segment music. Now we will present some premises used to guide our objectives.

Music has emotional information [22]. Music is characterized by distinct music features (e.g., rhythm and melody). The systematic variation of these features is closely related to variations in listeners' emotional states. So, music affective content can be changed, through the transformation of music features, to evoke intended emotions. Relations between emotions and music features are grounded on a state of the art done in areas of Music Psychology.

Music induces emotional states. In situations, where we are playing computer games, specifically the ones which have action, when a sudden sound/music is perceived, an emotion can be induced. Roughly speaking, after being perceived, this sound/music is transmitted to our brain nerve cells, which will communicate with our limbic system that will interact with our motor system to send signals to specific parts of our body. There are some patterns that can be detected by using psychophysiological techniques, like Electromyography, Galvanic Skin Response and Heart Rate allowing us to predict induced emotion.

Music can be a way of healing. As it was said before, music can be therapeutic by healing your mind (cognition and emotion) and body (physical). For instance, music can be used to stimulate our body to dance, and as a result cause the motion of our body in ways that can heal it. This premise can also be supported through the use psychophysiological techniques.

Our work, when compared with works described in the previous section, intends to bring together the following ideas:

1. Build a knowledge base with relations between emotions and musical features that evolve in such a way that can be used by Music Psychologists/Music Therapists;
2. Create an autonomous DJ-like application;
3. Produce music with appropriate emotional content;
4. Establish a music production framework that can be used by musicians;
5. Use music to psychomotor therapy through the induction of appropriate emotional states.

3.2 Scope

Both emotions and music are of multidimensional nature. This work is focused on music content, so other dimensions are not studied. Social variables like context, human listener experience and other sociopsychological variables are not considered. Moreover, editorial and cultural metadata and songs' lyrics are not meant to be analysed. The central attention of this work is on the role of high level features (acoustic metadata) in induction of emotions.

3.3 Computational Approach

Our computational approach deals with the problem of inducing emotions with music. A brief overview of our approach is presented with the aid of figure 1.

The input is the description of the emotional experience that the system is intended to induce in the listener. A Knowledge Base with mappings between emotions (calm, anger, sadness, happiness, fear, among others) and musical features (harmony, melody, rhythm, dynamics, tempo, texture, loudness, among

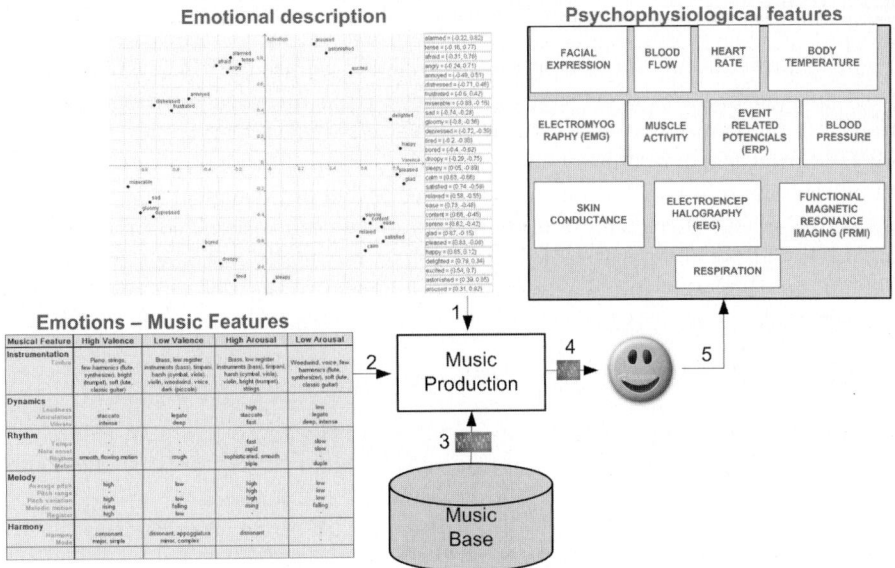

Fig. 1. Computational Approach

others) allows the system to retrieve the more appropriate music from the music base. Then, music is played and the emotional state of the listener can be analysed using psychophysiological and/or self-report measures.

Models. A computational model used to control affective in music production will be designed. There are some studies of computational models in Music Cognition and Music Performance that can be helpful in the development of our model. Honing [23] proposed 3 criteria for model selection (goodness-of-fit, model simplicity and surprisingness) when comparing kinematic and perception-based models in a Music Cognition case study. Widmer and Goebl [24] studied computational models for the emotional expression in Music Performance.

Techniques and Algorithms. The Knowledge Base (KB) is like a white box module with mappings between emotions and musical features. This means that all represented mappings are always visible. This option derives from the fact that this KB can be used in the future by Music Psychologists and Therapists. Both Case-Based and Rule-Based techniques are known to be adequate for this kind of representation. Semantic networks and frame/analogy-based systems can also be helpful.

Some algorithms will be developed: music transformation, music sequencing and music remixing. Others will be adapted from third party software/ algorithms: music composition, music selection (energy, timbre, etc.), music mosaicing (automatic remixing) and music synthesis. All these algorithms take into account the control of music affective content.

3.4   Validation

Figure 2 presents the assessment methodology to be used in this system. Music with specific features is selected according to the intended emotions descriptions and then emotional playlists are generated. Musical features are previously selected from the mappings of the intended emotion. After the play of the emotional playlist, emotions are identified using psychophysiological and self-report measures. Then, there will be a comparisons between recognized and intended emotions. These comparisons will be used to refine the mappings in the KB. Techniques that were previously refered are known to be adequate for this kind of operation.

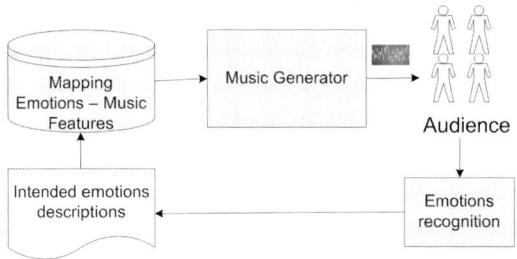

Fig. 2. Validation

Sessions planning. For each session we need to define the number of participants and what affective states we intend to evoke. To decrease the effect of exogenous variables each participant rests a period of time before the experiment. Then, each participant is subjected to a number of musical stimuli that induces one affective state (e.g., happiness). Later, other musical stimuli are used to induce other affective states (sadness, tenderness, etc.) sequentially. For these stimuli, both audio and MIDI music will be used. Playlists that will be used can comprise music chunks that last more than 20 seconds and less than 10 minutes. These music chunks will be automatically taken from the music base.

The audience is not limited to any stage of human development. However, it will be easier to do some tests with people in stages of adolescence or early adulthood, which are almost non-musicians.

4   Emotions Representation

A 2 dimensional emotion space (valence and arousal) is being considered in this work like in [25] and [26]. The user will describe the intended emotion by selecting a region in the emotional plane. Another useful dimension that can be considered is the emotional intensity. This dimensional approach seems to be intuitive for the user, but rises some problems in the mapping of the user input to the discrete descriptions of emotions in the KB. Actually, it is not clear whether there is an

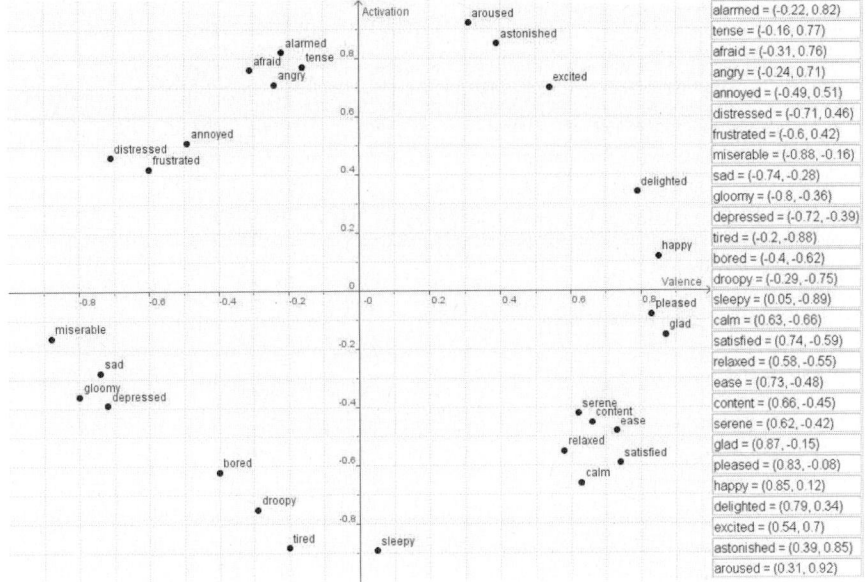

Fig. 3. Affective Space (adapted from Russel's circumplex model)

obvious matching between some regions in the cartesian plane and descriptions of emotions.

Another open possibility is to let the user represent the input by a set of lexical terms that represent affective states. This last approach can be aided by an ontology of types of affect [2]. These types can be emotions (e.g., sad), moods (e.g., depressed), interpersonal stances (e.g., cold), preferences (e.g., loving) and affect dispositions (e.g., anxious). Currently there is not a unifying model of affective states. Nevertheless, EARL [27] was recently proposed as an XML-based representation language for emotions. This proposal takes into account limitations of similar works.

Figure 3 illustrates a possible 2 dimensional affective space that can be used in our work. This space has the representation of 28 affective states. For each of these states we can see on the right side of this figure their approximate coordinates.

5   Affective Music Knowledge Base

The Knowledge Base (KB) mappings are grounded on reviewed Music Psychology research works that studied ways to establish mappings between emotions and musical features (e.g., [25] and [22]). Literature usually uses lexical terms to represent musical features. Feature extraction algorithms usually represent the result as a value. Therefore, literature terms need to be mapped to (fuzzy)

Musical Feature	High Valence	Low Valence	High Arousal	Low Arousal
Instrumentation				
Timbre	Piano, strings, few harmonics (flute, synthesizer), bright (trumpet), soft (lute, classic guitar)	Brass, low register instruments (bass), timpani, harsh (cymbal, viola), violin, woodwind, voice, dark (piccolo)	Brass, low register instruments (bass), timpani, harsh (cymbal, viola), violin, bright (trumpet), strings	Woodwind, voice, few harmonics (flute, synthesizer), soft (lute, classic guitar)
Dynamics				
Loudness	-	-	high	low
Articulation	staccato	legato	staccato	legato
Vibrato	intense	deep	fast	deep, intense
Rhythm				
Tempo	-	-	fast	slow
Note onset	-	-	rapid	slow
Rhythm	smooth, flowing motion	rough	sophisticated, smooth	-
Meter	-	-	triple	duple
Melody				
Average pitch	high	low	high	low
Pitch range	-	-	high	low
Pitch variation	high	low	high	low
Melodic motion	rising	falling	rising	falling
Register	high	low	-	-
Harmony				
Harmony	consonant	dissonant, appoggiatura	dissonant	-
Mode	major, simple	minor, complex	-	-

Fig. 4. Knowledge Base Mappings

values in the knowledge base. For instance, a slow tempo is about 60 Beats Per Minute (bpm), while a rapid tempo can be 120 bpm.

Both audio and MIDI music will be used. Some mappings are only applied to audio or MIDI as there are some unshared features among them. Figure 4 illustrates a table with mappings established between affective states (valence and arousal) and high level musical features (instrumentation, dynamics, rhythm, melody and harmony). These mappings were established having a dimensional approach as a background. Nevertheless, we also established mappings with an approach based on categories where we used 10 affective states (sadness, happiness, anger, tenderness, fear, solemnity, depressed, dreamy, excitement and surprise).

6   Emotional Output Validation

Human listeners are stimulated with music that is appropriate to the emotional description given in stage 1. The system output is assessed using qualitative and quantitative criteria. To validate quantitatively the results we intend to analyse psychophysiological data from the listeners, like the changes in heart rate, blood pressure, skin conductance, temperature and respiration. Some classifier algorithms [28] can be used to help this analysis task. The qualitative validation can be done using self-report measures [25] and experimental methods from Psychology and Cognitive Science fields. Gestures and body motion are also important factors to detect emotional expression, however we do not meant to use them. Lastly, a comparison is made between the intended and the induced emotion.

7   Conclusion

This research reviewed affective and psychophysiological foundations relevant to a computational model that can foster the expansion of Affective Computing, namely in the domain of automatic music production according to an emotional description. We intend to foster a computational systematization of the relations between emotions and music, which can contribute to a high affective control in the selection and transformation of both structural (e.g., harmonic mode) and performing features (e.g., beat accent). This can contribute to a systematized scientific research for psychologists and health scientists working in Music Psychology and Music Therapy.

We intend to tune our system with users to promote a reliable induction and expression of emotions by using music. This way, our system can be applied in areas that intend to produce music given an emotional input. The production of soundtracks for arts, movies, dance, theater, virtual environments, computer games and other entertainment activities are some examples. Another one is Music Therapy as a way of emotional, cognitive and physical healing. Musicians can also benefit from this system as an affective music production tool or as an autonomous affective DJ-like application.

References

1. Scherer, K.: On the nature and function of emotion: A component process approach. Approaches to emotion, 293–317 (1984)
2. Scherer, K.: Psychological models of emotion. The Neuropsychology Of Emotion, 137–162 (2000)
3. Friberg, A.: A fuzzy analyzer of emotional expression in music performance and body motion. Music and Music Science (October 2004)
4. Taylor, R., Boulanger, P., Torres, D.: Visualizing emotion in musical performance using a virtual character. In: Butz, A., Fisher, B., Krüger, A., Olivier, P. (eds.) SG 2005. LNCS, vol. 3638, Springer, Heidelberg (2005)
5. Haag, A., Goronzy, S., Schaich, P., Williams, J.: Emotion recognition using biosensors: First steps towards an automatic system. In: André, E., Dybkjær, L., Minker, W., Heisterkamp, P. (eds.) ADS 2004. LNCS (LNAI), vol. 3068, pp. 36–48. Springer, Heidelberg (2004)
6. Vyzas, E.: Recognition of Emotional and Cognitive States Using Physiological Data. PhD thesis, Massachusetts Institute Of Technology (1999)
7. Leman, M., Camurri, A.: Musical content processing for expressive gesture applications in interactive multimedia. Conference on Interdisciplinary Musicology (April 2004)
8. Leman, M., Vermeulen, V., De Voogdt, L., Taelman, J., Moelants, D., Lesaffre, M.: Correlation of gestural musical audio cues and perceived expressive qualities. In: Camurri, A., Volpe, G. (eds.) GW 2003. LNCS (LNAI), vol. 2915, pp. 40–54. Springer, Heidelberg (2004)
9. Castellano, G.: Experiments, analysis, and models of motor activation as a component of an emotional process. Master's thesis, University of Genoa (2004)
10. Scherer, K., Zentner, M.: Emotional effects of music: Production rules. Music and emotion. Theory and research, 361–392 (2001)

11. Chiu, P., Kumar, A.: Music therapy: Loud noise or soothing notes? International Pediatrics 18(4), 204–208 (2003)
12. Hilliard, R.: Music therapy in hospice and palliative care: a review of the empirical data. Evidence-based Complementary and Alternative Medicine 2(2), 173–178 (2005)
13. Erkkilä, J., Lartillot, O., Luck, G., Riikkilä, K., Toiviainen, P.: Intelligent music systems in music therapy. Music Therapy Today 5 (2004)
14. Liljedahl, M., Sjömark, C., Lefford, N.: Using music to promote physical well-being via computer-mediated interaction. Musicnetwork Open Workshop 5, 5 (2005)
15. Wingstedt, J., Liljedahl, M., Lindberg, S., Berg, J.: Remupp: An interactive tool for investigating musical properties and relations. New Interfaces For Musical Expression, 232–235 (2005)
16. Fagerlönn, J.: A prototype using music responding to heart rate for stress reduction. Master's thesis, Luleá University of Technology (June 2005)
17. Nakra, T.: Inside the Conductors Jacket: Analysis, Interpretation and Musical Synthesis of Expressive Gesture. PhD thesis, Massachusetts Institute of Technology (1999)
18. Nakra, T.M., Picard, R.: Analysis of affective musical expression with the conductors jacket. Col. Musical Informatics 12 (1998)
19. Healey, J., Picard, R., Dabek, F.: A new affect-perceiving interface and its application to personalized music selection. Workshop Perceptual User Interfaces (November 1998)
20. Casella, P., Paiva, A.: Magenta: An architecture for real time automatic composition of background music. In: de Antonio, A., Aylett, R., Ballin, D. (eds.) IVA 2001. LNCS (LNAI), vol. 2190, pp. 224–232. Springer, Heidelberg (2001)
21. Chung, J., Vercoe, G.: The affective remixer: Personalized music arranging. Conference on Human Factors in Computing Systems, 393–398 (2006)
22. Gabrielsson, A., Lindström, E.: The influence of musical structure on emotional expression. Music and emotion: Theory and research, 223–248 (2001)
23. Honing, H.: Computational modeling of music cognition: A case study on model selection. Music Perception 23(5), 365–376 (2006)
24. Widmer, G., Goebl, W., Intelligence, A., Vienna, A.: Computational models of expressive music performance: The state of the art. Journal of New Music Research 33(3), 203–216 (2004)
25. Schubert, E.: Measurement and Time Series Analysis of Emotion in Music. PhD thesis, University of New South Wales (1999)
26. Friberg, A.: pdm: An expressive sequencer with real-time control of the kth music-performance rules. Computer Music Journal 30(1), 37–48 (2006)
27. Schröder, M., Pirker, H., Lamolle, M.: First suggestions for an emotion annotation and representation language. International Conference On Language Resources And Evaluation, pp. 88–92 (May, 2006)
28. Lim, T., Loh, W., Shih, Y.: A comparison of prediction accuracy, complexity, and training time of thirty-three old and new classification algorithms. Machine Learning 40(3), 203–228 (2000)

Sound Design for Affective Interaction

Anna DeWitt and Roberto Bresin

KTH, CSC School of Computer Science and Communication
Dept. of Speech Music and Hearing, Stockholm, Sweden
dewitt@kth.se, roberto@kth.se
http://www.speech.kth.se/music

Abstract. Different design approaches contributed to what we see to-day as the prevalent design paradigm for Human Computer Interaction; though they have been mostly applied to the visual aspect of interaction. In this paper we presented a proposal for sound design strategies that can be used in applications involving affective interaction. For testing our approach we propose the sonification of the Affective Diary, a digital diary with focus on emotions, affects, and bodily experience of the user. We applied results from studies in music and emotion to sonic interaction design. This is one of the first attempts introducing different physics-based models for the real-time complete sonification of an interactive user interface in portable devices.

1 Introduction

Being in the world and acting in an everyday setting puts us in special perspective regarding sounds, we move around the world without realizing that sounds take a great part of the reality which we inhabit. Sounds influence us, some of them in a positive and enriching way, while others are almost disturbing or even exhausting. Humans act their everyday life in a sound continuum, a soundscape [1], but their attention may not be always engaged with the sound per se. Our attention is turned to sounds when they communicate something important for our interaction with the environment, such as alarm sounds, sounds of moving objects, or sounds produced by human actions. In everyday listening [2] sounds are embedded in the world and constitute an important part of humans' interaction with it.

Sound is not tangible, not visible but still very much real. Sound in its natural expression is a phenomenon which is situated in the world, and in the moment in which it is originated. It origins from a source which we may perceive as a tangible and probably visual reality, it expands in a medium, the air, to reach our perceptual apparatus and it exists until it disappears from our perception domain. Sound is a multichannel information carrier. It informs about the event that caused it and therefore provides cues for the listener's interpretation of the environment in which they manifest. As an example, the footstep sounds of a person walking on a wooden floor tell us about the gender, age, size, and emotional intention of the person, and hardness and material of both shoes and floor [3].

A. Paiva, R. Prada, and R.W. Picard (Eds.): ACII 2007, LNCS 4738, pp. 523–533, 2007.
© Springer-Verlag Berlin Heidelberg 2007

Sonification is a recent field of research that explores the use of sound as information display in parallel or as complementary to visualization. In particular sonic interaction is called the field in which sonification is applied in human-machine interaction. In the present work we want to propose the use of sound models based on sonic interaction in applications focusing on affective interaction.

2 Sonic Interaction Design in an Ecological and Embodied Perspective

Different design approaches contributed to what we see today as the prevalent design paradigm for Human Computer Interaction; though they have been mostly applied to the visual aspect of interaction. The field of sound and music computing has reached significant results and developments in terms of new theories, techniques, and models during the last fifteen years [4][1]. The increasing computer power and its constantly diminishing costs allow for real-time sophisticated sound synthesis models which were unthinkable only ten years ago. All this opens for the new possibilities of including sound in the human-machine interaction loop.

The urgent need for interpreting and displaying the increasing amount of information, and for looking at new ways of expression has lead in the last 10 year to the use of sound as a new dimension to be considered. The development of the sonification discipline has been influenced by the ecological approach [5]. In psychoacoustics, Bill Gaver [2]took the ecological approach to everyday listening. His studies in sound perception, sound analysis and design contributed considerably to extend the boundaries of human-computer interaction especially by offering possible alternatives to the dominant visual displays. Consequently to Gaver's studies other researchers came on with considerations about the context in which sounds are produced. Sound is resulting from actions during a certain time interval and it is often connected to human gestures. An important aspect is the coupling between action and sound. A further step in Gaver's direction has been the the Sounding Object project [6]. This project provided new sound models, running in real-time and based on physics-based modeling, which can be controlled for generating sounds in a natural and dynamic way in human-machine interaction (HMI) applications. Because of their physical nature, these sound models can communicate properties such as size, material of an object, and information on user's manipulation effort on it. These sounding objects can therefore inform users with feedback about their actions on different objects, such as virtual objects on the screen, sensor-enabled devices, etc. These new sound models are used in the present work as explained in the following sections.

---

[1] The Sound and Music Computing Roadmap: http://www.soundandmusiccomputing. org/filebrowser/roadmap/pdf

3 A Proposal for Sound in Affective Interaction

We aim to show how the utilization of sound models introduced in previous section allow for a more natural humane-machine interaction, meaning that they make easier to exploit familiar patterns of everyday human action. We want also take an approach to design and to analysis of interaction that takes embodiment as central aspect. The use of real-time sound synthesis in HMI may be a way to narrow the gap between the embodied experience of the world that we experience in reality and the virtual experience that we have when we interact with machines. We envisage the possibility to use sound synthesis models for interaction that would enhance the users' possibilities to extract meanings and use those meanings to express themselves.

3.1 Embodiment

In a virtual experience, users are mainly observers and do not inhabit the environment. They try to making sense of the interaction interface by constantly checking if the results of their interaction were the expected ones. This is a disconnected way of interaction with the virtual environment. In the real world instead, users inhabit the interaction, are bodily present in the world, and are directly connected with the action. This is what it is called Embodied Interaction. According to Paul Dourish [7] embodied phenomena occurs "in real time and real place", and therefore "embodied interaction is the creation, manipulation and sharing through engaged interactions with artifacts". We argue that the perceptual discrepancy that exists between the real world and the virtual one is wider for the visual or haptic domain, while the auditory domain contains properties in itself that fit better for the application of the embodied interaction definition. As an example consider the difference between writing with a pen or writing with a word processor. Writing with pen and paper implies the use of real world objects, i.e. the execution of an action that is regulated by physical events during time, and with results perceivable in real-time while the action evolves. The pen and paper objects afford the user's action in a direct way. Writing with a word processor forces the user to understand the metaphor given by the system. The pen-pressing action leaves ink on the paper as a direct translation of user's intention. The key-pressing action is instead mediated by the system which shows on the screen the result of the action. The user's experience of the system is that of disembodiment, action and its result are disconnected from each other.

The sonic environment instead has properties that constrain the representational models to provide for unmediated connection between the sound (both real or virtual) and the user (i.e. the listener). If sound events are not synchronized with the event that generated them, the listener will perceive them as unnatural. Sound perception mechanisms also constrain sound models to a tightly coupled connection between the event, the sound and the listener. It is therefore necessary to use sound models which promptly respond to user's actions.

3.2   Sound Models

The results were models for sound synthesis. The sound models tend to become really complex if the aim is to reach the perfect reproduction of a sound.

In the present work we decided to use sound models developed in the above mentioned Sounding Object project. For computational reasons, these models are a simplified version of pure physics-based sound models which would provide hyper realistic sounds. The simplified sound models emphasize only the main features of the sound that they model, thus creating a cartoon of the sound. Cartoon sound models give the sense of a living sound, and at the same time differentiate from the real sound. Since these sound models are physically informed, it is possible to control them in real-time through their parameters, thus allowing for their direct manipulation. These features make these sound models the ideal candidate for the design of interactive sonification in HMI applications. These sound models sustain the design paradigm of the user's continuous flow of action, i.e. the Embodied Interaction paradigm that puts the user in control of the entire course of events.

In the present work, the role of the interaction designer is to provide the user with sounding objects, modeled by their physical and perceptual parameters, with a priori parameters settings depending on the real world rules of interaction.

3.3   Emotions

Emotions are part of the experience in the world and they are necessary for physically prepare the individual to an action, they are determined by real life conditions and they occur in social interactions that have some implication for the individuals' life [8]. Sonification design can address to the ideas of using the sound as an interface that could provide for emotion as interaction. When including emotions in HMI applications the designer should consider the cultural context and the dynamic experience. The user interface should help people to understand and experience their own emotions. This can be achieved by extending the boundaries of the cognitive model traditionally adopted by the HMI community. Emotion and cognition should not construed as private phenomena and restricted to the boundaries of the body. Emotions are tightly connected to the social context they manifest themselves in, they are qualities related to an experience, like narrative qualities that develop in time.

It has been demonstrated that at a certain extent emotions can be observed and modeled. Active fields of research in this sense have been those of speech and music. Models for the analysis and synthesis of emotions in both speech and music has been developed in the last years with a increased attention during the last 10 years [9] [10] [11]. In the present work we start from studies on expressive music performance for designing our models of emotions in sound and music.

Music listening can differ from other emotion producing conditions in which the emotional situation usually involves a social context and the use of verbal interaction. Emotional reactions are reported for music listening done in isolation, for example at home or in an experimental session [8].

As we have written above, humans listen to sound in both everyday listening and musical listening [2]. This implicates that the perceptive attention shifts from the need to hear properties of the sound source, and the need to interpret the situation that generated the sound, the "mood of the environment". In the present work, as we will see in the following, we applied results from studies in music and emotion to sonic interaction design. We also tried to model emotional understanding of sounds starting from studies on the perception of expressive sounds [3].

4   Sonic Interaction in the Affective Diary

In this section we present some sound models for the interactive sonification of Affective Diary (AD), a digital diary with focus on emotions, affects, and bodily experience of the user [12]. AD is a system developed by researchers at SICS, Stockholm, in collaboration with Microsoft Research, Cambridge.

AD is a software tool for organizing the digital information that a typical teenager collects during her everyday experience via portable devices such as mobile phones, mp3 players, digital cameras. Digital information can be SMS and MMS messages, photographs, and bluetooth IDs of other people devices. This information is complemented with data from wearable sensors that the user wears during the day. Sensors collect body temperature, number of steps, heart beat, and also environmental sounds. All these data are automatically organized in the form of a "story of the day" along a time line from early morning to late night.

The main idea behind AD is that of inviting the user to focus on and re-experience her emotional, social and bodily experience. Data collected by portable devices are presented as they are, while sensor data are plotted using an abstract colourful body shape.

AD runs on table-pc and smart phones. The latter in particular is character-ized by the small dimension of the graphical display. This is the ideal situation for introducing the auditory channel as information channel in the design of AD, i.e. when it is difficult to see, it is still possible to hear! In the present work we propose a design for an interactive sonification of AD.

A more detailed description of AD is beyond the scope of this paper. For further information about AD please refer to the project website[2].

All sound models presented in the following work in real-time, are reactive to users gestures and to AD events. The sound models are developed in Pure Data (PD), a multi-platform system for the sound synthesis and analysis[3]. PD communicates with AD via network protocol.

4.1   Sonification of SMS Messages

In AD the SMS messages are visualized as concentric circles and appear on the timeline at the moment they were received. The SMS text appears when tipping or pointing on its graphical representation (i.e. the concentric circles).

---

[2] Affective Diary: http://www.sics.se/interaction/projects/ad/
[3] Pure Data: http://www.puredata.info

In order to attribute a sonic metaphor to the event of an "incoming" SMS many ideas were considered, but the idea of a container and content was the one that felt more prone to provide with coupling and affordance. It finds its counterparts in other studies, as for example in the Tangible Bits [13] or the Marble Answering Machine where the idea was of small marbles representing incoming messages for a telephone answering machine. An SMS event can be illustrated as a little marble falling into a container. The container is the metaphor for the handheld device. When an SMS is received it will sound as an impact of the marble into the container. We used a sound model for impact sounds that can be configured to infer the idea of material, weight and impact force [14] [15]. In that way it is possible to personalize the sender of the message by associating sound attributes that distinguish her, such as different material and/or size. Or possibly the sender will set up his own attributes. The users feel free to construct the affective implications of the sound they produce by interacting with the sonic interface almost in the same way they would do if they were using real marbles in real box. The affective component of the synthesized impact sounds is given by the simulation of different materials, sizes, frequencies (spectral centroid). For instance an important message could be represented by the sound of an heavy and large steel marble, that of an happy message by a light, bouncing, wooden marble.

An interesting aspect of this idea is that the metaphor continues to live during the interaction with the device. For determining how many SMS messages are in the hardware device running AD, the user could shake it and would get a sonic feedback representing the marbles shaking into the "virtual" container. In this way it would be possible to get an idea about the number of messages in the device, and who send them (if different sizes and materials have been used in the modeling). The aim of this design is to make possible for the user to ascribe a meaning to the sound that she produces by interacting with the device and consequently to provoke the utilization of the information in the user's behavior.

If the case that SMS messages are accompanied by a pictures, such as in MMS messages, it has been shown that sound and music can enhance the emotional communication embedded in the text message [16].

A sound example can be find at this address:
http://www.speech.kth.se/ roberto/acii2007/sounds/pebblesfew.wav

4.2   Sonification of Bluetooth Presence

In AD, the presence of Bluetooth devices in the environment the user moves in is designed as abstract shapes on the screen of the portable device. The shapes become highlighted in correspondence of the timestamp when the user has approached a Bluetooth device during the day. The identifier of a Bluetooth device (i.e. the user name or the device name) appears on the screen by tipping on its abstract shape.

For the sonic representation of Bluetooth presence we thought of using the sound of footsteps of people passing by. The main reason for this choice is that identifiers of Bluetooth devices represent people that the AD user encountered during the day when moving/walking in different environments, such as public or working spaces.

Previous studies on the modeling of footstep sounds [17] and on the analysis of expressive walking sounds [3] inspired the idea of designing a model for the synthesis of emotionally expressive human footsteps.

Footstep sounds can be characterized by modifying the control parameters of their sound model such as impact force, distance, step velocity, and the ground textures which can be distinguished in soft or hard (see Figure 1). Special combinations of this control parameters allow for the direct manipulated of walker parameters such as age, gender, weight, size, ground texture, pace, and emotion. The synthesis of the footsteps then becomes malleable to the emotional influence of the user that manipulates the interface. Bluetooth presences could thus be represented by the description of a human presence going by with walking sounds if it was a longer presence, or with running sounds it was a shorter presence.

Here are some sound examples of walking sounds:

http://www.speech.kth.se/ roberto/acii2007/sounds/glasswalking.wav
http://www.speech.kth.se/ roberto/acii2007/sounds/steelwalking.wav
http://www.speech.kth.se/ roberto/acii2007/sounds/woodwalking.wav

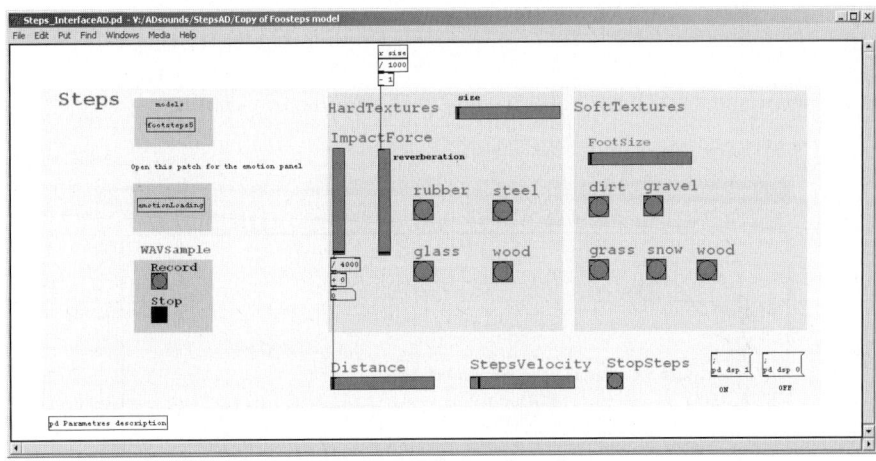

Fig. 1. Pure Data interface for the control of footstep sounds

4.3   Sonification of scribble events

The user of AD can write some comments using a pen on a Tablet PC or on a smart phone. This will produce freehand scribbles appearing on the AD display. The generated scribbles will be saved automatically and will reappear if that particular moment of the day will be revisited by the user.

When writing the user acts on the display and consequently gets the haptic and auditory feedback in a natural way. Because of this, the direct sonification of the event of writing on the AD display could be disregarded, however sometimes the auditory feedback could be too soft or the user could be wearing headphones preventing her from hearing it.

The sonic representation of the scribble is created as the friction sound of a pen on a surface. Even in this case the sound is produced in real-time by using a physics-based model, a model of friction sounds [18], and by modulating the parameters that define the pen sound. The user interaction is coupled to the real-time synthesis model. The parameters which control the sound model are saved so that the sound of a particular scribble can be retrieved and re-synthesized when the scribble reappears on the screen. This happens when the user browses AD. The user could browse AD without watching it and just listening to the sound feedback for identifying the scribble position. Sounds textures that has been created simulates sounds of pencil, chalk and felt-tip pen (see Figure 2). These textures are meant to express different efforts and to map different graphical properties of the pen (i.e. wide line for a felt-tip pen, thin line for pencil). The writing gesture of the user is also mapped into the sound, providing feedback on the user gesture, which can be for example gentle or nervous. In this way, affective gestures of the user are directly reflected in the synthesized sound.

At the following links are some sound examples of writing sounds:

http://www.speech.kth.se/ roberto/acii2007/sounds/chalckWriting.wav
http://www.speech.kth.se/ roberto/acii2007/sounds/pencilWriting.wav
http://www.speech.kth.se/ roberto/acii2007/sounds/touschWirting.wav

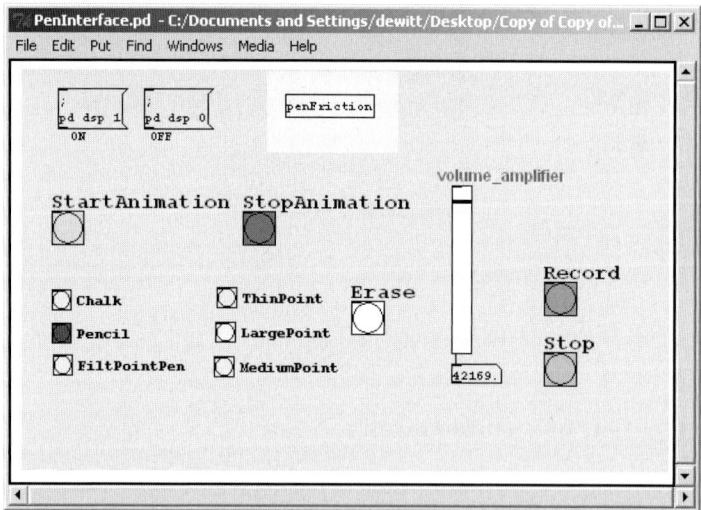

Fig. 2. Pure Data interface for the control of writing sounds

4.4   Sonification of Photo Events

The AD user receives and/or takes photos during the day and they are embedded in diary in correspondence to their timestamp.

As in the case of scribbles, we want to raise the user attention when she is browsing AD and a photo appears in a specific moment of the day. The event of taking a picture has already its own well established sonification standard. The click sound of a mechanical camera have been indeed replicated into digital cameras for providing feedback to users. Think for example to digital cameras in mobile phones. The sound is always the same, since it is meant to be generated by a fixed mechanical action. Therefore, in this case a sampled sound is the natural choice for sonifying photo events.

Another possibility would be that of using ambient sound recorded at the same time when the photo was taken. This would help the user in remembering the situation if she was taking the photo by herself or in enhancing her sense of presence in the environment where the photo was taken.

4.5   Sonification of the Abstract Body Shape

The movie event is an automatic scroll of the day stored in AD. The timeline scrolls on as the screen shows the daily events in the order they happened. It is possible to stop and pause the movie and to modify the shapes on the screen according to the actual affective and bodily experience of the user(see Figure 3). One of the functions of the timeline is to display during the playing of the movie the data collected by the wearable sensors. These are visualized as abstract shapes with different body postures and colors, representing movement

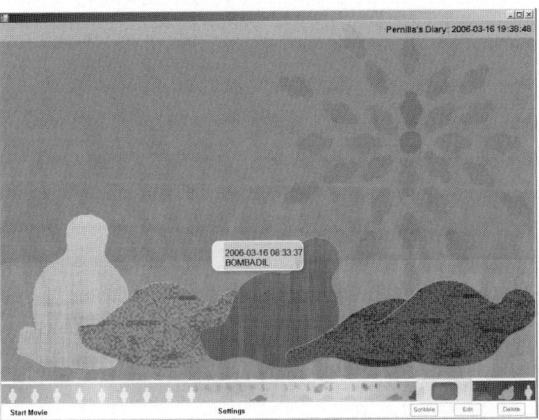

Fig. 3. Affective Diary: representation of a body shapes during a moment of the day. Note the Start Movie button at the bottom-left corner of the figure. The white cursor at the bottom-right indicates the current position during the scrolling of the day that is display at macro-level in the main panel above.

and arousal. As those characters follow each other as in a sort of narrative path it would be natural to propose a musical comment to the development of the story. What we felt was a supporting sonification for the narrative of the timeline is the computer-controlled expressive performance of music files stored in AD (e.g. ringtones, MIDI or mp3 files) [11]. The abstract shapes are used for controlling the real-time performance of the chosen score. Energy in the body is mapped into energy of the music performance. For example high energy of the body, corresponding to red colour of the silhouette, us mapped into high energy of the music performance (i.e. loud sound level, more legato articulation, etc.). Movement of the body is mapped into kinematics of the music performance. For example if the abstract shape represents high quantity of body motion (raised body), this will produce a music performance with fast tempo and more staccato articulation [19].

5 Conclusion

In this paper we have presented a proposal for sound design in affective interaction. At the best of our knowledge this is one of the first attempts introducing different physics-based models for the real-time complete sonification of an interactive user interface in portable devices. This is a work in progress and user tests have been started in June 2007. Results of the tests will be presented at the conference.

Acknowledgements

In its first phase this project was supported by Affective Diary, a project financed by Microsoft Research, Cambridge, UK. Special thanks to Kristina Höök, Martin Svensson, Anna Ståhl, Petra Sundström and Jarmo Laaksolathi, SICS, for providing us with the Affective Diary system, which was the system sonified in the work presented in this paper.

References

1. Schafer, R.M.: The Soundscape. Our Sonic Environment and The Tuning of the World. Destiny Books, Rochester, Vermont (1994)
2. Gaver, W.W.: What in the world do we hear? an ecological approach to auditory event perception. Ecological Psychology 5(1), 1–29 (1993)
3. Giordano, B., Bresin, R.: Walking and playing: What's the origin of emotional expressiveness in music? In: Baroni, M., Addessi, A.R., Caterina, R., Costa, M. (eds.) ICMPC9 - 9th International Conference on Music Perception & Cognition, Bologna, p. 149. Bonomia University Press (abstract) (August 2006)
4. VVAA: A Roadmap for Sound and Music Computing. The S2S^2 Consortium (2007), http://www.soundandmusiccomputing.org/roadmap
5. Gibson, J.J.: The Ecological Approach to Visual Perception. Lawrence Erlbaum, Mahwah

6. Rocchesso, D., Bresin, R., Fernstrm, M.: Sounding object. IEEE Multimedia Magazine 10(2), 42–52 (2003)
7. Dourish, P.: Where the Action Is: The Foundations of Embodied Interaction. The MIT Press, Cambridge (2001)
8. Krumhansl, C.: An exploratory study of musical emotions and psychophysiology. Can J. Exp. Psychol. 51(4), 336–353 (1997)
9. Schröder, M.: Emotional speech synthesis: A review. In: Eurospeech, vol. 1, pp. 561–564 (2001)
10. Juslin, P.N., Laukka, P.: Communication of emotions in vocal expression and music performance: Different channels, same code? Psychological Bulletin 129(5), 770–814 (2003)
11. Bresin, R., Friberg, A.: Emotional coloring of computer-controlled music performances. Computer Music Journal 24(4), 44–63 (2000)
12. Lindström, A., Ståhl, A., Höök, K., Sundström, P., Laaksolathi, J., Combetto, M., Taylor, A., Bresin, R.: Affective diary: designing for bodily expressiveness and self-reflection. In: CHI '06. CHI '06 extended abstracts on Human factors in computing systems, pp. 1037–1042. ACM Press, New York (2006)
13. Ishii, H., Ullmer, B.: Tangible bits: towards seamless interfaces between people, bits and atoms. In: CHI '97. Proceedings of the SIGCHI conference on Human factors in computing systems, pp. 234–241. ACM Press, New York (1997)
14. Rocchesso, D., Ottaviani, L., Fontana, F.: Size, shape, and material properties of sound models. In: Rocchesso, D., Fontana, F. (eds.) The Sounding Object, Mondo Estremo, Florence, Italy, pp. 95–110 (2003)
15. Rath, M., Fontana, F.: High-level models: bouncing, breaking, rolling, crumpling, pouring. In: Rocchesso, D., Fontana, F. (eds.) The Sounding Object, Mondo Estremo, Florence, Italy, pp. 173–204 (2003)
16. Luis, I.F., Bresin, R.: Influence of expressive music on the perception of short text messages. In: Baroni, M., Addessi, A.R., Caterina, R., Costa, M. (eds.) ICMPC9 – 9th International Conference on Music Perception & Cognition (2006) 244 abstract only
17. Fontana, F., Bresin, R.: Physics-based sound synthesis and control: crushing, walking and running by crumpling sounds. In: XIV Colloquium on Musical Informatics, XIV CIM 2003, Florence, Italy, pp. 109–114 (2003)
18. Avanzini, F., Serafin, S., Rocchesso, D.: Interactive simulation of rigid body interaction with friction-induced sound generation. IEEE Transactions on Speech and Audio Processing 13(5), 1073–1081 (2005)
19. Friberg, A.: pDM: an expressive sequencer with real-time control of the KTH music performance rules movements. Computer Music Journal 30(1), 37–48 (2006)

Explanatory Style for Socially Interactive Agents*

Sejin Oh[1], Jonathan Gratch[2], and Woontack Woo[1]

[1] GIST U-VR Lab.
Gwangju, 500-712, S.Korea
{sejinoh,wwoo}@gist.ac.kr
[2] Institute for Creative Technolgies, Univiersity of Southern California
13274 Fiji Way, Marina del Rey, CA 90292, U.S.A.
gratch@ict.usc.edu

Abstract. Recent years have seen an explosion of interest in computational models of socio-emotional processes, both as a mean to deepen understanding of human behavior and as a mechanism to drive a variety of training and entertainment applications. In contrast with work on emotion, where research groups have developed detailed models of emotional processes, models of personality have emphasized shallow surface behavior. Here, we build on computational appraisal models of emotion to better characterize dispositional differences in how people come to understand social situations. Known as *explanatory style*, this dispositional factor plays a key role in social interactions and certain socio-emotional disorders, such as depression. Building on appraisal and attribution theories, we model key conceptual variables underlying the explanatory style, and enable agents to exhibit different explanatory tendencies according to their personalities. We describe an interactive virtual environment that uses the model to allow participants to explore individual differences in the explanation of social events, with the goal of encouraging the development of perspective taking and emotion-regulatory skills.

1 Introduction

Imagine you have two friends that just lost their jobs at the same company. Although the company gave no explanation, Robert attributes the firing to the incompetence of his manager, and quickly applies for other positions. Jim becomes convinced his performance was inadequate. He becomes paralyzed, wondering about where he failed and sinks into depression. You've probably experiences a similar situation: the same event explained in very different ways with noticeable consequences for each individual's emotional ability to cope. In social psychology, these individuals are said to differ in their *explanatory styles*, or how they explain good or bad consequences to themselves [1]. Explanatory styles are associated with certain personality differences. For example, pessimists like Jim tend to internalize failure and externalize success. Pessimistic style, carried to the extreme, can be maladaptive and have negative

---

* This research was supported in part by the UCN Project, the MIC 21C Frontier R&D Program in Korea, and in part by the U.S. Army Research, Development, and Engineering Command (RDECOM).

A. Paiva, R. Prada, and R.W. Picard (Eds.): ACII 2007, LNCS 4738, pp. 534–545, 2007.
© Springer-Verlag Berlin Heidelberg 2007

consequences for socio-emotional development and physical health. Explanatory style can also be changed through cognitive behavioral therapy, a standard psychoanalytic technique that treats depression by teaching patients to alter their habitual ways of explaining social events. In our research, we consider how to model differences in explanatory styles, both to concretize psychological theories of emotional disorders such as depression, and to inform the behavior of interactive applications that can allow users to explore explanatory differences and encourage the development of perspective taking and emotion-regulatory skills.

In contrast with scientific explanations of physical events, people's explanations of social situations are particularly susceptible to multiple interpretations. Social explanations involve judgments not only of causality but epistemic factors such as intent, foreknowledge, free will and mitigating circumstances. For example, when being hit from behind by another vehicle, one driver might assume it was a simple accident, whereas another might assume it was a malicious intentional act and responded with rage. Faithfully modeling explanatory style requires a system that can produce such social explanations and bias them systematically depending on the personality one is attempting to model.

Unlike much of the work on modeling personality that has focused on surface behavior, a model of explanatory style attempts to characterize differences in underlying perceptions and thoughts that motivate behavior. Hayes-Roth, et al. developed synthetic actors showing relevant behavioral tendencies with respect to their personalities [2]. Gebhard, et al. adjusted the intensity of an agent's emotion based on personality traits [3]. Pelachaud, et al. introduced Greta, as a conversational agent, assigning different degrees of importance of certain goals according to its personality [4]. Paiva, et al. regulated an agent's emotional threshold and decay rate in accordance with the personality in an interactive system, called FearNot! [5]. While they have modeled an agent's different behavioral tendencies according to the agent's personality, they have hardly considered an agent's dispositional differences in understanding of social events based on the personality. Thus, we aim to concretize how an agent appraises social situations differently according to personality factors and how the appraisal differences influence the agent's emotional abilities to cope with the situations.

In this paper, we begin by introducing psychological explanatory styles and individual differences on the styles according to personality. Then, we present how to recast these theoretical explanatory styles to a computational framework. We also develop an interactive virtual environment that uses the model to allow participants to explore individual differences in the explanation of social events, a step toward the ultimate goal of developing applications that encourage the advancement of perspective taking and emotion-regulatory skills. Finally, we summarize our work and discuss future researches.

2   Explanatory Styles for Appraisals

Research about individual differences in expressional, logical, and emotional aspects has been studied extensively in psychology. Most psychological approaches structure personality in terms of abstract traits such as extroversion or neuroticism – e.g., The

Big-Five model [6]. Traits are abstract constructs that have broad impact over many aspects of cognition and behavior, and an individual is characterized as some combinations of different levels of intensity of different traits. On the other hand, some psychologists have studied specific personality differences in greater detail, attempting to elucidate the underlying factors that produce these differences – e.g., explanatory styles [1].

In this paper, our goal is to make an agent understand situations differently according to its own personality. To achieve the goal, we base our studies on psychological explanatory styles, especially the work of Peterson and Seligman [1]. They define an explanatory style as a cognitive personality variable that reflects how people habitually explain the causes of events. They insist that a person's mental and physical health is affected by the person's explanatory style in important ways. Explanatory styles are closely associated with clinical disorder, e.g. depression, and help to predict whether a person will succeed in a wide variety of tasks [7] [8]. In addition, explanatory styles are straightforwardly investigated through several measurements, e.g., Attributional Style Questionnaire (ASQ), Content Analysis of Verbatim Explanation technique (CAVE), Expanded ASQ, etc [9]. The measured styles are exploited for cognitive behavioral therapy helping to improve the confidence and well-being of individuals.

To explain events, people basically answer the following questions: Who causes the situation? How long will the situation last? How much of my life does the situation affect? That is, explanatory styles are differentiated by three factors: Personalization, permanence, and pervasiveness[1]. *Personalization* shows the extent to which the explanation is internal ("it's me.") versus external ("it's someone else."). *Permanence* indicates a stable event ("it will last forever.") versus an unstable event ("it's short-lived"). *Pervasiveness* denotes an event as global ("it's going to affect everything that happens to me") versus specific ("it's only going to influence this").

People differ in their habitual explanatory tendencies based on their own personalities [1]. Especially, the tendencies clearly can be differentiated with pessimists or optimists. Pessimists have negative explanatory styles to explain events in their lives. They believe that negative events are caused by them (internal), always happens (stable), and affect other all areas in their life (global). They see that positive events are caused by things outside their control (external), probably will not happen again (unstable), and are isolated (specific). In contrast, optimists have positive explanatory styles. They explain negative events as not being their fault (external), and consider them as being isolated (unstable) that have nothing to do with other areas of their lives or future events (specific). They consider positive events as having happened because of them (internal). They see them as evidence that more positive things will happen in the future (stable), and in other areas of their lives (global).

3 Computational Framework for Explanatory Style

In recasting psychological explanatory styles to a computational framework for socially interactive agents, we model core conceptual variables underlying the

---

[1] We quote terms indicating key factors of an explanatory style from Seligman's book [10].

explanatory styles. To make the agents present different explanatory tendencies on situations according to their personalities, we design the algorithm to regulate degrees of explanatory variables based on the personality factors. Then, we specify how the variables have influence on the agent's explanatory process and the assignment of emotional states. To provide a solid framework for modeling differences in explanatory styles, we base our work on a computational appraisal theory of Gratch and Marsella [11], and especially theoretical developments on modeling social attribution [12]. Thus, an agent appraises the significance of events in its environment in terms of its relationships to its beliefs, desires and intentions. Then, the agent explains the situation based on the assessment, and reflects the explanation to emotion selection about the circumstance. Fig. 1 shows an overview of our computational framework.

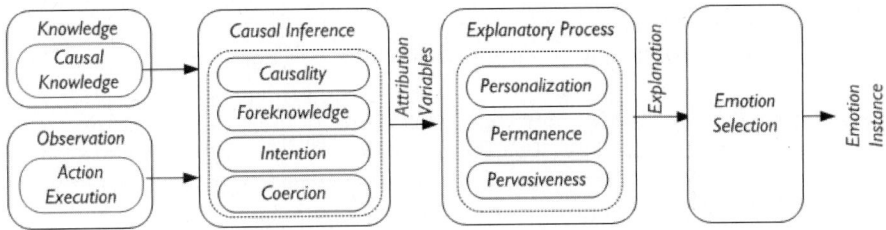

Fig. 1. An overview of our computational framework. An agent infers causal information about an event, explains the event according to its explanatory style, and changes an emotional state by reflecting the explanation.

3.1 Causal Inference

To make an agent infer causal information about an event, we need to represent the agent's mental state concerning actions and states [11]. An action consists of a set of preconditions and effects, and is associated with a performer (an agent that performs the action) and an authorizer (an agent that possesses the authority over the action). For example, if a student wishes to use the toilet, and needs to ask the teacher for permission, the student is the performer and the teacher is the authorizer. In addition, each state can be assigned a numerical value in the interval [-100, 100] denoting the agent's preference (utility) for the state. In our approach, the preference implies how much the state contributes to achieve the goal [13]. Thus, a state associated with positive value of preference is desirable for helping the agent accomplish its intended goal. In addition, the relationship between actions and states is represented by causal establishment or threat relation, i.e. the effect of action can establish or threaten the goals. A plan to achieve the intended goal is composed of a set of actions, states and their relationships. Moreover, each state is appraised, in accordance with computational appraisal theory in terms of appraisal variables: Relevance, likelihood, controllability, changeability, etc., and can result in an emotional response (see [11]).

An agent deduces causal information, i.e., causality, foreknowledge, intention, and coercion, about circumstances from causal evidence in social interaction. The agent judges who causally contributes to the occurrence of an event, and whether the agency has foreknowledge about the event. It also decides if the outcome is coerced or intended by some other agents. In this paper, it is beyond the scope of this paper to describe algorithms on how to infer the causal information. However, detailed axioms and inference algorithms can be found at [12].

3.2 Explanatory Variables

Psychological explanatory styles have considered human's habitual dispositions on explanations about their situations through three key variables: Personalization, permanence and pervasiveness. In this paper, our goal is to build a computational model describing explanatory styles of socially interactive agents. Thus, we embody theoretical variables of explanatory styles into our model, and associate them with specific aspects of an agent's tendencies to appraise the situations.

Personalization refers to who causes a situation. It is closely related to the assignment of responsibility for the occurrence of an event. Especially, it is associated with the blame or the praise for the outcome. If an agent has internal personalization, it tends to blame or credit itself for the situation. Contrastively, if the agent externalizes the situation, it shows a tendency to explain the consequence by attributing the blame or the credit to some other agents or other external factors.

Permanence determines how long this situation will last. It has an effect on the appraisal of the persistence of an event. It is correlated with the assessment of controllability and changeability about a situation. Controllability is a measure of an agent's ability to control the circumstance. Changeability indicates how likely the situation will be changed without any intervention. Thus, if an agent thinks an outcome is persistent, the agent considers that the consequence is not changeable (low changeable) and the agent itself does not have any controllability (low controllable). On the other hand, the agent considers a variable circumstance as high changeable and high controllable.

Pervasiveness is a measure of how much a situation affects other aspects. It takes effect on judgments of other events. In our approach, it corresponds to an agent's appraisal biases for other circumstances. When an agent regards a previous effect as pervasive, it makes the agent hold a biased view. Accordingly, the agent evaluates other events toward similar appraisals of prior outcomes. For example, if an agent thinks of a bad circumstance as global, the agent tends to evaluate other consequences on negative lines. Meanwhile, if the agent considers the situation as specific, it does not show any influence on other appraisals.

3.3 Explanatory Process

We have developed an explanatory process, as shown in Fig.2, which allows an agent to appraise a situation differently with respect to its own personality. We have extended Mao's framework for social explanations [12] to incorporate biases on a function of the agent's personality. We design to assign different tendencies on an agent's explanatory variables in accordance with personality factors. Thus, based on a dispositional personalization, an agent attributes responsibility for the occurrence of an event, and blames or credits for the circumstance in different ways. As the agent has different inclinations to evaluate the persistence of the situation, it assigns different degree of controllability and changeability of appraisals on the outcome. The agent also adjusts the extent of influence of previous circumstances by the degree of pervasiveness. Therefore, same situation can be evaluated differently according to the agent's different explanatory propensities.

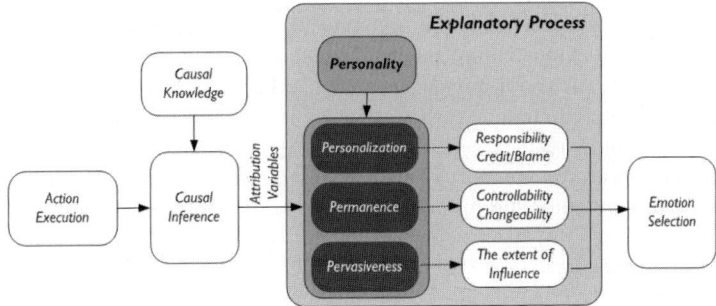

Fig. 2. An agent's different explanation depending on its explanatory tendencies. An agent differentiates to assign the responsibility, evaluate controllability and changeability, and determine the extent of influence of the situation based on the agent's personality.

According to an agent's explanatory characteristic on personalization, it differentiates the assignment of responsibility for the state. Furthermore, based on an agent's desirability on the circumstance, the agent blames or praises responsible agents for the situation. The assignment begins with a primitive action causing a set of effects. For an undesirable outcome, a pessimistic agent is biased to blame itself for the outcome. At first, the pessimistic agent judges whether it causally contributes to achieve the outcome or compels other agents to perform an action achieving the consequence. If the agent has any causality or coercion for the effect, the agent accuses itself for the undesirable state. On the other hand, an optimistic agent turns the responsibility of the negative outcome over to some other agents. So, when others who have causalities or coercions for the undesirable circumstance exist, the agent blames the consequence on them. In contrast, for a desirable effect, it shows an opposite way to assign the responsibility. That is, a pessimistic agent has a tendency to praise some other agents, such as indirect agencies or coercers, for the consequence. But an optimistic agent is apt to praise itself for the desirable outcome when the agent has causality or coercion on achieving the effect. For example, the project your friend is in charge of is a great success. If your friend has a pessimistic explanatory style, the friend applauds other teammates as they devoted time and energy to the project. Contrastively, if your friend has an optimistic explanatory style, the friend takes credit to himself or herself in the success – e.g. self-admiration for good management of the project.

An agent's habitual tendency to assess the permanence of an effect is closely related to evaluate the persistence of the effect. Thus, the explanation is associated with appraisals of controllability and changeability for the circumstance. A pessimistic agent assigns high permanence (low controllability and low changeability) for an undesirable outcome, and low permanence (high controllability and high changeability) for a desirable outcome. Meanwhile, an optimistic agent attributes low controllability and low changeability for an undesirable state, and high controllability and high changeability for a desirable circumstance.

The agent's disposition on pervasiveness influences appraisal biases for other outcomes. In our model, it corresponds to the adjustment of the intensity of emotion instances associated with other appraisals. For an undesirable outcome, a pessimistic agent considers that the negative consequence affects all other appraisals. Thus, it increases the intensity of negative emotions (e.g. distress, shame, reproach, etc), while it decreases the intensity of positive emotions (e.g. joy, pride, admiration, etc) in other appraisals. Reversely, since an optimistic agent thinks of the undesirable consequence as isolated, it does not show any influence on other appraisals. However, when an agent has a desirable outcome, a pessimistic agent does not necessarily carry over the circumstance. Contrastively, as an optimistic agent regards the positive effect as pervasive, it increases the intensity of positive emotions and decreases the intensity of negative emotions in other appraisals.

3.4 Emotion Selection

In our approach, another concern is how an agent's explanation influences on the assignment of an emotional state. The explanation contains information related to appraisal variables [11], especially desirability, controllability, and changeability, associated with an effect, and responsibility of the effect, the blame or the credit of the responsibility. Thus, we map the information into emotion instances based on OCC Model [14]. In OCC Model, responsibility has relevance to attribution emotions, e.g., pride, admiration, shame, reproach, etc. Accordingly, we define rules to assign the attribution emotions based on responsibility and the blame or the praise of the responsibility for an outcome. In addition, since desirability is related to assign the event-based emotions, e.g., joy, distress, etc, we list conditions for attributing the emotions. We append changeability and controllability to conditions for assigning the event-based emotions. Table 1 describes our basic principles to assign an emotion instance according to agent (p)'s perspective for the outcome e. Pride arises when p is responsible for producing a desired outcome e. Meanwhile, shame arises when p has the responsibility for causing an undesired state e. Respect arises when some other agent has the responsibility on achieving a desired state e, and p is praiseworthy for e. On the other hand, Reproach arises when some other agents are responsible for an undesired state e, and p is blameworthy for e. Distress occurs when agent p has low controllability in undesirable state e, which is seldom changed. Joy arises when p has a desirable state e which is unchangeable.

Table 1. Mapping explanations into emotion instances

Explanation configuration	Emotion instance
responsible agent(e) = p, causal attribution (p, e) = praiseworthy	Pride
responsible agent(e) = p, causal attribution (p, e) = blameworthy	Shame
responsible agent(e) = q ($\neq p$), causal attribution (p, e) = praiseworthy	Respect
responsible agent(e) = q ($\neq p$), causal attribution (p, e) = blameworthy	Reproach
desirability (p, e) < 0, controllability(p, e) = low, changeability (p, e) = low	Distress
desirability (p, e) > 0, changeability (p, e) = low	Joy

4 Implementation

We have developed an interactive environment that uses our model to allow participants to explore individual differences in the explanation of social events, a step toward the ultimate goal of developing applications that encourage the advancement of perspective taking and emotion-regulatory skills. As illustrated in Fig. 3, it makes participants experience flower gardening with a bluebird as a team. In this environment, there are two actors, gardener (participant) and guidance (bluebird), who worked as a team. A participant has an authority over a bluebird and orders commands, such as sprinkling water, etc, via a simple GUI. The bluebird actually carries out the commands in a virtual gardening environment, and then the virtual flower presents the effects of executed commands. Thus, the participants can learn the influence of the commands for flower gardening. Furthermore, the bluebird provides the participant with guidance through its own emotional responses to the status of the virtual flower.

Fig. 3. An interactive environment with a bluebird. Participants can select a specific command through left GUI window. The bluebird executes the command and the virtual flower shows the effect of the selected command in this interactive environment.

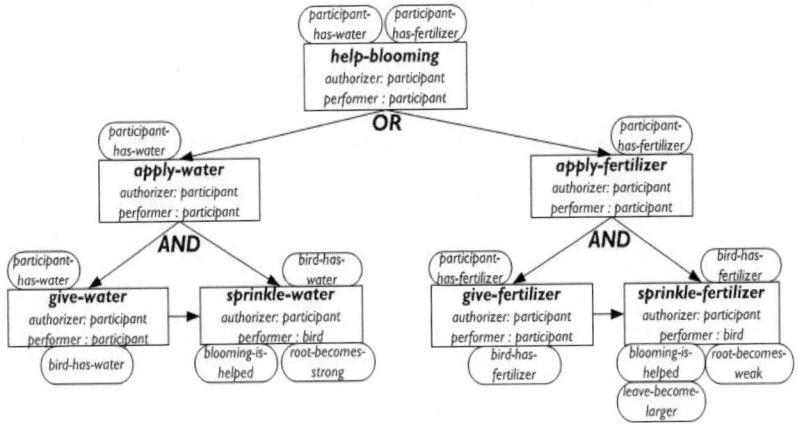

Fig. 4. A task structure of *help-blooming* in our interactive environment

We used our model to enable the bluebird to explain social situations in different ways depending on its personality factors. Before interacting with the bluebird, a participant can predetermine the bluebird's explanatory style - e.g. pessimistic, neutral, and optimistic style. Then, selected style has an impact on the bluebird's explanatory tendencies for social interaction with the participant. In this environment, a participant has a *help-blooming* mission to achieve the goal *blooming-is-helped*. As shown in Fig. 4, there are two methods to achieve this: *apply-water* and *apply-fertilizer*. *Apply-water* consists of primitive actions; *give-water* and *sprinkle-water*, and *apply-fertilizer* is composed of *give-fertilizer* and *sprinkle-fertilizer*. *Sprinkle-water* and *sprinkle-fertilizer* have the effect *blooming-is-helped* which is a desirable goal to a bluebird and a participant. However, *sprinkle-fertilizer* has an undesirable side effect for the bluebird, which is that *root-becomes-weak*.

Let's imagine that a participant predetermined a bluebird's explanatory style as optimistic and coerced the bluebird to perform *sprinkle-fertilizer*. Then, an undesirable outcome *root-becomes-weak* occurred. Fig. 5 shows how our computational model

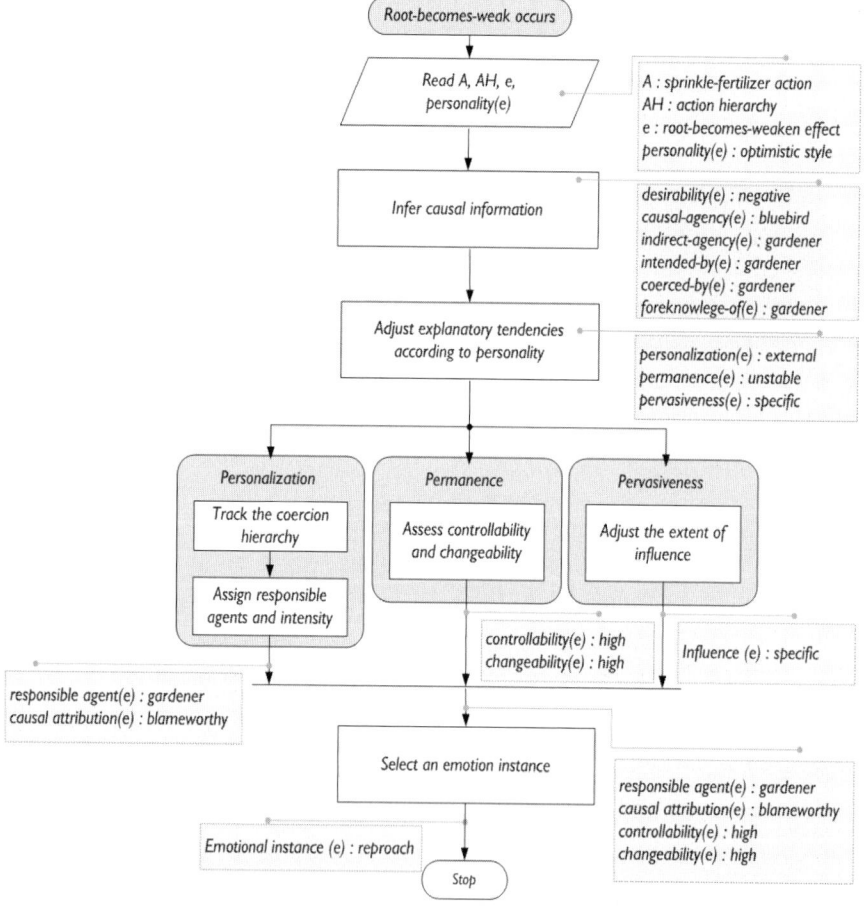

Fig. 5. An optimistic bluebird's explanation about a negative outcome *root-becomes-weak*

informs the bluebird's explanation for the undesirable effect. Firstly, a bluebird knows that it is a causal agency and a participant is an indirect agency for the effect. The bluebird infers that the participant has foreknowledge about the effect and intends to achieve the consequence because the participant coerced the bluebird to perform *sprinkle-fertilizer* causing the negative outcome. According to a bluebird's optimistic explanatory style, the bluebird externalizes an undesirable state. Thus, it finds some other blameworthy agents, e.g., indirect agency, coercer, etc. Because the outcome is forced by a participant, the bluebird attributes the responsibility to the participant. Moreover, since the bluebird regards *root-becomes-weak* as unstable, it attributes high controllability and high changeability to the state. As the bluebird thinks of the negative outcome as isolated, it does not have any influence on other appraisals. Finally, the bluebird reproaches the participant for being blameworthy on the undesirable state *root-becomes-weak* according to our principles for determining an emotional state.

Fig. 6 shows examples of a bluebird's different emotional responses to same events according to its explanatory tendencies. Since participants can interact with a bluebird as a team, it enables them to explore other team members' different explanatory styles when there is teamwork in the interactive environment. As a result, we can study how different explanatory styles of teammates influence the other teammate's performance of teamwork in team task environments. Ultimately, we can expect possibilities of applications that encourage the advancement of participants' perspective taking and emotion-regulatory skills in interactive environments.

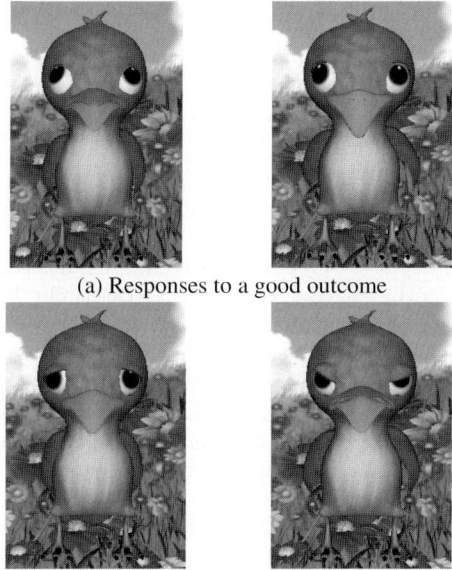

(a) Responses to a good outcome

(b) Responses to a bad outcome

Fig. 6. Different emotional responses to same situation depending on its explanatory style. Left figures show a pessimistic agent's expression to a good or bad outcome, and right ones describe an optimistic agent's expression.

5   Summary and Future Work

In this paper, we presented a computational framework which allowed an agent to exhibit different explanatory tendencies for social events according to personality. Building on the framework, we modeled key conceptual variables underlying psychological explanatory styles, and designed to assign different explanatory tendencies depending on an agent's personality. We also specified how the variables inform the agent's explanatory process and the assignment of emotional states in social situations. Finally, we built an interactive virtual environment that used our framework to allow participants to explore individual differences in the explanation of social events, with the goal of encouraging the development of perspective taking and emotion-regulatory skills.

This work is still in its early stages. The current framework has focused on simple common sense rules which are sufficient and efficient for our practical application. Future research must extend our framework with more general rules for pervasiveness in explanatory styles. Since the implemented bluebird limits to exhibit its explanation through facial expression and simple movement, it is not enough to allow participants to understand a bluebird's explanations about social events. Therefore, we are planning to combine additional modalities, e.g., sound, etc, to improve participants' understanding about the bluebird's explanation. We are also planning to evaluate the effectiveness of our proposed framework through a comparative study with other research. Furthermore, we will measure how participants' explanatory tendencies influence their comprehensions of the bluebird's explanations of social events in interactive edutainment systems.

References

1. Buchanan, G., Seligman, M.E.P.: Explanatory Style. Erlbaum, Hillsdale, N.J (1995)
2. Rousseau, D., Hayes-Roth, B.: A Social-Psychological Model for Synthetic Actors. In: Agents' 98, pp. 165–172 (1998)
3. Gebhard, P.: ALMA – A Layered Model of Affect. In: AAMAS'05, pp. 29–36 (2005)
4. de Rosis, F., Pelachaud, C., Poggi, I., Carofiglio, V., De Carolis, B.: From Greta's mind to her face: modeling the dynamics of affective states in a conversational embodied agent. International Journal of Human-Computer Studies, 81–118 (2003)
5. Paiva, A., Dias, J., Sobral, D., Aylett, R., Zoll, C., Woods, S.: Caring for Agents and Agents that Care: Building Empathic relations with Synthetic Agents. In: Kudenko, D., Kazakov, D., Alonso, E. (eds.) Adaptive Agents and Multi-Agent Systems II. LNCS (LNAI), vol. 3394, pp. 194–201. Springer, Heidelberg (2005)
6. Digman, J.: Personality Structure: Emergence of the Five-Factor Model. Annual Review of Psychology 41, 417–440 (1990)
7. Alloy, L.B., Peterson, C., Abramson, L.Y., Seligman, M.E.P.: Attributional style and the generality of learned helplessness. Journal of Personality and Social Psychology 46, 681–687 (1984)
8. Peterson, C., Vaidya, R.S.: Explanatory style, expectations, and depressive symptoms. Personality and Individual Differences 31, 1217–1223 (2001)
9. Fernandez-Ballesteros, R.: Encyclopedia of Psychological Assessment. Sage, Thousand Oaks (2002)

10. Seligman, M.E.P.: Learned optimism: How to change your mind and your life. Random House, New York (1998)
11. Gratch, J., Marsella, S.: A Domain-independent framework for modeling emotion. Journal of Cognitive Systems Research 5(4), 269–306 (2004)
12. Mao, W.: Modeling Social Causality and Social Judgment in Multi-agent interactions. Ph.D Dissertation (2006)
13. Gratch, J., Marsella, S.: Technical details of a domain independent framework for modeling emotion, from http://www.ict.usc.edu/ gratch/EMA_Details.pdf
14. Ortony, A., Clore, G.L., Collins, A.: The cognitive structure of emotion. Cambridge University Press, Cambridge, UK (1988)

Expression of Emotions in Virtual Humans Using Lights, Shadows, Composition and Filters

Celso de Melo and Ana Paiva

IST-Technical University of Lisbon and INESC-ID,
Av. Prof. Cavaco Silva, Taguspark,
2780-990 Porto Salvo, Portugal
cdemelo@gaips.inesc-id.pt, ana.paiva@inesc-id.pt

Abstract. Artists use words, lines, shapes, color, sound and their bodies to express emotions. Virtual humans use postures, gestures, face and voice to express emotions. Why are they limiting themselves to the body? The digital medium affords the expression of emotions using lights, camera, sound and the pixels in the screen itself. Thus, leveraging on accumulated knowledge from the arts, this work proposes a model for the expression of emotions in virtual humans which goes beyond embodiment and explores lights, shadows, composition and filters to convey emotions. First, the model integrates the OCC emotion model for emotion synthesis. Second, the model defines a pixel-based lighting model which supports extensive expressive control of lights and shadows. Third, the model explores the visual arts techniques of composition in layers and filtering to manipulate the virtual human pixels themselves. Finally, the model introduces a markup language to define mappings between emotional states and multimodal expression.

Keywords: Expression of Emotions, Virtual Humans, Expression in the Arts, Light Expression, Screen Expression.

1 Introduction

"The anger which I feel here and now (...) is no doubt an instance of anger (...); but it is much more than mere anger: it is a peculiar anger, not quite like any anger that I ever felt before"

In Collingwood's passage [1], the artist wishes to express an emotion. He feels 'anger'. But not just any anger. This is a unique anger. Thus, he seeks, in whichever medium need be, to understand the feeling. When he succeeds, he has expressed it using words, sounds, lines, colors or textures. So, we observe, first, artists express emotions through art. In fact, for many, emotions are important for appreciating and attributing value to the arts [2]. Second, in order to express the full complexity of their feelings, artists need flexible media.

Digital technology is a flexible medium for the expression of emotions. In particular, four expression channels can be distinguished: camera [3], lights [4][5], sound [6], and screen [5][7]. Their manipulation for the purpose of expression of

A. Paiva, R. Prada, and R.W. Picard (Eds.): ACII 2007, LNCS 4738, pp. 546–557, 2007.

emotions is inspired, in many ways, in the arts [8] such as theatre, cinema, photography, painting and music.

Virtual humans, which are embodied characters inhabiting virtual worlds [9], introduce yet a new expression channel. Effectively, with embodiment comes the possibility of simulating the kind of bodily expression we see in humans. Such is the case for the expression of emotions through postures, facial expression and voice modulation. But, of course, the expression of emotions in virtual humans need not be limited to the body.

This work proposes to go beyond embodiment and explore the expression of emotions in virtual humans using lights, shadows, composition and filters. The focus lies in two expression channels: light and screen. Regarding the first, a pixel-based lighting model is defined which supports control of lights and shadows. Regarding the second, acknowledging that, at a meta level, virtual worlds and virtual humans are no more than pixels in a screen, composition and filtering from the visual arts is explored. Finally, with respect to emotion synthesis, the Ortony, Clore and Collins [10] cognitive appraisal emotion theory is integrated.

The rest of the paper is organized as follows. Section 2 provides background on expression of emotions in the arts, in the digital medium and in virtual humans, detailing how it can be achieved using lights, shadows, composition and filters. Section 3 presents the virtual human emotion expression model using lights, shadows, composition and filters. Section 4 describes our results with the model. Finally, section 5 draws conclusions and discusses future work.

2   Background

2.1   Arts and Emotions

There are several conceptions about what expression in the arts is. First, it relates to beauty as the creative expression of beauty in nature [11]. Second, it relates to culture as the expression of the values of any given society [12]. Third, it relates to individuality as the expression of the artists' liberties and creativity [13]. Finally, it relates to emotions as the expression of the artists' feelings [2].

In fact, many acknowledge the importance of emotions for appreciating and attributing value to the arts. From the perspective of the creator, expression in the arts is seen as a way of understanding and coming to terms with what he is experiencing affectively [1]. From the perspective of the receiver, through its empathetic emotional responses to a work of art, it is seen as means to learn about the human condition [14].

This work proposes a solution to the problem of expressing emotions in virtual humans which capitalizes on the accumulated knowledge from the arts about expression of emotions. Precisely, the work introduces a model which supports expression of emotions using lights, shadows, composition and filters.

2.2   The Digital Medium and Emotions

Digital technology is a flexible medium for the expression of emotions. Here, four expression channels can be used to express emotions: *camera, lights, sound,* and *screen*. The camera [3] defines the view into the virtual world. Expressive control, which inspires on cinema and photography, is achieved through selection of shot, shot transitions, shot framing and manipulation of lens properties. Lights [4][5] define which areas of the scene are illuminated and which are in shadow. Furthermore, lights define the color in the scene. Expressive control, which inspires in the visual arts, is achieved through manipulation of: light type, placement and angle; shadow softness and falloff; color properties such as hue, brightness and saturation. Sound [6][7] refers to literal sounds (e.g., dialogues), non-literal sounds (e.g., effects) and music. Expressive control, which inspires in drama and music, is achieved through selection of appropriate content for each kind of sound. Finally, the screen [5][7] is a meta channel referring to the pixel-based screen itself. Expression control, which inspires on cinema and photography, is achieved through manipulation of pixel properties such as depth and color. This work shall focus on the light and screen expression channels.

2.3   Virtual Humans and Emotions

Virtual humans are embodied characters which inhabit virtual worlds [9]. First, virtual humans look like humans. Thus, research draws on computer graphics for models to control the body and face. Second, virtual humans act like humans. Thus, research draws on the social sciences for models to produce synchronized verbal and nonverbal communication as well as convey emotions and personality. With respect to emotion synthesis, several cognitive appraisal theories of emotion have been explored, the Ortony, Clore and Collins (OCC) [10] being one of the most commonly used. With respect to emotion expression, research tends to focus on conveying emotions through synchronized and integrated gesture [15], facial [16] and vocal [17] expression. In contrast, this work goes beyond the body using lights, shadows, composition and filters to express emotions.

A different line of research explores *motion modifiers* which add emotive qualities to neutral expression. Amaya [18] uses signal processing techniques to capture the difference between neutral and emotional movement which would, then, be used to confer emotive properties to other motion data. Chi and colleagues [19] propose a system which adds expressiveness to existent motion data based on the effort and shape parameters of a dance movement observation technique called Laban Movement Analysis. Hartmann [20] draws from psychology six parameters for gesture modification: overall activation, spatial extent, temporal extent, fluidity, power and repetition. Finally, closer to this work, de Melo [21] proposes a model for expression of emotions using the camera, light and sound expression channels. However, this model did not focus on virtual humans, used a less sophisticated light channel than the one proposed here and did not explore screen expression.

2.4   Lighting and Emotions

This work explores *lighting* to express virtual humans' emotions. Lighting is the deliberate control of light to achieve expressive goals. The functions of lighting include [4][5][7]: illumination; modeling; focus; visual continuity; aesthetics; and, expression of affective states. This work focuses on the latter two. These are achieved through manipulation of the following elements of light [4][5][7]: (a) *type*, which defines whether the light is a point, directional or spotlight; (b) *direction*, which defines the angle. Illumination at eye-level or above is neutral, whereas below eye-level is unnatural, bizarre or scary; (c) *color*, which defines color properties. Color definition based on hue, saturation and brightness [22] is convenient as these are, in Western culture, regularly manipulated to convey emotions [23]; (d) *intensity*, which defines exposure level; (e) *softness*, which defines how hard or soft the light is. Hard light, with crisp shadows, confers a harsh, mysterious, environment. Soft light, with soft transparent shadows, confers a happy, smooth, untextured environment; (f) *decay*, which defines how light decays with distance; (g) *throw pattern*, which defines the shape of the light.

Shadows occur in the absence of light. Though strictly related to lights, they tend to be independently controlled by artists. The functions of shadow include [4][5][7]: defining spatial relationships; modeling; contextualizing; revealing and concealing parts of the scene; aesthetics; and, expression of affective states. This work focuses on the latter two. These are achieved through manipulation of the following elements of shadow: (a) *softness*, which defines how sharp and transparent the shadow is. The denser the shadow, the more dramatic it is; (b) *size*, which defines the shadow size. Big shadows confer the impression of an ominous, dramatic character. Small shadows confer the opposite impression.

Lighting transitions change the elements of light and shadow in time. Transitions can be used to [4][5][7]: decorate; reveal or conceal parts of the scene; simulate the dynamics of indoors and outdoors light sources; change focus; and, relevant for this work, change the mood or atmosphere of the scene.

Digital lighting introduces new possibilities for expressive control of light. Lighting becomes more akin to painting as the artist can, besides controlling the elements of light and shadow, explicitly manipulate the final image. Furthermore, the artist is free to *cheat*, for instance, creating more light sources than the ones motivated by the scene. Specific elements of digital lighting relevant for the expression of emotions include [5]: (a) *composition and effects*, which explicitly manipulate the pixels of the final image. Subsection 2.5 overviews this element; (b) *separate light components*, which refers to independent manipulation of ambient, diffuse and specular components of light; (c) *selective lights*, which constraint illumination to a subset of the objects; (d) *shadow color*, which defines shadow color. If set to white, shadow is omitted; (e) *shadows-only lights*, which don't illuminate the objects but, create shadows.

This work proposes a model which supports the elements of light and shadow as well as transition mechanisms. Specialized techniques for characters and scenes which build on these elements, such as the three-point lighting technique [4], are only implicitly supported.

2.5   Composition and Emotions

At a meta level, virtual humans and virtual worlds can be seen as pixels in a screen. Thus, as in painting, photography or cinema, it is possible to manipulate the image itself for expressive reasons. In this view, this work explores composition and filtering for the expression of emotions. *Composition* refers to the process of arranging different aspects of the objects in the scene into layers which are then manipulated and combined to form the final image [5]. Here, *aspects* refer to the ambient, diffuse, specular, shadow, alpha or depth object components. Composition has two main advantages: increases efficiency as different aspects can be held fixed for several frames; and, increases expressiveness as each aspect can be controlled independently. Composition is a standard technique in film production. *Filtering* is a technique where the scene is rendered into a temporary texture which is then manipulated using *shaders* before being presented to the user [7]. Shaders replace parts of the traditional pipeline with programmable units [24]. Vertex shaders modify vertex data such as position, color, normal and texture coordinates. Pixel shaders modify pixel data such as color and depth. Filtering has many advantages: it has constant performance independently of the scene complexity; it can be very expressive due to the variety of available filters [25]; and, it is scalable as several filters can be concatenated.

3   The Model

This work proposes a model for the expression of emotions in virtual humans based on the light and screen expression channels. Regarding the former, a pixel-based lighting model is defined which supports control of lights and shadows. Regarding the latter, composition and filtering is supported. Regarding emotion synthesis, the Ortony, Clore and Collins [10] (OCC) model is used. Finally, a markup language – Expressive Markup Language (EML) – is proposed to control multimodal expression. The model also supports bodily expression [26], however, this will not be addressed here. Figure 1 summarizes the model.

3.1   Light Expression Channel

Light expression relies on a local pixel-based lighting model. The model supports multiple sources, three light types and shadows using the shadow map technique [24]. Manipulation of light and shadow elements (subsection 2.4) is based on the following parameters: (a) *type*, which defines whether to use a directional, point or spotlight; (b) *direction* and *position*, which, according to type, control the light angle; (c) *ambient, diffuse* and *specular colors*, which define the color of each of the light's components in either RGB (red, green, blue) or HSB (hue, saturation and brightness) space [22]; (d) *ambient, diffuse* and *specular intensity*, which define the intensity of each of the components' color. Setting intensity to 0 disables the component; (e) *attenuation, attnPower, attnMin, attnMax*, which simulate light falloff. Falloff is defined as $attenuation^{attnPower}$ and is 0 if the distance is less than *attnMin* and, ∞ beyond a distance of *attnMax*; (f)

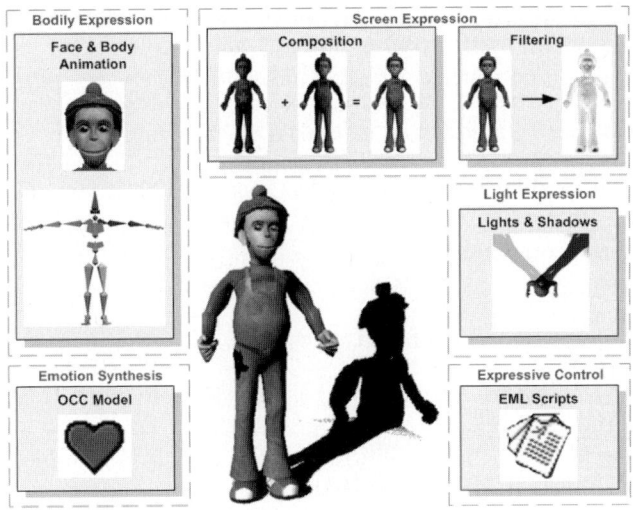

Fig. 1. The virtual human model supports bodily, light and screen expression. EML scripts control expression and the OCC model is used for emotion synthesis.

throw pattern, which constraints the light to a texture using component-wise multiplication; (g) *shadow color*, which defines the shadow color. If set to grays, shadows become transparent; if set to white, shadows are disabled; (h) *shadow softness*, which defines the falloff between light and shadow areas; (i) *shadow map size*, which defines the size of the texture used for the shadow map. The greater the size, the more precise is the shadow. Finally, sophisticated lighting transitions (subsection 2.4), such as accelerations and decelerations, are supported based on parametric cubic curve interpolation [24] of parameters.

The lighting model's equation is defined as follows:

$$\mathbf{f}_{tot} = \sum_{l \in lights} lerp(\mathbf{f}_{ds}^l \beta^l, \mathbf{f}_{ds}^l \otimes \mathbf{c}_\beta, 1 - \beta^l) + \mathbf{f}_a^l + \mathbf{m}_e \tag{1}$$

Where: $\mathbf{f}_{tot}$ is the pixel final color; *lerp* is the linear interpolator, used here to simulate light softness; $\mathbf{f}_{ds}^l$ is the diffuse and specular contribution from light l; β^l is the shadow factor for light l; $\mathbf{c}_\beta$ is the shadow color; $\mathbf{f}_a^l$ is the ambient contribution from light l; $\mathbf{m}_e$ is the material's emissive component.

The diffuse and specular contribution, $\mathbf{f}_{ds}$, is defined as follows:

$$\mathbf{f}_{ds} = spot \times attn(\mathbf{f}_d + \mathbf{f}_s) \tag{2}$$

Where: *spot* defines a spotlight cone [24]; *attn* defines a distance-based attenuation [5]; $\mathbf{f}_d$ is the diffuse contribution; $\mathbf{f}_s$ is the specular contribution.

The diffuse component, $\mathbf{f}_d$, is defined as follows:

$$\mathbf{f}_d = \mathbf{i}_d \otimes \mathbf{c}_d \otimes \max(\mathbf{n} \cdot \mathbf{l}, 0)\mathbf{m}_d \tag{3}$$

Where: $\mathbf{i}_d$ is the diffuse intensity; $\mathbf{c}_d$ is the diffuse light color; $\mathbf{n}$ is the normal; $\mathbf{l}$ is the light vector; $\mathbf{m}_d$ is the diffuse material component.

The specular component, $\mathbf{f}_s$, is defined as follows:

$$\mathbf{f}_s = \mathbf{i}_s \otimes \mathbf{c}_s \otimes \max(\mathbf{n} \cdot \mathbf{h}, 0)^{shi} \mathbf{m}_s \qquad (4)$$

Where: $\mathbf{i}_s$ is the specular intensity; $\mathbf{c}_s$ is the specular light color; $\mathbf{n}$ is the normal; $\mathbf{h}$ is the Blinn-Phong [24] half vector; shi is the shininess exponent; $\mathbf{m}_s$ is the specular material component.

The ambient component, $\mathbf{f}_a$, is defined as follows:

$$\mathbf{f}_a = \mathbf{i}_a \otimes \mathbf{c}_a \otimes \mathbf{m}_a \qquad (5)$$

Where: $\mathbf{i}_a$ is the ambient intensity; $\mathbf{c}_a$ is the ambient light color; $\mathbf{m}_a$ is the ambient material component.

The shadow factor, β, which lies in the range $[0, 1]$ determines the amount of shadow per-pixel. It is set to 0 if the pixel is in shadow and to 1 if it is fully light. Values within the range $]0, 1[$ occur in the transition between light and dark areas. The algorithm to calculate β corresponds to a variation of the shadow map technique [24] as described in [25].

3.2   Screen Expression Channel

Screen expression explores composition and filtering. Filtering consists of rendering the scene to a temporary texture, modifying it using shaders and, then, presenting it to the user. Innumerable filters have already been developed [25]. Some have been used in digital art to express emotions [7]. This work explores a subset of such filters. However, the focus here is not in presenting a basic set of filters but, to call attention to its expressiveness. For illustration purposes, some of the filters explored are: (a) the *contrast filter*, Fig.2-(b), which controls virtual human contrast and can be used to simulate exposure effects [4]; (b) the *motion blur filter*, Fig.2-(c), which simulates motion blur and is usually used in film to convey nervousness; (c) the *style filter*, Fig.2-(d), which manipulates the virtual human's color properties to convey a stylized look [23]; (d) the *grayscale filter*, Fig.3-(c), which totally desaturates the virtual human, rendering him in grayscale, thus, forcing the audience to immerse emotionally in the action [7]. Filters can be concatenated to create compound effects and, its parameters interpolated using parametric cubic curve interpolation [24].

Composition refers to the process of [5]: arranging different aspects of the objects in the scene into layers; independently manipulating the layers for expressive reasons; combining the layers to form the final image. A layer is characterized as follows: (a) *Is associated with a subset of the objects* which are rendered when the layer is rendered. These subsets need not be mutually exclusive; (b) *Can be rendered to a texture or the backbuffer*. If rendered to a texture, filtering can be applied; (c) *Has an ordered list of filters* which are successively applied to the objects. Only applies if the layer is being rendered to a texture; (d) *Is associated with a subset of the lights in the scene*. Objects in the layer are only affected by

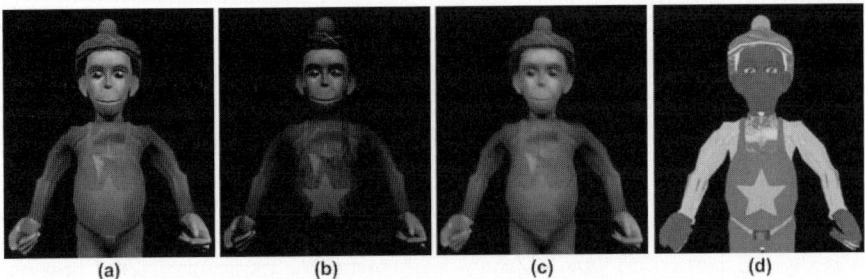

Fig. 2. Filtering manipulates the virtual human pixels. In (a) no filter is applied. In (b) the contrast filter is used to reduce contrast and create a more mysterious and harsh look [4]. In (c) the motion blur is used to convey nervousness [7]. In (d) the style filter, which is less concerned with photorealism, conveys an energetic look [23].

these lights; (e) *Defines a lighting mask*, which defines which components of the associated lights apply to the objects.

Finally, layer combination is defined by order and blending operation. The former defines the order in which layers are rendered into the backbuffer. The latter defines how are the pixels to be combined. This work uses a standard blending equation [24]:

$$\mathbf{p} = \odot(\mathbf{p}_s \otimes \mathbf{b}_s, \mathbf{p}_d \otimes \mathbf{b}_d) \tag{6}$$

Where: $\mathbf{p}$ is the output pixel, i.e., an RGBA value; $\odot$ is one of the following operations: addition, subtraction, max or min; $\mathbf{p}_s$ is the source layer pixel; $\mathbf{b}_s$ is the source blend factor, which can be one of the following: zero, one, the source color, the destination color, the source alpha or the destination alpha; $\mathbf{p}_d$ is the destination layer pixel; $\mathbf{b}_d$ is the destination blend factor.

3.3   Emotion Synthesis

Virtual human emotion synthesis is based on the Ortony, Clore and Collins (OCC) model [10]. All 22 emotion types, local and global variables are implemented. Furthermore, emotion decay, reinforcement, arousal and mood are also considered. Emotion decay is, as suggested by Picard [27], represented by an inverse exponential function. Emotion reinforcement is, so as to simulate the saturation effect [27], represented by a logarithmic function. Arousal, which relates to the physiological manifestation of emotions, is characterized as follows: is positive; decays linearly in time; reinforces with emotion eliciting; and, increases the elicited emotions' potential. Mood, which refers to the longer-term effects of emotions, is characterized as follows: can be negative or positive; converges to zero linearly in time; reinforces with emotion eliciting; if positive, increases the elicited emotions' potential, if negative, decreases it. Further details about the implementation of this emotion synthesis model can be found in [21].

3.4   Expressive Control

A markup language, called *Expression Markup Language (EML)*, is used to control multimodal expression. The language supports arbitrary mappings of emotional state conditions and synchronized body, light and screen expression. The language is structured into modules. The *core* module defines the main elements. The *time and synchronization* module defines multimodal synchronization mechanisms based on the W3C's SMIL 2.0 specification [28]. The *body*, *gesticulation*, *voice* and *face* modules control bodily expression [26]. The *light* module controls light expression, supporting modification of light parameters according to specific transition conditions. The *screen* module controls screen expression, supporting modification of the filter lists associated with composition layers. Finally, the *emotion* module supports emotion synthesis and emotion expression. Regarding emotion synthesis, any of the OCC emotion types can be elicited. Regarding emotion expression, the module supports the specification of rules of the form: {*emotionConditions*}∗ →{*bodyAction* | *lightAction* | *screenAction* | *emotionAction* }∗. Emotional conditions – *emotionConditions* – evaluate mood, arousal or active emotions' intensity or valence. Expressive actions – *bodyAction*, *lightAction* and *screenAction* – refer to body, light or screen actions as defined by its respective modules. Emotion actions – *emotionAction* – elicit further emotions.

4   Results

Consider a scenario were a virtual human expresses emotions using the proposed model. Initially, the emotional state is neutral and no emotion is expressed through any of the expression channels. The light setup follows the standard *three-point lighting* technique [4]. The *key light*, which defines the main illumination angle, is placed to the virtual human's right and above. The *fill light*, which softens and extends the key light, is placed to the virtual human's left and above. A point light is chosen for the key light and a directional light for the fill light. Both irradiate white light. Furthermore, in accord with standard practices [5], the key light is set with a higher intensity than the fill light and, only the key light is set to cast shadows. Besides being softened by the fill light, shadows are set to have a soft falloff. Finally, with respect to screen expression, two layers are defined, one for each light source. Layer combination is set to simple addition. No filtering is applied. Fig.3-(a) presents the virtual human in the initial state.

Suppose that, for some reason, the OCC anger emotion is elicited. As the emotion intensity increases, the key light color fades into an intense red, as it is known that, in Western culture, warm colors tend to be associated with excitement and danger [5][7]. Furthermore, the camera approaches so as to increase drama [3]. Finally, with respect to bodily expression, the face is set to express anger. Fig.3-(b) presents the virtual human in the anger state.

To conclude the scenario, consider that it is revealed to the virtual human that the cause of his anger is more serious than anticipated and, furthermore,

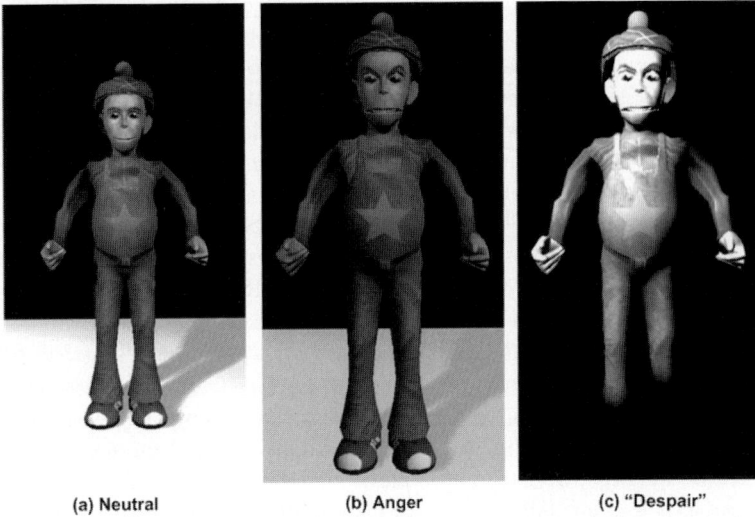

(a) Neutral   (b) Anger   (c) "Despair"

Fig. 3. The virtual human expressing emotions using light and screen expression. In (a) no emotions are being expressed. In (b) anger is expressed by changing the lights' color to a bright red. In (c) anger, fear and distress are being expressed by total desaturation of the scene and an overexposure effect.

that there is nothing he can do to prevent it. In this case, besides anger intensifying, the virtual human starts to feel sad and afraid (thus, eliciting the OCC sadness and fear emotions). Now, suddenly, the key light shadows harden, its falloff increases and its intensity sharply increases creating an overexposure effect [4] which overwhelms the virtual human with light; the fill light layer is faded out, thus reducing overall scene brightness and increasing contrast; finally, the grayscale filter is applied to the scene, thus, removing all chromatic color. The scene is now a perfect example of the photographic *chiaroscuro* lighting type which emphasizes contrasts, thus, increasing overall dramatic effect [4]. Furthermore, the absence of chromatic color is said to, according to the desaturation theory, "induce the audience to participate in the event, to look *into* rather than merely *at* it" [7]. Fig.3-(c) presents the virtual human in this "desperate" complex affective state.

5   Conclusions and Future Work

This work proposes a model for the expression of emotions in virtual humans using lights, shadows, composition and filters. Regarding light expression, a pixel-based lighting model is defined which provides several control parameters. Parameter interpolation based on parametric cubic curves supports sophisticated lighting transitions. Regarding screen expression, filtering and composition are explored. Filtering consists of rendering the scene to a temporary texture, manipulating it using shaders and, then, presenting it to the user. Filters can be concatenated to generate a combined effect. In composition, aspects of the scene objects are separated into layers, which are subjected to independent lighting constraints and filters, before being combined to generate the final image. Regarding emotion synthesis, the OCC emotion model is integrated. Finally, the model also proposes a markup language to control multimodal expression as well as define rules mapping emotional states to light and screen expression.

Regarding future work, light expression could be enhanced if lighting techniques were explored. For instance, the *chiaroscuro*, *flat* and *silhouette* lighting styles are known to convey specific moods [4][7]. Regarding screen expression, more filters could be explored. Many are already available [25]. However, first, their affective impact should be clarified; second, only filters suitable for real-time execution should be explored, since timing constraints on virtual humans are very tight. Regarding control of multimodal expression, this work proposes a language which supports definition of rules. There are, in fact, several rules and guidelines for effective artistic expression [7]. However, the expression of emotions in the arts is essentially a creative endeavor and artists are known to break these rules regularly [8]. Thus, a model which relies on rules for the expression of emotions is likely not to be sufficient. A better approach should rely on machine learning theory, which would support automatic learning of new rules and more sophisticated mappings between emotional states and bodily, environment and screen expression. Finally, the digital medium has immense potential and further expression modalities should be explored. Two obvious extensions to this work include exploring the camera and sound expression channels of which much knowledge already exists in the arts [3][6][7].

References

1. Collingwood, R.: Art and Craft. In: Feagin, S., Maynard, P. (eds.) Aesthetics, pp. 215–220. The Oxford University Press, New York, USA (1997)
2. Bell, C.: The Metaphysical Hypothesis. In: Feagin, S., Maynard, P. (eds.) Aesthetics, pp. 158–159. The Oxford University Press, New York, USA (1997)
3. Arijon, D.: Grammar of the Film Language. Silman-James Press, California, USA (1976)
4. Millerson, G.: Lighting for Television and film, 3rd edn. Focal Press, Oxford, UK (1999)
5. Birn, J.: [digital] Lighting and Rendering, 2nd edn. New Riders, California, USA (2006)
6. Juslin, P., Sloboda, J.: Music and Emotion: theory and research. Oxford University Press, New York, USA (2001)
7. Zettl, H.: Sight Sound Motion: Applied Media Aesthetics. Wadsworth Publishing, California, USA (2004)
8. Sayre, H.: A World of Art, 5th edn. Prentice-Hall, Englewood Cliffs (2007)
9. Gratch, J., Rickel, J., Andre, E., Badler, N., Cassell, J., Petajan, E.: Creating Interactive Virtual Humans: Some Assembly Required. IEEE Intelligent Systems 17(4), 54–63 (2002)

10. Orthony, A.: The Cognitive Structure of Emotions. Cambridge University Press, New York, USA (1990)
11. Batteux, A.: The Fine Arts Reduced to a Single Principle. In: Feagin, S., Maynard, P. (eds.) Aesthetics, pp. 102–104. The Oxford University Press, New York, USA (1997)
12. Clifford, G.: Art as a Cultural System. In: Feagin, S., Maynard, P. (eds.) Aesthetics, pp. 109–118. The Oxford University Press, New York, USA (1997)
13. Kant, I.: Art and Genius. In: Feagin, S., Maynard, P. (eds.) Aesthetics, pp. 180–192. The Oxford University Press, New York, USA (1997)
14. Elliot, R.: Aesthetic Theory and the Experience of Art. In: Feagin, S., Maynard, P. (eds.) Aesthetics, pp. 278–288. The Oxford University Press, New York, USA (1997)
15. Cassell, J.: Nudge, Nudge, Wink, Wink: Elements of Face-to-Face Conversation for Embodied Conversational Agents. In: Cassell, J., Sullivan, J., Prevost, S., Churchill, E. (eds.) Embodied Conversational Agents, pp. 1–27. The MIT Press, Massachusetts, USA (2000)
16. Noh, J., Neumann, U.: A Survey of Facial Modeling and Animation Techniques. USC Technical Report 99-705 (1998)
17. Schroder, M.: Speech and emotion research: an overview of research frameworks and a dimensional approach to emotional speech synthesis. PhD thesis. vol. 7 of Phonus, Research Report of the Institute of Phonetics, Saarland University (2004)
18. Amaya, K., Bruderlin, A., Calvert, T.: Emotion from motion. In: Proceedings Graphics Interface'96, pp. 222–229 (1996)
19. Chi, D., Costa, M., Zhao, L., Badler, N.: The EMOTE model for effort and shape. In: Proceedings of SIGGRAPH 2000, pp. 173–182 (2000)
20. Hartmann, B., Mancini, A., Pelachaud, C.: Implementing Expressive Gesture Synthesis for Embodied Conversational Agents. In: Gibet, S., Courty, N., Kamp, J.-F. (eds.) GW 2005. LNCS (LNAI), vol. 3881, Springer, Heidelberg (2006)
21. de Melo, C., Paiva, A.: Environment Expression: Expressing Emotions through Cameras, Lights and Music. In: Tao, J., Tan, T., Picard, R.W. (eds.) ACII 2005. LNCS, vol. 3784, pp. 715–722. Springer, Heidelberg (2005)
22. Hunt, R.: The Reproduction of Colour, 6th edn. John Wiley & Sons, Ltd., Sussex, UK (2004)
23. Fraser, T., Banks, A.: Designer's Color Manual: The Complete Guide to Color Theory and Application. Chronicle Books, California, USA (2004)
24. Moller, R., Haines, E.: Real-Time Rendering, 2nd edn. AK Peters Ltd., Massachusetts, USA (2002)
25. St-Laurent, S.: Shaders for Game Programmers and Artists. Thomson Course Technology, Massachusetts, USA (2004)
26. de Melo, C., Paiva, A.: Multimodal Expression in Virtual Humans. Computer Animation and Virtual Worlds Journal. 17(3), 239–248 (2006)
27. Picard, R.: Affective Computing. The MIT Press, Massachusetts, USA (1997)
28. SMIL: Synchronized Multimedia Integration Language (SMIL) (2007), http://www.w3.org/AudioVideo/

Pogany: A Tangible Cephalomorphic Interface for Expressive Facial Animation

Christian Jacquemin

LIMSI-CNRS & Univ. Paris 11, BP 133, 91403 ORSAY, France
Firstname.Name@limsi.fr

Abstract. A head-shaped input device is used to produce expressive facial animations. The physical interface is divided into zones, and each zone controls an expression on a smiley or on a virtual 3D face. Through contacts with the interface users can generate basic or blended expressions. To evaluate the interface and to analyze the behavior of the users, we performed a study made of three experiments in which subjects were asked to reproduce simple or more subtle expressions. The results show that the subjects easily accept the interface and get engaged in a pleasant affective relationship that make them feel as sculpting the virtual face. This work shows that anthropomorphic interfaces can be used successfully for intuitive affective expression.

1 Anthropomorphic Devices for Affective Communication

We have designed and built a head-shaped tangible interface for the generation of facial expressions through intuitive contacts or proximity gestures. Our purpose is to offer a new medium of communication that can involve the user in an affective loop [1]. The input to the interface consists of intentional and natural affective gestures, and the output is an embodiment of the emotional content of the input gestures. The output is either a facial expression or a smiley, it is used as a feedback to the user so that she can both tune her interactions with the interface according to the output (cognitive feedback), and feel the emotions expressed by the virtual actor or the smiley (affective feedback). The input device is a hollow resin head with holes and an internal video camera that captures the positions of the fingers on the interface. The output is an interactive smiley or an expressive virtual 3D face (see figure 1). The user can control a wide range of expressions of the virtual avatar through correspondences between finger contacts an a set of basic expressions of emotions. The interface is used as a means to display ones own expressions of emotions as well as a means to convey emotions through the virtual face.

We take advantage of the anthropomorphic shape of the input, a stylized human head, to establish easily learnable correspondences between users contacts and expressed emotions. Even though a doll head was used in an "early" design of tangible interfaces in the mid-90s [2], human shapes are more widely used as output interfaces (e.g. Embodied Conversational Agents) than as input devices. Through our study we show that anthropomorphic input interfaces

A. Paiva, R. Prada, and R.W. Picard (Eds.): ACII 2007, LNCS 4738, pp. 558–569, 2007.

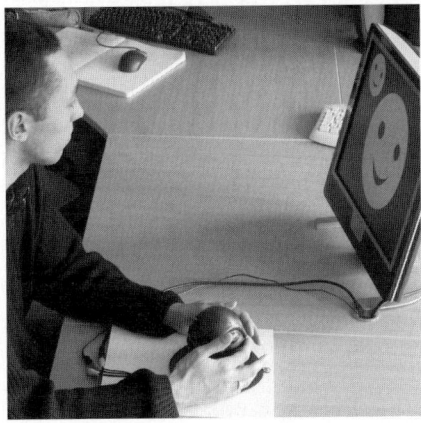

Fig. 1. Experimental setup

are experienced as an engaging and efficient means for affective communication, particularly when they are combined with a symmetric output that mirrors the emotions conveyed by the input interface.

2   Anthropomorphic Input/Output Device

We now examine in turn the two components of the interface: the physical tangible input device, and the virtual animated face together with the mapping between gestures and expressions. Three experimental setups have been proposed: two setups in which strongly marked expressions can be generated on an emoticon or a 3D virtual face, and a third and more attention demanding experiment in which subtle and flexible expressions of the 3D face are controlled by the interface. At this point of the development, no social interaction is involved in our study in order to focus first on the interface usability and on the ease of control of the virtual agent's expressions.

2.1   Input: Cephalomorphic Tangible Interface

The physical and input part of the interface is based on the following constraints:

1. it should be able to capture intuitive gestures through hands and fingers as if the user were approaching someone's face,
2. direct contacts as well as gestures in the vicinity of the head should also be captured in order to allow for a wide range of subtle inputs through distant interactions,
3. as suggested by the design study of *SenToy* [3], the shape of the physical interface should not have strongly marked traits that would make it look like a familiar face, or that would suggest predefined expressions,

4. the most expressive facial parts of the interface should be easily identified without the visual modality in order to allow for contact interaction: eyes, eyebrows, mouth, and chin should have clearly marked shapes.

The first constraint has oriented us towards *multi-touch interaction* techniques that can detect several simultaneous contacts. Since the second constraint prohibits the use of pressure-sensitive captures that cannot report gestures without contacts, we have chosen a vision-based capture device that is both multi-touch and proximity-sensitive. The interface is equipped with a video camera, and 43 holes are used to detect the positions of the fingers in the vicinity of the face (figure 2). In order to detect the positions and gestures of both hands, right and left symmetric holes play the same role in the mapping between interaction and facial animation.

The holes are chosen among the 84 MPEG4 key points used for standard facial animation [4]. The points are chosen among the mobile key points of this formalism, for instance points 10.* and 11.* for ear and hair are ignored. The underlying hypothesis for selecting these points is that, since they correspond to places in the face with high mobility, they also make sensible capture points for animation control.

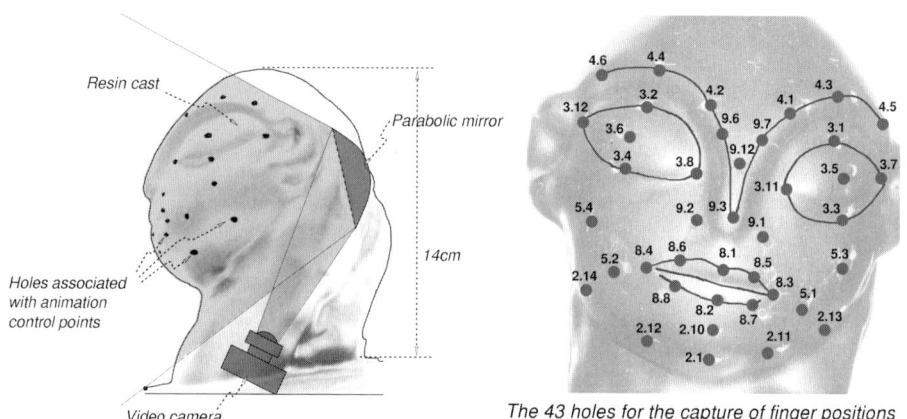

Fig. 2. Cross section of the physical interface and list of capture holes

The third constraint has oriented us towards an abstract facial representation that would hardly suggest a known human face. Since we wanted the interface to be however appealing for contact, caress or nearby gestures, its aesthetics was a concern. Its design is deliberately soft and non angular; it is loosely inspired by *Mademoiselle Pogany*, a series of sculptures of the 20th century artist Constantin Brancusi (figure 3). The eye and mouth reliefs are prominent enough to be detected by contact with the face (fourth constraint). The size of the device (14cm high) is similar to a joystick, and is about three times smaller than a human face.

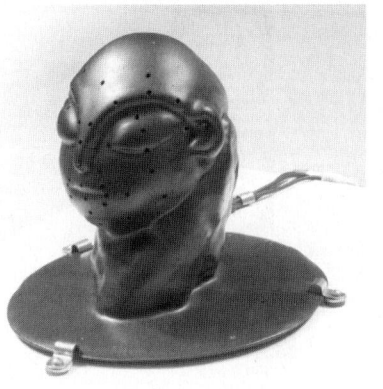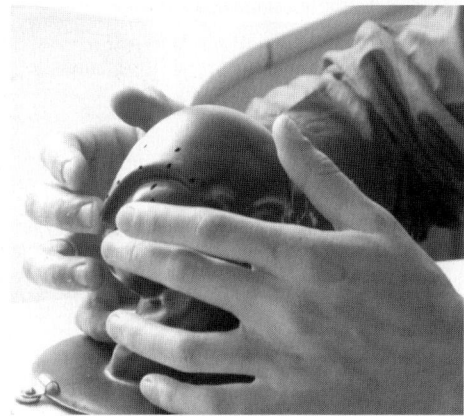

Fig. 3. Overview of the physical interface and bimanual interaction

All the tests have been done with bare hands and normal lighting conditions (during day time with natural light and in the evening with regular office lighting).

2.2   Output: Expressive Smiley or Virtual 3D Face

A straightforward way to provide users with a feedback on the use of the interface for affective communication is to associate their interactions with expressions of emotions on an animated face. We have used two type of faces: a smiley and a realistic 3D face with predefined or blended expressions. Of course other types of correspondences can be established and we do not claim that the physical interface should be restricted to control facial animation. Other mappings are under development such as the use of the interface for musical composition. In a first step, we however found it necessary to check that literal associations could work before turning to more elaborated appliances.

The association of interactions with facial animations is performed in two steps. First the video image is captured with the *ffmpeg* library[1] and transformed into a bitmap of gray pixels. After a calibration phase, bitmaps are analyzed at each frame around each hole by computing the difference between the luminosity at calibration time and its current value. The activation of a capture hole is the ratio between its current luminosity and its luminosity at calibration time. The activation of a zone made of several holes is its highest hole activation.

In a second step, zone activations are associated with facial expressions. Each expression is a table of keypoint transformations, a Face Animation Table (FAT) in MPEG4. The choice of the output expression depends on the rendering mode. In the *non-blended mode*, the expression associated with the highest activated zone is chosen. In the *blended mode*, a weighted interpolation is made between the

---

[1] http://ffmpeg.mplayerhq.hu/

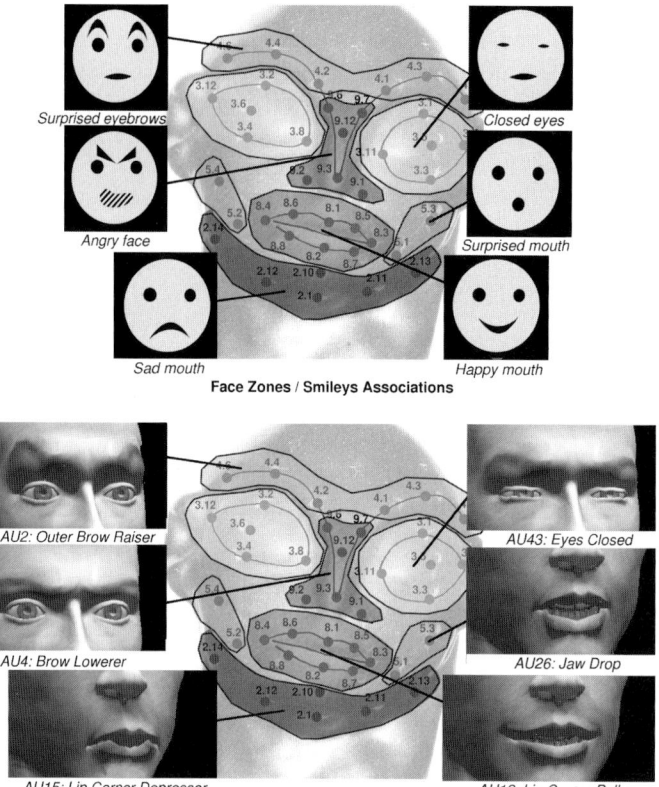

Fig. 4. Mapping between face zones and emoticons or virtual face expressions

expressions associated with each activated zone. Facial animation is implemented in *Virtual Choreographer* (VirChor)[2], an OpenSource interactive 3D rendering tool. VirChor stores the predefined FATs, receives expression weights from the video analysis module, and produces the corresponding animations.

2.3   Basic and Blended Facial Expressions

The mapping between interactions and expressions relies on a partitioning of the face into six symmetrical zones shown in the center part of the two images in figure 4. Each zone is associated with a single basic expression and the level of activation of a zone is the percentage of occlusion of the most occluded key point in this zone. Thus hole occlusion by fingers is used to control expressions on the virtual faces (smiley or 3D face). All the zones are symmetrical so that right- and left-handed subjects are offered the same possibilities of interactions.

---

[2] http://virchor.sf.net/

Two sets of 6 basic facial expressions were designed for the smiley and for the 3D face that the users could identify and reproduce quickly. For the smiley, the 6 expressions correspond to 5 basic emotions and a non expressive face with closed eyes: *angry face, surprised eyebrows, surprised mouth, happy mouth, sad mouth, closed eyes* (see upper part of figure 4). Only the *angry face* expression involves both the upper and the lower part of the face.

Each *basic expression* of the 3D face (lower part of figure 4) is associated with an Action Unit (AU) of Ekman and Friesen's Facial Action Coding System [5]: a contraction of one or several muscles that can be combined to describe the expressions of emotions on a human face. Only 6 of the 66 AUs in this system are used; they are chosen so that they have simple and clear correspondences with expressions of the smiley. The only noticeable difficulty is the correspondence between the *angry face* smiley, which involves modifications of the upper, lower, and central part of the face, and the associated 3D expression of AU4 (*Brow Lowerer*) that only involves the upper part of the face.

3D basic face expressions are deliberately associated with AUs instead of more complex expressions in order to facilitate the recognition of *blended expressions* in the third task of the experiment. In this task, the users have to guess what are the basic expressions involved in the synthesis of complex expressions resulting from the weighted interpolation of AUs. Through this design, only a small subset of facial expressions can be produced. They are chosen so that they can be easily distinguished. More subtle expressions could be obtained by augmenting the number of zones through a larger resin cast with more holes or through this version of the interface with less holes in each zone.

The 3D animation of each basic expression is made by displacing the MPEG4 key points. Since these expressions are restricted to some specific parts of the human face, they only involve a small subset of the 84 MPEG4 key points. For example, the basic expression associated with AU2 (*Outer Brow Raiser*) is based on the displacement of key points 4.1 to 4.6 (eye brows), while the expression of AU12 relies on key points 2.2 to 2.9 (inner mouth) and 8.1 to 8.8 (outer mouth).

We now turn to the study of the interface usability in which the users were asked to reproduce basic or blended expressions of emotions on a virtual face through interactions with the physical interface.

3   Usability Study: Control of Emoticons or Facial Expressions Through Pogany

As for the *SenToy* design experiment [3], our purpose is to check whether a user can control a virtual character's expressions (here the face) through a tangible interface that represents the same part of the body. Our usability study is intended to verify that (1) users can quickly recognize facial expressions from a model, and (2) that they can reproduce them at various levels of difficulty. Last, we wanted to let the users express themselves about their feelings during the experiment and their relationship to the device.

3.1 Experiment

22 volunteers have participated to the experiment: 12 men and 10 women aged between 15 and 58 (average 29.1). Each experiment lasts between 30 and 50 minutes depending on the time taken by the subject to train and to accomplish each task. Each subject is first introduced by the experimenter to the purpose of the experiment, and then the tasks are explained with the help of the two zone/expression association schemas of figure 4.

The experiment consists of three tasks in which users must use the physical interface to reproduce models of facial expressions. Each task corresponds to a different mapping between users' interactions and facial expressions. In task T_1, the visual output is a smiley, and in task T_2 and T_3, the output is a 3D animated face. In task T_2 only basic expressions of the virtual face are controlled, while in task T_3 blended expressions are produced through the interactions of the user.

The tasks are defined as follows:

1. Task T_1: The face zones on the interface are associated with smileys as shown in the upper image of figure 4. If several zones are occluded by the user's hand(s) and finger(s), the zone with the strongest occlusion wins.
2. Task T_2: The face zones of the interface are associated with basic expressions as shown in the bottom image of figure 4. The same rule as in 1. applies for zone-based occlusion: highest occluded zone wins.
3. Task T_3: The face zones are associated with the same expressions as in 2. But zone activation is now gradual (from 0 inactive to 1 maximally active) and several zones can be activated simultaneously. Each zone weight is equal to the percentage of occlusion of the most occluded key point. The resulting facial animation is made of blended expressions as described in 2.3.

Tasks T_1 and T_2 could be easily implemented through keyboard inputs. We have chosen a tangible interface as input device because we wanted the user to get used to the interface on simple tasks T_1 and T_2 before experiencing the more complex task T_3. We also wanted to observe the user, and check the usability and the quality of affective communication through this interface even on simple tasks. To make a simple parallel with other types of interactions: even though firing bullets in a FPS game could also be performed by pressing a keyboard key, most players certainly prefer to use the joystick trigger.

In tasks T_1 and T_2, the subject faces a screen on which a target expression is shown and she must reproduce the same expression on the smiley (task T_1) or on the virtual face (task T_2) by touching the interface on the corresponding zones. 20 expressions are randomly chosen among the 6 basic ones. They are shown in turn and change each time the user holds the finger positions that display this expression for at least 0.5 second. Before each task begins, the subject can practice as long as she needs until she feels ready. The experimental setup for task T_1 is shown in figure 1 given at the beginning of the article. For the tasks T_2 and T_3, the output is a 3D face instead of a smiley.

In task T_3, the generated expressions are composed by blending the expressions associated with each zone (weights are computed from zone activation as

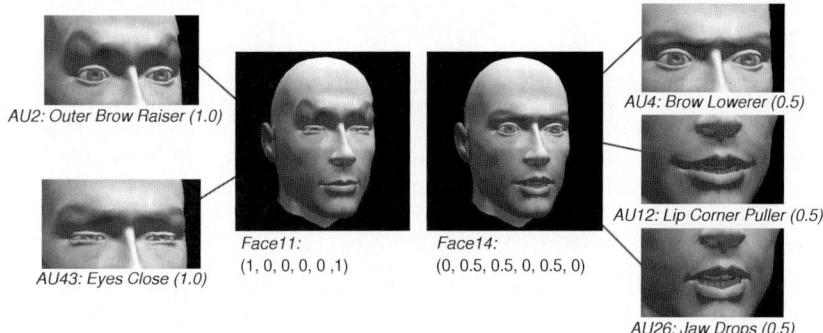

Fig. 5. Two blended expressions of emotions (Face11 and Face14 of task T_3)

explained above). The blended expressions are implemented as weighted combinations of elementary expressions as in [6]. Two such blended expressions, Face11 and Face14, are shown in figure 5. They can be described as 6-float weight vectors based on the 6 basic expressions and associated AUs of figure 4: AU2, AU4, AU12, AU15, AU26, and AU43. Each vector coordinates are in [0..1]. The vector of Face11 is $(1, 0, 0, 0, 0, 1)$ because it is a combination of AU2 and AU43 fully expressed. Similarly, the vector of Face14 is $(0, 0.5, 0.5, 0, 0.5, 0)$ because it is a combination of AU4, AU12, and AU26 partially expressed.

The 15 target blended expressions are designed as follows: 6 of them are basic expressions (weight 1.0), 6 are combinations of 2 basic expressions (weights 1.0 and 1.0, see Face11 in figure 5), and 3 are combinations of 3 partially weighted expressions (weights 0.5, 0.5 and 0.5, see Face14 in figure 5). Blended expressions are obtained by pressing simultaneously on several zones in the face. For example, Face14 is obtained through the semi-activation of three zones: the nose (AU4), the lips (AU12), and the jaws (AU26).

The difficulty of task T_3 comes from the combination of expressions, possibly in the same part of the face, and from the necessity to control simultaneously several zones in the face. In task T_3, we let the user tell the experimenter when she is satisfied with an expression before turning to the next one. We use self-evaluation because automatic success detection in this task is more delicate than for T_1 and T_2, and because we are interested in letting the user report her own evaluation of the quality of her output. Contrary to previous experiments on conversational agents in which the users are asked to tell which expressions they recognize from an animation sequence [7], we evaluate here the capacity to reproduce an expression at a subsymbolic level without any explicit verbalization (no labelling of the expression is required).

Table 1 summarizes the definition of the tasks and gives the quantities measured during these tasks: the time to reproduce an expression for the three tasks and, for T_3, the error between the expression produced on the virtual face and the target expression.

Before starting the experiment, the experimenter insists on three points: the subject should feel comfortable and take as much time she needs to practice

Table 1. Task definition

Task	Avatar	Target	Measures	Success detection
T_1	Smiley	Emoticons	Time	Hold target emoticon 0.5 sec.
T_2	3D face	Basic expressions	Time	Hold target expression 0.5 sec.
T_3	3D face	Blended Expressions	Time & error	Self-evaluation

before starting, speed is not an issue, and the final and anonymous questionnaire is an important part of the experiment. The subject can handle the interface as she wants: either facing her or the other way round. She is warned that when the interface faces her, the color of her cloths can slightly disturb finger contact recognition due to the video analysis technique.

3.2   Quantitative Results

Tasks T_1 and T_2: The average time taken by the subjects to complete the tasks is very similar for the first two tasks: 7.4 and 7.5 sec. per target expression with standard deviations of 3.6 and 3.3. Even though the target expressions are defined on very different face models (smiley vs. 3D face), the similar modes of interaction (winning zone defines the expression) make the two tasks very similar for the subjects. They rate these two tasks as easy: 1.6 and 1.7 with standard deviations of 0.7 and 0.6 on a scale of 1 (easy) to 3 (difficult).

Task T_3: The figures are very different for task T_3, in which the difficulty is due to the blended combination of expressions. It requires (1) to analyze an expression and guess its ingredients, and (2) to progressively tune the weights of each ingredient in order to obtain a resulting expression as close as possible to the proposed target. For T_3, the subjects have taken an average time of 26.9 sec. to reproduce each expression, with a high standard deviation of 13.7. Half a minute is however not very long for such a complex task when compared with the complexity of the input (43 holes, several sites for finger positioning on the physical input, and complex output made of interpolations between basic expressions).

The error between an achieved face and the required target is the sum of the distances between the coordinates of the face performed by the user and the target face in the 6-dimensional space of the facial expressions. For example, if the user produces a blended face weighted by $(0.2, 0.6, 0.5, 0.1, 0.8, 0.0)$, its distance to Face14 $(0.0, 0.5, 0.5, 0.0, 0.5, 0.0)$ is $0.2 + 0.1 + 0 + 0.1 + 0.3 + 0 = 0.7$.

Surprisingly, the time taken to make an expression for task T_3 does not depend on the composition of the expression (28 sec. for basic expressions, 26 sec. for dual expressions, and 25 sec. for triple expressions). The average error (1.79) on binary expressions made of two fully weighted expressions such as Face11 is higher than single expressions (1.23) or partially weighted triple expressions such as Face14 (1.31). This result suggests that mildly blended expressions are easier to reproduce than heavily blended ones. Task T_3 has been unanimously rated as difficult (2.77 in a 1-3 scale with only one subject rating it as easy).

Role of Expertise: In the questionnaire, the subjects were asked questions about their level of expertise: average use of a computer, musical instrument practice, use of 3D devices, and gaming. We now investigate whether expert subjects perform better or quicker than non-expert ones.

The two leftmost histograms of figure 6 analyze the average time taken to accomplish tasks T_1 and T_2 for each level of expertise. Each group of bars is associated with a time range and each bar is associated with a level of expertise (low, medium, or high). The height of a bar represents the percentage of subjects with this level of expertise that have performed the experiment in this time range. The histograms show that the expert subjects are quicker in the smiley experiment than the two other categories. In the second experiment, all the subjects take approximately the same time. This is probably because the time taken to identify the facial expressions does not vary with the expertise of the subject, and therefore increases the duration for expression recognition and reproduction for expert subjects.

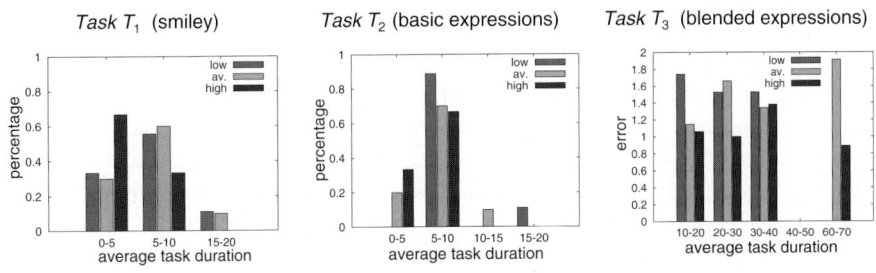

Fig. 6. Duration and error as a function of expertise

In the histogram for the third task (rightmost histogram in figure 6), the height of a bar represents the error of the blended faces realized by the subjects in comparison with the target face. Bars are grouped by time duration intervals as for the two other tasks. These histograms show that expert subjects are not quicker than non expert ones for task T_3, but they get better quality: average error for low or average experts is 1.67 and 1.40, and 1.15 for highly expert subjects. Incidentally, this histogram also shows that the slowest subjects do not perform significantly better than the fastest ones.

3.3   Subjective Evaluation

The questionnaire contained several fields in which subjects could write extended comments about the experiment. All but one of the subjects have positively rated their appreciation of the interface: 3 or 4 on a scale of 1 (very unpleasant) to 4 (very pleasant). Their appreciations concern the tactile interaction, and the naturalness and the softness of the correlation between kinesthetics and animation. They appreciate that the contact is soft and progressive: *natural, touch friendly, reactive, simple* are among the words used by the subjects to qualify the positive aspects of this interface. Users also appreciate the emotional transfer to the virtual avatars that make the smiley and the face more "human". Some of the subjects have even talked to the interface during T_3, rather kindly, such as *Come on! Close your eyes.*

The questionnaire asked the subjects whether the face was conveying expressions of emotions and whether they would have preferred it with another shape. They qualify the face as expressionless, calm, placid, quiet, passive, neutral... and have positive comments about the aesthetics of the interface. One of them finds that *it looks like an ancient divinity.* It confirms our hypothesis that a neutral face is appreciated by the users for that type of interface.

Some users feel uncomfortable with the interface, because it requires a tactile engagement. But for the subjects who accept to enter in such an "intimate" experience with the interface, the impression can become very pleasant as quoted by a 43 years old male subject: *The contact of fingers on a face is a particular gesture that we neither often nor easily make. [...] Luckily, this uncomfortable impression does not last very long. After a few trials, you feel like a sculptor working with clay...*

Depreciative comments concern the difficulty to control accurately the output of the system because of undesirable shadows on neighboring zones, and the smallness of the tactile head that makes the positioning of the fingers on capture holes difficult. Some subjects have however noticed the interest of the video capture by using distant positions of the hand for mild and blended expressions. Criticism also concerns the limits of the experimental setup: some users would have liked *to go a step further in the possibility of modifying the facial expressions* and control *an output device as innovative as the input interface.*

To sum up, depreciative comments concern mainly technical limitations of the interface that should be overcome by using gestures (sequences of hole occlusions) instead of static contacts. Positive comments concern mostly the perspectives for affective communication opened by this new type of interface.

4   Conclusion and Future Developments

The evaluation on the usability of the interface reported here shows that a head-shaped interface can be successfully used by expert and non-expert subjects for affective expressions. Comments in the questionnaire show that, for most of the users, this type of interaction is a very positive and pleasant experience.

Our future work on this interface will follow three complementary directions. At the technical level, Hidden Markov Models are currently implemented so that gestures can be recognized in addition to static interactions. Since tactile communication relies on a wide palette of caresses and contacts, it is necessary to capture pressure, speed, and directions of gestures. At the application level, we intend to design new experiments in which more than one subject will be involved in order to study the communicative properties of this interface in situations of intimate or social relationship. Last we will improve the quality of facial rendering to generate more realistic expressions [8].

Acknowledgement

Many thanks to Clarisse Beau, Vincent Bourdin, Laurent Pointal and Sébastien Rieublanc (LIMSI-CNRS) for their help in the design of the interface; Jean-Noël Montagné (Centre de Ressources Art Sensitif), Francis Bras, and Sandrine Chiri (Interface Z) for their help on sensitive interfaces; Catherine Pelachaud (Univ. Paris 8) for her help on ECAs and for her detailed comments on a draft version of this article. This work is supported by LIMSI-CNRS *Talking Head* action coordinated by Jean-Claude Martin.

References

1. Sundström, P., Ståhl, A., Höök, K.: In situ informants exploring an emotional mobile meassaging system in their everyday practice. Int. J. Hum. Comput. Stud. 65(4), 388–403 (2007) Special issue of IJHCS on Evaluating Affective Interfaces.
2. Hinckley, K., Pausch, R., Goble, J.C., Kassell, N.F.: Passive real-world interface props for neurosurgical visualization. In: CHI '94. Proceedings of the SIGCHI conference on Human factors in computing systems, pp. 452–458. ACM Press, New York (1994)
3. Paiva, A., Andersson, G., Höök, K., Mourão, D., Costa, M., Martinho, C.: Sentoy in FantasyA: Designing an affective sympathetic interface to a computer game. Personal Ubiquitous Comput. 6(5-6), 378–389 (2002)
4. Ostermann, J.: Face animation in MPEG-4. In: Pandzic, I.S., Forchheimer, R. (eds.) MPEG-4 Facial Animation, pp. 17–55. Wiley, Chichester, UK (2002)
5. Ekman, P., Friesen, W.V.: Facial action coding system: A technique for the measurement of facial movement. Consulting Psychologists Press, Palo Alto, CA, USA (1978)
6. Tsapatsoulis, N., Raouzaiou, A., Kollias, S., Crowie, R., Douglas-Cowie, E.: Emotion recognition and synthesis based on MPEG-4 FAPs. In: Pandzic, I.S., Forchheimer, R. (eds.) MPEG-4 Facial Animation, pp. 141–167. Wiley, Chichester, UK (2002)
7. Pelachaud, C.: Multimodal expressive embodied conversational agents. In: MULTIMEDIA '05. Proceedings of the 13th annual ACM international conference on Multimedia, pp. 683–689. ACM Press, New York (2005)
8. Albrecht, I.: Faces and Hands: Modeling and Animating Anatomical and Photorealistic Models with Regard to the Communicative Competence of Virtual Humans. Ph. D. Thesis, Universität des Saarlandes (2005)

SuperDreamCity: An Immersive Virtual Reality Experience That Responds to Electrodermal Activity

Doron Friedman[1], Kana Suji[2], and Mel Slater[3]

[1] Interdisciplinary Center, Herzliya, Israel
doronf@idc.ac.il
[2] Dream Products Co.
dreamproductsco@yahoo.co.uk
[3] ICREA-Universitat Politecnica de Catalunya, Spain
and Department of Computer Science, UCL
m.slater@cs.ucl.ac.uk

Abstract. In this paper we describe an artistic exhibition that took place in our highly-immersive virtual-reality laboratory. We have allowed visitors to explore a virtual landscape based on the content of night dreams, where the navigation inside the landscape was based on an online feedback from their electrodermal response. We analyze a subset of the physiology data captured from participants and describe a new method for analyzing dynamic physiological experiences based on hidden Markov models.

1 Introduction

This study is part of a research that assumes an experimental paradigm where a person is exposed to stimuli that induce physiological changes (such as changes in heart rate (HR), heart rate variability (HRV), electrodermal activity (EDA), and similar autonomous responses). A computer program monitors how the physiology changes over time and in response to sequences of visual stimuli. The automated decisions related to the presentation of the visual stimuli are planned to have some desired impact on the participant's physiological state.

Such research could be considered complementary to traditional biofeedback. "Classic" biofeedback involves measuring a subject's bodily processes such as blood pressure or galvanic skin response (GSR) and using a machine to convey this information to him or her in real-time in order to allow him or her to gain control over physical processes previously considered automatic [3,9]. Biofeedback thus has a number of therapeutic uses in helping people learn how to achieve and control positive mental states such as concentration or relaxation, and has been used with people with anxiety, depression and attention problems [19]. Our view is that we can now revisit traditional biofeedback taking into account advances in online signal processing, intelligent computation, and various types of

A. Paiva, R. Prada, and R.W. Picard (Eds.): ACII 2007, LNCS 4738, pp. 570–581, 2007.

feedback, such as, in this case, highly-immersive virtual reality (VR). Our approach is almost the inverse: in our case the machine is the one supposed to do the learning and adaptation, and not the person.

In this study we report on an early step where we integrated a highly immersive Cave-based experience with real-time feedback based on skin conductance [1]. While this was not a scientifically controlled experiment, we show how the results can be systematically analyzed.

2   Background

GSR, also sometimes called electrodermal activity (EDA), is measured by passing a small current through a pair of electrodes placed on the surface of the skin and measuring the conductivity level. Skin conductance is considered to be a function of the sweat gland activity and the skin's pore size. The real-time variation in conductance, which is the inverse of the resistance, is calculated. As a person becomes more or less stressed, the skin's conductance increases or decreases proportionally [1]. There are two measures associated with GSR: one is overall level, called the tonal level, which gives the overall level of arousal, and the other is skin conductance response (SCR), which gives arousal in response to specific events (or unknown random internal events). In our study we have used the tonal level.

The idea of closed-loop VR has already been addressed by the sci-art community. One of the classic VR art pieces of all times is Osmose [5], where the participants' experience depends on the analysis of their breathing. Another, more recent art piece related with body-centered interaction in VR include Traces by Simon Penny[1]. These art projects are highly influential in raising discussions regarding interface design practices. However, there is no attempt for any scientific analysis of the experience, in terms of the human-machine feedback loop, and no analysis of the data. Some interactive applications or games using biofeedback have proved useful for relaxation (as an example based on EEG see [10]).

We have come upon such man-machine loop issues in our recent studies in brain-computer interfaces (BCI) in highly-immersive VR [8,14]. Such BCI includes training human subjects to control a computer system by "thought", based on real-time analysis of electroencepalogram (EEG). It involves two complex, interdependent systems: the brain and the machine, and in order for the BCI to be successful they both need to learn. The solution typically adapted, is to allow each of the systems to learn in separate, while the other is kept constant [13]. The research proposed here similarly suggests studying this issue of mutual adaptation, but in a different context.

Picard [15] coined the term *affective computing*: this includes computers that both recognize and exhibit emotions. Picard, as well others in this area of research, have demonstrated devices based on real-time analysis of autonomic responses, such as: affective jewelry and accessories, affective toys, affective tutoring systems, computer responses to user frustration, and visualization of

---

[1] http://www.medienkunstnetz.de/works/traces

the user's emotional state [15]. Recognition of emotions is addressed by several means, physiological responses being one of them.

Bersak et al. coined the term *affective feedback*, which means that "the computer is an active intelligent participant in the biofeedback loop" [2]; where both player and game are affected by the actions of the other. Prendinger and his colleagues have developed and evaluated a closed-loop virtual agent that responds to users' emotions. The valence and intensity of emotions are recognized based on skin-conductance level and electromiography [17,18,16].

The so-called *affective loop* has also been described by Hook and colleagues; see for example [22]. It has been shown in systems like SenToy [12], eMoto [22], Affective Diary [11] and Brainboll [21] that it is indeed possible to involve users in affective loops, but that the design needs to be carefully crafted to the specific demands of the application functionality in order for the application to work.

3   The VR Experience as an Experiment

3.1   Scientific Objective

The objective of the study is to test whether the physiological state of a VR participant may be manipulated systematically over time, during a VR experience. In addition, we suggest methods for analyzing the data and inspecting whether the manipulation was achieved.

Such intelligent systems for physiological manipulation may be based on several computation paradigms.

Our approach in this paper is based on reinforcement loops – Such an approach would try to use positive and negative feedback loops; these were investigated as early as the middle of the twentieth century [23]. Positive loops may be used to drive an existing trend to an extreme, and negative loops may be used to extinguish existing trends.

Specifically, our assumption is that we can induce positive feedback loops by leading participants into positive spaces when they are relaxed and into negative spaces when they are stressed (or aroused). If the system is successful, we would see two types of patterns: in one case participants will mostly visit positive spaces, and their overall GSR levels would remain flat, or even decrease. In the other case, participants would mostly visit negative places and their overall GSR level will increase significantly during the experience.

This assumption can be broken into two hypotheses:

1. Negative places would have a significantly different impact on GSR tonal level than positive places – specifically, the GSR level would increase after negative places and decrease after positive places; and
2. An analysis of the dynamics of transitions between positive and negative places would reveal the existence of positive feedback loops.

3.2   The VR System

The study was carried out in a four-sided ReaCTor system that is similar to a Cave [4]. The UCL Cave is a 2.8x3x3 meter room with stereo projection on three walls and on the floor. The participant wears light-weight shutter glasses and an Intersense IS900 wireless head-tracker. The result is that the participant is free to move around the room and is (almost) surrounded by the virtual landscape.

3.3   The Virtual Environment

The content of the virtual environment (VE) is based on work by the second author, who is a London-based artist. She is in the (fictional) business of buying dreams: she pays people one Great British Pound each so that they tell her about their night dreams. Then she models the dreams in 3D, and adds them into DreamCity – an online version, where people are able to browse among other people's dreamscapes (http://www.dreamproductsco.com).

For the London Node (Networked, Open, Distributed Event) media-art festival, March 2006, we decided to create a unique version of DreamCity, called SuperDreamCity. First, rather then displaying the models on a desktop computer, we adapted DreamCity for the Cave. Second, we decided that the participants will explore the dreamscape using their physiological responses.

For SuperDreamCity the second author selected several "dreams" into one VE where all the dreamscapes were randomly scattered around (see Figure 1); we have only used static models in this version. Most of the dream sites includes sound files that played when the participant was in the site vicinity. The VE included a low-volume background music playing in a loop, for the purpose of "atmosphere building" – this was a dream-like electronic music (by musician Laurie Anderson).[2]

3.4   Real-Time Physiology

We wanted to allow the participants to explore the VE in a way that would depend on their internal bodily responses to the environment, as reflected in their autonomous nervous-system responses. We have selected GSR as a single measurement, since this is easily measured by a small sensor placed on two fingers, which is easy and quick to fit; this was important as we were attempting a quick turnover of visitors. We have used the raw GSR values (the tonal GSR level) as a single feature in affecting the navigation.

We have carried out previous work in real-time neurophysiology in the Cave [8]. It was relatively straightforward to convert the system to use for real-time GSR. In this case we used the g.Mobilab system (g.Tec, Austria), which includes sensors, a small amplifier, and software. GSR was sampled at 32 Hz, and the signal was obtained from electrodes on two fingers. The g.Mobilab software is

---

[2] A video is available online in http://www.cs.ucl.ac.uk/staff/d.friedman/sdc/ sdc.mov

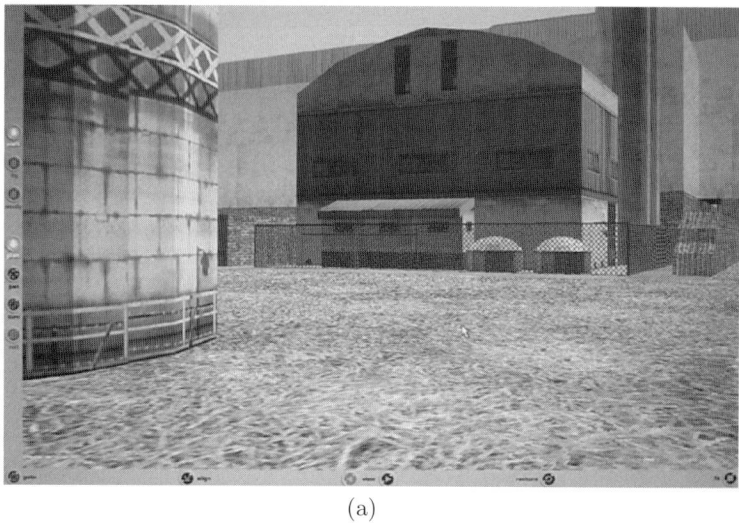

(a)

(b)

Fig. 1. (a) A screenshot of an industrial area from a dream, as viewed online. (b) A participant in the VR Cave experiencing the same industrial area in SuperDreamCity. Note that this image is for illustration: in the actual experience the participant would not be holding the navigation wand (as they navigate based on GSR) and the image would be stereoscopic.

easy to modify – it includes a Matlab/Simulink model for the device. We have used Simulink to extract the raw GSR value, pass it to a dynamically-linked library (DLL) and over the network using the Virtual Reality Peripheral Network (VRPN)[3]. On the Cave Irix system, a VRPN client would intercept the raw GSR values and feed them into the VR application. The VR software was implemented on top of the DIVE software [7,20]. The DIVE application would then implement the navigation logic based on the real-time GSR value (this is scripted in TCL).

3.5 Method

For the show, the artist re-created the VE with 20 of her own dreams modeled in 3D, 10 having positive associations and 10 having negative associations. As an example of a positive dream consider an amusement park, and as a negative dream consider industrial areas. The emotions were expressed with choice of colors and sound effects. In this case the emotional interpretation of the dreams was given by the artist or by the dreamer; clearly, in a controlled scientific experiment, this emotional interpretation needs to be validated.

Rather than a low-level mapping of GSR into navigation, we have opted for a high-level mapping. We decided to split the experience into stages. First, all subjects find themselves floating over one of the positive dream sites. Then, in each stage of the experience they start floating from one dream site towards another site. The decision to what site to navigate is based on the trend of the GSR[4].

For the art exhibition, we decided to explore positive feedback loops, i.e., the system would try to reinforce the participant's physiological trend. If the GSR value increased from the previous section, a random negative dream site was targeted. If overall GSR decreased, a random positive site was selected. Navigation speed was also modified — for every selection of a negative site the speed was increased by 10% of the baseline speed, and, correspondingly, for every selection of a positive site the speed decreased by 10%. Thus, our expectation was that this VE would create a positive feedback loop with the participant – i.e., we expected that some participants will keep visiting negative sites, which would increase their GSR, so that overall they would mostly visit negative sites and become increasingly stressed throughout the experience. We expected that for other subjects there would be a relaxation loop, such that their GSR would gradually decrease as they keep visiting positive sites and floating in a slower and more relaxed fashion. In the next session we explore how this was evaluated scientifically, and report the results.

4   Experimental Procedure

Our assumption was that, under some conditions, an exhibition open to the public can serve as a scientific experiment (for another example see [6]); in the least case, the data collected can serve as useful insight for future research.

---

[3] http://www.cs.unc.edu/Research/vrpn/

[4] In states of increased excitement people sweat more, which should result in a higher GSR as compared with a relaxed state.

The London Node Festival took place over a whole month, included dozens of events in different locations around the city, and advertised online. We have advertised our exhibition, in our VR lab, to be open to the public for a few hours each day over three consecutive days (over the weekend), and required people to register in advance online. Each registered person received a time slot to show up in the lab (with 20 minutes allocated per person).

During the exhibition there were at least three people working in the lab. One person was necessary to fit the GSR device and operate the systems. Another person stayed outside the lab space, and managed the queue of people. Finally, the artist greeted each person into the experiment. She was dressed as a businesswoman, handed them her business card, explained to them about her (fictional) business buying dreams, and explained to them that they are about to experience a dreamscape that would respond to their physiology.

When participants were led into the Cave room they were fitted with the GSR sensor and goggles, and placed inside the dark Cave. they were instructed to wait there. Then there was a period of at least 60 seconds, after which the VR experience began – this duration was used for measuring GSR baseline. Participants stayed in the Cave for varying durations of 5-15 minutes, based on the queue outside. Most participants loved the experience and would have stayed more if they were allowed.

5   Results

During the three exhibition days we had 35 participants in the Cave. We collected data for all participants, but most of the sessions had to be discarded. Because this was an art exhibition, participants behaved in quite different ways than subjects would behave in a typical scientific experiment in our Cave. Some of them talked a lot, moved a lot, tried to jump, or even, in one case, lie down on the Cave floor. In some cases we had a long queue outside and had to allow more than one person into the Cave. All these sessions were discarded. Out of the remaining sessions, 15 sessions included valid GSR data (these were most of the "good" sessions), and these were analyzed as described below.

Each session is characterized by a number of events – an event is the point in time when the system decided to navigate into another dream site, either negative or positive. The duration elapsing between two events varies, as it depends on varying navigation speeds and on variable distances among the pairs of dream sites. The duration between events was always at least 20 seconds, sometimes up to one minute. Thus each session included a different number of events, ranging from 7 to 35.

First, we want to test whether positive dreamscapes affect GSR in a different way than negative dreamscapes and examine the trends in GSR tonal level around the events. This is tested using an analysis of covariance (ANOCOVA). We take the time around the events (from 20 seconds before the event to 20 seconds after the event) to be the predictor x, the GSR level to be the response variable y, and a binary variable c for the dream category. If our hypothesis is correct then we expect the coefficient of the positive dreams to be significant with a negative slope, the coefficient of the negative dreams to be significant with a positive slope, and the Anova value for $x \cdot c$ to be significant.

A case by case study reveals that the hypothesis was correct for 5 out of the 15 subjects: cases where the slope was significantly different between the two events, and the trend for negative dreams was higher than for positive dreams (this includes cases such as in Figure 2, where both trends were decreasing, but the positive dreams decreased faster). For 9 subjects the results were not significant, and for one subject the results were significant, but they were the opposite of our prediction: the positive dreams resulted in an increase in GSR and the negative dreams in a decrease.

After normalizing the GSR values for all subjects, we can perform the same analysis for the data taken from all subjects together. Our hypothesis is not supported, i.e., the experience, taken over all subjects, did not cause increase and decrease in GSR levels as predicted.

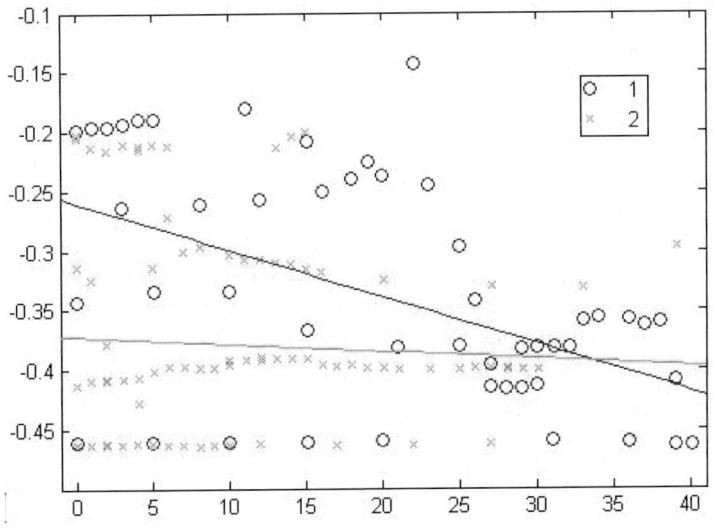

Fig. 2. The analysis of variance plot for one subject, showing GSR as a function of time around the events. In this case we see that both event categories resulted in a decreasing trend of GSR, but positive (blue) decreased more than negative (green). For this subject the difference is significant. Note that we do not care about the intercept of the regression line, only the slope (since each event starts in a different level). To make the results apprehensible each is the average of 50 GSR samples.

Our main interest is in the dynamics of the experience. Since the first hypothesis was not fully supported we did not expect to find the dynamics we expected, but we still describe how we suggest to analyze such data. We model each session as a stochastic process over state transitions. There are two states: P (positive)

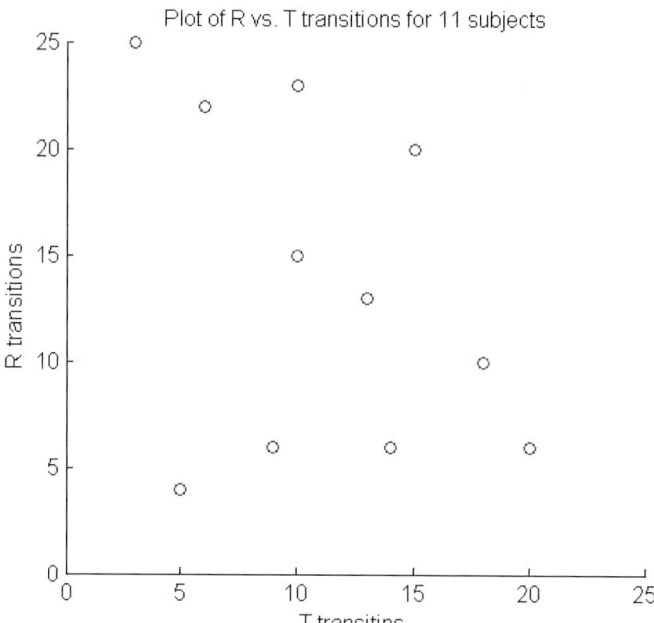

Fig. 3. A plot of the ratio of the state-preserving transitions (PP and NN) vs. the state-change transitions (PN and NP) for 11 out of 15 subjects (for four subjects the number of transitions in the session was too small). We see that the scatter seems uniform inside the lower left triangle part of the space, as expected from a random process. If, as we expected, the experience would have had a positive-loop impact, we would expect the points to be concentrated near the axes of the diagrams. If the experience would have enforced negative feedback loops we would have expected the points to be around the diagonal $y = x$.

and N (negative), according to the two types of dreams. Accordingly, there are four types of transition types: PP, PN, NP, and NN. Furthermore, we can distinguish between two types of transitions: T transitions that keep the current trend (NN and PP) and R transitions – trend reversal transitions (NP and PN).

Figure 3 illustrates that, indeed, the state transitions seem random. More formally, the data from each session can be modeled as a hidden Markov model (HMM): we observe a sequence of emissions, and our goal is to recover the state information from the observed data.

Our HMM includes two states: P and N. We know the emission matrix for the model: when the system is in state P there is a probability of 0.1 for events $1 - 10$ to occur and a probability of 0 for events $11 - 20$ to occur. Conversely, when the system is state N there is a probability of 0 for events $1 - 10$ to occur and a probability of 0.1 for events $11 - 20$ to occur. For each session we know the state path and the emission sequence. Based on these parameters we can estimate the transition matrix, which is the only unknown parameter, for each session. For each transition from state S_1 to state S_2 the estimation of the transition probability is given by the number of transitions from S_1 to S_2 in the sequence divided by the total number of transitions from S_1 in the sequence.

In our case there are two states only, so the transition matrix has two free parameters: if we denote by α the probability for a transition from P to P then clearly the probability for moving from P to N is $1 - \alpha$; similarly, we denote by β the probability for a transition from N to P and then the probability for a transition from N to N is $1 - \beta$.

Thus, For each session we have two observations, resulting in two response variables: α and β. In our case α is in the range $0 - 0.8$ with mean 0.38 and β is in the range $0.25 - 1$ with mean 0.63^5. Most importantly, an Anova test reveals that for both variables we cannot reject the null hypothesis, i.e., we have an indication that both α and β are random. We note that trying to estimate the emission matrix of our model does result in a rejection of the null hypothesis, i.e., the probabilities for selecting an event based on a state are not arbitrary. This indicates that our analysis should have revealed a pattern in the transition matrix if there was one.

6   Discussion

We are interested in studying the dynamics of human physiology when participants are placed inside immersive environments that respond to this physiology. We have described how this dynamics was implemented and studied in the scope of an artistic exhibition.

There is growing interest in such affective-loop systems, for various applications, including training, psychological treatment and entertainment. However, the dynamics of such closed-loop systems is rarely studied in a systematic way. It would be of both theoretic and practical interest to have a better understanding of the way media systems, providing sensory inputs, may affect people's autonomous responses over time, especially in the context of a closed-loop system.

One of our main lessons from this study is that while it is now feasible to create this type of biofeedback application, even using highly-immersive VR, it is not easy to create a meaningful experience that fully exploits the possibilities of biofeedback in highly-immersive VR. In our case our analysis revealed that the feedback loop did not take place as expected (unless, possibly, for 5 out of 15 subjects whose data was analyzed). For most participants the biofeedback part of the experience was probably meaningless, in the sense that the experience had no systematic effect on the participant's physiology. This is probably the case in many similar art projects, but these do not even report the results, let alone analyze the data.

There are several lessons and ways to go forward. For example, raw GSR is not necessarily the best feature to use for such neurophysiological experiences. It is probably better to use SCR (the number and/or amplitude of peaks in GSR as a response to a new stimulus), heart rate, or some combination of these features.

---

[5] The fact that $\alpha + \beta \cong 1$ is only a coincidence.

As a result of this study, we are currently revisiting the same questions, using a similar approach, in the context of a more scientific methodology. Obviously, such experiments would first validate the effects of the selected stimuli, before studying their dynamics. We suggest studying such experiences, based on real-time physiology, and analyze the degree of success using HMMs.

Acknowledgements

This work has been supported by the European Union FET project PRESENC-CIA, IST-2006-27731. We would like to thank David Swapp and other members of the VECG lab in UCL for their support. We would also like to thank Christoph Guger for his support with the gMobilab system.

References

1. Andreassi, J.L.: Psychophysiology: Human Behavior & Physiological Response. Laurence Elbaum Associates (2000)
2. Bersak, D., McDarby, G., Augenblick, N., McDarby, P., McDonnell, D., McDonal, B., Karkun, R.: Biofeedback using an immersive competitive environment. In: On-line Proceedings for the Designing Ubiquitous Computing Games Workshop, Ubi-comp 2001 (2001)
3. Blanchard, E.B., Young, L.D.: Clinical applications of biofeedback training: A review of evidence. Archives of General Psychiatry 30, 573–589 (1974)
4. Cruz-Neira, C., Sandin, D.J., DeFanti, T.A., Kenyon, R.V., Hart, J.C.: The CAVE: Audio visual experience automatic virtual environment. Comm. ACM 35(6), 65–72 (1992)
5. Davies, C., Harrison, J.: Osmose: Towards broadening the aesthetics of virtual reality. ACM Computer Graphics [special issue on Virtual Reality] 30(4), 25–28 (1996)
6. Eng, K., Klein, D., Babler, A., Bernardet, U., Blanchard, M., Costa, M., Delbruck, T., Douglas, R.J., Hepp, K., Manzolli, J., Mintz, M., Roth, F., Rutishauser, U., Wassermann, K., Whatley, A.M., Wittmann, A., Wyss, R., Verschure, P.F.M.J.: Design for a brain revisited: The neuromorphic design and functionality of the interactive space Ada. Reviews in the Neurosiences 14, 145–180 (2003)
7. Frecon, E., Smith, G., Steed, A., Stenius, M., Stahl, O.: An overview of the COVEN platform. Presence: Teleoperators and Virtual Environments 10(1), 109–127 (2001)
8. Friedman, D., Leeb, R., Guger, C., Steed, A., Pfertscheller, G., Slater, M.: Navigating virtual reality by thought: What is it like? Presence: Teleoperators and Virtual Environments 16(1), 100–110 (2007)
9. Gaarder, K.R., Montgomery, P.: Scientific foundation of biofeedback therapy. In: Gaarder, K.R., Montgomery, P. (eds.) Clinical Biofeedback, pp. 3–30. Williams & Willkins (1981)
10. Hjelm, S.I., Eriksson, E., Browall, C.: BRAINBALL - Using brain activity for cool competition. In: Proc. First Nordic Conf. on Human-Computer Interaction 2000 (2000)
11. Lindstrom, M., Stahl, A., Hook, K., Sundstrom, P., Laaksolahti, J., Combetto, M., Taylor, A., Bresin, R.: Affective diary - Designing for bodily expressiveness and self-reflection. In: Proc. ACM SIGCHI Conf. Computer-Human Interaction, ACM Press, New York (2006)

12. Paiva, A., Chaves, R., Piedade, M., Bullock, A., Andersson, G., Hook, K.: Sentoy: A tangible interface to control the emotions of a synthetic character. In: AAMAS '03: Proceedings of the second international joint conference on Autonomous agents and multiagent systems, pp. 1088–1089 (2003)
13. Pfurtscheller, G., Neuper, C.: Motor imagery and direct brain computer communication. Proc. of the IEEE 89(7), 1123–1134 (2001)
14. Pfurtshceller, G., Leeb, R., Keinrath, C., Friedman, D., Neuper, C., Guger, C., Slater, M.: Walking from thought. Brain Research 1071, 145–152 (2006)
15. Picard, R.W.: Affective Computing. MIT Press, Cambridge (1997)
16. Prendinger, H., Becker, C., Ishizuka, M.: A study in users' physiological response to an empathic interface agent. Int'l J. Humanoid Robotics 3(3), 371–391 (2006)
17. Prendinger, H., Ishizuka, M.: Human physiology as a basis for designing and evaluating affective communication with life-like characters. IEICE Trans. Inf. & Syst. E88-D(11), 2453–2460 (2005)
18. Prendinger, H., Morib, J., Ishizuka, M.: Using human physiology to evaluate subtle expressivity of a virtual quizmaster in a mathematical game. Int. J. Human-Computer Studies 62, 231–245 (2005)
19. Schwartz, M.S.: Biofeedback: A Practitioner's Guide. Guilford Press, New York (1995)
20. Steed, A., Mortensen, J., Frecon, E.: Spelunking: Experiences using the DIVE system on CAVE-like platforms. In: Immersive Projection Technologies and Virtual Environments, vol. 2, pp. 153–164. Springer, Heidelberg (2001)
21. Sundstrom, P., Stahl, A., Hook, K. In: situ informants exploring an emotional mobile meassaging system in their everyday practice. Int. J. of Human-Computer Studies
22. Sundstrom, P., Stahl, A., Hook, K.: emoto: affectively involving both body and mind. In: CHI '05: CHI '05 extended abstracts on Human factors in computing systems, pp. 2005–2008 (2005)
23. Wiener, N.: Cybernetics, or Control and Communication in the Animal and the Machine. MIT Press, Cambridge (1961)

Stoop to Conquer: Posture and Affect Interact to Influence Computer Users' Persistence

Hyung-il Ahn, Alea Teeters, Andrew Wang, Cynthia Breazeal,
and Rosalind Picard

MIT Media Laboratory,
20 Ames Street, Cambridge, MA 02139, USA
{hiahn,alea,zephyrus,cynthiab,picard}@media.mit.edu

Abstract. RoCo, a novel robotic computer, has the capability to move its monitor in subtly expressive ways that respond to and promote its user's postural movement. Motivated by Riskind's "Stoop to conquer" research where it was found that postures congruous to the type of outcome a person received (e.g. slumping following a failure or sitting up proudly following a success) led to significantly better performance in a subsequent cognitive task than incongruous postures (e.g. sitting up proudly following a failure or slumping following success), we performed two experiments where RoCo was used to manipulate its user's posture. Our results show that people tend to be more persistent on a subsequent task when RoCo's posture is congruous to their affective state than when it is incongruous. Our study is the first to show that a computer's "pose," congruous or incongruous to a user's affective state, can influence factors such as persistence in problem solving tasks.

Keywords: User Studies, Robotic Computer (RoCo), Affective Interaction, Posture and Emotion, Human-Robot Interaction.

1 Introduction

Everyone knows that how you feel can influence what you think and do. However, many people do not know that there is a growing body of findings from psychology, cognitive science, and neuroscience where more subtle affective states have been shown to systematically influence cognition [10,12,13,19]. In particular, a number of studies have explored the effect of body posture on affect and cognition [16,17,5,21]. An example is the theory in Riskind's "stoop to conquer" research [16,17], where it was found that incongruous postures, such as slumping after a success, negatively affected subsequent performance, while congruous postures, such as slumping after a failure, helped to mitigate the effects of failing.

Motivated by Riskind's "stoop to conquer" research, we performed two experiments examining the interaction of posture and affect on persistence, creativity, and comfort, and report the persistence effects here. While Riskind's experiments were conducted over 22 years ago with pencil, paper and directly human-manipulated postures, we modified the experiment, adapting it to computer users, whose posture

A. Paiva, R. Prada, and R.W. Picard (Eds.): ACII 2007, LNCS 4738, pp. 582–593, 2007.

can be indirectly influenced either by the position of a static monitor, or by one that can move smoothly, like the new RoCo.

This paper is organized as follows. First we present a brief description of the new RoCo robotic computer platform to motivate this new desktop technology that moves and can get people to shift their posture naturally while working. Next we offer a summary of relevant psychological literature with respect to body, affect, and cognition interaction effects that informs and guides our work. We then present two novel user studies adapting Riskind's experiment to the RoCo platform. Finally we discuss the findings and conclusions, and suggest future directions.

2   RoCo: A New Robotic Computer Platform

RoCo is designed to lie within a continuum that might be loosely described as having ordinary fixed desktop computers at one end, and humanoid robots at the other end. In between is a huge unexplored space, where one can begin to animate the things in the office environment that usually do not move on their own: computers, chairs, and more. With increasing interest in promoting healthy activity, we are starting with the desktop computer, considering how it might move in ways that get the person using it to move more. RoCo was carefully designed to look like an ordinary computer, but to move in ways that are completely paradigm changing. RoCo has no face or body that attempts to evoke humanoid or animal characteristics: it has a regular monitor, keyboard, and box, which are sessile. However, it also has motors that give it quiet, smooth, expressive, articulated movement.

The physical RoCo robot has five degrees of freedom (DoFs) that manipulate its mechanical "neck" with a LCD screen as its "face" and "head." See Figure 1. Two DoFs move the mechanical neck (base yaw and base pitch) and three DoFs (head yaw, head pitch, and head roll) move the LCD display. These five degrees allow RoCo to perform a wide variety of simple motions, including nodding, shaking its head, and leaning forward. The motions happen at life-like speeds, and thus can implement a wide variety of immediacy behaviors. For example, if you lean toward RoCo, perhaps to read something tiny on the screen, it could meet you halfway. At the same time, we are designing RoCo with sensors to monitor your facial and postural movements so that it does not move in ways that distract you. Inspired by examining how and when humans move naturally, we are currently aiming to have

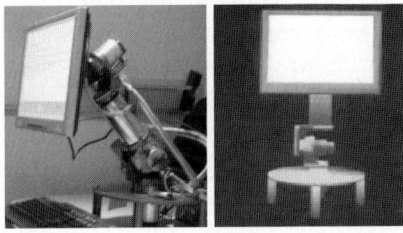

Fig. 1. RoCo: a robotic computer (left) and its graphical simulator for designing new behaviors (right)

RoCo hold very still while you are attentive to the screen, but to look for natural breaks to maximize your movement without distracting or annoying you. For example, if you have been slumping for a while, and then turn away your gaze, then when you return your gaze, you might find RoCo has "stretched" upward, subtly encouraging you to adjust your posture upward. However, as we show in this paper, there is more to consider than your attention and your posture.

In this paper we wish to isolate how its posture interacts with and influences the person using it. In fact, for this paper, we will pre-set RoCo's postures so that the novelty of a computer moving does not enter into our results. We do this as the first set of experiments with this new technology, to carefully control the variables influencing the outcomes.

3 Body, Affect and Cognition Interaction

3.1 Affect and Cognition Interactions

Studies from psychology, cognitive science, and neuroscience indicate that affect and emotional experience interact with cognition in significant and useful ways. Current understanding is that emotion plays a useful role in regulating learning, creative problem solving, and decision making. For example, Isen shows that a positive mood promotes a tendency toward greater creativity and flexibility in negotiation and in problem solving, as well as more efficiency and thoroughness in decision making [10]. These effects have been found across many different groups, ages, and positive affect manipulations. Other specific influences of affect on cognition have also been found for negative affective states, e.g., Schwartz argues that being in a sad mood enables better performance on certain kinds of analytic tests [19].

Emotion not only influences cognition, but it also interacts with information in the environment in ways that can enhance or hinder your ability to perform. Cliff Nass and colleagues, while trying to decide if a voice in the automobile driver's environment should sound subdued and calm or energetic and upbeat, ran an experiment trying both kinds of voices [13]. Importantly, they also looked at the two conditions where drivers were either upset or happy (having just viewed disturbing or funny films.) In a total of four conditions, the happy or upset drivers drove in a simulator with either an energetic voice or a subdued voice talking to them and asking them questions. On multiple measures of driving performance and cognitive performance, happy drivers did better overall than upset drivers. But there was also an important and interesting interaction, highly relevant to the work in this paper. When the voice was congruous with the driver's state (energetic/upbeat for happy drivers, subdued/calm for upset drivers) then performance was significantly better than in the two incongruous conditions. The worst performance of all four conditions occurred when the upset drivers were paired with the energetic and upbeat voice. It is this kind of effect – where performance is improved by mood congruent interaction – that we explore in this paper. However in this paper, we induce the congruence condition in an entirely new way.

3.2 Body and Affect Interactions

According to Riskind's [16] "appropriateness hypothesis", slumped or upright physical postures are not just passive indicators of mental states but can reciprocally affect the mental states and behavior. The results suggest that "inappropriate" postures, such as slumping after a positive success, can undermine subsequent motivation and feelings of control, while "appropriate" postures, such as slumping after a failure, help to mitigate the effects of failing. His findings suggest that it is therefore not beneficial after a failure to sit with chin up as if proud, despite that people often tell children to do that.

In Riskind's original experiment, all the subjects were first asked to perform a cognitive task (e.g. a tracing puzzle task). The affective manipulation (positive/ negative affect) was handled by the experimenter who informed the subject of his or her "score" on the task. A high score (success) was designed to elicit a positive affect in the subject, while a poor score (failure) to elicit a negative affect. After this first task, the subjects were escorted to a different room and assisted to take one of three postures reflecting appropriateness (neutral/slumped/upright) under the false pretense of a biofeedback experiment. The subjects were required to hold this posture for 8 minutes before relaxing it and performing a subsequent cognitive task (e.g. additional puzzle tracing tasks). Riskind found that subjects in incongruous postures (stooped/slumped following success, upright following failure), felt like they had less control, showed less motivation in persistence tasks, and reported higher depression than subjects in congruous postures. His study suggested that a slumped versus upright posture orientation can guide and moderate information processing and responses to positive and negative mood-relevant stimuli.

4   Our Purpose, Hypothesis and Predictions

In this paper, we explore whether a computer's "posture" can influence its user's subsequent posture, and if the congruence of the user's body state with their affective state during a task leads to improved task measures, such as persistence in problem solving. This research serves as a baseline study to investigate RoCo's ability to manipulate both the user's posture and the user's cognitive and affective state, illuminating the capabilities of this new technology. The key question, therefore, is how we design new technologies to beneficially influence the interactions between a human user's body, affective, and cognitive states. We wish not only to provide an ergonomic experience, but also to foster healthful computer usage and improved task outcomes.

Our study expands on the appropriateness hypothesis [17], predicting that congruous posture guides an individual towards self-regulating behaviors while incongruous posture leads to self-defeating behavior. Taking advantage of the unique RoCo research platform, our experiment introduces a different posture manipulation method that allows the subject to perform dependent measure tasks on a computer while in the manipulated posture. Thus, while Riskind measured the effect of a prior posture on a subsequent cognitive task, we can now measure the effect of the posture concurrent with the task. Our prediction is that RoCo will be an effective agent for manipulating posture and inducing the "stoop to conquer" effect.

In Riskind's original experiment, subjects were asked to either slump or sit upright under the false pretense of a biofeedback experiment. In his study, a human experimenter was responsible for direct posture manipulation. While this kind of manipulation is useful for detecting the "stoop to conquer" effect, it is not practical in real applications that aim to utilize this effect in a more natural way. However, when a user works on the RoCo platform, by changing RoCo's posture, we have been able to get RoCo to subtly lure the user into a target posture without seriously interrupting his or her workflow. While the postures are not always perfectly held (see below) for the duration of the experiment, there is still a significant influence. Also, in our experiment, since RoCo is responsible for posture manipulation instead of a human experimenter, this change makes the manipulation significantly more subtle and unobtrusive than in the Riskind experiment.

5 Experiments and Results

5.1 Experiment 1

This experiment measured persistence on a helplessness task, creativity on a word association task, and general spatial cognition on a puzzle task as a function of congruous and incongruous postures following affect manipulation [3, 20]. In this paper we will focus on the results about persistence. The results of other dependent measures can be found in our previous publication [3].

Subjects. Seventy-one naive subjects were recruited from our school and the surrounding area. Subjects were given a $10 gift certificate to Amazon.com as compensation for their participation. In this study there were six control conditions each of which involved a mood manipulation (success / failure) and one of RoCo's posture states (slumped / neutral / upright). Subjects were assigned to one of the six conditions based on the order that they signed up to participate in the study.

Preliminaries. When subjects arrived they were first greeted by the experimenter then led to a standard PC. The experimenter read the following standard set of instructions aloud to the subject: "Please be seated. In front of you is a standard computer setup with mouse, keyboard, monitor and a pen tablet for use in the tracing puzzles. You may arrange these components on the desk any way you like. Please read the instructions carefully as you go. The height of the chair is adjustable with a lever underneath the seat. I will be outside the curtains, if you have any questions or get confused, but in general, please try do as much on your own as possible." The experimenter then left the area while the subject was shown a two minute video clip previously shown to induce neutral affect [18].

Success-Failure Manipulation. Half of the six conditions involved inducing a feeling of success, while the other half involved inducing a feeling of failure. This was accomplished as follows. Subjects were given a series of four tracing puzzles to solve. They had two minutes to solve each puzzle. To solve a puzzle, the subject must trace over the design without lifting a pen from the puzzle or retracing any lines. In this case, the puzzles were presented on a standard LCD screen and pen tracing is done with a computer pen and tablet input device. The puzzles used are the same set used by Riskind [16] in his studies as well as by Glass and Singer [7]. To create a success condition, all four puzzles were solvable. Generally each subject was able to solve at least three out of the four. Unsolved puzzles were usually the result of not carefully reading the instructions beforehand or difficulty using the pen and tablet interface. Regardless of how the subject actually performed, a results chart was displayed and subjects were told they scored an 8 out of 10. For the failure condition, the first and last puzzles were insolvable. The sense of failure was further reinforced by displaying the same results chart as in the success condition, except in this case they were told that they scored a 3 out of 10.

Posture Manipulation. Following the success-failure manipulation, the subject's chair, the height of which was adjusted by each subject for comfortable "neutral" viewing using the first PC, was rolled over a few feet to RoCo, the position of which had already been preset to slumped, upright, or neutral, relative to the first PC. These positions are shown in Figure 2. Notice that they are not quite the same as can be obtained with the typical degrees of freedom on a desktop monitor, although people certainly are capable of slumping or sitting up straight in front of an ordinary desktop monitor. The poses of RoCo are somewhat exaggerated to more strongly encourage sitting up or slumping relative to the neutral position. The subject, while seated in the same calibrated-height chair, was then asked to perform another series of puzzles, this time on RoCo. The subject was video taped as a manipulation check.

Fig. 2. RoCo's postures: neutral (left), slumped (center), upright (right)

Dependent Measures. The experiment examined three dependent measures: persistence, spatial cognition, and creativity. Here we will report on the persistence.

Insolvable Tracing Task to Test Persistence: The subject was given four mathematically insolvable tracing puzzles with a time limit of two minutes for each. This task assumes that the fewer the number of tries in the allotted time, the lower the subject's tolerance for a frustrating task. Some of the puzzles are the same as those used in Riskind's original study. Additional puzzles were created by transforming some solvable into insolvable.

Debriefing. Following the dependent measure tests, each subject was given a full debriefing. As a check on the success-failure manipulation, subjects were asked how well they thought they performed in part one. All subjects in the failure manipulation responded with answers like "not well", "below average", and "ok", suggesting that the manipulation was successful. Similarly, most subjects in the success case responded with answers such as "well" and "above average". Four subjects in the success condition who had trouble with the tracing puzzles in part one reported that they did not do well. Their data were omitted since the manipulation was not successful. Following the manipulation check, the details of the study were disclosed including the impossibility of some of the tracing puzzles and the fabricated test results in part one. We learned that four subject knew the mathematical rule for solvability ahead of time, enabling them to distinguish solvable from insolvable puzzles; the data for these four subjects also had to be dropped, leaving 63 subjects with valid data for analysis in the persistence task (Tables 2 and 3 and Fig. 3 below).

Main Results. 1. *RoCo posture's influence on the user posture:* Separately from the analysis on task persistence, an outside hypothesis-blind person coded the changing user posture for video data collected from 61 of the 71 subjects. This number differs from the one above because of technicalities with data collection (7 videos were missing and in 3 the subjects were not completely visible) and because the interest here is mainly on the interaction between Roco's posture and the user's posture, regardless of any manipulation. Based on the states of the chin, shoulder and back of the user, the coder classified the user posture into three basic states (Slumped / Neutral / Upright) every 30 seconds. The video analysis shows that RoCo's posture is strongly associated with the user's posture (See Table 1). The most frequently occurring posture state during the subsequent tasks was used for counting the user posture in these tables. Most subjects (about 70% of all subjects) tended to keep the dominant posture for over 80% of the task time. Also, about 15% of all subjects changed the posture state every 5~7 minutes. 2. *Persistence on Task:* As predicted, the two-way analysis of variance (ANOVA) on the persistence on the insolvable puzzles data (summarized in Tables 2 and 3 and shown in Figure 3) did reveal a statistically significant interaction effect, $F(2, 57) = 4.1$, $p < 0.05$. Further simple effects analysis by success-failure outcome revealed that success subjects exhibited more persistence when they used RoCo in its upright position ($M = 11.97$) after their success than when they used RoCo in its neutral position ($M = 8.32$), or in its slumped position ($M = 8.15$), $F(2, 57) = 7$, $p < 0.01$, where M is the mean number of tracing attempts. However, unlike in Riskind's study, failure subjects showed no statistical difference across postures, $F(2, 57) = 0.1$. We address this in the discussion and in Experiment 2. Also, there were no main effects for either the success-failure or the posture manipulations, $F(2, 57) < 2$, $p < 0.2$ and $F(2, 57) < 3$, $p < 0.07$ respectively.

Table 1. RoCo posture's influence on the user posture (for 61 subjects, the number of subjects are shown)

RoCo / User	Slumped	Neutral	Upright
Slumped	16	6	3
Neutral	6	10	0
Upright	0	0	20

Table 2. (Success condition). Average number of tracing attempts (for 30 subjects).

Groups	Slumped	Neutral	Upright
N	10	11	9
Average	8.15	8.32	11.97
SD	2.43	3.50	3.26

Table 3. (Failure condition). Average number of tracing attempts (for 33 subjects).

Groups	Slumped	Neutral	Upright
N	12	10	11
Average	8.33	8.75	8.41
SD	2.59	1.65	1.79

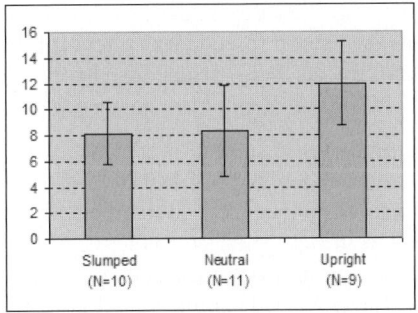 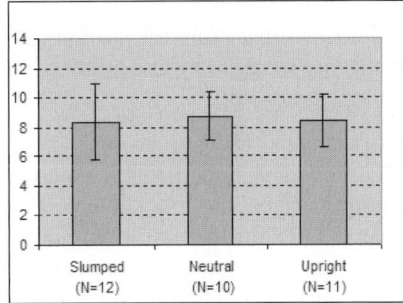

Fig. 3. Average number of tracing attempts: success (left) and failure (right) conditions (error bars show the standard deviation)

Discussion. We adapted a number of factors from Riskind's original study to work with RoCo, which may explain why our results differ for the failure condition. In Riskind's study, subjects were taken to a separate room and told to hold the assigned posture for approximately eight minutes under the pretense of a biofeedback experiment. They then performed the second set of tasks without controlling for posture. However, in our study, the user is free to adopt any posture as long as he or she can still read the screen. The video footage shows that users seemed to adjust their posture, particularly while sitting back and thinking about possible solutions. They tended to move more in the slumped conditions where they reported lower comfort (especially the failure-slumped condition, which can also foster a sense of malaise). While thinking, the primary posture manipulation was relaxed. Thus, our subjects who encountered the slumped condition of RoCo did not slump as consistently as Riskind's subjects did, as his were directly forced to hold the slumped position for 8 minutes, without moving. In sum, one possible explanation for why we are seeing the positive-upright effect but not the "negative-stooped" effect in our study may be that subjects did not sustain the stooped posture for a sufficiently long period of time. We designed Experiment 2 to address this problem.

5.2 Experiment 2

Experiment 2 was designed to see if having the subject hold the slumped position after failure would produce the "stoop to conquer" effect. Here, the posture-manipulation portion of the task was re-designed to require more reading on the screen, giving a person less time to sit back and think. The task this time was a decision-making (gambling) task that had instructions and content written in a small font size on the LCD monitor in order to encourage the subject to stay in a position focused on the monitor. This task did appear (from videos) to keep subjects in the desired posture for a longer time than Experiment 1 because they had to scrutinize details on a screen for 8 minutes.

Subjects. Thirty-seven naive subjects were recruited from our school and surrounding area, each between 18 and 40 years old. Subjects were randomly assigned to one of the three conditions (failure-upright/failure-neutral/failure-slumped).

Procedure. The same procedure as in Experiment 1 was performed, except that they performed the 8-min decision-making task before the other dependent measure tasks. Since our primary interest in Experiment 2 was the "stoop to conquer" effect on the persistence measure in the failure conditions, all subjects were assigned to the failure manipulation..

Debriefing. Following the dependent measure tests, the 37 subjects were given a full debriefing as in Experiment 1. We found 7 of the subjects did not feel bad after the failure manipulation: four subjects did not feel bad in spite of the low score, and three subjects believed that the low score given for the manipulation was not true (failed mood manipulation). Thus, their results were excluded from all our analysis, and we see 30 subjects in Tables 4 and 5. In Table 6, we found we had to omit an additional 12 subjects: after the video analysis, we found that two subjects' posture did not match with RoCo's conditioned posture (failed posture manipulation). Also, one subject reported that she had much trouble in using the pen tablet for the tracing puzzles, and nine subjects knew the rule for whether a tracing puzzle was solvable or not. While these problems did not interfere with the mood manipulation (as verified in the debriefing), they would make comparisons of persistence unfair, because the subjects who knew the rule skipped puzzles, so they are omitted from Table 6. Since the sample size is small, we risk false acceptance or rejection of the null hypothesis. Thus, below, we report all the averages and standard deviations as well as results of statistical tests.

Main Results. 1. *RoCo posture's influence on the user posture:* RoCo's posture was strongly associated with the user's posture. Also, compared with the failure condition of Experiment 1, the 8 minute cognitive task helped the user keep a constant posture longer (See Tables 4 and 5). *2. Persistence on Task:* One-way ANOVA analysis was applied to the persistence measure from the insolvable puzzles data (summarized in Table 6 and shown in Figure 4). The result shows a statistically significant posture effect on the persistent measure, $F(2, 15) = 3.70$, $p < 0.05$. Subjects showed higher persistence when they used RoCo in its slumped position ($M = 9.75$, $SD = 2.50$) after their failure than when they used RoCo in its neutral position ($M = 7.36$, $SD = 1.58$), or in its upright position ($M = 6.85$, $SD = 1.60$). Thus, the better persistence of the matched combinations supports the appropriateness hypothesis.

Discussion. Experiment 1 showed that people tended to be more persistent on a subsequent task when they used RoCo in its upright position after success than when they used RoCo in its neutral or slumped position. However, Experiment 1 did not show a significant "stoop to conquer" effect on the same persistence measure in the negative mood conditions. We hypothesized that these results were mainly caused by the fact that subjects did not keep the target posture for a significant period of time while doing the subsequent task on RoCo. Thus, Experiment 2 was designed to encourage subjects to hold the target posture longer before doing subsequent tasks. This new experiment allowed us to observe that people in the negative mood were more persistent using RoCo's slumped posture than using its neutral or upright postures, thus achieving the "Stoop to Conquer" effect. Therefore, Experiment 1 and 2 show that a computer's "pose" congruous or incongruous to a user's affective state can influence performance factors such as task persistence. Also, we find that holding the target posture before doing other dependent measure tasks may be critical in utilizing the "stoop to conquer" effect. This makes sense if the slumping helps a person to process their negative state, and thus go on to better performance.

Table 4. RoCo posture's influence on the user posture for the initial 8 minutes (for 30 subjects, the number of subjects are shown)

RoCo / User	Slumped	Neutral	Upright
Slumped	11	0	0
Neutral	2	8	0
Upright	0	0	9

Table 5. RoCo posture's influence on the user posture for the total task time (for 30 subjects, the number of subjects are shown)

RoCo / User	Slumped	Neutral	Upright
Slumped	10	3	0
Neutral	3	5	0
Upright	0	0	9

Table 6. (Failure condition). Average number of tracing attempts (for 18 subjects).

Groups	Slumped	Neutral	Upright
N	6	7	5
Average	9.75	7.36	6.85
SD	2.50	1.58	1.60

Since we first wanted to observe the "stoop to conquer" effect on the RoCo platform without involving any other effects between RoCo and the human subject, the experiments in this paper did not engage RoCo's dynamic movements of responding

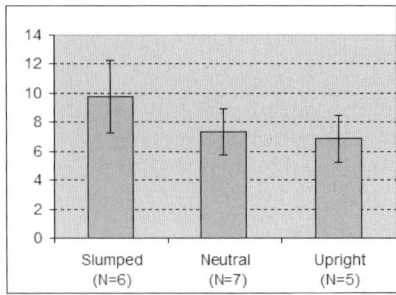

Fig. 4. (Failure condition). Average number of tracing attempts (error bars show the SD).

appropriately to the user's affective state. When RoCo uses these dynamic behaviors, there might be additional emotion contagion effects between RoCo and the user. Thus, we sampled these behavioral positions by exposing users to three different fixed points: slumped, neutral, upright. There was probably still a novelty effect of using a monitor with wires running up it, but this effect was constant across all conditions.

RoCo is an entirely new kind of system, which can greet its user socially and move during natural interaction much like people move. Suppose the user greets RoCo cheerily, then sits and slumps. Our findings support the theory that an upright posture (congruent with cheery mood) could help this user be more productive [16,17]. RoCo can begin to move upward, subtly, without being distracting. More likely, RoCo will observe that you are already slumped, and then choose movements to respond best to your wishes, which may include increased productivity. The three positions tested so far (and the 8min timing) provide the first proof of concept that posture-mood interaction matters in HCI. This now opens the door to investigating what timings and positions are most effective.

6   Conclusion

We used RoCo in a novel user study to explore whether a computer's "posture" can influence its user's subsequent posture, and if the interaction of the user's body state with their affective state during a task leads to improved task measures, such as persistence in problem solving. These findings lend support to the theory of embodied cognition where invoking a cognitive concept invokes an associated bodily (and/or affective) state, and vice-versa. When the states are congruent, there is less conflict, and more resources to devote to task performance. This paper is the first to show that mood-posture interactions influence performance for a person sitting in a chair using a computer monitor.

Research in computer-human interaction has long ignored human feelings, conducting experiments that (effectively) assume users are in a neutral mood. Our findings suggest that it might be important to bias users into multiple moods, and then measure outcomes. The field of economics has found that this makes a big difference in matching theory to real behavior (e.g., [12], where the endowment effect is reversed dependent on mood.) We suggest that the field of human-computer interaction may similarly find that measuring affective state is important, and can lead to measurably different outcomes. Persistence and perhaps many other cognitive variables are likely to be influenced by body and affective states.

Acknowledgments. This work was supported by NSF SGER award IIS-0533703.

References

1. Argyle, M.: Bodily Communication. Methuen and Co. Ltd., New York, NY (1988)
2. Breazeal., C.: Designing Sociable Robots. MIT Press, Cambridge, MA (2002)
3. Breazeal, C., Wang, A., Picard, R.: Experiments with a Robotic Computer: Body, Affect, and Cognition Interactions. In: Proceedings of HRI, Washington DC (2007)
4. Chirstensen, L., Menzel, K.: The linear relationship between student reports of teacher immediacy behaviors and perception of state motivation, and of cognitive, affective, and behavioral learning. Communcation Education 47, 82–90 (1998)
5. Duclos, S., Laird, J., Schneider, E., Sexter, M., Stern, L., Van Lighten, O.: Emotion-specific effects of facial expressions and postures on emotional experience. Journal of Personality and Social Psychology 57, 100–108 (1989)
6. Faiks, F., Reinecke, S.: Investigation of spinal curvature while changing one's posture during sitting. Contemporary Ergonomics (1998)
7. Glass, J., Singer, J.: Urban Stress. Academic Press, New York (1972)
8. Hartup, W.: Cooperation, Close Relationships, and Cognitive Development. Cambridge University, Cambridge (1996)
9. Hatfield, E., Cacioppo, J., Rapson, R.: Emotion Contagion. Cambridge University Press, New York (1994)
10. Isen, A.M.: Positive affect and decision making. In: Lewis, M., Haviland, J. (eds.) Handbook of Emotions, 2nd edn., Guilford, New York (2000)
11. D. K. Isen, A., Nowicki, G.: Positive affect facilitates creative problem solving. Journal of Personality and Social Psychology 52, 1122–1131 (1987)
12. Lerner, J., Small, D., G., L.: Heart strings and purse strings: Carryover effects of emotions on economic decisions. Psychological Science 15(5), 337–341 (2004)
13. Nass, C., Jonsson, I.-M., Harris, H., Reeves, B., Endo, J., Brave, S., Takayama, L.: Improving automotive safety by pairing driver emotion and car voice emotion. In: Proceeding of the CHI 2004 Proceedings, Portland, Oregon (2004)
14. Reinecke, S., Bevins, T., Weisman, J., Krag, M., Pope, M.: The relationship between seating postures and low back pain. In: Rehabilitation Engineering Society in North Ameriac, 8th Annual Conference (1995)
15. Richmond, V., McCroskey, J.: Immediacy, Nonverbal Behavior in Interpersonal Relations. Allyn and Bacon, Boston, MA (1995)
16. Riskind, J.: They stoop to conquer: Guiding and self-regulatory functions of physical posture after success and failure. Journal of Personality and Social Psychology 47, 479–493 (1984)
17. Riskind, J., Gotay, C.: Physical posture: Could it have regulatory or feedback effects upon motivation and emotion? Motivation and Emotion 6, 273–296 (1982)
18. R. R. Rottenberg, J., Gross, J.: Emotion elicitation using films. Oxford University Press, New York (2004)
19. Schwartz, N.: Situated cognition and the wisdom in feelings. In: Barrett, L.F., Salovey, P. (eds.) The Wisdom in Feeling, pp. 144–166. The Guilford Press (2002)
20. Wang, A.: Physically Animated Desktop Computer for Ergonomic & Affective Movement. MIT Master Thesis (May 2006)
21. Wilson, V., Peper, E.: The effects of upright and slumped postures on recall of postive and negative thoughts. Applied Psychophysiology and Biofeedback 29, 189–195 (2004)

Video Affective Content Representation and Recognition Using Video Affective Tree and Hidden Markov Models

Kai Sun and Junqing Yu

Computer College of Science & Technology, Huazhong University of Science & Technology,
Wuhan 430074, China
sunkai@smail.hust.edu.cn, yjqing@hust.edu.cn

Abstract. A video affective content representation and recognition framework based on Video Affective Tree (VAT) and Hidden Markov Models (HMMs) is presented. Video affective content units in different granularities are firstly located by excitement intensity curves, and then the selected affective content units are used to construct VAT. According to the excitement intensity curve the affective intensity of each affective content unit at different levels of VAT can also be quantified into several levels from weak to strong. Many middle-level audio and visual affective features, which represent emotional characteristics, are designed and extracted to construct observation vectors. Based on these observation vector sequences HMMs-based video affective content recognizers are trained and tested to recognize the basic emotional events of audience (joy, anger, sadness and fear). The experimental results show that the proposed framework is not only suitable for a broad range of video affective understanding applications, but also capable of representing affective semantics in different granularities.

1 Introduction

Digital video systems are creating many new opportunities for rapid access to content archives. In order to explore these collections using search applications, the content must be annotated with significant features. An important and often overlooked aspect of human interpretation of video data is the affective dimension, which is an important natural component of human classification and retrieval of information. Imagine life without emotion: There would be no joy associated with great art. A vicious crime elicits no anger or disgust. Watching our favorite sports team never leads to "the thrill of victory or the agony of defeat." Sadness does not follow the death of a loved one because we would not experience love. Without emotion, life would be listless and colorless, like a meal in need of seasoning. Recognizing multimedia content contributing to this dimension and using it to automatically label the significant affective features potentially allow a new modality for user interaction with video content.

Intensive research efforts in the field of multimedia content analysis in the past 15 years have resulted in an abundance of theoretical and algorithmic solutions for extracting the content-related information from audiovisual information [1]. However, due to the inscrutable nature of human emotions and seemingly broad affective gap

A. Paiva, R. Prada, and R.W. Picard (Eds.): ACII 2007, LNCS 4738, pp. 594–605, 2007.

from low-level features, the video affective content analysis is seldom addressed [2]. Several research works have been done to extract affective content from video. One method is to map low-level video features into emotion space. Hanjalic and Xu found in literature connections between some low level features of video data streams and dimensions of the emotions space and made algorithmic models for them [2]. The relations they found for the arousal dimension were a motion component, rhythm component and a sound energy component. The motion component measures the amount of motion in video frames. The more motion in the video the more exciting this part is. The rhythm component is obtained by measuring the shot lengths along the video. The shorter the shot length the more arousing this part is. In the end the total energy of the sound track is measured. Again the more energy is in the sound track the more arousing the part of the video is. Using these three components they modeled a curve, named arousal time curve, to represent intensity of audience's excitement. Although this method can be used to locate video affective content or highlights effectively, the recognition of specific affective category is beyond its ability. Moreover, in implementation it's very difficult to choose the appropriate Kaiser Window's parameters according to the different video, i.e., there are not a set of constant parameters suited to all kinds of video. Another method is using HMMs to recognize video affective content [3]. In this method, empirical study on the relationship between emotional events and low-level features was performed and two HMM topologies were created. However, it can't measure the affective intensity and discriminate fear and anger due to the lack of proper low-level features (e.g. audio affective features).

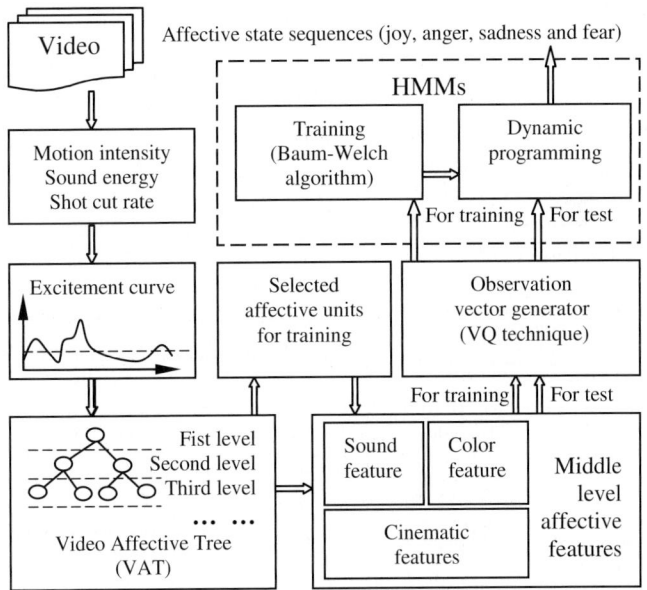

Fig. 1. Proposed Video affective representation and recognition framework

Taken these results into account, a novel video affective content representation and recognition framework is proposed, which is illustrated by Fig. 1. Firstly, video affective content units in different granularities are located by excitement curve and then mapped to be a Video Affective Tree (VAT). The affective intensity of affective content units in VAT is quantified into several levels from weak to strong (e.g. weak, median and strong) according to the intensity of excitement curve. Video affective content can be conveniently represented by VAT at different granularities. Next, middle-level affective features that represent emotional characteristics are extracted from these affective content units and observation vectors are constructed subsequently by combining these features. Finally, HMMs-based affective recognizer are trained and tested to recognize the basic emotional events (joy, anger, sadness and fear) using these observation vector sequences.

2 Affective Features Extraction

Little is known regarding the relations between the low-level features and affect. The most extensive investigations on this open issue in the context of affective video content analysis were presented in [2] and [3]. Their research results show that features about motion, shot length and sound energy are generic and robust in measuring the excitement level of film affective content; therefore these features are

Table 1. Basic emotion and middle-level audio affective features

Feature / Emotion Type		Joy	Anger	Sadness	Fear
Audio Features	**Speech Rate**	Faster or slower	Slightly faster	Slightly slower	Much faster
	Pitch average	Much higher	Very much higher	Slightly lower	Very much higher
	Pitch Range	Much wider	Much wider	Slightly narrower	Much wider
	Sound energy	Higher	Higher	Lower	Normal
	Silence ratio	Small	Small	Big	Big
Cinematic Features	**Color features**	Bright colors	NA	Dark, Low saturated	Dark and blue, sometimes dark and red, Low saturated
	Camera motion (Phase/ Intensity)	NA/ Large	Zoom, tilt, dolly /Large	No camera motion/ Small	Zoom, tilt, dolly /NA
	Shot cut rate	NA	Fast	Slow	Fast

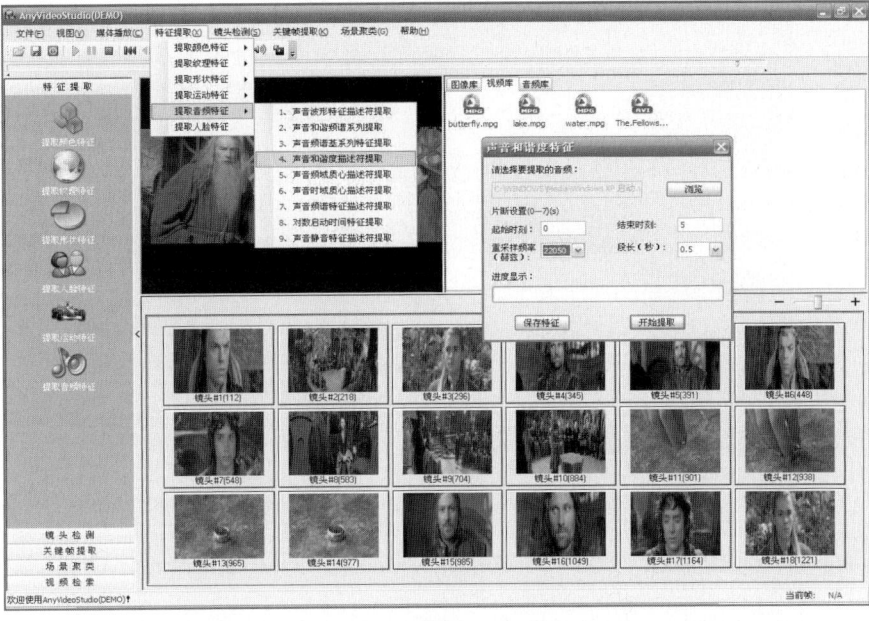

(a)

(b)

Fig. 2. (a) Our experimental prototype system. (b) Some extracted audio features.

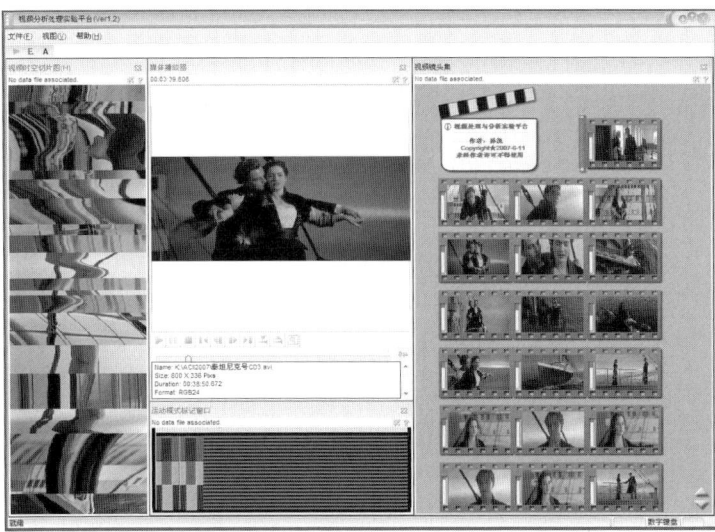

Fig. 3. Video temporal slices (800 frames) extracted by our experimental prototype system

also adopted to construct the excitement curve in our proposed framework. To effectively recognize the basic emotion type, we extract middle-level audio and visual affective features from video shots based on the information listed in Table 1.

The audio features in Table 1 are designed according to the work of Murray and Arnott [4]. In our implementation, these audio features are extracted based on MPEG-7 audio content description [5]. Several MPEG-7 high-level tools designed to describe the properties of musical signals are also implemented. These high-level tools include Timbre Description Scheme, Melody Description Scheme and Tempo Description Scheme. The aim of the MPEG-7 Timbre DS is to describe some perceptual features of musical sounds with a reduced set of descriptors. These descriptors relate to notion such as "attack", "brightness" or "richness" of a sound. The Melody DS is a representation for melodic information which mainly aims at facilitating efficient melodic similarity matching. The music Tempo DS is defined to characterize the underlying temporal structure of musical sound. Some extracted audio features are showed in Fig. 2 (a) and (b), which are the GUI's snapshots of our experimental prototype system. Visual features (including color and cinematic features) are designed and extracted based on the analysis of video temporal slices which are extracted from the video by slicing through the sequence of video frames and collecting temporal signatures [6,7]. While traditional approaches to video frame sequences analysis tend to formulate computational methodologies on two or three adjacent frames, video temporal slices provide rich visual patterns along a larger temporal scale and are very suitable for video affective content analysis. Fig. 3 gives an example about the temporal slices, which was extracted by our experimental prototype system and its duration is 800 frames.

To apply HMM to the time-sequential video shots which are basic units of film affective content unit, the features of each video shot mentioned above must be transformed to observation vector sequences in training and recognition phase. We use vector quantization technique in generating observation vector sequences. Once the model topology and observation vectors are determined, the next step is to train the model and determine the initial, state-transition and emission probabilities. Parameter estimation for the HMM is done using Baum-Welch algorithm [8].

3   Generation of Video Affective Tree (VAT)

The excitement time curve indicates how the intensity of the emotional load changes along a video, and depicts the expected changes in audience's excitement while watching that video. In this sense, the excitement time curve is particularly suitable for locating the "exciting" video segments. Our excitement time curve is inspired by the arousal time curve proposed in [2]. Computing the arousal values over time results in the excitement time curve $E(k)$, which is defined as a function of N basic components $f_i(k)$, i.e., $E(k) = F(f_i(k), i = 1, ..., N)$. The function $f_i(k)$ models the variations in the excitement level over the video frame k induced by the stimulus represented by the feature i. It is assumed that all of the N features are selected to reliably represent the stimuli which influence the affective state of the audience. Each function $f_i(k)$ can be seen as an elementary excitement time curve or the primitive of the overall excitement time curve $E(k)$, while $E(k)$ is obtained by integrating the contributions of all component $f_i(k)$ using a suitable function F. The definition of the function F is a weighted average of the three components, which is then convolved with a sufficiently long Kaiser window in order to merge neighboring local maxima of the components. Then we can get the excitement time curve by scaling the results into the 0–1 range. Here $N = 3$, and the values of $f_1(k)$, $f_2(k)$ and $f_3(k)$ are computed according to the features including motion intensity, shot cut rate and sound energy.

On the basis of the excitement time curve we can generate a group of affective content units in different granularities. Namely, given the excitement time curve, affective highlights can be extracted by analyzing the values of the curve at different levels and those video segments that are likely to excite the audience most should be extracted. To explain how to select video affective content units, we illustrate the main ideas in Fig. 4 and Fig. 5, which can be depicted as follows:

1. Convolve the whole video excitement time curve with a Kaiser window and locate all the local maximums in the smoothed curve.
2. Select the time-sequential video shots around each of the local maximums as video affective content unit at first level, whose affective intensity is labeled according to the value of the local maximum. Here, the values of the excitement time curve are quantified into three levels: weak, median and strong.
3. All the local minimums of the smoothed curve are located and the whole video is divided into several parts at each shot which includes the local minimums (Fig. 4(a)).
4. Reduce the size of the Kaiser window (to make the excitement curve more detailed) and repeat step 1, step 2 and step 3 on every part of the video until the number of shots in each sub-part is below the designated threshold (Fig. 4(b)).
5. Assemble all the video affective content units from the first level to the last level and the video affective tree (VAT) is generated (Fig. 5).

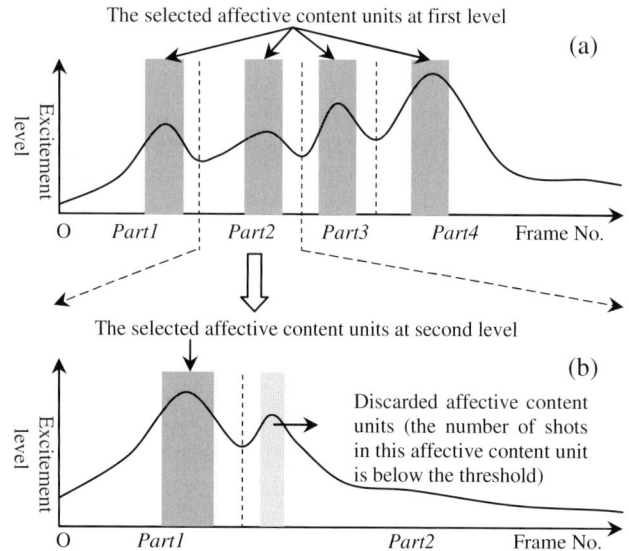

Fig. 4. Illustration of the generation of affective content units

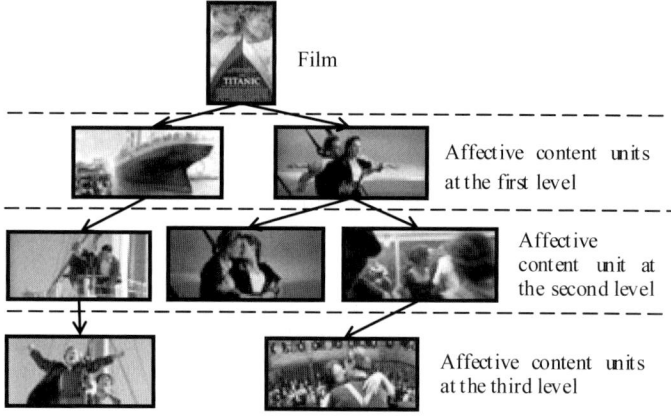

Fig. 5. Illustration of the generation of the Video Affective Tree

4   HMM Based Affective Recognizer

Hidden Markov models (HMMs) are powerful tools for characterizing the dynamic temporal behavior of video sequences. An HMM is a doubly stochastic model whose observable symbol probability distribution for each state captures the intra-state variability of the observable symbols, and the state transition probability describe the underling dynamic structure of the observable symbols.

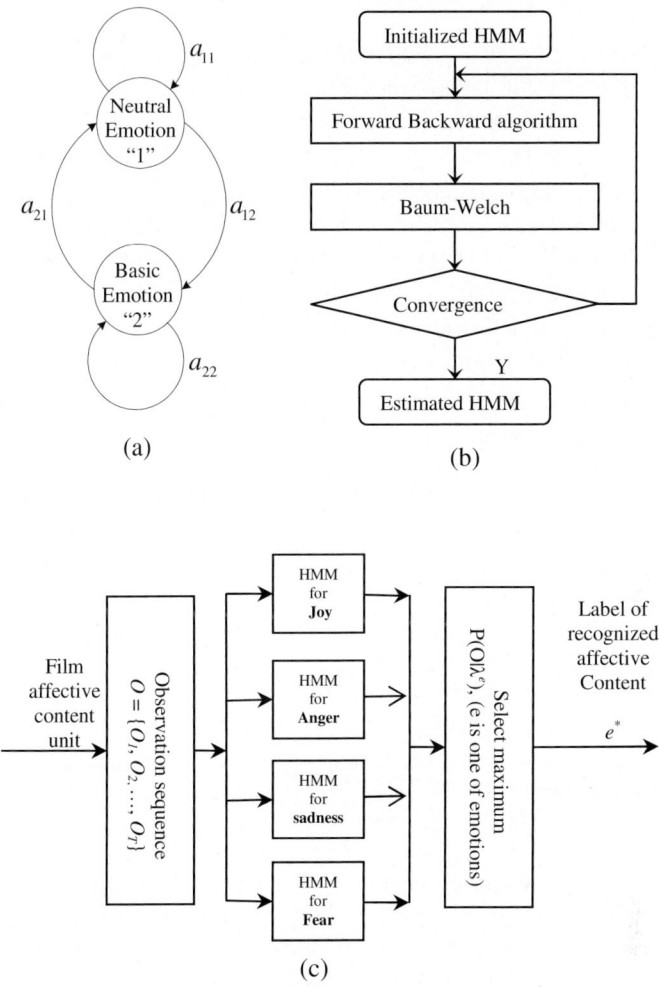

Fig. 6. (a) 2-state HMM topology for modeling the basic emotion. (b) The training scheme for affective recognizer. (c) Block diagram of affective recognizer based on HMMs.

We aim to utilize HMM in two distinct ways for video affective content recognition: (*i*) given a sequence of observations extracted from an affective content unit, to determine the likelihood of each model (every basic emotion has its own HMM model) for the input data, (*ii*) given the observation sequences, to train the model parameters. The first problem can be regarded to score how well a given model matches a given observation sequence. The second problem is attempting to optimize the model parameters in order to best describe how a given observation sequence comes about. The observation sequence used to adjust the model parameters is called a training sequence since it is used to "train" the HMM. The training problem is the crucial one for our HMMs-based affective recognizer, since it allows us to optimally adapt model parameters to observed training data, i.e., to create best models for real phenomena.

Therefore, in order to recognize affective content, our affective recognizer contains two components: training and recognizing. For each basic emotion e, we build an ergodic 2-state HMM λ^e, whose topology is shown in Fig. 6(a). We must estimate the model parameters (A, B, π) that optimize the likelihood of the training set observation vectors for the basic emotion e. The training scheme is shown in Fig. 6(b). For each affective content unit which is to be recognized, the processing listed in Fig. 6(c) should be carried out, namely measurement of the observation sequence $O = \{O_1, O_2, ..., O_T\}$ (T is the number of the shots within a affective content unit), via the feature analysis of section 2; followed by calculation of model likelihoods for all of possible models, $P(O \mid \lambda^e)$, $e \in \{joy, anger, sadness, fear\}$; followed by selection of the basic emotion type whose model likelihood is the highest, i.e., $e* = \underset{e \in \{joy, anger, sadness, fear\}}{\arg \max} \{p(O \mid \lambda^e)\}$. The probability computation step is performed using the Viterbi algorithm (i.e., the maximum likelihood path is used).

5   Experimental Results and Discussion

Preliminary experiments have been done to demonstrate the performance of our affective content recognizer. We made a data set from ten feature films such as "Titanic", "A Walk in the Clouds", "Love Letter", "Raiders of the Lost Ark", "Con Air", "Pirates of the Caribbean", "Scary Movie", "Spider-Man", "Lord of the Rings" and "the Lion King". Firstly, the excitement time curves for all the films were computed. The algorithms for generating the excitement time curve have been realized in our previous work [9]. Next, we utilized these excitement time curves to construct the Video Affective Tree for each film. The ground truth for the four basic affective events (joy, anger, sadness and fear) was manually determined within the extracted video affective units at different levels. The scenes that belong to four emotional events were labeled by 30 students. If one of the video scenes was labeled with the same emotional event by at least 21 of 30 students, we assigned the scene as having one of four emotional events. Shot boundary detection and key frame extraction were based on the analysis of video temporal slices and our previous work [10]. To compute color features, we transformed RGB color space into HSV color space and then quantized the pixels into 11 culture colors such as red, yellow, green, blue, brown, purple, pink, orange, gray, black and white [11]. For a key frame of each shot, we computed the histogram of 11culture colors. We also computed the saturation(S), value (V), dark colors, and bright colors. So, 15 color features were extracted from each shot. The motion phase and intensity for each shot was also computed. The audio features, such as speech rate, pitch average, pitch range and short time energy, were computed using our experimental prototype system (Fig. 2). By fusing all of these audio and visual features, observation vectors are generated by vector quantization.

Our problem is to classify observed middle-level feature sequences into affective events. Unlike most classical pattern classification problems, the data to be classified is time series data. At first, we applied several traditional machine learning algorithms to the features extracted from the dataset mentioned above in the Weka3.5 workbench [12]. Due to the poor experimental results, we adopted Hidden Markov Models (HMMs) because HMMs are widely used probabilistic models for time series data. In addition, several works using HMMs show good potential for video parsing or segmentation [13-15]. We also designed Several HMMs topologies to address our problem. Finally, HMMs topologies like Fig. 6(a) were adopted in spite of its simple structure, because its overall performance is the best one. Leave-one-out cross-validation is a good choice to measure the error rate of our HMMs-based affective recognizer, because the amount of data for training and testing is limited. Leave-one-out cross-validation is simply n-fold cross-validation, where n is the number of instances in the dataset. Each instance in turn is left out, and the learning method is trained on all the remaining instances. It is judged by its correctness on the remaining instance – one or zero for success or failure, respectively. The results of all n judgments, one for each member of the dataset, are averaged, and that average represents the final error estimate. Our experimental results are shown in Table. 2. From the results, it can be easily found that most of the affective contents are recognized exactly.

Table 2. Experimental results

Affective events / Results	Joy	Anger	Sadness	Fear
Number of Affective content units	87	105	152	213
Recognized	76	78	124	153
False alarms	18	54	47	102
Precision	80.9%	59.1%	72.5%	60.0%
Recall	87.4%	74.3%	81.6%	71.8%
F-Score	84.0%	65.8%	76.8%	65.4%

Affective content is a subjective concept which relies on audience's perceptions. Talking about affect (feeling, emotion and mood) inevitably calls for a discussion about subjectivity. There are many implementation issues for our proposed video affective representation and recognition framework. For example, finding a representative training data set in the affective domain is a very difficult task for us. The main problem lies in the fact that the variety of content that can appear in joy, anger, sadness or fear is practically unlimited. Therefore, it's difficult to compare our experimental results with the other reported results.

6 Conclusion and Future Work

In this paper, we propose a novel video affective content representation and recognition framework based on Video Affective Tree (VAT) and Hidden Markov Models (HMMs). VAT is a new proposed idea, which inspired by the arousal time curve proposed in [1]. The limitation of the arousal time curve is that the parameters of the Kaiser Window vary according to different video, while VAT can efficiently represent the affective content at different granularities profiting from the non-linear tree structure. The proposed framework is not only suitable for a broad range of video affective understanding applications, but also capable of modeling affective semantics in different granularities. The experimental results on feature films show our framework is promising.

Much work remains to be done in this largely unexplored field. First, with regards the shortcomings of our work, the low recognition rate of "Fear" and "Anger" shows up the inherent limitation of low-level cues (especially visual) in bridging the affective gap. This is also a well known problem for emotion theories that categorize emotions in the arousal-valence space. Both fear and anger are in the area of high arousal and negative valence. This problem is typically solved in 3-dimensional models, which use "dominance" as the third axis: fear has low dominance, whereas anger has high dominance. Therefore, in the immediate future, we intend to implement more complex intermediate-level cues to represent the "dominance" of emotions and further improve present results. Second, the existence of multiple emotions in the affective content unit requires a more refined treatment. Finally, we will also investigate the possibility of using the main actors' face expressions to recognize the film affective contents.

Acknowledgments. We gratefully acknowledge the granted financial support from China Postdoctoral Science Foundation (20060400847) and Huawei Foundation (YJCB20060471N).

References

1. Hanjalic, A.: Extracting Moods from Pictures and Sounds: Towards truly personalized TV. IEEE Signal Processing Magazine 3, 90–100 (2006)
2. Hanjalic, A., Xu, L.-Q.: Affective video content representation and modeling. IEEE Trans. Multimedia 2, 143–154 (2005)
3. Kang, H.-B.: Affective Content Detection using HMMs. In: Proceedings of the eleventh ACM international conference on Multimedia, vol. 259, pp. 2–8 (November 2003)
4. Murray, I.R., Arnott, J.L.: Implementation and testing of a system for producing emotion-by-rule in synthetic speech. Speech Communication 16, 369–390 (1995)
5. Information Technology—Multimedia Content Description Interface—Part 4: Audio, ISO/IEC CD 15938-4 (2001)
6. Ngo, C.W., Pong, T.C., Chin, R.T.: Video partitioning by temporal slice coherency. IEEE Trans. Circuits Syst. Video Technol. 11(8), 941–953 (2001)
7. Ngo, C.W., Pong, T.C., Zhang, H.J.: Motion-based video representation for scene change detection. Int. J. Comput. Vis. 50(2), 11 (2002)

8. Rabiner, L.: A tutorial on hidden Markov models and selected applications in speech recognition. Proc. IEEE 77(2), 256–286 (1989)
9. Junqing, Y., Yunfeng, H., Sun, K., Zhifang, W., Xiangmei, W.: Semantic Analysis and Retrieval of Sports Video. In: Proceeding of Japan-China Joint Workshop on Frontier of Computer Science and Technology, Aizu-Wakamatsu, pp. 97–108 (2006)
10. Sun, K., Junqing, Y., Ning, W.: Shot Boundary Detection and Key-frames Extraction Based on MPEG-7 Visual Descriptors. In: Proceeding of 3rd Conference on Intelligent CAD and Digital Entertainment (November 2006)
11. Goldstein, E.: Sensation and Perception. Brooks/Cole (1999)
12. Witten, I.H., Frank, E.: Data Mining: Practical machine learning tools and techniques, 2nd edn. Morgan Kaufmann, San Francisco (2005)
13. Boreczky, J., Wilcox, E.: A Hidden Markov Model Framework for Video Segmentation Using Audio and Image Features. In: Proc. ICASSP' 98 (1998)
14. Eickeler, S., Muller, S.: Content-based Video Indexing of TV Broadcast News Using Hidden Markov Models. In: Proc. ICASSP'99 (1999)
15. Naphade, M., Garg, A., Huang, T.: Audio-Visual Event Detection using Duration dependent input output Markov models. In: Proc. IEEE CBAIBL'01, Kauai, HI (2001)

I Know What I Did Last Summer: Autobiographic Memory in Synthetic Characters

João Dias[1], Wan Ching Ho[2], Thurid Vogt[3], Nathalie Beeckman[4],
Ana Paiva[1], and Elisabeth André[3]

[1] INESC-ID and IST, Tagus Park
Av. Prof. Cavaco Silva, 2780-990 Porto Salvo, Portugal
[2] University of Hertfordshire
School of Computer Science
Hatfield, Hertfordshire, AL10 9AB, UK
[3] University of Augsburg
Multimedia concepts and applications
Eichleitnerstr. 30, 86159 Augsburg, Germany
[4] University of Utrecht
Department of Information and Computing Sciences
Princetonplein 5, 3584 CC Utrecht, The Netherlands

Abstract. According to traditional animators, the art of building believable characters resides in the ability to successfully portray a character's behaviour as the result of its internal emotions, intentions and thoughts. Following this direction, we want our agents to be able to explicitly talk about their internal thoughts and report their personal past experiences. In order to achieve it, we look at a specific type of episodic long term memory. This paper describes the integration of Autobiographic Memory into FAtiMA, an emotional agent architecture that generates emotions from a subjective appraisal of events.

1 Introduction

The concept of believability [2] in synthetic characters has been (and is still being) widely studied since traditional animators first started creating animated characters. Thomas and Johnston, creators of the well-known Disney characters, started to explore emotional expressivity and personality to achieve believability. They identified three important requisites in order to express emotions. One of them was that "emotions affect the reasoning process and consequences should be noticeable in the actions of the characters"[17]. Another concept also adopted by researchers (e.g. Blumberg's work [3]) to build believable characters is Daniel Dennett's intentional stance[7]. According to the intentional stance, if we can perceive a creature's beliefs and desires we can predict what will be its actions.

These two complementary notions suggest that if a viewer can predict a character's actions based on his perception of the character's emotional state, beliefs and desires, then it will become more believable to the viewer, thus allowing the suspension of disbelief. The same applies if, working backwards one can understand the actions of a given character as being influenced by its internal state.

A. Paiva, R. Prada, and R.W. Picard (Eds.): ACII 2007, LNCS 4738, pp. 606–617, 2007.
© Springer-Verlag Berlin Heidelberg 2007

For this reason, great part of the art in building believable characters resides in the ability to successfully portray this link between the character's internal thoughts and its external actions. The work presented in this paper tries to explore the following: making it easier for the viewer to infer the character's intentions and emotional state by having the character explicitly talking about them and report its past experiences (as we humans do to close friends). In order to achieve this, the character must have some kind of awareness over his internal thoughts and emotions, thus allowing it not only to remember past events but also what he felt at past time, and what he was planning to do.

Therefore, the main question we will be dealing is: how can we give an agent the ability to report what happened in a past experience, including his personal subjective experience? Our answer lies in a specific type of long term memory, strongly associated with the concept of self. This type of memory is called autobiographic memory. This paper describes the integration of autobiographic memory into FAtiMA[9], an emotional agent architecture based in OCC Appraisal Theory. The autobiographical memory together with the agent's ability to generate emotions from a subjective appraisal of events is used to generate summary descriptions of what happened in a past episode of the life of our characters. This summary provides the user with information about the agent's personal experience. We hope that this feature will make the user create a stronger empathic[6,16] relation with the agent and make the agent more believable.

The rest of this paper is organized as follows: We start by an analysis of autobiographic memory, and its relation with personal experiences. The next section describes how the Autobiographic Memory is implemented and integrated into FAtiMA. Afterwards we depict the application of the resulting features into an interactive system and its effect in the interaction with the users. The last section presents some final remarks and future work.

2   Autobiographic Memory

In Psychology, autobiographic memory is a specific kind of episodic memory that contains significant and meaningful personal experiences for a human being [15]. It serves important function in providing the basis for social interaction, maintenance of a dynamic self-concept as well as the representation of the meaning of concepts [4].

2.1   Memory and Emotion

It has been widely acknowledged, in research literatures about memory, that events associated with emotional experiences partly constitute highly available memory. Psychologists and cognitive scientists also propose that when experiencing an event with emotion, humans' cognitive system is more fully engaged to processing that event, in comparison with processing of events which are not associated with emotional experience. This view can be further elaborated in that high level emotionally intense events may also be related with high frequency of rehearsal – making a piece of memory more generally available for retrieval.

Personally significant events which are directly involved in the self memory structure, like first time experiences, can bring stronger impacts to humans' lives by creating a pre-existing knowledge structure for the rest of similar events [4]. These life events, together with events with emotions, indicate that central knowledge structures relating to the self have been employed in representing autobiographical memory.

2.2 Autobiographic Agents

Theoretically, an autobiographic agent is an embodied agent which dynamically reconstructs its individual history (autobiography) during its life-time [5]. This individual history helps autobiographic agents to develop individualised social relationships and to form communications, which are characteristic of social intelligence, and it may also lead to more appealing and human-like engaging interactions, making them more pleasant and acceptable to humans.

Different types of computational memory architectures for Artificial Life autobiographic agents have been developed and experimentally evaluated in our previous research work (e.g. [11]). These architectures include typical human memory modules which are commonly acknowledged in Psychology: short-term, long-term, and positively and negatively categorised memories. Agents embedded with these computational autobiographic memories outperform Purely Reactive agents that do not remember past experiences in surviving in both static and dynamic environments.

In the paradigm of developing synthetic agent architectures, we proposed that 1) knowledge representations in the computational autobiographic memory can be based on general episodes that agents have experienced and 2) goal structure, emotion, and attention processes, support and are influenced by the autobiographic knowledge [12]. Autobiographic knowledge may also support a long-term development and learning in synthetic agents as they gain new experience from acting in each new situation.

3   Integrating Autobiographic Memory in FAtiMA

This section describes the integration of Autobiographic Memory (AM) into FAtiMA and how the subjective appraisal of events helps in storing the agent's personal experience into memory. In order for the reader to understand this section we will provide a brief overview of FAtiMA. For a more detailed description please refer to [9,8].

3.1   FAtiMA Overview

FAtiMA (**F**earNot! **A**ffective **M**ind **A**rchitecture) is an Agent Architecture where emotions and personality take a central role in influencing behaviour. The concept of emotion used stems from OCC cognitive theory of emotions, where emotions are defined as valenced (good or bad) reactions to events. The assessment of this relationship between events and the character's emotions is called the appraisal process. This appraisal is clearly subjective and is made regarding the agent's goals, standards and attitudes. The same event can be positive for one character and negative for another.

The architecture incorporates two distinct levels in both appraisal and action-selection mechanisms. The first level (reactive level) provides a fast mechanism to appraise and react to a given event, and generates reactive behaviours such as crying when very distressed (which cannot be considered as planned). The deliberative level takes longer to react but allows a more sequentially complex and goal-oriented behaviour.

Whenever an external event or action is perceived, the reactive appraisal process tries to match the event with a set of predefined emotional reaction rules. These rules represent the character's standards and attitudes and assess how generic events are appraised by defining values for OCC's appraisal variables: desirability of the event, desirability for other (used when the event references another character other than self), praiseworthiness of the action. These variable are then used according to OCC to generate a wide range of emotions from Joy and Distress to Pity and Anger. Reactive behaviour is defined by action rules: each contains a set of preconditions that must be true to execute the action and an emotion that will trigger the action tendency.

In addition, when the event is appraised, the deliberative level checks if any goal has become active, and if so, an intention to achieve the goals' success conditions is created generating initial Hope and Fear emotions. The agent then tries to build a plan to achieve the goal and updates such emotions accordingly. This is done using a continuous planner [1] that was extended to include emotion-focused coping[14] strategies and generates Partially Ordered Plans. Instead of executing a plan, the agent may decide to give up a plan or goal because he is scared or he is not confident it will work. This type of coping is called emotion-focused coping. If the agent succeeds or fails in achieving a goal the corresponding emotions (ex: Satisfaction, Disappointment) are also generated.

3.2 AM Structure

In FAtiMA, AM is organized as a set of independent episodes. Each episode stores several actions or events that happened at a particular location and at a given time. Inspired from the research on narrative structure in life stories for humans [13], the knowledge structure representing each episode has three main components: **Abstract**, **Narrative** and **Evaluation**. Within an episode, there can be more than one important *cause-effect* action. Cause-effect actions represent actions that eventually bring a considerable impact to the agent's emotional states. Therefore, actions that do not have an emotional impact are not considered relevant. This causal-effect association between an action and the experienced emotion allows the agent to report its feelings, but also to select the representative actions from an episode and to generate appropriate episode evaluations.

The mechanisms that decide how the contents of each component are, are described as follows:

1. **Abstract:** Describes the type of episode, constructed by information from **Details** and **Feeling** fields from **Narrative**. If an episode contains more than one cause-effect action, the actions that create the highest emotional intensities will be selected to complete the Abstract field. Thus an agent will remember the situation (**Details** and **Feeling**) that has strongest emotional impact to itself as the rough abstract for a given episode.

2. **Narrative:** Detailed descriptions of the event, including who, when, where and how does this event happen, as well as the emotional intensities the agent had while experiencing the event.
   - To achieve flexibility while generating episode summaries, the **Time** field will record three different types of data:
     (a) *Real time* (RT) is the time that represents the real world; it will be used for calculating the time difference when the software is used over a long term with a user.
     (b) *Narrative time* (NT) indicates the virtual time when an episode takes place in the whole story.
     (c) *Event sequence* (ES) simply shows the order of the event in time, e.g. the first or second event.
   - The field **Details** shows all cause-effect actions that have brought emotional impact to the agent within an episode. Consequently, each action in the field **Details** is corresponding to one set of emotional impacts in the field **Feeling**.

3. **Evaluation:** Agent's psychological interpretations as evaluations of each cause-effect action in the episodes. This essentially shows the action's consequence(s) in terms of inter-personal relationships remembered in an agent's memory.

A similar narrative structure for stories remembered by bottom-up Artificial Life agents in their autobiographic memory has been implemented and evaluated in [11]. Example in Figure 1 shows abstracted autobiographic episode structure with sample contents.

3.3   Storing Personal Experience into AM

At a given time, there is always an active episode in AM. This episode represents the present, i.e. what is currently happening. When a new event is perceived it is necessary to determine whether to store that information in the current active episode, or create a new episode to store it. An episode in AM is strongly associated with a location and time, thus whenever the agent's location changes or if nothing happens for a certain amount of time, a new episode is created and is selected as the active one.

When the event is first perceived, it is stored into the current active episode and the corresponding emotional appraisal is associated to the event. The appraisal process might generate more than one emotion (e.g. being insulted might

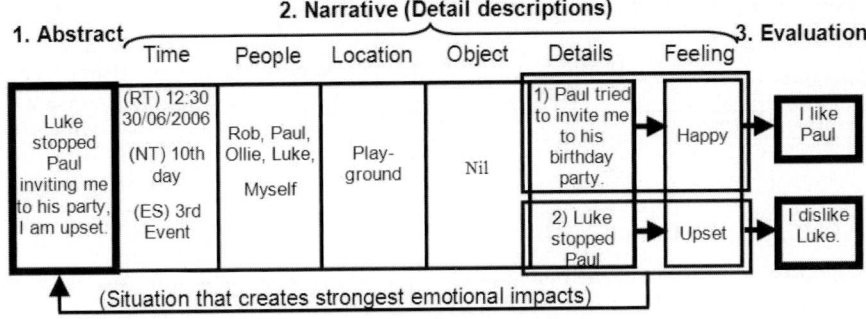

Fig. 1. Details of an episode

generate distress and anger), but only the strongest emotion is stored and associated to the event, like if the strongest one suppresses the others. The rationale for this choice is that although the agent can experience more than one emotion, it should express a clearly defined emotional state. As Thomas and Johnston put it *"the emotional state of the character should be undoubtedly perceived by the audience; emotions can be accentuated or exaggerated to be better understood;"*[17].

The subjective appraisal in FAtiMA (where the appraisal variables are specified differently for each character) gives rise to the subjective emotional experience for the character. This means that one character will remember that event with a given emotion, while another character will experience something quite different. Furthermore, the same event might be important for the first one and irrelevant to the second.

Although storing the emotional experience already gives a part of personal experience, we wanted to explore this feature further. Inspired by Dennett's intentional stance, we believe that providing explicit information about the agent's intentions will help us creating an even more believable characters. Fortunately, FAtiMA already models explicitly the activation, failure and success of intentions and activates the corresponding appraisal process. As such we can easily include that information into AM. In order to separately access the influence of this type of information in the character's believability we decided to distinguish between these two different type of events, classifying them as:

- **External Events:** all actions that happen in the virtual environment perceived by the agent.
- **Internal Events:** events associated to the intentions/goals of the agent. These are called internal because only the agent knows about them. At the moment, the internal events stored in FAtiMA are:
  - *Activation of an intention*
  - *Success in achieving an intention*
  - *Failure to achieve an intention*

Table 1. Mapping event information into the narrative structure supported by AM

	Who?	**What?**	**Whom?**	**How?**
External Event	action's subject	action's name	action's target	action's parameters
Intention Activation	SELF	activate	intention's name	intention's parameters
Intention Success	SELF	succeed	intention's name	intention's parameters
Intention Failure	SELF	fail	intention's name	intention's parameters

Nevertheless, this taxonomy of event types is completely transparent to the AM. An internal event is treated in the same way as an external event. When an internal event is generated, it is stored into AM according to what is defined in Table 1. The subject of an internal event its always the agent itself, the action corresponds to the activation, success or failure of the intention, the target of the event is the intention or goal referenced. Finally, the parameters stores additional information about the intention. For instance, if the intention is to insult John, the intention's name corresponds to "insult" and the intention's parameters corresponds to "John".

3.4   Generation of Summaries

When the agent wants to generate a summary of a past episode, it first needs to get the corresponding event from the AM. The memory retrieval process is able to retrieve a past episode by specifying a set of search keys. For instance one may want to get an episode that happened at a specific location or with a specific set of characters.

Once the episode is selected, the system is then able to retrieve the necessary information in order to generate the summary. The summary of an episode consists in the following information:

- **Location:** the location where the episode happened.
- **Time:** narrative time elapsed since the episode happened.
- **EventDescription:** a list of the most relevant events that happened in the episode, ordered by event sequence.

The location and time attributes are taken directly from the information stored within the episode. However, it is necessary to determine the most relevant events to report, since we don't want the agent to tell everything that happened, as there might exist events that are not important at all. The more relevant events are considered to be the ones that have generated a stronger emotional impact in the agent, and thus are determined by selecting the events with the strongest emotions associated to them. At the moment, we choose randomly the number of events to report (from three to five), just in order to get a higher variability in the generation of summaries. The chosen events are then ordered by event sequence, so that the summary generated follows a coherent narrative flow.

In order to provide the user with information on the agent's personal experience about the past episode, we need to add to the event's description the emotion experienced when the event was appraised (e.g. "Luke attacked me and I felt upset"). After some initial tests, we realized that describing the emotions for all events was repetitive and seemed unnatural. Furthermore, this was also causing difficulties in giving the user the most relevant emotions. For these reasons, only the strongest emotions are reported (at the moment, only the strongest two since the summary is short).

Once the information about the summary is gathered, it is sent to a natural language System (Language Engine). This module used by FAtiMA is responsible for generating proper English or German utterances for a requested speech act. A speech act is a special type of action used to perform speech related actions. When an agent wants to perform a communicative speech to another agent, lets imagine saying hello, it gathers the type of speech act he wants to perform (greeting in this case), the sender of the speech act, the receiver of the speech act. Afterwards it sends this information to the Languange Engine getting a specific utterance of the requested type (e.g. "Hello!" or "Hi"). The Speech Act with all information (including the generated utterance) is then sent to the virtual world and perceived by other agents. The episode summary is a special type of speech act because it includes additional information (as specified above) necessary to build the summary description. Nevertheless, after being generated the summary speech act is executed by the agent as any other speech act.

For the transformation of the information in the episode summaries into text, the LanguageEngine makes use of the semantic parser SPIN [10]. This is originally a parser for language analysis, but it can be — and has been [10] — also used for language generation. In this original direction, input words are parsed into a semantic type representation. Semantic parsers perform no deep syntactic analysis, so, as there is no detailed syntactic representation to generate the summaries from, this approach is very appropriate here also for generation. The task is then to map input type structures onto one result type containing the sequence of words to be returned.

A SPIN parser is built from three knowledge bases: an ontology, a lexicon and a rule set. The ontology specifies all available types, the features which are allowed for each type and the type hierarchy. The rules match type structures and define how they are replaced. In the lexicon additional information for words is defined, like stem, part of speech, semantic class and the semantic value.

In order to generate the summary text, an extract of the AM is split into events consisting of one action and subject, and optional location, time, target, parameter and emotion elements. The text of an event is then generated by transforming these elements into text and combining them through rules. The single utterances are concatenated using a set of connectional phrases like "and", "then", or "did you see that". By providing alternatives for the transformations of each element, a set of possible textual representations is generated for each summary from which the result is picked randomly. This ensures that successive summaries with similar events are not partly identical.

Extract of autobiographical memory	Text representation
$Time$(count:2, value:hour) $Location$(value:playground) $Event$(subject:Ollie, action: party-invitation, target: me) $Emotion$(value:joy, intensity: normal)	Ollie invited me to his party this morning at the playground which made me feel glad.
$Event$(subject: Luke, action: partyinvitationsabotagehost, target: Ollie) $Emotion$(value:distress, intensity: normal)	Then Luke didn't want me to go the party. I was feeling upset,
$Event$(subject:Ollie, action: party-invitationwithdraw, target:me)	next Ollie didn't want me to come anymore.

Fig. 2. Example of the transformation of an extract of the AM into a text representation

Figure 2 illustrates the transformation of a summary with an example. The mechanism is the same for English and for German. For German, additional information in the lexicon is used to observe case, number and gender agreement of words.

4 Results

To test our approach and the AM, we have embedded it into one particular example of a pedagogical system. FearNot![8] is a computer application developed to tackle and eventually help to reduce bullying problems in schools. Bullying has associated with it a wide variety of behaviours such as hitting, or kicking, in the case of direct bullying, or, in relational bullying, social exclusion or malicious rumour spreading. Thus, the overall objective of the development of FearNot!, was to build an anti-bullying demonstrator in which children age 8 to 12 experience a virtual scenario where they can witness (from a third-person perspective) bullying situations. The application runs like this: a child sees one episode where a bullying situation occurs (see Fig. 3-a). After such episode, the child is able to interact with the victim, acting as an invisible friend to a victimized character, discussing the problems that arise and proposing coping strategies. The coping strategy suggested by the user is taken into account by the victim, and will try to apply it in the next episode.

An improved version of FearNot!, FearNot! 2.0 (Fig. 3) is being developed in the context of an EU funded project (eCIRCUS). Among other features, one of the improvements over FearNot! 1.0 is the introduction of autobiographic memory into the agents. The agents store all events from previous episodes in

 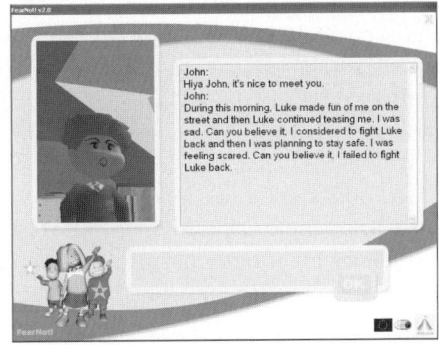

(a) Bullying episode seen by the user

(b) Interaction - John is describing what happened in the previous episode: *"During this morning. Luke made fun of me on the street and then Luke continued teasing me. I was sad. Can you believe it. I considered to fight Luke back and then I was planning to stay safe. I was feeling scared. Can you believe it. I failed to fight Luke back."*

Fig. 3. FearNot! 2.0 snapshots

the AM and are able to describe to the user what happened. Thus, in FearNot! 2.0 at the beginning of the interaction, the victim starts to describe a summary of the previous episode, giving the user its personal experience on what happened. This feature is important as it helps children not only to realize what happened in a past episode (that may have happened a week before for example), but also understand if the victim tried to follow their previous suggestion or not.

As an illustrative example consider Figure 3-b. It shows a description of the application of a suggested coping strategy. In an initial interaction with John (the victim), the user suggested him to fight back Luke (the bully). The next episode displayed another bullying situation where Luke provoked and teased John. However, John did nothing to prevent it or fight back as advised by the child. So, when John interacts with the user again, he will then explain that he did actually considered to fight back, but was afraid to be hurt. That made him remain passive.

The inclusion of the kind of dialogue with explanation of actions and memory experiences will allow for a more natural interaction similiar to one that close friends have.

5   Final Remarks and Future Work

This paper describes our current work within FAtiMA. Our aim is to give our agents the ability to talk about their past personal experiences. This is achieved in our work through the integration of Autobiographic Memory together with a subjective appraisal model. The AM associate past events with the emotions experienced when they were initially perceived. This emotional information has the additional advantage of giving us what is relevant in an past episode and it is worth retelling. In addition, the agent's are also capable of remembering their internal intentions and associated emotional states.

We believe, that this feature makes the link between the character's internal state and its external behaviour more easily understandable by observers. This, in turn, strengthens the empathic relation between the observer and the agent, and allows for a more natural interaction.

We are planning to evaluate the influence of the AM and the summary generation in the empathic relation created between the user and the victim. We will test whether the children experience the same kind of emotions the agent is feeling. The level of empathy will be determined and compared between four different kind of agents that we want to test. Therefore we will test four different situations:

- One where agents do not have an AM component whatsoever,
- One where agents only store External Events into AM,
- One where agents only store Internal Events into AM,
- One where agents store both External and Internal Events into AM.

We expect the agents that report both external and internal events from AM to be the ones evoking most empathy by the child users. The reason lies in the summary that they are able to generate about their past significant experiences, including the emotions that were involved in that episode and their internal intentions.

Acknowledgments

This paper is supported by the eCIRCUS (Contract no. IST-4-027656-STP) and HUMAINE (Contract no. 507422) projects carried out with the provision of the European Community in the Framework VI Programme, and by a scholarship (SFRH BD/19481/2004) granted by the Fundação para a Ciência e a Tecnologia. The authors are solely responsible for the content of this publication. It does not represent the opinion of the European Community or the Fundação para a Ciência e Tecnologia, which are not responsible for any use that might be made of data appearing therein.

References

1. Aylett, R., Dias, J., Paiva, A.: An affectively driven planner for synthetic characters. In: Proceedings of International Conference on Automated Planning and Scheduling ICAPS06, UK (2006)
2. Bates, J.: The role of emotion in believable agents. Communications of the ACM 37(7), 122–125 (1994)

3. Burke, R., Isla, D., Downie, M., Ivanov, Y., Blumberg, B.: Creaturesmarts: The art and architecture of a virtual brain. In: Proceedings of the Game Developers Conference, pp. 147–166 (2001)
4. Conway, M.A.: Autobiographical Memory: An Introduction. Open Univ. Press, Buckingham (1990)
5. Dautenhahn, K.: Embodiment in animals and artifacts. In: AAAI FS Embodied Cognition and Action, pp. 27–32. AAAI Press, Stanford, California, USA (Technical report FS-96-02) (1996)
6. Davis, M.: Empathy: a social psychological approach. Dubuque: Brown and Benchmark Publishers (1994)
7. Dennett, D.: The Intentional Stance. MIT Press, Cambridge (1987)
8. Dias, J.: Fearnot!: Creating emotional autonomous synthetic characters for empathic interactions. Master's thesis, Universidade Técnica Lisboa, Instituto Superior Técnico (2005)
9. Dias, J., Paiva, A.: Feeling and reasoning: a computational model for emotional agents. In: Bento, C., Cardoso, A., Dias, G. (eds.) EPIA 2005. LNCS (LNAI), vol. 3808, pp. 127–140. Springer, Heidelberg (2005)
10. Engel, R.: SPIN: A semantic parser for spoken dialog systems. In: Proceedings of IS-LTC, Ljubljana, Slovenia (2006)
11. Ho, W.C., Dautenhahn, K., Nehaniv, C.L.: A study of episodic memory-based learning and narrative structure for autobiographic agents. Proceedings of Adaptation in Artificial and Biological Systems, AISB 2006 conference 3, 26–29 (2006)
12. Ho, W.C., Watson, S.: Autobiographic knowledge for believable virtual characters. In: Dumke, R.R., Abran, A. (eds.) IWSM 2000. LNCS, vol. 2006, pp. 383–394. Springer, Heidelberg (2001)
13. Linde, C.: Life Stories: The Creation of Coherence. Oxford University Press, Oxford (1993)
14. Marsella, S., Johnson, L., LaBore, C.: Interactive pedagogical drama. In: Proceedings of the Fourth International Conference on Autonomous Agents AAMAS, pp. 301–308. ACM Press, New York (2000)
15. Nelson, K.: The psychological and social origins of autobiographical memory. Psychological Science 4, 7–14 (1993)
16. Plutchik, R.: Empathy and its Development, chapter Evolutionary bases of empathy. Cambridge University Press, Cambridge (1987)
17. Thomas, F., Johnston, O.: Disney Animation: The Illusion of Life. Abbeville Press, New York (1981)

Creative Industrial Design and Computer-Based Image Retrieval: The Role of Aesthetics and Affect

S.J. Westerman, S. Kaur, C. Dukes, and J. Blomfield

University of Leeds
Leeds LS2 9JT
s.j.westerman@leeds.ac.uk

Abstract. A study is reported that examined the effectiveness of computer-based image retrieval as a support tool for creative industrial design. Participants were given a design brief for a concept car, and asked to retrieve images from the web that would provide inspiration for this design task. They then rated various aesthetic, affective, and inspirational aspects of the images, and a second sample of participants rated the search terms that they had used. Emotional inspiration was important to designers, arising in part from a broad semantic theme and in part from the inspirational values of the more 'fundamental' image properties of colour and layout. The pattern of results suggested that some designers adopted a more risky (less efficient) search strategy in order to access emotional image content. Aesthetic and affective aspects of the retrieved images predicted inspirational value.

1 Introduction

Computer-based image retrieval is an important component of many applied tasks (e.g., accessing medical records, journalism, archiving museum collections). It is a complex process influenced by various factors some of which depend on the nature of the task being supported. In this paper we consider image retrieval in the context of creative industrial design and, in particular, car design. Images are an important source of inspiration for industrial designers [1][2]. They are sometimes incorporated into 'image boards' or 'mood boards' that provide a 'reference point' for a design and assist in the communication of design ideas to colleagues or clients. The empirical work reported here focuses on specific inspirational content, and affective and aesthetic assessments of images in relation to retrieval strategy and the overall inspirational value of retrieved images.

1.1 The Image Retrieval Process

When considering computer-based image retrieval two key aspects of the process can be identified: i) the method of input; and, ii) the method of retrieval. There are two broad classes of input method available through which users can express a query to an image retrieval system. They can use physical exemplars to express their requirements. This could take the form of a sketch or an example image or portion of an image [3]. This approach can be used to provide relevance feedback to the system,

A. Paiva, R. Prada, and R.W. Picard (Eds.): ACII 2007, LNCS 4738, pp. 618–629, 2007.

allowing searches to be refined, e.g., [4]. Alternatively users can provide verbal descriptors as a means of defining a query. These terms can vary in their level of abstraction. They might be relatively concrete, as for example, when the user is searching for an image that incorporates a specific target object, such as an 'estate car'; or they might be relatively abstract as, for example, when the user is searching for an image that coveys a broader semantic construct such as 'sportiness' or a particular emotion or mood [5].

There are also two possible retrieval methods [6][7]. First, retrieval can be based on text that accompanies images, either in the form of metadata or other surrounding material, e.g., text on a website that contains the image. Various algorithms are available that permit assessment of semantic distance between a query and a set of documents. Alternatively Content Based Image Retrieval (CBIR) algorithms are being developed that can associate physical characteristics of images and queries - see e.g., [8]. The study reported in this paper used the Google image search engine which is based on 'verbal description' as a means of input and 'associated text' as a means of retrieval.

1.2 Creativity and Information Retrieval

A key issue for image retrieval systems is the 'semantic gap', i.e., the semantic distance between the query and the retrieved items [9]. The success or otherwise of information retrieval systems in closing the semantic gap is 'traditionally' assessed on the basis of the measures of recall and precision - see [10]. Recall refers to the extent to which a search (an information retrieval system) retrieves all relevant items. Precision refers to the extent to which a search (an information retrieval system) avoids retrieving irrelevant items. So, a system with perfect recall and precision would retrieval all relevant items and only relevant items.

However, closing the semantic gap can be more difficult for some types of material such as emotion-related queries [5]. Potentially this is exactly the sort of material that would be useful to creative designers [11][12]. Perhaps related to this, a degree of diversity can also be advantageous in the context of creative industrial design. Diversity of concepts features in several models of creativity - e.g., [13], it can arise from serendipitous identification of material (see [14]), and is an important contributor to processes of analogy and contrast, on the basis of which creative solutions can be generated [11]. Consistent with this, in interviews car designers have indicated that they find structured diversity in sources of inspirational materials (e.g., magazines) beneficial [15]. Consequently, when conducting computer-based searches for inspirational materials, creative designers may adopt search strategies that generate a degree of diversity in their results - cf. [16]. In this paper we pay particular attention to the following four possible search strategies that are relevant to the specified methods of search input and retrieval (i.e., 'verbal description' and 'associated text') and that may produce affective and/or diverse results. It should be noted that these strategies are not mutually exclusive. First designers might query the system by using emotionally evocative search terms. It is not clear how well search engines are able to handle such affective queries, so one of the aims of this study is to examine this issue. Second, designers may use search terms that are diverse to the target of their design task (i.e. cars). Third, designers may deliberately 'under-specify' a search query, using fewer rather than more search terms, or using abstract rather than concrete search terms. Finally, designers may use semantically diverse combinations of search terms.

1.3 Inspiration, Emotion, Aesthetics, and Information Retrieval

There are a number of cognitive and affective assessments that system users make of retrieved images that impact on their creative and inspirational value. These include judgments on the aesthetic properties of images, the emotions that they evoke, and the degree of interest they engender. However, forming such judgments is a complex and somewhat idiosyncratic process and it is not clear that this aspect of image retrieval will be well represented by current search algorithms. In the study reported here we examine the contribution of these constructs to inspirational value and also consider the potential for curvilinear associations. It may be that for images to be considered inspirational they must exceed a threshold with regard to values on constructs such as aesthetic beauty; or even that high and low levels of aesthetic or affective properties are inspirational. The Benetton advertisements are a well documented and discussed example of images that evoke a negative affective response that may have creative value. If curvilinear associations are evident in the current context this would have implications for the assessment and development of search algorithms that adequately support creative design tasks. The position would contrast with the nature of 'traditional' information retrieval algorithms, for which 'good' exemplars rerieved on the basis of search queries tend towards the average. As far as we are aware, there is limited existing literature that bears on these issues that can be used to guide the development of computer-based support facilities for creative designers.

1.4 Experimental Aims

Taking the context of creative industrial design, the reported study examines the influence that assessments of specific inspirational, affective, and aesthetic content of images have on their overall inspirational value. In related work [12] we have found that designers' ratings of the emotional inspirational qualities of an image made a substantial contribution to the prediction of the overall inspiration value of that image. Here we seek to replicate and extend this finding. In particular we are interested to examine:

1.   The extent to which the use of emotionally evocative search terms results in the retrieval of emotionally evocative images.
2.   The extent to which specific inspirational content of images ('Shape', 'Colour', 'Layout', 'Emotion', and 'Theme') contributes to overall inspirational value.
3.   The nature of the association between the affective and aesthetic impressions of the image, on the one hand, and inspirational value, on the other. Related to this, we wanted to examine the possibility that the association between some of these image properties and overall inspirational value is curvilinear.
4.   Whether associations between specific search strategies and specific search outcomes can be identified. In particular, we wanted to examine the role of a number of identified factors that could be used to promote search diversity.

To address these issues a sample of participants was given a design brief for a concept car and asked to conduct a search for inspirational images using the Google image search engine. A second sample rated the search terms that were used.

2 Method

2.1 Participants

Component 1 - Retrieving and Rating Images: Twenty-four participants (14 female and 10 male) were recruited. All were second year, final year or post-graduate students from a variety of design-related disciplines. The mean age of the sample was 22.12 years. Two participants had worked in industry, with experience ranging from 1 year to 5 years.

Component 2 - Assessing the Attributes of Search Terms: A second sample of six participants (all female) was recruited to provide ratings of the search terms used by the first sample when retrieving the images (mean age=26.5). Data from one participant were excluded from analysis for reliability reasons (see below). English was the first language of all participants.

2.2 Procedure

Component 1 - Retrieving and Rating Images: The first sample of participants were presented with a design brief for a concept car (including information on physical requirements, branding, target users, and market sector). Participants were given a few minutes to consider the design brief and to think of 1-3 term(s) that they would use to search for inspirational images. They then performed a search using the Google image search engine. Participants were given a maximum of 20 seconds to look at the first eight images retrieved (sometimes fewer images were retrieved) and decide which images they found inspirational. While performing this task participants' eye movements were monitored using an infrared eye tracker. These results are not reported here. Following this, the retrieved images were presented sequentially and participants responded to a series of items (using a 7-point rating scale) relating to inspirational, affective, and aesthetic properties of the retrieved images. Finally, participants were asked to circle parts of the images they found inspirational and indicate whether they would include each image on an image board when designing the car.

The items used to assess images included four terms relating to affective and aesthetic qualities: 'Beautiful', 'Energetic', 'Unpleasant', and 'Boring'; five items relating to specific inspirational properties: 'Shape', 'Colour', 'Layout', 'Emotion', and 'Theme'; an item relating to overall inspirational value; and an item relating to overall utility of the image. The utility of an image is potentially something more than its inspirational value. An image may provide a reference point – conveying essential information about the design – possibly used for communicating with colleagues or clients.

Component 2 - Assessing the Attributes of Search Terms: The second sample of participants rated the search terms that the first sample had generated to indicate the degree to which they were: i) emotionally evocative; ii) concrete-abstract; iii) related to cars. Finally, all possible combinations of two search terms for each of the sets generated were rated for semantic proximity, one to the other. So, if three search terms were used by a participant then three pairings of terms would be possible and three ratings of semantic distance obtained. If two search terms were used only one pairing would arise, and if only one search term was used then no pairings were possible. Based on inter-rater reliability data for one participant from the second sample were not included in the final analysis. Correlations with all other participants for some ratings approximated zero.

3 Results

A correlation matrix was calculated for the responses of the first participant sample to the image questionnaire items (inspirational, aesthetic, and affective). Associations between responses to these items were generally moderate to strong. Of particular relevance, there was a moderately strong correlation between 'emotional inspiration' and 'overall inspiration' (r=0.58). 'Overall inspiration was very strongly correlated with 'Usefulness' (r=0.87), and is the primary focus of this report. When considering aesthetic and affective assessments, correlations between beautiful and inspirational value and between energetic and inspirational value were particularly strong (r=0.69 and r=0.61, respectively), while the correlation with 'Unpleasant' was relatively weak (r=-0.27). The specific affective image properties (Beautiful, Energetic, Unpleasant, and Boring) were relatively independent of one another (-0.10 < rs < 0.48). It would seem that participants were able to distinguish these affective and aesthetics concepts one from another.

3.1 The Association Between Specific Inspirational Content and Overall Inspirational Value of Images

A linear regression equation was used to examine the extent to which specific inspirational content contributed to overall inspirational value (see Table 1).

Table 1. Regression of overall inspirational value onto ratings specific inspirational properties (n=183)

	B	Std Error	Beta	t	p
Constant	-0.56	0.20		-0.28	
Shape	0.38	0.05	0.38	7.11	<0.001
Colour	0.11	0.05	0.11	2.36	<.05
Layout	0.22	0.05	0.22	4.06	<.001
Emotion	0.05	0.05	0.05	1.01	
Theme	0.28	0.06	0.28	4.71	<0.001

Note: R^2=0.75, $F_{(5,177)}$=106.93, p<.001.

Seventy-five percent of the variance in ratings of 'Overall inspirational value', was accounted for, with 'Shape', 'Colour', 'Layout', and 'Theme' all making a significant contribution. Only ratings for 'Emotional inspiration' did not contribute unique variance, although, as noted above, there was a moderately strong correlation between 'Emotional inspiration' and 'Overall inspiration'. It would seem that this variance is being accounted for by these other predictors. To examine this further, ratings for 'emotional inspiration' were regressed onto those for other specific inspirational properties (see Table 2). 'Colour', 'Layout', and 'Theme' contributed significantly to the equation, which accounted for 70% of the variance.

Table 2. Regression of emotional inspiration onto ratings of other inspirational properties (n=183)

	B	Std Error	Beta	t	p
Constant	0.45	0.29		1.57	
Shape	-0.06	0.08	-0.06	-0.82	
Colour	0.20	0.07	0.20	3.10	<.01
Layout	0.39	0.07	0.38	5.26	<.001
Theme	0.31	0.08	0.31	3.78	<.001

Note: $R^2=0.70$, $F(4,178)=78.34$, $p<.001$.

3.2 The Influence of Search Strategy

Ratings from the second sample of participants were averaged across participants to produce scores for each set of search terms that reflected assessments of: i) emotional evocativeness; ii) concrete-abstract; iii) relatedness to cars; iv) semantic relatedness of individual search terms.

Each participant in the first sample produced only one set of search terms but retrieved up to eight images. Therefore, to examine the association between the two sets of scores ratings for sets of images were averaged within participants. However, this results in a between-subjects variable and individual differences in the use of rating scales would have an undue impact on scores. Therefore scores were standardised for each participant based on their responses to all questionnaire items (relating to image properties). The average of these standardised scores were correlated with ratings from the second sample for the search terms that produced the images (see Table 3).

There was a tendency that just failed to reach significance (p=0.051) for searches that used more semantically congruent search terms to retrieve images that were rated as being less unpleasant (more pleasant). Although the effect is rather weak, it is an interesting one that might be pursued in further research.

There was a significant positive correlation between the average rating (for each set of images) for emotional inspiration and the average rating for how emotionally evocative the search terms were. There was also a significant negative correlation between ratings for emotionally evocative search terms and the rated utility of the retrieved images. A similar correlation for overall inspirational value of the images approached significance (p=0.061). It would seem that, on average, images retrieved using emotionally evocative search terms were less useful and perhaps less inspirational.

Table 3. Correlations between ratings of affective properties of images and properties of search terms (n. obs.=24)

| Image properties | Search term properties | | | |
	Emotionally evocative	Concrete - abstract	Related to cars	Search terms related
Shape	-0.01	-0.03	-0.24	-0.11
Colour	0.19	0.02	-0.05	-0.21
Layout	-0.19	-0.14	0.10	-0.05
Emotion	0.49 *	0.21	-0.54 **	0.04
Theme	0.01	-0.17	-0.04	-0.23
Overall insp	-0.39	-0.07	0.43 *	-0.15
Useful	-0.46 *	-0.14	0.59 **	0.05
Beautiful	-0.09	0.13	0.07	0.35
Energetic	0.14	-0.01	0.12	0.21
Unpleasant	-0.09	0.14	-0.21	-0.42
Boring	0.14	-0.05	0.03	0.26

Note: * $p<.05$, ** $p<.01$.

To examine the possibility that the use of emotionally evocative search terms results in more varied results in terms of overall inspirational value and utility correlations with the standard deviations for ratings for each set of retrieved image (each participant's results) were calculated (see Table 4). There was a significant positive correlation between emotionally evocative key words and the variability of overall inspirational value of results, such that variability was greater when relatively more emotionally evocative terms were used. There was a non significant trend in the same direction when considering the utility of the retrieved images.

Table 4. Correlations between variability of ratings of overall inspirational value and utility of images and properties of search terms (n. obs.=24)

| Image properties | Search term properties | | | |
	Emotionally evocative	Concrete - abstract	Related to cars	Search terms related
Inspiration	0.44 *	0.09	-0.17	-0.09
Utility	0.32	0.17	-0.13	-0.18

Note: * $p<.05$

The effect that the number of search terms used had on the propertics of images retrieved was tested using a series of ANOVAs in which the ratings of image properties were the dependent measures and the number of search terms (1, 2, or 3) was the independent variable. There were 16 images retrieved with one search term, 75 with two search terms, and 92 with three search terms. This corresponds to 2 participants using one search term, 10 participants using two search terms, and 12 participants using three search terms. Results are shown in Table 5. As can be seen, there was a significant effect of the number of search terms on rating of the emotional inspiration provided by images, with emotional inspiration decreasing as the number of search terms increased. There was also a significant effect for ratings of image beauty. For this dependent measure the optimal number of search terms was two.

Table 5. Effects of number of search terms on ratings of inspirational, affective, and aesthetic properties of images

| | Number of search terms | | | | | | | |
| | 1 | | 2 | | 3 | | | |
	M	SD	M	SD	M	SD	F	p
Shape	3.69	1.62	4.43	1.90	3.97	1.80	1.82	
Colour	5.00	1.55	4.22	2.01	4.26	1.69	1.27	
Layout	4.00	1.79	3.93	1.94	3.65	1.61	0.64	
Emotion	4.69	1.70	3.87	1.86	3.26	1.70	5.57	<.01
Theme	3.81	1.87	3.79	1.82	3.48	1.82	0.67	
Overall Insp.	4.25	1.73	4.19	1.86	3.79	1.75	1.17	
Useful	3.75	1.98	4.12	1.87	3.90	1.85	0.41	
Beautiful	3.68	1.62	3.91	1.95	3.23	1.49	3.21	<.05
Energetic	4.56	2.44	3.67	1.92	3.90	1.62	1.63	
Unpleasant	2.81	2.01	2.29	1.79	2.14	1.38	1.26	
Boring	2.44	1.63	3.07	1.95	2.61	1.49	1.84	

3.3 The Association Between Affective and Aesthetic Image Properties and Inspirational Value

To test the possibility that the association between affective and aesthetic responses to images and their inspirational value of images was non-linear, regressions were calculated for the items 'Beautiful', 'Energetic', 'Unpleasant', and 'Boring' that included quadratic and cubic terms.

The only significant improvement beyond the linear regression equation was found for 'Beautiful', with scores being better described by a quadratic equation (see Table 6). It would seem that the effects of 'Beautiful' on inspirational value are greatest when assessed beauty is low. As rating rise asymptote is reached (see Figure 2).

Table 6. Regression of ratings for overall inspirational value onto linear and quadratic terms for ratings of 'Beautiful' (n=183)

	B	Std Error	Beta	t	p
Beautiful	1.63	0.26	1.56	6.37	<.001
Beautiful**2	-0.12	0.03	-0.89	-3.62	<.001
Constant	0.07	0.43		0.17	

Note: R^2=0.52, F(2,182)=96.20, p<.001.

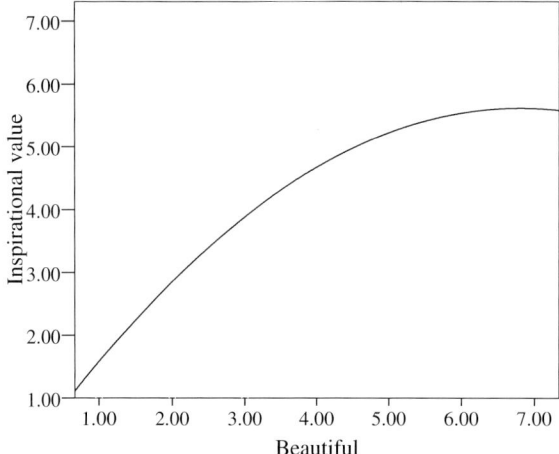

Fig. 1. Line of best fit for the quadratic regression of Inspirational value on to ratings for the item 'Beautiful'

The association between aesthetic and affective responses to images and assessments of overall inspirational value was examined with a further linear regression equation. Given the quadratic association between 'Beautiful' and inspiration, effects of this variable may be underestimated.

Table 7. Regression of overall inspirational value onto ratings of emotional and aesthics properties (n=183)

	B	Std Error	Beta	t	p
Constant	1.35	0.36		3.76	<.001
Beautiful	0.49	0.06	0.47	8.65	<.001
Energetic	0.36	0.05	0.37	7.25	<.001
Unpleasant	0.00	0.06	0.00	0.06	
Boring	-0.18	0.06	-0.17	-3.06	<.01

Note: $R^2=0.64$, $F(4,178)=78.34$, $p<.001$.

The regression equation accounted for 64% of the variance in ratings of 'Overall inspirational value'. Ratings for 'Beautiful', 'Energetic', and 'Boring' contributed significantly (see Table 7).

4 Discussion

The reported study examined the influence of the inspirational, affective, and aesthetic properties of images in the context of creative industrial design. Participants generated a key word search to retrieve images related to a specified design brief for a concept car. They then rated the aesthetic, affective, and inspirational properties of retrieved images. An independent sample of participants rated the search terms used by the first sample on several criteria.

4.1 The Influence of Emotional Inspiration

As predicted, there was a moderately strong positive association between the rated emotional inspirational value of images and their overall inspirational value [12]. There was also a significant correlation between ratings (by the second sample) of how emotionally evocative the search terms were and ratings (by the first sample) of the emotional inspiration value of images. These results validate the capacity of this type of information retrieval process ('verbal/semantic' input and retrieval based on 'associated text') to identify emotionally relevant material. Given the potential importance of emotional inspiration to the design process, these associations could be the target of further research designed to improve the performance of information retrieval systems in this regard. It should be noted that the extent to which the emotional content specified in the key words was congruent with the emotional content of the retrieved images has not been tested here.

Following from this, it is somewhat surprising that when a multiple regression equation was calculated, in which overall inspirational value for images was regressed onto items assessing other specific sources of inspiration ('colour', 'shape', 'layout', 'emotion', and 'theme'), the association with emotional inspiration did not contribute significant unique variance. To clarify the position, a second regression equation was conducted in which ratings of emotional inspiration for images were regressed onto ratings for these other specific inspirational properties. This equation indicated that 'Theme' is an important predictor in both cases, but also that inspiration arising from the colour and layout of images makes a direct contribution to participants' assessments of emotional inspiration. Emotional inspiration being as part of a broader semantic construct ('theme') is consistent with a qualitative assessment of the search terms used. Participants used affective terms as part of a group of keywords that conveyed a more general semantic theme, e.g., "Fast + Unique + Lively". Given the nature of the algorithms for text-based matching of search terms and information content this theme-based characterisation of queries may have beneficial effects on retrieval accuracy for affective content - cf. [17]. However, these results also suggest it may be possible to identify affective image content on the basis of more 'fundamental' physical image properties that may be relatively amenable to algorithmic assessment.

4.2 Trading Precision for Recall to Generate Emotionally Inspirational Material

The use of fewer search terms resulted in the retrieval of more emotionally inspirational images. This is consistent with emotionally inspiring images being retrieved by a less specified and more diverse search. The negative association between the use of emotionally evocative search terms and the usefulness of the retrieved images – and the similar correlation with overall inspirational value of images that approached significance is, at first sight somewhat counter intuitive, given the positive association between ratings of individual image emotional inspiration and overall inspirational value. However, this can be explained with reference to the effectiveness of the information retrieval process. It is possible that the quality of the retrieved images when using emotionally evocative search terms is more varied. This could result in retrieval of a few images that are deemed to be emotionally inspirational and that are regarded as having high overall inspirational value, but the majority of the retrieved set not being highly valued. To test this, ratings of emotional evocativeness of search terms were correlated with standard deviations for ratings of overall inspiration and usefulness for each of the image sets. Results indicated that, consistent with prediction, there was a significant association between ratings of emotionally evocative search terms and variability of inspirational quality. However, the association for the variability of image utility, although in the predicted direction, was not significant.

4.3 Aesthetics and Affect as Predictors of Inspiration

Correlations between the aesthetic and affective constructs were relatively modest, indicating a good deal of independence. This interpretation was supported by the results of a multiple regression equation in which 'Beauty', 'Energy', and 'Boring' all contributed to the prediction of inspirational value. Tests for non-linear associations identified the quadratic term for 'Beauty' as improving prediction for this construct. It seems that there may be a threshold for beauty, above which improvement has very little impact on inspirational value. The strongest effects of beauty are for images with relatively lower values. The other aesthetic and affective variables were appropriately described by linear association. Given this pattern of associations, it does seem that, for this particular task context, automatic identification of certain image features, relating to aesthetic and affective content, might produce generic benefits if incorporated as part of a retrieval algorithm.

4.4 Conclusions

The affective content of images was an important contributor to the overall inspirational value of images. This effect was exerted, in part, through thematic influences, but also seemed to be related to more fundamental physical image characteristics. In identifying images that were emotionally inspirational participants may adopt the strategy of making their search less specific (in this instance use fewer keywords). However, this is a risky strategy that produces greater variability in the inspirational quality of retrieved items.

Acknowledgements. Part of the work reported here was supported by the TRENDS project, which is funded under the EC FP6.

References

1. Goldschmidt, G., Smolkov, M.: Variances in the impact of visual stimuli on design problem solving performance. Design Studies 27, 549–569 (2006)
2. Malaga, R.A.: The effect of stimulus modes and associative distance in individual creativity support systems. Decision Support Systems 29, 125–141 (2000)

3. Niblack, W., Barber, R., Equitz, W., Flickner, M.D., Glasman, R.H., Petkovic, D., Yanker, P., Faloutsos, C.: QBIC project: querying images by content, using color, texture, and shape. Storage and Retrieval for Image and Video Databases, SPIE, vol. 173 - 187 (1993)
4. Heesch, D., Yavlinsky, A., Ruger, S.: Performance comparison of different similarity models for CBIR with relevance feedback. In: Bakker, E.M., Lew, M.S., Huang, T.S., Sebe, N., Zhou, X.S. (eds.) CIVR 2003. LNCS, vol. 2728, pp. 456–466. Springer, Heidelberg (2003)
5. Wang, S., Wang, X.: Emotion semantics image retrieval: A brief overview. In: Tao, J., Tan, T., Picard, R.W. (eds.) ACII 2005. LNCS, vol. 3784, Springer, Heidelberg (2005)
6. Li, B., Goh, K., Chang, E.: Confidence-based dynamic ensemble for image annotation and semantics discovery. In: Proceedings of Multimedia 2003, ACM, New York (2003)
7. Wang, W., Zhang, A.: Extracting semantic concepts from images: A decisive feature mining approach. Multimedia systems 11, 352–366 (2006)
8. Rummukainnen, L., Koskella, M.: An efficiency comparison of two content-based image retrieval systems, GIFT and PicSOM. In: Bakker, E.M., Lew, M.S., Huang, T.S., Sebe, N., Zhou, X.S. (eds.) CIVR 2003. LNCS, vol. 2728, pp. 500–510. Springer, Heidelberg (2003)
9. Enser, P., Sandom, C.: Toward a comprehensive survey of the semantic gap in visual image retrieval. In: Bakker, E.M., Lew, M.S., Huang, T.S., Sebe, N., Zhou, X.S. (eds.) CIVR 2003. LNCS, vol. 2728, pp. 291–299. Springer, Heidelberg (2003)
10. Baeza-Yates, R., Ribeiro-Neto, B.: Modern Information Retrieval. Addison Wesley, Harlow (1999)
11. Lubart, T.I., Getz, I.: Emotion, metaphor, and the creative process. Creativity Research Journal 10, 285–301 (1997)
12. Westerman, S.J., Kaur, S.: Supporting creative industrial design with computer-based information retrieval. Paper to be presented at the European Conference on Cognitive Ergonomics. Covent Garden, London (2007)
13. Pereira, F.C., Cardoso, A.: Conceptual blending and the quest for the holy creative process. In: Proceedings of the 2nd Workshop on Creative Systems. ECAI 2002, Lyon, France (2002)
14. Beale, R.: Supporting serendipity: Using ambient intelligence to augment user exploration for data mining and web browsing. International Journal of Human-Computer Studies 65, 421–433 (2007)
15. Kaur, S., Westerman, S.J., Mougenot, C., Sourbe, L., Bouchard, C.: Computer-based support for creativity in Industrial Design. In: Poster presented at the First International Symposium on Culture, Creativity, and Interaction Design (2006)
16. Bonnardel, N., Marmeche, E.: Toward supporting evocation processes in creative design: A cognitive approach. International Journal of Human-Computer Studies 63, 422–435 (2005)
17. Lew, M.S., Sebe, N., Djeraba, C., Jain, R.: Content-based multimedia information retrieval: State of the art and Challenges. ACM Transactions on Multimedia Computing and Applications 2, 1–19 (2006)

Interactive Storytelling with Literary Feelings

David Pizzi, Fred Charles, Jean-Luc Lugrin, and Marc Cavazza

School of Computing, University of Teesside TS1 3BA, United Kingdom
{d.pizzi,f.charles,j-l.lugrin,m.o.cavazza}@tees.ac.uk

Abstract. In this paper, we describe the integration of Natural Language Processing (NLP) within an emotional planner to support Interactive Storytelling. Our emotional planner is based on a standard HSP planner, whose originality is drawn from altering the agents' beliefs and emotional states. Each character is driven by its own planner, while characters are able to operate on their reciprocal feelings thus affecting each other. Our baseline story is constituted by a classic XIXth century French novel from Gustave Flaubert in which characters feelings play a dominant role. This approach benefits from the fact that Flaubert has described a specific ontology for his characters feelings. The objective of NLP should be to uncover from natural language utterances the same kind of affective elements, which requires an integration between NLP and the planning component at the level of semantic content. This research is illustrated with examples from a first fully integrated prototype comprising NLP, emotional planning and real-time 3D animation.

Keywords: Aesthetic computing, literary analysis, interactive storytelling, emotional NLP.

1 Introduction

Narratives traditionally depict emotions and feelings, and are similarly meant to elicit comparable ones in the mind of their readers (or spectators). This is why this issue has been addressed by research in Interactive Storytelling (IS). For instance, Cheong and Young have described how suspense could be elicited from formal properties of a sequence of narrative actions [11]. Previous research in IS has mostly addressed Ekmanian feelings, in particular fear [1] [15]. Fear is traditionally important as part of narratives: it can be depicted as experienced by characters and can also be elicited in the spectator, which contributes to realism as well as empathy.

However, studies of narrative aesthetics tend to uncover more sophisticated feelings. A study on a corpus of French novels has for instance uncovered over 128 such feelings [27] such as *ambition, complicity, gratitude, guilt, loneliness, pride, shame, tact...* Of course, literary feelings have no claim to psychological validity: they constitute a fine-grained semantics, which is very much related to aesthetic properties of the narrative. Their description is connected to other current topics in AI such as aesthetic computing [23], in which AI techniques are confronted with the processing of sophisticated cultural content, as in IS or the computational analysis of literary texts [3]. The distinction between psychological and literary feelings is another example of the duality between

A. Paiva, R. Prada, and R.W. Picard (Eds.): ACII 2007, LNCS 4738, pp. 630–641, 2007.
© Springer-Verlag Berlin Heidelberg 2007

cognitive and semiotic approaches to cultural content, which, in the specific case of storytelling has been revisited by Christian and Young [12].

The majority of IS research prototypes have embraced planning as their core technology to control the behaviour of virtual actors, and drive the IS. In addition, the necessity to relate plan progression to dramatic elements has led to the adoption of emotional planning approaches, which will be discussed in the next section.

1.1 System Overview and Architecture

Our experimental system presents itself as a real-time 3D computer animation featuring virtual actors, which express themselves via animation and speech synthesis. The baseline story is adapted from a XIXth century novel, *Madame Bovary* by Flaubert [13]. Only a small fragment of the original novel has been represented, more specifically chapters 9-12 of Part II [13]. The IS engine is based on a multi-threaded planner controlling each character independently. 3D animations are generated by the graphics engine from the grounded actions produced by the planner. During story visualisation, the system accepts NL input through the keyboard, which is analysed to update characters' beliefs and emotional state (i.e. by modifying character's mental states). In this way, the user interacts with the evolution of the narrative by influencing the selection of the next narrative action, albeit indirectly.

From a system architecture perspective (Figure 1), visualisation is provided by the Unreal Tournament™ game engine with which the planner communicates via UDP sockets. The communication between the planner and the visualisation engine takes place in both directions to acknowledge execution of actions in the virtual world by returning the resulting value (i.e. action success or failure). The planner itself is a C++ implementation of the Heuristic Search Planner (HSP) approach (described in the next section) [4] [5]. The NLP module consists of an integrated parser (syntax and semantics) and is developed in Allegro Common Lisp: it communicates with the planner only, to which it sends new facts corresponding to the semantic interpretation of the utterance, also via a UDP socket.

With respect to previously described IS systems, this prototype relies on a baseline plot from an actual novel thus providing a realistic framework to explore the nature and consistency of interaction-driven alternatives.

2 Emotional Planning for Interactive Storytelling

The majority of IS research prototypes have relied on planning techniques for their narrative engine, generating action sequences as the story backbone [6] [24] [29]. Among the factors having favoured the adoption of planning was a tendency to present narratives as some kind of problem solving which is typical in epics, tales and certain genres such as the crime novel (e.g., plans to commit crimes such as robbery [30]).

The inclusion of emotions in IS systems has been extensively described by Gratch et al. [15] [17] and follows the development of emotional planning by Gratch [16]. They introduced the two central notions of *appraisal* (evaluating the emotional significance of events) and *coping* (maintaining the relationship between the agent and its social environment). However, in their approach emotions derive from an anticipation of plan evolution, for instance the anticipation of plan failure due to possible threats. In that sense, emotions do not belong to the planning domain itself.

If we now consider different narrative genres, emotions and feelings can actually be central to the plot itself and determine characters situation at every stage. We thus wanted to explore another approach, which consists in i) basing the plan domain itself on characters' feelings and ii) adopting a weaker representational model, in which planning is only used to drive action selection towards certain long-term objectives (rather than equating the story itself with a plan). Our planning component is based on a standard HSP approach, which provides additional flexibility in the generation of action sequences. The planning domain is composed of a list of characters' emotions and mental states characteristic of the novel. Some are represented on Figure 1, e.g. `reputation`, `embarrassment`, `loneliness`.

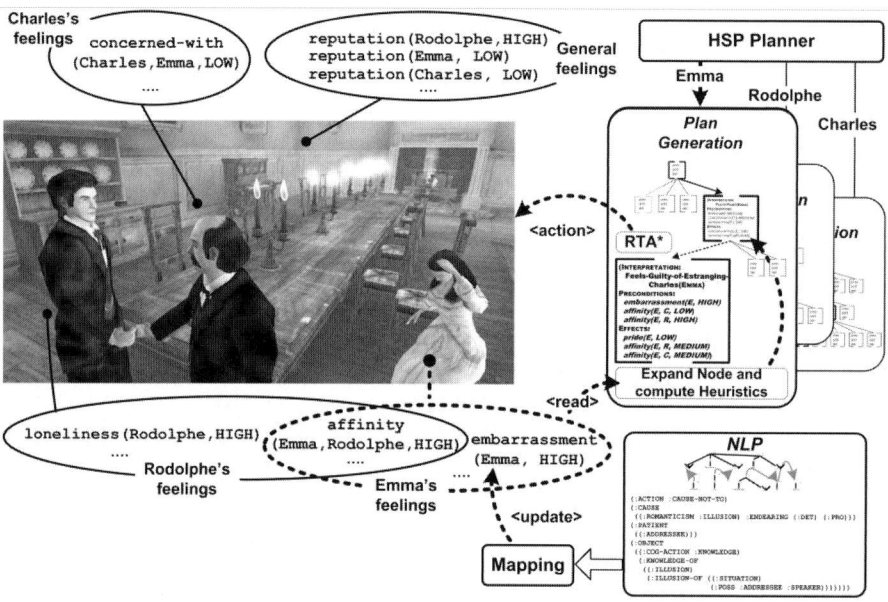

Fig. 1. System Architecture. The IS engine is based on a planning system whose domain is described in terms of characters' feelings. Characters can be influenced via Natural Language input.

These states admit various intensity values {LOW, MEDIUM, HIGH}, which are modified by planning operators, themselves corresponding to feelings, which govern the evolution of mental states. These operators have been classified in three categories. *Interpretation operators* update a character's feelings to respond to a change in the state of the world, as with the following `Disappointed-in` or `Regrets-Falling-for` (this being prompted by another character's actions or by the provision of new information, e.g. through user interaction). Figure 2 shows such an operator (`Emboldened-by-love`), which corresponds to a feeling of increased self-confidence for Emma Bovary. *Character interaction operators* intentionally modify another character's mental states and correspond to narrative actions such as invitations, arguments, and declarations (e.g. Accepts-Conversation, Makes-Love-Declaration, etc.). Finally, *physical operators* correspond to necessary physical actions such as changing location to interact with another character (the low-level details of motion planning and animation are automatically generated in the 3D environment from the corresponding action primitive). From the above description, it appears that the planning environment, in which each character influences other characters' feelings, is naturally dynamic, even more so considering the potential for user intervention at anytime. This is why we have opted for a "real-time" version of HSP by implementing RTA* [19] as its underlying search algorithm. Our implementation generates the next operator to be executed for each character, thus searching at a depth of one, without using look-ahead, and with a computational threshold of 500 ms. Finally, we use the simple Value Iteration (VI) method as described by Liu et al. [22] to calculate the heuristic function from the content of operators and the goal ("driver") definition. There is potential for further optimisation, for instance by using more sophisticated methods to calculate the heuristic function such as PINCH [22].

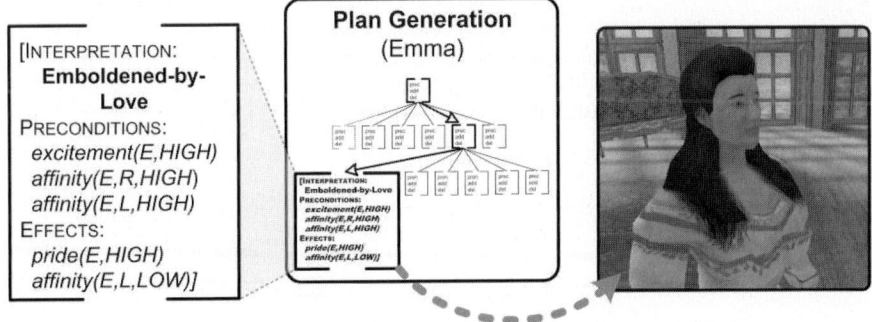

Fig. 2. An example Interpretation Operator: its contents are mental states and feelings relating the various characters (E = Emma, L = Léon, R = Rodolphe)

3   Narrative Formalisation: From Feelings to Planning Domains

Character psychology and feelings permeate traditional forms of narratives such as XIXth century novels. Gustave Flaubert's 1856 classic novel *Madame Bovary* is such an example. Further to placing significant emphasis on the characters' psychology, Flaubert's preliminary studies for the novel contain a description of the plot in the form of elementary plans and scenarios, together with an extensive description of the characters' psychology at various stages of the plot [21]. This description is actually based on his inventory of characters' feelings, accurate enough to constitute the basis for an "ontology".

Examples of such feelings described by Flaubert for Emma Bovary include *feeling-of-emptiness, boredom* [21, p.17]; *pride-of-having-a-lover, poetic-feelings* [21, p.48] *emboldened-by-love* (developing an attitude), *jealousy-curiosity* [21, p. 48]; *feels-hatred-for-Charles* [21, p. 49]; *irritated-by-vice* [21, p.50]; *bitter-love-feelings* [21, p.50]. Over 30 such feelings have been described by Flaubert in his preliminary plans and scenarios. This is a rather unique case of content formalisation provided by an author himself: it constitutes a formidable starting point for the design of an emotional planner, whose objective is to operate on the characters' feelings and mental states. These feelings range from traditional ones (e.g. *boredom*) to fairly specific ones. In deriving a planning domain from their inventory, we have first defined a set of ground mental states (such as `affinity` between characters, `pride`, `womanhood`), which were derived from the traditional feelings. Whereas the more specific feelings have been associated with *Interpretation operators*, which actually express the consequences of that literary feeling, and decompose it into ground mental states within the expression of the operator (both pre-conditions and effects).

Table 1. The definition of emotional (Interpretation) operators for virtual actors following the ontology feelings identified by Flaubert himself for *Madame Bovary*

Feelings from Flaubert ([21])	Description	Operator

Pride-of-Having-a-Lover (p. 48)	The relationship between Emma and Rodolphe is strong, and she fulfils her dreams of living a passionate love.	`[Interpretation:`
		`Joy-of-Love (Emma)`
		`Preconditions:`
		`affinity(E, R, HIGH)`
		`pride(E, HIGH)`
		`womanhood(E, HIGH)`
		`Effects:`
		`satisfaction(E, HIGH)]`

Irritated-by-Vice (p. 50)	Emma has doubts about their relationship prompted by a letter from her father enquiring about her well-being.
	At the same time, Rodolphe behaviour is increasingly rude and Emma is suffering from it.
		`[Interpretation:`
		`Regrets-Falling-for-Rodolphe (Emma)`
		`Preconditions:`
		`embarrassment(E, HIGH)`
		`affinity(E, C, MEDIUM)`
		`power-over(R, E, HIGH)`
		`Effects:`
		`affinity(E, R, LOW)`
		`anger(E, R, HIGH)`
		`affinity(E, C, HIGH)]`

This "ontology" plays a central role in the integration of AI technologies in our system, as it will be used to specify not only the planning domain but also the main semantic domains targeted by NL interpretation, as described in the next sections. When considering Flaubert's descriptions, there appears to be some kind of continuity between elementary mental states such as *anger* or *pride*, and the more sophisticated feelings of the type illustrated by Table I, which we have precisely termed "*literary feelings*". While Flaubert in his description does not explicitly formalise complex feelings in terms of elementary ones, this is an additional step we had to take to make the whole approach computational: this explains the above formalisations, in which mental states tend to feature as *fluents* belonging to operators' preconditions, while operators themselves have been associated to *literary feelings*.

4   Emotional NLP for Interactive Storytelling

The ability to incorporate Natural Language in IS remains a major challenge that has received comparatively less attention than other aspects such as action generation. Language is an important element of the aesthetics of narratives: in the case of IS it plays a dual role by being both part of the staged drama, and the privileged modality for user interaction. For that reason, and from the long-term perspective of explicitly addressing *literary feelings* in IS, it is important to lay some foundations for its investigation.

Previous IS systems having incorporated NLP (under written [25] or spoken [6] [31] form) can be divided into two categories depending on whether user utterances are actually meant to form part of the staged IS or not. In the latter case [6], they support intervention from a spectator who influences the characters from a God-like perspective: as such, they follow normal user expressions and are unrelated to narrative aesthetics. However, the most challenging case consists of utterances, which, because they should also be part of the (interactive) narrative's dialogues, have to contribute to the aesthetics of the narrative. Emotional NLP in the context of these aesthetic expressions is thus faced with the double challenge of parsing complexity, because the style will often be literary rather than common, and the extraction of implicit or figurative meaning, which will ultimately have to be interpreted in terms of characters' feelings. We have used sentences derived from the English translation of *Madame Bovary* to experiment with NL input. Despite variations in style in the translations [32] they presented similar characteristics in terms of style and implicit meaning, including emotional aspects.

To a large extent, it can be said that the whole objective of the NLP step is to uncover feelings from the semantic content of the utterance, which are part of the planners' domain. To address this challenge, we propose to direct the whole NLP step towards the identification of specific feelings by using a highly contextual approach to the lexicon directly inspired from Textual Semantics [28].

Textual Semantics posits that the relevant semantic content of the lexicon actually corresponds to highly contextual categories rather than generic ones (this differs from the introduction of generic emotional tags [33] and corresponds to specific types of applications). This leads to a redefinition of lexical content in context, based on the identification of the most relevant semantic domains. In the case of *Madame Bovary*, one can identify dimensions such as /boredom/ vs. /enjoyment/, /illusion/ vs. /reality/, /fear-for-reputation/ vs. /acceptance-of-risk/, etc. Rastier [27] has in particular demonstrated that the concept of /boredom/, whilst central to *Madame Bovary* was however not lexicalised in the novel's text (only 4 occurrences in the whole of the original text) and constituted instead a semantic category into which a variety of words would be indexed. This encourages us to identify semantic categories corresponding to the novel main topics (as in the above semantic oppositions).

The potential of this approach can be compared to previous work on NLP in IS. It has been generally based on the identification of dialogue acts which were then mapped to specific narrative functions (or in certain cases even equated to them). The number of speech acts varies but can be reduced to evaluative dimensions such as *agree/disagree* [9] [25].

Let us consider the utterance [13]:

"And I shall remain tonight, tomorrow, all other days, all my life!" (S1)

A traditional speech act interpretation would categorise this utterance as a "promise" and more specifically in the romantic context of the novel, an "eternal love promise". This would assume a corresponding narrative function in the IS system, but the main difficulty would be to identify such a speech act from either the surface form or the semantic content. However, it can also be interpreted in terms of semantic features such as */lover-presence/* and */duration/*, which can then be mapped directly to the planning domain. The principle behind that mapping, which follows from early work described in [7] consists in identifying feelings as collections of semantic features [27]. Similar principles have been described more recently: by Basili and Marocco [2] using co-occurrence analysis and Latent Semantic Analysis [20] and by Gliozzo [14] using semantic domains, which are equivalent to the semantic classes of Textual Semantics [28].

We have attempted a first small-scale implementation of these principles. The linguistic coverage is both limited and specific to certain constructs encountered in our sample corpus. However the principles aim at being generic (the only large-scale NLP system used in IS has been described by Mateas [26] as "author-intensive", suggesting a strong intertwining of linguistic and narrative representations, probably justified by the fact that the *Façade* narrative is essentially dialogue-based). Our NLP component aims at constructing a feature structure based on (contextual) semantic features associated to the lexicon.

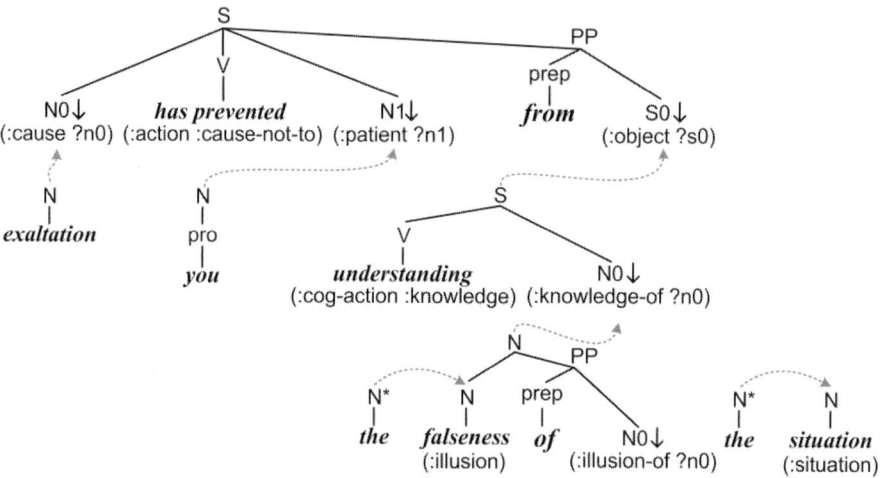

Fig. 3. Partial representation of the parsing of an actual sentence from the novel with a lexicalised grammar

The construction of such a semantic structure is driven by syntactic analysis. We have developed an ad-hoc lexicalised grammar covering some major syntactic forms encountered in the set of dialogues and monologues occurring in the novel. This lexicalised grammar is derived from a simplified version of the Tree-Adjoining Grammar (TAG) [18] formalism in which adjunction is replaced with the operation of furcation [8]. The use of TAG also facilitates the processing of idiomatic constructs, which are frequent in that literary genre. The parser we used is adapted from an earlier implementation [8], which integrates syntactic and semantic processing, as its main purpose is to construct a semantic structure. Parsing proceeds bottom up, as adjacent trees of compatible types are combined through substitution and furcation. During furcation, semantic features are propagated from the auxiliary to the target tree to progressively build up a semantic structure (Figure 3). Substitution establishes semantic relations between the related trees, creating a nested feature structure. In those cases where the parser is unable to produce a complete parse, the semantic structures obtained from the various partial parses are merged into a single structure. In other words, parsing is not about identifying named entities or even uncovering (narrative) action structure but establishing the recurrence of semantic features associated to feelings.

The Emotional NLP module operates in three steps: i) the TAG parser assembles a semantic structure whilst processing the sentence. In case no single parse of head S can be produced, the semantic structures for partial parses are merged into one; ii) this semantic structure is interpreted, not as a logical formula or as a case structure, but as a *resource* for the extraction of semantic patterns based on emotional categories (feelings) for the novel and; iii) these semantic patterns are mapped to the planning domain using association rules. Certain patterns can actually take part in the preconditions of certain operators: for instance an inventory of properties (*illusion, selfishness, prodigality*) can be mapped to certain key feelings such as embarrassment when brought to the attention of Emma's consciousness.

To illustrate this let us consider the analysis of the following sentence:

"This charming exaltation has prevented you from understanding the falseness of our future situation" (S2)

The complexity of this sentence in terms of interpretation makes it challenging for traditional NLP techniques to extract an appropriate (implicit) meaning and map it subsequently to the planning domain. However, if we assign as a goal to the parser to construct an integrated semantic feature structure, it can support the identification of feature patterns that map onto feelings in the planning domain.

Part of the parsing process is represented on Figure 3 and the resulting feature structure on Figure 4.

```
(:ACTION :CAUSE-NOT-TO)
(:CAUSE
 ((:ROMANTICISM :ILLUSION) :ENDEARING (:DET) (:PRO)))
(:PATIENT
 ((:ADDRESSEE)))
(:OBJECT
 ((:COG-ACTION :KNOWLEDGE)
  (:KNOWLEDGE-OF
   ((:ILLUSION)
    (:ILLUSION-OF ((:SITUATION) (:POSS :ADDRESSEE :SPEAKER)))))))
```

Fig. 4. Semantics Structure obtained for sentence 2

Its analysis results in a fairly complex and redundant semantic structure formed by the aggregation of features and establishment of case relations (Figure 4). The central point is how semantic description through a very focussed set of features corresponding to the novel's main dimensions (:illusion, :illusion-of) supports further interpretation which would otherwise be beyond reach. In the semantic structure, :speaker and :addressee are first replaced by Rodolphe and Emma. The key expression (:illusion-of ((:situation (:poss Emma Rodolphe))))) together with the recurrence of the :illusion feature can be mapped to domain facts such as embarrassment(Emma, HIGH). We have defined a small number of rules for that mapping, which embody the main narrative dimensions (as illustrated in section 2). Semantic features associated to lexical entries are described using differential semantics [28], i.e. by identifying salient features within semantic classes (equivalent to "Synsets", although with a stronger focus, which makes them "minimal" meaning classes [28]). These classes themselves derive from an identification of emotional vocabulary in French novels, which obviously apply to the current context [27].

5   Prototype Integration and Example Results

A first version of the prototype has been implemented comprising a total of 70 operators and 150 logical atoms in the Planner's domain. At its present stage of development, the system has not been the object of formalised evaluation which, in the general case of IS, remains a research topic in itself [10]. The system has however been tested for the generation of variants of the baseline plot from different initial conditions and is able to produce multiple stories of an average duration of 4 minutes.

Figure 5 illustrates the impact of an utterance on the story unfolding from the perspective of the central character, Emma Bovary. The initial situation corresponds to Emma and Rodolphe meeting just after she has decided to reach happiness (which is translated in the planning domain by adding a new local goal represented by the feeling satisfaction(E, HIGH)). Emma is estranging her husband Charles (Disappointed-in-Charles), after he fell into disrepute due to medical malpractice, and she is ready to take any risk (accepts-adultery-risk(E, C, HIGH)) to escape from a life she sees as miserable. In absence of influence (left hand side of the figure), Emma will fulfil her goal by letting Rodolphe seduce her. She engages first in a romantic conversation (Accepts-Conversation-Rodolphe and Say-Sthg-in-Confidence-Rodolphe) before falling for her new lover and showing him affection signs (Kissed-by-Rodolphe, Physical-Contact-with-Rodolphe). She is now living in a new relationship and starts to enjoy it (In-Love-Attitude and Emboldened-by-Love), which will make her forget about Leon (her ex-lover who moved away). At the end, she will not hesitate to risk her financial situation for him (Offer-Gifts-to-Rodolphe) before at last being proud of this new lover (Joy-of-Love). This to a large extent corresponds to a generation of the original storyline by the system, which would be a first indication that the planning domain is consistent.

Conversely, the right-hand side of the figure shows alternative story evolutions from exactly the same initial conditions, under the influence of a Natural Language utterance introduced at different stages. This utterance is entered by the user on behalf of Rodolphe (S2 or "you should not be one of those frivolous women"). This type of criticism is most likely to generate Embarrassment. However, depending on the stage at which this utterance is introduced, Emma will react differently. At an early stage, where her feelings for Rodolphe are not that strong (marked as A and B of Figure 5), she will soon return to her family (Emphasises-Motherhood and Joy-of-Family), eventually feeling compassion for Charles (Commiseration). However, at a more advanced stage of her relation (Figure 5 C), following her first affection signs to Rodolphe (Kissed-by-Rodolphe, Physical-Contact-with-Rodolphe), Emma will experience feelings of *guilt* (Feels-Guilty-of-Estranging-Charles) and will hesitate between her husband and her lover (Love-Ambivalence). In absence of new seduction acts from Rodolphe, she will also return to her family (Emphasises-Motherhood and Joy-of-Family). The same utterance at a later stage of their relation (Figure 5 D), will upset Emma about the power that actually Rodolphe has gained over her (Regrets-Falling-for-Rodolphe), prompting her to return to her family, more as a rejection of Rodolphe.

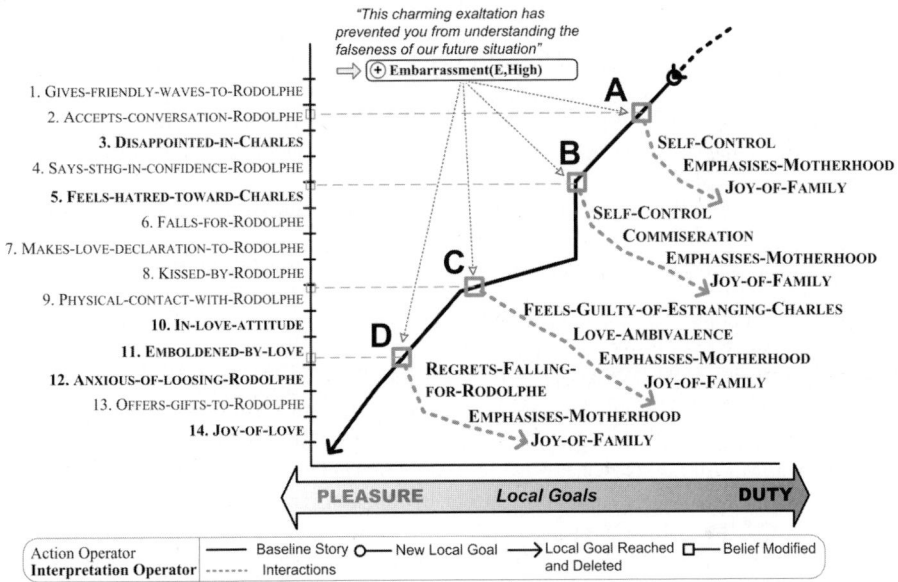

Fig. 5. The influence of a NL utterance on the unfolding of the story (see text for details)

If however this utterance takes place once their affair has transformed Emma's personality (Emboldened-by-Love), it will have no effect on Emma's subsequent behaviour, as she will reach happiness through this new love (Joy-of-Love).

6 Conclusion

We have presented an approach to IS based on characters' feelings and the use of such feelings to implement the planning domain of the IS engine. This integration has emphasised content and knowledge representation aspects, as can be expected for an application processing aesthetic content. While this is largely a research prototype of moderate scale, it could form the basis for new IS technologies. In particular a more flexible interpretation of NL input could circumvent the inevitable limitations of parsing for utterances extracted from literary texts, as well as the difficulties of specific speech acts identification, thereby facilitating integration with storytelling engines based on planning technologies. This approach falls under the generic distinction between the *cognitive* and the *narrative* (See also [12] for a specific discussion in the context of IS).

Acknowledgments. This work has been funded in part by the Department of Trade and Industry, via the Technology Programme BARDS Project, in collaboration with Eidos Interactive Ltd.

References

1. Aylett, R., Louchart, S., Dias, J., Paiva, A., Vala, M.: FearNot! - An Experiment in Emergent Narrative. In: Panayiotopoulos, T., Gratch, J., Aylett, R., Ballin, D., Olivier, P., Rist, T. (eds.) IVA 2005. LNCS (LNAI), vol. 3661, pp. 305–316. Springer, Heidelberg (2005)
2. Basili, R., Marocco, P.: A geometrical approach to literary text analysis. In: Proceedings of the LREC 2006 Workshop "Towards Computational models of Literary Analysis", Genova, Italy (May 22, 2006)
3. Basili, R.: Toward Computational Models of Literary Analysis. In: Proceedings of the LREC 2006 workshop, Genova, Italy (2006)
4. Bonet, B., Geffner, H.: Planning as Heuristic Search: New Results. In: Biundo, S., Fox, M. (eds.) ECP 1999. LNCS, vol. 1809, pp. 360–372. Springer, Heidelberg (2000)
5. Bonet, B., Geffner, H.: Planning as Heuristic Search. Artificial Intelligence Special Issue on Heuristic Search 129(1), 5–33 (2001)
6. Cavazza, M., Charles, F., Mead, S.J.: Interacting with Virtual Characters in Interactive Storytelling. In: Alonso, E., Kudenko, D., Kazakov, D. (eds.) Adaptive Agents and Multi-Agent Systems. LNCS (LNAI), vol. 2636, pp. 318–325. Springer, Heidelberg (2003)
7. Cavazza, M., Martin, O., Charles, F., Mead, S.J., Marichal, X.: Interacting with Virtual Agents in Interactive Storytelling. In: International Conference on Intelligent Virtual Agents (2003)
8. Cavazza, M.: An Integrated Parser for TFG with Explicit Tree Typing. In: Proceedings of the Fourth TAG+ Workshop, University of Pennsylvania (1998)
9. Cavazza, M., Martin, O., Charles, F., Mead, S.J., Marichal, X., Nandi, A.: Multi-modal Acting in Mixed Reality Interactive Storytelling. IEEE Multimedia 11(3) (July-September 2004)
10. Charles, F., Cavazza, M.: Exploring the Scalability of Character-based Storytelling. In: AAMAS'2004, pp. 872–879. ACM Press, New York (2004)
11. Cheong, Y.-G., Young, R.M.: A Computational Model of Narrative Generation for Suspense. In: The AAAI 2006 Workshop on Computational Aesthetics (2006)
12. Christian, D.B., Young, R.M.: Comparing Cognitive and Computational Models of Narrative Structure. In: AAAI 2004. Proceedings of the Nineteenth National Conference on Artificial Intelligence, pp. 385–390 (2004)
13. Flaubert, G.: Madame Bovary. La revue de Paris (ed.) France(1856) (in French)
14. Gliozzo, A.M.: Semantic Domains and Linguistic Theory. In: Proceedings of the LREC 2006 workshop "Toward Computational Models of Literary Analysis", Genova, Italy (2006)

15. Gratch, J., Marsella, S.: Tears and fears: Modeling emotions and emotional behaviors in synthetic agents. In: Proceedings of the Fifth International Conference on Autonomous Agents, pp. 278–285 (2001)

16. Gratch, J.: Why you should buy an emotional planner. In: Proceedings of the Autonomous Agents, Workshop on Emotion-based Agent Architectures, EBAA'99 (1999)

17. Gratch, J., Marsella, S., Mao, W.: Towards a Validated Model of "Emotional Intelligence". In: AAAI06. Twenty-First National Conference on Artificial Intelligence, Boston, MA (2006)

18. Joshi, A.K., Schabes, Y.: Tree-adjoining grammars and lexicalized grammars. In: Nivat, M., Podelski, A. (eds.) Tree Automata and Languages. Elsevier Science, Amsterdam (1992)

19. Korf, R.E.: Real-time heuristic search. Artificial Intelligence 42(2-3), 2–3 (1990)

20. Landauer, T.K., Dumais, S.T.: A solution to Plato's problem: the Latent Semantic Analysis theory of acquisition, induction and representation of knowledge. Psychological Review 104(2), 211–240 (1997)

21. Leclerc, Y. (ed.): Plans et Scenarios de Madame Bovary, CNRS edn., France (1995) (in French)

22. Liu, Y., Koenig, S., Furcy, D.: Speeding Up the Calculation of Heuristics for Heuristic Search-Based Planning. In: Proceedings of the Eighteenth National Conference on Artificial Intelligence, AAAI2002, pp. 484–491 (2002)

23. Liu, H., Mihalcea, R.: Computational Aesthetics: Artificial Intelligence Approaches to Beauty and Happiness. In: AAAI Workshop. Technical Report WS-06-04. American Association for Artificial Intelligence, Menlo Park, California, pp. 8–15 (2006)

24. Magerko, B., Laird, J.E., Assanie, M., Kerfoot, A., Stokes, D.: AI Characters and Directors for Interactive Computer Games. In: Proceedings of the Nineteenth National Conference on Artificial Intelligence, pp. 877–883 (2004)

25. Mateas, M., Stern, A.: Natural Language Understanding in Façade: Surface-Text Processing. In: Göbel, S., Spierling, U., Hoffmann, A., Iurgel, I., Schneider, O., Dechau, J., Feix, A. (eds.) TIDSE 2004. LNCS, vol. 3105, pp. 3–13. Springer, Heidelberg (2004)

26. Mehta, M., Dow, S., Mateas, M., MacIntyre, B.: Evaluating a Conversation-Centered Interactive drama. In: AAMAS'07. Proceedings of the Sixth International Conference on Autonomous Agents and Multiagent Systems, Honolulu, Hawaii, USA (2007)

27. Rastier, F.: La sémantique des thèmes - ou le voyage sentimental. In: Rastier, F. (ed.), L'analyse thématique des données textuelles. L'exemple des sentiments. Didier, Paris, pp. 223–249 (1995) (in French)

28. Rastier, F., Cavazza, M., Abeille, A.: Semantics for Descriptions: From Linguistics to Computer Science. CSLI Lecture Notes 138, University of Chicago Press (2001)

29. Riedl, M.O., Young, R.M.: An Intent-Driven Planner for Multi-Agent Story Generation. In: AAMAS'04, pp. 186–193. ACM, New York (2004)

30. Riedl, M.O., Young, R.M.: From Linear Story Generation to Branching Story Graphs. IEEE Computer Graphics and Applications 26(3), 23–31 (2006)

31. Swartout, W., Gratch, J., Hill, R., Hovy, E., Marsella, S., Rickel, J., Traum, D.: Toward Virtual Humans. AI Magazine 27(1) (2006)

32. Uzuner, Ö., Katz, B.: Capturing Expression Using Linguistic Information. In: AAAI 2005. Proceedings of the Twentieth National Conference on Artificial Intelligence, pp. 1124–1130 (2005)

33. Valitutti, A., Strapparava, C., Stock, O.: Lexical Resources and Semantic Similarity for Affective Evaluative Expressions Generation. In: Tao, J., Tan, T., Picard, R.W. (eds.) ACII 2005. LNCS, vol. 3784, pp. 474–481. Springer, Heidelberg (2005)

Children's Emotional Interpretation of Synthetic Character Interactions

Lynne Hall[1], Sarah Woods[2], Marc Hall[1], and Dieter Wolke[3]

[1] ENTICE Research Group, School of Computing and Technology,
University of Sunderland, Sunderland, UK
{lynne.hall,marc.hall}@sunderland.ac.uk
[2] School of Psychology, University of Hertfordshire, Hatfield, Herts, UK
s.n.woods@herts.ac.uk
[3] School of Psychology, University of Warwick, UK
dieter.wolke@warwick.ac.uk

Abstract. Using synthetic characters to support children's personal, social and emotional education requires that the emotional response elicited from the children is that desired by educators and stakeholders. This paper discusses an approach to understanding children's emotional interpretation of character's behaviour in a complex social situation. We outline this approach based on Theory of Mind concepts, that we have developed to enable us to understand and analyse children's emotional interpretation of synthetic characters involved in bullying scenarios in a virtual school. We discuss an empirical study of 345 children, aged 8-11 years, and concluded that our approach enabled us to gain a greater understanding of children's emotional interpretations. Results from the study identified that overall children did make appropriate emotional interpretations of characters and story, highlighting the potential of synthetic characters for exploring personal, social and emotional issues.

Keywords: Synthetic characters, Theory of Mind concepts, virtual learning environments, personal, social and emotional learning, emotional interpretation.

1 Introduction

Children's personal, social and emotional learning is an important factor for academic and non-academic success [14]. Synthetic characters offer high potential for providing such learning and a number of applications have been developed for classroom use. However, it remains difficult to identify and understand children's emotional interpretations of such interactions, and to evaluate whether these interactions do result in the desired personal, social and emotional learning outcomes required by educators and stakeholders.

In earlier work using Classroom Discussion Forums [5], a technique that has been used successfully to help children in vocalising and discussing their views and perspectives, we found that 8-12 year old children had relatively little to say about emotions, either those of the characters or their own emotions. To further understand children's emotional interpretation we have developed an alternative approach

A. Paiva, R. Prada, and R.W. Picard (Eds.): ACII 2007, LNCS 4738, pp. 642–653, 2007.

focusing on story and character comprehension using concepts from Theory of Mind (ToM) methods that we discuss in this paper.

This research is occurring as part of a European project, eCIRCUS (Education through Characters with Emotional-Intelligence and Role-playing Capabilities that Understand Social interaction). eCIRCUS will support social and emotional learning within Personal and Social Education through virtual role-play with synthetic characters in a 3D environment that establishes credible and empathic relations with the learners. Our particular focus is on empathy and supporting children in empathic interactions and learning outcomes.

Empathy is essential for personal, social and emotional learning [8] and requires the ability to represent the mental states (thoughts, feelings, desires, hopes) of others. These skills are often referred to as 'Theory of Mind' or mentalising [7]. Being able to represent the internal mental state of another is assumed to play an important role in the activation of affective empathy.

Theory of Mind (ToM) is a concept closely interlinked to empathy and can be used to determine user's perceptions and interpretations of synthetic character behaviours. ToM methods offer considerable potential for determining whether a child has appropriately interpreted the emotional message of an interaction. In this paper we discuss a ToM approach to investigate children's emotional interpretation of interactions with FearNot (Fun with Empathic Agents to Reachout Novel Outcomes in Teaching), a virtual learning environment, populated by synthetic characters.

FearNot focuses on exploring bullying and coping strategies for 8-12 year olds, and here, we focus on relational bullying, which is bullying typified by social exclusion, verbal and emotional harassment and isolation [2]. In FearNot interactions we are aiming for the child to have an emotional response that indicates not only that they can correctly interpret a character's emotional state and intent, but additionally that they engage and empathise with this.

In looking at children's emotional interpretation of various relational bullying interactions within FearNot, we aim to identify if children understand and correctly interpret the actions and behaviours of the synthetic characters. In addition, we are interested in identifying if children's real-world bullying roles (e.g. victim, bully, neutral) have an impact on emotional interpretation, with research suggesting there could be differences in Theory of Mind responses dependant on children's bullying role [1].

Section 2 briefly outlines the FearNot scenario used for the empirical study with 345 children. Section 3 discusses the analysis approach we developed that aimed to understand children's emotional interpretations. Section 4 presents the empirical study and results. Section 5 discusses these results and outlines future work. Finally some brief conclusions are provided.

2 FearNot: The Relational Bullying Scenario

The scenario begins with the characters, school and situation being presented to the children, providing them with the context of the bullying. The children then watch an episode, where Frances (the victim) is relationally bullied by Sarah (bully) and Janet (bully assistant), with the bullying involving verbal harassment and social exclusion (see figure 1a).

After the bullying incident, Frances goes to the school library, where she opens up a dialogue with the user. Within the initiated dialogue the user selects an advice from a list of coping strategies (shown as a drop down menu). The user also explains her selection and what she thinks will happen after having implemented the selected strategy, by typing it in.

Children then view Martina (the bystander) offering Frances (the victim) help (see figure 1b), with Frances accepting an offer of friendship. At the end of the scenario, a universal educational message is displayed pointing out that "telling someone" is always a good idea.

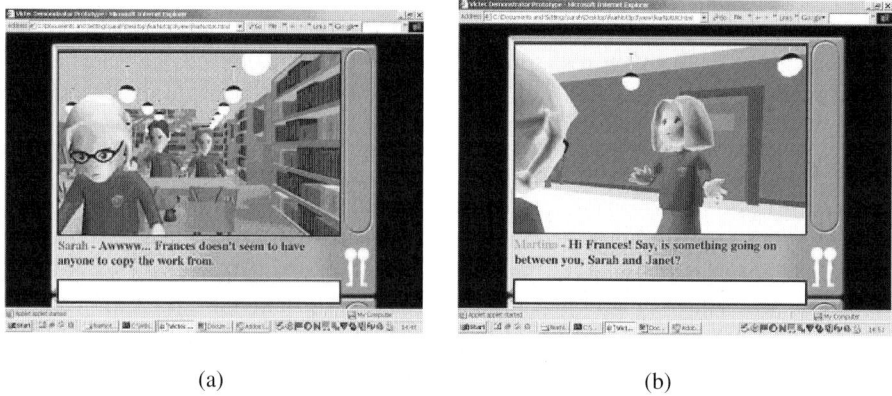

(a)   (b)

Fig. 1. FearNot: the Relational Bullying Scenario

3   Investigating Children's Emotional Interpretation of FearNot

Although we have found that children were unwilling to verbally discuss emotions, the few comments received did appear to identify that they were emotionally interpreting the activities in the scenarios. In that verbal discussions were unsuccessful at gaining information about emotional interpretation, here, we discuss how we have sought to gain further insight into children's emotional interpretations using Theory of Mind with the following analysis approach.

3.1   Theory of Mind Questions

A series of ToM questions based on Happe and Frith (1996)'s first order and second order false belief questions were devised [6]. The questions were presented electronically to the children immediately after interacting with FearNot and were supported with FearNot screen shots, acting as aide memoirs to the characters names and situations within the interaction. The ToM questions required children to infer the emotions, mental states and intentions of the synthetic characters, with responses including selection and free text entry. For the selection questions, children were presented with 5 emotional responses (neutral, sad, happy, fearful, angry) using facial representations. The child was instructed to click on the face that they thought represented the feelings of the character they are being asked about. They were then asked 'which emotion to you mean?' to clarify their interpretation of emotions.

The questions asked children to select how they thought the characters felt (by selecting the appropriate face) followed by a question asking them to explain why the characters might feel like this (free text). Children were asked about their emotional interpretation of characters feelings at specific times in the scenario: at the beginning of the scenario (before bullying had occurred); directly after the main bullying incident(s); and at the end of the scenario after coping strategies had been applied.

3.2 Analysing Free Text

Extending earlier work [4], here we have focused not only on the generation of frequency and percentage data from the ToM questions, but also on examining the children's free text responses. A content analysis scheme[1] was developed to code children's text-based responses for the following questions based on first order and second order theory of mind story comprehension: 1) What do you think is happening in the story you have seen?, 2) What does Sarah (bully) think about Frances (victim)? 3) What does Frances (victim) think about Sarah (bully)? 4) If you were Frances (victim), why do you think that Sarah (bully) is doing this? 5) If you were Sarah (bully), why do you think that Sarah is doing this to Frances (victim)? Questions 1-3 relate to first order theory of mind questions, whilst questions 4 and 5 consider second order theory of mind concepts.

Subsequently, each question was blindly and independently rated by two post-graduate coders. Each rater was supplied with a copy of the coding criteria and had to code each child's response to the above questions. Kappa coefficients were then computed for each of the questions to ascertain the degree of inter-rater reliability. Kappa statistics of 0.6 or greater are considered highly adequate and indicate high levels of reliability. Table 1 illustrates the kappa coefficient values obtained for each of the questions. High levels of reliability were found for all questions. Therefore, no changes were required to the coding and subsequent analytical framework.

Table 1. Inter-rater reliability values for the story comprehension questions

Question	Kappa Coefficient Value
1. What do you think is happening in the story you have seen?	0.79
2. What does Sarah think about Frances?	0.81
3. What does Frances think about Sarah?	0.72
4. If you were Frances, why do you think that Sarah is doing this?	0.77
5. If you were Sarah, why do you think that Sarah is doing this to Frances?	0.79

3.3 User Bullying Characteristics and Theory of Mind

FearNot has been developed for exploring bullying and coping strategies. As part of our investigation we have sought to determine whether user bullying characteristics

---

[1] Available at: http://osiris.sunderland.ac.uk/~cs0lha/tom.htm

are reflected in interactions, in terms of mental representations as provided through the Theory of Mind. Children's bullying characteristics were categorized into bullying roles using the School Relationships Questionnaire [11, 12]. Using this data, children were classified as 'pure' bullies, 'pure' victims, bully/victims or neutral children for both direct and relational bullying behaviour.

Children were classified according to physical bullying roles (bully, victim, neutral) and relational bullying roles (bully, victim, neutral). Table 2 illustrates that a similar proportion of children were classified as physical or relational bullies, victims and neutral.

Table 2. Peer nominated physical and relational bullying roles (%) (N: 319)

	Bully	Victim	Neutral
Physical	55 (17.2)	53 (16.6)	211 (66.1)
Relational	60 (18.8)	46 (14.4)	213 (66.8)

3.4 Emotional Interpretation: Scale of Correctness

A 5-point emotion identification scale ranging from 1 = most correct to 5 = least incorrect was constructed to analyse children's responses of what the characters in the relational scenario were feeling at various stages throughout the story (Table 3). To construct the scale, 6 people independently watched the scenario and rated the emotional response in relation to each of the emotion related questions. High consensus was found, which allowed the scale to be developed based on what was deemed to be a correct emotional response through to an incorrect interpretation. This scale was subsequently used to investigate for possible differences in emotional interpretations of the characters, and bullying roles.

Table 3. Emotion identification scale ranging from 1 = most correct to 5 = least incorrect

Question	Angry	Fearful	Happy	Sad	Neutral
Q2 How does Sarah feel at beginning of story?	2	3	1	4	5
Q3 How does Janet feel at beginning of story?	2	4	1	5	3
Q4 How does Frances feel at beginning of story?	3	2	4	1	5
Q5 How does Sarah feel after calling Frances names?	3	4	1	5	2
Q6 How does Janet feel after calling Frances names?	3	4	1	5	2
Q7 How does Frances feel after Sarah and Janet have called her names?	3	2	4	1	5
Q12 How does Frances feel at the end of the story?	3	2	4	1	5
Q13 How does Sarah feel at the end of the story?	2	4	1	5	3

4 Empirical Study and Results

The data used to investigate the children's emotional interpretation of the synthetic characters in FearNot, was collected during a large-scale evaluation with 345 children participating. 172 male (49.9%) and 173 female (50.1%). The sample age range was 8 to 11, mean age of 9.95 (SD: 0.50) and comprised of children from a range of local primary schools. Here, we focus on the relational bullying scenario, with the data relating to the physical bullying scenario having already been partially presented in [4].

4.1 Character Emotional Interpretation

No significant differences emerged between children's physical and relational bullying roles and emotional interpretation for the characters throughout the relational bullying story.

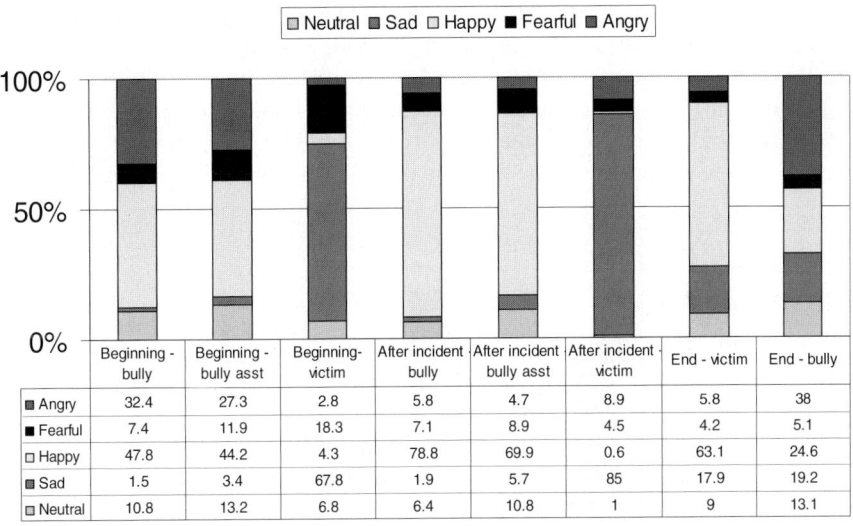

Fig. 2. Character Emotional Interpretation

Figure 2 illustrates the descriptive data for children's emotion interpretation responses for the three main characters in the story, Sarah the bully, Frances, the victim and Janet, the bully assistant. Responses were analysed at the beginning of the story, after a bullying incident had occurred, and at the end of the story.

Nearly 50% of children stated that the bully felt happy at the beginning of the story, followed by feeling angry or neutral. Only 1.5% of children stated that the bully felt sad at the beginning of the story. A similar pattern was found for children's emotion interpretations for the bully assistant, with 44% stating that she felt happy, followed by 27% stating that she felt angry at the start of the story. Nearly 70% of children interpreted the victim as feeling sad at the beginning of the story, followed by just under 20% stating that the victim felt fearful.

Just under 80% of children responded that the bully character felt happy after having called the victim names, and a similar response pattern emerged for the bully assistant, although to a slightly lesser degree. 85% of children correctly interpreted that the victim felt sad after being called nasty names. With regards to how the characters felt at the end of the story, 63% of children responded that the victim felt happy, whilst just under 20% interpreted that the victim felt sad. The emotional interpretation for the bully character at the end of the story was less distinguishable. 38% stated that the bully felt angry at the end of the story, followed by 25% who said that she felt happy.

4.2 Understanding Emotions in the Scenarios

Using the content analysis scheme, children's responses were analysed to see whether there was any relationship with bullying roles, and gender. Although no association was found between bully role and emotional inferences on the theory of mind questions, a number of significant gender differences were found.

Children's responses to what was happening overall in the story were classified according to 4 categories: 1) bullying, being bullied, 2) being nasty, being picked on, teasing, 3) other reason, 4) don't know/no comprehension. Chi-square analysis revealed a significant association (X^2 (3, 320) = 14.38, p = .002). More boys compared to girls did not understand the overall storyline, and more girls than boys identified the specific nature of the bullying in the form of name-calling, see figure 3.

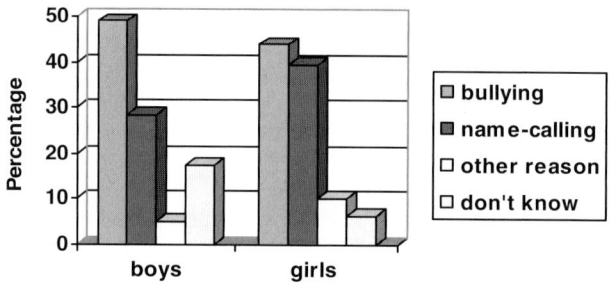

Fig. 3. Storyline comprehension and relationship to gender (N: 320)

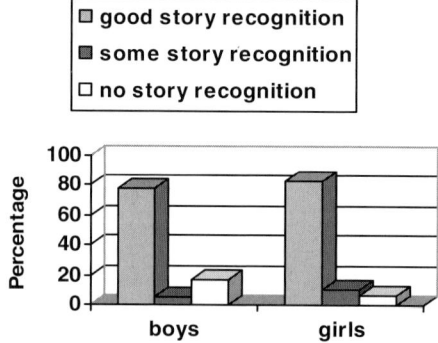

Fig. 4. Storyline comprehension and relationship to gender (N: 320)

Children were initially asked about their interpretation of the events that had happened in the bullying story. These detailed text-based responses were coded according to three categories – good story recognition, some story recognition, no story recognition, see figure 4. Significant gender differences emerged (X^2 (2, 320) = 11.43, p = .003). Males had significantly poorer overall story recognition of the relational bullying scenario compared to females.

A significant relationship was uncovered between gender and children's responses to the first order theory of mind question 'What does Sarah (bully) think about Frances (victim)?' (X^2 (3, 296) = 7.40, p = 0.05).

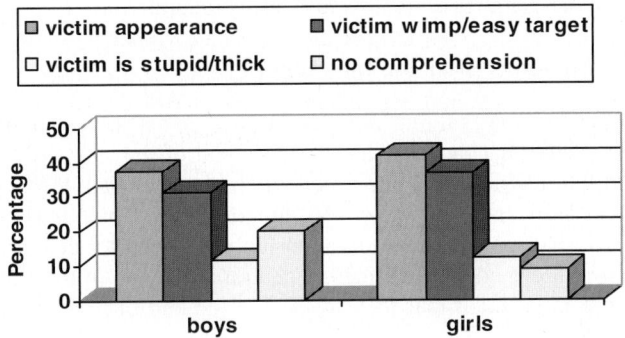

Fig. 5. Relationship between children's responses to the question 'What does Sarah (bully) think about Frances (victim)?' and gender (N: 320)

Responses were related to the appearance of the victim (smelly, ugly, stinks, dirty), that the victim was a wimp and an easy target, that the victim was stupid and thick, or no story comprehension. The same pattern of findings emerged with more boys not fully understanding this question compared to girls. Girls were more likely to respond that the bully thought that the victim was a wimp/easy target, or had something wrong with their appearance (ugly, spotty, stinks, dirty) (see figure 5).

A significant trend was revealed between gender and the first order theory of mind question 'What does Frances (victim) think about Sarah (bully)?' (X^2 (3, 320) = 6.86,

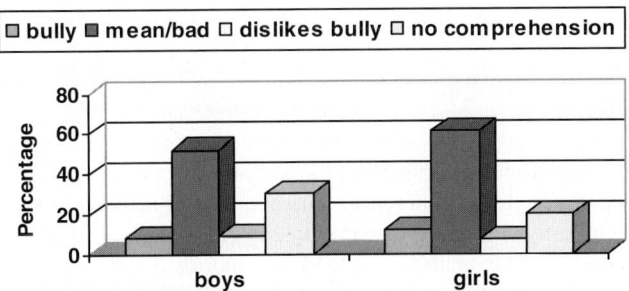

Fig. 6. Relationship between children's responses to the question 'What does Frances (victim) think about Sarah (bully)?' and gender (N: 320)

p = 0.07). Responses to this question were coded according to Frances thinking that Sarah is a bully, that the bully is mean, selfish, bad, that the victim dislikes the bully, or no story comprehension. Boys were less likely to fully comprehend the question, and girls were more likely to state that Frances thought that Sarah was selfish, mean, unfair and horrible compared to boys (See figure 6).

No further significant relationships were found between gender and children's responses to the second order theory of mind questions 'If you were Frances (victim), why do you think that Sarah (bully) is doing this?' and 'If you were Sarah (bully), why do you think that Sarah is doing this to Frances (victim)?'

4.3 Children's Emotions After the Interaction

At the end of the relational bullying story, children were asked to state how they felt. 57% of children stated that they felt happy at the end of the story, followed by just under 20% who felt neutral at the end. 14% of children felt sad, 8% angry, and 2% felt fearful. No significant association was found between bullying roles and end emotions felt. However, a significant relationship was found for gender (X^2 (4, 311) = 10.26, p = 0.04). More boys stated feeling neutral at the end of the story compared to girls, and more girls stated that they felt sad at the end of the story compared to boys.

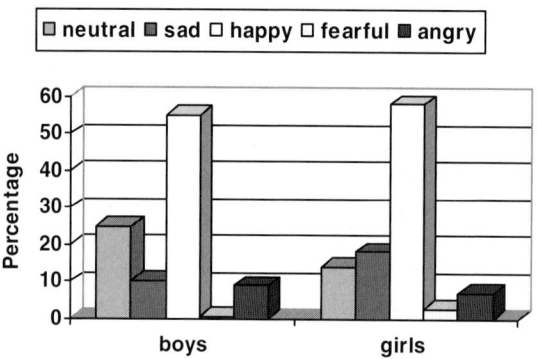

Fig. 7. End of story emotion in association with gender (N: 311)

5 Discussion

With FearNot, appropriate emotional interpretation is essential to permit the children to develop empathy with the characters. The approach discussed in this paper aimed to enable us to investigate children's emotional interpretation of the characters and the scenarios of FearNot. Our analysis focused on emotional interpretation intending to identify whether children were engaging, empathized and understanding the nature of the relational bullying scenario. Through this application of concepts from Theory of Mind methods we are able to identify that overall there was good emotional interpretation, with children understanding the story and how the characters felt at various points of the story. However, a number of our results were unexpected and require further consideration.

Although we anticipated a relationship between bullying roles and emotional interpretation of the characters involvement in the story, we found no significant differences. Emotional interpretations of the story were relatively correct and equivalent across bullying type and roles, a finding counter to the perspective that bullying roles are associated with different levels of emotional understanding and interpretation [1, 9, 10]. We hypothesised that victims would have lower emotion interpretation scores, and theory of mind abilities compared to bullies and neutrals, and that bullies would have superior theory of mind skills compared to victims and neutral children. Further, we have recently found that victims have difficulties detecting the emotions of others [13]. As emotion processing and theory of mind abilities are closely interlinked, in this study we anticipated that victims could have problems interpreting the emotions and intentions of the characters in the relational bullying scenario. However, the results from this present study do not provide any evidence to support these hypotheses.

For the first order theory of mind questions, there were significant gender differences. Fewer boys than girls understood the overall storyline and less boys than girls identified the specific nature of the bullying (name calling). In general girls revealed a deeper, more insightful understanding of the story, rather than broader, more general interpretations as identified by the boys. However, a surprising finding was that no gender differences emerged for the second order theory of mind questions, which asked children why they thought the bully was doing this and why the victim would think the bully was behaving in this way.

Extensive previous research [3] has consistently found that males are usually poorer at recognising and interpreting emotional information, however, here there appeared to be no difference. This result could be due to the greater experience that boys have of interpreting digital media than girls; or possibly that the immersive nature of interacting with FearNot reduces the boys' levels of distraction and thus allows them to focus on emotional interpretation. However, further empirical work is needed, firstly to see if these results can be replicated and if they can, to try to understand the contributory factors underlying this result.

The results presented in this paper identify that our approach to dealing with a complex, challenging issue such as bullying, is an appropriate one for children in this age group. However, we recognize that a one-day lab interaction with FearNot does not provide us with sufficient data to determine if FearNot can actually have an impact on bullying behaviour. To address this issue in eCIRCUS we will be conducting a large longitudinal study of FearNot in the classroom situation over the next year, in the UK and Germany. This study includes an adapted version of the Theory of Mind framework discussed here, with modifications reflecting long-term use of FearNot.

The approach we have used, based on Theory of Mind concepts, provided us with considerably more information relating to children's emotional interpretation than other approaches we have used, such as questionnaires, interviews and group discussions. It has enabled us to investigate children's emotional interpretation of the scenarios and characters of FearNot, with the results indicating clear understanding and emotional interpretation from the children. We found that children are exhibiting appropriate emotional interpretations and responses to the behaviours of synthetic characters in complex social situations. Our results offer further support for the use of synthetic characters for personal, social and emotional learning.

6 Conclusion

Children's emotional interpretation of interactions with synthetic characters are difficult to determine. The approach outlined here, using questions based on Theory of Mind concepts offers considerable potential for investigating children's emotional interpretations and their comprehension of characters and the story. For FearNot, this approach has resulted in several unanticipated results relating to the impact of both gender and bullying role on children's emotional interpretation of synthetic character interactions. Through use of this approach we have identified that children can understand and emotionally interpret synthetic character behaviours in the complex social situation of relational bullying.

References

[1] Arsenio, W.F., Lemerise, E.A.: Aggression and moral development: Integrating social information processing and moral domain models. Child Development 75, 987–1002 (2004)

[2] Crick, N.R., Grotpeter, J.K.: Relational aggression, gender, and social-psychological adjustment. Child Development 66, 710–722 (1995)

[3] Fischer, A.H.: Gender and emotion: Social psychological perspectives. Cambridge University Press, Paris (2000)

[4] Hall, L., Woods, S., Aylett, R., Paiva, A.: Using Theory of Mind methods to investigate empathic engagement with synthetic characters. International Journal of Humanoid Robotics 3, 351–370 (2006)

[5] Hall, L., Woods, S., Dautenhahn, K.: FearNot! Designing in the Classroom. presented at British HCI, Leeds, UK (2004)

[6] Happe, F., Frith, U.: Theory of mind and social impairment in children with conduct disorder. British Journal of Developmental Psychology 14, 385–398 (1996)

[7] Leslie, L.M.: Pretense and representation: The origins of theory of mind. Psychological Review 94, 412–426 (1987)

[8] Payton, J.W., Wardlaw, D.M., Gracyzk, P.A., Bloodworth, M.R., Tompsett, C.J., Weissberg, R.: Social and Emotional Learning: A Framework for promoting mental health and reducing risk behaviours in children and youth. Journal of School Health 70, 179–185 (2000)

[9] Sutton, J., Smith, P.K., Swettenham, J.: Bullying and 'theory of mind': A critique of the 'social skills deficit' view of anti-social behaviour. Social Development 8, 117–127 (1999)

[10] Sutton, J., Smith, P.K., Swettenham, J.: Social cognition and bullying: Social inadequacy or skilled manipulation? British Journal of Developmental Psychology 17, 435–450 (1999)

[11] Wolke, D., Stanford, K.: Bullying in school children. In: Wolke, D., Stanford, K. (eds.) Developmental Psychology, Arnold Publisher, London (1999)

[12] Woods, S., White, E.: The association between bullying behaviour, arousal levels and behaviour problems. Journal of Adolescence 28, 381–395 (2005)

[13] Woods, S., Wolke, D., Nowicki, S., Hall, L.: Emotion recognition abilities and empathy in bullies and victims, Social Development, in submission

[14] Zins, J.E., Bloodworth, M.R., Weissberg, R.P., Walberg, H.J.: The Scientific Base Linking Social and Emotional Learning to School Success. In: Zins, J.E., Bloodworth, M.R., Weissberg, R.P., Walberg, H.J. (eds.) Building Academic Success on Social and Emotional Learning: What Does the Research Say?, Teachers College Press, New York (2004)

Visual Femininity and Masculinity in Synthetic Characters and Patterns of Affect

Agneta Gulz[1], Felix Ahlner[1], and Magnus Haake[2]

[1] Div. of Cognitive Science, Lund University, Sweden
Agneta.gulz@lucs.lu.se, Felix_ahlner@idgmail.se
[2] Dept. of Design Sciences, Lund University, Sweden
Magnus.haake@design.lth.se

Abstract. It has been shown that users of a digital system perceive a more 'masculine-sounding' female voice as more persuasive and intelligent than a corresponding but more 'feminine-sounding' female voice. Our study explores whether a parallel pattern of affectively colored evaluations can be elicited when *femininity and masculinity* are manipulated via *visual* cues instead of via voice. 80 participants encountered synthetic characters, visually manipulated in terms of femininity and masculinity but with voice, spoken content, linguistic style and role of characters held constant. Evaluations of the two female characters differed in accordance with stereotype predictions – with the exception of competence-related traits; for the two male characters evaluations differed very little. The pattern for *male* versus *female* characters was slightly in opposite to stereotype predictions. Possible explanations for these results are proposed. In conclusion we discuss the value of being aware of how different traits in synthetic characters may interact.

1 Background

As Reeves, Nass and collaborators [16] have shown, many of the *affective responses* that human beings evoke in one another are likewise evoked by different kinds of media, as soon as the media involves a social cue such as natural language interaction, voice, something face-like, etc. In response to these social cues, humans tend to experience, for instance, various degrees of trust, irritation and empathy, feeling flattered, humiliated, distanced, and so on. Furthermore, [16] documents how certain *response patterns*, known from social psychology, are paralleled in responses towards media. As an example, extroverted people tend to respond more positively towards others that speak relatively loud with varied pitch than those who speak quietly and with little variation in pitch, and the opposite is the case for introverted people. This pattern can be reproduced towards a computer application with a voice interface [16].

An explicitly anthropomorphic form of digital media is that of synthetic characters. These characters populate the digital society in increasing number, and there is no doubt that they do evoke affective responses. But to what extent does the embodiment in the sense of a *visualized* humanlike character influence the affective responses that *appear already* towards the same system without this visualized character? And can

A. Paiva, R. Prada, and R.W. Picard (Eds.): ACII 2007, LNCS 4738, pp. 654–665, 2007.

affective response patterns known from social psychology be elicited by manipulating only the *static visual appearance* of the character, while controlling for voice, content and visual dynamics such as movements and facial expressions?

1.1 The Role of Static Visual Characteristics

In line with Ruttkay and collaborators' [17] analysis of the *physical appearance* of a synthetic character we distinguish between:

– *static visual characteristics,* including: (i) degrees of anthropomorphism and degrees of visual naturalism/realism; (ii) basic physical properties such as body-type, face properties, skin, hair and hair-cut, clothes and attributes – characteristics that, furthermore can make up representations of age, gender and ethnicity
– *dynamic visual characteristics* such as facial expressions, body and hand gestures, postures, movements, etc.

Whereas visual dynamics have been extensively researched, relatively little attention has been paid to the static visual appearance or *look* of synthetic characters [7, 8], even though there are important exceptions [3, 4, 11, 14, 22, 24][1]. It is, however, well established in the case of *human-human* interaction that static visual appearance plays an important role for the eliciting of affective responses and evaluations. In an encounter with another person, visual cues as to the persons face, body shape, height, ethnicity, hair, dressing, etc. are immediately picked up and exploited to guide our approach to this person [18]. Among those very quick, and affectively colored, evaluations are, for instance, estimates of how friendly, how trustworthy, how dominant, and how similar to oneself somebody is [7, 14]. Our focus is on an aspect that is crucial for socio-affective responses and interaction in a human-human context, namely *gender*.

1.2 Gender and Affective Responses

One of the very first things we do when we encounter someone is to determine whether the person is female or male. This categorization, in turn, colors several consequent responses and evaluations. Analyses reveal, that peoples' evaluations of an identical proposal, narrative, message etc. as presented by a man versus by a woman (for instance, by a female or a male author; in a woman's or in a man's voice) often differ in accordance with gender stereotypes [1, 5]. A content mediated by a man is perceived as more credible than the same content mediated by a woman, and a male mediator is perceived as more competent than a female mediator[2].

That such evaluative patterns can also be replicated towards computer-based systems has been shown by Reeves, Nass and collaborators. In one study [16], participants perceived a (visually non-present) digital tutor as significantly more competent

---

[1] Furthermore, in [3] and [24], just like in the study to be presented, aspects of visual femininity are addressed and manipulated. Baylor and collaborators [3] compare responses towards a feminine-looking and a "geek"-looking (virtual) female engineer. Waern and collaborators [24] vary body shape and clothing in terms of 'hypersexuality' in female avatars.
[2] This is the case for 'neutral' content. Patterns look different with respect to contents that are considered to belong to 'typically female domains' (c.f. [16]).

and credible when it had a male voice than when it hade a female voice. Participants were more satisfied and found the praise from the tutor more valuable and trustworthy when the tutor had a male voice than when it had a female voice.

Other gender aspects, applicable both to males and females, are degrees of *femininity* and of *masculinity*. Here, Reeves, Nass and collaborators [16, 23] performed a study where screen depictions of six women were accompanied by female voices electronically altered to be either 'feminine-sounding' or 'masculine-sounding'. The former were amplified in the higher and reduced in the lower frequencies and were played at softer volume. For masculine voices, the lower frequencies were amplified, the higher ones dampened, and the voices were made louder than average. Participants encountered three screen depictions with a feminine-sounding voice and three with a masculine-sounding voice. Results were that the evaluative patterns reproduced patterns known from social psychology. Masculine-sounding women were perceived as significantly more persuasive and intelligent than feminine-sounding women.

As to the visual images used in the study, theses are neither included nor described in the thesis [23], and thus we know nothing about femininity/masculinity as *visually* represented in these images. It is, however, precisely this aspect that is the focus of the present study: Can femininity/masculinity *as visually coded* influence affective evaluations regarding persuasiveness, intelligence, empathy, warmth etc. of synthetic characters? In contrast to the [23] study we focus on evaluations of animated characters (even though the *manipulated* aspect is the underlying static visual character).

1.3 Issues Addressed in the Study

The inspiration to our study came from the above-mentioned study [23] in combination with our own line of research. Its primary goal was to investigate whether a gender stereotypical pattern of affective evaluations could be elicited when degrees of femininity and masculinity were manipulated visually instead of via voice cues. Would evaluations of intelligence, empathy, warmth, trustworthiness, etc. also in this case vary according to gender stereotypes known from human-human interaction?

Table 1. The parameters used in the questionnaire (*translated from Swedish*), categorized into five groups and ordered as opposites with stereotypic feminine traits (to the left) vs. stereotypic masculine traits (to the right). The order also corresponds to the order used in Table 2, 3 & 4.

Trustworthiness / Expertise	**Personality (Communication)**
ignorant vs. knowledgeable (L1)	personal vs. impersonal (L3)
non-expert vs. expert (L4)	subjective vs. objective (L11)
un-experienced vs. experienced	
undecided vs. decided (L13)	**Intelligence (talent)**
non-persuasive vs. persuasive	non-intelligent vs. intelligent (L6)
Personality (Empathy)	**Self-confidence**
warm vs. cold (L5)	unsure of oneself vs. self-confident
empathic vs. non-emphatic (L16)	submissive vs. dominant (L8)
friendly vs. unfriendly (L18)	
pleasant vs. unpleasant (L20)	

In addition to the parameters 'intelligence' and 'persuasiveness' used in [22] we included twelve additional parameters (se above) for which peoples' conceptions and attitudes are known to relate to gender stereotypes [1, 5, 15]. Thus, the question was whether our manipulations of degree of femininity/masculinity via visual cues would be reflected in evaluations of the synthetic characters with respect to the gender stereotypical traits listed in Table 1.

2 The Study

2.1 Study Design

To address these issues we created eight conditions, which each consisted of an encounter with one female and one male synthetic character. The female character should be either a feminine-looking character (F+) or a more neutral, slightly masculine-looking, female character (F-). The male character should be either a masculine-looking male character (M+) or and a slightly feminine-looking male character (M-).

Both characters should speak about a similar, gender-neutral, topic divided in two subsequent parts. After listening to each character, the participants should report their impressions of the character by means of a Likert scale questionnaire.

The participants were randomly assigned one of the eight conditions: [M+ F-], [M+ F+], [M- F+], [M- F-], [F+ M-], [F+ M+], [F- M-], [F- M+].

2.2 Materials

Visual characters: A number of images for each character were designed on the basis of the *SitePal* on-line demo design tool [19]. The images were further manipulated in *Photoshop*, to establish an image set consisting of: a body, about 10 different views of the face and about 10 different mouth shapes. The animation (including lip synchronization) was done in *Flash* using frame-by-frame animation. The experiment was run on a web page, with the animation incorporated as a *Flash* movie.

The design of the characters, exploited a number of visual cues, as follows:

– *Feminine character (F+):* Manipulated with feminine attributes such as: the *baby-face* scheme (rounded head shapes, bigger eyes, smaller nose, narrower shoulders); long (colored) hair and make up, that pronounces feminine attributes by enlarging the eyes, making them rounder and more distinct and making the lips fuller.
– *Weak feminine character (F-):* Manipulated with masculine attributes such as: broader head, a more angular and pronounced jaw, a high for-head; paler colors as to eyes, mouth and hair, which weakens the impact of these female attributes; overall paler color scheme reducing the number of distinct features and thus weakening any categorization of gender – whether feminine or masculine.
– *Weak masculine character (M-):* Manipulated with feminine attributes such as: rounder and less pronounced shapes of head, jaw and nose; narrower shoulders; slightly red lips in combination with an overall paler color scheme, that weakens any distinct categorization of gender.
– *Masculine character (M+):* Manipulated with masculine attributes such as: broader, angular and more pronounced head shapes; broader shoulders, a distinct

Adam's apple, pronounced, dark eye brows; neatly done hair; a more prominent color scheme which produces distinct features and strengthens the categorization with respect to gender.

Fig. 1. Screen shots of the four characters used in the study. Upper left: (F+); upper right: (F); lower left: (M-); lower right: (M+).

Since we were interested in unreflective and affectively mediated evaluations, we wanted to avoid the use of over-explicit visual stereotypes – i.e. *extremely* feminine-, non-feminine-, masculine- or non-masculine-looking characters – since these are liable to initiate conscious deliberation as to what is an 'appropriate' answer, etc.

The characters were pre-evaluated in order to ensure that they were perceived as intended in terms of femininity and masculinity. Forty subjects were presented with pictures of one male and one female character, without voice, animation and background. They were asked whether they thought the male character looked masculine, neutral or non-masculine, and whether they thought the female character looked feminine, neutral or non-feminine. Results were that 14 out of 20 categorized M+ as masculine; 1 did so with M-. For the female characters, 11 out of 20 categorized K+ and 4 categorized K- as feminine. In this pre-study, note, no subject saw both females or both males. In a brief follow-up 13 additional subjects were shown all four characters and were asked which female character they thought looked more feminine and which male character they thought looked more masculine. Twelve unhesitatingly categorized the characters according to our prediction. One categorized K- as more feminine, explaining that "she looks more like a mother". A limitation of the pre-validation was that (for practical reasons) all subjects were 20 years and older, whereas half of the participants in the main study were teenagers.

An issue brought up in the pre-validating process was this: What counts as an appropriate and satisfactory pre-validation of a character design when the target is not conscious and deliberate responses towards it, in this case specifically towards visual femininity/masculinity – but instead unreflective and non-deliberate responses? These kinds of responses, note, are known to differ considerably from one another [6, 18].

Animations: Frame-by-frame animations makes it difficult and time consuming to produce exact and identical movements in shifts of head position, lip movements (synchronization), eye blinking, and breathing – nevertheless these parameters have been considered and are more or less the same for all four characters (see demo [25]).

Voice: Since we wanted to keep femininity/masculinity aspects as mediated through voice constant, one and the same female voice was to be used for the F- and F+ characters, and one and the same male voice for the M- and M+ characters. However, *inconsistencies* in virtual characters can disturb and irritate users. It was therefore important to choose a female voice that would fit *both* female characters, and a male voice that would fit *both* male characters (especially since we were interested in affectively coloured evaluations and did not want to over-layer those with affect in terms of irritation or confusion due to a mismatch between voice and visual design). The challenge was thus to find: (i) a female voice that was neither pronouncedly feminine nor pronouncedly non-feminine; and (ii) a male voice that was neither too masculine nor too non-masculine. We consulted two speech therapists (whereof one specialized in voice and gender) that arranged a contact with two people, with voices suitable according to our criteria.

Script: The verbal script had two parts, and the aim was to have them as equivalent as possible with respect to masculinity/femininity. The subject domain chosen was medicine, which within Swedish culture is a relatively gender-neutral subject domain. The original text was taken from a Swedish popular science magazine [21], and was adapted in order to be suitable for oral presentation. Furthermore, the text was modified in order to obtain equivalence in the two parts in terms of length, number of facts and of linguistic style, especially with respect to differences in male versus female linguistic styles [2, 15]. The script parts were then pre-tested and validated in the sense that a number of readers and listeners could not decide whether they were written by a man or a woman. The final script parts were each about 2 minutes in length.

Questionnaire: The questionnaire consisted of a series of twenty 7-point Likert-type scales with opposite traits on the two poles. Since some of the trait pairs include one more negative and one more positive trait, the positive traits were evenly placed to the left and to the right, respectively. *Fourteen* of the twenty scales concerned the gender stereotype related traits that we were interested in – those presented in table 1.

The six scales omitted here relate to a parallel study on perceived attractiveness, which is outside the scope of the present article. For reference, see [12].

2.3 Participants

Forty adolescents (aged 13-18) and 40 adults (aged 25-65) participated in the study. Within each age group there were an equal number of females and males.

2.4 Procedure

A laptop was used, and the sessions took place at different, but always calm and quiet locations with only the participant and the experimental leader present. Sessions lasted on average 25 minutes. The participants were informed that they would get to listen to two computer characters speaking about diurnal rhythm and on what happens in the body during shift work. They were told that they would first listen to doctor Elm and thereafter to doctor Ask, and that after having listened to each doctor character they would be asked questions about their impressions. Participants were also told that there would be no memory or knowledge tests, but that we were only interested in their impressions and opinions. Furthermore, they were told that they could interrupt their participation at any time. Which of the 8 conditions (order and combination of characters) was assigned to a participant was decided according to a random table. Observe that no participant encountered the two female, or the two male characters but always one male and one female character. Upon each of the two presentations, the participants filled out the (identical) questionnaire. When the second and last questionnaire had been filled out, a brief interview was carried out with the participant on masculinity and femininity. At this stage, all four visual characters were shown to the participant, and finally she/he was debriefed about the aim of the study.

3 Results

3.1 Female Characters - More or Less Feminine

The five largest differences (a-e) – three significant (a-c), two nearly significant (d,e) – all follow the direction predicted by gender stereotypes. The more feminine-looking woman is evaluated as significantly more personal, warm and pleasant than the less feminine-looking and also as more subjective and friendly, as well as slightly more emphatic, submissive and uncertain of herself. (And in 12 out of all 14 traits the difference in evaluation goes in stereotype-direction, even though several of the differences are not statistically significant).

Table 2. Evaluation of the feminine character (F+) vs. the weak feminine character (F-). The mean values correspond to the bipolar Likert type scales presented in Table 1.

	L1	L3	L4	L5	L6	L7	L8	L9	L11	L13	L16	L17	L18	L20
m(F+)	5,75	4,05	5,15	3,45	5,35	5,23	3,28	5,38	5,48	5,63	3,48	5,65	2,38	2,28
m(F-)	5,95	5,23	5,30	4,83	5,05	5,60	3,65	5,28	6,05	5,73	3,90	5,78	2,88	3,30
p	0,46	0,00	0,60	0,00	0,41	0,30	0,29	0,76	0,10	0,75	0,25	0,66	0,13	0,00
		a		b					d				e	c

If we instead look at the traits with the *smallest* differences in evaluations between the two characters, these are: decisiveness, experience, persuasiveness, expertise and knowledge – which all belong to the heading of expertise/trustworthiness[3] (Table 1).

---

[3] This, furthermore, is the only of the five larger categories with clearly non-significant differences between evaluations of the two female characters.

Intelligence, furthermore, is one of the *two* traits that does not follow gender stereotype predictions. The more feminine-looking woman is evaluated as more intelligent than the more masculine-looking one.

3.2 Male Characters - More or Less Masculine

In the evaluations of the two male characters we find much less divergence. They are very evenly evaluated, with no significant differences. If we, nevertheless, look at the four *somewhat* larger differences, they are all consistent with gender stereotypes. The more masculine-looking male is evaluated as more decisive, more expert, more dominant and more objective (less subjective) than the less masculine-looking male.

Table 3. Evaluation of the masculine character (M+) vs. the weak masculine character (M-). The mean values correspond to the bipolar Likert type scales presented in Table 1.

	L1	L3	L4	L5	L6	L7	L8	L9	L11	L13	L16	L17	L18	L20
m (M+)	6,00	4,60	5,05	4,00	5,35	5,20	3,75	5,10	5,40	5,45	3,73	5,28	2,75	2,70
m (M-)	5,90	4,75	4,73	4,25	5,10	5,30	3,48	5,20	5,15	5,03	3,80	5,18	2,65	2,55
p	0,72	0,71	0,32	0,49	0,48	0,79	0,42	0,78	0,45	0,23	0,84	0,79	0,76	0,61

3.3 And How About Male vs. Female?

Our focus was on *masculinity and femininity within* the categories of males and females, respectively. However, since we had the data, we also wanted to analyze the evaluations of *male* versus *female* characters. As described in section 1.2., studies have shown that when a female and a male voice are exchanged for one another in a digital system, patterns of evaluations tend to correspond to gender stereotype patterns known from social psychology. For example in the study [16] where participants found praise from a digital tutor with a male voice more credible and valuable.

Table 4. Evaluation of the female characters (F+ & F-) vs. the male characters (M+ & M-). The mean values corresponds to the bipolar Likert type scales presented in Table 1.

	L1	L3	L4	L5	L6	L7	L8	L9	L11	L13	L16	L17	L18	L20
m (F)	5,85	4,64	5,23	4,14	5,20	5,41	3,46	5,33	5,76	5,68	3,69	5,71	2,63	2,79
m (M)	5,95	4,68	4,89	4,13	5,23	5,25	3,61	5,15	5,28	5,24	3,76	5,23	2,70	2,63
p	0,61	0,89	0,12	0,96	0,92	0,53	0,54	0,46	0,04	0,06	0,77	0,04	0,75	0,45
			d						a	c		b		

In our study, as well, we had a female versus a male voice, but additionally also visual representations of male versus female characters. Given this, we expected similar results as in [16] – i.e. results corresponding to gender stereotypes. However, quite to the contrary to our expectation, evaluations of male and female characters were very *uniform* (see table 4). They were perceived as *equally* warm, intelligent, emphatic, friendly, knowledgeable, personal and pleasant. The four significant or close to significant differences found – in expertise, objectiveness, decisiveness and persuasiveness – were all *contrary* to gender stereotypes, in the sense that the female characters were held to be more objective, decisive, experts and persuasive.

4   Discussion

4.1   More and Less Feminine-Looking Female Characters

The result indicates that manipulation of visual appearance of female virtual characters as to how feminine-looking they are may influence users' evaluation of the characters in accordance with gender stereotypes. Furthermore, this can, apparently, be achieved through *relatively subtle* visual cues.

The latter statement may seem depressing. Are humans really that sensitive to stereotype mechanisms? Do they really associate a *slightly* more feminine-looking female synthetic character with higher degrees of warmth, subjectivity and empathy than a *slightly* less feminine-looking one? It does seem so. One should remember, though, that stereotypes often operate non-consciously in evaluations and expectations [6, 10, 18]. When *asked,* many people deny that one or another gender stereotype cues could make any difference to them or that they would even notice them.

In the actual study, there was, however, also one cluster of traits where the evaluations of the female characters were not in line with gender stereotypes, namely those concerning the characters' decisiveness, experience, persuasiveness, expertise and knowledge. The more and the less feminine-looking characters scored more or less even on these traits. In fact, *all four* characters were very similarly, and highly, rated on these traits. A possible explanation, we suggest, is that *gender* stereotypes are here overridden by a *medical doctor stereotype*[4]. In the Swedish society this is a high status profession, with its practicians ascribed expertise, knowledge and intelligence.

4.2   More and Less Masculine-Looking Male Characters

The evaluations of the two male characters followed one another quite closely. In other words, the two characters did not elicit differences in accordance with gender stereotype patterns. The reason for this can only be speculated about at this stage. Perhaps more explicit visual cues in the degree of masculinity are required in order to elicit gender stereotypes for male characters. Perhaps there are inadequacies in the visual designs of the two male characters that level away evaluative differences (*e.g.* too large differences in the color schemes, potentially influencing evaluations of warmth and empathy). Note that such possible explanations are compatible with a pre-validation of the characters with M+ being categorized as more masculine than M-, since conscious evaluations as answers to explicit questions about gender may not necessarily match unconscious interpretations and evaluative effects.

4.3   Male Characters Versus Female Characters

The results of the comparison between male and female characters at first seemed puzzling. Here we had *two unmistaken females,* as to their voices as well as looks (even if one slightly more and one slightly less feminine-looking). Similarly, we had *two unmistaken males* as to their voices and looks (even if one slightly more and one

---

[4] Such an interaction between role-of-character effects and visual-appearance-of-character effects would fall in line with other studies [9] indicating interdependence of (i) user responses to visual appearance and (ii) the roles of synthetic characters.

slightly less masculine-looking). Yet, the differences in how the male versus the female characters were evaluated did not at all correspond to gender stereotypes and evaluative patterns known from social psychology. Instead, the evaluations were very *uniform* – with the exception of four (statistically or nearly statistically significant, yet not very large) differences. These, though, all went in the *opposite direction* than the direction predicted by gender stereotypes.

In order to seek an explanation of this, in our view, puzzling result, we decided to repeat the study with a number of (new) participants, but this time using only the voices and no visually appearing synthetic characters[5]. Eighteen adults took part in this follow-up-study. Again, the male and the female (now only mediated via voices) were very uniformly evaluated, and for the few differences, these were *contrary* to gender stereotypes. In other words, again we had a result quite contrary to social psychology studies and to studies reported in [16]. At this stage one of the article authors suggested that the puzzling results might be due to the somewhat differing *dialects* in the male and the female voices – the woman speaking something like standard Swedish, and the man speaking a regionally colored dialect from southern Sweden (yet quite refined or mild).

According to dialect research [20], standard Swedish is associated with high status and authority. It is held to be neutral and clear, and is often used by politicians, company directors, actors and newscasters in national media. It is also perceived as credible and trustworthy, yet somewhat machinelike and cold. This, then, was the dialect of the female character(s) – in the original as well as the follow-up study. A participant in the follow-up-study indeed commented that the female voice sounded "monotonous but informative". Another participant said, that "she sounds like a newscaster or a spokesman for something".

Turning to regional dialects, someone who speaks a regional dialect is often perceived as kinder, duller, slower and more naïve than someone who speaks standard Swedish [20]. Some participants in the follow-up-study described the male voice, in contrast to the female voice, as "less professional", "milder" and "more easy-going".

In sum, in our experimental setup a *woman's* voice with high-status dialect, associated with professionalism, neutrality, facts, distance, credibility etc. (i.e. 'male' traits), had been compared to a *man's voice* with a low-status dialect, associated with naïveté, niceness, non-professionalism, non-intelligence, subjectivity and commonplaceness (i.e. 'female' traits). In light of this, the 'out-leveled' results in the original as well as in the follow-up study – in the sense that males and females were valued very similarly on a number of gender stereotypical traits – may be due to the fact that dialect and gender stereotypes in this case counteracted one another.

5   Conclusion

In an empirical study like this, one often strives to focus on and isolate specific parameters, while controlling the rest. In this case the focus has been on *femininity and masculinity in the visual static appearance* of synthetic characters. The results support

---

[5] Regarding the role of the virtual characters as medical doctors, participants were, just as in the original study, *told* that they would listen to medical doctor Elm and medical doctor Ask.

the proposal that this is, indeed, a design aspect of these characters that plays a role for users' perceptions and evaluations of them. More importantly, influences seem to appear also when no obvious or extreme visual categories or stereotypes are involved, indicating that, perhaps, the static visual representation of synthetic characters is *never* socio-affectively neutral.

However, for any complex digital product, a number of factors are there to (potentially) explain users' affective responses (cf. [13, 17]). As already pointed out, a synthetic character has, of course, more to it than its visual gender. There is an inevitable complexity in which any given design parameter will interact with others. In the present study, for instance, *visually mediated gender aspects* seemed to interact in particular with dialects and roles of characters[6], in an unforeseen way that interfered with the set-up where we had aimed at controlling critical parameters.

A possible lesson to draw is that user studies, such as this one, from the outset should be framed as *iterative studies* to be repeated in different versions. *Which* aspects – in settings, tasks and various character traits – that should be modified and manipulated throughout the series of studies is however not to be settled at the start, but instead be allowed to emerge during the process. Within a more pragmatic design tradition such an explorative and iterative approach is self-evident. We hold that it can also be useful within an academic context [cf. 13]. Furthermore, we think that results from collected sets of user studies can be used as design heuristics – not that designers of synthetic characters can thereby refrain from (iterative) user evaluations, but as a means to start the navigation in the immense design space at the outset, and influence the design of the initial materials supplied for the first user evaluations.

With respect to the issue of *gender perception*, specifically, we believe it is useful to realize that a character is here being loaded by several parameters. Furthermore, we think that insight into how dialect stereotypes, gender stereotypes and role stereotypes can be combined as to strengthen, weaken or override each other, can be useful for designers of synthetic characters. In particular while these are artifacts with a seemingly enormous potential to elicit affective responses in users.

Acknowledgements

Our thanks to Dan Holmér and to ACII reviewers for valuable comments.

References

1. Adelsvärd, V.: Kvinnospråk och fruntimmersprat – Forskning och fördomar under 100 år. Brombergs, Stockholm (1999)
2. Argamon, S., Koppel, M., Fine, J., Shimoni, A.: Gender, Genre, and Writing Style in Formal Written Texts. Text 23(3), 321–346 (2003)
3. Baylor, A., Rosenberg-Kima, R., Plant, E.: Interface Agents as Social Models: The Impact of Appearance on Females' Attitude Toward Engineering. CHI 2006, pp. 526–531 (2006)
4. Baylor, A.: Preliminary Design Guidelines for Pedagogical Agent Interface Image. IUI 2005, 249–250 (2005)

[6] Most certainly there is also interaction with user characteristics.

5. Bem, S.: Lenses of Gender: Transforming the Debate on Sexual Inequality. Yale University Press, New Haven, CT (1993)
6. Cook, M.: Perceiving Others – The Psychology of Interpersonal Perception. Methuen & Co Ltd, London/New York (1979)
7. Gulz, A., Haake, M.: Design of Animated Pedagogical Agents – A Look at Their Look. Int. J. of Human-Computer Studies 64(6), 322–339 (2006a)
8. Gulz, A., Haake, M.: Visual Design of Virtual Pedagogical Agents: Naturalism versus Stylization in Static Appearance. 3rd Int. Design and Engagability Conference NordiChi 2006 (2006)
9. Haake, M., Gulz, A.: A Look at the Roles of Look & Roles in Virtual Pedagogical Agents (Submitted).
10. Haake, M., Gulz, A.: Visual Stereotypes and Virtual Pedagogical Agents (Submitted).
11. Hall, L., Woods, S.: Empathic Interaction with Synthetic Characters: The Importance of Similarity. In: Ghaoui, C. (ed.) Encyclopaedia of HCI, IDEA Group (2005)
12. Holmér, D.: Stereotyper i den virtuella världen: Hur visuella intryck påverkar deltagares uppfattningar av virtuella agenter. Master Thesis, Lund university, Lund (2006)
13. Höök, K.: User-centered Design and Evaluation of Affective Interfaces. In: Ruttkay, Z., Pelachaud, C. (eds.) From Brows to Trust, pp. 127–160 (2004)
14. Isbister, K.: Better Game Characters by Design. Elsevier, Amsterdam (2006)
15. Koppel, M., Argamon, S., Shimoni, A.: Automatically Categorizing Written Texts by Author Gender. Literary and Linguistic Computing 17(4), 401–412 (2003)
16. Reeves, B., Nass, C.: The Media Equation. Cambridge University Press, New York (1996)
17. Ruttkay, Z., Doorman, C., Noot, H.: Embodied Conversational Agents on a Common Ground. In: Ruttkay, Z., Pelachaud, C. (eds.) From Brows to Trust, pp. 27–66 (2004)
18. Schneider, D.: The Psychology of Stereotyping. Guildord Press, New York (2003)
19. SitePal, http://www.oddcast.com/home/sitepal
20. Skogsberg, Y.: Styr fördomar om andra människor vår uppfattningar om dialekter? Dept. of Lingustics, Stockholm University, Stockholm (2004)
21. Snaprud, P.: Få klarar att vända på dygnet. Forskning & Framsteg 7, 37–39 (2005)
22. Van Vugt, H., Hoorn, J., Konijn, E., de Bie Dimitriadou, A.: Affective Affordances: Improving Interface Character Engagement through Interaction. Int. J. of Human-Computer Studies 64(9), 874–888 (2006)
23. Voelker, D.: The Effects of Image Size and Voice Volume on the Evaluation of Represented Faces. PhD Thesis. Stanford University, Palo Alto, CA (1994)
24. Waern, A., Larsson, A., Néren, C.: Who Wants Them? Advances in Computer Entertainment Conference, Valencia, Spain (2005)
25. Demo, http://wwwold.eat.lth.se/Personal/Magnus/default_eng.htm

The Dynamics of Affective Transitions in Simulation Problem-Solving Environments

Ryan S.J.d. Baker[1], Ma. Mercedes T. Rodrigo[2], and Ulises E. Xolocotzin[1]

[1] Learning Sciences Research Institute, University of Nottingham, Nottingham, UK
[2] Department of Computer Science, Ateneo de Manila University, Quezon City, Philippines
ryan@educationaldatamining.org, mrodrigo@ateneo.edu,
lpxux@nottingham.ac.uk

Abstract. We analyze the antecedents of affective states in a simulation problem-solving environment, The Incredible Machine: Even More Contraptions, through quantitative field observations of high school students in the Philippines using that system. We investigate the transitions between affective states over time, finding that several affective states, including flow, boredom, and frustration, but not surprise, tend to persist over for relatively long periods of time. We also investigate how students' usage choices influence their later affect, finding that gaming the system leads to reduced confusion but increased boredom.

1 Introduction

In recent years, researchers of intelligent tutoring systems and interactive learning environments have investigated ways in which these systems can be made to recognize and respond to differences in students' affect. Researchers in these areas have developed systems which attempt to recognize differences in student affect, using a variety of types of data, from biometric sensors [1,6], to posture data [15], to interaction patterns in system logs [11]. Work towards developing systems that can reliably detect affect has sparked progress in developing systems that can respond to differences in affect. For instance, pedagogical agents have been designed with social intelligence that takes account of a learner's emotional state [13], in order to guide the learner to an optimal emotional state for learning [4]. The goal of learning environments that respond to differences in affect is to influence and improve each student's affect, and through doing so boost students' learning gains and enhance their overall learning experience.

However, until recently, there has been relatively little consideration of the natural dynamics and shifts in students' affect, in learning environments that do not explicitly attempt to monitor and alter affect. Understanding affective dynamics in non-affective learning environments will be useful to researchers in many fashions. First of all, it will help us set goals for the design of affective learning environments. For instance, the elimination of common affective transitions, where both the start and end affective states are considered negative (what D'Mello et al. [10] refer to as vicious cycles), may be as important as creating positive affective transitions. In addition, if we know which transitions between negative and positive affective states are reasonably common, we may more easily be able to improve students' affect by strengthening naturally occurring beneficial affective transitions, as opposed to attempting to create transitions which seldom occur naturally.

A. Paiva, R. Prada, and R.W. Picard (Eds.): ACII 2007, LNCS 4738, pp. 666–677, 2007.

Second, understanding and modeling affective dynamics will provide a baseline to use in understanding the impact of systems that attempt to influence affect. If a common affective transition disappears or a previously unseen transition develops in an affective learning environment, it will be easier to infer how the environment has influenced students' affect.

Third, a model of affective dynamics will provide evidence on the base rate of an affective state in a given situation beyond just the overall frequency of that affective state. Understanding affective dynamics may therefore make it possible to develop more successful detectors of affect.

Hence, modeling and understanding affective dynamics may lead to the development of more accurate and useful affective learning environments.

However, there has only been limited research, thus far, into affective dynamics. In one early paper on this subject, Guastello and his colleagues [12] studied the dynamics of a single affective state, flow [8], over time. Two more recent papers have investigated specific aspects of affective dynamics. D'Mello, Taylor, and Graesser [10] studied the transition between affective states in an intelligent tutoring system, AutoTutor. They computed the likelihood that learners would transition between a set of affective states thought to be relevant to learning: boredom, flow, confusion, frustration, delight, and surprise. They found that learners experiencing negative affective states such as boredom and frustration were likely to remain in these states. They were not likely to transition out of them and into more positive states such as flow or delight, nor to potentially more positive states such as confusion or surprise.

A second recent paper, by Rodrigo et al. [16], examined the relationship between these same affective states and a set of potential usage choices drawn from [3]: on-task, on-task conversation, off-task conversation, off-task solitary, inactive, and gaming the system, focusing on how affective states influence later usage choices. Baker, et al. [3] define gaming the system as "attempting to succeed in an educational environment by exploiting properties of the system rather than by learning the material and trying to use that knowledge to answer correctly." This study, conducted within a simulation problem-solving environment, The Incredible Machine, found that boredom, confusion, and the affective state coded as neutral were antecedents to gaming. Frustration, flow, and delight were not found to be antecedents to gaming the system.

The findings from [10] and [16] lead to further questions: Are the affective state transitions found in D'Mello et al. [10] generalizable? Are they particular to intelligent tutoring systems, or do they hold true for other types of interactive learning environments? And, do usage choices influence affective states to the same extent that affective states influence usage choices?

In this paper, we study these questions within the context of a simulation problem-solving environment, The Incredible Machine. We will consider data relevant to these questions, and discuss the implications for the design of affective learning environments.

2 Study Methods

We studied affective dynamics within a high school mathematics class in a private school in urban Manila, in the Philippines. Student ages ranged from 14 to 19, with an average age of 16. Thirty-six students participated in this study (17 female, 19 male).

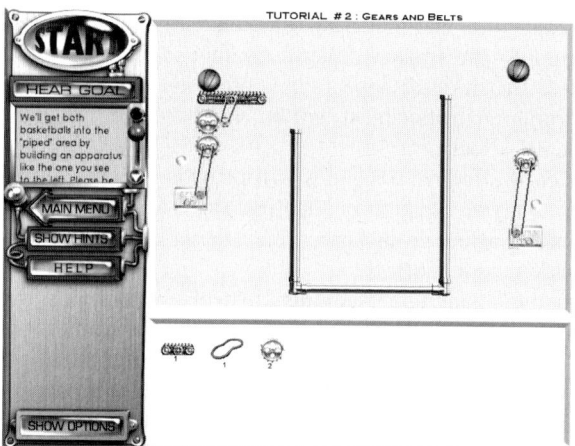

Fig. 1. A screen shot from The Incredible Machine: Even More Contraptions

Each student used The Incredible Machine: Even More Contraptions [18] (shown in Figure 1), a simulation environment where the user completes a series of logical "Rube Goldberg" puzzles. In each puzzle, the student has a pre-selected set of objects to use, such as scissors, ropes, and pulleys, electrical generators, and animals. The student must combine these objects in order to accomplish a pre-defined goal, such as lighting a candle or making a mouse run. If a student is stuck, he or she can ask for a hint; hint messages display where items should be located in a correct solution to the current problem (but do not show which item should be placed in each location).

Each student used The Incredible Machine for ten minutes, and each student's behavior and affect was observed several times as he or she used The Incredible Machine. The observations were conducted using a method which incorporated aspects of Baker et al's [3] quantitative field observations of student behavior categories, and Craig et al's [7] laboratory observations of affect. The observations were carried out by a team of six observers, working in pairs. The observers were Masters students in Education or Computer Science, and all but one had prior teaching experience. Observations were conducted according to guide that gave examples of actions, utterances, facial expressions, or body language that would imply a behavior or an affective state, and practiced the coding categories in another school prior to this study.

As in Baker et al., each observation lasted twenty seconds, and was conducted using peripheral vision, i.e. observers stood diagonally behind or in front of the student being observed and avoided looking at the student directly, in order to make it less clear exactly when an observation was occurring. If two distinct behaviors were seen during an observation, only the first behavior observed was coded, and any behavior by a student other than the student currently being observed was not coded.

During the laboratory sessions in which the data was gathered, it was not possible for the entire class to use the software at the same time, due to the size of the school computer laboratory; hence, students used the software in groups of nine (one student per computer), during their class time. Each pair of observers was assigned to three students and alternated between them. Since each observation lasted twenty seconds, each student was observed once per minute.

Observing students more frequently than in [3,7] made it possible to directly analyze the relationship between a student's affective state at a given time and their usage choices shortly thereafter.

Within an observation, each observer coded both the student's behavior and affective state, using coding schemes developed in prior research. The observers trained for the task through a series of pre-observation discussions on the meaning of the usage and affective categories.

The usage categories coded were adapted from [3], and are as follows:

1. **On-task** – working within The Incredible Machine
2. **On-task conversation** – talking to the teacher or another student about The Incredible Machine, or its puzzles
3. **Off-task conversation** – talking about any other topic
4. **Off-task solitary behavior** – behavior that did not involve The Incredible Machine or another person (such as reading a magazine or surfing the web)
5. **Inactivity** – instead of interacting with other students or the software, the student stares into space or puts his/her head down on the desk.
6. **Gaming the System** – sustained and/or systematic guessing, such arranging objects haphazardly or trying an object in every conceivable place. Also, repeatedly and rapidly requesting help in order to iterate to a solution.

The affective categories coded were drawn from [9,10]. Since many behaviors can correspond to an emotion, the observers looked for students' gestures, verbalizations, and other types of expressions rather than attempting to explicitly define each category. The categories coded were:

1. **Boredom** – behaviors such as slouching, and resting the chin on his/her palm; statements such as "Can we do something else?" and "This is boring!"
2. **Confusion** – behaviors such as scratching his/her head, repeatedly looking at the same interface elements; statements such as "Why didn't it work?"
3. **Delight** – behaviors such as clapping hands or laughing with pleasure; statements such as "Yes!" or "I got it!"
4. **Surprise** – behaviors such as jerking back suddenly or gasping; statements such as "Huh?" or "Oh, no!"
5. **Frustration** – behaviors such as banging on the keyboard or pulling at his/her hair; statements such as "This is annoying!" or "What's going on?!?"
6. **Flow** – complete immersion and focus upon the system [cf. 8]; behaviors such as leaning towards the computer or mouthing solutions to him/herself while solving a problem
7. The **Neutral** state, which was coded when the student did not appear to be displaying any of the affective states above, or the student's affect could not be determined for certain.

Some of these affective categories may not be mutually exclusive (such as frustration and confusion), though others clearly are (delight and frustration). For tractability, however, the observers only coded one affective state per observation.

Past research has suggested that brief observations can be reliable indicators of a student's affective state, whether carried out live [9] or by watching screen-capture videos [11]. 706 observations were collected, for an average of 19.6 observations per student. Inter-rater reliability was acceptably high across all observations — Cohen's [4] κ=0.71 for usage observations, κ=0.63 for observations of affective state.

3   Prior Research with this Data Set

Data from this study was previously used in order to analyze how affect influences students' behavior [16]. In this section, we will briefly recapitulate the results reported in that paper, in order to inform the analyses we present within the current paper.

Within this data, the most common affective state was flow, coded in 61% of the observations. The dominance of the flow state was similar to results seen in prior studies of affect in students using intelligent tutoring systems [7,10]. The second most common category was confusion, observed 11% of the time. Boredom (7%), frustration (7%), delight (6%), and the neutral state (5%) were each seen in a small but definite proportion of the observations. Boredom was less common than in previous work studying affect in intelligent tutoring systems [7,10], but frustration was more common. Surprise was the rarest category, but was still observed (3%).

The two most common behaviors observed were working on-task with the software (80% of observations), and talking on-task (9% of observations). Gaming the system was the third most common category of behavior, observed 8% of the time. Off-task conversation and off-task solitary behavior were quite rare, occurring 0.5% and 0.3% of the time — this frequency is much lower than the frequency of off-task behavior in intelligent-tutor classrooms [3] but comparable to the frequency of off-task behavior among students playing non-educational action games [20].

Gaming the system was strongly associated with boredom and confusion — a student who was bored or confused was significantly more likely to game the system both at the time he or she was bored/confused, and one minute afterwards. Frustration significantly co-occurred with gaming, but was not associated with later gaming. The neutral state was associated with gaming one minute later, but did not co-occur with gaming. Delight never co-occurred with gaming or preceded gaming.

4   The Antecedents of Affective States

In this section, we will analyze how affect and usage choices influence a student's later affect, specifically looking at how given affective states and usage choices influence the probability of a student being in a specific affective state one minute later.

In conducting these analyses, it is important to take into account the base rates of each affective category. Flow was the dominant category within our observations; hence, flow is likely to be the most common affective state that follows *any* other affective state. In order to appropriately account for the base rate of each affective category in assessing how likely a transition is, we adopt D'Mello et al's [10] transition likelihood metric, *L*, which is statistically equivalent to Cohen's [5] κ. D'Mello et al's *L* gives the probability that a transition between two affective states will occur, given the base frequency of the destination state, and is computed:

$$L = \frac{\Pr(NEXT \mid PREV) - \Pr(NEXT)}{(1 - \Pr(Next))}$$

L is scaled between 1 and - ∞. A value of 1 means that the transition will always occur; a value of 0 means that the transition's likelihood is exactly what it would be given only the base frequency of the destination state. Values above 0 signify that the transition is more likely than it could be expected to be given only the base frequency of the destination state, and values under 0 signify that the transition is less likely than it could be expected to be given only the base frequency of the destination state.

For a given transition, we calculate a value for L for each student, and then calculate the mean and standard error across students. We can then determine if a given transition is significantly more likely than chance (0), given the base frequency of the next state, using the two-tailed t-test for one sample.

4.1 Transitions Between Affective States

In this section, we will examine how a student's affective state at a given time influences their affective state at a later time, within the Incredible Machine. Within the data, four transitions were significantly or marginally significantly (p<0.10) more likely than chance, and five transitions were significantly or marginally significantly less likely than chance. Ten transitions did not occur with sufficient frequency for it to be possible to compute a standard error value, and thus will be excluded from formal statistical analysis (however, it can therefore be inferred that these transitions are quite rare). With seven affective states, 49 transitions are theoretically possible. Nine of the 39 transitions with sufficient data were significant or marginally significant; by chance, one would expect 3.9 transitions to be significant or marginally significant. The probability of 9 of 39 transitions being significant or marginally significant is 0.014 (computed by Monte Carlo simulation [14], 100,000 runs), so it appears quite unlikely that the pattern of results is due to chance.

One very clear pattern that emerged from the data is that affective states are persistent — if a student is in a given affective state at a given time, he or she is likely to be in that state one minute later as well. This pattern is true of the transition boredom → boredom (Mean L = 0.26, SE = 0.11, t(7)=2.27, p=0.06), confusion → confusion (Mean L = 0.10, SE = 0.06, t(20)=1.68, p=0.11), delight → delight (Mean L = 0.10, SE = 0.06, t(14)=1.71, p=0.11), flow → flow (Mean L = 0.20, SE = 0.12, t(33)=1.75, p=0.09), and neutral → neutral (Mean L = 0.41, SE = 0.09, t(5)=4.59, p=0.01). It is not clearly true of the transition frustrated → frustrated (Mean L = 0.12, SE = 0.08, t(12)=1.56, p=0.14), and appears not to be true of the transition surprised → surprised (Mean L = 0.03, SE = 0.06, t(7)=0.54, p=0.61). Interestingly, D'Mello et al. [10] found a similar degree of persistence and for more or less the same affective states, studying affective transitions within an intelligent tutoring system. Both our results and D'Mello et al's results found persistent transitions for boredom → boredom, flow → flow, confusion → confusion, and delight → delight (at the edge of marginal significance in both studies), and did not find significant persistent transitions for frustrated → frustrated and surprised → surprised.

Beyond the state-to-itself transitions, six relationships were significant or marginally significant. The neutral state was significantly more likely than chance to transition to boredom (Mean L = 0.23, SE = 0.10, t(5)= 2.44, p=0.06), but significantly less likely than chance to transition to flow (Mean L = -1.22, SE = 0.37, t(5)= -3.29, p=0.02). Flow was significantly less likely than chance to transition to boredom (Mean L = -0.05, SE = 0.02, t(33)= -3.10, p<0.01), confusion (Mean L = -0.04, SE = 0.02, t(33)= -1.86, p=0.07), or delight (Mean L = -0.03, SE = 0.01, t(33)= -2.18, p=0.04). Frustration was significantly less likely than chance to transition to delight (Mean L = -0.05, SE = 0.01, t(12)= -6.50, p<0.001). None of these relationships were significant in D'Mello et al's study of affective transitions within an intelligent tutor. The complete pattern of transitions is shown in Table 1.

Table 1. The transitions between affective states. Horizontal rows represent previous affective states, and vertical columns represent affective states one minute later. The first number in each cell is the mean value of D'Mello's L across students, the number in parantheses is the standard error. Cells with insufficient sample size are left blank (but can be inferred to be quite rare). Statistically significant relationships are in dark grey. Marginally significant relationships are in light grey.

	BOR	CON	DEL	FLO	FRU	NEU	SUR
BOR	0.26	0.00	-0.03	-0.58	0.01	0.03	
	(0.11)	(0.13)	(0.03)	(0.42)	(0.06)	(0.08)	
CON	0.03	0.10	0.00	-0.23	-0.03	-0.03	0.03
	(0.05)	(0.06)	(0.03)	(0.23)	(0.02)	(0.02)	(0.03)
DEL		-0.02	0.10	0.33			-0.01
		(0.08)	(0.06)	(0.23)			(0.02)
FLO	-0.05	-0.04	-0.03	0.20	0.03	0.01	0.00
	(0.02)	(0.02)	(0.01)	(0.12)	(0.03)	(0.03)	(0.01)
FRU	0.00	0.15	-0.05	-0.29	0.12		
	(0.05)	(0.11)	(0.01)	(0.32)	(0.08)		
NEU	0.23	-0.02		-1.22	-0.03	0.41	
	(0.10)	(0.07)		(0.37)	(0.04)	(0.09)	
SUR			-0.02	0.09	0.09	0.06	0.03
			(0.04)	(0.38)	(0.12)	(0.12)	(0.06)

4.2   Usage Choices as an Antecedent to Affect

In this section, we will analyze how a student's choice of how to use a learning environment at a given time influences their affective state at a later time. In our earlier work [16], we found that certain affective states are antecedents to certain usage choices. Specifically, boredom, confusion, and the neutral state served as antecedents to the choice to game the system, and that delight and flow are negative antecedents to the choice to game the system (i.e. a student in flow or delight is less likely to game one minute later). In the analysis presented here, we ask: Does a student's current usage choice influence his or her affect, the next time it is observed?

Within the data from our study on students using The Incredible Machine, one antecedent relationship was significantly more likely than chance, and three antecedent relationships were significantly or marginally significantly less likely than chance. Sixteen antecedent relationships did not occur with sufficient frequency for it to be possible to compute a standard error value, and thus will be excluded from formal statistical analysis (though these relationships can be inferred to be quite rare). With 7 affective states and 6 usage categories, 42 antecedent relationships are theoretically possible. Four of the 26 antecedent relationships with sufficient data were significant or marginally significant; by chance, one would expect 2.6 antecedent relationships to be significant or marginally significant. The probability of 4 of 26 antecedent relationships being significant or marginally significant is 0.28 (computed by Monte Carlo simulation [14], 100,000 runs), so it appears that the pattern of results could be due to chance. However, it is still possible to trust that an individual antecedent relationship is significant if that antecedent relationship is still significant after applying a Bonferroni procedure [17], which takes the number of tests run into account. In this case, we find that p must be less than 0.0018 for the test to be truly significant. Antecedent relationships which are not significant, given a Bonferroni procedure, must be considered suggestive rather than statistically significant.

As mentioned, four antecedent relationships are statistically significant or marginally statistically significant. Two involve gaming the system. First, a student who games the system is significantly less likely to be confused a moment later; this result is significant even after the Bonferroni procedure is applied (Mean $L = -0.11$, SE $= 0.02$, $t(11) = -6.37$, $p<0.001$). Since confusion is an antecedent to gaming behavior, this suggests that a student who is confused games the system to get past a confusing problem and that the gaming strategy generally succeeds in bypassing the confusing problem, enabling a transition out of the confused affective state.

A student who games the system also appears to be more likely to be bored a moment later, though this second result does not hold after applying the Bonferroni procedure (Mean $L = 0.26$, SE $= 0.12$, $t(11) = 2.18$, $p=0.05$). If this relationship is confirmed by later studies, it will have interesting implications. Since boredom is also an antecedent to gaming behavior, this result would suggest that a student who is bored games the system to alleviate their boredom, but that this strategy backfires, because the student's chance of being bored a minute after gaming is actually increased relative to the general incidence of the affective state.

It is worth noting that a student who games the system does not appear to be more likely to be frustrated a moment later (Mean $L = 0.005$, SE $= 0.05$, $t(11) = 0.12$, $p=0.91$). In our earlier work, we found that frustration is also not an antecedent to gaming behavior, but that gaming behavior and frustration co-occur more than would be expected by chance. If frustration neither proceeds nor follows gaming, but co-occurs with gaming, it may be the case that that a student who attempts to game the system but does not immediately succeed becomes frustrated until he or she succeeds in gaming the system, and that his or her frustration ends as soon as the attempt to game the system is successful.

Two other antecedent relationships are marginally statistically significant — both involve students who are on-task, working with the system. On-task behavior is marginally significantly negatively associated with a reduction in both frustration (Mean $L = -0.026$, SE $= 0.014$, $t(34) = -1.85$, $p=0.07$) and delight (Mean $L = -0.020$, SE $= 0.012$, $t(34) = -1.68$, $p=0.10$). Neither of these results hold after applying the Bonferroni procedure. The complete pattern of transitions is shown in Table 2.

Table 2. Usage choices as antecedents to affective states. Horizontal rows represent usage choices, and vertical columns represent affective states one minute later. The first number in each cell is the mean value of D'Mello's L across students, the number in parantheses is the standard error. Cells with insufficient sample size are left blank (but can be inferred to be quite rare). Statistically significant relationships are in dark grey. Marginally significant relationships are in light grey.

	BOR	CON	DEL	FLO	FRU	NEU	SUR
GAMING THE SYSTEM	0.26 (0.12)	-0.11 (0.02)	-0.02 (0.04)	-0.47 (0.29)	0.01 (0.05)	0.09 (0.08)	
STARING INTO SPACE	0.03 (0.11)	-0.05 (0.08)	0.15 (0.21)	-0.90 (0.50)	0.21 (0.21)	0.05 (0.11)	
SOLITARY OFF-TASK							
TALKING OFF-TASK							
ON-TASK	0.00 (0.02)	0.00 (0.03)	-0.02 (0.01)	0.06 (0.12)	-0.03 (0.01)	0.01 (0.03)	0.00 (0.01)
ON-TASK CONVERS.	-0.03 (0.05)	-0.07 (0.05)	0.10 (0.07)	-0.14 (0.24)	0.04 (0.06)	-0.01 (0.03)	0.02 (0.04)

5 Discussion and Conclusion

In this exploratory study, we have investigated the antecedents of affective states, both in terms of how affective states precede other affective states, and in terms of how usage choices influence later affective states, within the context of the use of a simulation-based learning environment, The Incredible Machine: Even More Contraptions. The first of these issues, how affective states influence later affective states, was previously studied by D'Mello and his colleagues [10], in the context of a very different type of learning environment, an intelligent tutoring system, and using quite different experimental methods. Their main finding was that if a student is in any affective state at a given time, they are likely to be in the same affective state a minute later. We replicated this finding over the majority of the affective states studied: flow, boredom, confusion, frustration, and delight (both studies found that delight → delight was almost significant). At the same time, both our study and D'Mello et al's study found that being surprised at a given time is *not* associated with being surprised a moment later. This result is not counter-intuitive — how long can someone genuinely be surprised? — but this result suggests that it is probably mistaken to conceptualize surprise as being part of the same category of affective states as flow, boredom, confusion, frustration, and delight. Instead, perhaps surprise should be conceptualized as a "transient affective state", as distinguished from other "durable affective states".

An interesting area for future research will be to determine if the other five affective states are all persistent to the same degree — if some affective states predominate for 20 minutes in a row whereas others tend to dissipate after 3 or 4 minutes, it will suggest that some affective states may actually be "moods" [cf. 17; personal communication, Sidney D'Mello], which last for considerably longer than other types of affective states. The data used in this paper was neither lengthy enough nor did it have a large enough sample to answer this question; addressing this question will be an important focus of future research in the field. It will be interesting, as well, to determine if the distinctions between moods and affective states apply across multiple types of learning environments, as the distinction between surprise and other affective states did.

The second major issue investigated in this paper, how usage choices within interactive learning environments influence later affect, has not to our knowledge been explicitly addressed in prior research, though the converse question, how affective states influence usage choices, was studied in [16]. Our results in this paper found that relatively few usage choices appeared to influence later affect. This forms an interesting contrast to the pattern of results in [16], where almost every affective state significantly influenced whether a student would later game the system. The combined pattern of results suggests that affect and usage choices may form a mostly one-way relationship — affect appears to influence usage much more than usage influences affect. However, we should obtain data similar to the data obtained in this paper for a system where off-task behavior is a more common choice (such as intelligent tutors [cf. 3]) before concluding that this pattern is generally true; off-task behavior may have stronger implications for future affect than the usage choices common in the Incredible Machine.

However, the primary relationships between usage choice and affect found in this study provide insight as to the implications of students' usage choices. Given existing knowledge that both boredom and confusion lead to the choice to game the system [16], it is interesting that gaming the system is positively associated with future boredom but negatively associated with future confusion. This result suggests that gaming the system can be an effective strategy for alleviating confusion (albeit a strategy that carries with it the cost of significantly poorer learning [3]), but not an effective strategy for alleviating boredom. To the extent that students game the system for different reasons, and with different results, a system's responses to gaming behavior should likely vary depending on why the student is gaming.

If we acknowledge that gaming the system does relieve students' confusion, perhaps we can develop systems to take advantage of the engagement with the task that confusion implies, and that attempt to respond to gaming by helping students to find more constructive ways to alleviate their confusion (such as, for instance, supplementary exercises [2]). On the other hand, since gaming the system does not successfully alleviate boredom, perhaps a system faced with a bored student should attempt to prevent gaming behavior entirely by taking immediate measures to alleviate the student's boredom. Since such a system may address boredom more effectively than the student could by gaming, this approach could completely eliminate bored students' incentive to game the system.

Overall, by studying how affect changes over time, and how usage choices and affect influence one another, we will be able to come to a full and rich picture of learners' experiences as they use interactive learning environments. This knowledge will be essential to the project of developing intelligent affective environments which can assess differences in students' affect and behavior and can respond to those differences in effective and constructive fashions.

Acknowledgements. We would like to thank Maria Carminda Lagud, Sheryl Ann Lim, Alexis Macapanpan, Sheila Pascua, Jerry Santillano, Leima Sevilla, Jessica Sugay, Sinath Tep, and Norma Jean Viehland for their assistance in organizing and conducting the studies reported here. We would also like to thank Sidney D'Mello for a very valuable conversation and suggestions. The work presented in this paper was funded in part by research fellowships from the Learning Sciences Research Institute, at the University of Nottingham.

References

1. Amershi, S., Conati, C., Maclaren, H.: Using feature selection and unsupervised clustering to identify affective expressions in educational games. Proceedings of the Workshop. Motivational and Affective Issues in ITS. In: conjunction with ITS, 8th International Conference on Intelligent Tutoring Systems (2006), Jhongli, Taiwan (2006)
2. Baker, R.S.J.d., Corbett, A.T., Koedinger, K.R., Evenson, E., Roll, I., Wagner, A.Z., Naim, M., Raspat, J., Baker, D.J., Beck, J. Adapting to When Students Game an Intelligent Tutoring System. In: Proceedings of the 8th International Conference on Intelligent Tutoring Systems, pp. 392-401 (2006)
3. Baker, R.S., Corbett, A.T., Koedinger, K.R., Wagner, A.Z.: Off-Task Behavior in the Cognitive Tutor Classroom: When Students Game the System. In: Proceedings of ACM CHI: Computer-Human Interaction, pp. 383--390 (2004)
4. Chaffar, S., Frasson, C.: Using and Emotional Intelligent Agent to Improve the Learner's Performance. In: Proceedings of the Workshop on Social and Emotional Intelligence in Learning Environments. In conjuction with Intelligent Tutoring Systems, Maceio, Brazil (2004)
5. Cohen, J.A.: Coefficient of Agreement for Nominal Scales. Educational and Psychological Measurement~20, 37--46 (1960)
6. Conati, C., Chabbal, R., Maclaren, H.: A: study on using biometric sensors for detecting user emotions in educational games. In: Proceedings of the Workshop Assessing and Adapting to User Attitude and Affects: Why, When and How? In: conjunction with UM '03, 9th International Conference on User Modeling, Pittsburgh, PA, U.S.A (2003)
7. Craig, S.D., Graesser, A.C., Sullins, J., Gholson, B.: Affect and learning: an exploratory look into the role of affect in learning with AutoTutor. Journal of Educational Media~29(3), 241--250 (2004)
8. Csikszentmihalyi, Flow, M.: The Psychology of Optimal Experience. Harper and Row, New York (1990)
9. D'Mello, S.K., Craig, S.D., Witherspoon, A., McDaniel, B., Graesser, A.: Integrating affect sensors in an intelligent tutoring system. In: Affective Interactions: The Computer in the Affective Loop Worksho. In: conjunction with International conference on Intelligent User Interfaces, pp. 7-13 (2005)
10. D'Mello, S., Taylor, R.S., Graesser, A.: Monitoring Affective Trajectories during Complex Learning. In: Proceedings of the 29th Annual Meeting of the Cognitive Science Society (in press),

11. de Vicente, A., Pain, H.: Informing the detection of the students' motivational state: an empirical study. In: Proceedings of the 6th International Conference on Intelligent Tutoring Systems, pp. 933--943 (2002)
12. Guastello, S.J., Johnson, E.A., Rieke, M.L.: Nonlinear Dynamics of Motivational Flow. Nonlinear dynamics, psychology, and life sciences~3(3), 259--274 (1999)
13. Johnson, W.L., Kole, S., Shaw, E., Pain, H.: Socially Intelligent Learner-Agent Interaction Tactics. In: Proceedings of Artificial Intelligence in Education: Shaping the Future of Learning through Intelligent Technologies, pp. 431--433 (2003)
14. Metropolis, N., Ulam, S.: The Monte Carlo Method. Journal of the American Statistical Association~44, 335 (1949)
15. Mota, S., Picard, R.W.: Automated posture analysis for detecting learner's interest level. Workshop on Computer Vision and Pattern Recognition for Human-Computer Interaction, CVPR HCI (2003)
16. Rodrigo, M., Baker, R., Lagud, M., Lim, S., Macapanpan, A., Pascua, S., Santillano, J., Sevilla, R., Sugay, J., Tep, S., Viehland, N.: Affect and Usage Choices in Simulation Problem-Solving Environments. In: Proceedings of the 13th International Conference on Artificial Intelligence in Education (in press). Available online via Google Scholar,
17. Rosenthal, R., Rosnow, R.L.: Essentials of Behavioral Research: Methods and Data Analysis, 2nd edn. McGraw-Hill, Boston (1991)
18. Sierra Online, Inc, The Incredible Machine: Even More Contraptions (2001)
19. Thayer, R.E.: The biopsychology of mood and arousal. Oxford University Press, New York (1989)
20. Ziemek, T.: Two-D or not Two-D: gender implications of visual cognition in electronic games. In: Proceedings of the 2006 Symposium on Interactive 3D graphics and games, pp. 183--190 (2006)

Investigating Human Tutor Responses to Student Uncertainty for Adaptive System Development

Kate Forbes-Riley and Diane Litman

Learning Research and Development Ctr, Univ. of Pittsburgh, Pittsburgh, PA 15260

Abstract. We use a χ^2 analysis on our spoken dialogue tutoring corpus to investigate dependencies between uncertain student answers and 9 dialogue acts the human tutor uses in his response to these answers. Our results show significant dependencies between the tutor's use of some dialogue acts and the uncertainty expressed in the prior student answer, even after factoring out the answer's (in)correctness. Identification and analysis of these dependencies is part of our empirical approach to developing an adaptive version of our spoken dialogue tutoring system that responds to student affective states as well as to student correctness.

1   Introduction

Within research on spoken dialogue systems, promising results have been reported for automatically detecting user affect (e.g., [1,2,3,4]). The larger goal of such work is to improve dialogue system quality by automatically adapting to affect; however, to date not a lot of work has focused on the affect adaptations themselves. This difficult task involves developing appropriate responses, determining when to apply them, and evaluating the responses with real users. In some domains, it seems plausible to start with intuitively useful adaptations. For example, [5]'s health assessment system responds with empathy to user stress. [6]'s gaming system responds with sympathy and apology to user frustration. In both studies, users preferred the adaptive system over non-adaptive versions.

In contrast, in the tutoring system domain, where student learning is the primary metric of system performance, it is not clear a priori what system responses to student affective states will be most useful (for improving learning). We take an empirical approach to developing affect adaptations for our spoken dialogue tutoring system. Our approach is to develop system adaptations to student affective states based on analysis of our *human* tutor responses to those states. For this analysis, we use a previously collected human tutoring corpus that corresponds to our system corpora, except the tutor is human (Section 2.1).

We target student uncertainty as our first affective state for adaptation for two reasons. First, it occurs more often than other affective states in our tutoring dialogues [9]. Second, although most tutoring systems respond based only on student correctness, tutoring researchers are showing interest in also responding

A. Paiva, R. Prada, and R.W. Picard (Eds.): ACII 2007, LNCS 4738, pp. 678–689, 2007.

to student uncertainty, hypothesizing that uncertainty and incorrectness each create an opportunity for the student to engage in constructive learning [8,10].

In this paper, we use the χ^2 test to investigate dependencies between uncertain student answers (Section 2.2) and 9 dialogue acts (Section 2.3) that our human tutor uses to respond to these answers. Our dialogue acts include Feedback Acts (Positive or Negative), Question Acts (Short and Hard Answer), and State Acts (Hints, Bottom Outs, Restatements, Recaps and Expansions).

Our results (Section 3) show significant dependencies between uncertain student answers and the human tutor's use of some dialogue acts in his response, even after factoring out the answer's (in)correctness. Within incorrect answers, the tutor's responses contain a Bottom Out significantly more than expected after uncertain answers. Within correct answers, the tutor's responses contain Positive Feedback significantly more than expected, and contain Expansions and Short Answer Questions significantly less than expected, after uncertain answers. This work builds on our and other prior work in this area (Section 4). Identification and analysis of these dependencies is part of our empirical approach to developing an adaptive version of our spoken dialogue tutoring system that responds to affective states[1] in student answers as well as their correctness.

2   Data and Annotations

2.1   Human Tutoring Spoken Dialogues

Our data consists of a human tutoring spoken dialogue corpus of 128 transcribed and annotated dialogues between 14 students and one human tutor. Each dialogue contains 47 student turns and 43 tutor turns on average. This corpus was collected in tandem with a computer tutoring corpus using our ITSPOKE spoken dialogue tutoring system; the human tutor and ITSPOKE performed the same task [11]. Each dialogue consists of a question-answer discussion between tutor and student about one qualitative physics problem. First, the student types an essay answer. The tutor analyzes the essay, then engages the student in a dialogue to correct misconceptions and incompleteness. The student then revises the essay, thereby ending the dialogue or causing another round of dialogue/essay revision. Figure 1 shows a dialogue excerpt from the human tutoring corpus.

The experimental procedure for collecting our corpora was as follows: each student 1) took a pre-test, 2) used a web and voice interface to work through 5 to 10 physics problems with the tutor, and 3) took a post-test. Before working the problems, students read a small document of background physics material[2].

---

[1] We use "affect" to cover emotions and attitudes. Some argue for separating the two, but some speech researchers find the narrow sense of "emotion" too restrictive since it excludes states in speech where emotion is not full-blown, including arousal and attitude [7]. Some tutoring researchers also combine emotion and attitude (e.g. [8]).

[2] In the human corpus, the pretest was given before the reading. In the computer corpus, it was was moved after the reading, to measure learning gains caused only by the tutoring. Also, in the computer corpus, students work only 5 problems.

TUTOR₃₇: Is there any other force on the- on these objects? *[SAQ]*
STUDENT₃₈: Uh no, just gravity. *[non-uncertain, correct]*
TUTOR₃₉: Now why do you say that? *[HAQ]*

< *...further discussion ...*>

TUTOR₅₃: Ok, they have been dropped in vacuum, so gravity is the only force acting on them. And uh, what is the motion called when gravity is the only force, uh, acting? *[RCP, SAQ]*
STUDENT₅₄: ... Freefall? *[uncertain, correct]*
TUTOR₅₅: Uh freefall, yes, so these two balls are in freefall. *[RST, POS, RST]*
STUDENT₅₆: Right *[non-uncertain, NA]*
TUTOR₅₇: What is the essential characteristic of objects that are in freefall? *[SAQ]*
STUDENT₅₈: Uh... Mass? *[uncertain, incorrect]*
TUTOR₅₉: Mass of course is an intrinsic property of the object. Uh, but if they are in freefall then there is something which is in common in for all objects that are in freefall? *[POS, RST, SAQ]*
STUDENT₆₀: Ok, uh, the weight. The gravitational force. *[non-uncertain, incorrect]*
TUTOR₆₁: Gravitational force we have already recognized is different for both of them. It's not the same. *[HINT]*
STUDENT₆₂: Oh, ok, um... no, I don't know. *[uncertain, incorrect]*
TUTOR₆₃: Well, all objects in freefall have the same acceleration. *[BOT]*

< *...further discussion ...*>

TUTOR₇₅: Now, there is a letter which is used for representing acceleration due to gravity. What is that letter? *[EXP, SAQ]*
STUDENT₇₆: Um, A? *[uncertain, incorrect]*
TUTOR₇₇: No, G-G in the lower case is, uh, used for representing acceleration due to gravity. *[NEG, BOT]*

Fig. 1. Annotated Human Tutoring Corpus Excerpt (at 5.2 min. into dialogue)

2.2   Student Uncertainty and Correctness Annotations

In our human tutoring corpus, each student answer has been manually labeled by a paid annotator for uncertainty [9]. Here we distinguish two labels[3]: the *uncertain* label is used for answers expressing uncertainty or confusion about the material being learned, and the *non-uncertain* label is used for all other answers. The same annotator also manually labeled each student answer for correctness, based on the human tutor's response to the answer [11]. Here we distinguish two labels[4]: the *correct* label is used for answers the tutor considered to be wholly or partly correct, and the *incorrect* label is used for answers the tutor considered to be wholly incorrect. Labeled examples are shown in Figure 1.

---

[3] A second annotator labeled a subset of the human tutoring corpus (505 student turns), yielding inter-annotator agreement of 0.61 Kappa for these two labels. See [9] for further discussion of this inter-annotation. Two annotators also labeled an IT-SPOKE corpus with these labels, yielding inter-annotator agreement of 0.73 Kappa.
[4] A second annotator also labeled a subset of the corpus (507 student turns) with these labels, yielding inter-annotator agreement of 0.85 Kappa.

Note that although student uncertainty and (in)correctness are related, they cannot be equated. First, prior work has shown that an uncertain answer may be correct or incorrect [8]. This is also true in our data. As discussed in Section 3.2, our dataset consists of 1985 student answers. Table 1 shows the distribution of our uncertainty and (in)correctness labels across these answers. For example, in our data 412 uncertain answers are correct, while 341 uncertain answers are incorrect. However, when we apply the χ^2 test to this data (as discussed in Section 3.2), we find a highly significant positive dependency between uncertainty and (in)correctness: uncertain answers are incorrect significantly more than expected by chance alone - or equivalently, uncertain answers are correct significantly less than expected by chance (χ^2 value = 78.47 (df=1)).

Table 1. Distribution of Student Answers in terms of Uncertainty and (In)Correctness

	correct	incorrect	total
uncertain	412	341	753
non-uncertain	912	320	1232
total	1324	661	1985

Uncertainty and incorrectness also differ in terms of what they convey to the tutor. Incorrectness conveys that there is a misconception in the student's knowledge. Uncertainty - in both a correct and a incorrect answer - conveys that the student *perceives a possible misconception* in their knowledge. If that answer is correct, a misconception does not actually exist; if that answer is incorrect, a misconception does exist. Our analyses of the dependencies presented in Section 3 suggest that our human tutor responds both to an answer's (in)correctness and to the student's perceived misconception; our system responses to uncertainty over correctness can thus be modeled based on these human tutor responses.

2.3   Tutor Dialogue Act Annotations

In our human tutoring corpus, each utterance in each tutor turn has been manually labeled by a paid annotator for tutoring dialogue acts [11][5]. Our annotation is based on similar schemes from other tutorial dialogue projects (e.g. [12]). Here we distinguish 9 labels, which are defined in Figure 2 and illustrated in Figure 1. Note that some definitions relate to the prior student answer's correctness. "Feedback Acts" label feedback based on lexical items in the tutor turn. These labels often coincide with the prior student answer's correctness, but can also convey encouragement, or relate to the discourse level or to the student's earlier essay. "State Acts" summarize or clarify the current state of the student's argument, based on the prior student turns(s). "Question Acts" label the type of question asked, in terms of its content and the type of answer required.

---

[5] A second annotator labeled these dialogue acts in a subset of our corpus (8 dialogues containing 548 utterances), yielding agreement of 0.48 Kappa.

- **Tutor Feedback Acts**
  - Positive Feedback **(POS)**: positive feedback word/phrase present in turn
  - Negative Feedback **(NEG)**: negative feedback word/phrase present in turn
- **Tutor State Acts**
  - Restatement **(RST)**: repetitions and rewordings of prior student statement
  - Recap **(RCP)**: summarize overall argument or earlier-established points
  - Bottom Out **(BOT)**: full answer given if student answer is incorrect
  - Hint **(HINT)**: partial answer given if student answer is incorrect
  - Expansion **(EXP)**: novel details related to answer given without being queried
- **Tutor Question Acts**
  - Short Answer Question **(SAQ)**: concerns basic quantitative relationships
  - Hard Answer Question **(HAQ)**: requires definition/interpretation of concepts or reasoning about causes and/or effects

Fig. 2. Tutor Dialogue Acts

3   Student Uncertainty-Tutor Response Dependencies

3.1   Extracting Student Answers and Tutor Responses

Here we are investigating dependencies between uncertain student answers and 9 dialogue acts that our human tutor uses to respond to these answers. However, while our computer tutoring dialogues follow a strict Tutor Question-Student Answer-Tutor Response format, our human tutoring dialogues are more complex. In particular, not all student turns contain an answer to a tutor question; instead (see Figure 1, STUDENT$_{56}$), they may contain a backchanneling or grounding, or a clarification question, or they may be related to the situation rather than the physics content (e.g. "How do I submit my essay?"). All student turns that do not contain an answer are labeled "NA" in our correctness annotation scheme. In this study we exclude these non-answer student turns from our analysis, because they don't exist in our computer tutoring corpus. In other words, we only investigate dependencies between actual student answers (labeled correct or incorrect) and tutor responses to them. We do this by extracting from our human tutoring corpus all bigrams consisting of a student answer turn followed by a tutor response turn, yielding 1985 student answer-tutor response bigrams.

3.2   The χ^2 Analysis

We use a χ^2 analysis to investigate dependencies between uncertain student answers and each of the 9 dialogue acts that may be present in our human tutor's responses to these answers. We investigate each dialogue act separately, because most tutor turns contain multiple dialogue acts (see Figure 1) and there are no limits on their combination. Thus, treating each tag combination as a unique response would yield a data sparsity problem for our dependency analysis.

We performed 9 dependency analyses, one for each dialogue act D. For each analysis, we first took our dataset of student answer-tutor response bigrams and replaced all tutor responses containing D with only **D**, and replaced all tutor responses not containing D with only **notD**.[6] Next, we applied four χ^2 tests to this dataset. To illustrate the analysis, we refer to Table 2, which shows the results of the analysis of the BOT ("Bottom Out") dialogue act response.

The first χ^2 test investigates the dependency between uncertain student answers and the tutor's use of D in his responses. We compute a χ^2 value for the dependency between a binary student answer variable with two values: *uncertain or non-uncertain*, and a binary tutor response variable with two values: *D or notD*.[7] For example, the first data row of Table 2 shows a significant dependency between uncertain answers and the tutor's use of BOT in his responses: the χ^2 value is 13.70, which exceeds the critical value of 3.84 (p≤0.05, df=1).[8] This row also shows the observed (112) and expected (86) counts, whose comparison determines the dependency's sign. The "+" indicates that BOT occurs significantly more than expected after uncertain answers. A "-" indicates a dependency where the observed count is significantly less than expected. An "=" indicates a non-significant dependency (observed and expected counts are nearly equal).

This first χ^2 test does not tell us whether there is also a dependency between (in)correctness and the tutor's use of D in his response. Dependencies are expected for those D labels defined in relation to correctness (Section 2.3). Our second χ^2 test thus computes a χ^2 value for the dependency between a new binary student answer variable with two values: *correct or incorrect*, and the same tutor response variable with its two values: *D or notD*. For example, the second data row of Table 2 shows that BOT occurs significantly more than expected after incorrect answers. For discussion, the third data row shows the counts for BOTs after correct answers, but both rows express the same dependency.

Because uncertainty and incorrectness co-occur significantly more than expected (Section 2), the first two χ^2 tests cannot tell us whether a dependency between uncertainty and D exists independently of (in)correctness. Thus, for our third and fourth χ^2 tests, we first factor out the answers' correctness value, and then investigate the dependency between uncertainty and the use of D in the tutor's responses. More specifically, the third χ^2 test is applied only to the incorrect answers, and the fourth χ^2 test is applied only to the correct answers. For these tests, the student answer variable and tutor response variable have the same values as in the first test. For example, the second-to-last data row of Table 2 shows that even within the incorrect answers, there is a significant positive dependency between uncertainty and the tutor's use of BOT in his responses. However, the last row shows that this is not true of correct answers.

---

[6] We also used this method in our prior work [9], as discussed in Section 4.

[7] The χ^2 test arrays the variables' values along the row and column axes of a table. Each cell C contains the observed count of that row and column value co-occurring. C's expected count = *(C's row total*C's column total)/(overall total)*, and the χ^2 value = *(C's observed total - C's expected total)^2/C's expected total*. The overall χ^2 value for the dependency is computed by summing the χ^2 values over all cells.

[8] The critical χ^2 value accounts for the degrees of freedom (df = (#rows-1)*(#columns-1)) between the variables and the probability of exceeding a sampling error (e.g., p≤0.05). A dependency's significance increases as its χ^2 value increases.

3.3   Results

Tables 2-5 show uncertainty dependencies that do (or do not) remain significant after factoring out *incorrectness*. First, as discussed above, Table 2 shows that the tutor uses Bottom-Outs significantly more than expected after uncertain answers, incorrect answers, and uncertain answers within the incorrect answers.

Table 2. Student Answer $\sim$ BOT Dependencies (p$\leq$.05: critical χ^2=3.84 (df=1))

Dependency		Obs.	Exp.	χ^2
Uncertain $\sim$ BOT	+	112	86	13.70
Incorrect $\sim$ BOT	+	139	76	88.76
Correct $\sim$ BOT	-	89	152	88.76
Uncertain within Incorrect $\sim$ BOT	+	82	72	3.86
Uncertain within Correct $\sim$ BOT	=	30	28	0.30

The χ^2 test is not a causal test; however, we can formulate hypotheses about the reasons underlying dependencies, to help guide the development of our system adaptations. The strong *Incorrect $\sim$ BOT* dependency is not surprising, given that BOT by definition is the act of supplying a complete answer after an incorrect answer[9]. It is somewhat surprising that the tutor also uses BOT more than expected after uncertain answers; one might intuitively expect a HINT here. We hypothesize that the tutor uses BOT after uncertainty (overall and within incorrects) to respond to the student's perceived misconception conveyed by his/her uncertainty. [10] argues that uncertainty and incorrectness are both types of *learning impasses*: opportunities for students to learn what they are wrong and/or uncertain about (i.e., to resolve a misconception). However, the learning event requires first perceiving and then bridging the impasse. For uncertain incorrect answers, where an impasse is already perceived, the tutor may use BOT to provide this bridge. For non-uncertain incorrect answers, he may equally employ some other technique to help students first perceive the impasse. However, the relative weakness of the *Uncertain within Incorrect $\sim$ BOT* dependency suggests that for some non-uncertain incorrect answers, the tutor expects BOT to enable the student to both perceive and bridge the impasse.

Table 3 suggests what this other technique for non-uncertain incorrect answers may be. The tutor uses Hints significantly more than expected after incorrect answers, but not after uncertain answers (overall or within incorrects). Again, the strong *Incorrect $\sim$ HINT* dependency is not surprising; HINT is defined as the act of supplying help after an incorrect answer. Taken with the BOT results, the HINT results suggest that HINTs, unlike BOTs, aren't used as a specific response to uncertainty because uncertain students already perceive a learning impasse; rather, the tutor may often employ a HINT to ensure incorrect students first perceive (and possibly bridge) a particular impasse.

---

[9] BOTs, HINTs and NEGs after correct answers are cases where the answer was only partly correct or the tutor felt it should be filled out in some way.

Table 3. Student Answer $\sim$ HINT Dependencies (p$\leq$.05: critical χ^2=3.84 (df=1))

Dependency		Obs.	Exp.	χ^2
Uncertain $\sim$ HINT	=	170	160	1.26
Incorrect $\sim$ HINT	+	227	141	101.32
Correct $\sim$ HINT	-	195	281	101.32
Uncertain within Incorrect $\sim$ HINT	=	115	117	0.12
Uncertain within Correct $\sim$ HINT	=	55	61	0.91

Table 4. Student Answer $\sim$ NEG Dependencies (p$\leq$.05: critical χ^2=3.84 (df=1))

Dependency		Obs.	Exp.	χ^2
Uncertain $\sim$ NEG	+	87	64	14.39
Incorrect $\sim$ NEG	+	154	56	278.09
Correct $\sim$ NEG	-	15	113	278.09
Uncertain within Incorrect $\sim$ NEG	=	81	79	0.08
Uncertain within Correct $\sim$ NEG	=	6	5	0.56

Table 5. Student Answer $\sim$ RST Dependencies (p$\leq$.05: critical χ^2=3.84 (df=1))

Dependency		Obs.	Exp.	χ^2
Uncertain $\sim$ RST	-	199	252	26.88
Incorrect $\sim$ RST	-	71	221	229.58
Correct $\sim$ RST	+	593	443	229.58
Uncertain within Incorrect $\sim$ RST	=	30	37	2.78
Uncertain within Correct $\sim$ RST	=	169	184	3.44

Table 4 shows that the tutor uses Negative Feedback significantly more than expected only after uncertain answers and incorrect answers overall. Thus the uncertainty dependency is wholly accounted for by the stronger incorrectness dependency. The tutor may use NEG equally after all incorrect answers to assert his recognition of a learning impasse, e.g. before using a BOT or HINT.

Table 5 shows that the tutor uses Restatements significantly less than expected after uncertain answers and incorrect answers overall, but not after uncertain within incorrect answers. Again, the uncertainty dependency is wholly accounted for by the stronger incorrectness dependency. It is not surprising that the tutor is unlikely to restate or reword an incorrect answer; the tutor's increased use of RST appears to be a response to all types of correct answers.

Tables 6-8 show uncertainty dependencies that are significant even after factoring out *correctness*. The tutor uses Positive Feedback significantly more than expected after uncertain answers, correct answers, and uncertain within incorrect answers; the latter two dependencies are very strong. We hypothesize that the human tutor uses POS to respond to uncertainty over correctness as a direct

Table 6. Student Answer $\sim$ POS Dependencies (p$\leq$.05: critical χ^2=3.84 (df=1))

Dependency		Obs.	Exp.	χ^2
Uncertain $\sim$ POS	+	241	211	9.86
Incorrect $\sim$ POS	-	20	185	305.88
Correct $\sim$ POS	+	535	370	305.88
Uncertain within Incorrect $\sim$ POS	=	12	10	0.58
Uncertain within Correct $\sim$ POS	+	229	166	57.20

Table 7. Student Answer $\sim$ EXP Dependencies (p$\leq$.05: critical χ^2=3.84 (df=1))

Dependency		Obs.	Exp.	χ^2
Uncertain $\sim$ EXP	-	126	146	5.31
Incorrect $\sim$ EXP	-	96	128	14.77
Correct $\sim$ EXP	+	288	256	14.77
Uncertain within Incorrect $\sim$ EXP	=	51	50	0.11
Uncertain within Correct $\sim$ EXP	-	75	90	4.42

Table 8. Student Answer $\sim$ SAQ Dependencies (p$\leq$.05: critical χ^2=3.84 (df=1))

Dependency		Obs.	Exp.	χ^2
Uncertain $\sim$ SAQ	=	211	226	2.21
Incorrect $\sim$ SAQ	=	206	198	0.67
Correct $\sim$ SAQ	=	389	397	0.67
Uncertain within Incorrect $\sim$ SAQ	=	107	106	0.01
Uncertain within Correct $\sim$ SAQ	-	104	121	4.94

method of bridging the perceived learning impasse: Positive Feedback asserts that the students' perceived misconception does not exist.

Table 7 shows that the tutor uses Expansions significantly less than expected after uncertain answers, incorrect answers, and uncertain answers within the correct answers. It is not surprising that the tutor is more likely to expand on a correct answer than an incorrect one. However, the *Uncertain within Correct* $\sim$ *EXP* dependency suggests the tutor's strategy may be to address perceived (false) misconceptions without adding novel (and possibly confusing) information to his response.

Table 8 shows that the tutor uses Short Answer Questions significantly less than expected after uncertain within correct answers. Like Expansions, this dependency suggests that the tutor's strategy may be to address perceived (false) misconceptions without asking for further basic information in his response.

Finally, we found no significant dependencies involving the tutor's use of Hard Answer Questions (HAQs) or Recaps (RCPs). Overall our results suggest that some dialogue acts used in our tutor's response do depend on the prior student answer's uncertainty after factoring out correctness, but that these are not the only factors governing their use. For example, his use of Recaps and Hard Answer questions may instead depend on larger units of discourse structure, such as the number or type of topics covered so far, and/or larger units of uncertainty, such as the total overall uncertainty (within (in)correctness) seen so far. Moreover, the content of these dialogue acts may also depend on uncertainty; e.g. when the tutor uses a Short Answer Question that moves on to a new topic, versus when he uses a Short Answer Question that further queries the current topic. Although the current analysis is a step towards identifying human tutor responses to uncertainty, it does not capture such additional factors.

4   Related Work

This work builds on our prior work [9], where we also used χ^2 to investigate dependencies between uncertain student answers and dialogue acts used in the human tutor's response to these answers. There are numerous differences in this current work. First, here we distinguish uncertain and non-uncertain answers, because our current focus is on developing adaptations only for uncertain answers. In [9] we also distinguished neutral, certain, and mixed answers. Second, here our dataset is restricted to student answer turns, because in our ITSPOKE dialogues all student turns answer a tutor question. In [9] we included all student turns as a preliminary analysis. Third, in [9] we examined only uncertainty dependencies; here we also examine (in)correctness dependencies and uncertainty dependencies after factoring out (in)correctness. Fourth, in [9] we used a different version of our dialogue act tags. The version used here better corresponds to the dialogue acts used by our computer tutor. Here we also further develop the conclusions from this prior work. In particular, in [9] we also found that BOTs occur more than expected after uncertainty; here we showed this is actually only the case for uncertainty within incorrectness. Similarly, in [9] we also found that EXPs occur less than expected after uncertainty; here we showed this is actually only the case for uncertainty within correctness. We found similar clarifications of the tutor's use of the other dialogue acts by factoring out (in)correctness.

Our work also builds on related tutoring research developing system adaptations to student affect based on human tutor dialogue act responses. For example, [8] used a frequency analysis to extract two tutor responses to uncertain answers from a human tutoring corpus, then implemented and evaluated them in the SCoT-DC tutor. These adaptations, "paraphrasing" after uncertain+correct answers and "referring back to past dialogue" after uncertain+incorrect answers, were found to increase learning when used after all correct and incorrect answers, but not when used only after the uncertain answers. Other examples include researchers who have focused on developing computer tutor Feedback Acts that respond to affect as well as correctness. [13] developed a set of positive feedback responses based on a frequency analysis of the human tutor's responses in a spoken tutoring dialogue corpus, which included praising acknowledgments after uncertain+correct student turns, and implemented these responses in their

Memory Game computer tutor. Students rated the system that used these positive feedback responses more highly than a version without. Such research suggests that human tutors adapt the content and presentation of their response to student uncertainty over and above correctness, and that these human tutor responses can be mined to develop effective computer tutor responses. However, none of these adaptations have yet shown a positive impact on student learning, which suggests that further research on affect adaptations is worthwhile. Moreover, our approach differs in that we use a statistical method of determining significant differences in how the human tutor responds to uncertainty, rather than a less rigorous frequency analysis.

5   Current Directions

We used χ^2 tests to identify and analyze dependencies between uncertain student answers and 9 dialogue acts the human tutor uses in his response to these answers. Within incorrect answers, we found that the tutor gives a Bottom Out significantly more than expected after uncertain answers. Within correct answers, the tutor gives Positive Feedback significantly more, and gives Expansions and ShortAnswer Questions significantly less, than expected after uncertain answers. We hypothesized that these dependencies reflect tutor methods of resolving learning impasses after students express perceived misconceptions.

Our next steps will be to develop and implement responses to uncertainty over correctness in ITSPOKE, based on analyses such as discussed here, and also on our recent work investigating contexts in our ITSPOKE corpora that are strongly associated with uncertainty [14]. For example, in [14] we found that uncertainty occurs significantly more than expected after Hard Answer Questions. Here we found BOT used significantly more than expected after uncertain and incorrect answers. Together these results suggest that ITSPOKE can use BOTs to respond to uncertain and incorrect answers to HAQs. This context-dependent approach to affect adaptation is described further in [14]. After developing and implementing our uncertainty adaptations, we will conduct a controlled experiment to test whether they improve student learning. More generally, our empirical approach can be used to develop adaptations for other dialogue systems and other user affective states, such as frustration, by analyzing dependencies between those states and human responses in annotated human-human dialogue corpora.

In general, it is common for dialogue system researchers to model systems on human behavior; as discussed in Section 4, this is particularly true for tutoring systems. Of course, this approach assumes that the human tutor's behavior can have a positive impact on the learning process. In our case, this assumption is supported by the fact that our human tutor had significant prior tutoring experience and our students learned significantly with our human tutor [11]. In future work we can examine this assumption further by running correlations between learning and the dependencies analyzed here (as in [9]). Although we have only analyzed the behavior of one human tutor, as discussed in [9], tutors have different teaching styles and skill levels; thus studying multiple tutors will not necessarily yield consistent generalizations about the "best" adaptive strategies. More generally, it is still an open question in the tutoring literature as to the "best" method of responding to uncertainty (and other affective states) [8,10].

Acknowledgements

This material is based upon work supported by NSF (0328431 & 0631930) and ONR (N00014-04-1-0108). We thank the ITSPOKE Group.

References

1. Litman, D., Forbes-Riley, K.: Recognizing student emotions and attitudes on the basis of utterances in spoken tutoring dialogues with both human and computer tutors. Speech Communication 48(5), 559–590 (2006)
2. Lee, C.M., Narayanan, S.: Towards detecting emotions in spoken dialogs. IEEE Transactions on Speech and Audio Processing 13(2) (2005)
3. Vidrascu, L., Devillers, L.: Detection of real-life emotions in dialogs recorded in a call center. In: Proceedings of INTERSPEECH, Lisbon, Portugal (2005)
4. Batliner, A., Fischer, K., Huber, R., Spilker, J., Noth, E.: How to find trouble in communication. Speech Communication 40, 117–143 (2003)
5. Liu, K., Picard, R.W.: Embedded empathy in continuous, interactive health assessment. In: CHI Workshop on HCI Challenges in Health Assessment. (2005)
6. Klein, J., Moon, Y., Picard, R.: This computer responds to user frustration: Theory, design, and results. Interacting with Computers 14, 119–140 (2002)
7. Cowie, R., Cornelius, R.R.: Describing the emotional states that are expressed in speech. Speech Communication 40, 5–32 (2003)
8. Pon-Barry, H., Schultz, K., Bratt, E.O., Clark, B., Peters, S.: Responding to student uncertainty in spoken tutorial dialogue systems. International Journal of Artificial Intelligence in Education 16, 171–194 (2006)
9. Forbes-Riley, K., Litman, D.: Analyzing dependencies between student certainness states and tutor responses in a spoken dialogue corpus. In: Dybkjaer, L., Minker, W. (eds.) Recent Trends in Discourse and Dialogue, Springer, Dordrecht (2007)
10. VanLehn, K., Siler, S., Murray, C.: Why do only some events cause learning during human tutoring? Cognition and Instruction 21(3), 209–249 (2003)
11. Litman, D.J., Forbes-Riley, K.: Correlations between dialogue acts and learning in spoken tutoring dialogues. Journal of Natural Language Engineering: Special Issue on Educational Applications 12(2), 161–176 (2006)
12. Graesser, A., Person, N., Magliano, J.: Collaborative dialog patterns in naturalistic one-on-one tutoring. Applied Cognitive Psychology 9, 495–522 (1995)
13. Tsukahara, W., Ward, N.: Responding to subtle, fleeting changes in the user's internal state. In: Proceedings of the SIG-CHI on Human factors in computing systems, pp. 77–84. ACM Press, New York (2001)
14. Forbes-Riley, K., Rotaru, M., Litman, D., Tetreault, J.: Exploring affect-context dependencies for adaptive system development. In: Proc. NAACL-HLT (2007)

Generalized "Stigma": Evidence for Devaluation-by-Inhibition Hypothesis from Implicit Learning

Haotian Zhou[1,2,*], Lulu Wan[1,2,*], and Xiaolan Fu[1,**]

[1] State Key Laboratory of Brain and Cognitive Science,
Institute of Psychology, Chinese Academy of Sciences,
Beijing 100101, China
{zhouht,wanll,fuxl}@psych.ac.cn
[2] Graduate School, Chinese Academy of Science, Beijing 100039, China

Abstract. Recently, a new fundamental discovery has been made of the relationship between attentional system and affective system of human brain, giving rise to the devaluation-by-inhibition hypothesis. It is shown that selective attention has an affective impact on an otherwise emotionally bland stimulus. Particularly, if a neutral stimulus was inhibited by selective attention in a prior task, it would be valued less in a subsequent affective evaluation task than it would otherwise have been. In the present study, we extend this line of research on the affective consequence of attention and demonstrate that prior attentional states (attended or inhibited) associated with a group of neutral stimuli (character strings) can even influence subsequent preference judgment about previously-unseen stimuli if these new stimuli share certain basic features (e.g., follow the same rule) with those encountered in a previous stage.

Keywords: Affective evaluation, attentional inhibition, implicit learning, artificial grammar learning.

1 Introduction

People from all walks of life would agree that emotion is an integral part of human existence [16]. The important role played by emotion in our daily life is wide-ranging and cannot be overestimated. During the past several decades, emotion as an academic subject has been studied intensely by psychologists, computer scientist, biologists, and the likes. According to Cacioppo and Gardner [4], one of the major focuses of the scientific endeavor to unravel the mystery of emotion is centered on the interaction between emotion and cognition. Considerable effort goes into addressing issues such as how emotion influences decision-making, memory and creativity [1][2][13]. Nevertheless, much of the insight we have gained into the interaction

---

* These two authors contributed equally to this paper.
** Corresponding author.

A. Paiva, R. Prada, and R.W. Picard (Eds.): ACII 2007, LNCS 4738, pp. 690–697, 2007.

between emotion and cognition comes from the studies dealing with the interplay between emotion and attention.

1.1   Emotion Influences Attention

Given the significance of both attention and emotion to the survival of human race, it is not surprising that substantial evidence has been accumulated showing that emotional state exert great impact on attentional process. Research has demonstrated that affective stimuli (e.g. faces with expressions, sexually-relevant pictures, et al.) attract attention compared with neutral or meaningless stimuli. For instance, Hao and colleagues showed that compared with neutral target, emotionally-salient target is located faster amongst multiple neutral distracters [8]. Other studies have found that the scope of attention can be modulated by the subjective emotional states. For example, in Rowe's recent experiment [13], participants in negative mood were less likely to be influenced by the interference from nearby distracters than their counterparts in positive mood. Moreover, some researchers have found that emotional disorders can profoundly alter one's selective attention [10]. In fact, one would be hard-pressed to find one study which contradicts the general finding that attention is subject to the influence of emotion.

1.2   Attention Influences Emotion

A number of functional imaging studies have discovered that the neural substrates underlying attention and emotion are not only connected but also, in some cases, they reside in the same brain regions (e.g. [3]). Thus, one should expect a reciprocal relationship between attention and emotion. However, for quite a long period, the situation is lopsided in terms that much of the effort has been devoted to deciphering the possible influence of emotion on attention while little has been done about the flipping side of the question—how attention affects emotion [6].

Recently, this long over-looked question has been taken up by Fenske and Raymond. In a series of studies [7][11], they made an important discovery that selective attention—the process of selecting a subset of stimuli from amongst many potentially available ones to focus on—is capable of swaying affective judgment of stimuli in a systematic way. Specifically, they propose a devaluation-by-inhibition hypothesis which asserts that the attentional state (attended or inhibited) assigned to a stimulus when it is first encountered can influence subsequent affective judgment of the same stimulus [7]. For example, if an emotionally bland stimulus served as distracter in the initial task (hence must be inhibited), it will be rated less cheerful than its target counterpart, which is neutral in nature, in a following evaluation task. In other words, attentional inhibition can depreciate the value of a given stimulus.

1.3   Stigmatized Representation

In their conceptualization, Raymond and colleagues suggest that the attentional inhibition associated with a stimulus functions very much like a stigma and is attached to the representation of the stimulus [11]. Therefore, whenever the representation is activated again, this inhibition-based stigma is also invoked and devalues the stimulus automatically. Such a stigma analogy is reminiscent of the activation of social stereotype from social psychology. Yet, in social stereotype, the stigma is attached to the representation of a group on the basis of certain common traits possessed by group members, whereas in Raymond and Fenske's studies, the stigma is attached to the representation of each individual exemplar [6]. A natural question to ask, hence, is: Can the inhibition-based stigma proposed by Raymond and Fenske attach to a group-level representation so that a stimulus, which in itself has not been subject to attentional inhibition but nevertheless shares certain commonalities with those inhibited stimuli, will be devalued once encountered in an evaluation task.

As a matter of fact, abstraction and generalization are important coping strategies for us to manage and organize the huge amount of information stored in our brains so that we will not be overwhelmed. It is clear that if the number of stimuli being inhibited exceeds certain numbers and all the stimuli share certain common diagnostic traits, then it is far more efficient to store a single inhibition-based stigma with an abstracted representation of the group than to store each individual stimulus along with their associated stigma. For example, if a person has some unpleasant encounter with a dog, it is very likely he will develop some aversion toward not that specific dog but dogs as a group.

In the present study, we seek to examine whether the devaluating effect of attentional inhibition can be spread to previously unseen stimuli which share certain diagnostic features with those inhibited stimuli.

2 Method

In this experiment, a variant of the artificial grammar learning (AGL) paradigm devised by Tanaka et al. [17] was adopted to address the research question (see section 2.3). AGL is a classical paradigm for the investigation of implicit learning [12]. A typical AGL procedure comprises two stages [5]. During the first stage (training stage), participants are required to memorize (i.e. rote learning) some character strings all of which follow the same rule (or grammar); then in the second stage (testing stage), they are required to classify whether the test items (unseen in the training stage) follow the same rule as those appeared in the first stage. Past studies using AGL have repeatedly shown that people can abstract the common complex rule underlying all the memorized items independent of conscious attempts to decipher such a rule and largely in the absence of explicit knowledge of what has been acquired [15]. Therefore, AGL provide us with the basic rationale for exploring the possibility that the affective consequence of attentional inhibition can be spread to new stimuli from the same family as those being inhibited. In specific, supposing that participants can acquire the rules underlying both the attended and inhibited strings in the training stage, we can test our hypothesis by examining whether the affective value of an unseen strings would be affected by its membership (i.e. to which rules— attended or inhibited—this new stimulus conforms) in a fashion as would be predicted from devaluation-by-inhibition hypothesis.

2.1 Participants

26 participants (6 males, 20 females) were recruited from the China Agriculture University. Participation was voluntary and all participants were reimbursed. They

were naive to the experimental hypothesis and have normal or corrected-to-normal vision.

2.2   Apparatus and Stimuli

The experiment was conducted with a Pentium-IV computer connected to a 17-inch monitor. E-Prime 1.2 was used to control the stimuli presentation and response recording [14]. Participants were seated about 60 cm from the monitor. All stimuli appeared on a uniform 50%-gray field.

Strings of five to nine characters in length were generated according to one of the three different artificial grammars, Grammar D (GD), Grammar V (GV), and Grammar K (GK). GD was used by Dienes et al. [5], GV by Vokey et al. [18], and GK was a modified version of that used by Knowlton et al. [9]. To ensure that the strings from each grammar were comparable at the perceptual level, all three grammars consist of the same letter set, M, R, T, V, and X.

A total of 39 non-repeating GD strings were generated, of which 15 were used in training stage and the remainders in evaluation stage. This was the same case with GV strings. In addition, a total of 48 non-repeating strings were generated from GK, but were used solely in the evaluation stage.

2.3   Design and Procedure

In the training stage (Fig. 1A), each trial began with an 800-ms fixation point and was followed by the presentation of two character strings of the same length with one from GD and the other from GV. The two partially-overlapped strings of different colors (black and white) were presented simultaneously. The misalignment of the two strings was done in such a way that, in order to read one string of the pair correctly, the participants had to inhibit the interference from the other. The participants were instructed to type the string of the cued position (front or back) into the computer as fast as possible and then pressed the "Enter" key to proceed to next trial. The cue is a Chinese character meaning either front or back and displayed on the left of the string pair. Both the cue and the string pair would stay on screen until the onset of next trial. If participants submit a copy with error, the program would notice them to type again until the correct one was submitted. There were eight blocks in the training stage. Each block comprises 15 trials. Each of the 15 different GV-GD string pairs was presented once in each of the eight blocks with the position being determined randomly at the onset of each block.

Unbeknownst to the participants, throughout the whole stage, the strings to be typed were all conform to GD. Yet, their color (black or white) and position (front or back) were counterbalanced across the eight blocks.

In the evaluation stage (Fig. 1B), participants were instructed to complete a preference judgment task. In each trial, two strings of equal length were presented simultaneously and participants were required to indicate which one of the two they liked better by click on corresponding buttons on the screen. That is, if one prefers the string in the upper position, one should click the "U (up)" button, and if the one favors the string in the lower position, one should click the "D (down)" button. There were 48 trials in the evaluation stage.

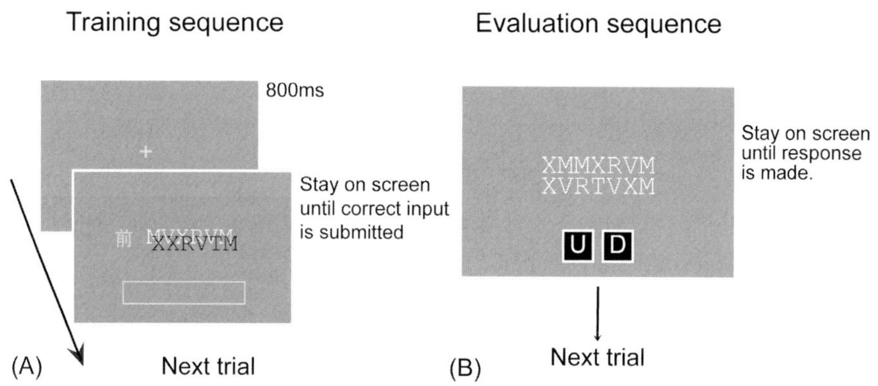

Fig. 1. (A) Time sequence of a single trial in training stage. The Chinese character on the left of the string pair indicates which string to copy. If the character is " 前 (meaning front)", participants need to type in the string in the foreground. On the other hand, if it is "后 (meaning back)", participants need to type in the back one. Participant's input will be shown in the rectangular box below the string pair. (B) Time sequence of a single trial in evaluation stage. Participants choose the preferred string by click either one of the two buttons at the bottom of the screen.

Unbeknownst to the participants, in half of the trials, the string pair comprises a GV string and a GK string; and in the other half, it comprises a GD string and a GK string. The position of GK (upper or lower) was randomly determined at the onset of each trial.

2.4 Data Analysis

Two preference scores (PSs) were calculated for each individual participant based on their choices in the evaluation stage. PS-GD corresponds to the proportion of the 24 GD-GK trials in which GD was favored by the participant, while PS-GV corresponds to the proportion of the 24 GV-GK trials in which GV was favored by the participant. Hence, a PS-GD of over 0.5 means that GD strings were preferred by the participant over GK strings. In a similar vein, a PS-GV of over 0.5 means that GV strings were preferred by the participant over GK strings.

3   Results

A one t-test was conducted on the PS-GD scores to determine whether their mean was significantly different from 0.5, the expected value if the choice was made by chance. The result shows that the mean of PS-GD is significantly larger than 0.5 ($M = 0.58$, $SD = 0.15$), $t(25) = 2.9$, $p = 0.008$.

A one t-test was conducted on the PS-GV scores to determine whether their mean was significantly different from 0.5, the expected value if the choice was made by chance. The result shows that the mean of PS-GV is significantly larger than ($M = 0.42$, $SD = 0.18$) which is significantly smaller than 0.5, $t(25) = -2.4$, $p = 0.025$.

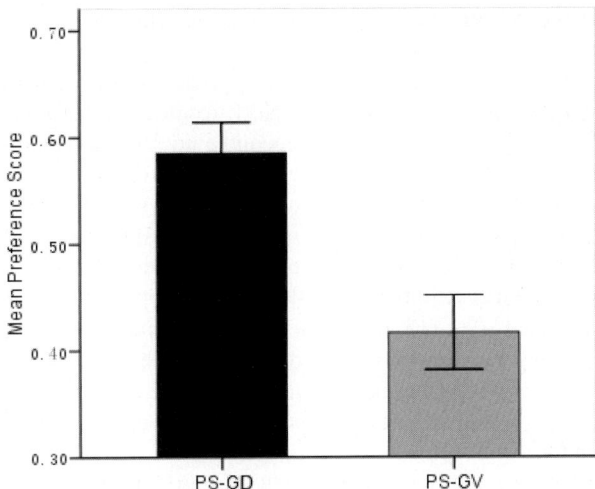

Fig. 2. Mean preference score for GD strings (PS-GD) and mean preference score for GV (PS-GV). Vertical bars indicate plus or minus one standard error of mean.

Taken together (Fig. 2), the results from the present study indicate that if the unseen, emotionally-bland stimuli belong to the same family as the previously *attended* stimuli (i.e. GD strings), they were more likely to become the preferred ones when pitted against other unseen, emotionally-bland stimuli based on a novel rule (i.e. GK strings). However, if the unseen, emotionally-bland stimuli belong to the same family as the previously *inhibited* stimuli (i.e. GV strings), they were less likely to be favored by participants when pitted against other unseen, emotionally-bland stimuli based on a novel rule (i.e. GK strings).

4   Discussion

In this experiment, we measure the affective evaluation of a meaningless character string conforming to the same rule as either the attended strings or inhibited strings in a prior implicit learning task. A previous artificial grammar learning study using a similar design provided evidence that participants could acquire abstract rules underlying both the attended strings and the inhibited ones simultaneously [17]. Therefore, assuming participants extracted the rules of both GD strings (attended) and GV strings (inhibited) unconsciously, the novel and important finding of current experiment is that even previously unseen stimuli can be subject to the devaluating effect of attentional inhibition as long as these stimuli share certain commonalities (e.g. underlying grammars in the present study) with those previously inhibited stimuli and these commonalties have been successfully learned by participants. In other words, we showed that the "dislike" toward previously inhibited stimuli can be spread to previously unseen stimuli of the same family. This new discovery about the interaction between three major systems—affective system, attentional system, and information acquisition system in the human brains—will no doubt have far-reaching implication for the design and evaluation of both affective system and affective agents.

Note that in this study, participants showed greater liking toward GD (attended rule) strings than GK (novel rules) strings. Such result could easily be explained by the perceptual fluency theories without recourse to the devaluation-by-inhibition hypothesis. Perceptual fluency theories assert that prior experience with a given stimuli makes future process of the same stimuli less taxing, hence leads to positive affect during subsequent encounter [20]. However, the result concerning GV (inhibited rule) strings stands in stark contrast with the prediction from perceptual fluency theories. In the present study, GV strings, though inhibited by attentional system, were exposed 120 (15 trials $\times$ 8 blocks) times more than GK strings, providing a great opportunity for stimuli of this grammar to develop fluency, hence would have led to positive affect in the evaluation stage compared to string of novel grammar. Yet, they were still devalued significantly, which is more in line with distracter devaluation effect [6].

Two potential problems might undermine the validity of the conclusion drawn from present study. First, the assumption that participants acquired both the attended and the inhibited rules may not hold true. Though an above-chance preference score (mean PS-GD = 0.58) for the GD (attended rule) strings may indicate that participants have obtained knowledge about GD [19], there is little support from available literature suggesting that a below-chance preference score can also be taken as the evidence of the acquisition of abstract rule by participants. Therefore, it is a priority for future studies to investigate whether people is capable of extracting rule from inhibited strings under the same experimental condition. Second, since all the participants in the current experiment were required to attend to GD strings while inhibiting GV ones, the preference scores obtained may simply have been caused by this systematic bias. Though in theory, the intrinsic affective values of the strings used in this experiment should not differ as a function of their underlying grammars, future study is nevertheless needed to address this possible confounding effect.

Acknowledgments. This research was supported by grants from 973 Program of Chinese Ministry of Science and Technology (#2006CB303101), and the National Natural Science Foundation of China (#60433030).

References

1. Anderson, A.K., Wais, P.E., Gabrieli, J.D.E.: Emotion Enhances Remembrance of Neutral Events Past. PNAS 103, 1599–1604 (2006)
2. Bechara, A.: The Role of Emotion in Decision-making: Evidence from Neurological Patients with Orbitofrontal Damage. Brain and Cognition. 55, 30–40 (2004)
3. Bush, G., Luu, P., Posner, M.I.: Cognitive and Emotional Influences in Anterior Cingulate Cortex. Trends in Cognitive Sciences. 4, 215–222 (2000)
4. Cacioppo, J.T., Gardner, W.L.: Emotion. Annual Review of Psychology, pp. 191–192 (1999)
5. Dienes, Z., Altmann, G.T.M., Kwan, L., Goode, A.: Unconscious Knowledge of artificial grammars is applied strategically. Journal of Experimental Psychology: Learning, Memory, and Cognition 21, 1322–1338 (1995)

6. Fenske, M.J., Raymond, J.E.: Affective Influences of Selective Attention. Current Directions in Psychological Science. 15, 312–316 (2006)
7. Fenske, M.J., Raymond, J.E., Kessler, K., Westoby, N., Tipper, S.P.: Research Report Attentional Inhibition Has Social-Emotional Consequences for Unfamiliar Faces. Psychological Science. 16, 753 (2005)
8. Hao, F., Zhang, H., Fu, X.: Modulation of Attention by Faces Expressing Emotion: Evidence from Visual Marking. In: Tao, J., Tan, T., Picard, R.W. (eds.) ACII 2005. LNCS, vol. 3784, Springer, Heidelberg (2005)
9. Knowlton, B.J., Squire, L.R.: Artificial Grammar Learning Depends on Implicit Acquisition of Both Rule-based and exemplar-based information. Journal of Experimental Psychology. 1150, 169–181 (1996)
10. McCabe, S.B., Gotlib, I.H.: Selective Attention and Clinical Depression: Performance on a Deployment-of-attention Task. J Abnorm Psychol. 104, 241–245 (1995)
11. Raymond, J.E., Fenske, M.J., Westoby, N.: Emotional Devaluation of Distracting Patterns and Faces: A Consequence of Attentional Inhibition During Visual Search? Journal of Experimental Psychology: Human Perception and Performance 31, 1404–1415 (2005)
12. Reber, A.S.: Implicit learning of synthetic languages. Journal of Verbal Learning and Verbal Behavior. 6, 855–863 (1967)
13. Rowe, G., Hirsh, J.B., Anderson, A.K.: Positive Affect Increases the Breadth of Attentional selection. PNAS 104, 383–388 (2007)
14. Schneider, W., Eschman, A., Zuccolotto, A.: E-Prime User's Guide: Psychology Software Tools (2002)
15. Stadler, M.A., Frensch, P.A.: Handbook of implicit learning: Sage Publications. Sage Publications, Thousand Oaks, CA (1998)
16. Strongman, K.T.: The Psychology of Emotion: From Everyday Life to Theory, 5th edn. Wiley, Chichester (2003)
17. Tanaka, D., Kiyokawa, S., Yamada, A., Shigemasu, K.: Investigating the Role of Selective Attention in Implicit Learning Using Overlapping Letter Strings. Paper presented at the 28th Annual Conference of the Cognitive Science Society, Vancouver, British Columbia, Canada (2006)
18. Vokey, J.R., Brooks, L.R.: Salience of Item Knowledge in Learning Artificial Grammars. Journal of Experimental Psychology: Learning, Memory, and Cognition 18, 328–344 (1992)
19. Whittlesea, B.W., Wright, R.L.: Implicit (and explicit) learning: acting adaptively without knowing the consequences. Journal of Experimental Psychology: Learning, Memory, and Cognition. 23, 181–200 (1997)
20. Winkielman, P., Schwarz, N., Fazendeiro, T., Reber, R.: The Hedonic Marking of Processing Fluency: Implications for Evaluative Judgement. The psychology of Evaluation: Affective Processes in Cognition and Emotion, 189–117 (2003)

Early Prediction of Student Frustration

Scott W. McQuiggan, Sunyoung Lee, and James C. Lester

Department of Computer Science, North Carolina State University, Raleigh, NC 27695
{swmcquig,slee7,lester}@ncsu.edu

Abstract. Affective reasoning has been the subject of increasing attention in recent years. Because negative affective states such as frustration and anxiety can impede progress toward learning goals, intelligent tutoring systems should be able to detect when a student is anxious or frustrated. Being able to detect negative affective states early, i.e., before they lead students to abandon learning tasks, could permit intelligent tutoring systems sufficient time to adequately prepare for, plan, and enact affective tutorial support strategies. A first step toward this objective is to develop predictive models of student frustration. This paper describes an inductive approach to student frustration detection and reports on an experiment whose results suggest that frustration models can make predictions early and accurately.

1 Introduction

Affect has begun to play an increasingly important role in intelligent tutoring systems. Recent years have seen the emergence of work on affective student modeling [6], detecting frustration and stress [5, 22], modeling agents' emotional states [1, 9], devising affectively informed models of social interaction [10, 13, 19, 21], detecting student motivation [7], and diagnosing and adapting to student self-efficacy [3, 14]. All of this work seeks to increase the fidelity with which affective and motivational processes are modeled and utilized in intelligent tutoring systems in an effort to increase the effectiveness of tutorial interactions and, ultimately, learning. One such effort is to detect and provide support to students experiencing negative affect.

Intelligent tutoring systems should provide support that helps students cope with emotions such as anxiety and frustration and, if possible, increasing their tolerance for frustrating learning situations. Because feelings of anxiety or frustration can divert students' attention from learning tasks by causing them to become fixated on the source of frustration or causing them to worry excessively about failure, it is important that learning environments employee mechanisms to diagnosis situations that are likely to create anxious or frustrated students. Early detection of negative affective states could permit ITSs sufficient time to enact corrective "affective scaffolding" strategies. In this paper we focus on accurately predicting student frustration as early as possible by utilizing established affective computing techniques for obtaining student affective state information, including physiological response data [5, 6, 14, 22] and student self-reports [6, 7, 14].

This paper is structured as follows. Section 2 discusses affect recognition and the role of anxiety and frustration in learning. The modeling techniques used to detect

A. Paiva, R. Prada, and R.W. Picard (Eds.): ACII 2007, LNCS 4738, pp. 698–709, 2007.

frustration are described in Section 3. Section 4 introduces CRYSTAL ISLAND, our interactive learning environment test bed and describes the study. The results of the study are presented and discussed in Section 5, followed by concluding remarks and directions for future work in Section 6.

2 Background

2.1 Affect Recognition

Affect recognition is the task of identifying the emotional state of a user from a variety of physical and behavioral cues, which are produced in response to affective changes in the individual [20]. However, because affect is fundamentally a cognitive process in which the user appraises the relationship between herself and her environment [9, 24], affect recognition models should take into account both physiological and environmental information. For task-oriented and goal-oriented learning environments, affect recognition models can leverage knowledge of task structure and user goals to effectively reason about users' affective states. In particular, for such learning environments, affect recognition models can use appraisal theory [12] to recognize users' emotions generated in response to their assessment of how their actions and events in the environment relate to their goals.

2.2 Anxiety and Frustration

Frustration occurs when something or someone impedes an individual's progress towards a particular goal. As an emotional response, frustration is not fundamentally different from another negative affective response common to a variety of situations, anxiety. Anxiety is often more than merely an emotional response; it also consists of behavioral, cognitive, and physiological responses [23]. However, because our work focuses on interactive task-oriented learning environments [17], where the construction and achievement of goals is critical to student learning episodes, we primarily focus on frustration. Both anxiety and frustration can lead students to fixate on the impeding source of frustration, diverting attention from, and in some cases causing students to ignore, the task at hand. Anxiety particularly arises when students affectively respond to their focus on planning contingencies for potential future events. Detecting situations that will likely lead to student anxiety or frustration that in turn may eventually lead to student impasses would allow learning environments to intervene early, i.e., before the emotion is fully realized as the student approaches her threshold for the particular emotion.

Several strategies can be employed to identify levels of anxiety and frustration that are not detrimental to learning. Setting realistic expectations based on a student's abilities and observed past performance can contribute to student successes. Encouragement, and specific feedback directed at particular behaviors, not merely global performance assessments, may help motivate students and provide them with guidance so that they can improve their self-assessment and help them cope with frustration and anxiety [18]. The central questions that must be answered are, "How can we detect and monitor anxiety and frustration levels so that our learning environments have sufficient time to plan and execute appropriate scaffolding?" and,

"With what computational mechanisms can we draw inferences about the student, the task, and the environment to accurately predict student frustration?"

3 Modeling Frustration

To create models that make accurate predictions of student frustration as early as possible, we first collect training data by observing students interacting with an intelligent tutoring system. From this training data, we then induce n-gram models to make early predictions of student frustration. Models based on n-grams models are useful for early prediction because they are induced from sequences of observations, making predictions with each new observation until they arrive at the final observation of the sequence. In the final observation, concrete evidence of student affect (used as the class label) is obtained. Each prediction from an n-gram model is attempting to determine the affective state of the student recorded in this final observation of the sequence. In many cases, n-gram model predictions will converge on the correct affective state early in a sequence of observations. The point at which an n-gram model first begins making the correct prediction and then continues to make a correct prediction for the remainder of the sequence is known as the *convergence point*.

While sequential models such as n-grams allow us to make early predictions, they are not computationally well suited to large multidimensional data. To address this issue, we investigate three non-sequential modeling techniques: naïve Bayes, decision trees, and support vector machines. To enable non-sequential models to make early predictions, we exploit the results of the n-gram models. Utilizing convergence point information, we construct data sets that contain only those observations preceding the convergence point. Thus, models induced from the newly constructed datasets are able to make predictions of student affect long before the observation in which the student's affective state was recorded.

Section 3.1 presents n-gram frustration modeling, followed by Section 3.2's description of naïve Bayes, decision tree, and support vector machine frustration modeling techniques. Section 3.3 then describes the training data, which are observations of students interacting with the CRYSTAL ISLAND learning environment.

3.1 n-Gram Models for Early Prediction of Frustration

Given an observation sequence $O_1, O_2, ..., O_n$, the objective of affect recognition is to identify the student's most likely affective state E^* (i.e., frustrated or not frustrated) such that:

$$E^* = \arg \max P(E \mid O_1, O_2, O_3, ..., O_n)$$
$$= \arg \max P(E \mid O_{1:n})$$

where each O_i is an observation encoding the user's goals, user's action, the location at which action was performed, and physiological responses such as heart rate and galvanic skin responses. The observation sequence $O_1, O_2, ..., O_n$, is denoted by $O_{1:n}$. Applying Bayes rule and the Chain Rule, the equation becomes:

$$E^* = \arg\max P(O_n \mid O_{1:n-1}, E) P(O_{n-1} \mid O_{1:n-2}, E)$$
$$\cdot P(O_{n-2} \mid O_{1:n-3}, E) \ldots P(O_1 \mid E) P(E)$$

However, estimating these conditional probabilities is impractical – it would require exponentially large training data sets – so we make a Markov assumption that an observation O_i depends only on the affective state E and a limited window of the preceding observations.

We explore two n-gram affect recognition models for detecting student frustration, a unigram model and a bigram model. The unigram model is based on the assumption that, given the affective state E, O_i is conditionally independent of all other observations. Thus, the affect recognition formula for the unigram model can be simplified to:

$$E^* = \arg\max P(E) \prod_{i=1}^{n} P(O_i \mid E)$$

The bigram model is based on the assumption that, given the affective state E and the preceding observation O_{i-1}, O_i is conditionally independent of all other observations. Thus, the affect recognition formula for the bigram model can be simplified to:

$$E^* = \arg\max P(E) \prod_{i=1}^{n} P(O_i \mid O_{i-1}, E)$$

The resulting formulae for the unigram and bigram models are very efficient because updating the affect prediction for each new observation only requires computing the product of the probability returned by the previous prediction and the current conditional probability.

During training, we estimate $P(E)$, $P(O_i|E)$, and $P(O_i| O_{i-1}, E)$ using training data acquired with an interactive learning environment as described below. Because training data is necessarily sparse, i.e., we are unlikely to observe all possible combinations of actions, locations, goals, and physiological response levels, the unigram and bigram models employ a standard smoothing technique (a flattening constant and simple Good-Turing frequency estimation [8] to re-evaluate zero-probability and low-probability n-grams.

3.2 Naïve Bayes, Decision Tree, and SVMs for Modeling Frustration

Naïve Bayes, decision tree, and support vector machine classifiers are effective machine learning techniques for generating preliminary predictive models. Bayes classification approaches produce probability tables that can be implemented in runtime systems and used to continually update probabilities for predicting student affective states, and, in the approach proposed here, for predicting whether students are frustrated or not. Decision trees provide interpretable rules that support runtime decision making. The runtime system monitors the condition of the attributes in the rules to determine when conditions are met for diagnosing particular student emotions. Support vector machines (SVM) are also particularly effective at handling high-dimensional data. SVMs search for hyperplanes that linearly separate data into classes (affective states).

These classification techniques are particularly useful for inducing models with large multidimensional data, such as the data gathered in the user study described below. Because it is unclear precisely which runtime variables are likely to be the most predictive, naïve Bayes and decision tree modeling provide useful analyses that can inform more expressive machine learning techniques (e.g., Bayesian networks) that also leverage domain experts' knowledge. We have used the WEKA machine learning toolkit [25] to analyze naive Bayes, decision tree, and SVM approaches for generating models of student affect to predict student frustration as early as possible.

3.3 Training Data

Accurately modeling user affect requires a representation of the situational context that satisfies two requirements: it must be sufficiently rich to support assessment of changes in affect, and it must be encoded with features that are readily observable at runtime. Because affect is fundamentally a cognitive process in which the user appraises the relationship between herself and her environment [9, 24] affect recognition models should take into account both physiological and environmental information. In task-oriented interactive learning environments, task structure is often explicit. To effectively reason about students' affect, affect models can leverage this knowledge of task structure as well as the state of the student's progress through a learning episode and physiological responses to unfolding events. In particular, affect models can rely on concepts from appraisal theory [12] to recognize student emotional responses generated from their assessment of their progress in the learning task. Thus, affect models can leverage representations of the information observable in the learning environment – note that this is the same information that students may use in their own appraisals – to predict student emotion, particularly frustration.

Therefore we employ an expressive representation of all activities in the learning environment, including those controlled by users and the interactive system, by encoding them in an observational attribute vector, which is used in both model induction and model usage. During model induction, the observational attribute vector is passed to the affect learner for model generation; during runtime operation, the attribute vector is monitored by runtime components that utilize knowledge of user affect to inform effective pedagogical decisions. The observable attribute vector represents four interrelated categories of features for making decisions:

- **Temporal Features:** The interactive learning environment continuously tracks the amount of time that has elapsed since the student arrived at the current location, since the student achieved a goal, and since the student was last presented with an opportunity to achieve a goal. Temporal features are useful for measuring the persistence of the student on the current and past tasks.
- **Locational Features:** The interactive learning environment continuously monitors the location of the student's character. It monitors locations visited in the past, and locations recently visited. There are 45 designated locations in the interactive learning environment test bed (e.g., the laboratory, the living room of the men's quarters, and the area surrounding the waterfall). Locational features are useful for tracking whether students are in locations where learning tasks and current goals are achievable. When a student arrives in a location where a learning objective can be completed, combined temporal attributes and

locational features can inform the prediction of students' learning task progression and associated affective responses.

- **Intentional Features:** The interactive learning environment continuously tracks goals being attempted (in the interactive learning environment described below goals are explicitly presented to students by an onscreen textual display), goals achieved, the rate of goal achievement, and the effort expended to achieve a goal (as inferred from recent exploratory activities and locational features). These features enable models to incorporate knowledge of potential and student-perceived valence (positive and negative perceptions) of a given situation. Here we circumvent the problem of goal recognition [4, 16] through explicit delivery of student goals. Integrating goal recognition and affect recognition is a promising direction for future work.

- **Physiological Response:** The interactive learning environment continuously tracks readings from a biofeedback apparatus attached to the student's hand. Blood volume pulse and galvanic skin response readings are monitored at a rate of approximately 30 readings/second to accurately track changes in the student's physiological response. Blood volume pulse readings are used to compute student's heart rate and changes in their heart rate.

During training sessions later used for model induction, a continuous stream of physiological data is collected and logged approximately 30 times per second. In addition, an instance of the observational attribute vector is logged every time a significant event occurs, yielding, on average, hundreds of vector instances each minute. We define a significant event to be a manipulation of the environment that causes one or more features of the observational attribute vector to take on new values. At runtime, the same features are continuously monitored by the respective environment.

4 Evaluation

4.1 Crystal Island

To serve as an effective "laboratory" for studying user affect recognition in an interactive task-oriented learning environment, a test bed should pose the same kinds of challenges that affect recognition modelers are likely to encounter in future runtime learning environments. It should offer users a broad range of actions to perform and provide a rich set of tasks and goals in a nontrivial task-oriented virtual learning environment. The goals should exhibit some complexity, and the environment should be populated by manipulable artifacts and be inhabited by multiple characters. To this end, we have devised CRYSTAL ISLAND, a task-oriented learning environment test bed featuring a science mystery in the domain of genetics. The mystery is set on a recently discovered volcanic island where a research station has been established to study the unique flora and fauna. The user plays the role of the daughter (or son) of a visiting scientist who is attempting to discover the origins of an unidentified illness at the research station. The environment begins by introducing the student to the island and the members of the research team for which her father serves as the lead scientist.

As members of the research team fall ill, it is her task to discover the cause of the outbreak. She is free to explore the world to collect physical evidence and interact with other characters. Through the course of her adventure she must gather enough evidence to correctly choose among candidate diagnoses including botulism, cholera, salmonellosis, and tick paralysis as well as identify the source of the disease relying on her knowledge of microbiology to solve the mystery.

The task-oriented learning environment of CRYSTAL ISLAND, the semiautonomous characters that inhabit it, and the user interface were implemented with Valve Software's Source™ engine, the 3D game platform for Half-Life 2. In CRYSTAL ISLAND, the user can perform a broad range of actions including performing experiments in the laboratory, interacting with other characters, reading "virtual books" to obtain background information on diseases, and collecting data about the food recently eaten by the members of the research team. Throughout the mystery, users can walk around the island and visit the infirmary, the lab, the dining hall, and the living quarters of each member of the team. In the current test bed, there are 20 goals users can achieve, three hundred unique actions the user can carry out, and over fifty unique locations in which the actions can be performed.

4.2 User Study

There were 5 female and 31 male participants varying in age, race, and marriage status. Approximately 44% of the participants were Asian, 50% were Caucasian, and 6% were of other ethnicities. Participants' average age was 26.0 (SD=5.4).

After filling out a consent form and demographic survey, participants began training sessions by first completing a practice task. The practice task allowed them to become familiar with the keyboard and mouse controls as well as interacting in a 3D virtual environment. Following the practice task, participants were presented a controlled backstory for CRYSTAL ISLAND situating them on the island and providing details about their task. For reference, participants had access to a cast of agents found in the CRYSTAL ISLAND environment as well as an overview map. Participants then interacted with the environment to solve the science mystery. The training test bed provided them with specific goals to focus on, guiding them through the solution to the mystery.

Self-reporting mechanisms are frequently used in studies to obtain information about a subject's affective state [6, 7]. In the study reported here, periodically (every 75 seconds) a "self-report emotion dialog" box would appear requesting input from participants about their affective state. They were asked to select the emotion, from a set of six emotions (*excitement, fear, frustration, happiness, relaxation,* and *sadness*), that best summarized their own feelings since they were previously asked to assess their emotional state. This set of emotions was chosen to cover the affect space [11] so that most subjects would easily be able to relate their feelings during interaction to one of the six affective states. In addition to periodic reports, participants had the ability to trigger the self-report emotion dialog if they felt compelled to report a change in their affective state. This functionality proved in practice to be used sparingly. After solving the science mystery, participants completed a post-experiment survey before exiting the training session.

5   Results

Unigram, bigram, naïve Bayes, decision tree, and SVM affect recognition models for detecting student frustration were learned from the collected datasets.

The *n*-gram models were evaluated using the following the criteria [4]:

- *Accuracy*: Ratio of correct predictions to the total number of observations.
- *Converged*: Percentage of observation sequences in which the goal recognizer's final prediction is correct.
- *Convergence Point*: For observation sequences which converged, the point within the sequence when the affect recognizer started making the correct prediction and continued to make the correct prediction for the remainder of the sequence.
- *Average Observations of Converged*: Average number of observations contained in observation sequences in sequences which converged.

The induced n-gram models were tested using the standard k-fold cross validation evaluation methodology [15], with k=10. (In each fold, nine segments are used for training and one, which is held out of training, is used for testing.) The results of n-gram affect recognition models are presented in Table 1. Figure 1 shows a bigram convergence graph depicting the amount of data (actions) required by the model to converge on the correct affective state and the associated probability of that emotion classification. Note that the bigram model utilizing a flattening constant converged after consuming 6.5% of the records leading up to the student self-reported affective state (the class label). In instances where n-gram models converged the models were able to correctly classify whether the student was frustrated, on average, 35 seconds prior to the self-report.

The results of the naïve Bayes, decision tree, and support vector machine (SVM) affect recognition models are presented in Table 2. Using the results of the n-gram analysis in which bigram models converged after 6.5% of observations contained in a defined window, we constructed datasets containing only these records for naïve Bayes, decision tree, and SVM model induction. Let us consider the observations O_1, O_2, ..., O_n, as the observations leading up to a student self-reported affective state used by n-gram model induction. The data set consisting of observations O_1, O_2, ..., O_m, where m equals n × 0.065, leading to each self-report are then used to induce naïve Bayes, decision tree, and SVM affect models. Thus, all induced models are able to

Table 1. *n*-gram Results

	Unigram Flattening Constant	Unigram Good-Turing	Bigram Flattening Constant	Bigram Good-Turing
Accuracy	68.5%	73.4%	73.6%	73.5%
Converged	39.7%	67.1%	67.8%	67.2%
Converged Point	22.6%	7.1%	6.5%	6.9%
Average Observations of Converged	54.3	51.7	51.8	51.8

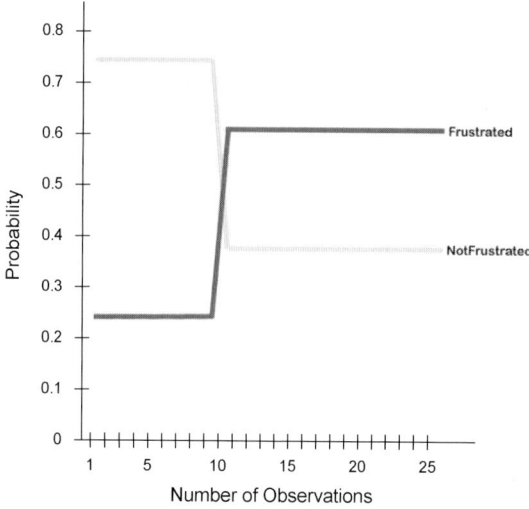

Fig. 1. Bigram convergence graph

Table 2. Induced model results

	Unigram Flattening Constant	Unigram Good-Turing	Bigram Flattening Constant	Bigram Good-Turing	Naïve Bayes	SVM	Decision Tree
Accuracy	68.5%	73.4%	73.6%	73.5%	75.7%	82.2%	88.8%
Precision	60.1%	60.3%	61.6%	60.8%	76.3%	82.2%	88.7%
Recall	52.6%	59.6%	60.3%	59.9%	75.7%	81.9%	88.9%

predict student affective states (i.e., whether students are frustrated or not) early, i.e., long before we receive confirmation of the student's affective state from self-reports. These early prediction datasets contain the same data n-gram models consumed up to the convergence point. The constructed dataset allows induced models to make the same early predictions as the n-gram models, approximately 35 seconds prior to the self-reported affective state.

Below ANOVA statistics are presented for results that are statistically significant. Because the tests reported here were performed on discrete data, we report Chi-square test statistics (χ^2), including both likelihood ratio Chi-square and the Pearson Chi-square values. To analyze the performance of induced models we first establish a baseline level. Because six affective states were reduced to a two-class predictive classifier (frustrated vs. not frustrated), we consider chance as a baseline measure of performance. If our baseline model were to predict the most frequent classifier (not frustrated, n=3859), then the model would correctly predict a student's frustration state 65% of the time. Using this model as a baseline, we observe that all induced models outperform the baseline model. The lowest performing induced model, a unigram model using a flattening constant accurately predicted 68.5% of instances correctly in testing. This performance is statistically significantly better than the baseline (likelihood ratio, χ^2

= 16.075, p = 6.089 × 10^{-5}, and Pearson, χ^2 = 16.067, p = 6.1 × 10^{-5}, df = 1). Thus, the performance of all induced models is a statistically significant improvement over the baseline. On the high performing end, the induced decision tree model performed best, accurately predicting 88.8% of all test instances. This is statistically significant compared to the baseline (likelihood ratio, χ^2 = 980.87, p = 2.6 × 10^{-215}, and Pearson, χ^2 = 943.92, p = 2.8 × 10^{-207}, df = 1), and is also statistically significant compared to the next highest performing model, the induced SVM model (likelihood ratio, χ^2 = 105.28, p = 1.06 × 10^{-24}, and Pearson, χ^2 = 104.49, p = 1.58 × 10^{-24}, df = 1).

The experiment has two important implications for the design of runtime student frustration modeling. First, by monitoring student physiological response, the student's learning task, and events unfolding in the learning environment, induced models can make early, accurate predictions of forthcoming student frustration. Second, using models that can make early predictions of student frustration creates a significant window of opportunity for the learning environment to take corrective action; early-prediction models offer an improvement over traditional approaches that predict affective states and self-reports on a moment-by-moment basis.

6   Conclusion and Future Work

Recent advances in affective reasoning have demonstrated that emotion plays a central role in human cognition and should therefore play an equally important role in the human-computer interaction, especially in intelligent tutoring systems. To support effective, enjoyable tutorial interactions, affect-informed systems must be able to accurately and efficiently recognize user affect from available resources, including negative affect. Following appraisal theory, representations of users' actions and goals enable affect recognition models to consider the same relationship that users continually assess in order to predict their affective states.

This paper has introduced an inductive approach to generating affect recognition models for early detection of student frustration. In this approach, models are induced from observations of students interacting within a task-oriented learning environment in which student actions, locations, goals, and temporal information are monitored. After problem-solving traces have been recorded, affect recognition models are induced that are both accurate and efficient.

The findings reported here contribute to the growing body of work on affective reasoning for learning environments. In the future, it will be useful to investigate the issue of individual differences in tolerance levels for anxiety and frustration. Because students can tolerate different levels of anxiety and frustration, in the future, learning environments should be equipped to adapt to this variance in students' negative affect thresholds. To determine how much frustration a student can persist through, it may be possible to utilize models of student self-efficacy [14]. Self-efficacy has been identified as a predictor of persistence and levels of student effort [2]. Determining frustration thresholds may allow learning environments to monitor students' persistence, intervening only when necessary, so that student efficacy and affect are maintained at levels that best support effective learning. Extending early predictive models to a broader range of emotions could contribute to more comprehensive models of student affect. Evaluating the resulting models as runtime control components in task-oriented learning environments is a critical next step in investigating affect-informed interactive learning.

Acknowledgements

The authors would like to thank the members of the IntelliMedia Center for Intelligent Systems at North Carolina State University for their contributions to the implementation of Crystal Island. The authors also wish to thank Valve Software for authorizing the use of their Source™ engine and SDK. This research was supported by the National Science Foundation under Grant REC-0632450. Any opinions, findings, and conclusions or recommendations expressed in this material are those of the authors and do not necessarily reflect the views of the National Science Foundation.

References

1. André, E., Mueller, M.: Learning affective behavior. In: Proceedings of the 10th International Conference on Human-Computer Interaction, pp. 512–516. Lawrence Erlbaum, Mahwah, NJ (2003)
2. Bandura, A.: Self-efficacy: The exercise of control. Freeman, New York (1997)
3. Beal, C., Lee, H.: Creating a pedagogical model that uses student self reports of motivation and mood to adapt ITS instruction. In: Workshop on Motivation and Affect in Educational Software, in conjunction with the 12th International Conference on Artificial Intelligence in Education (2005)
4. Blaylock, N., Allen, J.: Corpus-based, statistical goal recognition. In: Proceedings of the Eighteenth International Joint Conference on Artificial Intelligence, Acapulco, Mexico, pp. 1303–1308 (2003)
5. Burleson, W., Picard, R.: Affective agents: Sustaining motivation to learn through failure and a state of stuck. In: Proceedings of the ITS Workshop of Social and Emotional Intelligence in Learning Environments, Maceio, Alagoas, Brazil (2004)
6. Conati, C., Mclaren, H.: Data-driven refinement of a probabilistic model of user affect. Tenth International Conference on User Modeling. New York, NY, pp. 40–49 (2005)
7. de Vicente, A., Pain, H.: Informing the detection of the students' motivational state: an empirical study. In: Proceedings of the 6th International Conference on Intelligent Tutoring Systems, pp. 933–943. Springer, New York (2002)
8. Gale, A., Sampson, G.: Good-Turing frequency estimation without tears. Journal of Quantitative Linguistics 2(3), 217–237 (1995)
9. Gratch, J., Marsella, S.: A domain-independent framework for modeling emotion. Journal of Cognitive Systems Research 5(4), 269–306 (2004)
10. Johnson, L., Rizzo, P.: Politeness in tutoring dialogs: Run the factory, that's what I'd do. 7th International Conference on Intelligent Tutoring Systems, Maceio, Brazil, pp. 67-76 (2004)
11. Lang, P.: The emotion probe: Studies of motivation and attention. American Psychologist 50(5), 285–372 (1995)
12. Lazarus, R.: Emotion and Adaptation. Oxford University Press, New York (1991)
13. McQuiggan, S., Lester, J.: Learning empathy: A data-driven framework for modeling empathetic companion agents. In: Proceedings of the 5th International Conference on Autonomous Agents and Multiagent Systems, Hakodate, Japan, pp. 961–968 (2006)

14. McQuiggan, S., Lester, J.: Diagnosing self-efficacy in intelligent tutoring systems: An empirical study. In: Proceedings of the 8th International Conference on Intelligent Tutoring Systems, Jhongli, Taiwan, pp. 565–574 (2006)
15. Mitchell, T.: Machine Learning, McGraw-Hill, OH (1997)
16. Mott, B., Lee, S., Lester, J.: Probabilistic goal recognition in interactive narrative environments. In: Proceedings of the Twenty-first National Conference on Artificial Intelligence, Boston, MA, pp. 187–192 (2006)
17. Mott, B., Lester, J.: Narrative-centered tutorial planning for inquiry-based learning environments. In: Proceedings of the 8th International Conference on Intelligent Tutoring Systems, Jhongli, Taiwan, pp. 675–684 (2006)
18. Ormrod, J.: Educational Psychology: Developing Learners, 4th edn. Prentice Hall, Upper Saddle River, NJ (2002)
19. Paiva, A., Dias, J., Sobral, D., Aylett, R., Woods, S., Hall, L., Zoll, C.: Learning by feeling: evoking empathy with synthetic characters. Applied Artificial Intelligence 19, 235–266 (2005)
20. Picard, R.: Affective Computing. MIT Press, Cambridge, MA (1997)
21. Porayska-Pomsta, K., Pain, H.: Providing cognitive and affective scaffolding through teaching strategies: applying linguistic politeness to the educational context. Seventh International Conference on Intelligent Tutoring Systems, Maceio, Alagoas, Brazil, pp. 77–86 (2004)
22. Prendinger, H., Ishizuka, M.: The empathic companion: a character-based interface that addresses users' affective states. Applied Artificial Intelligence 19, 267–285 (2005)
23. Seligman, M., Walker, E., Rosenhan, D.: Abnormal psychology, 4th edn. W.W. Norton & Company, Inc, New York (2001)
24. Smith, C., Lazarus, R.: Emotion and adaptation. In: Pervin (ed.) Handbook of Personality: theory & research, pp. 609–637. Guilford Press, NY (1990)
25. Witten, I., Frank, E.: Data Mining: Practical machine learning tools and techniques, 2nd edn. Morgan Kaufman, San Francisco, CA (2005)

A Novel Feature for Emotion Recognition in Voice Based Applications

Hari Krishna Maganti, Stefan Scherer, and Günther Palm

Institute of Neural Information Processing, University of Ulm, Germany

In the context of affective computing, a significant trend in multi modal human-computer interaction is focused to determine emotional status of the users. For a constructive and natural human-computer interaction, the computers should be able to adapt to the user's emotional state and respond appropriately. This work proposes few simple and robust features in the framework of determining emotions from speech. Our approach is suitable for voice based applications, such as call centers or interactive voice systems, which are dependent on telephone conversations. For a typical call center application, it is crucial to recognize and classify agitation (anger, happiness, fear, and disgust) and calm (neutral, sadness, and boredom) callers, for the systems to respond appropriately. For instance, in a typical voice based application, the system should be able to either apologize or appreciate the problem of the caller suitably, if necessary by directing the call to the supervisor concerned.

In [1], the basic emotions were grouped into two categories and features based on fundamental frequency, energy, speaking rate, first three formants, and their bandwidths, along with their vital statistics were used. However, commonly used features such as pitch, energy, and statistics of these may not suffice to extract the relevant information needed to classify emotions accurately [2]. Therefore in this work, a simple feature extraction approach is proposed, which is based on the long term modulation spectrum of speech. The performance of the proposed approach is comparatively accurate, robust and close to real-time, potentially irrespective of the speaker, gender, and speech acquisition channel.

In the first step, the Fast Fourier Transform (FFT) of the input speech signal is computed. Then, the Mel-scale transformation, which imitates the human auditory system, is applied to these vectors. In the second step, the modulations of the signal for each band are computed by taking the FFT, resulting in a sequence of modulation vectors. It is observed that most of the prominent energies are within the frequencies between 2 to 16 Hz. After the computation of the modulation spectrum energy for each band, the median values of these energies are used as features. In our work, the Euclidean distance between the prototypes and the presented feature vectors are considered for classification in a KNN classifier.

All the emotion recognition experiments were performed on a subset of the Berlin Database of Emotional Speech[1], comprising utterances in seven different

---

[1] Optainable at: http://pascal.kgw.tu-berlin.de/emodb/

A. Paiva, R. Prada, and R.W. Picard (Eds.): ACII 2007, LNCS 4738, pp. 710–711, 2007.

emotions recorded from professional actors. The complete details, specification, and structure of the corpus are fully described in [3].

In an earlier work by Petrushin, the basic emotions were grouped as agitation (anger, happiness, and fear) and calm (neutral and sadness) [1]. In the context of a call center application, the best classification, resulting in an accuracy of around 77% was achieved with ensembles of neural networks. However, the simple features based on long term modulation spectrum of speech proposed in this work were efficient in classifying calm and agitated emotions with more than 88% accuracy. Note that, we included seven emotions in "calm" and "agitation", whereas Petrushin [1] considered only five different emotions.

Additionally to the classification results our experiments reveal similarities to the studies by Murray and Arnott, where the relationship between emotion and speech parameters were investigated. This further indicates, that the new features proposed in this work are suitable for emotion recognition [4].

The earlier studies are based on large number of features, and more so prosodic type such as pitch, energy, duration, etc, their variants at frame level and different combinations of the same. The feature extraction process is time-consuming and computational intensive. Apart from requiring huge quantities of data, time, and computational resources, the problem of robustness against unforeseen conditions is an issue of training based approaches. The proposed approach, based on simple features, with the performance close to real-time is independent of gender, speaker, and speech acquisition channel.

In the present work, a novel feature, based on modulation spectrum of speech for emotion recognition, intended for voice based applications is proposed. These simple features as motivated by human auditory system formed the input for classifiers, which performed close to real-time. The performance of automatic emotion recognizers was compared to earlier studies, in which a large set of features, based on pitch, energy, etc were used. The results outperformed earlier work and offer the possibility of extending the experiments further to recognize emotions such as happiness, fear, disgust, anger, boredom, neutral, and sadness separately. Additionally, the proposed features can also be used along with the standard approaches and more sophisticated classifiers to improve the recognition performance, which would be the subject of future research [5].

References

1. Petrushin, V.: Emotion in speech: recognition and application to call centers. In: Proceedings of Artificial Neural Networks in Engineering (1999)
2. Scherer, K.R., Johnstone, T., Klasmeyer, G.: Vocal expression of emotion. In: Handbook of Affective Sciences, pp. 433–456. Oxford University Press, Oxford (2003)
3. Burkhardt, F., et al.: A database of German emotional speech. In: Proceedings of Interspeech (2005)
4. Murray, I.R., Arnott, J.L.: Toward the simulation of emotion in synthetic speech: A review of the literature on human vocal emotion. The Journal of the Acoustical Society of America 93(2), 1097–1108 (1993)
5. Scherer, S., Schwenker, F., Palm, G.: Classifier fusion for emotion recognition from speech. to be published in Proc. of IE07 (2007)

Asymmetry of Left Versus Right Lateral Face in Face Recognition*

Wenfeng Chen[1], Chang Hong Liu[2], and Xiaolan Fu[1]

[1] State Key Laboratory of Brain and Cognitive Science,
Institute of Psychology, Chinese Academy of Sciences, Beijing 100101, China
{chenwf, fuxl}@psych.ac.cn
[2] Department of Psychology, University of Hull, Cottingham Road, Hull, HU6 7RX, UK
c.h.liu@hull.ac.uk

1 Introduction

Prior research has found that the left side of the face is emotionally more expressive than the right side [1]. This was demonstrated in a study where the right and the left halves of a face image were combined with their mirror-reversed duplicates to make composite images. When observers were asked which composite face appeared more emotional, they selected the left-left over the right-right composite more often.

According to Nicholls et al., this asymmetrical display of facial expression may be a part of an innate code for facial expressions [1]. The identity of the face, on the other hand, requires learning or a process of familiarization. There has been evidence that recognition facial identify can be influenced by recognition of facial expressions [2]. The present research attempts to resolve an unanswered question in this literature: can the hardwired asymmetry in facial expression affect the learning of facial identities? Faces in reality are often seen from the left or right views. Because recognition of novel faces is viewpoint dependent, we ask whether the face can be recognized more easily from the left or right views.

2 Methods

Twenty two undergraduates participated in the experiment. A total of 84 faces were chosen from a 3D face database [3]. Nine of these were used a practice session. The models were rendered and converted to 2D grayscale images with black background. Each face had 3 different poses (frontal/0°, 30° to the left, and 30° to the right), and 7 facial expressions (happiness, sadness, disgust, surprise, anger, fear, and neutral).

Each trial of the experiment consisted of two sequentially displayed faces, a learn face and a test face. Participants were asked to judge whether the two faces are of the same person. They were told to respond as quickly and as accurately as possible. The learn face was either shown in six frontal images of different facial expressions that appeared successively (multiple-image condition), or a single frontal image with an emotional or neutral expression (one-image conditions). The face in all these

---

* This research was supported in part by grants from 973 Program (2006CB303101), the NSFC (60433030, 30500157, and 30600182) and China-UK Science Networks.

A. Paiva, R. Prada, and R.W. Picard (Eds.): ACII 2007, LNCS 4738, pp. 712–713, 2007.

conditions was shown for 3*s*. The test face was always shown in a neutral expression, and was presented in a different view and size from the learned face. Half of the test faces faced left, and the remaining half faced right.

3   Results and Discussion

Face recognition performance based on the right side of the face was superior to the left side (see the accuracy results in figure 1). However, this asymmetry in face recognition demonstrates a right-face advantage, which is the opposite of the left-face advantage for facial expressions [1].

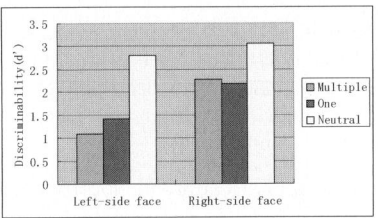 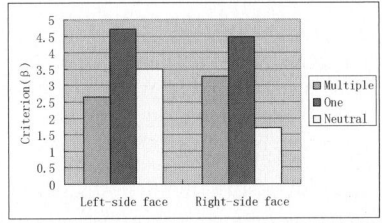

Fig. 1. Means of accuracy (d') and criterion (β) data in the face matching task

Our finding may result from a side effect of the left-face advantage for facial expressions. Because the stronger expression from the left side of the face is attributable to a greater difference between the emotional and neural expressions on this side, the larger physical difference between learned and tested faces should make this side of the face more difficult to recognize. If this is true, the asymmetry should vanish in the neutral expression condition where no expression change occurred. Our analysis of data support this explanation: the asymmetry effect appeared only when expressions changed between learning and test. However, McCurdy observed that the right side of the face is noticeably more like the whole face than the left side [4]. This may be an alternative explanation that focuses on a possible, inherent advantage of the right side for face identity. More rigorous design is needed to test these theories. For example, using left/right composite faces in future studies should allow precise estimation of the contribution from the two halves of the face in recognition tasks.

References

1. Nicholls, M.E.R., Wolfgang, B.J., Clode, D., Li, A.K.: The effect of left and right poses on the expression of facial emotion. Neuropsychologia. 40, 1662–1665 (2002)
2. Ganel, T., Goshen-Gottstein, Y.: Effects of Familiarity on the Perceptual Integrality of the Identity and Expression of Faces: The Parallel-Route Hypothesis Revisited. Journal of Experimental Psychology: Human Perception and Performance 30, 583–597 (2004)
3. Yin, L., Wei, X., Sun, Y., Wang, J., Rosato, M.J.: A 3D facial expression database for facial behavior research. 7th International Conference on Automatic Face and Gesture Recognition (FGR06), pp. 211–216.
4. McCurdy, H.G.: Experimental notes on the asymmetry of the human face. Journal of Abnormal Psychology. 44, 553–555 (1949)

Simulating Dynamic Speech Behaviour for Virtual Agents in Emotional Situations

Artemy Kotov

Institute of Linguistics, Russian State University for Humanities, Moscow, Russia
kotov@harpia.ru
http://www.harpia.ru/english.html

Abstract. In this article we demonstrate the application of a linguistic model of d/r-scripts to simulate the speech behaviour of artificial agents in virtual emotional situations. We apply the model to animate speech behaviour of a virtual agent for a term of about 10-30 seconds. This behaviour can be controlled by short emotional states, expressed in communication – *microstates*.

In our work we apply linguistic model of d/r-scripts [1] to simulate speech behaviour of computer agents in emotional situations. The model includes a list of reactive mechanisms (scripts) for processing of an external situation or an incoming text. We distinguish two sets of scripts, competing during text analysis: *d-scripts* (dominant scripts) for emotional processing and *r-scripts* (rational scripts) for "rational", neutral processing of incoming texts or other stimuli.

A d-script contains *starting* and *target models*, it activates as soon as the starting model is recognised in an incoming text or in the structure of a surrounding situation – and goes to the target model: behavioural reaction or specific speech output. Starting models describe semantic components, appearing in emotional texts. For "positive" d-scripts these are "pleasant" meanings, used in compliments and advertising ('X cares about Y' corresponds to CARE d-script, 'X – is the best' – to SUPR "superiority" d-script, etc.). For "negative" d-scripts – these are "terrible" meanings ('deception' corresponds to DECEPT, 'inadequate actions' – to INADEQ, etc.). The general list contains 13 negative and 22 positive d-scripts.[1] Starting model of a d-script has a number of slots, which can be distributed between the members of communication in different ways, resulting conflict (*You* make all the trouble!), self-accusation (*I* always make trouble!) or other types of emotional communication. We consider this as different *segments* in a situation.

To simulate speech behaviour for computer agents we have collected replies of about 500 participants of different age and professional groups [2] in several situations of Rosenzweig picture frustration test (PFT) [3]. This is a projective text suggesting to the participant a list of emotional situations (e.g. coming late to a date, being splashed by a car, breaking the favourite vase of the addressees mum) and asking for a possible speech reaction. The replies were marked up with the help of d/r-scripts. Further, we applied the model and the database of PFT replies to simulate speech behaviour for computer agents, similar to game or cartoon agents. In a proposed simulated scenario two cartoon agents (Grey and Green) interact in a

---

[1] For the list of negative d-scripts, refer to: http://www.harpia.ru/d-scripts-en.html

A. Paiva, R. Prada, and R.W. Picard (Eds.): ACII 2007, LNCS 4738, pp. 714–715, 2007.

number of emotional situations: Green is asked to jump up on the upper platform or to turn on the light, he fails (falls down or get an electric shock) and has to react to the event and/or to the request of the Grey agent. In our model Green is constructing a large list of possible speech reactions, which can be (i) filtered to select just one phrase for reply or (ii) arranged in sequence to provide an "emotional monologue" – speech animation for 10-30 seconds. The arrangement or filtering of phrases can be controlled by three factors: (a) selection of a particular segment (e.g. who is treated as causing the trouble in the situation, AGGR), (b) selection of a particular d/r-script (e.g. do we treat the situation as 'deception' or 'danger') and (c) filtering (we can freely express extreme positive or negative appraisals in our speech reactions or not).

For example, speech behaviour may be controlled through the manipulation of segments. During the simulation - the agent, which follows the sequence of segments in it's speech behaviour seems like "observing" or "realizing" the surrounding situation. For an agent, falling from an upper platform, the protocol may look as follows (added introduction fragments are underlined, fragments required to be updated for the situation to meet it's semantics are dotted-underlined):

- [Seg_6] *Oh! Bother!*
- [Seg_1] *I failed, as always!*
- [Seg_3] *I'm so sorry! You were counting on me and I failed you!*
- [Seg_4] *And for you there is no need to turn on the water works!*
- [Seg_7] *In fact, check where you are telling me to jump. Did you deliberately climb that high?*
- [Seg_8] *All, right. That's not your fault. Sorry.*

To simulate changes in emotional state during agent's monologue we have introduced the notion of a *microstate* – a short emotional state, linked with a certain type of expression in speech and represented by a number of utterances in the PFT base. For example, an agent may experience and express in speech several consecutive microstates while preparing to jump onto the upper floor (like fear and then – inspiriting), and following frustration (like being upset and then – quieting).

To control speech behaviour of the virtual agent we operate with a multi-component model, where (i) structure of a particular situation and (ii) microstates – together control: (a) segmentation of a situation, (b) selection of a particular d-script (emotional meaning to assign to the situation) and (c) filtering of emotional appraisals in speech. The model allows us to animate an artificial agent for the term of 10-30 seconds and make it's speech behaviour more vivid and natural from the point of view of an observer.

References

1. Kotov, A.A.: D-scripts model for speech influence and emotional dialogue simulation. In: Proceedings of the 7th Annual Colloquium for the UK Special Interest Group for Computational Linguistics, pp. 134–140. University of Birmingham (2004)
2. Kotov, A.A.: Application of Psychological Characteristics to D-Script Model for Emotional Speech Processing. In: Tao, J., Tan, T., Picard, R.W. (eds.) ACII 2005. LNCS, vol. 3784, pp. 294–302. Springer, Heidelberg (2005)
3. Rosenzweig, S.: Aggressive behavior and the Rosenzweig Picture-Frustration. Journal of Clinical psychology. 34(4), 885–891 (1976)

A Definition Approach for an "Emotional Turing Test"

Dirk M. Reichardt

BA Stuttgart - University of Cooperative Education
D-70180 Stuttgart, Germany
reichardt@ba-stuttgart.de

Abstract. There are lots of modelling approaches for emotional agents. Can they be compared in any way? The intention of this work is to provide a basis for comparison in a small but consistent environment which focuses on the impact of emotions in the decision making of agents. We chose the public goods game with punishment option as a scenario. Why? In this scenario it has been proven that humans show emotional, *non-rational* reactions. An emotional agent should therefore be able to show the same emotions and the underlying models should be capable *of explaining* them! The simulation and test environment is designed to allow any emotional agent model. Eventually, human players should not be distinguishable from artificial emotional agents.

1 Introduction and Theoretical Fundament

The well known Turing test decides whether a machine is capable of thinking. In this test, already, the lack of emotion could disclose that the communication partner is a machine. Nevertheless, if we want to isolate the emotional reaction, a more focused test setup is required. Note that the original imitation game setup leads to a decision according to *statistics* rather than to *individual* classifications [1]. The "emotional Turing test" uses a similar criterion. The idea is to consider groups of humans and of artificial emotional agents as basis for comparison. Is it possible to determine which group consists of humans and which group does not? How do we guarantee, that emotional reactions play the key role in the test setup?

As a basis for the test we chose the well known *public goods game* (PGG) scenario. The idea of the game: The player has to decide how much to invest in a public project which is bearing interest. The sum of all contributions plus interest is distributed among the players in equal shares. According to game theory the rational decision is not to contribute. The punishment option allows each player to punish a defector. However, punishing is not free of cost. Fehr and Gächter [2] repeat the game with the condition that the group composition changes from period to period: the punishment decision becomes *altruistic*. The experiments showed a significant correlation between *emotion* and the punishment decisions. This is the key point for the "emotional Turing test". Will artificial emotional agents perform comparable to humans in this setting? If we assume that the human behaviour is caused by emotional effects, the observation of this behaviour would be a sign for emotional human-like agents.

A. Paiva, R. Prada, and R.W. Picard (Eds.): ACII 2007, LNCS 4738, pp. 716–717, 2007.
© Springer-Verlag Berlin Heidelberg 2007

2   Scenario Definition

In order to provide emotional agent groups for the test we need a number of *different* instances of the same emotional agent model. Moreover, the PGG should be considered a closed world to exclude any emotional impact of anything outside the game constellation. The configuration of the public goods game is chosen as follows: four players form a group, each player gets the amount of 20 Euro. The public project is bearing 60 % interest. A player can invest up to 10 Euro to punish any of the other players. Each invested Euro results in a 3 Euro deduction from the account of the punished player. The game is repeated for n rounds in the same constellation before groups are recombined. Each player carries a record in which account balance, number of punishments received and imposed is revealed to the other players. After each session, the players are informed about the overall performance of their own group and of the other groups in terms of average income per player and average cost for punishment per player. The simulation consists of m consecutive sessions with m depending on the overall number of agents. Both, n and m are *not* communicated to the participating agents to avoid last game effects. Group constellations are formed by random, therefore it is possible that two players meet again during the test. The test environment is implemented as a distributed system. The core component of the environment handles the login of the participants, the group distribution, the accounting and the communication with the players. Every player component can log in via network using a common communication interface. The player agent – which can be instantiated by any agent architecture – only has to provide the communicative acts for the defined communication protocol.

As a test candidate we develop an own agent to fit into this environment. This agent is based upon the model by Ortony, Clore and Collins (OCC) and combines it with a personality model which provides mood control functions (see [3]), as well as the standards, goals and eliciting functions. Using different personalities for the agents involved in the experiment, we achieve exactly the requirement of having a number of different instances of the same emotional agent model.

Our aim is to apply different models of emotion to this experimental scenario and to compare their performance in terms of human-like "social" behavior. After a scientific discussion of this scenario – which we intend to start with this paper – we plan to provide the test environment on the university website and to encourage researchers to use it and add an implementation of their model.

References

[1] Turing, A.: Computing Machinery and Intelligence. Mind LIX(236), 433–460 (1950)
[2] Fehr, E., Gächter, S.: Altruistic Punishment in Humans. Nature 415, 137–140 (2002)
[3] Reichardt, D.: Will Artificial Emotional Agents Show Altruistic Punishment In The Public Goods Game. In: Reichardt, D., Levi, P., Meyer, J.-J. (eds.) Proceedings of the 1st Workshop Emotion and Computing – Current Research and Future Impact. 29th Annual German Conference on Artificial Intelligence, Bremen, (ISBN 3-88722-664-X), (2006)

Interpolating Expressions in Unit Selection

Marc Schröder*

DFKI GmbH, Saarbrücken, Germany

In expressive speech synthesis, a key challenge is the generation of flexibly vary-ing expressive tone while maintaining the high quality achieved with unit se-lection speech synthesis methods. Existing approaches have either concentrated on achieving high synthesis quality with no flexibility, or they have aimed at parametric models, requiring the use of parametric synthesis technologies such as diphone, formant or HMM-based synthesis.

This extended abstract reports on on-going work exploring the addition of a certain degree of control over expressivity in a unit selection context. Rather than merely choosing *one* unit selection voice database in order to determine the expression contained in the generated speech, we use technology from the voice conversion domain to flexibly interpolate between *two* voice databases. This provides us with the possibility to generate a *continuum* of expressive tones between the two extremes defined by the two voice databases.

Spectral Interpolation Algorithm

The spectral interpolation method employed here has previously been used to interpolate diphone voices with different vocal effort [1]. The method is based on a linear predictive coding (LPC) paradigm of speech representation, using line spectral frequencies (LSFs) as a representation of LPC coefficients with good interpolation properties [2].

The method works as follows. Two utterances with the same phoneme chain are mapped to each other on the time axis. For each analysis frame in a given phoneme in the source utterance, the corresponding frame in the target utterance is determined by linearly scaling the phoneme durations. Analysis frames can be either pitch-synchronous or at a fixed frame rate. Both frames are represented as LSFs plus residual. Interpolation between these two frames is performed indi-vidually for each LSF. With LPC prediction order p, let lsf_m^S be the m-th LSF of the source frame, and lsf_m^T the m-th LSF of the target frame, for $1 \leq m \leq p$. Then we compute the interpolated output LSF

$$lsf_m^O = (1 - r) \cdot lsf_m^S + r \cdot lsf_m^T \tag{1}$$

where r is the mixing ratio, $0 \leq r \leq 1$. Higher r means a larger contribution of the target signal in the interpolated spectrum.

* This work was supported by the projects HUMAINE (IST-507422) and PAVOQUE.

A. Paiva, R. Prada, and R.W. Picard (Eds.): ACII 2007, LNCS 4738, pp. 718–720, 2007.
© Springer-Verlag Berlin Heidelberg 2007

Before re-synthesising audio with the interpolated LPC filter, we need to scale the source residual with a gain factor computed by interpolating gain in the energy domain. In LPC analysis, the *prediction gain* is defined as the square root of the total energy of the prediction error, i.e. of the residual. From the gain of the source and target frames, g^S and g^T, the gain factor is computed as

$$gainfactor = (1/g^S)\sqrt{(1-r) \cdot (g^S)^2 + r \cdot (g^T)^2} \qquad (2)$$

One frame of audio is resynthesised by filtering the gain-corrected residual of the source with the LPC filter defined by the interpolated LSFs lsf_m^O. Frames are combined into the resulting audio stream using a standard overlap-add mechanism.

Application in Unit Selection Synthesis

We have integrated the interpolation algorithm into our unit selection speech synthesis platform MARY (http://mary.dfki.de), in a way that makes it easy to use the interpolation from markup.

Two unit selection voices can be interpolated by writing as input markup: <voice name="voice1 with XY% voice2">, where voice1 and voice2 are existing unit selection voices, and XY is a number between 0 and 100, indicating the relative weight of the spectrum from voice2 to be used in the interpolation. Thus, "voice1 with 0% voice2" corresponds to the original voice1, whereas "voice1 with 100% voice2" is a combination of the LPC residual from voice1 with the spectral envelope from voice2.

The algorithm first selects and concatenates units for each of the two voices separately; in the subsequent interpolation step, the unit durations serve as phoneme labels for the frame mapping.

We have tested the algorithm using two limited domain voices from the same speaker, generating "neutral" and "excited" soccer announcements. The "neutral" voice states the results in a rather matter-of-fact tone; the "excited" voice resembles the style of announcements made in soccer stadiums: high pitch, high vocal effort, and a relatively fast speech rate.

First informal listening tests confirm that the synthetic utterances generated with this interpolation algorithm are of good quality, with gradually changing spectral characteristics as the interpolation weight is changed. Noticeable distortions could be heard under two circumstances. Noise-like sounds were generated for some plosives when merging the excited spectrum into the neutral voice, probably due to different timing of silence vs. burst within the plosive units. This could be avoided by analysing the substructure of plosives with respect to acoustically similar sections, which would allow for a more appropriate time alignment. A weaker but noticeable type of distortion occurred when merging the neutral spectrum into the excited voice: at mixing ratios around 50%, some vowels were accompanied by a faint buzz noise. Despite these minor distortions, however, the overall degradation to intelligibility and naturalness seems very limited, and the interpolated voice exhibits vocal characteristics between the two original synthetic voices.

References

1. Turk, O., Schröder, M., Bozkurt, B., Arslan, L.: Voice quality interpolation for emotional text-to-speech synthesis. In: Proc. Interspeech 2005, Lisbon, Portugal, pp. 797–800 (2005)
2. Paliwal, K.K.: Interpolation properties of linear prediction parametric representations. In: Proc. Eurospeech'95, Madrid, Spain, pp. 1029–1032 (1995)

Induction and Evaluation of *Affects* for Facial Motion Capture

Gaspard Breton[1], Florence Février[2], Eric Jamet[2], and Géraldine Rouxel[2]

[1] Orange Labs TECH/IRIS/IAM
gaspard.breton@orange-ftgroup.com
4 rue du Clos Courtel
35512 Cesson-Sévigné, France
[2] CRPCC - University of Rennes II Haute Bretagne,
{florence.fevrier,eric.jamet,geraldine.rouxel}@uhb.fr
Place du Recteur Henri Le Moal
35043 Rennes, France

In this study, we are interested in capturing the facial configuration of *Affects* in order to use them for Embodied Conversational Agents. In order to create a believable ECA, it is necessary to capture natural *Affects* that can be learnt and replayed. However, until now, animation data are extracted from videos and their description is far from being sufficient to generate realistic facial expressions. It seems that believable results cannot be obtained without using 3D motion capture. This is why in this study we tried to set up a protocol for *Affects* induction in a motion capture situation with manipulated subjects who are unaware of the real goals. Similarly from [1], we induce natural *Affects* in order to capture the related facial expressions.

The protocol we have developed is inspired by the *Social Interactions* technique [2]. This technique postulates that the behavior of other people has an effect on our own emotional state. In this study [3], we have chosen to put the subjects into a video conversation situation where they have to sell theatre seats for a play. They have been told that they were here to test the ergonomics of the software. The customer is actually an associate who plays a predefined *scenario*. This protocol was first conducted on videos only, the subject being recorded by the webcam. Once the protocol proved its efficiency, it was adapted to motion capture. Fourteen subjects were equipped with 99 markers glued onto their faces. The make up took almost an hour during the one subjects had time to get used to the equipment and to forget the markers stuck on with an very elastic glue. The subjects were told the same things as in the first experiment and the need for the markers was explained by the fact that the customer was not seeing a video but a real time animated character thanks to their faces. Five *scenarii* *scenario* selected: Satisfaction, Amusement, Embarrassment, Misunderstanding and Surprise.

The sequences have been auto-evaluated by the subjects and are being evaluated by 80 independent judges. When considering the auto-evaluations the *Affect* which was generally most experienced was the target *Affect* but it is composite most of the time. For example, for the Satisfaction *Affect*, subjects describe a feeling made up of Joy, Satisfaction and Amusement. Moreover, the *Activation*

A. Paiva, R. Prada, and R.W. Picard (Eds.): ACII 2007, LNCS 4738, pp. 721–722, 2007.

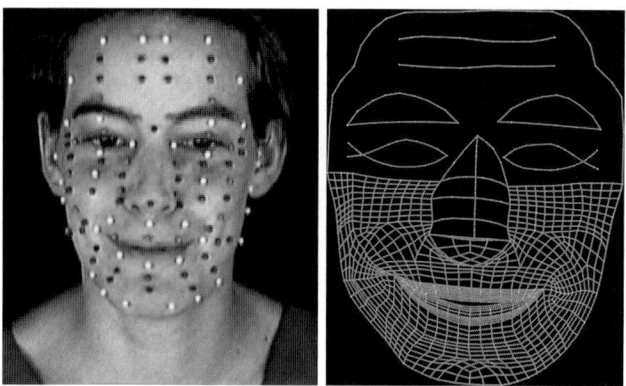

Fig. 1. Subject with markers on and the corresponding 3D motion captured data

levels are not very intense, but rather moderate. It is possible that the subjects have been impressed by the equipment and maybe held back their feelings. Some subjects also reported that they really wanted to achieve the task seriously and that it was not very professional to express his feelings. For the independent evaluations, it has been decided to present the sequences to be evaluated under four different modalities. The three first ones use the *Point Lights* paradigm [4] and the fourth one is the raw video with the markers. The three *Point Lights* sequences are built into assumed increasing intelligibility levels. Results show that it is not easy to capture and replay subtle *Affects*. In many cases, the selected *Affects* were not really recognized by judges. However, they could be clustered into two *meta*-groups according to their positive or negative *Valence*. Also, we obtained rather low *Activation* levels showing that the *Affects* were not fully expressed. This certainly comes from the fact that we are not studying basic emotions like many authors do. This is particularly obvious when considering the Surprise *Affect*, for which the expression is different from the common description found in literature.

References

1. Aubergé, V., Rilliard, A., Audibert, N.: De E-Wiz à E-Clone : Méthodologie Expérimentale pour la Modélisation des Emotions et Affects Authentiques. Proceedings of WACA Grenoble France (2005)
2. Westerman, R., Spies, K., Stahl, G., Hesse, F.W.: Relative Effectivness of Mood Induction Procedures : A Meta Analysis. European Journal of Social Psychology 16, 557 580 (1996)
3. Février, F., Jamet, E., Rouxel, G., Dardier, V., Breton, G.: Induction d'émotions pour la motion capture dans une situation de vidéo-conversation. In: Proceedings of WACA Toulouse, France (2006)
4. Johansson, G.: Visual Perception of Biological Motion and a Model for its Analysis. In: Jansson, G., Bergström, S.S., Epstein, W. (eds.) Perceiving events and objects (1973)

Ontology-Driven Affective Chinese Text Analysis and Evaluation Method

Linhong Xu and Hongfei Lin

Department of Computer Science and Engineering,
Dalian University of Technology, Dalian, China 116024
qingniao1203@163.com,hflin@dlut.edu.cn
http://ir.dlut.edu.cn

Abstract. This paper studies text affective analysis from three different levels: words, sentences and discourses. Firstly, affective lexicon ontology is constructed by employing the manual and automatic classification methods referred to the present emotional classification. Then affective analysis of sentences and discourses is completed by emotional information of affective lexicon ontology. For sentential recognition, the lexical emotion information and semantic features are appended into Condition Random Fields, and the emotional chain of a text document is generated. Finally affective structure of a text document is evaluated by two different methods as single sentence evaluation and joint sentence evaluation. In analyzing the discourses, affective tone is acquired through Emotional Largest Chain method and Support Vector Machine method.

1 Introduction

In the year 2000, Pero Subasic presents that fuzzy semantic is employed to recognize affective text analysis, and exploit rather than reducing the word's ambiguity [1]. Three years later, Hugo Liu in MIT discusses visualizing the affective structure of a text document [2]. In 2005, Chunling Ma in the University of Tokyo employs the syntactical sentence-level processing and keyword spotting technique to analyze emotions [3], and, Fuji Ren in the University of Tokushima recognizes the emotion from text based on the constructed emotion thesaurus [4].

2 The Model of Affective Text Analysis

This paper studies text affective analysis from three different levels: words, sentences and discourses. Firstly, basic emotional information of words is provided by affective lexicon ontology which includes 10,200 entries now.

Secondly CRF is used to analyze sentences' emotion in literatures, and semantic features of emotional information of the sentence are chosen as follows: affective word feature; emotional class feature; words with negative meanings; the adversative conjunction; modal feature of sentence; whether it is the first sentence of the article; the length of the sentence; the type of sentence; lexical repetitive degree in a sentence.

A. Paiva, R. Prada, and R.W. Picard (Eds.): ACII 2007, LNCS 4738, pp. 723–724, 2007.
© Springer-Verlag Berlin Heidelberg 2007

Finally, this paper adopts two methods to acquire affective tone of the discourse. One is Emotional Largest Chain method. It chooses the one emotion which sustains the longest time in the emotional chain of the recognition of sentences, namely that one emotion occurs continuously in chain and has the longest sub chain. Another method firstly obtains the tf*idf values of every affective words of the article accord to affective lexicon ontology, and then uses SVM to classify, finally gets affective tone of the discourse by the result of SVM.

Two evaluation methods of affective analysis are used. The first evaluation method (single sentence evaluation): the number of the correct tagged sentences divides the number of all sentences in an article; The second evaluation method (joint sentence evaluation): the emotional consistency is evaluated by the accuracy of the multivariable emotion co-occurrence.

3   Conclusion and Further Work

This paper studies text affective analysis from three different levels of words, sentences and discourses. Affective recognition of sentences is evaluated one by one, and then the emotion recognition of the discourse is completed. The result with CRFs is better than the result with tagging the emotion directly on the accuracy of micro average and the consistency of emotion. In the analysis of affective tone of the discourse, the Emotional Largest Chain method is better than Support Vector Machine on both total accuracy and respective accuracy of every emotion class, especially when the distribution of the corpus is not well-distributed.

Acknowledgments. This work is supported by grant from the Natural Science Foundation of China (No.60373095 and 60673039) and the National High Tech Research and Development Plan of China (2006AA01Z151).

References

1. Subasic, P., Huettner, A.: Affect Analysis of Text Using Fuzzy Semantic Typing, Fuzzy Systems, pp. 483–496 (2000)
2. Liu, H., Selker, T., Lieberman, H.: Visualizing the affective structure of a Text Document. Conference on Human Factors in Computing Systems, 740–741 (2003)
3. Ma, C., Helmut, P., Mitsuru, I.: Emotion estimation and reasoning based on affective textual interaction. Affective computing and intelligent interaction, 622–628 (2005)
4. Zhang, Y., Li, Z., Ren, F., Kuroiwa, S.: Semi-automatic Emotion Recognition from Textual Input Based on the Constructed Emotion Thesaurus. Natural Language Processing and Knowledge Engineering, 571–576 (2005)

Modeling the Dynamic Nonlinear Nature of Emotional Phenomena

Luís Morgado[1,2] and Graça Gaspar[2]

[1] Instituto Superior de Engenharia de Lisboa
Rua Conselheiro Emídio Navarro, 1949-014 Lisboa, Portugal
lm@isel.ipl.pt
[2] Faculdade de Ciências da Universidade de Lisboa
Universidade de Lisboa, Campo Grande, 1749-016 Lisboa, Portugal
gg@di.fc.ul.pt

Abstract. The study of emotional phenomena, particularly the development of emotion models for intelligent agent implementation, has been mainly based on a perspective of emotion as a human phenomenon and on the assumption that emotions can be divided into discrete and independent categories. We propose an alternative model that emphasizes the continuous nonlinear nature of emotion processes, where emotional phenomena are rooted not on high level cognitive or even nervous structures, but on biophysical principles that are pervasive among biological organisms.

1   Introduction

In the evolutionary continuum there is no evidence of a discontinuity in what regards the existence of emotional phenomena. On the contrary, it is well known that some simple organisms, even unicellular organisms, can present remarkable behaviors for organisms without nervous system, which from an observer point of view are easily classified as emotional [1]. Although almost unexplored, these observations give rise to the possibility that emotional phenomena are rooted not on cognitive or even on nervous structures, but on biophysical principles that are pervasive among biological organisms. In our work we explore this line of research by defining an emotion model that is inspired on the view that "basic biological organization is brought about by a complex web of energy flows" [2]. In our model, called *flow model of emotion*, an agent is modeled as a dissipative structure [3], i.e. an open system governed by the interchange of energy with the environment and able to maintain itself in a state far from equilibrium, yet keeping an internally stable overall structure.

2   The Flow Model of Emotion

In a dissipative structure, the maintenance of an internal stability in spite of environmental changes is done through feedback networks that motivate the system to act. The maintenance of a basic life support energy flow can be seen as a base motivation. However motivations can take various forms according to the cognitive

A. Paiva, R. Prada, and R.W. Picard (Eds.): ACII 2007, LNCS 4738, pp. 725–726, 2007.
© Springer-Verlag Berlin Heidelberg 2007

context (e.g. drives, desires). In any case, to achieve its motivations an agent must apply an internal potential to be able to produce the adequate change in the environment. However the concretization of the intended change depends on the characteristics of the current environmental situation that, from a thermodynamic point of view, can be modeled as an agent-environment coupling conductance. Therefore, the agent-environment relation can be modeled as a relation between an agent's internal potential, its *achievement potential*, and the agent-environment coupling conductance, the *achievement conductance*. The achievement potential represents the potential of change that the agent is able to produce in the environment to achieve the intended state-of-affairs. The achievement conductance represents the degree of the environment's conduciveness or resistance to that change, which can also mean the degree of environment change that is conducive, or not, to the agent intended state-of-affairs.

From a thermodynamic point of view, the achievement potential can be viewed as a force (P) and the achievement conductance as a transport property (C). The behavioral dynamics of an agent can therefore be characterized as a relation corresponding to a flow, called *achievement flow* (F), which results from the application of a potential P over a conductance C. The forces that arise from this relation between achievement potential and achievement conductance, expressed as energy flows, generate behavioral dynamics that underlie the cognitive activity of an agent. In our model we consider emotional phenomena as the expression of those dynamics [4].

Although inspired by biophysical analogies, the main aim of the proposed model is to support the development and implementation of agents, independent of their kind or level of complexity. Therefore the base notions of the model are concretized in a computationally tractable way, namely the notion of energy. In thermodynamics, energy is usually defined as the capacity to produce work. In the context of the proposed model, energy is defined as the capacity of an agent to act or, in a wide sense, to produce change. Considering an agent as a dissipative structure, that change is oriented towards the achievement of motivations driven by internal potentials and expressed through energy flows. That is, both the agent and the environment can be modeled as a composition of multiple energetic potentials with different characteristics. This notion of energetic potential serve as a unifying support to explore the existence of specific emotional patterns and, at the same time, to explain the continuous nonlinear nature of emotion processes.

References

1. Staddon, J.: Adaptive Dynamics: The Theoretical Analysis of Behavior. MIT Press, Redmond, Washington (2001)
2. Bergareche, A., Ruiz-Mirazo, K.: Metabolism and the Problem of its Universalization, Biosystems, vol. 49 (1999)
3. Morgado, L., Gaspar, G.: Emotion Based Adaptive Reasoning for Resource Bounded Agents. In: Proceedings of the 4th International Joint Conference on Autonomous Agents and Multi-Agent Systems (2005)
4. Morgado, L., Gaspar, G.: Adaptation and Decision-Making Driven by Emotional Memories. In: Bento, C., Cardoso, A., Dias, G. (eds.) EPIA 2005. LNCS (LNAI), vol. 3808, Springer, Heidelberg (2005)

Deception Detection Via Blob Motion Pattern Analysis⋆

Fan Xia, Hong Wang, and Junxian Huang

State Key Laboratory of Intelligent Technology and Systems
Department of Computer Science and Technology, Tsinghua University
Beijing, 100084, P.R. China

Deception dectection is one of the most difficult problems in affect recognition and expression research area. Recently, non-verbal methods of detecting deception have appeared to be promising. Thomas[1] presented a proof-of-concept study based on the blob analysis of some suspects' interviews and mock experiments video clips. In this paper, we present our recent research work in the direction of developing an automated deception detection system. We propose a blob motion pattern analysis approach to solve this problem.

Our approach consists of the following steps: (a) using skin-color based technology to detect body blobs, i.e. head and hands, and calculating the in-frame and cross-frame features. (b) segmenting the training videos into small clips with a fixed duration where each clip contains only one blob motion pattern, and automatically clustering these patterns into groups. (c) using HMM-based method to model the pattern sequences and estimating the latent subject's state.

During the body blobs detection process, we first take an off-line training phase to set up a lookup table to determine the probability of each color vector c_i being skin-colored. Then a standard connected components labeling algorithm is applied to yield different skin-colored regions. Size filtering on the derived connected components is performed to eliminate small, isolate blobs that do not correspond to body blobs. An ellipse fitting algorithm is also applied to find the right position of body blobs. We calculate the in-frame and cross-frame features include position, shape, distance between blobs, velocity, etc. and denote each blob as a vector $b = \{position, size, velocity, \ldots\}$.

Due to the space-time nature of blob motion patterns, we adopt a discrete scene event based feature representation approach considering that each clip contains only one blob motion pattern. The blob motion pattern in a clip can be represented as $P = \{f_1, f_2, \ldots, f_T\}$, where T is the number of frames in the video clip and $f_i = \{b_{head}, b_{left-hand}, b_{right-hand}\}$.

Now the deception detection problem can be redefined formally. Consider the training data set D consists of N patterns with a fixed duration, $D = \{P_1, P_2, \ldots, P_N\}$, where P_i is the pattern vector defined as above. The subject's behavioral state can be considered as a discrete time series of patterns. Using these patterns as observations we can train an HMM to estimate the latent subject's state. We assume that there are 3 hidden states in the model, denoted as $S = \{agitation, normal, over - control\}$ This assumption comes from the

---

⋆ Supported by the National Natural Science Foundation of China (60433030).

A. Paiva, R. Prada, and R.W. Picard (Eds.): ACII 2007, LNCS 4738, pp. 727–728, 2007.

fundamental theories IDT[2] and EVT[3]. All training video clips are manually labeled. However, there are considerable quantity of patterns. The key point of the problem to be addressed is to cluster these patterns. Based on the clustering result, each patterns can be automatically labeled with the group it belongs to.

We adopt the Guassian Mixture Model (GMM) to classify the pattern vectors of training data set into K classes. A Bayesian Information Criterion (BIC) process is applied as an automatic model order selection to determine which value is proper for K.

When a new video query comes in, we segment it into several clips with a fixed duration and calculate the pattern vectors. Then the trained GMM is used to label each of these unseen patterns as one of the known K pattern classes. Finally, an HMM is trained upon these patterns and used to estimate the most likely latent state through Viterbi decoding.

We collect some videos containing deception scenes from an experiment whose design has drawn some inspiration from the popular Mafia Game[4]. We've tested 19 deceptive clips and 18 truthful clips from the experiment. Finally, we've got 17 deceptive clips and 16 truthful clips given correct recognition result. For those clips not recognized correctly, we find that some of them are even hard to distinguish by human.

Our current research is focusing on macro blob movement analysis, future research should involve some work focusing on micro blob movement, such as finger movement and eyebrow movement, etc.. A more accurate and fast blob detection method is another target. An automated deception detection system that synthesize these technologies and tools is our final goal.

This work is a part of the Research on Affective Computing Theory and Approach, which is a key research project of National Natural Science Foundation of China (NSFC). We would like to thank Prof. CAI Lianhong and Prof. FU Xiaolan and other members of the project group for their invaluable discussion and help.

References

1. Meservy, T.O., Jensen, M.L., Kruse, J., et al.: Deception detection through automatic, unobtrusive analysis of nonverbal behavior. IEEE Intelligent Systems 20(5), 36–43 (2005)
2. Buller, D.B., Burgoon, J.K.: Interpersonal deception theory. Communication Theory 6, 203–242 (1996)
3. George, J.F., Biros, D.P., Burgoon, J.K., Nunamaker Jr., J.F.: Training Professionals to Detect Deception. NSF/NIJ Symposium on Intelligence and Security Informatics, Tucson, AZ (2003)
4. Mafia game introduction, http://en.wikipedia.org/wiki/Mafia_Game.htm

Combining Audio and Video by Dominance in Bimodal Emotion Recognition*

Lixing Huang, Le Xin, Liyue Zhao, and Jianhua Tao

National Laboratory of Pattern Recognition (NLPR),
Institute of Automation, Chinese Academy of Sciences
{lxhuang,xinle,lyzhao,jhtao}@nlpr.ia.ac.cn

Abstract. We propose a novel bimodal emotion recognition approach by using the boosting-based framework, in which we can automatically determine the adaptive weights for audio and visual features. In this way, we balance the dominances of audio and visual features dynamically in feature-level to obtain better performance.

1 Introduction

Since it is the nature of human beings to speak and exhibit facial expressions simultaneously, multimodal emotion recognition, especially through the tightly coupled modalities of sound and sight, has been emphasized recently. The decision-level fusion and feature-level fusion methods are two main approaches. The former combines the results from acoustic classifier and visual classifier by rules, while the latter classifies the bimodal feature vectors combined from audio and visual channels into different emotions directly. The decision-level fusion takes advantage of the assumption that audio and visual channels play different roles in human perception of different emotions; however the feature-level fusion is close to the nature of human. To integrate the advantages of both methods and avoid their drawbacks, we propose a novel bimodal fusion approach by using the boosting-based framework.

2 System Description

Our system consists of three modules, as shown in Fig.1, two input modules, including visual and audio features extraction, and one output module, using the boosting-based framework to fuse the features from two input modules.

The output module contains a series of classification and regression tree (CART) models, which are built under the framework of boosting. These models are combined linearly and allow emphasizing audio and visual features differently.

---

* The work is supported by the National Natural Science Foundation of China (No. 60575032) and the 863 Program (No. 2006AA01Z138).

A. Paiva, R. Prada, and R.W. Picard (Eds.): ACII 2007, LNCS 4738, pp. 729–730, 2007.

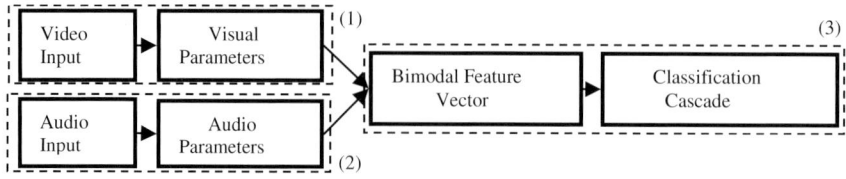

Fig. 1. The system of our bimodal emotion recognition

3 Boosting-Based Algorithm

The boosting based algorithm has been discussed in [2]. Since it is difficult to integrate sample weights into the training of CART, we use the distribution of weights in a resampling way. That is, a sample with higher weight will duplicate itself in the training set. Fig.2. shows the change of sample percentages and the change of feature dominances. It is clear that the dominances of features vary with respect to the changes of the sample percentage of each emotion, which means that our boosting-based bimodal emotion recognition method intends to select the most dominant features in the classification of each emotion inherently.

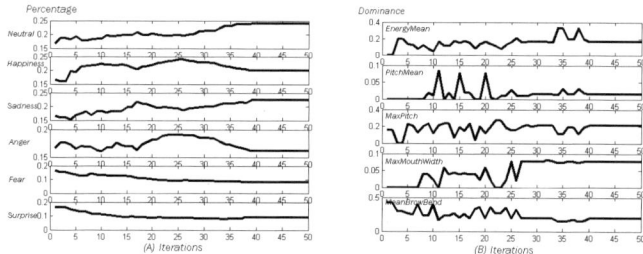

Fig. 2. (A) The change of sample percentage with respect to iterations (B) The change of feature dominance with respect to iterations

References

[1] Huang, T.S., Chen, L., Tao, H.: Bimodal emotion recognition by man and machine. In: Proc. ATR Workshop on Virtual Communication Environments, Japan (April 1998)

[2] Schapire, R.E., Singer, Y.: Improved boosting algorithms using confidence-rated prediction. Machine Learning 37, 297–336 (1999)

[3] Silva, D., Miyasato, T., Nakatsu, R.: Facial emotion recognition using multi-modal information. In: Proc. International Conference on Information and Communications Security, pp. 397–401 (1997)

[4] Chen, C.Y., Huang, Y.K., Cook, P.: Visual/Acoustic emotion recognition. In: Proc. International Conference on Multimedia and Expo, pp. 1468–1471 (2005)

Metric Adaptation and Representation Upgrade in an Emotion-Based Agent Model*

Rodrigo Ventura and Carlos Pinto-Ferreira

Institute for Systems and Robotics
Instituto Superior Técnico, TULisbon
Av. Rovisco Pais, 1; 1049-001 Lisbon, Portugal
{yoda,cpf}@isr.ist.utl.pt

The research presented here follows a biologically inspired approach, based on the hypothesis that emotions contribute decisively for humans to cope with complex and dynamic environments. This hypothesis is founded on neurophysiological findings showing that damage in the emotion circuitry of the brain cause inability to handle simple, common life tasks [1]. Inspired by these findings, an emotion-based agent model was previously presented [2], proposing a double-processing of stimuli: a simple representation termed *perceptual image*, designed for fast processing and immediate response to urgent situations, and a complex representation termed *cognitive image,* thus slow to process, are extracted from each stimulus reaching the agent. These two representations are extracted and processed, simultaneously, by the two levels of the architecture: the perceptual and the cognitive levels. The parallelism of the processing is essential, so that quick response to urgent situations is not compromised by the slow processing of the cognitive level. These two representations are then associated and stored in memory. Once the agent faces a new situation, it matches the incoming stimulus with the agent memory, thus retrieving the associated images.

The agent model hypothesizes that the representations matching mechanism proceeds according to two steps. In the first step, a perceptual image is obtained from the stimulus and matched against the perceptual images in memory. For the ones yielding a closer match, the agent, in the second step, matches the cognitive image extracted from the stimulus with those indexed by the closest perceptual images. This mechanism is termed *indexing.* Considering that the cognitive matching mechanism is an operation more complex than the perceptual one, this mechanism allows for a narrowing of the candidate cognitive images, thus providing an efficient algorithm to find cognitive matches. This indexing mechanism was previously formulated and theoretically analyzed, under the assumption that the matching of the cognitive and perceptual images are performed in metric spaces [3]. The goal of the indexing mechanism is then to find the memory pair which cognitive image minimizes its distance to the one extracted from the stimulus, employing the perceptual representation to do so in an efficient manner.

---

* This work was partially supported by FCT (ISR/IST plurianual funding) through the POS_Conhecimento Program that includes FEDER funds.

A. Paiva, R. Prada, and R.W. Picard (Eds.): ACII 2007, LNCS 4738, pp. 731–732, 2007.

With the issue of indexing efficiency in mind, the research presented here concerns the following problem: how to construct a perceptual representation (and metric) with the goal of optimizing the indexing efficiency. In other words, the ideal perceptual representation and metric are the ones that yield small perceptual distances iff the corresponding cognitive distances are also small. To do so, two strategies are explored. One corresponds to adapting a perceptual metric, via a set of parameters, such that cognitive proximity implies perceptual nearness, in a given environment. The second strategy addresses the improvement of the perceptual representation, in the following sense. Assuming that the perceptual representation is a vector of features extracted from stimuli, when these features are not sufficiently representative, the goal is to upgrade the perceptual representation with new, more representative, features. Both of these strategies are approached using Multidimensional Scaling (MDS) techniques [4].

We propose to perform a gradient descent, within the framework of the nonmetric MDS w.r.t. a parameterization of the perceptual metric, instead of w.r.t. the point coordinates. These parameters can, for instance, assign a degree of relevance to each feature of the perceptual representation. Regarding the construction of additional perceptual features, we propose to append each perceptual image with a pre-specified amount of additional components. These components represent the values that the new features ought to take, for each one of the perceptual images in the training set. Their values are randomly initialized, and subject to gradient descent as in the nonmetric MDS. Concerning the obtainment of those added components for new stimuli, the idea we advance is to utilize the obtained values to construct a regression model. That regression model can then be used to obtain the new features values for new stimuli. Details concerning the methodology and the adaptation algorithm can be found in the companion paper [5].

Experimentation have shown interesting results [5], illustrating the proposed methodology. Both metric adaptation and the inclusion of new features were experimented with, using a synthetic world as testbed. Performance evaluations showed a clear benefit in terms of improved indexing efficiency.

References

1. Damásio, A.R.: Descartes' Error: Emotion, Reason and the Human Brain. Picador (1994)
2. Ventura, R., Pinto-Ferreira, C.: Emotion-based agents. In: Proceedings of the 15th National Conference on Artificial Intelligence, Cambridge/Menlo Park, p. 1204. AAAI Press and The MIT Press, Cambridge (1998)
3. Ventura, R., Pinto-Ferreira, C.: A formal indexing mechanism for an emotion-based agent (Special session on Automated Reasoning: Perception and Emotions). In: Proceedings of International Conference on Artificial Intelligence and Applications 2002 (IASTED), Malaga, Spain, pp. 34–40. ACTA Press (Special issue on Automated Reasoning: Perception and Emotions) (2002)
4. Cox, T.F., Cox, M.A.A.: Multidimensional Scaling. Chapman & Hall, London, UK (1994)
5. Ventura, R., Pinto-Ferreira, C.: Indexing by metric adaptation and representation upgrade in an emotion-based agent model. In: Proceedings of the 3rd International Conference on Natural Computation (to appear 2007)

Combining Global and Local Classifiers for Lipreading

Shengping Zhang, Hongxun Yao, Yuqi Wan, and Dan Wang

School of Computer Science and Engineering, Harbin Institute of Technology,
Harbin, 150001, China

Lipreading has become a hot research topic in recent years since the visual information extracted from the lip movement has been shown to improve the performance of automatic speech recognition (ASR) system especially under noisy environments [1]-[3], [5]. There are two important issues related to lipreading: 1) how to extract the most efficient features from lip image sequences, 2) how to build lipreading models. This paper mainly focuses on how to choose more efficient features for lipreading.

Feature extraction is very important for lipreading. Many feature extraction methods have been proposed in the literature. In general, variant feature extraction methods can be divided into two kinds: 1) pixel-based features derived directly from the image transforming such as Discrete Fourier Transform (DFT), Discrete Cosine Transform (DCT) [2] [6], Principal Component Analysis (PCA) [3], Linear Discriminant Analysis (LDA) [6], Gabor Wavelets Transform(GWT) [4], Local Binary Pattern (LBP)and so on. 2) model-based features by tracking lip contours to describe its movement [5]. Some experiment results show that pixel-based method is more efficient than model-based method [2] [5].

In those pixel-based feature extraction methods mentioned above, DFT and DCT extract the global features in the mouth images; GWT and LBP extract local features. Global features consider the mouth image as a whole and it is easy to reflect the whole difference of mouth images. Local features, on the other hand, are computed at multiple points in the mouth images and are more robust to the variations between the images of the same mouth due to illumination and viewing direction. Although both global and local features work well to some extent, each is limited by the fact that it ignores other information that may also be very important.

Most lipreading systems tent to use either global or local features. Some psychological evidences show that people use both global and local features for object recognition, in some extent, people use global features before analyzing the image in detail [7] [8]. Local features could result in much better performance than global ones. Motivated by this study, this paper presents a novel method of combining global and local classifiers to form a more powerful classifier for lipreading. The global classifier uses Discrete Fourier Transform (DFT) to extract global features. The local classifier uses block-based Gabor Wavelets Transform (BGWT) to extract local features. Both global and local classifiers use Hidden Markov Models (HMM) to model. These two classifiers are then

A. Paiva, R. Prada, and R.W. Picard (Eds.): ACII 2007, LNCS 4738, pp. 733–734, 2007.

combined to form the final classifier which not only uses the global information but also the local information.

We investigate and compare several current popular global and local feature extraction methods such as Discrete Cosine Transform (DCT), Discrete Fourier Transform (DFT), block-based Gabor wavelets Transform (BGWT) and Local Binary Pattern (LBP) as well as several combination methods between them. The experiment results reveal that the performance of single global or local classifier is around 77%. Among these classifiers, the one based on LBP performs worse than others. The reason is that LBP is implemented in spatial domain and extracted global features are not more efficient than other features which are extracted in frequency domain. In all of the combinations of global and local classifiers, the combination of DFT classifier and Gabor classifier (DFT+BGWT) gained the highest accuracy up to 82.45% which not only surpasses each of the individual classifiers but also the other combinations, in other words, the global DFT features can compensate the local Gabor features much better. The combination of DCT classifier and Gabor classifier gains worse recognition rate than DFT+BGWT. In fact, DCT coefficients can be derived from the real part of DFT coefficients, and DFT features have more powerful capability to reflect the intensity variations in an entire image. The performance of combination of DFT and LBP is better than LBP but worse than DFT. The reason is that LBP features have worse discriminability than DFT features. When they are used together, the test samples which will be recognized right by DFT may be recognized wrong with the influence of weaker LBP classifier.

References

1. Morishima, S., Ogata, S., Murai, K., Nakamura, S.: Audio-visual speech translation with automatic lip synchronization and face tracking based on 3D head model. Proc. IEEE Int. Conf. Acoustics, Speech,and Signal Processing 2, 2117–2120 (2002)
2. Potamianos, G., Graf, H.P., Cosatto, E.: An image transform approach for HMM based automatic lipreading. In: Proc. Int. Conf. Image Process, Chicago, pp. 173–177 (1998)
3. Dupont, S., Luettin, J.: Audio-visual speech modeling for continuous speech recognition. IEEE Trans. On Multimedia 2, 141–151 (2000)
4. Shen, L., Bai, L.: Gabor feature based face recognition using kernel methods. AFGR, pp. 170–176 (2004)
5. Matthews., et al.: Extraction of Visual Features for Lipreading. IEEE Trans. on Pattern Analysis and Machine Intelligence 24(2) (2002)
6. Duchnowski, P., et al.: Toward movement-invariant automatic lip-reading and speech recognition. In: Duchnowski, P. (ed.) Proc. Int. Conf. Acoust. Speech Signal Process, Detroit, pp. 109–111 (1995)
7. Navon, D.: Forest before the trees: the precedence of global features in visual perception. Cognitive Psychology 9, 353–383 (1977)
8. Biederman, I.: On the semantics of a glance at a scene. In: Kubovy, M., Pomerantz, J. (eds.) Perceptual organization, pp. 213–253. Erlbaum (1981)

The Personality-Enabled Architecture for Cognition (PAC)

Stephen Read[1], Lynn Miller[2], Anna Kostygina[2], Gurveen Chopra[1],
John L. Christensen[1], Charisse Corsbie-Massay[1], Wayne Zachary[3],
Jean-Christophe LeMentec[3], Vassil Iordanov[3], and Andrew Rosoff[3]

[1] Department of Psychology, University of Southern California,
Los Angeles, CA 90089, USA
{read,gchopra,jlchrist,corsbiem}@usc.edu
[2] Annenberg School for Communication, University of Southern California,
Los Angeles, CA 90089, USA
{lmiller,kostygin}@usc.edu
[3] CHI Systems, Inc., Suite 300, 1035 Virginia Drive, Ft. Washington, PA 19034, USA
{wzachary,jclementec,viordanov,arosoff}@chisystems.com

The Personality-enabled Architecture for Cognition (PAC) is a new modeling architecture designed to create Intelligent Virtual Agents (IVAs) with specific personality traits. PAC integrates theory and empirical data from personality psychology, social psychology, cognitive science, and neuroscience to build a model of personality that is based on fundamental underlying human motivational systems.

In PAC, motives are controlled through a hierarchy of motivational systems, with broad approach (BAS) and avoidance (BIS) systems influencing more specific motives. Individual agents differ in parameters for broad Approach, Avoidance, and Disinhibition/ Constraint systems, as well as differing in baseline activations for specific motives. The resulting motive dynamics give rise to persistent individual behavioral tendencies: Agents varying in specific personalities result.

Recent work in personality has led to the Big Five: Neuroticism, Extraversion, Openness to Experience, Agreeableness, and Conscientiousness (McCrae & John, 1992). However, this work offers little insight into the internal processes that give us personality.

Two lines of research helped us fill this gap. First, Read and Miller (1989; Miller & Read, 1991) identified cognitive constructs underlying personality, noting that traits could be represented as configurations of motives, plans and beliefs, tying the Big Five to motives. Second, recent neuroscience findings (Clark & Watson, 1999; Depue, 1996; Pickering & Gray, 1999), suggest that the motives central to personality are organized into two levels; specific (*level one*) emotional/motivational systems and broader, overarching (*level two*) motivational systems. *Level one emotional /motivational systems* handle people's major adaptive challenges, such as social bonding, or self-protection.

At a more general level are *level two overarching motivational systems* – a Behavioral *Approach* System (BAS), which governs sensitivity to reward, and a Behavioral *Inhibition* System (BIS), which governs sensitivity to punishment and *avoidance* of threatening stimuli (Depue, 1996; Gray, 1987). There is evidence that these two systems provide a biological basis for two dimensions of personality: Extroversion and Neuroticism.

A. Paiva, R. Prada, and R.W. Picard (Eds.): ACII 2007, LNCS 4738, pp. 735–736, 2007.
© Springer-Verlag Berlin Heidelberg 2007

A third system, the Disinhibition/ Constraint system (DCS) provides a more general level (*level three*) of inhibitory control for the other systems (Watson & Clark, 1993). Inhibition enforces selectivity among motives by enhancing differential activation, governing the extent to which the system is motive-focused versus situationally reactive.

Motive activations are influenced by situational factors, by innate individual differences in baseline motive activations, and by overall sensitivities of the BIS and BAS. And, the entire activity of the system is further focused (or defocused) by the DCS.

Knowledge is represented in a set of story structures that are used both to generate behavior and to interpret behavior of others. The general representation of a story is as a collection of Plot Units, inspired by Lehnert (1981), which capture pieces of the story.

The personality mechanism controls the process by which traits are exhibited. The Motive Interpreter calculates the motive activations for each motive as each Action is processed during the story. It operates on three types of data: (1) *motive implications* from the current action structure –values between 0 and 1 indicating the relevance of an action to a motive, (2) individual motive *baseline activations* representing the tendency of the individual to pursue that motive and (3) *sensitivity levels* for the BIS, BAS, and DCS.

For each motive, the motive interpreter calculates its level of activation R using:

$$R = 1 - \frac{1}{1 + \gamma\left[I + S - D \, v \, C\right]_+}$$

Where: $[x]_+ = x$ if $x > 0$ and $[x]_+ = 0$ if $x <= 0$; I is the motive implication as provided by the current action structure, S is the individual baseline for this motive, γ is the gain for either the BIS or BAS depending on the type of motive. This formula adjusts the activation levels to meet the opportunities afforded in the current Action Structure.

More extensive discussion of PAC is in Zachary et al (2005b) and Read, et al., (2006), where we demonstrated that PAC-based IVAs in military settings would generate a range of plausible behavior simply based on their underlying personalities. Here we tested PAC in a more complex and realistic social situation, a "pick up" scenario in a bar.

Based on previous research we developed a list of dating-related behaviors that might be observed in a bar setting and organized them into a narrative graph structure. We then identified a set of motives (e.g., Achieve Physical/Sexual Intimacy, Achieve Social Interaction, Avoid Physical Harm) judged to be central to the dating scenario, and rated each action for the extent to which it either inhibited or facilitated each of the woman's motives. In simulations we showed that manipulating the BIS and BAS parameters, as well as the chronic baseline activation for individual motives, yielded individual differences in behavior. For example, when the BIS parameter was low and the BAS high, the woman was more likely to engage in approach behaviors, for example kissing the man and going home with him. In contrast, when BIS was high and BAS low, the woman was more likely to avoid risks; she refused to dance and refused to kiss the man.

These simulations demonstrate that PAC can be used to create agents with different personality characteristics, who make different choices as a function of differences in their underlying motivational system. This and other work we have done shows that it is possible to model human personality in terms of underlying motivational systems.

Rules of Emotions: A Linguistic Interpretation of an Emotion Model for Affect Sensing from Texts

Mostafa Al Masum Shaikh[1], Helmut Prendinger[2], and Ishizuka Mitsuru[1]

[1] Department of Information and Communication Engineering, University of Tokyo,
7-3-1 Hongo, Bunkyo-ku, 113-8656 Tokyo, Japan
mostafa@mi.ci.i.u-tokyo.ac.jp, ishizuka@i.u-tokyo.ac.jp
[2] Digital Contents and Media Sciences Research Division, National Institute of Informatics,
2-1-2 Hitotsubashi, Chiyoda-ku, 101-8430 Tokyo, Japan
helmut@nii.ac.jp

Abstract. This paper aims to interpret the cognitive theory of emotions known as the OCC emotion model from the computational linguistic standpoint. Since the OCC emotions are associated with several cognitive variables, in this paper we explain how the values could be assigned to those by analyzing and processing natural language components.

1 Characterization of the OCC Emotions

There are two kinds of variables, namely, emotion inducing variables (event, agent and object based) and emotion intensity variables. The event-based variables are usually calculated with respect to the event which is usually a verb-object pair found in the sentence. For example, the sentence, *John bought Mary an ice-cream*, gives an event as (buy, ice-cream).

The OCC emotion model specifies 22 emotion types and 2 cognitive states. The cognitive and appraisal structure of the OCC emotion types can be characterized by some rules interplaying with several variables. For example, literal definitions of "Happy-for" and "Fear" emotion are respectively, "Pleased about an event Desirable for a Liked agent" and "Displeased about Negative Prospect of an Undesirable Unconfirmed event".

2 Assigning Values to the Variables

The values for the variables self_presumption (sp) and self_reaction (sr) are set "Desirable" or "Undesirable", and "Pleased" or "Displeased" towards an event if the valence of that event is positive or negative, respectively. In the example above, the event *"buy ice-cream"* gets a positive valence (+8.433), and hence the values for sp and sr for this event are "Desirable" and "Pleased", respectively. But, for the sentence *"A terrorist escaped from the Jail"* the value for other_presumption (op) for the event *"escape jail"* is presumably "Desirable" for the agent *"terrorist"* but it is usually "Undesirable" and "Displeased" for sp and sr, respectively. Hence, the value for op is set "Undesirable" if an event of negative or positive valence is associated with an agent/object having positive (e.g., *the police was sacked*) or negative (e.g., *the*

A. Paiva, R. Prada, and R.W. Picard (Eds.): ACII 2007, LNCS 4738, pp. 737–738, 2007.
© Springer-Verlag Berlin Heidelberg 2007

criminal was taken to trial) valence respectively. The value for cognitive_strength (*cs*) indicates how closely the program considers selfness. This value is set as "Self" if the agent described in the text is a first person (i.e., *I or We*); otherwise it is set as "Other". If the tense of the verb is present or future, the value for status (*stat*) is set as "Unconfirmed" (e.g., *I am trying to solve it.*); and if it is past or modal without a negation, *stat* is set "Confirmed" (e.g., *I succeeded.*), but if with a negation, *stat* is set "Disconfirmed" (e.g., *I did not succeed.*). If the valence of the agent/object is positive, "Like" is set for *af* and *of* variables. The value for self_appraisal (*sa*) is set "Praiseworthy" if a positive value or zero is assigned for the event; otherwise "Blameworthy" is set. The value of object_appealing (*oa*) indicates whether an object is "Attractive" or "Unattractive". "Attractive" is set if the object has a positive valence with a familiarity score higher than a threshold value. The familiarity score is obtained from the ConceptNet by calculating the percentage of nodes (out of 300000 concept-nodes) linking the given object/concept. For example, the familiarity score for "restaurant" is 0.4872%. The value for valenced_reaction (*vr*) is obtained from the SenseNet's valence analysis. We consider *vr* to be "True" if the sentiment-valence become above than 4 or less than -4. The value for intensity variable event_deservingness (*ed*) is "High" for an event having positive valence or "Low" for negative one. If an action is qualified with an adverb (e.g., *He worked very hard.*) or target object qualified with an adjective (e.g., *I am looking for a quiet place.*) without a negation the value for effort_of_action (*eoa*) is set "Obvious". The variable expected_deviation (*edev*) indicates the difference between the event and its actor. For example, in the sentence *"The police caught the criminal finally."*, the actor *"police"* and the event *"catch criminal"* don't deviate because the action is presumably expected by the actor. We set the value for *edev* as "Low" if ConceptNet returns any semantic relationship between the actor and event. The values "Common" or "Uncommon" are set for event_familiarity (*ef*) according to the familiarity score obtained from ConceptNet for the event.

For example, the sentence *"I suddenly got to know that my paper won the best paper award."*, may output the following sets of emotions: {Joy, Satisfaction, Surprise, Pride, Gratification}. In the example the event, *"win award"* and object *"best paper award"* set the values for *cs* to "Self", *of* to "Like", *sr* to "Pleased", *sp* to "Desirable", *pros* to "Positive", *stat* to "Confirmed", *unexp* to true (because of token 'suddenly') and *vr* to "True". In order to reduce the number of emotions we can consider the intensity variables and thus we can output {Satisfaction, Surprise, Pride} for this example sentence because "Joy" doesn't have any intensity variable, but on the contrary the intensity variables *ed* and *edev* are set to "High".

Reference

1. Ortony, A., Clore, G.L., Collins, A.: The Cognitive Structure of Emotions. Cambridge University Press, Cambridge (1988)

The Role of Internal States in the Emergence of Motivation and Preference: A Robotics Approach

Carlos Herrera, Alberto Montebelli, and Tom Ziemke

University of Skövde, School of Humanities and Informatics, 54128 Skövde, Sweden
{carlos.herrera,alberto.montebelli,tom.ziemke}@his.se

In order to explain and model emotion we need to attend to the role internal states play in the generation of behavior. We argue that motivational and perceptual roles emerge from the dynamical interaction between physiological processes, sensory-motor processes and the environment. We investigate two aspects inherent to emotion appraisal and response which rely on physiological process: the ability to categorize relations with the environment and to modulate response generating different action tendencies.

The motivational character is explained because physiological internal states have intrinsic meaning for an agent's well being – an embodied system, natural or artificial, proper functioning will depend on the state of its body. "Homeostasis" refers to variables essential for the system that need to remain within certain limits for the organism to function and survive [1]. An adaptive agent must incorporate mechanisms that ensure deviations from that viability zone are balanced during adaptive interaction, thus producing emergent motivations.

Coupling with the environment implies that for an agent there is a need, not only to balance its internal states, but also to balance its relationship with the environment – maintaining internal homeostasis can only be possible given a balanced relationship with the environment. Internal states can therefore be signals of great significance for the appraisal of environmental relations. *Embodied appraisal* theory argues that internal states can be an essential factor in a control architecture to realize environmental factors [2].

Changes in the physiological substrate modulate behavior and ongoing relationships to the environment. Such changes can be considered control parameters of agent-environment relations – we interpret the emotion theory term *action tendency* to refer to changes in the attractor space. The integration of these motivational, perceptual and modulatory roles of internal states in an autonomous system allows for the emergence of emotion. The aim of the experimental section is not to produce a model of emotion, but to provide a simple robotic implementation that demonstrates these roles.

Consider a robot which needs to maintain acceptable levels of energy by periodically returning to a recharging station. The station is marked with a light, but there are other lights in the environment which do not mark a station. Energy levels decrease linearly, and are required for the functioning of the system – they are homeostatic variables and thus energy maintenance is a constant motivation. Categorization and preference of a light depends on current battery levels – they can be representative of relational features. Response is generated within a basin of attraction that is modulated by internal states. We demonstrate that internal states can be part of a categorization task for a neural controller in which different behaviors are realized through modulatory effects of internal states (related to parametric bias modulation [3]).

A. Paiva, R. Prada, and R.W. Picard (Eds.): ACII 2007, LNCS 4738, pp. 739–740, 2007.
© Springer-Verlag Berlin Heidelberg 2007

We evolved Khepera robots controlled by a feedforward network biased by current energy levels to exhibit such behavior (fig 1). An analysis of behavioral attractor dynamics shows how internal states can modulate behavior in a coupled system and give rise to motivation and preference. The method is to feed the previous controller with discrete, steady levels of energy. This allows us to identify different behavioral attractors, based on general morphology and spectral characteristics (for details see [4]).

A. Robots that are motivated to seek light and can disambiguate lights that mark energy source from other lights.
B. Robots that are motivated to seek light but cannot disambiguate.
C. Robots that are not motivated to seek light.

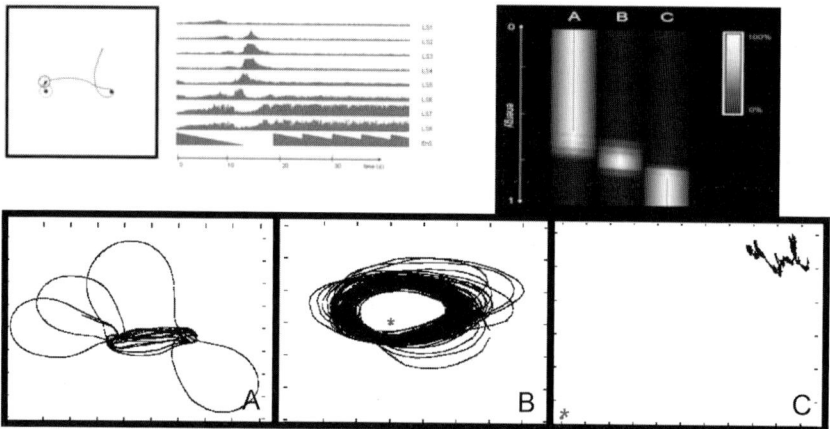

Fig. 1. Top left: Interactive behavior. Top right: Relative frequency of behavioral attractors for different levels of energy. Bottom: Examples of spatial trajectories for three behavioral groups.

Acknowledgement. Work supported by an EU grant to the project *"Integrating Cognition, Emotion and Autonomy"* (ICEA, IST-027819, www.iceaproject.eu).

References

1. Ashby, W.: Design for a Brain: The Origin of Adaptive Behavior. Chapman & Hall, Sydney, Australia (1960)
2. Prinz, J.: Embodied Emotions, in Thinking about Feeling. Contemporary Philosophers on the Emotions, 44–59 (2004)
3. Ito, M., Tani, J.: On-line Imitative Interaction with a Humanoid Robot Using a Dynamic Neural Network Model of a Mirror System. Adaptive Behavior 12(2), 93 (2004)
4. Montebelli, A., Herrera, C., Ziemke, T.: An analysis of behavioral attractor dynamics. In: Proceedings of ECAL'07 (in press)

Feature Combination for Better Differentiating Anger from Neutral in Mandarin Emotional Speech

Tsang-Long Pao[1], Yu-Te Chen[1], Jun-Heng Yeh[1], Yun-Maw Cheng[1],
and Charles S. Chien[2]

[1] Department of Computer Science and Engineering, Tatung University
[2] School of Management and Development, Feng Chia University
{tlpao,kevin}@ttu.edu.tw, {d8906005,d9306002}@ms2.ttu.edu.tw,
scchien@fcu.edu.tw

Extended Abstract

Just as written language is a sequence of elementary alphabet, speech is a sequence of elementary acoustic symbols. Speech signals convey more than spoken words. The additional information conveyed in speech includes gender information, age, accent, speaker's identity, health, prosody and emotion [1].

Affective computing, which is currently a very attractive research topic, aims at the automatic recognition and synthesis of emotions in speech, facial expressions, or any other biological signals [2]. Recently acoustic investigation of emotions expressed in speech has gained increased attention partly due to the potential value of emotion recognition for spoken dialogue management [3-4]. Imagine for example a call-center system that can detect complain or anger due to unsatisfied services about user's requests, could deal it smoothly by transferring the user to human operator. However, in order to reach such a level of performance we need to extract a reliable acoustic feature set that is largely immune to inter- and intra-speaker variability in emotion expression. Within the field of affective computing, this paper addresses how far we can go to use feature combination (FC) to concatenate different features to improve the accuracy of differentiating anger from neutral emotion in Mandarin speech.

We selected the pitch, log energy, formants, linear predictive coefficients (LPC), linear prediction cepstral coefficients (LPCC), mel-frequency cepstral coefficients (MFCC), log frequency power coefficients (LFPC), perceptual linear prediction (PLP), relative spectral PLP (Rasta-PLP), jitter and shimmer as the base features. We also added velocity and acceleration information for pitch and MFCCs, respectively, to take the speaking rate into account and model the dynamics of the corresponding temporal change of pitch and spectrum.

Feature combination is a well-known technique [5]. During the feature extraction of speech recognition system, we typically find that each feature type has particular circumstances in which it excels, and this has motivated our investigations for combining separate feature streams into a single emotional speech recognition system. However, it is forbiddingly time consuming to perform exhaustive search for the subset of features that give best classification. Due to the highly redundant information in the concatenated feature vector, a forward feature selection (FFS) or backward feature selection (BFS) should be carried out to extract only the most representative features, thereby orthogonalizing the feature vector and reducing its dimensionality.

A. Paiva, R. Prada, and R.W. Picard (Eds.): ACII 2007, LNCS 4738, pp. 741–742, 2007.
© Springer-Verlag Berlin Heidelberg 2007

The used corpus in this paper is constructed by MIR lab at National Tsing Hua University in Taiwan. They invite one female to portray two emotions, including anger and neutral. Finally, they obtained 2000 utterances that were recorded in 16-bit PCM with a sampling frequency of 16k Hz including 1000 angry and 1000 neutral utterances.

The Mandarin emotion recognition system was implemented using "MATLAB" software run under a desktop PC platform. The correct recognition rate was evaluated using leave-one-out (LOO) cross-validation which is K-fold cross validation taken to its logical extreme, with K equal to the number of data points.

The task of the classifier component proper of a full system is to use the feature vector provided by the feature extractor to assign the object to a category. To recognize emotions in speech we tried the following approaches: linear discriminant analysis (LDA), support vector machine (SVM), and back-propagation neutral network (BPNN), as they had been applied successfully in previous researches and achieved high accuracy [6-7].

The experimental results show that Rasta-PLP is the most important feature in LDA and BPNN classifiers and accMFCC is the most important one in SVM classifier. The velMFCC or accMFCC that model the dynamics of the corresponding temporal change spectrum can achieve better accuracy than MFCC. Jitter is the most irrelevant feature among these classifiers. Contrary to [6], the pitch and energy were not shown to play a major role in this paper. By Adopting feature selection and combination, the recognition rates can improve 2.1%, 7.8% and 20.6%, respectively. The best accuracy of differentiating anger from neutral can be achieved 99.10% by using accMFCC, LFPC, LPC, PLP, and RASTA-PLP feature streams and the support vector machine classifier. Although BPNN achieved the lowest recognition rate among all classifiers, it benefited most by feature combination in our system.

References

1. Rabiner, L.R., Juang, B.H.: Fundamentals of Speech Recognition. Prentice-Hall, Englewood Cliffs, NJ (1993)
2. Picard, R.W.: Affective Computing. MIT Press, Redmond, Washington (1997)
3. Lee, C.M., Narayanan, S.: Towards detecting emotion in spoken dialogs. IEEE Trans. on Speech & Audio Processing (in press)
4. Cowie, R., Douglas-Cowie, E., Tsapatsoulis, N., Votsis, G., Kollias, S.: Emotion Recognition in Human-Computer Interactions. IEEE Sig. Proc. Mag. 18, 32–80 (2001)
5. Ellis, D.: Stream combination before and/or after the acoustic model. In: Proc. of the Int. Conf. on Acoustics, Speech, and Signal Processing (2000)
6. Kwon, O.W., Chan, K., Hao, J., Lee, T.W.: Emotion Recognition by Speech Signals. In: Proceedings of EUROSPEECH, pp. 125–128 (2003)
7. Bhatti, M.W., Wang, Y., Guan, L.: A Neural Network Approach for Human Emotion Recognition in Speech. In: Proceedings of the 2004 International Symposium, vol. 2, pp. 1184–1811 (2004)

Affect-Insensitive Speaker Recognition by Feature Variety Training

Dongdong Li and Yingchun Yang[*]

Department of Computer Science and Technology,
Zhejiang University, Hangzhou, P.R. China, 310027
{lidd,yyc}@zju.edu.cn

A great deal of inner variabilities such as emotion and stress are largely missing from traditional speaker recognition system. The direct result is that the recognition system is easily disturbed when the enrollment and the authentication are made under different emotional state. Reynolds [1] proposed a new normalization technique called feature mapping. This technique achieved big successes in channel robust speaker verification. We extend the mapping idea to develop a feature variety training approach for affective-insensitive speaker recognition.

The feature variety training algorithm could be implemented by two processes: model parameters shift and feature transformation. First, the transformations are learned by examining how model parameters shift after MAP adaptation which builds the emotional depended models from the background one. Then different emotional types of generated features are obtained for speaker model building.

Model parameters shift: An emotional independent background model (UBM) is trained using all available emotional data including the neutral speech. Next, emotional specific models (EDM) are derived by MAP adaptation with emotional specific data that is also used to generate the UBM. All models are derived with a common background, which lead to a correspondence between Gaussian components in the models. Let $E_i = [e_{i1}, e_{i2}, ..., e_{iN}]$ be the ith type of specific affective feature used to construct EDMi, where N is the frame number of training data E_i. The top-1 decode Gaussian j_i for the ith type of emotional speech is determined by

$$j_i = \arg\max_{1 \le k \le M} \sum_{n=1}^{N} 1_k^{EDM_i}(e_{in}) = \arg\max_{1 \le k \le M} \sum_{n=1}^{N} \omega_k^{EDM_i} p_k^{EDM_i}(e_{in}) \tag{1}$$

where $p_k^{EDM_i}(e_{in}) = N(\mu_k^{EDM_i}, \sigma_k^{EDM_i})$ is the kth mixture component of the GMM EDM_i and M is the orders of the Gaussian mixture model.

Feature transformation: Let $\mu_{j_i}^{EDM_i}$ and $\sigma_{j_i}^{EDM_i}$ be the mean and the standard deviation of the top-1 order with the maximal likelihood in the EDMi. Given enrollment speech x, the transformed feature of the ith type of emotional space y_i, is then given by

$$y_i = FT_i(x) = (x - \mu_{j_i}^{UBM}) * \sigma_{j_i}^{EDM_i} / \sigma_{j_i}^{UBM} + \mu_{j_i}^{EDM_i} \tag{2}$$

---

[*] Corresponding author.

A. Paiva, R. Prada, and R.W. Picard (Eds.): ACII 2007, LNCS 4738, pp. 743–744, 2007.

where $\mu_{j_i}^{UBM}$ and $\sigma_{j_i}^{UBM}$ is the mean and the standard deviation of the corresponding order j in the UBM. The ith type of emotional speaker model is trained with the generated feature y_i.

The enrollment speech is used to generate the target emotion speech of all types with the feature transformation function. The speaker models (SM) of different emotional types are established. For the authentification process, the log likelihood of the test (identified or verified) utterance is computed against the most likely type of emotional speaker model (SM). The maximum likelihood rule is applied.

The experiments are conducted with the Mandarin Affective Speech Corpus (MASC) [2]. Two protocols are defined to evaluate the performance of speaker authentication. In Protocol I, both the SM training and the pre-build model (like the UBM and the EDM) training data are drawn from the same speaker sets. For Protocol II, the learned model parameters are totally separated from the test set of the system. In each strategy, the Hamming windows size is 32 ms. The feature vector is composed by 16 dimensional mel-cepstral and its Delta. The silence and unvoiced segments are discarded based on an energy threshold. The models are 1024 order Gaussian Mixture Models. ALIZE [3] is used as the interface in our source code. Table 1 reports the identification rate (IR) of the speaker authentication system observed over different types of affective speech compared with the GMM-UBM in two protocols.

Table 1. The identification rate of the system(%)

IR	GMM-UBM		Feature Variety Training	
	Protocol I	Protocol II	Protocol I	Protocol II
Neutral	0.9243	0.9483	0.9450	0.9712
Anger	0.3004	0.3738	0.3195	0.3933
Elation	0.3265	0.4067	0.3357	0.4300
Panic	0.2599	0.3567	0.2710	0.3733
Sadness	0.5114	0.6029	0.5331	0.6238

It is significant to note that similar profits of performance in protocol I and protocol II are achieved compared the baseline and feature variety training strategy, while in the second protocol the training and test data of the speakers is totally separated from the UBM and EDM training data. The encouraging result demonstrates that feature variety training could be learned in advance from the prior affective speech irrelevant to the registered users by the proposed technique.

Acknowledgments. This work is supported by NSFC_60525202/60533040, 863 Program_2006AA01Z136, PCSIRT0652, ZPNSF_Y106705, NCET-04-0545.

References

1. Reynolds, D.A.: Channel robust speaker verification via feature mapping. ICASSP'03 2, 53–56 (2003)
2. Wu, T., Yang, Y.C., Wu, Z.H., Li, D.D., MASC,: A Speech Corpus in Mandarin for Emotion Analysis and Affective Speaker Recognition, The IEEE Odyssey, pp. 1–59 (2006)
3. Bonastre, J.F., Wils, F., Meignier, S.: ALIZE, a free toolkit for speaker recognition, IEEE International Conference on Acoustics, Speech, and Signal Processing. In (ICASSP '05), March 18-23, vol. 1, pp. 737–740 (2005)

Expressing Complex Mental States Through Facial Expressions

Xueni Pan[1], Marco Gillies[1], Tevfik Metin Sezgin[2], and Celine Loscos[1,3]

[1] Department of Computer Science, University College London, London, UK
s.pan@cs.ucl.ac.uk
[2] Department of Computer Science, Cambridge University, Cambridge, UK
[3] Departament d'Informtica i Matemtica Aplicada, Universitat de Girona, Spain

A face is capable of producing about twenty thousand different facial expressions [2]. Many researchers on Virtual Characters have selected a limited set of emotional facial expressions and defined them as basic emotions, which are universally recognized facial expressions. These basic emotions have been well studied since 1969 and employed in many applications [3]. However, real life communication usually entails more complicated emotions. For instance, communicative emotions like "convinced", "persuaded" and "bored" are difficult to describe adequately with basic emotions. Our daily face-to-face interaction is already accompanied by more complex mental states, so an empathic animation system should support them. Compared to basic emotions, complex mental states are harder to model because they require knowledge of temporal changes in facial displays and head movements as opposed to a static snapshot of the facial expression. We address this by building animation models for complex emotions based on video clips of professional actors displaying these emotions.

The first step of our work is to extract the facial and head movements from video clips. We have adopted the recognition framework proposed by [4] to recognize head and facial displays, which allows facial displays to be based on not just the current facial action, but also on a pre-determined number of previous facial actions. Using the framework in [4], a commercial face tracker is used to locate and track 24 landmarks on the face. These are then mapped into facial actions and displays using Hidden Markov Models (HMMs) trained on video clips from the Mind Reading DVD compiled by researchers at the University of Cambridge Psychology Department [1].

The likelihoods of the facial displays, computed by the HMMs from the input video sequences, are used to drive the animation of our virtual characters. Six head action displays(*head tilt, head turn, head forward, head backward, head shake* and *head nod*) and three three facial displays (*lip pull, lip pucker,* and *brow raised*) are extracted for every frame and applied on the Virtual Character. The first four of the HMM outputs for head movement were translated directly into rotation about a single axis whereas *head shake* and *head nod* were translated into periodic animations. The facial displays are applied on the Virtual Characters as morph targets.

As described above complex mental states differ from basic emotions in that they cannot be effectively recognized from static facial expressions, only from

A. Paiva, R. Prada, and R.W. Picard (Eds.): ACII 2007, LNCS 4738, pp. 745–746, 2007.

Fig. 1. Animation result of the emotion *interest*

facial movements over time. This implies that we must use different animation techniques, ones based on time series rather than static methods such as morph targets or principal component analysis. The approach we take in this paper is to base our animations on a corpus of capture facial motion data using a data structure called a motion graph[5]. A motion graph enables new animations to be generated from a corpus of animation data by resequencing animation clips in different orders. It is a directed graph structure in which edges are motion clips and nodes are possible transition points between clips. These transition points are chosen so that they ensure smooth transitions between different clips. New animations are created by walking the graph. We use a dynamic programming method to calculate a value function over edges which is used to generate graph walks that give a good representation of the desired mental state.

Six communicative complex mental states were chosen based on their importance in giving feedback during conversations: *agreement, disagreement, concentration, interest, thinking* and *uncertainty.* We used eighteen video clips, three for each emotion, from the Mind Reading database. We first extracted the facial movements for each video clip, then applied those on the Virtual Character as separated animations. From the eighteen animations we then created a motion graph labeled with the six emotions. Finally, from the motion graph, we constructed animations for each of the six complex emotions by walking the graph. Figure 1 is an example of our final results of the emotion *interest.*

References

1. Baron-Cohen, S., Golan, O., Wheelwright, S., Hill, J.: Mind-reading: The interactive guide to emotions (January 2004)
2. Birdwhistell, R.L.: Kinesics and context: essays on body motion communication. Allen Lane The Penguin Press (1971)
3. The Duy Bui. Creating Emotions And Facial Expressions For Embodied Agents. PhD thesis (2004)
4. el Kaliouby, R., Robinson, P.: Real-time inference of complex mental states from facial expressions and head gestures. Real-time vision for HCI, 181–200 (2005)
5. Kovar, L., Gleicher, M., Pighin, F.: Motion graphs. ACM Transactions on Graphics 21(3), 473–482 (2002)

Metaphor and Affect Detection in an ICA

T.H. Rumbell, C.J. Smith, J.A. Barnden, M.G. Lee, S.R. Glasbey,
and A.M. Wallington

School of Computer Science, University of Birmingham, Birmingham, B152TT, UK
A.M.Wallington@cs.bham.ac.uk

Abstract. We discuss an aspect of an affect-detection system used in edrama by intelligent conversational agents, namely affective interpretation of limited sorts of metaphorical utterance. We discuss how these metaphorical utterances are recognized and how they are analysed and their affective content determined.

1 Introduction

In [1], we described a system for text-based, on-line, improvisational, role-playing (*e-Drama*) containing an ICA, EMMA (EMotion, Metaphor and Affect), that plays a minor character and uses NLP techniques to extract affect (i.e. emotions/moods e.g. embarrassment, hostility and evaluations of goodness, importance, etc) from the other characters' utterances in order to make largely content-free, but affectively sensitive, responses Although metaphor was noted as major conveyer of affect in edrama and generally (see [2]), analysing it for affect was not fully investigated nor implemented. We now report a start, with the implementation of certain types of metaphor analysis.

2 Processing Metaphor for Affect

Metaphor has been largely ignored by ICA research and there are few computational treatments elsewhere (c.f. [3]). We describe here the processing of two limited but important types of metaphorical phenomena found in edrama transcripts.

1) Casting someone as either: a special type of human without claiming literal truth (e.g. 'you baby,' 'you freak'); or a monster, mythical or supernatural creature, etc. (e.g 'Lisa is an angel'); or an animal. Note, the latter often conveys affect -negative or positive- but interestingly the young form ('piglet', 'pup' etc.) may be affectionate, even when the adult form is negative. EMMA deals with cases with a conventional metaphorical sense but also with those without one, for one might still determine a particular affective sense, e.g. from the young form, or size. The latter is because of:

2) The metaphorical use of size adjectives. 'A little X' often conveys affective qualities of X such as unimportance and contemptibility, but may convey affection, even if the X is usually negative as in 'little devils' for children. 'Big X' can convey the importance of X ('big event') or intensity of X-ness ('big bully'). See [4].

Our approach splits processing into two: (A) recognition of potential metaphors and (B) analysis of recognised elements to determine affect. The basis for (A) is a list of phrases and syntactic structures, observed in edrama scripts and elsewhere, which

A. Paiva, R. Prada, and R.W. Picard (Eds.): ACII 2007, LNCS 4738, pp. 747–748, 2007.

often include metaphors or have metaphors as collocates. We currently focus on three syntactic structures, 'X is/are a Y', 'You Y' and 'like [a] Y' and on the lexical strings, 'a bit of a', 'such a' and 'look[s] like'. These structures/phrases are found by parsing the actors' utterances for Grammatical Relations (GR) using the RASP parser.

Once the (X and) Y nouns have been recognised, WordNet is used to analyse them, checking for example whether Y is a kind of animal. In simple cases (e.g. with 'cow') Y has an alternative sense (or synset) as an 'unpleasant person'. However, 'person' senses are not always found, in which case Y is still marked as a metaphor but the affect labelled 'positive or negative'. Further processing may determine which. We illustrate here the process with examples (1) 'Lisa is an angel' and (2) 'You piglet'.

1a. The metaphor detector recognises the 'X is a Y' signal, with the 'Y' as 'angel'.
1b. The metaphor analyser finds that 'angel' is a hyponym of 'supernatural being'.
1c. It finds that for another synset the word is a hyponym of 'person'.
1d. The hypernym tree of the 'person' synset also passes through 'good person' which expresses positive affect and the metaphor is labelled as positive.
1e. The metaphor is labelled as a supernatural being metaphor that is positive.
2a. The metaphor detector recognises the 'You Y' signal with 'Y' as 'piglet'.
2b. The metaphor analyser detects 'piglet' is a hyponym of 'animal'.
2c. 'Piglet' has no alternative synset with 'person' as a hypernym. So the analyser retrieves its gloss from WordNet.
2d. It finds 'young' in the gloss and retrieves all of the words that follow it. In this example the gloss is 'a young pig' so 'pig' is the only following word.
2e. The analysis process is repeated for each of the words captured from the gloss and the metaphor labelled with the appropriate polarity.
2f. This example would result in the metaphor being labelled as an animal metaphor which is negative but affectionate with the affection label having a higher numerical confidence weighting than the negative label.

Other analyses involve checking and comparing the hypernym trees of both X and Y.

Acknowledgments. Supported by EPSRC grant EP/C538943/1 and ESRC grant RES-328-25-0009.

References

1. Zhang, L., Barnden, J.A., Hendley, R.J., Wallington, A.M.: Exploitation in Affect Detection in Improvisational E-Drama. In: Gratch, J., Young, M., Aylett, R., Ballin, D., Olivier, P. (eds.) IVA 2006. LNCS (LNAI), vol. 4133, pp. 68–79. Springer, Heidelberg (2006)
2. Kövecses, Z.: Metaphor and Emotion: Language, Culture and Body in Human Feeling. Cambridge University Press, Cambridge (2000)
3. Barnden, J.A.: Artificial Intelligence, Figurative Language and Cognitive Linguistics. In: Kristiansen, G., et al. (eds.) Cognitive Linguistics: Current Applications and Future Perspectives, pp. 431–459. Mouton de Gruyter, Berlin (2006)
4. Sharoff, S.: How to Handle Lexical Semantics in SFL: A Corpus Study of Purposes for Using Size Adjectives. System & Corpus: Exploring Connections. Equinox, London (2006)

An Emotional Model for Synthetic Characters with Personality

Karim Sehaba, Nicolas Sabouret, and Vincent Corruble

Laboratoire d'Informatique de Paris 6
Université Pierre et Marie Curie University
104, Avenue du Président Kennedy, 75016 Paris, France
{Karim.Sehaba,Nicolas.Sabouret,Vincent.Corruble}@lip6.fr

1 Background

In recent years, emotional computing has found an important application domain in the field of interactive synthetic characters. Interesting examples of this domain are computer games, interface agents, human-robot interaction, etc. However, few systems in this area include a model of personality, although it plays an important role in differentiating agents and determining the way they experience emotions and the way they behave.

Some work explicitly take into account the personality of the characters. In [3], personality is viewed as a number of weights on different goals of agents. [1] uses formulas that determine how personality influences the way an agent experiences emotion. However, these papers do not focus on how personality influences the feeling and the expression of emotions at every step of the emotional process. In our work, we introduce an emotional model for synthetic characters that relies on a formal model of personality. We use studies from the field of psychology, regarding emotions, personality and the correlation between them in order to define a character able to express appropriate emotions in response to various situations.

Several personality models have been defined in psychology research. These models consist of a set of factors, where every factor is a specific property of the personality. Emotions have already been widely studied in psychology. Much research work, related to *cognitive appraisal theory*, proposes various criteria in order to distinguish emotions (see for example *OCC Model* [4]). However, the emotional process defined in these models is not complete [2], i.e. it does not specify how the personality factors influence the feeling of emotions. Moreover, links between emotions and their intensity, and the intensity thresholds corresponding to the activation of each emotion are not defined.

2 Proposed Model

We propose an emotional model based on an explicit representation of personality and emotions and the correlation between them. This correlation represents the influence of each personality factors on the sensitivity to emotion categories.

A. Paiva, R. Prada, and R.W. Picard (Eds.): ACII 2007, LNCS 4738, pp. 749–750, 2007.

The emotional process, that we have developed, lists steps that characters follow from the initial categorization of an event to the resulting emotional state. Thus, in the first stage, the character evaluates the event in order to define the emotion categories affected and their potentials. In the second stage, we calculate the influence of this emotional potential on the character emotions taking into account its personality. This emotional value will interact with the current emotional state of the character stored in the emotional memory. In this process, we also take into account the decay of emotions over time.

Formally, we represent the personality factors with a vector p of n dimension and the emotional state at time t by a vector $e(t)$ with m dimension. The influence of each personality factor $(p_i \in p)$ on the sensitivity of each emotional category $(e_j \in e)$ is represented by a function $f(p_i, e_j)$. Thus, a matrix M_{n*m} of functions is formed representing all influences of each personality factor on each emotional categories. With this matrix, we can calculate the influence on the character of the emotional potentials of the environmental stimuli.

We consider the decay of each emotion with a decreasing monotonous function whose pace depends on the personality and which tends towards the baseline emotion intensity of the character. The updating of the emotional state combines the influence of stimuli and the decay of previous emotions.

In order to validate our model, we have developed a tool for the simulation of emotional processes. We have created three characters with different personalities. Thereafter, we have submitted each one of these three characters to the same scenario. Our evaluation shows significative differences in emotional reactions according to each character personality.

3   Perspectives

We are currently working on the influence of the emotional state on the dialog and the decision-making process. It consists in generating behavior adapted to the situation and the character's emotional state.

References

1. Bui, D., Heylen, D., Poel, M., Nijholt, A.: ParleE: An Adaptive Plan Based Event Appraisal Model of Emotions. In: Jarke, M., Koehler, J., Lakemeyer, G. (eds.) KI 2002. LNCS (LNAI), vol. 2479, pp. 129–143. Springer, Heidelberg (2002)
2. El-Nasr, M.S., Yen, J., Ioerger, T.R.: FLAME: Fuzzy Logic Adaptive Model of Emotions. Autonomous Agents and Multi-Agent Systems 3(3), 219–257 (2000)
3. Rosis, F., Pelachaud, C., Poggi, I.: From Greta's mind to her face: modelling the dynamics of affective states in a conversational embodied agent. International Journal of Human-Computer Studies 59(1-2), 18–118 (2003)
4. Ortony, A., Clore, G.L., Collins, A.: The cognitive structure of emotions. Cambridge University Press, Cambridge (1988)

A Tool for Experimenting with Theories of Emotion in MultiAgent Systems
(Extended Abstract)

Maria R. Cravo[1] and Énio M. Pereira[2]

[1] Instituto Superior Técnico, Dep. Eng. Informática,
GIA Lisbon, Portugal
[2] Altitude Software, Portugal
mrcravo@gia.ist.utl.pt, enio.pereira@altitude.com

In order to synthetize affective states, computer systems use emotion theories from psychology, that provide guidelines for deciding what kind of emotion, and with what intensity, should be elicited in a given situation. According to most theories, the emotions of an agent depend on the subjective appraisal of situations. While they provide essential knowledge for the generation of synthetic emotions, these theories do not specify all aspects necessary for the design of computational systems that implement them. So, when designing computational agents that "experience" affective states, computer scientists have a long way to go, and many decisions to make, to produce the information necessary to theories of emotion. When all these difficulties are overcome, still a lot of experimenting is necessary to make adjustments to the formulas and algorithms used.

We present an implemented system for experimenting with emotion theories.[1] The system simulates the evolution of a virtual world populated with agents. As the agents evolve in the world, they "experience" affective states, sometimes towards other agents. Several aspects, including the underlying emotion theory, may be easily changed, so as to allow for extensive experimentation.

Each agent has its particular goals, abilities, personality, etc. As long as it has goals, it selects one of these goals, makes a plan to achieve it, and tries to execute that plan. Agents receive percepts about their environment, incorporate those percepts in their beliefs, decide what to do next, and eventually act upon their environment.

For the generation of emotions, several steps are needed: 1) the generation of the appraisal information; 2) the generation of values for the appraisal variables; 3) the generation of emotions. We now briefly describe each of these steps.

To generate the appraisal information, the agent starts by determining what changed from the previous situation to the present one. Then, it determines how these changes affect its goals and current plan. We consider three ways in which the agent's goals may be affected: 1) a goal may become attained; 2) a previously attained goal, may become "unattained"; 3) a goal may become impossible to achieve. We consider two ways in which the agent's current plan may be affected:

---

[1] This work was partially supported by IDMEC (Institute of Mechanical Engineering - Intelligent Systems Center - Lisbon) and the EC project HUMAINE.

A. Paiva, R. Prada, and R.W. Picard (Eds.): ACII 2007, LNCS 4738, pp. 751–752, 2007.

some action(s) may become unnecessary, and/or some other action(s) may have to be added to the plan.

The appraisal information just described is then used to determine the values for the appropriate appraisal variables. To illustrate the system we use the OCC theory [1]. Due to lack of space, we only briefly describe the determination of the value of *desirability*. Nonzero values of this variable may elicit the emotions of joy and distress. The value of this variable is the sum of the partial desirability of each of the goals and actions that were affected. Attained goals and unnecessary actions contribute with positive values of desirability, while unattained/impossible goals and necessary actions contribute with negative values. The absolute values depend on the importance of the affected goals, and on the cost of the actions.

Finally, we turn our attention to the determination of emotions from the values of the appraisal variables.[2] Each agent has, as part of its internal state, its emotional information. This information includes the agent's personality, which is set by the user, its history of emotions, and its mood. These last two items are updated by the system, each time the agent "experiences" an emotion. The underlying emotion theory is defined through a hierarchy of classes of emotions, in a XML file. The description of each class includes, among other things, the names of the appraisal variables that influence the potential, and the potential and threshold formulas. The formulas used may be specified in the file defining the structure of the emotions or, alternatively, in another XML file, as explained below. This is especially useful when the same formula is used for several purposes; It can be defined once in the file containing the formulas, given a name, and then this name can be used as many times as necessary.

To allow for easy experimentation, several formulas can also be specified in an XML file. There is a simple language that provides several operators to define formulas, e.g. `+`, `-`, `*`, `/`, `max`, `min`, `average`, `sum`, `if`. In addition, several useful parameters can be used in formulas. E.g., `mood` represents the mood of the agent whose emotions are being determined; `ClassVal` represents the valence (1 or -1) of the emotion whose potential is being computed; `DPot[i]` represents the decayed potential of the i-th emotion of the agent under consideration. The names of the personality traits defined in the personality XML file can also be used in formulas. For the system to work, the following formulas have to be specified: 1) the formula for the emotions' potentials; 2) the formula for the decay of emotions' potentials with time; 3) the formula used to update the mood of agents. As we have said before, the formulas used in the definition of the hierarchy of emotions, can either be defined in the file describing this hierarchy, or in the file describing the formulas.

Reference

1. Ortony, A., Clore, G., Collins, A.: The Cognitive Structure of Emotions. Cambridge University Press, Cambridge (1988)

---

[2] Our thanks to R. Santos and M. Nascimento for their contribution to this component.

Displaying Expression in Musical Performance by Means of a Mobile Robot

Birgitta Burger[1,2] and Roberto Bresin[1]

[1] KTH, CSC School of Computer Science and Communication,
Dept. of Speech Music and Hearing, Stockholm, Sweden
[2] University of Cologne, Dept. of Systematic Musicology, Germany

1 Introduction

In recent times several attempts have been made to give a robot or broader spoken a computer some kind of feelings in order to understand and model human capacities. The main idea of our work was the design of expressive robot movements for the display of emotional content embedded in the audio layer in both live and recorded music performance. Starting from results in studies on musicians' body in emotional expressive music performance (see [3]), we tried to map different movement cues (e.g. speed, fluency) to movements of a small mobile robot. The robot had constraints of sensors and motors, so the emotions were implemented taking into account only the main characteristics of musicians' movements. We implemented movements for the three emotions happiness, anger and sadness. Subjects were asked to judge in a perceptual test which emotional intentions were communicated by the movements.

2 The M[ε]X Robot and Its Emotional Behaviour

We used the Lego Mindstorms NXT System to build our robot called M[ε]X (short for **M**usical **EX**pression). Fig. 1 shows the final version of M[ε]X.

The implementation of the emotional behavior is based on literature on how emotion is communicated by acoustical cues [4], on how musicians communicate emotional intentions by body movements during performance [3], and on how emotional intention is expressed by shapes of 3-d objects [5].

The movements for *happiness* consisted of two interleaved circular structures: one big circle was interrupted by smaller circles (round shapes convey a positive emotion [5]).

Fig. 1. M[ε]X

The movements for *anger* were very fast, jerky, irregular, asymmetrical and unpredictable (jerky movements in music performance communicate anger [3]; sharp and spiky objects convey a negative emotion [5]).

The movements for *sadness* were very slow, smooth (i.e. neither jerky or irregular) and the amount of gestures was small.

A. Paiva, R. Prada, and R.W. Picard (Eds.): ACII 2007, LNCS 4738, pp. 753–754, 2007.

3   Experiments

We conducted two experiments, one in Stockholm, and another one in Cologne. The movement stimuli were presented with and without musical background that were conveying the same emotional intention. The aim was to investigate if a musical input supports the perception of the movements. For more information about the musical stimuli see [1]. The experiment was divided into 2 sections, section 1 containing only the movements of the robot, while in section 2 the movements were combined with the musical stimuli. In the first experiment 15 subjects were asked to rate each stimulus on the *happy, angry, sad, neutral* and *expressive* scales on a questionnaire. Each scale was divided into 7 steps (from *not ...* to *very ...*). The results of the first experiment show that the intended emotion happiness was better recognized when presented with music. When presented without music the subjects could not distinguish between happy and angry movements. The movements for displaying anger were not perceived as angry, independently from the musical input. Sad movements were perceived well both with and without music. 36 subjects took part to the second experiment. For happiness the same results as in Experiment 1 occurred: a better recognition in combination with music. When presented without music the subjects could not distinguish between *happy* and *angry* stimuli. The intended emotion anger was better recognized when presented without music. When presented with music the subjects rated the movements rather happy. *Sad* stimuli were again perceived well with and without music. (Detailed analysis of both experiments: [2]).

4   Discussion and Future Work

Different musical stimuli could be tested in further experiments – e.g. different melodies for each emotion. Further work could be done on the distinction between happiness and anger, since the subjects rated high on the *expressive* scale, but seemed to have problems distinguishing between *happiness* and *anger*. The experiment could be also repeated with another kind of robot. A robot capable to directly translate the emotion in the music into expressive movements instead of using predefined movements.

References

1. Bresin, R.: What is the color of that music performance? In: ICMC, pp. 367–370 (2005)
2. Burger, B.: Communication of Musical Expression from Mobile Robots to Humans. Master's Thesis (in preparation)
3. Dahl, S., Friberg, A.: Visual perception of expressiveness in musicians' body movements. In: Music Perception, vol. 24(5) (in press)
4. Friberg, A., Schoonderwaldt, E., Juslin, P.N.: CUEX: An algorithm for extracting expressive tone variables from audio recordings. In Acoustica united with Acta Acoustica. 93(3), 411–420 (2007)
5. Isbister, K., Höök, K., Sharp, M., Laaksolahti, J.: The Sensual Evaluation Instrument: Developing an Affective Evaluation Tool. In: CHI, pp. 1163–1172 (2006)

Gradient or Contours Cues? A Gating Experiment for the Timing of the Emotional Information

Nicolas Audibert and Véronique Aubergé

GIPSA Lab - Institut de la Communication Parlée - UMR 5216 CNRS/INPG/UJF/Stendhal,
Université Stendhal - 1180, av. Centrale - BP25 - 38040 Grenoble Cedex 9, France
{Nicolas.Audibert,Veronique.Auberge}@gipsa-lab.inpg.fr

Abstract. This work aims at measuring the anticipated perception of emotions on minimal linguistic units, to evaluate if the underlying cognitive processing is compatible with the hypothesis of gradient contours. Selected monosyllabic stimuli extracted from an expressive corpus and expressing anxiety, disappointment, disgust, disquiet, joy, resignation, sadness and satisfaction, were gradually presented to naïve judges in a gating experiment. Results strengthen the hypothesis of gradient processing by showing that identification along successive gates of most of expressions follow a linear pattern typical of a contour-like processing, while expressions of satisfaction present distinct gradient values that make possible an early identification of affective values.

Keywords: Expressive speech, prosody; morphology, contours, gradient cues.

A central question arises when modeling the morphology of vocal expressions of affects, which is to understand how these different cognitive affects processing (summarized by the push vs. pull effect in Scherer's model [8]) are implemented in the same acoustic material. In a previous study [2], we have showed that distinct fundamental frequency (F0) contour shapes appear with different emotional values. We hypothesize that, for involuntary as well as social affects, both processes are used together in a gradient contour processing, in which values and relative weights of those processes vary with the type of affect expressed and can be tuned according to different expressive strategies [3].

If one considers that a gradient processing is involved in the cognitive decoding of emotional expressions, an interesting question would be to determine to what extend this gradient processing makes possible an anticipated identification of emotion values, and the location of possible gradient cues. The gating paradigm [6], which consists in gradually presenting auditory stimuli cut according to fixed points called gates, was used for evaluating the amount of affective information carried by different parts of stimuli. 27 stimuli expressing anxiety, disappointment, disgust, disquiet, joy, resignation, sadness and satisfaction, as well as neutral expressions on the French monosyllabic utterances *jaune*, *rouge* and *vert*, extracted from the E-Wiz expressive corpus [1] and showing no other prosodic variation than emotional variation, were used to generate 162 gated stimuli filled with white noise. Emotional expressions were chosen as matching those used in a previous experiment [4]. Kohler [7] found in German different communicative values for the same stimuli according to the late, medial or late position of the F0 peak. Thirds of vowels were subsequently retained as

A. Paiva, R. Prada, and R.W. Picard (Eds.): ACII 2007, LNCS 4738, pp. 755–756, 2007.
© Springer-Verlag Berlin Heidelberg 2007

a base unit for the definition of gates. 6 gates were defined relatively to hand-labelled phoneme boundaries, from the first 3rd of the vowel to the end of the stimulus. The 162 generated stimuli were evaluated by 20 naïve judges in a closed-choice perception task. The stable identification point was defined for each judge*stimulus pair as the number of the gate from which one of the emotional labels of the correct cluster is chosen, without a change of answer in any of the following gates, except for expressions of sadness not significantly identified over chance and discarded from analysis. While patterns of identification along gates for all other expressions are quite linear with a correct identification rate at gate 1 below chance level, showing a progressive identification with no salient cues, the expressions of satisfaction show a different pattern, with a correct identification rate as high as 60.7% at gate 1.

Expressions of joy and satisfaction share the same F0 contour shapes, with a much larger F0 range for satisfaction. As affective information on expressions of joy and satisfaction was found to be mainly carried by F0 contours [4], these contours can therefore be considered as a reliable cue to the affective information presented at different gates. Comparative analysis of those contours show that gradient values of satisfaction are known from the 1st gate and can yield early identification of the expressed affect, while listeners have to wait until the contour shape of joy is known to discriminate it from other expressions. Since activation on the expressions of satisfaction vs. joy is clearly higher, our results support Bänziger and Scherer's [5] hypothesis that F0 level and range vary strongly with emotional activation. However their claim that F0 contours carry little information should be revisited: though the scope of this study remains limited due to the number of stimuli, most of the tested expressions appear as decoded using the contours shapes rather than gradient values.

References

1. Aubergé, V., Audibert, N., Rilliard, A.: E-Wiz: A Trapper Protocol for Hunting the Expressive Speech Corpora in Lab. In: Proceedings of the.4th International Conference on Language Resources and Evaluation (LREC), Lisbon, Portugal, pp. 179–182. Portugal (2004)
2. Aubergé, V., Audibert, N., Rilliard, A.: Acoustic morphology of expressive speech: What about contours? In: Proceedings of the 1st International Conference on Speech Prosody, Prosody, Nara, Japan, pp. 91–95 (2004)
3. Aubergé, V.: A gestalt morphology of prosody directed by functions: the example of a step by step model developed at ICP. In: Proceedings of the 1st International Conference on Speech Prosody, Aix-en-Provence, France, pp. 151–155 (2002)
4. Audibert, N., Aubergé, V., Rilliard, A.: The prosodic dimensions of emotion in speech: the relative weights of parameters. In: Proceeding of the 9th European Conference on Speech Communication and Technology (Interspeech), Lisbon, Portugal, pp. 525–528 (2005)
5. Bänziger, T., Scherer, K.R.: The role of intonation in emotional expressions. Speech Communication 46, 252–267 (2005)
6. Grosjean, F.: Spoken word recognition processes and the gating paradigm. Perception & Psychophysics. 28, 267–283 (1980)
7. Kohler, K.J.: Timing and Communicative Functions of Pitch Contours. Phonetica 62, 88–105 (2005)
8. Scherer, K.R.: Appraisal considered as a process of multi-level sequential checking. In: Scherer, K., Schorr, A., Johnstone, T. (eds.) Appraisal processes in emotion: Theory, Methods, Research, pp. 92–120. Oxford Univ. Press, Oxford (2001)

Exploring Manipulative Hand Movements During a Stressful Condition

Miguel Bruns Alonso, Michel Varkevisser, Paul Hekkert, and David V. Keyson

ID-StudioLab, Faculty of Industrial Design Engineering, TU Delft
Landbergstraat 15, 2628 CE Delft, The Netherlands
{m.bruns,m.varkevisser,p.p.m.hekkert,d.keyson}@tudelft.nl

1 Introduction

By observing the way people who are stressed interact with objects one may be able to interpret how they feel (Krauss et al., 1996). For instance, at a presentation a nervous presenter can often be seen fidgeting with a pen or pointer. This has shown to be true even if people are actively trying to suppress or hide these feelings (Ekman & Friesen, 1967). The behaviors when manipulating objects during a stressful event appear to be qualitatively different from manipulations during boring or neutral events (Kenner, 1984). Yet, no studies were found in which a categorization was made in the types of manipulative hand movements during different arousing and non-arousing conditions. The goal of this study was to explore what manipulative hand movements are evoked when using a pen during a stressful event as compared to a neutral event.

2 Method

Fourteen subjects (10 women and 4 men; mean age 20.93 ± 2.27 years) participated voluntarily in the experiment. A paper version of the Raven Advanced Progressive Matrices (RAPM) test was implemented as the stressor. They were also told to solve Sudoku puzzles in the pre- and post-stress conditions, requiring similar solving strategies as the RAPM. Hand manipulations with a pen, which had to be used throughout the experiment, were scored by the classification of Elliott & Connolly (1984) and grouped by *simple synergies*, *reciprocal synergies*, and *sequential patterns*. While dynamic tripod can be considered as writing, which would be relevant behavior, it was scored separately from the simple synergies. Furthermore, when subjects changed the pen from one hand to the other, or the pen was relocated it would be marked as a *re-grasp*. For every condition, movements were summed per movement and an index was calculated, showing the relation between relevant and irrelevant movements, i.e. dividing the sum of irrelevant movements between the total of relevant movements.

3 Results

Significant decreases in both relevant and irrelevant movements were found during the stressful condition, except for simple synergies and re-grasp (see Table 1). Also a

A. Paiva, R. Prada, and R.W. Picard (Eds.): ACII 2007, LNCS 4738, pp. 757–758, 2007.

Table 1. Means for manipulations during the three conditions and Repeated Measures ANOVA outcomes

	Pre-stress	RAPM	Post-Stress	F_{value}	$df_{1,2}$	p_{value}
Simple Synergies	2.93±3.67	1.07±1.73	1.86±2.48	1.98	2,26	0.16
Reciprocal Synergies	29.00±7.13	11.35±8.25	21.86±10.70	18.94	2,26	0.00
Sequential Patterns	6.64±6.13	2.71±3.24	6.50±6.64	3.56	2,26	0.06
Re-grasp	4.21±2.89	4.50±3.18	4.93±5.01	0.12	2,26	0.86
Sum Irrelevant	42.79±10.97	19.64±9.92	35.14±18.38	12.50	2,26	0.00
Relevant	14.21±8.39	1.64±0.50	12.57±7.21	21.56	2,26	0.00
Index Irrelevant/Relevant	3.42±2.36	12.36±6.75	3.03±1.90	19.76	2,26	0.00

significant increase was found for irrelevant behavior in relation to relevant behavior during the stressful condition.

4 Discussion

The goal of this study was to investigate hand manipulations when using a pen during a stressful condition as compared to a neutral condition, to determine which manipulations are primary indicators of stress. It was shown that there is an inverse relation between hand manipulations and stress. Overall, during the stressful event fewer manipulations were observed than in the neutral conditions. These findings are consistent with results found in previous studies on behavior during stressful conditions (Kenner, 1984). The decrease in relevant behavior could be because the RAPM task was more difficult and subjects responded less frequently than when solving a puzzle. However, the ratio of relevant and irrelevant movements during the RAPM task was significantly higher during the stressful condition compared with the pre-stress and post-stress conditions. This would argue for calculation of a ratio index when measuring stressful behavior instead of a categorization in specific movements.

Future research in our laboratory will focus on quantifying the observed movements by implementing sensors in a pen or similar object that invokes the suggested movements. The frequency and intensity of the movements will be measured. Equipping products with sensors and technology could help detecting behavioral stress and continuously communicate it to systems that support in relaxing the users in order to develop intelligent stress relieving systems.

References

1. Ekman, P., Friesen, W.V.: Detecting deception from body or face. Journal of Personality and Social Psychology 29, 288–298 (1974)
2. Elliott, J.M., Connolly, K.J.: A classification of manipulative hand movements. Developmental Medicine and Child Neurology 26(3), 283–296 (1984)
3. Kenner, A.N.: The effect of task differences, attention and personality on the frequency of body-focused movements. Journal of Nonverbal Behavior 8(3), 159–171 (1984)
4. Krauss, R.M., Chen, Y., Chawla, P.: Nonverbal behavior and nonverbal communication: What do conversational hand gestures tell us? In: Zanna, M. (ed.) Advances in experimental social psychology, pp. 389–450. Academic Press, San Diego, CA (1996)

Real Emotion Is Dynamic and Interactive

Margaret McRorie and Ian Sneddon

School of Psychology, Queen's University, University Road,
Belfast, N.Ireland
m.mcrorie@qub.ac.uk

Abstract. This paper discusses a data driven pilot study, designed to explore the expression of emotion in a natural situation. Short sequences of natural behaviour were transformed into still photos and compared with examples of acted behaviour using a FeelTrace type analysis. Results indicate that rapid transitions are more common in natural than in acted behaviour.

Keywords: Naturalistic data, databases, facial expression.

1   Introduction

Popular understanding of facial expressions of emotion is sympathetic to the research of Ekman [4]. Based on this research, facial expressions of the basic emotions are seen as universal in humans. However the methodology typically used (ability to recognize still photographs of actors instructed to portray an emotion) has been criticized as lacking in ecological validity [1]. Authors have remarked on the paucity of natural data [2] in emotion research. Yet development of affective computing systems relies on accurate data on human emotional expression.

   Past research has tended to rely on acted sequences, despite growing evidence that natural emotional expression may differ markedly. Acted emotions seem to fail to capture the dynamic and interactive way in which one emotion may cross into another and the facial expressions that intervene during this transition. Preliminary research indicates this may be due to more rapid transitions in natural than in acted behaviour. Such rapidity of transition in natural emotion has been noted by teams working on television databases [3], and for that reason, transition is included as a descriptive category in the HUMAINE database. It has not however yet been demonstrated that this effect truly exists. The major motivating factor in gathering our own data was to provide a statistically valid means of sampling behaviour, and to test this effect. Our focus on the rapidity of changing facial expression is linked to a component model of emotion [6] as opposed to the theory of facial affect programs [5]. If facial behaviours are a direct outcome of component processes, we would expect more static and less varying expression of emotion in acted than in natural behaviour.

2   Method

Participants used a 'Feeltrace' type instrument to rate emotion in a series of still pictures derived from short sequences of natural and acted behaviour. Although it was

A. Paiva, R. Prada, and R.W. Picard (Eds.): ACII 2007, LNCS 4738, pp. 759–760, 2007.

deemed impossible to match the precise content of the natural and acted sequences, a range of emotions were present in both.

3 Data Analysis

Results show a greater degree of change between adjacent frames of natural photos, indicating more rapid transitions in natural than in acted behaviour.

4 Discussion

Our data confirm the hypothesized rapidity of transition in natural emotion. The effect is linked to suggestion [7] that we need to change the span of attention when analyzing emotion. Changes seem to come from tracking external events rapidly, e.g. surprise may give way to fear/horror, which may in turn be replaced by relief/humour. Future databases will thus be required to represent these behaviours instead of relying on actors portraying basic emotions. Our observations point to the intricacy of connections between person and context, and highlight important distinctions between observed and unobserved behaviour. Social mix is also important, but how such differences translate into the subtleties of emotional expression is not obvious. The emotional colouring which pervades behaviour seems to have a more ambiguous landscape than clear cut emotional episodes. In addressing this, the task of emotional analysis will require awareness of the dynamic and interactive nature of real emotion.

References

1. Carroll, J.M., Russell, J.A.: Facial expressions in Hollywood's portrayal of emotion. Journal of Personality and Social Psychology 72, 164–176 (1997)
2. Cowie, R., Douglas-Cowie, E., Cox, C.: Beyond emotion archetypes: databases for emotion modelling using neural networks. Neural Networks 18, 371–388 (2005)
3. Devillers, L., Cowie, R., Martin, J-C., Douglas-Cowie, E., Abrilian, S., McRorie, M.: Real life emotions in French and English TV video clips: an integrated annotation protocol combining continuous and discrete approaches. LREC (2006)
4. Ekman, P.: The Face of Man: Expressions of Universal Emotions in a New Guinea Village, New York, Garland (1980)
5. Ekman, P.: An argument for basic emotions. Cognition and Emotion 6, 169–200 (1992)
6. Scherer, K.R.: On the nature and function of emotion: A component process approach. In: Scherer, K.R., Ekman, P. (eds.) Approaches to Emotion, Hillsdale, NJ: Erlbaum (1984)
7. Scherer, K.R., Ceschi, G.: Lost luggage: A field study of emotion-antecedent appraisal. Motivation and Emotion 21(3), 211–235 (1997)

Perception of Emotions from Static Postures
(Extended Abstract)

Ahmad S. Shaarani and Daniela M. Romano

Department of Computer Science
Regent Court, 211 Portobello Street
Sheffield, S1 4DP, UK
{shaarizan,d.romano}@dcs.shef.ac.uk
http://www.shef.ac.uk/dcs/research/groups/graphics

Human synthetic characters in any computer simulated environment need to be capable of behaving the appropriate way of expressing emotion like normal human do. If the characters fail to express the suitable emotional expression, they will likely to break the users mood and belief. These imply that the key problem in designing synthetic characters is to make them believable in their overall behavior. Therefore the study was directed to construct human synthetic characters that can improve humans respond as well as identify intensity rating of emotions. Ekmans six emotional expressions [1], which are happiness, sadness, anger, surprise, fear and disgust were used because these basic emotions are clear, widely accepted and sufficient. An experiment was conducted to measure believable emotional expression from static images. Sets of virtual human static images of posed expressions of emotions were shown to the subjects. A total of 36 thirty-six volunteers (18 men and 18 women) took part in the experiment. The mean age was 29 years old. The subjects were asked to recognize the expressions by grouping them into six basic emotions and provide the level of emotion for each posture to study the intensity-rating tasks.

Since the purpose of this study is to evaluate the perception of emotions from just the human body, all the faces of human images were removed. This is to make sure that the judgment of emotions is not influence by the face. The images of human figures were developed using Curious Lab Poser 5 animation packages. Five images were conceived as possible bodily expression for each of the six emotion categories. The human postures were created based on two main source: (i) from the literature (mostly in the psychology studies) that offer more or less descriptions of emotional postures [2], [3], [4], [5] and (ii) from the database collection of images in the web pages that can be found with a Google[1] search. The subjects were asked to complete two main tasks in this experiment. In the first task, they have to group all 30 cards of images representing human expression into six categories of emotions.

Based on the groups of images created in the first task, the subjects were then have to rearrange all the cards in the same group from the lowest to the highest level of emotion, for each of the category on the given board. The users rated the

---

[1] www.google.com

A. Paiva, R. Prada, and R.W. Picard (Eds.): ACII 2007, LNCS 4738, pp. 761–762, 2007.
© Springer-Verlag Berlin Heidelberg 2007

perceived emotion conveyed by each of the picture using a 5-point Likert scale, where 1 represents the lowest level of emotion and 5 represent the highest level of emotion. In this experiment, the non-parametric Friedman test [6] has been used to measure if significantly different levels of empathy for each emotion have been identified. Friedmans test was chosen since this type of analysis is suitable to analyst group of data with quantitative response variables.

A similar study on the attribution of emotion to static body posture of a wood mannequin has been conducted by Coulson [3]. The difference between this study and Coulsons study is that Coulson uses a wooden stick figures but this study use the images of static characters that look mostly like real human. By doing this, the detail of the body part such as fingers and foot position can be shown to the participants. Further more, Coulson did not relate his study with the intensity of emotion as emphasis in this study. The main result of this experiment shows that subjects could distinguish between different postures of expressive emotions. In general, happiness gains the highest percentage of recognition. This is follow closely by anger. The most difficult emotion to recognise by the subjects is disgust. The second findings from this experiment is, there appear to be different intensity level of emotion for each posture in the same group. By using Friedman analysis, the level of acceptance has been measured as well as the order of sequence and intensity level for each posture has been identified. The result presented here indicates that subjects can differentiate the basic emotion of human figures by just observing the posture of static body expression. The finding from this stage will be used in the next phase of the research that is to develop and experiment with the dynamic synthetic characters. The intention is to find out whether the level of recognition of emotion in synthetic characters can be improved using the dynamic postures.

References

1. Ekman, P.: An Argument For Basic Emotions. Cognition and Emotion 6(3-4), 169–200 (1992)
2. Montepare, J., Koff, E., Zaitchik, D., Albert, M.: The Use of Body Movements and Gestures As Cues to Emotions in Younger and Older Adults. Journal of Nonverbal Behaviour 23(2), 133–152 (1999)
3. Coulson, M.: Attributing Emotion to Static Body Postures: Recognition, Accuracy, Confusions and Viewpoint Dependence. Journal of Nonverbal Behavior 28(2), 114–139 (2004)
4. Wallbott, H.G.: Bodily Expression of Emotion. European Journal of Social Psychology 28, 879–896 (1998)
5. Boone, R.T., Cunningham, J.G.: Children's Decoding of Emotion in Expressive Body Movement: The Development of Cue Attunement. Development Psychology 34, 1007–1016 (1998)
6. Greene, J., D'Oliveira, M.: Learning to Use Statistical Tests in Psychology, 2nd edn. St Edmundsbury Press Ltd, Suffolk, UK (2001)

Sound for A-Life Agents

Melanie Baljko[1], John Kamevaar[3], and Nell Tenhaaf[2]

[1] Department of Computer Science and Engineering
mb@cse.yorku.ca
[2] Department of Visual Arts, York University, Toronto, Canada
tenhaaf@yorku.ca
[3] Independent Artist, Toronto, Canada

The artwork *Swell* (2003), by Tenhaaf with sound by Kamevaar, has a pod-like amorphous shape and affords the feeling to people that they are dealing with an entity. It has been dubbed by some interactants as a "baby" robot, despite the fact that it has no moving parts and only one ultrasonic distance sensor for detecting its environment (and thus is not robotic). But it has "baby talk" suitable for a machine: sound as pure signal, that could have no other origin than electronic signal flow itself. Interactants set off electronically-manipulated microphone feedback sounds when proximal to *Swell* — sounds that become louder and more intense when the interactant moves away and softer as she or he comes closer. The generated sounds are layered: several sounds playing at once generate the assault of noise, whereas a single sound is almost melodic. Through its sound, *Swell* both commands its space and directs people's movements; it is thereby perceived as having the potential to mature into a more autonomous entity. The idea of the work is not to elicit beliefs that one is seeing life emerging artificially, but rather to elicit a willingness to talk to this entity.

Flo'nGlo [2005], also by Tenhaaf and Kamevaar, consists of two physical entities (*Flo* and *Glo*) that interact with one another in rudimentary conversation. Each of the two agents "vocalizes" using an embedded speaker and senses the other's acoustic articulations directly (as opposed to sensing the environment more generally). *Flo*'s sound is a compellingly relentless flow of "scrubbed" source files (a quick movement back and forth in the timeline of the sound), whereas *Glo* occasionally articulates discernible words. Those words are her power: she causes *Flo* to shrink in consternation when she utters them, while otherwise her attempts to butt in on *Flo*'s chatter are thwarted. After this back-and-forth has gone on for a while, *Glo* calls on her optimizing swarm algorithm, to the tune of a chorus of "granularized" voices. Upon convergence of the algorithm, the exchange begins again. The two voices are central to the agents' behaviour, not an add-on to it; this emphasizes that the affective domain which is generated by sound is not a flourish, but is at the core of elicitation and response. From this de-centralized behaviour, conversational turn-taking is emergent.

A central notion in our current project (a collaboration of the three authors, since 2005) is *agent population*. Whereas *Flo'nGlo* form a *homogeneous* population of agents, we are concerned with *heterogeneous* populations. More specifically, we are focused on populations in which (1) the human interactants acquire a presence as human-representative agents (see [3]) and (2) the embodiments of

A. Paiva, R. Prada, and R.W. Picard (Eds.): ACII 2007, LNCS 4738, pp. 763–765, 2007.

the artificial agents are characterized by minimal "articulators", such as those in the form of light clusters (displayed in arrays of LEDs) and abstract electroacoustic sound — what we term *low-fidelity* embodiments. Thus, the architecture for such agents is predicated on greatly constrained modes of sensory-perception and articulation (the "voice" as described below).

We are building A-life sculptural installations and evaluating the elicited interactions. A scientific goal of this work is to test the hypothesis that conversational turn-taking can emerge even in the interactions between humans and low-fidelity artificial agents. An artistic goal is to expand the concept of the interface and established methods of interactivity. This is cross-disciplinary work: Tenhaaf and Kamevaar are artists (electronic media and electroacoustic sound, respectively), and Baljko is a computer scientist (multimodal communication).

In the artwork, the construction of the human-representative agents (the representations of the human interactants in the hetereogenous population, which are human-driven) is separated from the instantiation of the artificial agents, each with its own locally-autonomous architecture for action. Human interactants must come to realize which of their modes of articulation can be perceived by the other, artificial agents in the population (we have based previous systems on the mode of torso gesture and position; we are presently using proxemics). The human-representative agents are differentiated from the artificial agents by colour in the LED displays and by sound or their "voice". The sounds are taken from the natural and media world, but micro-sampled (broken down into very small segments) and extensively processed. The voice of the human-representative agent is unpitched (percussive), whereas for the artificial agents, it is pitched (tonal), as musical notes are. The artificial agent architecture implements the basic mechanisms of turn-taking (i.e., the sensing and constructing of turn-relevant points and the various responses to them; see [1]).

Our goal is for "conversation" (i.e., characterized by the free exchange of "turns" [1]) to be elicited among the agents in the mixed population without overt explanation. A conversational exchange will be manifested as a sound progression, combining the two different types of sounds. We hypothesize that the manipulation of this progression will become a goal to the human interactant, even if only tacit. As such, the resulting sound becomes the product of the combined effort among all agents in the population (which may be as small as two). It is possible for the human interactant to learn, to an extent, what different sounds designate, but the overall ambiance of the sound is one of fragmentation and conjoining of disparate elements. "Successful" interaction with the artwork implies a recognition that the sound progression co-produced by both types of agent in the population bridges the difference between them. This dynamic establishes the affective realm of the interactive experience as a whole.

We have implemented and evaluated a version of the artwork in which the agent architecture implements collaborative "herding" behaviours [3] (as opposed to turn-taking behaviours). The sound in this version uses a sequence of oscillators based on the quarter-tone scale, mapping the locations of human interactants only. At present, we are evaluating this version as an installation

in the Ontario Science Centre, and testing our hypotheses with children interactants, as opposed to adults. Our next stage of work is to transition to the
turn-taking agent architecture, to transition from its current software form to
sculptural form, involving prototyping and fabrication phases. Installation of the
artwork in various spaces will be the final phase, along with data-gathering and
analysis. For further information, please refer to `www.lo-fi.ca`.

References

1. Sacks, H., Schegloff, E.A., Jefferson, G.A.: A simplest systematics for the organization of turn-taking in conversation. Language 50, 696–735 (1974)
2. Clark, H.H.: Using Language. Cambridge University Press, Cambridge (1996)
3. Baljko, M., Tenhaaf, N.: Different experiences, different types of emergence: A-life
   sculpture designer, interactant, observer. In: Proc. of AAAI Fall 2006 Symposium
   on Interaction and Emergent Phenomenon in Societies of Agents, Arlington, VA

I-Sounds

Emotion-Based Music Generation for Virtual Environments

Ricardo Cruz[1], António Brisson[1], Ana Paiva[1], and Eduardo Lopes[2]

[1] Instituto Superior Técnico
Intelligent Agents and Synthetic Characters Group, INESC-ID, Lisboa, Portugal
[2] Universidade de Évora, Music Department, Évora, Portugal
{ricardo.cruz,antonio.brisson,ana.paiva}@gaips.inesc-id.pt
el@uevora.pt

Abstract. I-Sounds aims to increase the Affective Bandwidth of an Interactive Drama system called I-Shadows, implementing a fully emergent system that generates affective music, based on musical theory and on the emotional state of the characters.

Keywords: Automatic music generation, sound, emotions, affective computing.

1 Music Generation Systems

We can identify two major approaches to music generation. Assisted composition uses pre-composed musical elements and/or user parameterization, such as Nakamura's [1] and Downie's [2] work. The alternate approach is the synthesis of composition algorithms based on musical knowledge and composition theory elements, the case of Herman [3,4]. Some relevant research focuses on music performance rather than music generation to convey emotions. Roberto Bresin's work [5] is a reference in this field.

2 The I-Sounds System

The I-Sounds system defines its own affective model and domains (e.g. a music score representation). Integration with applications is possible trough the coding of an "I-Sounds driver". This mechanism assures the independence and generality of I-Sounds. By allowing programmers to extend I-Sounds models we intend to improve the system's flexibility. The system divides into three levels. The first includes the I-Sounds driver described above responsible for translating the input of the application into the I-Sounds domain. The second divides into an affective module which receives affective input from the driver and uses it to evolve an affective context and a composition module, an asynchronous music generation pipeline whose filters (stages) implement the composition heuristic, fed with information provided by the affective context of the previous module

A. Paiva, R. Prada, and R.W. Picard (Eds.): ACII 2007, LNCS 4738, pp. 766–767, 2007.

transforming it into a music score. Finally the third level is responsible for the output of musical scores (e.g. MIDI sequences).

I-Sounds mapping heuristic will be mainly focused on rhythm. Lopes [6] develops in his PhD thesis a theory about rhythm and metre based on the two basic rhythmic qualities of pulse salience and kinesis. Pulse salience refers to the "emphasis" that a single pulse has on a rhythmic sequence, resulting from three components, the pulse's metric position, agogic accentuation and rhythmic cell accentuation. Kinesis is related with motion induction. There is an inverse relation between kinetic potential and the metrical stability of a pulse. In what respects to melody, we will be using only the first five degrees of the diatonic scale, enough to use the diatonic major and minor modes closely related with happiness and sadness respectively.

In spite of being a general system able to integrate with different applications under different environments, I-Sounds will be tested in a specific context, more precisely in an interactive narrative environment called I-Shadows, [7] which is being developed in our research group at INESC-ID [7]. One of the goals of I-shadows is to provide an environment where children learn how to create stories and act them out in character in front of an audience, in an expressive way. We expect I-Sounds to enlarge the Affective Bandwidth between the System and the Users adding another Affective Channel to the interaction, Sound.

3 Future Work

I-Sounds is currently a work in progress. We think that using a tested musical theory will provide a solid scientific basis to the system. Future work may contemplate; the use of the whole scale degrees as well as other scales and modes, extended affective models with complex emotions and exploring I-Sounds output in different ways (e.g. putting a synthetic character dancing a generated sequence) rather than producing audible signals.

References

1. Nakamura, J., Kaku, T., Hyun, K., Noma, T., Yoshida, S.: Automatic background music generation based on actors' mood and motions. he Journal of Visualization and Computer Animation 25(5), 247–264 (1998)
2. Downie, M.: Behavior, animation, music: the music and movement of synthetic characters. Master's thesis, Massachusetts Institute of Technology (2001)
3. Quincey, A.: Herman. Master's thesis, University of Edinburgh (1998)
4. Stapleford, T.: The harmony, melody, and form of herman, a real-time music generation system. Master's thesis, University of Edinburgh (1998)
5. Bresin, R.: Virtual Virtuosity, Studies in Atomatic Music Performance. PhD thesis, Kungliga Tekniska Högskolan, Stockholm (2000)
6. Lopes, E.: Just in Time: Towards a theory of rhythm and metre. PhD thesis, University of Southampton (2003)
7. Brisson, A., Fernandes, M., Paiva, A.: Children as affective designers. In: HUMAINE WP9 workshop, Kista, Sweden (2006)

A Computational Model of Goal Appraisal

William Jarrold

SRI International
Menlo Park, CA, USA
jarrold@ai.sri.com

Abstract. *Goal appraisal* is formulated as a specific sub-problem of cognitive appraisal. A computational model of goal appraisal is built via a knowledge-based system. An empirical validation study compared model versus human performance by eliciting believability judgments from naive human raters. Results showed that computer model goal appraisals were, in most cases, as believable as human-generated appraisals.

1 Background

The model of cognitive appraisal explicated in Ortony, Clore, and Collins (1988), also known as OCC, is an important foundation in computational affective modeling. *Desirability* is an important parameter in OCC. *Desirability* is an essential appraisal component to about one-third of OCC, i.e., the EVENT BASED (e.g., joy, fear, disappointment) emotions. OCC states that an agent's goals, the relationships among these goals, and the attainment statuses of these goals are important mediators of the appraisal process that determines *desirability*. However, specifics such as an ontology of attainment statuses or inference-capable knowledge representations defining them are left as future work. The present work aims to extend and refine this part of OCC.

2 Method

Goal appraisal is defined as the problem of inferring whether a typical agent of a given type would feel happy, indifferent, or sad given an arbitrary situation, a focal goal, and some assumed typical background goals. Solving this is considered a stepping-stone to the more general problem of inferring OCC *desirability* in the context of EVENT BASED emotions.

The aim of the present study was to evaluate a computer model of goal appraisal by mimicking three kinds of appraisal patterns uncovered via two prior studies (Jarrold, W., 2004) involving human participants. Rules defining so-called Type I, II, and III appraisals were engineered into a knowledge-based system known as The Knowledge Machine (Clark & Porter, 1999) or KM. KM's ability to produce English explanations was also leveraged. The resulting implementation was used to automatically generate English appraisals of the scenarios used in the prior two studies. These machine-generated appraisals were rated by a group of 130 students participating for course credit.

A. Paiva, R. Prada, and R.W. Picard (Eds.): ACII 2007, LNCS 4738, pp. 768–769, 2007.

The purpose of the present study was to test whether there is an insignificant difference in believability between computer-model versus human-generated appraisals. Because of the problematic nature of proving no significant difference, a benchmark significant difference was needed in order to test for insignificant differences between human- and computer-generated appraisals. This benchmark difference was achieved by experimentally manipulating the valence of appraisals. This manipulation, known as reversal, occurred at three levels – *un-reversed*, *slightly reversed*, and *strongly reversed*. By illustration, if an un-reversed appraisal item had a valence of *happy* in the un-reversed condition, it would have a valence of *sad* in the strongly reversed condition. Reversal was hypothesized to significantly decrease believability within the three goal appraisal types.

3   Results

Reversal works as predicted. As Table 1 indicates, reversal significantly decreased believability with both computer- and human-generated items. In addition, only un-reversed items had a mean believability greater than neutral (i.e., 3.0). Thus, even slight changes in valence lowered believability.

Table 1. Effect of Reversal within Each Level of Source

Appraisal Source	Means(sd)			$F(df)$	p
	Un-Reversed	Slightly Reversed	Strongly Reversed		
Human Generated	4.0(1.2)	2.8(1.2)	1.8(1.0)	161.20(2,227)	<.0001*
Computer Generated	3.7(1.2)	3.0(1.3)	2.0(1.2)	85.59(2,206)	<.0001*

$p < .05$.

Results showed that the computer model created affective evaluations that were, in most cases, as believable as human-generated evaluations. A more fine-grained analysis of results indicates that Type II (also known as Goal Substitution) appraisals are the most in need of better modeling.

References

Clark, P.B.: The knowledge machine 1.4: Users manual. [computersoftwareandmanual]. Retrieved from, April 4, 2001 (1999), http://www.cs.utexas.edu/users/mfkb/RKF/km.html

Jarrold, W.: Towards a Theory of Affective Mind: Computationally Modeling the Generativity of Goal Appraisal, University of Texas (2004)

Ortony, A., Clore, G., Collins, A.: The cognitive structure of emotion. Cambridge University Press, Cambridge, UK

Affective Video Data Collection Using an Automobile Simulator

Tevfik Metin Sezgin and Peter Robinson

University of Cambridge, Computer Laboratory, Cambridge UK CB3 OFD
Metin.Sezgin@cl.cam.ac.uk
Peter.Robinson@cl.cam.ac.uk

1 Introduction

The correlation between driver status and safety has increased interest in automated systems that can infer the physical and mental state of drivers [2,3]. So far, most research on automated recognition of driver state has focused on physical state. More recently, researchers have proposed inferring the mental states of drivers by extracting drivers' facial expressions from video data. Although systems that infer physical state have been evaluated in simulators or in real driving conditions, this has not been the case for systems inferring mental states which rely primarily on video data. Consequently, issues regarding the design of an experimental setup to collect such affective data have not been explored. Here, we describe our experimental setup for collecting video data from drivers.

2 Experimental Setup

We used a state of the art car simulator to subject four drivers to three drives designed to trigger a number of driving-related mental states. Fig. 1 shows examples of the first driver showing confusion.

The goal of our experiment was to observe how the drivers would behave when subjected to conditions intended to trigger complex mental states relevant to driving. Using the emotion taxonomy of Baron-Cohen et al. [1], a set of complex mental states were chosen based on driving behaviour research. The chosen mental states were discomfort, uncertainty, nervousness, boredom, drowsiness, comfort, surprise, concentration, thinking.

Fig. 1. Examples of the first driver expressing confusion

A. Paiva, R. Prada, and R.W. Picard (Eds.): ACII 2007, LNCS 4738, pp. 770–771, 2007.

3   Results

To measure the effectiveness of our experimental setup in eliciting mental states, we administered a questionnaire and collected drivers' subjective evaluation of how they felt at different times of the trial. The questionnaires have revealed that our setup was successful in putting the drivers into bothered, upset, bored and drowsy mental states.

Our experiments also allowed us to gauge the utility of a car-simulator in collecting affective video data. Our analysis revealed a number of issues regarding the effectiveness our experimental setup and the challenges of collecting video data of good quality. For example, we found that certain events triggered stronger facial expressions compared to others. Also some conditions worked well for some subjects and drew unexpected responses from others. Our experiments also revealed the difficulty of capturing clear frontal views of the driver's face due to physical space limitations.

4   Related and Future Work

We collected affective data from drivers using a car simulator. Our evaluation focused on eight driving-related mental states and allowed us to explore the challenges in eliciting and collecting affective video data. The above aspects of our work collectively distinguish it from the existing related work including work by Lisetti and Nasoz [3] and Healey and Picard [2] who carried out similar experiments in real and simulated driving conditions, but mainly focused on the analysis of physiological data.

There are two main directions that we would like to explore. First, we would like to analyse the videos in more depth and annotate interesting parts to include the corresponding facial actions and mental states. We also we would like to investigate how the knowledge of drivers' mental state can be effectively used to facilitate driver-automobile communication, enhance road safety and the overall driving experience.

Acknowledgements

We would like to thank Dr. Rana el Kaliouby for making her mental state analysis software available to assess the quality of the face tracking. We also thank the TRL staff for their input in the design and execution of the data collection.

References

1. Baron-Cohen, S., Golan, O., Wheelwright, S., Hill, J.J.: Mind Reading: The Interactive Guide to Emotions. Jessica kingsley publishers, London (2004)
2. Healey, J.A., Picard, R.W.: Detecting stress during real-world driving tasks. IEEE Tran. on Intelligent Transportation Systems 6(2), 156–166 (2005)
3. Lisetti, C.L., Nasoz, F.: Affective intelligent car interfaces with emotion recognition. In: HCI 2005, Las Vegas, USA (July 2005)

Mixed Feelings About Using Phoneme-Level Models in Emotion Recognition

Hannes Pirker

Austrian Research Institute for Artificial Intelligence (OFAI), A-1010 Vienna, Austria

Abstract. This study deals with the application of MFCC based models for both the recognition of emotional speech and the recognition of emotions in speech. More specifically it investigates the performance of phone-level models. First, results from performing forced alignment for the phonetic segmentation on GEMEP, a novel multimodal corpus of acted emotional utterances are presented, then the newly acquired segmentations are used for experiments with emotion recognition.

The *Geneva Multimodal Emotion Portrayals* corpus (GEMEP) [1] is a novel corpus that contains 2 pseudo-linguistic utterances (type1: *Né kal ibam soud molén!* and type2: *Koun sé mina lod bélam?*) produced with 18 different emotions and varying levels of intensity by 10 actors, resulting in altogether 3815 such sentences. This highly controlled, uniform segmental content provides a promising basis for investigating the acoustic correlates of emotions in detail. Phonetic segmentation using forced alignment was thus to be performed for this corpus in order to support fine grained analysis of temporal and spectral features in the future. This way it also was to be tested on how well standard segmentation techniques, i.e. Hidden Markov Models (HMM) with Mel Frequency Cepstral Coefficients (MFCC) [2], would deal with the variability of manner and voice quality found in emotional speech. The third goal was to shed some light on the conflicting requirements on MFCCs. They are used in speech recognition for discriminating speech sounds and for their robustness against variation in intonation and voice quality. But they are also used for emotion recognition, though then they should be indifferent to the underlying speech sounds. As the identity of the speech sounds is a major influencing factor on MFCC, first experiments with phone-level models for emotion recognition were performed.

Models for segmentation were trained on 505 manually labelled sentences of type1 and tested on 220 sentences. Simple global models performed better than speaker-specific and gender-specific models. For type1 sentences, 84% of the automatically derived phoneme boundaries were located with less than 10ms error, 89% with less than 20ms error, for type2 the figures were 59% for 10ms and 70% for 20ms errors[1]. The current automatic segmentations provide a reasonable basis for manual corrections, which are still clearly necessary though. Persistent alignment problems can e.g. be observed in flustered speech with its weakly articulated formant structures. Soft speech, even of very low intensity, as well

---

[1] For more detailed results cf. http://www.ofai.at/~hannes.pirker/gemep

A. Paiva, R. Prada, and R.W. Picard (Eds.): ACII 2007, LNCS 4738, pp. 772–773, 2007.

Table 1. Correctly classified sentences (%) for phoneme-level (left) and sentence-level HMMs

States per PHO	3
Gaussian Mixtures	5
18 emotions	28.5
6 emotions	48.2

States per SENT	22	1		
Gaussian Mixtures	5	5	128	512
18 emotions	52.5	29.6	57.2	64.9
6 emotions	72.7	53.9	75.5	81.7

as loud or even shouted speech are less critical. Intermingled laughter is another example which poses severe problems to any aligner.

For emotion recognition the corpus was split into 2940 sentences for training and 875 for testing different HMMs. To allow better comparability with other studies also a subset of 6 emotions (anger, joy, fear, sadness, pleasure, interest) was used (1129 training and 388 test sentences). For each phoneme and each emotion a separate left to right 3-state HMM, using 12 MFCC, energy, delta and acceleration was trained. Alternatively two sentence-level HMM typologies were tested: an 'elongated' version of the phone-level model with 22 states, and a 1-state HMM, equivalent to a Gaussian Mixture Model.

Table 1 shows that phoneme-level models clearly performed inferior to models that were trained on whole sentences, which show quite high results given they are speaker independent and no pre-selection of 'nice' samples whatever was performed. But still these results are not yet to be interpreted conclusively in complete disfavor of the segment-based approach. Because the segmental content is identical for all the sentences, phoneme-based models lose their implicit advantages in this context. On the other hand errors in the automatic alignment have a strong influence on them, e.g. surprisingly /s/ provided the best classification results of all phonemes, which is, because fricatives are most suitable for the aligner. The study on emotion recognition was not aimed to come up with impressive recognition rates, which could be easily boosted by using e.g. 10fold-cross-validation, a-priori probabilities etc., but to provide a first orientation for future experiments. The availability of validated phonetic segmentations in the near future will provide a solid basis for further investigations.

Acknowledgements. I am very much indebted to Klaus Scherer and his group, especially to Tanja Bänziger, for designing, creating and sharing their GEMEP corpus. This work has been funded by the EU Network of Excellence HUMAINE (IST 507422) and by the Austrian Funds for Research and Technology Promotion for Industry (FFF 808818/2970 KA/SA).

References

1. Bänziger, T., Pirker, H., Scherer, K.: GEMEP - GEneva Multimodal Emotion Portrayals: A corpus for the study of multimodal emotional expressions, LREC'06 Workshop Corpora for Research on Emotion and Affect, Genoa, Italy, pp. 15–19 (2006)
2. Young, S., Evermann, G., Kershaw, D., Moore, G., Odell, J., Ollason, D., Povey, D., Valtchev, V., Woodland, P.: The HTK Book (version 3.4). Cambridge University Engineering Department, Cambridge UK (2006)

Emotional Faces in Peripheral Crowding

Tian Ran[1,2], Wenfeng Chen[1], and Xiaolan Fu[1,*]

[1] State Key Laboratory of Brain and Cognitive Science,
Institute of Psychology, Chinese Academy of Sciences,
Beijing 100101, China
[2] Graduate School of the Chinese Academy of Sciences, Beijing 100049, China
`{rant,chenwf,fuxl}@psych.ac.cn`

Crowding effect refers to the deficit in identifying viewed targets, such as letters, numerals, line segments, or grating patches, when other shapes are nearby. This effect is reduced when distractors have a different color, contrast, or binocular disparity than that of the target. With feature singleton targets, the crowding effect decreases dramatically with an increasing number of distractors for both simple orientation and more complex letter identification tasks [4]. With a target that is not a salient feature singleton, however, the increasing number of distractors worsens rather than improves the perception of the target [2].

The present study uses the popular paradigm of crowding effect to explore whether the emotional schematic faces are salient in the peripheral visual field, and can affect the crowding effect by bottom-up salience of target. For the emotional faces have the ability of attention capture [1][3], we expected to see a normal crowding effect with the target crowding by a single ring of distractors, and performance would be recovered as the distractors increasing. In other words, if the positive or negative expression can 'pop-out' in the parafovea, we expect to see, with emotional singleton targets, the crowding effect may decrease even with an increasing number of distractors (neutral schematic faces).

Three undergraduates (2 women and 1 man) were paid to participate in the experiment. Participants' task was to judge the emotional face (either positive or negative expression) among neutral expression is red or green and press the corresponding key.

A target was presented at a fixed eccentricity, 60 mm either to the left or to the right of the fixation point, which was at the centre of display (Fig. 1). From a viewing distance of approximately 57 cm, this eccentricity corresponded to 6 deg of visual angle. Distances (center to center) between rows and columns of objects were 16 mm. Distractors (if present) formed a square matrix comprising 1×1 (a target alone), 3×3, 5×5, or 7×7 objects with the target in the center. Examples of stimuli for experiment were given in Fig. 2A, B, and C.

ANOVA of reaction times were conducted and the results showed that responses were fastest for no distractor condition ($M = 255$ ms,

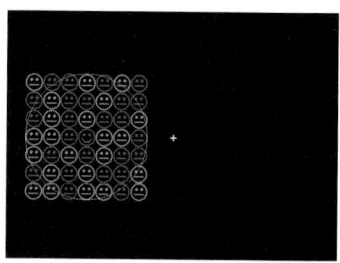

Fig. 1. An example of display

---

* Corresponding author.

A. Paiva, R. Prada, and R.W. Picard (Eds.): ACII 2007, LNCS 4738, pp. 774–775, 2007.
© Springer-Verlag Berlin Heidelberg 2007

SEM = 6 ms). A single ring of distractors caused the responses significantly slow down (*M* = 422 ms, *SEM* = 6 ms). And by increasing the number of distractors, response times were even slower, 496 ms for 24 distractors (*SEM* = 7 ms) and 548 ms for 48 distractors (*SEM* = 7 ms). The results of correct proportions showed the similar trend of results of reaction time, which suggests the perception of emotional faces might be affected by the distractors.

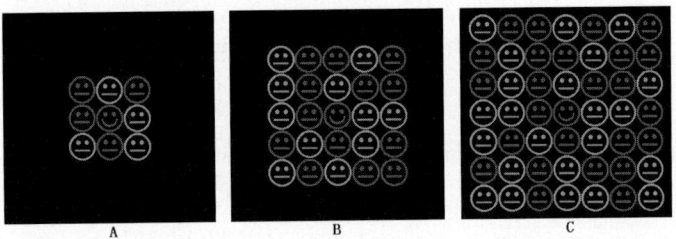

Fig. 2. Examples of stimuli used in the present study: (A) 3×3 matrix, (B) 5×5 matrix, and (C) 7×7 matrix. The stimuli were presented unpredictably either to the left or to the right of the fixation point (eccentricity ≈ 6 deg).

In the present experiment, the reaction time and accuracy data show that judgment is fastest and nearly perfect when there is a single ring of distractors, but as the increasing of rings of distractors, the judgment slows down with more errors. These are not consistent with the results of previous studies on crowding effect (e.g., [4]). The findings of this study suggest that the emotional features may not be very salient in the parafovea. This account requires further evidences to explore whether the recovered performance will be observed when the distractors increasing in the fovea.

Acknowledgement

This research was supported in part by grants from 973 Program (2006CB303101) and the National Natural Science Foundation of China (60433030, 30500157, and 30600182).

References

1. Dolan, R.J.: Emotion, cognition, and behavior. Science. 298, 1191–1194 (2002)
2. Felisberti, F.M., Solomon, J.A., Morgan, M.J.: The role of target salience in crowding. Perception 34, 823–833 (2005)
3. Hao, F., Zhang, H., Fu, X.: Modulation of Attention by Faces Expressing Emotion: Evidence from Visual Marking. In: Tao, J., Tan, T., Picard, R.W. (eds.) ACII 2005. LNCS, vol. 3784, pp. 195–201. Springer, Heidelberg (2005)
4. Poder, E.: Crowding, feature integration, and two kinds of "attention". Journal of Vision. 6, 163–169 (2006)

Affect Related Acoustic Features of Speech and Their Modification*

Dandan Cui, Fanbo Meng, Lianhong Cai, and Liuyi Sun

Department of Computer Science and Technology, Tsinghua University,
Beijing 100084, P.R. China
cuidd02@mails.tsinghua.edu.cn

Abstract. This paper presents our recent work on the investigation of affect related acoustic features of Mandarin speech and their modification. A syllabic F0 contour model so called "Gravity Model" is proposed, which can describe the detailed changes of the F0 contour on the syllable level between different emotions. Then, different representations of spectrum, together with different modification methods, are also tried and compared; a maximal-mean amplitude representation proves to be the best, with its corresponding modifying method.

1   Introduction

Acoustic features are very important for affective speech research. However, during our preliminary analyzing, converting, and modifying, we found the conventional features are facing many problems [1] [2]: utterances with the similar acoustic features may have different emotions; features may conflict during modification. This paper investigates acoustic features and their modification methods, especially for the purpose of affect conversion. The work is based on the affective speech corpus ACCorpus_SA developed in Tsinghua University, which includes 11 typical emotional categories that can cover all the octants of PAD space: exuberant, relaxed, docile, disdainful, disgusted, angry, fearful, anxious, surprised, sad and neutral [2].

2   Investigation on Prosodic Features: Gravity Model

To describe the detailed changes of F0 contour between different emotions, taking the principle of Pitch Target Model for reference but giving the F0 contour more variability and stability, we proposed a more detailed syllabic F0 model. First, referring to the SPiS [3], we use 6 parameters to build up the F0 framework of a syllable: B for MinF0, H for MaxF0, N_1 for the position of B, N_2 for the position of H, F for the start position of F0 contour, and E for the end. The kernel of

---

* The work in this paper is supported by National Science Foundation of China (No. 60433030, No. 60418012) and the Special Funds for Major State Basic Research Program of China (973 Program) (No. 2006CB303101).

A. Paiva, R. Prada, and R.W. Picard (Eds.): ACII 2007, LNCS 4738, pp. 776–777, 2007.

the whole model is to portray the difference between the shapes of F0 between emotions. We take 2 kinds of changes into account and model them by 3 kinds of Gravity Effects. In modification experiment, Gravity Model is superior to Pitch Target Model and conventional stat. features in both objective and perceptive measures. With the Gravity Affects, more details of F0 contour are concerned. At the same time, the framework insures our model wont produce unreasonable outputs like Pitch Target Model does, even if the emotions are really extreme, or the style is pretty free.

3   Characterization and Modification of Spectrum

After trying several approaches including Spectral Centroid, we suppose that: the affect related information may be embedded more in the distribution along amplitude-axis, rather than along the frequency-axis. So, the representation of spectrum is revised as follows: The maximal amplitude of spectrum (SpecMax), i.e. the range of spectrum; the average amplitude of spectrum (SpecMean), i.e. the major distribution of spectrum, which is modulated nonlinearly within the range of spectral amplitude. Perceptive test shows that introducing spectral features into conversion and taking the amplitude-axis oriented method in its characterization and modification, the perceptive distance between the modified and target speech is reduced. Besides, the two features we selected can be both easily calculated and modified.

4   Conclusion

As stated above, this paper presents our recent work on the investigation of affect related acoustic features of Mandarin speech and their modification. A syllabic F0 contour model so called Gravity Model is proposed, which can describe the detailed changes of the F0 contour on the syllable level between different emotions. Then, spectral features are also introduced: a maximal-mean amplitude representation proves to be the best, with its corresponding modifying method. The work is a basis of our succeeding affective speech modeling and system building.

References

1. Cui, D., Cai, L., Wang, Y., Zhang, X.: Investigation on pleasure related acoustic features of affective speech. In: Huo, Q., Ma, B., Chng, E.-S., Li, H. (eds.) ISCSLP 2006. LNCS (LNAI), vol. 4274, pp. 67–78. Springer, Heidelberg (2006)
2. Cui, D., Cai, L.: Acoustic and physiological feature analysis of affective speech. In: Huang, D.-S., Li, K., Irwin, G.W. (eds.) ICIC 2006. LNCS, vol. 4113, pp. 912–917. Springer, Heidelberg (2006)
3. Jianhua Tao. The prosodic modeling in Mandarin TTS. [PhD dessertation]. Beijing: Tsinghua University (2001)

Author Index

Printing: Mercedes-Druck, Berlin
Binding: Stein + Lehmann, Berlin

Lecture Notes in Computer Science

Sublibrary 6: Image Processing, Computer Vision, Pattern Recognition, and Graphics

Vol. 4141: A. Campilho, M. Kamel (Eds.), Image Analysis and Recognition, Part I. XXVIII, 939 pages. 2006.

Vol. 4122: R. Stiefelhagen, J.S. Garofolo (Eds.), Multimodal Technologies for Perception of Humans. XII, 360 pages. 2007.

Vol. 4109: D.-Y. Yeung, J.T. Kwok, A. Fred, F. Roli, D. de Ridder (Eds.), Structural, Syntactic, and Statistical Pattern Recognition. XXI, 939 pages. 2006.

Vol. 4091: G.-Z. Yang, T. Jiang, D. Shen, L. Gu, J. Yang (Eds.), Medical Imaging and Augmented Reality. XIII, 399 pages. 2006.

Vol. 4073: A. Butz, B. Fisher, A. Krüger, P. Olivier (Eds.), Smart Graphics. XI, 263 pages. 2006.

Vol. 4069: F.J. Perales, R.B. Fisher (Eds.), Articulated Motion and Deformable Objects. XV, 526 pages. 2006.

Vol. 4057: J.P.W. Pluim, B. Likar, F.A. Gerritsen (Eds.), Biomedical Image Registration. XII, 324 pages. 2006.

Vol. 4046: S.M. Astley, M. Brady, C. Rose, R. Zwiggelaar (Eds.), Digital Mammography. XVI, 654 pages. 2006.

Vol. 4040: R. Reulke, U. Eckardt, B. Flach, U. Knauer, K. Polthier (Eds.), Combinatorial Image Analysis. XII, 482 pages. 2006.

Vol. 4035: T. Nishita, Q. Peng, H.-P. Seidel (Eds.), Advances in Computer Graphics. XX, 771 pages. 2006.

Vol. 3979: T.S. Huang, N. Sebe, M.S. Lew, V. Pavlović, M. Kölsch, A. Galata, B. Kisačanin (Eds.), Computer Vision in Human-Computer Interaction. XII, 121 pages. 2006.

Vol. 3954: A. Leonardis, H. Bischof, A. Pinz (Eds.), Computer Vision – ECCV 2006, Part IV. XVII, 613 pages. 2006.

Vol. 3953: A. Leonardis, H. Bischof, A. Pinz (Eds.), Computer Vision – ECCV 2006, Part III. XVII, 649 pages. 2006.

Vol. 3952: A. Leonardis, H. Bischof, A. Pinz (Eds.), Computer Vision – ECCV 2006, Part II. XVII, 661 pages. 2006.

Vol. 3951: A. Leonardis, H. Bischof, A. Pinz (Eds.), Computer Vision – ECCV 2006, Part I. XXXV, 639 pages. 2006.

Vol. 3948: H.I. Christensen, H.-H. Nagel (Eds.), Cognitive Vision Systems. VIII, 367 pages. 2006.

Vol. 3926: W. Liu, J. Lladós (Eds.), Graphics Recognition. XII, 428 pages. 2006.

Vol. 3872: H. Bunke, A.L. Spitz (Eds.), Document Analysis Systems VII. XIII, 630 pages. 2006.

Vol. 3852: P.J. Narayanan, S.K. Nayar, H.-Y. Shum (Eds.), Computer Vision – ACCV 2006, Part II. XXXI, 977 pages. 2006.

Vol. 3851: P.J. Narayanan, S.K. Nayar, H.-Y. Shum (Eds.), Computer Vision – ACCV 2006, Part I. XXXI, 973 pages. 2006.

Vol. 3832: D. Zhang, A.K. Jain (Eds.), Advances in Biometrics. XX, 796 pages. 2005.

Vol. 3736: S. Bres, R. Laurini (Eds.), Visual Information and Information Systems. XI, 291 pages. 2006.

Vol. 3667: W.J. MacLean (Ed.), Spatial Coherence for Visual Motion Analysis. IX, 141 pages. 2006.

Vol. 3417: B. Jähne, R. Mester, E. Barth, H. Scharr (Eds.), Complex Motion. X, 235 pages. 2007.

Vol. 2396: T.M. Caelli, A. Amin, R.P.W. Duin, M.S. Kamel, D. de Ridder (Eds.), Structural, Syntactic, and Statistical Pattern Recognition. XVI, 863 pages. 2002.

Vol. 1679: C. Taylor, A. Colchester (Eds.), Medical Image Computing and Computer-Assisted Intervention – MICCAI'99. XXI, 1240 pages. 1999.